lonely planet

Egypt

Andrew Humphreys
Siona Jenkins

LONELY PLANET PUBLICATIONS
Melbourne • Oakland • London • Paris

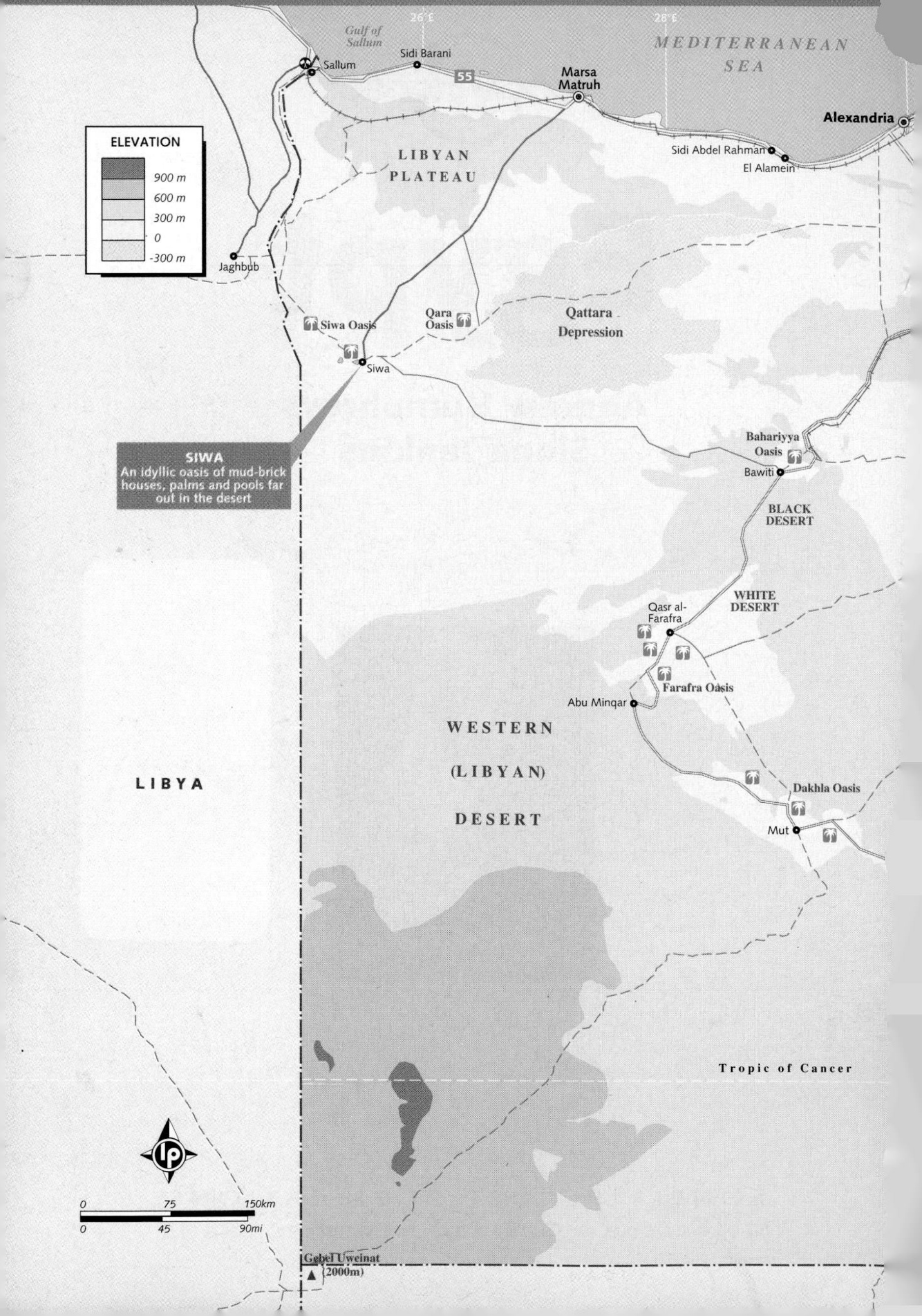
26°E
28°E
Gulf of Sallum
MEDITERRANEAN SEA
Sallum
Sidi Barani
55
Marsa Matruh
Alexandria
Sidi Abdel Rahman
El Alamein
ELEVATION
900 m
600 m
300 m
0
-300 m
LIBYAN PLATEAU
Jaghbub
Siwa Oasis
Qara Oasis
Qattara Depression
Siwa
SIWA
An idyllic oasis of mud-brick houses, palms and pools far out in the desert
Bahariyya Oasis
Bawiti
BLACK DESERT
WHITE DESERT
Qasr al-Farafra
Farafra Oasis
Abu Minqar
WESTERN (LIBYAN) DESERT
LIBYA
Dakhla Oasis
Mut
Tropic of Cancer
0
75
150km
0
45
90mi
Gebel Uweinat (2000m)

Contents – Text

Contents – Maps

CAIRO

AROUND CAIRO

NILE VALLEY – BENI SUEF TO QUS

NILE VALLEY – LUXOR

NILE VALLEY – ESNA TO ABU SIMBEL

WESTERN OASES

ALEXANDRIA & THE MEDITERRANEAN COAST

SUEZ CANAL

RED SEA COAST

DIVING THE RED SEA

SINAI

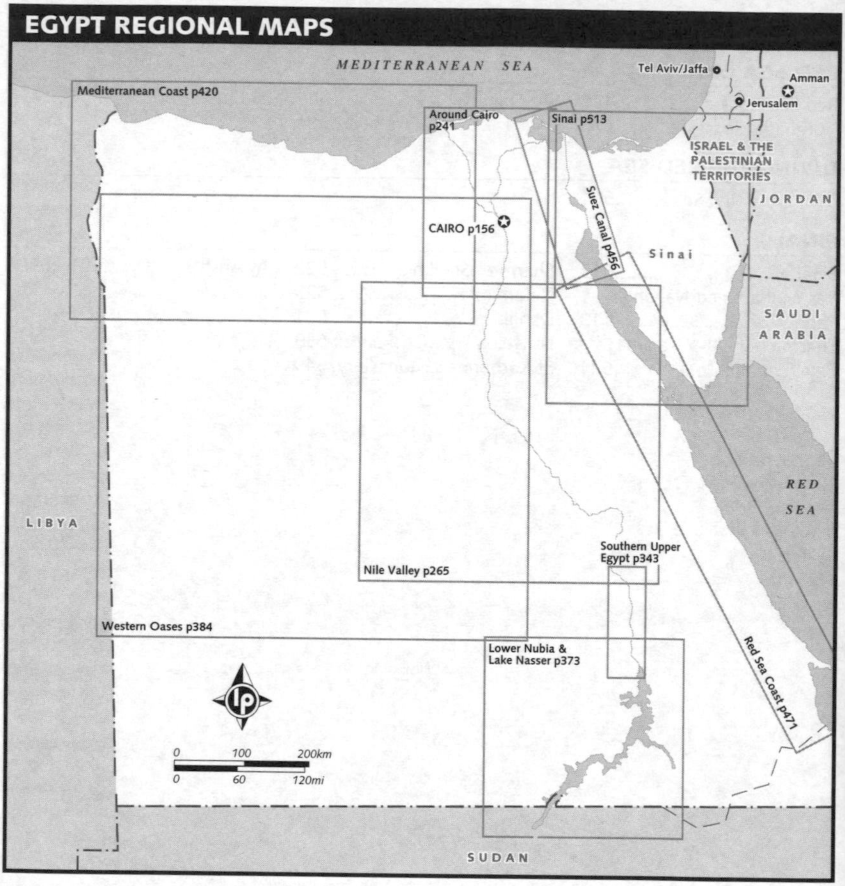
EGYPT REGIONAL MAPS
MEDITERRANEAN SEA
Tel Aviv/Jaffa
Amman
Jerusalem
Mediterranean Coast p420
Around Cairo p241
Sinai p513
ISRAEL & THE PALESTINIAN TERRITORIES
JORDAN
Suez Canal p456
CAIRO p156
Sinai
SAUDI ARABIA
RED SEA
LIBYA
Southern Upper Egypt p343
Nile Valley p265
Western Oases p384
Lower Nubia & Lake Nasser p373
Red Sea Coast p471
0 100 200km
0 60 120mi
SUDAN

The Authors

Andrew Humphreys & Gadi Farfour

Andrew has been living, travelling and working in the Middle East on and off since 1988 when he arrived in Cairo on holiday and took three years to leave. Originally trained in London as an architect, he slid into writing through a growing fascination with Islamic buildings. Following a spell in mainstream journalism based for several years in the Baltic States, Andrew hooked up with Lonely Planet for a return to the Middle East and has since authored or coauthored Lonely Planet guides to Russia, Central Asia, the Middle East, Israel & the Palestinian Territories, Jerusalem, Cairo and Syria.

Born of Egyptian-Estonian parents, Gadi grew up spending summers in Tallinn and the rest of the year in Alexandria. A designer by profession, she has accompanied Andrew on all his research trips, using her formidable language skills to reach the places he could never go.

Andrew and Gadi are two of the co-founders of the *Cairo Times*, an Egypt-based, English-language newspaper. They currently live in London but wonder for how long.

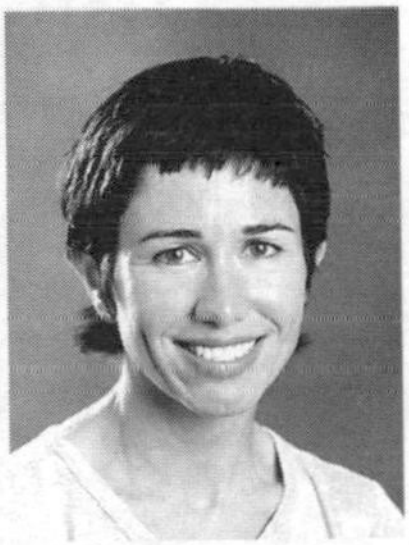

Siona Jenkins

Siona Jenkins arrived in Cairo for six months of Arabic language study in 1989 and is still based there. She is now a freelance journalist, writing for the *Irish Times* and a number of magazines when not writing guidebooks for Lonely Planet or helping to produce documentary films.

Dr Joann Fletcher

Fascinated with Egypt since she was a small child, Joann Fletcher's first visit to the country in 1981 only confirmed her decision to make it her career. A degree in Egyptology was followed by a PhD in the same subject, and undertaking scientific research on everything from royal mummies to ancient hair dyes, she has also excavated in Egypt. Having lectured around the world, she regularly appears on television and, as well as writing archaeology features for *The Guardian* newspaper and the BBC online history service, she has written six books to date. She lives with her Egyptian family on Luxor's West Bank when not at home on the Yorkshire coast, close to her English family, or in Normandy.

FROM THE AUTHORS

Andrew Humphreys Big thanks to co-contributors Siona and Joann, to Fiona Sibald, Paul Geday and the *Egypt Almanac*, and most of all to Gadi who, uncomplaining, continues to accept a life governed by publishers' deadlines.

Siona Jenkins Whether writing as a journalist or a travel writer, one is constantly indebted to people who go out of their way to help. These include Amr Shannon for more Western Desert lore; John Grainger for his commitment to Sinai's environment and the best stir-fry in St Katherine; Abdullah Baghi and Mounir Neamatallah for their efforts to keep Siwa special; Hani Derbala for going beyond duty at the Red Sea GIS unit; and officials at tourist information offices, particularly Hakeem Hussein in Aswan, Omar Ahmed in Dakhla and Mahdi Hweiti in Siwa. A big thank you also to John O'Carroll for Dakhla, Carol for the best desert trip of the new millenium, and to James for traipsing around hotels and keeping overzealous officials at bay. Lastly, special thanks and a big kiss to Leo, who deserves a medal for putting up with his mother's constant travel.

Dr Joann Fletcher Thanks to both families for their constant support – Garry, Susan and Katherine, Ali, Ahmed, Jamalat, Mohammed, Abu el-Naga, Ragab, Nagwa and Mahmoud – and of course Stephen and Joan who have always shared my feelings for this magic place.

This Book

Scott Wayne researched and wrote the first two editions of *Egypt & the Sudan* and Damien Simonis researched the 3rd edition. Leanne Logan and Geert Cole researched the 4th edition of *Egypt*; the 5th edition was researched by Andrew Humphreys, Gadi Farfour and Siona Jenkins. This 6th edition was also researched and written by Andrew Humphreys, Gadi Farfour and Siona Jenkins; Dr Joann Fletcher went over the book's Pharaonic content with a fine-tooth comb and wrote the Pharaonic Egypt special section and the boxed texts 'Making Mummies' and 'Tomb Building' in the Luxor chapter.

From the Publisher

This edition of *Egypt* was edited in Lonely Planet's Melbourne office by Lynne Preston with assistance from Bethune Carmichael, Melanie Dankel, Justin Flynn, John Hinman, Nancy Ianni, Jenny Mullaly and Isabelle Young. Amanda Sierp coordinated the mapping and design with assistance from Anna Judd, Heath Comrie and Sarah Sloane. Quentin Frayne and Emma Koch organised the language chapter. Illustrations were drawn by Trudi Canavan, Golo, Kelli Hamblet, Martin Harris, Margaret Jung and Geoff Stringer. Thanks to Hunor Csutoros for the climate charts, Simon Bracken for designing the front cover, Leonie Mugavin for checking and sourcing information in the Getting There & Away chapter. Thanks also to Kerryn Burgess, who assisted in layout, Lara Morcombe, who compiled the index, and Rod Zandbergs, for generating the index and contents. Brigitte Ellemor, Michelle Glynn, Brett Moore and Maree Styles guided the book through all the stages of its production.

THANKS
Many thanks to the travellers who used the last edition and wrote to us with helpful hints, advice and interesting anecdotes. Your names appear in the back of this book.

Foreword

ABOUT LONELY PLANET GUIDEBOOKS

The story begins with a classic travel adventure: Tony and Maureen Wheeler's 1972 journey across Europe and Asia to Australia. Useful information about the overland trail did not exist at that time, so Tony and Maureen published the first Lonely Planet guidebook to meet a growing need.

From a kitchen table, then from a tiny office in Melbourne (Australia), Lonely Planet has become the largest independent travel publisher in the world, an international company with offices in Melbourne, Oakland (USA), London (UK) and Paris (France).

Today Lonely Planet guidebooks cover the globe. There is an ever-growing list of books and there's information in a variety of forms and media. Some things haven't changed. The main aim is still to help make it possible for adventurous travellers to get out there – to explore and better understand the world.

At Lonely Planet we believe travellers can make a positive contribution to the countries they visit – if they respect their host communities and spend their money wisely. Since 1986 a percentage of the income from each book has been donated to aid projects and human rights campaigns.

Updates Lonely Planet thoroughly updates each guidebook as often as possible. This usually means there are around two years between editions, although for more unusual or more stable destinations the gap can be longer. Check the imprint page (following the colour map at the beginning of the book) for publication dates.

Between editions up-to-date information is available in two free newsletters – the paper *Planet Talk* and email *Comet* (to subscribe, contact any Lonely Planet office) – and on our Web site at www.lonelyplanet.com. The *Upgrades* section of the Web site covers a number of important and volatile destinations and is regularly updated by Lonely Planet authors. *Scoop* covers news and current affairs relevant to travellers. And, lastly, the *Thorn Tree* bulletin board and *Postcards* section of the site carry unverified, but fascinating, reports from travellers.

Correspondence The process of creating new editions begins with the letters, postcards and emails received from travellers. This correspondence often includes suggestions, criticisms and comments about the current editions. Interesting excerpts are immediately passed on via newsletters and the Web site, and everything goes to our authors to be verified when they're researching on the road. We're keen to get more feedback from organisations or individuals who represent communities visited by travellers.

Lonely Planet gathers information for everyone who's curious about the planet – and especially for those who explore it first-hand. Through guidebooks, phrasebooks, activity guides, maps, literature, newsletters, image library, TV series and Web site we act as an information exchange for a worldwide community of travellers.

Research Authors aim to gather sufficient practical information to enable travellers to make informed choices and to make the mechanics of a journey run smoothly. They also research historical and cultural background to help enrich the travel experience and allow travellers to understand and respond appropriately to cultural and environmental issues.

Authors don't stay in every hotel because that would mean spending a couple of months in each medium-sized city and, no, they don't eat at every restaurant because that would mean stretching belts beyond capacity. They do visit hotels and restaurants to check standards and prices, but feedback based on readers' direct experiences can be very helpful.

Many of our authors work undercover, others aren't so secretive. None of them accept freebies in exchange for positive write-ups. And none of our guidebooks contain any advertising.

Production Authors submit their manuscripts and maps to offices in Australia, USA, UK or France. Editors and cartographers – all experienced travellers themselves – then begin the process of assembling the pieces. When the book finally hits the shops, some things are already out of date, we start getting feedback from readers and the process begins again …

WARNING & REQUEST

Things change – prices go up, schedules change, good places go bad and bad places go bankrupt – nothing stays the same. So, if you find things better or worse, recently opened or long since closed, please tell us and help make the next edition even more accurate and useful. We genuinely value all the feedback we receive. A well-travelled team reads and acknowledges every letter, postcard and email and ensures that every morsel of information finds its way to the appropriate authors, editors and cartographers for verification.

Everyone who writes to us will find their name listed in the next edition of the appropriate guidebook. They will also receive the latest issue of *Planet Talk*, our quarterly printed newsletter, or *Comet*, our monthly email newsletter. Subscriptions to both newsletters are free. The very best contributions will be rewarded with a free guidebook.

We may edit, reproduce and incorporate your comments in all Lonely Planet products, such as guidebooks, Web sites and digital products, so let us know if you don't want your comments reproduced or your name acknowledged.

Send all correspondence to the Lonely Planet office closest to you:

Australia: Locked Bag 1, Footscray, Victoria 3011
USA: 150 Linden St, Oakland, CA 94607
UK: 10a Spring Place, London NW5 3BH

Or email us at: talk2us@lonelyplanet.com.au

For news, views and updates see our Web site: www.lonelyplanet.com

HOW TO USE A LONELY PLANET GUIDEBOOK

The best way to use a Lonely Planet guidebook is any way you choose. At Lonely Planet we believe the most memorable travel experiences are often those that are unexpected, and the finest discoveries are those you make yourself. Guidebooks are not intended to be used as if they provide a detailed set of infallible instructions!

Contents All Lonely Planet guidebooks follow roughly the same format. The Facts about the Destination chapters or sections give background information ranging from history to weather. Facts for the Visitor gives practical information on issues like visas and health. Getting There & Away gives a brief starting point for researching travel to and from the destination. Getting Around gives an overview of the transport options when you arrive.

The peculiar demands of each destination determine how subsequent chapters are broken up, but some things remain constant. We always start with background, then proceed to sights, places to stay, places to eat, entertainment, getting there and away, and getting around information – in that order.

Heading Hierarchy Lonely Planet headings are used in a strict hierarchical structure that can be visualised as a set of Russian dolls. Each heading (and its following text) is encompassed by any preceding heading that is higher on the hierarchical ladder.

Entry Points We do not assume guidebooks will be read from beginning to end, but that people will dip into them. The traditional entry points are the list of contents and the index. In addition, however, some books have a complete list of maps and an index map illustrating map coverage.

There may also be a colour map that shows highlights. These highlights are dealt with in greater detail in the Facts for the Visitor chapter, along with planning questions and suggested itineraries. Each chapter covering a geographical region usually begins with a locator map and another list of highlights. Once you find something of interest in a list of highlights, turn to the index.

Maps Maps play a crucial role in Lonely Planet guidebooks and include a huge amount of information. A legend is printed on the back page. We seek to have complete consistency between maps and text, and to have every important place in the text captured on a map. Map key numbers usually start in the top left corner.

Although inclusion in a guidebook usually implies a recommendation we cannot list every good place. Exclusion does not necessarily imply criticism. In fact there are a number of reasons why we might exclude a place – sometimes it is simply inappropriate to encourage an influx of travellers.

Introduction

'There'll be no such thing as normal for quite a while now': so spoke celebrity traveller Michael Palin touching down in Egypt on his televised voyage 'Around the World in 80 Days'. 'No such thing as normal' could almost be the country's tagline, because Egypt is the most extraordinary place. Herodotus, the ancient Greek historian, noted as much more than a century before the birth of Christ when he wrote 'Concerning Egypt I will now speak at length, because nowhere are there so many marvellous things, nor in the world besides are there to be seen so many things of unspeakable greatness...' It's not just the Pyramids and the immense wealth of awe-inspiring temples and monuments left by the pharaohs (which are what Herodotus had witnessed and which were already ancient wonders in his time, oggled by Classical-era tourists), but also the legacy of the Greeks and Romans, the churches and monasteries of the early Christians, and the overwhelming profusion of art and architecture accumulated from centuries of successive Islamic dynasties, whose domains stretched to encompass all the Near East and the Arabian Peninsula.

Added to what the visitor can see is the allure arising from the knowledge that there are more, possibly even greater, riches still to be discovered. Archaeologists are unearthing a vast horde of mummies out in the Western Desert, while others are exploring what may well be Cleopatra's palace on the sea bed beneath the waters of Alexandria's harbour.

In between and around these ancient wonders day-to-day life goes on, with Egyptian society and culture offering just as much intrigue and magic as the country's historical treasures, whether it's the voice of diva Umm Kolthum wafting from a busy coffeehouse at dusk, or taking passage on a local Nile ferry to reach a small family restaurant on the far bank.

Added to all this is the incredible beauty of the country. Although it's the legacy of the pharaohs that has traditionally proved to be the big draw, increasingly visitors to

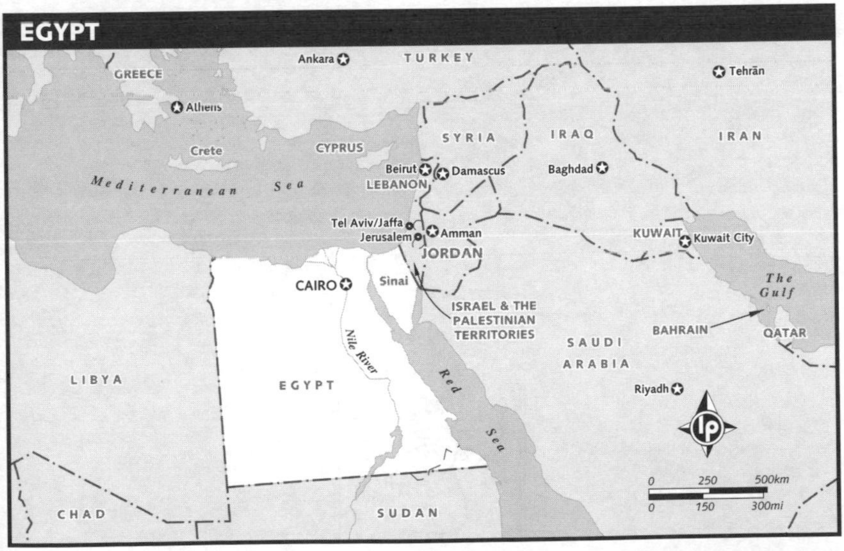

Egypt are skipping the old stones altogether. The fine white sand, clean clear water, and purple mountain backdrops of the Sinai and the Red Sea coasts have long been known to divers, who come for offshore reefs with sheer drop-offs that plummet to unknown depths, for coral-encrusted shipwrecks, and for the abundance of marine life all this supports. But in recent times divers have had to share their secret with the increasing numbers of sun-seekers who now flock to Egypt's beaches as an exotic alternative to Greece or Turkey.

Just as other-worldly as the underwater landscapes are the vast expanses of blinding white sand and rippling dunes of the Western Desert, now being made ever-more accessible by a growing number of desert safari outfits. Through such developments – and shaped by expensive advertising campaigns abroad – the image of Egypt is changing. It's no longer just a monuments and museums destination. It's fun and sun on the beach; it's adventure, diving wrecks and treks across the sands on a camel; it's culture with Aida at the Pyramids; it's spiritual, with the promotion of a new 'holy pilgrimage route' tracing the path of the Holy Family up the Nile; it's even sporty, with a baffling profusion of golf resorts currently under development all over the country. Golf? In a country where for much of the year it's too hot to walk unshaded? Where water is scarce and usable land even scarcer? Well, like the man said, in Egypt things are far from normal.

Facts about Egypt

HISTORY

The history of Egypt is inextricably linked to the Nile. Back in 'prehistory' the savanna lands of the Sahara began to dry up, forcing the region's nomadic populations to gradually migrate towards the river. Its ever-fertile banks gave birth to the world's first nation-state. It also spawned some of the most important achievements in human history, since Egypt was the place where writing was invented, the first stone monuments erected and an entire culture set in place that would remain largely unchanged for thousands of years. All of this was made possible by the regular rhythms of the river and, in contrast to the vast areas of barren desert known as *deshret* (red land), the narrow banks of the Nile were known as *kemet* (the black land), after the rich silt deposited by the annual floods.

Ever since the earliest known communities settled its valley, the Nile River has inspired and controlled the religious, economic, social and political life of the Egyptians. For many centuries the narrow, elongated layout of the country's fertile lands hampered the fusion of those early settlements which held fast to their local independence. But with the river as a common highway providing an avenue for commercial traffic and communication, those barriers were eventually broken. The small kingdoms developed into two important states: Upper Egypt was comprised of the long thin valley, from its furthest navigable reaches at Aswan north to the Delta (or to the future site of Cairo); Lower Egypt consisted of the flat marshy Delta itself.

The unification of these two states by Narmer (also known as Menes) in around 3100 BC, set the scene for the greatest era of ancient Egyptian civilisation. Known as the Dynastic Period, more than 30 royal dynasties ruled over a period of some 3000 years, divided into Old, Middle and New Kingdoms separated by intermittent periods of unrest when the country briefly divided into north and south. Following the end of the New Kingdom, Egypt was ruled by a series of foreign invaders from Libya, Nubia, Persia, Macedonia and Rome, the start of a long period of foreign rule that was only to end with the Revolution of 1952.

Obviously, it's not within the scope of this book to cover this history in anything but the broadest of strokes. Bearing that in mind, the 5000 years from the time of Menes/Narmer can be divided roughly into seven periods:

Pharaonic Egypt	3100–332 BC
Alexander & the Ptolemaic Era	332–30 BC
Roman Rule	30 BC–AD 638
Arab Conquest	640–1517
Ottoman Turkish Rule	1517–1882
British Occupation	1882–1952
Independent Egypt	1952 onwards

Pharaonic Egypt

Little is known of the immediate successors of Menes/Narmer except that, attributed with divine ancestry, they promoted the development of a highly stratified society, patronised the arts and built many temples and public works. Their capital, founded by Menes, was Memphis, which lay 24km south of what is now modern Cairo, a site which at that time marked the meeting point of Upper and Lower Egypt. The city survived for 3½ millennia as the cradle of Pharaonic civilisation, where writing and administration, art and architecture were nurtured and developed. Though little of the greatest ancient Egyptian city remains, we can get an idea of the size and importance of Memphis by the remarkable funerary complexes that were created for its pharaohs. Foremost of these is the necropolis of Saqqara, which spread over 7km and which has as its centrepiece a stepped pyramid, the earliest of the many pyramids to follow.

The Narmer Palette, dating from about 3100 BC, represents the unification of the two states of Upper (south) and Lower (north) Egypt for the first time under one ruler.

Dating from about 2650 BC, the Step Pyramid, built for a pharaoh by the name of Zoser (Djoser), was not only a striking testimony to his power and the prosperity of the period but marked the start of a whole new trend.

The Old Kingdom For the next 500 years, a period which Egyptologists refer to as the Old Kingdom, the power of Egypt's pharaohs would seem to have greatly increased, judging by the scale and ambition of their monuments. Most of these drew their direct inspiration from Zoser's imposing structure, earning this period its other name, 'the Age of the Pyramids'.

First came Sneferu, the most prolific of the pyramid builders, who presided over the raising of the Bent and Red (North) Pyramids at Dahshur near Saqqara, and possibly of the Pyramid of Meidum in Al-Fayoum, too. His son, Khufu (Cheops), and grandson, Khafre (Chephren), were responsible for the two largest of the Pyramids at Giza. Khufu took the throne when the Old Kingdom was reaching the apex of its prosperity and culture and, if his colossal pyramid is any indication, he must have been one of the greatest of all the pharaohs. Its sheer size and mathematical precision is not only a monument to the extraordinary development of Egyptian architecture, it also suggests through the enormous labour and discipline involved that the era of Khufu saw the emergence, for the first time in human history, of an organisational principle.

As the centuries passed and the 5th dynasty (c. 2494–2345 BC) began, there were changes in the power and rule of the pharaohs. One of the first indications of this was the comparatively small pyramids built at Abu Sir, 12km south of Giza. The pharaohs had begun to delegate power to various high officials and nobles in the vast bureaucracies they had created, so unlike their predecessors they were not quite the absolute monarchs they once were and did not have the same resources for the construction of immense funerary monuments.

Control became even more diffuse during the 6th dynasty (2345–2181 BC) before the fall of the Old Kingdom resulted in the formation of a number of small local principalities. During the 7th and 8th dynasties (2181–2125 BC) a second rival capital was established at Heracleopolis, near present-day Beni Suef, while at the same time the south was controlled by rulers of the 11th dynasty (2125–1985 BC) based at Thebes (now Luxor). Both power bases had their own private armies, and small wooden models of the Egyptian and Nubian troops employed in Asyut at this time are on display in Cairo's Egyptian Museum.

The anarchy and civil war of the First Intermediate Period (2181–2055 BC) only ended when the Thebans finally defeated the pharaohs of Heracleopolis and

Chronology of the Pharaohs

This is not a complete listing but it does include all of the important rulers mentioned throughout this book. Gaps in some dates are accounted for by the pharaohs not listed.

Dynasty	Period (BC)
Early Dynastic Period 3100–2686	
1st Dynasty	**3100–2890**
Menes (Narmer)	c. 3100
2nd Dynasty	**2890–2686**
3rd Dynasty	**2686–2613**
Zoser	2667–2648
Sekhemket	2648–2640
Old Kingdom 2686–2181	
4th Dynasty	**2613–2494**
Sneferu	2613–2589
Khufu (Cheops)	2589–2566
Djedefra	2566–2558
Khafre (Chepren)	2558–2532
Menkaure (Mycerinus)	2532–2503
Shepseskaf	2503–2498
5th Dynasty	**2494–2345**
Userkaf	2494–2487
Sahure	2487–2475
Neferirkare	2475–2455
Shepseskare	2455–2448
Raneferef	2448–2445
Nyuserre	2445–2421
Unas	2375–2345
6th Dynasty	**2345–2181**
Teti	2345–2323
Pepi I	2321–2287
Pepi II	2278–2184
First Intermediate Period 2181–2055	
7th & 8th Dynasties	**2181–2125**
9th & 10th Dynasties	**2160–2025**
11th Dynasty (Thebes only)	**2125–2055**
Middle Kingdom 2055–1650	
11th Dynasty	**2055–1985**
Montuhotep II	2055–2004
Montuhotep III	2004–1992
12th Dynasty 1985–1795	
Amenemhat I	1985–1955
Sesostris I (Senwosret)	1965–1920
Amenemhat II	1922–1878
Sesostris II	1880–1874
Sesostris III	1874–1855
Amenemhat III	1855–1808
Amenemhat IV	1808–1799
13th & 14th Dynasties	**1795–1650**
Second Intermediate Period 1650–1550	
15th–17th Dynasties	**1650–1550**
New Kingdom 1550–1069	
18th Dynasty	**1550–1295**
Ahmose	1550–1525
Amenhotep I (Amenophis)	1525–1504
Tuthmosis I (Tuthmose)	1504–1492
Tuthmosis II	1492–1479
Tuthmosis III	1479–1425
Hatshepsut	1473–1458
Amenhotep II	1427–1400
Tuthmosis IV	1400–1390
Amenhotep III	1390–1352
Akhenaten (Amenhotep IV)	1352–1336
Tutankhamun	1336–1327
Horemheb	1323–1295
19th Dynasty	**1295–1186**
Ramses I	1295–1294
Seti I	1294–1279
Ramses II	1279–1213
Seti II	1200–1194
20th Dynasty	**1186–1069**
Ramses III	1184–1153
Ramses IV	1153–1147
Ramses V	1147–1143
Third Intermediate Period 1069–747	
21st Dynasty	**1069–945**
Psusennes I	1039–991

made Thebes the capital. Under Montuhotep II the north and south were again united under the leadership of a single pharaoh, marking the beginning of what Egyptologists refer to as the Middle Kingdom.

The Middle Kingdom The return to political order was marked by another spurt of tomb and temple building. The Middle Kingdom pharaohs saw their country thrive. The art of this time is regarded as the 'classical' period of Egyptian culture and they built extensively throughout the land, erecting their pyramids at Dahshur, Hawara and Al-Lahun, all of which are near Al-Fayoum and Saqqara. At the same time, the boundaries of Egyptian rule were also pushed southwards into the land of Nubia, where the pharaohs built huge mud-brick fortresses (now submerged beneath Lake Nasser) to maintain control of the region. The pharaohs centralised their government by replacing provincial governors with a vast bureaucracy of officials, many of them 'Asiatics' from Palestine who had settled peacefully and had been absorbed into Egyptian society. By gradually infiltrating the government this way they were able to take advantage of the instability caused by the 70 or so short-lived pharaohs of dynasties 13 to 14 (1795–1650 BC) and eventually took the throne around 1650 BC.

These new rulers were known as the Hyksos, a corruption of *hekaw-khasut* meaning 'rulers of foreign lands', and they were to provide the full stop to the Middle Kingdom. Yet the south was never fully conquered and Thebes remained a bastion of resistance throughout a century of Hyksos rule (which marks what's known as the Second Intermediate Period). By 1550 BC the Theban warlords once again triumphed to reunite their country and drive the Hyksos out, following this up with vigorous campaigning as far as the Euphrates and down into Nubia. This marks the beginning of the New Kingdom (1550–1069 BC) and a lineage of power that would continue more or less unbroken for almost 500 years.

The New Kingdom Beginning with Ahmose (1550–1525 BC), more than 30 monarchs from three successive dynasties ruled through what is commonly regarded as the golden age of the pharaohs. Most of the incredible monuments to be seen at Luxor date from the period of the New Kingdom. Thebes was the religious and political centre of the kingdom, while the age-old capital of Memphis took care of the practical affairs such as administration. For this new age came a new god, and Amun-Ra became Egypt's state god. He was a composite of a Theban god, Amun, and the great sun god of Heliopolis, Ra. Great temples were built in his honour, particularly at Karnak, which soon became the religious capital and power base, swelling in size as the empire expanded. Each successive pharaoh of the 18th and 19th dynasties added a room, hall or pylon, replete with intricately carved hieroglyph inscriptions.

Significant expansion of the empire began with the reign of Tuthmosis I when he grabbed Upper Nubia (now part of Sudan). On his death, he was also the first pharaoh to be entombed in the Valley of the Kings on the West Bank across from Thebes, although the Theban area had been in use as a necropolis since the end of the Old Kingdom (Montuhotep II, first ruler of the Middle Kingdom, had already built an impressive funerary temple at Deir al-Bahri).

The daughter of Tuthmosis I was Hatshepsut, the most famous of the female pharaohs. She had a spectacular funerary temple built for herself at Deir al-Bahri, next to and dwarfing that of Montuhotep.

Hatshepsut was married to her half-brother Tuthmosis II and, on his death, his child by a minor wife was to become pharaoh. As Tuthmosis III was still young when his father died, Hatshepsut became regent and later crowned herself pharaoh, sharing the regency with Tuthmosis III. Tuthmosis III became the sole ruler in around 1458 BC, and was Egypt's greatest conqueror, expanding the empire beyond Syria and into western Asia. His son and successor Amenhotep II shared his warlike nature, unlike the next pharaoh Tuthmosis IV. His policy of diplomacy was inherited by his son Amenhotep III, whose long, peaceful reign marks the zenith of ancient Egyptian power. The resulting prosperity made possible a huge building program, including Luxor Temple and the pharaoh's enormous funerary temple of which the Colossi of Memnon are just about all that remains.

While Amenhotep III is regarded as the most splendid of Egypt's pharaohs, astutely managing to reduce the power of the priests of Amun, his son and successor Amenhotep IV irreversibly changed the course of Egyptian history with his disastrous policies. Alienating the priests completely, he abandoned the traditional gods and also closed down their temples, diverting all their revenues to the crown, while at the same time losing his grip on the empire. He also changed his name to Akhenaten which means 'one who is beneficial to the Aten', the sun disc, which Akhenaten raised to the status of Egypt's main god. The so-called 'heretic pharaoh' also spurned Thebes and, along with his powerful wife Nefertiti, moved further north to establish a new but short-lived capital called Akhetaten (Horizon of the Aten) at Tell al-Amarna near Minya.

After Akhenaten's death his successor, who many now believe to be Nefertiti, returned to Thebes and prepared the throne for Akhenaten's son Tutankhaten. Changing his name to Tutankhamun (and known today chiefly for the discovery of his treasure-filled tomb in 1922), he restored the old gods along with their temples while the Aten was phased out, until the memory of Akhenaten's rule (known today as 'the Amarna Period' after the site of the new capital) was finally obliterated by the next generation of pharaohs.

For the next few centuries, Egypt was ruled by military men such as Horemheb, Seti I, Ramses II and III. Keen to establish their Pharaonic credentials, they built massive monuments at Abydos, Abu Simbel and Thebes, greatly expanding Amun-Ra's temple at Karnak. They also waged war to reclaim Egypt's empire abroad and fought against the Hittites and Libyans to successfully defended Egypt's borders.

Following the reign of Ramses III (1184–1153 BC) the glory days were finally over and Egypt's fortunes began to decline. As the empire shrank away, it was subject to attack from outsiders until the north was occupied piecemeal when Libyans captured parts of the Delta and ruled as the 22nd and 23rd dynasties from 945 BC to 715 BC. The Kushites moved up through Nubia to occupy much of southern Egypt, forming the 25th dynasty (747–656 BC) which in turn ended after the Assyrian invasions in 671 BC and 669 BC. The Persians ruled Egypt for more than a century (525–404 BC) until the native dynasties reasserted themselves for the last time between 404–343 BC and Persia once again took over. Yet this second Persian period was short-lived and after only 10 years they and their entire empire were taken over by Alexander the Great of Macedonia in his conquest of the ancient world.

Alexander & the Ptolemaic Era

Due to the unpopularity of Persian rule, the Egyptians greeted Alexander (332–323 BC) as a liberator. He was crowned pharaoh by the priests of Memphis before choosing to found a new city on the Mediterranean coast, named for himself. His creation of Alexandria opened up Egypt to the rest of the world, changing its outlook forever from conservative to cosmopolitan. Although Alexandria soon eclipsed both Memphis and Thebes in its importance, Alexander never lived to see the city he had founded, although his body was eventually buried here by his Ptolemaic successors.

At Alexander's death one of his generals, Ptolemy, took over and founded a highly successful dynasty which lasted three centuries (323–30 BC). Although they were

Macedonian Greeks, the Ptolemies would come to assimilate much of Egypt's heritage, adopting Pharaonic dress, reworking Egyptian gods into a new Graeco-Egyptian pantheon and, most visibly, adopting Pharaonic building styles: the temples of Dendara, Edfu, Esna, Kom Ombo and Philae all date from the time of the Ptolemies.

The Ptolemies made Alexandria the greatest city of the ancient world in terms of both wealth and scholarship, and they did everything in their power to hold out against the growing power of Rome.

The last of their line, Cleopatra VII (*the* Cleopatra of asp, Liz Taylor and great eyeliner fame) was a brilliant politician who kept Egypt independent by allying herself with Julius Caesar, whom she married and gave a son. After his assassination she married Marc Antony (with whom she had three more children), their combined forces a serious threat to Caesar's nephew Octavian who now wielded power in Rome.

Alexander the Great ruled as pharaoh over Egypt and was greeted as a liberator by the Egyptian people. He founded the city of Alexandria in 331 BC.

After their naval forces were defeated in 31 BC at the battle of Actium, Antony committed suicide. Rather than face capture, Cleopatra followed suit.

Roman Rule

Taking the title Augustus Caesar and becoming the first emperor of Rome, Octavian also had himself portrayed as pharaoh in Egypt, although he and his successors ruled from Rome through governors. They did little to develop the country, which served largely as the granary of the Roman Empire, but they established trading posts down the Red Sea coast and out across the Western (Libyan) Desert to link up with their territories in Cyrenaica (now Libya). They also established a fortress on the site of a Pharaonic river crossing near Memphis, 10km to the east of the Pyramids. Controlling the access to the upper Nile, the fortress of Babylon-in-Egypt, as it became known, grew to become a busy port and major frontier stronghold.

To ensure their rule of the native population, the Romans continued to build temples in a Pharaonic style, worship Egyptian gods and keep Egyptian traditions such as mummification. When Christianity arrived in Egypt in AD 40 with the preachings of St Mark, the Romans regarded the new religion as a potential threat and although Christians were persecuted it nevertheless flourished. When the Romans finally accepted Christianity as their official religion in AD 323, they went on to close down 'pagan' temples all across the empire in AD 394. As the last hieroglyphic inscription was carved at the Temple of Philae on 24 August AD 394, ancient Egyptian culture finally died.

Yet soon Egyptian Christianity, known as 'Coptic' Christianity, ran into trouble with the church in Rome, since its Monophysitic doctrine held that Christ was divine, rather than both human and divine. The Egyptians were therefore declared heretical and expelled from the rest of the Christian world.

Within Egypt the Roman overlords continued to persecute the local population.

This oppressive state of affairs came to an end in AD 640 with the arrival of an army of mounted warriors riding out of the deserts of the Arabian peninsula.

The Arab Conquest

The Arab conquest brought Islam to Egypt. By AD 642 the new rulers had established a base immediately north of the walls of the Roman fortress of Babylon. This encampment, called Fustat, was the precursor of the city of Cairo. From this point on, the history of Egypt becomes largely synonymous with the history of Cairo.

From the arrival of Islam onwards, all of Egypt's existing historical capitals (Memphis, Thebes, Alexandria) were allowed to decline and, in a relatively short space of time, all became thinly populated backwaters. Their monuments served as quarries for the stone needed for the walls, palaces and religious buildings of the new Islamic capital.

Like Christianity before it, Islam, though still in its infancy, was already subject to splinter factions and dynasties. In AD 658 the Umayyads, an Arab dynasty based in Damascus, became rulers, or caliphs, of the whole Muslim world, including Egypt. They were supplanted by the Abbasids of Baghdad, whose influence also extended to the lands of the Nile from AD 750. As a distant province far removed from the seat of power, neither caliphate made much of a physical mark on Egypt. The exception was when an ambitious governor sent from Baghdad made the country his independent fief adorning it with great palaces (long gone) and a splendid mosque named for himself, the Mosque of Ibn Tulun, which still stands to this day. Sweeping changes came with the next rulers, the Fatimids, a dynasty that came out of North Africa to establish a counter-caliphate to the Abbasids. They conquered Egypt in AD 969 and made Cairo their capital.

As Alexander and the invading Arab army had after him, the Fatimids chose not to base their authority in any existing city. Instead they marked out territory to the north of Fustat. The fortified walled city they built formed the core of Al-Qahira, 'the Victorious', a name later corrupted by European merchants to Cairo. The Fatimids, though, were not popular rulers. They held themselves aloof from the country's indigenous Egyptian citizens, whom they kept outside the city walls. The division was made even greater by the fact that the Fatimids were Shiites, a brand of Islam at odds with the traditional orthodox Sunnism of Egypt and the eastern Mediterranean.

Around this time the Christians of Western Europe took up arms against the 'heathen' armies in occupation of the holy sites of the Bible. Their prime goal was to wrest Jerusalem from the Muslims, and this they achieved in 1099. By 1168, having bloodily rampaged through Palestine, the Crusaders advanced into Egypt. They got as far as the Delta before they were driven off by the Seljuks of Damascus, a powerful warrior dynasty to whom the Fatimids had appealed for help. The Seljuks were Sunni Muslims and once in Cairo they promptly deposed the Shiite dynasty they had come to aid and sent the Fatimids into exile.

The restorer of Sunni rule and the new overlord of Cairo was Salah ad-Din al-Ayyoub, known to the Crusaders, and later to the West, as Saladin, who established a new dynasty, the Ayyubids (1171–1250). A soldier foremost, Saladin made his mark on Cairo by looping it with a great defensive wall and by establishing the Citadel that still dominates the city's eastern skyline today.

The Ayyubid line ran to only four rulers before a vicious bout of scheming and betrayals resulted in the seizure of power by a group of former mercenaries, the Mamluks.

The Mamluks A Turkish slave-soldier class, the Mamluks' (AD 1250–1517) military service had been rewarded by Saladin with gifts of land. They were organised in a quasi-feudal manner, with groups of Mamluks each attached to their own lord or emir. The purchase of new young slaves maintained the groups. There was no system of hereditary lineage, instead it was rule by the strongest. Rare was the sultan who died of old age.

Natural born soldiers, the military prowess of the Mamluks led to a series of successful campaigns that gave Egypt control of all of Palestine and Syria. At the same time, while renowned for their savagery, the Mamluks also endowed Cairo with the most exquisite architectural constructions and, during their 267-year reign, the city was the intellectual and cultural centre of the Islamic world. The contradictions in the constitution of the Mamluks are typified in the figure of Qaitbey, who was bought as a slave-boy by one sultan and witnessed the brief reigns of nine more before he himself clawed his way to the throne. As sultan he rapaciously taxed all his subjects and dealt out vicious punishments with his own hands, once tearing out the eyes and tongue of a court chemist who had failed to transform lead into gold. Yet Qaitbey marked his ruthless sultanship with some of Cairo's most beautiful monuments, notably his mosque which stands in the Northern Cemetery.

The funding for the Mamluks' great buildings came from trade. A canal existed that connected the Red Sea with the Nile at Cairo, and thus the Mediterranean, forming a vital link in the busy commercial route between Europe and India and the Orient. In the 14th and 15th centuries, the Mamluks, in partnership with Venice, virtually controlled east-west trade and grew fabulously rich off it.

The end of these fabled days came in the closing years of the 15th century when Vasco da Gama discovered the sea route around the Cape of Good Hope, so freeing European merchants from the heavy taxes raked in by Cairo and Venice. At around the same time the Ottoman Turks of Constantinople were emerging as a mighty new empire looking to unify the Muslim world, a goal that included the conquest of Egypt. In 1516 the Mamluks, under the command of their penultimate sultan Al-Ghouri, were obliged to meet the Turkish threat. The battle, which took place at Aleppo in Syria, resulted in complete defeat for the Mamluks. In January of the following year the Turkish sultan Selim I entered Cairo.

Ottoman Turkish Rule

Egypt's days as a great imperial centre were at an end. Under the Ottoman Turks the country was once again, as it had been under the Romans, reduced to the level of a far-flung province. What trading revenues there were went back to Constantinople (İstanbul), as did the taxes that were squeezed from the local population.

Although the Mamluk sultanate had been abolished, the Mamluks themselves lived on in the form of lords known as *beys* and maintained considerable power. Over time the Turkish hold on Egypt became weaker as the Ottoman Empire went into decline. In 1796 one of the Mamluk beys was confident enough to take on the Turkish garrison in Cairo, defeat them and dispatch the Ottoman governor back to Constantinople. But the Mamluks' re-emergence was short-lived. Within two years they were unseated again, not by the Turks but by a new force in Egypt: Europeans, in the form of Napoleon and the French army.

Napoleon & *Description de l'Egypte*

Napoleon and his musket-armed forces blew apart the sword-wielding Mamluk cavalry, supposedly as a show of support for the Ottoman sultanate. In reality, Napoleon wanted to strike a blow at Britain, with whom the French were at war, by gaining control of the land and sea routes to the British colony of India.

The diminutive general established a French-style government, revamped the tax system, implemented public works projects and introduced new crops and a new system of weights and measures. Napoleon was also accompanied by 167 scholars and artists who were set to work making a complete study of Egypt's monuments, crafts, arts, flora and fauna, and of its society and people. The resulting

MARGARET JUNG

During his short time in Egypt, Napoleon Bonaparte brought in scholars who produced the fascinating *Description de l'Egypte*.

work was published as the 24-volume *Description de l'Egypte*; it's still in print today, albeit in a radically slimmed-down, one-volume edition.

Anthropological efforts aside, Napoleon's Egyptian adventure seemed doomed from the beginning. Less than a month after he arrived, the British navy under Admiral Nelson appeared off the coast of Alexandria and destroyed the French fleet. Then the Ottoman sultan sent an army which, though trounced by the French, put paid to any pretence that the French were in Egypt with the complicity of Constantinople. Relations between the occupied and occupier deteriorated rapidly and uprisings in the capital could only be quashed by shelling which left 3000 Egyptians dead.

Sitting on a powder keg in Cairo with the British and Turks allying in Syria, the French forces readily agreed to an armistice and in 1801 departed the way they had come, via Alexandria.

Mohammed Ali Although brief, the French occupation had significantly weakened Egyptian political stability. Turkish rule was reinstated but it was tenuous and masked great internal strife. A lieutenant in an Albanian contingent of the Ottoman army named Mohammed Ali took advantage of the melee. Within five years of the departure of the French he had fought and intrigued his way to become the pasha (governor) of Egypt, nominally the vassal of Constantinople but in practice looking on the country as his own.

The sultan in Constantinople was too weak to challenge this usurpation and the only possible threat to Mohammed Ali's power could have come from the Mamluk beys. Any danger here was swiftly and viciously snuffed out by a very deadly dinner invitation. On 1 March 1811 Mohammed Ali had 500 Mamluk leaders attend a grand day of feasting and revelry at the Citadel in honour of his son's imminent departure for Mecca. When the feasting was over the Mamluks mounted up on their lavishly decorated horses and were led in procession down the narrow high-sided defile below what's now the Police Museum towards the Bab al-Azab. But as they approached, the great gates were swung closed before them. Gunfire rained down from above. After the scything fusillades, Mohammed Ali's soldiers waded in with swords and axes to finish the job. Not one Mamluk escaped alive.

There is a popular legend that tells of how one Mamluk survived by jumping his horse over the Citadel walls (a scene depicted in a fine painting hung at the Manial Palace) but in fact the character in question kept his life because he didn't turn up for the feast that bloody day.

Although Mohammed Ali's means of achieving his ends could be barbarous, his reign is pivotal in the history of Egypt, as under his uncompromising rule the country underwent a transition from medieval-style feudalism to something approaching industrialisation. Mohammed Ali is credited with introducing a public education system and with planting Egypt's fields with the

The Discovery of the Orient & its Subsequent Plunder

In the decades following Napoleon's doomed expedition and the wonders portrayed in *Description de l'Egypte,* Egypt attracted attention like no place ever before. During the 1820s, '30s and '40s the country was visited by a stream of adventurers and intrepid early travellers, including Mark Twain, Gustave Flaubert, Florence Nightingale and Richard Burton, translator of *The Thousand and One Nights.* The resulting accounts and journals were eagerly devoured by Western audiences enraptured by tales of temples in the sand, veiled harems and the bare-breasted women of the slave markets.

Artists too found Egypt a rich source of material and several made the journey to set up their easels in backstreets and before temples to record images little changed since the medieval days of the Mamluks. The most prolific was a Scot, David Roberts, who produced an immense body of work from Egypt and the Holy Lands that ensured him a fortune in his lifetime.

As a result of this import of fantastic images and texts, Europe and the 'civilised' world was swept by Egyptomania. Sphinxes and Pharaonic motifs adorned architecture from Melbourne to Chicago, operas were written around ancient Egyptian themes and a new vogue in painting was inspired. Known as Orientalism, this drew heavily on scenes of sensuous figures depicted against sumptuously ornate backgrounds, all usually a product of the artist's imagination aided by studio props and models, but lent an air of authenticity by the ultrarealist manner in which the canvases were painted. Now widely derided for its imperialistic and exploitative undertones, the Orientalist movement at the time attracted well-known practitioners including the respected French painters Ingres and Renoir.

The appetite for all things Egyptian didn't halt with words and images. The imperial powers had to have antiquities. Intent on dragging his country into the industrial age, Mohammed Ali, ruler of Egypt, readily gave away the obelisks that now adorn the Place de la Concorde in Paris, London's Embankment and Central Park in New York.

While some antiquities were presented as gifts, the core of the great collections of Egyptian antiquities at the British Museum in London, the Louvre in Paris, Germany's Berlin Museum and the Metropolitan Museum in New York were being built up with pieces hauled back as booty by wealthy traveller-collectors and treasure hunters. The most famous, an Italian circus strongman named Giovanni Belzoni, supplied the British with a huge bust of Ramses II looted from the Ramesseum, which now rests in the British Museum. The same museum also houses the famed Rosetta stone, originally discovered by the French but claimed by the British as spoils of war.

In recent years there have been requests from the Egyptian government for the return of key pieces including the Rosetta stone, a bust of Nefertiti held by the Berlin Museum and some statues of Hatshepsut held in New York. But although the Western fascination with 'Oriental' Egypt has long since abated, the chances of these treasures being returned is very slight.

valuable cash crop of cotton. While Egypt's ruler had a mania for all things new and foreign, conversely, during his reign, a growing number of foreigners became ever more fascinated by Egypt and all things 'Oriental': see the boxed text 'The Discovery of the Orient & its Subsequent Plunder'.

On his death, Mohammed Ali's preoccupations were taken up by his heirs who continued the work of implementing reforms and social projects, foremost of which were the establishment of the railway system, factories and a telegraph and postal system that was one of the first in the world. Egypt's fledgling cotton industry boomed as production in America was disrupted by civil war, and revenues were directed into ever grander schemes. Grandest of all was the Suez Canal, which opened to great fanfare and an audience composed of most of the crowned heads of Europe in 1869.

Egypt was attracting increasing numbers of foreign tourists. As early as 1860 Thomas Cook had begun leading organised tours down the Nile. Cairo had gained a large foreign population who were involved in running businesses and conducting trade and the place almost had the character of a gold rush town. The pickings were particularly rich for the European bankers who, with the connivance of their governments, bestowed lavish loans upon the Egyptian khedive Ismail for his grandiose schemes. They advanced the kind of money Egypt could never conceivably repay, at insatiable rates of interest, providing a convenient excuse for Britain to intervene in 1882 and announce that until such time as Egypt could repay its debts, it was taking control.

British Occupation

The British allowed the heirs of Mohammed Ali to remain on the throne but all real power was concentrated in the hands of the British agent. It has been written that the British viewed their role in Egypt as a stern sort of paternalism, acting for a country that couldn't look after itself but, more honestly, at the heart of the matter was the desire to ensure the security of the Suez Canal for continued British use. And while the British introduced a form of Egyptian legislative assembly and many local landowners benefited from the improved administration, the bottom line was that this was occupation by might. In this were sown the seeds of a national movement toward independence.

The Egyptians' desire for their self-determination was strengthened by the Allies' use of the country as a glorified barracks during WWI. Popular national sentiments were articulated by riots in 1919 and, more eloquently, by the likes of Saad Zaghloul, the most brilliant of an emerging breed of young Egyptian politicians, who said of the British, 'I have no quarrel with them personally but I want to see an independent Egypt'.

As a sop to the independence movement, the British allowed the formation of a nationalist political party, called the Wafd (Delegation), and granted Egypt its sovereignty. But this was very much an empty gesture; 'King' Fuad enjoyed little popularity among his people and the British kept tight hold of the reins. Moreover, they came in ever greater numbers with the outbreak of WWII. The war wasn't all bad news for the Egyptians, certainly not for the shopkeepers and businessmen who saw thousands of Allied soldiers pouring into the towns and cities with money to burn on 48-hour leave from the desert.

There was a vocal element that saw the Germans as potential liberators. Students held rallies in support of Rommel and in the Egyptian army a small cabal of officers, which included future presidents Nasser and Sadat, plotted to aid the German general's advance on their city.

Rommel pushed the Allied forces back almost to Alexandria, which had the British hurriedly burning documents in such quantity that the skies over Cairo turned dark with the ash, but the Germans did not break through. Instead, the British were to remain for almost 10 more years until a day of flames was to drive them out for good.

Independent Egypt

On Saturday, 26 January 1952, 'Black Saturday', Cairo was set on fire. After years of demonstrations, strikes and riots against foreign rule, the storming by the British of a rebellious Egyptian police station in the Suez Canal zone provided a spark that ignited the capital. Shops and businesses owned or frequented by foreigners were put to the torch by mobs and all the landmarks of 70 years of British rule were reduced to charred ruins within the space of a day.

The British must have realised that as far as they were concerned Egypt was ungovernable, so when just a few weeks later a group of young army officers seized power in a coup it was accepted as a *fait accompli*. On 26 July 1952, the Egyptian puppet-king

Farouk, descendant of the Albanian Mohammed Ali, departed Alexandria harbour aboard the royal yacht, leaving Egypt to be ruled by Egyptians for the first time since the pharaohs.

Colonel Gamal Abdel Nasser, leader of the revolutionary Free Officers, ascended to power and was confirmed as president in elections held in 1956. With the aim of returning Egypt to the long put-upon Egyptian peasantry, in an echo of the events of Russia in 1917, the country's landowners were dispossessed and their assets nationalised. This applied equally, if not more so, to foreigners, so while the country's huge foreign community was not forced to go, they nevertheless began to hurriedly sell up and stream out of the country.

The same year of his inauguration, the colonial legacy was finally and dramatically shaken off in full world view when Nasser successfully faced down Britain and France over the Suez Canal. To finance the building of a great dam that would control the flooding of the Nile, Nasser had announced his intention to nationalise the Suez Canal. The military attempt by the two former occupiers of Egypt to seize the waterway resulted in diplomatic embarrassment and undignified retreat, leaving Nasser the hero of the developing world, a sort of Robin Hood and Ramses rolled into one.

SARAH JOLLY

Colonel Gamal Abdel Nasser became the first president of an independent Egypt in 1956, ending a long-term colonial legacy.

Egypt became a beacon for all those countries in Africa and Asia that had recently thrown off European colonial administrations, and in particular to those of the Arab world, from Algeria to Iraq and Yemen. Nasser became the lauded spokesman of pan-Arabism.

War & Peace with Israel Little more than 10 years later, the brave new Egypt came crashing down. On 5 June 1967, Israel wiped out Egypt's airforce in a surprise attack. With it went the confidence and credibility of Nasser and his nation.

Relations with Israel had been hostile ever since its founding in 1948. Egypt had sent soldiers to aid the Palestinians in fighting the newly proclaimed Jewish state and ended up on the losing side. Since that time, the Arabs had kept up a barrage of anti-Zionist rhetoric. Although privately Nasser acknowledged that the Arabs would probably lose another war against Israel, for public consumption he gave rabble-rousing speeches about liberating Palestine. But he was a skilled orator and by early 1967 the mood engendered throughout the Arab world by these speeches was beginning to catch up with him. Soon, other Arab leaders started to accuse him of cowardice and of hiding behind the UN troops stationed in Sinai since the Suez Crisis. Nasser responded by ordering the peacekeepers out and blockading the Straits of Tiran, effectively closing the southern Israeli port of Eilat. He gave Israel reassurances that he wasn't going to attack but meanwhile massed his forces east of Suez. Israel struck first.

When the shooting stopped six days later Israel controlled all of the Sinai peninsula and had closed the Suez Canal which didn't reopen for another eight years. A humiliated Nasser offered to resign but in a spontaneous outpouring of support the Egyptian people wouldn't accept it and he remained in office. It was to be for only another three more years though as, abruptly in November 1970, the president dropped dead of a heart attack.

Anwar Sadat, Egypt's second president, instigated a complete about-face; where Nasser looked to the USSR for his inspiration, Sadat looked to the US. Out went socialist principles, in came capitalist opportunism. After a decade-and-a-half of keeping a low profile the wealthy resurfaced and were joined by a large, new moneyed middle class grown rich on the back of Sadat's much-touted *al-infitah* or 'open door policy'. Sadat also believed that to truly revitalise Egypt's economy he would have to deal with Israel. But first he needed bargaining power, a basis for negotiations.

On 6 October 1973, the Jewish holiday of Yom Kippur, Egypt launched a surprise attack across the Suez Canal. Its army beat back the much better armed Israelis and although these initial gains were later reversed, Egypt's national pride was restored. Sadat's negotiating strategy had succeeded.

In November 1977, Sadat travelled to Jerusalem to begin negotiating a peace with Israel, a process that ended two years later with the cosigning of the Camp David Agreement. Israel agreed to withdraw from Sinai while Egypt recognised Israel's right to exist. This was a complete abandonment of Nasser's pan-Arabist principles and Sadat's peace was viewed by the Arab world as no less than a betrayal. It cost Sadat his life: on 6 October 1981 as he observed a parade in commemoration of the 1973 War, one of his soldiers broke from the marching ranks and sprayed the presidential stand with gunfire. Sadat was killed instantly.

Islamic Extremism Sadat's assassin belonged to what are usually described for convenience as 'Muslim fundamentalists', a loose term for a collection of Islamic groups with a different vision for the state. Mass round-ups of Islamists and suspected Islamists were immediately carried out based on the orders of Sadat's successor Hosni Mubarak, a former air force general and vice president.

Less flamboyant than Sadat and less charismatic than Nasser, Mubarak has often been criticised as being both unimaginative and indecisive. Nevertheless, he managed to carry out a balancing act on several fronts, abroad and at home. To the irritation of more hardline states such as Syria and Libya, Mubarak was able to rehabilitate Egypt in the eyes of the Arab world, without abandoning the treaty with Israel. The Arab League headquarters, which was removed to Tunis in 1979 in protest at Sadat's recognition of the Jewish state, was returned to Cairo in 1990. And for almost a decade he managed to keep the lid on the Islamist extremists.

But in the early 1990s the lid blew off. Despite its use of religious symbolism the Islamists is essentially a political movement that has grown out of harsh socioeconomic conditions. In the 1980s discontent had been brewing among the poorer sections of society. Government promises had failed to keep up with the population explosion and a generation of youths were finding themselves without jobs and living in squalid, overcrowded housing with little or no hope for the future. With a repressive political system that allowed little chance to legitimately voice opposition, the only hope lay with the Islamic parties and their calls for change.

Denied recognition by the state as a legal political entity, the Islamists turned to force. There were frequent attempts on the life of the president and his ministers and frequent clashes with the security forces. Perhaps even more alarmingly, the matter escalated from a domestic issue to a matter of international concern when the Islamists began to target one of the state's most vulnerable and valuable sources of income: tourists.

Several groups of foreign tourists were shot at or bombed in the last months of 1992 and at the start of 1993 resulting in a handful of deaths. The government responded with a heavy-handed lightning crackdown arresting thousands and introducing the death penalty for terrorism. Egypt, after all, remains a police state, if a less repressive one than others in the region. Justice here is not for the squeamish. Human rights groups were up in arms at the mass arrests and reports of confessions extracted by torture and other police brutalities but by the mid-1990s the violence had receded from the capital, retreating to the religious heartland of middle Egypt. The Egyptian government proclaimed the Islamist extremists 'utterly crushed'.

Egypt Today

Egypt is on a slow but gradual climb. Over the last decade or so the country's public debt has fallen. Foreign currency reserves have climbed. Inflation is under control. Population growth has been checked. The Egyptian president is a respected guarantor of peace and is a vital ally of the West in the Middle East. On the home front, the government looks stable. But as anyone who wasn't on Mars in late 1997 knows, terrorist violence is far from being completely a thing of the past in Egypt. The sickening one-two of the fire bomb attack on a tour bus outside the Egyptian Museum in Cairo, followed a few weeks later by the massacre of holiday-makers at the Temple of Hatshepsut in Luxor, stunned the whole world. The world responded by staying away and tourism figures quickly plummeted.

Since that time Egypt has been frantically wooing back the holiday-makers with high profile events such as opera at the Pyramids and shopping festivals and millions spent on tourist office advertising. It is a strategy that seems to have paid off; over five million tourists visited in 2000, the highest number ever, and at the time of writing Egypt's international profile is all pharaohs and frolicking at the Red Sea. It's an attractive combination but one that's very much at odds with the Egypt experienced by the majority of the 65-plus million people who actually live there. Until more is done to bridge this disparity the sunny outlook of the tourist posters is bound to remain tinged with the threat of dark clouds.

History Updates

There's not a year goes by without one or more significant finds being made in Egypt, all adding to the sum of historical knowledge of this ancient region. Since the last edition of this guide the big find has been at the Western Desert oasis of Bahariyya where a fantastic cache of mummies was unearthed, many adorned with gilded golden masks (see the boxed text 'Mummies of Gold' in the Western Oases chapter). Less spectacular, but of immense value for what they reveal about the lives of the men and women who built the Pyramids, are the Workmen's Tombs and Village currently being excavated at Giza. One of several new Old Kingdom tombs recently discovered includes a curse painted on the wall that threatens thieves with death by hippo, crocodile and snake. Meanwhile, off the Mediterranean coast east of Alexandria (where diving continues on what may or may not be Cleopatra's sunken palace: see the boxed text 'Cleopatra's Palace' in the Alexandria & the Mediterranean Coast chapter) the nautical archaeologists have rediscovered the Ptolemaic cities of Canopus, Herkaleion and Menouthis beneath the bay of Abu Qir. Monumental statues stand in front of ruined temples 10m below the surface, along with the ghostly shapes of shops and houses, all shedding light on this complex period of Egyptian history.

According to Egypt's most famous Egyptologist, Zahi Hawass, the finds are set to continue: 'You never know what the sands of Egypt might hold. We have discovered only 30% of our monuments. Still 70% remains buried.'

With thanks to the *Egypt Almanac*

GEOGRAPHY

For most Egyptians the Nile Valley is home. Although the country covers roughly one million square kilometres, some 90% of the population is confined to the narrow carpet of fertile land bordering the great river. To the south the river is hemmed in by mountains and the agricultural plain is narrow, but as it flows north the land becomes flatter and the valley widens to 20km to 30km in width.

To the east of the valley is the Eastern (Arabian) Desert, a barren plateau bounded on its eastern edge by a high ridge of mountains that rises to more than 2000m and extends for about 800km. To the west is the Western (Libyan) Desert, which comprises two-thirds of the land surface of Egypt, but if you ignore the political boundaries on the map it stretches right across the top of North Africa under its better-known name of the Sahara Desert. Suffering extremes of temperature, barren and forbidding, the desert is not completely devoid of life. A series of wind-sculpted depressions allow water to come to the surface, thereby creating a string of cultivatable oases.

In addition to the Nile, the capital, Cairo, also demarcates Egyptian geography. It lies roughly at the point where the Nile splits into several tributaries and the valley becomes a 200km-wide delta, a vast green fan of fertile countryside running into the Mediterranean Sea. Burdened with the task of providing for the whole of the rest of the country, this delta region ranks among the world's most intensely cultivated lands. Everything north of Cairo is known as 'Lower Egypt', while everything to the south is loosely known as 'Upper Egypt'.

To the east, across the Suez Canal, is the triangular wedge of Sinai. A geological extension of the Eastern Desert, terrain here slopes from the high mountain ridges, which include Mt Sinai and Mt Katherine (or Gebel Katarina, the highest mountain in Egypt, at 2642m) in the south, to desert coastal plains and lagoons in the north.

CLIMATE

Egypt's climate is easy to summarise. Hot and dry. This holds for most of the country for most of the year, with the exception of the winter months of December, January and February, which can be quite cold in the north. Average temperatures range from 20°C (68°F) on the Mediterranean coast to 26°C (80°F) in Aswan. Maximum temperatures for the same places can get up

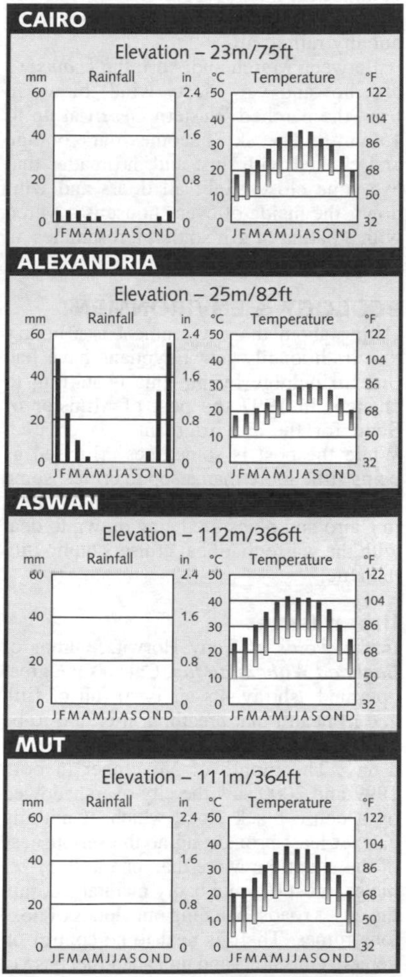

to 31°C (88°F) and 50°C (122°F) respectively. At night in winter the temperature sometimes plummets to as low as 8°C in Cairo and along the Mediterranean coast. In the desert it's even more extreme – often scorching during the day and bitterly cold at night.

Alexandria receives the most rain, approximately 19cm a year, while far to the south in Aswan, the average is about 10mm every five years. Kharga in the Western Desert once went 17 years without any rain at all.

Between March and April the *khamsi* (a dry, hot and very dusty wind) blows in from the parched Western Desert at up to 150km/h. The sky becomes dark orange and choked with dust and, no matter that everyone closes tight all doors and windows, the inside of every house is covered with a patina of grit so that it resembles an undisturbed tomb.

ECOLOGY & ENVIRONMENT

Caring about the environment is a luxury that traditionally few Egyptians have had time to indulge in, but this is starting to change. In 1997 the post of Minister of State for the Environment was created. While the post is sometimes criticised as being little more than a sop to critics, some action has been taken on industrial polluters in Cairo and plans are being drawn to deal with the waste that boat cruisers dump into the Nile.

Urban Issues

In the words of Tony Horwitz, author of *Baghdad Without a Map*, Cairo is the great upturned ashtray. Its air is so full of filth and ill health that breathing it is said to be equivalent to smoking a packet of cigarettes a day. The month of November in both 1999 and 2000 saw the city overshadowed by a dense black cloud which, if nothing else, at least brought home the seriousness of the situation. More than one million vehicles, most old and badly maintained, jam the city's roads, belching out clouds of noxious fumes. There is next to no control on vehicle emissions and unleaded fuel has yet to catch on. Add to that the factories on the edge of town that spew crap into the air and the net result is that Cairo may well be the world's second–most polluted urban centre after Mexico City. The US Agency for International Development (USAID) reports that Cairo has the world's highest levels of lead and suspended solid particles (the main cause of respiratory problems), accounting for somewhere between 10,000 and 25,000 deaths per year.

The government is finally sufficiently alarmed to do something about all this: factories are now required to install filters (reportedly, few have done so); there are now several thousand taxis running on liquid natural gas; and a US$200 million USAID-sponsored air improvement project has been launched. But it's very little and for the time being residents of Cairo are forced to resign themselves to the incredibly nasty habit of passive smoking.

The other big problem is overcrowding. Although the latest census results show that Egypt's population growth rate is falling, some 90% of the population is squeezed into about 5% of the country's total land mass. The Nile Valley is in danger of becoming one large sprawling city. Cairo alone holds 14 to 16 million people. By the government's own admission, parts of the city continue to house the densest number of people per kilometre anywhere in the world. The strain placed on the city's decaying infrastructure is enormous and more than it can cope with. The result is one of the world's most lethal public transport systems with a regular roll call of train wrecks and bus smashes; as well as cities of hastily thrown up buildings which all too frequently crash to the ground again, with horrific consequences.

Country-Wide Issues

Ill-planned touristic development remains one of the biggest threats to the Red Sea coast and Sinai. The construction of a new airport halfway between Al-Quseir and Marsa Alam is expected to unleash a frenzy of development along this wild coastline. There are fewer than 15 places along here where people can enter the sea without stepping on coral. Environmentalists are worried that the 100-plus hotels planned for this area will simply dump sand on the coral to let their guests swim more easily.

In Sinai, the coast north of Nuweiba is already the site of a building boom and a wall of resorts is connecting the town to the border crossing of Taba. Whether or not the businessmen investing in the area will make good on their promises to protect the reefs around the area remains to be seen. Given their past record there is little reason to believe them.

So far, though, the solid waste generated by the thousands of visitors who come here remains one of the peninsula's biggest problems. In Dahab, for example, periodic cleanups of the beaches and reefs have been rendered useless by the municipality's refusal to allocate land for a dump (at the moment all the area's garbage is put at the end of a wadi prone to flooding; what is not blown away by the constant wind is periodically swept down into the sea with flash floods, choking coral and marine life).

It may be impossible to repair dead corals but existing hotels that were built without consideration for their environment can be improved. New 'green' guidelines for running hotels are being trialled under a joint US-Egyptian Red Sea Sustainable Tourism Initiative (RSSTI). Recommendations focus on energy use, water conservation and handling and disposal of waste, including simple measures such as installing foot pedal taps at sinks that make it harder to leave water running. Pilot hotels in the scheme include the Sheraton Miramar at Al-Gouna, the Soma Bay Sheraton, the Shams Allam and Kahramana resorts in Marsa Allam and the Utopia Beach Club in Al-Quseir.

Responsible Tourism

Tourism is vital to the Egyptian economy and the country would be in a mess without it but, at the same time, millions of visitors a year can't help but add to the ecological and environmental overload. As long as outsiders have been stumbling upon or searching for the wonders of ancient Egypt, they have also been crawling all over them, chipping bits off or leaving their own contributions engraved in the stones. This is no longer sustainable. The organised menace of mass tourism threatens to destroy the very monuments that visitors come to see. At sites such as the Valley of the Kings, thousands of visitors a day mill about in cramped tombs designed for one occupant. The deterioration of the painted wall reliefs alarms archaeologists whose calls for limits on the numbers of visitors have largely fallen on deaf ears. Even the Pyramids, which have so far survived 4500 years, are suffering. Cracks have begun to appear in inner chambers and in this case, authorities have been forced to limit visitors and to close the great structures periodically to give them a bit of rest and recuperation. It can only be a matter of time before similar measures are enforced elsewhere.

In the meantime, it's up to you, the tourist, to behave responsibly. Don't be tempted to baksheesh guards so you can use your flash in tombs. Don't clamber over toppled pillars and statues. Don't touch painted reliefs. It's all just common sense.

The same goes with adventuring off-road in protected areas such as Ras Mohammed. True, you're in the middle of nowhere and who's going to know anyway? But it's illegal to drive off the beaten tracks and the fragile desert environment needs you to enforce this law.

Few places in Egypt are likely to win a tidy-town award: inadequate waste disposal and little regard for the environmental issues that are popular in the West produces some ugly sights. But some of the refuse – plastic mineral water bottles for instance – is actually recycled, so don't be too quick to point an accusing finger at the Egyptians. More than one traveller has reported being disgusted by the garbage left behind by visitors climbing Mt Sinai. Try not to add to it.

Now that the Ministry of Tourism, not known for its attention to environmental considerations, is actively promoting the Western Desert and the oases as a tourist destination, this is another area that is coming increasingly under threat from environmental damage. A boom in so-called adventure tourism in this remote place is already leaving its mark on the landscape: garbage can sometimes be seen rolling over the dunes of the Great Sand Sea and visitors have made off with many of the fossil remains that lie throughout the area. Despite crackdowns on illegal desert hunting, parties of Gulf Arabs and others continue to arrive with high-tech weaponry and shoot the species that they have decimated in their own lands – sometimes with the Egyptian military acting as a guide.

There have been some positive developments too. At the end of 1997 Nuweiba saw the establishment of a recycling program to deal with its solid waste problem. Moreover, there are now five protected areas in Sinai. A National Parks office has also been created in Hurghada and it is hoping to rein in some of the more grandiose development plans in the Marsa Alam area. Finally, the government is looking into environmentally friendly tourism as a marketing strategy and Egypt's first ecolodge has been built in Siwa Oasis and is expected to be the prototype for more sensitive touristic development.

FLORA & FAUNA

Egypt is often described as being about 94% desert. Such a figure conjures up images of vast, barren wastelands where nothing can live. But that's not the case. While there are areas that are extremely arid and incapable of supporting life, there are also plenty of desert regions where fragile ecosystems have adapted over millennia to extremely hostile conditions. For more information on desert flora, see the boxed text 'Balancing Sinai's Ecosystem' in the Sinai chapter. You could also pick up *Natural Selections: A Year of Egypt's Wildlife*, written and illustrated by Richard Hoath and published locally by the American University in Cairo Press; it's a passionate account of the birds, animals, insects and marine creatures that make Egypt their home.

Flora

The lotus that symbolises ancient Egypt can be found, albeit rarely, in the Delta area, but the papyrus reed, depicted in ancient art as vast swamps where the pharaohs hunted hippos, has been lost. Except for one clump found in 1968 in Wadi Natrun, papyrus can only be found in botanical gardens.

More than a hundred kinds of grasses thrive in areas where there is water, and the date palm is to be seen in virtually every cultivable area. Along with tamarisk and acacia, the imported jacaranda and poinciana (red and orange flowers) have come to mark Egyptian summers with their vivid colours. You'll also see a water hyacinth, known as the 'Nile rose', choking parts of the Nile and many canals.

In Ras Mohammed National Park in Sinai, there is a stand of mangroves which, according to environmentalists, is the second most northerly mangrove group in the world. These trees live in salt water and are extremely important to the area's ecosystem.

Fauna

Mammals Egypt is home to about a hundred types of mammals. There are still a few exotic species about, however, the most common critters are house mice, black and brown rats, and bats. You'll be lucky to see anything other than camels, donkeys and, to a lesser extent, domesticated horses and buffaloes.

Egypt's deserts used to be sanctuaries for an amazing variety of larger mammals, such as the leopard, cheetah, oryx, aardwolf (which feeds on termites), striped hyena and caracal (a desert lynx with long black ear tufts). All of these, however, have been brought to the brink of extinction through hunting. In fact, there's only one known family of cheetah still living in Egypt, and many years have passed since a leopard was sighted. Other creatures such as the sand cat (the soles of their feet are covered in fur to aid hunting), the Fennec fox (the world's smallest vulpine) and the Nubian ibex (the males of this species have long, backswept horns) are very occasionally sighted.

There are three types of gazelle in Egypt: the Arabian, Dorcas and White. The first species is thought to be extinct, and of the other two groups only individual sightings are made these days, despite the fact that herds of Dorcas gazelle were, up until 30 or so years ago, common features of the desert landscape.

The zorilla, a kind of weasel, lives in the Gebel Elba region, while in Sinai you may see rock hyrax: small creatures about the size of a large rabbit which, like elephants (whom they're most closely related to), live in large groups and are extremely sociable.

Birds About 430 species have been sighted in Egypt, of which about one-third actually breed in Egypt, while most of the others are passage migrants or winter visitors. Each year an estimated one to two million large birds migrate via certain routes from Europe to Africa through Egypt. Most large birds, including flamingo, stork, crane, heron, and all large birds of prey are protected under Egyptian law.

The most ubiquitous birds are the house sparrow and the hooded crow; one of the most distinctive is the hoopoe. This bird, which has cinnamon tones, has a head shaped very much like a hammer and, when excited, it extends its crest. Hoopoes are often seen hunting for insects in gardens in central Cairo, though they're more commonly found in the countryside.

For information on bird-watching, see Activities in the Facts for the Visitor chapter.

Marine Life See Marine Life in the Diving the Red Sea chapter for details on Egypt's marine life.

Other Creatures Some 34 species of snakes live in Egypt. The best known is the cobra, which featured on the headdress of the ancient pharaohs. Another one to see is the horned viper, a thickset snake that has horns over its eyes to keep the sand out when it buries itself.

There are plenty of scorpions throughout the country and, although some are capable of a fatal sting, they're largely nocturnal and rarely seen. Be careful if you are lifting up stones as they like to burrow into cool spots.

Once plentiful up and down the length of the Nile, crocodiles have been extinct north of the Aswan Dam since 1891 when the last one was shot by a British officer. These days they are protected and live only in Lake Nasser south of the High Dam near Aswan.

GOVERNMENT & POLITICS

Egypt has been a republic since 1952, when the army overthrew the monarchy. The bulk of power is concentrated in the hands of the president (present incumbent, Mohammed Hosni Mubarak), who is nominated by the People's Assembly and elected by popular referendum for six years. In September 1999 Mubarak was re-elected for a fourth term with a mandate of 94% – not so much an absolute endorsement of the candidate, more a reflection of the fact that there are no alternatives. The president himself admits democracy in Egypt is 'limited' and it would be fair to say that the country operates under a benign dictatorship. There are no serious opposition parties to Mubarak's ruling National Democratic Party (NDP). The most important group is the Muslim Brotherhood, which in the late 1980s and early '90s built up a massive following, particularly among the poor, and was subsequently banned. In the last elections most seats were contested by rivals from within the NDP.

The president appoints vice presidents and ministers, as well as 10 members of the 454-member People's Assembly and 70 of the 210-member Majlis ash-Shura (Advisory Council).

ECONOMY

The four pillars of the Egyptian economy are oil and gas, Suez Canal revenues, remittances from Egyptians working abroad and tourism. The oil comes from fields in the Red Sea, and more oil and gas finds in the Western Desert have boosted hopes of continuing export profits to be made from that sector. An estimated 7% of the world's cargo passes through the world's oldest trans-sea canal and the dues paid pour close to US$2 billion per year into the Egyptian state coffers. Meanwhile, Egyptians working abroad in Libya, Iraq, and particularly in Gulf countries such as Kuwait and Saudi Arabia send home some US$3 billion a year from jobs abroad. The top earner though is tourism, which is Egypt's fastest growing sector. According to the Egyptian Ministry of Tourism, the country hosted five million visitors in 1999/2000, which represents a doubling of numbers in a little over five years. Tourist spending is currently worth $4.3 billion a year to Egypt. Plans are to double the number of tourist arrivals to a massive 9.5 million by 2005.

Egypt also remains a big exporter of cotton, the crop introduced to the country in the 19th century by its reformist-minded ruler Mohammed Ali. It also exports large quantities of maize, wheat, fruit and vegetables.

POPULATION

Egypt is the most populous country in the Arab world and has the second highest population in Africa after Nigeria. Its population has, in a sense, become its greatest problem – see Urban Issues under Ecology & Environment earlier in this chapter. From about 6.5 million people at the first census in 1882, the population was counted at 65.5 million in 2000. With annual growth of about 1.8%, or more than a million new bodies every year, it hardly seems to matter what Egypt does to improve its economic situation, the gains are always eaten up by the extra mouths to feed and people to house.

Despite efforts to spread the population over as wide an area as possible, the major cities (in particular Cairo and Alexandria) continue to become ever more densely packed. Some 14 to 16 million people, or almost a quarter of the entire country's population, lives in the Greater Cairo area alone. There are more Cairenes than there are Austrians, Belgians or Greeks. There are about a further five million in Alexandria and outlying zones.

One result of the rapid population growth is that half the population is now under 18 years; a quarter is aged 10 or under. This could potentially fuel an economic resurgence except that the government is unable to construct schools and train teachers quickly enough to keep up.

PEOPLE

According to anthropologists, the ancestors of the Egyptians include many races and ethnic groups. Most Egyptians will proudly tell you that they are descendants of the ancient Egyptians, and while there is a strand of truth in this, any Pharaonic blood still flowing in modern veins has been seriously diluted. The country has weathered numerous invasions of Libyans, Persians, Greeks, Romans and, most significantly, the 4000 Arab horsemen who invaded Egypt in AD 641, all of whom have been assimilated. Following the Arab conquest, there was significant Arab migration and intermarriage with the indigenous population. The Mamluks, rulers of Egypt between the 13th and 16th centuries, were of Turkic and Circassian origins, and then there were the Ottoman Turks, rulers from 1517 until the latter years of the 18th century. They all also intermarried with the locals, especially with its elite ranks. There's even a particular kind of fair-skinned, blue-eyed, blonde-haired Egyptian girl, known as 'Rashidi' (after the Mediterranean port) who, the myth goes, is a descendent of unions between Egyptian women and Napoleon's French soldiers.

Beside the Egyptians, there are a handful of separate indigenous groups with ancient roots, notably the Bedouin, Berbers and Nubians.

Bedouins

The ancestors of Egypt's Bedouins migrated from the Arabian Peninsula. They settled the harshest, most desolate parts of the Western and Eastern Deserts and Sinai. The numbers of Bedouin in Egypt these days are around 500,000, but their nomadic way of existence is under threat as the interests of the rest of the country are increasingly intruding into their previously isolated domains (see the boxed text 'Sinai's Bedouin' in the Sinai chapter).

Berbers

A small number of Berbers who settled in the west of the country, particularly in and around Siwa, have retained much of their own identity. They are quite easily distinguished from other Egyptians by, for instance, the dress of the women – usually in *meliyyas* (head-to-toe garments with slits for the eyes). Although many speak Arabic, they have preserved their own language.

Nubians

Tall and with darker skin than the average Egyptian, the Nubians are the bridge between Egypt and Africa. They originate from Nubia, the region between Aswan in the south of Egypt and Khartoum in Sudan, a land that almost completely disappeared in the 1970s when the High Dam was created and the subsequent build-up of water behind it drowned their traditional lands (see the Lower Nubia & Lake Nasser section in The Nile Valley – Esna to Abu Simbel chapter).

EDUCATION

Although nine years of primary school education are supposedly compulsory in Egypt, and about 97% of children from six to 15 attend school, the adult illiteracy rate is estimated to be around 37% for men and over 60% for women. Those who are literate have usually received inferior education because classes are often too large for individual attention.

Secondary education lasts for six years, beginning at 11 years of age. Only 7.3% of the population emerges with a university degree. Even so, many graduates do not find active employment in their field of training and it's not uncommon to find lawyers, engineers and other professionals working for their brother's factory or driving taxis. Many professionals (and a good number of the less educated) are compelled to seek work in other Arab countries, which at least has the beneficial effect of boosting Egypt's national revenue.

Egyptian men have to do three years' military service. If they complete high school it's reduced to two years; if they go through university it's dropped to one. Only sons are exempt from service.

ARTS

Literature

Awarded the Nobel Prize for Literature in 1988, Naguib Mahfouz can claim to have single-handedly shaped the nature of Arabic literature this century. Born in 1911 in Cairo's Islamic quarter, Mahfouz began writing when he was 17. His first efforts were very much influenced by European models, but over the course of his long writing career he developed a voice that was uniquely of the Arab world and that drew its inspiration from the talk in the coffeehouses and the dialect and slang of Cairo's streets. His ability to write was savagely ended in 1994 by a knife attack that left the author partially paralysed.

His masterpiece is usually considered to be *The Cairo Trilogy*, a generational saga of family life set in the districts of Mahfouz's youth, but also well worth reading are *Midaq Alley*, a soap operatic portrayal of life in a poor back-alley in Islamic Cairo, and *The Harafish*, perhaps the definitive Mahfouz book, written in an episodic, almost folkloric style that owes much to the tradition of *The Thousand and One Nights*.

On the strength of what's available in English it's all too easy to view Egyptian literature as beginning and ending with Mahfouz, but he's only the best known of a canon of respected writers that includes Taha Hussein, a blind author and intellectual who spent much of his life in trouble with whichever establishment happened to

Recommended Reading

If you're new to Egyptian writers then the following is a shortlist of 10 must-read books, all of which are (or have been) available in English-language translations.

Beer at the Snooker Club by Waguih Ghali. Fantastic novel that deserves to be far better known; the Egyptian *Catcher in the Rye*.

A Daughter of Isis by Nawal al-Saadawi. Autobiographical work that has completely divided critics over the author's sour take on the world.

The Golden Chariot by Salwa Bakr. Inmates in a women's prison exchange life stories; surprisingly upbeat, funny, even bawdy.

The Harafish by Naguib Mahfouz. The desert-island choice if we were allowed only one work by Mahfouz, but everything he's done is worth reading.

The Map of Love by Ahdaf Soueif. Bestselling (in the UK) historical novel about love and clashing cultures.

No One Sleeps in Alexandria by Ibrahim Abdel Meguid. An antidote to Durrell; wartime Alexandria as viewed by two poor denizens of the city.

Proud Beggars by Albert Cossery. Egyptian but resident in Paris since 1945. His novels are widely available in French, less so in English, not at all in Arabic.

Rings of Brass & Other Stories by Yousef Idris. Some absolute crackers in here.

The Tent by Miral al-Tahawy. Bleak but beautiful tale of the slow descent into madness of a crippled Bedouin girl.

Zayni Barakat by Gamal al-Ghitani. Intrigue, backstabbing and general Machiavellian goings-on in the twilight of Mamluk-era Cairo.

be in power, the Alexandrian Tewfiq Hakim, and Yousef Idris, a writer of powerful short stories based on his own life experiences. Unfortunately, none of these authors has gained anything like the international attention they deserve and they're only published in English-language editions by the AUC Press, a small Cairo-based academic publishing house.

Curiously, though under-represented at home, Egypt's women writers are arguably enjoying more international success than the men. Nawal al-Saadawi's fictional work *Woman At Point Zero* has been published, at last count, in 28 languages. An outspoken critic on behalf of women, she is very much marginalised at home – her nonfiction book *The Hidden Face of Eve*, which considers the role of women in the Arab world, is banned in Egypt and for many years Saadawi was also forced to stay out of the country after Islamists issued death threats against her.

Equally as forthright and uncompromising is Salwa Bakr, another writer who tackles taboo subjects such as sexual prejudice and social inequality. All of which is a world away from Egypt's current best known cultural export, Ahdaf Soueif. Though Egyptian, born and brought up in Cairo, she's something of an anomaly in that she writes in English. She lives and is published in London, where she's very much part of the UK literary scene. So far, most of her work has yet to appear in Arabic. Her 790-page coming-of-age (and highly autobiographical) novel about a middle-class Cairene girl *In the Eye of the Sun* and her two short-story collections *Aisha* and *Sandpiper* flit between grey, drizzly Britain and the close, muggy city of her birth. The predominant theme of much of her work is, unsurprisingly, the notion of foreignness. Her latest novel *The Map of Love* was shortlisted for the UK's most prestigious literary prize, the Booker. Although she didn't win, her profile is sky high and the book remains on the bestseller lists.

Painting

While Egypt has produced one or two outstanding painters, contemporary art is very much in the doldrums. The problem stems from the Egyptian art school system, where a student's success largely depends on their ability to emulate the artistic styles favoured or practiced by their professors. Nepotism reigns over originality and as a result much of what finds its way into the galleries is of very dubious merit. Unsurprisingly, some of the most interesting work comes from artists with no formal training at all. Such artists are often shunned by the state-run galleries but there are several private exhibition spaces that are happy to show nonconformist work. Anyone seriously interested in contemporary art should visit the Cairo-Berlin, Mashrabia or Townhouse galleries in Cairo (see that chapter for addresses and opening times).

Things have not always been so stagnant and it is worth paying a visit to Cairo's National Museum of Modern Egyptian Art in the Opera House grounds in Gezira. In particular look out for the work of Abdel Hady al-Gazzar, a true one-off, who painted Egypt as a kind of colourful but slightly freakish circus. The rich, warm portraits of Alexandrian Mahmoud Said, several of which hang in the museum, are also strikingly beautiful. Said also has a museum devoted to his work in his home city (see Mahmoud Said Museum in the Alexandria & the Mediterranean Coast chapter).

For more information there's a good book by Lilliane Karnouk, *Modern Egyptian Art*, or pick up Fatma Ismail's *29 Artists in the Museum of Egyptian Modern Art*; both are available at the art museum and at the Mashrabia gallery in Cairo. There's also a Web site (W www.elzamzamy.com) with a growing gallery of contemporary Egyptian art accompanied by brief biographies.

Music

Unlike literature and painting, which are take-it-or-leave-it affairs, there's no getting away from music in Egypt. Taking a taxi, shopping or just walking the streets; the routines of daily life are played out to a constant musical accompaniment blasted from wheezing, tinny cassette players. The music you hear can be broadly divided into two categories: classical and pop. Down in the south of the country you're also likely to come across some more regional music types – see the boxed texts 'Saidi Music' in the Nile Valley – Luxor chapter and 'Nubian Music' in the Nile Valley – Esna to Abu Simbel chapter.

Classical In the 1940s and '50s, classical Arabic music peaked. It fitted the age. These were the golden days of a rushing tide of nationalism and then, later, of Nasser's rule when Cairo was the virile heart of the Arab-speaking world. Its singers were icons and through the radio their impassioned words captured and inflamed the spirits of listeners from Algiers to Baghdad. Chief icon of all was Umm Kolthum, the most famous Arab singer of the 20th century. Her protracted love songs and *qasa'id* (long poems) were the very expression of the Arab world's collective identity. Egypt's love affair with Umm Kolthum was such that on the afternoon of the first Thursday of each month, streets would become deserted as the whole country sat beside a radio to listen to her regular live-broadcast performance.

She had her male counterparts in Abdel Halim Hafez and Farid al-Attrache but they

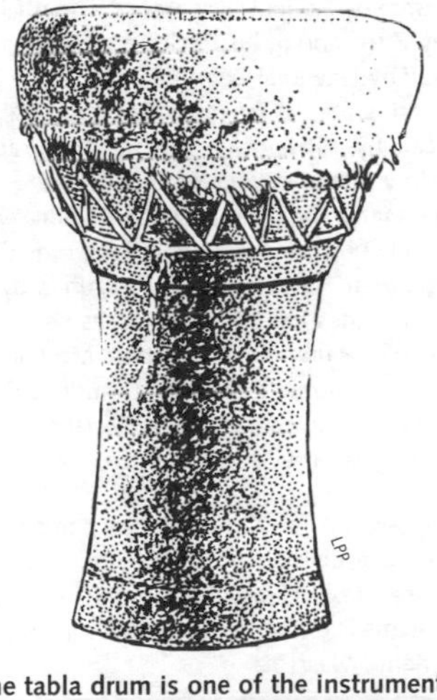

The tabla drum is one of the instruments used in classical Arabic music.

never attracted anything like the devotion accorded to 'Al-Sitt' (the Lady). She sang well into the mid-1970s, and when she died in 1975 her death caused havoc with millions of grieving Egyptians pouring out onto the streets of Cairo.

Her cassettes still sell as well now as any platinum pop and her presence is strongly felt in the media, including a radio station that broadcasts four hours of her music daily. Her appeal hasn't been purely confined to the Arab world either. In an article in *Vanity Fair* magazine in 2000, Elvis Costello nominated an Umm Kolthum anthology as one of his '500 albums you need,' while former Led Zeppelin vocalist Robert Plant has said that one of his lifetime ambitions is to reform the Middle Eastern Orchestra, Umm Kolthum's group of backing musicians (he and Jimmy Page have toured backed by an Egyptian orchestra). The kind of orchestra in question is a curious cross-fertilisation of East and West, with the instruments familiar to Western ears augmented by the *oud* (a type of lute), *nai* (reed pipe), *qanun* (zither) and tabla (a small hand-held drum).

Pop Although to this day the likes of Umm Kolthum and Abdel Halim Hafez are still eulogised and revered, as Egypt experienced a population boom and the mean age decreased, a gap in popular cult-

Recommended Listening

The following 10 tapes/CDs together will give you a pretty good taster of what Egyptian music is about. You never know, you might even get to like it. Some of these are available internationally on CD.

Aho by Hakim. 'Hey People' – a loud, anthemic shout rooted in a traditional *shaabi* (popular) sound.

Awadouny by Amr Diab. Slick, slick, slick – Spanish guitars and huge sing-along choruses from Egypt's answer to Ricky Martin.

Inta Omri by Umm Kolthum. Sixty minutes long and an absolute classic. Also try Fakharuni and Al-Atlal.

Khosara by Abdel Halim Hafez. The riff from this song was apparently ripped off by US rapper Jay-Z for one of his tracks.

Layali by Nawal al-Zoghby. She may be Lebanese but she's huge in Egypt, helped no end by fronting a local TV campaign for Pepsi.

Lo Laki by Ali Hameida. Pivotal 1988 track that set the formula for much of the Egyptian pop to follow. Listen at your peril.

Maatadarsh by Shaaban Abdel Rahim. A former ironing man and the shaabiest of shaabi singers, hugely popular for singing the words that few others in the public spotlight would dare say.

Nagham al-Hawa by Warda. Algerian by birth but an honorary Cairene by residency. This double CD includes her best, 'Batwanes Beek'.

Fi'Ishq al-Banat by Mohammed Mounir. Latest album by the thinking person's pop star, a Nubian who fuses traditional Arabic music with jazz.

Zahma by Ahmed Adawiyya. Social comment (the title means crowded) from the 1970s when Adawiyya's irreverent backstreet sound was at the peak of its popularity.

Also look out for *Yalla* (1990) a compilation of Egyptian street music released by Mango Records, which is a division of Island. Also, *Songs From The City Victorious*, a collaboration between Jaz Coleman (ex-Killing Joke), Anne Dudley (ex-Art of Noise) and a bunch of Egyptian musicians. The Egyptians like it so much that it's all over state TV. It's available on cheap cassette in Egypt under the name *Masryat*.

ure developed which the memory of the greats couldn't fill. Enter Ahmed Adawiyya, who did for Arabic music what punk did in the West. Throwing out traditional melodies and melodramas, his backstreet, streetwise and, to some, politically subversive songs captured the spirit of the times and dominated popular culture throughout the entire 1970s.

Adawiyya set the blueprint for a new kind of music known as *al-jeel* (the generation), characterised by a clattering, handclapping rhythm overlaid with synthesised twirling and a catchy, repetitive vocal. Highly formularised, poorly recorded and mass-produced on cheap cassettes, this form of Egyptian pop was always tacky and highly disposable. That's changing fast as in recent years the Cairo sound is getting ever more chic and slickly produced as the big name artists look toward the international market. Head of the pack is Amr Diab, the chubby foremost purveyor of Western-style pop.

Adawiyya's legacy also spawned something called *shaabi* (from the word for popular), which is considered the real music of the working class; it's much cruder than al-jeel and its lyrics are often satirical or politically provocative. The acceptable face of shaabi is TV-friendly Hakim, whose albums regularly sell around the million mark. However, most other shaabi artists are considered too close to the bone and kept well away from state media.

But while the greatest names in 20th-century Arabic music were nearly all Egyptian, that's not the case in the 21st. The majority of current big sellers in Cairo cassette shops hail from Lebanon, Syria, Tunisia and even Iraq. It's something of a sore point. The consolation is that Egypt still provides the best backing musicians, song writers and production facilities in the Arab world, not to mention the biggest audiences.

UK-Egypt Remix

An Anglo-Arab with her roots in Egypt and Morocco, Natacha Atlas is an ethno-techno diva whose work fuses traditional Egyptian songwriting, orchestrations and vocals with a London dance club sensibility. Although she can be guilty of over-playing the Oriental card and indulging in unnecessary warbling, she nonetheless has a cult following and has worked with a number of cutting-edge artists including TransGlobal Underground, David Arnold and Nitin Sawhney. She's released four albums to date recorded jointly in Cairo and London: *Diaspora* (1995), *Halim* (1997), *Gedida* (1998) and *Ayeshteni* (2000).

Belly Dance

Tomb paintings in Egypt prove that the tradition of formalised dancing goes back as far as the pharaohs. During medieval times dancing became institutionalised in the form of the *ghawazee*, a cast of dancers who travelled with storytellers and poets and performed publicly or for hire, rather like the troubadours of medieval Europe. Performances were often segregated, with women dancers either performing for other women or appearing before men veiled.

The arrival of 19th-century European travellers irrevocably changed this tradition. Religious authorities, outraged that Muslim women were performing for 'infidel' men, pressured the government to impose heavy taxes on the dancers. When the high prices failed to stop the Western thrill seekers, the dancers were banished from Cairo. Cut off from most of their clientele, many turned to prostitution to survive. For intrepid male travellers, this only increased their allure and they went out of their way to fulfil their erotic fantasies. One of the most famous was Gustave Flaubert, whose infamous account of his journey to Esna in pursuit of a well-known dancer/prostitute (in *Flaubert in Egypt*) titillated Victorian Europeans and helped cement the less-than-respectable reputation of Egyptian dance.

Belly dancing as we see it today began to gain credibility and popularity in Egypt with the advent of cinema, when dancers were lifted out of nightclubs and put on the screen before mass audiences. The cinema imbued belly dancing with glamour and made household names of a handful of dancers. It also borrowed liberally from Hollywood, adopting Tinseltown's fanciful costumes of hip-hugging bikini bottoms and swathes of diaphanous veils.

Also imported from the Western movie industry was the modern phenomenon of the belly dancer as a superstar capable of commanding Hollywood-style fees for an appearance. Dancers such as Samia Gamal and Tahia Carioca, who became the stars of black-and-white films of the 1930s and '40s, can still be seen today as the old films are endlessly rerun on Egyptian TV. Such is the present-day earning power of the top dancers that in 1997 a series of court cases was able to haul in E£900 million in back taxes from 12 of the country's top artists.

Despite its long history and the wealth of some of its practitioners, belly dancing is still not considered completely respectable and, according to many aficionados, is slowly dying out. In the early 1990s, Islamist conservatives patrolled weddings in poor areas of Cairo and forcibly prevented women from dancing or singing, cutting off a vital source of income for lower-echelon performers. In an attempt to placate the religious right, the government joined in and declared that bare midriffs, cleavage and thighs were out. At the same time a number of high-profile entertainers donned the veil and retired, denouncing their former profession as sinful. Since then, bellies have once more been bared but the industry has not recovered. For information on where to see belly dancing see Entertainment in the Cairo chapter.

Away from the glitz of the professional scene, dance in Egypt survives at a grassroots level where it is known as *raqs sharqi* (Eastern dancing). Visit the humblest of weddings and you'll witness the unmarried girls moving to the tabla beat, hands clasped above their heads and pelvises gyrating in a blatant attempt to attract a groom of their own.

Also keeping the dance alive is its popularity abroad: Belly dancing is the one native Egyptian art form to have been successfully exported worldwide, reaching nightschools and community centres where Tutankhamun has yet to be heard of. There is now an annual belly-dance festival held in Cairo every July. For more information on this style of dance visit W www.joyofbellydancing.com, which has heaps of articles, news and links.

Folk Dance

Belly dancing and raqs sharqi are exclusively female pursuits but there is also a male dance performed with wooden staves. Called *tahtib*, it looks something like a stylised, slow motion martial art. It can be seen at *moulids* (religious festivals) in Upper Egypt and is often part of the folkloric shows on the five-star hotel circuit.

Sufi Dancing

In its true form this isn't dancing but a form of worship. The Sufis are adherents of a Muslim mystic order who spin and whirl to attain a trance-like state of devotion. There's a Sufi troupe that performs regularly in Islamic Cairo (see Entertainment in the Cairo chapter for details).

Film

In the halcyon years of the 1940s and 1950s Cairo's film studios would be turning out more than 100 movies annually, filling cinemas throughout the Arab world. These days, the average number of films made is around 20 a year. The chief reason for the decline, according to the producers, is excessive government taxation and restrictive censorship. Asked what sort of things they censor, one film industry figure replied, 'Sex, politics, religion – that's all'. However, at least one Cairo film critic has suggested that another reason for the demise of local film is that so much of what is made is trash. The ingredients of the typical Egyptian film are shallow plot lines, farcical slapstick humour, over-the-top acting and perhaps a little belly dancing.

There are exceptions. Every year one or two films come out which do display artistic skill and quite often handle social themes of a controversial nature. The one director who consistently stands apart from the mainstream detritus is Yousef Chahine. Born in 1926, he has directed 37 films to date in a career that defies classification. Accorded messiah-like status by critics in Egypt (though he's far from being a huge hit with the general public), he has been called Egypt's Fellini and he was honoured at Cannes in 1997 with a lifetime achievement award. Chahine's films are also some of the very few Egyptian productions that are ever subtitled into English or French, and they regularly do the rounds of international film festivals. His most recent works are 1999's *Al-Akhar* (The Other), 1997's *Al-Masir* (Destiny) and from three years earlier *Al-Muhagir* (The Emigrant), effectively banned in Egypt because of Islamist claims that it portrays scenes from the life of the Prophet. Others to look out for are *Al-Widaa Bonaparte* (Adieu Bonaparte), a historical drama about the French occupation, and *Iskandariyya Ley?* (Alexandria Why?), an autobiographical meditation on the Mediterranean city of Chahine's birth.

For anyone wondering what happened to Omar Sherif, star of *Dr Zhivago* and *Lawrence of Arabia*, he's living in Cairo making very poor films for the local market and appearing in TV ads pushing ceramic tiles.

Architecture

The rich heritage of Pharaonic-era buildings is discussed at length throughout this book, as well as specifically in the special section 'Pharaonic Egypt', but there is another side to monumental Egypt that often passes less noticed: Cairo is one of the greatest repositories in the world of medieval Islamic architecture.

Medieval Islamic Starting with the earliest existent Islamic structure in Cairo,

EDDIE GERALD

Billboards for Egyptian films are a regular and colourful backdrop in Cairo's streets. In the golden era of the 1940s and 1950s, Cairo's film studios made more than 100 films a year. Nowadays about 20 films a year are produced.

which is the Mosque of Amr ibn al-As (AD 827), it's possible to trace the unbroken development of Muslim architecture through more than a thousand years and a succession of dynasties.

The earliest Islamic constructions inherited much from Christian and Graeco-Roman models. However, various styles soon developed that owed increasingly less to their architectural forebears. The Fatimids (969–1171), for example, were the first to introduce the use of the dome and the keel arch, the pointed arch that has come to typify Islamic architecture. They also introduced the use of heavy stone masonry, where previously mud-brick and stucco had been the main building materials. The Ayyubids (1171–1250) did little to advance on these techniques, though Saladin made good use of stone in constructing the walls of the Citadel.

From these beginnings, the vocabulary of Islamic architecture quickly became very sophisticated and expressive, reaching its apotheosis under the Mamluks (1250–1517). The Mamluks extended the types of buildings to include not only mosques, walls and gates but also madrassas (theological schools), *khanqahs* (Sufi monasteries) and mausoleum complexes. Their buildings are typically characterised by the banding of red and white stone (a technique known as *ablaq*) and by the elaborate stalactite carvings *(muqarnas)* and patterning around windows and in the recessed portals. The Mamluks were also responsible for the transformation of the minaret from a squat, stubby, often square tower, into the slender cylindrical form that is the typical Cairo minaret. As well, they nurtured stone dome carving into a fine art (shown at its best in some of the monuments in the Northern Cemetery in Cairo).

When the Ottoman Turks defeated the Mamluks and took control of Egypt in 1517, they brought their own architectural styles from Constantinople. But there were to be no grand mosques like that city's Haga Sophia or Blue Mosque. Egypt was a distant province and as such any new buildings were small in scale: practical structures such as houses, merchants' hostels and public works such as fountains and schools. Cairo's handful of Ottoman-era mosques are modest, though instantly recognisable by their slim pencil-shaped minarets. This imported style fell out of favour toward the end of the 19th century as Egypt pulled free of Constantinople, and since that time the Mamluk style has regained popularity as the model for the design of new mosques.

SOCIETY & CONDUCT

There's no simple definition of Egyptian society. On the one hand there's traditional conservatism, reinforced by poverty, in which the diet is one of fuul, ta'amiyya and vegetables; women wear the long, black, all-concealing *abeyyas* and men wear *galabiyyas* (men's robes); cousins marry; going to Alexandria constitutes the trip of a lifetime; and all is 'God's will'. On the other hand, there are sections of society who order out from McDonald's; whose daughters wear little black slinky numbers and flirt outrageously; who think nothing of regular trips to the USA; and who never set foot in a mosque until the day they're laid out in one.

While this latter group is definitely in the minority, due to their money and status they exert an influence on society vastly disproportionate to their numbers. Occasionally there is a backlash, as in 1997 when around 80 sons and daughters of the Westernised elite were rounded up on charges of Satan worshipping. They were accused of drinking the blood of rats, digging up corpses and burning the Quran when in reality all they had done was listen to Western music, dress like kids of the MTV generation, and enjoy access to satellite TV and the Internet. Within two weeks they were all released without charges.

The bulk of the Egyptian populace falls somewhere between these two extremes.

City Life

The make-up of Egypt's towns and cities is predominantly working class. The typical family lives in the hemmed-in side streets of an overcrowded suburb in a six-floor breeze-block apartment building with cracking walls and dodgy plumbing. If they're lucky they may own a small Fiat or Lada which will be 10 or more years old. Otherwise the husband will take the metro to work or, more likely, fight for a handhold on one of the city's sardine-can buses. He may well be a university graduate (about 40,000 people graduate each year), although that is no longer any guarantee of a job. He may well also be one of the million-plus paper-pushing civil servants, earning a pittance to while away each day in an undemanding job. This at least allows him to slip away from work early each afternoon to borrow his cousin's taxi for a few hours and bring in some much needed supplementary income. His wife remains at home each day cooking, looking after the three or more children, and swapping visits with his mother, her mother and various other family members.

The aspirations of this family are to move up the social scale. With no class system as such or aristocracy, movement upwards is completely dependent on money. In the 1970s, Sadat's free market policies resulted in a rapid influx of wealth, which laid the foundations for a 'middle class' that had never previously existed in Egyptian society.

At the other end of the scale are the masses of fellaheen (subsistence farmers), who traditionally have moved to the city to escape the poverty of working the land. They end up living in 'unplanned housing', makeshift shanty towns that fringe Egypt's bigger cities. If they're lucky they find employment as construction labourers or as *bawwabs*, doormen to middle-class apartment blocks.

Country Life

Just over half of Egypt's population lives in rural areas, and the popular image of the countryside is of galabiyya-clad peasant farmers, the fellaheen, working the land much as they have since the time of their Pharaonic forebears, holding onto their traditions in the face of Egypt's growing Westernisation. Reality is less simple.

Life in rural Egypt at the end of the 20th century is undergoing an immense transformation. The population density on Egypt's agricultural land, on which most cities and villages are built, is one of the highest in the world. What little land remains is divided into small plots averaging just 0.6 hectares, which does not support even a medium-sized family. As many as 50% of the rural population no longer make their living off the land. For those who do, the small size of their plots prevents the mechanisation needed to increase yields and they increasingly rely on animal husbandry or are forced to look for other ways of surviving. So the fellah you see working his field is probably spending his afternoons working as a labourer or selling cigarettes in a home-made kiosk in an effort to make ends meet. He knows there's no hope of finding work in the cities; the migration to urban areas that took place in the 1970s and 1980s has all but stopped and the country's 5000 villages have swollen to an average population of 10,000.

Still, for all the changes, the countryside remains the repository of traditional culture and values. Large families are still the norm, particularly in Upper Egypt, where government family planning campaigns have had far less effect than in the rest of the country. Extended families still live together in the same house, building additions as sons get married and have children. The houses used to be made of mud brick and sheltered animals as well as people, but increasingly peasants are building in red brick and concrete with separate pens for animals.

Rural traditions are at their strongest when it comes to women. High rates of female illiteracy are the norm in much of the countryside and women dress conservatively, often with long black overdresses worn on top of long dresses. Heads are almost always covered, although among peasants the headscarf is worn to protect hair and is often worn by Christians as well as Muslims.

Whether all this will change with the steady diet of urban Cairene values and Western soap operas that is currently beamed into village cafes and farmhouses each night remains to be seen.

Dos & Don'ts

Dress Although this is dealt with under Women Travellers in the Facts for the Visitor chapter, dressing prudently is just as much a male issue. In places less used to tourists, the sight of a man in shorts is considered offensive while, in Cairo, you'll be looked at like someone who's forgotten to put his trousers on. Count the number of Egyptian men in shorts.

Drink While alcohol is haram (forbidden) in the eyes of many Muslims, it is tolerated by most, drunk by a fair few, and quite freely available throughout most of the country. That said, getting blasted is not a widespread national pastime. It is advisable not to go reeling around Egypt's streets otherwise you may end up cooling your heels in a police cell.

RELIGION

About 90% of Egypt's population are Muslim; most of the rest are Coptic Christians. Generally speaking the two communities

The Mosque & How it Functions

The *mihrab* (niche indicating the direction of Mecca)

Embodying the Islamic faith and representing its most predominant architectural feature is the mosque, or *masgid* or *gamaa*.

The house belonging to the Prophet Mohammed is said to have provided the prototype for the mosque. The original setting was an enclosed oblong courtyard with huts (housing Mohammed's wives) along one wall and a rough portico providing shade. This plan developed with the courtyard becoming the *sahn*, the portico the arcaded *riwaqs* and the houses the *haram* or prayer hall.

Typically divided into a series of aisles, the centre aisle in the prayer hall is wider than the rest and leads to a vaulted niche in the wall called the *mihrab*, which indicates the direction of Mecca, which Muslims must face when they pray.

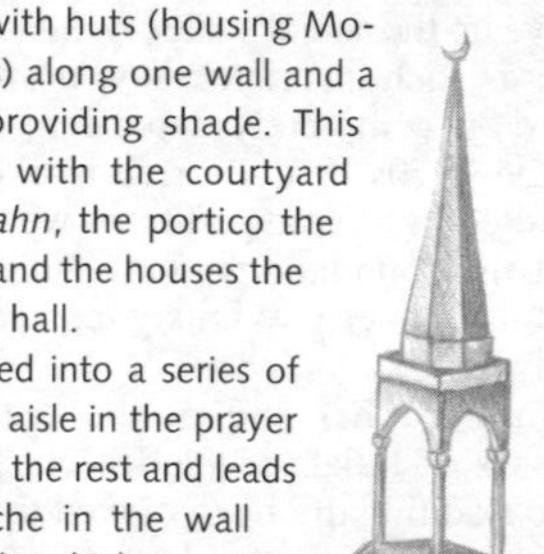

The *minbar* (pulpit)

Islam does not have priests as such. The closest equivalent is the mosque's *imam*, a man schooled in Islam and Islamic law. He often doubles as the *muezzin*, who calls the faithful to prayer from the tower of the minaret – except these days recorded cassettes and loud speakers do away with the need for him to climb up there. At the main Friday noon prayers, enjoy a more or less easy coexistence. Though Western newspapers from time to time run stories claiming that Copts are a persecuted minority, virtually all prominent Christians in Egypt insist they are neither persecuted nor a minority. Intermarrying between Christians and Muslims is not common.

Islam

Islam is the predominant religion of Egypt. It shares its roots with two of the world's other major monotheistic religions: Judaism and Christianity. Adam, Abraham (Ibrahim), Noah, Moses and Jesus are all accepted as Muslim prophets, although Jesus is not recognised as the son of God. Muslim teachings correspond closely to the Torah (the foundation book of Judaism) and the Christian Gospels. The essence of Islam is the Quran (or Koran) and the Prophet Mohammed who was the last and truest prophet to deliver messages from Allah to the people.

Islam was founded in the early 7th century by Mohammed, who was born around AD 570 in Mecca (now in Saudi Arabia). Mohammed received his first divine message at about the age of 40. The revelations continued for the rest of his life and they were transcribed to become the holy Quran. To this day not one dot of the Quran has been changed, making it, Muslims claim, the direct word of Allah.

The Mosque & How it Functions

the imam gives a *khutba* (sermon) from the *minbar*, a wooden pulpit that stands beside the mihrab. In older, grander mosques these minbars are often beautifully decorated.

Before entering the prayer hall and participating in the communal worship, Muslims must perform a ritual washing of hands, forearms and face. For this purpose mosques have traditionally had a large ablutions fountain at the centre of the courtyard, often carved from marble and worn by centuries of use. These days, modern mosques just have rows of taps.

The mosque also serves as a kind of community centre, and often you'll find groups of children or adults receiving lessons (usually in the Quran), people in quiet prayer and others simply dozing – mosques provide wonderfully tranquil havens from the chaos of the street.

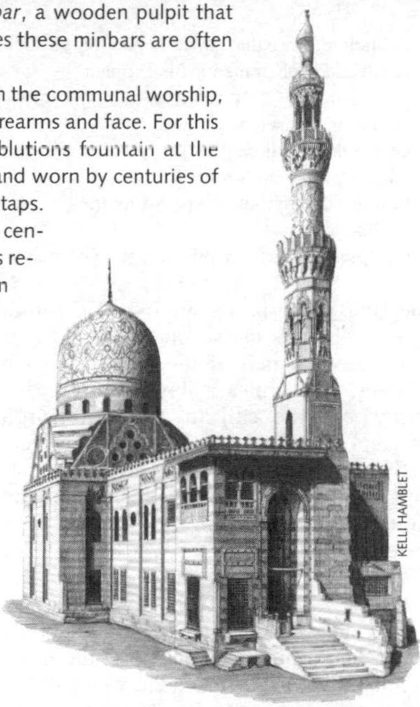

View of the Mosque of Qaitbey in Cairo.

Visiting Mosques

With just a couple of exceptions, non-Muslims are quite welcome to visit any mosques in Egypt at any time other than during Friday prayers. (Two of the mosques that cannot be entered by non-Muslims are the mosques of Sayyida Zeinab and Sayyldn al-Hussein in Cairo.) You must dress modestly. For men that means no shorts; for women that means no shorts, tight pants, shirts that aren't done up, or anything else that might be considered immodest. You must also either take off your shoes or use the shoe coverings that are available at most mosques for just a few piastres.

Mohammed's teachings were not an immediate success. He started preaching in AD 613, three years after the first revelation, but could only attract a few dozen followers. Having attacked the ways of Meccan life, especially the worship of a wealth of idols, he made many enemies. In 622 he and his followers retreated to Medina, an oasis town some 360km from Mecca. This hejira, or migration, marks the start of the Muslim calendar.

Mohammed died in AD 632 but the new religion continued its rapid spread, reaching all of Arabia by AD 634 and Egypt in AD 642.

Islam means 'submission' and this principle is visible in the daily life of Muslims. The faith is expressed by observance of the five so-called pillars of Islam. Muslims must:

1. Publicly declare that 'there is no God but Allah and Mohammed is his Prophet'.
2. Pray five times a day: at sunrise, noon, mid-afternoon, sunset, and night.
3. Give zakat, alms, for the propagation of Islam and to help the needy.
4. Fast during daylight hours during the month of Ramadan.
5. Complete the haj, the pilgrimage to Mecca.

The first pillar is accomplished through prayer, which is the second pillar. Prayer is an essential part of the daily life of a believer. Five times a day the muezzins bellow out the call to prayer through speakers on top of the minarets. It is perfectly permissible to pray at home or elsewhere; only the noon prayer on Friday should be conducted in the mosque. It is preferred that women pray at home. (For information about Islamic holidays and festivals, see Public Holidays & Special Events in the Facts for the Visitor chapter.)

The fourth pillar, Ramadan, is the ninth month of the Muslim calendar, when all believers fast during the day. Pious Muslims do not allow *anything* to pass their lips in daylight hours. Although many Muslims do not follow the injunctions to the letter, most conform to some extent. However, the impact of the fasting is often lessened by a shift in waking hours: many only get up in the afternoon when there are just a few hours of fasting left to observe. They then feast through the night until sunrise. The combination of abstinence and lack of sleep means that tempers are often short during Ramadan.

Although there are no public holidays until Eid al-Fitr (see Public Holidays & Special Events in the Facts for the Visitor chapter), it is difficult to get anything done because of erratic hours. Almost everything closes in the afternoon or has shorter daytime hours; this does not apply to businesses that cater mostly to foreign tourists but some restaurants and hotels may be closed for the entire month. Although non-Muslims are not expected to fast it is considered impolite to eat or drink in public during fasting hours. The evening meal during Ramadan, called *iftar* (breaking the fast), is always a celebration. In some parts of town tables are laid out in the street as charitable acts by the wealthy to provide food for the less fortunate. Evenings are imbued with a party atmosphere and there's plenty of street entertainment which often goes throughout the night until sunrise.

The ultimate Islamic authority in Egypt is the Sheikh of Al-Azhar, a position currently held by Mohammed Sayyed Tantawi. It is the role of the supreme Sheikh to define the official Islamic line on any particular matter from organ donations to heavy metal music.

Coptic Christianity

Egyptian Christians are known as Copts. The term is laden with history. It's the Western form of the Arabic *qibt*, which is derived from the Greek *aegyptios* (Egyptian). In turn this is a corruption of the ancient Egyptian *hi-kuptah* (the castle of the ka of Ptah); Ptah is an ancient name for the Pharaonic capital Memphis. Hence, the claims by some Egyptian Christians you may meet to be the true direct descendants of the pharaohs.

Before the arrival of Islam, Christianity was the predominant religion in Egypt

St Mark, companion of the apostles Paul and Peter, began preaching Christianity in Egypt around AD 40 and although it did not become the official religion of the country until the 4th century, Egypt was one of the first countries to embrace the new faith.

Egyptian Christians split from the Orthodox church of the Eastern (or Byzantine) Empire, of which Egypt was then a part, after the main body of the church described Christ as both human and divine. Dioscurus, the patriarch of Alexandria, refused to accept this description. He embraced the theory that Christ is totally absorbed by his divinity and that it is blasphemous to consider him human.

The Coptic Church is ruled by a patriarch (presently Pope Shenouda), other members of the religious hierarchy, and an ecclesiastical council of laypeople. It has a long history of monasticism and can justly claim that the first Christian monks, St Anthony and St Pachomius, were Copts. The Coptic language is still used in religious ceremonies, sometimes in conjunction with Arabic for the benefit of the congregation. It has its origins in several Egyptian hieroglyphs and ancient Greek. Today, the Coptic language is based on the Greek alphabet with an additional seven characters taken from hieroglyphs.

The Copts have long provided something of an educated elite in Egypt, filling many important government and bureaucratic posts, and they've always been an economically powerful minority. Internationally, the most famous Copt today is the former United Nations secretary-general, Boutros Boutros Ghali.

Other Creeds

Other Christian denominations are represented in Egypt, each by a few thousand adherents, or sometimes fewer. In total, there are about one million members of other Christian groups. Among Catholics, apart from Roman Catholics of the Latin rite, the whole gamut of the fragmented Middle Eastern rites is represented, including the Armenian, Syrian, Chaldean, Maronite and Melkite rites. The Anglican communion comes under the Episcopal Church in Jerusalem. The Armenian Apostolic Church has 10,000 members, and the Greek Orthodox church is based in Alexandria.

Egypt was formerly home to a significant number of Jews but, from an all-time peak of 80,000 in the early 20th century, they now number no more than 200. Historical sources record that there were 7000 Jews living in Cairo as far back as 1168 and in Mamluk times there was a Jewish quarter, Haret al-Yahud, in the vicinity of the Al-Azhar mosque. The first four decades of the 20th century constituted something of a golden age for Egyptian Jews as their numbers expanded and they came to play a bigger role in society and the affairs of state. Jews were responsible for the modernisation of the country's finances, including the founding of the national bank, the founding of most of Cairo's great department stores, plus major financial involvement in new urban developments.

The reversal began with the creation of Israel in 1948. Not long after, the exodus received further impetus with the nationalisation that followed Nasser's seizure of power. In the present climate of media-led anti-Israeli hysteria mention of the 'J' word in connection with Egypt is virtually taboo but there is incontrovertible evidence of the Jewish presence in Cairo's Ben Ezra and Shar Hashamaim Synagogues, and in synagogues in Alexandria and Minya.

LANGUAGE

Arabic is the official language of Egypt. However, the Arabic spoken on the streets differs greatly from the standard Classical Arabic written in newspapers, spoken on the radio or recited in prayers at the mosque all throughout the Arab world. Egyptian Colloquial Arabic (ECA) is a dialect of Arabic, but so different in many respects to Classical Arabic as to be virtually another language. As with most dialects, it is the everyday language that differs the most from that of Egypt's other Arabic-speaking neighbours. More specialised or educated language tends to be pretty much the same across the Arab world, although pronunciation may vary considerably. An Arab from, say, Jordan or Iraq, will have no problem having a chat about politics or literature with an Egyptian, but might have trouble making himself understood in the bakery.

For further information on Egyptian Colloquial Arabic, plus a vocabulary and pronunciation guide, see the Language chapter at the back of this book.

Pharaonic Egypt

HIGHLIGHTS of PHARAONIC EGYPT

The monuments of ancient Egypt have enthralled travellers for centuries, and the legacy of the pharaohs can still be seen in their ruined temples (eg, the Luxor Temple, title page), statues (eg, the Colossi of Memnon, top), pyramids (eg, the Step Pyramid of Zoser, middle) and buried tombs (eg, the Valley of the Kings). Although every site is different, they all reflect the richness of Egyptian religion and culture.

Title Page & Top Photo: Greg Elms
Middle Photo: Bethune Carmichael
Bottom Photo: Anders Blomqvist

One of the most underrated sites in Luxor, arguably second only to Karnak, is the temple complex at Medinat Habu, with the Temple of Ramses III (top) as its centrepiece.

Abu Simbel is the site of the imposing Temple of Ramses II and the adjacent Temple of Hathor (middle), devoted to Ramses II's beloved wife Nefertari.

Possibly the most enigmatic of all the ancient monuments, the famous Sphinx at Giza (bottom) has suffered the loss of its beard and nose over time, but still attracts the crowds.

Top Photo: Anders Blomqvist
Middle Photo: Chris Mellor
Bottom Photo: Mason Florence

Deir al-Bahri (top) appears to rise out of the limestone cliffs from which it was carved. Montuhotep II, Tuthmosis III and Hatshepsut all built temples here, though the best preserved and most famous is that of Hatshepsut.

Equally impressive is the great hypostyle hall at Karnak (bottom). The temple complex of Karnak is the largest in Egypt.

Photos: Anders Blomqvist

INTRODUCTION

The words 'Pharaonic Egypt' immediately conjure up images of mummies, pyramids and the treasures of Tutankhamun, images that are so frequently churned out by the media it is often difficult to see beyond them. Yet there is so much more to ancient Egypt than these cliched themes. The ancient Egyptians left behind them a great legacy of amazing achievements no less important than the renowned innovations of Greece or Rome.

Recent discoveries indicate that writing began in ancient Egypt, where it gave rise to a highly efficient bureaucracy able to organise the world's first nation state. The Egyptians also devised the 365-day calendar, created a sophisticated legal system, made great advances in the fields of science and medicine and excelled in all areas of craftsmanship. The abundant harvests that were gathered as taxes provided the wealth to fund the construction of the world's first stone monuments, ambitious building projects that for many symbolise ancient Egyptian culture.

Ironically, the survival of huge stone temples and tombs, not to mention mummies, has left a totally misleading impression that the ancient Egyptians were a morbid bunch obsessed with religion and death. In reality they simply loved life so much that they went to enormous lengths to ensure its survival for eternity.

The depth of this conviction permeated every aspect of their lives, and gave their culture its incredible coherence and conservatism.

BETHUNE CARMICHAEL

In this detail of an inscription at the Temple of Horus at Edfu (inset & bottom), the goddess Wadjet of Lower Egypt (left) and Nekhbet of Upper Egypt (right) crown Ptolemy VI with the red and white crowns respectively. The two crowns worn together represent a united Egypt.

Inset Photo: Bethune Carmichael

With their numerous gods and the pharaoh as the gods' representative on earth ruling by divine approval, absolute monarchy was integral to their culture.

Their entire history was based around the regnal years of their pharaohs, starting from year one with each new ruler. A total of 30 royal dynasties reigned over a period of some 3000 years, divided into Old, Middle and New Kingdoms. These kingdoms were separated by intermittent periods of unrest (known as intermediate periods) when the country divided into north (Lower Egypt) and south (Upper Egypt).

Even when threatened from abroad, Egyptian culture was so all-pervading that invaders could not escape its influence and adopted many traditional Egyptian ways. The Greeks were so impressed by what they found that they regarded Egypt as the 'cradle of civilisation', and even the occupying Romans adopted Egyptian gods. Only when the Roman Empire embraced Christianity did the traditions of ancient Egypt finally die, the 'pagan' script of hieroglyphs becoming obsolete by the late 4th century AD.

LPP

Discovered in the town of Rosetta (Rashid) and now on display in the British Museum, the Rosetta Stone (above) i considered one of the key finds of Egyptology Inscribed from top to bottom in Egyptian hieroglyphs, demotic Egyptian (a cursive forn of hieroglyphs, and Greek, the French scholar Champollion wa able to decipher the meaning of hieroglyphs

For the next 1500 years ancient Egypt lay silent until unwittingly resurrected by the international politics of the early 19th century. In his war with the British, Napoleon's invasion of Egypt included an army of scholars as well as soldiers. The Rosetta Stone – the key to unlocking the culture of ancient Egypt – was discovered by the French at a fort in the Delta. Inscribed in Greek and Egyptian, it proved to be the key that allowed the French scholar Champollion to decipher the meaning of hieroglyphs in 1822.

These events marked the birth of Egyptology. Almost all that is known about Egypt's more than 5000-year history has been gathered in only two centuries. Egyptology is still developing at an amazing rate, and new discoveries are constantly being made in excavations, laboratories and even underwater. Computers and microscopes are increasingly replacing the pick and the shovel in the rush to discover ever more about this great ancient culture.

TEMPLE ARCHITECTURE

The ancient Egyptians built their temples on sites they considered sacred, and as each successive temple occupied the same ground, traces of the original structures are rare. Egypt's earliest known temple site at Hierakonpolis remained free of later additions, but most temples were rebuilt by pharaohs keen to demonstrate their piety by adding their own contribution to existing structures. This can be seen most clearly at the enormous temple complex of Karnak in modern-day Luxor, whose succession of buildings are the culmination of at least 2000 years of architectural reconstruction. The Egyptians' highly conservative nature meant that temple design changed little over the millenia. Even the 'newest' temples built in the Graeco-Roman period are stylistic imitations of earlier structures.

Initially temples and houses were built along similar lines, both rectangular in plan and constructed from bundles of plant stems and other natural materials. The temples were distinguished from the houses by their large size and by their characteristic flagpoles. The flagpoles remained a standard feature throughout the Pharaonic period, and the flag symbol even formed the hieroglyph sign for 'god' *(netjer)*.

Developments in royal funerary architecture led to corresponding changes in temple architecture, and by around 2650 BC both were made in the more permanent medium of stone. The transition between reed and stone can be seen at the Saqqara funerary complex of the pharaoh Zoser, the site of the world's oldest stone monument. One of the most fascinating things about this place is that it is possible to see the architects' innovative experiments with the new medium, in the

ANDERS BLOMQVIST

The buildings at the Temple of Karnak in Luxor (inset & bottom) were reconstructed over 2000 years. Due to the conservative nature of the ancient Egyptians, temple design barely changed during this time.

Inset Photo: Troy Flower

way that they cut the limestone blocks relatively small and carved the surfaces of the temple's walls and columns in imitation of the plant materials previously employed.

In contrast to the stone used to house both the gods and the dead, homes for the living, regardless of status, continued to be made in perishable materials. Indeed, early scholars assumed that royalty must have lived inside the stone temples, and had considerable difficulty accepting that pharaohs really did live in mud-brick structures just like the rest of the population – albeit on a far grander scale.

LEE FOSTER

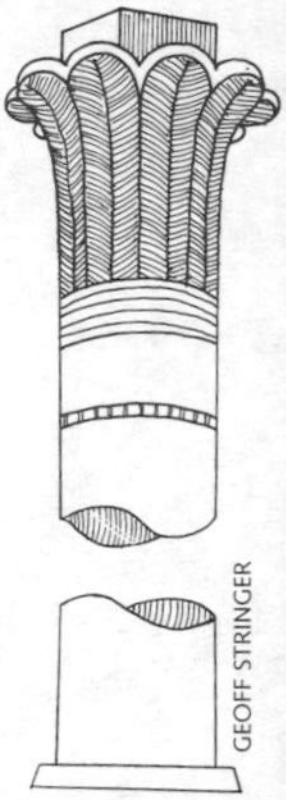

GEOFF STRINGER

The Palm Column

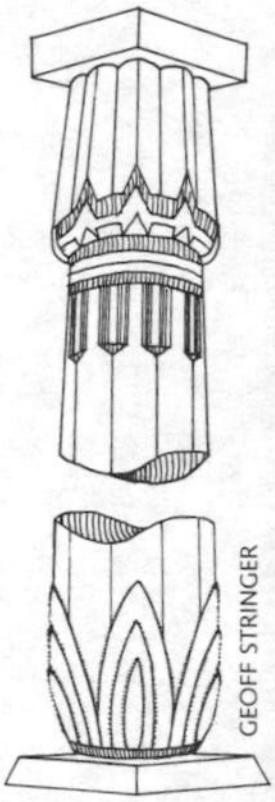

GEOFF STRINGER

The Papyrus Column

This composite capital at the Temple of Philae (middle) has been carved in an imitation of bound palm fronds with lotus and papyrus flowers in between. The capital is the most elaborate part of the column, and is useful in identifying its architectural style.

Typical Temple Layout

In terms of temple architecture, mud brick was only used for the huge walls that surrounded the consecrated ground and for subsidiary buildings such as workshops and storehouses. The storehouses at Ramses II's funerary temple (the Ramesseum) retain their arched, tunnel-like structure (see photo on page 60). Forming the centre point of each settlement, Egyptian temples were not only religious institutions, but acted as town hall, college, library, medical centre and warehouse.

Another key feature of each complex was the sacred lake used for ritual ceremonies and the regular ablutions of the clergy. As priests and priestesses had to bathe twice a day and twice a night for reasons of purity, it is no surprise that their houses were located very close to the sacred waters.

The priesthood were known as 'servants of the gods', and as their rituals did not involve public participation they had no congregation. Only authorised personnel could be admitted into the temples, and although the pharaoh was regarded as the supreme high priest and the intermediary between gods and humans, he reasonably delegated his

GEOFF STRINGER

The Lotus Column

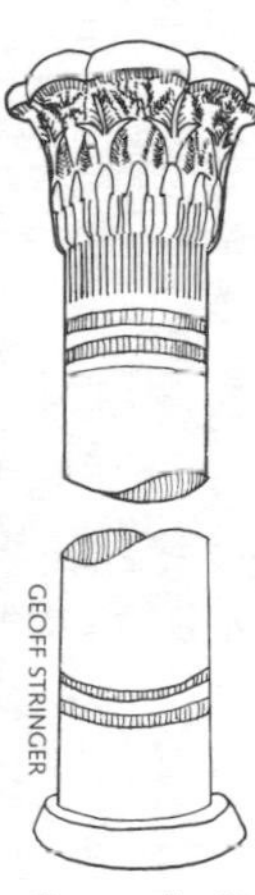

GEOFF STRINGER

he Composite Capital

SIMON BRACKEN

powers to each temple's high priest. Each high priest in turn headed a hierarchy of male and female clergy, from the lector priests who read out the ritual texts, to the stablehand who tended the sacred cattle and cleaned out the temple cowsheds. Access to the various areas of the temple was based on status. Many personnel were restricted to the outer buildings, and only the pharaoh and high priest were allowed to progress into the temple's innermost parts.

The approach to most temples was along a paved processional way, often bordered by sphinxes, and set on either side with formal gardens. The massive entrance formed by a pylon gateway, and originally sealed by a pair of huge cedar doors, was flanked with traditional flagpoles whose enormous niched supports can still be seen. Obelisks were also set up in pairs in front of the pylon. The pinnacles of these tall, tapered stone columns were originally covered with gold or electrum, designed to catch the first rays of the morning sun and transmit its life-giving powers into the temple – a bit like an esoteric lightning conductor.

SARA-JANE CLELAND

Obelisks, such as the ne remaining in front of the Temple of Luxor (top), were set up in pairs in front of massive pylons that formed the temple entrance. These ylons featured reliefs of the pharaoh and gods, uch as at the Temple of Horus at Edfu (bottom).

The surfaces of the pylons themselves generally featured gigantic reliefs of the pharaoh poised to execute Egypt's foes in the presence of the gods. Originally a riot of colour rather than the dusty beige we see today, these painted reliefs were not primarily decorative but were a form of effective propaganda demonstrating the power of the pharaoh and his divine connections.

The art in both temples and tombs was integral to the building's purpose and was meant to be functional. In scenes visible to all on the exterior walls, the pharaoh repeatedly performs public duties and defeats the volatile forces of chaos; inside, on the hidden, inner walls, the repetitive, orderly scenes emphasise his intimate relationship with the gods. Reflecting the function of each part of the temple, the scenes were meant to continually re-enact the rituals they depict.

Many rituals were processional in nature and dictated that most temples were designed along a single east-west axis. The first set of pylons generally led into an open-air peristyle courtyard surrounded on

ANDERS BLOMQVIST

Standing over 19m high the huge columns of the Colonnade Court of Amenhotep III at Luxor Temple (bottom) formed the prototype for the later great hypostyle hal built by Seti I at Karnak.

two or three sides by a covered colonnade, beyond which lay the three other main temple areas: the hypostyle hall, the inner chambers and the sanctuary *(naos)* containing the god's statue. The approach to the sanctuary was made as atmospheric as possible using a series of ancient 'special effects'. The sun-filled peristyle court gave way to succeeding rooms purposefully made smaller, darker and more mysterious by raising floors, lowering ceilings and narrowing doorways.

The hypostyle hall was one of the most imposing parts of the temple. It was filled with a forest of towering stone columns designed to resemble the primeval marshes that surrounded the mound of creation. The columns were positioned so that when viewed from certain angles there seems to be no space between them. Their capitals and bases were decorated with aquatic plants and the ceiling was covered in stars. Tiny clerestory windows positioned high in the walls did little to alleviate the darkness. The mysterious atmosphere would have been further heightened by clouds of incense caught in the narrow shafts of sunlight – think medieval cathedral sights, sounds and smells and you're halfway there.

Behind the hypostyle hall lay further dimly lit chambers, including small, often columned, halls in which the priests prepared the daily offerings of food, wine, flowers and perfume. Representations of the same types of offerings were shown on the surrounding walls. Side doors generally led off via a maze of corridors into subsidiary chapels and storage rooms, which once held ritual texts, priestly vestments and ritual equipment. There were also stairways that led up to the flat roof and down into the crypts.

In the most remote part of the temple lay the sanctuary itself. Representing the primeval mound of creation, this was the domain of the god. Within its dark interior stood the statue believed to house the

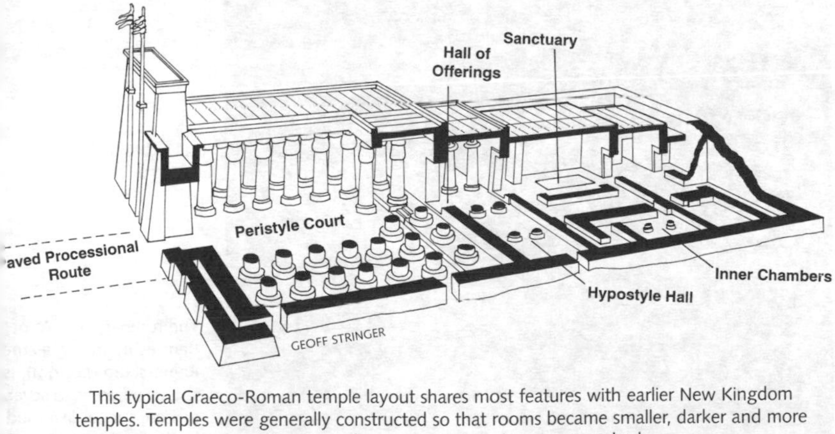

This typical Graeco-Roman temple layout shares most features with earlier New Kingdom temples. Temples were generally constructed so that rooms became smaller, darker and more mysterious as the sanctuary *(naos)* was approached.

god's actual spirit, which was encouraged to remain with daily offerings made to musical accompaniment. In a reciprocal arrangement, the priests could then use these divine powers, redirecting them through rituals for the benefit of the country. The statues were also taken out in procession inside portable boat-shaped barques during state festivals, accompanied by music, dancing and plenty of wine.

Cult & Funerary Temples

As well as more general cult temples devoted to the worship of Egypt's many gods, there were also smaller numbers of funerary (mortuary) temples, built to house the spirits of Egypt's pharaohs and perpetuate their worship after death. Originally, a funerary temple was attached to each pharaoh's tomb, but the need to avoid robbers finally led to it being separated from the tomb around 1500 BC. Over time, the low-key design of these ritual buildings became increasingly elaborate and individualistic.

This is best illustrated on the West Bank at Luxor, where the pharaohs of the New Kingdom (1550–1069 BC), who were buried in secret tombs in the remote Valley of the Kings, had huge funerary temples built on the other side of the cliffs close to the cultivated area. Their funerary temples, called 'Mansions of Millions of Years' by ancient Egyptians, are set in a line. The most important include Ramses III's temple at Medinat Habu; Amenhotep III's once vast temple, today marked only by the Colossi of Memnon; the Ramesseum, temple of Ramses II; and the best known of all the funerary temples, built by Hatshepsut into the cliffs of Deir al-Bahri.

DR JOANN FLETCHER

The funerary temple of Ramses II, known as the Ramesseum (bottom), is shown adjacent to sever… arched, tunnel-like mud brick storehouses.

GODS & GODDESSES

Egyptian gods and goddesses initially represented aspects of the natural world and were worshipped at a local level, gradually becoming more complex with the passage of time. They began to blend together, taking on each other's characteristics, and their ability to appear in many guises can make their identification rather difficult. To complicate matters further, the Egyptians had numerous myths relating to their gods. Never ones to throw out a good story, they preserved each as equally valid, retaining at least three versions of the Creation Story. However, the following brief descriptions should help identify at least some of the hundreds of gods and goddesses you will meet while visiting Egypt's monuments and museums.

Amun Originally the local god of Thebes (Luxor) who absorbed the war god Montu and fertility god Min, Amun eventually combined with the sun god Ra to create Amun-Ra, King of the Gods. He is generally portrayed as a man with a double-plumed crown and sometimes the horns of his sacred animal, the ram.

Anubis God of mummification, patron of embalmers and guardian of cemeteries. He is generally depicted as a black jackal.

Apophis The huge snake embodying darkness and chaos. As enemy of the sun god Ra, Apophis threatened to destroy him every night until Ra triumphed to bring light back to the world.

Aten The solar disc itself whose rays end in outstretched hands. Although first appearing around 1900 BC, this briefly became the chief deity during the Amarna period (c. 1360–1335 BC).

his detail (inset) shows the head of Horus, the falcon god of the sky d representative of the ruling pharaoh.

Inset Photo: Anders Blomqvist

Illustrations of gods: Geoff Stringer

Amun

Anubis

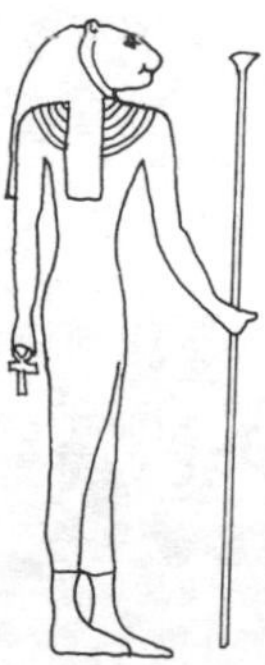

Bastet

Atum Creator god of Heliopolis who rose from the primeval waters and ejaculated (or sneezed depending on the myth) to create both gods and humans. Generally depicted as a man wearing the double crown, Atum is identified with the sun god Ra and represented by the setting sun.

Bastet Cat goddess whose cult centre was Bubastis. Ferocious when defending her father Ra, she was more often regarded as a friendly deity, personified by the domestic cat.

Bes Benign dwarf god, fond of music and dancing. His grotesque appearance frightened away evil from the home and protected women in childbirth.

Geb God of the earth. He is generally depicted as a reclining green man lying under the arched figure of his sister-wife Nut, the sky goddess, supported by their father Shu, god of air.

Hapy God of the Nile flood. As the plump embodiment of fertility, he appears as an androgynous figure, wearing a headdress of aquatic plants.

Hathor Goddess of love and pleasure. She is represented as a woman, a cow or a woman with cow's horns and sun disc in her guise as a daughter of Ra. Patron of music and dancing whose cult centre was Dendara, she was known as both 'she of the beautiful hair' and 'lady of drunkenness'.

Horus Falcon god of the sky and son of Isis and Osiris. He avenged his father to rule on earth and was personified by the ruling pharaoh. Horus generally appears as a falcon or as a man with a falcon's head, and his eye *(wedjat)* was a powerful amulet.

Hathor

Horus

Maat

Isis Goddess of magic, protector of her brother-husband Osiris and their son Horus. She also protected the dead with her sister Nephthys. As symbolic mother of the pharaoh, Isis appears as a woman with the throne symbol on her head, or sometimes the cow horns of Hathor.

Khepri God of the rising sun. Khepri is represented by the scarab beetle, whose habit of rolling balls of dirt was equated with the sun's journey across the sky.

Khnum Ram-headed god who created life on a potter's wheel, controlled the Nile flood from Aswan and was worshipped at Esna.

Khons Young god of the moon, and son of Amun and Mut of Thebes. He is generally depicted in human form wearing a crescent moon crown and 'sidelock-of-youth' hairstyle.

Maat Goddess of cosmic order, truth and justice. She is depicted as a woman wearing an ostrich feather on her head or simply by the feather alone.

Mut Amun's consort and one of the symbolic mothers of the pharaoh. Her name means both 'mother' and 'vulture' and as such she is generally shown as a woman wearing a vulture headdress.

Nekhbet Vulture goddess of Upper Egypt. Worshipped at Al-Kab, she often appears with her sister-goddess Wadjet, the cobra, to protect the pharaoh.

Nut Sky goddess usually portrayed as a woman whose star-spangled body arches across the ceilings of tombs and temples. She swallows the sun each evening to give birth to it each morning.

Ptah

Geb, Nut & Shu are often depicted together. The sky goddess, Nut, is supported by Shu, god of air and light, who separates her from Geb, the reclining earth god.

Osiris God of regeneration, he is portrayed in human form and was worshipped mainly at Abydos. The first mummy to be created, he was then magically restored by Isis to produce their son Horus, who took over the earthly kingship while Osiris became ruler of the underworld and symbol of eternal life.

Ptah Creator god of Memphis who thought the world into being. He is patron of craftsmen and wears a tight cap and clutches a tall sceptre (which can often look like a 1950s microphone).

Ra Supreme sun god of Heliopolis. He is generally shown as a man with a falcon's head topped by a sun disc, although he can take many forms (eg, the Aten, Khepri) and others merge with him to enhance their powers (eg, Amun-Ra, Ra-Atum). Ra travelled through the skies in a boat, sinking down into the underworld each night in the west before re-emerging in the east at dawn to bring light.

Sekhmet Lioness goddess of Memphis whose name means 'the powerful one'. As a daughter of Ra and as a vengeful form of her benign alter-ego Hathor, Sekhmet was capable of great destruction; since she brought pestilence, her priests also functioned as doctors.

Seth God of chaotic forces. He is represented by a mythological, composite animal. Seth murdered his brother Osiris but after his subsequent defeat by Horus, Seth's great physical strength was harnessed to defend Ra in the underworld.

Sobek Crocodile god representing the might of the pharaoh. He is worshipped at Kom Ombo and at Al-Fayoum.

Taweret Hippopotamus goddess whose threatening appearance scared away evil forces around the home and protected women in childbirth.

Thoth God of wisdom, writing and patron of scribes, worshipped in the form of an ibis or baboon at his cult centre Hermopolis.

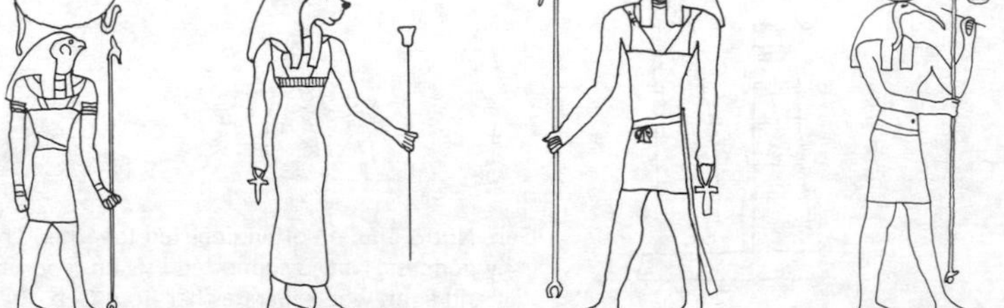

Ra Sekhmet Seth Thoth

HIEROGLYPHS

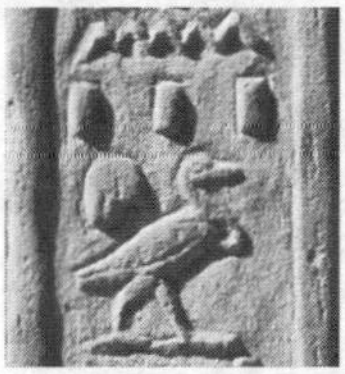

Hieroglyphs are the pictorial script first developed by ancient Egyptians as a means of recording produce. Recent discoveries of such texts at Abydos dating to around 3250 BC make them the earliest form of writing yet found, even predating that of Mesopotamia.

The impact of hieroglyphs on Egyptian culture cannot be overestimated, and their use strongly influenced the means by which the state took shape. A civil service made up of scribes working on the pharaoh's behalf collected taxes and organised vast workforces to exploit resources. As less than one per cent of the population was literate, scribes were considered to be society's elite.

Within a few centuries, day-to-day transactions were undertaken in a shorthand version of hieroglyphs known as hieratic, whereas hieroglyphs remained the perfect medium for monumental inscriptions. Hieroglyphs were in constant use for over three and a half thousand years. The very last example was carved at the Temple of Philae on 24 August AD 394. Covering every available tomb and temple surface, hieroglyphs were regarded by the Egyptians as 'the words of the Thoth', the ibis-headed god of writing and patron deity of scribes, who is shown holding the reed pen and ink palette. The word hieroglyph actually means 'sacred carving' in Greek.

is detail (inset) is from wall of hieroglyphs at the Temple of Karnak.

lthough vowels as we know them were not art of the hieroglyphic phabet, modern translations include them for convenience. Several ns also had commonly used alternatives. (The phabet is illustrated at the bottom of this and the following pages.)

Inset Photo: Vito Vampatella

Illustrations of hieroglyphs: Martin Harris

The small figures of humans, animals, birds and symbols that populate the script were believed to infuse each scene with divine power. Certain signs were considered so potent that they were even shown in two halves to prevent them causing havoc should they magically reanimate. Yet the ancient Egyptians also liked a joke, and their language was often onomatopoeic; for example, the word for cat is 'miw', and the word for wine was 'irp', after the noise made by those who drink it!

b

Evolving from a handful of basic signs, more than 6000 hieroglyphs have been identified, although less than a thousand were in general use. Although they may at first appear deceptively simple, the signs themselves operate on several different levels and can best be understood if divided into three categories – logograms (ideograms), determinatives and phonograms. While logograms represent the thing

a

a

ch

d

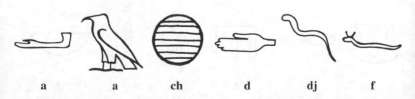

dj

f

VITO VAMPATELLA

they depict (eg, the sun sign meaning 'sun'), and determinatives are simply placed at the ends of words to reinforce their meaning (eg, the sun sign in the verb 'to shine'), phonograms are less straightforward and are the signs that represent either one, two or three consonants. The 26 signs usually described in simple terms as 'the hieroglyphic alphabet' are the single consonant signs (eg, the owl pronounced 'm'). Another 100 or so signs are biconsonantal (eg, the bowl sign read as 'nb'), and a further 50 are triconsonantal signs (eg, 'nfr' meaning 'good' or 'beautiful').

m

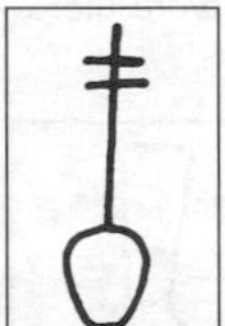

nfr

Unfortunately there are no vowels as we would recognise them. The absence of any punctuation can also prove tricky, especially since the signs can be arranged either vertically, to be read down, or horizontally, to be read left to right or right to left, depending on which way the symbols face.

The majority of hieroglyphic inscriptions are simply endless repetitions of the names and titles of the pharaohs and gods, surrounded by protective symbols. Names were of tremendous importance to the ancient Egyptians. It was sincerely believed that to speak the name of the dead was to make them live, and was as vital to an individual's existence as their soul (*ka*). The loss of an individual's name meant their permanent obliteration from history. Those unfortunate enough to experience the eradication of their names due to official censure included commoners and pharaohs. At times it even occurred to the gods themselves, a fate that befell the 'state' god Amun during the reign of the 'heretic' pharaoh Akhenaten,

Hieroglyphs were an integral part of Egypti culture, and were usec for over three and a h thousand years. Often covering every availab wall and surface of temples and tombs, su as on this wall at the Temple of Karnak (top hieroglyphs were cons ered 'the words of Thoth', the god of writing.

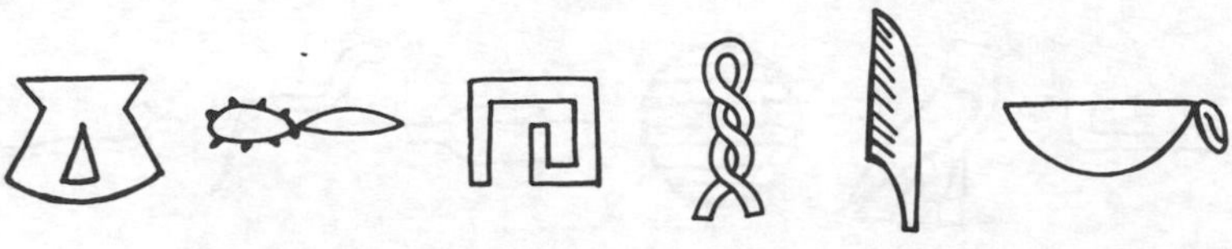

g **h** **h** **h** **i** **k**

CHERYL CONLON

This cartouche of Ramses III (top), inscribed on a wall at his temple at Luxor, was carved deeply into the rock to prevent it being carved over by his successors.

who in turn suffered the same fate together with his god, the Aten, when Amun was later restored.

life, prosperity, health

In order to prevent obliteration, names were sometimes carved so deeply into the rock it is possible to place an outstretched hand inside each hieroglyph, as is the case with Ramses III's name and titles at his funerary temple at Medinat Habu.

Royal names were also followed by epithets such as 'life, prosperity, health', comparable to the way in which the name of the Prophet Mohammed is always followed by the phrase 'peace be upon him'. For further protection, royal names were written inside a rectangular fortress wall known as a *serekh*, which later developed into the more familiar oval-shaped cartouche (the French word for cartridge).

prenomen

nomen

Although each pharaoh had five names, cartouches were used to enclose the two most important ones, the prenomen or 'King of Upper and Lower Egypt' name assumed at the coronation (written with the symbol of a bee and a sedge plant), and the nomen 'Son of Ra' name which was given at birth (and written with a goose and a sun sign).

As an example, Amenhotep III is known by his nomen, or 'Son of Ra' name, Amenhotep (meaning 'Amun is content'), although his prenomen, or 'King of Upper and Lower Egypt' name, was Nebmaatre

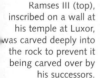

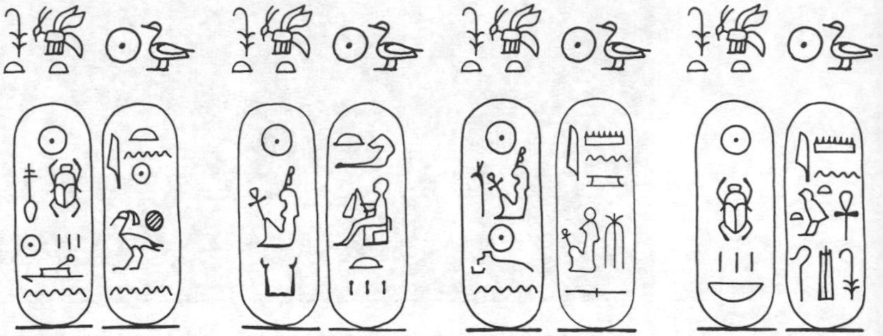

Akhenaten Hatshepsut Ramses II Tutankhamun

(meaning 'Ra, Lord of Truth'). His grandson had the most famous of all Egyptian names, Tutankhamun, which literally translates as 'the living image of Amun', yet he had originally been named 'Tutankhaten', meaning 'the living image of the Aten', a change in name which reflected the shifting politics of the time.

Amenhotep III

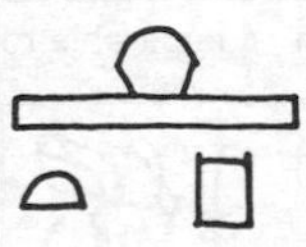

hotep

Gods were also incorporated into the names of ordinary people, and as well as Amenhotep there was also Rahotep, 'the sun god Ra is content' and Ptahhotep, 'the creator god Ptah is content'. The use of *mose* (meaning 'born of') instead of *hotep* (meaning 'content') ensured the names Amenmose, Ramose and Ptahmose meant that these men were 'born of' these gods.

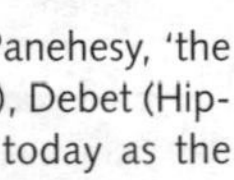

mose

In similar fashion, goddesses featured in women's names. Hathor, goddess of love and pleasure was a favourite, with names such as SitHathor (daughter of Hathor). Standard names could also be feminised by the simple addition of 't', so Nefer, (meaning good or beautiful), becomes Nefert, which could be further embellished with the addition of a verb, as in the case of the famous name of Nefertiti, (meaning 'beauty has come').

Others were known by their place of origin, such as Panehesy, 'the Nubian', or were named after flora and fauna: Miwt (Cat), Debet (Hippopotamus) and Seshen (Lotus), which is still in use today as the name 'Susan'.

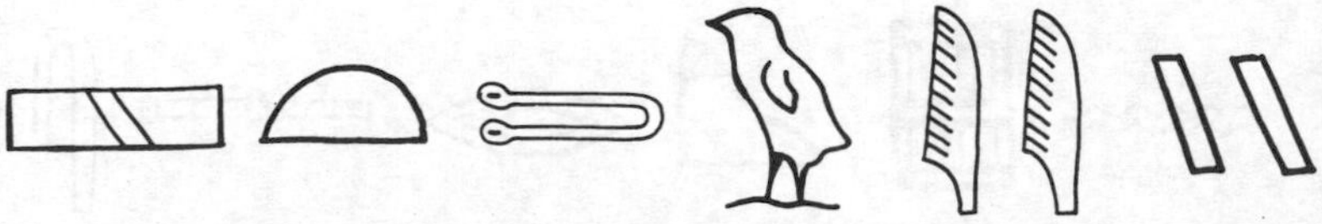

ART

Ancient Egyptian art is instantly recognisable and its distinctive style remained largely unchanged for more than three millennia. Its basic characteristics were already in place at the beginning of the Pharaonic period (c. 3100 BC). For example, the pharaoh smiting his enemies before the gods on the Narmer Palette, Egypt's earliest historical document, is a motif that was still found in Roman times.

Yet despite the familiar appearance of items that are described in modern terms as 'works of art', the reasons for their production are still very much misunderstood. Whereas most cultures create art for decorative purposes, Egyptian sculpture and painting was primarily functional. This idea can best be conveyed when gazing at the most famous and perhaps most beautiful of all Egyptian images, Tutankhamun's death mask, which was quite literally made to be buried in a hole in the ground.

Indeed, the great majority of Egyptian artefacts were produced for religious and funerary purposes and, despite their breathtaking beauty, would have been hidden away from public gaze, either within a temple's dark interior or, like Tut's mask, buried in a tomb with the dead. This only makes the objects – and those who made them – even more remarkable. The artisans were obviously motivated by something other than the need for personal adulation, as only once or twice in 3000 years did an artist actually sign their work. They seem to have regarded the things they made more as pieces of machinery designed to do a job than as works of 'art' in the modern sense of the term.

This concept also explains the appearance of carved and painted wall scenes, whose deceptively simple appearance and lack of perspective

In tomb paintings, such as those in the Tomb of Nefertari in the Valley of the Queens (bottom & inset), figures were shown with all key features – eyes, nose and mouth – clearly illustrated. This was to ensure that an individual's ka, their life force or double, could see, breathe and eat in the afterlife.

LEANNE LOGAN

MARK ECCLESTON

CAROLINE MCGREGOR

reinforces their functional purpose. The ancient Egyptians believed it was essential that the things they portrayed had every relevant feature shown as clearly as possible, so that when these objects were magically reanimated through the correct rituals they would be able to function effectively, protecting and sustaining the unseen spirits of the gods and the dead.

Figures were given a clear outline, with a profile of nose and mouth to allow them to breathe, and the eye shown whole as if seen from the front, to allow the figure to see. Eyes were often shown on the sides of coffins to allow the dead to see out, and certain figures had their eyes scratched out to prevent them seeing who was desecrating their tomb. Others had their nose and mouth damaged to prevent them taking in 'the breath of life' to live again. This same belief caused certain hieroglyphs, such as snakes or figures of the enemy, to be shown in two halves in order to prevent them causing damage when reactivated.

Inanimate objects were likewise shown as clearly as possible. Vast quantities of food and drink offered in temples and tombs were duplicated on the surrounding walls to ensure a constant supply of life-giving sustenance for eternity. The offerings are shown piled up in distinct layers, sometimes appearing to float in suspension if the artist took this practice too far. In the same way, objects that would otherwise have been hidden from view if portrayed realistically appear to balance on top of the boxes that actually contained them.

While working within these restrictive conventions, the artists still managed to capture a real feeling of vitality. Inspired by the natural world around them, they selected images that often reflected the concept of life and rebirth, as embodied by the scarab beetles and tilapia fish that were thought capable of self-generation. Since images were believed to be able to transmit the life force they contained, fluttering birds, gambolling cattle and the speeding quarry of huntsmen were all favourite motifs. The life-giving properties of plants were also very much in evidence, with wheat, grapes, onions and figs stacked side by side with the flowers the Egyptians loved so

In tomb paintings food was often portrayed stacked in layers, as in this painting at the Tom of Nefer at Saqqara (to left), or the tomb owne was shown receiving food at an offering tabl such as at the Tomb of Sirenput II at Aswan (tc right). Large amounts c food and drink were painted on tomb walls sustain the ka, which could absorb the life-giving force of the fooc for eternity.

much. Particularly common are the ever-present lotus (waterlily) and papyrus, the heraldic symbols of Upper and Lower Egypt respectively, which were often shown entwined to symbolise a kingdom united.

Colour was also used as an important means of reinforcing an object's functional nature, and naturally occurring pigments achieved a wide range of bright colours. Egypt itself was represented politically by the white crown of Upper Egypt and the red crown of Lower Egypt, fitted together in the dual crown to represent the two lands brought together. The country could also be represented in environmental terms by the colours red and black, the red desert wastes of *deshret* contrasting with the fertile black land of *kemet*. For the Egyptians, black was very much the colour of life, which explains the choice of black in representations of Osiris, god of fertility and resurrection, in contrast to the redness associated with his brother Seth, god of chaos. However, colour cannot really be used to work out ethnic origins, since Osiris is also shown with green skin, the colour of vegetation and new life. Some of his fellow gods are coloured blue to echo the ethereal blue of the sky, and the golden-yellow of the sun is regularly employed for its deeply protective qualities. Even human figures were initially represented with different coloured skin tones, the red-brown of men contrasting with the paler, more yellowed tones of women. Although this was interpreted as indicating that men spent most of the time working outdoors whereas women led a more sheltered existence, changes in artistic

This scene from the Tomb of Nefer at Saqqara was painted during the Old Kingdom and shows the tomb owner with a much darker, redder skin tone than that of his wife. In later periods style changed and paintings depicted men and women with a similar skin colour.

CAROLINE MCGREGOR

convention meant everyone was eventually shown with the same red-brown skin tone.

The choice of material was also an important way of enhancing an object's purpose. Sculptors worked in a variety of different mediums, with types of stone often picked for their colours: white limestone and alabaster (calcite), golden sandstone, green schist (slate), brown quartzite and both black and red granite. Smaller items could be made of red or yellow jasper, orange carnelian, blue lapis lazuli or metals such as copper, gold or silver. Other less costly materials, such as wood or highly glazed blue faience pottery, were also utilised.

All these materials were used to produce a wide range of statuary, from 20m-high stone colossi to solid gold figurines only a few centimetres tall that once adorned both temples and tombs. Regardless of their dimensions, each figure was thought to be capable of containing the spirit of the individual it represented – useful insurance should anything happen to the mummy. Amulets and jewellery were another means of ensuring the security of the dead. While their beauty would enhance the appearance of the living, each piece was also carefully designed as a protective talisman or as a means of communicating status. Even when creating such small-scale masterpieces, the same principles employed in larger-scale works of art still applied, and very little of the work that the artisans of ancient Egypt produced was either accidental or frivolous.

CHRIS MELLOR

A detail from one of the small wooden boats from the tomb of the official Meketre that, along with models of his house, cattle and workshops, was designed for use in the afterlife. These models can be found in the Egyptian Museum in Cairo.

TOMB PAINTINGS

The ancient Egyptians used a standard repertoire of scenes in their funerary art, from the colourful images that adorn the walls of their tombs to the highly detailed vignettes that illuminate their funerary texts. Every single image, whether carved on stone or painted on papyrus, was designed to serve and protect the deceased on their journey into the afterlife.

The afterlife was initially restricted to royalty, and the texts meant to guide the pharaohs towards eternity were inscribed on the walls of their burial chambers. Since the rulers of the Old Kingdom were buried in pyramids, the accompanying funerary writings are therefore known as the Pyramid Texts.

In the hope of sharing in their royal masters' afterlife, Old Kingdom officials built their tombs close to the pyramids. When the pharaohs lost power at the end of the Old Kingdom, these officials, no longer reliant on the pharaohs' favour, began to use the royal funerary texts for themselves and had them inscribed on their coffins. These so-called 'Coffin Texts' were therefore a Middle Kingdom version of the earlier Pyramid Texts, adapted for nonroyal use.

ANDERS BLOMQVIST

This development, known by Egyptologists as the 'democratisation of the afterlife', evolved even further when the Coffin Texts were literally brought out in paperback; they were inscribed on papyrus and made available to the masses during the New Kingdom. Collectively called *The Book of the Dead*, these texts were also known to the ancient Egyptians as *The Book of Coming Forth by Day*, with related texts including *The Book of Gates, The Book of That Which is in the Underworld* and *The Book of Breathing*.

MARK ECCLESTON

this detail of a painted coffin interior from the 22nd dynasty (middle), the deceased priest offers floral bouquets to the gods. Later versions of these Coffin Texts were also inscribed on papyrus, though this ene (bottom), from the *ook of That Which is in e Underworld*, is in the omb of Tuthmosis III in the Valley of the Kings.

BOTH PHOTOGRAPHS BY CAROLINE MCGREGOR

Set out in chapters sometimes referred to as spells, the separate sections included a 'spell for not dying a second time', 'spell not to rot and not to do work in the land of the dead' and 'spell for not having your magic taken away'. The texts also gave various visions of paradise – joining the sun god Ra in his journey across the sky, joining Osiris in the underworld or rising up to become one of the imperishable stars – the variety of final destinations reflecting the ancient Egyptians' multifaceted belief system.

These spells and instructions acted as a kind of guidebook to the afterlife, with some of the texts accompanied by maps and numerous scenes portraying the kinds of things the dead should expect, including the gods and demons encountered en route and the correct forms of addressing them.

The same scenes were also portrayed on tomb walls. The royal tombs of the New Kingdom were decorated with highly formal, ritual scenes showing the pharaoh in the company of the gods and all forces of darkness defeated. Since the pharaoh was always the pharaoh, and treated as such even in death, there was no room for the informality and scenes of daily life that can be found in the tombs of lesser mortals. This explains the big difference between the formal scenes in the royal tombs in the Valley of the Kings and the much more relaxed, almost eclectic nature of nonroyal tomb scenes that feature everything from eating and drinking to dancing and hairdressing. Yet here too these apparently random scenes of daily life carry the same message found throughout Egyptian art – the eternal continuity of life and the triumph of order over chaos. As the pharaoh is shown smiting the enemy and restoring peace to the land, his subjects also contribute to this continual battle of opposites in which order must always triumph for life to continue.

The Tomb of Prince Montuhirkhopshef (son of Ramses IX) is illustrated with figures of himself before the gods and inscribed with sections from the *Book of the Dead*. The scene on the top left shows Montuhirkhopshef pouring a libation, while on the top right is a detail of the image of the god Ra-Horakhty.

In one of the most common nonroyal tomb scenes, the tomb owner hunts on the river. Although generally interpreted on a simplistic level as the deceased enjoying a day out boating with his family, the whole scene is actually far more complex than it first appears. The male tomb owner, shown in a central position in the prime of life, strikes a formal pose as he restores order amid the chaos of nature all around him. In his task he is supported by the female members of his family, his small daughter and his wife who stands serenely beside him. Dressed far too impractically for a mere hunting trip on the river, his wife wears an outfit more in keeping with a priestess of Hathor, goddess of love, beauty and sensual pleasure. Yet Hathor is also the protector of the dead, and is capable of great violence as defender of her father, the sun god Ra, in his eternal struggle against the chaotic forces of darkness.

As the scene continues to unfold, the cat that often accompanies the family, and usually described as a kind of 'retriever' (whoever heard of a retriever cat?), is actually one of the creatures who was believed to defend the sun god on his nightly journey through the underworld. Similarly, the river's teeming fish were regarded as pilots for the sun god's boat and were themselves potent symbols of rebirth. Even the abundance of lotus flowers in these scenes is significant since the lotus, whose petals open each morning, is the flower that symbolised rebirth.

While tomb paintings for a pharaoh were always formal, nonroyal tomb scenes were almost casual in comparison, such as in this haircutting scene (top left) in the Tomb of Userhet, one of Amenhotep II's royal scribes. A more formal scene is the funerary procession depicted in the Tomb of Ramose (bottom). Both of these are found in the Tombs of the Nobles in Luxor.

BOTH PHOTOGRAPHS BY DR JOANN FLETCHER

So once the coded meaning of ancient Egyptian art is understood, such previously silent images almost scream out the idea of 'life'.

Another common tomb scene is the banquet at which guests enjoy generous quantities of food and drink. Although no doubt reflecting some of the pleasures the deceased had actually enjoyed in life, the food portrayed in these scenes was also meant to sustain their souls, as would the accompanying scenes of bountiful harvests. Even the music and dance performed at the banquets indicate more than that the party was in full swing. The lively proceedings were believed to be yet another way of reviving the deceased by awakening as many of their senses as possible.

The culmination of this idea can be found in the funeral scenes of both pharaohs and commoners alike, when the all-important 'Opening of the Mouth' ceremony was performed by the heir, either the next pharaoh or the eldest son. It was a ceremony designed to reanimate the soul (ka) which could then go on to enjoy eternal life once the individual's senses had been restored. Noise and movement were believed to reactivate hearing and sight, while the sense of smell was restored with incense and flowers. The essential offerings of food and wine then sustained the soul that resided in the mummy as it was finally laid to rest inside its tomb.

Dr Joann Fletcher

Dr Joann Fletcher is an Egyptologist, writer and consultant to museums and the media.

In this scene, three female musicians play the harp, lyre and pipes in a banquet-scene deta[il] from the Tomb of Nakh[t] who was temple astronomer during the reign of Amenhotep III. The scene was designed to awaken the senses of the deceased so the ka could function in the afterlife.

DR JOANN FLETCHER

Facts for the Visitor

HIGHLIGHTS

A perusal of the hundreds of letters that Lonely Planet receives from travellers on the subject of Egypt reveals that the sites and places most raved about are

1. Karnak and the West Bank monuments at Luxor
2. The Pyramids
3. Egyptian Museum, Cairo
4. Abu Simbel
5. Dahab and the Red Sea
6. Siwa

Other Egyptian experiences that continue to be rated highly include snorkelling (diving if you have the cash) at Ras Mohammed; watching the sun rise from the top of Mt Sinai; sleeping out in the White Desert on an overnight trip from Farafra; and taking a two- or three-day trip on a felucca (Egyptian sailing boat) from Aswan.

Also, check our own highlights, at the start of each chapter.

SUGGESTED ITINERARIES

Egypt is a big country and, unless you have the money to fly, getting around takes time. If you hit the ground running you can cover a lot, though if you're on a particularly tight schedule then it's better to limit yourself to one or two places and save the rest for next time.

The following itineraries assume that you're not taking internal flights.

One Week

Two days in Cairo allows you to take in the Pyramids and the Egyptian Museum, after which you could take the overnight train to Luxor and spend the next couple of days visiting the ancient necropolis of Thebes and the East Bank temples. Jump on a morning bus to Aswan (five hours) and you'll be able to spend the afternoon sailing on a felucca on the Nile. At a push, the next day you could fit in a trip to Abu Simbel before hightailing it by train or bus back to Cairo.

AEO

Ancient Egyptian Overload (AEO) is the curse of the time-constrained traveller. So many monuments, so little time, resulting in temple after temple after temple after temple – and that's just before lunch. By the end of day two, it's so many monuments, so what? Recently a Lonely Planet editor making her first trip to Egypt got AEO so bad in Luxor that a planned trip to Abu Simbel was cancelled. What a tragedy! One of the world's most stunning monuments, so close, but just a colossus too far – she had already overdosed on the works of Ramses and fellow pharaohs.

What to do? Well, for a start, don't try and do everything. Set yourself reasonable sightseeing goals. Pick your monuments and intersperse the worthy stuff with time spent relaxing, drifting on the Nile, lying by the pool, hanging out in cafes. After all, this stuff's been there for 4000 years or more, and it will still be around when you come back.

Two Weeks

A fortnight is an ideal amount of time. Take three days in Cairo, using the third day to explore the medieval quarters of Islamic Cairo. Take a train straight down to Aswan to see Abu Simbel and the Temple of Isis at Philae, before moving into relaxation mode with two nights on a felucca sailing up to Edfu from where you can move on to Luxor. Take two or three days to see the Pharaonic sights before catching a bus across the Eastern Desert to Hurghada and onward by bus or ferry to Sharm el-Sheikh in southern Sinai where you can delight in the underwater world before climbing to the top of Mt Sinai.

Or, if you're not interested in beaches and snorkelling or diving, head west from Luxor on a circuit of the oases of Bahariyya, Farafra, Dakhla and Kharga, finishing up in Cairo. Or return directly to Cairo from Luxor and head west via Alexandria to Siwa.

One Month

In a month you could cover most of Egypt's main sites, but you'd still have to travel at a steady pace. Spend four or five days in and around Cairo before hightailing it west to Siwa. After two days in this tranquil haven, backtrack along the Mediterranean coast to Alexandria, which is worth an overnight stay at the least. Take an early morning train to Cairo and you'll be in time to get the bus on to Bahariyya or Farafra, where you can arrange an overnight trip in the White Desert. From the oases you can bus it to the Nile Valley, and then split a week between Luxor, Aswan and the neighbouring sites. Head east to Hurghada on the coast for the ferry across the Red Sea. You'll then have another six or so days to explore Sinai.

PLANNING

When to Go

The best time to visit Egypt depends very much on where you want to go. June to August is unbearable almost anywhere south of Cairo, especially around Luxor and Aswan, where daytime temperatures soar up to 40°C. Summer in Cairo is almost as hot, and the combination of heat, dust, pollution, noise and crush makes walking the city streets a real test of endurance. On the other hand, a scorching sun might be exactly what's wanted for a week or two of slow roasting on the beaches of southern Sinai.

For visiting somewhere like Luxor, winter (December to February) is easily the most comfortable time – though hotel rates are at a premium. However, in Cairo from December to February skies are often overcast and evenings can be chilly, while up on the Mediterranean coast, Alexandria is subject to frequent downpours resulting in flooded, muddy streets. Even Sinai's beaches are a little too chilly for sunbathing in January.

The happiest compromise for an all-Egypt trip is to visit in spring (March to May) or autumn (September to November).

Religious Holidays & Festivals Most of Egypt's religious and state holidays (for dates see Public Holidays & Special Events later in this chapter) last only one or two days at most and should not seriously disrupt any travel plans. Buses, though, may be fully booked around the two *eids* (feasts) and on Sham an-Nessim, the spring holiday. Ramadan, the Muslim month of fasting, is seriously disruptive. During daylight hours many cafes and restaurants are closed, while bars cease business completely for the duration. Offices also operate reduced and very erratic hours.

Upgrade This Book

UPGRADE ONLINE

The world can change a lot in a day. Borders may open, hotels close or currencies crash. So before you leave home, check out Upgrades on the LP Web site (W www.lonelyplanet.com/upgrades) for significant changes that might have occurred since this book went to press. View or download them, print them and fold them to fit inside the guidebook.

Upgrades are available for over 60 guidebooks, including our most popular titles and those covering countries or regions that are changing rapidly. They are revised every six months until the new, thoroughly updated edition of the book is published.

Maps

Lonely Planet does a handy, slide-it-in-your-back-pocket *Cairo City Map*, produced on laminated card and combining maps of the city centre, Islamic Cairo, the Pyramids and the metro, along with an index of all streets and sights.

Otherwise, the pick of the other commercially available maps is Kümmerly & Frey, which covers all of Egypt on a scale of 1:950,000. The same company also produces a separate map of Sinai and a pictorial (but fairly useless) map of the Nile. Similarly good is the Freytag & Berndt map, including a plan of the Great Pyramids of Giza and covering all of Egypt except the western quarter at a scale of 1:1,000,000. It includes small insets of Cairo and central Alexandria.

Nelles Verlag has one of the most complete, though dated, general maps of Egypt (scale 1:2,500,000) including, on the reverse side, a map of the Nile Valley (scale 1:750,000) and a good enlargement of central Cairo.

Map of Egypt (scale 1:1,000,000), published by Macmillan, includes a map of the Nile Valley and a small map of the country, plus good maps of Cairo and Alexandria and a variety of enlargements and temple plans.

Clyde Surveys, of England, has an excellent map of eastern Egypt titled *Clyde Leisure Map No 6: Egypt & Cairo*. It covers the Nile region from the coast to Aswan, and has detailed maps of Cairo, Alexandria, Luxor and Thebes, and the Pyramids, with notes in English, French and German.

The Bartholomew *World Travel Map of Egypt* (scale 1:1,000,000) is a bit simplistic and it's missing a large part of the Western Desert. On the same scale is the French IGN map that concentrates on the Nile Valley. Michelin map No 954 (scale 1:4,000,000) covers north-east Africa as well as parts of the Middle East.

Falk produces a detailed map of Cairo (scale 1:13,000) with a small Alexandria addition and a booklet packed with details about the two cities, but you have to appreciate Falk's style of unravelling map.

Many of these maps are available in Egypt, as is an ever-increasing range of local products. There are several Cairo maps, the best of which is the *City Map of Cairo* (1:25,000) which, despite the small scale, is clear and has larger-scale inserts of Downtown and Heliopolis. It's conveniently pocket-sized and cheap at E£5. If you're spending a long time in Cairo you may find the *Cairo A-Z* (E£40) helpful, although at 150 pages it is bulky and quite heavy. There's a slimmer (32 pages), handier booklet, *Cairo Maps* (E£20), produced by the AUC Press.

In addition, once in Egypt you'll be able to pick up good maps of Saqqara, Aswan, Luxor, Alexandria, the Western Desert and Sinai.

What to Bring

There is very little that you might need that you won't be able to find in Egypt, but the choice might be more limited than at home. So bring sunglasses, a torch (flashlight), sunscreen (anything above factor 8 is hard to find anywhere in Egypt), a hat, flat drain stopper, pocket knife, sleeping sheet, small sewing kit and a moneybelt or pouch. If you're a light sleeper you may also want to bring earplugs – Cairo is a noisy city, and throughout the country dawn is accompanied by the amplified voice of the muezzin calling the faithful to prayer. If you are visiting during winter then a sweater is useful in the evenings, especially in desert areas.

Although most toiletries can be found in city pharmacies and supermarkets (and at major hotels), certain items can be difficult to get, and expensive, so you may want to bring your own contact lens solution, tampons (Tampax are about the only kind available) and contraceptives (Tops condoms are available – to men – but apparently have a distressingly high failure rate). Women living in Egypt suggest it is better to bring your own sanitary pads and panty liners, although they are available.

TOURIST OFFICES

The Egyptian government has tourist information offices throughout the country, some of which are better than others. The usefulness of the offices depends largely on the staff – while they are usually pleasant and well-meaning, they're not always that knowledgeable. Also, government-produced reference material, such as maps and brochures, tends to be out of date and too general. However, there are exceptions – the Aswan, Dakhla and Siwa offices are staffed by people who have wide-ranging local knowledge and will go out of their way to help you.

Egyptian tourist offices abroad tend to be well stocked with brochures, free maps and booklets and have fairly helpful staff.

Following is a selected list of tourist offices outside Egypt:

Australia
(☎ 02-6273 4260, fax 6273 4629) Press & Information Bureau of the Arab Republic of Egypt, 1 Darwin Ave, Yarralumla, Canberra, ACT 2600

Canada
(☎ 514-861 4420, fax 861 8071) Egyptian Tourist Authority, Suite 250, 1253 McGill College Ave, Montreal, Quebec H3B 2Y5

France
(☎ 01 45 62 94 42, fax 01 42 89 34 81) Bureau de Tourisme, Ambassade de la RAE, 90 Ave des Champs Élysées, Paris
Germany
(☎ 69-25 23 19, fax 23 98 76) Aegyptisches Fremdenverkehrsamt, 64A Kaiserstrasse, 60329, Frankfurt-am-Main
Italy
(☎ 396-482 79 85) Egyptian Tourist Authority, Via Bissolati 19, Rome
Spain
(☎ 341-559 21 21) Oficina de Turismo Egipto, Torre de Madrid Planta 5, Oficina 3, Madrid
UK
(☎ 020-7493 5283, fax 7408 0295, ⓔ egypt@freenetname.co.uk) Egyptian Tourist Authority, 3rd floor West, Egyptian House, 170 Piccadilly, London W1V 9DD
USA
Chicago: (☎ 312-280 4666, fax 280 4788) Egyptian Tourist Authority, Suite 829, 645 North Michigan Ave, Chicago, IL 60611
Los Angeles: (☎ 213-781 7676, fax 653 8961) Egyptian Tourist Authority, San Vincente Plaza, Suite 215, 8383 Wilshire Boulevard, Beverly Hills, CA 90211
New York: (☎ 212-332 2570, fax 956 6439) Egyptian Tourist Authority, Suite 1706, 630 Fifth Ave, New York, NY 10111

VISAS & DOCUMENTS

Passport

Make sure that your passport remains valid well beyond the period of your intended stay. If it's just about to expire, Egyptian immigration may not let you into the country. Also, make sure that you have at least one free page for the visa.

Visas

All foreigners entering Egypt, except nationals of Malta, South Africa and Zimbabwe must obtain visas from Egyptian consulates overseas or at the airport or port on arrival. As a general rule, it is cheapest to get a visa at Cairo airport, where the whole process takes only a few minutes; the required stamps are bought from one of the 24-hour bank exchange booths just before passport control and no photo is required. The cost is US$15/UK£12, payable in foreign currency.

Elsewhere, processing of visa applications varies. In the USA and the UK, processing takes about 24 to 48 hours if you drop off your application in person, or anything from 10 days to six weeks if you mail it.

A single-entry visa is valid for three months and entitles the holder to stay in Egypt for one month. Multiple-entry visas (for three visits) are also available but although good for presentation for six months, they still only entitle the bearer to a total of one month in the country.

Costs at embassies and consulates vary depending on your nationality and the country where you apply. As an example, a single-entry tourist visa costs most Western applicants the equivalent of UK£15 (about US$22) in the UK.

If you are on the road elsewhere in the Middle East, neighbouring countries Israel & the Palestinian Territories, Jordan, Sudan and Libya all have Egyptian representations where you can get a visa (see Embassies & Consulates later in this chapter for contact details). In Jordan there's an embassy in Amman and a consulate in Aqaba. At the embassy, drop your passport off in the morning and collect the visa that same afternoon; in Aqaba, visas are issued on the spot. The cost is JD17 and you need one photo.

You can also get a visa in Nuweiba on arrival by ferry but the Egyptian officials make a bit of a song and dance about it, and will want payment in US dollars.

If you are coming from Israel & the Palestinian Territories, you *cannot* get a visa on the Israeli-Egyptian border. Instead, you have to get the visa beforehand at either the embassy in Tel Aviv or the consulate in Eilat. At both places the visa is issued the same day and costs 60NIS (US$18).

Sinai Permits It is not necessary to get a full visa if your visit is confined to the area of Sinai between Sharm el-Sheikh and Taba (on the Israeli border), including St Katherine's Monastery. Instead you are issued with an entry stamp, free of charge, allowing you a 14-day stay. Points of entry where these visa-free stamps are issued are Taba, Nuweiba (port) and Sharm el-Sheikh (airport or port).

Visas for Onward Travel

For travel to another country from Egypt, contact the relevant embassy for visas (for embassy addresses, see Embassies & Consulates in Egypt later in this chapter). The requirements for the following destinations are:

Ethiopia You need a letter of recommendation from your embassy and two photos, and you must be able to show a return air ticket. If you fulfil these requirements the visa is issued the next day and costs US$63. Hours are from 8.30am to noon Saturday to Thursday.

Jordan Visas cost from nothing for Australians to E£63 for UK citizens, E£77 for Americans and E£91 for Canadians. Apply in the morning and collect the visa at 2pm. You need one photo. Hours are from 9am to 3pm Sunday to Thursday.

Kenya Visas valid for three months and good for travel for one month cost E£26 for most Western nationalities. You need one photo. Hours are from 8am to 2pm Monday to Friday.

Lebanon Apply in the morning and collect your visa the same afternoon. You need a photocopy of the information pages of your passport plus one passport photo. Cost is E£123 for all nationalities. Hours are from 9.30am to noon Saturday to Thursday.

Libya Do not count on getting a Libyan visa in Cairo. The embassy has to contact Tripoli and there is little likelihood of permission being given.

Saudi Arabia The place to get your Saudi visa is a consular building in Garden City near the Canadian embassy, which will issue transit visas for those passengers on a boat from Suez to Eritrea via Jeddah. Phone the embassy for the address. The consulate in Suez also supposedly issues transit visas.

Sudan Obtaining a visa for Sudan in Cairo would seem to be governed by cloud formations, coffee grinds or the Nikkei index. The consul himself said it would take at least a month to commune with Khartoum on the question of a visa, but a German girl, along with an American friend, got their visas in less than a week. To make the application you need four passport-size photos and a letter of recommendation from your embassy. If successful you pay US$64 cash (no other currency accepted) on receipt of the visa, valid for use within a month and for a month's stay.

Syria Visas are issued the same or next day depending on how early in the morning you get your application in. You need two photos. For Australians the visa is free, US citizens pay E£116, UK citizens pay E£210 and most other nationalities pay E£185. Hours are from 8am to 1pm Saturday to Thursday.

Visa Extensions & Re-Entry Visas Beyond the first month, visa extensions can easily be obtained for anything up to 12 months and cost E£8.50 (for the form) plus E£3.10 for stamps. You need photocopies of the pages in your passport with your picture and with your visa, one photograph and a modicum of patience. There are passport offices where visas can be extended in Cairo, Alexandria, Luxor, Aswan and Al-Tor in Sinai.

If you do not have a multiple-entry visa, it is also possible to get a re-entry visa, valid to the expiry date of your visa and any extensions, at most passport offices. A single/multiple re-entry visa costs E£10/14.

There is a two-week grace period beyond the expiry date of your visa. In other words, a one-month stay is to all intents and purposes six weeks. If you stay beyond that, a fine of E£60 is imposed on exit, and there are also the costs and hassles of getting an extension. If you are caught at the airport in this situation, you could well have to kiss your flight goodbye.

Travel Permits

Travel permits *used* to be required for travel west beyond Marsa Matruh or to Siwa but as a result of warmer relations between Egypt and Libya since 1989, this is no longer the case. That said, continued good neighbourliness can never be taken for granted and the need for permits could quickly be reimposed if the two countries again find themselves at loggerheads.

Military permits issued by the Ministry of the Interior in Cairo are required for travel south of the Shams Alam, 50km south of Marsa Alam on the Red Sea coast. They are very hard to come by, particularly as long as Egypt and Sudan continue to squabble about the Halaib region.

Travel Insurance

A travel insurance policy to cover theft, loss and medical problems is a good idea. Some policies offer lower and higher medical-expense options; the higher ones are chiefly for countries such as the USA, which have extremely high medical costs. There is a wide variety of policies available, so check the small print. Some policies specifically exclude 'dangerous activities', which can include scuba diving, motorcycling, even trekking. A locally acquired motorcycle licence is not valid under some policies.

You may prefer a policy that pays doctors or hospitals directly rather than you having to pay on the spot and claim later. If you have to claim later make sure you keep all documentation. Some policies ask you to call back (reverse charges) to a centre in your home country where an immediate assessment of your problem is made.

Check that the policy covers ambulances or an emergency flight home.

Driving Licence & Permits

If you plan to drive in Egypt you should obtain an international driving permit from your local automobile association before you leave home – you'll need a passport photo and a valid licence. For information about driving in Egypt, see Car & Motorcycle in the Getting Around chapter.

Hostel Cards

Some Egyptian hostels don't require you to be a Hostelling International (HI) member, but often charge a pound or two less if you have a card. Occasionally they'll issue a membership card on the spot, otherwise cards are available at the HI office in Cairo (see the Accommodation section later in this chapter for contact details).

Student & Youth Cards

For years, it has been notoriously easy to get a legitimate International Student Identification Card (ISIC) in Cairo. That situation has now changed. Proof of student status is now required before an ISIC card will be issued. That proof must be an ID card or letter from your own college or university. ISIC now works exclusively in Egypt with Egyptian Student Travel Services (ESTS) in Cairo. ESTS issues the ISIC, the International Teacher Identity Card (ITIC) and the International Youth Travel Card (IYTC). It also provides a full range of student travel services. For more information, contact ESTS (☎ 02-531 0330, fax 363 7251, ⓔ ests@rusys.eg.net) at 23 Sharia al-Manial in the Medical Faculty of Cairo University.

Most of Cairo's backpacker hotels and budget travel agencies can also get the cards but require proof of your student status.

In Luxor, if you're under 30 years old (or have proof of student status) you can get an ISIC card from an office next to the Venus Hotel (☎ 095-372 625). You need a photo, your passport and E£40, and the process can take as little as 15 minutes. The office is open from 8.30am to 11pm.

It is well worth having a student card as it entitles you to a 50% discount on admission to nearly all the antiquities and museums, as well as significant reductions on train travel.

Travellers have reported using a wide range of other cards to get student discounts for museum entry and transport, from HI cards to Eurail cards.

Vaccination Certificates

You'll need proof that you have been vaccinated against yellow fever and/or cholera only if you are coming from an infected area (such as most of sub-Saharan Africa and South America). Yellow fever is not endemic in Egypt.

Copies

All important documents (passport data page and visa page, credit cards, travel insurance policy, air/bus/train tickets, driving licence etc) should be photocopied before you leave home. Leave one copy with someone at home and keep another with you, separate from the originals.

EMBASSIES & CONSULATES

Egyptian Embassies & Consulates

Following are the addresses and telephone numbers of Egyptian embassies and consulates in major cities around the world:

Australia (☎ 06-273 4437/8) 1 Darwin Ave, Yarralumla, Canberra, ACT 2600
Consulate in Melbourne: (☎ 03-9654 8869/8634) 9th floor, 124 Exhibition St, Melbourne, Vic 3000
Consulate in Sydney: (☎ 02-9332 3388) 112 Glenmore Rd, Paddington, NSW 2021

Canada (☎ 613-234 4931/35/58) 454 Laurier Ave East, Ottawa, Ontario K1N 6R3
Consulate in Montreal: (☎ 514-866 8455) 1 Place Ville Marie, 2617 Montreal, Quebec H3B 4S3

France (☎ 01 47 23 06 43, 01 53 67 88 30) 56 Ave d'Iena, 75116 Paris
Consulate in Marseille: (☎ 04 91 25 04 04) 166 Ave d'Hambourg, 13008 Marseille
Consulate in Paris: (☎ 01 45 00 49 52, 01 45 00 77 10) 58 Ave Foch, 75116 Paris

Germany (☎ 228-956 83 11/2/3) Kronprinzenstrasse 2, Bad Godesberg, 53173 Bonn
Embassy branch: (☎ 30-477 10 48) Waldstrasse 15, 13156 Berlin
Consulate in Frankfurt: (☎ 69-59 05 57/8) Eysseneckstrasse 34, 60322 Frankfurt-am-Main

Ireland (☎ 01-660 6566, 660 6718) 12 Clyde Rd, Dublin 4

Israel (☎ 03-546 4151/2) 54 Rehov Basel, Tel Aviv
Consulate in Eilat: (☎ 07-597 6115) 68 Afraty St, Bna Betkha, Eilat

Italy (☎ 06-844 0191, e amb.egi@pronet.it) Villa Savoia, Via Salaria 267, Rome
Consulate in Milan: (☎ 02-951 6360) Via Gustavo Modena 3/5, Milan

Jordan (☎ 06-605202, fax 604082) Karbata Ben al-Dawar St, 4th floor, Amman, PO Box 35178
Consulate in Aqaba: (☎ 03-316171/81) Al-Wahdat al-Jarbiyya, Al-Istiqlal St, Aqaba

Libya (☎ 61-92488, fax 96291) Omar Khayyam Hotel, 5th floor, Benghazi

Netherlands (☎ 070-354 2000) Badhuisweg 92, 2587 CL, The Hague

Spain (☎ 91-577 6308, e egyptemb@teleline.es) Velazquez 69, 28006 Madrid

Sudan (☎/fax 11-778741) Sharia al-Gama'a, al-Mogran, Khartoum
Consulate in Khartoum: (☎ 11-772191) Sharia al-Gomhurriya, Khartoum

UK (☎ 020-7499 2401) 26 South St, Mayfair, London W1
Consulate in London: (☎ 020-7235 9777/19) 2 Lowndes St, London SW1

USA (☎ 202-895 5400) 3521 International Court NW, Washington, DC 20008
Consulate in Chicago: (☎ 312-828 9162/4/7) Suite 1900, 500 N Michigan Ave, Chicago, IL 60611
Consulate in Houston: (☎ 713-961 4915/6) Suite 2180, 1990 Post Oak Blvd, Houston, TX 77056
Consulate in New York: (☎ 212-759 7120/1/2) 1110 Second Ave, New York, NY 10022
Consulate in San Francisco: (☎ 415-346 9700/2) 3001 Pacific Ave, San Francisco, CA 94115

Embassies & Consulates in Egypt

Most embassies and consulates are open from around 8am to around 3pm Sunday to Thursday. The addresses of some of the foreign embassies and consulates in Egypt are listed below. If you need to ask directions to find an embassy say 'Feyn sifarat [country name]'. Country names in Arabic are given in brackets in the following list:

Australia (Australia; ☎ 02-575 0444, fax 578 1638) World Trade Centre, 11th floor, 1191 Corniche el-Nil, Cairo

Canada (Kanada; ☎ 02-794 3110, fax 796 3548) 5 Al-Saraya al-Kubra, Garden City, Cairo

Denmark (Dinmark; ☎ 02-735 2503, fax 736 1780) 12 Hassan Sabry, Zamalek, Cairo

Your Own Embassy

It's important to realise what your own embassy – the embassy of the country of which you are a citizen – can and can't do to help you if you get into trouble. Generally speaking, it won't be much help in emergencies if the trouble you're in is remotely your own fault. Remember that you are bound by the laws of the country you are in. Your embassy will not be sympathetic if you end up in jail after committing a crime locally, even if such actions are legal in your own country.

In genuine emergencies you might get some assistance, but only if other channels have been exhausted. For example, if you need to get home urgently, a free plane ticket is exceedingly unlikely – the embassy would expect you to have insurance. If you have all your money and documents stolen, it might assist with getting a new passport, but a loan for onward travel is out of the question.

Some embassies used to keep letters for travellers or have a small reading room with home newspapers, but these days the mail-holding service has usually been stopped and even newspapers tend to be out of date.

Ethiopia (Ethiopia; ☎ 02-335 3696, fax 335 3699) 6 Abdel Rahman Hussein, Doqqi, Cairo
France (Faransa; ☎ 02-570 3916, fax 571 0276) 29 Sharia al-Giza, Giza
Consulate in Alexandria: (☎ 03-486 7950) 2 Midan Orabi, Mansheya, Alexandria
Consulate in Cairo: (☎ 02-393 4645) 5 Sharia Fadl, off Talaat Harb, Cairo
Germany (Allemagne; ☎ 02-736 0015, fax 736 0530) 8 Hassan Sabry, Zamalek, Cairo
Ireland (Irlanda; ☎ 02-735 8264, fax 736 2863) 7th floor, 3 Abu al-Feda, Zamalek, Cairo
Consulate in Alexandria: (☎ 03-485 2672, fax 484 3320) 9 Rue al-Fawatem, Azarita, Alexandria
Israel (Israi'il; ☎ 02-361 0528, fax 361 0414) 18th floor, 6 Ibn al-Malek, Giza, Cairo
Consulate in Alexandria: (☎ 03-544 9501, fax 544 8136) 15 Rue Mina Kafr Abdou, Rushdy, Alexandria
Italy (Italia; ☎ 02-794 0658, fax 794 0657) 15 Abd al-Rahman Fahmy, Garden City, Cairo
Jordan (Al-Ordun; ☎ 02-348 5566, fax 360 1027) 6 Al-Shaheed Bassem al-Katab, Doqqi, Cairo
Kenya (Kenya; ☎ 02-345 3907, fax 344 3400) 7 Sharia al-Mohandis Galal, Doqqi, Cairo
Lebanon (Libnan; ☎ 02-738 2823) 22 Mansour Mohammed, Zamalek, Cairo
Consulate in Alexandria: (☎ 484 6589, fax 480 1902) 64 Tariq al-Horreyya, Alexandria
Libya (Libya; ☎ 02-735 1864, fax 735 0072) 7 Sharia Salah ad-Din, Zamalek, Cairo
Netherlands (Hollanda; ☎ 02-735 1936, fax 736 5249) 18 Hassan Sabry, Zamalek, Cairo
Consulate in Alexandria: (☎ 03-482 9044) 3rd floor, 18 Tariq al-Horreyya, Alexandria
New Zealand (New Zealanda; ☎ 575 5326) 4th floor, 2 Talaat Harb, Cairo
Saudi Arabia (Al-Saudiyya; ☎ 02-349 0757, fax 349 3495) 2 Ahmed Nessim, Giza
Consulate in Alexandria: (☎ 03-482 9911) 9 Sharia Batalsa, Alexandria
Consulate in Suez: (☎ 062-222 461) Port Tawfiq (around the corner from the tourist office), Suez
Spain (Espanya; ☎ 02-735 6437, fax 735 2132) 41 Ismail Mohammed, Zamalek, Cairo
Sudan (Al-Sudan; ☎ 02-794 5043, fax 794 2693) 4 Sharia al-Ibrahimy, Garden City, Cairo
Consulate in Cairo: (☎ 02-354 9661) 1 Mohammed Fahmy as-Said, Garden City, Cairo
Syria (Suriya; ☎ 02-337 7020, fax 335 8232) 18 Abdel Rahim Sabry, Doqqi, Cairo
UK (Brittanya; ☎ 02-794 0850, fax 794 0959) 7 Ahmed Ragheb, Garden City, Cairo
Consulate in Alexandria: (☎ 03-546 7001) 3 Sharia Mena, Rushdy, Alexandria
USA (Amrika; ☎ 02-795 7371, fax 797 3200, W www.usembassy.egnet.net) 5 Sharia Latin America, Garden City, Cairo
Consulate in Alexandria: (☎ 03-486 1009) 3 Sharia al-Pharaana, Alexandria

CUSTOMS

The duty-free limit on arrival is 1L of alcohol, 1L of perfume, 200 cigarettes and 25 cigars. On top of that, you can buy another 3L of alcohol (4L in Alexandria) plus a wide range of other duty-free articles once in the country but this must be done within 24 hours of arrival at one of the special Egypt Free shops.

A grand total of E£1000 can be imported into or exported out of the country. There are no restrictions on the import of foreign currencies, although you are supposed to declare all you have when you enter, and you aren't supposed to take out more than you have brought in and declared. This is all highly theoretical and we've never heard of anyone being asked to declare any currency.

Sometimes the Customs Declaration Form D is given to arriving tourists to list all cameras, jewellery, cash, travellers cheques and electronics (personal stereos, computers, radios, VCRs etc). No-one seems to be asked for this form on departure, and few tourists are given it on arrival. Travellers are, however, regularly asked to declare their video cameras and some have reported being hit with a hefty 'import tax'.

There are prohibited and restricted articles including books, printed matter, motion pictures, phonographs and materials that the government considers 'subversive or constituting a national risk or incompatible with the public interest'. Articles for espionage, or 'intelligence activities', and explosives are banned.

Duty-Free Shops

You can make duty-free purchases at branches of the Egypt Free Shops Company. These shops stock imported spirits, wine, beer and cigarettes, plus a range of electrical goods and other items. Wine costs from US$8 to US$20, whisky, gin and vodka from US$12 upwards and a carton of 24 cans of Heineken beer is US$16. Take your passport. Branches can be found at the following places:

Alexandria (☎ 03-586 8546) 513 Tariq al-Horreyya; (☎ 03-483 3429) 16 Sharia Salah Salem

Cairo (☎ 02-348 9059) Cairo Sheraton, Doqqi; (☎ 02-349 7094) 106 Sharia Gamiat ad-Dowal al-Arabiyya, Mohandiseen; (☎ 02-393 1985) 19 Sharia Talaat Harb, central Cairo – alcohol and cigarettes are not sold at this branch; (☎ 02-391 5134) 17 Sharia al-Gomhuriyya, Central Cairo

Luxor Off Sharia al-Karnak, one block north of the Emilio Hotel

Port Said (☎ 066-325 151) Sharia al-Gomhuriyya

It is also possible to purchase duty free in Aswan (on the Corniche), Hurghada (opposite Banque Masr on the resort strip), Na'ama Bay (at the Aquamarine Hotel) and in Nuweiba (in the port area).

MONEY

Currency

The official currency is the Egyptian pound (E£) – in Arabic, a *guinay*. One pound consists of 100 piastres (pt). There are notes in denominations of 25pt, 50pt, E£1, E£5, E£10, E£20, E£50, E£100 and E£200. Coins in circulation are for denominations of 10, 20 and 25pt.

Prices can be written in pounds or piastres; for example, E£3.35 can also be written as 335pt.

There is a severe shortage of small change in Egypt. The 25pt, 50pt and E£1 notes, which are useful for tipping, local transport (taxis especially) and avoiding the painfully repetitious incidence of not being given the correct change, are not always easy to come by. Make sure you hoard them.

Exchange Rates

Bad news for Egypt but a boon for travellers: in 2000 the longtime stable Egyptian pound wobbled and devalued, dropping against all major currencies. From a traditional 3.4-ish to the US dollar it fell to as low as four to the dollar. It recovered slightly but at the time of writing has yet to return to strength. Economists reckon it is unlikely to make a full recovery any time soon.

Exchange rates for a range of foreign currencies were as follows when this book went to print:

country	unit		Egyptian pound
Australia	A$1	=	E£2.16
Canada	C$1	=	E£2.73
Euro zone	€1	=	E£3.75
Israel	1NIS	=	E£0.99
Japan	¥100	=	E£3.43
Jordan	JD1	=	E£5.95
New Zealand	NZ$1	=	E£1.78
UK	UK£1	=	E£5.98
USA	US$1	=	E£4.20

Exchanging Money

Cash Money can be officially changed at American Express (AmEx) and Thomas Cook offices, commercial banks, foreign exchange (forex) bureaus and some hotels. Rates don't tend to vary much especially on the US dollar but if you're keen to squeeze out the last piastre then the forex bureaus generally offer slightly better rates than the banks and usually don't charge commission.

Most hard currencies can be changed in Egypt although in smaller places US dollars and UK pounds are easiest. Look at the money you're given when exchanging and don't accept any badly defaced, shabby or torn notes (there are plenty of them around) because you'll have great difficulty offloading them later. The same goes for transactions in shops, taxis etc.

Egyptian pounds can be changed back into hard currency at the end of your stay at some banks, forex bureaus and Thomas Cook and AmEx offices. See Business Hours later in this chapter for opening hours of banks and other institutions.

Travellers Cheques While there is no problem cashing well-known brands of travellers cheques at major banks, such as Banque Masr or the National Bank of Egypt, many forex bureaus don't take them. Cheques issued on post office accounts (common in Europe) or cards linked to such accounts cannot be used in Egypt.

Banks sometimes have a small handling charge on travellers cheques, usually about 50pt per cheque, plus E£2 to E£3 for stamps. Always ask about commission as it can vary. Forex bureaus that take cheques tend not to charge any commission.

In addition, AmEx and Thomas Cook travellers cheques can also be cashed at one of their offices, found in Cairo, Alexandria, Luxor, Aswan, Hurghada (Thomas Cook only) and Sharm el-Sheikh/Na'ama Bay. There's a small handling charge. Some souvenir shops and hotels will also accept payment with travellers cheques, but check with them beforehand.

There's a small handling charge. Some souvenir shops and hotels will also accept payment with travellers cheques, but check with them beforehand.

ATMs It's almost possible to travel in Egypt now relying solely on plastic, as ATMs are becoming more and more widespread. Cairo is saturated with cash dispensers, Alexandria has several, there are plenty in Hurghada and Sharm el-Sheikh, and a handful each in Aswan and Luxor. Where you will be hard pushed to find ATMs is anywhere between Cairo and Luxor (the towns of Minya and Asyut have just the occasional one) and out in the oases.

However, of the numerous types of ATMs in Egypt, not all are compatible with Western-issued cards. Those belonging to Banque Masr, CIB, Egyptian American Bank (EAB) and HSBC are good. If you have your PIN then these machines will dispense cash on Visa and MasterCard and any Cirrus or Plus compatible cards.

Credit Cards AmEx, Visa and MasterCard are becoming ever more useful in Egypt and are now accepted quite widely in shops and restaurants – though away from tourist establishments they are far less common and in remote areas they remain useless.

Make sure you retain any receipts to check later against your statements as there have been cases of shop owners adding extra noughts – it's a dumb, easily detected crime, but the swindlers are playing on the fact that they will only be found out once the victim has returned home and is thousands of kilometres from Egypt.

Visa and MasterCard can be used for cash advances at Banque Masr and the National Bank of Egypt, as well as at Thomas Cook offices. Banque Masr does not generally charge commission for cash advances, but does set a limit of E£1500.

To report lost cards in Egypt, call AmEx (☎ 02-570 3411); MasterCard and Visa (☎ 02-357 1148/9); or Diners Club (☎ 02-333 2638).

International Transfers Western Union, the international money transfer specialist, operates jointly in Egypt with Masr America International Bank and IBA business centres. You can receive money at all the following branches, but you can only send money from the Downtown, Garden City and Heliopolios branches in Cairo.

Alexandria (☎ 03-420 1148) 281 Tariq al-Horreyya; (☎ 03-492 0900) 73 Tariq al-Horreyya
Cairo (☎ 02-393 4906) 19 Qasr el-Nil, Downtown; (☎ 02-357 1385) 1079 Corniche el-Nil, Garden City; (☎ 02-355 7071) 8 Ibrahim Naguib, Garden City; (☎ 02-331 3500) 24 Sharia Syria, Mohandiseen; (☎ 02-249 0607) 67 Sharia Hegaz, Heliopolis; (☎ 02-258 8646) 6 Sharia Boutros Ghali, Heliopolis
Dahab (☎ 062-640 320) Nesima Hotel & Diving Centre
Hurghada (☎ 065-442 772) Redcon Mall, Unit 19, Sheraton Rd
Luxor (☎ 095-372 292) Mina Palace Hotel, Corniche el-Nil
Port Said (☎ 066-326 404) Sonesta Shopping Centre, Unit 621
Sharm el-Sheikh (☎ 062-602 222) Rossetta Hotel, Na'ama Bay

The opening hours for these offices are the same as those of the banks. For details call the Western Union hotline on ☎ 02-355 5023.

It is also possible to have money wired to you from home through AmEx. This service operates through most of its branches, and can be used by anyone, regardless of whether you have an AmEx card or not. The charge is about US$80 per US$1000, payable in the country from which the money is sent.

Black Market For hard currency, the black market is negligible and few travellers can be bothered hunting it out for the fraction of the difference it makes.

Security

With the growing proliferation of ATMs and increasing acceptance of credit cards, it is no longer necessary to carry large amounts of cash. Whenever we travel to Egypt we take just enough to cover the first day or two then top up via the plastic whenever necessary. If you do come armed with a wad of notes, then do not leave it in your hotel room – see the warning in Dangers & Annoyances later in this chapter. Instead, carry your money with you, preferably in a moneybelt or pouch secured about you. Keep a small stash of cash in your wallet or purse for immediate use.

Costs

By international standards Egypt is still fairly cheap. It is possible to get by on US$15 a day or maybe less if you are willing to stick to the cheapest hotels (you can get a bed for as little as E£7, or US$1.80), eat the staple snacks of *fuul* (mashed fava beans) and *ta'amiyya* (felafel), and limit yourself to one historical site per day. At the other end of the scale, Cairo has plenty of accommodation where you can pay upwards of US$100 a night for a room, and some of the better restaurants will set you back US$20 per person or more.

Taking a middle route, if you stay in a modest hotel and have a room with a fan and private bathroom, eat in the type of low-key restaurants locals frequent, with the occasional splurge, and aim to see a couple of sites each day, you'll be looking at between US$20 and US$30 a day.

To give some idea of daily costs, a fuul or ta'amiyya sandwich costs about 35pt (around US$0.10), while a Big Mac goes for E£5.95 (US$1.75). A meal in a cheap restaurant will cost around E£15 (US$4) but if you prefer to go a little upmarket you can eat very well for E£20 to E£35 (US$5.50 to US$10). A cup of coffee is between 50pt and E£2 (US$0.14 to US$0.50), a beer retails for around E£6.50 (US$1.70), and a bottle of mineral water is E£1.50 (US$0.40).

Getting around the country is cheap: the 10-hour train ride between Cairo and Luxor can cost as little as E£31 (just under US$10) in 2nd class.

The major expense is going to be the entry fees to tourist sites. Foreigners are seen as dollars on legs so places where they flock tend to be pricey. A complete visit to the Pyramids costs E£90 (US$24) in admission charges, and if you want to see the

Backhand Economy – The Art of Baksheesh

Tipping in Egypt is called baksheesh. It's a word you'll become very familiar with very quickly. It is more than just a reward for services rendered. Salaries and wages in Egypt are much lower than in Western countries, so baksheesh is an often essential means of supplementing income. To a cleaner in a one- or two-star hotel who might earn only about E£150 per month, daily tips can be the mainstay of his or her salary. It's far from a custom exclusively reserved for foreigners. Egyptians have to constantly dole out the baksheesh too – to park their cars, receive their mail, ensure they get fresh produce at the grocers and to be shown to their seat at the cinema.

For travellers who are not used to continual tipping, demands for baksheesh for doing anything from opening doors to pointing out the obvious in museums can be quite irritating. But it is the accepted way in Egypt. Just use your discretion and don't be intimidated into paying baksheesh when you don't think the service warrants it. At the same time, remember that more things warrant baksheesh here than anywhere in the West.

In hotels and restaurants, a 12% service charge is included at the bottom of the bill, but the money goes into the till; it's necessary therefore to leave an additional tip for the waiter. Services such as opening a door or carrying your bags warrant 50pt. A guard who shows you something off the beaten track at an ancient site should receive a pound or two. Baksheesh is not necessary when asking for directions.

One tip is to carry lots of small change with you and also to keep it separate from bigger bills; flashing your cash will lead to demands for greater baksheesh.

mummies at the Egyptian Museum, the combined fee is E£60 (US$16).

A service charge of 12% is applied in restaurants and hotels to which a 5% to 7% sales tax is added. In other words, the price you are quoted at a hotel or read on a menu could be almost 20% higher when it comes to paying the bill.

Bargaining

Bargaining is part of everyday life in Egypt and almost everything is open to haggling, from hotel rooms to the price of imported cigarettes. Even in shops when prices are clearly marked, many Egyptians will still try to shave something off the bill. Of course, when buying in souqs such as Cairo's Khan al-Khalili, bargaining is unavoidable unless you are willing to pay well over the odds (see the boxed text 'The Art of Bargaining' under Shopping, later in this chapter).

POST & COMMUNICATIONS

Post

Postcards and letters up to 15g cost E£1.25 to most countries and take four or five days to get to Europe and a week to 10 days to the USA and Australia. Stamps are available at post offices, and some souvenir kiosks, shops, newsstands and the reception desks of major hotels. Sending mail from the post boxes at major hotels instead of from post offices seems to be quicker. If you use the post boxes, blue is international air mail, red is internal mail and green is internal express mail.

Post offices are generally open from 8.30am to 3pm Saturday to Thursday. Poste restante in Egypt functions remarkably well and is generally free (though in Alexandria there's a small fee to collect letters). If you plan to pick up mail there, ensure that the clerk checks under Mr, Ms or Mrs in addition to your first and last names.

If you receive a package, you'll get a card (written in Arabic) directing you to some far-flung corner of the city to collect it. Take your passport, money and patience.

Parcels Packages going by normal sea mail or air mail are sent from the main post office, although in Cairo they can only go from the huge post traffic centre at Midan Ramses. As an indication of fees, a parcel to Australia costs E£32.50 per kilogram for air mail; E£16 to the UK. Sea mail to both is E£8.35 (and arrival times are impossible to guess). Parcels of more than 20kg for Western Europe and Africa, and 30kg to the USA, will not be accepted. Parcels should also not be bigger than 1m long and deep, and 50cm wide.

There is usually a long and complicated process of customs inspection and form filling – don't close the parcel until the procedures are over. You may have to get export licences or have goods inspected, depending on what they are. Printed matter and audio and visual material will be checked and foodstuffs (except dried food) and medicines also need clearance.

The easiest way to send a package is to pay someone else a small fee and have them do it for you. Some shopkeepers will provide this service, especially if you've bought the article in their bazaar. It should include obtaining an export licence, packaging and mailing.

Express Mail It is possible to send a letter of up to 500g by Express Mail Service (EMS). There are several branches of this service around the main cities. An express letter to the UK costs E£57.50 or to Australia E£66 and arrival is guaranteed within two days. For packages weighing from 500g to 1kg rates to the UK are E£75.70 and to Australia E£90.

In addition to EMS, Egypt has DHL, Federal Express, TNT Skypack and various other courier services. Their addresses are listed under Post in the Information sections of individual city entries.

Telephone

Since the last edition of this book phoning abroad from Egypt is a whole lot easier, not to mention cheaper. The national phone system has recently benefited from a massive shake up in which the government has allowed the private sector in on the telecommunications game. Two companies are currently engaged in a battle to plant international-call cardphones on every street corner in Egypt. Leading the contest by a clear mile is Menatel (a subsidiary of France Telecom), with their distinctive yellow-and-green booths. Cards are sold at a multitude of shops and kiosks bearing the little Menatel sticker and come in units of E£10, E£20 and E£30. Rates for calling Europe via Menatel are E£4.40 (US$1.20) for the first minute and then E£4.80 (US$1.25) for each additional minute. Calls to the USA are slightly cheaper, while to Australia it's about 25% more expensive. Using a 20-unit card gives a 20% discount on all calls.

The old central telephone and telegraph offices, known as *centrales*, still exist. At these places you give the number you want to call to an operator behind a desk, tell them how long you want (there is a three-minute minimum), and pay upfront. You then wait your turn to be connected. It's a slow process and also very frustrating as Egyptian minutes always seem to be far shorter than the international norm. Happily, there is no longer any reason to use the centrales since the arrival of Menatel.

Area Codes & Important Numbers

Telephone area codes are given at the start of each city or town section. The country code for Egypt is ☎ 20, and the international access code (to call abroad from Egypt) is ☎ 00.

Following are some telephone numbers you may find useful:

ambulance	☎ 123
directory inquiries in Cairo	☎ 140
directory inquiries outside Cairo	☎ 10
fire service	☎ 125
International inquiries	☎ 144
police	☎ 122
tourist police	☎ 126

Collect Calls Collect (reverse charge) calls can be made from Egypt, but only to countries – such as Canada, Italy, South Korea, the UK and the USA – that have set up Home Country Direct phones. With this service, you can get through to an operator in one of the previously mentioned countries and then reverse the charges or, depending on the service, charge the call to a credit card. At the time of writing, this service was offered by only a few places – all in Cairo – such as the Marriott or Semiramis Inter-Continental hotels, the telephone office in the departure hall at the new airport terminal, or at British Airways (calls to the UK only).

International Calling Cards The following cards can be accessed through these Cairo numbers: AT&T ☎ 02-510 0200; MCI ☎ 02-355 5770; and Global One & Sprint ☎ 02-356 4777.

Mobiles Egypt's mobile phone network works on the GSM system, like Europe (and unlike North America). If your phone works on GSM and your account allows you to roam, you can use it in Egypt. Keep in mind, though, that anyone trying to contact you from within Egypt will have to make an international call. Check with your mobile phone company back home to find out its charges for roaming.

There are two mobile phone companies in Egypt: Mobinil and Click. The latter is a joint venture with Vodaphone and has better coverage internationally.

Mobile rates are more expensive in Egypt than in most European countries. Getting a permanent line is tricky without a work permit but you can rent temporary mobile phone lines from both Mobinil and Click, although only the former is good for short-term use. There are supposedly Mobinil agencies at the airport. If not, you can go to any Mobinil shop and rent a line (but not the phone itself). The service is called Allo Hallo and the linc costs about E£50. It is good for a maximum of 20 days, and includes a E£10 phone credit. For more credit, simply buy a card available at shops all over town. For information, call Mobinil customer service ☎ 02-302 8004 or 575 7100.

Click does not have a cheap short-term rental and charges a whopping E£675 to rent a line for a maximum of 120 days (but for the last 30 you can only receive calls). The line rental calling credit is E£80. To increase this amount you buy cards, which are widely available. For more information call Click customer service ☎ 02-336 4591 or 293 1170.

Mobinil customer service centres include the following, all in Cairo:

Heliopolis (☎ 02-417 2054) 110 Mirghany
Ma'adi (☎ 02-516 3019) 49 Sharia al-Lasliky
Mohandiseen (☎ 02-302 8004/7) 39 Sharia Shehab

Phonophobia

It is tough to get phone numbers in Egypt. According to a report in a local paper, in one year the phone numbers in a particular part of the city were changed three times. Even more astounding is that the subscribers weren't always informed that they had new numbers. There is also a random element in making connections – just because you've dialled the right number it does not mean you're going to end up on the right line.

If you are sure that the number we have listed is inaccurate then you could try dialling directory inquiries, but if you can get through – the lines aren't busy and they decide to pick up – there's still no guarantee that you'll be given the correct number.

Fax & Telegraph

Fax machines are available for sending and receiving documents at the main centrales in the big cities, at EMS offices, at most three- to five-star hotels and at some of the smaller hotels as well. You can receive a fax for free at AmEx offices but it's not possible to send faxes from there.

From a telephone office, a one-page fax costs about E£14 to the UK or USA, and E£20 to Australia. Hotel rates are more. The minimum from the Nile Hilton to the UK is E£38.50, and to Australia it's E£51.25. Receiving a fax message costs E£6 at a telephone office, or E£5.50 at an EMS office.

Telegrams in English or French can also be sent from the centrales. The rates to the UK, USA and Europe are 67pt per word and to Australia it's 84pt per word. Each word in an address is also counted. Major hotels also offer this service but rates vary.

Email & Internet Access

Travelling with a portable computer is a great way to stay in touch with life back home, but unless you know what you're doing it's fraught with potential problems. If you plan to carry your notebook or palmtop computer with you, remember that the power supply voltage in Egypt may vary from that at home, which entails the risk of damage to your equipment. The best investment is a universal AC adaptor for your appliance, which will enable you to plug it in anywhere without frying the innards. More problematic is the issue of phone plugs. There is a mind-boggling variety of these in use in Egypt, and in some cases the phone cable is wired straight into the wall. All we can recommend is that you come pre-armed with a selection of adaptors, including a US RJ-11 telephone adaptor that works with your modem. You can almost always find an adaptor that will convert from RJ-11 to the local variety. For more information on travelling with a portable computer, see W www.teleadapt.com or W www.warrior.com.

Other issues are that your PC-card modem may or may not work once you leave your home country – and you won't know for sure until you try. The safest option is to buy a reputable 'global' modem before you leave home.

The good news is that Egypt has taken up the Internet in a big way and there are Internet cafes throughout the country including in Cairo, Alexandria, Aswan, Dahab, Hurghada, Ismailia, Sharm el-Sheikh and Luxor. Many budget and mid-range hotels provide online terminals for the use of guests, free or otherwise. Unfortunately, Internet connections can be infuriatingly slow, a result of too much demand on insufficient international bandwidth.

If you do intend to rely on Internet cafes or public access points to collect your mail, you'll need to carry three pieces of information with you to enable you to access your Internet mail account: your incoming (POP or IMAP) mail server name, your account name and your password. Your Internet Service Provider (ISP) or network supervisor will be able to give you these. Armed with this information, you should be able to access your Internet mail account from any Internet-connected machine in the world, provided it runs some kind of email software (remember that Netscape and Internet Explorer both have mail modules).

Service Providers There are more than 30 ISPs in Egypt. Of these, companies that we've had good word on include Internet Egypt (☎ 02-796 2882, e info@internetegypt.com, W www.ic-cg.com), which is the largest private ISP in the country, Soficom (☎ 02-342 1954, W www.soficom.com.eg) and Gega Net (☎ 02-414 9700, W www.gega.net). Account rates that were formerly expensive are now becoming much more reasonable; InternetEgypt, for example, offers unlimited dial-up accounts at E£49 (US$13) a month or E£499 (US$130) a year.

DIGITAL RESOURCES

The World Wide Web is a rich resource for travellers. You can research your trip, hunt down bargain air fares, book hotels, check on weather conditions or chat with locals and other travellers about the best places to visit (or avoid).

At the Lonely Planet Web site (W www.lonelyplanet.com) you will find succinct summaries on travelling to most places on earth, postcards from other travellers and the Thorn Tree bulletin board, where you can ask questions before you go or dispense advice to others when you get back. You can also find travel news and updates to many of our guidebooks, and the subWWWay section links you to the most useful travel resources elsewhere on the Web.

Alternatively, entering the word 'Egypt' into one of the many Net search engines will result in several thousand links, offering everything from prayer times to theories on who built the Pyramids. Narrowing the field down a little, the following are some of our recommendations, ranging from very general to more specific information about Egypt:

Egypt: The Complete Guide The official site of Egypt's Ministry of Tourism is surprisingly good; it's updated regularly with magazine-type features, news and a huge range of resources and links.
W touregypt.net

All of Egypt Confusing site that tries to be all things to everybody, from tourist site descriptions to business directories, but well worth a browse to see what you can find.
W www.allofegypt.com

Al-Bab An incredible Arab World gateway site ('Al-Bab' means 'The Gate'); the Egypt page includes links to dozens of news services, country profiles, travel sites, maps, people profiles etc. It is a fantastic resource.
W www.al-bab.com/arab/countries/egypt.htm

Cairo Cafe Lively site devoted to what's on in the Big Mango. It includes new openings, restaurant reviews and an events calendar, and is particularly good on nightlife. It's updated regularly.
W www.cairocafe.com.eg

Alexandria 2000 The name could do with an update but that aside this is a pretty good compendium of information on Egypt's second city, kept up to date with regular postings.
W www.alexandria2000.com

Red Sea Guide & Search Engine This site does exactly what it says: provides heaps of travel tips and water sports information and links.
W www.red-sea.com/main.html

Al-Ahram Weekly Electronic version of the weekly English-language newspaper. Just about the whole paper is online and the archives are fully searchable and free.
W www.ahram.org.eg/weekly

Egypt Today Electronic version of the glossy monthly mag with a selection of features and departments but no access to past issues.
W www.egypttoday.com

The Plateau The official Web site of Zahi Hawass, Undersecretary of State for the Giza plateau, that is, the man who looks after the Pyramids. This is one of the best places to go for news on recent discoveries and news on what is happening with the Pharaonic sites around Cairo.
W guardians.net/hawass/index.htm

The Pyramids of Egypt & Mars Just one of the many, many sites devoted to the whacky science of pyramidology. One of the more technically adept examples, this is run by the Watcher Ministries who believe that angels built the Pyramids and Sphinx – and a parallel city on Mars.
W www.mt.net/~watcher/pyramid.html

BOOKS

The following is a very short, personal list of recommended reading. Many of these titles can be found at bookshops in Egypt, particularly at the excellent American University in Cairo (AUC) bookshop. Outside Egypt you may have to order them.

Most books are published in different editions by different publishers in different countries. As a result, a book might be a hardcover rarity in one country while it's readily available in paperback in another. Fortunately, bookshops and libraries search by title or author, so your local bookshop or library is best placed to advise you on the availability of the following recommendations.

Lonely Planet

As well as this book, Lonely Planet also publishes a separate guide, *Cairo*, that deals with the Egyptian capital in much greater depth, complemented by colour street maps. There is also an *Egyptian Arabic Phrasebook* and a diving guide, *Diving & Snorkeling Red Sea*. Other guides to the region include *Middle East*, *Israel & the Palestinian Territories*, *Jordan*, *Libya* and *Africa*.

Guidebooks

There are numerous locally produced guidebooks available in Egypt devoted to every square centimetre of the country, from Siwa Oasis in the west to the dive sites of the Red Sea in the east.

We highlight a few guidebooks in relevant places in the text but a few others to look out for include:

Cairo: The Practical Guide by Claire E Francy. Published locally by the AUC Press, this book is aimed at people setting up home in the city and focuses on matters such as finding a flat and a school for the kids, but it also contains a wealth of information of use to the visitor, such as a very comprehensive shopping section.

A Guide to the Nubian Monuments on Lake Nasser by Jocelyn Gohary. The most comprehensive guide to the temples and tombs of the Lake Nasser area.

Islamic Monuments in Cairo by Richard B Parker. Scholarly and comprehensive work on the city's Islamic heritage organised around walks (with accompanying maps) so you can also use the book as a guide.

Mount Sinai by Joseph J Hobbs. A wide-ranging and eclectic view of Mt Sinai, examining its history, religious significance, ecology and the threats posed to it by tourism.

Siwa Oasis by Ahmed Fakhry. This exhaustive look at the history and archaeology of Egypt's most beautiful oasis is still the best, despite being written in 1973.

The Western Desert of Egypt by Cassandra Vivien. Excellent, detailed background on the history, culture, and geography of the Western Desert and the oases that dot it. The book should not replace a human guide to off-road destinations, however, because many of the directions are misleading or even wrong.

Travel

Surprisingly little travel literature has appeared in recent times concerning Egypt. However, a great many entertaining 19th-century accounts continue to be reprinted. The following list runs in roughly chronological order with the earliest travelogues first:

Flaubert in Egypt by Gustave Flaubert. Reprints extracts from diaries Flaubert kept when he visited the country for a few months in 1849. The Pyramids receive short shrift as Flaubert prefers to focus on his exploits in the bathhouses and bordellos.

A Thousand Miles up the Nile by Amelia Edwards. A thousand miles was a long way on a *dahabiyya* (houseboat) and Victorian adventuress Amelia Edwards evidently had a lot of time on her hands – her famous book runs to more than 1000 pages, or a page per mile. Still, it gives a good idea of travel in Egypt before air-con buses and aeroplanes turned it into a five-day jaunt from Europe.

Letters from Egypt by Lucy Duff Gordon. Letters written by a famous 19th-century consumptive who lived inside Luxor temple before it was cleared for the admiration of tourists. There she was able to get to know her neighbours and portrayed them far more sympathetically than most other travellers of the time.

The Nile: A Traveller's Anthology by Deborah Manley (ed) and ***Egypt: A Traveller's Anthology*** by Christopher Pick (ed). These are collections of literary titbits from some of Egypt's more illustrious visitors, including Lawrence Durrell, EM Forster, Mark Twain and Agatha Christie.

Beyond the Pyramids by Douglas Kennedy. Written in the 1980s the book is now badly dated, but as one of the very few travel books written exclusively about Egypt in recent years, it's still worth picking up.

In an Antique Land by Amitav Ghosh. A wonderfully observed account of the author's lengthy stay in a Delta village; entertaining, educational and one of the few travel books that is not patronising towards its subject.

From Giza to Galipolli by Garrie Hutchinson. An Aussie's account of a pilgrimage to WWI and WWII battlefields throughout the Middle East, which kicks off in Egypt. It's very much a first-impressions book but the research is solid and it's an entertaining read.

The Pharaoh's Shadow by Anthony Sattin. Subtitled 'Travels in Ancient and Modern Egypt' this is travel literature with a twist as Sattin searches for 'survivals' of Pharaonic traditions and practices in the Egypt of today, encountering along the way magicians, snake catchers, mystics and sceptics.

Travels with a Tangerine by Tim Mackintosh Smith. Not strictly about Egypt, this is a modern account of a journey in the footsteps of Ibn Battuta, a 13th-century Arab Marco Polo, which spends a few enjoyable chapters in Cairo.

Pharaonic Egypt

The catalogue of Egyptological works is immense with more appearing almost weekly. The following are some accessible titles that don't assume any prior knowledge:

Ancient Egypt: The Great Discoveries by Nicholas Reeves. A lavishly illustrated, chronological account of the most important finds of Egyptology, beginning with the Rosetta Stone and taking in Tutankhamun and coming up to date with such recent discoveries as the Valley of the Golden Mummies, Cleopatra's Palace and KV5.

The British Museum Book of Ancient Egypt by Stephen Quirke & Jeffrey Spencer (ed). Gives an authoritative overview of ancient Egypt, although it's surprisingly short on plans and diagrams of monuments.

The Complete Pyramids by Mark Lehner. Everything you ever wanted to know about pyramids

– not just those at Giza but the other 80 or more scattered throughout the country.

The Complete Valley of the Kings by Nicholas Reeves & Richard H Wilkinson. Lively compendium of information accompanied by many photos and specially drawn illustrations. Companion volume to *The Complete Pyramids* – both are highly recommended.

Egypt's Sun King by Joann Fletcher. An intimate life study of one of the greatest of pharaohs, Amenhotep III, builder of Luxor Temple. The writing is lively with great details, such as the name of his cat, and it's accompanied by well-chosen illustrations.

The Lost Tomb by Kent Weeks. Engrossing account of the discovery in the Valley of the Kings of KV5, the largest Egyptian tomb ever discovered, written by the archaeologist who made the discovery.

Mummies of Gold by Zahi Hawass. Beautifully produced coffee-table tome about the famous Bahariyya mummies by the archaeologist who dug them out of the ground.

The Mummy in Ancient Egypt: Equipping the Dead for Eternity by Aidan Dodson & Salima Ikram. The most comprehensive book yet on mummies, mummification and our morbid fascination with the subject by two of the world's foremost experts.

The Mysterious Fayoum Portraits: Faces from Ancient Egypt by Euphrosyne Doxiadis. Beautifully produced study of the incredibly lifelike Graeco-Roman funerary portraits. Expensive but worth the money.

The Penguin Guide to Ancient Egypt by William J Murnane. One of the best overall books on the life and monuments of ancient Egypt. There are plenty of illustrations and descriptions of almost every major monument in the country.

The Rape of the Nile: Tomb Robbers, Tourists and Archeologists in Egypt by Brian M Fagan. The title says it all – a lively account of the damage done to Egypt's heritage, particularly in the last 200 years.

General History

Egypt's span of history is so immense and diverse that there's not one book that really covers it all. Instead there are numerous excellent works on specific periods and cities.

Alexandria 1860-1960 by Robert Ilbert & Ilios Yannakakis (ed). An absorbing collection of essays on various facets of the city in its cosmopolitan heyday. There's also a good companion volume, *Alexandria Third Century BC*.

Alexandria Rediscovered by Jean-Yves Empreur. An exploration of Graeco-Roman Alexandria including sections on the Pharos and the search for Alexander's tomb, written by the archaeologist currently leading the underwater excavations in the city's harbour.

Cairo: The City Victorious by Max Rodenbeck. An entertaining and prodigiously researched anecdotal meander through 5000 years of history of the Mother of the World, written by the Egypt correspondent for the *Economist*.

A History of Egypt by PJ Vatiokis. The single best introduction to the history of Egypt, though the emphasis is firmly on the 19th and 20th centuries and the new social order that has evolved since the 1952 Revolution.

A Short History of Modern Egypt by Afaf Lutfi al-Sayyid Marsot. A concise, if dry, history of Egypt from AD 639 onwards written by one of Egypt's foremost historians.

Zarafa by Michael Allin. The charming story of a giraffe (Zarafa) sent as gift from the ruler of Egypt to the king of France overlies a fascinating study of the meeting between Age of Enlightenment Europe and an Egypt barely out of the Middle Ages. Very readable and a surprising bestseller on its publication in 1998.

Culture & Society

There's no one primer on Egyptian culture and society that encompasses strands as diverse as Western educated business communities and Bedouin tribes yet to encounter computers. Bear in mind all the following titles focus only on single aspects and in no way present a particularly full picture.

Egypt: Moulids, Saints and Sufis by Nicholas Biegman. One of the best nonacademic books on the subject, written by a former Dutch ambassador to Cairo. Biegman has also produced a coffee-table book, *Egypt's Sideshows*, with photos of *moulids* (religious festivals), weddings and other traditional occasions.

The Hidden Face of Eve by Nawal al-Saadawi. Considers the role of women in the Arab world and is banned in Egypt. For more on Al-Saadawi see the Arts section in the Facts about Egypt chapter.

Khul-Khaal: Five Egyptian Women Tell their Stories by Nayra Atiya (ed). Five women from different backgrounds tell their stories. An often harrowing but revealing portrait of women's lives in Egypt, it could use an update in light of the effect of Islamism on Egyptian society.

No God but God: Egypt and the Triumph of Islam by Geneive Abdo. One of the best books on the Egyptian Islamist movements in recent years. Examines the Islamist movement as a response to increased piety and the ineptitude of governance in the post-Nasserist era.

Shahhat: An Egyptian by Richard Critchfield. This book has become an anthropology classic, even though much of its content was recently debunked as a copy of a 1930s ethnographic study. So long as you keep this in mind it's still a good read if you're spending time on Luxor's West Bank.

Veiled Sentiments: Honour and Poetry in a Bedouin Society by Lila Abu Lughod. A study of the Awlad Ali tribe in the Western Desert and how they speak their mind through poetry. A great insight into a Bedouin society.

Fiction

With a vivid history stretching back some 5000 years encompassing pyramid builders (human or otherwise), Hammer horror caliphs, the enchantment of *The Thousand and One Nights*, colonial hi-jinks and romance, and the modern day tinderbox that is the Middle East, little wonder that Egypt has provided a perfect backdrop for the imaginings of writers.

In addition to the following list, for books to do with Alexandria see the boxed text 'Literary Alexandria' in the Alexandria & the Mediterranean Coast chapter; for literature by Egyptian writers see Arts in the Facts about Egypt chapter.

Baby Love by Louisa Young. Smart, hip novel by a young Londoner that shimmies between Shepherd's Bush in west London and the West Bank of Luxor, as an ex-belly dancer, now single mother skirts romance and violence. There are also a couple of follow-ups, *Desiring Cairo* and *Tree of Pearls*.

City of the Horizon*, *City of Dreams*, *City of the Dead by Anton Gill. Highly readable mystery trilogy set in the turmoil of post-Akhenaten Egypt.

Death on the Nile by Agatha Christie. Draws on Christie's experiences of a winter in Upper Egypt. She writes in the introduction, 'When I read it now I feel myself back on the steamer from Aswan to Wadi Halfa'. An absolute must if you're booked on a cruise.

The English Patient by Michael Ondaatje. Although it has little to do with the film of the same name and has a highly impressionistic sense of history, this story of love and destiny in WWII remains a beautifully written, poetic novel. And a bit of it is set in Egypt.

The Eye of Ra by Michael Asher. An Indiana Jones meets the X-Files type tale of missing corpses, multiple murders, hidden tombs, psychic Bedouin characters and other gung-ho malarkey. Still, it's terrific fun and Cairo is well described. Plus it's not half as absurd as its follow up, *Firebird*.

The Face in the Cemetery by Michael Pearce. The 14th and latest in a highly entertaining series of lightweight, period mystery novels featuring the Mamur Zapt, head of Cairo's secret police. It reads a bit like Tintin but without the pictures.

Into the Mummy's Tomb by John Richard Stephens (ed). Anthology of mummy related pieces mixing fiction by Anne Rice, Bram Stoker and Edgar Allen Poe with historical accounts of tomb exploration by the likes of Howard Carter and Rudyard Kipling.

The Levant Trilogy by Olivia Manning. Cairo during the war serves as the setting for the trials and traumas of a dislikable bunch of ex-pats. It was filmed by the BBC as *Fortunes of War* starring Kenneth Branagh and Emma Thompson.

The Map of Love by Ahdaf Soueif. Booker-prize shortlisted, bestselling historical novel about love and clashing cultures. Jumps between Egypt's early 20th-century nationalist foment and the contemporary era. For more on Soueif, see Literature under Arts in the Facts about Egypt chapter.

The Mummy or Ramses the Damned by Anne Rice. Best known for her best-selling vampire books, this is a credible stab at a modern horror rooted in ancient Egypt.

The Photographer's Wife by Robert Sole. One of three historical romances by this French journalist set in late 19th-century Egypt (the others being *Birds of Passage* and *The Alexandria Semaphore*). They're a little slow going but worth persevering with for the fine period detail and emotive stories.

Ramses: The Son of Light by Christian Jacq. First of a five-volume trashy and immensely popular hagiography of the famous pharaoh. Prose is simplistic, with long descriptions of rippling muscles and Nefertari's diaphanous robes, but Jacq is an Egyptologist so it must be true.

A Woman of Cairo by Noel Barber. One of those historical novels of breathtaking sweep in which dynasties crash and fall about star-crossed lovers. In this, British and Egyptian neighbours are in the run-up to the Revolution; King Farouk, Nasser and Sadat all get walk on parts.

FILMS

The meticulously painted backdrops of 1998's animated *Prince of Egypt* aside, it's quite some time since Egypt has been seen at the cinema. True, a large part of the Oscar-sweeping *The English Patient* (1996) was set in the Western Desert and Cairo, but this was silver-screen trickery, achieved with scenic doubles – the Egyptian locations were actually Tunisia and, in the case of some interiors, Venice.

It's not that Egypt is unphotogenic – quite the opposite. Its deserts, temples and colourful bazaars appear beguilingly seductive on a wide screen. So much so, that the country experienced a surge in tourism in the wake of *The English Patient*, despite the best attempts of the Tunisian tourist authority to set the record straight. But extortionate taxes levied on foreign film companies keep the cameras away. It wasn't always so, and the 1970s and 1980s, in particular, resulted in a number of films on location in Egypt, most of which you should still be able to find down the local video library.

The Awakening (1980) Lame, ineffective horror about an ancient Egyptian queen possessing modern souls, loosely based on Bram Stoker's *The Jewel of the Seven Stars* and starring Charlton Heston.

Cleopatra (1963) Best remembered for the on-set affair between Richard Burton and Liz Taylor, shooting for part of this four-hour-long dreary spectacle took place in the Egyptian desert.

Death on the Nile (1978) Agatha Christie whodunnit, with Poirot investigating the murder of an heiress on board on a Nile cruiser. Gorgeous scenery but the real mystery is how the boat manages to sail from Aswan down to Karnak and back up to Abu Simbel all in the same day.

The Mummy Rises, Again & Again & Again

In 2001 the mummy returned to Egypt. He first walked abroad in 1932 when Universal pictures made *The Mummy* to cash in on the Egyptomania generated by the end of the decade-long excavation of Tutankhamun's tomb. Boris Karloff was the priest Imhotep brought back to life and appearing unwrapped for most of the movie as he searched for a way to resurrect his long dead love. A sequel, *The Mummy's Hand* (1940), set the formula for future horrors: unwitting archaeologists trespass in a tomb, the wrath of the long-dead is invoked and they rise, fully bandaged, to lurch around, with arms outstretched, through shaky tombs and dusty museums, until banished by some intoned magical text. Sticking to the set ingredients, more sequels followed in rapid succession, including *The Mummy's Tomb* (1942), *The Mummy's Ghost* (1944) and *The Mummy's Curse* (1945).

The menace of the bandaged creature was then largely put to rest until revived by the British Hammer studios in 1959 (with Christopher Lee as the creature). They kept the franchise going with a further three films made over the next 12 years. But measured against 1970s film shockers such as *The Exorcist* and *The Omen*, a monster that looked more like a lost patient from a 3000-year-old casualty department no longer delivered. Hence the reinvention of 1999's *The Mummy* as a *Raiders of the Lost Ark*-type romp with thrills, spills, self-depreciating humour and a monster that could morph into howling sandstorms. It did big-time at the box office, but not in Egypt. There the film was banned. According to the censor it contained 'dialogue and scenes that denigrate ancient Egyptian history'. Two years later the sequel *The Mummy Returns* hit screens worldwide. This time round a committee of public figures, including leading Egyptologist Zahi Hawass, was set up to pass judgement on the new film. While it found the film 'depressing' and 'full of historical and geographical mistakes' the committee concluded that a ban achieved nothing. So even if Egyptians found little in the film they recognised, they did get to see their mummy.

Five Graves to Cairo (1943) Wartime espionage thriller with a British corporal holed up in a Nazi-controlled hotel in the Western Desert directed by Billy Wilder *(Some Like It Hot)*.

Gallipoli (1981) Aussie film about the fateful WWI battle with an extended middle section devoted to the young soldiers' training in Egypt in the shadow of the Pyramids.

Ice Cold in Alex (1958) Classic wartime thriller with a British ambulance officer and crew fleeing Rommel's forces across the Western Desert and dreaming of an ice-cold beer in a little bar in Alexandria.

Ruby Cairo (1992) One of the last Hollywood productions to brave the bureaucracy, this is a limp tale of a wife who tracks down her missing-presumed-dead husband to a hideaway in Egypt. Headlined by Andie MacDowell and Liam Neeson but the real star of the film is Cairo, where no cliche is left unshown, including camels, pyramids, moulids and feluccas.

Sphinx (1980) Adapted from a bestselling novel by Robin (Coma) Cook, this is a tale about antiquities smuggling shot entirely in Cairo and Luxor, but from which no-one emerges with any credit, except the location scout.

The Spy Who Loved Me (1977) The Pyramids, Islamic Cairo and Karnak provide Martini-glamorous backdrops for the campy, smirking antics of Roger Moore as James Bond.

NEWSPAPERS & MAGAZINES

The *Egyptian Gazette* is Egypt's awful daily English-language newspaper. It serves largely as a press puff for the office of the president, although it does offer great entertainment for lovers of typos and seriously screwed-up headlines. The Saturday issue is called the *Egyptian Mail*. The French-language equivalents are the daily *Le Progrés Egyptien* and Sunday's *Progrés Dimanche*.

Al-Ahram Weekly, *Cairo Times* and *Middle East Times* all appear every Thursday and do a much better job of keeping English-readers informed of what's going on. Of the three, the *Cairo Times* is the most readable and is great for news analysis, but the *Weekly* is the most comprehensive and particularly good on coverage of current events, including restaurant openings, cultural performances or sports. *Al-Ahram* also puts out a weekly French edition, *Hebdo*.

Egypt Today is an ad-saturated, general interest glossy with excellent listings but its monthly schedule means that in this most unpredictable of countries, much of the information has a certain hypothetical quality. It also has several sister publications including the monthly *Sports & Fitness* and *Business Today*, and the quarterly *Sinai Today* and *Red Sea Today*.

An extremely broad range of Western newspapers and magazines is sold at hotel bookshops and street-side newsstands. Papers are just a day old and monthly magazines usually make it within a week of their home publication dates, but expect to pay up to twice the cover price. Censorship is still in force and it's not unusual to find a page has been neatly sliced from your copy of *Time* magazine, usually because a model in an ad had a little bit too much flesh on display.

Of the local Arab-language press, the venerable state-owned *Al-Ahram* remains the best known of the national dailies, though the journalism is very stilted and conservative compared with some of the newer publications such as the progressive business-focused *Al-Alam al-Yom* and the Egyptian edition of the Arab world daily *Al-Hayat*.

RADIO & TV

Radio-wise, FM95 broadcasts news in English on 557kHz at 7.30am, 2.30pm and 8pm daily. This is the European-language station and, in addition to English-language programs, it has programs in French, German, Italian, and Greek. BBC and Voice of America (VOA) broadcasts can be picked up on medium wave at various times of the morning and evening. The BBC can be heard on both 639kHz and 1320kHz, and VOA on 1290kHz.

Despite a firm state stranglehold, Egyptian TV is booming. In the last few years the traditional three channels have been supplemented by half a dozen or more, as throughout the country every governorate gets in on the act with their own station. Nile TV, which is based in Cairo, broadcasts news and current affairs exclusively in English and French from 7am each day until past midnight. Otherwise, there's little for non-Arabic speakers, apart from the occasional old American movie (the Saturday night Cine Club on

Channel One sometimes screens the odd good one) and a nightly English-language news bulletin on Channel Two at 8pm.

Satellite has made a big splash (check the number of dishes on the city skylines), and cable to a lesser extent. Many hotels have satellite TV, even some of the budget places. MTV seems to be a staple at fast-food joints all over the country.

Check the *Egyptian Gazette* for the day's TV (both local and satellite) and radio program information. There are also a couple of special monthly program-listing magazines for satellite and cable.

PHOTOGRAPHY & VIDEO

Egypt is full of opportunities for great photography. Early morning and late afternoon are the best times as during the rest of the day, the sunlight can be too bright and the sky too hazy, resulting in washed-out photos. There are a few remedies for this. A polarisation filter will cut glare and reflection off sand and water and a lens hood will cut some of the glare. Kodachrome film with an ASA of 64 or 25 and Fujichrome 50 and 100 are good slide films to use when the sun is bright.

Cameras and lenses collect dust quickly in Egypt. Lens paper and cleaner are difficult to find, so bring your own. A dust brush is also useful.

Film & Equipment

Film generally costs as much as, if not more than, it does in the West; for example, Kodacolor 100/200 (36 exposures) costs about E£22, while for Kodachrome 100 slide film, you'll pay E£24 (36 exposures). If you buy film in Egypt, always check the expiry date and don't buy from anywhere that keeps its stock in direct sunlight.

Colour-print processing costs from E£2 to E£5 depending on whether it's a one-hour or overnight service, plus from 50pt to 135pt per print depending on print size. B&W processing is not recommended, but colour processing is usually adequate for nonprofessional purposes. Developing a roll of slide film costs between E£10 and E£13. There are quite a few labs and one-hour processing places in the big cities and tourist centres.

Restrictions

Be careful when taking photos of anything other than tourist sites. It is forbidden to photograph bridges, train stations, anything military, airports and any other public works; a photographer friend of ours had her film confiscated for shooting pictures of public telephones, while another spent a day at a police station for inadvertently snapping a factory. If anyone kicks up a fuss because of your picture taking, apologise and get the message across that you're just a 'dumb tourist' who doesn't know any better.

Egyptians are also sensitive about the negative aspects of their country. It is not uncommon for someone to yell at you when you're trying to take photos of things

Photography & Video-Camera Fees

Photography is allowed at all ancient sites, but flash photography is banned in some of the tombs to help preserve the paintings. You can take photos of the interior of mosques and temples, although at an increasing number of sites the government now charges outrageous fees for the use of personal cameras and videos. Camera fees range from E£5 to E£15; the fees for using a video camera, which begin at E£25, are at some sites as high as E£100 or even E£150. These fees also apply to many museums and galleries throughout Egypt. At the Manial Palace Museum in Cairo, for instance, the fee is E£150 for a video camera.

If you are carrying a camera/video and baulk at the cost, promising the guards you aren't going to use your equipment doesn't cut the mustard. They will insist that you deposit the gear at the ticket office. If you don't like the thought of leaving possibly expensive equipment in surroundings of dubious security, then leave the stuff at your hotel.

like a crowded bus, a dilapidated building or a donkey cart full of garbage. Exercise discretion.

Photographing People

It can sometimes be tricky taking photos of people, so it's always better to ask first. Children will almost always say yes, but their parents or other adults might say no. Some Muslims believe that by taking photos of children you might be casting an 'evil eye' upon them. Similar attitudes sometimes apply to taking photos of women, especially in the countryside.

TIME

Egypt is two hours ahead of GMT/UTC and daylight saving time is observed (it begins in late April and ends on 30 September). So, without allowing for variations due to daylight saving, when it's noon in Cairo it is 2am in Los Angeles; 5am in New York and Montreal; 10am in London; 1pm in Moscow; and 7pm in Melbourne and Sydney.

ELECTRICITY

Electric current is 220V AC, 50Hz. Wall sockets are the round, two-pin European type (though for some strange reason the socket holes are often too narrow to accept European plugs). Adaptor plugs are easily found in city shops but bring a transformer if you need one as these are difficult to obtain in Egypt.

WEIGHTS & MEASURES

Egypt is on the metric system. Basic conversion charts are given on the inside back cover of this book.

LAUNDRY

There are a few self-service laundries around Cairo but virtually none elsewhere in the country. Most hotels can organise to have your washing done. Another option is to take your clothes to one of Egypt's many 'hole-in-the-wall' laundries where they wash and iron your clothes by hand. The process is fascinating to watch. The *makwagee* (ironing man) takes an ancient iron that opens at the top, places hot coals inside and then fills his mouth with water from a bottle on the table. The water is sprayed from his mouth over the clothes as he vigorously irons.

In a few of the places where travellers hang out, such as Luxor and Dahab, some of the cheaper hotels lure guests with advertisements about 'washing machines'. Don't be fooled into thinking they've got a Zanussi stashed away in a back room; the reality is a humble machine that lethargically twists your clothes around and leaves you to do the rinsing and wringing out. These machines are almost as laborious as your last – and most common – option, which is to do your own washing by hand.

TOILETS

Public toilets, when they can be found, are bad news: fly infested, dirty and smelly. Some toilets are still of the 'squat over a hole in a little room' variety. Only in mid-range and top-end hotels will toilet paper be provided; most toilets simply come equipped with a water squirter for washing yourself when you're finished. It's a good idea to adopt this practice if you can as toilets in Egypt are not capable of swallowing much toilet paper and it's not uncommon to find toilets in hotels frequented by Westerners absolutely choked with the stuff. If you do use toilet paper, put it in the bucket that's usually provided.

In cities it's a good idea to make a mental note of all Western-style fast-food joints, such as McDonald's and KFC, and of the five-star hotels, as these are where you'll find the most sanitary facilities.

While on the subject of ablutions, when trekking in the desert, climbing Mt Sinai or camping out on a beach somewhere, do not leave used toilet paper lying around. Burying it is no good either; sand is blown away in strong winds. So either take a plastic bag with you and put it in there, to be thrown in a bin later, or take some matches and burn it.

HEALTH

Travel health depends on your predeparture preparations, your daily health care while travelling and how you handle any medical problem that does develop. While the potential dangers can seem quite frightening, in reality few travellers to Egypt ever experience anything more than upset stomachs.

Predeparture Planning

It's a good idea to get medical advice at least six weeks before you travel. This is especially important if you are pregnant or if you are travelling with children, as the risks of illness in pregnancy and in children are often higher.

Immunisations Before you travel, make sure your vaccinations are up to date. Plan ahead for getting your vaccinations, as some require more than one injection, and some should not be given together. Discuss your individual requirements with your doctor. It's a good idea to carry proof of your vaccinations with you. You will need to show proof of yellow fever vaccination only if you are coming into Egypt from parts of the world where yellow fever is a risk (most of sub-Saharan Africa and parts of South America). There is no risk of yellow fever in Egypt. The following list gives some information about vaccinations you may need to have before you travel to Egypt; details about the diseases themselves are given later in this section.

Diphtheria & Tetanus Vaccinations for these two diseases are usually combined and are recommended for everyone. After an initial course of three injections (usually given in childhood), boosters are necessary every 10 years.

Polio Everyone should keep up to date with this vaccination, normally given in childhood. A booster every 10 years maintains immunity.

Hepatitis A This provides long-term immunity (possibly more than 10 years) after an initial injection and a booster at six to 12 months. Alternatively, an injection of gamma globulin can provide short-term protection against hepatitis A – two to six months, depending on the dose given. Gamma globulin is not a vaccine, it is a ready-made antibody collected from blood donations. It is reasonably effective and, unlike the vaccine, it is protective immediately, but because it is a blood product, there are current concerns about its long-term safety. **Hepatitis A** vaccine is also available in a combined form with hepatitis B vaccine. Three injections over a six-month period are required, the first two providing substantial protection against hepatitis A.

Typhoid Vaccination against typhoid may be required if you are travelling for more than a couple of weeks in Egypt. It is available either as an injection or as capsules to be taken orally.

Cholera The current injectable vaccine against cholera is poorly protective and has many side effects, so it is not generally recommended. However, in some situations it may be necessary to have a certificate as travellers are very occasionally asked by immigration officials to present one, even though all countries and the WHO have dropped cholera immunisation as a health requirement for entry.

Hepatitis B Travellers who should consider vaccination against hepatitis B include those on a long trip, as well as those visiting countries such as Egypt where there are high levels of hepatitis B infection, where blood transfusions may not be adequately screened or where sexual contact or needle sharing is a possibility. Vaccination involves three injections, with a booster at 12 months. More rapid courses are available if necessary.

Rabies Vaccination should be considered by those who will spend a month or longer in Egypt, especially if they are cycling, handling animals, caving or travelling to remote areas, and for children (who may not report a bite). Pretravel rabies vaccination involves having three injections over 21 to 28 days. If someone who has been vaccinated is bitten or scratched by an animal, they will require two booster injections of vaccine; those not vaccinated require more.

Malaria Medication There is a risk of malaria in the Al-Fayoum area only, with the highest risks from June to October.

Antimalarial drugs do not prevent you from being infected but kill the malaria parasites during a stage in their development and significantly reduce the risk of becoming very ill or dying. Expert advice on medication should be sought, as there are many factors to consider, including the area to be visited, the risk of exposure to mosquitoes that carry malaria, the side effects of medication, your medical history and whether you are a child or an adult or pregnant. Travellers going to isolated areas in high-risk countries may like to carry a treatment dose of medication for use if symptoms occur.

Health Insurance Make sure that you have adequate health insurance. See Travel Insurance under Visas & Documents earlier in this chapter for details.

Travel Health Guides Lonely Planet's *Healthy Travel Africa* is a handy pocket size and packed with useful information including pretrip planning, emergency first aid, immunisation and disease information and what to do if you get sick on the road. *Travel with Children* from Lonely Planet also includes advice on travel health for younger children. If you are planning to be away or travelling in remote areas for a long period of time, you may like to consider taking a more detailed health guide with you.

There are also a number of excellent travel health sites on the Internet. From the Lonely Planet home page there are links at W www.lonelyplanet.com/health/health.htm/hlinks.htm to the World Health Organization and the US Centers for Disease Control & Prevention.

Other Preparations Make sure you are healthy and that your teeth are OK before you start travelling. If you wear glasses take a spare pair and your prescription.

If you require a particular medication take an adequate supply, as it may not be available locally. Take part of the packaging showing the generic name rather than the brand, which will make getting replacements easier. It's a good idea to have a legible prescription or letter from your doctor to show that you legally use the medication to avoid any problems.

Basic Rules

The main concern in Egypt for most of the year is the heat. Drink plenty of fluids to prevent dehydration. Avoid sunburn by using sunscreen and wearing a hat, and protect your eyes with good quality sunglasses. For further details on how to recognise and combat heat-related problems see Heat Exhaustion later.

Food It pays to be a bit careful about what you eat in Egypt to help avoid the stomach problems that commonly afflict travellers here. Vegetables and fruit should be washed with purified water or peeled where possible. Beware of ice cream that is sold in the street or anywhere it might have been

Medical Kit Check List

Following is a list of items you should consider including in your medical kit – consult your pharmacist for brands available in your country.

- ☐ **Aspirin or paracetamol (acetaminophen in the USA)** – for pain or fever
- ☐ **Antihistamine** – for allergies, eg, hay fever; to ease the itch from insect bites or stings; and to prevent motion sickness
- ☐ **Cold and flu tablets, throat lozenges and nasal decongestant**
- ☐ **Multivitamins** – consider for long trips, when dietary vitamin intake may be inadequate
- ☐ **Antibiotics** – consider including these if you're travelling well off the beaten track; see your doctor, as they must be prescribed, and carry the prescription with you
- ☐ **Loperamide or diphenoxylate** – 'blockers' for diarrhoea
- ☐ **Prochlorperazine or metaclopramide** – for nausea and vomiting
- ☐ **Rehydration mixture** – to prevent dehydration, which may occur, for example, during bouts of diarrhoea; particularly important when travelling with children
- ☐ **Insect repellent, sunscreen, lip balm and eye drops**
- ☐ **Calamine lotion, sting relief spray or aloe vera** – to ease irritation from sunburn and insect bites or stings
- ☐ **Antifungal cream or powder** – for fungal skin infections and thrush
- ☐ **Antiseptic (such as povidone-iodine)** – for cuts and grazes
- ☐ **Bandages, Band-Aids (plasters) and other wound dressings**
- ☐ **Water purification tablets or iodine**
- ☐ **Scissors, tweezers and a thermometer** – note that mercury thermometers are prohibited by airlines
- ☐ **Sterile kit** – in case you need injections in a country with medical hygiene problems; discuss with your doctor

melted and refrozen; if there's any doubt (eg, a power cut in the last day or two), steer well clear. Shellfish such as mussels, oysters and clams should be avoided as well as undercooked meat, particularly in the form of mince. Steaming does not make shellfish safe for eating.

If a place looks clean and well run and the vendor also looks clean and healthy, then the food is probably safe to eat. In general, places that are packed with travellers or locals will be fine, while empty restaurants are always questionable. The food in busy restaurants is cooked and eaten quickly with little time to stand around and is probably not reheated.

Stay healthy by making sure your diet is well balanced. Cooked eggs, beans, lentils (*shurbat ads*, or lentil soup, is popular in Egypt) and nuts are all safe ways to get protein. Fruit you can peel (bananas, oranges or mandarins, for example) is usually safe and a good source of vitamins. Melons, however, can harbour bacteria in their flesh and are therefore best avoided. Try to eat plenty of grains (such as rice) and bread. Remember that although food is generally safer if it is cooked well, overcooked food loses much of its nutritional value. If your diet isn't well balanced or if your food intake is insufficient, it's a good idea to take vitamin and iron pills.

Water Most of the year Egypt is hot, so make sure you drink enough – don't rely on feeling thirsty to indicate when you should drink. Not needing to urinate or voiding small amounts of very dark yellow urine is a danger sign. Always carry a water bottle with you on long trips. Excessive sweating can lead to loss of salt and muscle cramping. Salt tablets are not a good idea as a preventative, but adding salt to food can help.

US embassy tests on local tap water have confirmed it to be safe – the funny taste is due to its high chlorine content, which makes it a great antiseptic for washing fruit and vegetables. However, if you are in Egypt on a short-term stay, it's best to stick to mineral water as it takes a while for digestive systems to adapt to even minor changes in water content. There are several good local brands widely available such as Baraka or Siwa. When you buy, check that the seal on the bottle is not broken – it's not unknown for shopkeepers to refill mineral water bottles with tap water.

Take care with fruit juice, particularly if water may have been added. Milk should be treated with suspicion as it is often unpasteurised, though boiled milk is fine if it is kept hygienically. Tea or coffee should also be OK, since the water should have been boiled.

Medical Problems & Treatment

Self-diagnosis and treatment can be risky, so you should always seek medical help. An embassy, consulate or five-star hotel can usually recommend a local doctor or clinic. Although we do give drug dosages in this section, they are for emergency use only. Correct diagnosis is vital. In this section we have used the generic names for medications – check with a pharmacist for brands available locally.

Note that antibiotics should ideally be administered only under medical supervision. Take only the recommended dose at the prescribed intervals and use the whole course, even if the illness seems to be cured earlier. Stop immediately if there are any serious reactions and don't use the antibiotic at all if you are not sure you have the

Everyday Health

Normal body temperature is up to 37°C (98.6°F); more than 2°C (4°F) higher indicates a high fever. The normal adult pulse rate is 60 to 100 per minute (children 80 to 100, babies 100 to 140). As a general rule the pulse increases about 20 beats per minute for each 1°C (2°F) rise in fever.

Respiration (breathing) rate is also an indicator of illness. Count the number of breaths per minute: Between 12 and 20 is normal for adults and older children (up to 30 for younger children, 40 for babies). People with a high fever or serious respiratory illness breathe more quickly than normal. More than 40 shallow breaths a minute may indicate pneumonia.

orrect one. Some people are allergic to ommonly prescribed antibiotics such as enicillin; carry this information (eg, on a racelet) when travelling.

octors, Dentists & Hospitals

t's best to inquire at your embassy for the atest list of recommended doctors and denists. The UK and US embassies also have ealth units that can direct people with speial problems, or who need immediate care, o suitable physicians. Doctors and hospials usually expect immediate cash payment or their services.

It may also be worth contacting SOS Asistance, especially if you are considering a ong stay in Egypt. This organisation can be ontacted care of Cairoscan (☎ 02-360 965), 35 Suleiman Abaza, Mohandiseen. ts policy offers full medical cover in case f emergency, including a flight out to the ountry of your choice under the SOS IEDEVAC scheme. Contact SOS Assisance for more information.

Pharmacies in Egypt (at least those in the igger cities) are surprisingly good and alnost anything can be obtained without a precription. In addition to Western products here are homegrown medications, some of vhich are extremely good. For example, mecta is a locally produced compound that s good for easing stomach complaints.

Where relevant, addresses of hospitals, nedical centres and pharmacies are given in ndividual city sections throughout this ook, or for pharmacy addresses, you can lso refer to the listings in the back of *Busiess Today* magazine and in the *Al-Ahram Veekly* newspaper.

nvironmental Hazards

eat Exhaustion & Heatstroke Dehyration and salt deficiency can cause heat xhaustion, which is a real risk in Egypt most f the year. Take time to acclimatise to high emperatures, drink sufficient liquids and on't do anything too physically demanding.

Salt deficiency is characterised by fatigue, ethargy, headaches, giddiness and muscle ramps; salt tablets may help, but adding xtra salt to your food is better.

Heatstroke is a serious, occasionally fatal, condition that can occur if the body's heat-regulating mechanism breaks down and the body temperature rises to dangerous levels. Long, continuous periods of exposure to high temperatures and insufficient fluids can leave you vulnerable to heatstroke.

The symptoms are feeling unwell, not sweating very much (or at all) and a high body temperature (39° to 41°C or 102° to 106°F). Where sweating has ceased, the skin becomes flushed and red. Severe, throbbing headaches and lack of coordination will also occur, and the sufferer may be confused or aggressive. Eventually the victim will become delirious or convulse. Hospitalisation is essential, but in the interim get victims out of the sun, remove their clothing, cover them with a wet sheet or towel and then fan continually. Give fluids if they are conscious.

Prickly Heat This is an itchy rash caused by excessive perspiration trapped under the skin. It usually strikes people who have just arrived in a hot climate. Keeping cool, bathing often, drying the skin and using a mild talcum or prickly heat powder or resorting to air-conditioning may help.

Sunburn In Egypt you can get sunburnt surprisingly quickly, even through cloud. Use a sunscreen, a hat, and a barrier cream for your nose and lips. Calamine lotion, a sting-relief spray or aloe vera are good for mild sunburn. Wear good quality sunglasses, particularly if you are going to be spending time near water or sand.

Infectious Diseases

Diarrhoea Simple things such as a change of water, food or climate can all cause a mild bout of diarrhoea, but a few rushed toilet trips with no other symptoms is not indicative of a major problem.

Dehydration is the main danger with any diarrhoea, particularly in children or the elderly as it can occur quite quickly. Under all circumstances *fluid replacement* (at least equal to the volume being lost) is the most important thing. Weak black tea with a

Bilharzia

Schistosomiasis, more commonly known as bilharzia, is a frighteningly debilitating disease carried in fresh water by minute worms. The worm enters through the skin and attaches itself to your intestines or bladder. The first symptom may be a general feeling of being unwell, or a tingling and sometimes a light rash around the area where it entered. Weeks later a high fever may develop. Once the disease is established, abdominal pain and blood in the urine are other signs. The infection often causes no symptoms until the disease is well established (several months to years after exposure) and damage to internal organs irreversible.

It's prevalent in the Nile Delta area and in the Nile Valley. To be on the safe side, do not drink, wash, paddle or even stand in water except swimming pools, the ocean or the oases pools out in the Western Desert. Above all, do not swim in the Nile.

Seek medical attention if you think you may have been exposed to the disease. A blood test is the most reliable way to diagnose the disease, but the test will not show positive until a number of weeks after exposure.

little sugar, soda water, or soft drinks allowed to go flat and diluted 50% with clean water are all good. With severe diarrhoea a rehydrating solution is preferable to replace minerals and salts lost. Commercially available oral rehydration salts (ORS) are very useful; add them to boiled or bottled water. In Egypt they are available in boxes of six sachets for a little more than E£1. Just ask for Rehydran. Add one sachet to about 250mL of water. In an emergency you can make up a solution of six teaspoons of sugar and a half teaspoon of salt to 1L of boiled or bottled water. You need to drink at least the same volume of fluid that you are losing in bowel movements and vomiting. Urine is the best guide to the adequacy of replacement – if you have small amounts of concentrated urine, you need to drink more.

Nonprescription diarrhoea remedies such as diphenoxylate or loperamide (many different brand names) can be used to bring relief from the symptoms, although they do not cure the problem. Only use these drugs if you do not have access to toilets, for example, if you *must* travel. Note that they are not recommended for children under 12 years. Do not use these drugs if you have a high fever or are severely dehydrated.

In certain situations you may need a course of antibiotics: severe diarrhoea, diarrhoea with blood or mucus (dysentery), any diarrhoea with fever, profuse watery diarrhoea or persistent diarrhoea not improving after 48 hours. These suggest a more serious cause and diarrhoea remedies should be avoided.

In these situations, a stool test may be necessary to diagnose the cause of your diarrhoea, so you should seek medical help urgently. Where this is not possible the recommended drugs for bacterial diarrhoea (the most likely cause of severe diarrhoea in travellers) are norfloxacin 400mg twice daily for three days or ciprofloxacin 500mg twice daily for five days. These are not recommended for children or pregnant women. The drug of choice for children would be a five-day course of co-trimoxazole with dosage dependent on weight. Ampicillin or amoxycillin may be given in pregnancy, but medical care is necessary.

Persistent Diarrhoea Two causes of persistent diarrhoea in travellers are giardiasis and amoebic dysentery. **Giardiasis** is caused by a common parasite. Symptoms include stomach cramps, nausea, a bloated stomach, watery, foul-smelling diarrhoea and frequent gas. Giardiasis can appear several weeks after you have been exposed to the parasite. The symptoms may disappear for a few days and then return; this can go on for several weeks.

Amoebic dysentery is characterised by a gradual onset of low-grade diarrhoea, often with blood and mucus. Cramping abdominal pain and vomiting are less likely than in other types of diarrhoea, and fever may not be present. It will persist until treated and can recur and cause other problems.

You should seek medical advice if you think you have giardiasis or amoebic dysentery, but where this is not possible, tinidazole or metronidazole are the recommended drugs. Treatment for giardiasis is a 2g single dose of tinidazole or 2g of metronidazole once daily for three days. For amoebic dysentery, treatment is either 2g of tinidazole once daily for three days or 600mg of metronidazole three times daily for six to 10 days.

Fungal Infections These occur more commonly in hot weather and are usually found on the scalp, between the toes (athlete's foot) or fingers, in the groin and on the body (ringworm). You get ringworm (which is a fungal infection, not a worm) from infected animals or other people. Moisture encourages these infections.

To prevent fungal infections wear loose, comfortable clothes, avoid artificial fibres, wash frequently and dry yourself carefully. If you do get an infection, wash the infected area at least daily with a disinfectant or medicated soap and water, and rinse and dry well. Apply an antifungal cream or powder. Try to expose the infected area to air or sunlight as much as possible and wash all towels and underwear in hot water, change them often and let them dry in the sun.

Hepatitis A general term for inflammation of the liver, hepatitis is a common disease worldwide. There are several different viruses that can cause hepatitis. Symptoms of hepatitis include fever, chills, headache, fatigue, feelings of weakness and aches and pains, followed by loss of appetite, nausea, vomiting, abdominal pain, dark urine, light-coloured faeces, jaundiced (yellow) skin and yellowing of the whites of the eyes. People who have had hepatitis should avoid alcohol for some time after the illness, as the liver needs time to recover.

Hepatitis A is transmitted by contaminated food and drinking water. You should seek medical advice, but there is not much you can do apart from resting, drinking lots of fluids, eating lightly and avoiding fatty foods. **Hepatitis E** is transmitted in the same way as hepatitis A; it can be particularly serious in pregnant women.

There are almost 300 million chronic carriers of **hepatitis B** in the world. It is spread through contact with infected blood, blood products or body fluids, for example through sexual contact, unsterilised needles and blood transfusions, or contact with blood via small breaks in the skin. Other risk situations include shaving, tattoo or body piercing with contaminated equipment. The symptoms of hepatitis B may be more severe than type A and the disease can lead to long-term problems such as chronic liver damage, liver cancer or a long-term carrier state. **Hepatitis C and D** are spread in the same way as hepatitis B and can also lead to long-term complications.

There are vaccines against hepatitis A and B, but there are currently no vaccines against the other types of hepatitis. Following the basic rules about food and water (hepatitis A and E) and avoiding risk situations (hepatitis B, C and D) are important preventative measures.

HIV & AIDS Infection with the human immunodeficiency virus (HIV) may lead to acquired immune deficiency syndrome (AIDS), which is a fatal disease. Any exposure to blood, blood products or body fluids may put the individual at risk. The disease is often transmitted through sexual contact or dirty needles – vaccinations, acupuncture, tattooing and body piercing can be potentially as dangerous as intravenous drug use. HIV/AIDS can also be spread through infected blood transfusions; some countries, including Egypt, cannot afford to screen blood used for transfusions.

If you do need an injection, ask to see the syringe unwrapped in front of you, or take a needle and syringe pack with you.

Intestinal Worms These parasites are most common in rural, tropical areas. The different worms have different ways of infecting people. Some may be ingested on food such as undercooked meat (eg, tapeworms) and some enter through your skin (eg, hookworms). Infestations may not show up for some time, and although they are generally not serious, if left untreated some can cause severe health problems later. Consider having a stool test when you return home to check for these and to determine the appropriate treatment.

Sexually Transmitted Infections HIV/AIDS and hepatitis B are transmitted through sexual contact – see Hepititis and HIV/AIDS earlier for more details. Other STIs include gonorrhoea, herpes and syphilis; sores, blisters or rashes around the genitals and discharges or pain when urinating are common symptoms. In some STIs, such as wart virus or chlamydia, symptoms may be less marked or not observed at all, especially in women. Chlamydia infection can cause infertility in men and women before any symptoms have been noticed. Syphilis symptoms eventually disappear completely but the disease continues and can cause severe problems in later years. While abstinence from sexual contact is the only 100% effective prevention, using condoms is also effective. The treatment of gonorrhoea and syphilis is with antibiotics. The different STIs each require treatment with specific antibiotics, so seek medical advice if you think you may be infected.

Typhoid Caused by contaminated water and food, typhoid fever is a dangerous gut infection. Medical help must be sought. In its early stages sufferers may feel they have a bad cold or flu on the way, as early symptoms are a headache, body aches and a fever which rises a little each day until it is around 40°C (104°F) or more. The victim's pulse is often slow relative to the degree of fever present – unlike a normal fever where the pulse increases. There may also be vomiting, abdominal pain, diarrhoea or constipation.

In the second week the high fever and slow pulse continue and a few pink spots may appear on the body; trembling, delirium, weakness, weight loss and dehydration may occur. Complications such as pneumonia, perforated bowel or meningitis may occur.

Insect-Borne Diseases

Dengue fever, leishmaniasis and typhus are insect-borne diseases, but they do not pose a great risk to travellers in Egypt (for more information see Less Common Diseases later).

Malaria This serious and potentially fatal disease is spread by mosquito bites. If you are travelling to the Al-Fayoum area it is extremely important to avoid mosquito bites and perhaps to take tablets to prevent this disease (discuss this with your doctor before you leave). Symptoms range from fever, chills and sweating, headache, diarrhoea and abdominal pains to a vague feeling of ill-health. Seek medical help immediately if malaria is suspected. Without treatment malaria can rapidly become more serious and can be fatal.

If medical care is not available, malaria tablets can be used for treatment. You need to use a malaria tablet that is different from the one you were taking when you contracted malaria. The standard treatment dose of mefloquine is two 250mg tablets and a further two six hours later. For Fansidar, it's a single dose of three tablets. If you were previously taking mefloquine and cannot obtain Fansidar, then other alternatives are Malarone (atovaquone-proguanil; four tablets once daily for three days), halofantrine (three doses of two 250mg tablets every six hours) or quinine sulphate (600mg every six hours). There is a greater risk of side effects with these dosages than in normal use if used with mefloquine, so medical advice is preferable. Be aware also that halofantrine is no longer recommended by the WHO as emergency standby treatment, because of side effects, and should only be used if no other drugs are available.

Travellers are advised to prevent mosquito bites at all times. The main messages are

- wear light-coloured clothing;
- wear long trousers and long-sleeved shirts;
- use mosquito repellents containing the compound DEET on exposed areas (prolonged overuse of DEET may be harmful, especially to children, but its use is considered preferable to being bitten by disease-transmitting mosquitoes);
- avoid perfumes or aftershave;
- use a mosquito net impregnated with mosquito repellent (permethrin) – it may be worth taking your own;
- consider impregnating clothes with permethrin, as this effectively deters mosquitoes and other insects.

Cuts, Bites & Stings

See Less Common Diseases for details of rabies, which is passed through animal bites.

Cuts & Scratches Wash any cut well and treat with an antiseptic such as povidone-iodine. Where possible avoid bandages and Band-Aids, which can keep wounds wet. Coral cuts are notoriously slow to heal and if they are not adequately cleaned, small pieces of coral can become embedded in the wound.

Bedbugs & Lice Bedbugs live in various places, but particularly in dirty mattresses and bedding, evidenced by spots of blood on bedclothes or on the wall. Bedbugs leave itchy bites in neat rows. Calamine lotion or antihistamine cream may help.

All lice cause itching and discomfort. They make themselves at home in your hair (head lice), your clothing (body lice) or in your pubic hair (crabs). You catch lice through direct contact with infected people or by sharing combs, clothing and the like. Powder or shampoo treatment will kill the lice and infected clothing should then be washed in very hot, soapy water and left in the sun to dry.

Bites & Stings Bee and wasp stings are usually painful rather than dangerous. However, in people who are allergic to them severe breathing difficulties may occur and require urgent medical care. Calamine lotion or antihistamine cream will give relief and ice packs will reduce the pain and swelling. There are some spiders with dangerous bites but antivenins are usually available. Scorpion stings are notoriously painful and in some parts of the Middle East can actually be fatal. Scorpions often shelter in shoes or clothing.

Avoid contact with jellyfish, as these sea creatures have stinging tentacles. Although some jellyfish stings are dangerous, stings from most jellyfish are simply rather painful. Seek local advice on avoiding and treating stings. Dousing in vinegar will deactivate any stingers that have not 'fired'. Calamine lotion, antihistamines and analgesics may reduce the reaction and relieve the pain.

Snakes To minimise your chances of being bitten by a snake, always wear boots, socks and long trousers when walking in places where snakes may be present. Don't put your hands into holes and crevices, and be careful when collecting firewood.

Snake bites do not cause instantaneous death and antivenins are usually available. Immediately wrap the bitten limb tightly, as you would for a sprained ankle, and then attach a splint to immobilise it. Keep the victim still and seek medical help, if possible with the dead snake for identification. Don't attempt to catch the snake if there is a possibility of being bitten again. Tourniquets and sucking out the poison are now comprehensively discredited.

Less Common Diseases

The following diseases pose a small risk to travellers, and so are only mentioned in passing. Seek medical advice if you think you may have any of these diseases.

Cholera This is the worst of the watery diarrhoeas and medical help should be sought. Outbreaks of cholera are generally widely reported, so you can avoid such problem areas. *Fluid replacement is the most vital treatment* – the risk of dehydration is severe as you may lose up to 20L a day. If there is a delay in getting to hospital, then begin taking tetracycline. The adult dose is 250mg four times daily. It is not recommended for children under nine years nor for pregnant women. Tetracycline may help shorten the illness, but adequate fluids are required to save lives.

Dengue Fever There is no prophylactic available for this mosquito-spread disease; the main preventative measure is to avoid mosquito bites. A sudden onset of fever, headaches and severe joint and muscle pains are the first signs before a rash starts on the trunk of the body and spreads to the limbs and face. After a further few days, the fever will subside and recovery will begin. Serious complications are not common but full recovery can take up to a month or more.

Leishmaniasis This is a group of parasitic diseases transmitted by sandflies, which are found in Egypt, as well as other parts of the world. Cutaneous leishmaniasis affects the skin tissue causing ulceration and disfigurement, and visceral leishmaniasis affects the internal organs. Seek medical advice, as laboratory testing is required for diagnosis and correct treatment. Avoiding sandfly bites is the best precaution. Bites are usually painless, itchy and yet another reason to cover up and apply insect repellent.

Rabies This fatal viral infection is found in many countries, including Egypt. Many animals can be infected (such as dogs, cats, bats and monkeys) and it is their saliva which is infectious. Any bite, scratch or even lick from an animal should be cleaned immediately and thoroughly. Scrub with soap and running water, and then apply alcohol or iodine solution. Medical help should be sought promptly to receive a course of injections to prevent the onset of symptoms and death.

Tetanus This disease is caused by a germ that lives in soil and in the faeces of horses and other animals. It enters the body via breaks in the skin. The first symptom may be discomfort in swallowing, or stiffening of the jaw and neck; this is followed by painful convulsions of the jaw and whole body. The disease can be fatal. It can be prevented by vaccination.

Tuberculosis (TB) This is a bacterial infection usually transmitted from person to person by coughing but which may be transmitted through consumption of unpasteurised milk. Milk that has been boiled is safe to drink, and the souring of milk to make yogurt or cheese also kills the bacilli. Travellers are not often at risk as close household contact with the infected person is usually required before the disease is passed on.

Typhus This disease is spread by ticks, mites or lice. It begins with fever, chills, headache and muscle pains followed a few days later by a body rash. There is often a large painful sore at the site of the bite and nearby lymph nodes are swollen and painful. Typhus can be treated under medical supervision. Seek local advice on areas where ticks pose a danger and always check your skin carefully for ticks after walking in a danger area. An insect repellent can help, and walkers in tick-infested areas should consider having their boots and trousers impregnated with benzyl benzoate and dibutylphthalate.

Women's Health

Gynaecological Problems Antibiotic use, synthetic underwear, sweating and contraceptive pills can lead to fungal vaginal infections, especially when travelling in hot climates. Fungal infections are characterised by a rash, itch and discharge. The usual treatment is antifungal pessaries (such as nystatin, myconazole or clotrimazole), although it can be treated with a vinegar or lemon-juice douche, or with plain yogurt. Maintaining good personal hygiene and wearing loose-fitting clothes and cotton underwear may help prevent these infections.

STIs are a major cause of vaginal problems. Symptoms include a smelly discharge, painful intercourse and sometimes a burning sensation when urinating. Medical attention should be sought and male sexual partners must also be treated. Remember that in addition to these diseases, HIV or hepatitis B may also be acquired during exposure. Besides abstinence, the best thing is to practise safe sex using condoms.

Pregnancy It is not advisable to travel to some places while pregnant as some vaccinations normally used to prevent serious diseases are not advisable during pregnancy. In addition, some diseases, such as malaria, are much more serious for the mother (and may increase the risk of a stillborn child) in pregnancy.

Most miscarriages occur during the first three months of pregnancy. They are not uncommon and can occasionally lead to severe bleeding. The last three months should also be spent within reasonable distance of good medical care. A baby born as early as 24 weeks stands a chance of survival, but only in a good modern hospital. Pregnant women should avoid all unnecessary medication, but vaccinations and malarial prophylactics should still be taken where needed. Additional care should be taken to prevent illness and particular attention should be paid to diet and nutrition. Alcohol and nicotine, for example, should be avoided.

WOMEN TRAVELLERS

Egyptians are conservative, especially about matters concerning sex and women; Egyptian women that is, not foreign women.

An entire book could be written from the comments and stories of women travellers about their adventures and misadventures in Egypt. A recent article in the UK's *Guardian* newspaper written by two female travellers reckoned Egyptian men were the 'creepiest on earth' with incessant chat-up lines such as 'I miss you like the desert misses the rain', which, they wrote, could have been funny had they not been so constant and intimidating. Most of the incidents are nonthreatening nuisances, like a fly buzzing in your ear: you can swat it away and keep it at a distance, but it's always out there buzzing around.

Attitudes Towards Women

Some of the biggest misunderstandings between Egyptians and Westerners occur over the issue of women. Half-truths and stereotypes exist on both sides: many Westerners assume all Egyptian women are veiled, repressed victims, while a large number of Egyptians just see Western women as sex-obsessed and immoral.

For many Egyptians of both genders, the role of a woman is specifically defined: she is mother and matron of the household. The man is the provider. However, as with any society, generalisations can be misleading and the reality is far more nuanced. There are thousands of middle and upper-middle class professional women in Egypt who, like their counterparts in the West, juggle work and family responsibilities. Among the working classes, where adherence to tradition is strongest, the ideal may be for women to concentrate on home and family, but economic reality means that millions of women are forced to work (but are still responsible for all the domestic chores).

The discomfiture of many Egyptians at this mixing of roles has been exploited by Islamists, who have politicised the issue of women and the family in their constant battle to undermine the government. Interspersed with the politics is a general wave of conservatism that has swept the country in recent years. The most visible sign of this return to 'traditional values' has been the huge number of women adopting more conservative dress and wearing the higab or headscarf. But again, the issue is more complex than first meets the eye. For every woman who adopts the higab for religious reasons, there are many others who wear it because it allows them to walk around freely – not many men would dare hassle a higab-wearing woman. Or because it means they don't have to worry about fashion, or, paradoxically, because it *is* the fashion (check out the different ways to wear a headscarf). It is also a socioeconomic phenomenon: only a fraction of wealthy upper-middle or middle-class women have their heads covered.

Away from dress, the issue of sex is where the differences between Western and Egyptian women are most apparent. Premarital sex (or, indeed, any sex outside marriage) is taboo in Egypt, although, as with anything forbidden, it still happens. Nevertheless, it is the exception rather than the rule – and that goes for men as well as women. However, for women the issue is potentially far more serious. With the possible exception of the upper classes, women are expected to be virgins when they get married and a family's reputation can rest upon this point. In such a context, the restrictions placed on a young girl – no matter how onerous they may seem to a Westerner – are to protect her and her reputation from the potentially disastrous attentions of men.

The presence of foreign women presents, in the eyes of some Egyptian men, a chance to get around these norms with ease and without consequences. This possibility is reinforced by distorted impressions gained from Western TV and, it has to be said, by

Tips for Women Travellers

- Wear a wedding band. Generally, Egyptian men seem to have more respect for a married woman.
- If you are travelling with a man, it is better to say you're married rather than 'just friends'.
- Avoid direct eye contact with an Egyptian man unless you know him well; dark sunglasses could help.
- Try not to respond to an obnoxious comment from a man – act as if you didn't hear it.
- Be careful in crowds and other situations where you are crammed between people as it is not unusual for crude things to happen behind you.
- On public transport, sit next to a woman if possible. This is not difficult on the Cairo metro where the first compartment is reserved for women only.
- If you're in the countryside (off the beaten track) be extra conservative in what you wear.
- Be very careful about behaving in a flirtatious or suggestive manner – it could create more problems than you ever imagined.
- If you need help for any reason (directions etc), ask a woman first.
- Be wary when horse or camel riding, especially at touristy places. It's not unknown for a guy to ride close to you and grab your horse, among other things. Riding with a man on a horse or camel is simply asking for trouble.
- Egypt is not the place for acquiring a full suntan. Only on private beaches in the top-end resorts along the Red Sea and in southern Sinai are you likely to feel comfortable stripping down to a bikini. Along the Mediterranean coast and in oases pools, you'll have to swim in shorts and a T-shirt at the very minimum, and even then you'll attract a flock of male onlookers. Egyptian women rarely go swimming on public beaches; when they do, they swim fully clothed, scarf and all.
- You may find it handy to learn the Arabic for 'don't touch me' (*la tilmasni*). Also worth memorising are: *ihtirim nafsak* (literally 'behave yourself') or *haasib eedak* (watch your hand). Stronger language will only make it worse.
- Being befriended by an Egyptian woman is a great way to learn more about life in Egypt and, at the same time, have someone totally nonthreatening to guide you around. Getting to know an Egyptian woman is, however, easier said than done. You won't find them in cafes or *ahwas (coffeehouses)* and fewer women speak English than men. Most encounters will come while using public transport or shopping. All we can say is seize on whatever opportunities you get.

the behaviour of some foreign women – as one young man in Luxor remarked when asked why he harassed every Western woman he saw, 'For every ten that say no, there's one that says yes'. So, as a woman traveller you can expect some verbal harassment at the very least. Sometimes it will go as far as pinching bottoms or brushing breasts but flashing and masturbating in front of the victim are much less common. Serious physical harassment and rape do occasionally occur, but more rarely than in most Western countries.

What to Wear

Away from the Sinai and Red Sea beaches, Egyptians are quite conservative about dress. Wearing shorts and a tight T-shirt on the street is, in some people's eyes, confirmation of the worst views held of Western women. Generally, if you're alone or with other women, the amount of harassment you get will be directly related to how you dress: the more skin exposed, the more harassment. You'll have fewer hassles if you don't dress for hot weather in the same way you might at home. Baggy T-shirts and loose cotton trousers or long skirts won't make you sweat as much as you think and will protect your skin from the sun as well as from unwanted comments. As with anywhere, take your cues from those around you: if you're in a rural area and all the women are in long concealing dresses, you should be conservatively dressed. If you're going out to a hip Cairo nightspot, you're likely to see middle- and upper-class Egyptian girls in the briefest designer gear and can dress accordingly – just don't walk there.

Unfortunately, although dressing conservatively should reduce the incidence of any such harassment, it by no means guarantees you'll be left alone.

What to Bring

For advice on the availability of sanitary towels etc, see What to Bring under Planning at the beginning of this chapter.

GAY & LESBIAN TRAVELLERS

Homosexuality in Egypt is no more or less prevalent than elsewhere in the world but it's a whole lot more ambiguous than in the West. Men routinely hold hands, link arms, give each other big slobbery kisses on greeting but don't misread the signals, this is not gay behaviour it's just a local take on male bonding. Beyond this though, a strange double-think goes on whereby an Egyptian man can indulge in same-sex intercourse but not consider himself gay because only the passive partner is regarded as queer. So it's not uncommon for foreign male visitors to receive blatant and crudely phrased propositions of sex from Egyptian men. It's not for nothing that Cairo has always had more than its fair share of European queens in residence. But if a lot of man-to-man sex goes on, there's not necessarily any sort of gay scene. The concept of 'gay pride' is totally alien, and bar the odd young (possibly foolhardy) crusader no Egyptian man would openly attest to being homosexual for fear of being shunned by society and labelled as weak and feminine.

While there is no mention of homosexuality in the Egyptian penal code, some statutes criminalizing obscenity and public indecency have been used against gay men in the past. Most recently, in May 2001, 55 Egyptian men were arrested when police raided a floating bar/restaurant moored on the Nile in Cairo. They were held and questioned on charges of 'exploiting religion to promote extreme ideas to create strife and belittling revealed religions' – whatever that means. The state prosecutor's office put it more bluntly when it labelled the men 'deviants'.

The bottom line is that Egypt is a conservative society that condemns homosexuality but at the same time plenty of same-sex intercourse goes on.

There are no national support groups or gay information lines but you could try searching the Web. The premier gay Egypt site is W www.gayegypt.com, or you could take a look at the Gay in Egypt Private Net Society (W www.geocities.com/westhollywood/5884/).

Although necessarily low key, there are a few places in Cairo that are recognised gay hang-outs. Chief of these is the Taverne du Champs de Mars in the Nile Hilton, Tahrir Square, which has a strong queer element most nights, some of which moves on later to Jackie's Disco in the same hotel. The Queens Boat moored opposite the Cairo Marriott also used to be heavily homo but since the raid who knows if the crowd is going to feel safe coming back. There also used to be a lot of activity at certain of the old *hammams* (bathhouses) in Islamic Cairo, particularly Hammam Beshtak (Souq as-Silah, 300m north of Ar-Rifai Mosque), but we heard a rumour this had also been clamped down on by the authorities and may now be closed.

DISABLED TRAVELLERS

Egypt is not well equipped for travellers with a mobility problem; ramps are few, public facilities don't necessarily have lifts, kerbs are high, traffic is lethal and gaining entrance to some of the ancient sites – such as the Pyramids of Giza or the tombs on the West Bank near Luxor – is all but impossible due to their narrow entrances and steep stairs. Despite all this, there is no reason why intrepid disabled travellers shouldn't visit Egypt. In general you'll find locals quite willing to assist with any difficulties. Getting around should not be too much of a problem as most places can be reached by comfortable internal flights, while anyone with a wheelchair can take advantage of the large hatchback Peugeot 504s, which are commonly used as taxis. One of these, together with a driver, can be hired for around US$30 per day. Chances are the driver will be quite happy to help you in and out of the vehicle.

Crusader Travel (W www.divers.co.uk), a UK-based tour company, does special Red Sea diving packages for the disabled, while Wind Sand & Stars (W www.windsandstars.co.uk), another UK company, inspired by the fact that many desert Bedouin are deaf, has run several trips to Sinai for deaf and hearing impaired people, accompanied by a BSL interpreter. For further contact details on both these companies, see Organised Tours in the Getting There & Away chapter.

Organisations

See the Access-Able Travel Source Web site (W www.access-able.com) for general information for disabled travellers. Before leaving home, disabled travellers can also get in touch with their national support organisation, listed here. Ask for the 'travel officer' who may have a list of travel agencies that specialise in tours for the disabled.

Access, The Foundation for Accessibility by the Disabled (☎ 516-887 5798) PO Box 356, Malverne, NY 11565, USA

CNFLRH (☎ 01 53 80 66 66) 236 Rue de Tolbiac, Paris, France

Radar (☎ 020-7250 3222, fax 7250 0212, W www.radar.org.uk) 12 City Forum, 250 City Rd, London EC1V 8AF, UK; produces holiday fact packs that cover planning, insurance, useful organisations, transport, equipment and specialised accommodation

Society for the Advancement of Travel for the Handicapped (SATH; ☎ 212-447 7284, W www.sath.org) 347 Fifth Ave, No 610, New York, NY 10016, USA

SENIOR TRAVELLERS

Egypt doesn't subscribe to the cult of youth worship that exists in the West, and traditionally its older citizens are accorded great respect. The family remains the single most important thing in the lives of most Egyptians and if you bring along some photos of your children and (even better) grandchildren, they'll act as a great icebreaker.

Respect yes, but concessions no; unlike in many Western countries, there are no discounts on public transport, museum admission fees and the like for senior travellers in Egypt. But when it comes to transport, you may well prefer to hire taxis by the day anyway. This should cost no more than about US$25 per day and is a good way of avoiding the rigours of Egypt's local transport systems. Alternatively, plenty of local tour operators arrange day trips, which can take some of the strain out of sightseeing.

The other major thing to be wary of is the heat. It can be crippling – not just to senior citizens but to travellers of any age. A lightweight folding stool might be a good idea if you are prone to tiring quickly. Some sites require a certain degree of fitness, such as the Valley of the Kings, with all its steep stairways and sloping passageways. Similarly the Pyramids can also require a bit of energy. However, there's plenty enough to see without having to tackle these tasks; the Pyramids are quite impressive enough without having to go inside, while there are many tombs at Luxor (such as those of the nobles) that don't have long flights of stairs. Plan ahead and don't try to do too much in too short a time – advice good for travellers of all ages.

TRAVEL WITH CHILDREN

Egypt is a very child-friendly place and having kids along with you can be a great icebreaker with locals. And with a little creativity, easily bored young people can also have fun visiting temples and antiquities. Seeking out gruesome temple reliefs (of which there are many) or searching for Tutankhamun's toys in the Egyptian Museum are both good ways to pique a child's interest. In Cairo, Dr Ragab's Pharaonic Village (☎ 02-571 8675, fax 568 9266, W touregypt.net/village) at 3 Sharia al-Bahr al-Aazam, Giza, is a theme park with boat rides that is usually a big hit with kids of all ages and it gives them an idea of what the pharaohs were about. You'll have to take a taxi to get there. It's open from 9am to 5pm daily and admission is E£40.

Bookshops at most five-star hotels in Cairo and the major tourist centres stock a wide variety of Egyptology-related children's books that will help kids relate to what they're seeing. Locally produced history books, such as Salima Ikram's *The Pharaohs* are excellent and reasonably priced. (Hoopoe Books is a local children's publisher with a great list of titles that make good souvenirs or presents, too. Visit its Web site at W www.hoopoebooks.com.) For something set in modern Egypt, look for *The Day of Ahmed's Secret*, a wonderful story of a day in the life of a small boy who delivers gas canisters in one of Cairo's poor neighbourhoods.

Away from antiquities there are the ever-popular camel or donkey rides. The stables around the Pyramids also have plenty of docile horses suitable for young people. Also for animal fans, Cairo Zoo is good in that it's one of the few zoos where children get to feed the animals – the keepers sell the appropriate foodstuffs.

Fagnoon (mobile ☎ 010-152 6715) is an art centre run by artist Mohammed Allam in the fields between Giza and Saqqara. Children can slosh paint around, model clay or hammer together some wood in a farm-type setting. Expect to pay about E£30 for canvases and other materials. You can bring your own food and drink, although coffee and water are usually on sale.

Swimming is a good way of getting rid of excess energy in the heat. Most four- and five-star hotels will let nonresidents pay to use their swimming pools and many let children in for free. If you're in Cairo you might want to check out one of the water parks on the outskirts of the city. Crazy Water has half a dozen or more water slides, a wave pool, a kiddies pool, and a playground area with sand, slides and tunnels. Admission is E£15, or E£12 for small fry. It's open from 10am to 10pm daily. To get there, drive 15km from the intersection of the Giza road and Cairo-Alexandria road, then turn left on the route to 6th of October City.

If you're looking for somewhere that's children-friendly to dine out in Cairo away from the ubiquitous McDonald's and Pizza Hut, then Andrea's (see Giza & Pyramids Rd under Places to Eat in the Cairo chapter for more details), an open-air restaurant out near the Pyramids, are great. The kids can roam around the gardens, and there are big climbing frames, swings and donkey rides. Children also enjoy the local restaurant chain, Felfela – most branches have caged birds and aquariums.

There are a couple of things to keep in mind while you're out and about with kids in Egypt. One is that child-safety awareness is minimal. Seatbelts are nonexistent in the back seats of most cars and taxis, and if you're renting a car remember to specify that you want them. Also, don't expect felucca or other boat operators to have children's lifejackets. If you can't do without them, bring your own. Likewise with helmets for horse riding.

Another potential worry is the high incidence of diarrhoea and stomach problems that hit travellers in Egypt. If your children get sick, keep in mind that they dehydrate far more quickly than adults and given the dry climate it is crucial to keep giving them liquids even if they just throw them up again. It's worth having some rehydration salts on hand just in case (they do double duty as effective hangover cures). These are available at all pharmacies (ask for Rehydran) and cost about 90pt for a box of six sachets. They can prevent a bad case of the runs from turning into something more serious. Just stir a packet into 200mL of water and keep giving it until the diarrhoea has passed. See Health earlier in this chapter for more details on preventing and dealing with potential problems.

DANGERS & ANNOYANCES

The amount of crime, violent or otherwise, in Egypt is negligible compared with most Western countries. (Crimes of passion are another thing. The *Egyptian Gazette* carries a column called 'Red Handed' that most days is filled with tales of murderous wives, revengeful jilted lovers, and assorted cases of fratricide, patricide and matricide. It makes fascinating reading.) Most visitors and residents would agree that Egyptian towns and cities are some of the world's safest places in which pedestrians can walk abroad, anywhere, at any hour of the day or night. Unfortunately, the hassle factor often means that this isn't quite the case for an unaccompanied foreign woman – see Women Travellers earlier in this chapter.

Apart from the issues discussed here, land mines are a risk in some areas of Sinai (see the boxed text 'Land Mines' in the Sinai chapter for more details). Remember, too, that the Egyptian authorities take a dim view of illegal drug use (see the boxed text 'Drugs & Dahab' in the Sinai chapter).

Terrorism

Is Egypt safe? Well, there's no absolute answer to that. The country was struck by a couple of particularly horrific acts of terrorist violence back in 1997 resulting in a great many deaths. For a couple of years tourists stayed away. But since then, nothing, and the tourists have returned in greater numbers than ever. Meanwhile security remains at an all-time high and while that in itself is no guarantee of no future terrorist atrocities, we'd say that Egypt is presently no more or less dangerous than any other country, your own included. For more on the issue see the boxed text 'Troubles in the Nile Valley' in the Nile Valley – Beni Suef to Qus chapter.

Theft

Theft never used to be a problem in Egypt but it seems to be becoming more so. In the past couple of years we've received a steady

Scams, Hustles & Hassle

Egyptians take hospitality to strangers seriously. You'll receive a steady stream of salaams and the odd *ahlan wa sahlan* inviting you to sit and have tea. A lot of this is genuine, particularly out in rural areas, where drink, food and transport are frequently offered with no expectation of remuneration. But in more touristy places – notably around the Egyptian Museum and Pyramids in Cairo and all over Luxor – a cheery 'Hello my friend' is doublespeak for 'This way, sucker'. You are a magnet attracting instant friends who coincidentally have a papyrus factory they'd like to show you. You are showered with helpful advice such as the museum is closed, take tea with me while you wait – of course the museum isn't closed and refreshments will be taken at a convenient souvenir shop. As an English-speaker you might be asked to spare a moment to check the spelling of a letter to a relative in the USA, and while you're at it how about some special perfume for the lady...

It's all pretty harmless stuff but it can become very wearing. Everyone works out their own strategy to reduce the hassle to a minimum. A colleague kept interest at bay by jabbing his finger at his chest accompanied by the words *Ya Russki* (I'm Russian). Not only would the hustlers be defeated by the language, everyone knew that the Russians had no money. But now that Egypt is a popular holiday destination for newly rich Muscovites, the street entrepreneurs are just as fluent in Slavic sales patter as they are in English, German, French, Dutch and Japanese.

About the only way to deal with unwanted attention is to be polite but firm and when you're in for a pitch cut it short with 'Sorry, no thanks'.

Aside from the hustling, there are countless irritating scams. The most common one involves touts who lie and misinform to get newly arrived travellers into hotels for which they get a commission – see the boxed text 'Cairo hotel Scams' in the Cairo chapter. Hustlers in Downtown Cairo loiter outside EgyptAir to intercept foreigners and redirect them across the road to a travel agency that they falsely claim is the only place non-Egyptians can buy tickets – and then they collect a commission on the sale. There are well-dressed guys who cruise Midan Tahrir offering their friendship as a smokescreen for whatever they can get out of it. One reader's letter confesses being taken in by a 'schoolteacher' named Omar who helped arrange a camel ride around the Pyramids for E£110 – a fair price would have been E£10.

If you do get stung, or feel one more 'Excuse me, where are you from?' will make you crack, simmer down, wise up, and beware acting brusquely and offending the majority of locals who would never dream of hassling a foreigner.

stream of letters from readers concerning money disappearing from locked hotel rooms. The obvious conclusion to draw is that staff are involved, but in the cases we've been alerted to management have been disinclined to take responsibility until threatened by the tourist police, at which point reimbursements were offered. Money has even 'disappeared' from hotel safes. The advice has got to be keep your cash and valuables on your person at all times.

But how about this tale in which a bag goes missing from the roof of a taxi:

> I was the victim of a well-practised coup which your readers should be on the guard for. Halfway through our journey from Giza to the hotel our taxi driver started tapping the dashboard and feigning irritation. He stopped, got out and went to the back of the vehicle. He opened the boot, thus blocking our view through the back window. It must have been at this point that he transferred one of the bags from the roof into the boot. At the end of the journey in the rush of the traffic and the argument about the fare (he was quite aggressive at this point) we unloaded what there was on the roof, saw that there was nothing left and assumed we had everything. Then with our taxi pulling away swiftly into the traffic we counted the bags. One was missing. Mine! What was in it? Almost everything: air ticket, passport, wallet and nearly all my clothes.
>
> **G Bernard**

Of course the bag could have fallen off the roof except that two days later in the early hours of the morning the thief dropped off the travel documents at the hotel. He kept the money and clothes.

There are also a few areas where pickpockets are known to operate, notably on the Cairo metro and the packed local buses from Midan Tahrir to the Pyramids. Tourists aren't the specific targets but be careful how you carry your money in crowded places.

Most unwary visitors are parted from their money through scams and these are something that you really do have to watch out for.

LEGAL MATTERS

Foreign travellers are subject to Egyptian laws and get no special consideration. If arrested, you have the right to immediately telephone your embassy. For information on driving laws, see Road Rules under Car & Motorcycle in the Getting Around chapter.

BUSINESS HOURS

Banking hours are from 8am or 8.30am to 2pm Sunday to Thursday. Many banks in Cairo and other cities open again from 5pm or 6pm for two or three hours, largely for foreign exchange transactions. Some of them also open on Friday and Saturday for the same purposes. During Ramadan, banks are open between 10am and 1.30pm. Foreign exchange offices are generally open throughout the day.

Most government offices operate from about 8am to 2pm Sunday to Thursday but tourist offices are generally open for longer.

Shops generally have different hours at different times of the year. In summer most shops are open from 9am to 1pm and from 5pm to 10pm or even later. Winter hours are from 10am to 6pm. Hours during Ramadan are from 9.30am to 3.30pm and 8pm to 10pm. There are no real hard and fast rules, however, and even on Fridays, shops are sometimes open for most of the day.

PUBLIC HOLIDAYS & SPECIAL EVENTS

Egypt's holidays and festivals are primarily Islamic or Coptic religious celebrations, although all holidays are celebrated equally by the entire population regardless of creed.

The Islamic, or Hejira (meaning 'flight', as in the flight of Mohammed from Mecca to Medina in AD 622), calendar is 11 days shorter than the Gregorian (Western) calendar. This means that Islamic holidays fall 11 days earlier each year. The 11-day rule is not entirely strict – the holidays can fall from 10 to 12 days earlier. The precise dates are known only shortly before they fall as they're dependent upon the sighting of the moon. See the Islamic Holidays table in this section for the approximate dates of the major holidays for the next few years.

Islamic Holidays

Hejira Year	New Year	Prophet's Birthday	Ramadan Begins	Eid al-Fitr	Eid al-Adha
1422	26.03.01	03.06.01	16.11.01	16.12.01	23.02.02
1423	15.03.02	23.05.02	05.11.02	05.12.02	12.02.03
1424	04.03.03	12.05.03	25.10.03	25.11.03	01.02.04
1425	22.02.04	01.05.04	14.10.04	14.11.04	21.01.05

The following are public holidays in Egypt:

New Year's Day 1 January – Official national holiday but many businesses stay open.

Christmas 7 January – Coptic Christmas is a fairly low-key affair and only Coptic businesses are closed for the day.

Eid al-Adha – Also known as Eid al-Kebir, the 'Great Feast', this marks the time of the haj, the pilgrimage to Mecca. Those who can afford it buy a sheep to slaughter on the day of the feast, which lasts for three days (although many businesses reopen on the second day). Many families also head out of town, so if you intend travelling at this time secure your tickets well in advance.

Ras as-Sana – Islamic New Year's Day. The entire country has the day off but celebrations are low key.

Easter March/April – The most important date on the Coptic calendar although it doesn't significantly affect daily life for the majority of the population.

Sham an-Nessim March/April – A Coptic holiday with Pharaonic origins, it literally means the 'Smell of the Breeze'. It falls on the first Monday after the Coptic Easter and is celebrated by all Egyptians, with family picnics and outings.

Sinai Liberation Day 25 April – Official national holiday celebrating Israel's return of Sinai in 1982.

May Day 1 May – Official national holiday.

Moulid an-Nabi – This is the birthday of the Prophet Mohammed. One of the major holidays of the year; the streets are a feast of lights and food.

Revolution Day 23 July – Official national holiday commemorating the date of the 1952 coup when the Free Officers seized power from the puppet monarchy.

National Day 6 October – Official national holiday celebrating Egyptian successes during the 1973 War with Israel. The day is marked by military parades and air displays and a long speech by the president.

Ramadan – Observant Muslims fast for a whole month during daylight hours. Everyone is tired, listless, hungry and bad tempered during the day, but they come back to life again when the sun goes down and they can feast and get festive. For more information, see Religion in the Facts about Egypt chapter.

Eid al-Fitr – A three-day feast that marks the end of Ramadan fasting.

Special Events

There aren't very many events on the cultural calendar and those that there are don't always take place. Much of what is there is also singularly underwhelming. In fact, the only events worth going out of your way to attend are possibly the moulids – see the boxed text 'The Moulid'.

January

Book Fair Held at the Cairo Exhibition Grounds over two weeks, this is one of the major events on the city's cultural calendar. It draws massive crowds, most of whom are there for a day out rather than because of any literary leanings. Far more burgers, soft drinks and balloons are sold than books.

February

Ascension of Ramses II One of the two dates each year (22 February) when the sun penetrates into the inner sanctuary of the temple at Abu Simbel, illuminating the statues of the gods within.

International Fishing Tournament Held at Hurghada on the Red Sea and attended by anglers from all over the world

Luxor Marathon Held on the West Bank with competitors racing around the main antiquities sites.

Nitaq Festival Excellent arts festival centred on Downtown Cairo with two weeks of exhibitions, theatre, poetry, and music at galleries, cafes and a variety of other venues. Only in its second year in 2001 but already one of the cultural highpoints of the annual calender.

April

South Sinai Camel Festival A new addition to the cultural calendar (if cultural is the right word), the first camel festival took place in 1999. Some 250 camels representing 17 different Bedouin tribes were present to take part in races.

June

Al-Ahram Squash Tournament International competitors play in glass courts set up for the occasion on the Giza plateau beside the Pyramids.

July

International Festival of Oriental Dance Held in Cairo, this is a festival of belly dancing in which famous Egyptian practitioners give showcase performances and lessons to international attendees.

August

Tourism & Shopping Festival A countrywide promotion of Egyptian products with participating shops offering discounted prices.

September

Alexandria Film Festival A very modest international film festival that's most notable for the blunders that take place each year.

Experimental Theatre Festival Held over 10 days, this theatre festival brings to Egypt a vast selection (40 at the last outing) of international theatre troupes and represents almost the only time each year that it's worth turning out for the theatre in Cairo.

October

Alexandrias of the World Festival A four-day celebration attended by delegations from all the cities bearing the name Alexandria (there are over 40 in the world).

Birth of Ramses The second date in the year (22 October) when the sun's rays penetrate the temple at Abu Simbel.

Pharaohs' Rally An 11-day, 4800km motor vehicle (4WDs and bikes) race through the desert beginning and ending at the Pyramids that attracts competitors from all over the world.

The Moulid

A cross between a funfair and a religious festival, a *moulid* celebrates the birthday of a local saint or holy person. They are often a colourful riot of celebrations with hundreds of thousands of people. Those from out of town set up camp in the streets close to the saints' tomb, where children's rides, sideshows and food stalls are erected. In the midst of the chaos, barbers perform mass circumcisions; snake charmers induce cobras out of baskets; children are presented at the shrine to be blessed and the sick to be cured. *Tartours* (cone-shaped hats) and *fanous* (lanterns) are made and sold to passers-by and in the evenings local Sufis usually hold hypnotic *zikrs* in colourful tents. A zikr (literally 'remembrance') is where the Sufis chant the name of Allah to achieve a trance-like state that brings them closer to god. The *mugzzabin*, meaning the 'drawn-in', stand in straight lines and sway from side to side to rhythmic clapping that gradually increases in intensity. As the clapping gains momentum, the zikr reaches its peak and the mugzzabin, having attained oneness with Allah, awake sweating and blinking. Other zikrs are formidable endurance tests where troupes of musicians perform for hours in the company of ecstatic dancers.

Most moulids last for about a week, and climax with the *leila kebira* (the big night). Much of the infrastructure is provided by 'professional' *mawladiyya*, or moulid people, who spend their lives going from one moulid to another.

For visitors, the hardest part about attending a moulid is ascertaining dates. Events are tied to either the Islamic or Gregorian calendars, and dates can be different each year. Also, you'll need to be prepared for immense crowds (hold onto your valuables or, better still, leave them behind) and women should be escorted by a male.

The country's biggest moulid, the Moulid of al-Badawi, is held in Tanta in October, while Cairo hosts three major moulids dedicated to Sayyida Zeinab, Al-Hussein and Imam ash-Shafi (held during the Islamic months of Ragab, Rabei al-Tani and Sha'aban, respectively). You'll need to ask a local for the exact dates in any particular year. There are a number of smaller moulids in the area around Luxor – see the boxed text 'Moulids Around Luxor' in the Luxor chapter for more details.

November

Arabic Music Festival A 10-day festival of classical, traditional and orchestral Arabic music held at the Cairo Opera House, early in the month. Programs are usually in Arabic only but the tourist office should have details.

December

Cairo International Film Festival This 14-day festival, held early in the month, gives Cairenes the chance to watch a vast range of recent films from all over the world. The main attraction, however, is that the films are all supposedly uncensored. Anything that sounds like it might contain scenes of exposed flesh sells out immediately.

ACTIVITIES

The heat and predominantly desert landscape greatly limit the types of activities available in Egypt but following is a brief listing of some of the possibilities.

Bird-Watching

Egypt is an ornithologists delight with a plethora of birds both native and migrant (see Flora & Fauna in the Facts about Egypt chapter for more details). The country boasts several excellent bird-watching areas. Prime among these is Lake Qarun in the Al-Fayoum region with birds ranging from spoonbills to marsh sandpipers. The saltwater lagoons in the northern Delta and the Zaranik Reserve on Lake Bardawil in northern Sinai are home to greater flamingoes, white pelicans and spoonbills (all winter visitors). It's also possible to see huge flocks of pelicans around the small lakes near Abu Simbel in southern Egypt. On star-filled nights in the desert you may see, or hear, eagle owls. In spring the cliffs at Ain Sukhna on the Red Sea coast offer opportunities for viewing eagles, vultures and other birds of prey spiralling on the thermals.

Anyone interested in the subject should read 'Nature Notes' in *Egypt Today*, an excellent monthly local wildlife column. There are also a couple of good reference works (notably *Birds of Egypt and the Middle East* and *Pharaohs Birds: Ancient and Present-day Birds in Egypt)*, both available at the AUC bookshop in Cairo. Or visit **W** www.birdingegypt.com, which is the Web site of the Egyptian birding community and an excellent resource, listing top birding sites, rarities reports and travel tips.

Cycling

High temperatures, a limited road network and some fairly dull landscape mean that Egypt is not the ideal place for cycle touring, but see the Getting Around chapter for making the best of what there is. There's also a club, the Cairo Cyclists (☎ 02-519 6078) that meets at 7am Friday and Saturday at the front gate of the Cairo American College on Midan Digla, in Ma'adi, a southern suburb of Cairo. The club also organises long-distance rides.

Desert Safaris

Desert safaris are fast becoming a growth area in tourism in Egypt. The options are the Western Desert with its fantastic sand landscapes, weirdly eroded rocks and Roman ruins, or the more rugged, rocky surrounds of Sinai. Western Desert trips can be arranged cheaply in the Oases (particularly Farafra) or, more expensively (involving 4WDs) in Cairo; for details see the boxed text 'Desert Safaris' in the Western Oases chapter.

Sinai safaris are perhaps easier to arrange. These typically involve a day or two (with overnight camping) trekking through desert canyons on foot, by camel or in a jeep. These expeditions can be organised on the ground at one of the south Sinai resorts such as Sharm el-Sheikh, Dahab or Nuweiba. Alternatively, you can book a complete holiday with a specialised Sinai outfit such as Wind, Sand & Stars (see Organised Tours in the Getting There & Away chapter for contact details).

Diving & Snorkelling

Many visitors to Egypt rarely have their heads above water. No wonder, as some of the best diving in the world is to be found along the Red Sea coast. The pick of the crop is along the southern stretch towards the border with Sudan and along the southern coast of the Sinai peninsula. Away from the expensive resort atmosphere, there are possibilities further north, such as in Dahab or you can cross the Gulf of Suez to Hurghada.

However, it isn't necessary to dive to enjoy the marine life of the Red Sea. You can see plenty with just a snorkel, mask and flippers. Along the Sinai coast the reefs are only 15m out and in some places you don't even need to go out of your depth to be among shoals of brightly coloured fish. The best places are Basata, Nuweiba and Dahab, all of which have equipment for hire for around E£10 a day (for more details see the Diving the Red Sea chapter).

Fishing

Other than the guys that regularly brave the spray on the rocks beside Fort Qaitbey in Alexandria, we've never seen much evidence of angling as a pastime in Egypt. In fact, the only serious fishing we know of occurs on Lake Nasser where a couple of outfits organise 'big game' fishing safaris for Nile perch – see the boxed text 'Fishing in the Desert' in the Nile Valley – Esna to Abu Simbel chapter. There is also an annual International Fishing Tournament every February in Hurghada; for more details contact the Egyptian Federation for Fishing (☎ 02-395 3953, fax 395 3516).

Golf

Bizarrely, given the desperate lack of usable land, the shortage of water and the blistering temperatures Egypt endures for most of the year, the Ministry of Tourism is actively promoting the country as a golfing destination. It's a sport introduced by the British in the 19th century but never taken up by the locals, until in 1996, when the first of the modern clubs opened its doors. Since then seven more resort courses have opened around the country, with another four in preparation. Egyptians have yet to take to the greens in any significant numbers (it's too expensive) but the idea is that these courses will broaden the appeal of Egypt as a tourist attraction beyond monuments and beaches.

The Cascades Golf Resort & Country Club (☎ 065-544 901, W www.thecascadessomabay.com) 48km on the Safaga Rd, Soma Bay, Red Sea coast. Gary Player designed this 18-hole links course south of Hurghada. There's a Sheraton beside the course that offers special golf packages.

Dreamland Golf & Tennis Resort (☎ 02-400 577, W www.dreamlandgolf.com) 6th of October City Rd, Dreamland City, Cairo. This is a sports resort on the outskirts of Cairo that also includes a theme park, shopping centre, equestrian riding centre, 16 cinema screens, nine hotels and the worlds largest clubhouse. The 18-hole, par-72 course designed by golf architect Karl Litten has spectacular views of the Pyramids.

Al-Gouna Golf Course (☎ 065-580 009, W www.elgouna.com) Al-Gouna Resort, Red Sea coast. A USPGA-sized 18-hole championship golf course designed by Gene Bates, associate of Fred Couples.

Jolie Ville Golf Resort (☎ 069-600 63, W www.moevenpick-sharm.com) Sharm el-Sheikh, South Sinai. An 18-hole championship course (a favourite of President Mubarak) that is attached to the Mövenpick Jolie Ville luxury hotel, where golf packages are available.

Mirage City Golf Course (☎ 02-408 5041, fax 408 5040) Intersection of the Cairo Ring Rd and the Cairo-Suez Highway. This is an 18-hole, par-72, rating-73 course. An adjoining Marriott is currently under construction to be completed some time in 2001 to house resident golfers.

Pyramids Golf & Country Club (☎ 049-600 953, fax 600 954, e amngolf61@hotmail.com) Cairo-Alexandria Desert Highway. This is part of a giant project intended to have no less than 99 holes. The first 27 are open for play, including the championship 18-hole course. The rest are slated to be fully operational by 2002.

Royal Valley Golf Club (☎ 02-414 6538, W www.royalvalley.com) Luxor. This is an 18-hole, par-72, rating-72 course on the outskirts of Luxor. Several of the Luxor resort hotels offer special golf packages.

Horse Riding

Horse riding is possible in Cairo around the Pyramids and in Luxor on the West Bank, where there are a couple of stables just up from the local ferry landing; see the relevant chapters for further details. There are also stables at the Sinai resorts of Sharm el-Sheikh, Dahab and Nuweiba that rent steeds to tourists by the hour.

Sadly, most of the animals are not very well looked after. A letter we had from a

British veterinary surgeon who had just holidayed in Egypt reckoned that perhaps only 30% of the horses he saw were fit to be ridden. Many animals are lame or emaciated. The vet also reported evidence of bad respiratory disease.

The following is a simple guide to hiring healthy horses that we advise prospective riders to observe for their own sake (a healthy horse is a better ride) and for the sake of the animals (if stable owners realise tourists will not ride neglected animals they may look after them better). If the answer to any of these pointers is yes, then pass on the horse and request another.

Is the horse too thin? Are the ribs visible? Are the pin bones prominent? These are the bones on either side of the rump behind the saddle. In a healthy horse they appear as a rounded bump; if a horse is too thin then muscle wastage will cause them to look angular and prominent.

Is the horse limping/lame? Ask the owner to walk then trot the horse up and down a couple of times.

Does the horse have diarrhoea? Is there staining on the back of its legs?

Does the horse have respiratory problems? Is it coughing? Does it gurgle when it breathes? Is there pus showing at its nostrils?

Are there any obvious wounds? If they are healing then this shouldn't be a problem, but also check under the saddle for open or weeping sores.

Windsurfing

Moon Beach in Sinai is reckoned to be one of the world's best windsurfing centres – see Water Sports at the start of the Sinai chapter for more details.

COURSES

Language

Several institutions in Cairo offer Arabic courses. The full-blown option is to sign up at the Arabic Language Institute (☎ 02-797 5055, fax 795 7565, ⓔ alu@aucegypt.edu), a department of the AUC, PO Box 2511, Cairo 11511. It offers intensive instruction in Arabic language at elementary, intermediate and advanced levels. The courses incorporate both Egyptian colloquial Arabic and classical Arabic – in other words, as well as learning to speak, you learn how to read and write. At the time of writing, the intensive, full-time course cost US$11,710 for a full year's tuition, or US$5905 per semester (20 hours per week over 14 weeks). The institute also offers intensive summer programs (20 hours per week for six weeks) for US$2920.

The Arabic Department (☎ 02-347 6118, fax 301 8348, ⓦ www.britishcouncil.org.eg) at the British Council, 192 Sharia el-Nil, Agouza, Cairo, also does colloquial and classical courses. Courses in the former are 12 hours a week (four mornings) over four weeks for E£1200, or six hours a week (two mornings) over four weeks for E£600. Classical Arabic is taught for eight hours a week over four weeks for E£800. There are also summer programs of two successive three-week terms costing E£1200 for 48 hours of tuition in colloquial Arabic or E£800 for 32 hours classical. The British Council in Alexandria also sometimes offers Arabic language courses.

The third and cheapest option is to study at one of the two (unconnected) International Language Institutes (ILI) in Mohandiseen (☎ 02-746 3087, fax 703 5624, ⓔ ili@starnet.com.eg) at 4 Sharia Mahmoud Azmy, Sahafayeen; or in Heliopolis (☎ 02-291 9295, fax 415 1082, ⓔ ili@idsc.net.eg) at 2 Sharia Mohammed Bayoumi, off Mirghani, a few minutes' walk east of the Baron's Palace (Qasr al-Baron). The Heliopolis school offers intensive courses with four sessions a week for four weeks or regular courses of two sessions a week spread over eight weeks. Costs in both cases are E£475 for colloquial Arabic and E£500 for classical Arabic. Private tuition can also be arranged from E£35 per hour. Contact the Mohandiseen school for its latest rates.

American University in Cairo

The AUC is one of the premier universities in the Middle East. In 2000 there were some 4900 students, the bulk of whom are Egyptian, studying at its cluster of campuses just off Midan Tahrir in the heart of Cairo. The curriculum, and one-third of the full-time faculty of over 300, are American and accredited in the USA.

The AUC offers degree, nondegree and summer-school programs. Any of the regular courses offered can be taken. Popular subjects include Arabic Language & Literature, Arab History & Culture, Egyptology, Islamic Art & Architecture, Middle East Studies and Social Science courses on the Arab world. Up to 15 unit hours can be taken per semester at the undergraduate level.

Summer programs offer similar courses. The term lasts from mid-June to the end of July. Two three-unit courses can be taken and several well-guided field trips throughout Egypt are usually included.

Applications for programs with the Arabic Language Institute (see under Language earlier) and undergraduate and graduate studies at the university are separate. Specify which you want when requesting an application form. A catalogue and program information can be obtained from the Office of Admissions (☎ 212-730 8800, fax 730 1600), The American University in Cairo, 420 Fifth Avenue, New York, NY 10018 2719; or you can write to PO Box 2511, Cairo 11511 (☎ 754 2964, fax 795 7565, W www.aucegypt.edu).

Egyptian Universities

It is also possible to study at Egyptian universities such as Cairo University, Al-Azhar (in Cairo), Ain Shams (in Cairo) and Alexandria. Courses offered to foreign students include Arabic Language, Islamic History, Islamic Religion, and Egyptology. For information on courses, tuition fees and applications contact the Cultural Counsellor, The Egyptian Educational Bureau (☎ 202-296 3888), 2200 Kalorama Rd NW, Washington, DC 20008. In London, contact the Cultural Affairs Office (☎ 020-7491 7720).

Diving

For information on the various dive courses offered in Egypt see the Diving the Red Sea chapter.

WORK

More than 40,000 foreigners live and work in Egypt. That figure alone should give you some idea of the immense presence foreign companies have in the country. It is possible to find work with one of these companies, especially if you begin your research before you leave home. *Cairo: A Practical Guide*, published by the AUC Press, has lists of foreign companies operating in Egypt. Once you have an employer, securing a work permit through an Egyptian consulate or from the Ministry of the Interior if you are in Egypt should not be difficult.

If you are looking for casual work to extend your stay in Cairo then teaching English at a cowboy school (see English Tutoring below) is probably the easiest way. It's also sometimes possible to find other types of work in the resorts. Dahab in particular has a relatively large number of travellers who find short-term work as bartenders or administrators in the many hotels and dive centres that dot the beach. There are also a few enterprising travellers who've financed their stay by setting up shop as masseurs, acupuncturists and herbalists. Windsurfing outfits occasionally need staff, although there are not enough of them for much turnover.

Away from the beaches, some of the larger hotels in Luxor and Aswan occasionally take on foreigners as entertainment directors, but many of the large chains have their own staff sent in from abroad.

English Tutoring

The most easily available work for native or fluent English speakers is teaching the language to the locals. The best places to do this are reputable schools such as the British Council, the ILI in Heliopolis and the Centre for Adult & Continuing Education (☎ 02-754 2964) at the AUC – see Courses earlier for AUC contact details. However, all of these places require qualifications and the minimum requirement is a Certificate in English Language Teaching to Adults (CELTA). This is what used to be known as TEFL. To get the qualification you need to attend a one-month intensive course, which you can do in your home country via an English-language training centre. In the UK, contact International House (IH; ☎ 020-7491 2598, w www.ihlondon.com), which runs more than a dozen courses a year (for UK£1010). The ILI (☎ 02-291 9295, fax 415 1082, e ili@idsc.net.eg) at 2 Sharia Mohammed Bayoumi, off Mirghani in Heliopolis, runs several one-month intensive CELTA courses each year and sometimes employs course graduates. The cost of the course is the equivalent of UK£650.

If you have no qualifications or experience, you could try one of the 'cowboy schools' such as the International Living Language Institute (ILLI) at 34 Talaat Harb, on the top floor above El-Abd bakery, in central Cairo. These are fly-by-night places (that said, the ILLI has been around for at least 15 years) that take on unqualified staff and work them hard for little financial return. But they do pay enough to allow you stay on and maybe earn enough to take the CELTA and gravitate to better-paid employment.

Some travellers also make ends meet by offering private tuition, which can be well paid; however, the difficulty is in finding your students.

Newspapers & Magazines

Another possible source of work for English speakers with a good sense of grammar is in copy-editing for one of Cairo's many English-language publications. *The Egyptian Gazette* and *Al-Ahram Weekly* are probably the best two places to inquire, although new English-language magazines are springing up all the time. The pay is nothing terrific but it could be enough to scrape by on.

Film & TV Extras

Europeans are often in demand to appear as background decoration in local TV commercials, dramas or even films. The work is far from glamorous and involves hanging around all day when often you're only required for five minutes of shooting. Still, it pays about E£40 to E£50 per session. Notices for persons wanted are sometimes posted at the hostels in the Tawfiqiyya Souq in Cairo or, more commonly, middlemen will tell you. They haunt Ash-Shams coffeehouse (see Entertainment in the Cairo chapter) at the top end of Talaat Harb.

Dive Instructors

If you are a dive-master or diving instructor you can find work in Egypt's diving resorts fairly easily. As many divers fund their travels through such work the turnover is high and you're likely to find an opening if you can hang around for a couple of weeks. Owners say that apart from the basic diving qualifications, they look for languages and an ability to get along with people. If you're interested in a job, a dive centre will usually take you along on a few dive trips to assess your diving skills and to see how you interact with others before offering you work.

ACCOMMODATION

Egypt offers visitors the full spectrum of accommodation, from the big international five-star chains to flea-ridden dives. There are hotels, flotels (Nile cruisers), pensions, youth hostels, a few camping grounds and even the odd ecofriendly resort. Some hotels offer half board, which includes accommodation, breakfast and dinner, while full board also includes lunch.

In mid-range and top-end hotels, rates often go up by around 10% at peak times, including the two big feasts (Eid al-Fitr and Eid al-Adha), New Year (20 December to 5 January) and sometimes for the summer season (approximately 1 July to 15 September). As a general rule there is a review of prices each year in October and, on average, prices rise by about 15%.

Residents in Egypt are often entitled to something closer to the local rate for rooms in the bigger hotels – yes, there is one rate for foreigners and another for locals. If you do have residency ask about resident rates, as they mean a considerable saving.

One thing that's available to everyone is bargaining. Just because a hotel has its rates displayed in a glass frame on the wall, it doesn't mean they are untouchable. In off-peak seasons haggling will often get you significant discounts, even in mid-range places. That said, at the time of writing numbers of tourists in Egypt are at an all-time high and hotel rates are at a similar peak.

Camping

Officially, camping is allowed at only a few places around Egypt, such as at Harraniyya near Giza in Cairo, Luxor, Aswan, Farafra and Ras Mohammed National Park. At official sites, facilities tend to be rudimentary. A few private hotels around the country also allow campers to set up in their backyard, such as at Abu Simbel, Kharga, Nuweiba, Basata, Qena and Abydos. Facilities in most of these places are extremely basic.

Hostels

Egypt has 15 hostels recognised by HI, in Cairo, Alexandria, Al-Fayoum, Aswan, Asyut, Damanhur, Hurghada, Ismailia, Luxor, Marsa Matruh, Port Said, Sharm el-Sheikh, Sohag, Suez and Tanta. They generally range in price from about E£4 to E£14. The one in Ismailia has beds as expensive as E£16 – it's virtually a hotel. In some cases the price includes breakfast. Having an HI card is not absolutely necessary as nonmembers are admitted, but a card will save you between E£2 and E£4, depending on the hostel. The youth hostels tend to be noisy, crowded and often a bit grimy. In some there are rooms for mixed couples or families, but on the whole the sexes are segregated. Reservations are not usually needed.

The offices of the Egyptian Youth Hostels Association (☎ 02-794 0527, fax 795 0329) at 1 Ibrahimy, Garden City, Cairo, can give you the latest information.

Budget Hotels

The two-, one- and no-star hotels form the budget group. Often the ratings mean nothing at all, as a hotel without a star can be as good as a two-star hotel, only cheaper. You can spend as little as E£10 a night for a clean single room with hot water or E£40 or more for a dirty double room without a shower. Generally, the prices quoted include any charges and, quite often, breakfast – but don't harbour any great expectations about breakfast as it is usually a couple of pieces of bread, a frozen patty of butter, a serving of jam, and tea or coffee.

Most hotels will tell you they have hot water when they don't. They may not even have warm water. Before paying, turn the tap on and check for yourself or keep an eye out for an electric water heater when inspecting the bathroom. If there's no plug in your bathroom sink and you forgot to bring your own, then try using the lid of a Baraka mineral-water bottle – according to one hip traveller, they fit 90% of the time.

Also, many budget establishments economise on sheets, putting only one, or sometimes none, between you and blankets that may never have seen the inside of a washing machine. If you aren't carrying your own sleeping sheet, then just ask for clean sheets – most hotels will oblige.

Mid-Range Hotels

While Egypt has plenty of reasonable budget hotels and a full complement of international five stars, the choices are often not so great when it comes to mid-range options. This is particularly so in Cairo and Alexandria, where foreign investment is channelled into top-end accommodation, while local establishments all too often pitch themselves as mid-range establishments but through inexperience, lack of funds or poor practices end up offering no-star facilities at three-star rates. Also, beware the extras. Breakfast is often compulsory and sometimes you are charged extra for the fridge and TV in your room. You can take an ordinary double room for E£50, add E£8 for breakfast, E£2 for the fridge you never used and E£2 for the TV you never turned on, whack 12% service on the whole lot and then 5% sales tax and possibly a government tax on top of that, and your E£50 room is suddenly costing you more than E£70.

Top-End Hotels

At the five-star end of the price range are hotels representing most of the world's major chains. While their prices (typically

Best Rooms

Looking for something different? Romantic? Chic? Memorable (in the nicest possible way, of course)? The concept of the boutique hotel hasn't yet taken hold in Egypt (there are just two), but the country does possess some wonderful old historic institutions, hangovers from the days when the country was a winter retreat for the rich and titled of Europe. Several of the Red Sea resorts are also striking, marrying attractive architecture with stunning locations. Unfortunately, most of our picks here are necessarily pricey. If you can't afford a room make a visit anyway and give yourself something to aspire to.

Adrére Amellal (Siwa) Ecolodge on the edge of the desert. Seemingly a million miles from civilisation – no electricity, no phones – but possessing stunning mud-brick architecture, breathtaking scenery, fantastic gourmet cuisine, clean air and quiet.

Basata (Sinai) Ecologically minded travellers' settlement of bamboo beach huts on a white sandy cove backed by purple mountains and fronted by gorgeous aquamarine sea with just-offshore reefs teeming with marine life.

El Moudira (Luxor) Traditional architecture with ethno-chic touches and palatial rooms decorated in a variety of themes. Arguably Egypt's quirkiest and most-charming hotel, made to order for a Conde Nast crowd.

Mövenpick Resort (Al-Quseir) Beautiful, environmentally friendly, self-contained resort set around an aquamarine bay. Rooms are pretty stone bungalows set around a gorgeous terraced pool area.

Oberoi Mena House (Cairo) Built in the shadow of the Great Pyramids in the 1860s as a hunting lodge for Khedive Ismail, the hotel's isolation from the city was seen as a distinct security advantage when in 1943 Roosevelt and Churchill met there to hammer out plans for the D-Day invasions.

Old Cataract Hotel (Aswan) In 1999 the *Times* newspaper ranked the Cataract one of the top hotels anywhere, stating that its terrace had 'possibly the greatest view in the world'.

Sheraton Miramar (Al-Gouna) This pastel-painted post-modernism creation designed by internationally renowned architect Michael Graves looks resplendent in its seaside desert setting.

Winter Palace (Luxor) At first it was reserved exclusively for the use of Egypt's royalty and nobility before being later opened to the public. Howard Carter's first announcement of his discovery of the tomb of Tutankhamun was a posting on the guests' bulletin board here.

starting at about US$120 per night, not including a series of taxes and service charges of between 19% and 23%) and amenities are usually up to international standards, service hardly ever is.

Although all five-star and many much cheaper hotels still quote prices in US dollars, it is usually no problem to pay in Egyptian pounds. Hotels quoting prices in dollars will accept most credit cards, particularly Visa, MasterCard and AmEx. Many smaller places also accept credit cards.

FOOD

While there are many wonderful things about Egypt, food is not one of them. Egyptian cuisine is crude: salads are typically boring, vinegary and often far from fresh; vegetables have the flavour boiled out of them; typical main dishes of potato, rice and meat are heavy and often oily. In fact, Egypt introduced the world to one of the most revolting dishes of all time in *molokhiyya*. Made by stewing the molokhiyya leaf in chicken stock, the resulting soup looks like green algae and has the consistency of mucus. The 11th-century caliph Al-Hakim found the stuff so repulsive he had the dish banned. Still, it has its fans.

All of this aside, it is possible to eat well (not to mention cheaply), if you can accept the lack of variety and pack your taste buds off on holiday.

Egyptian Staples

Fuul & Ta'amiyya Fuul is mashed fava beans, usually ladled into a piece of *shammy* bread (flat bread pocket similar to pitta) and sells for 35pt to 50pt; ta'amiyya is mashed fava beans and spices fried in a patty (it's known elsewhere as felafel) and stuffed into a piece of shammy with salad and tahini (sesame-seed paste). A ta'amiyya sandwich costs about 50pt and two make a substantial snack. Bright pink pickled vegetables, known as *torshi*, are usually served complimentary. Sit-down restaurants offer variations on the fuul and ta'amiyya theme serving them up with egg, garlic, butter, mincemeat or *basturma*, the Egyptian take on pastrami.

Kushari Next in national affections after fuul and ta'amiyya is *kushari*, a mix of noodles, rice, black lentils, fried onions and tomato sauce. The ingredients are served up together in a bowl (small, *sughayyer*; medium, *metawasit*; or large, *kebir*) for sit-down meals, or spooned into a polythene bag for takeaway. A medium serve, which is more than most people can eat, costs from E£1 to E£1.50. You can recognise kushari joints by the great tureens of noodles and rice in their windows.

Shwarma This is the Egyptian equivalent of the Greek *gyros* sandwich or the Turkish kebab. Strips of lamb or chicken are sliced from a spit, sizzled on a hotplate with chopped tomatoes and garnish, and then stuffed in a pocket of shammy. Unfortunately, the meat is often unappetisingly fatty and it's difficult to find decent shwarma.

Fiteer This is a kind of Egyptian pizza made with a flaky pastry base. The filling can be served as a topping or stuffed inside, and can be sweet or savoury. The place that serves *fiteer* is called a *fatatri*. Part of the attraction of eating fiteer is watching the dough being pounded, stretched and whirled around the cook's head like a lasso. At most fatatris all the toppings are arrayed in dishes around the cook and you can point to what you want; the typical mix is egg, cheese and chopped tomato. Avoid the meat as it's usually terrible. Sweet fiteer are usually sprinkled with icing sugar, coconut and raisins.

Starters & Side Dishes

Soup Choices are limited but most menus offer a *shurba* (soup) or two. The standard is some kind of vegetable broth, often with pearl pasta (which is about the size and shape of puffed rice). The other common item, especially in winter, is *shurba ads*, or lentil soup, often spiced with cumin.

Salads These are uninventive. Typically what you get is a mixed green salad of chopped tomatoes, lettuce and cucumber doused in a fairly over-powering vinegary dressing. You need to visit an upmarket restaurant to get anything more exciting.

Mezze Although the practice of dining on mezze isn't as ingrained as say with Lebanese cuisine, there are plenty of popular Egyptian side dishes. *Mahshi* is various vegetables, such as vine leaves (in summer), cabbage (in winter), peppers, or white and black aubergines, stuffed with minced meat, rice, onions, parsley and herbs and then baked. It's good when just cooked and hot but less so when cold. *Baba ghanoug* is puree made of grilled aubergine with tahini and olive oil, similar in appearance to hummus or tahini.

Egyptians are keen on offal. *Kebda firekh* (chicken livers) are often excellent – if done right they should be beautifully soft with an almost pâté-like consistency. Less appealing is *mokh*, or brains. This is served crumbed and deep fried or whole, garnished with salad. Lambs testicles are another delicacy, although these are rarely served alone and are usually included as part of a mixed grill.

Main Dishes

Kofta and kebab are two of the most popular dishes in Egypt. Kofta is ground meat peppered with spices, skewered and grilled. Kebab is skewered and flame-grilled chunks of meat, usually lamb (the chicken equivalent is called shish tawouq). The meat usually comes on a bed of *badounis* (parsley) and may be served in upmarket restaurants with grilled tomatoes and onions. Otherwise you eat it with bread, salad and tahini. Kofta and kebab are always ordered by weight; 250g (known as a *roba* kilo) is usually sufficient for one person and it typically costs from E£9 to E£12.

Firekh (chicken) is common, roasted on a spit and, in restaurants, ordered by the half. Takeaway spit-roasted whole chickens are available from many small restaurants for about E£8 to E£12 depending on the weight. *Hamam* (pigeon) is also extremely popular and usually served stuffed with rice and spices. It's also served as a stew cooked in a deep clay pot, known as a *tagen*, with onions, tomatoes, and rice or cracked wheat. In Alexandria, you'll also get quail.

Alexandria is also, not surprisingly, good for fish. Although there's not much variety and the cooking methods are not wildly inventive (baked or grilled), the quality of the

Fine Dining

Egyptian cuisine may not be up there with that of the Moroccans, Lebanese, Turks...or pretty much any other nation you care to name, but for foodies there are a few highlights. Some dishes to look out for include:

Fuul Protein for the poor, but consistently good. A great vehicle for all manner of vegetables and spices, served as accompaniment to a main meal or ladled into freshly baked pita bread as a snack.
Mahshi kurumb When correctly cooked with plenty of dill and lots of sinful semna, stuffed cabbage leaves are decadently delicious (incorrectly prepared they are tasteless).
Molokhiyya Many find it repulsive but if you want to test your mettle, this is the dish. Properly prepared with rabbit broth and plenty of garlic it's actually quite delicious.
Stuffed Pigeons Smaller than European pigeons and usually stuffed with fareek and rice, these popular birds are served at all traditional restaurants but can be a bit fiddly to eat. Beware the plentiful little bones.

Progress is slow but the restaurant scene is improving, particularly in Cairo, where welcome recent additions such as Abu as-Sid and Flux are raising the standards. Some other places to look out for include:

Sharia Safar Pasha A street in Alexandria's old Anfushi quarter lined with grills producing billowing clouds of aromatic smoke from sizzling seafood and meat served to diners at a multitude of open-air restaurants.
Siwa With its Berber culture and thousands of palms, coucous and dates feature heavily on restaurant menus and make for a delicious change from other Egyptian dishes. If you want to blow the budget, dine at Adrére Amellal, in Sidi Jaafar, where organically grown produce is turned into some of the most innovative and delicious food in the country.
West Bank Dining A handful of restaurants on Luxor's West Bank serve basic, home-cooked Upper Egyptian cuisine, such as tagens and duck. Simple but pleasing.

JULIET COOMBE

The names of spices may be spelt differently, but you'll recognise many of the flavours they create in Egyptian food. Spices are also a cheap and memorable souvenir.

catch is good. The most popular fish are something called *balti*, which is about 15cm long, flattish and grey with a light belly, and the larger, tastier *bouri*, which is about 30cm, thin and silver, darkening toward the top. You'll also commonly find sea bass, red and grey mullet, bluefish, sole, squid *(subeit)* and shrimp *(gambari)*. The choice is greater at the Sinai and Red Sea resorts, where we've enjoyed excellent rock-salt-baked fish.

Desserts & Sweets

Given the Egyptian addiction to sickly sweet sticky pastries it is no wonder that dentistry is such a popular profession – there is no shortage of needy clients. The generic term for these sugar-loaded confections is baklava, and it applies to a delicacy constructed of layers of wafer-thin filo pastry filled with crushed nuts and pistachios and drenched in syrup. It is baked in great trays and then typically sliced into small diamond-shaped pieces. *Kunafa* is another generic type; this is made by sieving liquid batter onto a hot metal sheet so it sets in vermicelli-like strands, which are quickly swept off so they remain soft. These are then piled on top of a soft cheese or cream base. Kunafa is often associated with feasts, and is always eaten at Ramadan.

When buying from a pastry shop order by weight – 250g is generally the smallest amount you can buy, and that's probably more than enough for one person.

Apart from pastries, desserts are surprisingly few in number. *Muhalabiyya* is a milk cream thickened by cornflour or ground rice, often flavoured with rose-water, and sprinkled with chopped almonds or coconut. It looks like blancmange. *Om Ali* is layers of pastry, filled with nuts and raisins, soaked in cream and milk, and baked in the oven. It's like an Egyptian version of bread and butter pudding and is said to have been introduced into the country by an Irish mistress of one of the khedives. *Roz bi laban* (rice with milk) is self explanatory, and it's served cold.

Vegetarian Meals

Vegetarians should have no trouble finding food to eat in Egypt, although the concept of vegetarianism is not understood at all.

A friend once ordered vegetable casserole off the menu at a Cairo restaurant and was served up a hunk of lamb in broth. When he complained about his order the waiter replied, 'But there are vegetables in there'.

Misconceptions aside, avoiding meat is easy as salads, dips, pulse-based dishes and rice-stuffed vegetables feature heavily on most restaurant menus. The basic staples of the Egyptian diet are wholly vegetarian too: fuul, ta'amiyya and kushari. If you can find it on menus, *musaga* is a great dish; it's a mixture of aubergines, tomatoes, garlic, oil and spices baked in the oven.

Self-Catering

For those who find themselves on long train or bus rides, it is also essential to know about bread and cheese – the easily transportable staples of the traveller. Bread, including pitta, is called *a'aish* (the word 'a'aish' also means 'life'). Most of what you'll eat is *a'aish baladi*, a round flat, plate-sized bread that is coarse and spongy. The other main type is called *a'aish fransawi*, or French bread, which are rolls in the European style.

There are two main types of cheese – *gibna beida*, or white cheese, which tastes like Greek feta; and *gibna rumi*, a hard, sharp-tasting, yellow cheese.

DRINKS

Nonalcoholic Drinks

Tea & Coffee *Shai* (tea) and *ahwa* (coffee) are both served strong and sugary. Tea is served in glasses at traditional Egyptian coffeehouses and in teacups at Western-style restaurants. At coffeehouses, the tea leaves are boiled with the water making a very black, tannin-loaded drink; the alternative is to ask for *shai libton*, 'Lipton' being the generic term for tea bag. Specify how much sugar you want on ordering, otherwise it'll be assumed that you want four or five spoonfuls. *Sukar shwaiyya* is 'with a little sugar', *minrheyer sukar* is without. If you want milk ask for *b'laban*, although it's much more refreshing taken with fresh mint *(b'naanaa)*.

If you ask for coffee, you will probably get *ahwa turki* (Turkish coffee), which comes in a small, two-sip cup. It is gritty and *very* strong. Let the grains settle before drinking. As with tea, specify how much sugar: *ahwa mazboot* is medium sweet; *ahwa saada* is without sugar. Coffee is often flavoured with cardamom. If you want Western-style coffee ask for 'neskaf'.

Fruit Juices Juice stands are common. At such places you can get a drink squeezed out of just about any fruit or vegetable in season. Standard *asiir* (juices) include: *moz* (banana); *guafa* (guava); *limoon* (lemon); *manga* (mango); *bortuaan* (orange); *rumman* (pomegranate); *farawla* (strawberry); and *asab* (sugar cane).

Depending on the type of fruit, a glass costs from 50pt to E£1.50. You can also take along an empty mineral-water bottle and get that filled up.

Alcoholic Drinks

For information on Egyptian attitudes to beer and alcohol see Society & Conduct in the Facts about Egypt chapter.

Beer For beer in Egypt say 'Stella'. It's been brewed and bottled in Cairo now for more than 100 years. It's a yeasty lager, the taste of which varies enormously by batch. Since 1998, the standard Stella (sold in dark green bottles at E£4 in shops and anywhere from E£6 to E£16 in bars) has been supplemented by sister brews including Stella Meister (a light lager) and Stella Premium (which tastes like a particularly rough home-brew). Most locals just stick to the unfussy basic brew – it's the cheapest and if served cold it's not bad. Since the late 1990s there's also been a rival brew on the market, called Saqqara, brewed at Al-Gouna on the Red Sea coast. It's not a bad beer and more reliable in quality than Stella. Unfortunately, as this book was in production, it was announced that Saqqara was in the process of being bought by ABC Breweries, producers of Stella, so its future looks highly uncertain.

Some bars in five-star hotels serve imported beers, but prices are always outrageous. The duty-free shops (see Customs earlier in this chapter) often have crates of imported beer.

Vine & Liquor Although the ancient
gyptians are supposed to have invented
vine, until recently it was all but absent
rom contemporary Egypt, at least in any
rinkable form. A government-owned com-
any produced red, rosé and white wines –
inegary bouquets that went by nicknames
uch as 'Chateau Migraine'. Most bottles
vere bought as one-off, never to be repeat-
d experiments by expats and tourists. That
ituation changed in 1999 with a buyout
nd relaunch. The new, revamped wines,
nade with grapes from the Delta and with
he assistance of a Bordeaux-based winery,
re quite drinkable. Bottles can be bought
t Al-Ahram beverage shops, where they
ell for about E£30. The wines are also
ffered at restaurants frequented by for-
igners (Egyptians account for only 20%
f wine sales). However, seriously up-
narket places usually have the real stuff,
nported and subject to outrageous taxes,
neaning prices are astronomic. Econom-
cs may dictate that you give the local
tuff a go.

The local liquor isn't just bad, it's poten-
ally lethal. Egypt produces its own gin,
vhisky, vodka and brandy. They all taste
oughly the same, which is to say dreadful.
musingly, the spirits are marketed to re-
emble foreign imports – the whiskies in-
lude Johnny Wadie and Robert Horse,
vhile bottles of Garden's Gin used to carry
bold claim to the effect that 'The Queen
rinks this'. What's less funny is that some
ocal liquor is truly poisonous. Tales have
ong circulated among Cairo folk of deaths
aused by drinking local spirits. The stories
vere always apocryphal until the Canadian
mbassy issued a circular, warning that two
eaths had proven to be as a result of drink-
ng local whisky. Leave this stuff well
lone.

NTERTAINMENT

or locals, entertainment depends on gen-
er and age. The great social activity for
lder males is hanging out at the ahwa (cof-
eehouse). For younger males it's the club
nd the cinema, while for women of all
ges, it's the club and visiting family.

The Ahwa

The coffeehouse or ahwa (in Arabic the word means both coffee and the place in which it's drunk) is one of the great Egyptian social institutions. Typically just a collection of cheap tin-plate-topped tables and wooden chairs in a sawdust strewn room open to the street, the ahwa is a relaxed and unfussy place where the average Ahmed hangs out for part of each day reading the papers, meeting friends, sipping tea and while away the time. The hubbub of conversation is usually accompanied by the incessant clacking of *domina* (dominoes) and *towla* (backgammon) pieces, and the burbling of smokers drawing heavily on their *sheeshas*, the cumbersome water pipes.

Ahwa-going is an all-male preserve. With few exceptions Egyptian women do not frequent ahwas. That said, there is absolutely no reason why a foreign women shouldn't do so – although if you are unaccompanied by a male choose a large busy ahwa in which you aren't going to stand out too much.

In the hot summer months many ahwa-goers forgo the tea and coffee for cooler drinks such as iced *karkadey*, a refreshing drink made from boiled hibiscus leaves, *zabaady* (yogurt) or *limoon* (homemade lemon squash). In the winter many prefer *sahleb*, a hot drink made with semolina powder, milk and chopped nuts, or *yansoon*, a medicinal-tasting aniseed drink.

With the sheesha, there's usually a choice of two types of tobacco: the standard *m'aasil*, which is soaked in molasses, or *tofah*, which is soaked in apple juice and has a sweet aroma but a slightly sickly taste. Filtered by the water in the glass bowl, the smoke is mild but the effort required to draw it can leave you light-headed. A good sheesha can last 15 to 20 minutes. When the tobacco is burnt out or the coals have cooled the *raiyis* (waiter) will change the little clay pot of tobacco (the *hagar* or stone) for a fresh one. Each hagar costs around E£1. Most Egyptians smoke two or three at a sitting.

When it comes time to pay catch the eye of the raiyis and shout *Filoos!* (Money!).

The Club

The *nadi* (club) is the other great keystone of Egyptian social life. Unfortunately, this is not so easy for the casual visitor to penetrate. Any local who can afford to do so and has the right connections is a member of a club, which gains them access to a private swathe of the city's precious greenery, along with whatever sporting facilities are on offer. Some of the clubs do allow day memberships and these are worth taking advantage of if you fancy swimming or jogging or simply spending a day away from traffic and crowds, surrounded by greenery.

Nightlife

Certain towns and cities such as Cairo, the southern Sinai resorts and to a certain extent Alexandria, have a great nightlife scene. Cairo, for instance, only comes to life with the setting of the sun. During the summer months, families don't head out to shop until 8pm or 9pm when the heat of the day is less intense, and the smarter set never make dinner reservations before 10pm. Bars get busy towards midnight and the witching hour is long past before any discos start to fill. It's after 1am before the bands kick in and the belly dancers take to their five-star stages, and 3am or 4am when the last ones bow out. For those still unwilling to call it a night, Cairo has places that just don't close at all.

Bars Not just in Cairo, but throughout Egypt you'll find plenty of local spit-and-sawdust bars. These places are euphemistically known as 'cafeterias', though the only food present is usually a small plate of *termis* (small yellow beans that you nip with your teeth and squeeze out through their skin), used to salt up the palate and quicken the down flow of beer. Such places are fairly discreet and don't advertise themselves, but if you know what you're looking for they're pretty easy to spot – saloon-type doors leading to a dark interior. A beer typically costs E£5 to E£6 and opening hours are usually from around 11am to anywhere between 1am and 4am.

Cairo also has an ever-increasing numbe of chichi bars catering for the city's youn moneyed crowd.

You should be aware that all bars excep those in hotels are closed for the duration o Ramadan (see Public Holidays & Specia Events earlier in this chapter).

Discos You'll find discos only in Cairc Hurghada and the southern Sinai resorts usually attached to upmarket hotels. The almost always have a ridiculously high doc charge and many have fairly strict dres codes and are no great shakes once you ge in. However, Cairo's African discos are riot – see under Entertainment in the Cair chapter for more details.

Outside the capital, the best nightlife ca be found in Sharm el-Sheikh and Hurghada Many young Egyptians gravitate there t have fun on weekends, and by Egyptia standards the scene is much wilder than i Cairo. The top venues in each place are de tailed in their respective chapters.

Live Music This stops at cabaret artists i hotel lounges backed by a perma-grin key boardist in an ultra-brite suit. There are few exceptions. In Cairo, there's live jazz a the Cairo Jazz Club.

In Aswan and the surrounding village it's possible to see Nubian artists but it's o a fairly ad hoc basis – see the Aswan sec tion for information.

In Luxor, there is a Saidi music festiva each spring and you can sometimes com across local musicians at weddings. I Sharm el-Sheikh, the Sanafir Hotel (☎ 60 197, fax 600 196, W www.sanafirhot .com) has started organising occasiona concerts in the Sinai Desert. There's n set schedule so check with the hotel or i Web site.

Nightclubs & Belly Dancing Nightclu in the Egyptian sense means a place to s down and eat, or possibly just drink, an watch a floor show. The floor show can fea ture folkloric dancing or a star singer, bu the ones that really pull in the crowds con centrate on belly dancing.

The best dancers perform at Cairo's five-ar hotels for well over E£200 per ticket, ut at the other end of the scale, it is possi-le to watch belly dancing for just a few ounds. There are several places Downtown lus plenty more along Pyramids Rd (gen-rally expensive rip-off joints) that cater ainly to Egyptians. These places are fairly edy and most of the dancers have the ap-earance and grace of amateur wrestlers, but can be fun especially when the inebriated atrons join in as they invariably do.

In Luxor, live nighttime performances ften include horse dancing and a round of aidi stick dancing. One of the best places see this, as well as the obligatory belly ancer, is the Hatshepsut Restaurant on the /est Bank – see the Luxor chapter for details.

If scantily clad Russian girls gyrating on stage is your thing, Hurghada is the place go. Kitsch cabarets are a dime a dozen ere – see the Red Sea chapter for details.

asinos Some five-star hotels throughout gypt have casinos, open to non-Egyptians nly (take your passport). All games are onducted in US dollars or other major for-gn currencies, with a minimum stake of S$1. Smart casual attire is required.

These casinos are not to be confused with cal *casinos*, the name given for certain staurants popular with families.

he Cultural Scene

inema In Egypt, cinema-going is boom-g. Old movie houses are being refur-shed while, in Cairo and Alexandria at ast, new multiplexes have either recently ened or are being built. Screens are split etween local output and the latest Holly-ood releases. Films are subtitled rather an dubbed. Being able to read what's oing on allows patrons to carry on their wn conversations. Egyptian cinema-goers e also big on participation – great fun if 's a no-brain adventure flick, but the hooping, cheering and applause can be a t distracting if you're trying to settle into mething a bit more subtle.

Films are subject to censorship. How eavy-handed this is depends on the mood of the moment, but even seemingly innocuous movies often arrive on screen with telltale hiccups indicating the cut of the scissors.

Beware – Egypt's antiterrorism laws mean that no-one, no matter how bad the film is, can leave a cinema before the screening ends.

Screenings are usually at 1.30pm, 3.30pm, 6.30pm and 9.30pm. A few cinemas have midnight shows on Friday and Saturday. Tickets range in price from E£8 to E£18 depending on the venue.

Theatre, Music & Dance Cairo Opera House (☎ 02-342 0598) on Gezira is the country's premier performing arts venue. Well-known international troupes some-times perform here; the Bolshoi Ballet vis-its almost annually and recitals by local companies, such as the Cairo Opera Ballet Company and the Cairo Orchestra, are worth catching too. In addition to a main hall and small hall, the Opera House has an open-air theatre and summer amphitheatre. Check *Egypt Today* and *Al-Ahram Weekly* for what's on, or pass by and pick up a pro-gram. Jacket and tie are required by males for main hall performances, but less well-dressed travellers have been known to bor-row them from staff.

There are often music recitals and plays of varying quality at Ewart Hall and Wal-lace Theatre, both part of the AUC campus. In Islamic Cairo, theatre performances and music evenings are held at the House of Zeinab Khatoun and the Al-Ghouri com-plex, especially during Ramadan. It's worth attending something at each of these places at least once, if only for the setting.

Weddings

Visitors often find themselves invited by locals to weddings, which are always rau-cous affairs with troupes of drummers and ululating women. But you don't necessar-ily need an invitation. Just head along to al-most any five-star hotel on a Thursday night. These are the prized venues for brides and grooms to flaunt their good for-tunes, and usually involves a procession up the staircase with relatives and guests showering the couple with confetti or rose petals. The entire process can last a good 30 minutes or so. Later in the evening the newly married couples head out for the photographs which, in the case of Cairo, are often taken on the 6th of October Bridge.

In Aswan, Nubian weddings are a huge and often public affair, with Nubian music and hundreds of guests. If you're lucky enough to be invited to one, don't be surprised if you're asked to pay; most guests contribute to the colossal cost of the fiesta. For more information, see Nubian Culture under Lower Nubia & Lake Nasser in the Nile Valley – Esna to Abu Simbel chapter.

SPECTATOR SPORTS

Football is king in Egypt. Of the Arab nations, Egypt is the one country with players of international capacity (Hazem Emam, formerly of Cairo club Zamalek now currently plays for Udinese of Italy). In conversation with any Egyptian male, premier teams Zamalek and Al-Ahly arouse greater passions than almost any other subject. Demand for tickets makes them hard to get, especially for derbies. The season begins in September and continues until May. The big matches are held in the Cairo Stadium in Medinat Nasr.

SHOPPING

Egypt is both a budget souvenir and a kitsch-shoppers' paradise. Tourists with shelf space to fill back home can indulge in an orgy of alabaster pyramids, onyx Pharaonic cats, sawdust stuffed camels, and the ubiquitous painted papyrus. Hieroglyphic drawings of pharaohs, gods and goddesses embellish and blemish everything from leather wallets to engraved brass tables. Every town and village in Egypt has a small market (or souq, as they're known in Arabic) but the greatest is Cairo's Khan al-Khalili bazaar – although you will have to be prepared to bargain hard.

Antiques

There are few real antique bargains around. Dealers here know what they're about and study the latest Sotheby's catalogues. It also illegal to export anything of antiqu value out of Egypt without a licence fro the Department of Antiquities. But you're interested then good places browse include Alexandria's Attareen di trict, a maze of narrow, antique-shop-line alleys; and the emporiums along Shar Hoda Shaarawi in Downtown, Cairo. F the true connoisseur, Osiris (☎ 02-39 6609) at 15 Sharia Sherif, opposite th Banque Masr, Downtown, is Cairo's be auction house and a place where the occa sional genuine bargain can be had. Au tions are held every few weeks, precede by three days of viewing.

The Art of Bargaining

All prices are negotiable in the souq and bargaining is expected. It can be a hassle for anyone not used to shopping this way, but keep your cool and remember it's a game not a fight.

The first rule is never to show too much interest in the item you want to buy. Second, don't buy the first item that takes your fancy. Wander around and price things up, but don't make it obvious otherwise when you return to the first shop the vendor knows that it's because he or she is the cheapest.

Decide how much you would be happy paying and then express a casual interest in buying. The vendor will state their price. So the bargaining begins. You state a figure somewhat less than that you have fixed in your mind. The shopkeeper will inevitably huff about how absurd that is and then tell you the 'lowest' price. If it is still not low enough, then be insistent and keep smiling. Tea or coffee might be served as part of the bargaining ritual but accepting it doesn't place you under any obligation to buy. If you still can't get your price, walk away. This often has the effect of closing the sale in your favour. If not, there are thousands more shops in the bazaar.

If you do get your price or lower, never feel guilty – no vendor, no matter what they may tell you, ever sells below cost.

ackgammon Boards & heeshas

ackgammon boards and sheeshas make ır great conversation pieces back home, ıd they're practical too. Well, maybe not.

plain backgammon box with plastic ›unters, similar to those used in many gyptian coffeehouses, goes for as little as £20. As the boards get more fancy the ice goes up – a board inlaid with bone ill set you back more than E£100.

Sheeshas start at around E£30 but if you ight actually use it and not just stick flow-'s in the top you need to buy a supply of e little clay tobacco holders and some to-ıcco. The entire package is bulky and ›avy. Khan al-Khalili is probably the best ace to buy them.

rass & Copperware

ates, coffeepots and a variety of other ob-cts make good gifts, and are often fairly ıeap. Engraved trays and plates start ound E£15, depending on their intricacy ıd age. Watch for the quality of any en-'aving work and be wary of claims that an ›ject is 100 years old – more often than ›t it rolled off the production line a couple ' weeks ago. The best place for this sort of thing is Khan al-Khalili, in Cairo, particularly around Street of the Coppersmiths, Sharia an-Nahassin.

Carpets & Rugs

You can find carpets and rugs all over the place, but if you have time and happen to be in the area of the Pyramids, visit some of the carpet and tapestry schools along Saqqara Rd. The Wissa Wassef Art Centre is particularly interesting (see under Giza in the Cairo chapter for details).

Far better are the rugs woven by Bedouin in Sinai and the Western Desert. The weekly market at Al-Arish in northern Sinai is a good place to immerse yourself in local colour while buying the rugs, where there's a plethora of shops selling cheap, colourful cotton rugs made by the Bedouins. Rugs from the Bedouin of the northern part of the Western Desert can be found in Siwa and in the small town of Hamaam, near Alexandria on the north coast.

Crafts

Applique The place to go for applique is the Street of the Tentmakers, or Sharia al-Khayamiyya, south of Bab Zuweila in Islamic Cairo, where a dozen or so workshops

ANDERS BLOMQVIST

Brass plates and trays for sale in markets around Egypt are a popular souvenir, though they're unlikely to be antiques.

That Special Something

There are few places on earth that beat Egypt when it comes to kitsch. How about taking home one or more of the following?

Belly-Dancing Outfits Sequined, spangled and bright, these flimsy little numbers are a great gift to anyone who likes to shake their midriff. They are available in every tourist bazaar at wildly fluctuating prices (expect to pay at least E£45).

Golden Pyramid Paperweight A clear resin pyramid that has a golden sphinx inside. When you shake it golden 'snow' rains down. It costs about E£20.

Nefertiti-Head Lamp Haven't you always wanted Nefertiti to light up your life? Now she can be yours in onyx/alabaster with a little lightbulb inside for only E£50.

King Tut Galabiyya This is just perfect for lounging in around the house. A short-sleeved, brightly coloured robe festooned with a giant iron-on reproduction of the famous death mask. It costs E£35 and up, depending on the size and brightness of Tut's face.

Gold Cartouche For the pharaoh in everyone: write your name and a goldsmith will translate it into hieroglyphics and fashion you a Pharaonic-style cartouche. It will cost you about E£200 and up, depending on the weight of the gold.

Hieroglyphic Sun Hat This white cotton sunhat is available at all outdoor antiquities sites and is covered in a mishmash of blue hieroglyphs and the word 'Egypt', just in case you don't get it. About E£10 to E£15, depending on your bargaining skills.

Tutankhamun Hologram Lamp White plaster bust of the famous boy-pharaoh that appears to float like a hologram when plugged in. Available in some museum shops and in Khan al-Khalili for a mere E£150.

Taxi-Cab Clutter Turn your car into a Cairo taxi: a red plastic heart with 'I love you' written across the middle and small lights that blink in time to your *al-jeel* cassette. To get one, ask a Cairo cab driver or go to a car accessories shop in Muski. It should cost around E£15.

are clustered in a medieval, covered market. The colours are bright and the patterns range from arabesques and calligraphy to more figurative dervish dancers or Pharaonic motifs. The price depends on the intricacy of the pattern (arabesques and calligraphy cost the most), the quality of the work and the size. As a guide, a small cushion cover costs E£20; a larger one is E£40. Wall hangings of about 1.5 sq metres range from E£80 to almost E£200.

Inlaid Boxes & Chess Boards Second in popularity only to papyrus as souvenir items are the inlaid boxes piled high in most of the shops in Cairo's Khan al-Khalil They are very inexpensive, a small one sel ing for as little as E£6. For that price yo will get poor quality (it will not be inlai with mother-of-pearl, as the shopkeep may tell you, but plastic), but for a highe price you can buy something beautifull crafted such as a mirror frame or jeweller casket. A mother-of-pearl chessboard tc gether with camel-bone pieces would se for E£240 to E£300.

Leather Another popular buy is leathe the best shops are concentrated in Cair Many shops will custom-make jackets, bag nd clothes for you at a fraction of what you /ill pay in the West, although the zips and astenings will usually be of poor quality. Beware of being offered items in the soft eather of gazelle hide as these creatures are rotected and are becoming rare in Egypt.

Mashrabiyya Virtually nobody these days still makes complete *mashrabiyya* (wooden lattice) screens. What you get are things that ook like magazine racks (actually Quran olders) or table bases. It is still possible to find large screens in some of the antique stores, but they'll be prohibitively expensive. The one exception is the National Art Development Institute for Mashrabiyya Nadim; ☎ 02-348 1075), a craftshop dedicated to keeping the art of mashrabiyya alive. It has all types of mashrabiyya products, screens included (from E£2000 to E£3000), and visitors are welcome to watch the artisans at work without any obligation o buy. It is on Sharia al-Mazaniyya in Cairo, off Sharia Sudan behind the Coca Cola factory.

Clothing

Egyptian cotton is famous the world over for its high quality and durability. Unfortunately, the best stuff (especially for sheets and towels) is exported, while Egyptian factories' outmoded equipment and poor design mean that what's available on the local market is rarely worth lugging home. However, there have been a few projects in recent years that have revived Egypt's artisanal weaving tradition and the results can be beautiful, if pricey. Handloomed cotton from Nagada, near Luxor, is available at the shop of the same name in Cairo. Cheaper than this (but still expensive) is the cotton and linen woven in Akhmin, a town in Sohag governorate. Some of this can be found in Al-Ain Gallery in Cairo, but one of the best outlets is in the Winter Palace Hotel in Luxor.

Cotton clothing is a better option if you're on a budget. Cheap cotton shirts and *galabiyyas* (the loose gowns worn by many Egyptians) can be made to your specifications. One of the best places to go for the fabrice is Auf in Khan al-Khalili. The area between Al-Azhar and Bab Zuweila in Cairo is teeming with shops selling galabiyyas, ready and tailor-made. You can also try at the village of Kerdassa, near the Pyramids. Many enterprising merchants in tourist souqs near antiquities sites have started selling ready-made galabiyyas too. The price will be inflated but the process of buying will probably be easier.

Western-style clothing is also on sale in most towns frequented by tourists. T-shirts abound all over the country and many travellers have suits and other clothes tailor-made in Egypt, at prices that are ridiculously low by Western standards.

In Dahab, Sinai, cotton trousers and printed shirts are popular. A pair of light, simple trousers will cost around E£15. The Bedouins also make traditional clothing for sale. Canvas bags are cheap and popular, at around E£8 depending on size and quality.

Jewellery

Gold and silver jewellery can be made to specification for not much more than the cost of the metal. A cartouche with the name of a friend spelt in hieroglyphs makes a good gift.

Although gold shops are concentrated in the centre of the Khan al-Khalili in Cairo, gold can be bought all over Islamic Cairo. It is generally sold by weight. Buying gold and jewellery is always a little fraught. The Assay Office in Birmingham, UK, says that hallmarking for gold of at least 12 carats and silver of 600 parts per thousand or more is compulsory in Egypt – verifying this is another matter. The hallmark contains a standard mark showing where a piece was assayed and a date mark in Arabic. Foreign goods cannot be resold, in the UK at least, unless they are first assayed there. Storekeepers have an irritating habit of weighing the gold out of sight. Insist that they put the scales on the counter and let you see what's happening. This doesn't eliminate the chances of cheating, but does reduce them. Another precaution may be to check the day's gold prices in the *Egyptian Gazette*.

Much the same cautionary rules apply to silver and other jewellery. An endless assortment of rings, bracelets, necklaces and the like can be found all over Islamic Cairo. Hunt around, and beware of the 'antiques' made to look so.

If modern designer jewellery with an Egyptian twist is your thing, there are a handful of boutiques in Cairo specialising in unique, handmade creations in both silver and gold. See the Cairo chapter for details.

Siwa is famous for its beautiful silver jewellery and although there is very little antique jewellery left, the modern replicas are just as good. The silver itself has a heavy metal content and is generally not sold by weight, so sharpen your bargaining skills. (See Siwa in the Western Oases chapter for more information.)

Music Cassettes

Locally produced cassettes sell for E£8 or E£9. Quality, needless to say, is bad. As well as Egyptian and other Arab artists (see Music under Arts in the Facts about Egypt chapter for some recommended listening) most places have a limited selection of pirate copies of Western artists. The biggest choice is at the shops along Sharia Shawarby in Cairo or, for Nubian music, see Nubian Culture under Lower Nubia & Lake Nassar in the Nile Valley – Esna to Abu Simbel chapter. A good selection of Saidi music can be found in Luxor (see the boxed text 'Saidi Music' in the Nile Valley – Luxor chapter).

Imported Western CDs and a growing number of CD recordings by Egyptian artists are available in Cairo (try Maestro and Juke Box both at the World Trade Centre on the Corniche el-Nil, Bulaq) but they're expensive at E£80 to E£90.

Musical Instruments

Traditional musical instruments such as an oud (lute), *kamaan* (violin), *nay* (flute), tabla (drum) and various others are made and sold in about a dozen shops in Cairo on Sharia Mohammed Ali, which runs southeast from Midan Ataba to the Museum of Islamic Art. Gamil Georges at No 170 sell ouds, for example, with prices ranging fron E£150 to E£300.

Papyrus

You can pick up cheap, poor-quality papyrus all over Egypt for virtually nothing Equally, you can pay large sums of money for exactly the same thing. Look long and hard at what you are getting. If you are considering buying an expensive piece i should be hand-painted not machine printed. And is it papyrus, which will not be damaged by rolling, or is it in fact banana leaf that will crack?

The name Dr Ragab has long been associated with papyrus, and he has several 'institutes' throughout Egypt. His stuff is good quality but it's also expensive.

Perfumes

Egypt is a big producer of many of the essences that make up French perfume hence it's no surprise that part of Cairo's Khan al-Khalili is devoted to a perfume bazaar. Here you can buy pure essence (anywhere from E£8 to E£20 an ounce) as

ANDREW MACCOLL

Handmade perfume bottles, in all shapes and sizes, are available in the perfume bazaar of Cairo's Khan al-Khalili.

well as cheaper substances diluted with alcohol or oil. Some of the perfume traders have price tags on their goods, but that doesn't mean you can't haggle.

Intricate perfume bottles are also popular. Again, there are expensive and cheap varieties. Small glass bottles start at about E£3; the heavier and more durable Pyrex bottles start at about E£10.

Spices

Every conceivable herb and spice, and many you will never have heard of or seen, can be bought in most markets throughout the country. Generally they are fresher and better quality than any of the packaged stuff you'll find in the West, and four to five times cheaper. Exactly how much cheaper will, of course, depend on your bargaining skills.

Getting There & Away

If you're heading to Egypt from Europe, you have the choice of either flying direct or, if you have plenty of time on your hands, travelling overland. If you're coming from any other continent, it can sometimes be cheaper to fly first to Europe, and then make your way to Egypt. There are also the overland combinations of bus, taxi and ferry from other African countries, and from Jordan, Kuwait, Saudi Arabia, Israel and Libya.

Whichever route you take there is always the inescapable search for the cheapest ticket and the certainty that no matter how great a deal you find, there's always someone out there with a better one.

Warning

The information in this chapter is particularly vulnerable to change: Prices for international travel are volatile, routes are introduced and cancelled, schedules change, special deals come and go, and rules and visa requirements are amended. Airlines and governments seem to take a perverse pleasure in making price structures and regulations as complicated as possible. You should check directly with the airline or a travel agency to make sure you understand how a fare (and ticket you may buy) works. In addition, the travel industry is highly competitive and there are many lurks and perks.

The upshot of this is that you should get opinions, quotes and advice from as many airlines and travel agencies as possible before you part with your hard-earned cash. The details given in this chapter should be regarded as pointers and are not a substitute for your own careful, up-to-date research.

AIR

Airports & Airlines

Egypt's international and national carrier is EgyptAir. It's not a particularly good airline – departures are too often delayed and in our experience the food is usually poor and the flight attendants are often surly. Neither are fares cheap and you can usually get a seat on a much better carrier for the same price if not less.

Egypt has a handful of airports but only six are international ports of entry: Cairo, Alexandria and, increasingly gaining status, the 'international' airports at Luxor, Aswan, Hurghada and Sharm el-Sheikh. Additional international airports are to be added at Taba in Sinai and Marsa Alam on the southern Red Sea coast. Facilities and services at secondary airports are poor. One letter to the travel pages of a UK newspaper recently described Sharm el-Sheikh as one of the most 'shameless' airports the reader had ever had the misfortune to visit: one immigration officer on duty, 20 tour reps, aimless queues, bags from three flights on one carousel, and 50 porters looking for baksheesh. The ordeal of leaving, he wrote, was even worse. Most air travellers, however, will continue to enter Egypt through Cairo. The other airports tend to be used by charter and package-deal flights, except for Alexandria, which handles the scheduled services of British Mediterranean, Lufthansa Airlines and Olympic Airways.

EgyptAir and Air Sinai have internal flights linking nine destinations within Egypt (see the Getting Around chapter).

Cairo International Airport The airport is 25km north-east of central Cairo. There are two terminals about 3km apart; Terminal II, the 'new' *(gedida)* terminal, services most international airlines, while Terminal I, the 'old' *(adimah)* terminal, is mainly used by EgyptAir for both domestic and international flights.

Arriving at Terminal II, you'll pass a couple of duty-free shops, exchange offices and several banks before arriving at customs control. The exchange offices are next to each other and their rates are about the same. They can also issue stamps for a visa

Warning

Many travellers arriving at Cairo airport are met by the infamous 'tourist officials'. For more on the tactics of these touts, see the boxed text 'Cairo Hotel Scams' in the Cairo chapter.

(see Visas & Documents in the Facts for the Visitor chapter for details). Similar banking facilities are available at Terminal I. There's also a (quite useless) tourist information office at Terminal II.

The departure lounge at Terminal II has a handful of duty-free shops and a post and telephone office. Cardphones and a Home Country Direct telephone are available, as are telex and telegraphic services.

Between the arrival and departure lounges is a left-luggage room that is open 24 hours. It charges E£3 for items less than 25kg, and E£6 for those weighing more.

Most major car rental companies have booths in the arrivals hall. Outside Terminal I is a lost-and-found booth.

For details on getting between the airport and central Cairo, see Getting Around in the Cairo chapter.

Buying Tickets

An air ticket alone can gouge a great slice out of anyone's budget, but you can reduce the cost by finding discounted fares. Stiff competition has resulted in widespread discounting – good news for travellers. The only people likely to be paying full fare these days are travellers flying in 1st or business class. Passengers flying in economy can usually manage some sort of discount, but unless you buy carefully, it is still possible to end up paying exorbitant amounts for a journey.

For long-term travel there are plenty of discount tickets that are valid for 12 months, allowing multiple stopovers with open dates. For short-term travel, cheaper fares are available if you travel midweek, stay away at least one Saturday night or take advantage of short-lived promotional offers.

When you're looking for bargain air fares, go to a travel agency rather than directly to the airline. From time to time, airlines have promotional fares and special offers, but generally they only sell fares at the official listed price. One exception to this rule is the expanding number of 'no-frills' carriers operating in the USA and north-west Europe that mostly sell direct to travellers. Unlike the 'full service' airlines, no-frills carriers often make one-way tickets available at around 50% of the return fare, meaning that it is easy to put together a return ticket when you fly to one place but leave from another.

The other exception is booking on the Internet. Many airlines, full-service and no-frills, offer some excellent fares to Web surfers. They may sell seats by auction or simply cut prices to reflect the reduced cost of electronic selling. Many travel agencies around the world have Web sites, which can make the Internet a quick and easy way to compare prices, a good start for when you're ready to start negotiating with your favourite travel agency. Online ticket sales work well if you are doing a simple one-way or return trip on specified dates. However, online superfast fare generators are no substitute for a travel agent who knows all about special deals, has strategies for avoiding layovers and can offer advice on everything from which airline has the best vegetarian food to the best travel insurance to bundle with your ticket.

The days when some travel agencies would routinely fleece travellers by running off with their money are, happily, almost over. Paying by credit card generally offers protection, as most card issuers provide refunds if you can prove you didn't get what you paid for. Similar protection can be obtained by buying a ticket from a bonded agency, such as one covered by the Air Travel Organisers' Licensing (ATOL) scheme in the UK. Agents who only accept cash should hand over the tickets straight away and not tell you to 'come back tomorrow'. After you've made a booking or paid your deposit, call the airline and confirm

Air Travel Glossary

Alliances Many of the world's leading airlines are now intimately involved with each other, sharing everything from reservations systems and check-in to aircraft and frequent-flyer schemes. Opponents say that alliances restrict competition. Whatever the arguments, there is no doubt that big alliances are the way of the future.

Baggage Allowance This will be written on your ticket and usually includes one 20kg item which can go in the hold, plus one item of hand luggage. Limits on size and weight of baggage is set by the airlines and may vary.

Bucket Shops These are travel agencies specialising in discounted airline tickets.

Bumped Just because you have a confirmed seat doesn't mean you're going to get on the plane (see Overbooking).

Cancellation Penalties If you have to cancel or change a discounted ticket, there are often heavy penalties involved; insurance can sometimes be taken out against these penalties. Some airlines impose penalties on regular tickets as well, particularly against 'no-show' passengers.

Check-In Airlines ask you to check in a certain time ahead of the flight departure (usually one to two hours on international flights). If you fail to check in on time and the flight is overbooked, the airline can cancel your booking and give your seat to somebody else.

Confirmation Having a ticket written out with the flight and date you want doesn't mean you have a seat until the agent has checked with the airline that your status is 'OK' or confirmed. Meanwhile you could just be 'on request'.

Courier Fares Businesses often need to send urgent documents or freight securely and quickly. Courier companies hire people to accompany the package through customs and, in return, offer a discount ticket which is sometimes a bargain. However, you may have to surrender all your baggage allowance and take only carry-on luggage.

Fares Airlines traditionally offer 1st class (coded F), business class (coded J) and economy class (coded Y) tickets. These days there are so many promotional and discounted fares available that few passengers pay full fare.

Lost Tickets If you lose your airline ticket, an airline will usually treat it like a travellers cheque and, after inquiries, issue you with another one. Legally, however, an airline is entitled to treat it like cash and if you lose it then it's gone forever. Take very good care of your tickets.

MCO An MCO, or 'miscellaneous charge order', is a voucher that looks like an airline ticket but carries no destination or date. It can be exchanged through any International Association of Travel Agents (IATA) member for a ticket on a specific flight. It's a useful alternative to an onward ticket in those countries that demand one, and is more flexible than an ordinary ticket if you're unsure of your route.

No-Shows No-shows are passengers who fail to show up for their flight. Full-fare passengers who fail to turn up are sometimes entitled to travel on a later flight. The rest are penalised (see Cancellation Penalties).

On Request This is an unconfirmed booking for a flight.

Air Travel Glossary

Onward Tickets An entry requirement for many countries is that you have a ticket out of the country. If you're unsure of your next move, the easiest solution is to buy the cheapest onward ticket to a neighbouring country or a ticket from a reliable airline which can later be refunded if you do not use it.

Open-Jaw Tickets These are return tickets where you fly out to one place but return from another. If available, this can save you backtracking to your arrival point.

Overbooking Since every flight has some passengers who fail to show up, airlines often book more passengers than they have seats. Usually excess passengers make up for the no-shows, but occasionally somebody gets 'bumped' onto the next available flight. Guess who it is most likely to be? The passengers who check in late. If you do get 'bumped', you are normally offered some form of compensation.

Promotional Fares These are officially discounted fares, available from travel agencies or direct from the airline.

Reconfirmation Some airlines require you to reconfirm your flight at least 72 hours prior to departure. Check your travel documents to see if this is the case

Restrictions Discounted tickets often have various restrictions on them – such as needing to be paid for in advance and incurring a penalty to be altered or cancelled. Others are restrictions on the minimum and maximum period you must be away.

Round-the-World Tickets RTW tickets give you a limited period (usually a year) in which to circumnavigate the globe. You can go anywhere the carrying airlines go, as long as you don't backtrack. The number of stopovers or total number of separate flights is decided before you set off and they usually cost a bit more than a basic return flight.

Stopovers These are overnight stays during your journey.

Ticketless Travel Airlines are gradually waking up to the realisation that paper tickets are unnecessary encumbrances. On simple one-way or return trips, reservations details can be held on computer and the passenger merely shows ID to claim their seat.

Transferred Tickets Airline tickets cannot be transferred from one person to another. Travellers sometimes try to sell the return half of their ticket, but officials can ask you to prove that you are the person named on the ticket. On an international flight, tickets are compared with passports.

Travel Agencies Travel agencies vary widely and you should choose one that suits your needs. Some simply handle tours, while full-service agencies handle everything from tours and tickets to car rental and hotel bookings. If all you want is a ticket at the lowest possible price, then go to an agency specialising in discounted fares.

Travel Periods Ticket prices vary with the time of year. There is a low (off-peak) season and a high (peak) season, and often a low-shoulder season and a high-shoulder season as well. Usually the fare depends on your outward flight – if you depart in the high season and return in the low season, you pay the high-season fare.

Waitlists If a flight you want to take is full you can be waitlisted in the event that a seat becomes available.

that the booking was made. It's generally not advisable to send money (even cheques) through the post unless the agency is very well established – some travellers have reported being ripped off by fly-by-night mail-order ticket agencies.

You may decide to pay more than the rock-bottom fare by opting for the safety of a better-known travel agency. Firms such as STA Travel, which has offices worldwide, Council Travel in the USA and Usit Campus (formerly Campus Travel) in the UK are not going to disappear overnight and they do offer good prices to most destinations.

If you purchase a ticket and later want to make changes to your route or get a refund, you need to contact the original travel agency. Airlines only issue refunds to the purchaser of a ticket – usually the travel agency that bought the ticket on your behalf. Many travellers change their routes halfway through their trips, so think carefully before you buy a ticket that is not easily refunded.

Travellers with Special Needs

Most international airlines can cater for people with special needs – travellers with disabilities, people with young children and even children travelling alone.

Travellers with special dietary preferences (vegetarian, kosher etc) can request appropriate meals with advance notice. If you are travelling in a wheelchair, most international airports can provide an escort from check-in desk to plane where needed. Ramps, lifts and facilities for disabled people such as toilets and phones are generally available.

Airlines usually allow babies up to two years of age to fly for 10% of the adult fare, although a few may allow them free of charge. Reputable international airlines usually provide nappies (diapers), tissues, talcum and all the other paraphernalia needed to keep babies clean, dry and half-happy. For children between the ages of two and 12, the fare on international flights is usually 50% of the regular fare or 67% of a discounted fare.

Departure Tax

Departure tax is factored into the cost of your ticket.

The USA

Discount travel agencies in the USA are known as consolidators (although you won't see a sign on the door saying 'Consolidator'). San Francisco is the ticket consolidator capital of the USA, although some good deals can be found in Los Angeles, New York and other big cities. Consolidators can be found through the *Yellow Pages* or the major daily newspapers. The *New York Times*, *Los Angeles Times*, *Chicago Tribune* and *San Francisco Examiner* all produce weekly travel sections in which you will find a number of travel agency ads. Ticket Planet is a leading ticket consolidator in the USA and is recommended. Visit its Web site at **W** www.ticketplanet.com.

Council Travel, the USA's largest student travel organisation, has around 60 offices in the USA; its head office (☎ 800-226 8624) is at 205 E 42 St, New York, NY 10017. Call it for the office nearest you or visit its Web site at **W** www.ciee.org. STA Travel (☎ 800-777 0112) has offices in Boston, Chicago, Miami, New York, Philadelphia, San Francisco and other major cities. Call toll free on ☎ 800 for office locations or visit its Web site at **W** www.statravel.com.

The cheapest way from the USA and Canada to the Middle East and Africa is usually a return flight to London and a cheap fare from there. A round-the-world (RTW) ticket including a stopover in Cairo is also a possibility.

EgyptAir flies from New York and Los Angeles to Cairo. The cheapest advance tickets are for a minimum stay of seven days and a maximum stay of two months. Regular fares from New York/Los Angeles are approximately US$1300/1800 in low season and US$1900/2200 in high season.

Lufthansa Airlines has connections to Cairo via Frankfurt from many cities in the USA. Advance fairs are available. From Los Angeles, the high season one-way/return fare is US$1750/2200 and from New

York it's US$1155/1600. These fares entail a minimum stay of seven days and a maximum of two months.

Canada

Canadian discount air ticket sellers are also known as consolidators. Their air fares tend to be about 10% higher than those sold in the USA. The *Globe & Mail*, *Toronto Star*, *Montreal Gazette* and *Vancouver Sun* carry travel agency ads and are a good place to look for cheap fares.

Travel CUTS (☎ 800-667 2887) is Canada's national student travel agency and has offices in all major cities. Its Web site is W www.travelcuts.com.

Australia

Cheap flights from Australia to Europe generally go via South-East Asian capitals, with stopovers at Kuala Lumpur, Bangkok or Singapore. If a long stopover between connections is necessary, transit accommodation is sometimes included in the price of the ticket. If it's at your own expense, it may be worth considering a more expensive ticket.

Quite a few travel offices specialise in discount air tickets. Some travel agencies, particularly smaller ones, advertise cheap air fares in the travel sections of weekend newspapers, such as the *Age* in Melbourne and the *Sydney Morning Herald*.

Two well-known agencies for cheap fares are STA Travel and Flight Centre. STA Travel (☎ 03-9349 2411) has its main office at 224 Faraday St, Carlton 3053, and offices in all major cities and on many university campuses. Call ☎ 131 776 Australiawide for the location of your nearest branch or visit W www.statravel.com.au. Flight Centre (☎ 131 600 Australiawide) has a central office at 82 Elizabeth St, Sydney, and there are dozens of offices in Australia. Its Web address is W www.flightcentre.com.au.

Expect to pay around A$1700 for a return flight from Australia during the low season or A$2050 during the high season. Star Alliance has RTW fares with a stopover in Cairo starting from A$2269 in the low season.

Neighbouring Countries

Israel & the Palestinian Territories There are two land routes, although at present only the one via Taba in Sinai is safe, or you can fly.

Jordan The options from Cairo are a bus to Nuweiba and then one of three ferries across the Red Sea to Aqaba, or by air.

Libya The slow, cheap way is to take a bus from Cairo or Alexandria, or now that international sanctions have been lifted you can fly from Cairo direct to Tripoli.

Sudan At the time of writing it was not possible to go from Egypt to Sudan overland, so the options are to fly or take the Wadi Halfa ferry from just south of Aswan.

New Zealand

Round-the-world fares for travel to or from New Zealand are usually the best value, often cheaper than a return ticket. Depending on which airline you choose, you may fly across Asia, with possible stopovers in India, Bangkok or Singapore, or across the USA, with possible stopovers in Honolulu, Australia or one of the Pacific Islands.

The *New Zealand Herald* has a travel section in which travel agencies advertise fares. Flight Centre (☎ 09-309 6171) has a large central office in Auckland at National Bank Towers (on the corner of Queen and Darby Sts) and many branches throughout the country. STA Travel (☎ 09-309 0458) has its main office at 10 High St, Auckland, and has other offices in Auckland as well as in Hamilton, Palmerston North, Wellington, Christchurch and Dunedin. The Web address is W www.sta.travel.com.au.

Return low-season fares from Auckland start from around NZ$2329, with fares in the high season starting from around NZ$2599.

The UK

London is one of the best centres in the world for discounted air tickets. If you start looking early and are prepared to phone around then you shouldn't have to pay more than about UK£240 for a return ticket, including all taxes. In recent times Air France, Alitalia and Olympic Airways have all offered fixed-date returns at this price. All these involve a change of flight in the national capital. Only British Airways and EgyptAir offer direct flights; these cost upwards of UK£350.

Start off by phoning Suleiman Travel (☎ 020-7244 6855) at 113 Earls Court Rd, London, which is a long-established Egypt specialist. Its prices are very competitive and it can sometimes come up with cheaper alternatives to scheduled Cairo flights, such as charters into Luxor or Sharm el-Sheikh in Sinai. Another good specialist often able to secure the cheapest fares is Egypt On The Go (☎ 020-8993 9993) at 81 Gunnersbury Lane, Acton Town, London W3 8HQ.

For students or travellers under 26, popular travel agencies in the UK include STA Travel (☎ 020-7361 6144, W www.statravel.co.uk), which has an office at 86 Old Brompton Rd, London SW7 3LQ, and other offices in London and Manchester. Usit Campus (☎ 0870-240 1010, W www.usitcampus.com), 52 Grosvenor Gardens, London SW1W 0AG, has branches through out the UK. Both agencies sell tickets to all travellers but cater especially to young people and students.

Other recommended travel agencies include: Trailfinders (☎ 020-7938 3939), 194 Kensington High St, London W8 7RG; Bridge the World (☎ 020-7734 7447), 4 Regent Place, London W1R 5FB; and Flightbookers (☎ 020-7757 2000), 177–178 Tottenham Court Rd, London W1P 9LF.

Middle East

If you have the time, travelling overland between Egypt and Israel, Jordan or Syria is much cheaper than travelling by air, and relatively simple. The only drawback is the time factor.

For the addresses of the following airlines see Getting There & Away in the Cairo chapter.

Israel & the Palestinian Territories Air Sinai and El Al Israel Airlines regularly fly between Cairo and Tel Aviv with five flights a week each. Fares are US$185 one way or US$265 return (valid for one month).

Jordan There are daily flights with Royal Jordanian Airlines and EgyptAir between Cairo and Amman, but there is no discounting. The fare from Egypt is US$245 one way and US$320 return with EgyptAir, or about E£80 cheaper with Royal Jordanian. There are no student reductions.

Syria Syrian Arab Airlines flies five times a week to Damascus for a one-way fare of US$220.

Africa

Despite the proximity, there is nothing cheap about travelling from Egypt into other parts of Africa. In fact, for most African capitals a ticket bought in London will be cheaper than one bought in Cairo. The best bet is to buy your African ticket with a stopover in Egypt.

For the addresses of the following airlines, see Getting There & Away in the Cairo chapter.

Ethiopia There are flights from Egypt to Addis Ababa twice a week (currently in the early hours of Saturday and Thursday mornings) with a fare of US$580 one way or US$824 return. However, one-way tickets can only be purchased if you can show a credit card or travellers cheques to cover the cost of a return ticket.

Kenya Kenya Airways flies to Nairobi three times a week for a one-way fare of US$622. From Nairobi there are onward connections to Rwanda (Kigali), Tanzania (Dar es Salaam), Democratic Republic of Congo (Zaïre; Kinshasa) and Zimbabwe (Harare).

Libya Until recently, international flights to and from Libya were still suspended as a result of the UN air embargo imposed on Libya over the Lockerbie affair. With the lifting of the sanctions, flights from Cairo to Tripoli have resumed.

Sudan EgyptAir and Sudan Airways both have two flights each week between Cairo and Khartoum (2½ hours). However, you won't be able to buy a one-way ticket unless you can show a ticket from Sudan back to your home country, and no ticket will be issued until you've obtained your Sudanese visa.

LAND

Israel & the Palestinian Territories

Rafah Traditionally the most direct way to travel overland between Egypt and Israel & the Palestinian Territories was to go via the border crossing at Rafah. An Israeli company (Mazada Tours) and an Egyptian company (Travco) cooperated in running a six-days-a-week service on this route connecting Cairo with Tel Aviv. But Rafah is situated on the edge of the Gaza Strip and over the last year or so it's been the scene of conflict and killing, hence Mazada/Travco have halted their service. We include their numbers here so you can call and inquire whether it has been resumed or not.

Mazada Tours
Jerusalem: (☎ 02-623 5777) 9 Koresh St
Tel Aviv: (☎ 03-544 4454) 141 Ibn Gvirol
Travco
(☎ 02-735 4650) 13 Mahmoud Azmy, Zamalek, Cairo

Theoretically, you can do the trip independently. From Cairo's Turgoman garage take a bus for Rafah, cross the border under your own steam and then pick up a service taxi to Gaza City where you change to another service taxi to Jerusalem. In reverse, once you cross the border into Egypt, take a service taxi to Al-Arish from where you'll be able to pick up a bus service to Cairo. However, given the volatile nature of the Gaza Strip at present, such a journey could put your life at risk. We do not recommend that you do this. Instead, you should travel via Taba.

Taba Taba is in the extreme east of Sinai, at the point where Egypt, Israel and Jordan almost come together. It's just a few kilometres from Eilat and Aqaba (Jordan).

Three buses daily run to Taba from Cairo at 7am (E£50), 9.30am (E£50) and 10pm (E£70), a journey of around 8½ hours. If you're at one of the south Sinai resorts, such as Dahab, Nuweiba or Sharm el-Sheikh, then there are plenty of buses heading north up the coast or you can jump in a service taxi.

Once at Taba you can walk across the border (which is open 24 hours) into Israel. Immigration formalities are painless and usually take no more than 30 minutes. An Israeli visa is not required for most nationalities but there is an Egyptian departure tax of E£7. Once across the border take a taxi (20NIS) or catch a bus (every 20 minutes between 7am and 9.30pm; 4NIS) to central Eilat where there are frequent buses to Jerusalem and Tel Aviv. Note that there are no buses operating in Israel on Friday evenings or before sundown Saturday, the Jewish holy day of Shabbat.

Coming the other way, from Israel to Egypt, you must have a visa in advance. If you don't have one there's an Egyptian consulate in Eilat (☎ 07-637 6882) at 68 HaAfroni St. It's open from 9am to 11am Sunday to Thursday. There's a 67NIS Israeli departure tax to be paid plus an Egyptian entry tax of E£17.

Libya

There are direct buses running between Cairo, Benghazi and Tripoli (At-Tarablus). You can also get buses to the same destinations from Alexandria. Fares from here tend to be slightly cheaper. For more details see Getting There & Away in the Cairo and Alexandria chapters. A more laborious, but cheaper, alternative would be to get local transport to Sallum in the far north-west of Egypt (there are buses from Alexandria) and a service taxi to the border. From there you can get Libyan transport heading west.

SEA

Europe

MenaTours acts as the agency for the limited passenger-ship services that operate between Port Said and various Mediterranean destinations, including Beirut (Lebanon) and Antalya (Turkey). There are no passenger boats operating between Egyptian ports and any ports in Europe at present. The last services between Alexandria and Athens ceased in 1997; boats between Port Said and Lebanon halted the same year.

Sudan

Via Wadi Halfa There is a ferry from the High Dam, south of Aswan, to Wadi Halfa in northernmost Sudan every Monday at around 3pm. It arrives in Wadi Halfa at about 8am Tuesday morning. The boat returns from Wadi Halfa every Wednesday, arriving in Aswan the following morning.

Buy tickets at the Nile Navigation Company in Aswan (☎ 097-303 348), next to the second tourist office, one block in from the Corniche. It's open from 8am to 2.30pm and closed Thursday and Friday. Note that it will not sell you a ticket unless you have a Sudanese visa in your passport.

Tickets cost E£142/88.50 in 1st/2nd class. In 1st class you get a small cabin with bunks; 2nd class means seats, if you can find one. The fare includes a meal: fuul in 2nd class or meat and rice in 1st class. If you've opted for 2nd class, you can still buy a 1st-class meal for E£3. It's a good idea to bring some food of your own too. Tea and soft drinks (sodas) are available on board.

You should be at the High Dam by noon, three hours before departure. As a foreigner, you should be ushered through the various customs and passport hurdles. Some of the Sudanese immigration formalities are carried out on the boat; they will ask for a yellow-fever certificate.

If you want to take a vehicle into Sudan, the Nile Navigation Company also has a cargo ferry that will carry up to five or six cars. However, there are no fixed departures and you have to pay for the entire boat, a whopping E£8000. There are no facilities on the boat (you are expected to bring your own food and sleep in your car) and the trip takes about two days. For more information call the Nile Navigation Company.

Via the Red Sea At present there are no scheduled ships heading from Egypt to Port Sudan. You can get a boat from Suez to Jeddah and then from Jeddah to Port Sudan, but your transit visa will only be issued if you ensure that the ship leaves the same day that you arrive from Suez. For more information call the MenaTours office in Suez (☎ 062-228 821) and see Getting There & Away under Suez in the Suez Canal chapter. You can also try to find a private yacht heading south, but there are very few and they may not be willing to take passengers. Mohammed Moseilhy at Damanhur Shipping Agency in Suez can sometimes help find willing yacht owners; call him on ☎ 062-330 418.

Jordan

There are three ferries between Nuweiba on Egypt's Sinai coast and Aqaba, the southernmost point in Jordan. The fastest and most comfortable boat is called the *Bridge*. It arrives in Nuweiba port (☎ 069-520 364) from Aqaba at about 1.15pm daily and leaves again at 3pm. The trip takes one hour. One-way tickets cost US$45 for adults, US$22.50 for five- to 12-year-olds and US$11.25 for three- to five-year-olds. Children under three years travel for free. The boat takes passengers only and you should be at the port at least one hour prior to departure. Tickets for this service are sold at the Coral Bay Hilton (☎ 069-520 320).

The other boats, the *Hoda* and the *St Katherine*, take three to four hours to make the trip and carry cars. One of the two leaves at noon each day, and in times of heavy traffic there is another laid on at 6pm although departure times are fluid and there are often delays. Tickets cost US$32 for foot passengers and US$150 and up for cars, depending on the size of the engine. You should be there about two hours before departure, but if you have a car, allow at least four hours for customs procedures. You may be asked to hand over your passport upon boarding; it will be returned to you upon arrival in Aqaba, or you can ask for it back during the voyage.

Tickets for these slower boats are issued by Damanhour Shipping (☎ 069-529 309, fax 520 149). Its office is beside the port entrance. Tickets must be paid for in US dollars, and visas can be obtained by most nationalities on arrival at Aqaba (however, check this if you are not an EU, US, Canadian, Australian or New Zealand citizen).

Visas for those arriving from Jordan are issued at the port, and Jordanian passport officials can issue visas on the boat.

For details of buses to Nuweiba see the Getting There & Away section of whichever city you're travelling from. You can book a ferry-and-bus combination ticket from Cairo or Alexandria through to Aqaba, or even on to Amman if you wish. From Cairo's Sinai terminal the trip to Amman is US$32 plus E£63.

Saudi Arabia & Kuwait

There are regular ferries between Suez and Jeddah (about 36 hours). Several lines compete on the route and fares can vary from one agency to another but, generally, tickets start at around E£145 for deck class to E£300 for 1st class. Most of the ferries on the route also carry cars, at a significant cost. Getting a berth during the haj is virtually impossible. You can get information at Masr Travel agencies, or buy a ticket directly from its office in Port Tawfiq, Suez – for more details see Getting There & Away under Suez and Safaga in the Suez Canal and Red Sea Coast chapters respectively.

There are also regular services between Hurghada and Port Safaga, both on the Red Sea coast, and Duba in Saudi Arabia, including what's known as the 'flying boat'. This departs Hurghada daily at noon, but you must be at the port at least three hours in advance. Tickets cost E£180 per person, and US$100 to US$200 per car. The trip takes three hours. If you're taking a car, be sure to allow a minimum of four hours for customs formalities. Call Hurghada-based Amco Tours (☎ 065-447 571) for more information.

The *Al-Salam al-Seoudi* leaves Safaga for Duba daily at 11pm. The trip takes about seven hours, depending on the state of the sea. Tickets for 1st class cost E£170, 2nd class is E£120, Pullman (ie, a seat) is E£100 and deck class is E£95. Cars cost US$100 to US$125, depending on the size of the engine. Tickets can be bought at the Salam Maritime Transport Office (☎ 065-252 315/6) in Safaga. Passengers should be at the port no later than 8pm for customs and passport formalities. If you have a car, you should allow at least five hours for customs procedures.

In the same way that a passage can be booked straight through to Aqaba and Amman, you can purchase tickets through to many destinations in the Gulf, either at Cairo's Turgoman garage or in Alexandria.

ORGANISED TOURS

There are any number of tour possibilities to Egypt, and there is a plethora of agencies dealing with everything from Nile cruises to overland safaris or diving trips – depending on what kind of tour you want, or the area of Egypt you want to cover. The programs on such trips are usually fairly tight, leaving little room for roaming around on your own, but advantages are that many of the time-consuming hassles, such as waiting around for public transport and finding decent accommodation each night, are taken care of, therefore maximising time for exploring and sightseeing. There's also the security that comes with being in a large group, which allows you to do things such as camping out in the desert or exploring off-the-beaten-track activities that might be unsafe for individuals or couples.

It pays to shop around. When considering a tour ask about what the price includes. Does it include flights? Visa fees? Site admission fees? Food? Some companies include these in their prices, while some companies don't, so you need to be aware of what you're paying for when you compare prices.

Following is a list of specialist operators that organise Egypt packages tailored for independently minded travellers looking for a bit more than just two weeks in the sun.

Australia

Gateway Travel (☎ 02-9745 3333, fax 9745 3237, ⓔ agent@russian-gateway.com.au) 48 The Boulevarde, Strathfield, NSW 2135. Gateway offers stopover Cairo packages, Cairo to Aswan tours (by train or air) and Nile cruises.

Peregrine Adventures (☎ 03-9663 8611, fax 9663 8618, ⓔ travelcentre@peregrine.net.au) 258 Lonsdale St, Melbourne, VIC 3000. Peregrine is an agent for the UK's Dragoman, Exodus and The Imaginative Traveller. It also has offices in Adelaide, Brisbane, Perth and Sydney.

Yalla Tours (☎ 03-9646 0277, fax 9646 6722, ⓔ yallamel@yallatours.com.au) Level 1, 40 Beach St, Port Melbourne, VIC 3207. Yalla offers a wide variety of pick 'n' mix package tours, private-arrangement tours and Nile cruises.

The UK

Bales Tours (☎ 01306-885 991, fax 740 048) Bales House, Junction Rd, Dorking, Surrey RH4 3HL. Bales Tours offers pricey upmarket tours utilising five-star accommodation.

Egypt On The Go (☎ 020-8993 9993, fax 8993 9900, ⓦ www.traveldeals.uk.com) 81 Gunnersbury Lane, Acton Town, London W3 8HQ. This company offers five-, nine- and 13-day tours of Egypt as well as PADI diving course holidays at Dahab.

Exodus (☎ 020-8675 5550, fax 8673 0779, ⓔ websales@exodus.co.uk, ⓦ www.exodustravels.co.uk) 9 Weir Rd, London SW12 OLT. Exodus offers several reasonably priced Egypt packages including a nine-day jaunt around Sinai (UK£455) and a 17-day expedition including a Nile cruise and romp through the Western Oases (UK£800).

Explore Worldwide (☎ 01252-760 000, fax 760 001, ⓦ www.exploreworldwide.com) 1 Fredrick St, Aldershot, Hampshire GU11 1LQ. This company offers three short tours: a Nile felucca sailtrek; a Nile cruise; and a Sinai tour. In addition there are longer itineraries departing throughout the year. Most trips average about UK£550, including flights and accommodation.

Hayes and Jarvis (☎ 0870-907 7737, fax 333 0069, ⓔ res@hayes-jarvis.com, ⓦ www.hayes-jarvis.com). Hayes House, 152 King St, London W6 OQU. Hayes and Jarvis is a respected Egypt specialist offering a large variety of mainstream holiday packages, including cruises.

The Imaginative Traveller (☎ 020-8742 8612, fax 8742 3045, ⓦ www.imaginative-traveller.com) 14 Barley Mow Passage, Chiswick, London W4 4PH. This company offers small group tours with at least 20 different Egypt itineraries from felucca trips and cruises to a Red Sea diving trip for beginners based in Hurghada. There's a particularly good-value 11-day trip for UK£295.

Top Deck (☎ 020-7244 8641, fax 7373 6201, ⓔ res@topdecktravel.co.uk, ⓦ www.topdecktravel.co.uk). 131–135 Earls Court Rd, London SW5 9RH Top Deck offers six basic Egypt trips of either eight or 15 days.

Travelbag Adventures (☎ 01420-541 007, fax 541 022, ⓔ mail@travelbag-adventures.co.uk, ⓦ www.travelbag-adventures.co.uk) 15 Turk St, Alton, Hants GU34 1AG. Travelbag Adventures offers small group tours – desert, Nile and family – with structured itineraries.

Voyages Jules Vernes (☎ 020-7616 1000, fax 7723 8629, ⓔ sales@vjv.co.uk, ⓦ www.vjv.co.uk) 21 Dorset Square, London NW1 6QG. This top class (and top price) tour operator offers no less than 17 seductively packaged itineraries, including Lake Nasser cruises and Aida at the Pyramids.

The USA & Canada

Abercrombie & Kent (☎ 1800-323 7308, fax 630-954 3324, ⓦ www.abercrombiekent.com) 1520 Kensington Rd, Suite 212, Oak Brook IL 60523-2141. This company offers classy packages using top-end hotels, domestic flights and its own custom-built Nile cruisers.

Adventure Center (☎ 1800-227 8747, fax 510-654 4200, ⓔ tripinfo@adventure-center.com, ⓦ www.adventure-center.com) 1311 63rd St, Suite 200, Emeryville, CA 94608. This company is an agent for the UK's Dragoman, Encounter Overland and Explore Worldwide.

Bestway Tours & Safaris (☎ 604-264 7378, fax 264 7774, ⓔ bestway@bestway.com, ⓦ www.bestway.com) Suite 206, 8678 Greenall Ave, Burnaby, BC, V5J 3M6. Bestway offers small group tours, including tours of Egypt that take in Libya and Tunisia as well.

Overseas Adventure Travel (☎ 1800-955 1925) 625 Mt Auburn St, Cambridge MA 02138. This company specialises in small group tours for mature travellers. The Egypt trip is 15 days, including a three-day Nile cruise and return flights from New York for US$3290.

Nile Cruises

Since militant activity in Middle Egypt has been preventing cruise ships from sailing between Cairo and Luxor, many overseas companies have dropped their Nile cruise packages, and one or two companies that specialised in Nile cruises have gone bust. However, it is still possible – and safe – to sail a three- or four-day stretch of the river south from Luxor (see Nile Cruises under Boat in the Getting Around chapter). Abercrombie & Kent and Hayes and Jarvis (see The USA & Canada and The UK earlier for details) both do good cruise packages, and you should also have no problem booking something through a high-street travel agency.

Adventure & Overland Safaris

In this kind of tour you travel in a specially adapted 'overland truck' with anywhere from 16 to 24 other passengers and your group leader-cum-driver/navigator/nurse/mechanic/guide/fixer/entertainer – much of the success of your trip rests on this person's shoulders. Accommodation is usually a mix of camping and budget hotels. Food is bought along the way and the group cooks and eats together. You are expected to muck in; cooking is done on a rota and everyone is expected to lend a hand when it comes to digging the truck out of sand. It's like *Big Brother* without the evictions.

When you are travelling in such a self-contained bubble, the success of the trip depends on group chemistry. It could be long party on wheels or six endless weeks of grin, bear it and bite your tongue. Significantly, one group leader we spoke to said that the thing that most overlanders remembered about the trip was the people they were with. Following are some adventure companies worth checking out:

African Trails (☎ 020-8742 7724, fax 8960 1414) 3 Flanders Rd, Chiswick, London W4 1NQ. African Trails offers a six-week Egypt to Turkey trip for UK£600.

Dragoman (☎ 01728-862 222, fax 861 127, W www.dragoman.co.uk) Camp Green, Debenham, Suffolk IP14 6LA. Dragoman is an overland specialist with numerous itineraries through North Africa and the Middle East.

Economic Expeditions (☎ 020-8995 7707, fax 8742 7707, e info@economicexpeditions.com, W economicexpeditions.com) 29 Cunnington St, Chiswick, London W4 5ER. This company does a five-week İstanbul to Cairo trip for a basic UK£380.

Exodus (☎ 020-8673 0859, fax 8673 0779, W www.exodustravels.co.uk) 9 Weir Rd, London SW12 OLT. Exodus offers Cairo to Nairobi (nine weeks) and Cairo to Cape Town (18 weeks) trips.

High Places (☎ 0114-275 7500, fax 275 3870, W www.highplaces.co.uk) Globe Works, Penistone Rd, Sheffield S6 3AE. Although there's nothing in Egypt on this company's 2001 program, in the past it has organised eight-day camel treks around Sinai.

Kumuka (☎ 020-7937 8855, fax 7937 6664, e sales@kumuka.co.uk, W www.kumuka.co.uk) 40 Earls Court Rd, London W8 6EJ. In addition to İstanbul to Cairo/Jordan to Cairo trips (both lasting three weeks), Kumuka also offers an Oases & Pharaohs expedition lasting two weeks and costing UK£375.

Oasis Overland (☎ 01258-471 155, fax 471 166, W www.travellersway.demon.co.uk) 5 Nicholsons Cottages, Hinton St Mary, Dorset DT10 1NF. This company offers an Egypt Encompassed tour of 10 (UK£300) or 14 days (UK£380).

Wind, Sand & Stars (☎ 020-7433 3684, fax 7431 3247, e office@windsandstars.co.uk, W www.windsandstars.co.uk) 2 Arkwright Rd, London NW3 6AD. This Sinai specialist organises trips involving climbing and walking, desert camping, bird-watching and snorkelling.

Diving Tours

While it's quite possible to just book yourself a basic package to Sinai or Hurghada and sort out your own diving arrangements with a local company when you get there (see Clubs in the Diving the Red Sea chapter), there are numerous agencies that specialise in Red Sea diving holidays. The following are just a few that we know of in the UK:

Crusader Travel (☎ 020-8744 0474, fax 8744 0574, e crusader@divers.co.uk, W www.divers.co.uk) 57 Church St, Twickenham TW1 3NR. Crusader Travel mainly offers diving packages in the Red Sea out of Eilat, Nuweiba and Taba. It also offers special diving for the disabled.

Destination Red Sea (☎ 020-8440 9900, fax 8440 9905, e sales@redsea.co.uk, W www.redsea.co.uk) 125 East Barnet Rd, New Barnet, Herts EN4 8RF. This company offers diving tours out of Sharm el-Sheikh, Hurghada and Port Safaga. It also offers live-aboard trips.

The Imaginative Traveller (☎ 020-8742 8612, fax 8742 3045, W www.imaginative-traveller.com) This company offers a Red Sea diving trip for beginners based in Hurghada, including a PADI open-water course.

Oonasdivers (☎ 01323-648 924, fax 738 356, e info@oonasdivers.com, W www.oonadivers

.com) 23 Enys Rd, Eastbourne BN21 2DG. Oonasdivers offers diving tours based out of the Oonas dive club at Na'ama Bay. It also offers Red Sea diving safaris from the Marsa Alam region and live-aboard trips. Its prices seem very reasonable.

Regal Holidays (☎ 01353-778 096, fax 777 897) 22 High St, Sutton, Ely, Cambridgeshire CB6 2RB. Regal Holidays offers diving tours out of Sharm el-Sheikh and Hurghada, and also some live-aboards. The accommodation is fairly upmarket but prices still seem reasonable.

Getting Around

Egypt has a very extensive public and private transport system. If you don't suffer from claustrophobia, and have plenty of patience and a tough stomach, you can travel just about anywhere in Egypt relatively cheaply.

AIR

EgyptAir is the main domestic carrier. Air Sinai, which to all intents and purposes is EgyptAir by another name, is the only other operator. Fares are expensive and probably out of the range of most budget travellers. However, travellers flying the international sectors of their journey with EgyptAir should receive a 50% discount on internal flights. Check with your travel agency at the time of booking. In general, it is only worth flying if your time is very limited.

During the high season (October to April), many flights are full so it's wise to book as far in advance as you can. Due to volatile exchange rates, these fares are likely to increase; check with the airline for the latest figures.

from	to	one way	return
Aswan	Abu Simbel	E£275.40	E£550.80
Cairo	Abu Simbel	E£822.80	E£1645.60
	Alexandria	E£204	E£408
	Aswan	E£627	E£1254
	Hurghada	E£472	E£944
	Luxor	E£459	E£918
	Sharm el-Sheikh	E£472	E£944
	Taba	E£547.40	E£890.08
Luxor	Aswan	E£199	E£398
	Hurghada	E£210	E£420
	Sharm el-Sheikh	E£393	E£786

For EgyptAir contact details see Getting There & Away under individual cities and towns.

BUS

Buses service just about every city, town and village in Egypt. Ticket prices are generally comparable with the cost of 2nd-class train tickets. Intercity buses, especially on shorter runs and in Upper Egypt, tend to become crowded, and even if you are lucky enough to get a seat in the first place, you'll probably end up with something or somebody on your lap.

Deluxe buses travel between some of the main towns. For instance, the Superjet and West Delta bus companies shuttle luxury buses between Cairo and Alexandria every day. Similar services are offered to other parts of the country, and comfortable, air-con buses run between Cairo, Ismailia, Port Said, Suez, St Katherine's Monastery, Sharm el-Sheikh, Hurghada and Luxor. Tickets cost a bit more than on standard buses but they're still cheap. Most buses running south of Cairo along the Nile tend to be more basic.

Often the prices of tickets for buses on the same route will vary according to whether or not they have air-con and video, how old the bus is and how long it takes to make the journey – the more you pay, the more comfort you travel in and the quicker you get there. However, there are a few serious drawbacks to luxury bus travel, foremost of which is the video. This goes on as soon as the bus is out of the station and plays throughout the journey at a ridiculous volume that totally precludes any reading or any chance of sleep.

Even in summer you might find a sweater or scarf handy on overnight buses as the air-con brings the temperature down to a level where, according to one traveller, 'polar bears would feel at home'. Also, *beware*, snacks are not included in the price of the ticket so, unless you want to pay E£10 or more for a cup of tea and a biscuit, decline the on-board service.

One other problem associated with all bus travel in Egypt is smoking. Egyptian men are prolific smokers and nonsmokers may find long journeys to be a hazy nightmare of endless smog, despite the fact that many buses actually sport 'no smoking' signs. Protesting may make the guy next to you stop, but it's unlikely to change the habits of the rest of those on board.

Tickets can be bought at the bus stations or often on the bus. Hang on to your ticket until you get off, as inspectors almost always board to check fares. It is advisable to book tickets in advance, at least on very popular routes (such as from Cairo to Sinai) and those with few buses running (out to the Western Oases from Cairo). There are no student discounts on bus fares. Where you are allowed to buy tickets on the bus, you generally end up standing if you don't have an assigned seat with a booked ticket. On short runs there are no bookings and it's a case of first on, best seated.

TRAIN

Although there are trains travelling along more than 5000km of track to almost every major city and town in Egypt, the system is badly in need of modernisation and most of the services are grimy and battered and a poor second option to the deluxe bus. The exceptions are the trains to Alexandria and the tourist trains down to Luxor and Aswan – on these routes the train is preferable to the bus.

If you have an International Student Identification Card (ISIC) discounts of about 33% are granted on all fares except those for wagons-lit (cars with deluxe sleeper compartments). Some travellers report receiving a discount with International Youth Hostel Federation cards and Youth International Educational Exchange cards. It is possible to travel from Cairo to Aswan for only a few pounds if you have an ISIC and are willing to suffer in the 3rd-class cars.

One advantage (for a change) of being a woman here is that you go straight to the head of the queue for train tickets.

Classes

Services range from relatively cheap (compared with the USA and Europe) 1st-class wagons-lit to 1st-class sitting, 2nd-class air-con and 2nd-class ordinary and the ridiculously cheap 3rd-class cars.

Wagons-Lit Trains with wagons-lit are the most comfortable and among the fastest in Egypt. The cars are the same as those used by trains in Europe. Two wagons-lit trains used to travel between Cairo, Luxor and Aswan every day, but the number dropped to one several years ago.

Wagons-lit trains are 1st class only, have air-con, are carpeted, and each compartment has towels, coat hangers, hot and cold water and Venetian blinds. There are lounge cars, and dinner and breakfast are served in the compartments.

Other Classes Regular night trains with and without sleeper compartments and meals included leave for Luxor and Aswan every day and cost much less than the wagons-lit. Reservations must be made in advance at Ramses Station in Cairo. Unless you specify otherwise, you'll be issued with a ticket that includes meals on board. For this you'll pay, for example, an extra E£10 on the trip from Cairo to Luxor. Many travellers have said the food is tasteless and, for what you get, a waste of money so you may want to flout the rules and bring your own. Both 1st- and 2nd-class compartments have air-con and they can get chilly at night; have something warm to put on.

Non air-con trains are next down the scale. Classes are divided into 2nd class ordinary, which generally has padded seats, and 3rd class, where seating is of the wooden bench variety. These trains tend to spend a lot of time at a lot of stations and can be subject to interminable delays.

TAXI

Service Taxi

Travelling by 'ser-vees' is one of the fastest ways to go from city to city. Service taxis are generally big Peugeot 504 cars that run intercity routes. Drivers congregate near bus and train stations and tout for passengers by shouting their destination. When the car's full, it's off. A driver won't leave before his car is full unless you and/or the other passengers want to pay more money. Fares are usually cheaper than either the buses or trains and there are no set departure times, you just turn up and find a car. The drawbacks are that with six or seven squeezed in, journeys tend to be a bit uncomfortable and there's little room for baggage. Service-taxi rides can also be a little hairy at times – the drivers tend to be overconfident and often tired from long shifts on the road. Accidents involving service taxis are all too common and for this reason using them is not recommended unless as a last resort.

Microbus

A slightly bigger version of the service taxi is the 'meecrobus', a Toyota van that would normally take about 12 people but in Egypt takes as many as 22. These run on the same principle as service taxis and cost about the same but operate on fewer routes.

Pick-Ups

Toyota and Chevrolet pick-up trucks cover a lot of the routes between smaller towns and villages off the main roads. The general rule is to get 12 inside the covered rear of the truck, often with an assortment of goods squeezed in on the floor. After that, it's a matter of how many can and want to scramble on to the roof or hang off at the rear.

CAR & MOTORCYCLE

Driving in Cairo is a crazy affair, so think seriously before you decide to rent a car there. However, driving in other parts of the country, at least in daylight, isn't so bad. Having a car – or better still a 4WD – opens up entire areas of the country where public transport is nonexistent.

Motorcycle would be an ideal way to travel around Egypt. The only snag is that you have to bring your own and the red tape involved is extensive. Ask your country's automobile association and Egyptian embassy about regulations.

Petrol is readily available. *Tamaneen* (normal) costs 90pt a litre but is tough on the engine. Better is the higher-octane super, or *tisa'een*, at E£1 a litre. Lead-free was introduced in 1995 but, with only a handful of pumps in Cairo (mainly in Mohandiseen, Zamalek and Ma'adi) and Alexandria, there might be a queue. When travelling out of Cairo, remember that petrol stations are not always that plentiful; when you see one, fill up. Although the fast increase in car ownership over the past five to ten years has improved petrol distribution in the country, many provincial stations still run out of the high octane tisa'een, so if you're worried about your engine, bring an extra can along with you.

Road Rules

Driving is on the right-hand side. The official speed limit outside towns is 90km/h (though it is often less in some areas) and 100km/h on four-lane highways such as the one between Cairo and Alexandria. If you're caught speeding the police confiscate your licence and you have to go to the traffic headquarters in the area to get it back – a lengthy and laborious process. A few roads, such as the Cairo-Alexandria Desert Highway, the Cairo-Fayoum road and the road through the Ahmed Hamdi Tunnel (which goes under the Suez Canal near Suez) are subject to tolls of about E£1.25.

Many roads have checkpoints where police often ask for identity papers, so make sure you've got your passport and driving licence on hand or you may be liable for a US$100 on-the-spot fine.

Although city driving may seem chaotic, there is one cardinal rule: whoever is in front has the right of way – even if a car is only 1cm ahead of you and cuts across your path suddenly, you'll be liable if you hit it. As long as you don't assume that anybody looks in his or her rearview mirror and you use your horn to announce your presence, you'll be fine.

When driving through the countryside, keep in mind that children and adults are liable to wander into your path, even on main roads. Drive very carefully and use your horn liberally – hitting someone, even if it was their own fault, can sometimes result in the driver being attacked by angry villagers. If you do have an accident, get to the nearest police station as quickly as possible and report what happened.

Rental

Several car rental agencies have offices in Egypt, including Avis, Hertz and Budget (for contact details see Getting Around in

Slow Down, Belt Up

There is a new regimen being introduced into the anarchy of driving in Egypt, with police cracking down in the wake of recently introduced traffic laws. Provisions include hefty fines for driving at night without lights, running red lights, unnecessary horn-honking and speeding – all traditionally favourite pastimes of Egyptian drivers. In the case of the latter, there are not always signs telling you what the speed limit actually is, but generally, on dual carriageways outside cities it is 100km/h; on two-lane highways 90km/h. If you are caught speeding, your license will be confiscated, to be retrieved at the place where the vehicle is registered. If you're driving a car with customs plates then tough luck, because you're probably then looking at a trip to Alexandria or Suez.

Apparently, in the first week after the new law was passed on 1 January 2001, more than one million tickets were handed out – including almost 17,000 slapped on cars heading the wrong way down one-way streets. Even if drivers manage to obey all the newly enforced laws, that's still no guarantee of avoiding penalties; one journalist reported encountering a motorist at the traffic department office loudly questioning the legitimacy of a ticket he'd been given for passing a red light. He had a point. On the street where he was accused of committing the offence there were no lights at all. The unimpressed clerk made him pay up anyway.

The new laws also mandate seatbelts for front passengers and helmets for motorcyclists. Adjusting to these new regulations has involved plenty of creative interpretations. At the time of research a good many taxis had homemade belts with no buckles – the useless strap is just dangled across the chest in a way that might hopefully fool a traffic officer. And if it seems that half the country has suddenly become employed in the building trade, it's just that bright yellow construction hard hats are considerably cheaper than crash helmets, but just as effective at warding off E£100 on-the-spot fines.

the Cairo chapter). Their rates match international charges and finding a cheap deal with local dealers is virtually impossible. No matter which company you go with, make sure you read the fine print.

An international driving permit is required and you can be liable to a heavy fine if you're caught renting a car without one. Drivers should be over the age of 25.

As an indication of prices, for a small car like a Suzuki Swift you will be looking at about US$33 to US$40 per day, plus up to US$0.20 for each extra kilometre. A Toyota Corolla is about US$56 to US$60 per day, plus around US$0.25 per kilometre. These prices generally include insurance and the first 100km, but check this before signing. For unlimited kilometres, you'll be looking at about US$47/70 per day respectively for the above cars. Some companies set a minimum of seven days for unlimited-kilometre rentals, in which case you'll be looking at about US$240 to US$275 per week for a Toyota Starlet. Remember there will be a 10% to 17% tax added to your bill. It's usually possible to pay with travellers cheques or by credit card.

Some companies, such as Europcar, offer the option of one-way rentals from, for example, Cairo to Sharm el-Sheikh. It's also possible to hire a car plus a driver for those who don't feel like tackling Egyptian roads.

Your Own Transport

Drivers of cars and riders of motorcycles will need the vehicle's registration papers, liability insurance and an international driving permit in addition to their domestic licence. Beware that there are two kinds of international permits; one is needed mostly for former British colonies. You will also need a *carnet de passage en douane*, which is effectively a passport for the vehicle, and acts as a temporary waiver of import duty. The carnet may also need to list any expensive spares that you're planning to carry with you, such as a gearbox. Contact your local automobile association for details about all documentation.

At the Egyptian border, you will be issued with a licence valid for three months (less if your visa is valid for less time). You can renew the licence every three months for a maximum of two years but you'll have to pay a varying fee each time. A recent reader's letter gave the fees for bringing in a car as E£142 for entry tax and E£291 for customs and insurance.

The Egyptians themselves give conflicting advice on whether or not diesel-powered vehicles may enter the country. People wishing to bring in 4WDs should check at an Egyptian embassy, as the rules governing these vehicles are contentious. For further information try contacting the Automobile and Touring Club of Egypt (☎ 02-574 3355) at 10 Qasr el-Nil in Cairo, which is open from 9am to 1.30pm Saturday to Thursday.

If you plan to take your own vehicle, check in advance what spares and petrol are likely to be available. In Egypt, lead-free petrol was introduced in 1995 but is available only in Cairo and Alexandria. You are also likely to have trouble finding some parts for your car.

BICYCLE

Apart from a few charity affairs, you meet very few cyclists touring Egypt. There's no reason why it shouldn't be possible, particularly in Sinai and along the Nile Valley. The major problem would be the heat. This is at its worst from June to August and cycling in these summer months is definitely not recommended. May to mid-June and September to October would be the best times for two-wheel touring, and even then, it would be necessary to make an early morning start and be finished with most of the pedalling by early afternoon.

Carrying a full kit with you (see Practicalities following) is recommended as spares are hard to come by, although in a pinch Egyptians are excellent 'bush mechanics'.

Practicalities

Carry a couple of extra chain links, a chain breaker, spokes, a spoke key, two inner tubes, tyre levers and a repair kit, a flat-head and Phillips screwdriver, and Allen keys and spanners to fit all the bolts on your bike. Check the bolts daily and carry spares. Fit as many water bottles to your bike as you can – it gets hot. Make sure the bike's gearing will get you over the hills, and confine your panniers to 15kg maximum. In your panniers include: a two-person tent (weighing about 1.8kg) that can also accommodate the bike where security is a concern; a sleeping bag rated to 0°C and a Therm-a-Rest; small camping stove with gas canisters; MSR cooking pot; utensils; Katadyn water filter (two microns) and Maglite. Wear cycling shorts with chamois bum and cleated cycling shoes.

Repairs

Members of Cairo Cyclists (☎ 02-519 6078) reckon the best place in town for repairs is Ghoukho Trading & Supplies near St Mark's Cathedral, 800m south of Midan Ramses. We've never gone looking for it but we're told that it's quite hard to find, so be prepared to ask for directions.

Contacts

If you are considering cycling Egypt but have a few pressing questions that first need answering, one place to go is the Thorn Tree on Lonely Planet's Web site (W www.lonelyplanet.com). Post your query on the Activities branch and there's a strong likelihood somebody will respond with the information that you're looking for.

Alternatively, you could contact the CTC (Cyclists' Touring Club; ☎ 01483-417 217, fax 01483-426 994, e cycling@ctc.org.uk, W www.ctc.org.uk), a UK-based organisation that, among other things, produces information sheets on cycling in different parts of the world. At the time of research it had a dossier on Egypt. The club also publishes a good, glossy bimonthly magazine that always carries one or two travel-type cycling pieces.

HITCHING

Hitching is never entirely safe in any country in the world, and it is not recommended. Travellers who decide to hitch should understand that they are taking a small but potentially serious risk. People who do choose to hitch will be safer if they travel in pairs and let someone know where they are planning to go. Women must not hitch on their own. The general assumption would be that she's a prostitute.

BOAT

Nile Cruises

For centuries taking a boat was the only way to travel in Egypt. The pharaohs would view their realm from the river, people would visit one another via the waterway, barges with precious cargo would traverse the length of the country. In death, ancient Egyptians would even take boats to the underworld. Travellers too have historically gazed out over the country from the deck of a boat. From the 5th century BC, when that most famous of travel writers, Herodotus, was wandering through Egypt, up to modern times, a trip to Egypt meant sailing up the Nile.

Thomas Cook changed all that at the end of the 1860s, when he launched steamboats on the Nile, in the process inaugurating package tourism in Egypt.

Unfortunately, the threat of terrorist attacks in Middle Egypt has meant that since the early 1990s there have been no cruise ships sailing the length of the Nile from Cairo to Aswan, or vice versa. However, there are currently more than 250 cruise boats plying the waters between Luxor and Aswan that still make for a relaxing, timeless way to take in the monuments in this part of the country. Most cruises involve a three- or four-day sail between the two towns, stopping at the temple sites along the way.

Most of the boats are rated as either four- or five-star hotels, although there are some three-star boats available. Cruises on a top level boat, with all meals and sightseeing for four days (three nights) start at around US$200 to US$300 per person, but if it's low season, you can get them for much less. The cheapest deals come from booking in advance in your home country but you can also (space permitting) book yourself onto a cruise once in Egypt.

The most reputable boats are managed by international hotel chains such as Sheraton or Mövenpick. Cairo-based travel agencies, including Abercrombie & Kent (☎ 02-394 7735) and Thomas Cook (☎ 02-574 3776), also have their own boats complete with excellent reputations.

Other operators include Masr Travel Co & Hilton International (☎ 02-383 3444), Presidential Nile Cruises (☎ 02-735 0517), Travcotels (☎ 02-735 0959) and Seti First Travel (☎ 02-736 9820).

Felucca

The ancient sailboats of the Nile are still a fairly common means of transport up and down the river. As far as getting around, many people use them for a trip between Aswan and Esna, Edfu or Kom Ombo – it's not the quickest way to travel but that's not the point. For more information on how to arrange a trip see The River under Aswan in the Nile Valley – Esna to Abu Simbel chapter.

Yacht

It is possible to take a yacht into Egyptian waters and ports. There are 12 designated ports of entry, including Alexandria, Port Said, Sharm el-Sheikh, Dahab, Nuweiba, Hurghada, Suez and Ismailia. A security permit is required to enter the Nile River, and transit fees of US$10 per person and US$20 per yacht need to be paid to negotiate the Suez Canal. These and other fees are liable to change.

You will need all the usual documentation for the yacht, plus six copies of the crew list. You will also need valid visas and a raft of other bits of paper, including a health certificate, a customs list of the yacht's equipment and an insurance policy (for the Suez Canal). You can get visas on arrival in your first port.

It is also possible to shelter in other 'nonentry' ports, but you cannot go ashore.

Fuel is available in all ports of entry, and navigational charts are available in Alexandria, Port Said and Suez (ask for 'Marinkart'). There are nine yacht clubs in Egypt. For more details, contact your own yacht club before heading for Egypt.

Before leaving Egypt, a departure permit has to be obtained from the coastguard and you are supposed to leave within 24 hours of obtaining it.

If you want to get a lift on a yacht heading down to the Red Sea or elsewhere, it's best to try in Suez or Port Said.

LOCAL TRANSPORT

As well as the local transport options described here, some cities and towns have their own – most are variations on the pony-and-trap theme.

Bus & Minibus

Cairo and Alexandria are the only cities in Egypt with their own bus systems and taking a bus in either place is an experience far beyond the simple notion of getting from A to B. First, there's getting on. Egyptians stampede buses, charging the entrance before the thing has even slowed down. Hand-to-hand combat ensues as they run alongside trying to leap aboard. If you wait for the bus to stop, the pushing and shoving to get on is even worse. Often several passengers don't quite manage to get on and they make their journey hanging off the back doorway, clinging perilously to the frame or to someone with a firmer hold.

The scene inside the bus in this case usually resembles a Guinness World Record attempt on the greatest number of people in a fixed space. There are times when, crammed up the back with exhaust fumes billowing around you and ever more people squeezing on, asphyxiation seems perilously close. At some point during the trip, a man will somehow manage to squeeze his way through to sell you your ticket, which is usually 25pt.

Just as the buses only ever slow to pick up passengers, so they rarely completely stop to let you off. You stand in the doorway, wait for the opportune moment and launch yourself onto the road.

Taking a minibus is an easier option. Passengers are not allowed to stand (although this rule is frequently overlooked), and each minibus leaves as soon as every seat is taken. It costs 25pt to 50pt (depending on your destination) for a seat.

Microbus

Privately owned and usually unmarked microbuses shuttle around all the larger cities. For the average traveller, they can be difficult to use, as it is quite unclear where most of them go; however, quite often there's a small boy hanging out of the doorway yelling the destination. In Cairo, you might have occasion to use a microbus to get out to the Pyramids, while in Alexandria they shuttle the length of Tariq al-Horreyya and the Corniche to Montazah. Most of the smaller cities and towns have similar microbuses doing set runs around town.

Metro

Cairo is the only city in Egypt (indeed in Africa) with a metro system (for more details see Getting Around in the Cairo chapter).

Tram

Cairo and Alexandria are also the only two cities in the country with tram systems. While Alexandria still has a fairly extensive and efficient network, Cairo now only has a handful of lines. See Getting Around in the two city chapters for more details.

Taxi

There are taxis in most cities in Egypt; in Cairo they're all black and white, while in Alexandria they're black and orange. Almost every second car is a taxi and they are by far the most convenient way of getting about. Stand at the side of the road, stick your hand out and shout your destination at any cab passing in the right direction. It doesn't matter if there is already someone inside because taxis are shared. When a taxi stops, restate where you want to go and if the driver's amenable, hop in.

Do not ask 'how much?' The etiquette is that you get in knowing what to pay and when you arrive, you get out and hand the money through the window. Make sure that you have the correct money (hoard E£1 bills) because getting change out of drivers is like having your teeth pulled. If a driver suspects that you don't know what the correct fare is then you're fair game for fleecing. If once you get in the taxi the driver starts talking money then just state a fair price (we give examples of correct fares

'Taxi!'

Taxis are at once a blessing and a curse. They're a remarkably convenient and easily affordable way of getting around the city but they can also be a frequent source of unpleasantness when it comes to paying the fare. The problem comes with the unmetered system of payment, which almost guarantees discontent. Passengers frequently feel that they've been taken advantage of (which they often have), while drivers are occasionally genuinely aggrieved by what they see as underpayment. So why don't the drivers use the meter? Because they were all calibrated at a time when petrol was ludicrously cheap. That time has long passed and any driver relying on his meter would now be out of pocket every time he came to fill up.

Taxi driving is far from being a lucrative profession. Of the more than 60,000 taxis on the road in Cairo it would be a safe bet to assume none of the drivers are yet millionaires. Average earnings after fuel has been paid are about E£8 per hour. Consider too, that many drivers don't even own their car and have to hand over part of their earnings as 'rent'.

Which isn't to say that next time you flag a taxi for a short hop across town and the driver hisses '10 bounds' that you should smile and say 'OK', but maybe you can see that from a certain point of view, it was worth his while trying.

throughout this book) and if it's not accepted, get out and find another car.

Often when you come to paying, a driver will demand more money, and may yell. Don't be intimidated and don't be drawn into an argument. As long as you know you're not underpaying (and the fares in this book are generous), just walk away. It's all bluster and the driver is playing on the fact that you're a *khwaga* (foreigner) and don't know better.

The big Peugeot 504 service taxis, sometimes marked 'special', charge more than other taxis. The advantage of these taxis is that you can get a group together and commandeer one for a long trip.

Pick-Ups

As well as servicing routes between smaller towns, covered pick-up trucks are sometimes used within towns as local taxis. This is especially so in some of the oases towns and smaller places along the Nile. Should you end up in one of these, there are a couple of ways you can indicate to the driver when you want to get out: if you happen to be lucky enough to have a seat, pound on the floor with your foot; alternatively ask one of the front passengers to hammer on the window behind the driver; or, lastly, use the buzzer that you'll occasionally find rigged up.

Cairo

☎ 02

Few countries can be so dominated by their capital: Cairo *is* Egypt. Both of them are known by the same name, Masr, and for Egyptians, to speak of one is to speak of the other at the same time. The city's stature spreads beyond borders – to millions of Arabic speakers, Cairo is the semimythical capital of the Arab world. One tale in *The Thousand and One Nights* begins with a circle of men in a mosque in Mosul talking of foreign lands and the marvels of cities. 'Baghdad is Paradise', says one, to which the eldest sagely counters, 'He who has not seen Cairo has not seen the world. Its dust is gold; its Nile is a wonder; its women are like the black-eyed virgins of paradise: and how could it not be otherwise, when she is the Mother of the World'.

These days, she is mother to around 16 million Egyptians, Arabs, Africans and sundry international hangers-on. She's overburdened with one of the world's highest densities of people per square kilometre, which makes for a seething compress of people, buildings and traffic, and all the attendant cacophony and jostling for space this brings.

Cairo's lack of room to develop or expand constantly throws up startling juxtapositions. In one central Nile-side district, less than 500m from a new computer superstore, there are mud-brick houses where goats wander through living rooms and water has to be obtained from spigots in the street.

Cairenes see nothing strange in this. They aren't driven by the Western obsession to update and upgrade; possibly as a result of living in such close proximity to the physical remains of 4½ millennia of history (the Pyramids are visible from the upper storeys of buildings all over the city). The resulting pervasive sense of timelessness is one of the city's great charms. It's possible to move from the medieval backstreets of Islamic Cairo to the Pharaonic monumentalism of the Pyramids, then take time out in a coffeehouse that looks identical to those portrayed in 19th-century prints. And what is really wonderful is that none of these places feels 'historical', they all just feel like Cairo. That's to say, they're chaotic, noisy, totally unpredictable and seething with humanity. It's an exhilarating city for those with the patience to appreciate it.

Highlights

- Visit the Pyramids – one of the ancient Seven Wonders of the World and an absolute must-see.
- Discover the badly displayed but magnificent treasures of the Egyptian Museum, including those of Tutankhamun.
- Explore over 800 Islamic monuments spanning more than a thousand years, crammed into the labyrinthine quarters of the old medieval city.
- Drift along the Nile on a felucca and watch the sun sink behind the city skyline – the perfect end to a day.
- Check out Cairo's *ahwa*, or coffeehouse, scene, as vital to Cairo as cafes are to Paris.

HISTORY

Cairo is not a Pharaonic city, though the presence of the Pyramids leads many to believe otherwise. At the time the Pyramids were built the capital of ancient Egypt was Memphis, 22km south of the Giza plateau.

The core foundations of the city of Cairo were laid in AD 969 by the Fatimid dynasty. There had been earlier settlements, notably the Roman fortress of Babylon and the early Islamic city of Fustat, established by Amr ibn al-As, the general who conquered Egypt for Islam in AD 642. Fustat became one of the wealthiest cities of the new Muslim world, its wealth drawn from Egypt's excessively rich soil and the taxes imposed on the heavy Nile traffic. Descriptions left by 10th-century travellers tell of a cosmopolitan

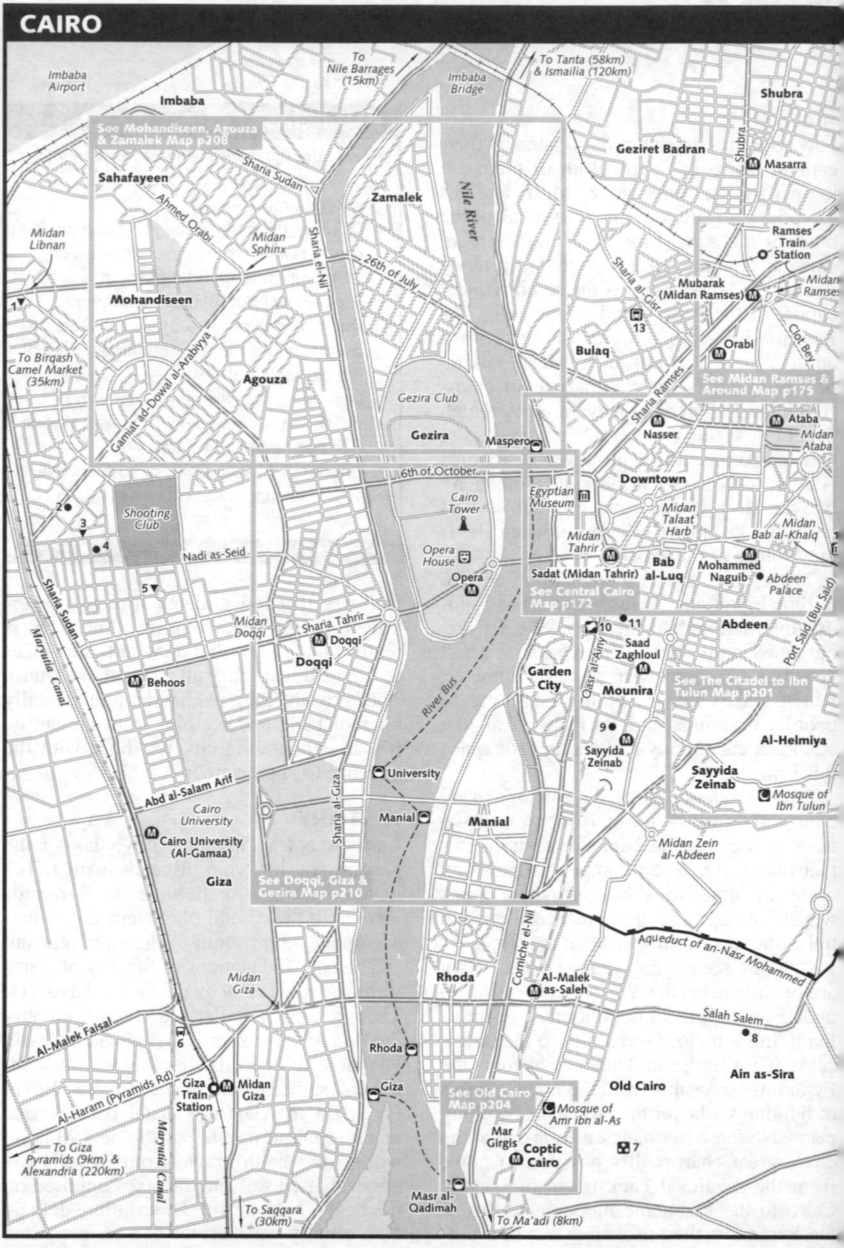
CAIRO
Imbaba Airport
Imbaba
To Nile Barrages (15km)
Imbaba Bridge
To Tanta (58km) & Ismailia (120km)
Shubra
See Mohandiseen, Agouza & Zamalek Map p208
Sharia Sudan
Sahafayeen
Ahmed Orabi
Zamalek
Nile River
Gezirat Badran
Shubra
Masarra
Midan Libnan
Midan Sphinx
Sharia el-Nil
26th of July
Ramses Train Station
Midan Ramses
Sharia al-Gisr
Mubarak (Midan Ramses)
Mohandiseen
13
Clot Bey
Orabi
Gamiat ad-Dowal al-Arabiyya
Bulaq
To Birqash Camel Market (35km)
Agouza
Gezira Club
Sharia Ramses
See Midan Ramses & Around Map p175
Gezira
Nasser
Ataba
Midan Ataba
Maspero
6th of October
Downtown
Egyptian Museum
Cairo Tower
Shooting Club
Midan Talaat Harb
Midan Bab al-Khalq
Opera House
Midan Tahrir
Nadi as-Seid
Bab al-Luq
Mohammed Naguib
Abdeen Palace
Opera
Sadat (Midan Tahrir)
See Central Cairo Map p172
Port Said (Bur Said)
Sharia Sudan
Midan Doqqi
Sharia Tahrir
Doqqi
10
11
Abdeen
Saad Zaghloul
Maryutia Canal
Doqqi
Garden City
Behoos
Qasr al-Ainy
Mounira
See The Citadel to Ibn Tulun Map p201
River Bus
Sayyida Zeinab
Al-Helmiya
University
Sayyida Zeinab
Abd al-Salam Arif
Mosque of Ibn Tulun
Cairo University
Manial
Manial
Cairo University (Al-Gamaa)
Sharia al-Giza
Midan Zein al-Abdeen
Giza
See Doqqi, Giza & Gezira Map p210
Aqueduct of an-Nasr Mohammed
Corniche el-Nil
Rhoda
Midan Giza
Al-Malek as-Saleh
Salah Salem
Al-Malek Faisal
Rhoda
Ain as-Sira
Giza Train Station
Midan Giza
Giza
Old Cairo
Al-Haram (Pyramids Rd)
See Old Cairo Map p204
Mosque of Amr ibn al-As
To Giza Pyramids (9km) & Alexandria (220km)
Mar Girgis
Coptic Cairo
Maryutia Canal
Masr al-Qadimah
To Saqqara (30km)
To Ma'adi (8km)

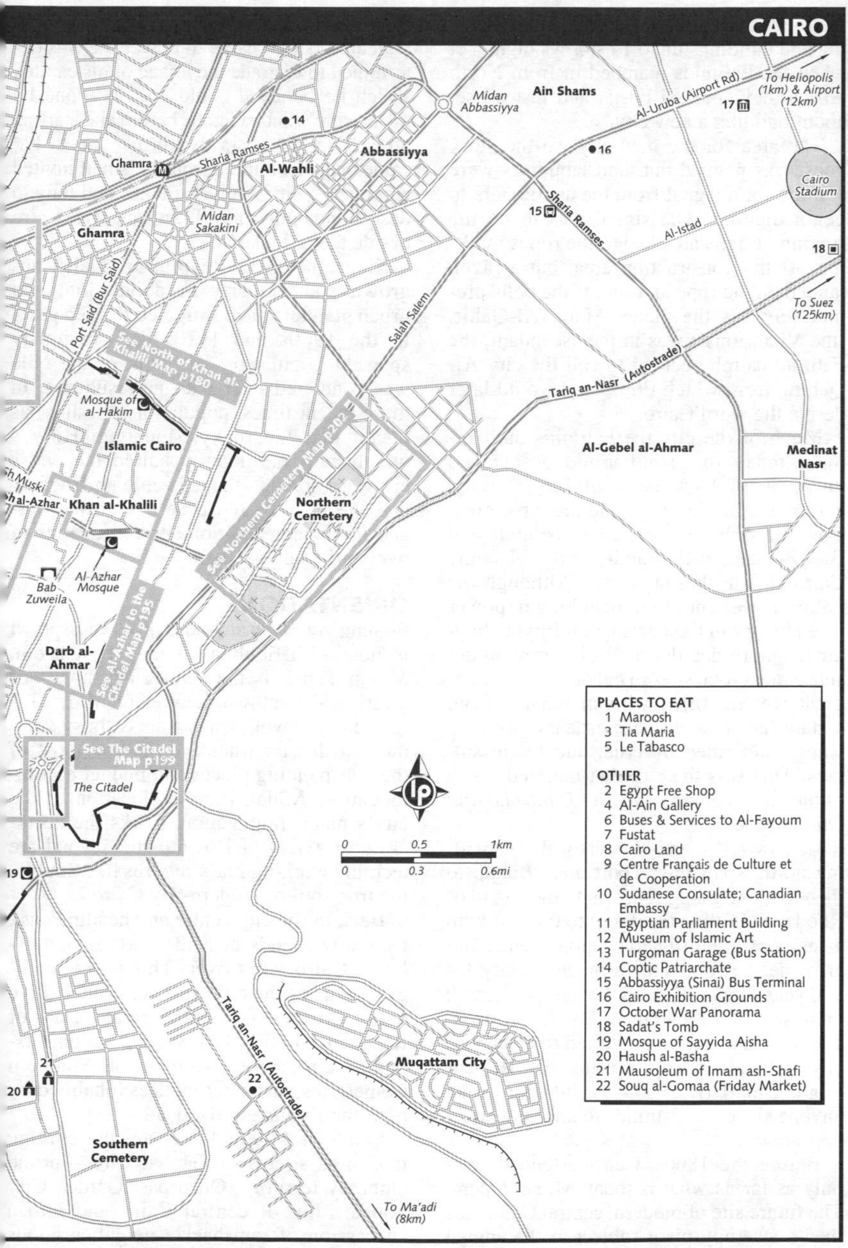
CAIRO
To Heliopolis (1km) & Airport (12km)
Ain Shams
Midan Abbassiyya
Al-Uruba (Airport Rd)
14
17
16
Sharia Ramses
Ghamra
Al-Wahli
Abbassiyya
Cairo Stadium
Midan Sakakini
Ghamra
15
Sharia Ramses
Al-Istad
18
Port Said (Bur Said)
Salah Salem
To Suez (125km)
See North of Khan al-Khalili Map p180
Tariq an-Nasr (Autostrade)
Mosque of al-Hakim
See Northern Cemetery Map p202
Islamic Cairo
Al-Gebel al-Ahmar
Medinat Nasr
Sh Muski
Sh al-Azhar
Khan al-Khalili
Northern Cemetery
Al-Azhar Mosque
Bab Zuweila
See Al-Azhar to the Citadel Map p195
Darb al-Ahmar
See The Citadel Map p199
The Citadel
0 0.5 1km
0 0.3 0.6mi
19
21
20
22
Tariq an-Nasr (Autostrade)
Muqattam City
Southern Cemetery
To Ma'adi (8km)
PLACES TO EAT
1 Maroosh
3 Tia Maria
5 Le Tabasco
OTHER
2 Egypt Free Shop
4 Al-Ain Gallery
6 Buses & Services to Al-Fayoum
7 Fustat
8 Cairo Land
9 Centre Français de Culture et de Cooperation
10 Sudanese Consulate; Canadian Embassy
11 Egyptian Parliament Building
12 Museum of Islamic Art
13 Turgoman Garage (Bus Station)
14 Coptic Patriarchate
15 Abbassiyya (Sinai) Bus Terminal
16 Cairo Exhibition Grounds
17 October War Panorama
18 Sadat's Tomb
19 Mosque of Sayyida Aisha
20 Haush al-Basha
21 Mausoleum of Imam ash-Shafi
22 Souq al-Gomaa (Friday Market)

metropolis with public gardens, street lighting and buildings up to 14 storeys high. Yet when the Fatimids marched in from North Africa they spurned Fustat and instead set about building a new city.

The area for the new city, so the story goes, was pegged out, and labourers were waiting for a signal from the astrologers to begin digging. The signal was to be the ringing of bells attached to the ropes marking off the construction area, but a raven landed on the rope and set off the bells prematurely. As the planet Mars (Al-Qahir, 'the Victorious') was in the ascendant, the Fatimid caliph decided to call the city Al-Qahira, from which Europeans would later derive the word Cairo.

Much of the city the Fatimids built remains today: the great Fatimid mosque and university of Al-Azhar is still Egypt's main centre of Islamic study; and the three great gates of Bab an-Nasr, Bab al-Futuh and Bab Zuweila still straddle two of Islamic Cairo's main thoroughfares. Although the Fatimids were not to remain long in power (see History in the Facts about Egypt chapter for more details) their city grew under subsequent dynasties to become a capital of great wealth, filled with merchants from distant lands, laden with bazaars of exotic wares, and ruled by cruel and fickle sultans. This was the city that inspired many of the tales that make up *The Thousand and One Nights*.

Cairo swelled and burst its walls, spreading north, spawning a port area, Bulaq, to the west, extending south on to the island of Rhoda, and filling the desert to the east with a series of grand funerary monuments. But at its heart it remained a medieval city for 900 years. It wasn't until the reign of Ismail, grandson of Mohammed Ali, in the mid-19th century that Cairo started to change in any significant way. During his 16-year reign, Ismail (r. 1863–79) did more than anyone since the Fatimids to alter the city's appearance.

Before the 1860s, Cairo extended west only as far as what is today Midan Opera. The future site of modern, central Cairo was then a swampy plain subject to the annual flooding of the Nile. When the French-educated Ismail came to power, he was determined to upgrade the image of his capital, which he believed could only be done by dismissing what had gone before and starting afresh. For 10 years the former marsh became one vast building site as Ismail invited architects from Belgium, France and Italy to design and build a new European-style Cairo beside the old Islamic city.

Since the 1952 Revolution, Cairo has grown spectacularly in population, and urban planners have struggled to keep pace. In the 1960s and 1970s the previously sparsely populated west bank of the Nile was concreted over with new suburbs. In more recent times, population pressure has meant that the rocky Muqattam Hills – which had traditionally halted the city's eastward spread – have been leap-frogged, and the once-barren desert is now a vast and messy construction site for a series of overspill-soaking satellite cities.

ORIENTATION

Finding your way around Cairo's vast sprawl is not as difficult as it may first seem. Midan Tahrir is the centre. North-east of Tahrir is Downtown. Centred on Midan Talaat Harb, Downtown is a noisy, busy commercial district where you'll find most of the cheap eating places and budget accommodation. Midan Ramses, location of the city's main train station, marks the northernmost extent of Downtown. Beyond are teeming working-class suburbs like Shubra, the true soul of modern-day Cairo.

Back in the city centre and heading east, Downtown ends at Midan Ataba and Islamic Cairo takes over. This is the medieval heart of the city, still very much alive today. At its centre is the great bazaar of Khan al-Khalili. Eastwards, beyond Islamic Cairo, are the Northern and Southern Cemeteries, vast necropolises inhabited by both the living and the dead.

South of Midan Tahrir are the curving tree-lined streets of Garden City – prime embassy territory. Once past Garden City you are out of central Cairo and into a succession of ramshackle neighbourhoods loosely termed Old Cairo. Buried in here is the small, walled enclave of Coptic Cairo, a feature on many tourist agendas.

West of all these districts is the Nile, which is obstructed by two sizable islands. The more central of these, connected directly to Downtown by three bridges, is Gezira, home to the Cairo Tower and the Opera House complex. The northern half of Gezira is an affluent, leafy suburb called Zamalek, historically favoured by the city's European residents and also home to many embassies. The southern island is known as Rhoda, although its northern part goes by the name of Manial.

The west bank of the Nile is less historic and much more residential than areas along the east bank. The primary districts from north to south are Mohandiseen, Agouza, Doqqi and Giza, all of which are heavy on concrete and light on charm. Giza covers by far the largest area of the four, stretching some 20km west either side of one long, straight road that ends at the foot of the Pyramids.

Arriving in Cairo

Cairo's airport lies on the north-eastern fringes of Heliopolis, some 25km from the city centre. For details of how to get from there to Downtown Cairo, see Getting Around later in this chapter. Travellers who arrive by bus will be dropped off either on Midan Abdel Moniem Riad, behind the Egyptian Museum, which is a short walk from Midan Tahrir, or at the Turgoman garage (bus station), from where you'll need to take a taxi. Trains come into Ramses Station on Midan Ramses, from where you can catch the metro three stops to the city centre.

INFORMATION

Visa Extensions

All visa business, including extensions, is carried out at the Mogamma, the 14-storey monolithic white building on Midan Tahrir. Not so long ago, to venture into this place was to see days of your life pass interminably while you waited on counter clerks and were bounced between desks, collecting stamps and signatures. That's all changed; processes have been simplified and streamlined, and if the place is not yet exactly user-friendly, you can at least usually get in and out within an hour.

Go up to the 1st floor, pass through the door on the right, then circle around to the left and walk straight down the corridor ahead (marked with a No 4). Go to window No 50 and ask for an extension or re-entry form. Hand in the completed form at window No 27, 28 or 29. For costs and other requirements see the Facts for the Visitor chapter. Re-entry forms are handed in at window No 16 or 17, again, you'll need one photograph. Single/multiple re-entry visas cost E£10/14.

The Mogamma is open from 8am to 2pm Saturday to Thursday.

Tourist Offices

Cairo's main tourist office (☎ 391 3454) is at 5 Sharia Adly, close to Midan Opera. Staff members can be helpful if they have nothing better to do, but even then, they're not particularly well clued-up. The office is open from 8.30am to 8pm daily (from 9am to 5pm during Ramadan).

There are tourist offices at Cairo international airport's Terminal I (☎ 667 475) and Terminal II (☎ 291 4255). The office at Terminal II should be open 24 hours, but don't bank on it.

There's also a tourist office (☎ 385 0259) at the Pyramids opposite the entrance to the Oberoi Mena House. It's usually open from 9am to 5pm daily. There are other small offices at the Manial Palace and Ramses train station.

The tourist police office (☎ 390 6028) is on the 1st floor of a building in the alley just to the left of the main tourist office on Sharia Adly.

Money

For general details about banks, foreign exchange bureaus and transferring funds, see Money in the Facts for the Visitor chapter. Information on banking hours is given under Business Hours in the same chapter, but it's worth knowing that the

Banque Masr branches at the Nile Hilton and Helnan Shepheard's hotels are open 24 hours a day. Hotel branches of the big banks are generally the best place to go to change your cash, but for slightly better rates you could try the city's forex bureaus, of which there are several along Sharia Adly, Downtown. They tend to close at 8pm.

ATMs For general details about the cards Cairo's ATMs accept, see Money in the Facts for the Visitor chapter. In central Cairo, ATMs are conveniently located on Talaat Harb (on the 1st floor of the concrete tower block across from the Felfela takeaway outlets); on Mahmoud Bassiouni, near Thomas Cook; on Qasr al-Ainy (200m south of Midan Tahrir); at the main entrance to the Al-Bustan Centre on Sharia al-Bustan; and in the foyers of all the five-star hotels.

American Express Offices of American Express (AmEx) are open from 8.30am to 5pm Saturday to Thursday. Their addresses in Cairo include:

Downtown (☎ 574 7991, fax 578 4003) 15 Qasr el-Nil; (☎ 578 5001/2) Nile Hilton
Giza (☎ 570 3411) Nile Tower Building, 21–23 Sharia Giza
Heliopolis (☎ 290 9158) 72 Omar ibn al-Khattab

AmEx also operates a handy 24-hour helpline (☎ 569 3299).

Thomas Cook Offices of Thomas Cook are open from 8am to 5pm daily. Addresses in Cairo include:

Downtown (☎ 574 3776) 17 Mahmoud Bassiouni
Giza (☎ 382 2688) Forte Grand Pyramids Hotel, Cairo-Alexandria Rd
Heliopolis (☎ 417 3511) 7 Sharia Baghdad
Mohandiseen (☎ 346 7187) 10 Sharia 26th of July

There's also an emergency hotline (☎ 010 140 1367), which operates from 5pm to 8am daily.

Post

Cairo's main post office, on Midan Ataba, is open from 7am to 7pm Saturday to Thursday, and from 7am to noon on Friday and public holidays. The poste restante is down the side street to the right of the main entrance, through the last door (opposite the Express Mail Service (EMS) fast mail office). It's open from 8am to 6pm Saturday to Thursday, and 10am to noon Friday and public holidays. Mail is held for three weeks.

To send a package abroad you must go to the post traffic centre at Midan Ramses. It is open from 8.30am to 3pm Saturday to Thursday. Set aside 30 minutes for this process and bring your passport. You'll need to go to the first big room to the left on the 2nd floor. At the counter get form No 13 (E£5), have the parcel weighed and pay for it. Probably customs will have a look at it (for details on these formalities see Packages under Post & Communications in the Facts for the Visitor chapter). After your package has been inspected, someone will wrap it for you (E£1.50 per metre of paper used plus E£1.60 for sealing).

Fast mail can be sent through the EMS main office (☎ 390 5874) down the side street beside the main post office. It's open from 8am to 7pm Thursday to Saturday. Most post offices also have an EMS counter.

In addition to EMS, Cairo also has a full complement of international courier services on offer:

DHL (☎ 393 8988) 34 Abdel Khalek Sarwat, Downtown; (☎ 795 7118) 20 Gamal ad-Din Abu al-Mahasin, Garden City; (☎ 636 0324) 35 Ismail Ramzy, Heliopolis
Federal Express (general inquiries ☎ 268 7888); (☎ 794 0520) 1079 Corniche el-Nil, Garden City; (☎ 331 3500) 24 Sharia Syria, Mohandiseen; (☎ 639 0607) 21 Mohammed Ghuneim, Heliopolis
TNT Skypak (☎ 748 8204) 33 Sharia Doqqi, Doqqi

Telephone & Fax

There are Menatel cardphones all over the city, although the policy of placing them on street corners means you can hardly ever hear the person on the other end of the line over the noise of passing traffic. For information on rates, making collect calls and telephone services in general, see Post & Communications in the Facts for the Visitor chapter. There are also a good many of the old telephone centrales around (where you pay the operator to make your international connection), most notably on Midan Tahrir.

Faxes can be sent to/from the telephone centrales on Midan Tahrir (fax 578 0979) and Sharia Alfy (fax 589 7662). You can also send and receive them from EMS (fax 393 4807) near the main post office on Ataba. Alternatively, you can receive faxes at AmEx (fax 574 7997) at the Qasr el-Nil office.

Email & Internet Access

The Internet business is booming in Cairo. Last edition of this guide there were all of four Internet cafes in town, two years on there are just too many to list. The most central include:

4U Internet Cafe (☎ 575 9304) 8 Midan Talaat Harb, 1st floor, Downtown; open from 9am to 10pm daily; E£8 per hour; six terminals

Buonanno Internet Cafe (☎ 395 6786) 20 Sharia Adly, Downtown; open from 10am to 9pm daily; E£10 per hour; newest hardware, fastest connections

InternetEgypt (☎ 356 2882) 2 Midan Simon Bolivar, ground floor, Garden City; open from 9am to 10pm Saturday to Thursday, 3pm to 10pm Friday; E£10 per hour; 10 terminals

Mohandiseen Cybercafe (☎ 305 0493) On a side street off Gamiat ad-Dowal al-Arabiyya between McDonald's and Arby's; open from 10am to midnight daily; E£12 per hour

Nile Hilton Cybercafe (☎ 578 0444 ext 758) Basement of the Nile Hilton shopping mall; open from 10am to midnight Saturday to Thursday, 10am to noon and 2pm to midnight Friday; E£12 per hour; eight terminals

Onyx Internet Cafe 26 Mahmoud Bassiouni, ground floor, Downtown; open from 9am to midnight daily; E£6 per hour

Palm Net Cafe (☎ 415 0685) 12 Sharia Ibrahim, 1st floor, next to Palmyra, Heliopolis; open from 10am to 10pm daily; E£7 per hour; six terminals

St@rnet Cyber Cafe (☎ 391 0151 ext 117) Basement of the Al-Bustan Centre, Sharia al-Bustan, Downtown; open from 10.30am to 10.30pm daily; E£10 per hour

An increasing number of budget hotels are also providing online terminals for the use of guests, including at present the Berlin Hotel, New Sun Hotel and Hotel Venice.

Travel Agencies

The area around Midan Tahrir is teeming with travel agencies but don't expect any amazing deals. In fact there are a lot of dodgy operators here; in particular, avoid Metro Travel and Wonder Travel. For tours of Cairo and surrounds and for trips down to Luxor or Aswan, try Hamis Travel (☎ 575 2757, fax 574 9276, e hamis @hamis .com.eg, w www.hamis.com.eg), with offices on the 1st floor in the annexe just south of the main booking hall at Ramses train station. The company is managed by Anny, a friendly Dutch lady who speaks excellent English. It's open from 9am to 9pm daily.

One of the best and most reputable agencies in town, though it's way down in the bedroom suburb of Ma'adi, is Egypt Panorama Tours (☎ 359 0200, fax 359 1199, e ept@link.net, w www.eptours .com) at 4 Road 79, just outside the Ma'adi metro station. They're good on cheap air fares and tours within Egypt and around the Mediterranean region. If you don't want to make the trip down to Ma'adi, Panorama takes bookings over the phone (staff members speak excellent English) and will courier the tickets to you.

The official Egyptian government travel agency, Masr Travel (☎ 393 0168, fax 392 4440), is at 7 Talaat Harb, Downtown.

Bookshops

Cairo has a reasonably good selection of bookshops, particularly if you are searching for Egypt-oriented titles. The best of the lot is the American University in Cairo (AUC) bookshop (enter the campus by the Mohammed Mahmoud gate, and it's in the building to the right). Being an academic outlet, it has stacks of material on the politics, sociology and history of Cairo, Egypt and the Middle East but it also has plenty of local guidebooks, coffee-table volumes and some fiction. It's open from 9am to 4pm Sunday to Thursday and from 10am to 3pm on Saturday. There is also a much smaller branch at the AUC Hostel at 16 Mohammed ibn Thakeb in Zamalek.

Other bookshops with very good selections of books about Cairo and Egypt are Lehnert & Landrock at 44 Sharia Sherif and Livres d'France at 36 Qasr el-Nil. The former has plenty of books in German and the latter has shelves of French titles. Lehnert & Landrock is also one of the better places for maps and it has a large collection of old postcards and prints. It's open from 9.30am to 2pm and from 4pm to 7.30pm daily (closed on Saturday afternoon and Sunday). Livres d'France is open from 10am to 7pm daily (closed on Saturday afternoon and Sunday).

Second-Hand Books There's a fairly large second-hand book market on the east side of the Ezbekiyya Gardens, reached from Midan Ataba in central Cairo. Many of its 40 or 50 stalls (cabins, actually) carry English-language books and magazines but half the stock is piled knee-high on the floor, and much of the rest sits on shelves with their spines to the wall making browsing something of a chore.

Newsstands Cairo's three best newsstands are across from each other on three corners of the junction of Sharia 26th of July and Hassan Sabry in Zamalek. You can get just about anything from these guys, provided there are no bare breasts or buttocks involved. Downtown, the places with the best selections include a stand on Midan Talaat Harb out the front of Groppi's cafe; the newsstand on Mohammed Mahmoud, opposite the entrance to the AUC; and the place on Midan Tahrir, next to TWA and opposite the Nile Hilton. Of the hotel bookshops, those at the Nile Hilton (in the garden court, not the one inside the hotel), Cairo Marriott and Semiramis Inter-Continental hotels are the best for periodicals and papers.

Libraries

For English readers the best libraries are at the British Council and American Cultural Center (see Cultural Centres following). Otherwise, the best public library is the new and very grand Greater Cairo Library (☎ 736 2280), housed in a villa at 15 Mohammed Mazhar, Zamalek. It's stocked with a fantastic collection of art, science and other reference books, mainly in English, and it also has newspapers and magazines for browsing. It's open from 9am to 7pm Tuesday to Sunday (10am to 8pm between June and August).

Cultural Centres

Bring your passport as many cultural centres require some ID before they'll allow you to enter. For details of events at the cultural centres check the local English-language press, particularly *Al-Ahram Weekly* or the monthly *Egypt Today*.

France

Centre Français de Culture et de Cooperation (☎ 795 3725) 1 Madrassat al-Huquq al-Fransiyya, Mounira; (☎ 419 3857) 5 Shafiq al-Dib, Ard al-Golf, Heliopolis. Both centres regularly put on films, lectures and exhibitions, have their libraries open to the public and screen French-language news from the satellite TV station TV5. The institute at Mounira also runs French and Arabic language courses. Both are open from 9am to 7pm Sunday to Thursday.

Germany

Goethe Institut (☎ 575 9877) 5 Sharia al-Bustan, Downtown. This centre presents seminars and lectures in German on Egyptology and other topics. There are also performances by visiting music groups, special art exhibitions and film screenings. The library has more than 15,000 (mainly German) titles. It is open from 1pm to 7pm Monday to Thursday and from 8am to noon on Friday.

Italy

Istituto Italiano di Cultura (☎ 735 8791) 3 Sheikh Marsafy, Zamalek. The centre has a busy program of films, lectures (sometimes in English), hosts art exhibitions and has a library. It's open from 10am to 1pm Sunday to Thursday.

Netherlands

Netherlands-Flemish Institute (☎ 738 2522) 1 Mahmoud Azmy, Zamalek. This centre hosts art exhibitions and is well known in the Cairo expatriate community for its weekly lectures – delivered on a wide variety of topics and usually in English. It is open 9am to 2pm Monday to Friday.

UK

British Council (☎ 347 6118, W www.britishcouncil.org.eg) 192 Sharia el-Nil, Agouza. The council's library carries an assortment of (dated) UK newspapers and has a vast library of books and periodical titles. Library membership costs E£60 but browsing is free. It's open from 10am to 8pm Monday to Thursday and 9am to 3pm Friday and Saturday.

USA

American Cultural Center (☎ 357 3529, W www.usembassy.egnet.net) 5 Latin America, Garden City. Part of the embassy complex, there's an American studies centre and library open here from 8.30am to 4.30pm Sunday to Thursday.

Film & Photography

There are plenty of labs in central Cairo. One Downtown place we recommend for both quality and price is the Photo Centre (☎ 392 0031) on the 1st floor at 3 Sharia Mahrany, a backstreet off Sherifeen, which itself is a side street off Qasr el-Nil. Also Downtown, there's a Kodak Express on Sharia Adly between Sherif and Mohammed Farid. In Zamalek there's a Kodak Express on Sharia 26th of July and an Agfa outlet at 22 Hassan Sabry. All of these places sell all kinds of film and offer all the services you would expect of a Western photo shop.

If you need quick, professional slide processing, the place to go is Antar Photostore (☎ 354 0786) at 180 Sharia Tahrir, just east of Midan Falaki, Bab al-Luq.

For passport photos, the cheapest option is to ask one of the photographers in front of the Mogamma. They will use an antique box camera to copy your passport photo or any other photo and make four copies (black-and-white only and usually out of focus) for E£4. For colour shots done quickly, your cheapest bet is the instant photo booth (E£6 for four photos) near the ticket windows in Sadat metro station under Midan Tahrir.

Medical Services

Hospitals Many of Cairo's hospitals suffer from antiquated equipment and a cavalier attitude to hygiene but there are several exceptions:

Anglo-American Hospital (☎ 735 6162/3/45) Sharia Hadayek al-Zuhreyya, to the west of the Cairo Tower, Gezira
As-Salam International Hospital (☎ 524 0250) Corniche el-Nil, Ma'adi; (☎ 302 9091) 3 Sharia Syria, Mohandiseen
Cairo Medical Centre (☎ 258 1003) Midan Roxy, Heliopolis

Pharmacies There is no shortage of pharmacies in Cairo and almost anything can be obtained without a prescription. Pharmacies that operate 24 hours include Isaaf (☎ 574 3369) on the corner of Sharias Ramses and 26th of July, Downtown; Zamalek Pharmacy (☎ 736 6424) at 3 Shagaret ad-Durr, Zamalek; and Al-Ezaby (☎ 418 0838) at 1 Ahmed Tayseer, Heliopolis.

The Anglo-Eastern Pharmacy, in the city centre, on the corner of Sharias Abdel Khalek Sarwat and Sherif is open from 10am to 3pm and 6.30pm to 10pm Saturday to Thursday.

Health-conscious folk might like to check out the Sekem Health Store (☎ 342 4979) at 6 Ahmed Sabry in Zamalek. It stocks organic fruit and vegetables, additive-free jams, honey, herbs and pulses, as well as a range of herbal and homoeopathic teas. It's open from 8am to 9pm daily.

Emergency

In the case of minor emergencies, such as theft, the first port of call should be the tourist police (☎ 126 or 391 9144). You stand a better chance of encountering someone who speaks English than if you go to the regular police. In the case of an accident and injury call the As-Salam International Hospital (see Medical Services earlier). For lost credit cards, see Money in the Facts for the Visitor chapter. For anything more serious contact your embassy.

THE PYRAMIDS

The sole survivors from the ancient Seven Wonders of the World, the Pyramids are the planet's oldest tourist attraction. Built by father, son and grandson, they were already more than 2500 years old at the time of the birth of Jesus Christ.

But, even more than their age, the wonder of the Pyramids is in their age-old mysteries, like how exactly were they built? And what are they all about? We know that they were massive tombs constructed on the orders of the pharaohs by vast teams of workers tens of thousands strong. This is supported by the recently discovered pyramid-builders' settlement, complete with areas of large-scale food production and medical facilities. Ongoing excavations at the Giza plateau are providing more and more evidence that the workers were not the slaves of Hollywood tradition, but a highly organised workforce of Egyptian farmers. During the season of the Inundation when the annual Nile flood covered their fields and made farm work impossible, the same farmers could have been redeployed by the highly organised bureaucracy to work on the pharaoh's tomb. So the Pyramids can almost be seen as a kind of ancient job-creation scheme, with the floodwaters also making it easier to transport building stone to the site.

Despite all the evidence, there are still those who won't accept that the ancient Egyptians were capable of such astonishing achievements. Pyramidologists – for the study of the vast structures has become a science in its own right – point to the carving and placement of the stones, precise to the millimetre, and argue the cosmological significance of the structures' dimensions as evidence that the Pyramids were variously constructed by angels, the devil or visitors from another planet. It's easy to laugh at such seemingly out-there ideas, but visit the Giza plateau and you'll immediately see why so many people believe such awesome structures could only have unearthly origins.

The Pyramids as Funerary Complex

It was neither an obsession with death, nor a fear of it, that led the ancient Egyptians to build such incredible mausoleums as the pyramids, rather it was their belief in eternal life and their desire to be one with the cosmos. The pharaoh as the son of the gods was also their intermediary, and his role was to conduct the gods' powers to his people. He was therefore honoured in life and worshipped in death, and set between the earth and the sky to connect the worlds mortal and divine. The pyramid was a fitting tomb for such an individual. A funerary temple attached to each pyramid allowed the pharaoh to be worshipped long after his death, with daily rounds of offerings to sustain his soul. A long covered causeway connected the funerary temple to a 'valley temple' built on the quayside where the annual flood waters would reach each season (there's a superb model illustrating all this on the 1st floor of the Egyptian Museum). The whole complex also provided a constant visible reminder of the eternal power of the gods and at the same time the absolute power of the pharaoh for whom it was built.

Giza Plateau Basics

There are two entrances to the Pyramids site. The main entrance is via a continuation of Pyramids Rd that runs up past the Oberoi Mena House hotel to the foot of the Great Pyramid of Khufu. If you come by public bus, or by taxi, this is the most likely approach to take. As you follow the road up to the plateau you'll pass the tourist office on your left, where you can check on the official rates for horse and camel rides. If anyone around here starts steering you towards the unmistakable stench of a stable, backtrack fast and ignore all the talk about them being able to get you onto the plateau area without a ticket. Just keep following the tarmacked road as it climbs and curves and you'll see the ticket office (a hut) off to your right. Only general site admission tickets are sold here; tickets to enter the Pyramids are sold at a separate office (see the Giza plateau map).

Note that the number of people allowed inside the two larger pyramids (Khufu and Khafre) is now limited to just 300 per day, with tickets issued on a first-come, first-served basis. As it stands, 150 tickets for each go on sale at 8am, and another 150 are released at 1pm. Note also that if you haven't

THE GIZA PLATEAU

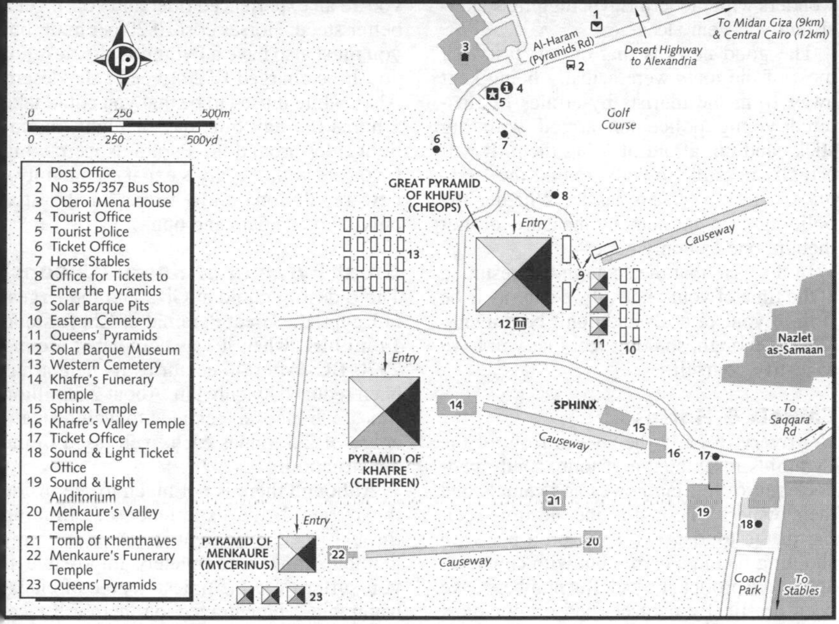

purchased a photography ticket (E£10) you will not be allowed to take your camera inside the pyramid. As there is nowhere to leave a camera, this could create problems if you're on your own, and might well involve a trek back to the ticket office to get the extra ticket. Readers have also complained of so-called 'officials' asking for additional money once inside the pyramids; this is a scam and you should not hand over any cash.

The other access to the site is via the village of Nazlet as-Samaan and through a gate directly in front of the Sphinx. If you arrive on a private tourist bus (or if your taxi driver's brought you via a perfume or papyrus shop), then this is the way you'll enter. There's another ticket office here, but again you'll have to buy Pyramid entry tickets elsewhere. There's an admission fee of E£20 for the plateau, plus another E£40 to enter the Great Pyramid, plus another E£20 for the Solar Barque Museum (plus E£10 for camera permits, and E£100 for video permits). The Pyramid site is open from 8am to 6pm daily. The Solar Barque Museum is open from 9am to 4pm October to May, and from 9am to 5pm June to September.

Be aware that the Pyramids close on a rotating basis, and only two are open for the public to clamber inside at any one time. This is to allow for necessary periodic restoration work.

The Hassle

Since the time of Mark Twain (who visited in 1866), and even before, tourists at the Pyramids have 'suffered torture that no pen can describe from the hungry appeals for baksheesh that gleamed from Arab eyes'. Every visitor to the Giza plateau has to run the gauntlet of camel and horse hustlers, souvenir and soft drink hawkers, would-be guides, agonisingly persistent shop owners and sundry beggars. As writer Tony Horwitz comments in *Baghdad Without a Map*, it's difficult to gaze in awe at these ancient wonders with modern Egypt tugging so persistently at your sleeve.

The good news is that on our last visit most of the touts were actually being kept away from the tourists by armies of flustered young policemen armed with big sticks and not afraid of using them. It was actually possible to walk around the Pyramids with next to no hassle. Whether the policing is a permanent measure or not though, one can only hope.

In the case that the scourge has resumed at the time of your visit, all we can say is be firm in your refusals and don't be drawn – 'No' is enough, so don't feel that you have to justify yourself.

Camels & Horses

Until very recently the area in front of the Pyramids resembled a chaotic, sandy paddock full of milling horses and camels and their owners who had a fine old time reeling in the tourists – a sport on a par with shooting fish in a barrel, but with considerably more profit to be had. But numbers have been drastically reduced, and on our most recent visit there were just a handful of animals. Word is authorities want to move them out altogether. In the meantime, if you do want to view the Pyramids from an elevated four-legged platform, beware – the camel owners are a pretty unscrupulous lot. Bargain fiercely and be sure of what you have agreed on. A camel should not cost more than E£15 an hour but more than a few people have found themselves paying ridiculous amounts of money at the end of the ride to be let *off* their mounts. Women should be particularly careful – *do not* allow the camel or horse owner to climb on the animal behind you.

Hiring a horse is a better option as once you're mounted you are away and off on your own. There are stables near the tourist office on Pyramids Rd but the animals here are often not in very good condition. For details on how to pick a healthy horse, see Horse Riding under Activities in the Facts for the Visitor chapter). It's better to head for either MG (☎ 358 3832) or AA (☎ 385 0531) by the coach park, two stables that look after their horses. Let them know that you're an experienced rider and you'll get a better steed. Horses cost E£20 per hour, but you must also have a Pyramids site ticket or you'll be charged E£20 to enter the desert. Also, while it used to be that you could take a horse out any time day or night (moonlight rides around the Pyramids were a big favourite with the city's expat community), new regulations allow riding in the area only between 6am and 6pm.

Great Pyramid of Khufu (Cheops)

The oldest pyramid at Giza and the largest in Egypt, the Great Pyramid of Khufu stood 146m high when it was completed around 2570 BC. After 46 centuries its height has been reduced by only 9m. About 2.3 million limestone blocks, reckoned to weigh an average of 2.5 tonnes each, were used in the construction.

Although there is not much to see inside the pyramid, the experience of climbing through such an ancient structure is unforgettable, though completely impossible if you suffer even the tiniest degree of claustrophobia. The entrance, on the north face, leads to a descending passage that ends in an unfinished tomb (usually closed) about 100m along and 30m below the pyramid. About 20m from the entrance, however, there is an ascending passage, 1.3m high and 1m wide, which continues for about 40m before opening into the Great Gallery, which is 47m long and 8.5m high. There is also a smaller horizontal passage leading into the so-called Queen's Chamber.

As you ascend the Great Gallery to the King's Chamber, notice how precisely the blocks were fitted together at the top. Unlike the rest of the pyramid, the main tomb chamber, which is just over 5m wide and 10m long, was built of red granite blocks. The roof, which weighs more than 400 tonnes, consists of nine huge slabs of granite, above which are another four slabs separated by gaps designed to distribute the enormous weight away from the chamber. There is plenty of air in this room, as it was built so that fresh air flowed in from two shafts on the north and south walls.

Climbing the outside of the Great Pyramid was, for centuries, a popular adventure despite the fact that every year a few people fell to their death. Scaling the pyramid is now forbidden.

On the eastern side of the pyramid are the Queens' Pyramids, three small structures about 20m high, which resemble little more than pyramid-shaped piles of rubble. They were the tombs of Khufu's wives and sisters.

Solar Barque Museum Along the eastern and southern sides of the Great Pyramid of Khufu are five long pits which once contained the pharaoh's barques. These solar barques (or boats) may have been used to bring the mummy of the dead pharaoh across the Nile to the valley temple, from where it was brought up the causeway and placed in the tomb chamber. The barques were then buried around the pyramid to provide transport for the pharaoh in the next world.

One of these ancient cedar-wood vessels, possibly the oldest boat in existence, was unearthed in 1954. It was restored and encased in a glass museum to protect it from damage from the elements. For the same reason, visitors to the museum must don protective footwear in order to keep sand out.

Pyramid of Khafre (Chephren)

South-west of the Great Pyramid, and with almost the same dimensions (it's 136m high), is the Pyramid of Khafre. At first it seems larger than that of Khafre's father, Khufu, but this is because it stands on higher ground and its peak is still capped with a limestone casing. Originally all three pyramids were totally encased with a polished

What They Said about the Pyramids

We will also mention the Pyramids...that idle and foolish exhibition of royal wealth. For the cause by most assigned for their construction is an intention on the part of those kings to exhaust their treasures, rather than leave them to successors or plotting rivals, or to keep the people from idleness.

Pliny the Elder, circa AD 50

Soldiers, forty centuries of history look down upon you from these Pyramids.

Napoleon, readying his forces for battle at Giza, 1798

Khafre's Pyramid seems to me inordinately huge and completely sheer; it's like a cliff, like a thing of nature, a mountain – as though it had been created just as it is, and with something terrible about it as if it were going to crush you.

Gustave Flaubert, 1849

The Pyramids looked as if they would wear out the air, boring holes in it all day long.

Florence Nightingale, 1840s

The Pyramids were a quarter of a mile away; it felt odd to be living at such close quarters with anything quite so famous – it was like having the Prince of Wales at the next table in a restaurant; one kept pretending not to notice, while all the time glancing furtively to see if they were still there.

Evelyn Waugh at the Mena House Hotel, 1929

I discovered that the marvels of the Pyramids at Gizeh and the Sphinx had been degraded into commodities for an enormous tourist trade.

Cecil Beaton, 1942

Very big. *Very* old.

camel owner, 1999

white limestone casing. They would have gleamed like giant crystals. Unfortunately, up until the 19th century successive builders in Egypt stripped away these outer blocks to build their palaces and mosques, exposing the Pyramid's softer inner core stones to the elements. Had it not been for this, the Pyramids might still stand today exactly as they were built, defying time to shift them.

The chambers and passageways of this particular pyramid are less elaborate than those in the Great Pyramid, but are almost as claustrophobic. The entrance leads down into a passage and then across to the burial chamber, which still contains the large granite sarcophagus of Khafre.

Back outside, to the east of the pyramid, are the substantial remains of Khafre's funerary temple, and the flagged flooring of the causeway that provided access from the Nile to the tomb.

Pyramid of Menkaure (Mycerinus)

At a height of 62m (originally 66.5m), this is the smallest of the great trio. A deep gash in the north face is the result of an attempt by Saladin's son Malek Abdel Aziz to dismantle the pyramid in AD 1186. He gave up after eight months having achieved little. Inside, a hall descends from the entrance into a passageway, which in turn leads into a small chamber and a group of rooms. There is nothing noteworthy about the interior, but at the very least you can have the thrill of exploring a seldom-visited site. Outside are the excavated remains of Menkaure's funerary temple and, further east, the ruins of his valley temple, still lying beneath the sand.

The Sphinx

Legends and superstitions abound about the Sphinx and the mystery surrounding its long-forgotten purpose is almost as intriguing as its appearance. English playwright Alan Bennett, however, was disappointed, noting in his diary, 'The Sphinx, like a personality seen on TV and then met in the flesh, is smaller than one had imagined'.

Known in Arabic as Abu al-Hol (Father of Terror), the feline man was called the Sphinx by the ancient Greeks because it resembled the mythical winged monster with a woman's head and lion's body who set riddles and killed anyone unable to answer them.

Carved from the natural bedrock at the bottom of the causeway to Khafre's pyramid, a recent geological and archaeological survey has shown that the Sphinx was most likely to have been carved during this particular pharaoh's reign, and it probably portrays his features, framed by the striped 'nemes' headcloth only worn by royal personages.

As is clear from the accounts of early Arab travellers, the nose was hammered off sometime between the 11th and 15th centuries, although some still like to blame Napoleon for the deed. Part of the fallen beard was carted off by 19th-century adventurers and is now on display in the British Museum in London.

These days the Sphinx has potentially greater problems than its ordinance-inflicted injuries of the past. It's suffering the stone equivalent of cancer and is being eaten away from the inside. By what, the experts don't quite know – pollution and rising ground water are the two likeliest diagnoses. A succession of restoration attempts were made throughout the 20th century, several of which disastrously sped up the decay rather than halting it. The Sphinx's shiny white paws are the result of the most recent effort.

Other Sites

Tomb of Khenthawes This rarely visited but imposing structure, opposite the Great Pyramid and south of Khafre's causeway, is the tomb of the powerful daughter of Menkaure. The tomb is a rectangular building cut into a small hill. You can go down a corridor at the back of the chapel room to the burial chambers, but the descent is a bit hazardous.

Cemeteries Private cemeteries with several rows of tombs are organised around the Pyramids in a grid pattern. Most of the tombs are closed to the public but those of Qar, Idu and Queen Meresankh III, in the

LEE FOSTER

EDDIE GERALD

RUSSELL MOUNTFORD

SARA-JANE CLELAND

Cairo is a fascinating mix of the modern and traditional, from its towering skyscrapers (top) and colourful billboards (middle left), to its bustling souqs (middle right) and street markets (bottom).

SARA-JANE CLELAND

JOHN BORTHWICK

CHRISTOPHER WOOD

BRETT SHEARER

Islamic Cairo has a character all of its own, with its winding, narrow streets and a skyline dominated by minarets and domes (top). Visitors can wander for days, exploring treasures such as the Mosque of Mohammed Ali (middle & bottom right) and the Madrassa & Mausoleum of Barquq (bottom left).

eastern cemetery, are accessible, although it's sometimes difficult to find the guard who has the keys.

The Tomb of Iasen, in the western cemetery, contains interesting inscriptions and wall paintings that present a glimpse of daily life during the Old Kingdom.

Sound & Light Show

The Sphinx takes the role of the narrator in this show, which is a little cheesy but worth attending to see the Pyramids by starlight. There are two or three shows an evening, each in a different language, and English features every night bar Sunday. Show times are 6.30pm, 7.30pm and 8.30pm in winter (October to May), two hours later in summer (June to September). At the time of research, the schedule was as follows:

day	show 1	show 2	show 3
Monday	English	French	
Tuesday	English	Italian	French
Wednesday	English	French	
Thursday	Japanese	English	Arabic
Friday	English	French	
Saturday	English	Spanish	
Sunday	Russian	French	German

The viewing terrace is close by the Sphinx, so you need to approach the site through the village of Nazlet as-Samaan. Tickets for the show cost E£33 (no student discounts). Performance times vary during Ramadan. Check the current schedules at W www.soundlight.egypt.com or call ☎ 386 3469.

Getting There & Away

The most comfortable way of getting to the Pyramids is to make use of the No 355/357 service, a big white, air-con bus (with CTA written on the side) that runs from Heliopolis via Midan Tahrir, where it picks up from beside the Egyptian Museum (see the Central Cairo map). There's no bus stand as such but there's usually a crowd to mark the spot, all waiting on various other buses (you should stand across from a sign that reads 'EMS'). Be alert: the bus doesn't automatically stop and you may have to flag it down. It runs every 20 minutes and costs E£2.

Alternatively, you can take a microbus from Midan Abdel Moniem Riad station. These depart from near the Ramses Hilton hotel – there are no signs, just ask for 'Haram' and somebody will point you to the right line of vehicles. The fare is 25pt and you'll be dropped off about 500m short of the Oberoi Mena House hotel (which is also where Nos 355 and 357 terminate).

Taking a taxi from Downtown costs E£15 one way. Or, to avoid the worst of the city centre traffic, take the metro out to the Giza stop (50pt), which lies at the foot of Pyramids Rd, from where a taxi to the Pyramids will cost only E£5.

AROUND THE PYRAMIDS

Kerdassa

Many of the scarves, *galabiyyas* (men's robes), rugs and weavings sold in the bazaars and shops of Cairo are made in this touristy village near Giza. There is one main market street along which you'll find all of the above as well as a hideous collection of stuffed animals such as gazelles, jackals and rabbits. In fact, Kerdassa is almost as well known for its illegal trade in Egyptian wildlife as it is for crafts. The Egyptian Environmental Affairs Agency periodically raids the bazaar to try to halt this.

To get to Kerdassa, head down Pyramids Rd, turn right at the Maryutia Canal, and follow the road for about 5km to the village. The minibus from Midan Tahrir to the Pyramids begins and ends its trips at the junction of the canal and Pyramids Rd, and a local microbus does the stretch along the canal for 25pt. You can also get bus No 116 from Midan Giza all the way to Kerdassa, the trip takes 20 minutes and costs 25pt.

Wissa Wassef Art Centre

This tranquil centre *(☎ 385 0746, Saqqara Rd, Harraniyya; admission free; open 9am-7pm daily)* is next to the Motel Salma in Harraniyya, on Saqqara Rd, about 4km south of Pyramids Rd. It specialises in woollen and cotton tapestries, as well as batiks and ceramics, and features a museum, workshops and sales gallery. The indigenous architecture of the complex is also very attractive. A visit here is best combined with a trip out to the archaeological site of Saqqara.

If you particularly want to see tapestries being woven, don't come on Friday when the workshops are closed. To get here, take a microbus for Abu Sir down the Saqqara Rd from Pyramids Rd. It's the same stop as for the Motel Salma.

CENTRAL CAIRO

Many travellers begin their Egyptian experience in the vicinity of Midan Tahrir and Talaat Harb. It's the bustling, noisy centre of Cairo where you'll find an amazing variety of shops as well as most of the budget hotels and eating places, banks, travel agencies and cinemas.

Midan Tahrir & Around

Midan Tahrir (Liberation Square) is the fulcrum of modern Cairo. All the city's main roads converge here, resulting in a round-the-clock jam of traffic and pedestrians. But the square is one of the few spaces that isn't tightly hemmed in by buildings or choked by overpasses, making it an excellent spot to stand back, have a look around and orient yourself.

One of the best buildings to use as a location aid is the **Nile Hilton**, the distinctive blue-and-white slab that stands between Midan Tahrir and the Nile. When it was built in 1959 it was the first modern hotel in Cairo, replacing a former British Army barracks. Immediately to the north of the Nile Hilton is the dusky pink neoclassical bulk of the **Egyptian Museum** (see the special section in this chapter), while south is the drab **Arab League Building**, occasional gathering place of the leaders of the Arab world.

Continuing around Midan Tahrir anticlockwise, the big white building is Cairo's monstrous, Kafkaesque monument to bureaucracy, the **Mogamma**, home to 18,000 semisomnolent civil servants – this is where you come for visa extensions. If the Mogamma is a symbol of Egypt's recent socialist-inspired past, then the next building around, across four-lane Qasr al-Ainy, is the beacon for the private-initiative-led future: The **American University in Cairo** (AUC) is the university of choice for the sons and daughters of Cairo's moneyed classes. The campus has an attractive courtyard and a good bookshop. Entrance (ID required, your passport will do) is via the gate on Mohammed Mahmoud, opposite the enterprisingly sited McDonald's.

About 50m north of the AUC is the **Ali Baba Cafeteria** which, until the 1994 knife attack that almost killed him, was a regular morning stop for Nobel Prize-winning author Naguib Mahfouz. It serves chilled Stella beer and the tables beside the window on the upper floor are a good place to watch the goings-on outside.

The buildings around Midan Tahir then break for Sharia Tahrir, which leads 250m east to a busy square (Midan Falaki) with a bus station in the middle. Continuing east brings you to Midan al-Gomhuriyya (Square of the Republic), an empty plaza skirted by speeding traffic. The great building to the east, dominating the square, is the Abdeen Palace, former residence of the rulers of Egypt.

Abdeen Palace Commissioned by the khedive Ismail and designed by the French architect Rosseau, the Abdeen Palace *(Mathaf Abdeen; ☎ 391 0042, Sharia al-Gamaa; Metro: Mohammed Naguib; admission E£10; open 9am-3pm Sat-Thur)* was started in 1863 and completed, 500 rooms later, in 1874. It served as the occasional residence of royalty until the abolition of the monarchy in 1952, when Abdeen became the presidential palace. The presidents have since moved out (Mubarak prefers Uruba Palace up in Heliopolis) and parts of the palace are now open to the public as a museum. Unfortunately, all the glitzy royal chambers are out of bounds and what you get to see instead is a series of halls filled with a vast array of weaponry, ranging from ceremonial daggers to howitzers. One for the boys.

Downtown

Downtown is the commercial heart of Cairo: its streets are packed with glitzy shops and above them is a beehive of countless thousands of small, dusty businesses. Talaat Harb and Qasr el-Nil are the two main streets and they intersect at **Midan Talaat Harb**, marked by a tarboosh-wearing statue of Mr Harb, founder of the National Bank. On the midan is **Groppi's**, once the most celebrated patisserie and tearoom this side of the Mediterranean. During the 1920s attendance at Groppi's society functions and nonstop concert dances was *de rigeur* for Cairo's smart set. The only glitter left today is in the beautiful mosaics around the doorway.

Just to the south of the midan, on Talaat Harb, **Cafe Riche** used to be a hangout for Egyptian writers and intellectuals. It's claimed Nasser met with his cronies here while planning the 1952 Revolution. Closed all through the 1990s, the Riche reopened in 2000 as an attractive cafe/restaurant that trades as much on nostalgia as on the quality of its food (see Places to Eat).

North of the midan, Qasr el-Nil is devoted to shops selling a drag queen's delight of footwear, but the street is redeemed by some particularly fine architecture, notably the **Italian Insurance building** on the corner of Qasr el-Nil and Sharia Sherifeen as well as the **Cosmopolitan Hotel** (see Places to Stay), hidden away just a block to the south of Qasr el-Nil. Talaat Harb is graced by the **Cinema Metro** building, a great 1930s movie palace which when it opened (with *Gone With The Wind*) also had a Ford showroom and a diner. That diner is now the Excelsior restaurant; the food isn't great these days but they serve cold Stella and the view from the large windows is more entertaining than whatever piece of Hollywood junk is being screened next door.

One block east of the Excelsior along Sharia Adly, the building that looks like it strayed from the Tomb Raider movie set, is the **Shar Hashamaim Synagogue**, the most visible testament to Cairo's once thriving Jewish community. The synagogue can be visited on Saturday, the Jewish holy day of Shabbat, when the caretaker opens up on the off chance there'll be somebody coming by to pray.

A block north of Adly is Sharia 26th of July, named for the date of abdication of Egypt's last king, Farouk. The street's major attraction as far as Cairenes are concerned is **El-Abd bakery** (corner of Sherif), which is packed out morning to midnight with folk jostling for cakes, sweets and the best pastries in town (there's a branch on Talaat Harb). Smoke-filled **Sharia Ezbekiyya**, one block north, is *the* street for kebabs. The pedestrianised **Sharia Alfy** is Downtown's nightlife centre, with several seedy bars, some dubious belly-dancing joints and a good 24-hour eating place in the Akher Sa'a (see Budget Dining in Places to Eat). The nearby **Tawfiqiyya Souq** is a late night fruit and vegetable market with several cheap eating places and a couple of good coffeehouses in the surrounding alleyways.

Heading east along Sharia 26th of July leads to **Midan Opera**, named for an opera house that burnt down in 1971 and now more notable for a great multistorey car park. Beyond the car park is Midan Ataba.

Midan Ataba This is the chaotic transition zone where the 'modern European' Cairo runs up against the old medieval Cairo of Saladin, the Mamluks and Ottomans. Normally it's one big bazaar, with all its corners filled with traders and hawkers, but for the past couple of years it's been more like one massive building site as engineers construct a tunnel meant to take cars under Islamic Cairo. In the south-west corner stands the domed **main post office**, with a pretty courtyard and an attached **Postal Museum** *(☎ 391 0011, 55 Abdel Khalek Sarwat, Midan Ataba; Metro: Ataba; admission 10pt; open 9am-1pm Sat-Thur)* with a vast collection of commemorative stamps and displays on the history of Egypt's postal service.

On the opposite side of Ataba, behind the big white theatre, is the **Ezbekiyya book market** (see Information earlier in this chapter) and north beyond that Midan Khazindar, where you should take a look in **Sednaoui**, one of Cairo's famed department stores from the early 20th century. Now state-owned and full of tat, the three-storey glass atrium interior remains glorious. Running north from Khazindar is **Sharia Clot Bey** (also known as Sharia Khulud) named after a French

CENTRAL CAIRO

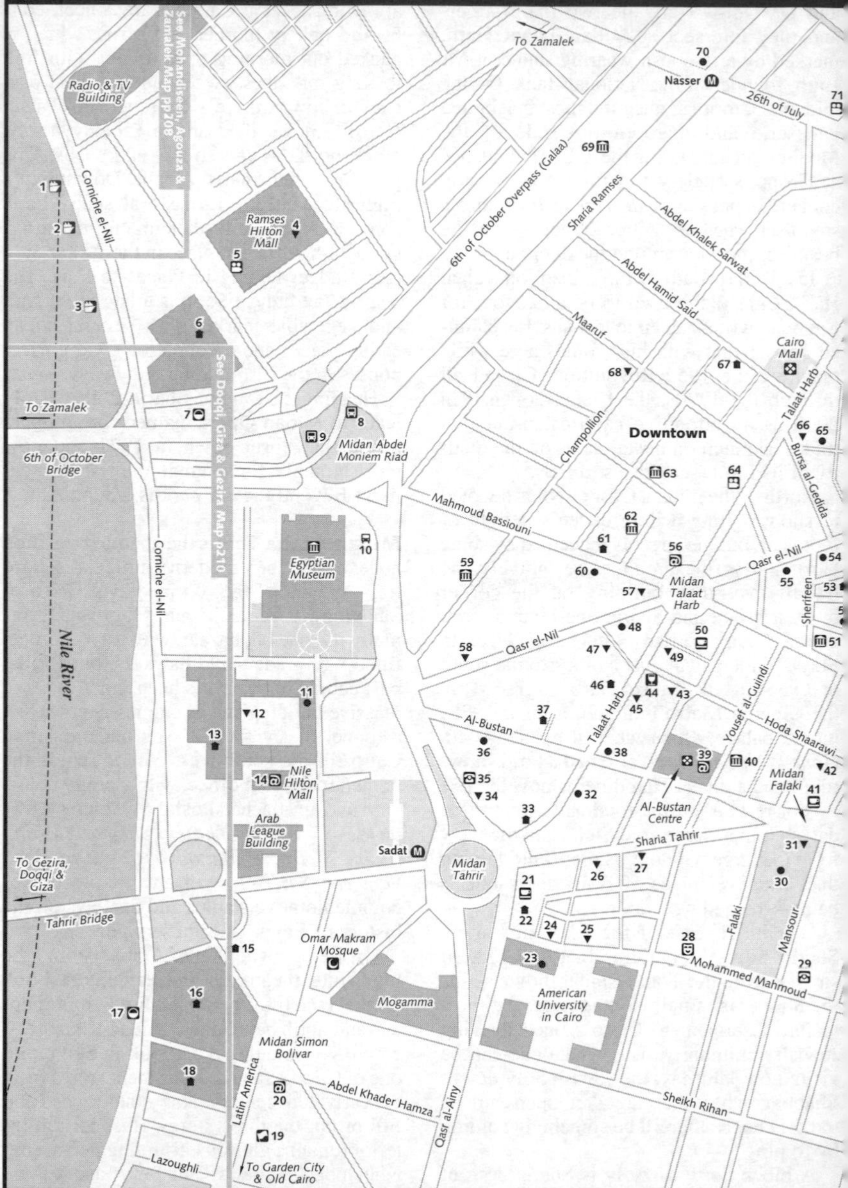

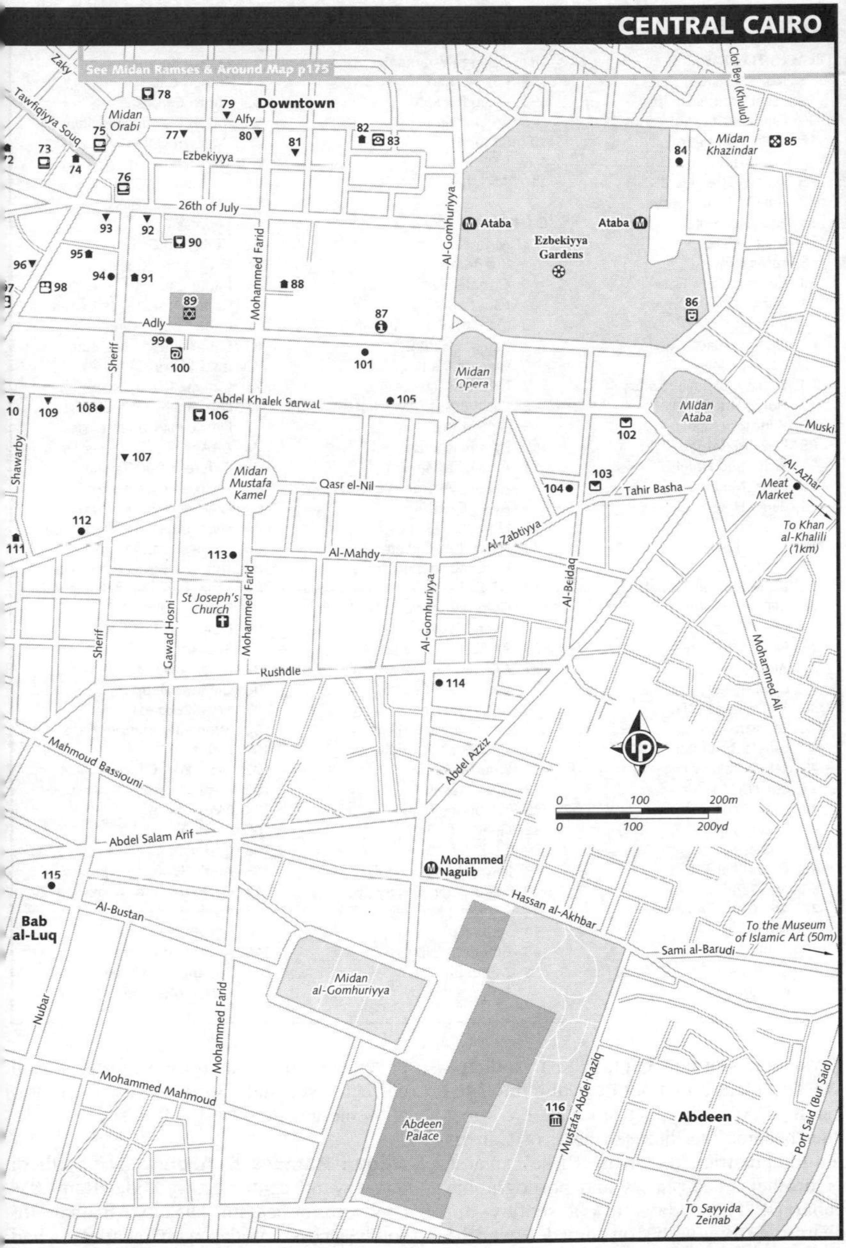
CENTRAL CAIRO
See Midan Ramses & Around Map p175
Zaky
Tawfiqiyya Souq
Midan Orabi
Downtown
Alfy
Ezbekiyya
26th of July
Clot Bey (Khulud)
Midan Khazindar
Al-Gomhuriyya
Ataba
Ataba
Ezbekiyya Gardens
Mohammed Farid
Adly
Sherif
Midan Opera
Abdel Khalek Sarwat
Midan Ataba
Muski
Al-Azhar
Meat Market
To Khan al-Khalili (1km)
Shawarby
Midan Mustafa Kamel
Qasr el-Nil
Tahir Basha
Al-Zabtiyya
Al-Mahdy
Al-Beidaq
St Joseph's Church
Gawad Hosni
Rushdie
Mohammed Ali
Abdel Azziz
Mahmoud Bassiouni
Abdel Salam Arif
Mohammed Naguib
Hassan al-Akhbar
Al-Bustan
Bab al-Luq
To the Museum of Islamic Art (50m)
Sami al-Barudi
Midan al-Gomhuriyya
Nubar
Mohammed Mahmoud
Abdeen Palace
Mustafa Abdel Raziq
Abdeen
Port Said (Bur Said)
To Sayyida Zeinab
0
100
200m
0
100
200yd
72
73
74
75
76
77
78
79
80
81
82
83
84
85
86
87
88
89
90
91
92
93
94
95
96
97
98
99
100
101
102
103
104
105
106
107
108
109
110
111
112
113
114
115
116

CENTRAL CAIRO

PLACES TO STAY
6 Ramses Hilton; Hertz
13 Nile Hilton; Cafe Ibis
15 Garden City House Hotel
16 Semiramis Inter-Continental; Hertz
18 Helnan Shepheard's
22 Ismailia House Hotel
33 New Sun Hotel
37 Magic Hotel
46 Lotus Hotel
53 Cosmopolitan Hotel
61 Dahab Hotel; Onyx Internet Cafe
67 Odeon Palace Hotel
72 Carlton Hotel
74 Sultan Hotel I-III; Safary Hotel; Hotel Venice
82 Windsor Hotel
88 Pension Roma
91 Richmond Hotel
95 Hotel Minerva
111 Berlin Hotel

PLACES TO EAT
4 McDonald's
12 Da Mario; Mc Donald's
24 KFC; Pizza Hut
25 McDonald's
26 Fatatri at-Tahrir
27 At-Tahrir
31 Lux Kushari
34 McDonald's, KFC
42 Le Bistro
43 Felfela Restaurant
45 Felfela Takeaway
47 Estoril
49 Cafe Riche
57 Groppi's
58 Arabesque
66 El-Abd Bakery
68 Abu Tarek
77 Alfy Bey; Shererazad Nightclub
79 Akher Sa'a
80 International Public Meal Kushari
81 Peking Restaurant
92 Lux Kushari
93 El-Abd Bakery
96 McDonald's
107 Simonds
109 KFC
110 At-Tahrir

OTHER
1 Maspero River Bus Terminal
2 Qanater Ferries (Government)
3 Qanater Ferries (Private)
5 Ramses Hilton Cinema I & II
7 Pyramids Services
8 Local Buses & Minibuses
9 Airport Bus
10 Pyramids' Bus
11 Air Malta; Air Sinai; Alitalia; American Express; Avis ; EgyptAir; Ethiopian Airlines
14 Nile Hilton Cybercafe
17 Felucca Mooring Point
19 US Embassy & Cultural Centre
20 InternetEgypt
21 Ali Baba Cafeteria
23 American University of Cairo Book Store
28 American University in Cairo Wallace Theatre
29 Telephone Centrale
30 Souq Mansour
32 Masr Travel
35 Telephone Centrale
36 Goethe Institut
38 EgyptAir
39 St@rnet Cyber Cafe
40 Cairo-Berlin Gallery
41 Cafeteria Horreyya
44 Stella Bar
48 American Express
50 Zahret al-Bustan Coffeehouse
51 Espace Karim-Francis Gallery
52 Photo Centre
54 Italian Insurance Building
55 Western Union Money Transfer
56 4U Internet Cafe
59 Mashrabia Gallery
60 Thomas Cook
62 Atelier du Caire
63 Townhouse Gallery
64 Radio Cinema
65 Centre Français de Culture et de Cooperation
69 Entomological Museum
70 Isaaf Pharmacy
71 Cinema Rivoli
73 Ash-Shams Coffeehouse
75 Leyaleena Coffeehouse
76 Al-Andalus Coffeehouse
78 Cafeteria Port Tawfiq
83 Telephone Centrale
84 Ezbekiyya Book Market
85 Sednaoui Department Store
86 Puppet Theatre
87 Tourist Information Office
89 Shar Hashamaim Synagogue
90 Palmyra Nightclub
94 Lehnert & Landrock Bookshop
97 Cinema Miami
98 Cinema Metro
99 Kodak Express
100 Buonanno Internet Cafe
101 EgyptAir
102 Main Post Office
103 Poste Restante
104 EMS Office
105 Senouhi
106 Cap d'Or
108 Anglo-Eastern Pharmacy
112 Livres d'France Bookshop
113 Osiris Auction House
114 Egypt Free Shop
115 Antar Photostore
116 Entrance to Abdeen Palace Museum

physician, Antoine Clot, who introduced Western ideas about public health into Mohammed Ali's Egypt. Ironically, the street later became the diseased heart of Cairo's red-light district, known as 'Birka'; an area of brothels, peepshows and pornographic cabarets. These days it's a shabby but charming street with stone arcades over the pavements sheltering dozens of sepia-toned coffeehouses and eating places. It eventually emerges onto Midan Ramses.

Midan Ramses & Around The northern gateway into central Cairo, Midan Ramses is a byword for bedlam. The city's main north-south access collides with overpasses and numerous arterial roads to swamp the square with an unchoreographed slew of minibuses, buses, taxis and cars. Commuters swarm from the train station to add to the melee.

In the middle of it all stands a Pharaonic-style **Colossus of Ramses II**. The original was discovered near Giza and erected here in 1955 but fears that the constant vibrations of the traffic and choking exhaust emissions were hazardous to the pharaoh's health led to the removal of the ancient statue and it was replaced by the present replica.

Ramses Station (Mahattat Ramses) is an attractive marriage of Islamic style and industrial-age engineering. At its eastern end it houses the **Egyptian National Railways Museum** (☎ *575 3555, Midan Ramses; Metro: Mubarak; admission E£1.50 Mon-Thur E£3 Fri & public holidays; open 8.30am-1pm Tues-Sun)*, which has a beautiful collection of old locomotives, including one built for Empress Eugénie on the occasion of the opening of the Suez Canal.

On the south side of the midan is Cairo's pre-eminent orientation aid, the **Al-Fath Mosque**. Completed in the early 1990s, the mosque's minaret is visible from just about anywhere in central and Islamic Cairo.

MIDAN RAMSES & AROUND

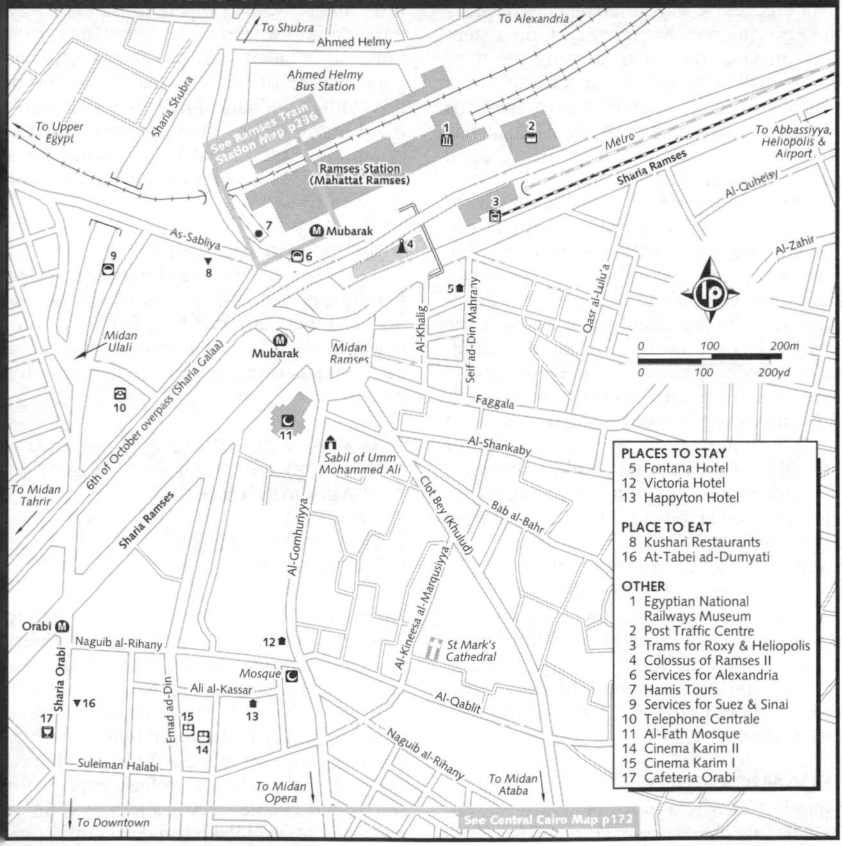

Garden City & Manial

Garden City was developed in the early 1900s along the lines of an English garden suburb. Its curving tree-lined streets were intended to create an air of tranquillity, while the proximity of the UK embassy no doubt provided a reassuring veneer of security. Many of the elegant villas that once characterised the area have fallen prey to quick-buck developers, however, enough grand architecture and palm, rubber and mango trees survive to make a walk through the streets still worthwhile. Alternatively, it's a pleasant walk south from the salmon-pink Semiramis Inter-Continental along the Nile-side Corniche, shaded by trees and cooled by river breezes. A walk of 20 minutes, passing the towering new Meridien Le Caire extension on your right and crossing the third bridge, will bring you to one of Cairo's least visited and most eccentric tourist sites, the **Manial Palace Museum** *(☎ 368 7495, Sharia al-Saray, Manial; admission E£10; open 9am-4.30pm daily).*

The palace was built in the early part of the 20th century as a residence for Prince Mohammed Ali Tawfiq, the uncle of King Farouk, Egypt's last monarch, . Apparently the prince couldn't decide which architectural style he preferred, so he went for the lot: Ottoman, Moorish, Persian and European rococo. Today the palace houses an assortment of collections in five main buildings including Farouk's huge horde of stuffed hunting trophies – not a sight for animal lovers. The largest building contains the prince's collection of manuscripts, clothing, silver objects, furniture, writing implements and other items dating from medieval times to the 19th century. A self-appointed guide likes to show you around this part of the museum, object by object – if you don't want his services let him know. If you don't want to walk to the museum, take a taxi from around Midan Tahrir (which should cost E£2.50); ask to go to 'Al-Mathaf al-Manial'.

ISLAMIC CAIRO

Islamic Cairo is almost another city altogether. Like Alice passing through her looking glass, as the visitor heads east from Midan Ataba all the familiar trappings of the modern world drop away, to be replaced by chaos and curiosities of a completely different nature.

The term Islamic Cairo is a bit of a misnomer, as the area is no more or less Islamic than most other parts of the city, but maybe the profusion of minarets on the skyline gives the impression of piety. Unchanged over the centuries to an astonishing degree, Islamic Cairo's neighbourhoods are full of twisting alleyways so narrow that the houses seem to touch at the top. Splendid mosques and crushes of medieval facades hedge in rutted streets on which little Suzuki vans compete for right of way with donkeys, carts and merchants with impossibly laden barrows. The sweet, pungent aromas of turmeric, basil and cumin mix with the odours of livestock and petrol. It's a mazelike area that is completely disorientating, the casual visitor easily loses not just any sense of direction but also any sense of time.

Visiting Islamic Cairo

With more than 800 listed monuments and few signposts or other concessions to the visitor, Islamic Cairo can be a fairly daunting place. We've divided it into six segments, each with its own map, and each making for a half-day's outing:

1. Al-Azhar & Khan al-Khalili	page 177
2. North of Khan al-Khalili	page 179
3. Al-Azhar to the Citadel	page 195
4. The Citadel	page 198
5. The Citadel to Ibn Tulun	page 200
6. Northern Cemetery	page 202

Appropriate dress is necessary for visiting this part of Cairo – legs and shoulders should be decently covered, otherwise custodians may baulk at allowing you inside mosques. Shoes have to be taken off before entering prayer halls so it might be wise to come in footwear that can be easily slipped off and on, but is also robust enough for rutted and rubble-strewn alleyways. Since a visiting official Pakistani delegation com-

Islamic Cairo Highlights

Exploring the whole of Islamic Cairo would take days, if not weeks, but if time is tight then following are the monuments and experiences not to be missed:

- Visit Al-Azhar Mosque, the keystone of Islam in Egypt, which has been a mosque and university for a thousand years.
- Find out how elegant and sophisticated life in 18th-century Cairo could be with a visit to Beit Suhaymi.
- Marvel at the Mosque of Qaitbey, the jewel of Mamluk architecture.
- Check out the Gayer-Anderson Museum, Cairo's quirkiest, most atmospheric museum and a set for Hollywood adventures.
- Visit Fishawi's Coffeehouse, even if it's the only *ahwa* (coffeehouse) you go to.

plained about having to pay money to get into mosques (they were Muslims), many admission charges have been dropped. However, you will be expected to tip guardians and caretakers, so carry lots of small change; E£2 is sufficient.

Also note that any given opening times should be interpreted as a rough guide only; caretakers are usually around from 9am until early evening but they follow their own whims. Most mosques are closed to visitors during prayer times.

If this whets your appetite you can find out much more in *Islamic Monuments in Cairo: A Practical Guide* published by the AUC Press (E£40). The Society for the Preservation of the Architectural Resources of Egypt (Spare) also puts out four semi-pictorial maps that are excellent tools for exploration; all are available from most Cairo bookshops.

Getting to Islamic Cairo Islamic Cairo covers a vast area, but the heart of it is Al-Azhar and Khan al-Khalili, which are easily reached from central Cairo. By foot, head for Midan Ataba then bear east along Sharia al-Azhar or Muski (see Sharia Muski later). Alternatively, it's a short taxi ride; ask for 'Al-Hussein' – the name of both the midan and the mosque at the mouth of the bazaar. The fare should be no more than E£3.50 from Downtown. Get out at the Al-Azhar mosque where a pedestrian subway burrows under the busy road to surface just off Midan Hussein. Almost all of the places we describe in the following pages can be reached from this point.

1. Al-Azhar & Khan al-Khalili

By far the best place to start becoming acquainted with Islamic Cairo is the area around the great bazaar, Khan al-Khalili. It's a place that panders perfectly to preconceptions of the Orient.

Al-Azhar Mosque Before diving into the bazaar, it is worth taking time out to visit one of Cairo's most historic institutions. Founded in AD 970, Al-Azhar *(Sharia al-Azhar; admission free; open 24 hrs daily)* is not only one of Cairo's earliest mosques, it's also the world's oldest surviving university. At one time it was the pre-eminent centre of learning, drawing scholars from Europe as well as from all over the Arab world. It continues to play a dominant role in Egyptian theological life to this day, with the Sheikh of al-Azhar being the country's ultimate religious authority. However, students are no longer taught in the mosque's courtyard; they attend one of nine campuses around the country.

Architecturally the mosque is a mixture of styles, the result of frequent enlargements over its thousand-year history. The central courtyard is the earliest part, while from south to north, the three minarets date from the 14th, 15th and 16th centuries. The tomb chamber, through a doorway on the left just inside the entrance, has a beautiful mihrab (niche indicating the direction of Mecca) and should not be missed.

Leaving the mosque and turning left and then left again brings you into an alley squeezed between the southern wall of Al-Azhar and a row of tiny shops housed in the vaults of a 15th-century merchants' building. At the top of this road (see the Al-Azhar to the Citadel map) is **Beit Zeinab al-Khatoun** *(House of Zeinab Khatoun;*

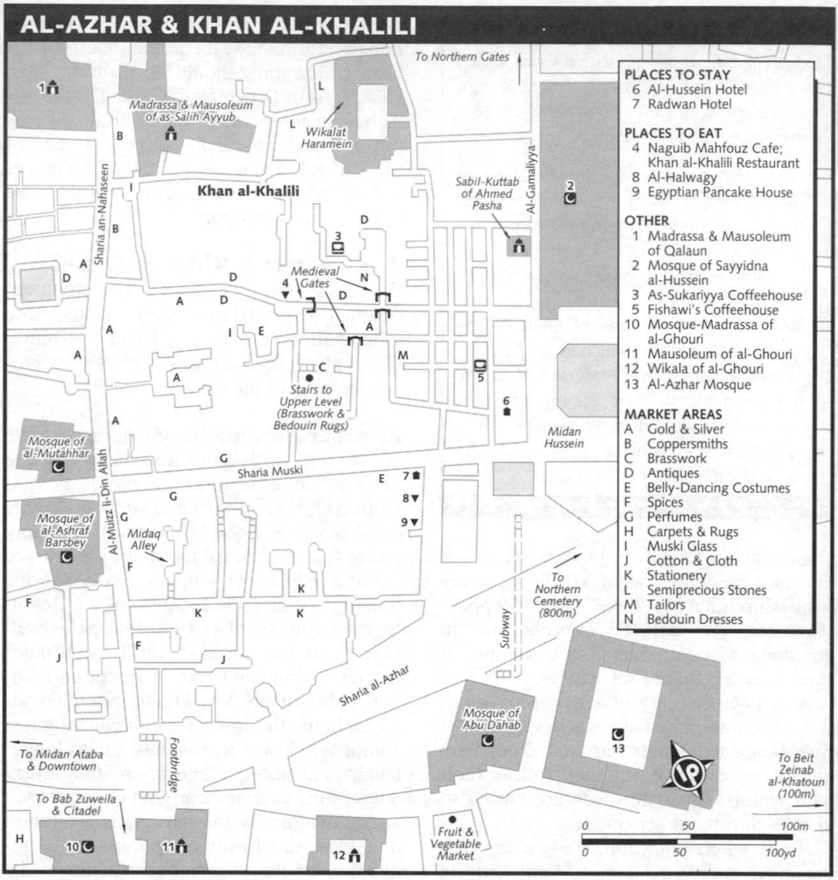

☎ *735 7001, Sharia al-Sheikh Mohammed Abdo; admission E£10; open 9am-9pm daily)*, a restored Ottoman-era house that now serves as a cultural centre and sometime gallery. Across a small garden is **Beit al-Harrawi** *(Harrawi House;* ☎ *735 7001, Sharia al-Sheikh Mohammed Abdo; admission E£10; open 9am-9pm daily)*, another fine piece of 18th-century vernacular architecture, but too sparse inside to really warrant the admission charge.

Midan Hussein This was one of the main squares of medieval Cairo, stretching between the two highly venerated mosques of Al-Azhar to the south and Sayyidna al-Hussein to the north. It's still an important space today, particularly at feast times, on Ramadan evenings, and during the *moulids* (religious festivals) of Al-Hussein and An-Nabi Mohammed (see the boxed text 'The Moulid' in the Facts for the Visitor chapter). At these times the midan is filled with vast crowds, bright lights and loud music, and the partying goes on until the early hours of the morning.

On the northern side, the **Mosque of Sayyidna al-Hussein** is one of the most sacred Islamic sites in Egypt. It contains a shrine under which the head of Ibn al-Hussein, grandson of the Prophet, is reputedly buried. Because of the importance of this holy relic, non-Muslims are not allowed inside the mosque. The building itself dates only from about 1870 (it replaces an earlier 12th-century mosque) and is not of great interest to travellers.

Khan al-Khalili Jaundiced travellers have been known to glibly dismiss Khan al-Khalili as a tourist trap, and it's true the tour bus-pleasing, travellers cheque-pulling element is well and truly present. But generations of Cairenes have lived their lives in these narrow, canvas-covered alleys, plying their trades since the founding of the Khan in the 14th century – the buying and selling did not begin with the arrival of the first tour group.

Today the Khan is an immense conglomeration of markets and shops (many of which are closed on Sunday), where it's possible to find everything from blankets and soap powder to books of magic spells and precious stones – as well as, of course, plenty of stuffed camels and alabaster pyramids. The clumsy 'Hey mister, look for free' touts aside, the merchants of Khan al-Khalili are some of the greatest salespeople and smooth talkers you will ever meet. Almost anything can be bought in the Khan, and if one merchant doesn't have what you're looking for, then he'll find somebody who does (for information on what's sold where within Khan al-Khalili, see the Al-Azhar & Khan al-Khalili map).

There are few specific things to see in the Khan but a stop off at **Fishawi's Coffeehouse** is a must. Hung with huge, ornately framed mirrors and packed day and night, it claims to have been open 24 hours a day for the last 200 years (which is not quite true because the place is closed mornings during the month of Ramadan, but it is indisputably old and, the holy month aside, it is usually open around the clock). Entertainment comes in the form of roaming salesmen, women and children who hawk wallets, cigarette lighters in the form of pistols, canes with carved tops, sheesha-style cigarette holders, and packet after packet after packet of Kleenex tissues. The coffeehouse is easily found: it fills a narrow alleyway with rickety tables and chairs just one block in off Midan Hussein.

Sharia Muski A congested market street, Sharia Muski runs parallel to Sharia al-Azhar from Midan Hussein, all the way west to Midan Ataba on the edge of Downtown. It is less overtly 'Oriental' than Khan al-Khalili but all the more vivid and boisterous for it. The goods on sale range from plastic furniture and party toys to items like wedding dresses and great mounds of bucket-sized bras at its western end.

2. North of Khan al-Khalili

From Midan Hussein take the road that leads up along the western side of Al-Hussein Mosque. Stick to it as it doglegs left and enters the district known as **Gamaliyya**. Sharia al-Gamaliyya, the main street you are following, was the second most important of medieval Cairo's thoroughfares. Today, it has the appearance of a back alley, rutted and unsealed, barely squeezing between the buildings. These buildings include some fine clusters of Mamluk-era mosques and madrassas, though many of them are partly obscured by forests of crude wooden scaffolding, there to shore up damage inflicted by the 1992 earthquake. Tragically, one of the district's most impressive monuments, the Musafirkhanah Palace, survived the earthquake only to be burnt to the ground in 1998.

Easily identified by its blindingly white new stone, the **Mosque of Gamal ad-Din** (1408) is one of the monuments that has been subject to the dubious attentions of the restorers (see the boxed text 'Fatimidland' later in this chapter). It's raised above a row of shops, the rent from which would have paid for the mosque's upkeep. Next door is the **Wikala of Bazara** *(Sharia al-Tombakshiyya, Gamaliyya; admission E£10; open 9am-7pm daily)*. A *wikala* (also called a caravanserai) is a medieval merchants' hostel; the traders slept in the upper rooms while the ground-floor rooms around the courtyard were used for the storage of goods and for stabling animals. The gates of the wikala were locked at night to protect the merchandise. In Ottoman times Cairo had more than 360 wikalas but now less than 20 remain. Until very recently the Wikala of Bazara lay in ruins but in recent years it has been almost completely rebuilt from scratch, opening to the public in early 2001. While undoubtedly attractive, there's little to see beyond a succession of small, empty rooms. The place cries out to be put to use and would make a fantastic boutique hotel.

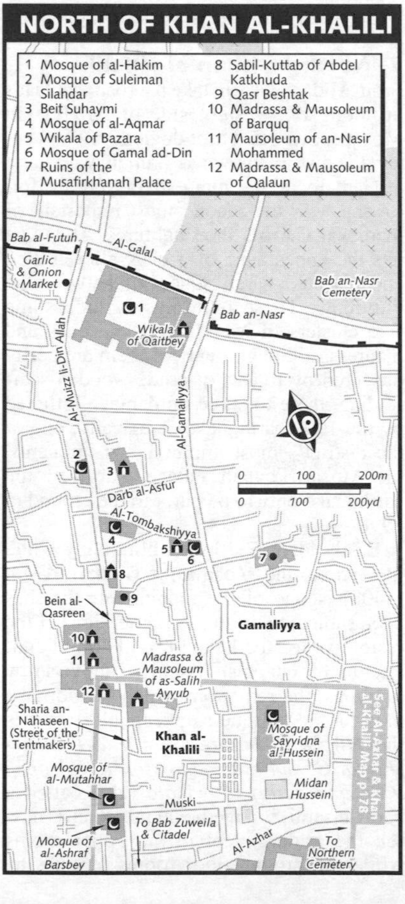

The Northern Walls & Gates The square-towered Bab an-Nasr (Gate of Victory) and the rounded Bab al-Futuh (Gate of Conquests) were built in 1087 as the two main northern entrances to the walled Fatimid city of Al-Qahira. Walk along the outside and you'll see what a hugely imposing bit of military architecture the whole thing is. In the past, visitors were able to get access to the top of the walls and explore inside the gates via the roof of the neighbouring Mosque of al-Hakim, but on our last visit this was no longer the case. Perhaps once restoration work has finished in the vicinity the walls may be open again and you can look for the inscriptions above the doorways which read 'Tour Lascalle' and 'Tour Milhaud', evidence that Napoleon's troops of occupation were once garrisoned here. You'll also be able to find the carved animals and Pharaonic figures that bear evidence that stone for Al-Qahira's fortifications was scavenged from the ruins of the ancient Egyptian city of Memphis.

Mosque of al-Hakim One of Cairo's older mosques, this place is as notable for its founder as its architecture. Al-Hakim was only 11 years old when his father died and he became the third Fatimid ruler of Egypt. His tutor nicknamed him 'Little Lizard' because of his frightening looks and behaviour. Hakim later got his revenge by having the tutor murdered. During his 24-year reign those nearest to him were in constant fear for their lives. A victorious general rushing unannounced into the royal apartments was confronted by a bloodied Hakim standing over a disembowelled page boy. The general was beheaded.

Hakim took a great interest in the affairs of his people and would patrol the city's streets on a donkey called Moon. He received petitions and complaints from the city folk and punished dishonest merchants by having them sodomised by a large black servant who accompanied him for this purpose. His death was as bizarre as his life. On one of his solitary nocturnal jaunts on Moon up onto the Muqattam Hills, Hakim disappeared and his body was never found.

To one of his followers, a man called Al-Darizy, this was proof of Hakim's divine nature. Al-Darizy travelled widely preaching and founded the sect of the Druze that continues to this day.

Completed in 1010, Hakim's mosque has rarely been used as a place of worship, instead it has been used as a prison to hold Crusaders, as a stable, as a warehouse by Napoleon, while Nasser made it into a boys' school. Most fittingly of all, it also served for a time as a madhouse.

Sharia al-Muizz li-Din Allah Al-Muizz li-Din (as it's often shortened to), which takes its name from the Fatimid caliph who conquered Cairo in AD 969, is the former grand thoroughfare of medieval Cairo. It was the city's main shopping street and a 15th-century description tells us that storytellers and entertainers, as well as stalls serving cooked food were to be found along its length. The garlic and onion market beside Al-Hakim's mosque was a slave market until the middle of the 19th century.

Heading south, the produce gives way to a variety of small places selling metal-worked accoutrements for coffeehouses and fuul vendors: *sheeshas* (water pipes), braziers and big, pear-shaped cooking pots. On the right, after about 200m, is the **Mosque of Suleiman Silahdar**, built comparatively late, in 1839 during the reign of Mohammed Ali and distinguished by its drain-pipe-thin minaret.

Beit Suhaymi Tucked down a small white-washed alley off Sharia al-Muizz li-Din Allah, Beit Suhaymi *(Darb al-Asfur; admission E£20; open 8am-8pm daily)* is Islamic Cairo's finest example of the traditional family mansion built throughout the

Fatimidland

Unesco, the cultural wing of the United Nations, includes Islamic Cairo on its select 'World Heritage list', a list that also includes tourist hotspots such as the Pyramids, the Great Wall of China, and Venice. But the shopping bazaar area of Khan al-Khalili aside, Islamic Cairo is an area that sees relatively few visitors. Why? Because unlike historic districts elsewhere in the world, which have been preserved, sterilised, and pickled, existing seemingly to provide sales opportunities for fast food outlets, Islamic Cairo has in the past made few concessions to the visitor. It could hardly do so given that it's home to a dense 21st-century population still living in what are essentially medieval quarters. As a consequence, Islamic Cairo retains a vital human presence that lifts it above being more than a mere open-air museum.

Recently, however, the attentions of Egypt's Ministry of Culture have turned to this neglected area. At the time of writing no less than 60 conservation projects are being carried out in the core of the medieval city, an area now officially designated 'Fatimid Cairo' by authorities worried that the word 'Islamic' (as in Islamic Cairo) might frighten away the tour buses. Results of the work can most clearly be seen around Beit Suhaymi, where the surrounding buildings and alley now positively gleam. If all goes to plan, the 21st-century version of Islamic Cairo, sorry, Fatimid Cairo, should see record numbers of visitors flocking to its streets. But it's a scheme not without controversy. For a start, the actual treatment of the monuments has been criticised as extreme – for example, the Northern Walls, which aren't so much being restored as rebuilt from scratch. There's also the question of reintegration: previously restored structures have remained empty and unused, quickly sliding back into disrepair. Ultimately, there is the worry that the upgrading, refacing and repackaging may result in the removal of the people and activities that give character to the area. In fact, just such a plan to relocate 50,000 residents elsewhere has already been unveiled. Should this go ahead, critics say, the authorities might be advised to consider a further rebranding, not Fatimid Cairo but 'Fatimidland', a more suitable name for what sounds suspiciously like the process of turning a living neighbourhood into a theme park.

city from Mamluk times to the 19th century. The *beit* (or house) presents a typically blank facade to the street but once through the tunnel-like entrance you emerge into a beautiful inner courtyard. Guests were received in an impressive reception room, or *qa'a*, left off the courtyard, graced with a polychrome marble fountain inset in the floor and a high, painted wooden ceiling. Upstairs are the family quarters, with the wooden-lattice windows known as *mashrabiyya*, which allowed the women to observe the goings on below without being seen themselves. The rooms are kept cool by devices called *malqaf*, angled wind catchers on the roof that direct the prevailing northerly breezes down into the building. The admission fee may seem a little steep but if you only shell out for one Islamic monument, then this should be it.

Back on Al-Muizz li-Din, just 50m south of the junction with Darb al-Asfar, is the petite **Mosque of al-Aqmar** (the Moonlit). Built in 1125 by one of the last Fatimid caliphs, it's important in terms of Cairo's architectural development because it's the oldest stone-facaded mosque in Egypt. Here, for the first time, appear several features that were to become part of the mosque builders' essential vocabulary: the stalactite carving; and the ribbing in the hooded arch.

Sabil-Kuttab of Abdel Katkhuda A *sabil* is a public fountain or tap from which passers-by can take a drink, and a *kuttab* is a Quranic school. So, a sabil-kuttab provides the two things commended by the Prophet: water for the thirsty and spiritual enlightenment for the ignorant. The building of a sabil-kuttab was a popular way for wealthy people to atone for their sins. This particular example was built in 1744 by a wealthy emir well known for his debauched behaviour. It has some nice ceramic work inside and it's worth finding the caretaker who has the key. He sits in the **Qasr Beshtak** (Beshtak Palace), which is found down the little alley that runs to the east (there's usually an orange seller on the corner), and right through the archway at the bottom. The ticket for the sabil-kuttab is E£6, which includes admission to the palace – largely ruined but with splendid rooftop views from the top floor.

Bein al-Qasreen The part of Al-Muizz li-Din immediately south of the sabil-kuttab is known as Bein al-Qasreen, which translates as 'Between the Palaces', a reference to two great royal complexes that flanked the street here during the Fatimid era. The palaces fell into ruin following the fall of the Fatimids, but Bein al-Qasreen remained a great public space and a favourite building place for subsequent rulers. Today, three great abutting Mamluk complexes line the west of the street, providing one of Cairo's most impressive assemblies of minarets, domes and towering facades.

Northernmost of the three is the **Madrassa & Mausoleum of Barquq**. Barquq seized power in 1382 as Egypt was reeling from plague and famine; his madrassa was completed four years later. It is entered through the bold black-and-white marble portal that leads into a vaulted passageway. To the right, the inner court has a colourful ceiling supported by four Pharaonic columns made of porphyry. Although this is called the Mausoleum of Barquq, it is actually his daughter who is buried in the splendid domed tomb chamber here; the sultan himself rests in the Northern Cemetery (see the Khanqah-Mausoleum of Ibn Barquq under Northern Cemetery later in this chapter).

South of the complex of Barquq is the **Mausoleum of an-Nasir Mohammed** (1304). The Gothic doorway was taken from a church in Acre (now Akko, Israel) when An-Nasir and his Mamluk army ended Crusader domination there in 1290. More foreign influence is discernible in the fine stucco on the minaret, which is North African in style. Buried in the mausoleum (on the right as you enter but usually kept locked) is An-Nasir's favourite son; the sultan himself is buried next door in the mausoleum of *his* father, Qalaun.

[Continued on page 195]

EGYPTIAN MUSEUM

More than 100,000 relics and antiquities from almost every period of ancient Egyptian history are housed in the Egyptian Museum. To put that in perspective, if you spent only one minute at each exhibit it would take more than nine months to see everything.

The nucleus of this collection was first gathered under one roof in Bulaq in 1858 by Auguste Mariette, the French archaeologist who had founded the Egyptian Antiquities Service. It was moved to its present purpose-built neoclassical home in 1902. Since then the number of exhibits has completely outgrown the available space and the place is virtually bursting at the seams. A persistent urban legend in Cairo has it that the building's storerooms are piled so high with uncatalogued artefacts that archaeologists will have to excavate their contents when the long-promised new museum is eventually built.

Beyond arranging the exhibits chronologically from the Old Kingdom to the Roman Empire, little has been done to present them in any sort of context or to highlight pieces of particular significance or beauty. In fact, since the museum's foundation a century ago, the displays have never been reorganised, despite the ever increasing number of artefacts. Labelling is poor or nonexistent, while the manner of display – mostly old wood-and-glass cases with no direct lighting – is hardly the last word in modern museum techniques. But this is slowly starting to change. Two new galleries opened in 1998 equipped with fibreoptic lighting and – taa daa! – labels. Also, new security and lighting systems have been installed following a sensational attempted robbery in 1996, when the authorities belatedly realised that the outmoded security system (basically barred windows and a dog making the rounds after closing) was insufficient protection for the museum's priceless contents. Still, the museum's eccentricity is part of its charm, and accidentally stumbling across treasures in its sometimes musty rooms is half the fun.

Practicalities

With so much to see, trying to get around everything in one go is liable to induce chronic 'Pharaonic phatigue'. The best strategy is to spread the exploration over at least two visits, maybe tackling one floor at a time. Unfortunately, there's no best time to visit as the museum is heaving with visitors throughout the day, although late afternoons can be a little quieter.

Queues start an hour before opening time and the four-fold admission procedure is as painfully slow as it sounds: (1) queue to pass through a metal detector and have your bags X-rayed; (2) queue to buy a ticket; (3) queue at the automatic ticket barriers to enter the building; and (4) queue to pass through a second metal detector and have your bags searched again.

This detail of a painted wooden coffin is from ie 22nd dynasty (inset).

Inset Photo: Anders Blomqvist

EGYPTIAN MUSEUM

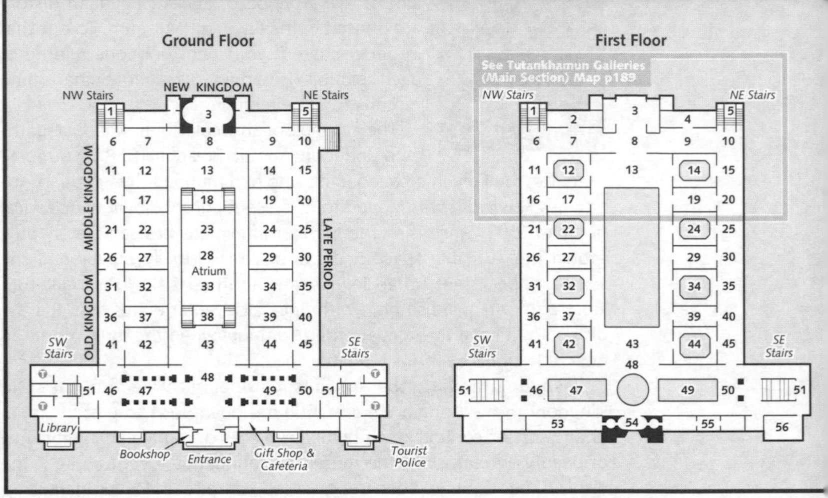

Admission to the museum is E£20 (E£10 for students), and it is open from 9am to 4.45pm daily. The museum (☎ 575 4319) is on Midan Tahrir and the closest metro station is Sadat.

Note that the Royal Mummy Room (for which tickets are bought inside the museum) closes a half-hour before the rest of the museum. Permission to use cameras (without flash) costs E£10; otherwise cameras must be left at the entrance. Use of a video camera costs E£100. There are official guides who will take you around for about E£40 per hour.

Highlights of the Egyptian Museum

For those people who do not have nine months to examine everything in the museum, the following is our list of the top 10 must-see exhibits (also highlighted in the following Museum Tour sections).

1. Tutankhamun Galleries (1st floor; pp189–91)
2. Royal Mummy Room (1st floor, room 56, p194)
3. Amarna Room (ground floor, room 3; pp187–8)
4. Graeco-Roman Mummies (1st floor, room 14; p192)
5. Royal Tombs of Tanis (1st floor, room 2; p192)
6. Old Kingdom Rooms (ground floor, rooms 42, 37 & 32; pp186–7)
7. Yuya & Thuyu Rooms (1st floor, room 43; p193)
8. Ancient Egyptian Jewellery (1st floor, room 4; p192)
9. Animal Mummies (1st floor, rooms 53 & 54; p194)
10. Pharaonic Technology (1st floor, room 34; p192–3)

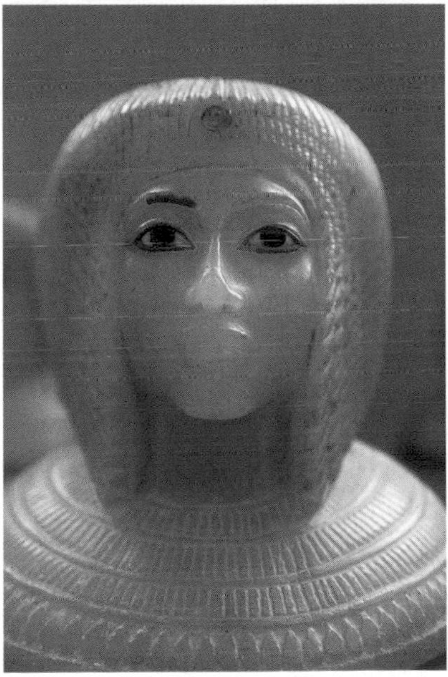

ALL PHOTOGRAPHS BY ANDERS BLOMQVIST

The Egyptian Museum (top), built in neoclassical style and opened in 1902, is home to more than 120,000 objects, including relics from the reign of the 'heretic pharaoh' Akhenaten, such as his statue bottom left) and the Canopic jar (bottom right) believed to portray Kiya, one of his minor wives.

ANDERS BLOMQVIST

SIMON BRACKEN

CHRIS MELLOR

DR JOANN FLETCHER

The treasures of Tutankhamun in the Egyptian Museum include a painted wooden chest (top) showing Tut as a sphinx trampling his enemies, his detailed throne (middle) and his spectacular gold death mask (bottom left). In a nearby room is the gold mask of Yuya (bottom right), Tut's great-grandfather.

Museum Tour: Ground Floor

Before entering the museum, wander through the garden; off to your left you'll find the tomb of Mariette (1821–1881), with a statue of the man, arms folded, shaded under a spreading tree. Mariette's tomb is also adorned with an arc of busts of other famous Egyptologists including Champollion, who cracked the code of hieroglyphs; Maspero, successor to Mariette as director of the Egyptian Antiquities Service; and Lepsius, the pre-eminent 19th-century German Egyptologist.

Once inside, the ground floor is laid out roughly chronologically in a clockwise fashion starting at the entrance hall. Following are a few of the things to look out for.

ROOM 48 – Early Dynastic Period

In glass cabinet No 16 is the near-life-size limestone seated **statue of Zoser (Djoser)**, the 3rd-dynasty pharaoh whose chief architect Imhotep designed the first pyramid, the Step Pyramid at Saqqara. The statue was discovered in 1924 in its serdab in the north-east corner of the pyramid (a replica now sits in its place) and is the oldest statue of its kind in the museum.

ROOM 43 – Atrium

The central atrium is the part of the museum that really feels like a warehouse, filled with a disordered miscellany of Egyptological finds large and small. In cabinet No 8, off to the right, is the double-sided **Narmer Palette**, which, although you'd never know it from the way it's presented, is one of the most significant artefacts in the whole museum. Dating from around 3100 BC it depicts the pharaoh Narmer (also known as Menes) wearing the crown of Upper Egypt on one side of the palette, and the crown of Lower Egypt on the other side, representing the first uniting of Upper and Lower Egypt under one ruler. This is ground zero – the event Egyptologists believe was the start of ancient Egyptian civilisation. Here begins over 3000 years of Pharaonic history, encompassing 170 or more rulers presiding over 30 dynasties, during which time almost every last exhibit in this building was fashioned. In effect, the Narmer Palette is the keystone of the Egyptian Museum.

At the far end of the atrium is a representation of all that the successors of Narmer would achieve in the form of a huge **colossus of Amenhotep III and Tiy**, his wife, with their small daughters at their feet. This particular pharaoh's lengthy reign (1390–1352 BC) represented the zenith of ancient Egypt's power and prestige. His rule was marked by great architectural achievements. Among his many projects Amenhotep built Luxor Temple and an even greater complex on the West Bank – possibly the greatest ever built in Egypt – but one that has completely vanished apart from the two lone guardians now known as the Colossi of Memnon.

ROOMS 47, 46 & 51 – Masterpieces of the Old Kingdom

Look for the three matching black schist triads that depict the pharaoh Menkaure (Mycerinus), builder of the smallest of the three Pyramids of Giza, flanked either side by a female figure. The figure to the pharaoh's right is the goddess Hathor, while each of the figures on his left represents a nome (district) of Egypt, the name of which is given by the symbol above their head. These triads (plus one other that is not held by this museum) were discovered at the pharaoh's valley temple, just east of his pyramid at Giza.

ROOMS 42, 37 & 32 – Old Kingdom Rooms

In the centre of Room 42 is what some consider to be the museum's masterpiece: a smooth, black, dioritic, larger than life-size **statue of Khafre (Chepren)**, builder of the second pyramid at Giza. He sits on a lion throne with the wings of the falcon god Horus wrapped around his head in a protective gesture. From the number of statueless bases discovered, archaeologists believe that this is just one of 23 such pieces that originally lined the hall of the pharaoh's valley temple on the Giza plateau.

Slightly to the left in front of Khafre is the **wooden statue of Ka-Aper** (No 14). Carved out of a single piece of sycamore (except for the arms), he's amazingly lifelike, especially the eyes which, set in copper lids, have whites of opaque quartz and corneas of rock crystal that have been drilled and filled with black paste to form the pupils. When they dug up this statue at Saqqara in 1860, local workmen named him Sheikh al-Balad (Headman), because they thought he resembled their own village chief.

Room 32 is dominated by the beautiful **statues of the royal couple, Rahotep and Nofret**, son and daughter-in-law of Sneferu, builder of some of the pyramids at Dahshur. Almost life-sized with well-preserved painted surfaces, the limestone sculptures' simple lines make them seem almost contemporary, despite having been around for a staggering 4600 years.

Another highlight in here, displayed in a cabinet off to the left, is the slightly bizarre tableau of the 'chief of the royal wardrobe' **Seneb** and his family. Seneb is a dwarf and he sits cross-legged, his two children strategically placed in front where an ordinary man's legs would be. His (nondwarf) wife Senetites has her arms protectively around his shoulders in an immediately recognisable expression of affection. The happy couple and their two kids have been used in recent Egyptian family planning campaigns.

Also in here is the panel known as the **Meidum Geese**. This is part of a wall painting that originates from a mud-brick mastaba at Meidum, near the oasis of Al-Fayoum (to this day, the lakes there are still host to a great variety of bird life). Though painted around 2600 BC, the pigments remain vivid and the degree of realism (while still retaining a distinct Pharaonic style) is astonishing – ornithologists have had no trouble identifying the bird types.

Room 37 is entered via Room 32; it contains finds from the Giza plateau **tomb of Queen Hetepheres**, including a carrying chair, bed, bed canopy and a jewellery box. Although her mummy was never found the remains of her internal organs are still inside her Canopic chest. A glass cabinet holds a mini statue of her son Khufu, found at Abydos. Ironically, at just 8cm or so high, it's the only surviving representation of the pharaoh who built Egypt's largest pyramid.

ROOM 26 – Montuhotep II

The seated statue on your right after leaving Room 32, with the black skin (which represents fertility and rebirth) and the red crown of Lower Egypt, is **Montuhotep II**, first new ruler of the Middle Kingdom period and the pharaoh who united the north and south. This statue was discovered by Howard Carter under the forecourt of the pharaoh's temple at Deir al-Bahri in Thebes in 1900 when the ground gave way under his horse – a surprisingly recurrent means of discovery in the annals of Egyptology.

ROOMS 21 & 16 – Sphinxes

These grey-granite sphinxes are very different from the great enigmatic Sphinx at Giza – in fact, they look more like the Lion Man from the Wizard of Oz, with a fleshy human face surrounded by a great shaggy mane and big ears. They were sculpted for the pharaoh Amenemhat III (1855–1808 BC) during the 12th dynasty and were later relocated to the Delta city of Tanis (see Tanis in the Around Cairo chapter), which is where they were discovered in 1863.

ROOM 12 – Hathor Shrine

The centrepiece of this room is a remarkably well-preserved sandstone chapel with a vaulted roof painted with reliefs of Tuthmosis III and his wife and daughters with the gods. It was part of the pharaoh's temple at Deir al-Bahri in Thebes, complete with the life-size representation of the goddess Hathor in cow form.

Hatshepsut, who was coregent for part of Tuthmosis III's reign, also built her temple at Deir al-Bahri. She took her position as regent a step further by having herself crowned pharaoh, and there's a life-size pink granite statue of the pharaoh queen to the left of the chapel. She's represented wearing a pharaoh's headdress and a false beard, but the face has definite feminine characteristics. The large reddish-painted limestone head in the corridor outside this room is also of Hatshepsut, and once belonged to one of her huge Osiris-type statues that adorned the pillared facade of her great temple at Deir al-Bahri.

ROOM 3 – Amarna Room

This room is devoted to Akhenaten (1352–1336 BC), the 'heretic pharaoh' who promoted the exclusive worship of the one god, the sun god Aten. A quick glance around the room is enough to see that artistic styles changed almost as drastically as the state religion during his 17-year tenure. Take a look at the great torsos and heads of the pharaoh and compare their strangely bulbous bellies, hips and thighs, their elongated faces, and thick, Mick Jagger-like lips with the sleek, hard-edged sculpture that you've just seen from the Middle Kingdom. Also worth a look are the stelae of the pharaoh and queen playing with their children, showing an informality and relaxed nature rarely seen in royal Pharaonic art.

Most striking of all is the **unfinished head of Nefertiti**, wife of Akhenaten. Worked in light brown quartzite, it's an incredibly delicate and sensitive portrait and shows the queen to be an extremely beautiful woman – unlike some of the relief figures of her elsewhere in the room, in which she appears with exactly the same strange features as her husband.

ROOM 10 – Ramses II

At the foot of the north-east stairs is a large, grey-granite representation of Ramses II, builder of the Ramesseum and Abu Simbel, but here depicted as a child with his finger in his mouth nestled against the breast of a great falcon, in this case the Canaanite god Horun. The pharaoh's figure actually spells out his name in sculpted form: *ra* (sun disc), *mes* (child) and *su* (the plant he holds).

ROOM 34 – Graeco-Roman Room

The lack of any kind of labelling is acutely felt in this room, which is full of fascinating pieces for which there's no explanation or context provided. But what is evident in many of the exhibits is the assimilation by Egypt's Greek, then Roman overlords of the indigenous Pharaonic style.

This is most obvious in the stelae on the back wall, and on the large sandstone panel on the right-hand wall that is inscribed in three languages: in hieroglyphics (the Egyptian literary language); demotic (the Egyptian popular language, a shorthand form of hieroglyphs); and, at the bottom, in Greek (the official language of the country's then rulers). This trilingually inscribed stone is similar in nature to the more famous Rosetta Stone (see the boxed text 'The Rosetta Stone' in the Alexandria & the Mediterranean Coast chapter), now housed in the British Museum in London (although there's a cast replica near the museum entrance in Room 48). Also, notice the bust immediately to the left as you enter this room: a typically Greek face with curly beard and locks, but wearing a Pharaonic-style headdress.

ROOMS 50 & 51 – Alexander the Great

On the official museum plan this area is labelled 'Alexander the Great' but currently there's nothing here that relates directly to the Macedonian conqueror who became pharaoh. However, there is an extremely beautiful small marble **statuette of the Greek goddess Aphrodite**, who the Egyptians identified with Isis. Carved in the 3rd or 2nd century BC, it was found in Alexandria.

Museum Tour: First Floor

The exhibits up here are grouped thematically and can be viewed in any order, but assuming that you've come up the south-east stairs (through Room 51), we'll go anticlockwise, entering the Tutankhamun Galleries at Room 45. This way, you'll experience the pieces in roughly the same order that they were laid out in the tomb (a poster on the wall outside Room 45 illustrates the tomb and treasures as they were found).

TUTANKHAMUN GALLERIES

Without doubt, the exhibit that outshines everything else in the museum is the treasure of the young and comparatively insignificant New Kingdom pharaoh Tutankhamun.

The tomb and treasures of this pharaoh, who ruled for only nine years during the 14th century BC (1336–1327 BC), were discovered in 1922 by English archaeologist Howard Carter. Its well-hidden location in the Valley of the Kings, below the much grander but ransacked tomb of Ramses VI, had prevented tomb robbers and archaeologists from finding it earlier. (For a more complete story see Tomb of Tutankhamun under West Bank in the Nile Valley – Luxor chapter). The incredible contents of this rather modest tomb displayed here can only make you wonder about the fabulous wealth looted from the tombs of pharaohs far greater than Tutankhamun.

About 1700 items are spread throughout a series of rooms – although, most of the 'rooms' are in fact sections of the museum's north- and east-wing corridors, and room numbers are not displayed, which sometimes makes it hard to find what you're looking for.

TUTANKHAMUN GALLERIES (MAIN SECTION)

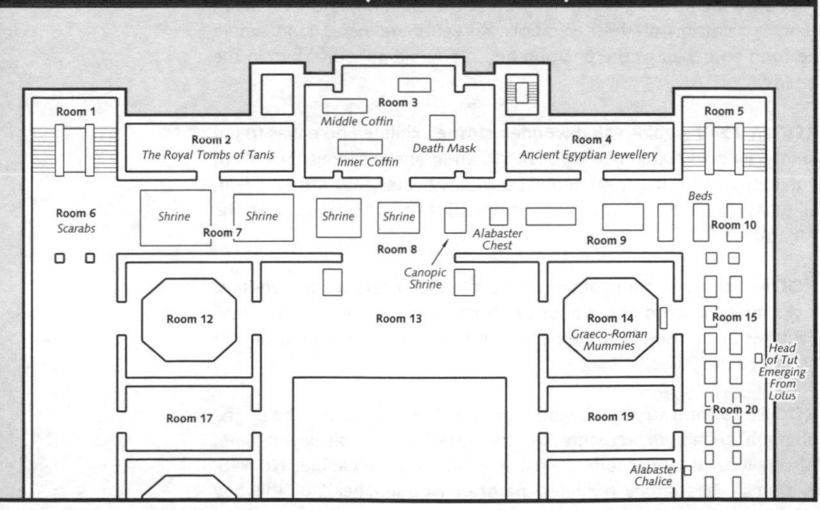

ROOM 45 Flanking the doorway as you enter are two life-size statues of the pharaoh found in the antechamber of the tomb. They served as sentries to the burial chamber (a large black-and-white photo on the wall shows the statues *in situ*). Made of wood, they are coated in bitumen – the black skin, identified with Osiris and the rich black river silt, symbolises fertility and rebirth.

ROOM 40 This area has a beautifully **painted chest** (contained in cabinet No 20) depicting the young pharaoh charging into battle in a chariot, his foes in disorganised chaos before him: Nubians on one side, 'Asiatics' from Syria and Palestine on the other. Although there is evidence that Tutankhamun was planning a foreign campaign just before he died, there's no record of him ever having fought such a battle. However, he did enjoy hunting, as depicted on the chest lid. When this chest was discovered it contained some of the necklaces and belts now displayed in Room 3.

ROOMS 35 & 30 The highlight here is the pharaoh's **lion throne**. Covered with sheet gold and inlaid with glass and semiprecious stones, the wooden throne is supported by spindly lions. The colourful tableau on the back of the chair depicts Tutankhamun's queen placing her hand on his shoulder under the rays of the sun (Aten), the worship of which was a hangover from his father and predecessor, Akhenaten, whose throne this may even once have been, as there is evidence of remodelling of both the figures and the names. Their robes are modelled in beaten silver and their hair is glass paste.

The many **golden statues** found in the tomb were all there to help the pharaoh on his journey in the afterlife. They include a series of 28 gilded wooden deities, meant to protect the pharaoh, and 413 ***shabti*** (only a selection of these symbolic servants are here) who would perform on behalf of the pharaoh any labours required of him in the afterlife.

ROOM 25 The gold-plated **wooden shrine** exhibited here was found empty, its gold statue having been stolen in ancient times. But it's of great interest for the royal domestic scenes beaten into the gold leaf, all of which are in an unconventional, realistic style evolved from the Amarna period.

ROOM 20 This room contains exquisite **alabaster jars and vessels**, including (just south of the door to Room 19) a lamp in which a small light has been inserted to demonstrate the delicacy of its translucent artwork.

ROOM 15 Intricate rigged **model barques** (boats), to be used by the pharaoh on his voyage through the afterlife, are displayed here. Also, almost unnoticeable against the back wall in cabinet No 118, is a small, beautifully rendered **painted wooden head** of the boy pharaoh emerging as the young sun god from a lotus flower – complete with pierced ears.

ROOMS 10 & 9 The northern end of this gallery is filled with the pharaoh's three elaborate **funerary couches**, one supported by two figures of the cow-goddess Mehetweret, one by two figures of the goddess of the underworld Ammut, 'the devourer' who ate the hearts of the damned, and the third by two lionesses. Although their exact purpose is unknown, it has been suggested that the couches would give the dead pharaoh access to the afterlife.

The alabaster chest contains four **Canopic jars**, the stoppers of which are in the form of Tutankhamun's head. Inside these jars were placed the four miniature gold coffins exhibited in Room 3 that, in turn, contained the pharaoh's internal organs. The whole chest and its gory contents was then placed inside the golden Canopic shrine with the four gilded goddesses: Isis, Neith, Nephthys and Selket, all portrayed with protective outstretched arms. If you look closely, you'll see that the alabaster chest is protected by the same four figures at its corners.

ROOMS 8 & 7 These galleries just barely accommodate the four huge **gilded wooden shrines** that fitted one inside the other like a set of Russian dolls, encasing at their centre the sarcophagi of the boy pharaoh.

ROOM 3 This is the room that everybody wants to see. At peak times you'll have to queue, and once inside it feels like you've entered the crush of the Khan al-Khalili bazaar. The central exhibit is the astonishing **death mask** of Tutankhamun. Made of solid gold and weighing 11kg, the mask was found covering the head of the mummy, where it lay inside a series of three sarcophagi. The mask is an idealised portrait of the young pharaoh; the eyes are fashioned from obsidian and quartz, while the outlines of the eyes and the eyebrows are delineated with lapis lazuli.

No less wondrous are the two **golden sarcophagi**. These are the inner two sarcophagi – the outermost coffin, along with the mummified remains of Tutankhamun, remains in place in his tomb in the Valley of the Kings. The smallest coffin is, like the mask, cast in solid gold and inlaid in the same fashion. It weighs 110kg. The slightly larger coffin is made of gilded wood.

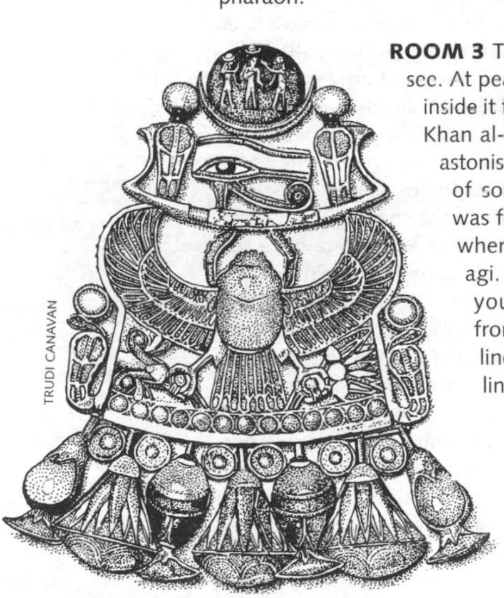

This elaborate pectoral made of gold, silver, semi-precious stones and glass was found in the linen wrappings of Tutankhamun's mummy.

ROOM 4 – Ancient Egyptian Jewellery

One of two galleries opened in 1998, this room has finds from all over the place including Saqqara and Giza. The jewellery includes belts, inlaid beadwork, necklaces, semiprecious stones and bracelets. Most beautiful of all is a diadem of Sit-Hathor-Yunet, a golden headband with a rearing cobra inset with semiprecious stones. As well as the Pharaonic cache there are finds from the Graeco-Roman period from the Western Oases and Red Sea areas including bracelets, another diadem and agate bowls.

ROOM 2 – Royal Tombs of Tanis

The second of the new galleries, this room contains a glittering collection of gold- and silver-encrusted amulets, gold funerary masks, daggers, bracelets, collars, gold sandals, and finger and toe coverings from five intact 21st- and 22nd-dynasty tombs found at the Delta site of Tanis. Unearthed by the French in 1939, their discovery rivalled Carter's finding of Tutankhamun's tomb, but it was overshadowed by the start of WWII and remains largely unknown. There's also the gold death mask of Psusennes I (1039–991 BC) and his silver inner coffin, with another silver coffin with the head of a falcon belonging to the pharaoh Shoshenq II (c. 890 BC).

ROOM 14 – Graeco-Roman Mummies

This room contains a small sample (over a thousand have been discovered) of the stunning portraits found on Graeco-Roman–period mummies, commonly refered to as 'Fayoum Portraits' (see the boxed text 'Portraits of the Past' in the Around Cairo chapter) after the place in which many were discovered. These images, whose large watchful eyes seem to follow you around the room, were painted onto wooden panels that were then placed over the mummys' embalmed faces; some were even painted directly onto the shrouds themselves. As few other painted portraits from the Graeco-Roman era have survived, this collection is unique both for the number of its paintings and the high quality of its images.

Although the cases are barely lit and are piled with dust, the beautiful and hauntingly realistic faces that stare out from behind the glass bring the personalities of their long-dead owners to life in a way that the stylised elegance of most ancient Egyptian art somehow can't. Take a look at the mummy in front of you as you enter the room; the portrait is of a woman with large brown eyes and it's so life-like you'd recognise her immediately if you saw her on the street. Make sure to walk through to area 13, where there's an extremely well-preserved tiny mummy of a young boy.

ROOM 34 – Pharaonic Technology

For gadget buffs, this room contains a great number of everyday objects that helped support ancient Egypt's great leap out of prehistory. Everything from combs and mirrors to fishing tackle, ploughs, hoes (that look exactly like the ones still used by Egypt's fellaheen today) and serious-looking blades and razors with their cases can be found here. Hunting paraphernalia includes Pharaonic boomerangs that were apparently used for killing birds. (Tutankhamun is depicted using one in the reliefs on the gold shrine in Room 25.)

ROOMS 32 & 27 – Middle Kingdom Models

The lifelike models that are contained in these rooms were mostly found in the tomb of Meketre, an 11th-dynasty chancellor in Thebes, and together the models constitute a fascinating portrait of daily life in Egypt almost 4000 years ago. The models include fishing boats (complete with fish in the nets), a slaughterhouse, a carpentry workshop, a loom and a model of Meketre's house (with figs on the trees and painted columns). Most spectacular is the 1.5m-wide scene of Meketre sitting with his sons, four scribes and various others, counting cattle. Painted wooden servant figures hold the animals by miniature ropes as they pass by the shaded dais on which Meketre sits.

ROOM 37 – Model Armies

Discovered in the Asyut tomb of the governor Meseheti and dating from about 2000 BC (11th dynasty), these are two sets of 40 wooden warriors marching in phalanxes. The darker soldiers are Nubian archers from the south of the kingdom, each wearing brightly coloured kilts of varying design, while the lighter-skinned soldiers are Egyptian pikemen.

ROOM 43 – Yuya & Thuyu Rooms

Before Tutankhamun, the discovery of the tomb of Yuya and Thuyu (the parents of Queen Tyi, and Tutankhamun's great-grandparents) was the most spectacular find in Egyptian archaeology. The tomb was discovered virtually intact in the Valley of the Kings in 1905 and contained a vast number of treasures including five ornate sarcophagi and the remarkably well-preserved mummies of the two commoners who became royal in-laws. Among the many other items on display here are such essentials for the hereafter as beds, sandals and a chariot, as well as two fabulous gilded death masks – Thuyu's mask is especially beautiful, fashioned with a broad smile.

ROOM 48 – Pyramid Model

There's an excellent large-scale model of one of the Abu Sir pyramids that perfectly illustrates the typical pyramid complex with its valley temple, high-walled causeway, mortuary temple and mini satellite pyramid – it's well worth studying before a trip to Giza.

ROOMS 53 & 54 – Animal Mummies

Before the rise of the Pharaonic dynasties in Egypt, animal cults proliferated, and the results can be seen in the battered and dust-covered little mummified cats, dogs, birds, rams and jackals in Room 53. More of these bizarre little trussed-up packages can be seen just outside in Room 54, where the better-preserved remains of a mummified falcon, a fish, a cat, an ibis, a monkey and a tiny crocodile are on show.

The museum is encouraging people to 'adopt' an animal mummy. On offer via the Internet at W www.animalmummies.com are everything from mummified snakes (donate US$50 to become a coparent) to ancient crocodiles (US$800). 'Parents' get a special information pack on their chosen animal while the money raised helps to pay for a climate-controlled room and special cases to conserve the poor desiccated beasts.

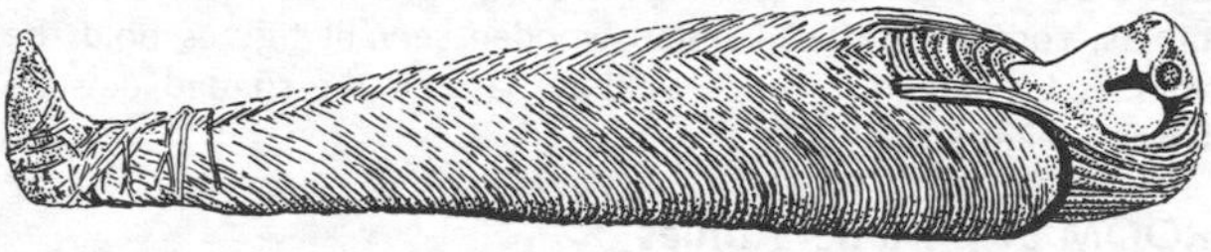

TRUDI CANAVAN

In ancient Egypt, falcons were considered sacred and were linked to Horus, the falcon god of the sky and representative of the pharaoh.

ROOM 56 – Royal Mummy Room

The Royal Mummy Room houses the bodies of 11 of Egypt's most illustrious pharaohs and queens from the 17th to 21st dynasties, who ruled Egypt between 1650 and 945 BC. They include the brave Seqenre II who died violently during the struggles to reunite the country in around 1560 BC, his arms still twisted by rigor mortis; Seti I; Tuthmosis II; Tuthmosis IV with his pierced ear and beautifully styled hair; Ramses II with his hair-dye job; and the partially unwrapped Ramses III, the model for Boris Karloff in Universal's 1932 version of *The Mummy*. The mummies all lie in individual glass showcases (kept at a constant temperature of 22°C) in a sombre, dimly lit environment reminiscent of a tomb. Talking above a hushed whisper is not permitted (although irreverent tour groups often need to be reminded of this); for this reason, tour guides are not allowed in, making it one of the most peaceful havens in the museum.

Note, taking young children into the Mummy Room could leave them with nightmares for months to come.

[Continued from page 182]

If you are only going to visit one of the complexes, make it the **Madrassa & Mausoleum of Qalaun**. The earliest of the trio, the Qalaun complex was completed in just 13 months in 1279. The mausoleum, on the right, is a particularly beautiful assemblage of inlaid stone and stucco patterned with stars and floral motifs, all lit by stained glass windows. The complex also includes a *maristan* (hospital). The Arab traveller and historian Ibn Battuta, who visited Cairo in 1325, recorded that Qalaun's hospital contained 'an innumerable quantity of appliances and medicaments'. Incredibly, a clinic still occupies part of the original building, maintaining a tradition of more than 700 years of medical care. Entrance is free to all three monuments.

Back to the City Centre Want to buy a minaret top? South of Bein al-Qasreen, the monuments give way to a string of shops filled with pots and pans and crescent-shaped finials, hence its more popular name: Sharia an-Nahasseen or the Street of the Coppersmiths. After a short stretch, copper gives way to gold, signifying that you have re-entered the precincts of Khan al-Khalili. At the junction with Muski, beside the two mosques, a left turn takes you back to Midan Hussein, while heading right will eventually take you to Midan Ataba (20 to 30 minutes' walk); straight ahead is Sharia al-Azhar, the best place to find a taxi.

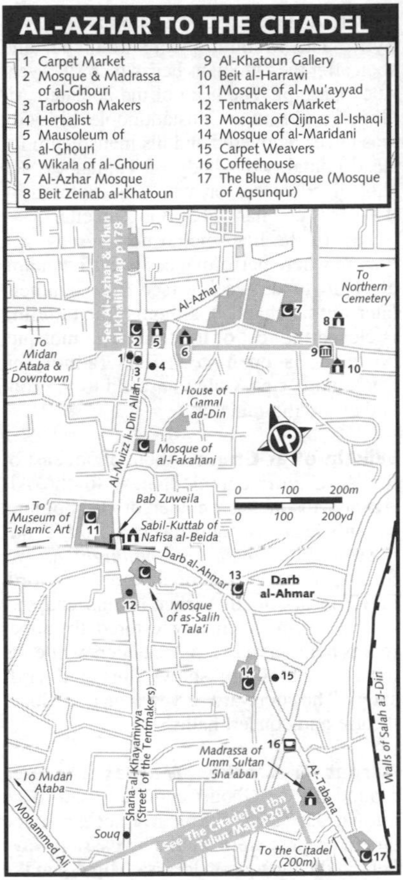

3. Al-Azhar to the Citadel

South of the main Al-Azhar road, Al-Muizz li-Din Allah continues as a busy market street running down to the twin-minareted gate of Bab Zuweila; it's a leisurely 10-minute walk. From the gate there are then two possible routes to the Citadel – east along Darb al-Ahmar, or south through Sharia al-Khayamiyya (Street of the Tentmakers). Either way it takes about another 20 minutes to reach the Citadel, where you can then have refreshments, enjoy the view, and exert yourself with a little more sightseeing before picking up a taxi back to town. Alternatively, turning right outside Bab Zuweila will take you the short distance to the Museum of Islamic Art.

Al-Ghouri Complex (Al-Ghouriyya) The grand pair of black-and-white buildings (dating from 1505) facing each other across the souq on the south side of Sharia al-Azhar are the mosque-madrassa (the one with the red-chequered chimneypot minaret) and mausoleum of Al-Ghouri. Together they form an exquisite monument to the end of the Mamluk era. Qansuh al-Ghouri, the penultimate Mamluk sultan, ruled for 16 years, before, at the age of 78, riding out at the head of his army to do battle with the Ottoman Turks in Syria. The Mamluks were trounced, and soon after the Ottomans began their 281-year rule of Egypt. The head of the defeated Al-Ghouri was sent to Constantinople; his body was never recovered and his mausoleum instead contains the body of Tumanbey, his short-lived successor, who was captured by the Turks and hanged at Bab Zuweila.

Part of the mausoleum now serves as a theatre where performances of Sufi dancing are held twice weekly (see Entertainment later in this chapter), although the building is closed the rest of the time. The mosque, however, is open to visitors (admission free) and it's possible to ascend to the roof and climb the minaret.

Wikala of al-Ghouri About 300m east of the Al-Ghouri complex, next to the Al-Azhar Mosque, is another of the doomed sultan's legacies, a wikala *(☎ 511 0472; admission E£6; open 8am-midnight daily)*. Similar to the Wikala of Bazara, (see North of Khan al-Khalili earlier in this chapter) but more sympathetically restored, the upper rooms here serve as artists' ateliers while the former stables are showrooms and craft shops. The courtyard serves as an occasional theatre and concert hall.

Carpet & Clothes Market The area around the Al-Ghouri complex used to be known as Cairo's 'Silk Market', a place where carpets were sold. The passageways behind the mosque-madrassa (slip down the side or enter from Sharia al-Azhar) are still filled with carpet sellers, although their wares are now made of wool or synthetics. South of the Ghouriyya, Al-Muizz li-Din Allah becomes a busy souq given over to household goods, cloth and cheap clothing. On the right, less than 50m south of the Ghouriyya are two of Cairo's last tarboosh (fez) makers. You can watch them shaping the hats on their heavy brass presses. Once worn by every respectable *effendi* (gentleman) the tarbooshes are now mainly bought by hotels and tourist restaurants. They sell for E£5 to E£30. Further along, on the opposite side of the street, is a herbalist whose shop front is hung with bunches of dried hedgehogs and lizards used in the preparation of healing compounds.

Bab Zuweila Built at the same time as the northern gates (10th century), Bab Zuweila is the only remaining southern gate of the old medieval city of Al-Qahira. Until the late 19th century it was still closed each evening. The area in front of the gate was one of the main public gathering places in Mamluk times. It was also the site of executions, which were a highly popular form of street theatre. A particularly vicious bunch, the Mamluks used to execute victims by publicly sawing them in half or crucifying them.

The two minarets atop the gate belong to the neighbouring **Mosque of al-Mu'ayyad** and were added 330 years after the gate was built. How the masons knew that the gate could take the extra weight is a mystery. Although closed for restoration at the time of our last visit, it used to be possible to climb the minarets (reached through the mosque) for one of the best views of the city. Hopefully, when the work is finished the minarets will be accessible again.

From Bab Zuweila, a right turn will take you towards town and the Museum of Islamic Art; left is Darb al-Ahmar and a 15-minute walk to the Citadel; straight ahead is the Street of the Tentmakers.

Street of the Tentmakers The street (in Arabic, Sharia al-Khayamiyya) takes its name from the artisans who traditionally worked here producing the brightly printed fabrics formerly used to adorn caravans. Nowadays these fabrics are used for the ceremonial tents that are set up for funerals, wakes, weddings and feasts. There's also a lot of applique work stitched and sold here. For more information see Shopping in the Facts for the Visitor chapter.

Continuing south beyond the covered market, Sharia al-Khayamiyya runs for almost a kilometre before intersecting with Sharia Mohammed Ali; a left turn here will take you to the great Mosque-Madrassa of Sultan Hassan and to the Citadel. However, if you intend walking to the Citadel, the Darb al-Ahmar route is more interesting.

Darb al-Ahmar This district, which takes its name from its main street, Darb al-Ahmar (Red Rd), was the heart of 14th- and 15th-century Cairo. During these centuries Cairo had a population of about 250,000, most of whom lived outside the city walls in tightly packed residential districts like this where more than half the narrow, twisting streets ended in cul-de-sacs. As the walled inner city of Al-Qahira was completely built-up, patrons of new mosques, grand palaces and religious institutions were forced to build outside the city gates; most of the structures around here date from the late Mamluk era. One of the best examples of architecture from this period is the **Mosque of Qijmas al-Ishaqi** (1481). Its plain exterior is quite deceptive, as inside there are beautiful stained glass windows, inlaid marble floors and stucco walls.

About 150m further on the right, the **Mosque of al-Maridani** (1339) is notable for incorporating architectural elements from several different periods: eight granite columns were taken from a Pharaonic monument; the arches were made from Roman, Christian and Islamic designs; and the Ottomans added a fountain and wooden housing. The lack of visitors, the trees in the courtyard and the attractive mashrabiyya screening make it a peaceful place to stop.

The Blue Mosque, more correctly known as the **Mosque of Aqsunqur**, gets its popular name from the combination of blue-grey marble on the exterior and the flowery tiling on the interior. The tiles, imported from Syria, were added in 1652 by a Turkish governor but the original and much plainer structure dates from 1347. The minaret affords an excellent view of the Citadel, while over to the east, just behind the mosque, you can see the remains of Saladin's (Salah ad-Din's) city walls, now largely covered with rubbish and the detritus of collapsed buildings.

From here it's about another 400m up hill to the Citadel.

Museum of Islamic Art

Overshadowed by the Pharaonic crowd-pulling power of the Egyptian Museum, this museum (☎ *390 9930, Sharia Port Said; Metro: Mohammed Naguib; admission E£16; open 8am-4pm daily)*, which has one of the world's finest collections of Islamic applied art, undeservedly receives few visitors.

It has to be said though, the museum doesn't do itself any favours. As in the Egyptian Museum, the labelling leaves a lot to be desired – 'Statue in the shape of a lion painted blue' reads the printed card beside a statue of a lion painted blue. We recommend that you spend some time walking around Islamic Cairo and visit one or two mosques before coming here to help supply the missing context.

Entrance is through the garden door off Sharia Port Said. This brings you into the central hall, which contains some of the most beautiful exhibits; we suggest you immediately turn right, saving the best for later. Rooms 8 and 9 contain woodwork, including some nice coffered ceilings. Room 11 contains metal work and room 12 contains Mamluk weaponry. Room 13 is for

MUSEUM OF ISLAMIC ART

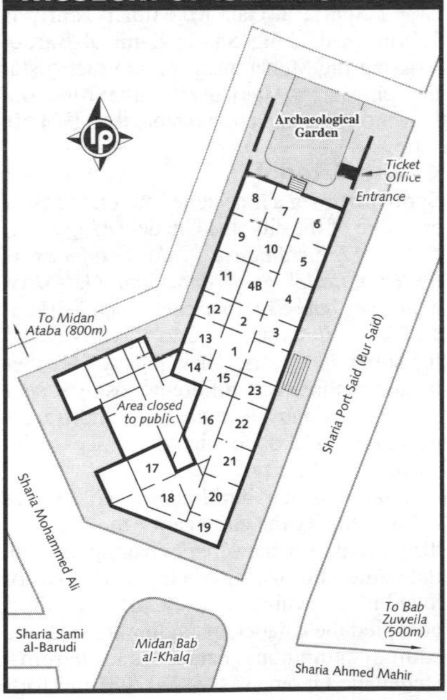

'masterpieces', which include a great door that originally belonged to the Sayyida Zeinab mosque. Beyond are rooms 14 to 16 which are given over to ceramics. There is no tradition of glazed tile making in Egypt, so most of what's on display here comes from Persia (modern-day Iran). The cone-topped fireplace in room 16, however, is from Anatolia (now central Turkey).

Walk through rooms 21 (glass) and 20 (Ottoman era) to room 19 which contains a small collection of illuminated manuscripts and ornate Qurans formerly owned by King Farouk. Now make your way back to rooms 4 and 4B which are divided by a row of carved Mamluk columns. The museum's centrepiece is in 4B: an Ottoman fountain combined with beautiful mashrabiyya and a carved wooden ceiling. There's another, more elaborate sunken fountain, dating from the time of the Mamluks, in room 5.

Getting There & Away The museum is about a 10-minute walk from Midan Ataba, straight down Sharia Mohammed Ali (also called Sharia al-Qala'a). Midan Tahrir is 1.5km west along Sharia Sami al-Barudi (passing the Mohammed Naguib metro station en route). Alternatively, a taxi to/from Downtown should cost no more than E£3.50.

4. The Citadel

Sprawling over a limestone spur on the eastern edge of the city, the Citadel *(Al-Qala'a; ☎ 512 1735, Midan al-Qala'a; admission E£20; Citadel open 8am-5pm Oct-May, 8am-6pm June-Sept; museums open 8.30am-4.30pm daily)* was home to Egypt's rulers for some 700 years. Their legacy is a collection of three very different mosques, several palaces housing some fairly indifferent museums, and a couple of terraces with views over the city.

Saladin began building the Citadel in 1176 to fortify the city against the threat of the Crusaders, who were rampaging through Palestine. Following their overthrow of Saladin's Ayyubid dynasty, the Mamluks occupied the Citadel, extending its area and adding sumptuous palaces and harems. Under the Ottomans (1517–1798) the fortress was further enlarged westwards and a new main gate, the Bab al-Azab, was added, while the Mamluk palaces were allowed to deteriorate. Even so, when Napoleon's French expedition took control of the Citadel in 1798, the emperor's savants regarded these buildings as some of the finest Islamic monuments in Cairo. Which didn't stop Mohammed Ali – who rose to power when the French left – from demolishing them. The only Mamluk structure left standing was a single mosque, which was used as a stable. Mohammed Ali completely remodelled the rest of the Citadel and crowned it with the Turkish-style mosque that currently dominates Cairo's eastern skyline.

After Mohammed Ali's grandson and heir, Ismail, moved the royal presence out of the Citadel (to Abdeen; see Abdeen Palace under Midan Tahrir & Around earlier in the chapter), it was used as a military garrison. The British Army was barracked here in WWII, to be replaced by Egyptian soldiers after 1952. The soldiers still have a small foothold, but now the Citadel has been given over almost entirely to the tourists.

The fortress – and indeed, the skyline of Cairo – is dominated by the **Mosque of Mohammed Ali**. Modelled along classic Turkish lines, it took 18 years to build (1830–48) and then the domes had to be demolished and rebuilt later. It's a building that has never found much favour with those who have written about Cairo and has been variously described as unimaginative, lacking in grace and resembling a great toad. Oblivious to the criticism, the mosque's patron Mohammed Ali lies in the marble tomb on the right as you enter. Note the chintzy clock in the central courtyard; this was a gift from King Louis Philippe of France in thanks for the Pharaonic obelisk that adorns the Place de la Concorde in Paris. It was damaged on delivery and has yet to be repaired.

Dwarfed by Mohammed Ali's mosque, the **Mosque of an-Nasir Mohammed** (1318) is the Citadel's sole surviving Mamluk structure. The interior is a little sparse because the Ottoman sultan Selim I had it stripped of its marble, but the twisted finials of the minarets are interesting for their covering of glazed tiles, something rarely seen in Egypt.

Facing the entrance of the An-Nasir Mohammed mosque is a mock Gothic gateway leading out onto a terrace that has superb views across Islamic Cairo to the tower blocks of Downtown and, on a clear day, the Pyramids at Giza. The **Police Museum**, at the northern end of the terrace, has an intriguing Assassination Room, with text and photos relating, among other things, to the various attempts on President Nasser's life. Curiously, the successful assassination of Sadat fails to get a mention. Immediately below the Police Museum, in the Citadel's Lower Enclosure (closed to the public), you can see the steep-sided roadway leading to the Bab al-Azab, which is where the infamous massacre of the Mamluks took place (see History in the Facts about Egypt chapter).

South of Mohammed Ali's mosque is another terrace with good views while off the terrace is the very dull **Gawhara Palace & Museum**, a lacklustre attempt to evoke 19th-century court life.

Northern Enclosure Entrance to the Northern Enclosure is through the 16th-century Bab al-Qalla, which faces the side of the An-Nasir Mohammed mosque. This brings you into a large area of lawn which, at its centre, contains a replica of the equine statue of Ibrahim that stands in Midan Opera. Beyond the statue, and the motley assortment of tanks and planes from the Arab-Israeli wars, is Mohammed Ali's one-time Harem Palace, now the **National Military Museum**. It's largely devoted to displays of ceremonial garb, but on the top floor is an excellent scale model of the Citadel.

East of the lawns a narrow road leads to a rather sparse area dotted with a few small, low buildings, one of which is the **Carriage Museum** containing a small collection of 19th-century horse-drawn carriages that might occupy five minutes of your time.

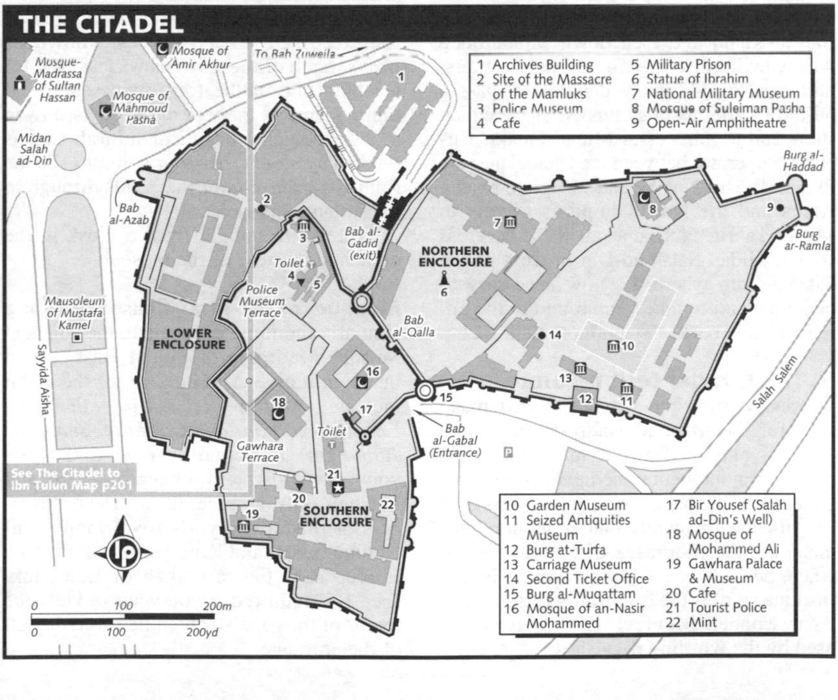

Devotees of Islamic architecture might appreciate the **Mosque of Suleiman Pasha** (1528), a beautiful little Ottoman-era structure topped by a cluster of domes. The painted woodwork inside has been lovingly restored over the past few years by a local art student.

From a point just behind the mosque it may still be possible to get up onto the wall ramparts and walk east towards the **Burg al-Haddad** (Blacksmith's Tower). If the way is now blocked, walk across the new, hideous concrete 'amphitheatre' towards the tower and its companion, the **Burg ar-Ramla** (Sand Tower). These are two of Saladin's towers and they can be entered at ground level. Although not officially permitted, it is still physically possible to walk either through the walls or along the ramparts around to the **Burg at-Turfa** (Masterpiece Tower).

Getting To/From the Citadel It's a good 3km walk from Downtown to the Citadel. From Midan Ataba go straight down Sharia Mohammed Ali, while from Midan Tahrir the best route is via Midan Falaki to Midan Bab al-Khalq and then down Mohammed Ali. A taxi will cost E£4. By public transport, bus No 174 from Midan Ramses passes by the Citadel as does bus No 173, which starts and terminates at Midan Falaki. Bus No 905 operates between the Citadel and the Pyramids. Bus Nos 57 and 951 go to Midan Ataba and the No 54 minibus travels to Midan Tahrir. Note that all these services stop at Midan Salah ad-Din in front of the Citadel from where it's now necessary to pick up a taxi to take you around to the entrance at the back. Pay no more than E£1.

5. The Citadel to Ibn Tulun

Anyone visiting the Citadel should make time for the Mosque-Madrassa of Sultan Hassan, one of Cairo's most awesome pieces of monumental medieval Islamic architecture. The backstreets around this area are filled with many smaller monuments, including the **Madrassa of Sunqur Sa'adi**, where behind a green door (with an Italian Institute sign) is the beautifully restored circular wooden Mevlevi Theatre formerly used by the whirling dervishes.

Mosque-Madrassa of Sultan Hassan Regarded as the finest piece of early Mamluk architecture in Cairo, this great structure *(Midan al-Qala'a; admission E£12; open 8am-5pm Oct-May, 8am-6pm June-Sept)* was built between 1356 and 1363 by Hassan who endured a troubled reign, taking the throne at the age of 13 and being deposed and reinstated no less than three times before being assassinated shortly before his mosque was completed. Such were the trials of power in the Mamluk era. Tragedy also shadowed the construction with one of the minarets collapsing, killing 300 or so onlookers. In later years, the mosque suffered substantial damage in cannon skirmishes between various warring Mamluk factions, and it was also shelled by Napoleon from the Citadel battlements when he sought to subdue an Egyptian uprising against French occupation. Nonetheless, it survives in an impressive form. The tall, recessed entrance is striking, and beyond this a dark passage leads through into a square inner courtyard with soaring walls punctured by four recessed arched arches, known as *iwans*. Each of these iwans was a space for teaching one of the four main schools of Sunni Isam. At the rear of the eastern iwan is an especially beautiful mihrab that is flanked by stolen Crusader columns. To the right is a bronze door that leads through to the sultan's mausoleum.

Tickets are bought from a kiosk in the garden at the rear of the mosque.

Mosque of Ar-Rifai Constructed on a similarly monumental scale to the adjacent Mosque-Madrassa of Sultan Hassan, and in an imitative Mamluk style, the Rifai mosque *(Midan al-Qala'a; admission E£12; open 8am-5pm Oct-May, 8am-6pm June-Sept)* is actually some 550 years younger. Construction began in 1867 and finished only as recently as 1912. Members of modern Egypt's royal family, including Ismail and King Farouk, are buried inside, as is the last Shah of Iran. Baksheesh is required if you want to view the tombs of the royals, which lie off to the left of the entrance.

THE CITADEL TO IBN TULUN

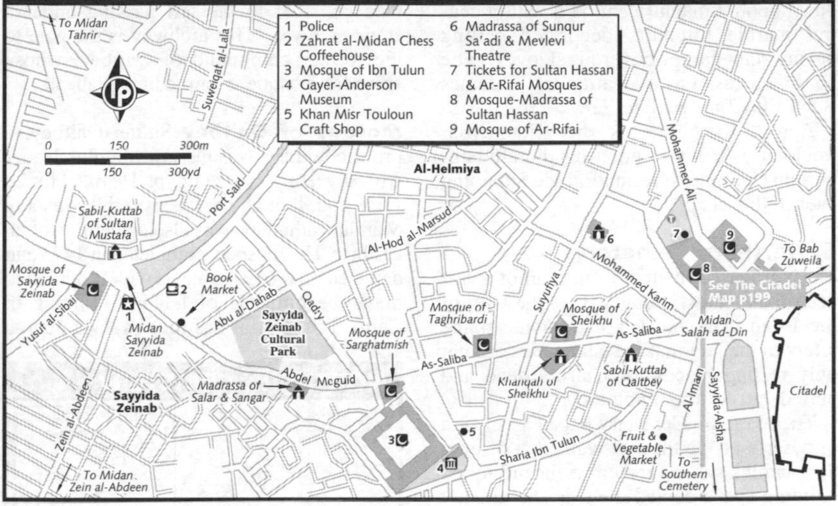

Mosque of Ibn Tulun Ibn Tulun was sent to rule Cairo in the 9th century by the Abbasid caliph of Baghdad. He had the mosque *(Sharia Ibn Tulun; admission E£6; open 8am-6pm daily)* built between AD 876 and 879, making it the city's oldest intact functioning Islamic monument. It's quite unlike any other mosque in Cairo mainly because the inspiration is almost entirely Iraqi – the ancient mosques of Samarra are the closest to it in style.

To the original Iraqi model, Ibn Tulun added some innovations of his own. According to architectural historians this is the first structure to use the pointed arch – a good 200 years before Christianity adopted it for the European Gothic arch. Constructed entirely of mud brick and timber, the mosque covers 6½ acres in area, large enough for the whole community to assemble for Friday prayers. Although the mosque is still in use, these days the congregation is much more modest and is usually accommodated in just the south-eastern arcaded sanctuary.

After wandering around the massive courtyard you should climb the spiral minaret reached from the outer, moat-like courtyard which, although originally created to keep the secular city at a distance, was at one time filled with shops and stalls. The top of the minaret is the best place to appreciate the grandeur and geometric simplicity of the mosque, and the views of the Citadel to the east and Cairo in general are magnificent.

Gayer-Anderson Museum This museum *(Beit al-Kretliyya; ☎ 364 7822, Sharia Ibn Tulun; admission E£16; open 8am-4pm Sat-Thur, 8am-noon & 1pm-4pm Fri)* is almost an annexe of the Ibn Tulun mosque, and can be reached from the outer court through a gateway to the south of the main entrance. The museum is actually two 16th-century houses joined together. It gets its current name from a British major, John Gayer-Anderson, who restored and furnished the houses between 1935 and 1942 and filled them with antiquities, artworks and Oriental artefacts that he acquired on his travels in the region. But the real attraction are the joined houses, their puzzle of rooms and the decor. There's a Persian room with exquisite tiling and a Damascus room with its walls and ceiling patterned with lacquer and gold. There's also an enchanting mashrabiyya gallery that looks down upon a magnificent qa'a with a central marble fountain, decorated ceiling beams and carpet-covered alcoves. The house was used as a location in the James Bond film *The Spy Who Loved Me*.

Across the street is the Khan Misr Touloun, which is a good handicrafts emporium (for more information see Shopping later in this chapter).

6. Northern Cemetery

The Northern Cemetery is one half of a vast necropolis known popularly as the City of the Dead. The lurid, arcade-game name refers to the fact that the cemeteries are not only resting places for Cairo's dead and buried, but for the living too.

The Northern Cemetery began as an area of desert outside the city walls that offered the Mamluk sultans and emirs the unlimited building space denied them in the already densely packed city. The vast mausoleum complexes they built were more than just tombs, they were also meant as places for entertaining. This is part of an Egyptian tradition that has its roots in Pharaonic times when people would picnic among the graves. Even the humblest of family tombs were designed to include a room where visitors could stay overnight. Naturally, the city's homeless took to squatting in the tombs. This was happening as far back as the 14th century, leading to the situation today where the living and dead coexist comfortably side by side. In some tomb-houses cenotaphs serve as tables and washing is strung between headstones. The municipality has running water, gas and electricity, and there's a local police station and even a post office. On Fridays and public holidays visitors flock here to picnic and pay their respects to the dead.

The easiest way to get to the Northern Cemetery is to walk east along Sharia al-Azhar from Al-Hussein. As you breast the top of the hill, bear right, under the overpass and straight on along the dusty road between the tombs. Follow this road to the left then right. You'll pass by the large crumbling domed Tomb of Emir Tashtimur on your left. About 100m further on a narrow lane goes off to the left passing under a stone archway. This archway is the gate to the former compound of Qaitbey, whose splendid mosque is immediately ahead.

Mosque of Qaitbey Sultan Qaitbey, a prolific builder, was the last Mamluk leader with any real power in Egypt. He ruled for 28 years and, though he was as ruthless as any Mamluk sultan, he was also something of an aesthete. His mosque, completed in 1474 and depicted on the E£1 note, is widely agreed to mark the pinnacle of Islamic building in Cairo. The interior has four iwans around a

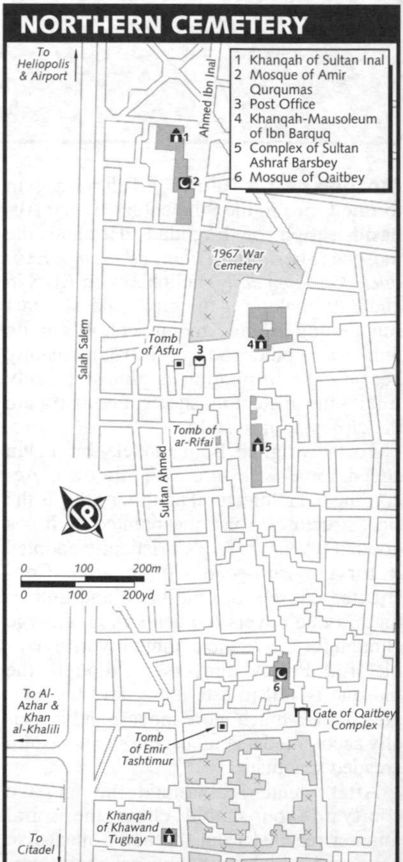

central court that is suffused with light from large, lattice-screened windows. It's one of the most pleasant places in Cairo to sit for a while and relax. The adjacent tomb chamber contains the cenotaphs of Qaitbey and his two sisters, as well as two stones that supposedly bear the footprints of the Prophet. The true glory, however, is above in the interlaced star and floral carving adorning the stone dome, which in its intricacy and delicacy was never surpassed in Cairo or anywhere else in the Islamic world – climb the minaret for the best view.

Other Monuments From Qaitbey cross the square and continue north. The cemetery has an almost village-like feel with small shops and street sellers, and sandy paths pecked by chickens and nosed around by goats. After about 250m the street widens out and on the right a stone wall encloses a large area of rubble-strewn ground that was formerly the **complex of Sultan Ashraf Barsbey**. Though not as sophisticated as the one topping Qaitbey, the dome here is carved with a beautiful star pattern. Inside, there is some fine marble flooring and a beautiful minbar (pulpit) inlaid with ivory. Look for the guard or have one of the children in the area find him; he'll let you in for baksheesh.

Two hundred metres further north is the **Khanqah-Mausoleum of Ibn Barquq**. *Ibn* means 'son of', and this is the mausoleum of Farag, son of Barquq, whose great madrassa and mausoleum stands on Bein al-Qasreen (see under North of Khan al-Khalili earlier this chapter). Completed in 1411, the *khanqah* (Sufi monastery) is an imposing fortress-like building with high, sheer facades, and twin minarets and domes. If you go through into the interior courtyard you can see the small monastic cells off the arcades. There's a tomb chamber under each dome, one for women, one for men. Both ceilings have been repainted in recent years and look great. It's also possible to get up onto the roof and climb the minarets.

Back to Al-Hussein North-west of Ibn Barquq are two large adjacent complexes, the **Mosque of Amir Qurqumas** (1507) and the **Khanqah of Sultan Inal** (1456), both of which have been the subject of extensive restoration work by a Polish team. Neither are accessible to the public just yet.

Rather than just retracing your steps, from Ibn Barquq, walk straight ahead from the entrance, passing the post office on your left, until you come to a small, elongated mausoleum (the Tomb of Asfur); turn left immediately after this and a straight walk of 1km down Sharia Sultan Ahmed will bring you back to the road leading to the underpass.

OLD CAIRO

Broadly speaking, Old Cairo (known in Egyptian as 'Masr al-Qadima', with a glottal stop 'Q') incorporates the entire area south of Garden City down to the quarter known to foreigners as Coptic Cairo. Most people visiting this area head straight to the latter, from where it is possible to explore sights further afield such as the Mosque of Amr ibn al-As and the Early Islamic-era Nilometer on the nearby island of Rhoda.

This is a very traditional part of Cairo and appropriate dress is essential. Visitors of either sex wearing shorts or with bare shoulders will not be allowed into churches or mosques.

Getting There & Away By far the easiest way of getting to Old Cairo is on the metro – Mar Girgis station is right outside the Coptic Cairo compound. The ride costs 50pt from Midan Tahrir and trains run every few minutes. There are buses running between Tahrir and Old Cairo but they are incredibly crowded. However, the bus trip back to Tahrir isn't as bad because you can get on at the terminal, beside the Amr ibn al-As mosque, before the bus fills up.

A slower but more pleasant way is to get a river bus from Maspero terminal near the radio and TV building, just north of the Ramses Hilton in central Cairo. Check it's going to Masr al-Qadima as not all do (see River Bus under Getting Around later in this chapter for route details). The ride takes about 50 minutes and costs 50pt. The last boat back to Maspero leaves at 4.15pm.

OLD CAIRO

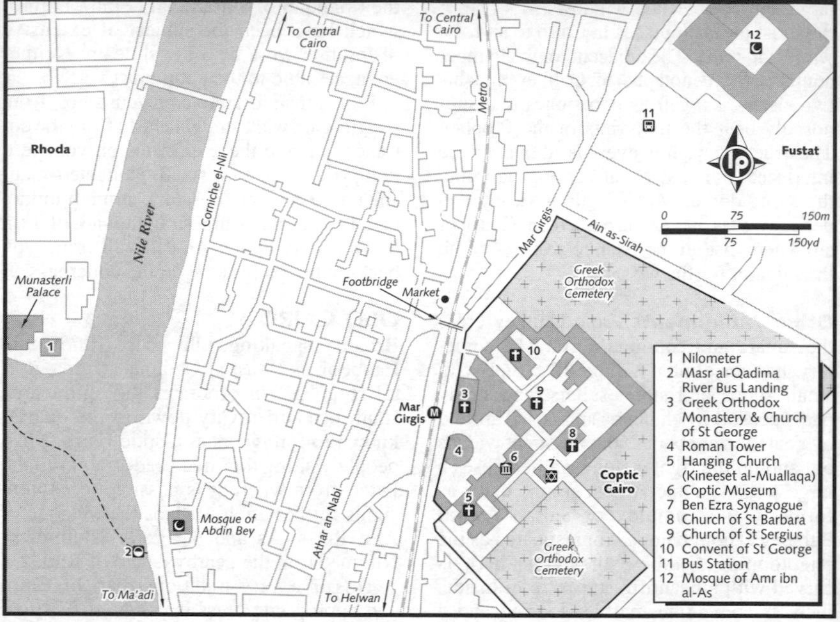

From the landing at Old Cairo cross the Corniche and head down the street with the Marlboro-emblazoned shop on the corner; at the end of the street turn left and walk straight along Sharia Athar an-Nabi for about 250m until you come to the footbridge over the metro line.

Coptic Cairo

Coptic Cairo is the heartland of Egypt's Christian community, as well as being the oldest part of modern-day Cairo. Seemingly oblivious to the growth and chaos that it has spawned, the tightly walled enclave remains a haven of tranquillity and peace.

Archaeologists claim that there was a small Nile-side settlement on this site as far back as the 6th century BC on which the Romans later established a fortress, called Babylon-in-Egypt, early in the 2nd century AD. The name Babylon is most likely a Roman corruption of 'Per-hapi-en-on' or 'Estate of the Nile God at On', a Pharaonic name for what was the former port of On (ancient Heliopolis).

Predating the arrival of Islam in Egypt, Babylon has always been a stronghold of Christianity (see History in the Facts about Egypt chapter). At one time there were more than 20 churches clustered within less than one square kilometre, although the number is down to just a handful today. They are linked by narrow cobbled alleyways running between high stone walls, and the feel of the place is quite similar to parts of the Old City of Jerusalem. In fact, after the Jews were exiled from their holy city in AD 70, some found refuge in Egypt and the country's oldest existing synagogue is here in Coptic Cairo.

There are two entrances to the Coptic Cairo compound: a sunken staircase beside the footbridge over the metro gives access to most churches and the synagogue, while the main entrance is used for visiting the Coptic Museum and Church of the Virgin.

Roman Towers The compound's main entrance is between the remains of the two round towers of Babylon's western gate. Built in AD 98 by Emperor Trajan, these were part of the waterside battlements and at the time, before it shifted west, the Nile would have lapped up right against them. Excavations on the southern tower have revealed part of the ancient quay, several metres below street level. The Greek Orthodox Monastery & Church of St George has been built on top of the northern tower.

Coptic Museum Founded in 1908, the museum *(☎ 363 9742, Sharia Mar Girgis; Metro: Mar Girgis; admission E£16; open 9am-5pm daily)* houses Coptic art from Graeco-Roman times to the Islamic era in a collection drawing not just from Cairo, but also from the desert monasteries and Nubia. It's split into two wings, the old and the new, but unfortunately the old wing is currently closed while damage sustained in the 1992 earthquake is repaired.

In the new wing the exhibits (stonework, woodwork, manuscripts, glass and ceramics) are housed on two floors and arranged in chronological order in an anticlockwise direction. Explanations are in French and English. The rooms themselves are very much part of the attraction, adorned with elaborately painted ceilings, fountains and mashrabiyya screens.

Hanging Church Dedicated to the Virgin Mary, this church *(Kineeset al-Muallaqa; Sharia Mar Girgis; Metro: Mar Girgis; admission free; Coptic mass Fri 8am-11am, Sun 7am-10am)*, which is still in use, is called the Hanging Church ('Al-Muallaqa', The Suspended) because it is built on top of the Water Gate of Roman Babylon. From ground level forecourt steep stairs climb to a 19th-century facade topped by twin bell towers, beyond which is a small inner courtyard, usually filled with sellers of taped liturgies and videos of papal sermons delivered by the present Coptic pope, Shenouda III.

The interior of the church, renovated many times throughout the centuries (and originally dating to the 9th century), has three barrel-vaulted, wooden-roofed aisles. Ivory inlaid screens hide the three altar areas, but in front of them, raised on 13 slender pillars that represent Christ and his disciples, is a fine pulpit, used only on Palm Sunday each year. One of the pillars is darker than the rest, symbolising Judas. In the baptistery off to the right a panel has been cut out of the floor through which you can look down on the Water Gate below; however, it's hard to make anything out in the gloom so also look out the window for a good view of one of the gate's twin towers and the green water stagnating about its foundations.

Monastery & Church of St George Back on Sharia Mar Girgis, the first doorway north of the main entrance leads through to the Greek Orthodox Monastery and Church of St George (in Arabic he's called Mar Girgis), named after one of the most popular Christian saints in the Middle East (later adopted by the English as their patron saint). He was a Palestinian conscript in the Roman army who was executed in AD 303 for tearing up a copy of the Emperor Diocletian's decree that forbade the practice of Christianity. There has been a church dedicated to him in Coptic Cairo since the 10th century, but this particular one dates from 1909. The interior is a bit gutted from past fires, but the stained glass windows are bright and colourful. The monastery next door is closed to the public.

Convent of St George If you descend the sunken staircase by the footbridge, then the first doorway on your left along the alleyway leads into the courtyard of the Convent of St George. The convent is closed to visitors but you can step down into the main hall and the chapel. Inside the latter is a beautiful, wooden door, almost 8m high, behind which is a small room still used for the chain-wrapping ritual that symbolises the persecution of St George during the Roman occupation. Visitors wishing to be blessed are welcome to be wrapped in chains by the patient nuns who will then intone the requisite prayers.

Churches of St Sergius & St Barbara

To get to St Sergius *(Abu Serga; open 8am-4pm daily)* leave the Convent of St George by the same door you entered, turn left and walk down the lane, following it around to the right and then take a left for the church entrance. This church is supposedly built over one of the spots where the Holy Family rested after fleeing from King Herod; the crypt in question is reached by descending some steps to the right of the altar but it's been flooded for some time now. Every year, on 1 June, a special mass is held here to commemorate the event.

Continuing on along the alley brings you to Ben Ezra Synagogue on the right and to the Church of St Barbara on the left. St Barbara's is dedicated to the saint who was beaten to death by her father for trying to convert him to Christianity. Her relics supposedly rest in a small chapel to the left of the nave.

If you walk on past the church, an iron gate on the right leads through to a large **Greek Orthodox cemetery**. The peace of this cemetery is usually shattered by the shouts and cheers from a neighbouring football pitch and sports field.

Ben Ezra Synagogue Egypt's oldest synagogue, Ben Ezra, dates from the 9th century, though it occupies the shell of a 4th-century Christian church. In the 12th century the synagogue was restored by Abraham Ben Ezra, Rabbi of Jerusalem, from whom it takes its name. Several legends are connected with the synagogue. It is said that the temple of the prophet Jeremiah once stood on the same spot and that this is where he gathered the Jews after they fled from Nebuchadnezzar, destroyer of their Jerusalem temple. There is also a spring that is supposed to mark the place where the pharaoh's daughter found Moses in the reeds, and where Mary drew water to wash Jesus.

Mosque of Amr ibn al-As

Although hardly any of the original structure remains, this mosque can claim direct descent from the first mosque ever built in Egypt. It was constructed in AD 642 by the victorious invader Amr (the general who conquered Egypt for Islam) and was founded on the site where he first pitched his tent. The original structure is said to have been made of palm trunks thatched with leaves, but it was rebuilt and expanded until it reached its current size in AD 827. The reconstruction didn't end there and the mosque has continued to be amended and reworked until as recently as 1983. There's little of interest to see inside, although of the 200 or so columns supporting the ceiling no two are said to be the same.

Nilometer

Located at the southern tip of the island of Rhoda, the Nilometer *(Sharia al-Malek as-Salah, Rhoda; admission E£8; open 9am-6pm daily)* was built in the 9th century to measure the rise and fall of the Nile, and thus predict the fortunes of the annual harvest. If the Nile rose to 16 cubits (a cubit is about the length of a forearm) this held great promise for the crops, and people would celebrate. The conical dome was added when the Nilometer was restored in the 19th century. The measuring device, a graduated column, is well below the level of the Nile in a paved area at the bottom of a flight of steps.

ZAMALEK & GEZIRA

Uninhabited until the mid-19th century Gezira (which means 'island') was a 3.5km by 1km strip of alluvial land rising up out of the Nile. Following the creation of a modern-day Downtown on the flood plain of the river's west bank, the khedive Ismail built a great palace on the island and had much of it landscaped as a vast royal garden. In the early years of this century, as Cairo was experiencing a land development boom, the palace grounds were partitioned, sold off and built upon.

The island today divides almost equally into two: the southern part is largely green and leafy and retains the name Gezira while the north is an upmarket residential district known as Zamalek.

Zamalek

Occupying the northern part of the island of Gezira, Zamalek is an attractive residential district with a Continental European tinge. It has few tourist sites but it's a pleasant place to wander and an even better place to eat (L'Aubergine, Abu as-Sid, La Bodega, Maison Thomas, Hana) or drink (Deals, L'Aubergine, or the Cairo Marriott garden).

The main street is Sharia 26th of July which cuts from east to west across the island. The junction of Sharias Hassan Sabry and Brazil is the focal point of the area. There's good shopping around here, and three of the city's best newsstands are located at the crossroads. Just a couple of doors east of Hassan Sabry on Sharia 26th of July is Simonds, the best cafe in town at which to read your papers – if you can get a seat.

At the eastern end of Sharia 26th of July, beside the bridge leading over to Bulaq, is the **Akhenaten Centre of Arts**, housed in a luxurious European-style villa built in the early 20th century by an aristocratic Egyptian family. There are always several different exhibitions on here, so it's worth dropping in; see Activities later in this chapter for details of the centre's opening hours.

Immediately south of Sharia 26th of July, overlooking the Nile, is the salmon-pink **Cairo Marriott** (see Places to Stay), occupying the premises of Ismail's former palace. It has a good bakery and an attractive garden, which is a good place for a beer. Behind the Marriott is a beautiful little neo-Islamic villa that opened in 1999 as the **Gezira Centre of Arts** *(☎ 736 8672, 1 Al Sheikh Marsafy, Zamalek; admission free; open 9am-1pm Sat-Thur)*. It houses a permanent exhibition of Islamic ceramics plus several galleries for temporary exhibitions of art.

Tales of the Riverbank

If it wasn't for the Nile, you'd go mad in Cairo. Cutting a swathe through the city north to south, the river ventilates – it is a channel free of the buildings through the heart of the metropolis that otherwise stifle breezes. It creates room to breathe, like a vast natural fire-break halting the smoky, choking urban sprawl and keeping it at bay. At the same time, it shows the city off at its best, allowing for miles of dramatic skyline along its banks.

The main place to appreciate all this is the waterside **Corniche** on the east bank. Planted with trees and set with benches it's the favourite spot for evening promenading. Any night of the week it will be crowded with families, kids licking ice cream, fathers cracking sunflower seeds bought from the roaming vendors; gangs of young students indulging in horseplay; and young lovers dangling their legs over the embankment wall, backs discreetly to the passers-by.

Across on Gezira, starting at the Qasr el-Nil bridge and running north to Zamalek is a new **pedestrian Corniche** down at water level. It opened in 1998 and was so popular that the authorities decided it was becoming untidy and promptly closed it to the public. Instead, strollers have to make do with the narrow strip of greenery up beside the road known as the **Andalusian Garden**, a small park, complete with Pharaonic obelisk, that costs 50pt to enter.

South of the Andalusian Garden, the bottom side of the bridge, is the **Casino el-Nil**, not a casino at all but a cafe-restaurant with plenty of riverside seating. Or if you have the cash, there are also restaurants at the **Gezira Sheraton** and **Meridien Le Cairo** at which you can take a table at the water's edge, not to mention the floating restaurants moored off Zamalek and boat-based **TGI Friday** down in Giza.

But absolutely the best way to appreciate the Nile is to take a **felucca**. From several landing stages on the Corniche it's possible to hire one of these graceful lateen-sailed boats (see Felucca Rides later in this chapter for further details), a type that has been plying the Nile since antiquity. Watching the sun set over the city skyline while languidly drifting on the river makes for a fantastically stress-relieving and cool end to a busy day's sightseeing.

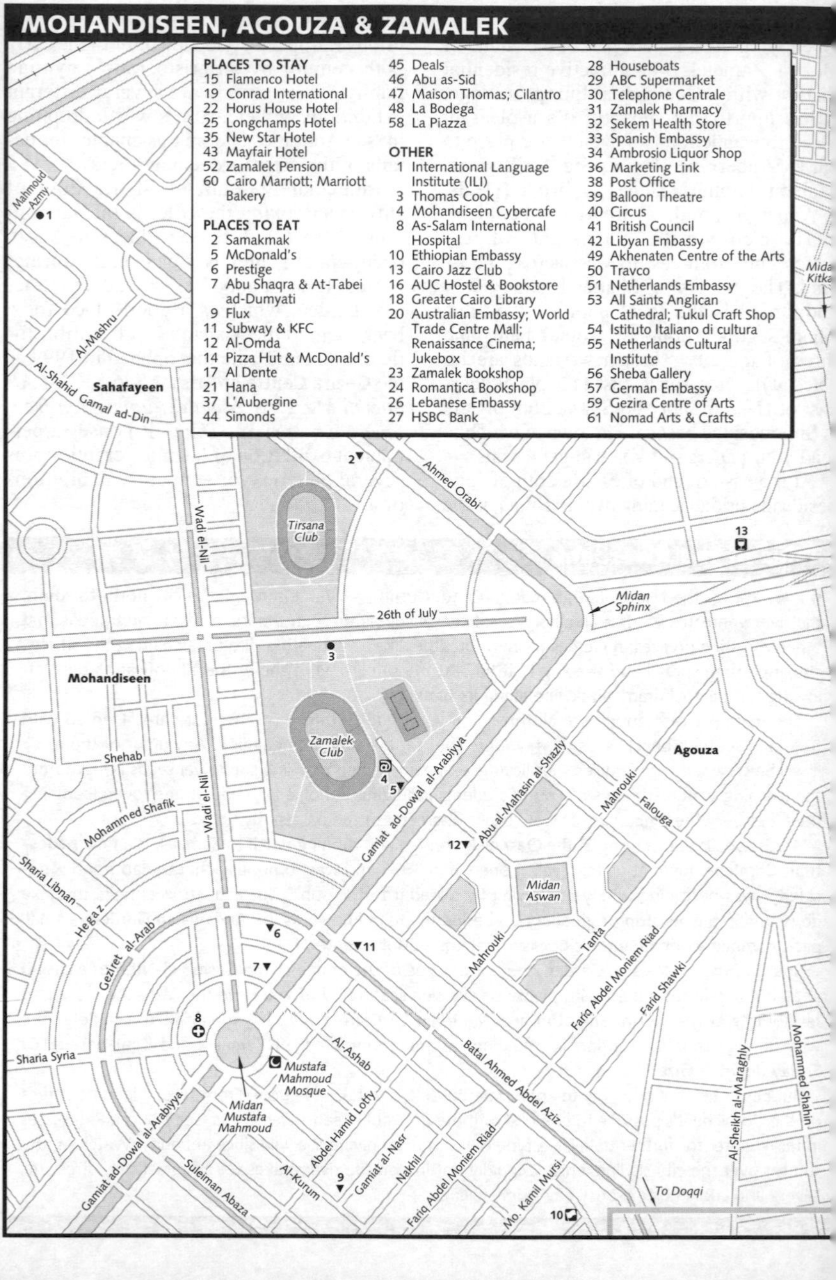
MOHANDISEEN, AGOUZA & ZAMALEK
PLACES TO STAY
15 Flamenco Hotel
19 Conrad International
22 Horus House Hotel
25 Longchamps Hotel
35 New Star Hotel
43 Mayfair Hotel
52 Zamalek Pension
60 Cairo Marriott; Marriott Bakery
PLACES TO EAT
2 Samakmak
5 McDonald's
6 Prestige
7 Abu Shaqra & At-Tabei ad-Dumyati
9 Flux
11 Subway & KFC
12 Al-Omda
14 Pizza Hut & McDonald's
17 Al Dente
21 Hana
37 L'Aubergine
44 Simonds
45 Deals
46 Abu as-Sid
47 Maison Thomas; Cilantro
48 La Bodega
58 La Piazza
OTHER
1 International Language Institute (ILI)
3 Thomas Cook
4 Mohandiseen Cybercafe
8 As-Salam International Hospital
10 Ethiopian Embassy
13 Cairo Jazz Club
16 AUC Hostel & Bookstore
18 Greater Cairo Library
20 Australian Embassy; World Trade Centre Mall; Renaissance Cinema; Jukebox
23 Zamalek Bookshop
24 Romantica Bookshop
26 Lebanese Embassy
27 HSBC Bank
28 Houseboats
29 ABC Supermarket
30 Telephone Centrale
31 Zamalek Pharmacy
32 Sekem Health Store
33 Spanish Embassy
34 Ambrosio Liquor Shop
36 Marketing Link
38 Post Office
39 Balloon Theatre
40 Circus
41 British Council
42 Libyan Embassy
49 Akhenaten Centre of the Arts
50 Travco
51 Netherlands Embassy
53 All Saints Anglican Cathedral; Tukul Craft Shop
54 Istituto Italiano di cultura
55 Netherlands Cultural Institute
56 Sheba Gallery
57 German Embassy
59 Gezira Centre of Arts
61 Nomad Arts & Crafts
Mahmoud Azmy
Al-Mashru
Al-Shahid Gamal ad-Din
Sahafayeen
Wadi el-Nil
Tirsana Club
Ahmed Orabi
Midan Sphinx
26th of July
Mohandiseen
Zamalek Club
Shehab
Mohammed Shafik
Gamiat ad-Dowal al-Arabiyya
Abu al-Mahasin al-Shazly
Mahrouki
Falouga
Agouza
Midan Aswan
Sharia Libnan
Hegaz
Geziret al-Arab
Tanta
Fariq Abdel Moniem Riad
Farid Shawki
Sharia Syria
Mustafa Mahmoud Mosque
Midan Mustafa Mahmoud
Al-Ashab
Batal Ahmed Abdel Aziz
Abdel Hamid Lotfy
Gamiat al-Nasr
Nakhil
Al-Kurum
Suleiman Abaza
Mo. Kamil Mursi
To Doqqi
Al-Sheikh al-Maraghly
Mohammed Shahin
Midan Kitka

MOHANDISEEN, AGOUZA & ZAMALEK

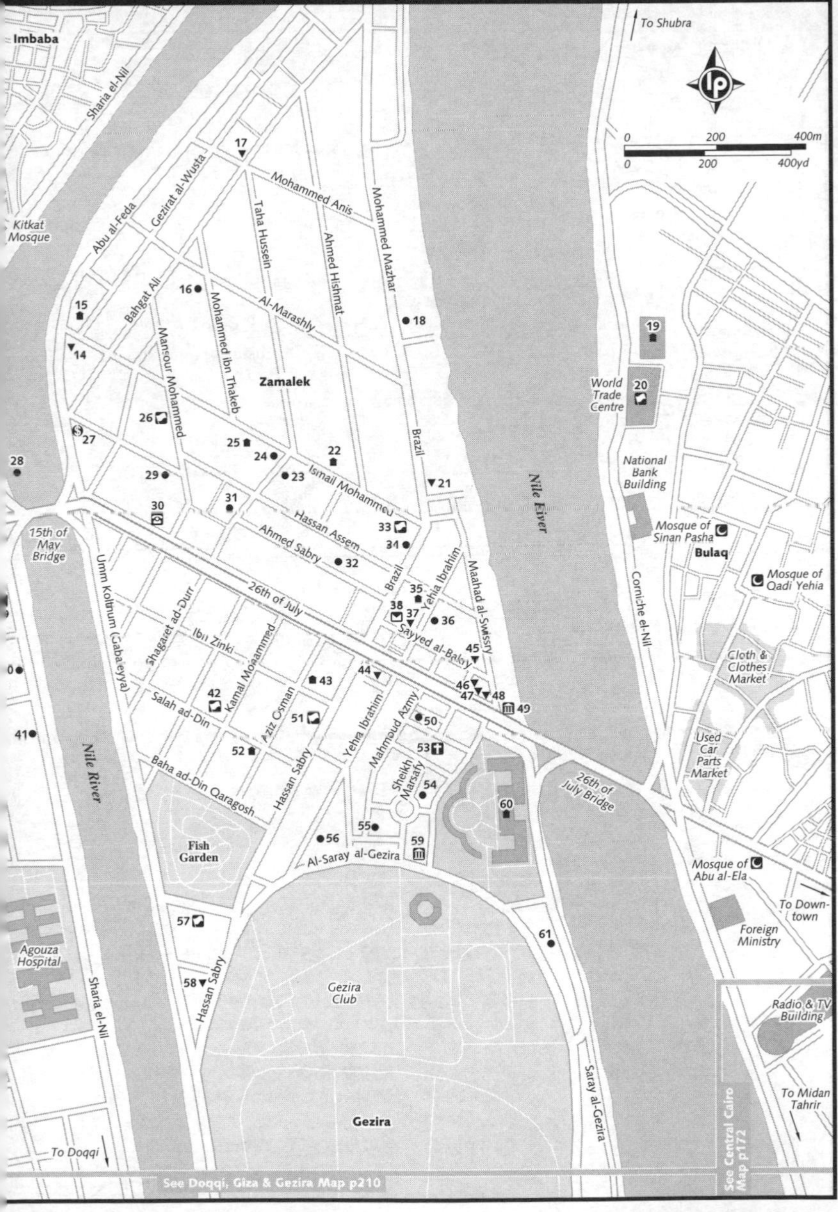

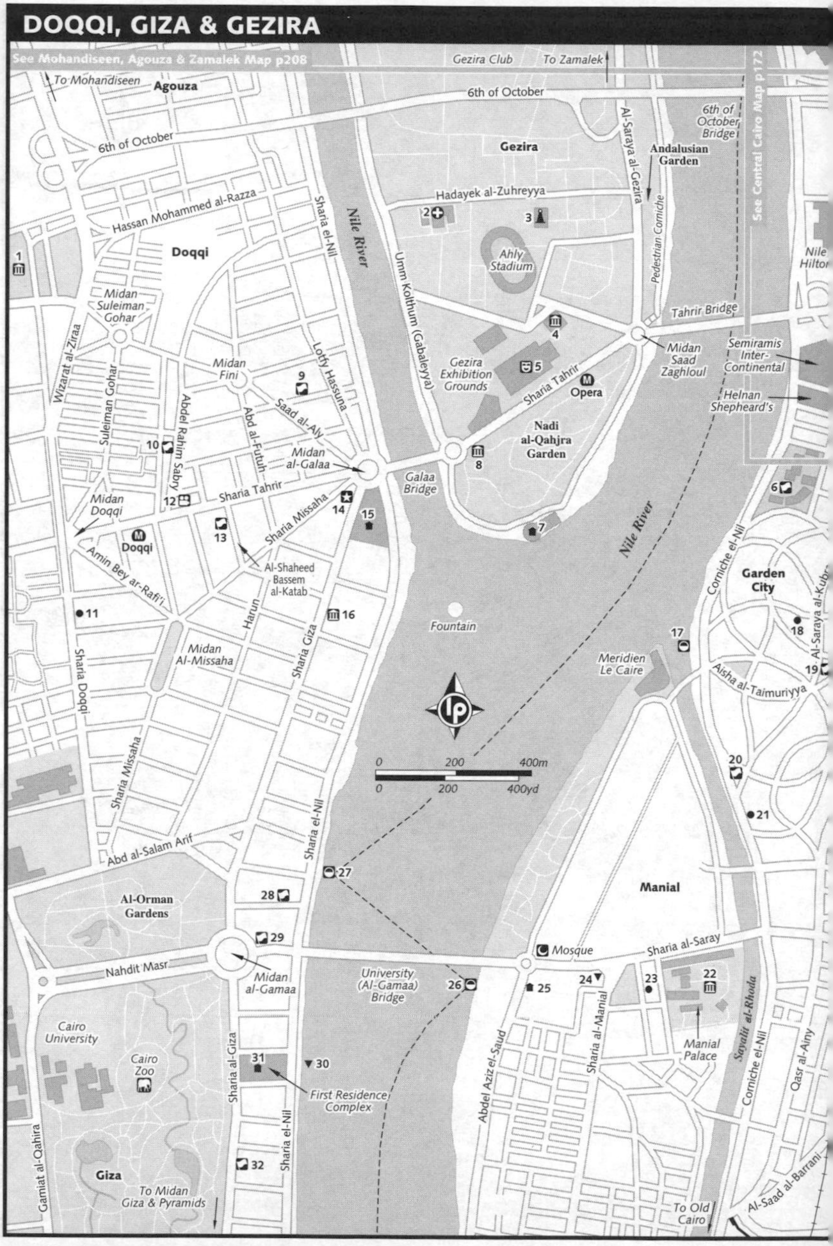
DOQQI, GIZA & GEZIRA
See Mohandiseen, Agouza & Zamalek Map p208
See Central Cairo Map p172
Gezira Club
To Zamalek
To Mohandiseen
Agouza
6th of October
6th of October Bridge
Gezira
Andalusian Garden
Al-Saraya al-Gezira
Pedestrian Corniche
Hadayek al-Zuhreyya
Hassan Mohammed al-Razza
Sharia el-Nil
Nile River
Doqqi
Ahly Stadium
Umm Kolthum (Gabaleyya)
Nile Hilton
Midan Suleiman Gohar
Tahrir Bridge
Midan Saad Zaghloul
Semiramis Inter-Continental
Helnan Shepheard's
Wizarat al-Ziraa
Suleiman Gohar
Midan Fini
Lotfy Hassuna
Gezira Exhibition Grounds
Sharia Tahrir
Opera
Abdel Rahim Sabry
Abd al-Futuh
Saad al-Aly
Nadi al-Qahjra Garden
Midan al-Galaa
Galaa Bridge
Midan Doqqi
Sharia Missaha
Doqqi
Amin Bey ar-Rafi'i
Al-Shaheed Bassem al-Katab
Corniche el-Nil
Garden City
Harun
Sharia Giza
Fountain
Midan Al-Missaha
Sharia Doqqi
Meridien Le Caire
Al-Saraya al-Kubra
Aisha al-Taimuriyya
0 200 400m
0 200 400yd
Sharia Missaha
Sharia el-Nil
Abd al-Salam Arif
Manial
Al-Orman Gardens
Mosque
Sharia al-Saray
Nahdit Masr
Midan al-Gamaa
University (Al-Gamaa) Bridge
Sharia al-Manial
Manial Palace
Sayalit el-Rhoda
Corniche el-Nil
Qasr al-Ainy
Cairo University
Cairo Zoo
Sharia al-Giza
First Residence Complex
Abdel Aziz el-Saud
Sharia el-Nil
Gamiat al-Qahira
Giza
To Midan Giza & Pyramids
To Old Cairo
Al-Saad al-Barrani
1 2 3 4 5 6 7 8 9 10 11 12 13 14 15 16 17 18 19 20 21 22 23 24 25 26 27 28 29 30 31 32

DOQQI, GIZA & GEZIRA

PLACES TO STAY
7 Gezira Sheraton
15 Cairo Sheraton; Cairo Sheraton Cinema
25 HI Manial Youth Hostel
31 Four Seasons Hotel

PLACES TO EAT
24 KFC
30 TGI Friday's

OTHER
1 Agricultural Museum
2 Anglo-American Hospital
3 Cairo Tower
4 National Museum of Egyptian Modern Art
5 Opera House
6 UK Embassy
8 Mahmoud Mokhtar Museum
9 Kenyan Embassy
10 Syrian Embassy
11 TNT Skypack
12 Cinema Tahrir
13 Jordanian Embassy
14 Police
16 Mahmoud Khalil Museum
17 Dok Dok Felucca Point
18 DHL
19 Canadian Embassy
20 Italian Embassy
21 Western Union; Federal Express
22 Manial Palace Museum
23 MSC (Student Cards)
26 Manial River Bus Stop
27 University River Bus Stop
28 Saudi Arabian Embassy
29 Israeli Embassy
32 French Embassy

Gezira

Gezira is best approached across the Tahrir Bridge from Midan Tahrir, which brings you to Midan Saad Zaghloul, presided over by a statue of a stout man in a tarboosh, representing Saad Zaghloul a nationalist leader of the 1930s. Immediately west are the immaculately groomed Gezira Exhibition Grounds, dominated by the centrepiece of the **Opera House** *(☎ 739 8144, Gezira Exhibition Grounds; Metro: Opera; open for performances only)*. Opened only in 1988, the building is a modern take on traditional Islamic design, and was a gift from the Japanese. You can only enter during performances (see Entertainment later this chapter) but the grounds are pleasant to walk around.

Across from the Opera House is the **National Museum of Egyptian Modern Art** *(☎ 736 6665, Gezira Exhibition Grounds; Metro Opera; admission E£10; open 10am-1pm & 5pm-9.30pm Tues-Sun)*, home to a fairly limited collection of 20th century Egyptian painting, some of which is certainly worth seeing, particularly the work of painters Abdel Hady al-Gazzar and Mahmoud Said. There are also two galleries in the grounds, both of which host ever changing temporary art exhibitions: the **Hanagar Art Centre** *(☎ 735 6861, Gezira Exhibition Grounds; Metro: Opera; free admission; open 10am-10pm Tues-Sun)*, behind the Opera House, and the **Arts Palace** *(☎ 736 7627, Gezira Exhibition Grounds; Metro: Opera; admission varies according to the exhibition; open 10am-1pm & 5pm-10pm Tues-Sun)*, just to the right of the main gate.

If you leave the Opera House grounds by the rear entrance, on the west of Gezira, near the Galaa Bridge, across the road you'll see a modest gate with a sign for the **Mahmoud Mokhtar Museum**. Mokhtar (1891–1934) was the sculptor laureate of Egypt; he was responsible for Saad Zaghloul on the nearby midan and for the Mother of Egypt statue outside the entrance to the Giza Zoo. Unfortunately, the museum has been closed for some years now and is unlikely to reopen during the lifetime of this edition of this book.

Cairo Tower North of the Museum of Modern Art and south of Hadeyek al-Zuhreya is the Cairo Tower. The story has it that the tower *(Burg al-Masr; ☎ 735 7187, Sharia Hadayek al-Zuhreya, Gezira; Metro: Opera; admission E£30; open 9am-midnight)*, completed in 1961 and looking like a 185m-high wickerwork tube, was built as a thumb to the nose at the Americans who had given Nasser the money used for its construction to buy US arms. After the Pyramids it's the city's most famous landmark. The view from the top is excellent; clearest in the early morning or late afternoon. There's an expensive revolving restaurant on top as well as a cheaper cafeteria. You might be greeted with quite a long queue at dusk.

MOHANDISEEN, AGOUZA & DOQQI

A map of Cairo in Baedecker's 1929 guide to Egypt shows nothing on the Nile's west bank other than a hospital and the road to the Pyramids. The hospital is still there, set back off the Corniche in Agouza, but it's now hemmed in on all sides by an unsightly rash of mid-rise housing blocks that shot up during the 1960s and 1970s when Mohandiseen, Agouza and Doqqi were created as new suburbs for Egypt's emerging professional classes. The three districts remain bastions of the middle classes, home largely to those families who made good during the years of Sadat's open-door policy. Unless you happen to find concrete and traffic stimulating, the sole attraction of these areas is that they contain many of the city's better eating places (see Places to Eat later in this chapter).

What little history there is here is on the river in the form of the **houseboats** moored off Sharia el-Nil just north of 15th of May Bridge. Known as *dahabiyyas*, these floating two-storey wooden structures used to line the banks of the Nile all the way up from Giza to Imbaba forming an extensive waterborne neighbourhood. During the 1930s they were something of a tourist attraction, especially when some of the boats were converted into casinos, music halls and bordellos. Many of the houseboats continue to be rented out and they're popular with teachers at the British Council, which is just a few hundred metres south down the street.

Nile-side attractions these days are a little more sedate: there's just the **Balloon Theatre**, a venue for farcical Egyptian plays, and the big top of the **Cairo Circus**. These are both in summer only (June to September), check with the tourist office or *Egypt Today* for more details.

Agricultural Museum

It sounds dull but this museum *(☎ 337 2933, Sharia Wizaret al-Ziraa, Doqqi; admission 10pt; open 9am-1.30pm Tues-Sun)* is actually quite fascinating, verging on the bizarre. Apart from stuff on life in Egyptian villages, it has giant plastic fruits, glass cases packed full of stuffed birds, and a Pharaonic-era mummified bull from Memphis. The gardens are also quite relaxing. The museum is just to the west of the 6th of October Bridge.

Mahmoud Khalil Museum

This museum *(☎ 336 2358, 1 Sharia Kafour, Doqqi; Metro: Doqqi; admission E£25, open 10am-5.30pm Tues-Sun)* houses one of the Middle East's finest collections of 19th- and 20th-century European art, including numerous sculptures by Rodin and a rich selection of French works by the likes of Delacroix, Gauguin, Lautrec, Monet and Pissaro. There are also some Rubens, Sisleys and a Picasso. The paintings are housed in a recently renovated, temperature-controlled (and what a pleasure that is on a hot summer's day) villa that used to be the home of Mohammed Mahmoud Khalil, a noted politician during the 1940s and was later taken over by President Sadat. It's just a few minutes walk south of the Cairo Sheraton.

GIZA

A former village on the west bank of the Nile, Giza is now a vast governorate in its own right. It stretches from the Nile 18km westwards to the Pyramids, adjoining Doqqi to the north and petering out into fields then desert to the south. To Cairenes it's best known as the home of their largest academic institution, **Cairo University**. The plaza in front of the domed main building is a favoured gathering point for demonstrations, directed more often than not against Israel which has an embassy about 500m east of here.

Cairo Zoo

Though bedraggled and short on funds, Cairo's zoo *(☎ 570 8895, Midan al-Gamaa, Giza; admission 10pt; open 8.30am-5pm daily)* has managed to struggle through more than 100 years of existence – it celebrated its centennial in 1994. It remains a popular excursion for local families and couples, especially on Friday and Saturday. It's not, however, a good place for anybody who cares about animals.

HELIOPOLIS

It's only a suburb of Cairo, but were it to stand alone as a town in its own right, Heliopolis (known to Egyptians as Masr al-Gedida, or 'New Cairo') would be considered one of the gems of North Africa. It was conceived in the early years of the 20th century as an exclusive 'garden city' in the desert, miles to the north-east of the squalor of Cairo, meant to house the colonial officials who ruled Egypt. The architectural style is a European fantasy of the Orient set in stone. Since the 1950s, however, overcrowding in Cairo has caught up with this not-so-distant neighbour and the former desert barrier was breached by a creeping tide of middle-income high-rises. Ranks of apartment buildings festooned with satellite TV dishes now greatly outnumber the graceful, old villas. Although there are no major sites as such, Heliopolis has a relaxed, almost Mediterranean air, and is a pleasant place for an evening's wandering, with a couple of interesting bars and a good many restaurants.

A Walk Around Heliopolis

If you're coming up by bus, alight opposite the **Uruba Palace**, formerly the Heliopolis Palace Hotel, and now occupied by the office of the Egyptian president. Running straight, up the side of the palace, is the main street, Sharia al-Ahram. At the first intersection, with the splendid Sharia Ibrahim Laqqany (detour left for some fantastic architecture) is the open-air cafeteria **Amphitrion**, while five minutes up the street and over the road is the **Palmyra**; both these cafes are as old as Heliopolis itself and were popular watering holes for the allied soldiers during WWI and WWII. Today they're two of the very few places in Cairo where it's possible to drink a beer without having to skulk in some dingy room away from public eyes. Both terraces serve food and are great places to relax and people watch on a balmy evening.

HELIOPOLIS

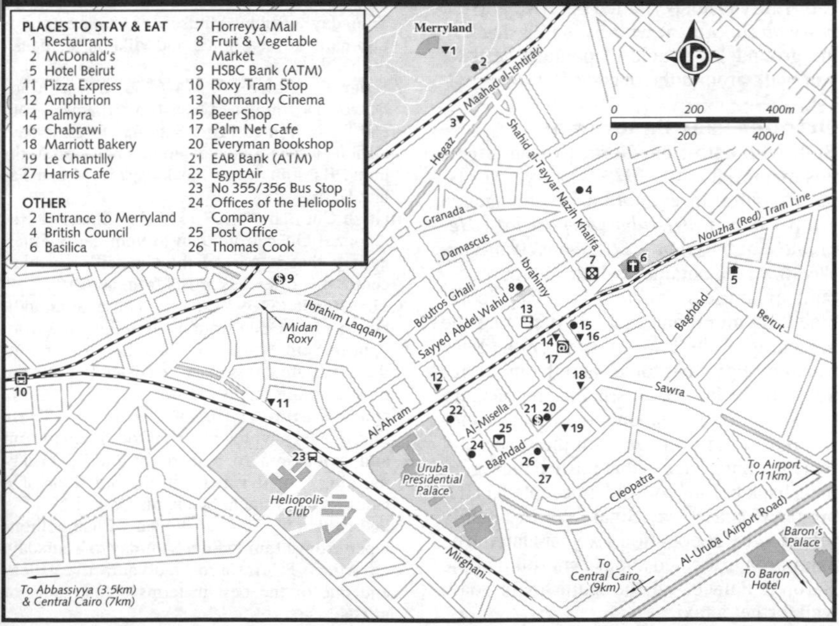

Two blocks further east on Al-Ahram is the **Basilica** designed as a miniature version of İstanbul's famous Aya Sofia. Its distinctive shape has caused it to be known as the 'jelly mould' by local expats. Baron Empain, the Belgian industrialist who founded Heliopolis, is buried in the crypt. Unfortunately, the place is usually kept locked. From the Basilica head south (right if you're facing the Basilica) down Sharia al-Shahid Tayyar Nazih Khalifa, which will bring you to the Airport Rd and, across it, the **Baron's Palace** (Qasr al-Baron), a Hindu-style temple looming up among the faceless apartment blocks. This was the personal residence of Baron Empain, modelled – for no known reason – on the temples of Angkor Wat in Cambodia. Three generations of the Empain family inhabited the palace until it was sequestered by the state in the 1950s and allowed to fall into ruin. While a rich collection of sandstone Buddhas, geishas, elephants and serpents still adorns the exterior, the interior has been gutted and is now home to large colonies of bats. Entry is not permitted but if you tip the *bawwab* (doorman; who lives in a shack in the grounds) a couple of pounds, he'll let you walk around the outside.

October War Panorama

Built with help from North Korean artists, this memorial to the 1973 'victory' over Israel is quite an extraordinary propaganda effort *(Sharia al-Uruba (Airport Rd), Heliopolis; admission E£10; open 9am-9pm Wed-Mon)*. Contained within the purpose-built cylindrical structure is a large combined 3D mural and diorama depicting the breaching of the Bar Lev Line on the Suez Canal by Egyptian forces and the initial retreats by the Israelis. A stirring commentary (in Arabic only) recounts the heroic victories but is short on detail on the successful Israeli counterattacks that pushed the Egyptians back before both sides accepted a UN-brokered cease-fire. Sinai was eventually liberated by negotiation six years later. The exhibition is located about 2km south of the Baron's Palace, on the same main road; walk or get a taxi.

Getting There & Away

The best way to get to Heliopolis is to take the airport bus (No 356) from Midan Abdel Moniem Riad, behind the Egyptian Museum. The ride takes about 30 minutes. Get off outside the Heliopolis Club (the first stop after reaching the street with tram tracks – look out for a Pizza Express on the left). The fare is E£2 and buses are usually every 20 minutes. Alternatively, there's the tram that goes from just north of Midan Ramses (see Getting Around later in this chapter).

ART GALLERIES

In addition to the National Museum of Egyptian Modern Art (see Gezira earlier this chapter) there are numerous small galleries around town where contemporary local and foreign artists and sculptors exhibit. The following places tend to show the most interesting stuff:

Akhenaten Centre of Arts (☎ 735 8211, 1 Maahad al-Swissry, Zamalek) Open from 10am to 1.30pm and from 5.30pm to 9pm Saturday to Thursday. Official Ministry of Culture exhibition halls housed in a grand villa on the banks of the Nile.

Atelier du Caire (☎ 574 6730, 2 Karim ad-Dawla, Downtown) Open from 10am to 1pm and from 5pm to 11pm Saturday to Thursday. Official artists' union exhibition halls, off Mahmoud Bassiouni, one block west of Midan Talaat Harb.

British Council (☎ 303 1514, 192 Sharia el-Nil, Agouza) Open from 9am to 9pm daily. Small gallery that is part of the Council's teaching centre that often has artists from abroad.

Cairo-Berlin (☎ 393 1764, 17 Yousef al-Guindi, Downtown) Open from noon to 3pm and from 5pm to 8pm Monday to Saturday. Along with the Mashrabia, this place consistently hosts the most exciting works in town.

Espace Karim-Francis (☎ 391 6357, 1 Sharia Sherifeen, Downtown) Open from 10am to 2pm and from 6pm to 9pm daily, closed Friday morning. Small gallery on the 3rd floor of a sidestreet apartment block, off Qasr el-Nil.

Mashrabia (☎ 578 4494, 8 Sharia Champollion) Open from 11am to 8pm Saturday to Thursday. Off Midan Tahrir Cairo's most attractive gallery and one of the best in terms of its stable of artists.

Townhouse Gallery (☎ 575 5901, Sharia Hussein Pasha, Downtown) Open from 10am to 2pm and from 6pm to 9pm, closed Thursday & Friday morning. Occupying three floors of an old 'townhouse', off Mahmoud Bassiouni, this is Cairo's most exciting gallery, showing two or three exhibitions at any one time and with a small sales space selling art and books.

BILLIARDS & BOWLS

Billiards (pool), snooker and tenpin bowling have really taken off in Cairo in a big way in the last few years. Most of the venues are in the wealthier suburbs away from the city centre, like Ma'adi and Medinat Nasr. But right in the middle of Downtown in the **Al-Bustan Centre**, there's bowling (E£12, 10 lanes) and pool (E£20 per hour) on the 9th floor, and more pool tables on the 2nd floor. Also, on the top floor of the **Ramses Hilton Mall** there's a snooker hall (E£25 per hour) and a pool hall (E£20 per hour), both of which serve beer. They're both open from 11am to 3am daily.

FELUCCA RIDES

Feluccas are the ancient broad-sail boats that are seen everywhere up and down the Nile. They can be hired out by the hour from several places along the Corniche. One of the most pleasant things to do in Cairo is to go out on a felucca with a supply of beer and a small picnic just as sunset approaches. The best spot for hiring is the Dok Dok landing stage on the Corniche at Garden City just north of the Meridien Le Caire. A boat and captain should cost about E£15 per hour irrespective of the number of people on board. This rate is, of course, subject to haggling. Other felucca mooring points are the southeast end of Gezira just north of the Tahrir Bridge; opposite the Helnan Shepheard's hotel (captains here tend to be more voracious in their demands for money); and in Ma'adi just north of the Felfela restaurant.

HORSE RIDING

A horse ride out by the Pyramids can be a great way to escape the clamour of Cairo and vent some pent-up aggro. For details, see The Pyramids earlier in this chapter.

SWIMMING

Finding a place to cool off is not easy in Cairo. Sporting clubs, the places that most Cairenes who can afford it go to swim, restrict access to members only for insurance reasons. The only option is to make for a hotel, most of which allow day use for nonguests at a price. Usage of hotel pools is generally restricted to 10am to 6pm, or similar. For addresses and phone numbers see the Places to Stay chapter.

At the cheaper end of the scale the Atlas Zamalek on Gamiat ad-Dowal al-Arabiyya in Mohandiseen has a high-rise postage stamp-sized plunge pool that costs E£30 per day. Even cheaper is the rooftop pool at the Pyramisa on Sharia Doqqi in Doqqi, charging E£20 per person. More expensive but worth splashing out for, the Meridien Le Caire has a fantastic Nile-side pool, accessible to all-comers at E£65 a day. The Semiramis Inter-Continental charges nonguests E£84, while at the Gezira Sheraton it's E£89. Both the Marriott (a lovely pool in the garden) and Conrad ask E£85 per person per day.

There are some excellent pools out at the hotels around the Pyramids, including at the Forte Grande, which has a big pool with island patio, for E£80 per day. To use the garden pool at the Oberoi Mena House, with its fantastic Pyramid views, you need to reserve a cabana (E£170 for two), and you can swim until sunset. The nearby Pyramids Park Inter-Continental (☎ 02-383 8666) on the Cairo-Alexandria Desert Rd has what's claimed to be the largest pool in the Middle East but it comes with the most expensive usage fee in town: E£256 per person, or E£306 for two.

Ask about discounts for kids or family packages.

ORGANISED TOURS

Some of the budget hotels in central Cairo arrange tours to various places around the city such as the Pyramids, Saqqara and Memphis. The price is usually about E£20 and includes transport only – there's no guide and admission is extra. The stories about these trips have often been negative, so forewarned is forearmed.

Salah Mohammed Abdel Hafez (☎ *298 0650, mobile 012-313 8446,* ⓔ *samo@intouch.com)* runs a full-day excursion to the already mentioned places, as well as to the Wissa Wassef Art Centre at Harraniyya, for E£18 per person (once again, lunch and admission prices are extra). If you're staying at one of the city centre hotels, he'll pick you up at around 9am. You'll need to arrange the tour at least one day in advance – leave a message on the answering machine if he's not there.

A third option is to go through a travel agency such as Masr Travel or American Express. They both do half-day sightseeing tours to the Pyramids and Sphinx, Memphis and Saqqara, Old Cairo, and the Egyptian Museum for between US$26 and US$30. See Information earlier in this chapter for contact details.

PLACES TO STAY

For general information about accommodation in Cairo see Accommodation in the Facts for the Visitor chapter.

PLACES TO STAY – BUDGET

Cairo's budget accommodation scene has seen little development in recent years. Since the demise of the notorious Oxford Hotel in the 1980s, the backpacker ghetto has been focused on one particular block at the top end of Talaat Harb, Downtown (where currently you'll find the Venice, Safary and Sultans I-III hotels). However, with travellers who prefer a modicum of comfort and privacy, the two continued favourites are at the bottom of Talaat Harb in the shape of the New Sun and Ismailia House. Lying somewhere in between, both geographically and in terms of cost, is the

Cairo Hotel Scams

The most perpetrated scam of all in Cairo is the one in which a local convinces the newly arrived traveller that the hotel they are heading for is closed, horrible or very expensive and leads them off to another 'better' place, for which your self-appointed 'guide' earns himself a commission.

The main culprits are the taxi drivers at Cairo airport. They have fixed commission rates with many of the Downtown hostels and will always take you to whichever is offering the best rate at that time. (Any hostel that refuses to pay the taxi drivers' commission can find itself blackballed and suffer a decline in trade as a consequence.) It's not just the taxi drivers. On arrival at the airport, if you're not with a group, you may be approached by a man or woman with an official-looking badge that says 'Egyptian Chamber of Tourism' or something similar. These people are not government tourism officials, they are hotel touts. There are also a couple of touts that ride the buses from the airport. As a final hurdle, there are also touts who attempt to latch onto new arrivals on the street; they'll offer to lead you to your hotel where they can 'check everything is OK' and, of course, unbeknown to you, claim credit and cash for bringing you in.

The problem with all of this is that, in the worst case scenario, you could be waylaid into checking into some very dodgy fleapit that may be way out of the centre. Added to which, whatever commission was paid out will ultimately find its way onto your bill. Worse still, often your 'local friend' will also negotiate a higher than normal price for the room, thus increasing their own cut.

The simple rule is do not be swayed by anyone who tries to dissuade you from going to the hotel of your choice. Hotels do not open and close with any great frequency in Cairo and if it's listed in this book then it is very unlikely to have gone out of business in the meantime. Some taxi drivers will stall by telling you that they don't know where your hotel is – in that case tell them to let you out at Midan Tahrir (or the Nile Hilton) from where it's a short walk to most of the budget hotels. If you find yourself with a new 'friend' walking you to your hotel, stop them at the door – if they begin to protest, then bear in mind that no decent, ordinary Egyptian would ever dream of accompanying a foreigner into their hotel.

CHRISTOPHER WOOD

JULIET COOMBE

JULIET COOMBE

EDDIE GERALD

For centuries Cairenes have lived in the 'City of the Dead', a series of mausoleum complexes built by the Mamluks in the 13th and 14th centuries. Today's residents continue to trade and play here, undaunted by the area's sombre history.

MASON FLORENCE

GAVIN ANDERSON

Cairo has expanded over the centuries and now encroaches upon the Pyramids of Giza, which were built over 4000 years ago, long before the capital was in existence. The Pyramids are a must-see for anyone visiting Cairo, and count as the world's oldest tourist attraction.

Dahab. We like the Berlin for its ultra-helpful manager, although the rates are really pushing up out of the budget category and into the mid-range. Pick of the crop, however, remains the Pension Roma, but unless you book well in advance you don't stand a chance of getting a room.

There are plenty of other cheapies that are not included in our listings, often for good reasons; Cairo is notorious for shyster operators, who enter the backpacker hotel business for the unrivalled opportunities it offers to fleece newly arrived foreigners.

Also, be aware that prices are often negotiable and you should consider the listed room rates as estimates. Although we give the rates quoted to us at the hotel receptions, at the same time we met other travellers who had paid less for the same accommodation, and some who'd paid more.

Camping

Motel Salma *(☎ 384 9152; fax 385 1010, Saqqara Rd, Harraniyya)* Camping E£7 per person, 2-person/4-person cabin E£30/40 without shower, with breakfast E£50. Although it's miles and miles from anywhere, this place is the only option when it comes to camping in Cairo. On the plus side, it does have views of the Pyramids from the back of the site. Overland tour companies occasionally stop here. Be prepared for a mosquito attack at sunset.

To get to the Salma, take a microbus for Abu Sir from Pyramids Rd (Sharia al-Haram). It's about a 4km trip; ask the driver about the best place to alight.

Hostels

HI Manial Youth Hostel *(☎ 364 0729, fax 398 4107, 135 Sharia Abdel Aziz as-Saud, Manial)* 3-bed/6-bed dorms E£12/8 for HI members, for nonmembers E£16/12. 11pm curfew. Cairo's only official youth hostel suffers from a lousy location well out of the centre. Neither is it such an attractive proposition that it's worth travelling for – while it's in reasonable nick with clean toilets, the beds are nothing great. It has dorm rooms only (sleeping three or six people) with no provision for couples or families. Breakfast is included in the price. Expect to spend lots of time in taxis.

Hotels & Pensions

The inexpensive hotels and pensions are concentrated Downtown, mainly on and around Talaat Harb (see the Central Cairo map). For those who like things a little less chaotic, there are also a few options in Zamalek.

Downtown This is the most convenient place to be for getting around, eating and entertainment. Most of the hotels are on the upper floors of old, and often fairly decrepit, apartment blocks. Rooms tend to be large, but are also musty and sparsely furnished. In this price range there is no air-con (except where noted), but sometimes there may be a ceiling fan. Shared bathrooms are the norm, usually with Pharaonic-era plumbing that delivers a highly erratic water supply.

The following list, while far from exhaustive, covers what we consider to be the better options. The cheapest options are given first.

Sultan Hotel I-III *(☎ 577 2258, 4 Tawfiqiyya Souq, Downtown)* Off the top of Talaat Harb, the three Sultan hotels plus the ***Safary Hotel*** *(☎ 575 0752, 4 Tawfiqiyya Souq, Downtown)* and ***Hotel Venice*** *(☎ 574 1171, 4 Tawfiqiyya Souq, Downtown)* all occupy one building on a colourful market street. Beds at these hotels start at E£9 on the 1st floor (Sultan I) and drop to E£6 up on the 5th floor (Sultan III and Safary), probably because there's no lift. There's little to choose between the five places; in all cases the word unsanitary springs to mind. Don't expect bed linen, hot water or privacy; do expect plenty of company of the six-legged kind. Venice is marginally better than the rest with a few private rooms (E£25) but still, it's recommended only for those on the tightest of budgets.

Dahab Hotel *(☎ 579 9104, 26 Mahmoud Bassiouni, Downtown)* Dorm beds E£15, singles/doubles E£20/25, with shower E£30/35. This hotel is a collection of whitewashed huts on a rooftop attempting to recreate the feel of a Sinai beach camp in unremittingly urban Downtown Cairo. It's not a bad attempt with cushioned communal spaces open to the sky, bamboo screens and Bob Marley on the cassette deck. Totally laid-back.

Hotel Minerva *(☎ 392 0600/1/2 39 Talaat Harb, Downtown)* Singles/doubles E£16/28, doubles with shower E£32. This hotel has a ground floor reception hidden down the alley opposite the Al'Américaine cafe, while the hotel itself occupies the 5th and 6th floors. The not-so-obvious location means this old place is often overlooked, but the rooms are kept clean, as are the communal showers and toilets, and it's good value.

Richmond Hotel *(☎ 393 9358, 41 Sharia Sherif, 7th floor, Downtown)* Singles/doubles/triples E£25/40/50. A new addition to the scene, this place has friendly management that is trying hard. Rooms are basic, and perhaps a little gloomy, but the shared showers and toilets are kept serviceable. It's about the only budget hotel to offer a double bed (just the one, mind).

Ismailia House Hotel *(☎ 356 3122, 1 Midan Tahrir, 8th floor, Downtown)* Singles/doubles/triples E£25/40/45, doubles with shower E£45. The location is tremendous at this hotel (west facing rooms have panoramic views over Cairo's main square and the Nile) but as far as we're concerned, the rooms and bathrooms are prohibitively grubby.

New Sun Hotel *(☎ 578 1786, ⓔ newsunhotel@yahoo.com, 2 Talaat Harb, 9th floor, Downtown)* Beds in 4-bed dorm E£15, singles/doubles E£25/40. In a good location just off Midan Tahrir, this hotel unfortunately doesn't have any views. Rooms are decent sized but dingy, although the shared bathrooms are commendably spotless.

Magic Hotel *(☎ 579 5918, 10 Sharia al-Bustan, 3rd floor, Downtown)* Singles/doubles with fans E£25/40. It used to be run by the same management as the New Sun and Ismailia House, but the bedrooms and bathrooms are that little bit cleaner at Magic Hotel, and the place has a cosier, less traveller-worn feel.

Pension Roma *(☎ 391 1088, fax 579 6243, 169 Mohammed Farid, 6th floor, Downtown)* Single/doubles/triples E£35/55/70, with private shower E£40/60/75. Down a side alley next to the Gattegno department store, this hotel is the city's most charming budget option. It is long popular for its old world elegance including shiny hardwood floors, antique furniture, a splendid breakfast room and proprietress Madam Cressaty herself. Reservations are necessary.

Berlin Hotel *(☎/fax 395 7502, ⓔ berlinhotelcairo@hotmail.com, 2 Sharia Shawarby, 4th floor, Downtown)* Singles/doubles/triples E£77/96/115. Off Qasr el-Nil, the Berlin is a little pricier than most other budget options, but you may consider it worth it for clean, air-con rooms all with their own shower cubicles. Rare among Cairo's budget hotels, the English-speaking owner/manager, Hisham Yousef, actually seems to care about keeping guests happy.

Zamalek For a different slant on Cairo, consider staying in Zamalek, which is a more relaxing and greener place than the city centre, with lots of good eating and drinking, yet it's still only a five-minute taxi ride from Downtown.

Mayfair Hotel *(☎ 735 7315, fax 735 0424, ⓔ mayfaircairo@yahoo.com, 9 Aziz Osman, Zamalek)* Singles/doubles E£25/30, with air-con & bath E£50/60. The Mayfair is quiet and tranquil with a pleasant shady breakfast terrace, and just a minute away is the buzzing shopping street, Sharia 26th of July.

Zamalek Pension *(☎ 340 9318, 6 Salah ad-Din, Zamalek)* Singles/doubles E£50/70. There are only about five rooms here and you feel like a house guest rather than a hotel resident. Also, it's located on a leafy street in an attractive neighbourhood. Pricewise it's really heading into the mid-range and there's a supplement for rooms with air-con.

PLACES TO STAY – MID-RANGE

The hotels in this section are organised by area then listed alphabetically.

Central Cairo

Carlton Hotel *(☎ 575 5022, fax 575 5323, 21 Sharia 26th of July, Downtown)* Singles

...and More Hotel Scams

A few more things to beware of. When checking in never pay in advance for your room. If reception asks for cash up front that should set warning bells ringing that there's something dodgy about the place – no decent hotel would ever make such a request. We've had letters from readers asked to stump up for two nights on arrival and then when they've decided to check out after one night (because of grotty toilets, no hot water, whatever), they've been unable to get a refund.

The big con of the moment is selling overpriced trips down to Luxor and Aswan. Many Cairo hotels do a hard sell on packages of three or four days in Upper Egypt, which include accommodation and a boat or felucca trip. The reason they're so keen is the commission they can make. If you contact the travel agency that organises these packages directly (and most hotels deal with a company called Amigo, at the Isis Hotel, Aswan; ☎ 097-324 722) you'll be offered an all-in price of around US$65. Buy the same thing through a Cairo hotel and you risk paying through the nose. We heard of one traveller who'd been taken for US$210, a mark up for the hotel in question of more than 300 percent. This practice is not restricted to budget places either; a few of the mid-range hotels are not above making a little extra through their 'travel desks'.

Our advice would be to skip the packages altogether. Accommodation is easy to find in Luxor and Aswan, and the hotels the tour agencies use are not particularly good. If you do want to take a package, at the very least call the agency yourself and cut out that expensive Cairo middleman.

US$15-25, doubles US$25-30. One for nostalgia buffs, the Carlton is stuck in a 1950s time warp and shows its age around the edges. But there are some good, recently renovated rooms with air-con and bathroom that are a good deal at the price. It also has a pleasant rooftop cafeteria, but no beer is served. It's located beside the Rialto cinema.

Cosmopolitan Hotel *(☎ 392 384, fax 393 3531, 1 Sharia ibn Taalab)* Singles/doubles US$42/54. Off Qasr el-Nil, right at the heart of Downtown, this is a gorgeous, old (1910) building with dark, lacquered antique furniture and tiled bathrooms with tubs, supplemented by mod-cons such as central air-con. Many of the rooms also benefit from a recent spruce up.

Garden City House Hotel *(☎ 794 4969, fax 794 8126, W www.geocities.com/garden77house, 23 Kamal ad-Din Salah, Garden City)* Singles US$11-15, doubles US$19-22. Opposite the back of the Semiramis Inter-Continental (look for the small sign at 3rd-floor level) is this longtime favourite among Egyptologists and Middle Eastern scholars, but now more popular with young students from the nearby AUC. It's noisy, a bit dusty and definitely overpriced, but a lot of people love it and keep coming back. Breakfast and supper are included in the price.

Lotus Hotel *(☎ 575 0966, fax 575 4720, 12 Talaat Harb, 7th floor, Downtown)* Singles/doubles US$20/25, with bath US$28/34. This is an old favourite that's now showing its age. Rooms have air-con and are clean, if shabby, but overpriced, yet the place remains popular. The hotel is reached via an elevator at the end of an arcade almost opposite the Felfela Takeaway.

Odeon Palace Hotel *(☎/fax 577 6637, 6 Abdel Hamid Said, Downtown)*. Singles/doubles US$34/43. Off Talaat Harb, is this very comfortable, upper mid-range hotel where all rooms have a mini-fridge, TV, telephone and air-con. Breakfast is E£10 extra. The rooftop 24-hour bar is popular with night owls.

Windsor Hotel *(☎ 591 5277, fax 592 1621, e wdoss@link.net, W www.windsorcairo.com, 19 Sharia Alfy, Downtown)* Singles/doubles from US$37/47. This was the British Officers' Club before 1952. It retains a colonial air, particularly in the reception area with its beautifully ornate lift, and in the lounge bar, which is one of the best spots in town for a beer. In 1991, former Monty Python member, Michael Palin, stayed here while filming the BBC series *Around the World in 80 Days*; he described the place as possessing an 'almost unreal individuality'. There's a wide variety of rooms with all combinations of bathroom types; cramped or the size of a tennis court, with or without shower/toilet/tub, newly tiled or well-worn antique, hot water or no water.

Around Midan Ramses

Midan Ramses is a little north of the city centre – about 10 minutes' walk or two stops on the metro.

Fontana Hotel *(☎ 592 2321, fax 592 2145, Midan Ramses)* Singles/doubles US$17/25. On the north-west corner of the midan, high above the traffic and fumes, the Fontana has clean rooms, a pleasant rooftop cafe/bar and a disco on the floor below. The views are great but the location is not really convenient for anywhere except the train station.

Happyton Hotel *(☎/fax 592 8600, 10 Ali al-Kassar, Downtown)* Singles/doubles with air-con US$16/20. Off Emad ad-Din, this is a relaxed, good-value-for-money option. Rooms are modern-ish and clean, although some are a little gloomy, so you might need to look at a couple before accepting. It's halfway between Midan Ramses and Downtown, about a 10-minute walk from the top of Talaat Harb, tucked away down a quiet backstreet behind the Karim Cinema.

Victoria Hotel *(☎ 589 2290, fax 591 3008, 66 Al-Gomhuriyya,* Singles/doubles US$20/25. For the price, the Victoria's air-con, three-star standard, well-kept rooms are an absolute steal, all with immaculate bathrooms and breakfast included. It's got to be Cairo's best accommodation bargain. And if the hotel is a little out of the way, the Ataba metro station is just a couple of minutes walk away, and then it's just two stops to Midan Tahrir.

Islamic Cairo

Islamic Cairo (see the Al-Azhar & Khan Al-Khalili map) is the liveliest and most fascinating part of the city, but noise levels are high and once you have managed to get off to sleep you're almost sure to be woken soon after by the early morning calls to prayer.

Al-Hussein Hotel *(☎ 591 8089, Midan Hussein)* Singles/doubles US$12/15, with air-con US$19/22. This hotel is institutional and grim, but almost the only option if you fancy a location right at the heart of the Khan al-Khalili bazaar.

Radwan Hotel *(☎ 590 1311, fax 592 5287, Sharia Muski, Khan al-Khalili)* Singles/doubles US$13/21 with bath. Few foreigners seem to stay here – a look at the registrations showed all Egyptian names – and it's easy to see why: the place is badly maintained and far from clean. We mention it only because options in the Islamic Cairo area are so few.

Zamalek

See Places to Stay – Budget earlier for some comments on Zamalek.

Flamenco Hotel *(☎ 735 0815, fax 735 0819, W www.flamencohotels.com, 2 Geziret al-Wusta, Zamalek)* Singles US$38-105, doubles US$43-125. The Flamenco is highly recommended for anyone who does not mind being a little out of the centre. It overlooks the branch of the Nile between Zamalek and Mohandiseen and the views from the balconies are excellent. The service is good and it has two OK bars and a good restaurant.

Horus House *(☎ 735 3634, fax 735 3182, 21 Ismail Mohammed, Zamalek)* Singles/doubles US$38/47. This is a small, friendly, family hotel in an apartment block. The place is kept immaculately clean and service is excellent.

Longchamps Hotel *(☎ 735 2311, fax 735 9644, 21 Ismail Mohammed, 5th & 6th floors, Zamalek)* Singles/doubles US$36/48. Oncc notorious for its raucous African disco, the Longchamps is much more sedate these days. Overseen by Heba Bakri and husband Chris, it's highly recommended for cleanliness, spotless air-con rooms with all new fixtures in the bathrooms, and wonderful, shady terraces. There's also a small bar and restaurant.

New Star Hotel *(☎ 735 0928, fax 735 3424, 34 Yehia Ibrahim, Zamalek)* Doubles

US$30. The rooms here are badly neglected, with peeling wallpaper, missing ceiling panels and leaky toilets, but they are big (some with reception areas and kitchens) and kept relatively clean. The quiet backstreet location might also be regarded as a plus.

Heliopolis

About 40 minutes north of the city centre by taxi, bus or tram, staying in Heliopolis is not a viable option for a casual visitor to Cairo, but if you have business up here or want to be close to the airport and don't wish to spend top dollar, then there are a couple of reasonable three-star options.

Baron Hotel (☎ *291 5757, fax 290 7077,* ⓔ *resvcai@baronhotels.com,* ⓦ *www baronhotels.com, 8 Mahaad al-Sahari)* Singles/doubles US$120/145. This is a modestly sized smart modern hotel with popular nightclub and bar, and pleasant conservatory cafe. Located off the Airport Rd, it overlooks the incredible Hindu-styled Baron's Palace.

Hotel Beirut (☎ *291 6048, 43 Sharia Baghdad)* Singles/doubles US$55/69. This hotel is a fairly sombre place, but it's very convenient for exploring central Heliopolis and the bar is popular with local expats.

PLACES TO STAY – TOP END

All of Cairo's five-star hotels come with the complete complement of amenities such as restaurants, bars, executive suites, business centres, shops and banks, plus a few Egyptian touches such as weekly wedding receptions in the foyer and nightclubs with belly-dancing. The following prices generally don't include breakfast and taxes (typically 19%).

Cairo Marriott (☎ *340 8888, fax 340 8240, Sharia Saray al-Gezira, Zamalek)* Singles/doubles from US$165. A former royal palace that has been tastefully extended, the Cairo Marriott boasts a classy reception, exquisite dining areas and a serene garden with bar, cafe, pool and tennis courts. While the location isn't great for sightseeing (you'll need to take taxis), Zamalek has good restaurants and bars, plus interesting boutiques, and lots of greenery.

Cairo Sheraton (☎ *737 3737, fax 336 4601,* ⓔ *sheratonegypt@starwoodhotels .com,* ⓦ *www.sheraton.com, Midan al-Galaa, Doqqi)* Singles/doubles US$152/176. The foyers and corridors that have to be negotiated to find reception make this a strangely soulless hotel. Plus it's on the wrong (western) side of the Nile, necessitating a long walk to get anywhere. And the whole thing is very 1970s and unattractive in appearance. Not a big favourite with us then, but the Sheraton name ensures that it's always busy nonetheless.

Conrad International (☎ *580 8000, fax 580 8080,* ⓔ *reservation@conradcairo .com.eg, 1191 Corniche el-Nil, Bulaq)* This is an attractive hotel that opened in 1999, but is a little devoid of life thanks to a location (Nile-side) some distance north of the city centre; too far to walk, though only a couple of minutes in a taxi. The in-house restaurants are good and next door is the World Trade Center, containing Cairo's most exclusive shopping mall and top restaurants.

Four Seasons (☎ *573 1212, fax 568 1616,* ⓦ *www.fourseasons.com, 35 Sharia Giza, Giza)* Singles US$220-300, doubles US$250-330. Cairo's newest luxury hotel is part of the exclusive First Residence complex, the most expensive real estate in the city. Levels of service are unmatched, although the location in Giza is not particularly convenient for anywhere.

Gezira Sheraton (☎ *7361 1333, fax 735 5056,* ⓔ *gzher@rite.com,* ⓦ *www.sheraton .com, Sharia al-Orman, Gezira)* Singles US$185-210, doubles US$210-250. This is on the very southern tip of the island of Gezira where views are superb both from the rooms and from the numerous riverside restaurants and bars.

Helnan Shepheard's (☎ *355 3800, fax 355 7284, Corniche el-Nil)* Singles/doubles US$90/105, fronting the Nile US$134/160. It benefits from a good location just south of Midan Tahrir but the hotel was built in the 1960s and hasn't aged well.

Oberoi Mena House (☎ *383 3222, fax 383 7414,* ⓔ *obmhofc@oberoi.com.eg,* ⓦ *www.oberoihotels.com, Pyramids Rd,*

Giza) Singles/doubles from US$150/180, for Pyramid views US$250/300. A former royal hunting lodge converted into a sumptuous luxury hotel, this has an unbeatable location right next door to the Pyramids. The interior is an opulent Oriental fantasy, and there are beautiful gardens with a large, swimming pool from which the Pyramids can be seen while floating on your back.

Meridien Le Caire *(☎ 362 1717, fax 362 1927, W www.lemeridien-hotels.com, Corniche el-Nil, Manial)* Singles US$165-250, doubles US$140-285. A location right on the northern tip of the island of Rhoda ensures that most of the rooms here have excellent views, which may or may not make up for the fact that you're far from the action and have to resort to taxis to get to and from the hotel. A massive new annexe dwarfing the original hotel opens in 2001, which should improve facilities that were starting to show their age.

Nile Hilton *(☎ 578 0444, fax 578 0475, e nhilton@brainy1.ie-eg.com, W www.hilton.com, Midan Tahrir, Downtown)* Singles/doubles from US$215/250, with Nile views US$240/275. Cairo's oldest five-star hotel is still a fine place to stay courtesy of the best location in the city, on Midan Tahrir next to the Egyptian Museum. It's very much a hub of social life; the terrace ***Ibis Cafe*** is popular with city residents and the hotel's secluded pool is one of the best in town.

Ramses Hilton *(☎ 574 4400, fax 575 7152, W www.hilton.com, 115 Corniche el-Nil)* Singles US$88-215, doubles US$111-230. Modern and towering (with good views all round), this particular Hilton is also bland and characterless. Worse still, it's surrounded by overpasses and is adjacent to a city bus station; unless you take a taxi from the door every time, walking anywhere involves negotiating at least half a dozen of Cairo's most lethal roads.

Semiramis Inter-Continental *(☎ 795 7171, fax 796 3020, e cairo@interconti.com, W www.interconti.com, Corniche el-Nil, Downtown)* Singles/doubles US$190/220, with Nile views US$210/240. This hotel benefits from a great riverside location just off Midan Tahrir, so it's close to the Egyptian Museum. The foyer is the most attractive of those of all the newer hotels, with lots of glass, greenery and Nile views.

PLACES TO EAT

For general descriptions of food types plus hints on ordering and prices, see the Food section in the Facts for the Visitor chapter.

Fast Food

Fast-food chains are mushrooming in Cairo quicker than you can say 'Big Mac and fries'. There are now more than 30 international franchises in town. There's even a Pizza Hut/KFC within swiping distance of the Sphinx's paws. The term fast food is something of a misnomer though, as young Egyptians spend hours at a time hogging the tables in these joints, which are considered some of the trendiest places in town to hang out. Mohandiseen's Gamiat ad-Dowal al-Arabiyya has become the street to cruise down – Cairo's smog-choked, six-lane, concrete Sunset Boulevard – largely because of its heavy concentration of fast-food outlets.

The following list of fast-food outlets covers only the Downtown branches.

KFC 9 Midan Tahrir; Mohammed Mahmoud, just off Midan Tahrir opposite the AUC; 21 Abdel Khalek Sarwat, just off Talaat Harb
McDonald's 13 Midan Tahrir; 42 Talaat Harb; Mohammed Mahmoud, just off Midan Tahrir opposite the AUC; Ramses Hilton Mall, 6th floor
Pizza Hut Mohammed Mahmoud, opposite the AUC

Vegetarian

Although there are few vegetarian restaurants (just two in fact), nonmeat-eaters shouldn't have too much trouble. The menus at places such as ***At-Tabei ad-Dumyati*** or ***Felfela Restaurant*** in central Cairo, ***Maroosh*** in Mohandiseen, or ***Chabrawi's*** in Heliopolis feature lots of nonmeat dishes (see elsewhere in Places to Eat for more information on all these places).

L'Aubergine *(☎ 735 6550, 5 Sayyed al-Bakry, Zamalek)* Mains E£17-30. Open

10am-2am daily. Cairo is short on dedicated veggie restaurants – in fact this is the only one – but luckily it's a good 'un. The menu is constantly changing but last time we visited it included things such as blue cheese and leek lasagne, aubergine moussaka and vegetables in coconut, ginger and green coriander sauce. There are also salads and soups, and beer is served.

Al-Omda *(☎ 345 2387, 6 Sharia al-Gazayer, Mohandiseen)* Dishes E£12-24. Open noon-2am daily. Located behind the Atlas Zamalek, Al-Omda is famous for its kebab and kofta, but beside the meaty restaurant is a branch specialising in salads only, supplemented by dips and other vegetarian mezze.

Budget Dining

North of Midan Talaat Harb There are plenty of small fuul and ta'amiyya places concentrated in the sidestreets around Tawfiqiyya Souq (where the cheapo backpacker hostels are), plus a couple of places around Cinema Miami on Talaat Harb where you can get shwarma.

Abu Tarek *(40 Sharia Champollion)* Dishes E£1.50-E£3. Open 8am-midnight daily. This is reckoned to be the best kushari joint in all Cairo; it's certainly the cleanest. It's perpetually packed and sometimes you have to queue for a table but it's worth it. For dessert ask for *roz bi'laban* – cold rice pudding.

Akher Sa'a *(8 Sharia Alfy)* Dishes E£3-4. Open 24 hrs daily. The sign is in Arabic only, but look for the Christian bookshop next door. This is a hugely popular fuul and ta'amiyya takeaway joint with a no-frills restaurant next door. The menu is limited but you can get things such as omelettes (with pasturma is good) and tahini and bread.

At-Tabei ad-Dumyati *(31 Sharia Orabi)* **Midan Ramses & Around map** Dishes E£3-8. About 200m north of Midan Ramses, this is absolutely one of the best places for a good cheap meal in Cairo. Like Akher Sa'a, it's basic (it resembles a canteen), but it's clean, the portions are large, the service is fast and friendly and the food is excellent. It's predominantly vegetarian and has a wonderful salad bar where you can choose from about 30 different prepared salads and mezze. Other specialities include fuul (numerous different types), ta'amiyya and a very tasty lentil soup.

At-Tahrir *(19 Abdel Khalek Sarwat)* Dishes E£1.50-3. Open 10am-midnight daily. Kushari only. Take a seat here and order small, medium or large – though small is usually more than most can finish. It also has a branch on Sharia Tahrir, off Midan Tahrir.

South of Midan Talaat Harb Sharia Tahrir, running down to Midan Falaki, is dotted with plenty of juice stands, bakeries, fuul and ta'amiyya, fiteer and kushari places, while Mohammed Mahmoud, which runs down the side of the AUC, is lined with fast food joints. For eating on the hoof, best bet are the ***Felfela takeaway outlets*** on Talaat Harb just around the corner from the sit-down restaurant (see below); one specialises in fuul, ta'amiyya and shwarma sandwiches, the other in seafood stuffed into bread.

Fatatri at-Tahrir *(166 Sharia Tahrir)* Dishes E£6-10. Close to Midan Tahrir, this is a 24-hour sit-down restaurant that specialises in fiteer, sweet or savoury.

Felfela Restaurant *(☎ 392 2751, 15 Sharia Hoda Shaarawi)* Meals E£20-30 for two. Open 8am-midnight daily. Perpetually packed with tourists and locals, Felfela nevertheless deserves its popularity. The quirky decor (tree-trunk tables, stuffed animals, aquariums and lanterns) creates a fun dining environment and, depending on your choices, the all-Egyptian food is excellent and moderately priced. Give the meat dishes a miss, as they are all overpriced and done better elsewhere. Instead order a selection of fuul, ta'amiyya, salads and other side dishes such as baba ghanoug and tahina. Beer is served.

Islamic Cairo This is not a good part of town in which to be looking for a feed. Although there are plenty of kebab-type places around Midan Hussein, the quality of food is generally poor.

Egyptian Pancake House *(Midan Hussein)* Small/medium fiteer E£10/12. You can choose from the following toppings: cheese, egg, tomato, olives and ground meat, or raisins, coconut and icing sugar. You'll probably want to avoid the 'turkey cock'.

Al-Halwagy *(☎ 591 7055, Midan Hussein)* Meals E£10-20 for two. Open 24 hrs daily. Just along from the Pancake House, this is a good ta'amiyya, fuul and salad place that has been around for nearly a century. You can eat at pavement tables or secrete yourself upstairs where one of the tables has a veiled view over the bazaar below.

Naguib Mahfouz Cafe *(☎ 590 3788, 5 Sikket al-Badestan, Khan al-Khalili)* Min charge E£15. Open 10am-2am daily. This cafe is located in the foyer of the Khan al-Khalili Restaurant (see Islamic Cairo under Restaurants earlier), where the extremely pleasant surroundings almost justify the grossly inflated prices of the tea, coffee, shwarma and sandwiches.

Zamalek Cheap dining is not one of Zamalek's fortes but there are a few possibilities.

Al Dente *(☎ 735 9117, 26 Bahgat Aly)* Dishes E£6-10. Open 10am-midnight daily. A tiny Italian place popular with students from the nearby AUC hostel, Al Dente specialises in pastas: you choose the type and the sauce. Portions are generous.

Maison Thomas *(☎ 735 7057, 157 Sharia 26th of July)* Pizzas E£15-20. Open 24 hrs daily. Cairo's only Continental-style deli, Maison Thomas does by far the best pizza in Cairo, and a 'regular' is easily enough for two. It also has excellent though pricey sandwiches and salads. Eat in or take out.

Heliopolis Traditional Egyptian fare such as kebab, kofta, shwarma and spit-roasted chicken is served at both ***Amphitrion*** and ***Palmyra***, the two terrace cafeterias on Sharia al-Ahram; and at ***Al-Kashef***, at the bottom of Sharia Damascus, near the intersection with Ibrahim Laqqany.

Chabrawi's *(Sharia Ibrahimy)* Dishes E£2.50-10. This is a fuul and ta'amiyya place with a 1st-floor dining room. It also has an extensive salad bar and serves some more unusual dishes such as egg-fried cauliflower and *agah*, which is a cross between a puffed-up omelette and a giant ta'amiyya. Other than pasturma the place is completely vegetarian. It's extremely clean, cheap and highly recommended.

Restaurants

Downtown Downtown isn't particularly good for fine dining, but if you're happy enough with grilled meats and Egyptian fare, then there are quite a few serviceable options.

Alfy Bey *(☎ 577 4999, 3 Sharia Alfy)* Mains E£9-16. Open 1pm-1am daily. Following a recent refurbishment this restaurant, in business since 1938, is still in good shape. The food, while basic, is very good and represents excellent value. Choose from dishes such as lamb chops, kebab, grilled chicken or stuffed pigeon; but there's no beer.

Arabesque *(☎ 574 7898, 6 Qasr el-Nil)* Mains E£25-30. Open 12.30pm-3.30pm & 7.30pm-12.30am daily. Between Midan Talaat Harb and Midan Tahrir, the Arabesque scores highly for its decor and surroundings – you enter through a small art gallery into a cosy dining area divided by mashrabiyya screens and columns with a small gurgling fountain as a centrepiece. Unfortunately the dishes – a mix of traditional Egyptian fare, seafood and steaks – are very hit and miss and it's wise to steer clear of anything ambitious.

Cafe Riche *(☎ 392 9793, 17 Talaat Harb)* Mains E£12-25. Open 8am-midnight daily. A survivor of pre-Revolution days that was extensively renovated in the 1990s, Cafe Riche serves traditional Egyptian fare in a room hung with portraits of Egypt's revered cultural pantheon. It's open for breakfast and still favoured as an intellectual's drinking den in the evenings. Try the chicken fatta: pieces of chicken on an oven-baked bed of rice and bread pieces in a garlicky sauce.

Da Mario *(☎ 578 0444, Nile Hilton, Midan Tahrir)* Mains E£18-25. Open noon-

1.30am daily. Out in the garden courtyard of the Nile Hilton, this is one of the better value five-star hotel restaurants. It serves a variety of very well presented pastas in gigantic portions.

Estoril *(☎ 574 3102, 12 Talaat Harb)* Dishes E£16-30. Open noon-2am daily. Tucked down an alley next to the AmEx office this is an old-style eatery with traditional Egyptian grills and salads plus Lebanese mezze. Quality is very variable but if you stick with a selection of starters accompanied by beer then you'll come away happy.

Le Bistro *(8 Hoda Shaarawi)* Dishes E£10-20. Open 11am-11pm daily. About 200m beyond the Felfela, Le Bistro has cooking that is sufficiently Gallic to ensure that the place is heavily patronised by Cairo's French-speaking community. The menu features some good salads and plenty of beef and chicken-in-sauce dishes. Busy at lunch, but like a morgue in the evenings.

Peking Restaurant *(☎ 591 2381, 14 Sharia Ezbekiyya)* Meals E£20-30. Don't be put off by the shabby exterior, inside the place is smart – if a little dark – and the predominantly Cantonese menu is reasonably authentic. If you've been in the country for any length of time it is refreshingly non-Egyptian.

Islamic Cairo Chronically short on decent dining Islamic Cairo, in fact, has really just the one restaurant.

Khan al-Khalili Restaurant *(☎ 590 3788, 5 Sikket al-Badestan)* Dishes E£24-40. Open 11am-midnight daily. In the heart of the bazaar, this is run by the Oberoi hotel people so, while it's certainly classy, the 'Disneyfied Orientalism' of resident musicians and chintzy decor can come across as a bit phoney. The menu is limited and the food, though good, is overpriced.

Zamalek For expats, moneyed Egyptians and anyone who eats to be seen, Zamalek is the place. Abu as-Sid and La Bodega are two of Cairo's best dining experiences, while L'Aubergine and Hana are tried and tested favourites.

L'Aubergine, described earlier under Vegetarian, also has some nonvegetareian elements on its ever-changing menu.

Abu as-Sid *(☎ 735 9640, 157 Sharia 26th of July)* Dishes E£24-50. Open noon-2am daily. One of Cairo's newest and most sumptuous restaurants, Abu as-Sid is decked out in stage-set Orientalia: padded cushions, brass lamps, and spangly bric-a-brac. Food is traditional Egyptian. Choose from the likes of *sharkassiyya* (chicken breast with walnut sauce), *sayadiyya* (fish with tomatoes, onions and red rice) or *molokhiyya*, the green-leaf soup, with rabbit. It's all exceptional. Reservations are necessary.

Deals *(☎ 736 0502, 2 Maahad al-Swissry)* Dishes E£16-30. Although primarily a bar, get here early enough and Deals is also a decent place to dine. Food ranges from burgers and chilli con carne to calamari and large salads. Check the blackboard for daily specials. As bar food goes, it's very good and not expensive, but if you're planning to eat make sure you get there before 8pm to stand a chance of finding some table space.

Hana *(☎ 341 3197, Sharia Brazil)* Mains E£20-30. Open 1am-11pm daily. About 400m north of Sharia 26th of July, Hana's is an unpretentious, smoky, little Korean restaurant that serves up fairly authentic South-East Asian food (the menu includes some Japanese and Chinese dishes). *Kimchi* (fermented pickles) comes complimentary, as does fruit at the end of the meal. Dishes are substantial. Beer is available.

La Bodega *(☎ 735 6761, 157 Sharia 26th of July)* Mains E£30-50. Open 7am-1am daily. Elegant and unusual, La Bodega is a restaurant, bar and cocktail lounge combination, the latter with the most fabulous decor. The menu ranges wide and includes Middle Eastern and international dishes. The selection of spirits is possibly the best in town, and the lounge even has its own cigar humidor.

La Piazza *(☎ 736 2961, 4 Hassan Sabry)* Dishes E£20-35. Open 12.30pm-12.30am daily. Part of a complex of restaurants under the collective title Four Corners, La Piazza has a light and airy dining room with plenty of greenery, and some of the items on the menu are quite good (though not the pastas). The onion soup is excellent as is the liver pâté mousse, and the salads are usually a good bet.

Mohandiseen & Doqqi Though bland and flavourless in appearance, Cairo's grey concrete suburbs contain some of the city's better restaurants and if you have the cash it's worth taxiing out here to eat.

***Abu Shaqra** (☎ 344 2299, 17 Gamiat ad-Dowal al-Arabiyya)* Dishes E£12-25. Open 9am-2am daily. Renowned for its (pricey) kebabs, this place also has a variety of other dishes, such as pigeon stuffed with rice and served with chips, and *fatta moza tagen* (lamb on a bed of baked rice with pieces of bread in a vinegary sauce). There's also a branch near Garden City at 69 Qasr el-Nil.

***Flux** (☎ 338 6601, 2 Sharia Gamiat al-Nasr)*. Dishes E£40-60 for two courses. Open 7pm-2am daily. Flux is Egypt's most stylish and chic restaurant, and one that wouldn't seem out of place in Soho. The food is international fusion, adventurous and, most of the time, successful.

***Prestige** (☎ 347 0383, 43 Sharia Geziret al-Arab)* Dishes E£12-40. Open noon-2am daily. Prestige is two restaurants in one – a cheerful, cheap pizzeria and a more expensive Italian-ish place specialising in steaks and fresh fish with pavement seating under large sun umbrellas. Beer is served, but only inside.

***Samakmak** (☎ 347 8232, 92 Ahmed Orabi)* Two courses E£40-50. Open 10am-6am daily. The Cairo branch of the respected Alexandrian fish restaurant has an extremely odd setting: on a paved terrace between two apartment blocks off a busy road. However, the fish and seafood are excellent – point out what you want from the iced display and tell the waiters how you want it cooked.

***Maroosh** (☎ 345 0972, 64 Midan Libnan)* **Cairo map** Dishes E£3-5. Open 8am-2am daily. Maroosh has excellent mezze that can be enjoyed while lounging in rattan chairs on a street-side terrace. Skip the main meat dishes (which shouldn't be too difficult in the case of the 'lamb scrotum sandwich') and fill the table with bread and dips. For those who don't know their tabouleh from their fatoush, everything is well described in English on the menu.

***Le Tabasco** (☎ 336 5583, 8 Midan Amman)* **Cairo map** Dishes E£25-40. Open noon-2am daily. In Doqqi and run by the same people as Zamalek's L'Aubergine, this is every bit as popular, especially with the city's smart young set. Again, the menu changes regularly, but ranges over a wider culinary field stretching beyond the Mediterranean to include, on occasion, dishes from Mexico and Eastern Europe. You usually need to make reservations to eat.

***Tia Maria** (☎ 335 3273, 32 Sharia Jeddah)* **Cairo map** Dishes E£12-20. Open noon-1am daily. Don't be put off by the incredibly chintzy interior here, all frilly, pink curtains and whatnot, because the Italian food is superb. We can thoroughly recommend the spaghetti carbonara, the seafood pasta, served in an enormous clam shell and the crespelle Argentine (crepes with ice cream smothered in caramel sauce).

Giza & Pyramids Rd There are very few places to eat in Giza itself. Pyramids Rd is lined with fast food joints. At the Pyramid end of the road there are several options but most of these are overpriced and not particularly good. One exception is the reliable ***Felfela*** (see Budget Dining, Downtown), which has a branch at 27 Cairo-Alexandria Desert Highway.

***TGI Friday's** (☎ 570 9690, 26 Sharia el-Nil)* Meals E£20-35, not including dessert. On a boat moored between the University and Giza bridges, this is a shamelessly manufactured American feel-good franchise and the Egyptians love it. The menu offers a broad range of American cuisine and reservations are recommended at the weekend when it's at its liveliest and loudest.

***Andrea's** (☎ 383 1133, 59-60 Maryoutia Canal Rd)* Meals E£20-30. Open noon-12.30am daily. Cairo's famous open-air chicken restaurant is 1.5km north of Pyramids Rd. Seating is out in a large garden, which would be quite pleasant if it weren't for the constant attention of clouds of mosquitoes – last time we were there, one of our party who'd come in sandals had to spend the evening with her feet in her handbag. There is no menu: it's spit-roasted chicken only (sometimes quail too) with a selection of very good mezze as starters. If you're taking a taxi here from central Cairo, you can expect it to cost about E£15 or about E£2 from the Mena House area.

Heliopolis Just to the west of central Heliopolis, Merryland is an ex-race course that's now an entertainment centre with a disco, nightclub, kiddies' rides and lots of places to eat, including a branch of Andrea's (see earlier), plus Lebanese, Egyptian and fish restaurants, soon to be joined by TGI Friday.

Le Chantilly *(☎ 290 7303, 11 Sharia Baghdad)* Meals E£25-35. Open 7am-midnight daily. After all these years, this is still about the best place to eat up here. The food is fine, if unexciting, but the surroundings are very pleasant if you can find seating in the garden at the back. Beer is served.

Pizza Express *(☎ 450 5871, 19 Sharia Mirghani)* Meals E£8.50-17. Open 11.30am-1am daily. On Mirghani, in front of the Heliopolis Club, is this franchise of the UK chain. It's several cuts above the likes of Pizza Hut, boasting a cool, classy interior and very good food – salads are crisp with good dressings and the pizzas (17 varieties) are made in view of the diners.

Cafes & Patisseries

Downtown The following are all European-style places, not to be confused with ahwas, the Egyptian coffeehouses, where food is not available

El-Abd *(35 Talaat Harb)* Open 8am-midnight daily. On the corner of Sharias 26th of July and Sherif, El-Abd serves the very best pastries and cakes in Cairo, as testified by the permanent crowds pushing to be served, but it's takeaway only.

Groppi's on Midan Talaat Harb used to be *the* place to take tea and cakes, but that was a long time ago. Now the offerings are poor and overpriced. For nostalgia buffs only.

Simonds *(Sharia Sherif)* Open 7am-8pm daily. This sister outlet to the much better place of the same name in Zamalek does a tolerable cappuccino.

Zamalek In addition to the list below, Zamalek also has a branch of the Harris Cafe (see Heliopolis) located at 18 Sharia al-Marashly, up near the AUC hostel.

Cilantro *(☎ 736 1115, 157 Sharia 26th of July)* Snacks E£4.50-15.50. Open 9am-2am daily. A stylish, new Continental-type cafe that does a range of healthy sandwiches, salads and pastries, as well as decent coffee.

Marriott Bakery *(☎ 735 8888, Cairo Marriott, Saray al-Gezira)* Open 6.30am-9pm daily. Croissants, all kinds of breads from walnut bread to toast, quiches, cakes and sandwiches are available.

Simonds *(112 Sharia 26th of July)* Open 7.30am-9.30pm daily. The closest thing you'll find to a real Italian cafe this side of the Mediterranean. In existence for more than 40 years serving up the city's best cappuccino, as well as fruit juices and savoury pastries.

Heliopolis In addition to the place below, Heliopolis also has a ***Marriott Bakery*** (see Zamalek) at the northern end of Sharia Baghdad.

Harris Cafe *(☎ 417 6796, 6 Sharia Baghdad)* Open until 12.30am daily. This is a pleasant Continental-style cafe, with outdoor seating; in addition to cappuccinos, hot chocolate and the like, it also does decent turkey, roast chicken, smoked salmon and club sandwiches.

Self-Catering

For fresh fruit and vegetables try the ***Tawfiqiyya Souq*** off the top end of Talaat Harb, Downtown or ***Souq Mansour***, off Midan Falaki and close to Midan Tahrir. Of the two, the Tawfiqiyya Souq has a larger range of produce and it's open until late at night. It's also home to several bakeries and numerous *ba'als*, the all-purpose grocers at which you can stock up on things such as bread, cheese and yogurt.

For bread, there are bakeries all over town, especially around the markets, but if you want something resembling the bread you buy at home try the bakeries at the Nile Hilton and Cairo Marriott hotels. For pastries and sweets the very best are found at ***El-Abd*** which has two branches Downtown, one at 35 Talaat Harb and one on the corner of Sharias 26th of July and Sherif. Both are open until midnight.

ENTERTAINMENT

Western-style discos, cinemas showing English-language films and nightclubs with floor shows abound in Cairo. With bucks to burn you can head to the casinos at many of the five-star hotels or, if you've already blown the budget, there are thousands of ahwas where you can while away the hours over a glass of *shai* (tea) and a few games of backgammon.

Ahwas

Other than in the newer suburbs such as Mohandiseen, Doqqi and Agouza, almost every street in Cairo has at least one ahwa. One of the oldest, and certainly the most famous, is ***Fishawi's***, a few steps off Midan Hussein in Khan al-Khalili. Despite frequently being swamped by foreign tourists and equally wide-eyed Egyptians from out-of-town, Fishawi's manages to shrug it all off (no waiters in fancy headgear or Fishawi keyrings for sale) and play the role of a regular ahwa, serving up tea, coffee and sheesha to all-comers. The place is open 24 hours a day, apart from Ramadan, and is especially alluring in the early hours of the morning.

Even more colourful than Fishawi's in terms of decor, if not atmosphere, is ***Ash-Shams***, tucked in a courtyard alleyway between Sharia 26th of July and Tawfiqiyya Souq, Downtown. It has walls adorned with gilt stucco and kitschy *faux*-classical paintings. However, because of its popularity with travellers from the neighbouring hotels, waiters have a bad tendency to overcharge and the sheesha here, frankly, is terrible. Much better is the nearby ***Al-Andalus***, tucked away behind the Grand Hotel on the corner of Talaat Harb and Sharia 26th of July. This place is kept spotlessly clean, prices are displayed (we've never been cheated by staff here) and, most unusually, upstairs is a 'family room' where women can go to smoke sheesha away from masculine eyes. Also good and in the vicinity is ***Leyaleena***, a new ahwa with rattan chairs and a very cultured, foreigner-friendly feel. It's just around the corner from the end of Tawfiqiyya Souq.

After Ash-Shams, the other big backpacker favourite is ***Zahret al-Bustan***, in the alleyway beside Cafe Riche off Sharia Talaat Harb. Formerly the haunt of intellectuals, journalists and writers, the place has now become a bit of a sleazy flytrap with papyrus sellers and assorted scamsters and hustlers greeting newcomers with 'Hello, my friend I been waiting you' and making offers of visits to villages, to papyrus factories, to cousins' weddings and whatever else they can improvise on the spot. Never again will you receive so many offers of instant friendship. And never will it cost you so dearly if you're suckered along. Nevertheless, hanging out here can be fun if you do so with your eyes open and wits about you.

Although *domina* (dominoes), *towla* (backgammon) and occasionally cards are the standard games played at ahwas, there are a couple of places popular with the chess crowd, notably the ***Cafeteria Horreyya*** on Midan Falaki in Bab al-Luq and ***Zahret al-Midan*** on Midan Sayyida Zeinab at the junction with Sharia Abdel Meguid.

Bars

Local Bars There are several local bars on and around Sharia Alfy in Downtown but they're fairly unwelcoming. Exceptions are ***Cafeteria Port Tawfiq*** *(Midan Orabi)* and ***Cafeteria Orabi*** (see Midan Ramses & Around map) just 150m north on the left-hand side of Sharia Orabi. ***Cap d'Or*** *(Abdel Khalek Sarwat)* is a little more salubrious and is possibly the best of central Cairo's local bars. The staff and regulars here are quite used to seeing foreigners. The same applies to the cramped ***Stella Bar*** on the corner of Hoda Shaarawi and Talaat Harb. None of these places are suitable for women on their own and the toilets are pretty foul in all of them (at the Stella you can at least nip a few doors down to use the ones at the Felfela Restaurant).

Although primarily a coffeehouse, ***Cafeteria Horreyya*** *(Midan Falaki)* also serves Stella (the cheapest in town at E£5.50), while on nearby Midan Tahrir ***Ali Baba Cafeteria*** is a great place to sink a cold one (E£6.50), especially if you can get the upstairs table by the window.

Western-Style Bars Like any other busy city, bars and hang outs open and close and go in and out of favour, but the place to go boozing (if you have the cash) is Zamalek, where there are several stylish bars within a short walk of each other.

L'Aubergine *(☎ 735 6550, 5 Sayyed al-Bakry, Zamalek)* Open until 2am daily. No longer quite as 'in' as it once was, upstairs at L'Aubergine still gets pretty crammed most evenings with an American University-type crowd (ie, young, rich and good looking). The atmosphere is cool jazz and candlelight. A beer costs E£12.50.

La Bodega *(☎ 735 6761, 157 Sharia 26th of July, Zamalek)* Open until 2am daily. Beside the restaurant of the same name is this swish lounge bar. You need to be dressed to impress to get in and a beer is going to set you back E£15, but if you want a glimpse of Cairo's nouveaux riches at play, this is the venue.

Cafe Riche *(☎ 392 9793, 17 Talaat Harb, Downtown)* Open until midnight daily. The management would probably prefer that you ate, but plenty of people use this cafe/restaurant as a bar.

Deals *(☎ 736 0502, 2 Maahad al-Swissry, Zamalek)* Open until 2am daily. A small cellar bar that gets too packed for comfort late in the evening and at weekends, Deals is pleasant enough at quieter times. There is also a branch in Heliopolis at 40A Sharia Baghdad.

Odeon Palace Hotel *(☎ 577 6637, 6 Sharia Abdel Hamid Said, Downtown)* Open 24 hrs. A rooftop bar, the Odeon is favoured by Cairo's heavy-drinking theatre and cinema clique for its unsociably good hours.

Windsor Bar *(☎ 591 5277, 19 Sharia Alfy, Downtown)* Open until 1am daily. One of the most relaxing places to drink in Cairo, the Windsor is favoured by guests of the hotel as well as by elderly locals. Solo women travellers should feel quite comfortable here. Beer is heading toward the E£10 mark.

Le Tabasco *(☎ 336 5583, 8 Midan Amman, Doqqi)* **Cairo map** Open until 2am daily. The music is usually good and the decor is smart and hip at Le Tabasco, which pulls in a young, trendy and mainly Egyptian crowd. The drawback is the hefty minimum charge and pricey beer.

Live Music Cairo's live music scene is next to nonexistent. It's largely limited to crooners doing covers in restaurants. For instance, every night at ***TGI Friday's*** (see Giza & Pyramids Rd under Places to Eat) at 10pm there's a live music spot; it's pretty unexciting stuff.

Cairo Jazz Club *(☎ 345 9939, 197 Sharia 26th of July, Agouza)*. Minimum charge E£30. Open 7pm-2am daily. The city's one blip of live music activity is here, with live jazz or blues every night.

Casinos

Nearly all of Cairo's five-star hotels have casinos, open to non-Egyptians only (take your passport). All games are conducted in US dollars or other major foreign currencies, with a minimum stake of US$1. Smart-casual attire is required. Don't confuse these casinos with local *casinos*, the name given for certain restaurants popular with families on a day out.

Cinemas

For general information on cinema-going in Egypt see The Cultural Scene under Entertainment in the Facts for the Visitor chapter. For details of what's showing, check the *Egyptian Gazette* or *Al-Ahram Weekly* newspapers. The following places regularly screen English-language films:

Cairo Sheraton (☎ 760 6081, Cairo Sheraton Hotel, Midan al-Galaa, Doqqi) The closest Cairo has to an art house cinema, in that it tends to forgo blockbusters for Merchant Ivory films and the like.

Karim I & II (☎ 591 6095, 5 Sharia Emad ad-Din, Downtown) A refurbished old cinema that typically screens action movies. Cheap tickets make it popular with young Egyptian males – it's not a place for women to go unaccompanied.

Metro (☎ 393 7566, 35 Talaat Harb, Downtown) Once Cairo's finest, now one of its scruffiest.

Normandy (☎ 258 0254, 32 Sharia al-Ahram, Heliopolis) One of Cairo's older cinemas, with open-air screenings in summer.

Radio (☎ 575 6562, 24 Talaat Harb, Downtown) See comments for Karim I & II.

Ramses Hilton I & II (☎ 574 7436, Ramses Hilton Mall, 7th floor, Midan Abdel Moniem Riad, Downtown) Two relatively new screens; they're well maintained, although II is a bit small.

Rennaisance (☎ 580 4039, World Trade Centre annexe, 1191 Corniche el-Nil, Bulaq) Central Cairo's newest and swishest cinema.

Tahrir (☎ 335 4726, 122 Sharia Tahrir, Doqqi) Comfortable, modern cinema where single females shouldn't receive any hassle.

Discos & Nightclubs

Crazy House Disco *(☎ 366 1082, 1 Salah Salem)* Admission E£50 Thur, E£25 Fri-Wed, includes two free beers. Open midnight-6am daily. Opened in 1998, this is part of a huge new entertainment complex called Cairo Land, bizarrely located on the edge of the city's ancient Southern Cemetery. The club (Cairo's only purpose-built dance venue) is huge with three dance floors. To get there you'll have to take a taxi (about E£5 from central Cairo).

Africana *(Pyramids Rd)* Admission E£25, includes one beer. Open from around midnight Thur-Sat. The Africana is interesting and fun; here sounds south of the Sahara make up the play list. This is a place for Cairo's huge communities of African students and refugees to let off steam, it's hot and sweaty with frequent brawls and 'high velocity chair shows' – but that's all part of the charm. The club is not easy to find: it's on the right as you head towards the Pyramids, beyond the Haram Theatre and then one block past KFC.

Belly Dancing The best dancers perform at Cairo's five-star hotels; nightclubs such as ***Alhambra*** *(☎ 336 9700, Cairo Sheraton)*, ***Haroun al-Rashid*** *(☎ 795 7171, Semiramis Inter-Continental)* and ***La Belle Epoque*** *(☎ 362 1717, Meridien Le Caire)* feature residencies by the big names. Names to look out for include Lucy, Dina and Fifi Abdou, but you'll have to phone around to find out who's currently performing where. Shows typically begin at around midnight and the main act probably doesn't take to the stage until around 2am or later. Admissions are steep; expect to shell out upwards of E£150, which will include a buffet but not drinks.

At the other end of the scale, it is possible to watch belly dancing for just a few pounds. There are several places in Downtown, plus plenty more along Pyramids Rd (generally expensive rip-off joints), that cater mainly to local Egyptians rather than the oil-rich Gulf Arabs who make up the five-star audiences. It has to be said that these places are fairly seedy and most of the dancers have the appearance and grace of amateur wrestlers, but it can be fun especially when the inebriated patrons join in as they invariably do.

Palmyra Admission E£3. Open 1am-4am daily. Just off Sharia 26th of July, this is a cavernous place with the full Arab music contingent, belly dancers and occasionally other acts such as acrobats. A Stella will cost you E£12.

Alternatively, there's also the ***New Arizona*** and the ***Nightclub***, both on Sharia Alfy (the latter is above the Alfy Bey Restaurant), but neither is as entertaining as the Palmyra.

Music, Theatre & Dance

Cairo Opera House *(☎ 342 0601, Gezira Exhibition Grounds; Metro: Opera)* The city's premier performing arts venue regularly plays host to famed international names and companies (the Bolshoi Ballet visits almost annually). At other times performances by local companies, such as the Cairo Opera Ballet Company and the Cairo Symphony Orchestra, are worth catching. In addition to a main hall and small hall, the Opera House also has an open-air amphitheatre. Check *Egypt Today* and *Al-Ahram Weekly* for what's on, or pass by and pick up a program. Jacket and tie are required by males for main hall performances, but less well-dressed travellers have been known to borrow them from staff.

American University in Cairo *(AUC; ☎ 797 5020 for information)*. There are often music recitals and plays of varying quality at the Ewart Hall and Wallace Theatre at the AUC. Events are advertised on boards at the campus entrance on Sharia Mohammed Mahmoud, off Midan Tahrir.

Beit al-Harrawi *(☎ 735 7001, Sharia al-Sheikh Mohammed Abdo, Islamic Cairo)* Admission free. On the first Thursday of every month at 8pm free classical Arabic music is played here. At other times, especially during Ramadan, the house, along with neighbouring ***Beit Zeinab al-Khatoun*** *(☎ 735 7001, Sharia al-Sheikh Mohammed Abdo, Islamic Cairo)*, is used for theatre, art exhibitions and music performances. If anything is going on during your visit (see the local press) then it's worth attending if only for the setting.

Sufi Dancing

Al-Tannoura Egyptian Heritage Dance Troupe *(Mausoleum of al-Ghouri, Islamic Cairo)* Admission free. On Wednesday and Saturday nights from 8pm (8.30pm in winter) this troupe gives a 1½ hour display of Sufi dancing. The troupe has toured overseas, and the colourful performances are extremely popular. It's advisable to come early, especially in winter, as the small auditorium can get quite crowded.

SHOPPING

Shopping in the Facts for the Visitor chapter gives some idea of what to look out for in Egypt. And if it's available anywhere in Egypt it will be found in Cairo.

Souqs & Markets

Khan al-Khalili is the place to head for the Cairo shopping experience par excellence. As well as tacky souvenirs, you'll also find copperware, blown glass, gold and silver, perfume, spices, clothing, fabrics, Bedouin dresses, semiprecious stones, antiques, belly-dancing costumes, and all manner of other nonessentials. The only way to shop the Khan successfully is to ignore unwanted overtures and, if you have a particular item in mind, to head for the section specialising in what you're after; the Khan al-Khalili map gives an indication of what's sold where.

In addition to Khan al-Khalili there are numerous other souqs and markets in Cairo, many worth a visit irrespective of whether you intend buying anything. On the east bank of the Nile opposite Zamalek, just north of Sharia 26th of July, ***Bulaq Market*** sells textiles, second-hand clothing, car parts and military surplus. An even odder mix is presented at the weekly ***Souq al-Gomaa*** *(Friday Market)*, held just south of the Citadel, where the trade is in bric-a-brac and animals. It starts early Friday morning and is over by midday. You'll need to take a taxi to get there. ***Ezbekiyya Market***, beside Ataba metro station, just north of Opera Square, Downtown, is a collection of cabins selling second-hand books and magazines, and much of the stock is in English.

Shopping Malls

Cairo has several moderately sized shopping centres mostly devoted to clothes and accessories. A lot of what's for sale is quite shabby, but look for branches of Safari, which sells good quality Egyptian cotton garments at prices considerably cheaper than back home. One of the most exclusive of malls is the ***World Trade Centre*** *(1191 Corniche el-Nil, Bulaq)*, which as well as shops has several upmarket eateries and clubs. Similarly chic is the ***First Residence Mall*** *(35 Sharia Giza)*, overlooking the zoo, which is where you'll find the likes of Louis Vuitton and Cartier. The ***Ramses Hilton Mall*** *(Midan Abdel Moniem Riad, Downtown)*, over the road from the hotel, is more family oriented, with lots of cheap clothing and shoes. On the top floor is a cinema and a snooker hall.

Souvenirs

Khan al-Khalili is full of incredible kitsch (including most of the items listed in the boxed text 'That Special Something' in the Facts for the Visitor chapter). But there are more worthwhile items. Attractive backgammon boards, such as those in use in Egyptian coffeehouses, at least have a practical purpose. They start at around E£20 for something quite plain, the price shooting upwards if you want it inlaid with mother-of-pearl (but why would you – they look terrible). Or you could buy your own water pipe (sheesha) – though you'll need to also stock up on the special tobacco and the small clay pots that it is stuffed into. Small jewellery boxes inlaid with mother-of-pearl are also quite pretty and very cheap. Painted papyrus at Khan al-Khalili is as cheap as you'll find it anywhere, but if you want something of quality you'd be better off visiting the ***Dr Ragab Papyrus Institute*** *(☎ 748 8177, Sharia el-Nil, Doqqi)*, which is between the Cairo Sheraton and University Bridge.

Handicrafts

Cairo has some excellent small handicraft galleries and boutiques that gather together items made in villages and oases all over Egypt.

Al-Ain Gallery *(☎ 349 3940, 73 Sharia al-Hussein, Doqqi)* Open 10am-9pm daily, closed Fri morning. This gallery is known for intricate 'Oriental' metalwork lamps by designer Randa Fahmy and gorgeous unique items of jewellery fashioned by sister Azza. Also assorted 'ethnic' clothing and furnishings, fabrics from Akhmin and rugs from Sinai.

Khan Misr Touloun *(☎ 365 2227, Sharia Ibn Tulun)* Open 10am-5pm Mon-Fri. Run by a French lady and her Egyptian husband and located opposite the mosque entrance, this is a beautiful shop that carries wooden chests, bowls and plates, marionettes, blown glass, clay figurines, scarves and woven clothing.

Al-Khatoun Gallery *(☎ 012-226 5329, Sharia al-Sheikh Mohammed Abdo, Islamic Cairo)* Open noon-9pm daily. Lying between Beit Zeinab al-Khatoun and Beit al-Harrawi behind Al-Azhar Mosque, this is a small place with an eclectic assortment of new (glassware, leatherwork, printed fabrics, wrought-iron furniture) and old (furniture, paintings, cigarette tins).

Marketing Link *(☎ 736 5123, W www.egyptcrafts.com, 27 Yehia Ibrahim, apartment 8, Zamalek)* Open 9am-8pm Sat-Wed, 9am-5pm Thur. This is a fair-trade shop with merchandise produced in income-generating projects throughout Egypt. Items on sale include Bedouin rugs from Sinai and the northern Western Desert, embroidery from Sinai, handmade paper from Muqattam, Bedouin beadwork and Upper Egyptian shawls. Prices are competitive.

Nagada *(☎ 594 3249, 8 Sharia Dar al-Shefa, 3rd floor, Garden City)* Beautiful handwoven textiles from the town of the same name (about 28km north of Luxor) are sold here, as well as handmade pottery from Al-Fayoum and clothes, lamps and jewellery. To get here head south along the Corniche and take the left immediately opposite the turn-off on the right for Meridien Le Caire hotel; follow the street that veers to the right, then take the first right and it's the second or third building along.

Nomad *(☎ 341 1917, 14 Saray al-Gezira)* Open 10am-3pm Mon-Sat. Up on the 1st floor of an apartment building down the street from the Cairo Marriott, this is a small, well-hidden gem of a place that specialises in jewellery and traditional Bedouin craft and costumes. It is well worth a look.

Senouhi *(☎ 391 0955, 54 Abdel Khalek Sarwat, 5th floor, Downtown)* Open 10am-5pm Mon-Fri, 10am-1pm Sat. This is a grotto-like apartment with a horde of antiques (jewellery, silver, and miscellanea) and handicrafts. It's worth a rummage for rugs, traditional clothing and artworks.

Sheba Gallery *(☎ 735 9192, 6 Sharia Sri Lanka, Zamalek)*. Contemporary gold and silver designs based on traditionally Yemeni jewellery are sold here, along with beautiful necklaces, bracelets, earrings and rings with semiprecious stones that are snapped up by chic Cairenes.

Tukul Craft Shop *(☎ 736 8391, All Saints Cathedral, Sheikh Marsafy, Zamalek)* Open 9am-4.30pm Mon-Thur & Sat, 11am-3pm Fri & Sun. This shop has bags, clothing and wall hangings from fabrics printed with original African designs made by displaced Sudanese to whom the profits go.

Carpets & Rugs

Unlike Morocco, Turkey or Iran, Egypt has no rich tradition of 'Oriental' carpet weaving. What you can find, however, are brown-and-beige striped, hard-wearing camel-hair rugs of Bedouin origin. The biggest selection is to be found in the Haret al-Fahhamin, a tight squeeze of alleys behind the Mosque of al-Ghouri, across the road from Khan al-Khalili in Islamic Cairo. Many of the places mentioned in Handicrafts, earlier, also carry Bedouin rugs.

In the area of the Pyramids, just off Saqqara Rd, the ***Wissa Wassef Art Centre*** *(☎ 385 0746, Saqqara Rd, Harraniyya)* specialises in very distinctive woollen rugs and wall hangings depicting rural and folkloric scenes. Wissa Wassef rugs are now very much imitated and you can buy similar ones at most souvenir shops but for the greatest choice – and choice pieces – visit the art centre (see Wissa Wassef Art Centre under Giza earlier in this chapter).

Jewellery

Egypt's gold and silver shops are concentrated in the centre of Khan al-Khalili. Jewellery is sold by weight, with a little extra added for workmanship. The day's gold prices are listed in the *Egyptian Gazette*. The most popular souvenirs are gold or silver car touches with your name engraved in hieroglyphs. Most of the shops in Khan al-Khalili can arrange to have this done. For something a bit different, visit ***Al-Ain Gallery*** (see Handicrafts opposite) to look at the work of Azza Fahmy. ***Nomad*** (see Handicrafts) also has interesting chunky Bedouin pieces.

Books, Tapes & CDs

Cairo bookshops are listed under Information earlier in this chapter. The best place to look for music cassettes is Sharia Shawarby, off Qasr el-Nil, Downtown, where there are maybe half a dozen tape shops in a short 200m stretch. For CDs (local and international) visit ***Jukebox*** *(☎ 578 2980, World Trade Centre, 1191 Corniche el-Nil, Bulaq)* or ***Mirage Megastore*** *(☎ 760 9793, 71 Gamiat ad-Dowal al-Arabiyya, Mohandiseen)*.

GETTING THERE & AWAY

See the Getting Around chapter for information on the best modes of transport between Cairo and the rest of the country.

Air

EgyptAir has a number of offices around town including Downtown on the corner of Talaat Harb and Sharia al-Bustan (☎ 393 0831), one at 6 Sharia Adly (☎ 390 0999), one in the garden courtyard of the Nile Hilton (☎ 579 3048), and one at 22 Ibrahim Laqqany up in Heliopolis (☎ 245 0270). All are open from 8am to 8pm daily. For general EgyptAir information call ☎ 390 0999.

For international air fare details see the Getting There & Away chapter; for domestic flights, see the Getting Around chapter. You can call Cairo airport for information on flights (☎ 291 4255). The addresses of some of the other airlines represented in Cairo are as follows:

Air France (☎ 575 8899) 2 Midan Talaat Harb, Downtown
Air Malta (☎ 575 6022) Nile Hilton, Midan Tahrir
Air Sinai (☎ 577 2949) Nile Hilton, Midan Tahrir
Alitalia (☎ 578 5823) Nile Hilton, Midan Tahrir
Austrian Airlines (☎ 735 2777) 22 Qasr el-Nil, Downtown
British Airways (☎ 578 0743) 1 Sharia al-Bustan, Midan Tahrir
El Al Israel Airlines (☎ 341 1429) 5 Elmakrizi St, Zamalek
Emirates (☎ 336 1555) Cairo Marriott, Zamalek
Ethiopian Airlines (☎ 574 0911) Nile Hilton, Midan Tahrir
Gulf Air (☎ 575 0852) 21 Mahmoud Bassiouni, Downtown
Kenya Airways (☎ 574 7004) 11 Qasr el-Nil, Downtown
KLM (☎ 574 7004) 11 Qasr el-Nil, Downtown
Lufthansa (☎ 739 8339) 6 Sheikh Marsafy, Zamalek
Middle East Airlines (☎ 574 7372) 12 Qasr el-Nil, Downtown
Olympic Airways (☎ 393 1277) 23 Qasr el-Nil, Downtown
Royal Jordanian Airlines (☎ 575 0875) 6 Qasr el-Nil, Downtown

Scandinavian Airlines (SAS) (☎ 575 3627) 2 Champollion, Midan Tahrir
Sudan Airways (☎ 578 7299) 1 Sharia al-Bustan, Midan Tahrir
Swissair (☎ 392 1522) 22 Qasr el-Nil, Downtown
Syrian Arab Airlines (☎ 392 8284) 35 Talaat Harb, Downtown
Turkish Airlines (☎ 395 8031) 3 Midan Mustafa Kamel, Downtown
TWA (☎ 574 9904) 1 Qasr el-Nil, Midan Tahrir

Cairo International Airport For information on the airport see the Getting There & Away chapter. For details of how to get from the airport to town and vice versa see Getting Around later in this chapter.

Bus

Bus Stations The city is in the process of being reordered and part of that process is the relocation of its bus stations. In an attempt to keep the big buses out of the Downtown area, a big new bus station is under construction in the Bulaq district, just north of the centre. Called the Turgoman garage (in Arabic, 'mo'af Turgoman'), it's located on Sharia al-Gisr, 1km north-west of the intersection of Sharias Galaa and Sharia 26th of July (see the Cairo map). It's an awkward location in that it's too far to walk to from central Cairo and the only way to get there is by taxi (E£2 from Downtown).

There's also a bus station on Sharia Ramses in the north-eastern suburb of Abbassiyya (see the Cairo map), known as the Sinai Terminal because, pre-Turgoman, this was where the Sinai buses departed from. Services still pick up from here and there is the odd bus that has Abbassiyya as its starting point. To get here you need to take bus No 983 or 948 or minibus No 32 from the station at Midan Abdel Moniem Riad. Alternatively, a taxi to/from Downtown should cost E£6. Sinai buses also usually stop at the Al-Mazar station in Heliopolis.

Alexandria & the Mediterranean Coast Superjet's comfy buses will whisk you from Turgoman garage to Alexandria's Sidi Gaber bus station in about 2½ hours. There are departures every 30 minutes from 5.30am to 5.30pm, thereafter hourly (roughly) until about 11pm. The fare is E£20 to E£25, rising to E£22 to E£31 after 5.30pm. Certain services (8am, 3.30pm, 5.30pm) are 'VIP buses' (more leg room), the fare on these is E£29.

West Delta also has services to Alexandria from Turgoman with hourly departures from 5.30am to 1.30am. Fares cost E£16 or E£20 depending on the type of bus. West Delta also has buses direct to Marsa Matruh (E£28 to E£36, five hours) nine times a day (roughly every half hour between 6am and 8.30am, then at 3.30pm, 5pm and 6pm) during the summer (June to September), dropping to three buses a day during winter (October to May).

The Nile Delta, Suez Canal & Red Sea Coast The East Delta Bus Co's white and yellow-green striped buses depart Turgoman garage every 30 minutes to Mansura (E£8.50, 2½ hours) and hourly to Damietta (E£10.50, 3½ hours) in the Delta. It has buses to Suez (E£6.50 to E£7.50, two hours) every half hour between 6am and 9pm; to Ismailia (E£6.50, two hours) every half hour between 6.30am and 8pm; and to Port Said (E£13 to E£15, three hours) at hourly intervals between 6.30am and 7pm.

To get to Tanta (E£6) and other smaller Delta destinations, you can take a Middle Delta Bus Co bus; they depart hourly between 7am and 9pm.

Hurghada (6½ hours) buses are run by Superjet and Upper Egypt Travel. Superjet has departures at 7.30am, 8.30am, 2.30pm and 11.15pm; fares are E£50 (E£55 on the overnight bus). Upper Egypt Travel has 18 services a day, departing at regular intervals between 7am and 1am. Fares are E£30 to E£50 depending on the type of bus. The noon, 5pm and 9pm buses go on to Safaga (E£55); the 1.30pm and 7.30pm buses go on to Marsa Alam (E£65).

Upper Egypt Upper Egypt Travel has luxury buses from Turgoman garage to Luxor (E£60, 10 to 11 hours) departing daily at 9pm and to Aswan (E£60, 12 hours) at 5pm. The same company's ordinary buses (cheap no-frills green buses) leave from the Ahmed

Helmy bus station behind Ramses train station and go to destinations such as Beni Suef (E£4.50), Minya (E£8 to E£11, four hours), Asyut (E£10 to E£15, six to seven hours), Luxor and Aswan. Buses to destinations such as Minya and Asyut run every 30 to 60 minutes from about 6am to 6pm.

Sinai East Delta has buses from Turgoman garage to Sharm el-Sheikh (E£50 to E£65, eight hours) 10 times per day between 6.30am and 11.30pm. The two overnight buses are the most expensive. The 7.30am, 1pm, 5pm and 11.30pm buses go on to Dahab (E£55, but E£70 on the 11pm bus, nine hours). Superjet also has a nightly service to Sharm el-Sheikh (E£55, seven hours) leaving at 11pm.

There are three East Delta buses daily to Nuweiba (eight hours) at 7am (E£50), 9.30am (E£50) and 10pm (E£55), all of which carry on to Taba (E£50, but E£70 on the 10pm bus, 8½ hours). There's just one bus to St Katherine's Monastery (E£35, 7½ hours) and that departs at 10.30am.

Western Oases All Western Oases buses also go from Turgoman. Timetables for these services have a slightly theoretical quality so it's a good idea to double-check times in advance. You also need to reserve to be sure of getting a seat anyway.

Note, there are no direct buses from here to Siwa – you have to take a bus to Alexandria or Marsa Matruh and change there.

To Bahariyya (E£12.50, five hours) there are buses at 7am, 8am and 6pm. On Friday there's one service only at 8am. Take some food and water as sometimes the oases buses don't stop anywhere useful for breaks.

For Farafra (eight hours) there are buses at 7am (E£25) and 6pm (E£27). The road linking Farafra and Bahariyya is still partly unpaved which makes this leg of the journey long and dusty.

To Dakhla (10 hours) there are buses at 7am (E£30) and 6pm (E£40) that travel via Bahariyya and Farafra, plus buses at 7pm and 8pm (both E£40, 12 hours) that go via Asyut and Al-Kharga. The evening services are supposedly direct and do not stop in Asyut itself.

To Al-Kharga (E£30, 10 hours) there are buses at 9am (E£23), 7pm, 8pm, 9pm and 10pm, all of which go via Asyut.

Al-Fayoum Buses for Al-Fayoum leave from the Ahmed Helmy bus station and a separate station in the vicinity of Midan Giza. For the latter, take a Pyramids minibus from Midan Abdel Moniem Riad and get off just after Midan Giza, immediately after passing under a railway bridge, then walk north along the canal; the bus station is 500m ahead. Alternatively, take the metro to the Giza stop. Al-Fayoum buses go every 15 minutes and the fare is E£3.50 on the newer air-con buses or E£2.50 on the old non air-con heaps.

Jordan Every Sunday and Wednesday Superjet has a bus to Amman (E£180, 20 hours) departing at 5am. On the same days there's also an East Delta Bus Co service for Aqaba departing Turgoman at 10pm; the fare, including the ferry, is US$45 plus E£34.

Libya Superjet has a daily 8am Libya service departing from the Turgoman garage. The fare to Benghazi (20 hours) is E£100, while to Tripoli (26 hours) it's E£205. The East Delta Bus Co has slightly cheaper seats to Tripoli (E£180) on its bus, which departs at 8am every Tuesday and Thursday.

Train

Ramses Station (Mahattat Ramses), on Midan Ramses, is Cairo's main train station and it's 100% pure confusion. If you need help there is a tourist office with tourist police just inside the main entrance on the left, open from 8am to 8pm daily. In a secondary entrance to the right is a small post office and next to it is the left-luggage area (marked 'cloak room'), which is open 24 hours and charges E£1 per piece.

For general details about the types of trains and tickets that are available, including student discounts, see Train in the Getting Around chapter. For travel information call ☎ 575 3555.

Luxor & Aswan If you can afford it, the wagons-lit sleeper is the way to travel (see the Getting Around chapter for a description of this service). It departs Cairo at 7.40pm each evening, arriving in Luxor at 5.30am the next morning (the perfect hour to head off sightseeing) and Aswan at 8.40am. An evening meal and early breakfast are included in the fare of E£362 one way or E£667 return. The same fare applies to both Luxor and Aswan. If you wish to get off at Luxor and continue to Aswan a few days later this must be specified when booking. There is no student discount.

There's also the option of travelling this luxury service on the cheap by taking a seat rather than a berth; this costs E£125 one way.

The wagons-lit booking office (☎/fax 576 1319) is in the main hall of the train station, beside the tourist police. Unfortunately, they don't take credit cards or travellers cheques – it's cash only (US dollars or Egyptian pounds). The office is open from 9am to 9pm daily. Tickets for same day travel must be purchased before 6pm, although in high season (from about October to April) it is best to book two or three days in advance. If you want to book your tickets in advance of your arrival in Egypt you could try using Hamis Travel (☎ 575 2757, fax 574 9276, ⓔ hamis@hamis.com.eg, Ⓦ www.hamis.com.eg).

Aside from the wagons-lit train, there are only two other services that foreigners are currently allowed to travel on down to Upper Egypt; these are the No 980, departing Cairo daily at 7.30 am, and the No 996, leaving at 10pm. Fares to Luxor on the night train are E£60/36 in 1st/2nd class, while to Aswan it's E£73/42. Fares on the morning train are E£4 cheaper. Students pay two-thirds of the full fare. On the night train there's also the option of travelling 'Nefertiti' class, which means newer, cleaner carriages; fares are E£70 to Luxor, E£80 to Aswan. However you go, the journey time is about 10 hours to Luxor and a further five on to Aswan.

Tickets can be bought from the ticket office beside platform 11, that is, on the other side of the tracks from the main hall (see the Ramses Station map). The trains themselves, at the time of writing, go from platform eight.

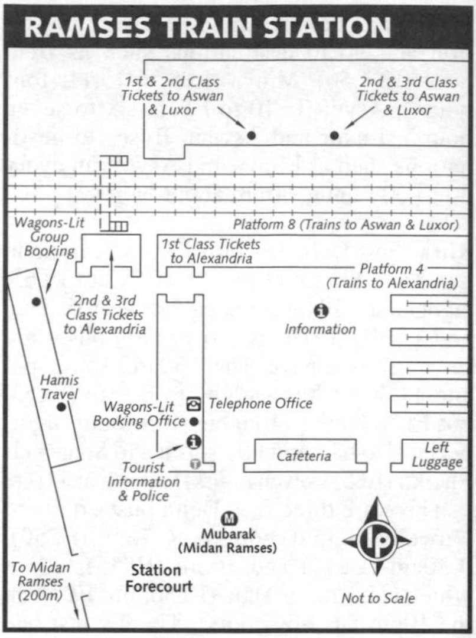

You must buy your tickets at least a couple of days in advance.

Alexandria & Northern Destinations

The best trains running between Cairo and Alexandria are the Turbini. They make only one stop, at Sidi Gaber station in Alexandria, and they take 2 hours 10 minutes. Second class in this train is about as good as 1st class in most others. You can't mistake the trains, they look a little like the high-speed European TGVs. They depart Cairo at 8am, 2pm and 7pm and tickets cost E£30/22 in 1st/2nd class with air-con.

Espani, the 'Spanish' services, are pretty much the same as the Turbini, fast and clean, departing Cairo at 9am, noon, 5pm and 10.30pm, which take 2½ hours, stopping at Benha, Tanta and Damanhur. Fares are the same as the Turbini.

All other Alexandria services (of which there are a further nine between 6am and 8pm) take three hours or more (fares are E£23/14 in 1st/2nd class).

For 1st-class tickets head for the windows directly in front of you in the main entrance, past the tourist office and the telephones. For 2nd-class ordinary tickets, bear left at the telephones, down the steps and into the small hall just off to the right.

Suez Canal & Eastern Destinations Five trains make the trip from Cairo to Port Said (four hours, E£16), stopping en route at Zagazig, Ismailia and Qantara. They leave at 6.25am, 8.45am, 11.30am, 2.35pm and 7.10pm. There are six other trains for Ismailia (three hours, E£11). Those making the fewest stops leave at 5.35am and 8.45am. There's no 1st class. Going by bus is a far better option.

Service Taxi

Most service taxis depart from lots around Ramses Station and Midan Ulali. Just north of Ulali, to the right of the Shubra road, is the area for Delta and Suez services. From here they depart for Mansura, Qantara, Damietta, Suez and Ismailia (E£5), Port Said (E£8), Al-Arish (E£12, five hours) and Rafah (E£15, six hours). Fares are determined by the distance, so keep an eye out for what others pay to get the set price.

Service taxis for Alexandria leave from in front of Ramses Station, at the time of research the set fare was E£10.

Taxis for destinations in and around Al-Fayoum (E£4) leave from the Al-Fayoum bus stop near Midan Giza (see Al-Fayoum under Bus earlier in this chapter).

GETTING AROUND

Overcrowded buses and minibuses are the most common form of transport for the majority of Cairenes, but for anyone who prefers breathing while travelling, taxis are the only option. By Western standards they are very cheap and there's never one far away. The only time when taxis aren't a good bet is when you are travelling a fair distance, say north to Heliopolis or south down to Ma'adi, in which case they become a little expensive. In such cases, the alternatives are the bus to Heliopolis or the metro to Ma'adi.

It's also wise to avoid taking taxis between about 2.30pm and 4pm (that's always supposing that you can find one free at this time of day) as this is when everyone slinks off home for the day and the roads are even more congested than usual.

To/From the Airport

Bus Don't believe anyone who tells you that there is no bus to the city centre – there are two, plus a minibus.

The best is the new No 356 airport service. These are big white, modern, air-con buses that run from Midan Abdel Moniem Riad behind the Egyptian Museum in central Cairo up via Abbassiyya and Heliopolis to Terminal II, where they stop for just a few minutes, then go on to Terminal I. The buses run at 20-minute intervals from 6am to 11pm and the fare is E£2, plus E£1 per large luggage item. To find the buses at either terminal, head out into the car park and you'll spot the stand, if not a waiting bus.

In addition to the No 356, there's local bus No 400 (25pt) and minibus No 27 (50pt), which both follow the same route as the No 356 airport service.

Taxi Cairo airport is not the easiest to get away from. Although there are bus services they are far from obvious and you may well just decide to grab a taxi. If you do, then the going rate to central Cairo is around E£30. Heading to the airport from the centre there are more taxis around so you can afford to bargain harder – you shouldn't pay more than E£25 to E£30. Avoid the large 'official' airport taxis as they have a fixed rate of E£46. It's generally better to get away from the arrivals hall and all the touts before starting to bargain with anyone. Walking away often tends to bring the price down. Triple-check the agreed fare, as there is an irritating tendency for drivers to nod at what you say and hit you with an out-of-the-world fare later on.

In the traffic-free early hours of the morning (when so many flights seem to arrive) the journey to central Cairo takes 20 minutes but at other, busier times of the day it can take well over an hour.

Bus & Minibus

See the Getting Around chapter for general information on Egypt's city buses.

Cairo's main local bus and minibus stations are at Midan Abdel Moniem Riad, behind the Egyptian Museum, where services leave for just about everywhere in the city.

Microbus

Increasingly, Cairenes are using private microbuses (as opposed to the public minibuses) to get around. Destinations are not marked in any language, so they are hard to use unless you are familiar with their routes. What you do is position yourself beside the road that leads where you want to go and when a microbus passes, yell out your destination – if it's going where you want to go and there are seats free it'll stop.

Metro

The metro system is startlingly efficient, and the stations are cleaner than any other public places in Cairo. It's also extremely inexpensive and, outside rush hours, not too crowded. At the time of writing there were two lines in operation. The main line, with 32 stations, stretches for 43km from the southern suburb of Helwan up to Al-Marg in the north. The second line connects the working class district of Shubra with Giza, stopping off at the Opera House complex en route. A planned third line will cross the city east to west linking Islamic Cairo with Zamalek and Mohandiseen.

Metro stations are easily identified by signs with a big red 'M' in a blue star.

It costs 50pt to ride up to nine stops; 70pt for up to 16 stops; 90pt for up to 22 stops; E£1.20 for up to 28 stops; and E£1.50 to ride the length of the line. The service starts at about 5am and closes about 11.30pm.

Men should note that the first carriage is reserved for women only. Women who want to ride in this carriage should make sure they're standing at the correct place on the platform (near where the front part of the train will stop) as the trains don't hang around in the station for long.

Tram

Most of Cairo's trams (known to Cairenes, confusingly, as 'metros') have been phased out. One of the few surviving lines a visitor might use is the one connecting central Cairo to Heliopolis. This runs from just north of Midan Ramses up to Midan Roxy on the southern edge of Heliopolis, at which point the line divides into three – Nouzha, Mirghani and Abdel Aziz Fahmy.

THE CAIRO METRO

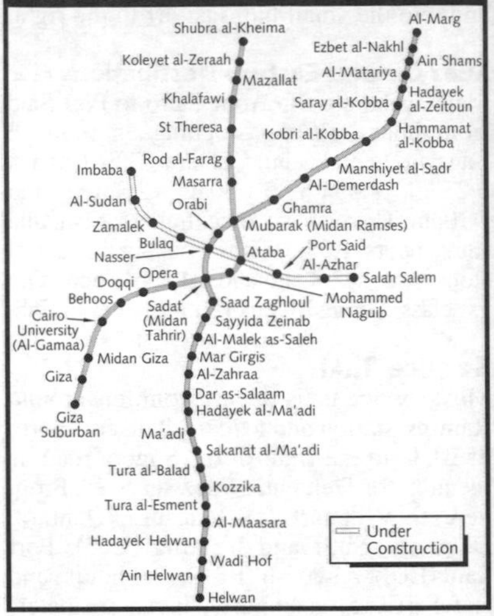

Car

Driving in Cairo is not for the faint-hearted. It's like the chariot race in Ben Hur only with Fiats. The roads are always crowded – the city's rush hour begins at about 8am each morning and doesn't slacken off until about midnight. Lane markings are ignored as Cairo drivers treat other vehicles like obstacles on a slalom, and a favourite manoeuvre is to suddenly sweep across multiple lanes of traffic to make a turn on the opposite side of the carriageway. Brakes are scorned in favour of the horn. Traffic lights are discretionary unless enforced by a policeman, who is equally likely to wave you through on a red light and halt you on green. Driving at night is particularly hazardous as headlights are reserved exclusively for flashing oncoming vehicles.

It is a wonder that the roads aren't strewn with shattered glass and crumpled bits of car bodywork. But in fact there are very few accidents. Cairo drivers have their own road rules, they look out for each other and they are extremely tolerant of the type of driving that anywhere else would spark an epidemic of road-rage. Things only tend to go awry when an inexperienced driver is thrown into the mix – something anyone considering driving here should bear in mind.

For more information see Road Rules in the Getting Around chapter.

Rental If you are crazy enough to want to battle the traffic in Cairo, there are a number of car rental agencies in the city, including the big three – Avis, Hertz and Budget.

You need to be over the age of 25 and have an international driving permit. However, the rental agencies don't care whether you have a permit or not and will rent you the car regardless but you can cop a heavy fine if you're caught driving without one.

As an indication of prices, for a small car such as a Suzuki Swift you'll be looking at about US$40 per day. A Toyota Corolla is about US$56 to US$60 per day, plus around US$0.25 per kilometre. Remember that a 10% to 17% tax will be added to your bill. It's usually possible to pay with travellers cheques or by credit card.

Avis (☎ 354 7400, fax 356 2464) 16 Mamal as-Sukkar, Garden City; (☎ 576 6432) Nile Hilton; (☎ 291 4288) Cairo international airport, ask for Avis; (☎ 291 0223) Heliopolis Sheraton; (☎ 290 5055) Meridien Heliopolis
Budget Rent-a-Car (☎ 340 0070, fax 341 3790) 5 Makrizy, Zamalek (head office); (☎ 340 6667) Cairo Marriott; (☎ 265 2395) Cairo international airport
Europcar (☎ 347 4712/3, fax 303 6123) 27 Sharia Libnan, Mohandiseen; (☎ 291 4288) Cairo international airport, ask for Europcar
Hertz (☎ 303 4241, fax 347 4172) 195 Sharia 26th of July, Mohandiseen; (☎ 574 4400) Ramses Hilton; (☎ 354 3239, fax 356 3020) Semiramis Inter-Continental; (☎ 291 4288) Cairo international airport, ask for Hertz.
J Car (☎ 335 0521, fax 360 3255) 33 Sharia Missaha, Doqqi; (☎ 291 4288) Cairo international airport, ask for J Car
Thrifty (☎/fax 266 3313) 1 Al-Entesar, Heliopolis; (☎ 265 2620) Cairo international airport

Taxi

If it's too far to walk, then the easiest way of getting around in Cairo is to flag down a taxi. They're cheap enough to make the hassle of the buses redundant. Use the following as a rough guide to what you should be paying for taxi rides around Cairo.

destination	cost
Downtown to the Airport	E£25-30
Downtown to Heliopolis	E£12-15
Downtown to Khan al-Khalili	E£3.50
Downtown to Zamalek	E£3.50
Midan Tahrir to the Citadel	E£5
Midan Tahrir to Midan Ramses	E£3
Midan Tahrir to the Pyramids	E£15

Note that these fares are generous and are more than a local would pay. For comprehensive information on taxi etiquette see the Getting Around chapter.

Hantour

These horse-drawn carriages and their insistent drivers hang around on the Corniche near the Helnan Shepheard's hotel and on Gezira near the Cairo Tower. They aren't a feasible means of getting around the city and are there for pleasure rides only.

River Bus

The river bus terminal is at Maspero, on the Corniche in front of the big round radio and TV building. From here, boats depart every 15 minutes or so between 6.30am and 3.45pm for University, a landing over on the Giza side of the river just north of the University Bridge. Every second boat continues south on to Manial, Rhoda, Giza and Masr al-Qadima (Old Cairo). The last stop is convenient for Coptic Cairo. The complete trip takes 50 minutes and the fare is 50pt.

Immediately south of the river bus terminal at Maspero is the departure point for boats to Qanater (see Nile Delta in the Around Cairo chapter).

Around Cairo

By Egyptian standards, Cairo, which at heart is a 10th-century city, is modern. But as the great and mysterious Pyramids at Giza attest, civilisation in the immediate vicinity dates back far, far earlier. Within just a short drive of the Cairo city limits are some of the oldest and most important ancient Egyptian sites in the country, including Memphis, the mighty capital of the Old Kingdom of Egypt, and its vast necropolis of Saqqara, site of the intriguing Step Pyramid and the eerie Serapeum. In the other direction, north of the city, in a depression on the edge of the desert are more pre-Islamic survivors in the form of the fortress-like monasteries of Wadi Natrun.

In addition to history, trips out to these places are highly appealing for the scenery. The overwhelming urbanity of Cairo ends surprisingly abruptly to be replaced by luscious green fields and palm groves.

Most of the destinations described in this chapter can be visited as day trips, the one exception being Al-Fayoum, where, if you don't have your own transport, you'll have to reckon on staying the night.

Highlights

- Feel like Indiana Jones as you explore the half-buried ruins at Saqqara in the peaceful solitude of the desert.
- Marvel at the pyramids of Dahshur, the older and smaller cousins of the Pyramids of Giza, but perhaps even more impressive on account of their remote location.
- Visit Birqash camel market for a wild contrast with Cairo city life; however, it's not for the squeamish.

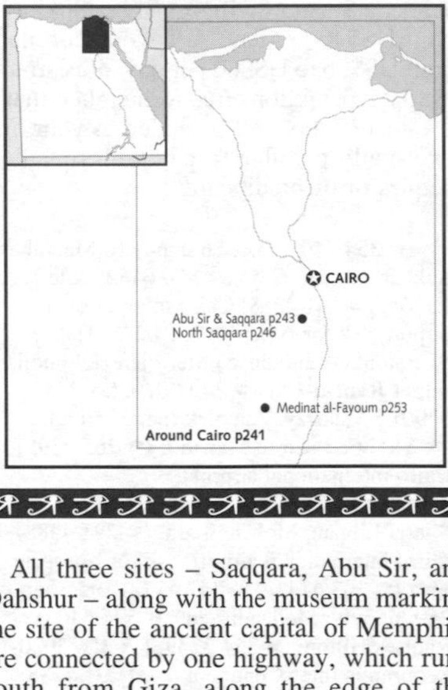

South of Cairo

While the world is familiar with the great Pyramids of Giza, what's less well known is that these are just three of the approximately 90 ancient pyramids spread throughout the country. Most of these pyramids are concentrated in the area just south of Cairo, stretching from the capital down to the oasis of Al-Fayoum. The must-see pyramid after Giza is the Step Pyramid at Saqqara, and then to the north and south are the associated pyramid fields of Abu Sir and Dahshur, also well worth a visit. All of these monuments predate the better-known temples of Luxor and Upper Egypt by several hundred years, and represent the formative steps of an architecture and art that would reach fruition at Karnak and in the Valley of the Kings.

All three sites – Saqqara, Abu Sir, and Dahshur – along with the museum marking the site of the ancient capital of Memphis, are connected by one highway, which runs south from Giza, along the edge of the fields, where they suddenly stop and the desert begins. They can be visited in a single day trip, although if you have the money and time we'd recommend spreading the sites over two days. Many of the city-centre hotels in Cairo arrange day-trip packages to Saqqara and Memphis, and occasionally Dahshur, for around E£70 (not including entrance fees), which is split between however many people sign up. Alternatively, you can arrange a day trip yourself.

AROUND CAIRO

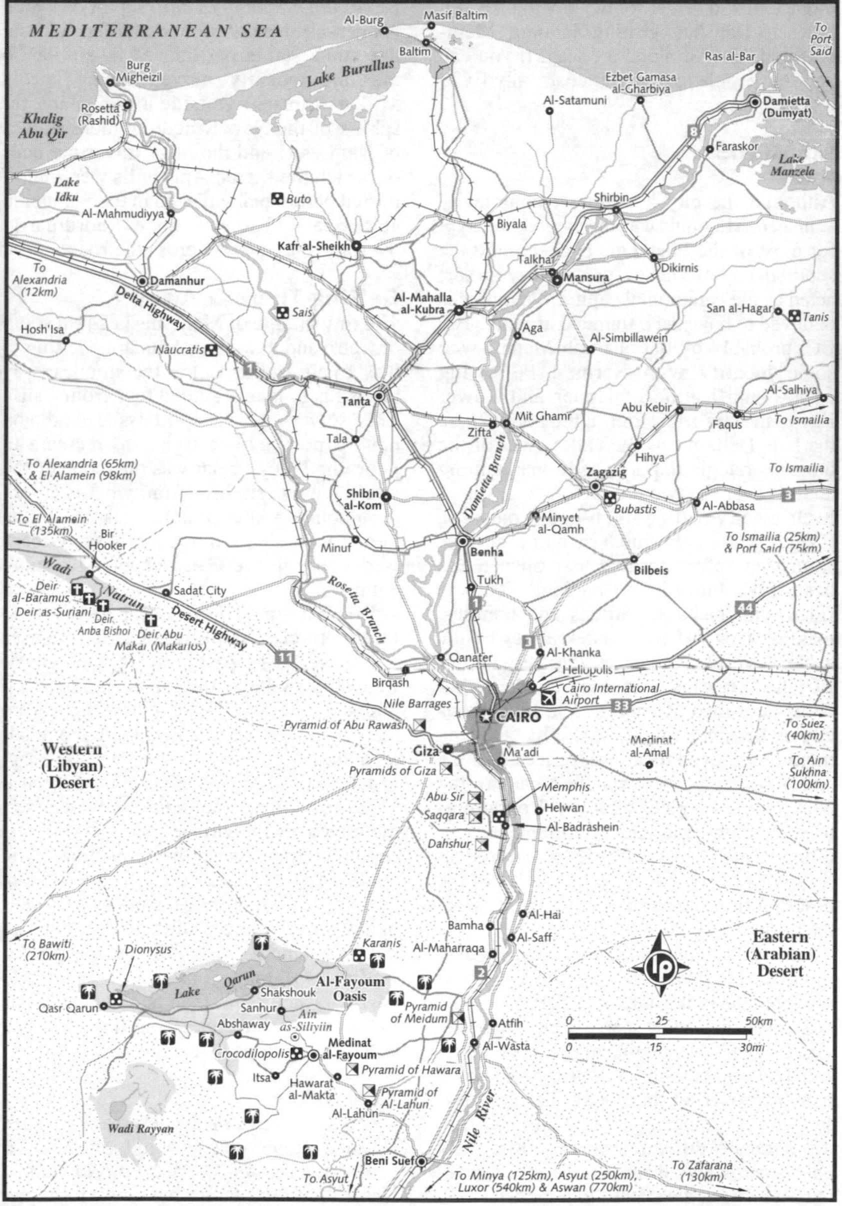
MEDITERRANEAN SEA
Al-Burg
Masif Baltim
Baltim
Lake Burullus
Burg Migheizil
Rosetta (Rashid)
Khalig Abu Qir
Lake Idku
Buto
Al-Mahmudiyya
Kafr al-Sheikh
Biyala
To Port Said
Ras al-Bar
Ezbet Gamasa al-Gharbiya
Al-Satamuni
Damietta (Dumyat)
Faraskor
Lake Manzela
Shirbin
Talkha
Mansura
Dikirnis
To Alexandria (12km)
Damanhur
Delta Highway
Sais
Al-Mahalla al-Kubra
Hosh'Isa
Naucratis
Aga
Al-Simbillawein
San al-Hagar
Tanis
Tanta
Al-Salhiya
Abu Kebir
Faqus
To Ismailia
Mit Ghamr
Zifta
Tala
Hihya
To Alexandria (65km) & El Alamein (98km)
Damietta Branch
Zagazig
To Ismailia
Shibin al-Kom
Bubastis
Al-Abbasa
To El Alamein (135km)
Bir Hooker
Minyet al-Qamh
To Ismailia (25km) & Port Said (75km)
Wadi Natrun
Minuf
Benha
Bilbeis
Deir al-Baramus
Deir as-Suriani
Deir Anba Bishoi
Deir Abu Makar (Makarios)
Sadat City
Desert Highway
Rosetta Branch
Tukh
Qanater
Al-Khanka
Heliopolis
Birqash
Nile Barrages
Cairo International Airport
CAIRO
Pyramid of Abu Rawash
To Suez (40km)
Western (Libyan) Desert
Giza
Ma'adi
Medinat al-Amal
To Ain Sukhna (100km)
Pyramids of Giza
Memphis
Abu Sir
Helwan
Saqqara
Al-Badrashein
Dahshur
Al-Hai
Bamha
Al-Saff
To Bawiti (210km)
Dionysus
Karanis
Al-Maharraqa
Eastern (Arabian) Desert
Lake Qarun
Shakshouk
Al-Fayoum Oasis
Qasr Qarun
Sanhur
Pyramid of Meidum
Ain as-Siliyiin
Atfih
Abshaway
0 25 50km
0 15 30mi
Crocodilopolis
Medinat al-Fayoum
Al-Wasta
Pyramid of Hawara
Itsa
Hawarat al-Makta
Pyramid of Al-Lahun
Al-Lahun
Wadi Rayyan
Nile River
Beni Suef
To Asyut
To Minya (125km), Asyut (250km), Luxor (540km) & Aswan (770km)
To Zafarana (130km)
1
8
3
44
11
33
2

AROUND CAIRO

For E£80 to E£100 you should be able to hire a taxi and driver for the day to take you down to Dahshur, visiting Saqqara, Memphis and Abu Sir along the way. If you can get four people together, it costs only E£20 to E£25 each.

MEMPHIS

☎ 02

Although the city has almost completely vanished, Memphis was the capital of Egypt for most of the Pharaonic period while the southern city of Thebes (present-day Luxor) acted as the ceremonial capital. Memphis is believed to have been founded around 3100 BC, probably by the pharaoh Menes, who some identify with Narmer. Following Menes' unification of Upper and Lower Egypt, the city's location, at the point where the Nile Delta meets the valley, was of the utmost strategic importance in maintaining control over the two regions.

Originally called Ineb-hedj, meaning 'White walls', the modern name derives from Men-nefer, meaning 'Established and beautiful'. Indeed, the ancient city was filled with palaces, gardens and temples, making it one of the greatest cities of the ancient world. As late as the 5th century BC, the Greek historian and traveller Herodotus described Memphis as 'a prosperous city and cosmopolitan centre'. Its enduring importance, even then, was reflected in the size of its cemetery on the west bank of the Nile, an area replete with royal pyramids, private tombs and sacred-animal necropolises. This city of the dead, centred at Saqqara, covers 35km along the edge of the desert, from Dahshur in the south to Giza in the north.

Centuries of annual floods have inundated Memphis with Nile mud – the once enormous temple of the creator god, Ptah, is now little more than a few sparse ruins frequently waterlogged due to the high water table. Other ancient buildings have long since been ploughed over so that today there are few signs of the grandeur of Memphis – in fact, it's extremely difficult to imagine that a city once stood where there is now only a small museum and some statues in a garden.

The **museum** *(Al-Badrashein; admission E£14; open 8am-5pm daily)*, part of which is open-air, is built around a fallen colossal limestone statue of Ramses II, similar to the one recently moved from Cairo's Midan Ramses. Outside is an alabaster sphinx of the New Kingdom, more statues of Ramses II and the huge travertine beds on which the sacred Apis bulls were mummified before being placed in the Serapeum at Saqqara. There is an extraordinarily overpriced cafeteria across the road.

Getting There & Away

The tiny village of Memphis is 24km south of Cairo and 3km from Saqqara. Getting to it is a pain in the neck – the simplest way to visit is to take a guided tour from Cairo. This solves the transport issue, and you have expert help in trying to recreate in your mind's eye what was once one of the world's greatest cities from what is a very disappointing site. Memphis can easily be tied in with a trip to Saqqara – see Organised Tours in the Cairo chapter for more details.

Doing it yourself, the cheapest way is to take a 3rd-class train from Cairo's Ramses Station to Al-Manashi, and get off at Al-Badrashein village; the trip takes about two hours (to go 24km!) and costs 35pt. From the village, you can then walk for about half an hour, catch a Saqqara microbus for 25pt or take a taxi. Ask for Memphis and you'll be dropped off at the museum, which is in the middle of the village.

Rather than catch the slow train, you could go via Helwan on the metro. From the station at Helwan, get a microbus (don't believe it if you're told there are none) to the boat landing (ask for the *markib lil-Badrashein*), take a boat across the Nile to Al-Badrashein, and then another microbus to Memphis from there. This, however, will still take you a good 1½ hours.

ABU SIR

Lying at the edge of the desert, surrounded by sand dunes, the pyramids of Abu Sir *(also rendered Abusir; Saqqara Rd; admission E£10; open 8am-4pm daily)* form part of the vast necropolis of Saqqara. Originally there were four Pharaonic pyramids, three more fragmentary pyramids for royal women and an unfinished pyramid that was possibly for Pharaoh Shepseskare. Most of what exists at the site today is badly worn; the pyramids are slumped and lack the geometric precision of their bigger, older brethren at Giza. For a long time few visitors ever bothered with Abu Sir, but at the beginning of 1999 the site was officially 'opened' and the enormous asphalt road leading to it is seeing an increasing number of big tour buses detouring by on their Giza-Saqqara-Memphis circuit.

Pyramid of Sahure

This is the most complete and the northernmost of the group. The entrance corridor is only half a metre high and slopes down to a small room. You then walk through a 75m-long corridor before crawling the last 2m on your stomach through Pharaonic dust and spider webs to get into the burial chamber.

The remains of Sahure's once impressive funerary temple complex stand on the east side of the pyramid. The temple once had black basalt-paved floors and red granite palm-style columns and walls embellished with 10,000 sq metres of superbly detailed reliefs. Although much is now in the museums of Cairo and Berlin, the scenes included the pharaoh waging war against Asiatics and Libyans, seafaring expeditions and Sahure in the company of the gods. Like most pyramid complexes, Sahure's funerary temple was connected by a long, similarly decorated causeway (almost 250m long), which sloped down to his valley temple. The temple was built at the edge of the cultivation and bordered by water, and too was embellished by beautiful relief scenes.

From this pyramid on a clear day, you can see as many as 10 other pyramids stretching out before you to the horizon.

Pyramid of Niuserre

This is the most dilapidated of the three complete pyramids at Abu Sir. Niuserre took over his father Neferirkare's causeway, which you can still see linking up with

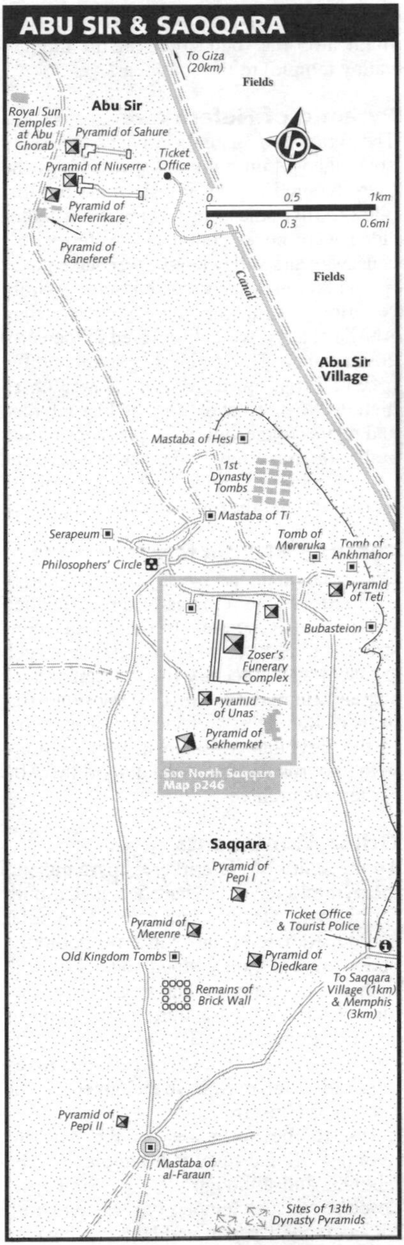

what's left of Niuserre's funerary temple (built atop the foundations of his father's valley temple) to the south-east.

Pyramid of Neferirkare

The pyramid of Sahure's brother Neferirkare now stands 45m high and it resembles the Step Pyramid at Saqqara, since the original plans to fill in the steps and make it smooth-sided were never completed. Neferirkare's causeway and valley temple were taken over by his son and successor Niuserre. Within Neferirkare's funerary temple, the so-called Abu Sir Papyri were discovered in the early 20th century. This highly important archive of Old Kingdom documents is written in hieratic, a shorthand form of hieroglyphs, and relates to the cult of the pharaohs buried at the site, recording important details of ritual ceremonies, temple equipment, priests' work rotas and the temple accounts.

Pyramid of Raneferef

On a diagonal, just west of Neferirkare's pyramid, are the remains of the unfinished Pyramid of Raneferef. In this hastily constructed mud-brick funerary temple, Czech archaeologists recently found fragments of statuary, including a superb limestone figurine of Raneferef protected by Horus (now in the Egyptian Museum in Cairo), along with papyrus fragments relating to the Abu Sir temple archives.

Other Monuments

To the south of Neferirkare's pyramid lies the **pyramid** recently identified as that built for his wife, Queen Khentkawes II, mother of both Raneferef and Niuserre. Although badly ruined, it once stood some 17m tall. In the nearby funerary temple, Czech archaeologists discovered a third set of papyrus archive documents. To the south of the queen's pyramid are two virtually destroyed pyramids that may have belonged to the queens of Niuserre.

Just to the north-west of the Abu Sir pyramids lie the **royal sun temples** at Abu Ghorab, and although the Abu Sir Papyri describe six such temples only the two built for Pharaohs Userkaf and Niuserre have so far been discovered. Both resemble the typical pyramid complex in layout, with a valley temple, causeway and an upper temple. As part of their solar focus, they originally featured a large obelisk of limestone blocks, which in Niuserre's case stood some 36m tall on a 20m-high base. In front of the obelisk, in the temple's court, the enormous alabaster altar can still be seen. Made in the form of a solar disc flanked by four 'hotep' signs, the hieroglyphic sign for 'offerings' and 'satisfied', the altar itself reads as 'The sun god Ra is satisfied'. Although it can easily be reached from Abu Sir, this enigmatic site is somewhat off the beaten track and is very rarely visited.

Getting There & Away

Lying some distance off the main Saqqara road, there's no way to reach Abu Sir by public transport. The only way to visit is as part of an organised tour, in a taxi (see under South of Cairo earlier in this chapter) or by car.

SAQQARA

The site of Saqqara was originally one huge cemetery for the inhabitants of the ancient city of Memphis, which was in use for more than 3500 years following the city's foundation. The necropolis is situated high above the Nile Valley's cultivation area, covering a 7km-stretch of the Western Desert. Deceased pharaohs and their families, administrators, generals and sacred animals were all interred here.

Although the Old Kingdom pharaohs were laid to rest within Saqqara's 11 major pyramids, their subjects were buried in the hundreds of smaller tombs that lie beneath the sands of the great necropolis. Apart from the Step Pyramid, most of Saqqara lay hidden until the middle of the 19th century when the great French Egyptologist, Auguste Mariette, discovered the Serapeum. Even the Step Pyramid's massive funerary complex was not discovered until 1924 and it is still being restored; French architect Jean-Philippe Lauer, who began work here in 1926, is still involved in its restoration an incredible 75 years later.

Saqqara Itinerary

With its vast size and huge collection of monuments and tombs there is too much at Saqqara to be seen in one visit. The following is a sample itinerary that includes the most important monuments:

- Enter through the hypostyle hall and gaze on the Step Pyramid. Built by the pharaoh Zoser (also rendered Djoser), it's the world's oldest pyramid.
- Wander around Zoser's funerary complex, through the huge great south court, into the Houses of the North and South and in front of the eerie serdab (cellar), where you can stare into the stone eyes of Zoser. Continue through the ruins of the funerary temple and around the back of the Step Pyramid.
- Walk south along the hill above the western edge of the funerary complex and down the causeway of Unas, where you can visit some of the beautiful tombs dotted on either side or peer into the huge boat pits.
- Head over to the Pyramid of Teti to see the famous Pyramid Texts.
- Descend into the Serapeum. Peer through the gloom and into the gigantic sarcophagi of the 25 huge Apis bulls that were entombed in this bizarre place.
- Walk over to the mastaba tomb of 5th-dynasty father and son Ptahhotep and Akhethotep, with its beautiful painted reliefs of animals, battle scenes and the two men receiving offerings.
- If you've still got the energy, visit the wonderful Mastaba of Ti, overseer of the Abu Sir pyramids and sun temples, with its fascinating tomb reliefs of daily life in the Old Kingdom that show people trading, building ships, milking cows and rescuing their livestock from the crocodiles.

A worthwhile visit to Saqqara will take more than one day. Because of its size, it seems that other visitors are few and far between, apart from the organised tour groups who are rushed through in the mornings. You'll find here, in the middle of the desert, a peaceful quality rarely found at other ancient sites in Egypt.

Orientation & Information

The main places of interest are in the area around the Step Pyramid, known as North Saqqara. Most travellers start their visit here and then, if they are up to it, continue by taxi, donkey or camel north to Abu Sir and/or down to South Saqqara. It's imperative to have some form of transport to get around as the tombs and sites are spread over a vast distance and walking is not feasible. Make sure you bring some water as it gets very hot. The site's rest house was recently pulled down because it was leaking water into the surrounding monuments, and although another one was planned at a new location, at the time of writing construction had not yet begun and there was nowhere to buy drinks.

Most of the pyramids and tombs at Saqqara can be 'officially' visited between 8am and 5pm daily. The guards start locking the monument doors at about 4.30pm, although some have been known to lock up even earlier – with tourists inside – to extract some baksheesh. The admission fee for all North Saqqara sights is E£20. There is a E£5 fee for using a camera, collected only at the entrance to the Step Pyramid. Before setting off, check at the ticket office to see which monuments are open.

Zoser's Funerary Complex

Constructed around 2650 BC by Imhotep, the pharaoh's chief architect who was later deified, the **Step Pyramid** of Pharaoh Zoser was Egypt's – and indeed the world's – earliest stone monument. It is still the most noticeable feature at Saqqara. Imhotep's brilliant use of stone, and his daring break from the tradition of building royal tombs as underground rooms topped with a mud-brick mastaba, was the inspiration for Egypt's future architectural achievements.

The pyramid began as a simple square mastaba but was transformed into its final form through six separate stages of construction and alteration. With each stage, the builders gained confidence in their use of the new medium and mastered the techniques

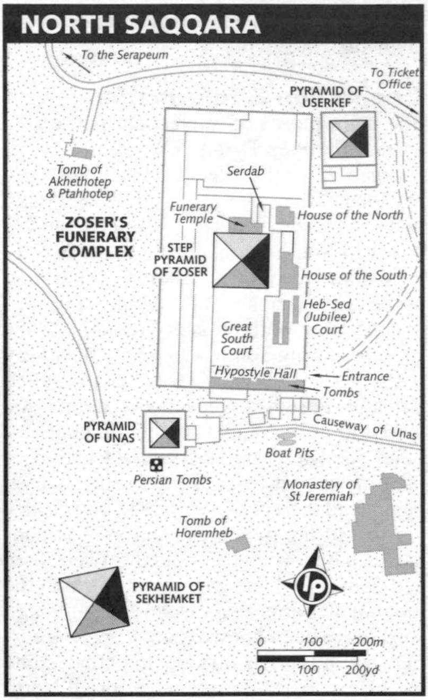

NORTH SAQQARA

required to move, place and secure the huge blocks. This first pyramid rose in six steps to a height of 60m and was encased in fine white limestone.

The Step Pyramid dominates Zoser's enormous funerary complex, which covers 15 hectares and is surrounded by a magnificent bastioned and panelled limestone wall 1645m long. The enclosure wall survives today at a height of about 5m, and a section at the south-east corner has been restored to its original 10m height. Fourteen false doors, carved and painted to resemble real wood, hinges and sockets, allowed the pharaoh's ka, or attendant spirit, to come and go at will. For the living, there is only one entrance into the pyramid, on the south-eastern corner, via a vestibule and along a colonnaded corridor into the broad hypostyle hall. The 40 pillars in the corridor are the original 'bundle columns', ribbed to resemble a bundle of palm or papyrus stems. The walls have been restored, but the protective ceiling is modern concrete. The roof of the hypostyle hall is supported by four impressive columns and there's a large, false, half-open ka door. Here, you will be accosted by a bevy of 'guides' eager to show you around.

Great South Court The hypostyle hall leads into the great south court, a huge open area flanking the south side of the pyramid, with a rebuilt section of wall featuring a frieze of cobras. The cobra, or uraeus, was a symbol of Egyptian royalty and represented the goddess Wadjet, a fire-spitting agent of destruction and protector of the pharaoh. A rearing cobra, its hood inflated, always appeared on the brow of a pharaoh's headdress or crown.

Near the base of the pyramid is an altar, and in the centre of the court two stone B-shaped boundary markers. These markers delineated the ritual race the pharaoh had to run to demonstrate his prowess and ability to rule. The race was part of the elaborate rituals of the Jubilee Festival, or Heb-Sed, which usually occurred after 30 years' reign and involved the pharaoh's symbolic rejuvenation and the recognition of his supremacy by officials from all over Egypt. The construction of Heb-Sed features within Zoser's funerary complex was therefore intended to perpetuate his revitalisation for eternity.

The buildings on the eastern side of the pyramid are also connected with the royal jubilee, and include the **Heb-Sed (Jubilee) Court**, the sides of which are lined with dummy structures. Those buildings on the east side represent the shrines of Lower Egypt, and those on the west represent Upper Egypt. All were designed to house the spirits of Egypt's gods when they gathered to witness the rebirth of the pharaoh during his jubilee rituals.

North of the Heb-Sed Court are the **House of the South** and **House of the North**, representing the two main shrines of Upper and Lower Egypt and symbolising the unity of the country. The heraldic plants of the two regions also form the column capitals; those in the House of the North are in the form of papyrus while in the House of the South the capitals are in lotus form.

The House of the South also features one of the earliest examples of tourist graffiti, written during the 47th regnal year of Ramses II, nearly 1500 years after Zoser's reign. Hadnakhte, the treasury scribe, records his admiration for Zoser while 'on a pleasure trip west of Memphis', his hieratic script written in black ink is preserved behind Perspex just inside the building's entrance.

Serdab A stone structure right in front of the pyramid, the serdab contains a slightly tilted wooden box with two holes drilled into its north face. Look through these and you'll have the eerie experience of coming face to face with Zoser himself. Inside is a life-size, lifelike painted statue of the long-dead pharaoh, gazing stonily out towards the stars. Although it's only a copy (original is in the Egyptian Museum), it's still quite haunting. Serdabs were designed so that a pharaoh's ka could communicate with the outside world.

The original entrance to the Step Pyramid is directly behind the serdab, and leads down to a maze of subterranean tunnels and chambers quarried for almost 6km through the rock. The pharaoh's burial chamber is vaulted in granite, and some of the other chambers are decorated with reliefs of the pharaoh performing the jubilee race and feature some exquisite blue faience tile decoration. Although the interior of the pyramid is unsafe and closed to the public, part of the blue-tiled decoration can be seen in the Egyptian Museum.

Pyramid of Userkef

To the north-east of the funerary complex is the Pyramid of Userkef. Although the removal of its limestone casing has left little more than a mound of rubble, this pyramid once rose to a height of 49m. Its funerary temple was once decorated with the most exquisite naturalistic relief carvings judging from one of the few remaining fragments showing birds by the river, which can now be found in the Egyptian Museum.

Pyramid & Causeway of Unas

What appears to be a another big mound of rubble, this time to the south-west of Zoser's funerary complex, is actually the Pyramid of Unas, the last pharaoh of the 5th dynasty (2375–2345 BC). Built only 300 years after the inspired creation of the Step Pyramid, and after the perfection of the Pyramids of Giza, this unassuming pile of loose blocks and debris once stood 43m high. Although it looks nothing special from the outside, the interior marks the beginning of a significant development in funerary practices. For the first time, the royal burial chamber was decorated, its ceiling adorned with stars and its white alabaster-lined walls inscribed with beautiful blue hieroglyphs. These are the funerary inscriptions now known as the 'Pyramid Texts', comprising 283 separate 'spells' chosen by Unas to protect his soul. The inscriptions include rituals, prayers and hymns, as well as lists of items, such as the food and clothing Unas would require in the afterlife. Unfortunately, deterioration of the interior led to the pyramid's permanent closure in 1998.

The 750m-long causeway running from the east side of Unas' pyramid to his valley temple (now marked by little more than a couple of stone columns at the side of the road leading up to the site) was originally roofed and decorated with a great range of painted relief scenes, including a startling image of people starving, now preserved in the Louvre in Paris.

The two 45m-long boat pits of Unas lie immediately south of the causeway, while on either side of the causeway are numerous tombs, more than 200 of which have been excavated. Of the several better-preserved examples usually open to visitors are the tombs of one of Unas' queens, Nebet, and that of Princess Idut, who was possibly his daughter. There are also several brightly painted tombs of prominent 5th- and 6th-dynasty officials. These include the Tomb of Mehu, the vizier; the Tomb of Nefer, the supervisor of singers; the joint Tomb of Niankhkhnum and Khnumhotep, overseers of the royal manicurists to Pharaoh Niuserre; the Tomb of Neferherenptah, the overseer of the royal hairdressers, which is also known as the Bird Tomb on account of its superbly drawn bird-hunting scene; and the Tomb of Irukaptah, overseer of the royal butchers, whose appropriate scenes support its title of the Butchers' Tomb.

Persian Tombs

Around the sides of the Pyramid of Unas are several large shaft tombs of the Saite (664–525 BC) and Persian (525–404 BC) eras. These are some of the deepest tombs in Egypt. Although their depth was an attempt to prevent grave robbers stealing their contents, the design failed to protect them, just as it did almost everywhere else. To the north of the pyramid is the enormous tomb shaft of the Saite general Amun-Tefnakht. On the south side of the pyramid is a group of three Persian tombs, where the entrance is covered by a small wooden hut to which a guard in the area has the key. If you don't have your own torch he'll lead you down a 25m-deep winding staircase to the vaulted tombs of three officials – the admiral Djenhebu to the west, chief royal physician Psamtik in the centre and Psamtik's son, Pediese, to the east. The sheer size of the tombs and the great stone sarcophagi within, combined with their sophisticated decoration, demonstrate that the technical achievements of the later part of Egyptian history were equal to those of earlier times.

Monastery of St Jeremiah

This monastery's half-buried remains date from the 5th century AD and are up the hill from the causeway of Unas, south-east of the boat pits. There's not much left of the structure as it was ransacked by invading Arabs in AD 950. More recently Egyptian antiquities officials took all the wall paintings and carvings to the Coptic Museum in Cairo.

Pyramid of Sekhemket

Although closed to the public because of the danger of a cave-in, the unfinished pyramid of Zoser's successor Sekhemket (2648–2640 BC) is a short distance west of the ruined monastery, near the south-west corner of Zoser's own pyramid. Although the project was abandoned for unknown reasons when the great limestone enclosure wall was only 3m high, the architects had already constructed the underground chambers in the rock beneath the pyramid, together with the deep shaft of the south tomb. An unused travertine sarcophagus was found in the sealed burial chamber, and a quantity of gold and jewellery in the south tomb. Recent surveys have also revealed another mysterious large complex to the west of Sekhemket's enclosure, but this remains unexcavated.

Tomb of Akhethotep & Ptahhotep

Akhethotep and his son Ptahhotep were top royal officials during the reigns of Djedkare (2414–2375 BC) and Unas at the end of the 5th dynasty. Akhethotep was vizier, judge, supervisor of pyramid cities and supervisor of priests. Most of his titles were inherited by his son, Ptahhotep, along with his tomb – father and son have a joint mastaba with two burial chambers, two chapels and a pillared hall.

The painted reliefs in Ptahhotep's section are particularly beautiful, and portray a wide range of animals, from lions and hedgehogs to the domesticated cattle and fowl, which were brought as offerings to the deceased. Ptahhotep himself is portrayed resplendent in a panther-skin robe inhaling perfume from a jar. Further on he is having his wig fitted, his feet massaged and his fingers manicured (although some Egyptologists prefer to interpret this detail as Ptahhotep inspecting an important document, which would be in keeping with his official status).

Philosophers' Circle

On the way to the Serapeum there is a group of Greek statues arranged in a semicircle – a collection of philosophers and poets set up as a wayside shrine by Ptolemy I (305–285 BC) as part of his patronage of learning. From left to right are Plato (standing), Heraclitus (seated), Thales (standing), Protagoras (seated), Homer (seated), Hesiod (seated), Demetrius of Phalerum (standing against a bust of Serapis) and Pindar (seated).

Serapeum

The sacred Apis bulls were by far the most important of the cult animals entombed at

SARA-JANE CLELAND

North-west of Cairo, camel traders tend to their charges at Birqash, Egypt's largest camel market.

GREG ELMS

This limestone colossus of Ramses II, over 12m long, is displayed inside its own museum at Memphis.

The Temple of Hathor at Dendara (left) is beautifully preserved and features towering columns and detailed reliefs. Scenes depicted in these reliefs include Thoth, the ibis-headed god of wisdom (top right), and figures laden with produce for temple offerings (middle & bottom right).

Saqqara. The Apis, it was believed, was an incarnation of Ptah, the god of Memphis, and was the calf of a cow struck by lightning from heaven. Once divinely impregnated, the cow could never again give birth and her calf was kept in the Temple of Ptah at Memphis and worshipped as a god. The Apis was always portrayed as black, with a distinctive white diamond on its forehead, the image of a vulture on its back and a scarab-shaped mark on its tongue. When it died, the bull was mummified on one of the large travertine embalming tables discovered at Memphis, then carried in a stately procession to the subterranean galleries of the Serapeum at Saqqara, and placed in a huge stone sarcophagus.

The first Apis burial took place in the reign of Amenhotep III (1390–1352 BC), and the catacombs were subsequently expanded up until 30 BC. The main corridor contained 28 side chambers for the bulls who died between the Saite and Ptolemaic periods (664–30 BC). The remaining 25 enormous granite and limestone coffins weigh up to 80 tonnes each, although only one was found intact when the Serapeum was first excavated in 1851.

Up until then, the existence of the sacred Apis tombs was known only from classical references. Having found a half-buried sphinx at Saqqara, and following the description given by the Greek historian Strabo in 24 BC, Auguste Mariette uncovered the avenue of sphinxes leading to the Serapeum. His great discovery sparked the extensive and continuing excavation of Saqqara.

A visit to the Serapeum is one of the definite highlights of Saqqara; it's very eerie to wander along galleries lit only by tiny lanterns that barely cast enough light to illuminate the enormous, macabre, black sarcophagi in the chambers. The largest and most elaborate sarcophagus, covered in hieroglyphs, is located at the end of the main gallery on the right. It would be wise to bring a torch, as the lighting has been known to be switched off for no apparent reason, only appearing to work again if small change is produced.

Mastaba of Ti

A few hundred metres north-east of the Philosophers' Circle is the mastaba Tomb of Ti, discovered by Auguste Mariette in 1865. It is perhaps the grandest and most detailed private tomb at Saqqara and one of the main sources of knowledge about life in the Old Kingdom of Egypt. Its owner, Ti, among other official titles, was overseer of the Abu Sir pyramids and sun temples during the 5th dynasty. The superb quality of his tomb is in keeping with his nickname, Ti the Rich. Like Zoser, he has a life-size statue of himself within a serdab in the tomb's offering hall (although, as with Zoser's, the original is in the Egyptian Museum). Ti's wife, Neferhetpes, was the priestess and 'royal aquaintance' and together with their two sons, Demedj (overseer of the duck pond) and Ti (inspector of royal manicurists), the couple appear throughout the tomb alongside endless scenes of daily life represented in the finest detail. As men and women go about their business working on the land, preparing food, fishing, building boats, dancing, trading and avoiding crocodiles, their figures are accompanied by chattering hieroglyphic dialogue, all no doubt familiar to Ti during his career as a royal overseer: 'Hurry up, the herdsman's coming', 'Don't make so much noise!', 'Pay up – it's cheap!'.

Pyramid of Teti

The avenue of sphinxes excavated by Mariette in the 1850s has again been engulfed by desert sands, but it once extended to the much earlier Pyramid of Teti. Teti was the first pharaoh of the 6th dynasty and his pyramid was built in step form and then filled and encased in limestone. Unfortunately, the pyramid was robbed both for its treasure and its stone, and little remains but a mound. However, the inside is well worth a visit and is very similar to that of the Pyramid of Unas (which is now closed), both in plan and also in that its walls are inscribed with Pyramid Texts. Within the intact burial chamber, Teti's basalt sarcophagus is also well preserved and represents the first instance of a sarcophagus with inscriptions on it.

Looking Good for Eternity

After visiting even just a few of Egypt's numerous temples and tombs, it can all start to get a bit much – endless wall scenes of pharaohs, all standing sideways presenting a never-ending line of gods with the same old offerings. But look more closely, and such scenes often produce a few surprises.

As the little figures on the wall strike their eternal poses, a keen eye can find anything from pharaohs ploughing fields to small girls pulling at each other's hair. There is also a whole range of activities that are regarded as modern to be found among the most ancient scenes, including hairdressing, perfumery, manicures and even massage. Certainly the tombs of important male officials sometimes contain rather unexpected representations. The treasury overseer Ptahhotep inhales deeply from a jar of perfume, then has his feet massaged and fingers manicured. There are similar scenes elsewhere at Saqqara, with a group of men in the Tomb of Ankhmahor enjoying both manicures and pedicures.

With the title 'Overseer of Royal Hairdressers and Wigmakers' commonly held by the highest officials in the land, hairdressing scenes can also be found in the most unexpected places. Not only does Ptahhotep have his wig fitted by his menservants, similar hairdressing scenes can even be found on coffins; the limestone sarcophagus of 11th-dynasty Queen Kawit in the Cairo Museum shows her wig being deftly styled.

Among its wealth of scenes, the Theban Tomb of Rekhmire (Tomb of the Nobles) shows a banquet at which the female harpist sings the lyrics 'Put perfume on the hair of the goddess Maat'. And then in the Deir el-Medina tomb of the workman Pashedu, his family tree contains relatives whose hair denotes their seniority, the eldest shown with the whitest hair as opposed to with wrinkles.

As in almost every representation of an ancient Egyptian figure, black eye make-up is worn by almost everyone, male and female, adult and child. As well as its aesthetic value, it was also used as a means of reducing the glare of the sun – think ancient sunglasses. Even manual workers wore it, with the Deir el-Medina Tomb of Ipy once containing a scene in which the men building the royal tombs were having their eyepaint applied while they worked – something pretty difficult to imagine on a building site today!

Dr Joann Fletcher

Tombs of Mereruka & Ankhmahor

Near the Pyramid of Teti is the mastaba of his highest official, Mereruka, vizier and overseer of priests. It is an enormous tomb, and its 32 chambers covering an area of 1000 sq metres make it the largest Old Kingdom courtier's tomb to be found so far. The 17 chambers on the east side belong to Mereruka, including a magnificent six-columned offering hall featuring a life-size statue of Mereruka appearing to walk right out of the wall to receive the offerings brought to him. The other rooms are reserved for his wife, Princess Seshseshat, Teti's daughter, and their eldest son, Meriteti (whose name means 'Beloved of Teti'). Much of the tomb's decoration is similar to that of the Mastaba of Ti, with an even greater number of animals portrayed – look out for the wide-mouthed, sharp-tusked hippos as you enter – along with a charming scene of domestic bliss as husband and wife are seated on a bed and Seshseshat plays them music on her harp.

A little further east, the tomb of the 6th dynasty vizier and palace overseer Ankhmahor contains further interesting scenes of daily life. These include men involved in a manicure and pedicure session and, most unusually, in the surgical procedures that give the tomb its alternative title, the Doctor's Tomb. As two boys are circumcised the hieroglyphic caption says, 'Hold him firmly so he does not fall'!

Mastaba of al-Faraun

This unusual funerary complex, known as the Mastaba of al-Faraun or Pharaoh's Bench belongs to the last 4th-dynasty pharaoh, the short-lived Shepseskaf (2503–2498 BC)

Inside an enclosure once covering 700 sq metres is the rectangular tomb built of limestone blocks. It was originally covered by a further layer of fine, white limestone and a lower course or lower layer of red granite. Inside, a 21m-long corridor slopes down to storage rooms and a vaulted burial chamber, which is possible to enter if you can find the guard.

Pyramid of Pepi II

A short distance north-west of the mastaba is the Pyramid of Pepi II (2278–2184 BC), whose 94-year reign at the end of the 6th dynasty must be something of a record. Despite his incredibly long reign, Pepi II's 52m-high pyramid was of the same modest proportions as those of his predecessor Pepi I. Although the exterior is little more than a mound of rubble, the interior is decorated with more excerpts from the Pyramid Texts.

Getting There & Away

Saqqara is about 25km south of Cairo. Although it is possible to get within 1.5km of the Saqqara ticket office using public transport, this is a very time-consuming business and, once there, you'll be stuck for getting around unless you try to hitch a ride up onto the plateau and then haggle for a camel or donkey. The site is best covered in a taxi, combined with a visit to Memphis and Dahshur. You'll have to arrange this option in Cairo as there are no taxis at the site.

If you're coming from Cairo or Giza, and are determined to do it on your own, you have several options.

Bus One of the cheapest ways of getting to Saqqara without going via Memphis is to take a bus or minibus (25pt to 50pt) to the Pyramids Rd (see Getting There & Away under The Pyramids in the Cairo chapter for more details) and get off at the Saqqara Rd stop. From there you can get a microbus to the turn-off to the Saqqara site (don't ask for Saqqara village as you'll end up in the wrong place), from where you'll probably have to walk the last 1.5km to the ticket office. Once at the ticket office, you'll have to try and hitch.

Train The 3rd-class train from Ramses Station in Cairo to the village of Al-Badrashein (see Getting There & Away under Memphis earlier in this chapter for more details) also goes to Dahshur; a taxi from either Al-Badrashein or Dahshur to North Saqqara should cost about E£5. You can arrange a microbus from Memphis to the turn-off to the Saqqara site on the Giza-Memphis road, from where it's about a 1.5km walk to the Saqqara ticket office. There is usually a bit of traffic along the Giza-Memphis road.

From Al-Badrashein, there are sometimes direct microbuses to Giza.

Getting Around

It is not feasible to explore Saqqara on foot and, as there are no taxis near the ticket office, your only option for getting around, if you do arrive independently, is to attempt to hitch or to hire (from near the Serapeum) a camel, horse or donkey. A trip around North Saqqara should cost, after bargaining, E£8 – but don't be surprised if it's more, as the handlers are well aware that you're in need of the extra legs so your bargaining power is diminished.

The only taxis you'll find around here are those coming from Cairo and they are usually already full.

DAHSHUR

Some 10km south of Saqqara in a quiet patch of desert, Dahshur *(admission E£10; open 8am-5pm daily)* is an impressive 3.5km-long field of 4th- and 12th-dynasty pyramids. The site was an off-limits military zone until mid-1996, and the camel drivers, guides and other touts who infest Giza and Saqqara have yet to find enough of a market here, so you can enjoy the monuments in peace.

There were originally 11 pyramids at Dahshur, although only the two Old Kingdom ones (the Bent and Red Pyramids) remain intact. Of the three Middle Kingdom pyramid complexes built by Amenemhat II (1922–1878 BC), Sesostris III (1874–1855 BC) and his son Amenemhat III (1855–1808 BC), only the oddly shaped Black Pyramid of Amenemhat III is worth a look. The tower-like structure appears to have completely collapsed due to the pilfering of its limestone outer-casing in Medieval times, but the mud-brick remains contain a maze of corridors and rooms designed to deceive tomb robbers. And while thieves did manage to penetrate its burial chambers, they left behind a number of precious funerary artefacts that were discovered in 1993.

However, the site is most famous for being home to Egypt's first true pyramid, the Red Pyramid, and its earlier version, the Bent Pyramid, both of which where built by Pharaoh Sneferu (2613–2589 BC), father of Khufu and founder of the 4th dynasty. It now seems that Sneferu was also responsible for building much of the Pyramid of Meidum before moving his court to Dahshur to found a new necropolis and embark on further pyramid building, making him the greatest of all Egypt's pyramid builders.

Bent Pyramid

Experimenting with ways to create a true, smooth-sided pyramid, Sneferu's architects began building with the same steep angle and inward-leaning courses of stone they had been using to create step pyramids. When this began to show clear signs of stress and instability around half way up its eventual 105m height, they had little choice but to reduce the angle from 54° to 43° and begin to lay the stones in horizontal layers. This explains why the structure has the unusual shape that gives it its name. Together with the Red Pyramid, which is the same height, these two pyramids are the third-largest in Egypt, after the two largest at Giza.

The Bent Pyramid is rare among the pyramids around Cairo in that most of its outer casing is intact. Inside there are two burial chambers, the highest of which retains its original ancient scaffolding of great cedar beams to counteract internal instability (although currently the interior is off limits to visitors). There is a small subsidiary pyramid to the south and the remains of a small funerary temple to the east. About halfway towards the cultivation to the east you can also see the ruins of Sneferu's valley temple, which yielded some interesting reliefs.

Red Pyramid

The world's oldest true pyramid is sometimes referred to as the North Pyramid, but more often as the Red Pyramid on account of the red tones of its limestone, exposed to weathering when the better-quality white limestone casing was removed. Alternatively others say the name derives from the red graffiti and construction marks scribbled on its masonry in ancient times. Having learnt from their experiences building the Bent Pyramid, the same architects carried on where they had left off, building the Red Pyramid at the same 43° angle as the Bent Pyramid's more gently inclining upper section.

Open to the public, the entrance is via 125 stone steps. A 63m-long passage takes you down to three chambers – two antechambers with stunning 12m-high corbelled ceilings and a 15m-high corbelled burial chamber in which fragmentary human remains, possibly of Sneferu himself, were found.

Getting There & Away

The simplest way to visit Dahshur is probably as part of a tour to Saqqara and Memphis. Alternatively, you could hire a taxi and a driver to take you here, visiting Abu Sir, Memphis and Saqqara on the way. For more details, see under South of Cairo at the start of this chapter.

AL-FAYOUM OASIS

☎ 084

About 100km south-west of Cairo is Al Fayoum, Egypt's largest oasis, covering an area about 70km wide and 60km long and including Lake Qarun (Birket Qarun). Home to more than two million people, it is an intricately irrigated and extremely fertile basin watered by the Nile via hundreds of capillary canals.

The region was once filled by Lake Qarun and during the reigns of the 12th-dynasty pharaohs Sesostris III and his son Amenemhat III a series of canals were built linking the lake to the Nile. Amenemhat also drained marshes in an early effort at land reclamation. Later, the Nile was diverted to the agricultural land and the lake, which lies 45m below sea level, suffers from increasing salinity; only a few varieties of fish remain and the water level is slowly decreasing.

The oasis was a favourite vacation spot for the pharaohs of the 13th dynasty, and many fine palaces were built in the area. The Greeks later called the area Crocodilopolis because they believed the crocodiles in Lake Qarun were sacred. A temple was built in honour of Sobek, the crocodile-headed god, and during Ptolemaic and Roman times pilgrims came from all over the ancient world to feed the sacred beasts.

These days, the region is revered as the garden of Egypt because of its lush fields of vegetables and sugar cane, and its groves of citrus fruits, nuts and olives, all of which produce abundant harvests. The lake, canals and vegetation support an amazing variety of birdlife. There isn't a whole lot to do here, but a couple of the archaeological sites (notably Qasr Qarun and the Pyramid of Meidum) are worth a visit, the vicinity of the lake is attractive, and the desert scenery around Wadi Rayyan, just beyond Al-Fayoum, is gorgeous.

Given that the oasis is so spread out, you really need your own transport. Ideally you would hire a taxi for a day in Cairo to bring you down here and chauffeur you around. Alternatively, get a bus to Medinat al-Fayoum from Giza (see Bus under Getting There & Away in the Cairo chapter for more details), and hire a taxi locally. Expect to pay about E£40 to E£50 for half a day.

Medinat al-Fayoum

All the tradition and fertility of Al-Fayoum Oasis surrounds the rather grimy Medinat al-Fayoum, or 'Town of the Fayoum', which sadly is a microcosm of everything that is bad about Cairo: horn-happy drivers, choking fumes and dust, crowded streets and a population of more than 400,000. It's a place to be avoided at all costs.

The canal acts as the city's main artery; most of the commercial activities take place

AROUND CAIRO

MEDINAT AL-FAYOUM

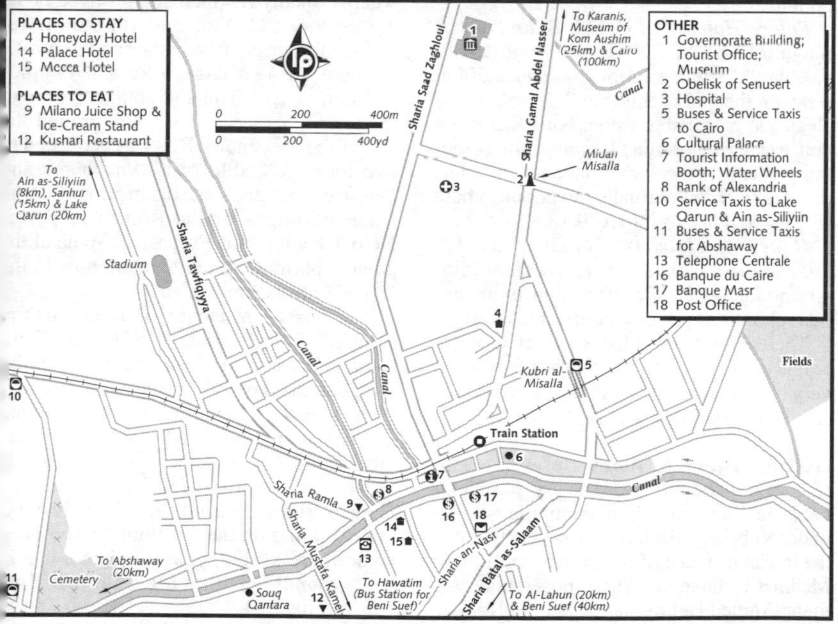

around it and the further you wander away from the canal, the quieter things become. The bus and taxi stations, unfortunately, are all a bit of a hike from the centre. There is a tourist office (☎ 342 313) on Sharia Saad Zaghloul at the rear of the governorate building. It's open from 8am to 2pm Saturday to Thursday.

As far as things to see go, there's the **Obelisk of Senusert**, which you'll pass coming in from Cairo at the centre of a roundabout to the north-east of town. Although it looks lost among the cars and buses, it's supposedly the only obelisk in Egypt with a rounded top, and it also features a cleft in which a golden statue of Ra was placed, reflecting the sun's rays in the four directions of the wind.

In the governorate building is a small **museum** *(☎ 342 313, Sharia Saad Zaghloul; open 8am-2pm Sat-Thur)* that has displays on the history and fauna of the oasis.

Places to Stay & Eat If you have to spend the night in town, there are a couple of options.

Palace Hotel *(☎ 351 222, Bahr Yousef)* Singles/doubles E£20/35, with bath E£30/45. On the south side of the canal, 200m west of the park, this hotel is relatively clean and reasonable value. For E£15 more you can have air-con. If you want something cheaper, the same management runs the ***Mecca Hotel***, virtually next door, where singles/doubles go for E£10/18.

Honeyday Hotel *(☎ 341 205, fax 340 105, Sharia Gamal Abdel Nasser)* Singles/doubles E£55/75. This is a more upmarket option; prices include breakfast.

There aren't any places to eat that we would recommend, but there are several very basic cafes and assorted eateries on the canal-side road just west of the park.

Getting There & Away Buses to Cairo (E£4, three hours) leave every half-hour between 7am and 7pm from the station under Kubri al-Misalla (the road bridge over the tracks just east of the railway station) in Medinat al-Fayoum. These buses take you to the Ahmed Helmy station behind Ramses train station in Cairo, stopping en route at Giza. From a separate station in an area called Hawatim to the south-west of Medinat al-Fayoum, buses leave regularly for Beni Suef (E£1, one hour) and twice daily for Minya (E£5.50).

For the 3rd-class train buff, there are four daily departures to Cairo (E£1.60). Progress is so slow as to be barely perceptible – the journey takes more than four hours.

Service taxis leave from the bus stations. To Cairo, they cost E£4 to Giza or E£5 to Midan Ramses. You can get to Beni Suef for E£1.50.

Getting Around The green-and-white minibuses cover all areas of Medinat al-Fayoum between the western and eastern bus stations and the centre of town *(wust al-Balad)* for 25pt.

Karanis

At the edge of the oasis depression, 25km north of Medinat al-Fayoum on the road to Cairo, are the ruins of the city of Karanis where Ptolemy II's mercenaries lived in the 3rd century BC. You can still see the remains of their bathhouse among the ruins.

There are two **Graeco-Roman temples** *(admission E£16)* in the southern part of the town. The larger one, built around the end of the 1st century BC, was dedicated to two local crocodile gods, Pnepheros and Petesouchos, and has inscriptions dating from the reigns of the Roman emperors Nero, Claudius and Vespasian. Some of the painted portraits found here are now in the Egyptian Museum in Cairo.

The nearby **Museum of Kom Aushim** *(Mathaf Kom Aushim; ☎ 501 825, Cairo road; admission E£6; open 8am-4pm daily)* has good displays of Old and Middle Kingdom objects, including sacred wooden boats, Canopic jars, and wooden and ceramic statuettes entombed to serve the deceased in the afterlife. Items from the Graeco-Roman period, and later history are exhibited on the 1st floor. If you need somewhere to stay, you can pitch a tent in the grounds of the Museum of Kom Aushim for E£4.

From Medinat al-Fayoum there are buses to Karanis (50pt) at 7am and 2.30pm, or simply take one of the Cairo-bound buses.

Pyramid of Hawara

About 12km south-east of Medinat al-Fayoum, off the road to Beni Suef, is the dilapidated mud-brick Pyramid of Hawara, which is actually the second pyramid of Amenemhat III (1855–1808 BC) – his other is the now tower-like Black Pyramid at Dahshur. It originally had a casing of white limestone covering the mud-brick core, which is all that is visible today. It has been suggested that like Pharaoh Sneferu 800 years before him, Amenemhat III built a second pyramid at a more gentle angle after the first at Dahshur showed signs of instability. Although the 58m-high exterior is now simply mud-brick, the interior reveals a series of sophisticated technical developments – corridors were blocked using a series of huge stone portcullises; the burial chamber is carved from a single piece of quartzite; and after the pharaoh's burial, the chamber was sealed by an ingenious device using sand to lower the roof block into place (as seen in the corny Hollywood movie *Land of the Pharaohs* in which a similar method is used to entomb Joan Collins).

Amenemhat's once vast funerary complex is now nothing but rubble, and even his temple, which had quite a reputation in ancient times, has suffered at the hands of stone robbers. Herodotus said the temple (300m by 250m) was a 3000-room labyrinth that surpassed even the Pyramids of Giza, while Strabo claimed it had as many rooms as there were provinces so that all the pharaoh's subjects could be represented by their local officials in the presentation of offerings.

The area was also used as a cemetery during the Graeco-Roman period, and although Egyptian mummification techniques continued to be used, the mummies' wrappings now incorporated a portrait-style face (see the boxed text 'Portraits of the Past'). After widespread excavations, pretty much all that is left are pieces of mummy cloth and human bones sticking up through the mounds of rubble. At the time of writing, it was not possible to go into the pyramid as rising ground water had blocked the entrance.

The buses between Beni Suef and Medinat al-Fayoum pass through Hawarat al-Makta; from here it's a short walk to the pyramid. Just ask the driver to let you off.

Portraits of the Past

Al-Fayoum may not be famous for much these days, but it was here that caches of what are some of the world's earliest portraits were found. These extraordinarily lifelike pictures, known as the 'Fayoum Portraits', were painted on wooden panels and put over the faces of the mummies, or painted directly onto the linen shrouds covering the corpses, in a fusion of ancient Egyptian and Graeco-Roman funerary practices.

Dating back to between 30 BC and AD 395, the portraits are executed in a technique involving a heated mixture of pigment and wax. They're remarkable for the superb skill of the anonymous artists who painted them; the beautifully rendered and eerily modern-looking faces bridge the centuries and, in some cases, look like they were painted only yesterday. The haunting images are made all the more poignant by their youth (some are only babies) – a reflection of the high mortality rates at the time.

More than a thousand of these portraits have been found, not just in Al-Fayoum but throughout Egypt. They now reside in numerous museums around the world, including the Egyptian Museum in Cairo.

Pyramid of Al-Lahun

About 10km south-east of Hawara, on the Nile side of the narrow fertile passage through the desert connecting Al-Fayoum to the Nile, are the ruins of another mud-brick pyramid. Once cased in limestone, it was built by the Middle Kingdom pharaoh Sesostris II (1880–1874 BC). The pyramid was stripped of all its treasures by ancient tomb robbers, but modern excavators found

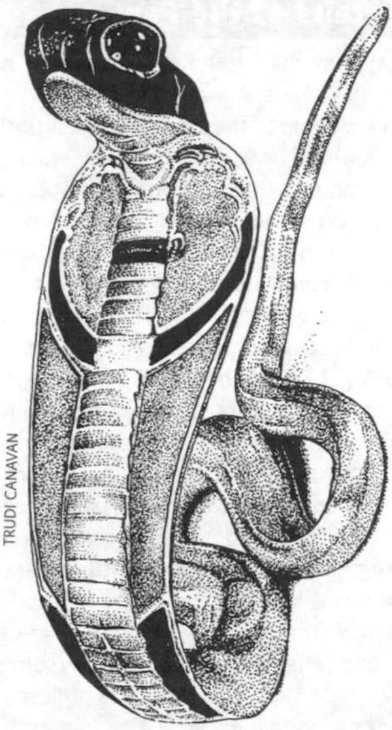

The 12th-dynasty Uraeus of Sesostris II was found at the pyramid of Al-Lahun. The uraeus was the serpent image of kingship and would have once been attached to a ceremonial headress or royal crown.

the one thing they missed: an amazing solid-gold uraeus (cobra), now displayed in the Egyptian Museum in Cairo.

Although there's not much left of the pyramid, you can climb to the top for a great view of the surrounding area. Be warned, to match the steep climb is an equally steep admission fee of E£20.

This pyramid is definitely off the beaten track. To get there, you can hitch from Beni Suef or Medinat al-Fayoum, or take the local bus between the two cities to the village of Al-Lahun from where it's a 2km walk to the site.

Ain as-Siliyiin

The spring waters and gardens of Ain as-Siliyiin *(admission 25pt)*, about 8km northwest of Medinat al-Fayoum, merit an excursion if only to see their location amid a lovely, lush valley. The spring water itself is sweet to taste and is said to help in the prevention of arteriosclerosis because of the traces of titanium found in it. There are a few cafes, restaurants and little stores where you can buy water, biscuits and the like. Farmers from the adjacent gardens sell their seasonal produce along the walkway.

From Medinat al-Fayoum, get a Sanhur service taxi or a bus (50pt, hourly) from the station in the west of the town and tell the driver where you want to get off.

Lake Qarun

This is a pleasant enough spot where there is really nothing to do, except sit at one of the lakeside cafes or hire a boat for about E£5 an hour.

Auberge du Lac *(☎ 700 002, fax 700 730, Lake Qarun)* Singles/doubles US$70/105. Arriving at the lake, this four-star hotel is the first place you will pass. World leaders met at the original hotel on this site after WWI to decide on the borders of the Middle East, and it later served as King Farouk's private hunting lodge. These days it is often taken over by hunting groups targeting ducks and geese, and by Cairenes looking for some fresh air. Prices include breakfast.

To get here, take a pick-up (E£1) from Sanhur to Shakshouk. When you see the lake and Auberge du Lac, you've arrived; get off wherever you choose. It's easy enough to get another pick-up going either way along the south-bank road.

Qasr Qarun

The ruins of the ancient town of Dionysus, once the starting point for caravans to the oasis of Bahariyya in the Western Desert, are just near the village of Qasr Qarun at the western end of Lake Qarun.

The **Ptolemaic temple** *(admission E£16)* erected in 4 BC to worship Sobek, the crocodile-headed god of Al-Fayoum, is just off to the left of the road shortly before the village. It was partly restored in 1956. You can ask to go down to the underground chambers (beware of snakes) and climb up to the top for a view of the desert, the sparse remains of Ptolemaic and Roman settlements, and the oasis.

Getting out here is a bit of an ordeal, considering the relatively small distances involved. From Medinat al-Fayoum, take a service taxi or pick-up to the town of Abshaway (55pt, one hour) and change there for Qasr Qarun (E£1.20, one hour). There are also some pick-ups plying the road along the south side of the lake to Qasr Qarun, but they are few and far between.

WADI RAYYAN

In the 1960s, the Egyptian authorities followed in the footsteps of their ancestors and carried out extensive irrigation works, creating three lakes in a depression called Wadi Rayyan, south-west of Lake Qarun. Filled with excess water from agricultural drainage, it was designed to be the first step in an ambitious land-reclamation project. But all has not gone to plan. One of the lakes has dried up and the other two are turning progressively more brackish; however, the surrounding area is now quite green and has become a major nesting ground for birds. One lake drains into the other, which is about a metre lower, at a spot rather grandly called 'the Waterfalls'.

Now a protected area, Wadi Rayyan has become a weekend picnic spot for Cairenes and there are a couple of small cafes near the Waterfalls and even a hut in which it's possible to bed down overnight, although you need to get permission in advance from the tourist police in Medinat al-Fayoum if you plan to do this.

While it's difficult to get here, it is worth the effort as the road in from Lake Qarun is spectacular – a thin black belt of tarmac snaking along the sides of sand hills. Last time we visited it was during high winds and we watched in amazement as rapidly shifting sands devoured the route ahead. Avoid Fridays and national holidays if you're hoping for peace.

Getting There & Away

There is no public transport to Wadi Rayyan so you'll either have to have your own vehicle or hire a taxi (from Medinat al-Fayoum expect to pay about E£40 for a half-day; from Cairo it will cost about E£120 for a full day). To get to Wadi Rayyan, follow the road to the end of Lake Qarun and take the wide asphalt road to the left just after you see the mud-brick domes of the village of Tunis (a rural retreat for Cairo's artists and Westernised intelligentsia) on a ridge to your left. An asphalt road leads right to the lake. There is an entrance fee of E£5 per person and E£5 per vehicle payable at a toll booth on the edge of the protected area.

WADI AL-HITTAN

Some 55km further south into the desert at Wadi al-Hittan (Whale Valley) are the fossilised skeletons of primitive whales that have been lying here for some 40 million years. To get out here is something of an expedition and it requires at least two 4WDs – one to help haul the other out in the event of getting stuck in the sand. Ask at Wadi Rayyan for directions.

PYRAMID OF MEIDUM

About 32km north-east of Medinat al-Fayoum and 45km north of Beni Suef, beyond the vegetation belt, is the ruin of the first true pyramid attempted by the ancient Egyptians. The Pyramid of Meidum *(admission E£16)* is impressive, although it looks more like a stone tower than a pyramid, rising abruptly as it does from a large hill of rubble. This is one case, however, where the apparent state of disrepair has not been caused by time or centuries of stone robbers, but rather it is the result of one instantaneous accident. The pyramid began as an eight-stepped structure; the steps were then filled in and the outer casing was added, forming the first true pyramid shell. However, there were serious design flaws and some time after completion (possibly as late as the time of the Ptolemaic rulers in the last few centuries BC) the pyramid's own weight caused the sides to collapse, leaving just the core that still stands today.

Although the pyramid was likely to have been started by Pharaoh Huni, his son Sneferu was responsible for its actual erection. Sneferu's architects obviously learnt from the mistakes that eventually led to the disaster of Meidum, as he also built the more successful Bent and Red Pyramids at Dahshur.

Ask the guard at the nearby house to unlock the entrance of the pyramid for you. You can follow the steps 75m down to the empty underground burial chamber.

Near the pyramid are the large mastaba tombs of some of Sneferu's sons and officials, including his son Rahotep and wife Nofret. The superb statues found in this Meidum tomb are in Cairo's Egyptian Museum.

Getting There & Away

It's actually much easier to get to the pyramid from Beni Suef, about 45km to the south, than from Medinat al-Fayoum. Get a pick-up (75pt, 45 minutes) from Beni Suef to Al-Wasta, and then another to Meidum village (35pt), from where you'll have to walk a couple of kilometres, unless you can get a ride.

Alternatively, you could get one of the service taxis or buses running between Beni Suef and Cairo and ask to be dropped off at the Meidum turn-off, from where you still have about 6km to go. The reverse of this is probably the easiest way to get back to Beni Suef (or to Cairo for that matter) – just flag down a service taxi, but be prepared to wait.

North-West of Cairo

North-west of Cairo is where the green fields of the Delta run up against the harsh, lifeless sands of the desert. Roughly demarcating this natural boundary is the Cairo-Alexandria Desert Hwy, the fastest and most direct road route between the country's two major cities. In recent times, this formerly desolate highway has become increasingly urbanised. The road is a life-support line off which have been hung several new satellite towns, including 6th of October City and Sadat City, designed to ease the population pressure on Cairo. Parts of the wide-open prairie-type expanses of the area have also been smoothly greened to create vast golfing resorts (see Golf in the Facts for the Visitor chapter). For the curious who have access to a car, such places are worth visiting for a glimpse into Egypt's vision of the future. For an insight into desert life of the past, try Wadi Natrun or the Birqash camel market. Both are accessible by public transport.

BIRQASH CAMEL MARKET

Egypt's largest camel market *(souq al-gamaal; admission E£3)* is held at Birqash, about 35km north-west of Cairo. Until 1995, this famous market was located among run-down tenements and overcrowded streets in Imbaba, one of Cairo's western suburbs. But a burgeoning population has made land, even on the city's periphery, a valuable commodity – too precious for camels – and so one of Cairo's age-old institutions was relocated to the edge of the Western Desert, an area deemed more suitable for camel trading.

The market is an easy half-day trip from Cairo but, like all Egypt's animal markets, it's not for animal lovers or the faint-hearted. Hundreds of camels are sold here every day, most having been brought up the 40 Days Rd from western Sudan to just north of Abu Simbel by camel herders (for more information, see the boxed text 'Taking Camels to Market' in the Nile Valley – Esna to Abu Simbel chapter). From here, most are sold to traders at the market in Daraw, from where they're hobbled and crammed into trucks for the 24-hour journey to Birqash. By the time they arrive, many are emaciated while others are fit only for the knacker's yard. Traders stand no nonsense and camels that get out of line are beaten relentlessly. The sound of bawling beasts is sickening.

In addition to those from Sudan, there are camels from various parts of Egypt (including Sinai, the west and the south) and sometimes from as far away as Somalia. They are traded for other livestock, such as goats, sheep and horses, or sold for farm work and for slaughter. If you're interested in buying a camel, smaller ones cost about

E£1500 while the bigger beasts fetch about E£3000. The market is most lively on Friday and Monday mornings, from about 7am to 9am. As the day wears on, the bargaining activity subsides and by early afternoon it becomes quite subdued.

Getting There & Away

Using public transport, the cheapest way involves getting yourself to the site of the old camel market at Imbaba, from where microbuses filled with traders and potential buyers shuttle back and forth to Birqash. To get to the old camel market take bus No 99 from Midan Abdel Moniem Riad, or minibus No 72 from Midan Ramses to Midan Libnan (in Mohandiseen), and then catch a microbus from there. Or, easier still, take a taxi from central Cairo all the way to the old site – ask for Imbaba airport *(matar Imbaba)* as it's the closest landmark. Expect to pay about E£5. Microbuses to Birqash (E£1) leave from a cafe (look for the sign 'Modern Cairo House') opposite the old souq site.

From Imbaba, the road winds through fields dotted with date palms, dusty villages and orange orchards before climbing the desert escarpment to the market. In all, it's a 45-minute taste of rural Egypt. Microbuses from Birqash back to Imbaba leave when full so, depending on the time of the day, you may have to wait an hour or so.

Alternatively, on Friday only, the New Sun Hotel (see Places to Stay – Budget in the Cairo chapter) organises a minibus tour to the souq, leaving from the hotel at 7am and returning at about noon. The charge is E£20 per person (minimum five people), and you must book a day or two in advance.

To hire a taxi yourself to take you all the way to the market and back is going to cost around E£70, depending on your bargaining skills.

WADI NATRUN

About 100km north-west of Cairo, Wadi Natrun is a partly cultivated valley now strongly connected with the Coptic Church. In ancient times, the valley was important to the Egyptians as it was a source of natron, used in the mummification process. Natron comes from large deposits of sodium carbonate that are left when the valley's salt lakes dry up every summer – those deposits are now used on a larger scale by the chemical industry.

A visit to the monasteries of Wadi Natrun should explain the endurance of the ancient Coptic Christian sect. It is the desert, in a sense, that has been the protector of the faith, for it was there that thousands of Christians retreated to escape Roman persecution in the 4th century AD. They lived in caves, or built monasteries, and developed the monastic tradition that was later adopted by European Christians.

The focal point of the monasteries was the church, around which were built a well, storerooms, a dining hall, kitchen, bakery and the monks' cells. These originally isolated, unprotected communities were fortified after destructive raids in AD 817 by Arabs who were on their way to conquer North Africa. Of the 60 monasteries that were scattered over the valley, only four remain. But the religious life they helped protect is thriving. The Coptic pope is still chosen from among the Wadi Natrun monks, and monasticism is experiencing a revival, with younger Copts once again donning robes and embroidered hoods to live within these ancient walls in the desert.

As well as for their solitude and serenity, the monasteries are also worth visiting for the Coptic art they contain, particularly Deir as-Suriani.

As a general rule, you can visit all of the monasteries with the exception of Deir Abu Makar (Makarios). If you wish to stay overnight, you'll need written permission from the monasteries' Cairo residences: Deir Anba Bishoi (☎ 02-591 4448); Deir as-Suriani (☎ 02-592 9658); Deir Abu Makar (☎ 02-577 0614); and Deir al-Baramus (☎ 02-592 2775). Generally, women are not allowed to stay overnight.

Deir Anba Bishoi

St Bishoi founded two monasteries in Wadi Natrun – this one (which bears his name) and the nearby Deir as-Suriani. Deir Anba Bishoi is built around a church that contains the saint's body, which is said to be perfectly preserved in its sealed, tube-like container. Each year on 17 July, the tube is carried in procession around the church, and, according to the monk who showed us around last visit, the bearers can quite clearly feel the weight of a whole body within the tube. Also in the church is St Bishoi's cell, where he used to tie his hair with a rope hooked to the ceiling in order to wake him if he fell asleep during prayers.

It's also worth exploring the monastery's massive fortified keep, entered over a drawbridge and containing a well, kitchens, church and storerooms that can hold enough provisions for a year. Up on the roof, trap doors open to small cells that acted as makeshift tombs for those who died while the tower was under siege, as it frequently was during the Middle Ages. The tower rooftop is a splendid place from which to watch the desert sunset.

Deir as-Suriani

Deir as-Suriani, or 'Monastery of the Syrians', is named after a group of wandering Syrian monks who bought the monastery, with the help of one of their wealthy countrymen, from the Copts in the 8th century. Since the 16th century, it has been occupied solely by Coptic monks. It's worth visiting for its superb art. A series of remarkable wall paintings has recently been discovered under the plaster in the monastery's Church of the Virgin. Some of the paintings can be viewed through small 'windows' cut into the plaster covering them.

Deir as-Suriani is about 500m north-west of Deir Anba Bishoi.

Deir Abu Makar (Makarios)

This monastery is nearly 20km south-east of Deir Anba Bishoi and was founded around the cell where St Makarios spent his last 20 or so years. Although structurally it has suffered worst at the hands of raiding Bedouin, it is perhaps the most renowned of the four monasteries, as over the centuries most of the Coptic popes have been selected from among its monks. It is the last resting place of many of those popes and also contains the remains of the 49 Martyrs, a group of monks killed by Bedouin in AD 444. It is also the most secluded of the monasteries, and permission even to visit must be requested in advance.

Deir al-Baramus

Deir al-Baramus was the most isolated of the Wadi Natrun monasteries until recently, when a good road was built between it and Deir Anba Bishoi to the south-east. Despite this, it still has an isolated feel, and is probably the best monastery to stay at, as it's a little less austere than the others. The special feature of St John's Church is a superb iconostasis of inlaid ivory.

Getting There & Away

You can get a West Delta bus to the village of Bir Hooker for E£3 from Cairo's Turgoman garage. Departures leave hourly from 6.30am. From the village, you have to negotiate for a taxi to make the rounds of the monasteries, along roads that have more potholes than surface. Expect to pay around E£20. If you go on a Friday or Sunday, when the monasteries are crowded with pious Copts, you shouldn't have any trouble picking up a lift.

If you have your own vehicle and you're coming from Cairo, take the Pyramids Rd and turn onto the Desert Hwy just before the Mena House. At about 95km from Cairo (just after the rest house) turn left into the wadi, go through the village of Bir Hooker and continue on, following the signs indicating the monasteries. The first one is Deir Anba Bishoi. Deir as-Suriani is about half a kilometre to the north-west, Deir Abu Makar is 20km further via a sealed road to the south-east, and Deir al-Baramus is off to the north-west.

The Nile Delta

If you have the time, it's well worth the effort to explore the lush, fan-shaped Delta of Egypt between Cairo and Alexandria. This is where the Nile divides into two branches to enter the Mediterranean at the old ports of Damietta and Rosetta (for coverage of Rosetta, see Rosetta in the Alexandria & the Mediterranean Coast chapter). The Delta is also laced with several smaller tributaries and is reputedly one of the most fertile and, not surprisingly, most cultivated regions in the world.

The Delta region played just as important a part in the early history of the country as did Upper Egypt, although few archaeological remains record this. While the desert and dryness of the south helped preserve its Pharaonic sites, the amazing fertility of the Delta region had the opposite effect. Over the centuries, when the ancient cities, temples and palaces of the Delta fell into ruin, they were literally ploughed into oblivion by the fellaheen (peasant farmers). The attraction of this area, therefore, is the chance of coming across communities rarely visited by foreigners, where you can gain a little insight into the Egyptian peasant farmer's way of life. If you do intend spending any time in this region, we strongly recommend that you read Amitav Ghosh's excellent *In An Antique Land*, an account of the author's lengthy stay in a Delta village.

Service taxis and buses crisscross the region from town to town, but if you want to explore this incredibly green countryside you'll have to hire a car. Theoretically, you're not supposed to leave the main roads, but in the unlikely event of being hassled by the police you can always say that you're lost.

NILE BARRAGES

The Nile Barrages and the city of Qanater (which simply means 'Barrages' in Arabic) lie 16km north of Cairo where the Nile splits into the eastern Damietta branch and the western Rosetta branch. On Fridays and public holidays this is *the* favourite spot for picnicking Cairenes who flock up here by boat. The barrages, begun in the early 19th century, were successfully completed several decades later. The series of basins and locks, on both main branches of the Nile and the two side canals, ensured the vital large-scale regulation of the flow of the Nile into the Delta region, and led to a great increase in cotton production.

The Damietta Barrage consists of 71 sluices stretching 521m across the river; the Rosetta Barrage is 438m long with 61 sluices. Between the two is a 1km-wide area filled with beautiful gardens and cafes. It's a decent place to rent a bicycle (E£2 per hour) or a felucca and take a relaxing tour.

The town of Qanater, at the fork of the river, is the official start of the Delta region.

To get to the barrages from Cairo, you can take a river bus for E£2 from the water-taxi station in front of the Radio & Television building (Maspero station), just north of the Ramses Hilton in central Cairo. The trip takes about 1½ hours. A faster but less relaxing way to get there is by taking bus No 930 from Midan Ataba bus station or No 950 from Ahmed Helmy bus station, behind the Ramses train station.

ZAGAZIG & BUBASTIS

Just outside Zagazig, founded in the 19th century, are the ruins of Bubastis, one of the most ancient cities in Egypt. There's not much to see in Zagazig itself, but as it's only 80km north-east of Cairo it's an easy day trip to the ruins (although there's also a hotel or two in town should you want to stay overnight). The train heading for Port Said from Cairo takes about 1½ hours to Zagazig, and a service taxi (E£4) from Midan Ahmed Helmy in Cairo takes about one hour.

The great deity of the ancient city of Bubastis was the elegant cat goddess Bastet. Festivals held in her honour are said to have attracted more than 700,000 revellers who would sing, dance, feast, consume great quantities of wine and offer sacrifices to the goddess. The architectural gem of Bubastis was the Temple of Bastet, which was built at a higher level to look down on it, between two canals surrounded by trees and encircled by the city. The temple was begun by the great pyramid-builders Khufu and Khafre during the 4th dynasty, and pharaohs of subsequent dynasties made their additions over about 17 centuries. The temple is now just a pile of rubble, and the most interesting site at Bubastis is the cat cemetery 200m down the road. The series of underground galleries, where many bronze statues of cats were found, is great to explore.

TANIS

Just outside the village of San al-Hagar, 70km north-east of Zagazig, are the ruins of the ancient city of Tanis. Many believe Tanis to be the biblical city where the Hebrews were persecuted by the Egyptians before fleeing through the Red Sea in search of the Promised Land. (It's also where Indiana Jones discovered the 'Lost Ark'.) Tanis was certainly of great importance to a succession of powerful pharaohs, all of whom left their mark through the extraordinary buildings or statues they commissioned. For several centuries Tanis was one of the largest cities in the Delta.

The site covers about 4 sq km, only part of which has been excavated. The monuments uncovered date from as early as the 6th-dynasty reign of Pepi I, around 2330 BC, through to the time of the Ptolemies in the 1st century BC. The excavation of the city so far has revealed sacred lakes, the foundations of many temples, a royal necropolis and a multitude of statues and carvings. There are a few royal tombs that can be visited (for an admission fee), although they're not particularly impressive and all the finds from the tombs are now on display in Cairo's Egyptian Museum.

Although it's less impressive than other archaeological sites in the country, the Egyptian government has been promoting Tanis as a tourist destination for the past few years.

TANTA

The largest city in the Delta, Tanta is 90km from Cairo and 110km from Alexandria. There's nothing much of interest here, although it is a centre for Sufism. There's a mosque here dedicated to Sayyed Ahmed al-Badawi, a Moroccan Sufi who fought the Crusaders in the 13th century, and the *moulid* (religious festival) held in his honour following the October cotton harvest is one of the biggest in Egypt, drawing crowds of over a million.

While there are no actual structural remains in this area of the western Delta, there are the sites of three ancient cities. North-west of Tanta, on the east bank of the Rosetta branch of the Nile, is **Sais**, Egypt's 26th-dynasty capital. Sacred to Neith, the goddess of war and hunting and protector of embalmed bodies, Sais dates back to the start of Egyptian history and once had palaces, temples and royal tombs.

West of Tanta, more then half way along the road to Damanhur, is the site of **Naucratis**, an ancient city where the Greeks were allowed to settle and trade during the 7th century BC. The city of **Buto**, north-east of Damanhur and north-west of Tanta, was the cult centre of Edjo, the cobra goddess of Lower Egypt, always represented on a pharaoh's crown as a uraeus.

Tanta is easily reached from Cairo, by service taxi from Midan Ahmed Helmy, by Middle Delta Bus Co buses from Turgoman garage, or on nearly all Cairo-Alexandria trains (except the Turbini).

MANSURA

Mansura is known as the 'City of Victory' for the part it played in Egypt's early Islamic history. In 1249, the Egyptians retreated from the coast and set up camp at Mansura after the Crusader forces, under Louis IX of France, had captured the port of Damietta. When the Crusaders decided to make their push inland, they charged straight through the Muslim camp, only to be cut down on the other side of Mansura by 10,000 Mamluk warriors. Louis himself was captured and ransomed for the return of Damietta.

In more recent times, Mansura has played an important role at the centre of Egypt's cotton industry. However, for the casual visitor there's absolutely nothing to see or do here.

There are regular train connections with Cairo, and a service taxi from Midan Ahmed Helmy costs E£8. The East Delta Co bus from Midan Ulali costs about E£7 and takes 2½ hours.

DAMIETTA

Damietta (Dumyat to the locals) was once a prosperous Arab trading port. Its fortunes suffered greatly with the construction of the Suez Canal and the subsequent development of Port Said. During the Middle Ages, its strategic position on the north coast of Egypt, at the mouth of the Nile, meant it was regularly being threatened by foreign armies. When it wasn't being attacked by marauding Crusaders, Damietta did a roaring trade in coffee, linen, oil and dates, and was a port of call for ships from all over the known world.

East Delta Co buses leave from Turgoman garage in Cairo (E£10) every hour from 6am to 6.30pm daily.

Nile Valley – Beni Suef to Qus

> He who rides the sea of the Nile must have sails woven of patience.
>
> **Egyptian Proverb**

Highlights

- Admire lithe dancing girls and muscular wrestlers in the finely painted tombs of Kheti and Amenemhat in Beni Hasan.
- Wander among the desolate remains of Tell al-Amarna, ancient Egypt's Sun City, capital of the heretic Akhenaten's brave new world.
- Gaze upon some of ancient Egypt's finest temple reliefs at the Temple of Seti in Abydos.
- Marvel at Dendara's magnificent Temple of Hathor, one of the best-preserved temple complexes in Egypt.
- Experience the shabby grandeur of Minya, the once-prosperous Upper Egyptian cotton centre.

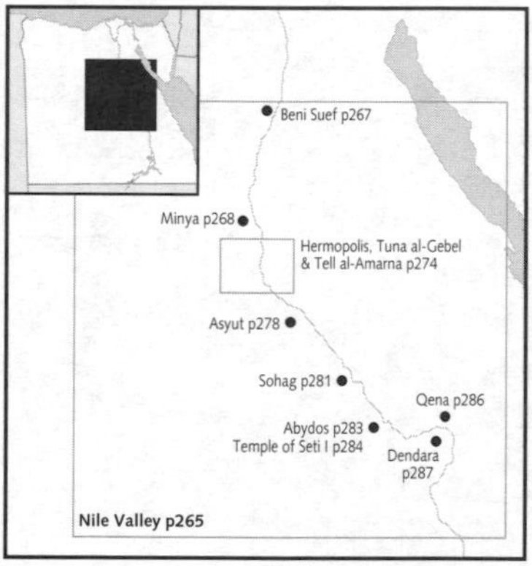

The ancient Greek traveller and writer Herodotus described Egypt as 'the gift of the Nile'; the ancient Egyptians likened their land to a lotus – the Delta being the flower, the oasis of Al-Fayoum the bud and the river and its valley the stem. Whichever way you look at it, Egypt is the Nile. The river is the lifeblood of the country and the fertile Nile Valley is its main artery.

As the world's longest river, the Nile cuts through an incredible 6680km of Africa as it winds its way north towards the Mediterranean. It begins its journey from two separate sources, 1500km apart: Lake Victoria in Uganda, from which the White Nile journeys almost 3000km; and Lake Tana in the Ethiopian Highlands. The two rivers converge at Khartoum in Sudan and the Nile then flows north without a single tributary contributing to the waters.

But Egypt is the main beneficiary of this mighty river. Rain seldom falls in the Nile Valley but in the past the river would break its banks each summer and flood the surrounding land, covering it with a rich layer of silt. As the waters subsided farmers would plant seeds on their newly fertilised land and wait for the crops to grow. As Herodotus (who had a sound bite for every occasion) put it, the Egyptians 'gather in the fruits of the earth with less labour than any other people'.

But while it may have been a relatively easy life for farmers, the Nile was not always reliable. Some years the river would not rise high enough to flood all the land, causing famine. At other times the flood would be too high, washing away villages and precious topsoil. So from the earliest times the Egyptians recognised that controlling the river's flow was the key to prosperity. To this end they developed a highly sophisticated irrigation system with a complex system of canals and reservoirs to try and conserve water and squeeze more than one crop out of the silt each year.

It was not until the completion of the High Dam at Aswan in 1971 (see High Dam in the Nile Valley – Esna to Abu Simbel chapter) that Egypt finally succeeded in controlling the river. And with the taming of the Nile, the countryside has seen a huge population explosion. The thousands of villages that dot the edges of the old flood plain are now the size of small towns in Europe. The provincial capitals, such as Minya, Asyut and Qena, are in many ways just large extensions of these villages.

Still, as you head south from Cairo, you are struck by the lush green fields contrasting with the desert beyond. Farmers still practise flood irrigation and occasionally you can catch a glimpse of a *sakia*, or waterwheel, being turned by a blindfolded donkey, or a *shadouf*, the age-old implement for lifting water. You also see peasants working the land by hand, often using tools modelled on designs thousands of years old.

All this makes the countryside extremely picturesque. But, as with so much in Egypt, there is another side to this rural idyll. Labour intensive as it may be, agricultural work cannot employ all of the area's burgeoning population and the lack of any real industrial base south of Cairo has caused severe economic hardship. Worst hit of all are young people, who suffer extremely high rates of unemployment and have little hope of finding long-term work. Add to this a historic distrust of the distant authorities in Cairo and a tradition of violent vendettas, and it is understandable how

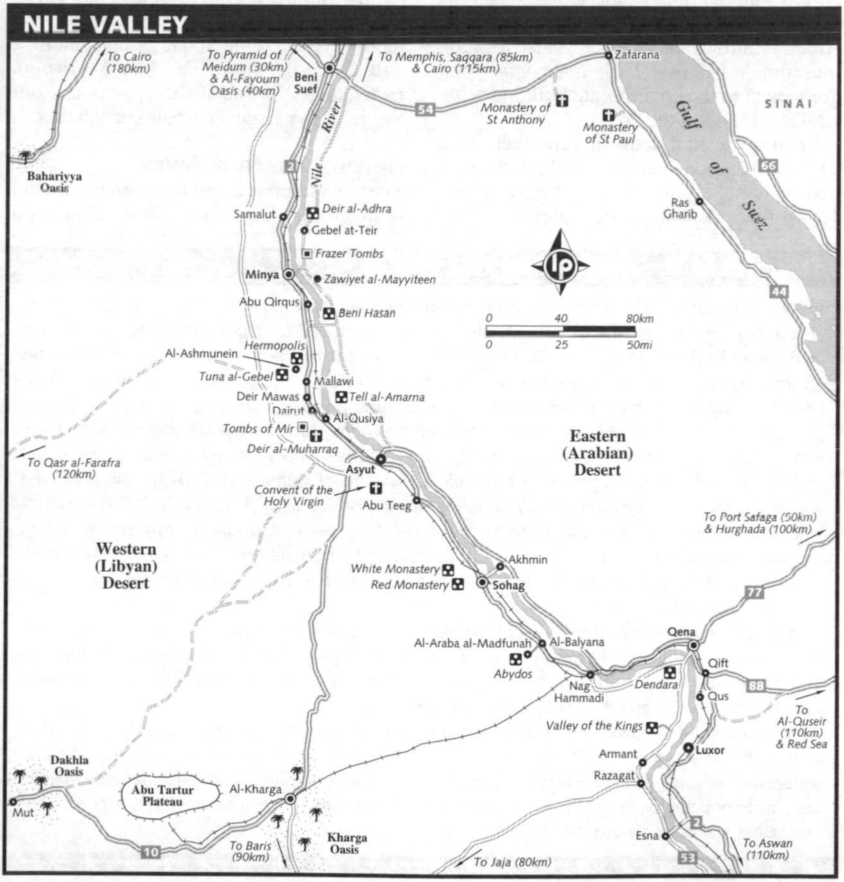

resentment against the state's perceived neglect of the area was exploited by Islamist leaders in the late 1980s and early 1990s, resulting in the violence that plagued parts of Middle and Upper Egypt until the late 1990s (see the boxed text 'Troubles in the Nile Valley').

BENI SUEF

☎ 082

Beni Suef is a provincial capital 120km south of Cairo. There's little to keep a traveller here these days; it is close to the Pyramid of Meidum and the oasis area of Al-Fayoum but both of these places can be just as easily visited from Cairo (see the Around Cairo chapter). There's also a **small museum** *(admission E£5; open 9am-4pm daily)* next to the governorate building with artefacts found in the area.

Should you find yourself here, there is a 24-hour telephone centrale in the train station building, a post office just past it, and yet another telephone office after that. The Bank of Alexandria has a branch just off the central Midan al-Gomhuriyya.

Places to Stay & Eat

Semiramis Hotel *(☎ 322 092, fax 326 017, Sharia Safiyya Zaghloul)* Singles/doubles E£32/45. This two-star hotel near the train station is the best place to stay in town. Rooms have bath and TV and breakfast is included in the price.

Hotel Rest House *(☎ 322 116, Sharia Port Said)* Singles/doubles E£14/16.50. This is not a great place but there's not much choice in Beni Suef. The slightly musty rooms with baths are reasonable and cheap.

There's not an awful lot to choose from food-wise. A filling kebab or chicken meal will cost you about E£15 at ***Semiramis Hotel***, or you'll find kushari places and fuul and ta'amiyya stands around the station.

Getting There & Away

The bus station is along the main road, south of town. Buses run from about 6am to 6pm

Troubles in the Nile Valley

In 1992, Islamist-instigated violence broke out in Cairo and Upper Egypt. Although massive police action crushed the movement's radical wings in Cairo, it proved far more difficult to do the same in the area between Minya and Qena. Easy escape routes to the desert and the hiding places afforded by crops such as sugar cane made it difficult for the police to fully control the area. Also, while the majority of the population never supported the violence, mass arrests and police brutality fuelled resentment against the government and the conflict took on aspects of a traditional feud, with police and militants as the opposing 'families'. Tourists who ventured here in the early and mid-1990s were often caught up in this violence, victims of Gama'a al-Islamiyya militants who wanted to target the government by crippling the tourism industry. By the late 1990s, few foreigners ventured this far although the state's iron-fist policies had all but destroyed the militant movement in the area. Ironically, it was in the supposedly safe area of Luxor that militants were able to pull off their most brutal attack, when they massacred 58 tourists at the Temple of Hatshepsut in November 1997.

In the aftermath of the attack, the police visibly tightened their protection on tourists throughout the country. Although the violence in the area between Minya and Qena had ceased, the area continued to be more or less off limits to foreigners. The few that went were forced to move about with heavily armed police escorts, hardly an inducement to visit.

In February 2001, however, the American Embassy in Cairo lifted its travel advisory to the area, stating that it was safe for tourists. In theory this should have resulted in an easing of travel restrictions for foreigners. In practice, it hasn't. So although the threat of violence has long abated, the police continue to control the movements of tourists, escorting them between towns and monuments and making individual travel frustrating.

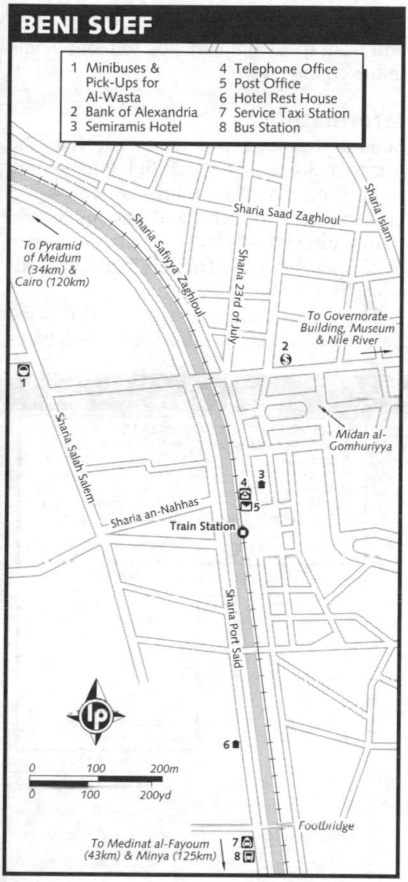

to Ahmed Helmy bus station behind Ramses Station in Cairo. There are also frequent buses to Minya and Al-Fayoum. Beni Suef is also a departure point for the trek across the desert to the Monastery of St Anthony, which is about 150km east, near the Gulf of Suez (see the Monastery of St Anthony in the Red Sea Coast chapter for details). There is a bus to Zafarana, the closest Red Sea town to the monastery, once a day.

There are frequent train connections north to Cairo and Giza, and to the south to Minya. There are also (slow) trains to Al-Fayoum.

GEBEL AT-TEIR & FRAZER TOMBS

The main feature of the small Christian hamlet of Gebel at-Teir, 93km south of Beni Suef, is **Deir al-Adhra** (the Monastery of the Virgin). Established as a church/monastery in the 4th century AD by the Roman empress Helena, it was built on one of the sites where the Holy Family supposedly rested while fleeing Palestine (see the boxed text 'The Holy Family in Egypt' later in this chapter). Gebel at-Teir and its church are perched on a hill 130m above the east bank of the Nile.

It is much more quickly reached from Minya, about 20km to the south, than from Beni Suef. If the police allow it, get a service taxi or microbus for between E£2 and E£5 from Minya to Samalut and from there take a pick-up to the Nile boat landing (50pt), where you can take the car ferry for E£1 or the felucca for the same. On the other side is a pick-up going to Deir al-Adhra, but you may find yourself paying about E£1 to get it moving, as not many passengers go that way. When you arrive, ask for the *kineesa*, or church, and someone will appear with the keys and give you a short tour. There are some interesting 400-year-old icons inside.

About 5km south of Gebel at-Teir are the Frazer Tombs, which date back to the 5th and 6th dynasties. These Old Kingdom tombs are hewn into the desert cliff on the east bank of the Nile and overlook the plain and fields. The four tombs are very simple, containing eroded statues and carved hieroglyphs but no colourful scenes. If you're attracted to places where other tourists rarely go, these are for you.

MINYA

☎ 086

It is called the 'Bride of Upper Egypt' (Arous as-Sa'id), as Minya more or less marks the divide between Upper and Lower Egypt. A semi-industrial provincial capital 245km south of Cairo, it is a centre for sugar processing and the manufacture of soap and perfume. In the 1990s it also acquired the unfortunate reputation of being a centre for Islamist opposition to the government. Because so many of the 'troubles' were based in the countryside around here, Minya became something of an armed fortress, with nervous policemen patrolling in tanks and personnel carriers. This police presence remains today, even though the threat of violence has abated. Even so, it remains a pleasant town with a long Corniche along the Nile and some great, if shabby, early-20th-century buildings testifying to its former prosperity as a centre of the cotton industry. Keep in mind that while you can usually (but not always) wander around the town relatively freely, the police will want to accompany you to monuments in the countryside.

Information

Should you need to extend your visa, the passport office is on the 2nd floor of the post office. There's a tourist office (☎ 343 500) on the Corniche and another in the train station (☎ 342 044) – the latter is open until 8pm. They are friendly but do not always have accurate information.

The Banque Masr branch on Midan as-Sa'a does Visa card cash advances – it takes

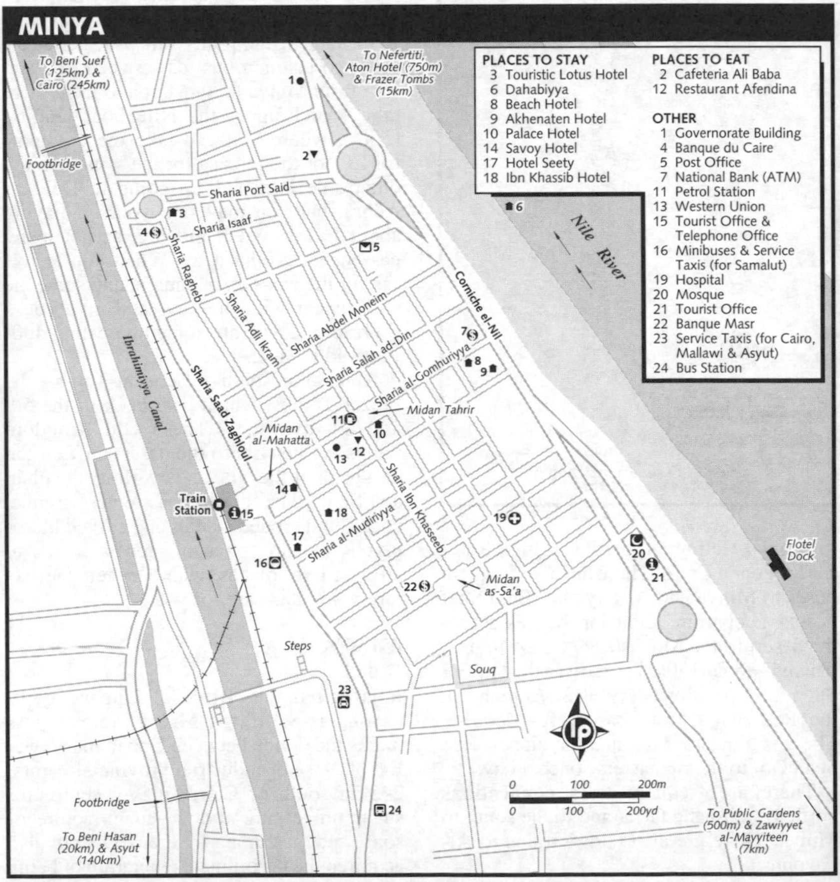

some time, though. The National Bank on the corner of Al-Gomhuriyya and the Corniche has an ATM and will exchange cash and travellers cheques. Western Union (☎ 364 905) has an office just past Midan Tahrir on Sharia al-Gomhuriyya.

The post office is open from 8am to 2pm Saturday to Thursday. The telephone office is in the train station and sells phone cards.

Things to See

Although Minya is a pleasant place the town itself doesn't have that much to see. Other than the interesting architecture in the town centre, there's the tree-lined Corniche along the Nile, which is a relaxing place for a picnic or a ride in a *hantour* (horse-drawn carriage). There is also a lively souq at the southern end of the town centre.

On the east bank is a large Muslim and Christian cemetery called **Zawiyyet al-Mayyiteen** (Place of the Dead) located about 7km south-east of the town. The cemetery consists of several hundred mud-brick mausoleums stretching for 4km from the road to the hills and is said to be one of the largest cemeteries in the world.

Places to Stay

Palace Hotel *(☎ 324 021, Midan Tahrir)* Singles/doubles E£15/20, with bath E£25/35. Fabulous high ceilings, hand-painted Pharaonic murals and time-warp atmosphere make this a great, if somewhat shabby, budget hotel. The huge Nefertiti mural and ancient posters alone make it worth a visit.

Hotel Seety *(☎ 363 930, 71 Saad Zaghloul)* Singles/doubles/triples E£12/15/18. Half a block south of the train station, despite its run-down appearance this hotel has relatively clean and comfortable rooms with bath.

Savoy Hotel *(☎ 363 270, Midan al-Mahatta)* Singles/doubles/triples E£15/25/30, with bath E£20/30/36. Directly opposite the train station, the Savoy exudes decrepit grandeur with a big hall and high, painted ceilings. The management claimed not to take tourists at the time of research, but this may change.

Ibn Khassib Hotel *(☎ 364 535, 5 Sharia Ragheb)* Singles/doubles E£30/38, with air-con & bath E£34/44. On a side street near the train station, is this other aged building. It has 18 gloomy rooms, all with high ceilings and Victorian-style furniture, but check the rooms first, some have tiny bathrooms/showers. There's a restaurant and bar with beer and a billiard area; breakfast is included in the price.

Beach Hotel *(☎ 322 307, Sharia al-Gomhuriyya)* Singles/doubles E£23/30, with bath E£30/40. Just in from the Corniche, Beach Hotel is a simple and reasonably clean place.

Akhenaten Hotel *(☎ 365 917/8, fax 365 918, Corniche el-Nil)* Singles/doubles E£55/80. This newly renovated, 48-room hotel is great value for money and Minya's most comfortable option if your budget won't stretch to the Nefertiti & Aton hotel. All rooms have air-con, satellite TV and fridges, and most have good Nile views.

Dahabiyya *(☎ 325 596, Corniche el-Nil)* Singles/doubles E£25/50. Dahabiyya is an old houseboat owned by the Coptic Evangelical Organisation with four newly renovated small rooms, and shared bathrooms with great old fixtures; prices include breakfast. There is also an open deck where you can watch the Nile flow by.

Touristic Lotus Hotel *(☎ 364 541, fax 364 576, 1 Sharia Port Said)* Singles/doubles/triples E£50/69.30/100.90. This hotel is about a 10-minute walk north of the train station. It used to be popular with German groups. All rooms have air-con and TV; prices include breakfast.

Nefertiti & Aton *(Etap; ☎ 331 515, fax 326 467, Corniche el-Nil)* Singles/doubles US$51/61. Still known locally as the Etap (its former incarnation), this is Minya's top hotel, located about 1km north of the town centre on the Corniche. Recently spruced up in hopes that tourism will return to Minya, it has three restaurants (although only one ever seems to be open), two bars, a pool and a tennis court. Of the 96 rooms, 72 have great Nile views – go for one of these and not one of the garden 'cabin' type rooms, which get too hot in summer.

Places to Eat

Minya doesn't have a huge selection of culinary delights. There are a lot of the usual cheap fuul and ta'amiyya stands and shwarma places scattered around Midan al-Mahatta, Midan Tahrir and along the market street stretching south off the latter. There is also a new, incongruous-looking KFC stuck by itself on the northern end of the Corniche.

Cafeteria Ali Baba *(Corniche el-Nil)* Dishes E£3-25. Satisfying meals of the usual favourites (kebabs or other meat dishes, salad, tahini and a soft drink) are served here for about E£15. This is also a good place for a morning coffee and a pastry.

Restaurant Afendina *(Midan Tahrir)* Dishes E£1-10. This thriving shwarma/roast chicken place offers the usual dips, salads, ta'amiyya and kushari.

Other than these two, most of the restaurants are at the hotels.

Green House Coffee Bar *(Nefertiti & Aton Hotel, Corniche el-Nil)* Meals E£20-40. It serves good pasta and Continental dishes, in addition to the usual Egyptian staples.

The restaurants on top of ***Touristic Lotus Hotel*** and ***Akhenaten Hotel*** both serve simple, filling meals for about E£15 to E£20. They also have good views. The restaurant at ***Ibn Khassib Hotel*** serves a large chicken followed by an orange for about E£12 and Stella beer for E£6.

Getting There & Away

Bus The police usually insist that foreigners travel only by train, but there is a bus station 500m south of the train station from where there's a service every hour to Cairo (E£8 to E£12, four hours) from 5am to 4pm. You can book ahead or try your luck on the day. Buses also depart for Asyut (E£5.50, two to three hours) every 30 minutes, for Beni Suef (E£7) every 20 to 40 minutes, and there's a daily bus to Hurghada (E£30). In summer there is a morning bus right through to Alexandria (E£35).

Train Trains to Cairo (three to four hours) have only 1st- and 2nd-class carriages that leave at 5.55am, 6.30am, 8.50am, 3.05pm (which goes on to Alexandria), and 6.50pm. First/2nd-class fares range from E£27/16 to E£31/20 (students E£14/13 to E£23/17). Trains heading south depart fairly frequently, with the fastest trains leaving Minya between about 11pm and 1am. Seven 1st-/2nd-class trains go all the way to Luxor and Aswan stopping at Asyut (E£13/8), Sohag (E£21/13) and Qena (E£31/19). They leave at 10.40am, 3.30pm, 7.25pm, 10pm, 11.30pm, 12.25am and 1.15am. First-/2nd-class fares to Luxor range from E£40/23 to E£44/28 (students E£26/19 to E£30/23), and to Aswan from E£51/30 to E£56/34 (students E£35/23 to E£39/27). Although foreigners are supposed

Travelling by 'ser-vees' or service taxi is one of the fastest ways to get from city to city in Egypt, though the ride can be uncomfortable and accidents are common.

to take only the two 'special' trains that come from Cairo, in practice no-one stops you from taking the one you want.

Service Taxi From Cairo, service taxis take three to four hours to Minya and cost E£10. From Minya, they still have departures as late as 8pm. There are also service taxis to Asyut and Mallawi, but you're unlikely to be allowed to take them as drivers will only take you on a taxi (as opposed to service taxi) basis, insisting, probably with reason, that otherwise they'll get in trouble with the police. Should the situation change, the depot is about a five-minute walk south from the train station (just past the bridge).

BENI HASAN

Beni Hasan *(admission E£12; open 7am-5pm daily)* is a necropolis on the east bank of the Nile about 20km south of Minya. It has a superb location, with the tombs cut into the cliffs that overlook the valley and the river. Of the 39 tombs here, most date from the 11th and 12th dynasties (2125–1795 BC) and belong to the local governors or 'nomarchs'. Many remain unfinished and only 12 are decorated. Only a few are accessible to visitors but they give a good idea of the general themes of decoration – trading, tax collecting, warfare, wrestling matches and even barbers at work, a mixture of daily life, funerary motifs and the political upheavals of the First Intermediate Period.

A guard will accompany you up the steps leading to the tombs and unlock the gates for you. Baksheesh (alms or tip) of E£2 or E£3 is expected. The view over the desert and the transition to cultivated land, with the Nile snaking through the middle, is stunning, but expect a heavy police presence.

Tomb of Kheti (No 17) Kheti, like his colleagues, was governor of the Oryx nome (district) during the 11th dynasty (c. 2000 BC), and his tomb scenes include hunting by the river and in the desert, linen production, playing board games, metal work, wrestling, acrobatics and dancing, farming, warfare, funerary offerings, and barbers at work (on the wall left of the entrance).

Tomb of Baqet (No 15) Baqet was the father of Kheti. His tomb has similar depictions, though less faded than Kheti's. They include Baqet and his wife on the left wall watching weavers and acrobats – mostly women in diaphanous dresses striking flexible poses, but also jugglers. Further along, scenes of animals, presumably possessions of Baqet, are being counted. A hunting scene in the desert includes mythical creatures among the gazelle. The back wall has clear depictions of wrestlers in wrestling moves that are still used today. The right wall shows scenes from daily life, with potters, metal workers and a flax harvest, among others.

Tomb of Khnumhotep (No 3) With its impressive facade and interior decoration, this tomb is the most impressive at Beni Hasan. Governor in the early 12th dynasty under the pharaoh Amenemhat III (c. 1820 BC), Khnumhotep's detailed 'autobiography' is inscribed on the base of walls that contain the most detailed painted scenes. The tomb is famous for its rich, finely rendered scenes of plants, animals and birds. On the left wall farmers are shown ploughing and harvesting their crops, while the back wall to the left of the shrine is a beautiful, stylised portrayal of Khnumhotep and his wife catching fish and birds in a papyrus swamp. On the other side of the shrine is another fishing scene, while the right hand wall has scenes of priests with Khnumhotep's wife and the lavish offerings made to the gods.

Tomb of Amenemhat (No 2) Khnumhotep's predecessor and governor, Amenemhat's tomb also has the same architectural layout with the standard scenes of farming, hunting, manufacturing and offerings to the deceased, who can also be seen with his dogs. Apart from the fine paintings, the tomb has a long, faded text in which he addresses the visitors to his chapel:

> You who love life and hate death, say: Thousands of bread and beer, thousands of cattle and wild fowl for the ka of the hereditary prince…the Great Chief of the Oryx Nome…

Many of the wall paintings show the cattle, beer and fowl as offerings, in addition to a voyage to Abydos and a painted false door. The destroyed statues in the shrine were of Amenemhat sitting between his wife and his mother.

If the police don't deter (or prevent) you, follow the cliffside track to the south-east for about 1.5km, then turn into a wadi where, about 500m along, is the rock-cut temple **Speos Artemidos** (Grotto of Artemis), known locally as Istabl Antar (the Stable of Antar, an Arab warrior-poet and folk hero). Dating back to the 18th dynasty, it was built by Hatshepsut and Tuthmosis III and dedicated to the lion goddess Pakht. There is a small hall with roughly hewn Hathor-headed columns and an unfinished sanctuary. On the walls are scenes of Hatshepsut making offerings and inscriptions describing how she restored order after the Hyksos were overthrown.

Getting There & Away

Almost the only way to get to Beni Hasan these days is in a private taxi with an accompanying phalanx of policemen. The taxi will charge about E£30 to E£50, depending on your bargaining skills and how long you stay. Should you avoid the excessive security, get a microbus to Abu Qirqus (E£1). There you take a pick-up (25pt) to the river. At the river you'll find an office, where return boat tickets cost E£6 if there are less than eight people, E£8 if you're by yourself. The price drops to E£2 per person if there are eight or more.

MALLAWI

Mallawi is 48km south of Minya and famous in Egypt as the home town of Sadat's assassin, Khalid al-Islambouli. A centre of foment and armed rebellion throughout the 1990s, the town remains a tense place, with a heavy police presence, resentful populace and blighted economy. There's little for the casual visitor to see here, even if the overzealous police allow a stop. Should this change, there's a small **museum** *(admission E£6; open 9am-4pm Sat-Tues & Thur, 9am-noon Fri)* that houses a collection of artefacts from Tuna al-Gebel and Hermopolis.

Food is limited to basic fuul and ta'amiyya places and trucker restaurants along the main road beside the Ibrahimiyya canal. There are no hotels.

Getting There & Away

At present you can only travel here with a police escort in a private taxi or your own vehicle. Should this change, all buses to or from Minya and Asyut stop here. A service taxi from Minya costs E£2; from Asyut it's about E£3 for the one-hour trip. Only the very slow 2nd- and 3rd-class trains stop at the station, which is on the east bank of the Ibrahimiyya Canal.

HERMOPOLIS

Hermopolis, 8km north of Mallawi near the town of Al-Ashmunein, is the site of the ancient city of Khmun, cult centre of Thoth, god of wisdom and writing whom the Greeks identified with their god Hermes and so referred to his city by its now more familiar name 'Hermopolis'.

Little remains of this ancient city. The most striking ruins are two colossal quartzite figures of Thoth set up by Amenhotep III, with the god represented as a baboon rather than his more familiar ibis-headed figure. The other main ruins are a Middle Kingdom temple gateway, a pylon of Ramses II built from stone plundered from nearby Tell al-Amarna and the extensive ruins of a Coptic basilica adapted from an earlier Ptolemaic temple on the site. There is also a small museum containing artefacts found at the site. However, it was closed at the time of writing.

Getting There & Away

If the police escort continues to be mandatory, you will have to take a private taxi to Hermopolis from Minya. Expect to pay about E£20 to E£30, depending on how long you take. If the situation changes, you can take a local microbus or service taxi from Mallawi to the village of Al-Ashmunein; the turn-off to the site is 1km from the main road. From the junction you can either walk the short distance to Hermopolis or coax your driver to go a bit further.

TUNA AL-GEBEL

Tuna al-Gebel *(admission E£12; open 7am-5pm daily)* was the necropolis of Hermopolis. It bordered Akhetaten, the short-lived capital of the pharaoh Akhenaten (see Tell al-Amarna following) and the area's oldest monument is one of 14 stelae that marked the boundary of the royal city – in this case the western perimeter of the city's farmlands and associated villages. Like the rest, the large stone stele is inscribed with Akhenaten's vow never to expand his city beyond these boundaries, nor to be buried anywhere else. To the left stand two damaged statues of the pharaoh and his wife Nefertiti holding offering tables on the sides of which are inscribed the figures of three of their daughters.

To the south of the stele, which is about 5km past the village of Tuna al-Gebel, are the **catacombs** and tombs of the residents and sacred animals of Hermopolis. The most interesting things to see are the dark catacomb galleries that once held millions (literally) of mummified ibis, the 'living image of Thoth', together with a smaller number of mummified baboons. Most of the animals have been destroyed by robbers, and in fact only one of the baboons was found fully intact by archaeologists. Most of the mummification was done in the Ptolemaic and Roman periods. The subterranean cemetery extends for at least 3km, but Egyptologists suspect it may stretch all the way to Hermopolis. You definitely need a torch if you're going to explore the galleries.

There's also the interesting **Tomb of Petosiris**, dedicated to a high priest of Thoth who was alive just before the arrival of Alexander the Great (c. 340 BC). It was built in the form of a small temple with wonderful coloured reliefs of traditional Egyptian scenes such as farming and the deceased given offerings, but all done in Greek style and the figures wearing Greek dress. Ancient graffiti, thought to be of pilgrims, covers many of the walls.

In a small two-storey building behind the Tomb of Petosiris is the **Tomb-Chapel of Isadora**. Isadora was a wealthy woman who drowned in the Nile during the rule of Antoninus Pius (AD 138–161), and whose tomb became the centre of a cult. Her **mummy** is extremely well preserved, with her teeth, hair and fingernails clearly visible. You'll need to give the guard a bit of baksheesh to see her.

Tuna al-Gebel is 7km west of Hermopolis. The very few tourists who come here these days are usually escorted by police from Minya. Make sure you check with the tourist office that it is open before you set out.

Getting There & Away

There's a fair amount of traffic between the Hermopolis junction and the village, so you could flag down a pick-up truck but as you'll probably be there with the police, they will take you there and back.

TELL AL-AMARNA

The scant remains of this once-glorious city, 12km south-east of Mallawi, are a little disappointing when compared with its fascinating, albeit brief, history.

In the 14th century BC, the pharaoh Akhenaten and his queen Nefertiti abandoned the gods, temples and priests of Karnak at Thebes to establish a new city and a new religion. At Akhetaten, as it was known, the pharaoh and his queen with their followers, worshipped Aten, god of the sun disc.

The city, in the area now known as Tell al-Amarna, was built on the east bank of the Nile on a beautiful, yet solitary, crescent-shaped plain, extending about 12km from north to south. Except for the side bounded by the river, the palaces, temples and residences of the city were surrounded by high cliffs, broken here and there by wadis. The royal couple named their city Akhetaten (Horizon of the Aten), and it served as the capital of Egypt for about 14 years.

It was abandoned for all time after Akhenaten's death, when his ephemeral successor (believed by some Egyptologists to be Nefertiti ruling as pharaoh) relocated to Thebes and restored the worship of traditional gods. As the priests of Karnak managed to regain their religious control, they desecrated the temples of Aten and did their

HERMOPOLIS, TUNA AL-GEBEL & TELL AL-AMARNA

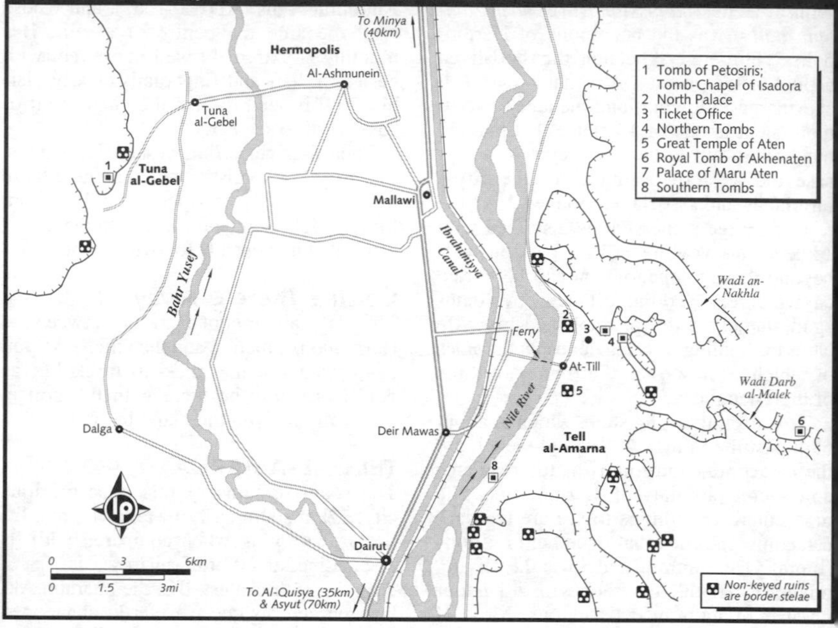

best to obliterate all record of the heretic pharaoh. Akhenaten's son (by a minor wife) and successor Tutankaten, or Tutankhamun as he became known, re-established the cult of Amun at Thebes, bringing to an end what is known as the 'Amarna Period'. Akhetaten fell into ruin, and the stones of its palaces and temples were used for buildings in Hermopolis and other cities.

Tell al-Amarna Necropolis

The Tell al-Amarna **necropolis** *(admission E£12; open 7am-4pm Oct-May, 7am-5pm June-Sept)* comprises two groups of cliff tombs, one at each end of the city, which feature colourful wall paintings of life during the Aten revolution.

The pricing system here is extremely confusing. To start with, you have three options to cross the Nile – the local passenger launch (50pt), the car ferry (50pt) or the blue tourist boat (E£4 return for one or two people; E£1 each for three or more). Tickets for the latter are bought from the ticket office on the east bank – you cross the river before paying for your ticket.

Once you've crossed the river, you pay the fee to enter the site at the tourist office. What you pay from here on depends on how many of you there are, which sites you wish to visit, and what mode of transport you used to cross the river. All payments are made to the staff at the tourist office except the admission fee to the north tombs that must be paid near the site.

For less than eight people, you'll be looking at E£8 for a two-hour bus tour around the northern tombs and the palace; for three or more people you each pay E£3.75. On arrival at the northern tombs, everyone must pay a E£12 (E£6 for students) entry fee.

Those wishing to take a bus tour to the southern tombs and the Great Temple of Aten must pay E£23 (shared among one to eight people) or E£3.75 each for groups of more than eight. It takes about 30 minutes to drive to the south tombs and you can supposedly stay as long as you want. To the Royal Tomb of Akhenaten it costs E£35 for the bus (one to eight people) or E£5 each when there are more than eight people.

The northern tombs are about 3km from the ferry crossing at At-Till, the southern ones about 8km away. Other remains of temples and private or administrative buildings are scattered about a wide area.

Tombs

In all, there are 25 tombs cut into the base of the cliffs, numbered from one to six in the north, and seven to 25 in the south. Those worth visiting are described here.

Tomb of Huya (No 1) Steward of Akhenaten's mother Queen Tiy, Huya's tomb contains two wonderful relief scenes either side of the entrance that show Tiy wining and dining with her son and his family. Over the door to the inner room is a scene with Tiy and her husband Amenhotep III and their son and daughter-in-law. Akhenaten also takes his mother to see a small temple he has built for her, and then he is shown together with Nefertiti in a carrying chair.

Tomb of Meryre II (No 2) Superintendant of Nefertiti's household, Meryre's tomb includes a nice scene of Nefertiti pouring wine for Akhenaten. Together with the Tomb of Huya, this is the most distant of the northern tombs and guides are often keen to skip them unless you really insist on visiting.

Tomb of Ahmose (No 3) Ahmose's title was 'Fan-bearer on the King's Right Hand'. Much of his tomb is unfinished with the initial ink outlines still to be seen. The royal couple drive their chariot to the Aten temple, followed by their armed guards – whose modern counterparts never seem very far away at Tell al-Amarna.

Tomb of Meryre I (No 4) High priest of the Aten, Meryre is shown being carried by his friends to receive rewards from the royal couple, who are also shown going to the temple driving their own chariots accompanied by Meryre in his capacity as high priest. A fascinating detail close to the Aten disc to the right of the doorway into the columned hall is the colourful depiction of a rainbow.

Tomb of Panehesy (No 6) Chief servant of the Aten in Akhetaten, Panehesy's tomb retains the decorated facade most of the others have lost. Inside the scenes repeatedly show the royal family, again Nefertiti driving her own chariot, and on the right side of the entrance passage there is even Nefertiti's sister Mutnodjmet, later married to Pharaoh Horemheb, together with her two dwarf servants. There are also two unfinished burial chambers intended for Panehesy and his family.

Tomb of Mahu (No 9) This southern tomb is one of the best preserved, and the wall paintings provide interesting details of Mahu's duties as Akhenaten's chief of police, including taking prisoners to the vizier, checking supplies and visiting the temple.

Tomb of Ay (No 25) This is the finest tomb at Tell al-Amarna. Although his titles were simply 'God's Father' and 'Fan-bearer on the King's Right Hand', Ay's wife Tiyi was Nefertiti's wet nurse and the couple may have been related to Queen Tiy's family. Scenes include Ay and Tiyi worshipping the sun and Ay receiving rewards from the royal family, including a pair of red leather riding gloves. Ay was never buried here, after he became pharaoh following Tutankhamun he was buried in the West Valley beside the Valley of the Kings back at Thebes.

Royal Tomb of Akhenaten Akhenaten's own tomb *(admission E£16)* is in a ravine about 13km up the Royal Valley (Wadi Darb al-Malek), the valley that divides the north and south sections of the cliffs and where the sun was seen to rise each dawn. The journey to the tomb is very bumpy, although the bleak valley with its tumbleweed and occasional sandstorm is incredibly atmospheric, as is the little-visited tomb itself. Recently restored and reopened to the public, very little remains of the tantalising wall reliefs that show Akhenaten and his family worshipping the Aten. A raised rectangular outline in the burial chamber once held the pharaoh's sarcophagus that is actually hidden away in the gardens of the Egyptian Museum in Cairo, held together with a rope and usually filled with litter. Yet it seems that Akhenaten himself was not buried here, and although there have been endless theories about his final resting place, the whereabouts of his remains are a mystery.

Getting There & Away

If police are escorting you, you'll have to take a taxi from either Asyut or Minya. Expect to pay about E£30 to E£50 for a return trip. If you've somehow evaded the police, you can get to Tell al-Amarna from Mallawi, by taking a service taxi or a covered pick-up from the south depot to the ferry crossing at At-Till. From Asyut, it's easiest to take a service taxi to Mallawi (about E£2.50) and then backtrack using one of the pick-ups from there.

When leaving, you may find you have to pay more for a pick-up from the west bank ferry landing back to either Mallawi or Deir Mawas as not many vehicles head in those directions after about 3pm.

DAIRUT

Dairut is about 10km south of Deir Mawas, but there is not a lot to interest most travellers here. It has a large Christian population and in the 1990s it was the scene of numerous bloody clashes. The police are unlikely to let you stay.

AL-QUSIYA

About 8km south-west of the small rural town of Al-Qusiya, 35km south of Mallawi, is the Coptic complex of Deir al-Muharraq (the Burnt Monastery). About 7km further north-west, on an escarpment at the edge of the desert, lie the Tombs of Mir. There are no hotels in Al-Qusiya, but there's a large guesthouse just outside the pseudo-medieval crenellated walls of Deir al-Muharraq and the monks sometimes allow groups of travellers to stay there (but not usually individuals). In any event, both sites can be visited in an easy day trip from Minya or Asyut providing you have your own wheels.

Deir al-Muharraq

The 100 or so monks who reside in Deir al-Muharraq claim that Mary and Jesus inhabited a cave on this site for six months and 10 days after fleeing from Herod into Egypt – their longest stay at any of the numerous places they are said to have rested during that flight. For 10 days every year (usually 18 to 28 June), thousands of pilgrims attend feasts to celebrate the consecration of the Church of al-Adhra (Church of the Virgin) that was built over the cave. Coptic Christians believe Al-Adhra to be one of the first churches in the world. (Remember to remove your shoes before entering.)

The religious significance of this place is, they say, given in the Old Testament;

> In that day there will be an altar to the Lord in the midst of the land of Egypt, and a pillar to the Lord at its border. It will be a sign and a witness to the Lord of Host in the land of Egypt; when they cry to the Lord because of oppressors he will send them a saviour, and will defend and deliver them. And the Lord will make himself known to the Egyptians; and the Egyptians will know the Lord in that day and worship with sacrifice and burnt offering, and they will make vows to the Lord and perform them.
>
> **Isaiah 19:19–21**

Next to Al-Adhra is a square tower, a 5th-century structure built for the monks to use as added protection in case of attack. It has four floors, an old sundial on an outer wall, and a church inside.

The Church of St George (or Mar Girgis), built in 1880, is behind Al-Adhra and is decorated with paintings of the 12 apostles and other religious scenes. Again, be sure to take off your shoes.

Guided tours *(donations appreciated)* usually finish with a brief visit to the new church built in 1940 and the nearby gift shop, and sometimes with a cool drink in the monastery's reception room.

Tombs of Mir

The necropolis of the governors of Cusae, or the Tombs of Mir *(admission E£16)* as they're also known, were dug into the barren escarpment during the Old and Middle Kingdoms. Nine of the tombs here are decorated and open to the public; six others were never finished and remain unexcavated.

Tomb No 1 and the adjoining tomb No 2 are inscribed with 720 Pharaonic deities but, during early Christian times, the Copts used the tombs as cells and many faces and names of the gods were destroyed. In tomb No 4 you can still see the original grid drawn on the wall to assist the artist in designing the layout of the tomb art. Tomb No 3 features a cow giving birth.

Getting There & Away

The Asyut to Minya bus will drop you at Al-Qusiya (E£1.25, 50 minutes from Asyut), otherwise, you could take a service taxi. From there, you may be able to get a local microbus to the monastery, or the police, worried about your welfare, may take you there themselves.

Few vehicles from Al-Qusiya go out to the Tombs of Mir, so you'll have to hire a taxi to take you there. Ideally, you could combine this with a visit to the monastery.

ASYUT

☎ 088

Asyut, 375km south of Cairo, was settled during Pharaonic times on a broad fertile plain bordering the west bank of the Nile. In ancient times, the town was named Zowty, and was capital of the 13th nome of Upper Egypt. An important trading post, it was the end of the line for the 40 Days Rd, one of Africa's great desert caravan routes that led from Sudan via Kharga Oasis. For centuries one of the main commodities traded here was slaves and as recently as 150 years ago the town boasted the largest slave market in Egypt.

However, this long history has been erased by the modern Assiutis, leaving an ugly agglomeration of high-rises that resemble an Eastern European new town rather than an ancient Egyptian entrepot and trading post. As a result, although Asyut is a transit point for people coming from the oases, few people bother to linger more than a few hours.

The one positive aspect of the place is its bustling air of prosperity, which may not make it interesting for visitors but no doubt means things are good for its inhabitants. This makes a change from 20 years ago, when Asyut had the unenviable reputation of being one of the earliest centres of Islamist foment in Egypt. There is a very large Coptic community in the area and

The Holy Family in Egypt

Biblical tradition holds that Joseph, Mary and the newly born infant Jesus fled to Egypt escaping persecution from King Herod of Judea who had embarked upon a 'massacre of the first born'. Here they remained for four years. Although the Bible has nothing to say on what they did during that time, Egyptian tradition makes a great deal of their stay. Theophilus, patriarch of the Coptic Church around AD 500, apparently had a dream in which the places where the Holy Family stayed in Egypt were revealed to him. So it is that a great many sites in the Delta and along the Nile Valley are linked to the Holy Family and the miracles they performed and inspired.

Most famous of the sites is the St Sergius church in Coptic Cairo, built over a cave in which the family purportedly took shelter. Also in Cairo, in the north-eastern suburb of Matariyya, is the Virgin's Tree, a gnarled sycamore supposedly descended from a tree that shaded Mary during a rest-stop. From Cairo the family took a boat bound for Middle Egypt where there are numerous sites linked to their sojourn. Asyut represents the furthest point south with any holy connections.

Whatever the truth, what is undeniable is that Middle Egypt has a long-standing Christian tradition, evidenced by the number of historic churches and monasteries in the region. Since the Christian millennium the Egyptian tourist authorities have been working hard to package and market this 'holy pilgrimage route' as a way of getting visitors back into Middle Egypt.

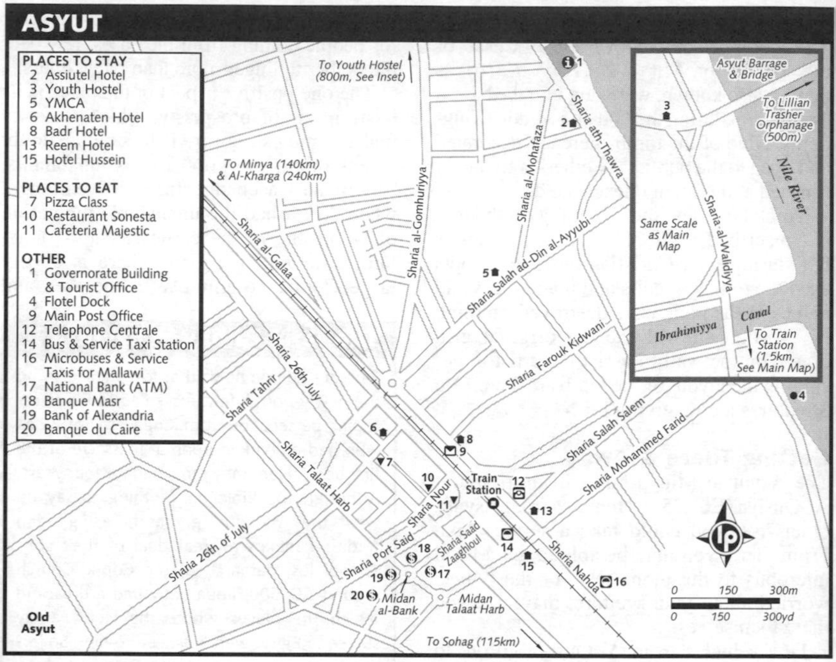

they were often the target of violence when Islamist militants began their terrorist campaign in the late 1980s. Although the town has been quiet for several years, the police continue to maintain a visible presence and hotels are obliged to inform the security forces of your presence, meaning that you are likely to find yourself with a police escort whether you want it or not.

Information

There is a tourist office (☎ 310 010) on Sharia ath-Thawra on the 1st floor of the governorate building. The staff are very friendly and willing to help but will insist on having police escort you everywhere. The office is open from 8.30am to 2pm Saturday to Thursday.

You can change money at the cluster of banks on Midan el-Bank. Banque Masr, which does Visa and MasterCard cash advances, has one branch with an ATM, and the Bank of Alexandria, good for changing Eurocheques, has one. Just up the road is the Banque du Caire.

The main post office is opposite the Badr Hotel behind the train station. The telephone centrale is to the right of the entrance of the train station.

Things to See

Banana Island (Gezirat al-Moz), at the end of Sharia Salah Salem, is a shady, pleasant place to picnic. You'll have to bargain with a felucca captain for the ride across.

At the northern edge of town is the 19th-century **Asyut barrage** that was built across the Nile, under British supervision, to regulate the flow of water into the Ibrahimiyya Canal and assist in the irrigation of the valley as far north as Beni Suef; it also serves as a bridge across the Nile. Taking photographs anywhere around here would be unwise.

On the east bank of the Nile, about 200m to the right after you've crossed the barrage, is the **Lillian Trasher Orphanage**. Born in Jacksonville, Florida, in the USA, Lillian Trasher came to Egypt in 1910 at the age of 23 and the following year she founded an orphanage in Asyut. It has since grown to be the biggest and most well known of its type in Egypt. Trasher never left, but died in her adopted country in 1961. The orphanage is something of a symbol of Christian charity in a city with a heavy concentration of Copts and welcomes interested visitors. Donations are appreciated. Microbuses will take you close to it from the centre of town for 50pt; a taxi will cost E£2. Ask for 'Malga Trasher'.

Places to Stay & Eat

Youth Hostel *(☎ 324 846, Lux Houses, 503 Sharia al-Walidiyya)* Beds in 8-bed dorm E£5.10. The entrance is off a side street.

YMCA *(☎ 323 218, Sharia Salah ad-Din al-Ayyubi)* Singles/doubles E£25/35. This place is a great deal on a quiet street with new rooms that feature air-con, TV, mini-fridge and private bath.

Hotel Hussein *(☎ 338 437, fax 352 599, Sharia Mohammed Farid)* Singles/doubles E£50/69. Overlooking the bus station, this small, new hotel is noisy but comfortable and convenient if you're changing buses or trains; prices include breakfast.

Akhenaten Hotel *(☎ 337 723, fax 331 600, Sharia Muhammed Tawfiq Khashba)* Singles/doubles E£40/50. Rooms are somewhat gloomy but clean and comfortable with bath, air-con, TV and friendly staff; prices include breakfast.

Reem Hotel *(☎ 311 421, fax 311 424, Sharia Nahda)* Singles/doubles E£39/60. This somewhat shabby three-star hotel is next to the railway tracks. The rooms overlooking the railway are very noisy.

Assiutel Hotel *(☎ 312 121, fax 312 122, Sharia ath-Thawra)* Singles/doubles E£114/129. Overlooking the Nile, this is the best hotel in town and has comfortable rooms with satellite TV, fridges and baths, as well as one of Asyut's few bars; breakfast is included in the price.

Badr Hotel *(☎ 329 811, fax 322 820, Sharia Nahda)* Singles/doubles E£100/170. This centrally located three-star hotel is overpriced and noisy because of its proximity to the station, it does boast a restaurant and a bar.

All the bigger hotels have their own restaurants. At the cheaper end of the scale, the air-con restaurant at ***Akhenaten Hotel*** does an escalope as well as good pizza and soup. Beer is also served. ***Cafeteria Majestic***, opposite the train station, has some decent food and there are a few of the usual fuul and ta'amiyya stands scattered around. The restaurant at ***Badr Hotel*** also offers reasonable food with the opportunity to have a beer or glass of wine to wash it down.

Pizza Class *(Sharia 26th July)* Meals E£2-6. This bright and cheerful fiteer restaurant is on a busy street corner.

Restaurant Sonesta *(☎ 342 778, Sharia Nour)* Dishes E£9-15. This is a reasonably good place with chicken and fillets in addition to a small selection of mezze.

Getting There & Away

Asyut is a major hub for all forms of transport but the police will encourage you to take the train.

Bus From Asyut buses depart for Cairo (E£17.50 to E£20.50, six to seven hours) almost every hour between 7.45am and 1.30am. There are buses to Alexandria (E£28, 10 hours) at 7am and 7pm and buses for Minya (E£3, two hours) every two hours from 6am to 5pm. There's a bus to Aswan (E£20) and Luxor (E£12.50) at 8am, as well as frequent departures to Qena (E£10) and Sohag (E£3 to E£5).

If you are heading out to the oases, there are eight daily buses to Kharga (E£7 to E£8), between 7am and 10pm, four of which go on to Dakhla (E£14 to E£16). There are also buses to Hurghada (via Qena) at 9am (E£20) and 8pm (E£30), and one to Sharm el-Sheikh at 3pm (E£50).

Train Trains arrive and depart for destinations north and south of Asyut frequently. There are about 20 trains throughout the day to Cairo and Minya, and about half that number to Luxor and Aswan. The 1st-/2nd-class fares to Cairo are E£33/19.

The same fares to Minya (two to three hours) are E£13/8 (E£9/6 for students). To Aswan (E£37/29, 10 to 12 hours) and Luxor (six hours) it costs E£29/19 (E£20/14). There are very slow regular trains to the next main centre down the line, Sohag, but the police are unlikely to let you get on.

Service Taxi Service taxis gather around the bus station, but most drivers will only accept foreigners as private taxis at the insistence of the police. Should this change, there are services to Cairo (E£15), Kharga (E£8) and to Minya (E£4.50, two hours). Microbuses and service taxis to Mallawi (E£2) leave from the big lot near the mosque.

AROUND ASYUT

Convent of the Holy Virgin

About 10km south-west of Asyut in an area known as Dirunka, is this convent, built near a cave that Coptic Christians believe the Holy Family sought refuge in during their flight into Egypt. Some 50 or so nuns and monks live at the convent, which is built into a cliff about 120m above the valley. One of the monks will happily show you around. During the Moulid of the Virgin (7 to 22 August), tens of thousands of pilgrims descend on the place and there are daily parades with portraits of Mary and Jesus carried around.

Rest house Dorm beds E£3, beds in smaller rooms E£5. Reception open 6am-6pm daily. Groups and individuals are welcome to stay at this rest house, which is just outside the main gate. No food is available.

SOHAG

☎ 093

The city of Sohag, 115km south of Asyut, is the administrative centre for the governorate of the same name and one of the major Coptic Christian areas of Upper Egypt. The main reason to visit is to see the White and Red Monasteries just outside Sohag, and the town of Akhmin across the river. However, as in Minya and Asyut, there is a strong police presence on the streets here. They take their job of protecting the few tourists who do pass through very seriously. If they know you're in town they will insist on escorting you everywhere and you'll probably be banned from leaving your hotel after dark. It's probably better to visit the sights as a day-trip from Luxor.

There's no tourist office but you can change cash or travellers cheques at the Bank of Alexandria or the Banque du Caire, both on Al-Gomhuriyya. The post office is a little way down the road from the Banque du Caire along the Nile.

White & Red Monasteries

The White Monastery *(Deir al-Abyad; open 8am-8pm daily),* 12km north-west of Sohag, was built in AD 400 by the Coptic saint Shenouda, with chunks of white limestone from a Pharaonic temple. It once supported a community of 2000 monks; today there are just four. Its fortress walls still stand, but most of the interior is in ruins, though you can see the several types of arches used in its construction.

The Red Monastery *(Deir al-Ahmar; open 8am-8pm daily)*, 4km south-east from Deir al-Abyad, is hidden at the rear of a village so you'll need to ask for directions. It was founded by Bishoi, a thief who converted to Christianity. He built this and two monasteries in Wadi Natrun and eventually became a Coptic saint. There are two chapels on the grounds, Santa Maria Chapel and St Bishoi Chapel. Be sure to see the remains of a 10th-century fresco in a frame on a side altar – it contains a 1000-year-old icon. There are interesting, though fading, frescoes on the walls, unusual pillars and old wooden peg locks on the doors.

To get to the monasteries you'll have to take a taxi (about E£15 there and back) unless you're visiting some time during the first two weeks of July, when you can catch a bus for about E£1 with the thousands of other pilgrims.

Akhmin

On the east bank of the Nile lies the town of Akhmin, known as Ipu to the ancient Egyptians. Built on the ruins of an older pre-dynastic settlement, it was dedicated to Min, a fertility god often represented by a giant phallus, equated with Pan by the Greeks (who later called the town Panopolis). Links to this ancient past were discovered in 1982 when excavations to build a new school in the centre of town led to the discovery of the 11m-high **statue of Meret Amun** *(admission E£10; open 9am-5pm daily)*. This is the tallest statue of an ancient queen to have been discovered in Egypt. Meret Amun (Beloved of the God Amun) was one of the daughters of Ramses II and wife of Amenhotep. She was also a priestess of the Temple of Min. Little is left of the temple itself, and the statue of Meret Amun now stands in a huge excavation pit among the houses in the middle of town. As the statue is so tall, you can get a good view of its rapidly fading colours without even entering the site.

Akhmin is also famed for its unique woven carpets and textiles. Opposite the statue of Meret Amun is a tiny post office and, across the road from this, a small **weaving factory**. It's the house with the green door – just knock to be led through to the showroom where you can buy handwoven silk and cotton textiles straight from the bolt or packets of ready-made tablecloths and serviettes. Ask to see the men and boys who make the products at work – you'll hear the 25 looms clattering away before you even climb the stairs.

A microbus from Sohag to Akhmin takes 15 minutes and costs 20pt.

Places to Stay & Eat

Travellers are discouraged from staying in Sohag. Some hotels will quote outrageous amounts in an effort to dissuade you from staying and others will simply refuse to take you. Wherever you do stay, you will probably be forbidden from going out after dark.

Andalous Hotel *(☎ 324 328, Sharia al-Mahatta)* Singles/doubles E£9/14, with bath E£12/18. Although directly across from the train station, this hotel isn't keen to have

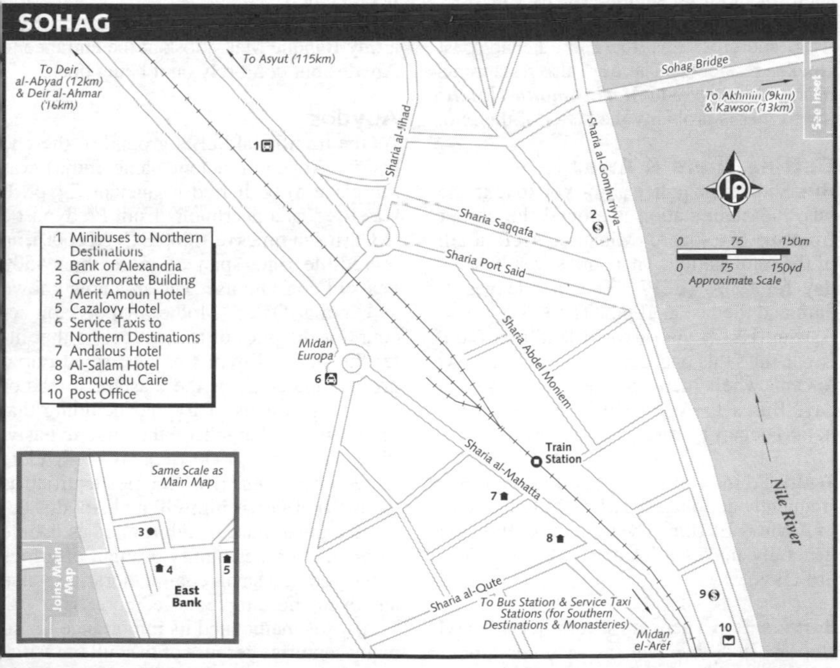

foreigners stay and some travellers have reported being charged as much as E£50 for a room.

Al-Salam Hotel *(☎ 333 317, Sharia al-Mahatta)* Singles/doubles E£15/25, with bath E£18/45. This is close to the train station but cleaner than the Andalous.

Merit Amoun Hotel *(☎ 601 985, fax 603 222, East Bank)* Singles/doubles E£70/88. This big three-star hotel on the east bank is one of the better options in town.

Cazalovy Hotel *(☎ 601 185, 601 170, East Bank)* Singles/doubles E£39/55. Also on the east bank, about 100m beyond the Merit Amoun, this hotel offers the best value in town. Soap and towels are provided and there is air-con in all rooms; prices include breakfast.

There's not much choice in the way of food in Sohag. As well as the usual fruit and vegetable stands, there are a few kushari and fuul and ta'amiyya places near the train station. If you follow Sharia al-Mahatta south of the train station (left as you walk out the entrance) to a big square, Midan el-Aref, and cross this, there is a kebab/roast chicken restaurant. There are also restaurants in the ***Cazalovy*** and ***Merit Amoun Hotels***; the former is probably the better of the two.

Getting There & Away

Bus Should the police allow you to take the bus, the main station is around the corner from the big square, Midan el-Aref, south of the train station. There are seven buses a day for Cairo (E£17). The first leaves at 5am and the last at 10pm. There is a bus to Aswan (E£13) via Luxor (E£6.50) at 6am. If you miss this one, get a bus or service taxi to Qena where there are many services each day. Buses to Asyut (E£2.75, 1½ to two hours) depart every 30 to 40 minutes.

Train Trains north and south stop fairly frequently at Sohag. The 1st-/2nd-class fare to Asyut is E£10/6. The train to Al-Balyana generally makes a lot of stops (E£1.50 in 3rd class).

Service Taxi There are several service taxi stations in Sohag but, as in other Upper Egyptian towns, you're likely to be forced to hire a private taxi because of the police. Should they lighten up, cars to Asyut and other northern destinations, including Cairo, can be found north of the train station on Midan Europa. Service taxis for Qena and Nag Hammadi leave from the southern depot, which is on the main road south, just after a canal. There are also stations for local taxis to the monasteries and to Akhmin – on some of these local routes wonderful vintage cars are used as service taxis.

AL-BALYANA

The only reason to go to this town is to visit the village of Al-Araba al-Madfunah, 10km away. There you'll find the necropolis of Abydos and the magnificent Temple of Seti, one of the most beautiful monuments in Egypt. The police here tend to be somewhat heavy-handed in their efforts to protect you and if you haven't been escorted thus far, you'll certainly pick up some policemen here.

Should you need to change money, there's a tiny Banque Masr kiosk at the entrance to Abydos but don't rely on it being open.

Abydos

As the traditional burial ground of the god Osiris, Abydos (ancient name Ibdju) was *the* place to be buried in ancient Egypt. It was used as a necropolis from Predynastic to Christian times (c. 4000 BC–AD 600), an incredible time span of more than 4500 years of constant use. The area now known as Umm al-Qa'ab (Mother of Pots), on account of the piles of ancient debris that litter the site, is Egypt's earliest royal burial ground and contains the mastaba tombs of the first pharaohs of Egypt, including that of the third pharaoh of the first dynasty, Pharaoh Djer (c. 3000 BC). By the Middle Kingdom his tomb had become identified as the tomb of Osiris himself, and Abydos became a great place of pilgrimage as people from all over the country brought offerings to the god, left small commemorative stelae and even chose to be buried here.

Abydos maintained its importance for so many centuries because of the cult of Osiris,

ABYDOS

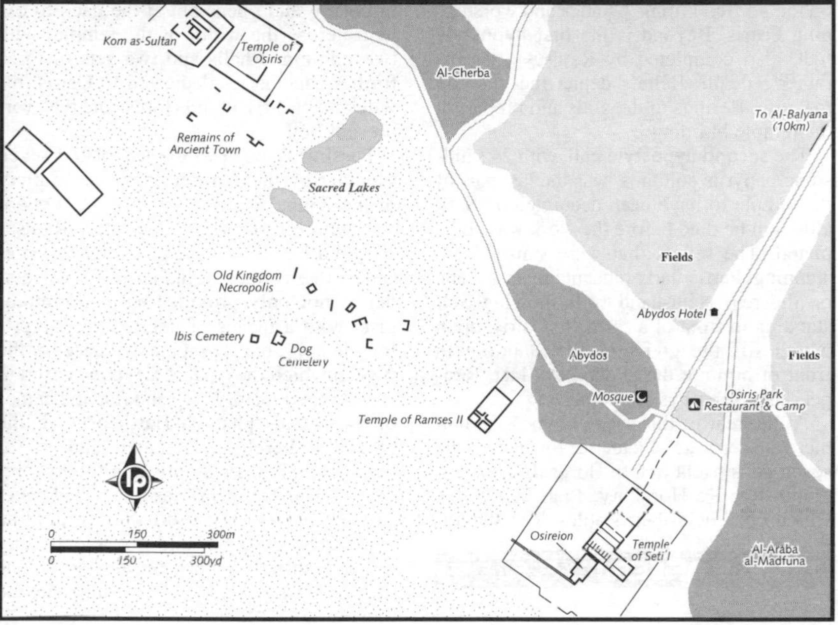

god of the dead. The area was a natural shrine for the worship of this ruler of the netherworld because, according to mythology, it was here that the head of Osiris was buried after his brother Seth had murdered him – see the boxed text 'The Cult of Osiris'. The temple at Abydos was the most important of the shrines to Osiris and became a place of pilgrimage that most Egyptians would try and visit in their lifetime much as Muslims try to get to Mecca today. If they didn't manage it they would be buried with small boats to enable their souls to make the journey after death.

Should you want more information, there's a booklet on sale at the Osiris Park Camp shop for E£10. There's also *Abydos – The Holy City in Ancient Egypt* written by a fascinating woman by the name of Dorothy Eady, better known to many as 'Umm Seti'. She was an English woman who believed she was a temple priestess and lover of Seti I and for 35 years, until her death in 1981, she lived at Abydos. *The Search of Umm Seti* by Jonathan Cott is a biography of her life there.

Temple of Seti I The first structure you'll see at Abydos is one of Egypt's most beautiful temples, also known as the Cenotaph or Great Temple of Seti I, which after a certain amount of restoration work is also one of the most complete. This great limestone structure, which unusually is L-shaped rather than rectangular, was dedicated to the six major gods – Osiris, Isis and Horus, Amun-Ra, Ra-Horakhty and Ptah – and also to Seti I himself. In the aftermath of the Amarna Period, it is almost as if Seti was trying to appease as many of the traditional gods as possible. As you roam through Seti's dark halls and sanctuaries a definite air of mystery, an almost tangible impression of ancient pomp and circumstance, surrounds you.

The temple is entered through a largely destroyed **pylon** and two **courtyards**, built by Ramses II, Seti I's son, who is depicted on the portico killing Asiatics and worshipping Osiris. Beyond is the **first hypostyle hall**, also completed by Ramses after his father's death. Reliefs depict the pharaoh making offerings to the gods and preparing the temple building.

The **second hypostyle hall**, with 24 sandstone papyrus columns, was the last part of the temple to have been decorated by Seti, although he died before the work was completed. The reliefs that were finished are stunning. Particularly outstanding is a scene on the rear right-hand wall showing Seti standing in front of a shrine to Osiris, upon which sits the god himself. Standing in front of him are the goddesses Maat, Renpet, Isis, Nephthys and Amentet.

At the rear of this second hypostyle hall there are separate sanctuaries for each of the seven gods (right to left: Horus, Isis, Osiris, Amun-Ra, Ra-Horakhty, Ptah and Seti), which once held their statues. The sanctuary of Osiris (third from right) is especially imposing and opens out at the back to extend across the width of the temple, with two columned halls and two sets of three further sanctuaries dedicated to Osiris, his wife and child, Isis and Horus, and the ever-present Seti.

TEMPLE OF SETI I

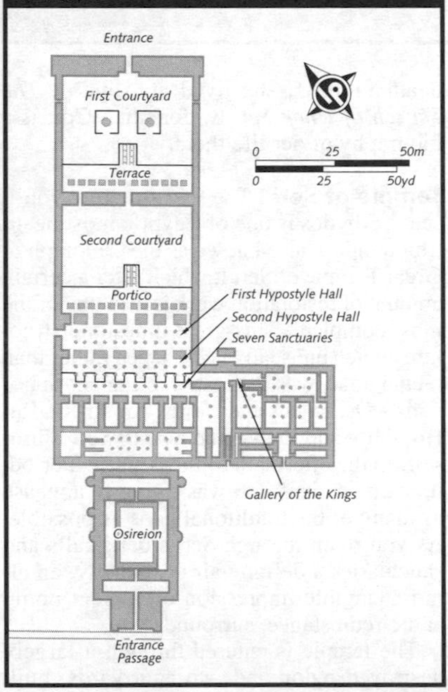

Passing through to the left of the seven sanctuaries, the corridor known as 'Gallery of the Kings' is carved with the figures of Seti with his eldest son, the future Ramses II, and a long list of the pharaohs who preceded them. Such valuable historical evidence not only provided early Egyptologists with a means of unravelling Egypt's long history, but is graphic evidence for the way in which the ancient Egyptians used to rewrite their history. Try and find the names of the female pharaoh Hatshepsut, or the so-called heretic Akhenaten and you'll draw a blank; they simply aren't there – removed from the records as if they had never existed. It seems that Seti and his hardline successors simply would not tolerate any more 'unusual' goings-on and from this time on the kingship would be run along the most orthodox lines.

The Osireion Directly behind Seti's temple is the Osireion, a weird, wonderful building interpreted as a cenotaph to Osiris. It was originally thought to be an Old Kingdom structure on account of the great blocks of granite used in its construction, and although now dated to Seti's reign (and completed by his grandson Merneptah), its design is said to be based on the rock-cut tombs in the Valley of the Kings. At the centre of its columned 'burial chamber', which lies at a lower level than Seti's temple, is a dummy sarcophagus originally surrounded by water. It's surrounded by water today as the Osireion is permanently submerged by the rising water table. If you want to visit be prepared to wade. This, together with the collapse of the roof, makes inspection of the funerary and ritual texts carved on its walls hazardous.

Temple of Ramses II Just to the northwest of Seti I's temple is the smaller and less well-preserved structure built by his

The Cult of Osiris

Osiris, the god of regeneration, is usually depicted as a mummy holding the royal crook and flail.

The most familiar of all ancient Egypt's myths is the story of Isis and Osiris, preserved in the writings of the Greek historian Plutarch (c. AD 46–126) following a visit to Egypt. According to Plutarch's version, Osiris and his sister-wife Isis had once been earthly rulers, civilising their people and bringing great peace and prosperity to the land. Their brother Seth, jealous of their success and happiness, invited Osiris to a banquet where he tricked his unsuspecting brother into trying out a coffin he had made. Once inside, Seth sealed up the coffin and threw it into the Nile to drown Osiris. Following the murder, the distraught Isis retrieved her husband's body, only to have it seized back by Seth who dismembered it, scattering the pieces far and wide. But Isis refused to give up, and taking the form of a kite she took to the skies with her sister Nephthys to locate the separate body parts. Then, according to Plutarch, they buried each piece wherever they found it, which explains why there are so many places that claim to be Osiris' tomb.

Yet in the traditional Egyptian version of the story, Isis actually kept the parts and reassembled them to create the first mummy, helped by Anubis, god of embalming. Then using her immense magic she restored Osiris back to life, reinvigorating him so successfully she conceived their son Horus, a miraculous act in which she quite literally created new life from death. Raised to avenge his father, Horus defeated Seth and became the living pharaoh on earth, represented by each pharaoh, while his resurrected father Osiris ruled as Lord of the Afterlife. He was a much-loved god, the salvation of all who die and the one who gives eternal hope, which explains why the names of the dead are often prefaced with Osiris's name, to show that they are with him in his kingdom.

son Ramses II (1279–1213 BC). Although taking the more standard rectangular plan of a traditional temple, there are sanctuaries for each of the gods Ramses considered important, including Osiris, Amun-Ra, Thoth, Min, the deified Seti I and, of course, Ramses himself. Although the roof is missing, the reliefs again retain a significant amount of their colour, clearly seen on figures of priests, offering bearers and the pharaoh anointing the gods' statues. You may have to get the guard to unlock the gate.

Places to Stay & Eat

You are unlikely to be allowed to stay in Al-Balyana, given the nervousness of the local police. Should the situation change, there are a few hotels and some cafes and food stands around the town.

Osiris Park Restaurant & Camp *(☎ 812 200, Abydos Temple)* Right in front of the temple, this was open for food at the time of research, but nobody was allowed to stay overnight. The food is overpriced and consists mostly of snacks, and it is best to bring your own from elsewhere. It's managed by Horus, a protege of Umm Seti.

Abydos Hotel *(☎ 812 102, Balyana)* Singles/doubles E£10/15. The only other accommodation option, this hotel is 200m before Osiris Park, on the way to the Temple of Seti I.

Getting There & Away

Al-Balyana is serviced by buses, trains and service taxis, and their respective stations are conveniently close to each other. However, you're unlikely to be given much choice in your mode of transport. If you haven't come in convoy, the police will usually take you to the train station. Occasionally they will stick you on the bus of a tour group coming from Luxor with an armed police escort. Arriving at Al-Balyana train station, you will be met by police who will put you in a local taxi and then escort you there and back. This costs about E£5.

QENA

☎ 096

Qena, a provincial capital 91km east of Al-Balyana and 62km north of Luxor, is at the intersection of the main Nile road and the road across the desert to the Red Sea towns of Port Safaga and Hurghada. A scruffy, overcrowded market town and provincial capital, it has little to recommend it. Unless you're on your way to or from the Red Sea and don't have a through connection, the only reason to stop is to visit the spectacular temple complex at Dendara, just outside the town, although this is usually done as a day trip from Luxor. There are two service taxi stations quite a long way apart from one another, one for northern destinations and places across the Nile, the other for southern destinations. Again, you are likely to be met by policemen here and could well be escorted to the temple and then put on the first train to Luxor. If you need money, there is a Bank of Alexandria and a Banque du Caire in town.

Dendara

Although built at the very end of the Pharaonic period, the wonderfully preserved Temple of Hathor *(admission E£12; open 7am-6pm daily)* at her cult site of Dendara

QENA

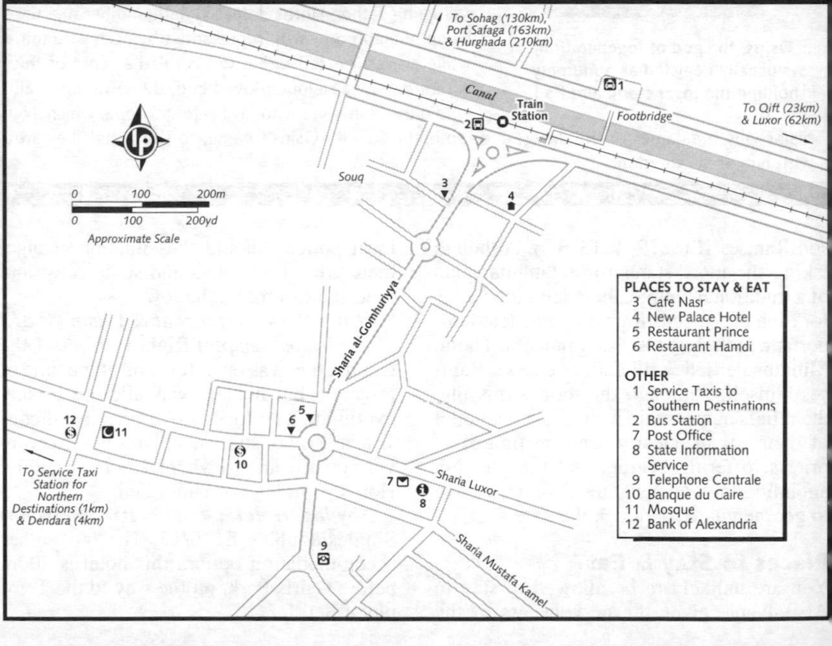

is a sight to behold. Its main building is virtually intact, with a great stone roof and columns, dark chambers, underground crypts and twisting stairways all carved with hieroglyphs.

Dendara itself was an important administrative and religious centre as early as the 6th dynasty (c. 2320 BC), when it also served as an important burial ground. Montuhotep II of the 11th dynasty built a small limestone chapel here (now in the Egyptian Museum in Cairo), although the great temple that dominates the site was begun in the 30th dynasty, with much of the building undertaken by the Ptolemies and completed during the Roman period. Yet it was almost certainly built on the site of earlier versions in which the goddess Hathor had been worshipped since the Old Kingdom.

Hathor was the goddess of love and sensual pleasures, patron of music and dancing, and as 'Lady of the West' was protector of the dead. Like most Egyptian deities Hathor was known by a range of titles, including 'the golden one', 'she of the beautiful hair' and 'lady of drunkenness', representing the joyful intoxication involved in her worship. She is generally represented as a woman, a cow, or a woman with a headdress of cow's horns and sun disc between to highlight her role as the daughter of the sun god Ra. Yet she was also a maternal figure and as wet nurse of Horus, by whom she also had the child Ihy, she shared attributes with the goddess Isis. The Greeks also associated Hathor with their goddess Aphrodite.

Dendara was the ritual location where Hathor gave birth to Horus' child, and her temple stands on the edge of the desert as if awaiting her return.

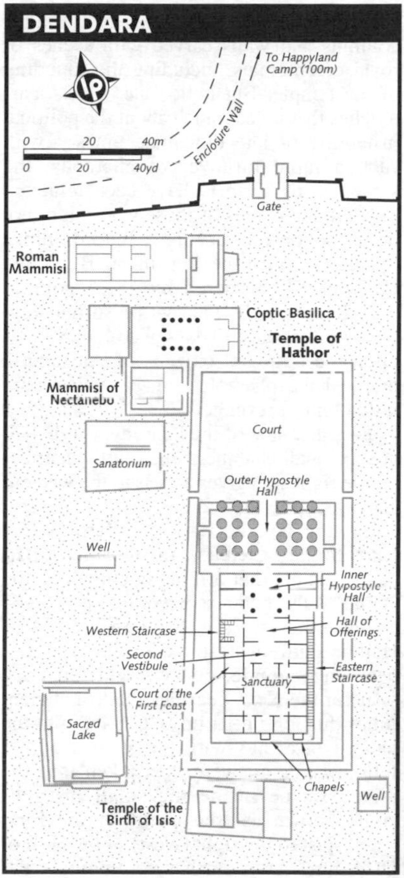

Touring the Temple Since the standard pylon gateway and entrance courtyard were never completed, the temple frontage is formed by the **outer hypostyle hall** built by the Roman Emperor Tiberius (AD 14–37). Visitors are greeted by the first six of its 24 great stone columns, each adorned on all four sides with Hathor's head. Although her features were defaced in Christian times they still present a most impressive sight. The walls inside are carved with highly detailed relief scenes of Tiberius and his successors in their role as pharaoh, presenting offerings to the goddess and her fellow gods, while the ceilings are decorated with relief scenes of the sun's journey through the heavens. The sky goddess Nut swallows the sun in the evening on the left (east) side while zodiac signs adopted from Babylonia are featured on the right (west) side.

Passing further into the rest of the temple built by the Ptolemies, the second smaller

inner hypostyle hall again has Hathor columns and walls carved with scenes of royal ceremonials, including the founding of the temple. But notice the 'blank' cartouches that reveal much about the political instability of late Ptolemaic times – with such a rapid turnover of pharaohs, the stonemasons seem to have been reluctant to carve the names of those who might not be in the job for very long. Indeed, things reached an all-time low in 80 BC when Ptolemy XI murdered his more popular wife Berenice III (who was also his stepmother) after only 19 days of co-rule, whereupon the outraged citizens of Alexandria dragged the pharaoh from his palace and killed him in revenge.

To either side of the inner hypostyle hall are six small chambers; the fourth chamber on the right side gives access to the western stairway up to the roof.

Beyond lies the **Hall of Offerings** that leads to the **sanctuary**, the most holy part of the temple that originally contained the statue of the goddess herself as portrayed on the sanctuary's wall reliefs. A further Hathor statue was stored in the crypt beneath her temple, and brought out each year for the New Year Festival (in ancient times this fell on 19 July). Carried into the hall of offerings with the statues of her fellow gods, all were then taken into the raised shrine inside the small open-air court known as 'the Court of the First Feast' just to the right (west) of the Hall of Offerings. After further ceremonials beneath the huge figure of Nut giving birth to the sun on the shrine's ceiling, the statues were then taken up to the roof via the western staircase, decorated with a procession of priests walking up the stairs. Placed inside the open-air kiosk on the south-west corner of the roof, they were then left to await the first reviving rays of the sun god Ra on New Year's Day. Once ceremonies were complete, the statues would be taken back down via the eastern staircase, with its carved priests appropriately walking downstairs.

The theme of reviving the gods is continued opposite the kiosk on the north-western corner of the **roof** and duplicated on the north-eastern corner, where two suites of rooms are dedicated to the revival of Osiris. Relief scenes show the means by which the god was restored by the power of his sister-wife, Isis, and in the centre room of the north-eastern suite is the famous 'Dendara Zodiac', or at least a plaster cast, since the original is now in the Louvre in Paris. Views of the surrounding countryside from the roof are magnificent. The graffiti on the edge of the temple was left by Napoleon's commander Desaix, and other French soldiers, in 1799.

The **exterior walls** of the temple feature lion-headed gargoyles to cope with the very occasional rain fall and are decorated along their length with highly detailed relief scenes of Ptolemaic pharaohs and their Roman successors paying homage to the gods. The most interesting scene of all can be found on the rear (south) wall, where none other than the great Cleopatra, stands with Ptolemy XV aka Caesarion, her son by Julius Caesar.

Facing this back wall is a small **Chapel** of Isis built by Cleopatra's great rival Octavian once he was the Emperor Augustus. Walking back toward the front of the Hathor temple on the west side, notice the now palm-filled Sacred Lake and the smaller well to its north that supplied the temple's water. To the north of the well lie the mud-brick walls of the **Sanatorium**, where the ill would seek a cure through the healing abilities of Hathor.

Finally there are the two **Mammisi** (Coptic for 'birth house'), the first built by the 30th dynasty Egyptian pharaoh Nectanebo I (380–362 BC) and decorated by the Ptolemies, and the one nearest the temple wall by the Romans and decorated by the emperor Trajan (AD 98–117). Such buildings were used as places to celebrate divine birth, both of the young gods and of the pharaoh himself as son of the gods. Between the mammisi is a **Coptic basilica**, built in the 5th century AD. It functioned as a church when Christianity took over from the old religion.

Getting There & Away Dendara is 4km south-west of Qena on the other side of the Nile. These days most people arrive here from Luxor in convoy. If you want to hire a service taxi from Luxor for the trip, it will cost you about E£120 to E£150 return. From Qena you can take a local microbus to the northern service taxi station, and from there another microbus along the main road. It drops you at the turn-off just after a new railway bridge, from where you have about a 20-minute walk to the temple. If you haven't already met up with the police, you will at the temple and they are likely to escort you back to town after your visit.

Places to Stay & Eat

If you must stay in Qena, there is limited choice.

Happyland Camp Singles/doubles E£30/45. About 100m from Dendara temple, this is basically a hotel with overpriced beds. If the police relax, there's a possibility of camping in its messy garden.

New Palace Hotel *(☎ 322 509)* Singles/doubles E£26/35. Near Sharia al-Gomhuriyya, this scruffy place is in a faded blue building just behind the Mobil petrol station, but it's the best of a bad lot.

Cafe Nasr *(Sharia al-Gomhuriyya)* Meals E£2.50-6. This workers' cafe serves cheap food such as spinach, tahini, salad (which should be avoided) and tea.

Restaurant Hamdi *(Sharia Luxor)* Meals E£7-15. Just off Sharia al-Gomhuriyya, this place serves full meals of chicken and vegetables.

Restaurant Prince *(Sharia al-Gomhuriyya)* Meals E£5-15. This restaurant serves more chicken and kofta and beer is reportedly on offer (although not at the time of research).

There are also several places to buy kushari, fuul and ta'amiyya along Sharia al-Gomhuriyya.

Getting There & Away

Bus The bus station (☎ 325 086) is in front of the train station. However, buses not originating or terminating here pass along the main road and drop (and might pick up) passengers at the bridge over the canal. There are two Superjet buses to Cairo (E£25) at 7am and 8pm. Eleven buses go to Aswan (E£7) from 6.30am to 7.45pm, and most stop in Luxor (E£2). A few other buses only go as far as Edfu or Luxor. There are nine buses to Hurghada and six of them go on to Suez (E£22 to E£38, nine to 10 hours). Superjet also has services to Hurghada (E£18) and Suez (E£41). There are also buses for coastal destinations such as Al-Quseir (E£6) and Port Safaga (E£7 to E£10).

Other buses serve Nile destinations such as Sohag, Asyut and Minya. Often, you can transfer from the Cairo buses for these. These buses all pass through Al-Balyana, where you can change for Abydos.

Train This is not a very practical way to get to and from Qena, as generally only the slower trains stop here. There are 1st- and 2nd-class air-con trains to Luxor (40 mins) and 2nd- and 3rd-class trains to Al-Balyana, if you want to visit Abydos.

Service Taxi Service taxis to destinations north of Qena leave from a T-junction 1km outside town. For destinations to the south of Qena, such as Luxor, service taxis leave from a taxi station that is on the other side of the canal from the train station.

Getting Around

There is a local microbus that shuttles from town to the northern service taxi station. You can pick it up near the train station or, if you're coming up from the south, at the canal bridge near the southern service taxi station. It costs 25pt.

QIFT

In Graeco-Roman times Qift was a major trading town on the Arabia-India trade route and an important starting point for expeditions to the Red Sea and Sinai. The town lost its importance as a trading centre from the 10th century onwards and is now little more than a sprawling village.

At the time of research the police were not letting foreigners visit Qift.

QUS

During medieval times this was the most important Islamic city in Egypt, after Cairo. Founded in 1083, it served as a port and transit point for goods coming and going between the Nile and Al-Quseir on the Red Sea. Today, the town is the site of a US$246 million Egyptian-German paper mill project that converts bagasse (the waste product of sugar-cane refining) into paper products.

At the time of research the police were not letting foreigners visit Qus.

Nile Valley – Luxor

☎ 095

Luxor is a place like no other on earth, a place where the grandeur of ancient Thebes sits comfortably alongside the modern town and its inhabitants. The sheer size and number of its wonderfully preserved monuments have made Luxor Egypt's greatest attraction after the Pyramids, with no fewer than eight of what we consider the 12 highlights of Pharaonic Egypt to be found in this small southern town. From the temples of Karnak and Luxor on its East Bank across to the temples of Deir al-Bahri and Medinat Habu, the Colossi of Memnon and the Valley of the Kings on its West Bank, there's an embarrassment of riches to be found in this fabulous place that is often described as the world's largest open-air museum.

Predynastic remains indicate that the area has been inhabited for at least 6000 years, and even tourists are nothing new. Travellers have been visiting Thebes for centuries to marvel at the monuments, with Greek and Roman tourists leaving graffiti to express their admiration of the things they saw. With 2000 years' worth of visitors hauling away whatever took their fancy, the monuments of ancient Thebes make up large parts of many of the world's great museum collections.

With such a huge proportion of the town's economy derived from tourism, Luxor was heavily hit by the massacre at Hatshepsut's temple in 1997. But after two years of empty rooms and slashed prices, the town is once again booming. However, while this is good news for the local economy it means that things are not so great for independent travellers who like to view monuments in peace. Most visitors come in groups and sweep from monument to monument in air-con buses. Sharing a stuffy tomb with 60 sweaty tourists and the booming voice of their guide is not most people's idea of fun.

Luxor also has the dubious distinction of being the hassle capital of Egypt. Travellers in Luxor complain of the almost incessant harassment from vendors, street hawkers and felucca middlemen. In the steamy summer months (May to September), when business is slack, it can be enough to tip a temper already frazzled by the heat. In winter, it's easier to bear in mind that they are

Highlights

- Lose yourself in the stone papyrus forest of the great hypostyle hall at Karnak.
- See how Egypt's ancient rulers tried to confound both thieves and mortality with spectacular tombs dug deep into the desert mountains in the Valley of the Kings.
- Marvel at the Temple of Hatshepsut at Deir al-Bahri, an architectural wonder carved out of the Theban hills for one of the few women to rule ancient Egypt.
- Get some idea of how Theban tombs looked before they were dulled by time and the breath of thousands of tourists by visiting the Tomb of Nefertari.
- Glide along the Nile in a felucca as you watch the sun set behind the mountains of Thebes.
- Wander between the colourful mud-brick houses of Gurna and see how modern Thebans coexist with the remains of their ancestors.

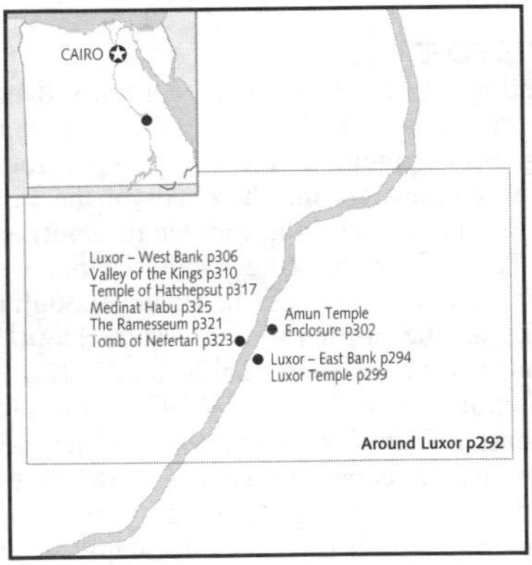

AROUND LUXOR

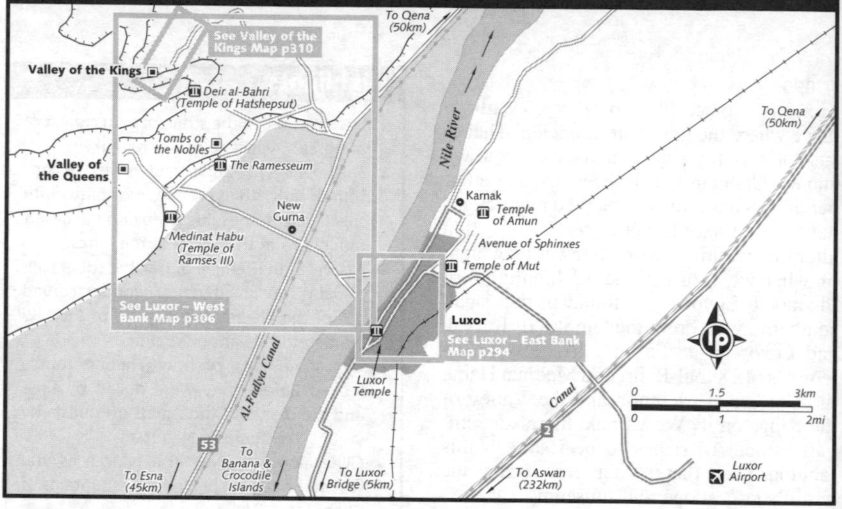

just trying to make a living. It can be hard to remember that behind the sleazy tourist facade, the town and its environs are filled with ordinary, friendly people.

HISTORY

Following the collapse of centralised authority at the end of the Old Kingdom, Egypt fragmented into a series of local power bases. During the chaos of the First Intermediate Period, the small southern village of Thebes (the ancient name was Waset) eventually became strong enough to take on the northern capital Heracleopolis and win under the capable leadership of Montuhotep II (2055–2004 BC) of the 11th dynasty. After reuniting the country and moving the capital to Thebes, Montuhotep initiated a series of great building works, including a temple to Thebes' local god Amun at his cult centre of Karnak and his own royal funerary temple complex at Deir al-Bahri. Although the 12th-dynasty pharaohs moved their capital back north, Thebes remained the capital of the south (Upper Egypt) and never lost its place as Egypt's ceremonial capital, a counterbalance to the administrative capital of Memphis.

Following a Second Intermediate Period (1650–1550 BC) Thebes once again emerged as the unifying power. Its ruling family drove out the foreign Hyksos pharaohs in the north, laying the foundations of Egypt's empire and all the glories of the New Kingdom (1550–1069 BC). For 500 years Thebes was at its peak, a great city with a population of many thousands, and it was during this time that most of its great monuments were constructed. Although most pharaohs continued to rule from the north, they visited Thebes on a regular basis to check on the progress of their massive building schemes and to lead the regular ceremonial events, when they stayed in the palaces attached to the temples.

The decline of Pharaonic rule was mirrored by Luxor's gradual slide into insignificance. Mud-brick settlements clung to the once mighty Theban temples, their stone walls the only protection against marauding tribespeople from the desert. Remains of these communities can still be seen at sites such as Medinat Habu on the West Bank.

As Christian rule gave way to Islamic, the area fell into obscurity and the only reminder of its once glorious past was the name given to it by its Arab rulers: Al-Uqsur, 'The Palaces'. By the time European travellers arrived here in the 18th century, Luxor was little more than a large Upper Egyptian village, known more for its famous saint, Abu al-Haggag, than for its half-buried temples and tombs.

Fast forward to the 19th century and the arrival of mass tourism. Luxor once again regained its place on the world map. Its temples were cleared and were visited by thousands. Since then, its lure has been dulled only by periodic political upheaval, most recently by the massacre of 58 tourists in 1997. The subsequent slump in tourism had a dramatic affect on the local economy but it has since rebounded and at the time of writing, Luxor was host to more visitors than ever before.

ORIENTATION

What most visitors today know as Luxor is actually three separate areas – the town of Luxor itself, the village of Karnak a couple of kilometres to the north-east, and the monuments and necropolis of ancient Thebes on the west bank of the Nile.

In Luxor town there are four main thoroughfares: Sharia al-Mahatta, Sharia Karnak, the Corniche el-Nil (also referred to as just 'the Corniche') and Sharia Televizyon, a bustling area around which are clustered many of the town's cheap hotels.

INFORMATION

Visa Extensions

The passport office (☎ 380 885) is almost opposite the Isis Hotel, south of the town centre. It's open from 8am to 8pm Saturday to Thursday. The best time to visit is before noon. Some travellers have commented that it's much easier to get a visa extension here than in Cairo.

Tourist Offices

The tourist police and tourist office (☎ 372 215, 373 294) are in the Tourist Bazaar on the Corniche, next to the New Winter Palace Hotel. The office is open from 8am to 8pm Saturday to Thursday, and 8am to 1pm Friday. Travellers can leave messages on a notice board next to the main information counter. There is another tourist office at the train station and a third at the airport. All have the same hours as the main office.

Money

The Bank of Alexandria has a branch on the Corniche, a little way up from the Hotel Mercure. Banque Masr is on Sharia Nefertiti, around the corner from the Mercure, and the National Bank of Egypt is down on the Corniche near the Old Winter Palace. Banks are usually open from 8.30am to 2pm and again for a few hours from 5pm or 6pm. In addition, the big hotels have various bank branches, and there is an exchange booth open quite long hours on the Corniche in front of the Tourist Bazaar.

ATM machines can be found at the Banque Masr beside Philippe Hotel, and at the Banque Masr branches just north of the Winter Palace Hotel, on Sharia Televizyon and just outside the doorway of Gaddis Hotel.

American Express (AmEx; ☎ 378 333) is at the Old Winter Palace Hotel and operates from 8am to 7pm, but closes at 3pm on Friday and Saturday, although the hours appear to be flexible. All the usual services are available.

There's also a Thomas Cook exchange office and travel agent (☎ 372 196, fax 376 502) across from AmEx; it's open from 8am to 7pm daily, closing at 3pm on Friday and Saturday.

Egyptian Exchange Company (☎ 388 257) has a branch on Sharia Karnak behind Luxor Temple and is open from 8am to 11pm daily.

Post & Telephone

The main post office, open from 8.30am to 2.30pm daily, is on Sharia al-Mahatta and there's a branch office in the Tourist Bazaar.

The central telephone office is on Sharia Karnak and is open 24 hours; there's another branch (open from 8am to 10pm) below the resplendent entrance of the Old Winter Palace Hotel and a third at the train station (open from 8am to 8pm).

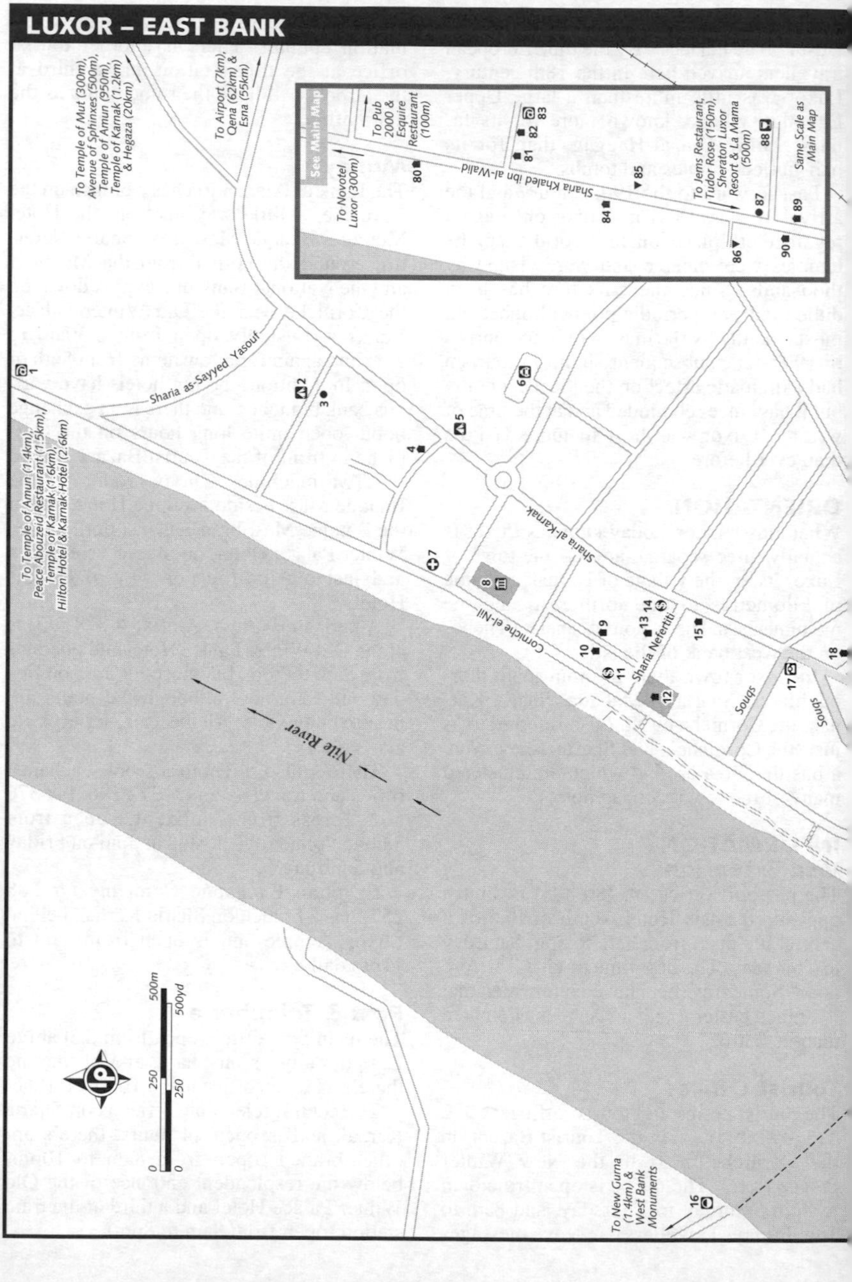
LUXOR – EAST BANK
To Temple of Mut (300m), Avenue of Sphinxes (500m), Temple of Amun (950m), Temple of Karnak (1.2km) & Hegaza (20km)
To Airport (7km) Qena (62km) & Esna (55km)
See Main Map
To Novotel Luxor (300m)
To Pub 2000 & Esquire Restaurant (100m)
Sharia Khaled ibn al-Walid
To Jems Restaurant, Tudor Rose (150m), Sheraton Luxor Resort & La Mama (500m)
Same Scale as Main Map
80
81
82
83
84
85
86
87
88
89
90
To Temple of Amun (1.4km), Peace Abouzeid Restaurant (1.5km), Temple of Karnak (1.6km), Hilton Hotel & Karnak Hotel (2.6km)
Sharia as-Sayyed Yasouf
Sharia al-Karnak
Corniche el-Nil
Sharia Nefertiti
Souqs
Souqs
Nile River
1
2
3
4
5
6
7
8
9
10
11
12
13
14
15
16
17
18
To New Gurna (1.4km) & West Bank Monuments
0
250
500m
0
250
500yd

LUXOR – EAST BANK

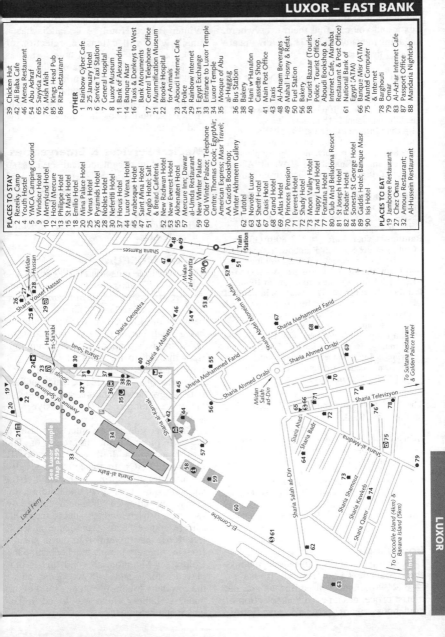

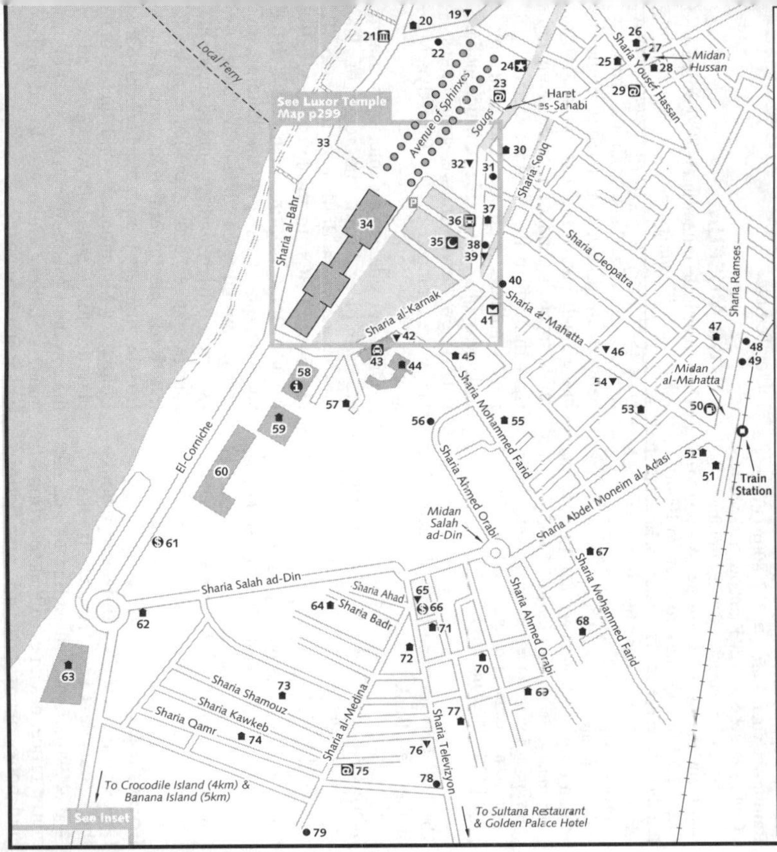

PLACES TO STAY
- 2 Rezeiky Camp
- 4 Youth Hostel
- 5 YMCA Camping Ground
- 9 Windsor Hotel
- 10 Merryland Hotel
- 12 Hotel Mercure
- 13 Philippe Hotel
- 15 St Mark Hotel
- 18 Emilio Hotel
- 20 Mina Palace Hotel
- 25 Venus Hotel
- 26 Pyramids Hotel
- 28 Nobles Hotel
- 30 Nefertiti Hotel
- 37 Horus Hotel
- 44 Luxor Wena Hotel
- 45 Arabesque Hotel
- 47 Saint Mina Hotel
- 51 Anglo Hotel; Salt & Bread Cafeteria
- 52 New Radwan Hotel
- 53 New Everest Hotel
- 55 Akhenaten Hotel
- 57 Mercure Inn; Dawar al-Umda Restaurant
- 59 New Winter Palace
- 60 Old Winter Palace; Telephone Centre; Thomas Cook; EgyptAir; American Express; Masr Travel; AA Gaddis Bookshop; Winter Akhmeem Gallery
- 62 Tutotel
- 63 Novotel Luxor
- 64 Sherif Hotel
- 67 Oasis Hotel
- 68 Grand Hotel
- 69 Atlas Hotel
- 70 Princess Pension
- 71 Everest Hotel
- 72 Shady Hotel
- 73 Moon Valley Hotel
- 74 Happy Land Hotel
- 77 Fontana Hotel
- 80 Club Med Belladona Resort
- 81 St Joseph Hotel
- 82 Flobater Hotel
- 84 Sonesta St George Hotel
- 89 Gaddis Hotel; Banque Masr
- 90 Isis Hotel

PLACES TO EAT
- 19 Jamboree Restaurant
- 27 Chez Omar
- 32 Amoun Restaurant; Al-Hussein Restaurant
- 39 Chicken Hut
- 42 Ali Baba Cafe
- 46 Mensa Restaurant
- 54 Abu Ashraf
- 65 Sayyida Zeinab
- 76 Mish Mish
- 85 Kings Head Pub
- 86 Ritz Restaurant

OTHER
- 1 Rainbow Cyber Cafe
- 3 25 January Hotel
- 6 Service Taxi Station
- 7 General Hospital
- 8 Luxor Museum
- 11 Bank of Alexandria
- 14 Banque Masr
- 16 Taxis & Donkeys to West Bank Monuments
- 17 Central Telephone Office
- 21 Mummification Museum
- 22 Brooke Hospital for Animals
- 23 Aboudi Internet Cafe
- 24 Police
- 29 Rainbow Internet
- 31 Egypt Exchange
- 33 Entrance to Luxor Temple
- 34 Luxor Temple
- 35 Mosque of Abu al-Haggag
- 36 Bus Station
- 38 Bakery
- 40 Hani w'Hanafon Cassette Shop
- 41 Main Post Office
- 43 Taxis
- 48 Al-Ahram Beverages
- 49 Mahal Hosny & Refat
- 50 Fuel Station
- 56 Bakery
- 58 Tourist Bazaar (Tourist Police, Tourist Office, Aboudi Bookshop & Internet Cafe, Marhaba Restaurant & Post Office)
- 61 National Bank of Egypt (ATM)
- 66 Banque Misr (ATM)
- 75 Mantel Computer & Internet
- 78 Barghouti
- 79 Omar
- 83 Al-Azhar Internet Cafe
- 87 Passport Office
- 88 Mandaria Nightclub

Email & Internet Access

Internet cafes spring up almost daily in Luxor and you can find them everywhere, including in many hotels. The following are some of the best:

Aboudi (☎ 327 390) Corniche el-Nil; (☎ 365 419) Sharia Karnak. These two Internet cafes have fast modems and air-con rooms. Both are open from 9am to 10pm. An hour costs E£12 and the minimum is 15 minutes (E£3).

Al-Azhar Internet Cafe (☎ 380 595) Sharia St Joseph. This quiet cafe, with six new computers and air-con, is convenient for people staying on Sharia Khaled Ibn al-Walid. Access costs E£10 per hour; it's open from 9am to 11pm.

Mantel Computer & Internet (☎ 374 015). This place is just off Sharia Medina al-Manawara; access costs E£10 per hour or E£3 for 15 minutes. It's open from 8.30am to 1am.

Rainbow Cyber Cafe (☎ 377 800) Officer's Club, Corniche el-Nil. Rainbow has two terminals; it's convenient if you're strolling at the northern end of the Corniche. Access costs E£12 per hour; it's open from 9am to 10pm.

Rainbow Internet (☎ 378 983) Sharia Yousef Hassan. This is Luxor's first Internet service provider, with seven terminals and fast connections in an air-con room. It's open from 9am to 11pm daily. An hour costs only E£6 and the minimum is 15 minutes for E£1.50. If you are staying in Luxor some time and want to open your own account, a month's service will cost you E£105; three months E£395.

The following are next door to each other on the West Bank:

Internet Business Centre (☎ 311 205). This is the slightly cheaper place of the two, charging E£12 per hour, E£3 for 15 minutes. It's open from 8.30am to midnight daily.

Osman International Phone Line (☎ 310 110). Close to the ferry landing in Gezira, Osman charges E£16 per hour and is open from 8am to midnight daily. It also has a photocopier and printer.

Bookshops

Luxor has the best English-language bookshops outside Cairo. Aboudi Bookshop (☎ 372 390), in the Tourist Bazaar near the tourist office, has an excellent selection of guidebooks, maps, postcards and fiction, including a good stock of second-hand novels. A few doors down towards the Old Winter Palace Hotel, AA Gaddis has a smaller, but still extensive, selection of books on Egypt. The larger hotels, such as the Mercure and the Sheraton also have bookshops, although their prices are often high. There are newsstands that stock reasonably up-to-date foreign newspapers in front of Aboudi Bookshop and outside the Old Winter Palace.

Medical Services & Emergencies

Luxor has few decent medical services, so you are limited to the General Hospital (☎ 372 025, 382 698) reserved for emergencies only. There is an ambulance service (☎ 123), but don't expect a speedy response.

The police station (☎ 372 350) is behind Luxor Temple.

LUXOR MUSEUM

This great little museum *(☎ 380 269, Corniche el-Nil; admission E£30; open 9am-1pm & 4pm-9pm Oct-Apr, 9am-1pm & 5pm-10pm May-Sept)* about halfway between the Luxor and Karnak Temples, has a small but well-chosen collection of relics from the end of the Old Kingdom right through to the Mamluk period, but mostly gathered from the Theban temples and necropolis. The displays, which include pottery, jewellery, furniture, statues and stelae, were arranged by the Brooklyn Museum of New York.

On either side as you enter the museum are two pieces from the reign of Tutankhamun's grandfather Amenhotep III (1390–1352 BC); to the left is a vividly coloured tomb painting (exhibit No 101) showing the seated pharaoh holding the crook, flail and mace while being fanned by two great ostrich feathers; and to the right, a huge granite head of the same pharaoh (No 126), one of numerous large statues from his funerary temple that lay behind the Colossi of Memnon. Beyond this is displayed a black-and-gold wooden head of the cow deity Mehit-Weret, an aspect of the goddess Hathor, which was found in Tutankhamun's tomb.

Beyond, in the 1st floor gallery, are two outstanding pieces among the museum's fine collection: exhibit No 61, a finely carved statue of Tuthmosis III (1479–1425 BC) from the Karnak temples and an alabaster group figure of Amenhotep III protected by the great crocodile god Sobek (No 107), found at the site of Sobek's temple at Dahamsah in 1967 at the bottom of a canal.

Moving up via the ramp to the 2nd floor, you come face to face with a seated granite figure of the legendary scribe Amenhotep (No 117), son of Hapu, the great official eventually deified in Ptolemaic times and who, as overseer of all the pharaoh's works under Amenhotep III, was responsible for many of ancient Thebes' greatest buildings.

One of the most interesting exhibits is the Wall of Akhenaten, a series of small sandstone blocks *(talatat)* that once made up part of Amenhotep IV's contribution to the temple complex at Karnak before he changed his name to Akhenaten and abandoned Thebes for Tell al-Amarna. After his death his buildings were demolished and these blocks were used to fill the inside of Karnak's ninth pylon, which is where they were found in the late 1960s. Now reassembled, they show Akhenaten, his wife Nefertiti and scenes of temple life. The museum also houses two fragmentary colossi of Akhenaten (Nos 156 and 171), also found at Karnak.

Further highlights on the 2nd floor are more treasures from Tutankhamun's tomb, including *shabti* (servant) figures, model boats, sandals, arrows and a series of gold rosettes from his funeral pall.

On the left, just before the exit, is the entrance to a relatively new hall, which contains 16 of 24 statues that were uncovered in Luxor Temple in 1989. The focus of this particular collection is an almost pristine quartzite statue of Amenhotep III, wearing a rather fetching pleated kilt.

MUMMIFICATION MUSEUM

This small museum *(☎ 381 501, Corniche el-Nil; admission E£20; open 9am-1pm & 4pm-9pm Oct-Apr, 9am-1pm & 5pm-10pm May-Sept)* housed in the former visitors centre on Luxor's Corniche, opposite the Mina Palace Hotel, has well-presented displays that tell you everything you ever wanted to know about mummies and mummification (although the explanations of the process itself could be a little more detailed). The well-preserved mummy of a 21st-dynasty official, Maserharti, as well as a host of mummified animals are on display; it would be fitting if some more of Luxor's ancient inhabitants could be brought back from their current home in Cairo's Egyptian Museum. In addition to the desiccated bodies there are exhibits showing the tools and materials used in the mummification process – check out the small, but particularly gruesome, spoon and metal spatula that were used for scraping the brain out of the skull. A number of artefacts that were crucial to the mummy's journey to the afterlife have also been included, as well as some picturesque painted coffins. Presiding over the entrance is a beautiful little statue of the jackal god, Anubis, who was considered to be the inventor of the mummification process.

LUXOR TEMPLE

Built by the New Kingdom pharaoh Amenhotep III (1390–1352 BC), this temple *(Corniche el-Nil; admission E£20; open 6am-9pm Oct-Apr, 6am-10pm May-Sept)* is a strikingly graceful piece of architecture on the banks of the Nile. Visit during the day but return at night when the temperature is lower and the temple is lit up, creating an eerie spectacle as shadow and light play off the reliefs and many structures.

The temple sits on the site of an older sanctuary built by Hatshepsut and dedicated to the Theban triad of Amun, Mut and Khons. Amun, one of the gods of creation, was the most important god of Thebes. As Amun-Ra, the fusion of Amun and the sun god Ra, he was also a state deity worshipped in many parts of the country. Once a year, from his temple at Karnak, the images of Amun and the other two gods in the triad – Amun's wife, the war goddess Mut, and their son, the moon god Khons – would journey up the Nile to Luxor Temple for the Opet

Making Mummies

Although the practice of preserving dead bodies can be found in cultures across the world, the Egyptians were the ultimate practitioners of this highly complex procedure that they refined over a period of almost 4000 years. Their preservation of the dead can be traced back to the very earliest times, when bodies were simply buried in the desert away from the limited areas of cultivation. In direct contact with the sand that covered them, the hot, dry conditions allowed the body fluids to drain away while preserving the skin, hair and nails intact. Accidentally uncovering such bodies must have had a profound effect upon those able to recognise people who had died sometimes years before, quite literally witnesses to eternal life in action.

As burial practices for the elite became more sophisticated, people who would once have been buried in a hole in the ground demanded purpose-built tombs befitting their status; however, this meant that instead of drying out in the sand, bodies rapidly decomposed. An artificial means of preserving the body was therefore required, and so began the long process of experimentation, with a good deal of trial and error. It wasn't until around 2600 BC that they finally cracked it, and began to remove the internal organs where putrefaction actually begins.

As the process became increasingly elaborate, all the organs were removed except the kidneys, which were hard to reach, and the heart. The heart was considered the source of intelligence rather than the brain, which in turn was removed by inserting a metal probe up the nose and whisking to reduce it to a liquid that could be easily drained away. All the rest – lungs, liver, stomach, intestines – were removed through an opening cut in the left flank.

The hollow body and its separate organs were then covered over with piles of natron salt and left to dry out for 40 days, after which they were all washed, purified and anointed with a range of oils, spices and resins. All were then wrapped in layers of linen, with the appropriate amulets set in place over the various parts of the body as priests recited the incantations needed to activate the protective functions of the amulets.

With each of the internal organs placed inside its own burial container (one of four Canopic jars), the wrapped body complete with its funerary mask was placed inside its coffin. It was then ready for the funeral procession to the tomb, where the vital 'Opening of the Mouth' ceremony reanimated the soul and restored its senses; offerings were given, while wishing the dead 'a thousand of every good and pure thing for your soul and all kinds of offerings on which the gods live'.

The ancient Egyptians also used their mummification skills to preserve animals, both as a means of preserving the bodies of much-loved pets to the far more widespread practice of mummifying animals to present as votive offerings to the gods with which they were associated. The Egyptians mummified everything from huge bulls to tiny shrews, with cats, hawks and ibis mummified in their millions by Graeco-Roman times, and recent research revealing that such creatures were killed to order.

Dr Joann Fletcher

Festival, during which the pharaoh 'met' with Amun in order to restore his own divine powers and reinvigorate himself – almost as if syphoning off some of the god's powers.

Amenhotep greatly enlarged Hatshepsut's shrine and rededicated the massive temple as Amun's southern ipet or harem, the private quarters of the god. The structure was further added to over the centuries by Tutankhamun, Ramses II, Alexander the Great and various Romans. The Romans constructed a military fort around the temple that the Arabs later called Al-Uqsur, 'The Palaces', giving modern Luxor its name. At one point the Arabs built a mosque in one of the interior courts, and there was also once a village within the temple walls. Excavation work has been going on since 1885, and has included removing the village and clearing the forecourt and first pylon of debris, and exposing part of the avenue of sphinxes leading to Karnak.

Walking Tour

The ticket office is on the Corniche and a path leads from it to the entrance of the temple complex. From here you proceed along a path that was once part of an **avenue of sphinxes** that ran all the way to the temples at Karnak 3km to the north. You find yourself standing before the enormous **first pylon** raised by Ramses II (1279–1213 BC) and decorated with his military exploits, including the Battle of Kadesh. In front of this 24m-high wall are some colossal **statues of Ramses II** and a pink granite **obelisk**. There were originally six statues, four seated and two standing, but only two of the seated figures and the westernmost standing one remain. The obelisk, too, was one of a pair; its towering counterpart now stands in the Place de la Concorde in Paris.

Beyond the pylon is another Ramses II addition to the main complex in the form of his **great court**. This is surrounded by a double row of columns with lotus-bud capitals, more reliefs of his deeds of derring-do and several huge statues. In the western corner of the court is the earlier triple-barque shrine built by Hatshepsut and her successor Tuthmosis III for Amun, Mut and

LUXOR TEMPLE

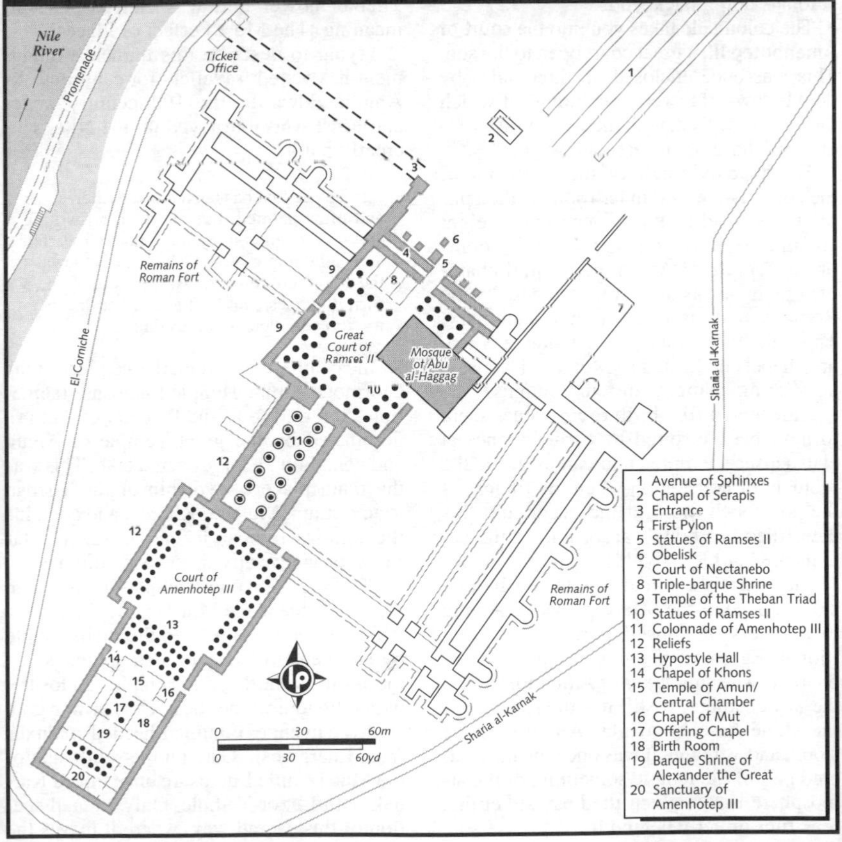

Khons when the gods' statues were brought from Karnak during the annual Opet Festival. On the south-east side is the 13th-century **Mosque of Abu al-Haggag**, dedicated to a local sheikh and holy man.

Beyond the court, 14 papyrus columns form the **colonnade of Amenhotep III**. The walls behind the splendid columns were decorated during the reign of the young pharaoh Tutankhamun and celebrate the return to Theban orthodoxy following the wayward reign of the previous pharaoh, Akhenaten. The Opet Festival is depicted in lively detail, with the pharaoh, nobility and common people joining the triumphal procession. Look out for the drummers and acrobats doing backbends.

The colonnade takes you into the **court of Amenhotep III**, a great court open to the sun. This was once enclosed on three sides by double rows of towering columns, of which the best preserved, with their architraves extant, are those on the east and west sides.

The **hypostyle hall**, on the south side of the court, is the first inner room of the temple proper and features four rows of eight columns each. Beyond are the main rooms of the **Temple of Amun**, the central chamber of which was once stuccoed over by the Romans and used as a cult sanctuary. Through this chamber, either side of which are chapels dedicated to Mut and Khons, is an **offering chapel** with four columns.

Amenhotep III's **birth room** scenes seem to have been inspired by earlier scenes at Hatshepsut's temple. You can even see the moment of conception when the fingers of the god touch those of the queen and 'his dew filled her body', according to the accompanying hieroglyphic caption.

Alexander the Great rebuilt the **barque shrine**, beyond the offering chapel, adding to it reliefs of himself portrayed in traditional Egyptian regalia in his role as pharaoh. The **sanctuary of Amenhotep III** is the last chamber; it still has the remains of the stone base on which Amun's statue stood, and although it was once the most sacred part of the temple something of the atmosphere is lost given the busy street that now runs directly behind it.

TEMPLES OF KARNAK

Karnak *(Sharia Karnak; admission E£20; open 6am-5.30pm Oct-Apr, 6am-6pm May-Sept)* is more than a temple, it is a spectacular complex of sanctuaries, kiosks, pylons and obelisks, all dedicated to the Theban gods and to the greater glory of Egypt's pharaohs. Everything here is on a gigantic scale – the site measures about 1.5km by 800m, large enough to contain about 10 cathedrals, while the first pylon is twice the size of the one at Luxor Temple. Built, added to, dismantled, restored, enlarged and decorated over a period of nearly 1500 years, Karnak was the most important place of worship in all Egypt during the height of Theban power and was called Ipet-Isut, meaning 'The Most Perfect of Places'.

Trying to describe this immense monument has vexed travellers for centuries. As Amelia Edwards, the 19th-century writer and artist who journeyed up the Nile, succinctly put it:

> It is a place that has been much written about and often painted; but of which no writing and no art can convey more than a dwarfed and pallid impression…The scale is too vast; the effect too tremendous; the sense of one's own dumbness, and littleness, and incapacity, too complete and crushing.

At the centre of this remarkable place is the enormous Amun Temple Enclosure (sometimes referred to as the Precinct of Amun), dominated by the great Temple of Amun and containing a large sacred lake. This was the main place of worship of the Theban triad (Amun, Mut and Khons), and contains the famous hypostyle hall, a spectacular forest of giant papyrus-shaped columns.

Flanking the Amun Temple Enclosure on the south side is the Mut Temple Enclosure, which was once linked to the main temple by an avenue of ram-headed sphinxes. To the north is the Montu Temple Enclosure, which honoured the local Theban war god. A paved avenue of human-headed sphinxes from Euergetes's Gate on the south side of the Mut Temple Enclosure once linked Karnak with Luxor Temple. Only a small section of this sacred way, where it leaves the great Temple of Amun and enters the forecourt of his Southern Harem, has been excavated. The rest of the 3km avenue lies beneath the town and paved roads of modern Luxor – bits of it are visible in places among the modern buildings.

Although the original sanctuary of the great Temple of Amun was built during the Middle Kingdom period, when the Theban pharaohs first came to prominence, the rest of the temples, pylons, courts, columns and reliefs were the work of New Kingdom rulers and their successors. The further into the complex you venture the further back in time you go.

The oldest parts of the complex are the White Pavilion of Sesostris I and the 12th-dynasty foundations of what became the most sacred part of the great Temple of Amun, the sacred barque sanctuary and central court of Amun (behind the sixth pylon). The limestone fragments of the demolished pavilion, or chapel, were recovered from the foundations of the third pylon, built five centuries after Sesostris's reign, and expertly reconstructed in the open-air museum to the north of the great court.

The major additions to the complex were constructed by pharaohs of the 18th to 20th dynasties, between 1570 and 1090 BC. The pharaohs of the later dynasties extended and rebuilt the complex, and the Ptolemies and early Christians also left their mark on it.

Wandering through this gigantic complex is one of the highlights of any visit to Egypt and it demands more than one visit if you want to make sense of the sometimes overwhelming jumble of ancient remains. Apart from its sheer size, the fact that almost every pharaoh left his (or her) mark here means that if you take the time you get a crash course in the evolution of ancient Egyptian artistic and architectural styles.

Amun Temple Enclosure – Main Axis

From the entrance you pass down the processional avenue of ram-headed sphinxes that originally flanked a canal connecting the temple to the Nile; this opened out into a rectangular dock that now lies beneath the present-day wooden entrance bridge. These lead to the massive unfinished **first pylon**, most likely built by Nectanebo I of the 30th dynasty. You used to be able to climb the stairs on your left to the top of the pylon's north tower, from where there is an amazing view of Karnak and the surrounding country but the stairs were closed off after a tourist fell from it and died.

Great Court You emerge from the first pylon into the Great Court, the largest area of the Karnak complex. To the left is the **Temple of Seti II**, dedicated to the Theban triad. The three small chapels held the sacred barques of Mut, Amun and Khons during the lead-up to the Opet Festival.

The north and south walls of the court are lined with columns with papyrus-bud capitals. The south wall is intersected by the **Temple of Ramses III**, a glorified trio of barque shrines or chapels for the Theban triad built in the form of a miniature temple. Obligatory scenes of the pharaoh as glorious conqueror adorn the pylon of this 60m-long temple that also features an open court, a vestibule with four columns, a hypostyle hall of eight columns and three barque chapels.

In the centre of the Great Court is the one remaining column of the **Kiosk of Taharqa**. A 25th-dynasty Nubian pharaoh, Taharqa built this open-sided pavilion of 10 columns, each rising 21m and topped with papyrus-form capitals. Only one of the columns remains, together with an alabaster altar.

The **second pylon** was originally built by Horemheb, an 18th-dynasty general who later became the last pharaoh of his dynasty. Ramses I and II added their names and deeds to the pylon above that of Horemheb. Ramses II also raised two colossal pink granite statues of himself on either side of the entrance.

Great Hypostyle Hall Beyond the second pylon is the awesome great hypostyle hall. It was built by Seti I, who decorated the northern half in delicate raised relief. Ramses II added the rest of the (sunken) relief work. Covering an area of 6000 sq metres (which is large enough to contain both

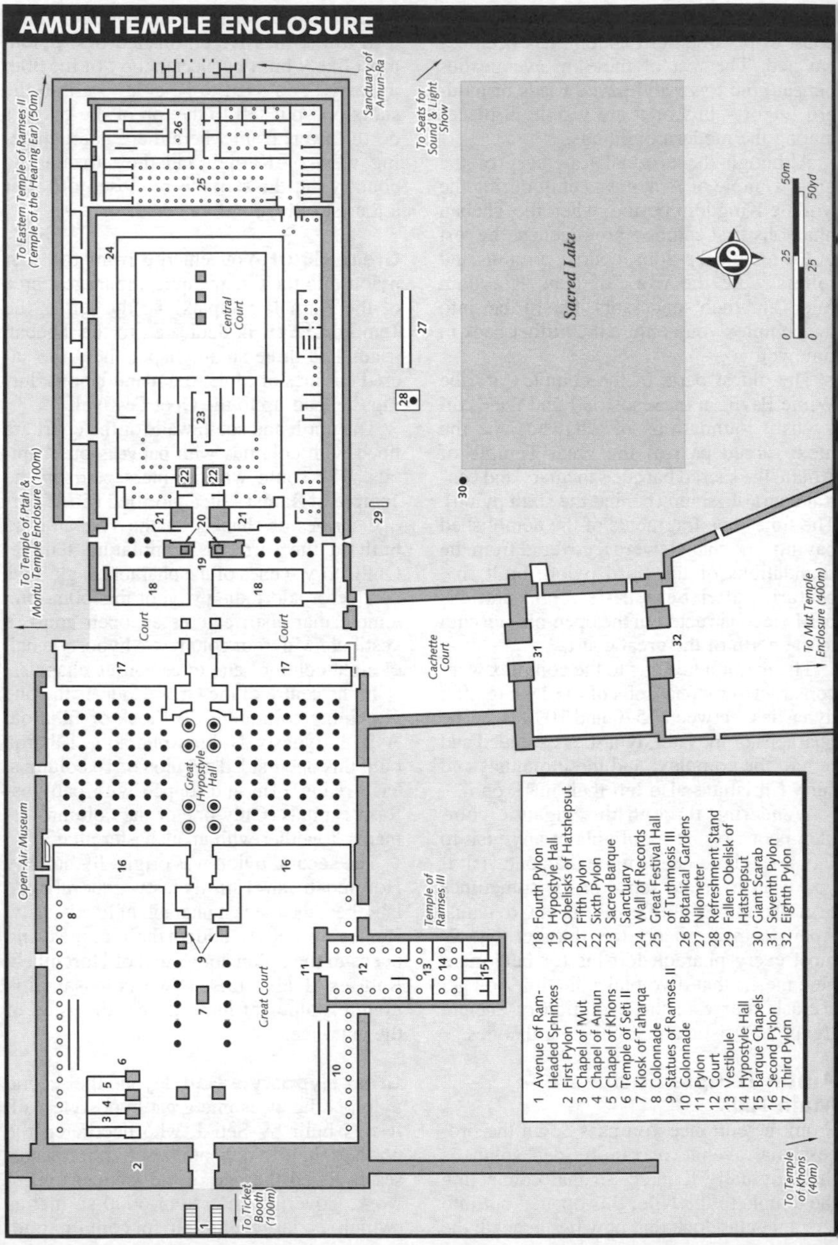
AMUN TEMPLE ENCLOSURE
To Eastern Temple of Ramses II (Temple of the Hearing Ear) (50m)
Sanctuary of Amun-Ra
To Seats for Sound & Light Show
To Temple of Ptah & Montu Temple Enclosure (100m)
Open-Air Museum
Great Court
Great Hypostyle Hall
Court
Central Court
Cachette Court
Temple of Ramses III
Sacred Lake
To Ticket Booth (100m)
To Mut Temple Enclosure (400m)
To Temple of Khons (40m)
0 25 50m
0 25 50yd
1 Avenue of Ram-Headed Sphinxes
2 First Pylon
3 Chapel of Mut
4 Chapel of Amun
5 Chapel of Khons
6 Temple of Seti II
7 Kiosk of Taharqa
8 Colonnade
9 Statues of Ramses II
10 Colonnade
11 Pylon
12 Court
13 Vestibule
14 Hypostyle Hall
15 Barque Chapels
16 Second Pylon
17 Third Pylon
18 Fourth Pylon
19 Hypostyle Hall
20 Obelisks of Hatshepsut
21 Fifth Pylon
22 Sixth Pylon
23 Sacred Barque Sanctuary
24 Wall of Records
25 Great Festival Hall of Tuthmosis III
26 Botanical Gardens
27 Nilometer
28 Refreshment Stand
29 Fallen Obelisk of Hatshepsut
30 Giant Scarab
31 Seventh Pylon
32 Eighth Pylon

St Peter's in Rome and London's St Paul's Cathedral), the hall is an unforgettable forest of 134 towering papyrus-shaped stone pillars. In its original form the whole would have been brightly painted and roofed, making it pretty dark. It is impossible to get an overall idea of this court; there is nothing to do but stand and stare up at the dizzying spectacle.

Between the **third pylon**, built by Amenhotep III, and the **fourth pylon**, raised by Tuthmosis I, is a narrow court. Tuthmosis I raised a pair of obelisks, and Tuthmosis III later raised another pair of obelisks in front of the fourth pylon, which was, during each of their reigns, the entrance to the temple proper. Only one of the four is still standing, but parts of the others lie in the court.

The Inner Temple Beyond the fourth pylon is the oldest preserved part of the complex, its 14 columns suggesting that it was originally a small hypostyle hall. It was constructed by Tuthmosis III in his attempt to eradicate or hide all signs of the reign of Hatshepsut, who was appointed regent when Tuthmosis III's father died (Tuthmosis III was too young to rule), and who later had herself appointed as pharaoh. In this hall, around the two magnificent **obelisks of Hatshepsut**, Tuthmosis III built a 25m-high sandstone structure. The upper shaft of one of the obelisks, which Hatshepsut raised to the glory of her 'father' Amun, lies on the ground by the sacred lake; the other obelisk still stands, reclaimed from the sandstone, in front of the fifth pylon. It is the tallest obelisk in Egypt, standing 29.2m high, and the tip was originally covered in electrum (a commonly used alloy of gold and silver).

The **fifth pylon** was constructed by Tuthmosis I, with little space between it and the now ruined sixth pylon (built at a later date). The latter, the smallest pylon at Karnak, was raised by Tuthmosis III, who is also responsible for the two pink granite columns in the vestibule beyond on which the emblems of Egypt are carved in high relief – the water lily of Upper Egypt on the north pillar and the papyrus flower of Lower Egypt on the south pillar. Nearby are two huge statues of Amun and his female counterpart Amunet, which date from the reign of Tutankhamun.

The original **sacred barque sanctuary** of Tuthmosis III was replaced by a granite one, which was built by Alexander the Great (332–323 BC); its well-preserved painted relief scenes were undertaken by his successor and half-brother Philip Arrhidaeus (323–317 BC).

Tuthmosis III's reputation as a great hero and empire builder is set in stone in the relief work on what is known as the **Wall of Records** on the north side of the central court. Though unrelenting in his bid for power, he had a penchant for being fairly just in his treatment of the people he conquered. This wall was a running tally of the organised tribute he exacted in honour of Amun from his subjugated lands.

Great Festival Hall of Tuthmosis III Tuthmosis' festival hall is an unusual structure with its uniquely carved stone columns imitating tent poles, perhaps a reference to the pharaoh's life under canvas on his frequent military expeditions abroad. A further reference to his foreign travels is the columned vestibule that lies beyond, generally referred to as the Botanical Gardens on account of the relief scenes of strange flora and fauna that 'his majesty encountered in the lands of Syria and Palestine' and brought back with him to Egypt.

For the many people not allowed inside the temple's sacred enclosure, Tuthmosis III also built a small **chapel** attached to the back of the temple wall behind his festival hall, at either side of which can be seen the enormous bases for two more of Hatshepsut's obelisks that once stood here. Beyond this, even further to the south-east, Ramses II built a similar chapel, the **Temple of the Hearing Ear**, again with a base for a single obelisk standing 32.2m tall and which Ramses usurped from Tuthmosis III. Removed from Karnak on the orders of the Emperor Constantine (AD 306–337) and bound for Constantinople, the obelisk was redirected to Rome to stand in the Circus Maximus; it was re-erected in 1588 on the orders of

Pope Sixtus V where it now stands, in front of the church of St John (Giovanni) Lateran.

Against the northern enclosure wall of the Amun Temple Enclosure is the cult **Temple of Ptah**, started by Tuthmosis III and finished by the Ptolemies and Romans. Access to the inner chambers is through a series of five doorways, which lead you to two of the temple's original statues. The headless figure of Ptah, the creator god of Memphis, is in the middle chapel behind a locked door – the custodian will unlock it for the usual remittance. To his left is the eerily beautiful black granite statue of his goddess-wife Sekhmet (the spreader of terror), bare-breasted and lioness-headed.

Amun Temple Enclosure – Southern Axis

The secondary axis of the Amun Temple Enclosure runs south from the third and fourth pylons. It is basically a processional way, bounded on the east and west sides by walls, and sectioned off by a number of pylons that create a series of courts. Just before the **seventh pylon**, built by Tuthmosis III, is the **cachette court**, so named because of the thousands of stone and bronze statues discovered there during excavation work in 1903. Seven of the statues, of Middle Kingdom pharaohs, stand in front of the pylon. Nearby are the remains of two colossal statues of Tuthmosis III.

The well-preserved **eighth pylon**, built by Queen Hatshepsut, is the oldest part of the north-south axis of the temple. Four of the original six colossi are still standing, the most complete being the one of Amenhotep I.

The **ninth** and **tenth pylons** were built by Horemheb, who used some of the stones of a demolished temple that had been built to the east by Akhenaten (before he decamped to Tell al-Amarna), now recovered, reassembled and displayed in Luxor Museum.

To the east of the seventh and eighth pylons is the **sacred lake**, where, according to Herodotus, the priesthood of Amun bathed twice a day and twice a night for ritual purity. On the north-west side of the lake is the top half of **Hatshepsut's fallen obelisk**, and a huge **stone statue of a scarab beetle** dedicated by Amenhotep III to Aten, the disc of the rising sun. Tour guides tell visitors to walk around the scarab – once for good luck, three times for marriage and seven times for a first child.

There are the ruins of about 20 other chapels within the main enclosure. In a fairly good state of repair in the south-west corner is the **Temple of Khons**, god of the moon, and son of Amun and Mut. The pylon faces Euergetes's Gate and the avenue of sphinxes leading to Luxor Temple, and provides access to a small hypostyle hall and ruined sanctuary. The temple was started by Ramses III, and added to by other Ramessids and later the Ptolemies.

Mut Temple Enclosure

From the 10th pylon an avenue of sphinxes leads to the partly excavated southern enclosure – the Precinct of Mut. The badly ruined Temple of Mut was built by Amenhotep III and consists of a sanctuary, a hypostyle hall and two courts. Amenhotep also set up an enormous number of black granite statues of the lioness goddess Sekhmet, Mut's northern counterpart. There were more than 700 of these statues and it has been suggested that they formed some sort of calendar, with two for every day of the year, receiving offerings each morning and evening.

Montu Temple Enclosure

A gate, usually locked, on the wall near the Temple of Ptah (in the Amun Temple Enclosure) leads to the Montu Temple Enclosure. Montu, the falcon-headed warrior god, was one of the original deities of Thebes. The main temple was built by Amenhotep III and modified by others. The complex is very dilapidated.

Open-Air Museum

Just before the second pylon, off to the left, is an open-air museum *(admission E£10, open 6am-5.30pm daily)* that contains a collection of statuary found throughout the temple complex. The ticket has to be purchased at the main Karnak ticket kiosk.

Sound-and-Light Show

Karnak's sound-and-light show is a 1½-hour, Hollywood-style extravaganza that recounts the history of Thebes and the lives of the many pharaohs who built sanctuaries, courts, statues or obelisks here in honour of Amun. The show starts at the avenue of ram-headed sphinxes, passes through the first pylon to the great court and on through the great hypostyle hall to the grandstand at the sacred lake for the show's finale. The overly dramatic text and booming music veer into kitsch for much of the show but it is almost worth the E£33 (no student discount) just for a specially lit night-time walk through the temple.

There are three or four performances each night, with sessions starting at 6.30pm, 7.50pm, 9.05pm and 10.20pm; or about one hour later in summer (May to September). The following schedule was correct at the time of writing but check at the tourist office, or at W www.sound-light.egypt.com or call ☎ 372 241, 371 228.

day	show 1	show 2	show 3	show 4
Mon	English	French	Spanish	–
Tues	Japanese	English	German	Arabic
Wed	German	English	French	German
Thur	English	French	Italian	Arabic
Fri	French	English	Spanish	–
Sat	French	English	Italian	–
Sun	German	English	French	–

Getting There & Away

To get to Karnak you can take a microbus from Luxor station or from behind Luxor Temple for 50pt, or you can hire a *hantour* (horse-drawn carriage) for around E£10. Give the driver baksheesh if you want him to wait. It's a quick bicycle ride to the temple or you can easily walk.

WEST BANK

Arriving on the West Bank of Luxor you meet with one of the most striking vistas in Egypt. As you pass through the lush green fields, desert mountains dotted with brightly coloured houses loom ahead. When you get closer you begin to make out gaping black holes among the houses and giant sandstone forms on the edge of the cultivation below. These are the tombs and temples of the necropolis of ancient Thebes, where magnificent monuments were raised to honour the cults of pharaohs entombed in the nearby cliffs. This is also where queens, royal children, nobles, priests, artisans and even workers built tombs that ranged in the quality of their design and decor from the spectacular to the ordinary.

From the New Kingdom onwards, the necropolis also supported a large living population. In an attempt to protect the valuable tombs from robbers, the artisans, labourers, temple priests and guards devoted their lives to the construction and maintenance of this city of the dead. They perfected the techniques of tomb building, decoration and concealment, and passed the secrets down through their families.

The desire for secrecy greatly affected tomb design. Instead of a single funerary monument such as a pyramid, which was both a venue to worship the immortal pharaoh and the resting place of his mummified remains, the New Kingdom Theban rulers commissioned their funerary monuments in pairs.

Magnificent funerary temples were built on the plains, where the illusion of the pharaoh's immortality could be perpetuated by the devotions of his priests and subjects, while the pharaoh's body and worldly wealth were laid in splendidly decorated secret tombs excavated in the hills. The prime location for the latter was an isolated canyon to the north-west, surrounded on three sides by high rugged cliffs.

However, although there was only one way into the Valley of the Kings and the tombs were well hidden, very few escaped the vandalism of the grave robbers.

Nowadays, ancient and modern coexist on the West Bank of Luxor, with several thriving communities built among the ancient ruins. The most famous of these is the colourful village of Gurna, which has existed here for hundreds of years and whose residents, some claim, continued the practice of grave robbing until well into the 20th century.

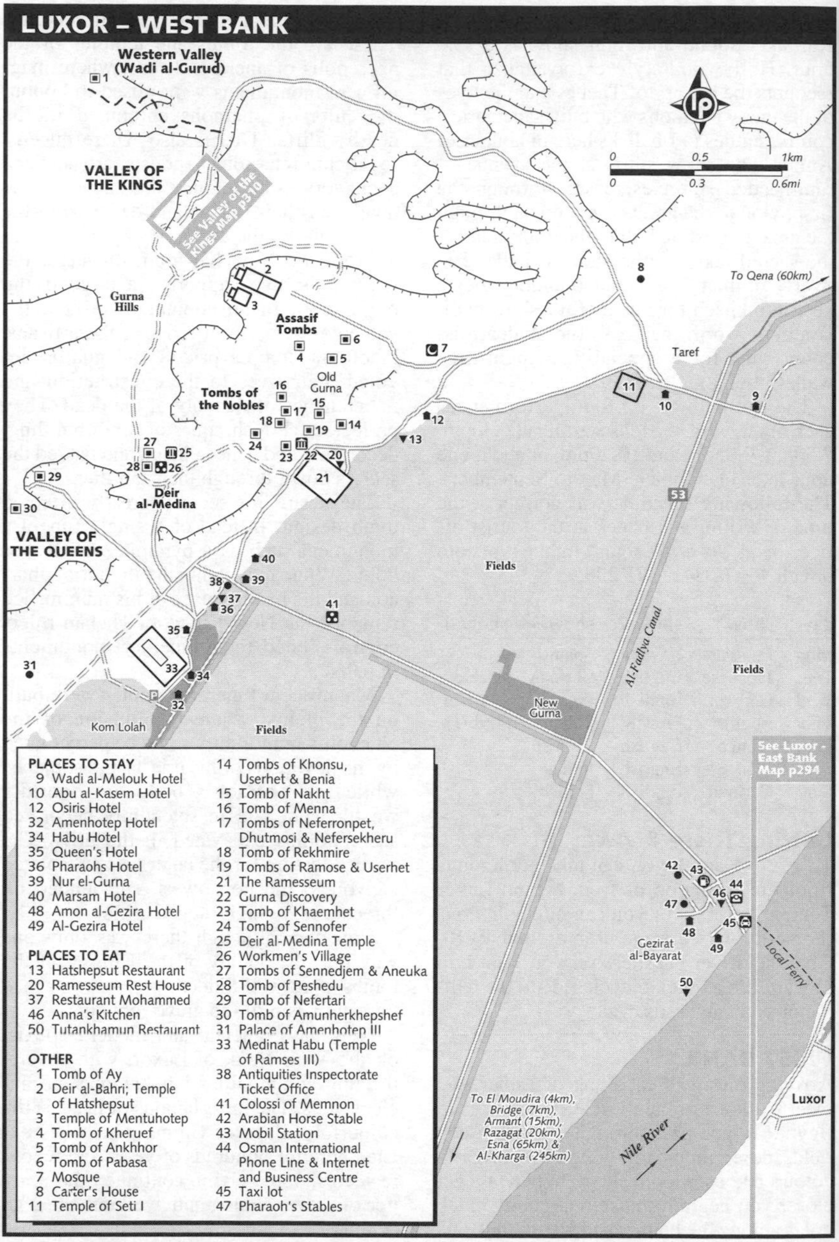
LUXOR – WEST BANK
Western Valley (Wadi al-Gurud)
VALLEY OF THE KINGS
See Valley of the Kings Map p310
Gurna Hills
Assasif Tombs
Old Gurna
Tombs of the Nobles
Deir al-Medina
VALLEY OF THE QUEENS
Taref
To Qena (60km)
0 0.5 1km
0 0.3 0.6mi
53
Fields
Al-Fadhya Canal
New Gurna
Kom Lolah
Fields
Fields
See Luxor - East Bank Map p294
Gezirat al-Bayarat
Local Ferry
Luxor
Nile River
To El Moudira (4km), Bridge (7km), Armant (15km), Razagat (20km), Esna (65km) & Al-Kharga (245km)
PLACES TO STAY
9 Wadi al-Melouk Hotel
10 Abu al-Kasem Hotel
12 Osiris Hotel
32 Amenhotep Hotel
34 Habu Hotel
35 Queen's Hotel
36 Pharaohs Hotel
39 Nur el-Gurna
40 Marsam Hotel
48 Amon al-Gezira Hotel
49 Al-Gezira Hotel
PLACES TO EAT
13 Hatshepsut Restaurant
20 Ramesseum Rest House
37 Restaurant Mohammed
46 Anna's Kitchen
50 Tutankhamun Restaurant
OTHER
1 Tomb of Ay
2 Deir al-Bahri; Temple of Hatshepsut
3 Temple of Mentuhotep
4 Tomb of Kheruef
5 Tomb of Ankhhor
6 Tomb of Pabasa
7 Mosque
8 Carter's House
11 Temple of Seti I
14 Tombs of Khonsu, Userhet & Benia
15 Tomb of Nakht
16 Tomb of Menna
17 Tombs of Neferronpet, Dhutmosi & Nefersekheru
18 Tomb of Rekhmire
19 Tombs of Ramose & Userhet
21 The Ramesseum
22 Gurna Discovery
23 Tomb of Khaemhet
24 Tomb of Sennofer
25 Deir al-Medina Temple
26 Workmen's Village
27 Tombs of Sennedjem & Aneuka
28 Tomb of Peshedu
29 Tomb of Nefertari
30 Tomb of Amunherkhepshef
31 Palace of Amenhotep III
33 Medinat Habu (Temple of Ramses III)
38 Antiquities Inspectorate Ticket Office
41 Colossi of Memnon
42 Arabian Horse Stable
43 Mobil Station
44 Osman International Phone Line & Internet and Business Centre
45 Taxi lot
47 Pharaoh's Stables

Getting There & Around

Most tourists cross to the West Bank on Luxor's controversial bridge, some 7km south of town. But if you want to cross the river by boat (still the quickest way to go), you have the choice of either the baladi ferry, or one of the small motor launches (called *lunches* locally) that moor all along the banks of the Nile. The baladi ferry costs E£1 for foreigners (10pt for locals) and leaves from a dock in front of Luxor Temple. Launches leave from wherever they can find customers and will take you across for E£5 or for E£1 per person if there are more than five in your group.

The advantage of the launches is that you can go immediately, rather than wait for an indeterminate period of time; on the other hand, sitting among the villagers on the ferry is a far more interesting experience.

Once you arrive on the West Bank, you have to walk up the hill to the new taxi lot, where you will be greeted by a cacophony of voices calling out the destinations of pick-up truck taxis. If you listen for Gurna you'll be on the right road to the ticket office (25pt). Lots of service taxis run back and forth between the villages, so you can always flag one down and find your way to one of the sites, although you might have to walk from the main road to the entrance.

Alternatively, if you haven't already been nabbed by the brother, cousin or friend of a taxi driver on the boat, you can also find Peugeot taxis at the ferry landing, but be prepared to bargain hard. If you want to rent one for the day, you'll be looking at anywhere between E£50 and E£100, depending on the season, the state of tourism and your bargaining skills.

If you walk up the hill from the ferry landing, you will find bicycles for rent for between E£6 and E£10, but keep in mind that you'll usually get a better deal, and a better bike, in town. Almost all of the sites on the West Bank can be seen by bicycle but it can get very hot during the day so don't push yourself. You will need plenty of water and a good hat.

Donkeys and camels with guides can be rented here – for more information, see under Donkey, Horse & Camel Rides later in this chapter.

To give you an idea of the distances involved, from the local ferry landing it is 3km straight ahead to the ticket office, past the Colossi of Memnon; 4km to the Valley of the Queens; and 8km to the Valley of the Kings.

Information

What to Bring You need to bring a torch (flashlight) and, more importantly, plenty of water because although drinks are available at some sites, they can be relatively expensive. At the noisy rest house just outside the Valley of the Kings, for instance, meals and drinks (including bottled water) are vastly overpriced.

Also, bring plenty of small change for baksheesh. Although it can be annoying when the tomb and temple guards tag along and give you explanations in broken English, remember that their salaries are pathetic and they are expected to augment their pay through tips. About 50pt will be enough to either get rid of them, or to open a door or shine a light on a particularly beautiful painting. Your other option is to destroy the ambience of the place completely by tagging along with a group in each tomb or temple.

Tickets If you wanted to see everything on offer in Thebes, you would end up spending more than US$65 on tickets (without a student card). Add to that the cost of the various sites on the East Bank and to the north and south of Luxor, and sightseeing can become prohibitively expensive for the traveller on a tight budget.

Tickets are available from the Antiquities Inspectorate ticket office, which is about 3km inland from the ferry landing. It is open from 6am to 4pm daily (until 5pm June to September). The various sites are officially open from 7am to 5pm December to February (though you can often get in from 6am) and from 6am to 7pm June to September. The exception to this is the Tomb of Nefertari, which has its own opening hours (see the Valley of the Queens later in this chapter for details).

Where First?

Because of the incredible heat and desolate mountain landscape around most of the archaeological remains, a series of early morning visits – ideally between sunrise and 1pm – is the best way to see the West Bank's many sites. Unfortunately, this is when everybody else goes and you can find yourself in a hot stuffy tomb with a busload of other tourists. Still, you'll have your afternoons free to loll beside a pool or have a siesta and you can visit Luxor and Karnak temples, or one of the museums, in the evening.

If you don't have the luxury of several days in Luxor, choosing what to miss can be difficult. If you only have one day (and a lot of energy), the best plan is to head over to the West Bank as early as possible. It is feasible to spend a couple of hours at the Valley of the Kings, have a quick visit to Deir al-Bahri and then head over to Medinat Habu. You can have a drink in one of the cafeterias before heading over to the Valley of the Queens and, if you can get a ticket, visit Nefertari's colourful tomb. Then you can head back to the East Bank for a quick look around Luxor Temple before heading to Karnak; try to arrive by 4.30pm and spend a couple of hours there before rounding off the day with the sound-and-light show.

If you've got more time, the itinerary suggested should be done over two or three days. You could add a hike over the mountain between the Valley of the Kings and Deir al-Bahri.

See the highlights at the beginning of this chapter for some more suggestions of things you could do in Luxor, time permitting.

Permits for taking photographs cost E£10 (E£5 for students) for *each* tomb, although many travellers have reported getting around this with a little baksheesh. Using a flash destroys the already deteriorating colours in the tombs and is not permitted; resist the temptation to use one.

With the exception of Tutankhamun's tomb, you cannot pay for admission at the sites, and individual tickets are required for each tomb, temple or group of sites, so you need to know exactly what you want to see before you set off. Tickets are valid only for the day of purchase and no refunds are given. They are numbered and priced (half for students) as follows:

1	Valley of the Kings (three tombs only)	E£20
2	Tomb of Tutankhamun	E£40
3	Deir al-Bahri (Temple of Hatshepsut)	E£12
4	Medinat Habu (Temple of Ramses III)	E£12
5	Ramesseum	E£12
6	Assasif Tombs (Kheruef & Ankhor)	E£12
7	Tombs of the Nobles (Menna & Nakht)	E£12
8	Tombs of the Nobles (Sennofer & Rekhmire)	E£12
9	Tombs of the Nobles (Ramose, Userhet & Khaemhet)	E£12
10	Deir al-Medina Temple & Tombs	E£12
11	Valley of the Queens (excluding Tomb of Nefertari)	E£12
12	Tomb of Nefertari	E£100
13	Temple of Seti I	E£12
14	Assasif Tombs (Tomb of Pabasa)	E£12
15	Tomb of Peshedu (Deir al-Medina)	E£10
16	Tomb of Ay (Western Valley)	E£10
17	Tombs of the Nobles (Neferronpet, Dhutmosi & Nefersekheru)	E£12
18	Tombs of the Nobles (Khonsu, Userhet & Benia)	E£12

Colossi of Memnon

The massive pair of statues known as the Colossi of Memnon are the first monuments that most tourists see when they arrive on the West Bank. Rising about 18m from the plain, the enthroned, faceless statues have kept a lonely vigil on the changing landscape, and are all that remains of what was once was the largest complex on the West Bank. Built by Amenhotep III as his funerary temple, some experts have recently worked out that it covered a larger area than Karnak. It was also filled with hundreds of statues, including the huge dyad of Amenhotep and Tiy that now dominates the central court of the Egyptian Museum in Cairo, most of which were later dragged off by other pharaohs (and many of which are in the British Museum, Turin etc). A stele, also

LUXOR

now in the Egyptian Museum, describes the temple as being built from 'white sandstone, with gold throughout, a floor covered with silver, and doors covered with electrum'.

The reason for the temple's complete disappearance is that it sat on the flood plain of the Nile and the annual inundation of water that used to occur has over the centuries eroded away almost all traces of the building.

The colossi alone have survived. They were among the great tourist attractions of Egypt during Graeco-Roman times because the Greeks believed they were actually statues of the legendary Memnon, a king of Ethiopia and son of the dawn goddess Eos, who was slain by Achilles during the Trojan War.

It was the northern statue that attracted most of the attention because each sunrise it would emit a haunting, musical sound that the Greeks believed was the voice of Memnon greeting his mother. Eos in turn would weep tears of dew for the untimely death of her beautiful son.

Actually, the phenomenon of the famous vocal statue was probably produced by the combined effect of a simple change in temperature and the fact that the upper part of the colossus was severely damaged by an earthquake in 27 BC. As the heat of the morning sun baked the dew-soaked stone, sand particles would break off and resonate inside the cracks in the structure. After a well-meaning Roman emperor repaired the statue in the 3rd century AD, Memnon's plaintive greeting to his mother was heard no more.

The colossi are just off the road, before you reach the Antiquities Inspectorate ticket office and are usually being snapped and filmed by an army of tourists – you won't miss them. There is a new archaeological project at the site, intended to open up what remains behind the colossi, so it will become a far more comprehensive place to visit than simply off the bus for a quick photo op.

Temple of Seti I

Seti I (1294–1279 BC), the second pharaoh of the 19th dynasty, continued his predecessor Horemheb's policies to restore Egypt's fortunes following the Amarna Period. His military campaigns re-established control abroad and won back much of the empire, and he undertook an ambitious building program at home, creating a superbly decorated temple at Abydos and at Thebes building Karnak's enormous hypostyle hall. He constructed a huge rock-cut tomb for himself in the Valley of the Kings, as well as this associated funerary temple, the most northerly and probably least visited of all the royal West Bank monuments.

Although the first two pylons and courts are in ruins, the temple itself is in reasonable repair and the surviving reliefs, in the hypostyle hall, chapels and sanctuary, are superbly executed and some of the finest examples of New Kingdom art. This temple, just off Sharia Wadi al-Melouk (the road to the Valley of the Kings) is seldom visited by tourists, so is well worth the effort.

Carter's House

On a barren hill, where the road from Deir al-Bahri to the Valley of the Kings meets the road from Seti's temple, there is a domed house where Howard Carter lived during his search for Tutankhamun's tomb. There is talk of turning this into a museum describing the process of finding the famous tomb but as yet nothing has come of it.

Valley of the Kings

Once called the Great Place or the Place of Truth, the canyon now known as the Valley of the Kings is at once a place of death – for nothing grows on its steep, scorching cliffs – and a majestic domain befitting the mighty pharaohs who once lay there in great stone sarcophagi, awaiting immortality.

The isolated valley, behind Deir al-Bahri, is dominated by the natural pyramid-shaped mountain peak of Al-Qurn (The Horn). It consists of two branches, the east and west valleys, with the former containing most of the royal burial sites.

In all, some 62 tombs have been excavated in the valley, although not all belong to pharaohs. Not all the tombs are open to the public and there are always a few that are closed for renovation work. Each tomb

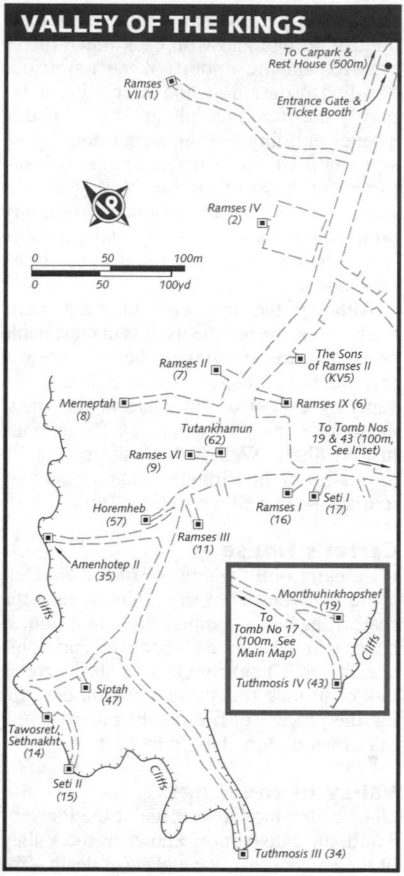

has a number that represents the order in which it was discovered. No 1 belongs to Ramses VII; it has been open since Greek and Roman times, and was mentioned in the *Description de l'Egypte*, dating from the late 18th century. No 62, Tutankhamun's famous tomb, which was discovered by Howard Carter in 1922, is the most recent.

Newly erected signs and maps make navigating the site far easier than before. Tomb plans and history have also been upgraded to help visitors understand better what they're seeing. It's worth having your own torch (flashlight) to illuminate badly lit areas. Sometimes the guards have the endearing habit of switching off the lights if you won't give them baksheesh – and they wait until you're halfway in to leave you in the dark.

The road into the Valley of the Kings is a gradual, dry, hot climb, so be prepared if you are riding a bicycle. There is a rest house before the entrance to the valley where you can buy mineral water, soft drinks and meals. It's expensive and usually crowded. There is a *tuf-tuf* – a noisy tractor dressed up to look like a train – which ferries visitors between the entrance and the tombs (it can be hot during summer). You're charged an absurd E£1 for the ride.

If you want to avoid the inevitable crowds that tour buses bring to the tombs, head for the tombs outside the immediate area of the entrance. There are many to choose from, but among the better ones are the Tombs of Ramses VI (No 9), Queen Tawosret/Sethnakt (No 14), Tuthmosis III (No 34) and Siptah (No 47).

You cannot buy tickets for the tombs at the entrance to the valley itself (for more details, see Tickets earlier in this chapter). Note that any one ticket is valid for three tombs only. If you want to visit more, you'll have to buy more tickets (and if you wanted to visit, say, four tombs, you'd still have to buy two tickets). The Tomb of Tutankhamun has been deemed worth a ticket on its own (E£40) and this can be bought at the entrance to the site.

The tombs that are usually open are described here in visiting order.

Tomb of Ramses IV (No 2) This is the second tomb on the right as you enter the Valley of the Kings. Its whereabouts was known even by the Ptolemies, as is evident from the graffiti dating back to 278 BC that can be seen on the walls. Only recently opened to the public, it's not one of the finest tombs – many of the paintings in the burial chamber have deteriorated, although the painting of the goddess Nut, stretched across the blue ceiling, is still in good condition. The mummy of Ramses IV was found in the Tomb of Amenhotep II (No 35) and is now in the Egyptian Museum in Cairo.

Tomb of Ramses IX (No 6) Opposite Ramses II, the Tomb of Ramses IX (1126–1108 BC) consists of a long, sloping corridor, a large antechamber decorated with animals, serpents and demons, then a pillared hall and short hallway before the burial chamber. The goddess Nut is the feature of the ceiling painting; she is surrounded by sacred barques full of stars. Just before the staircase down to the burial chamber are the cartouche symbols of Ramses IX.

Tomb of Ramses II (No 7) This tomb, the burial place of one of Egypt's longest reigning pharaohs (67 years, from 1279 to 1213 BC), has recently reopened after excavation by French archaeologists. It has been partly open since antiquity, but being near the valley floor it was subject to occasional but very heavy flooding, which accounts for its devastation. Based on the decorative scheme in his father Seti I's superb tomb, the walls of Ramses's tomb would once have been just as brightly coloured, the wall scenes featuring the *Litany of Ra*, *Book of Gates* etc. The recent French excavations have shown that Ramses II, following his father Seti, had his sarcophagus made from alabaster, although his mummy was eventually buried in a wooden coffin in the Deir al-Bahri tomb cache; it's now in the Egyptian Museum in Cairo.

Tomb of Merneptah (No 8) Because Ramses II lived so long, 12 of his sons died before he did, so it was his 13th son Merneptah (1213–1203 BC) who finally became pharaoh in his 60s. His tomb has been open since antiquity and has its share of classical graffiti. Reliefs of Isis and her sister Nepthys, guardians of coffins, adorn the entrance to this tomb. Although there is a certain amount of flood damage on the lower portions of the walls of the long, tunnel-like tomb, the scenes feature the *Litany of Ra*, *Book of Amduat* and *Book of Gates*. The pharaoh was originally buried inside four stone sarcophagi, three of granite (the lid of the second still in situ) and the fourth, innermost, sarcophagus of alabaster. His mummy was removed in antiquity and was found in Amenhotep II's tomb (No 35) – it's now displayed in the Egyptian Museum.

Tomb of Tutankhamun (No 62) The story behind the celebrated discovery of this, the most famous tomb in the Valley of the Kings, and the fabulous treasures it contained, far outshines its actual appearance, making it doubtful whether or not it warrants the E£40 charged for admission (half price for students).

Tutankhamun's tomb is neither large nor impressive and bears all the signs of a rather hasty completion and inglorious burial. In fact, for years archaeologists believed that if Tutankhamun was buried in the valley, his tomb would contain little of interest. The son of Akhenaten by a minor wife, he ruled relatively briefly (1336–1327 BC) and died young, with no great battles or buildings to his credit.

The Egyptologist Howard Carter, however, believed he would find the young pharaoh buried among his ancestors with his treasures intact. He slaved away for six seasons in the valley, excavating thousands and thousands of tonnes of sand and rubble from possible sites, until even his wealthy patron, Lord Carnarvon, tired of the obsession.

With his funding about to be cut off Carter made one last attempt at the only unexplored area that was left – a site covered by workers' huts just under the already excavated Tomb of Ramses VI.

The first step was found on 4 November, and on 5 November the rest of the steps and a sealed doorway came to light. Carter wired Lord Carnarvon to join him in Egypt immediately for the opening of what he believed was the completely intact Tomb of Tutankhamun.

The discovery proved sceptics wrong, and the tomb's priceless cache of Pharaonic treasures, which had remained undisturbed by robbers, vindicated Carter's dream beyond even his wildest imaginings. Three chambers were found crammed with furniture, statues, chariots, musical instruments,

Tomb Building

Tombs were initially created to differentiate the burials of the elite from those of the majority whose bodies continued to be placed directly into the desert. By about 3100 BC the mound of sand heaped over the grave was replaced by a more permanent structure of mud brick, whose characteristic bench shape is known as a 'mastaba' after the Arabic word for 'bench'.

As stone replaced mud brick, the addition of further levels to increase height gave birth to the pyramid, whose first incarnation at Saqqara is also the world's oldest stone monument. Its stepped sides soon evolved into the more familiar smooth-sided structure, of which the Pyramids of Giza are the most famous examples.

It was only when the power of the monarchy broke down at the end of the Old Kingdom that the afterlife became increasingly accessible to those outside the royal family, and as officials became increasingly independent they began to opt for burial in their home towns. Yet the narrow stretches of fertile land that make up the Nile Valley left little room for grand superstructures, so an alternative type of tomb developed, cut tunnel-fashion into the cliffs that border the valley and which also proved more resilient against robbery. Most were also built on the west side of the river, the traditional place of burial where the sun was seen to sink down into the underworld each evening.

These simple rock-cut tombs consisting of a single chamber gradually developed into more elaborate structures complete with an open courtyard, offering chapel and entrance facade carved out of the rock with a shaft leading down into an undecorated burial chamber.

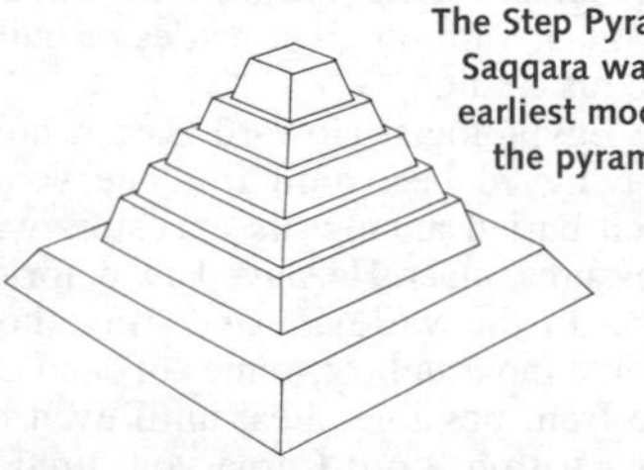

The Step Pyramid at Saqqara was the earliest model of the pyramid.

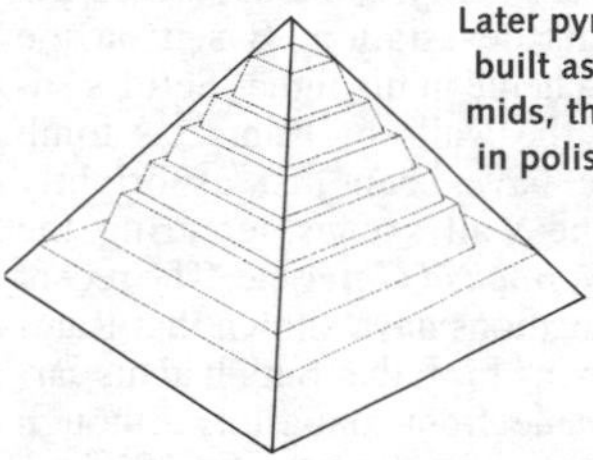

Later pyramids were built as step pyramids, then encased in polished stone.

weapons, boxes, jars and food, most of which are now in the Egyptian Museum in Cairo (a few items remain in Luxor at the museum in town).

Little remains to excite the modern visitor. The now empty tomb is small and only the burial chamber is decorated, with chubby figures on a yellow background similar to those in Ay's tomb (No 23). Only the outermost coffin of gilded wood, containing the decaying, mummified body of Tutankhamun, still lies within his red quartzite sarcophagus, inside the outermost of his three golden coffins.

Tomb of Ramses VI (No 9) The early excavation of this tomb forestalled the discovery of Tutankhamun's much smaller, earlier tomb that lay below it. The tomb was actually begun for the ephemeral Ramses V (1147–1143 BC) and continued by Ramses VI (1143–1136 BC), with both pharaohs apparently buried here. Its decoration has an emphasis on astronomical scenes and texts, which include the *Book of Gates, Book of Caverns*, *Books of the Heavens* and, for the first time, *Book of the Earth*. A superb double image of the sky goddess Nut decorates the ceiling of the burial chamber, where only part of the sarcophagi remain. Following the tomb's ransacking a mere 20 years after burial, the mummies of both Ramses V and Ramses VI were moved to Amenhotep II's tomb where they were found in 1898 and taken to Cairo.

Tomb Building

The most impressive rock-cut tombs were those built for the pharaohs of the New Kingdom (1550–1069 BC), who relocated the royal burial ground south to the remote desert valley now known as the Valley of the Kings. The first tomb here was created for Tuthmosis I by his architect Ineni, 'with no-one seeing, no-one hearing'. In a radical departure from tradition the offering chapel that was once part of the tomb's layout was built as a separate structure some distance away in an attempt to preserve the tomb's secret location. The tombs themselves were designed to resemble the underworld, with a long, inclined rock-hewn corridor descending into either an antechamber or a series of sometimes pillared halls, and ending in the burial chamber. All (except the newly discovered Tomb of the Sons of Ramses II) followed a similar plan, their variations largely due to structural difficulties or time constraints; the longer the life of the pharaoh, the longer the workers had to build the tomb.

The tomb builders lived in their own village of Deir al-Medina and worked in relays. The ancient week was 10 days (eight days on, two days off) and the men tended to spend the nights of their working week at a small camp located on the pass leading from Deir al-Medina to the eastern part of the Valley of the Kings. Then they spent their two days off at home with their families.

Once the tomb walls were created, decoration could then be added; this dealt almost exclusively with the afterlife and the pharaoh's existence in it. Many of the colourful paintings and reliefs are extracts from ancient theological compositions, now known as 'books', and were incorporated in the tomb to assist the deceased into the next life. Texts were taken from the *Book of the Dead*, the collective modern name for a range of works including the *Book of Amduat* (That which is in the Underworld), *Book of Gates*, *Book of Caverns* and *Litany of Ra*, all of which deal with the sun god's nightly journey through the darkness of the underworld, the realm of Osiris and home of the dead.

The Egyptians believed that the underworld was traversed each night by Ra, and it was the aim of the dead to secure passage on his sacred barque to travel with him for eternity. Since knowledge was power in the Egyptian afterlife, the texts give: 'Knowledge of the power of those in the underworld and knowledge of their actions, knowing the sacred rituals of Ra, knowing the hours and the gods and the gates and paths where the great god passes'.

Dr Joann Fletcher

Tomb of Ramses III (No 11) Ramses III (1184–1153 BC) was the last of Egypt's warrior pharaohs; he also built an impressive funerary temple at Medinat Habu. His tomb has been open since antiquity, and was originally started by Sethnakht (1186–1184 BC) who abandoned it when the tomb builders mistakenly cut through into the earlier Tomb of Amenmesse! By changing the corridor's course to the right, Ramses III carried on to create a huge tomb 125m long. The walls are decorated with colourful, painted sunken reliefs featuring the traditional ritual texts (*Litany of Ra*, *Book of Gates* etc) and Ramses before the gods but also, quite uniquely, a collection of secular scenes of foreign tribute, the royal armoury, boats and the harpists that gave the tomb its alternative name, Tomb of the Harpers. Ramses III's sarcophagus is now in the Louvre in Paris, its detailed lid is in Cambridge and his mummy – found in the Deir al-Bahri cache – is in the Egyptian Museum in Cairo.

Tomb of Horemheb (No 57) Horemheb (1323–1295 BC), a general of the Egyptian army in about 1320 BC, became the last pharaoh of the 18th dynasty. From the entrance, a steep flight of steps and an equally steep passage leads to a well shaft decorated with superb figures of Horemheb before the gods. Notice particularly Hathor's fabulous blue-and-black striped wig and Nefertem's lotus crown, all executed against a grey-blue background. This in turn leads

The Greatest Find Since Tutankhamun

In May 1995, American archaeologist Kent Weeks announced to the world his discovery of the largest tomb ever to be unearthed in Egypt. Believed to be the burial place of more than 50 sons of Ramses II – one of Egypt's most prolific pharaohs in terms of producing both offspring and monuments – it was immediately hailed as the greatest find since that of Tutankhamun. Or, as one London newspaper succinctly put it: 'The Mummy of all Tombs'.

The story of the tomb's discovery dates back to 1987 when the Egyptian Antiquities Organisation announced plans to level a hillside at the entrance to the Valley of the Kings in order to expand the paved car park. Weeks was familiar with the area and knew that there was a tomb entrance hidden somewhere in the hill. Indeed, Howard Carter had uncovered it earlier this century and partly cleared it as he suspected what it was but didn't have the resources to excavate at the time.

A year later, after moving mountains of rubble, Weeks finally located the entrance to the tomb, known only as KV5 (Kings Valley No 5). Together with his wife and a small team of workers, he then set about clearing the entrance chambers. Remnants of pottery, fragments of sarcophagi and, more importantly, wall decorations led Weeks to believe it was the tomb of the sons of Ramses II.

However, it wasn't until 1995 that Weeks unearthed a doorway leading to an incredible 110 chambers and corridors, making the tomb many times larger and more complex than any other found in Egypt. The symmetrical nature of many of the corridors leads Weeks to suspect that there are many more rooms still buried in debris. The mummified remains of four adult males have also been found. Although DNA testing is not allowed by the Egyptian government (DNA testing of Tutankhamun's mummy in 2000 was prevented at the last moment by a furore in the People's Assembly), X-ray studies will be carried out to help determine if the bodies could be related – if so, it will help to confirm Weeks' theory that these are the sons of Ramses II. If not, the mystery surrounding this astounding find will continue.

Weeks estimates it will take at least 10 years to study the tomb, although this is likely to increase along with the tomb's size. Apart from the time needed for excavation, the tomb's structure is weak, so extensive engineering work will have to be carried out, too. As for visitors, for the next few years they'll just have to be content with reading about KV5 in Weeks's book *The Lost Tomb* or following progress on the Web site, W www.kv5.com.

to an undecorated pillared hall, although the antechamber beyond is again decorated with more painted figures of the pharaoh and gods. A six-pillared burial chamber decorated with part of the *Book of Gates* is in an unfinished state revealing how the decoration was applied by following a grid system in red ink over which the figures were drawn in black prior to their carving and painting.

Tomb of Amenhotep II (No 35) One of the deepest structures in the valley, this tomb has more than 90 steps that take you down to a modern gangway built over a deep pit designed to protect the inner, lower chambers from thieves.

Stars cover the entire ceiling in the huge burial chamber and the walls feature, as if on a giant painted scroll, text from the *Book of Amduat*. While most figures are of the same stick-like proportions as in the tomb of Amenhotep's father and predecessor Tuthmosis III, this is the first royal tomb in the valley to also show figures of more rounded proportions, as on the pillars in the burial chamber showing the pharaoh before the gods Osiris, Hathor and Anubis.

Although in antiquity thieves breached the tomb and made off with valuable funerary items, they left its cache of royal mummies; when the huge tomb was excavated, by the French in 1898, a total of 13 mummies were found, including that of Amenhotep (1427–1400 BC) lying in his sarcophagus with a garland of flowers still around his neck. Nine of the other mummies, hidden there by priests, were also of royal blood, including those of Tuthmosis IV, Seti II, Amenhotep III, Merneptah, Ramses III, IV, V and VI, Seti II, Siptah and six other members of the New Kingdom royal family.

A word of warning – this tomb can sometimes be exceedingly hot and humid.

Tomb of Tuthmosis III (No 34) Hidden in the hills between high limestone cliffs and reached only via a steep staircase that crosses an even steeper ravine, this tomb demonstrates the lengths to which the ancient pharaohs went to thwart the cunning of the ancient thieves.

Tuthmosis III (1479–1425 BC) was one of the first to build his tomb in the Valley of the Kings. As secrecy was his utmost concern, he chose the most inaccessible spot and designed his burial place with a series of passages at haphazard angles and a deep shaft to mislead or catch potential robbers – all to no avail, of course.

The shaft, now traversed by a narrow gangway, leads to an antechamber supported by two pillars, the walls of which are adorned with a list of more than 700 gods and demigods. As the earliest tomb in the Valley to be painted, the walls appear to be simply giant versions of funerary papyri, with scenes populated by stick men (as also found in the tomb of Tuthmosis' son and successor Amenhotep II). The burial chamber itself has curved walls and is oval in shape; it contains the pharaoh's quartzite sarcophagus that is carved in the shape of a cartouche. Tuthmosis' mummy, which shows he was a short man of around 1.5m tall, was one of those found in the Deir al-Bahri cache and is now in the Egyptian Museum in Cairo.

Tomb of Siptah (No 47) Discovered in 1905, the entrance to this tomb is decorated with the sun disc and figures of the goddess Maat kneel on each side of the doorway. The entrance corridor features scenes from the *Litany of Ra* with an elaborately dressed Siptah before the gods, including Ra-Horakhty. With further scenes from the *Book of Amduat*, and figures of the black jackal god Anubis, the rest of the tomb is undecorated. Although the tomb contents were smashed up in antiquity, Siptah's mummy was found in Amenhotep II's tomb, and it clearly shows the pharaoh's left leg to be shorter than his right, his left foot severely deformed – Siptah (1194–1188 BC) had probably suffered from cerebral palsy.

Tomb of Tawosret/Sethnakht (No 14) Tawosret was wife of Seti II (1200–1194 BC) and after his successor Siptah she took power herself (1188–1186 BC). She began the tomb for herself and Seti II, but their burials were removed by her successor, the equally short-lived Sethnakht (1186–1184 BC) who completed the tomb by adding a second burial chamber where he himself was buried. The tomb has been open since antiquity and is decorated with images of both Tawosret and Sethnakht with the gods as well as scenes from the *Book of Gates*, *Book of Caverns* and *Book of Amduat* and it has astronomical ceiling decorations in both burial chambers.

Tomb of Seti II (No 15) Adjacent to Tawosret/Sethnakht's tomb is a smaller tomb where it seems Sethnakht buried Seti II (1200–1194 BC) after turfing him out of tomb No 14. Although the entrance area has some fine carved relief scenes, it was quickly finished in paint alone. Texts include the *Litany of Ra* and *Book of Gates* with the sky goddess Nut stretched out on the ceiling of the burial chamber. Seti II's mummy was found in the Amenhotep II tomb cache. This tomb was also used by Carter and his team as a conservation laboratory and photographic studio during their clearance of Tutankhamun's tomb.

Tomb of Ramses I (No 16) Although this tomb belongs to the founder of the 19th dynasty, it is a very simple affair because Ramses I only ruled for a year (1295–1294 BC). It has the shortest entrance corridor of all the royal resting places in the valley, leading to a single, almost square, burial chamber, containing the pharaoh's open pink-granite sarcophagus. The chamber is the only part of the tomb that is decorated; it features the pharaoh in the presence of deities such as Osiris, Ptah, Anubis and Maat set on a blue-purple background. The amount of decoration isn't large but the quality of the work is really superb. Although no trace of Ramses I's mummy was found, recent claims have stated it is actually in the Niagara Falls Museum in Ontario where it has lain for many years after being 'acquired' in the 1850s.

Tomb of Seti I (No 17) Discovered in 1817, the Tomb of Seti I (1294–1279 BC) is more than 120m long, making it one of the largest in the valley. Part of its superb painted reliefs of Seti with the goddess Hathor are now in the Louvre and Turin museums, while Seti's alabaster sarcophagus was brought to London – but the British Museum refused to pay the asking price, so it went to a private collector, Sir John Soane, in the basement of whose London house-turned-museum it can still be seen. Seti's mummy had been moved in antiquity and was found in the Deir al-Bahri mummy cache and is now in the Egyptian Museum. The first part of the pharaoh's burial chamber is decorated with texts from the *Book of Gates*, the *Book of the Divine Cow* and the *Book of Amduat* whereas the second part has the *Book of Amduat* and an astronomical ceiling.

At the time of writing, this tomb was closed for restoration (ongoing since 1991); it is due to open again in late 2001.

Tomb of Monthuhirkhopshef (No 19) The Tomb of Ramses IX's son, whose name translates as 'The Arm of Montu is Strong', is located high up in the valley's eastern wall. Its entrance corridor is adorned with life-sized reliefs of various gods, including Anubis and Horus, receiving offerings from the young prince, who is shown in all his finery, wearing exquisitely pleated fine linen and a blue-and-gold 'sidelock of youth' attached to his black wig – not to mention his gorgeous make-up (as worn by both men and women in ancient Egypt).

Tomb of Tuthmosis IV (No 43) This is one of the largest and deepest tombs constructed during the 18th dynasty. Discovered in 1903 by none other than Howard Carter (who less than 20 years later would find the tomb of Tuthmosis IV's great-grandson Tutankhamun), it is above the Tomb of Monthuhirkhopshef and accessed by a separate path (though the guardians will probably show you a short cut up the hill). Two long flights of steps lead down and around to the burial chamber where there's an enormous sarcophagus covered in hieroglyphs. Most of the walls in this tomb were never finished. However, there are two well-preserved painted sections where various gods, such as Osiris and Hathor, are shown presenting the pharaoh with the key of life.

Tomb of Ay (No 23)

This tomb is in the western valley, also known as Wadi al-Gurud (Valley of the Monkeys) after the baboons on the tomb walls. It is accessed by a rough dirt road leading off from the car park at the Valley of the Kings that winds for almost 2km up a desolate valley past sheer rock cliffs. It's well worth a visit if only to recapture something of the atmosphere (and silence) once to be found in the neighbouring Valley of the Kings. The well-hidden tomb dates from the 18th dynasty and is noted for its scenes of Ay hunting in the marshes (the sort of scene usually found in the tombs of nobles not royalty) and the wall featuring 12 baboons.

Before making your way up to this tomb, ask at the ticket office to ensure that it's open. If you're travelling by bicycle, note that it is not feasible to cycle up here unless you happen to have a good, sturdy mountain bike.

Walk to Deir al-Bahri

From the tombs of Seti I and Ramses I you can continue south-east and hike over the hills to Deir al-Bahri (or vice versa, of course). The walk takes about 45 minutes through an amazing lunar-type landscape.

From the top, there are various views of Deir al-Bahri, the Temple of Hatshepsut, in the amphitheatre setting below and excellent views across the plain towards the Nile.

In summer you should start this hike as early as possible, partly to catch the changing colours of the barren hills as the sun rises, but also because it gets mighty hot there later in the day. If you tire on the ascent there are donkeys available to carry you to the top. You're also likely to run into one of the many policemen who run the stations erected on strategic points of the mountain in the aftermath of the 1997 massacre at Deir al-Bahri. Sometimes they insist on following you, other times they'll leave you alone.

If you plan to visit the site, however, you will need tickets, which can only be obtained when the ticket offices open. There's also a much longer trail from the Valley of the Kings to the Valley of the Queens via Deir al-Medina.

Alternatively, if you're just hankering for a view, you can scramble up the hill from the Valley of the Kings to the viewpoint overlooking Deir al-Bahri then return to the valley.

Deir al-Bahri

Rising out of the desert plain, in a series of terraces, the **Temple of Hatshepsut** merges with the sheer limestone cliffs of the eastern face of the Theban mountain as if Nature herself had built this extraordinary monument.

The partly rock-cut, partly freestanding structure is one of the finest monuments of ancient Egypt, although its original appearance, surrounded by a variety of exotic trees and plants and garden beds and approached by a grand sphinx-lined causeway, must have been even more spectacular.

Excavations began in 1891, although it wasn't completely excavated until 1896 and it is still in the process of being restored.

Unfortunately, over the centuries the temple has been vandalised. Akhenaten removed all references to Amun, before taking his court off to Tell al-Amarna; and the early Christians who took it over as a monastery (hence the name Deir al-Bahri or 'Monastery of the North'), also defaced the pagan reliefs. Damage was also done by successors of Hatshepsut, who scratched out her name where they could. A similar fate befell other pharaohs who fell out of favour with future rulers.

The daughter of Tuthmosis I, Hatshepsut was married to her half-brother Tuthmosis II, whose son by a minor wife was to be his successor. As Tuthmosis III was still young when his father Tuthmosis II died, Hatshepsut was made regent. With the political support of the Amun priesthood, she ruled as pharaoh for 20 years, and for Egypt it was a time of peace and internal growth. In certain relief scenes, she is shown in the regalia of a pharaoh, including a false beard, while in other scenes she is clearly female. The fact that she was depicted as

TEMPLE OF HATSHEPSUT

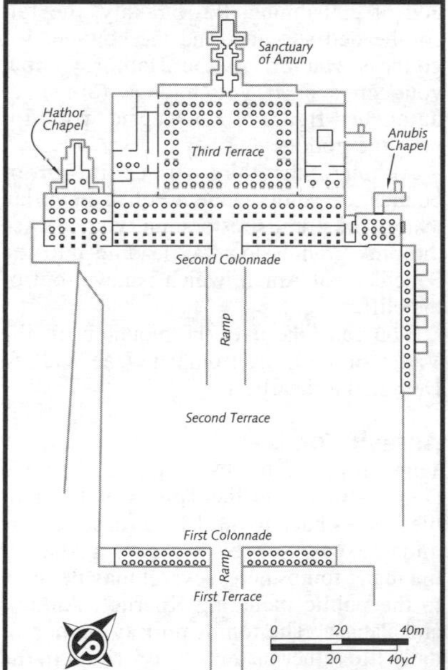

male in some scenes was more than likely a case of conforming with accepted decorum. After her death in 1458 BC Tuthmosis III became the sole ruler.

The temple's 37m-wide causeway leads onto the three huge terraced courts, each approached by ramps and separated by colonnades. The renowned delicate relief work of the lower terrace features scenes of birds being caught in nets, and the transport from the Aswan quarries to Thebes of a pair of obelisks commissioned by Hatshepsut.

The central court contains the best-preserved reliefs. There Hatshepsut recorded her divine birth and told the story of an expedition to the Land of Punt to collect myrrh trees needed for the precious incense used in temple ceremonies. There are also two chapels at either end of the colonnade. At the northern end the colourful reliefs in the Chapel of Anubis show the co-rulers, Hatshepsut and Tuthmosis III (with the female pharaoh's image again disfigured), in the presence of Anubis, the god of embalming, Ra-Harakhty, the falcon-headed sun god, and the cow-headed goddess Hathor. In the Hathor Chapel you can see (if you have a torch) an untouched figure of Hatshepsut worshipping the goddess.

Although the third terrace is out of bounds to visitors while a Polish-Egyptian team works on its restoration, you can see the pink granite doorway leading into the Sanctuary of Amun, which is hewn out of the cliff.

You can hike over the mountain to the Valley of the Kings from here (see Walk to Deir al-Bahri earlier).

Assasif Tombs

This group of tombs, situated between Deir al-Bahri and the Tombs of the Nobles, dates back to the 18th dynasty and is under excavation by archaeologists. Of the many tombs here, several may be open to the public including Kheruef, Ankhor and Pabasa. The tombs portray scenes of daily life rather than the heavy ritual in the royal tombs.

Tombs of the Nobles

The tombs in this area are some of the best, though least visited, attractions on the West Bank. Nestled in the foothills and among the houses of the old village of Gurna (Sheikh Abd al-Gurna) are more than 400 tombs that date from the 6th dynasty to the Graeco-Roman period.

Of the hundred or so tombs that have something of interest, 13 are highly recommended. They have been numbered and divided into five groups, each requiring a separate ticket (for details see Tickets earlier in this chapter). It's possible some of the tombs may be closed; the ticket office people will know.

There are no signs indicating the tombs, so you'll need to ask the locals or look out for the modern stone walls built around the entrances to some of the tombs. If you're on your own, most of the guardians here will give you a guided tour whether you want it or not.

Tombs of Khonsu, Userhet & Benia (Nos 31, 51 & 343) Khonsu was high priest of Tuthmosis III's funerary cult, and lived during the reign of Ramses II, when the dead pharaoh was still honoured. Inside his colourful tomb there is a scene of Khonsu offering flowers to Montuhotep II, who had been dead about 800 years but who was still honoured. The gods Osiris and Anubis are also honoured, and priests with shaved heads are shown carrying the barque of the war. Scenes inside his colourful tomb include a boat carrying the dead to Abydos and, before the final shrine, Khonsu offering incense to Osiris and Anubis. The ceiling is adorned with birds and eggs.

The Tomb of Benia, just behind that of Khonsu, is more colourful than its neighbour. Benia was a child of the royal nursery during the 18th dynasty. At the end of the tomb, there's a ka (spirit or double) statue of Benia flanked by his parents. Statues such as these are typical of tombs in this area, but the faces of this trio have been destroyed.

The Tomb of Userhet (not to be confused with Userhet No 56) was closed at the time of writing.

Tombs of Menna & Nakht (Nos 52 & 69) Situated close to the Tombs of Khonsu, Userhet and Benia, the wall paintings in the Tombs of Menna and Nakht (which may be closed to the public) emphasise rural life in the 18th dynasty. Menna was an estate inspector and Nakht was an astronomer of Amun. Their finely detailed tombs show scenes of farming, hunting, fishing and feasting. The Tomb of Nakht has a small museum area in its first chamber. Although this tomb is so small that only a handful of visitors can squeeze in at a time, the walls have some of the best known examples of Egyptian tomb paintings, including familiar scenes such as the three musicians that show up on a million T-shirts, posters, postcards and papyrus paintings.

Tombs of Ramose, Userhet & Khaemhet (Nos 55, 56 & 57) The Tomb of Ramose, who was a governor of Thebes during the reigns of Amenhotep III and Akhenaten, in the 18th dynasty, is fascinating. It's one of the few monuments dating from that time, when the cult power of the priests of Karnak was usurped by the Aten. Exquisite paintings and low reliefs grace the walls, showing scenes from the reigns of both pharaohs and the transition between the two forms of religious worship. The reliefs of Ramose, his wife and other relatives are extraordinarily lifelike and clearly show their affectionate relationships. The tomb was never actually finished because Ramose deserted Thebes to follow the rebel pharaoh Akhenaten to his new city at Tell al-Amarna.

The Tomb of Userhet, who was one of Amenhotep II's royal scribes, is next to Ramose's. Its distinctive features are the wall paintings depicting daily life in ancient Egypt. Userhet is shown presenting gifts to Amenhotep II; there's a barber cutting hair on another wall; other scenes include men making wine and people hunting gazelles from a chariot.

The third tomb belongs to Khaemhet, who was Amenhotep III's royal inspector of the granaries as well as court scribe. The scenes on the walls show Khaemhet offering sacrifices; the pharaoh depicted as a sphinx; the funeral ritual of Osiris; and images of daily country life as well as official business.

Tombs of Sennofer & Rekhmire (Nos 96 & 100) Prince Sennofer of Thebes worked for Amenhotep II as a supervisor of the gardens of the Temple of Amun. The most interesting parts of his tomb are deep underground in the main chamber. The ceiling there is covered with clear paintings of grapes and vines, while most of the scenes

Mummy Find

In 1881 the greatest mummy find in history was made just south of Deir al-Bahri in tomb No 320. After many antiquities began showing up in the marketplace the authorities realised someone had found, and was plundering, an unknown tomb (see also the boxed text 'Guardians or Thieves?' later in this chapter). After investigations they discovered a massive shaft containing the mummies of 40 pharaohs, queens and nobles.

It seems that the New Kingdom priests realised that the bodies of their pharaohs would never be safe from violation in their own tombs, no matter what precautions were taken against grave robbers, so they moved them after 934 BC to this communal grave, which was originally the family vault of the high priest Pinudjem II. The mummies included those of Amenhotep I, Tuthmosis I, II and III, Seti I and Ramses II and III, most of which are now on display at the Egyptian Museum in Cairo.

Their removal from the tomb and procession down to the banks of the Nile, from where they were taken by barge to Cairo, is said to have been watched by local villagers, with the black-clad women ululating to give a royal send-off to the illustrious remains. The episode makes for one of the most stunning scenes in Shadi Abdel Salam's 1975 epic *The Mummy (Al-Mumia)*, one of the best films ever to come out of Egypt.

Guardians or Thieves?

Surrounding and, in some cases, covering the hundreds of tombs lining the West Bank's barren mountainsides are the colourful houses that make up the village of Gurna. These bright mud-brick dwellings have been here for generations but if the authorities have their way they will soon be knocked down and their inhabitants moved to modern apartment blocks north of the road to the Valley of the Kings. Officialdom claims that the villagers steal antiquities and destroy the tombs, an accusation that goes back to the 19th century, when a then notorious tomb-robbing family, the Abdel Rassouls, discovered the cache of royal mummies near Hatshepsut's temple (see the boxed text 'Mummy Find' earlier in this chapter). Stunning amulets and cartouches found their way onto the black market but the suspicious antiquities officials could not discover the source until a disagreement resulted in a disgruntled family member leading them to the stash.

Nowadays, however, the Gurnawis insist that whatever tomb robbing may have existed is finished. They maintain that their presence protects the remaining monuments from unwanted intruders and believe that the government wants them out because it does not want tourists to see the poverty in which they live.

Attempts to relocate the village are not new. In the 1940s the government sponsored the then up-and-coming architect Hassan Fathy to create a new village for the Gurnawis. Using traditional materials and building techniques, Fathy built New Gurna, just off the main road to the east of the Colossi of Memnon. It still exists but you have to search through a forest of concrete in order to see the remaining domes and beautifully proportioned public buildings that he designed. Fathy himself acknowledged that New Gurna was a failure soon after it was built, although he blamed the authorities' disdain for the Gurnawis rather than any flaw in his rather naive attempts at social engineering.

Now it seems that history is repeating itself as officials try to force the villagers into tiny public housing units, disregarding the size of their extended families and their need for livestock pens to supplement meagre incomes. Most of the villagers are digging in and refusing to leave, knowing that the government will not risk using force and alienating the population in an area so important to tourism. Who will win this battle of wills remains to be seen.

on the surrounding walls and columns depict Sennofer with his sister. The guard usually has a kerosene lamp, but bring a torch just in case.

The Tomb of Rekhmire, a governor during the reigns of Tuthmosis III and Amenhotep II, is one of the best preserved in the area. In the first chamber, to the extreme left, are scenes of Rekhmire receiving gifts from foreign lands. The panther and giraffe are gifts from Nubia; the elephant, horses and chariot come from Syria; and the expensive vases come from Crete and the Aegean Islands.

Tombs of Neferronpet, Dhutmosi & Nefersekheru (Nos 178, 295 & 296)

This trio of tombs is not far from the Tombs of Khonsu, Userhet and Benia, and is surrounded by a new stone wall. Neferronpet, commonly known as Kenro, was an official scribe of the treasury. Discovered in 1915, the highlight of this brightly painted tomb is a scene showing Kenro overseeing the weighing of gold at the treasury. Next door, the Tomb of Nefersekheru is equally rich in yellow hues and, like Kenro's tomb, features a ceiling painted with a riot of geometric designs. From this long tomb, a small passage leads into the Tomb of Dhutmosi, which is in poor condition.

Gurna Discovery

Within Gurna, in a restored 1920s mud-brick house beside the Tomb of Ramose, is Gurna Discovery (*W www.sepcom.demon.co.uk/Hay/main.html; admission free but donations appreciated; open 7am-noon & 2pm-5pm Wed-Mon)*, a fascinating permanent exhibition of drawings of the village by early-19th-century British artist Robert Hay. His finely detailed works depicting ancient mud-brick structures that are now lost (one thought to be a medieval Coptic church) and, of course, the famous tomb houses, all show a life that has all but disappeared in the past 50 years. One constant, however, is that Gurnawis were, even in the 1820s, working as labourers for archaeologists.

Built around his works is a compelling description of Gurna's modern history highlighting the interplay between the village and tourism for over a century. The exhibition also addresses – in a diplomatic manner – the current problems facing the Gurnawis and suggests alternative solutions to their relocation. It ends with quotes from the villagers about how they would like to see the future.

The Ramesseum

This is yet another monument raised by Ramses II to the ultimate glory of himself. The massive temple was built to impress his priests, his subjects, his successors and of course the gods, so that he, the great warrior pharaoh, could live forever. Many of his other works were rather crudely constructed but in this, his funerary temple, he demanded perfection in the artisanship so that it would stand as an eternal testimony to his greatness.

Of course, it has done no such thing. It's mostly in ruins. This fact no doubt disappoints Ramses II more than it does present-day visitors. He dared all those who questioned his greatness in future centuries to gaze on the magnificence of his monuments in order to understand his power over life and death. The scattered remains of the colossal statue of the pharaoh and the ruins of his temple prompted the English poet Shelley to cut this presumptuous pharaoh

THE RAMESSEUM

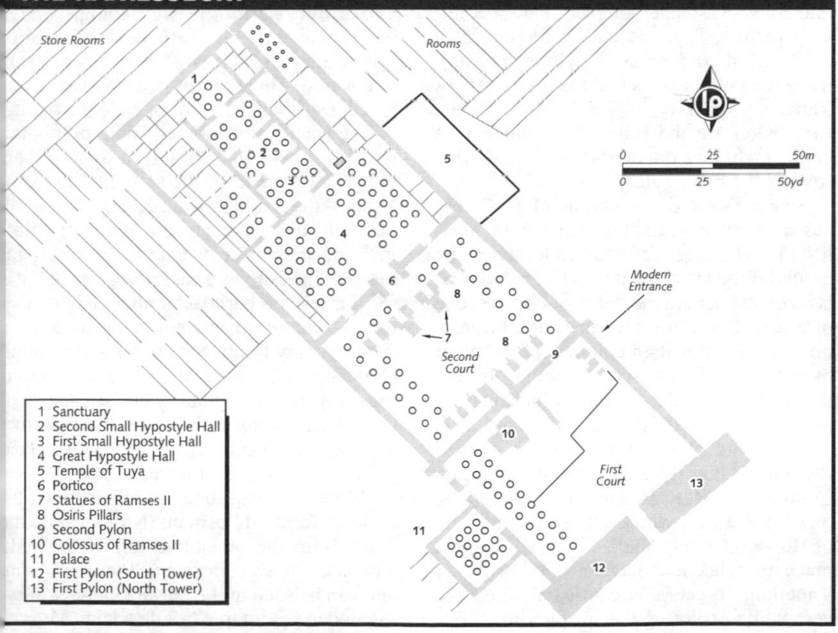

down to size by using the undeniable fact of Ramses's mortality to ridicule his aspirations to immortality.

> I met a traveller from an antique land
> Who said: Two vast and trunkless legs of stone
> Stand in the desert...Near them, on the sand,
> Half sunk, a shattered visage lies, whose frown,
> And wrinkled lip, and sneer of cold command,
> Tell that its sculptor well those passions read
> Which yet survive, stamped on these lifeless things,
> The hand that mocked them, and the heart that fed:
> And on the pedestal these words appear:
> 'My name is Ozymandias, king of kings:
> Look on my works, ye Mighty, and despair!'
> Nothing beside remains. Round the decay
> Of that colossal wreck, boundless and bare
> The lone and level sands stretch far away.

Although a little more elaborate than other temples, the fairly orthodox layout of the Ramesseum, with its two courts, hypostyle hall, sanctuary, accompanying chambers and storerooms, is uncommon in that the usual rectangular floor plan was altered to incorporate an older, smaller temple – that of Ramses's mother, Tuya, which is off to one side.

The **first and second pylons** measure more than 60m across and feature reliefs of Ramses's military exploits. Through the first pylon are the ruins of the huge **first court**, including the double colonnade that fronted the royal palace.

Near the western stairs is part of the **Colossus of Ramses II**, the Ozymandias of Shelley's poem, lying somewhat forlornly on the ground. When it stood, it was 17.5m tall. The head of another granite statue of Ramses, one of a pair, lies in the **second court**. Twenty-nine of the original 48 columns of the **great hypostyle hall** are still standing. In the smaller hall behind it, the roof, which features astronomical hieroglyphs, is still in place.

There is a rest house/restaurant next to the temple that is called, not surprisingly, ***Ramesseum Rest House***. It is owned by Sayyed Hussein, whose father was a friend of Howard Carter. The rest house is a great place to relax and have a cool drink or something to eat. You can leave your bike here while exploring the surroundings.

Deir al-Medina

About 1km off the road to the Valley of the Queens and up a short, steep paved road is Deir al-Medina (Monastery of the Town). It is named after a temple here that was occupied by early Christian monks. Near the temple is a ruined settlement known as the Workmen's Village, for it was here that many of the workers and artists who created the royal tombs lived and were buried. Although less frequently visited than many of the other tombs on the West Bank, some of the small tombs here have exquisite reliefs, making it well worth a visit.

Temple The small Ptolemaic temple of Deir al-Medina is just north of the Workmen's Village, along a rocky track. The temple was built between 221 and 116 BC by Ptolemy IV Philopator, Ptolemy VI Philometor and Ptolemy VIII Euergetes II. It was dedicated to Hathor, the goddess of pleasure and love, and to Maat, the goddess of truth and personification of cosmic order.

Workmen's Village Archaeologists have been excavating this settlement for most of this century and at least 70 houses have been uncovered. Three tombs in the village's terraced necropolis are now open to the public.

The beautifully adorned **Tomb of Inherka (No 359)** belonged to a 19th-dynasty servant who worked in the so-called Place of Truth – the Valley of the Kings. The tomb has only one chamber, but the wall paintings are magnificent. One of the most famous scenes shows a cat killing a snake; it's on the left of burial chamber. Right next to it is the **Tomb of Sennedjem (No 1)**, a 20th-dynasty tomb that contains two small chambers and some equally exquisite paintings. Due to the popularity and small size of both these tombs, only 10 people at a time are allowed inside; it's likely you'll find yourself in a sizable queue.

While you wait, take a look at the 19th-dynasty **Tomb of Peshedu (No 3)** just up the slope from the other two tombs. Peshedu was another servant in the Place of Truth and can be seen in the burial chamber praying under a palm tree beside a lake. Most of the other tombs in the area also belonged to the servants, overseers and labourers who worked in the valley.

Valley of the Queens

There are at least 75 tombs in the Valley of the Queens (Biban al-Harim). They belonged to queens of the 19th and 20th dynasties and other members of the royal families, including princesses and the Ramessid princes. Only tomb Nos 43, 44, 52, 55 and 66 are open.

Tomb of Nefertari (No 66) Hailed as the finest tomb in the Theban necropolis – and in all Egypt for that matter – the Tomb of Nefertari *(admission E£100; open 8.30am-noon & 1pm-4pm Oct-Apr, 7.30am-noon & 1pm-5pm May-Sept)* was first opened to the public in November 1995 and has been solidly booked ever since – a limit of 150 tickets are sold per day. It is by far the most expensive monument in Egypt.

Nefertari was one of the five wives of Ramses II, the New Kingdom pharaoh known for his colossal monuments of self-celebration. However, the tomb he created for his favourite queen is a shrine to her beauty and, without doubt, an exquisite labour of love. Every centimetre of the walls in the tomb's three chambers and connecting corridors is adorned with colourful scenes of Nefertari in the company of the gods and with associated text from the *Book of the Dead* nearby. Invariably, the 'Most Beautiful of Them', as Nefertari was known, is depicted wearing a divinely transparent white gown and a golden headdress featuring two long feathers extending from the back of a vulture. The ceiling of the tomb is festooned with golden stars.

Some of the best scenes in the tomb are in the side room off to your right at the bottom of the first set of stairs. In one panel here, the queen is shown with her arms outstretched next to the mummiform body of Osiris. At the top of the second staircase, which leads to the burial chamber, is another of the tomb's highlights – Nefertari offering two bowls of milk to Hathor, the goddess of pleasure and love.

TOMB OF NEFERTARI

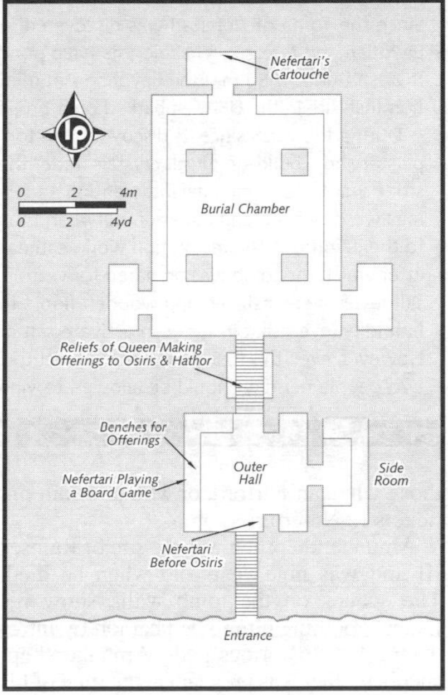

Like most of the tombs in the Valley of the Kings, this one had been plundered by the time it was discovered by archaeologists. Only a few fragments of the queen's pink granite sarcophagus remained.

In order to preserve the tomb's exquisite artwork, ticket sales are limited, so get to the ticket office early if you want to go; tickets go on sale at 6am and often sell out by 6:30am, even though the tomb doesn't open until 8am. Also, some readers have reported a scam whereby hustlers buy up a load of tickets and scalp them to tourists. Only 10 people are allowed in at any one time for a maximum of 15 minutes, and photography is strictly prohibited. You may be required to wear shoe covers and nose masks.

Tomb of Amunherkhepshep (No 55) Until the opening of Nefertari's tomb, the Tomb of Amunherkhepshep was the valley's showpiece. Now thoroughly overshadowed, it is still a worthwhile option for

Preserving Egypt's Finest Tomb

Since the Tomb of Nefertari was discovered in 1904 by Italian archaeologist, Ernesto Schiaparelli, Egyptian and foreign archaeologists have pondered the best way to restore and keep it preserved. It wasn't until 1986 that the Egyptian Antiquities Organisation, together with the Getty Conservation Institute in the USA, embarked on a program to safeguard this magnificent tomb.

During the years since its discovery, the tomb paintings had suffered due to dehydration of the plaster and a build-up of salt crystals under the paintings, causing the images to flake off the limestone walls. Using minimal intervention and ensuring the reversibility of materials used, the paintings were cleaned and adhesion between the plaster and rock reinforced. No colours were added to the paintings. The restoration work, estimated to cost about US$6 million, lasted for five years, after which the tomb was prepared for visitors. Devices to monitor the temperature, humidity and salt levels were installed and wooden floors to keep dust at bay were laid. As breathing can raise humidity levels that in turn can activate salt crystallisation, a limit of 150 visitors per day was set. However, even this figure has been subject to controversy, with some archaeologists believing only two people per day should be allowed to view Egypt's finest tomb.

those who can't afford, or who miss out on, tickets to Nefertari's tomb.

Amunherkhepshep was the son of Ramses III and was nine years old when he died. The scenes on the tomb walls show his father grooming him to be pharaoh by introducing him to various gods. Amunherkhepshep's mother was pregnant at the time of his death and in her grief she aborted the child and entombed it with Amunherkhepshep. A five-month-old mummified fetus was discovered there. Wall paintings also show Ramses leading his son to Anubis, the jackal-headed god of the dead, who then takes the young Prince Amunherkhepshep down to the entrance of the Passage of the Dead.

Medinat Habu

Second in size only to the temple complex at Karnak, the magnificent temple complex of Medinat Habu is one of the most underrated sites on the West Bank, and is usually bypassed by tourists in favour of the more famous Ramesseum. With the Theban mountains as a backdrop and the sleepy village of Kom Lolah in front, it is a wonderful place to spend a few hours.

The site was one of the first places in Thebes to be closely associated with the local god Amun. Although the complex is most famous for the large funerary temple built by Ramses III, Hatshepsut and Tuthmosis III also constructed buildings here. They were later added to and altered by a succession of rulers right through to the Ptolemies. At Medinat Habu's height there were temples, storage rooms, workshops, administrative buildings and accommodation for the priests and officials. It was the centre of the economic life of Thebes for several centuries and was still inhabited as late as the 9th century AD, when a plague was thought to have decimated the town. You can still see the mudbrick remains of the medieval town that gave the site its name (medina means 'town' or 'city') on top of the site's enclosure walls.

The original **Temple of Amun**, built by Hatshepsut and Tuthmosis III, was later completely overshadowed by the enormous **Funerary Temple of Ramses III**, which is the dominant feature of Medinat Habu.

Ramses III was inspired in the construction of his shrine by the Ramesseum of his illustrious forebear, Ramses II. His own temple and the smaller one dedicated to Amun are both enclosed within the massive outer walls of the complex.

Also just inside, to the left of the gate, are the **Tomb Chapels of the Divine Adorers**, which were built for the principal priestesses of Amun. Outside the eastern gate, one of only two entrances, was a landing quay for a canal that once connected Medinat Habu with the Nile.

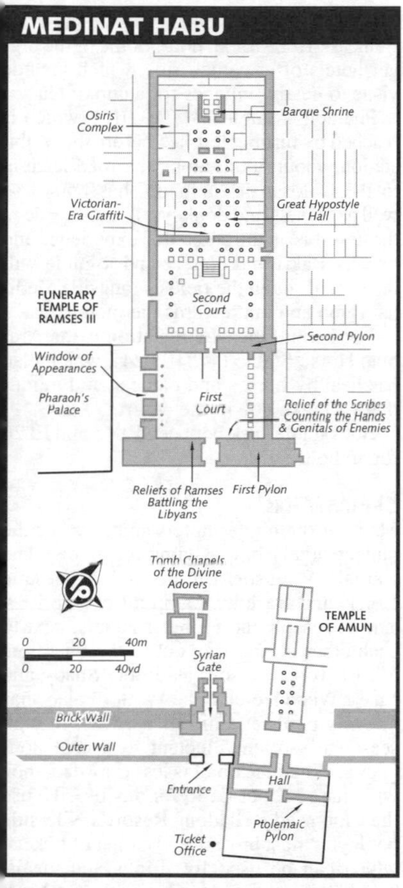

You enter the site through the unique **Syrian Gate**, a large two-storey building modelled after an Asiatic fortress. If you follow the wall to the left you will find a staircase leading to the upper floors. There's not much to see in the rooms but you get some great views over the village in front of the temple and across the fields to the south.

The well-preserved first pylon marks the front of the temple proper. Ramses III is portrayed in its reliefs as the victor in several wars. Most famous are the fine reliefs of his victory over the Libyans (who you can recognise by their long robes, sidelocks and beards). There is also a gruesome scene of scribes tallying the number of enemies killed by counting severed hands and genitals.

To the left of the **first court** are the remains of the **pharaoh's palace**; the three rooms at the rear were for the royal harem. There is a window between the First Court and the Pharaoh's Palace known as the **Window of Appearances**, which allowed the pharaoh to show himself to his subjects.

The reliefs of the **second pylon** feature Ramses III presenting prisoners of war to Amun and his vulture-goddess wife, Mut. Colonnades and reliefs surround the **second court**, depicting various religious ceremonies.

If you have time to wander about the extensive ruins around the funerary temple you will see the remains of an early Christian basilica as well as a small sacred lake.

Medinat Habu is off the road on your right as you return from the Valley of the Queens or can be reached by an asphalt road that turns off just east of the ticket office. After you have finished wandering around you come out in the small village of Kom Lolah, where Richard Critchfield's book *Shahhat: An Egyptian* is set.

New Gurna

For architecture buffs, Hassan Fathy's mud-brick architectural masterpiece, New Gurna, lies just past the railway track on the main road from the ferry to the ticket office. It was built to rehouse the inhabitants of Old Gurna (for more details, see the boxed text 'Guardians or Thieves?' earlier in this chapter) but most of them stayed where they were. The new, purpose-built village gradually filled up with the overflow from the surrounding area. Sadly, many of the domed mud-brick houses have been replaced with concrete buildings – Fathy did not plan his buildings to allow for extensions to accommodate growing extended families, sowing the seeds of the project's failure. However, the beautiful mud-brick mosque and theatre still survive, and you can still see the venerable architect's own house. Just ask for someone from the Abu al-Haggag family and they will show you around.

FELUCCA RIDES

One of the best things to do in Luxor in the late afternoon or early evening is to relax aboard a felucca. Local feluccas cruise the river throughout the day and cost from E£30 to E£50 per boat per hour, depending on your bargaining skills. Feluccas can be caught on either side of the Nile (below the Corniche or around the ferry landing).

An enjoyable outing is the trip upriver to Banana Island. The tiny isle, dotted with palms, is about 5km from Luxor and the trip takes two to three hours. Plan it in such a way that you're on your way back in time to watch a brilliant Nile sunset from the boat. A word of warning, though – some travellers have complained that the felucca captain has added money for 'admission' to the island; make sure you are clear about what is included in the price you agree.

BALLOONING

Two companies – Hod Hod Suleiman (☎ 370 116) and Balloons Over Egypt (☎ 376 515; owned by Britain's Virgin) – offer early-morning balloon flights over Luxor's West Bank. When the air is clear, the view over the monuments and the desert mountains is amazing. You also get a bird's-eye view of early morning village life. Changing winds mean that the trips are subject to cancellation at the last minute. It costs about US$250 for the flight plus a champagne breakfast and some folkloric dancing. Trips are usually arranged through hotels or travel agencies.

DONKEY, HORSE & CAMEL RIDES

Almost all the smaller hotels organise donkey treks around the West Bank. These trips, which start at about 7am (sometimes 5am) and finish about lunch time, cost a minimum of about E£30 per person, and may be more expensive. The hotels push these trips pretty hard, and although many travellers have reported being pleased with them, you can probably tailor your own trip with some hard bargaining when you cross the river.

If you just want to loll about on the back of a camel and take in the sights of the Nile, the boys at the local ferry dock on the West Bank ask E£25 for an hour. Some of the bigger hotels offer camel trips, which include visits to nearby villages for a cup of tea.

Pharaoh's Stables (☎ 310 015), which is reached by turning left just before the Mobil station, about 500m along the road leading to the Colossi of Memnon, has horses as well as camels and donkeys. A sunset ride in the desert is an unforgettable experience and owners Bakri and Nasser and a guide will take you through the fields, alongside Medinat Habu and out towards the mountains.

Just behind the Mobil station is the Arabian Horse Stable (☎ 310 024), which also has healthy horses and camels, and guides that will take you to the desert.

Both stables ask between E£15 and E£20 for an hour's ride.

SWIMMING

Many of the bigger hotels and some of the budget hotels have swimming pools. The Karnak, Windsor, Emilio and Arabesque Hotels and Rezeiky Camp all charge E£7. The St Joseph and Flobater Hotels, next to each other on the way out to the Sheraton, ask E£10 per person, as do the Shady and Luxor Wena Hotels. The Winter Palace has a lovely pool set amid its gardens. In high season it's often reluctant to accept non-guests. When the hotel is less crowded, they will charge about E£40 for day use. To use the Club Med Belladona Resort's Nile-side pool, you must buy a E£40 carnet of tickets which can be used for drinks and meals. The Sheraton, Isis and Mercure hotels all charge E£20.

ORGANISED TOURS

Masr Travel (☎ 373 551), Thomas Cook (☎ 372 1960) and other travel agencies around the Old Winter Palace organise half- and full-day tours to the West Bank in air-con buses. In summer this might be worth considering, as hefty reductions are offered. Otherwise, it's generally an expensive option at around US$40. Most of the small hotels aggressively promote their own tours. Some of these are better than others and there have been complaints by a

Moulids Around Luxor

At a *moulid* (religious festival) you can hear real Saidi music, see traditional Saidi stick dancing *(tahtib)*, or watch *mirmah*, where riders on Arabian horses gallop to and fro in what looks like a type of jousting.

There are a number of moulids in the Luxor area, most of them smaller and more manageable than the Moulid of Abu al-Haggag, which draws hundreds of thousands of visitors. Most take place in the month of Sha'aban, the month immediately before Ramadan. Although many take place outside the police *cordon sanitaire* around Luxor and are therefore all but impossible to visit these days, a few remain accessible.

Abu al-Gumsan, named after a religious man who died in 1984, is a small moulid that takes place on 27 Sha'aban near the West Bank village of Taref, just south of the road to the Valley of the Kings. **Sheikh Musa** and **Abu al-Jud** both take place in the sprawling village of Karnak, the latter on 30 Ashura. Other local moulids include **Sheikh Hamid** on 1 Sha'aban and **Sheikh Hussein** a couple of days later.

One of the only accessible Christian moulids is **Mar Girgis** (St George), which takes place at the monastery of the same name and has its climax on 11 November, although the celebrations go on for most of the week before. The monastery is at the village of Razagat, just south of Armant at the turn-off for the road to Kharga Oasis. Although this area is officially forbidden to foreigners, service taxis ferrying the hundreds of people attending the moulid will often avoid the checkpoint on the main road and go via a desert track.

Bakri, at Pharaoh's Stables (see under Donkey, Horse & Camel Rides earlier), often performs with his horses at moulids and he is more than willing to give you more information.

ıumber of travellers that they ended up eeing little more than papyrus shops and labaster factories from a sweaty car with ıo air-con. If you do decide to take one of hese tours, you're looking at about E£45 to E£65 per person.

The Novotel organises full-day cruises n its Lotus Boat to Dendara or Esna for E£150 per person, including lunch, guide nd admission fees. At the time of writing hey were planning to add a cruise to Abydos for about the same price.

SPECIAL EVENTS

The town's biggest traditional festival is the Moulid of Abu al-Haggag. One of Egypt's argest moulids, it is held in honour of Luxor's patron sheikh, Yousef Abu al-Haggag, a 12th-century Iraqi who settled in Luxor. The moulid takes place around the Mosque of Abu al-Haggag, the town's oldest mosque, which is actually on top of the orth-east corner of Luxor Temple. It's a aucous five-day event that takes place in he third week before Ramadan. See the boxed text 'Moulids Around Luxor' for details of other moulids in the area.

Around the end of February or beginning of March each year, a festival of Saidi music and culture, the Gourna Festival, is held in the village of Gurna on the West Bank. Each evening for five days, a different musician plays for an audience of villagers and foreigners. In 2001 tickets cost E£60 for each performance (locals go for free) – not cheap but well worth the price to see Sheikh Ahmed Berrin and others performing in a village setting to an enthusiastic audience (when we were there, villagers got up and began to move from side to side in a spontaneous *zikr* or devotional dancing – not something seen in the contrived folkloric shows at hotels). For more information, call ☎ 311 014, email **e** gourna@free.fr or check out the Web site, **w** gourna.free.fr.

In February each year a marathon is held on the West Bank. It begins at Deir al-Bahri and loops around the main antiquities sites before ending back where it began. You can ask at the tourist office for information.

PLACES TO STAY

Perhaps more than at any tourist destination in Egypt, the cost of accommodation in Luxor fluctuates seasonally. There is no hard-and-fast rule on how much rates might increase in winter or drop in summer. Some hotels drop their charges by 50% in the low season (summer), others barely alter them. In this section we've tried to give the high-season rate. Prices include taxes unless otherwise indicated.

PLACES TO STAY – BUDGET

Luxor has a good selection of budget places. Many boast both roof gardens and washing machines – although 'roof garden' can mean anything from an attractive rooftop restaurant to a concrete platform with chunks of cement and swirls of twisted iron all over the place. Most hotels offer breakfast, which usually means bread, butter, jam, cheese and maybe an egg, and a cup of tea or coffee. Unless stated otherwise, prices listed in this section include breakfast.

Another common feature of these places is the notice board. The quality of these varies considerably – some have a lot of useful information, others are more of a token effort.

Avoid the hotel touts who pounce on you as you get off the train or bus – they get a 25% to 40% commission for bringing you in which is added on your bill.

Camping

YMCA *(☎ 372 425, Sharia Karnak)* E£4 per night. This place was once popular with overland travel groups, but it has lost business to the more expensive Rezeiky Camp, further up the road towards the temple. The price includes the use of one of its 20 showers.

Rezeiky Camp *(☎ 381 334, fax 381 400, Sharia Karnak, W www.rezeikycamp.com)* Tent sites E£10 per person plus E£10 per vehicle, singles/doubles E£30/50. The camp is also a hotel with motel-style rooms with air-con, but you're paying for the privilege of having the pool on your doorstep. There's also an Internet cafe (50pt per minute), a large garden with a restauran and bar (E£6 for a beer), as well as a wash ing machine for which you pay E£10 for 4kg load. It's a reasonable deal but incon veniently located.

Warning

! Lone women travellers should use extreme caution when looking for budget accommodation in Luxor. Several have reported being sexually assaulted after being given spiked drinks by hotel staff.

Hostels

Youth Hostel *(☎ 372 139, fax 370 539* Members E£10.10, nonmembers E£11.10 The hostel is in a street just off Sharia Kar nak and has slightly dingy rooms with a least three beds and showers that tend to ge swampy. It is beside a school, which mean lots of early-morning noise. You can d better in town. Breakfast costs E£2.50.

Hotels – South of Sharia al-Mahatta

Anglo Hotel *(☎/fax 381 679, Midan al Mahatta)* Singles/doubles with fan & shared bath E£20/25; doubles with air-co & bath E£35. This hotel is very close to th station, and therefore noisy, but the room with air-con, private baths and telephone are a good deal.

Oasis Hotel *(☎ 381 699, Sharia Mo hammed Farid)* Singles/doubles E£7/13 Some rooms have baths and all have fans but hot water is not always available and th rooms are looking shabby. Travellers hav complained about the staff and the state c the rooms, so check carefully before com mitting to stay here.

Princess Pension *(☎ 373 997)* Dorr beds E£5. This is one of the cheapest place in town, even if it's not quite the cleanes It's off Sharia Ahmed Orabi.

Grand Hotel *(☎ 382 905, mobile 010 528 5865)* Singles/doubles with fan E£6 12, with air-con E£10/15. Off Sharia Mo hammed Farid, the Grand is clean and wel coming. It has a small rooftop terrace wit

ANDERS BLOMQVIST

At the village of Kom Lolah, near Luxor, fertile fields contrast with barren mountains.

THOMAS HARTWELL

The village of Gurna is built among Luxor's tombs.

CHRIS BARTON

Luxor market

DAVID ELSE

Many choose to ride a donkey over the rugged cliffs to the Valley of the Kings, near Luxor.

JOHN BORTHWICK

Funerary temple of Hatshepsut at Deir al-Bahri

TROY FLOWER

One of the sphinxes at Karnak

ANDERS BLOMQVIST

Statue of Ramses II with his daughter at Karnak

ANDERS BLOMQVIST

A black granite head of Ramses II at his funerary temple, known as the Ramesseum, at Luxor great views and decent shared bathrooms with hot water. The owner, a local schoolteacher named Nobi, is very friendly and keeps a room off the lobby where people can leave their belongings after checking out if they have a long wait for their train or bus. You can hire bikes here for E£6 per day.

Akhenaten Hotel *(☎ 373 979, Sharia Mohammed Farid)* Singles/doubles E£15/20, with bath E£15/25. The Akhenaten looks fancier on the outside than most other hotels and pensions around here, but has quite modest, cramped rooms.

Atlas Hotel *(☎ 373 514, fax 365 000)* Singles/doubles with fan E£15/20, doubles with air-con E£25. This is not a bad place and with 40 rooms (all with bath), it's rarely full. If you turn left into Sharia Ahmed Orabi (heading from the train station) and then right into the second dusty laneway, you'll find it.

Fontana Hotel *(☎ 380 663)* Beds in 4-bed room E£7, singles/doubles with air-con & bath E£15/30, doubles with fan & shared bath E£20. Off Sharia Televizyon, this 25-room hotel is popular with backpackers and has been known to reduce the prices for rooms with shared baths, as well as to raise the prices for the unwary – so sharpen your haggling skills. None of the bathrooms (all of which have full bathtubs as well as showers) are shared by more than three rooms, and toilet paper and towels are provided. The rooms are spotlessly clean and there's a kitchen (of sorts), rooftop terrace and washing machine for guests to use. The main complaint from travellers is that the owner can be a little too aggressive in promoting his tours.

Everest Hotel *(☎ 373 260, ⓔ everesthotel@hotmail.com, Sharia Nozha)* Singles/doubles E£10/25. On a small lane running off Sharia Televizyon, the Everest is a reasonable deal as the renovated rooms are OK and come with air-con or fan and bathrooms (with toilet paper). Like many other small hotels, the management is anxious to get you on one of its tours of the West Bank. They also have trips to Dendara for E£30 per person.

Sherif Hotel *(☎ 370 757, Sharia Badr)* Doubles with shared bath E£15, with air-con & bath E£20. This is a homey place on the west side of Sharia Televizyon. Run by a pleasant English teacher named Amr, it has 15 rooms, six with their own bathroom and four with air-con. It's a good deal and very conveniently located.

Moon Valley Hotel *(☎ 375 710, Sharia Shamouz)* E£10 per person. With decent-sized rooms with fans or air-con, plus private shower and toilet, as well as a common area with a VCR and selection of videos (should you feel like staying in), this is not a bad deal. However, some women readers have complained about the staff here.

Happy Land Hotel *(☎ 371 828, ⓔ happylandluxor@hotmail.com, Sharia Qamr)* Dorm beds with fan E£8, singles/doubles with bath E£25/30. The rooms here are spotless and toilet paper, soap and mosquito coils are provided. Happy Land claims to be the only budget hotel in town that offers cornflakes and real fruit with breakfast. It also has an Internet cafe (E£10 per hour). Some readers have complained about aggressive pushing of trips to the West Bank.

New Everest Hotel *(☎ 370 017)* Singles/doubles E£5/10, doubles with air-con & bath E£20. Close to the station, off Sharia al-Mahatta in a warren of side streets, this place has 12 clean rooms, four of which have air-con.

Hotels – North of Sharia al-Mahatta

Saint Mina Hotel *(☎ 375 409, fax 376 568)* Singles/doubles E£20/25, with bath E£25/35. Off Sharia Ramses, this is an excellent deal. The friendly hotel's 20 rooms are very clean, with air-con or fans, although some travellers have complained about noisy plumbing. These prices drop considerably in summer.

Nefertiti Hotel *(☎ 372 386)* Singles/doubles E£20/30. Off Sharia Karnak, the Nefertiti has been renovated and is under new management. It offers clean, air-con rooms and a roof terrace. It has been recommended by many travellers, despite the odd comment about pushing tours to the West Bank.

Nobles Hotel *(☎ 372 823, Midan Hassan)* Singles/doubles with fan E£20/30, with air-con E£25/40. With its less than friendly staff, Nobles is not quite as good as the other budget places but the rooms are reasonable.

Venus Hotel *(☎ 382 625)* Singles/doubles E£15/20. Across the road from Nobles, Venus has 30 reasonable rooms with bath and is popular with backpackers. It has a restaurant with blaring satellite TV and bar. There's also a 6th-floor terrace where you can down a cold Stella for E£6. They can also arrange donkey trips to the West Bank and have bicycles for rent at E£3 per day. However, at least one reader has complained about a peephole in the bathroom and staff pushing their donkey trips.

Pyramids Hotel *(☎ 373 243, Sharia Yousef Hassan)* Singles/doubles E£25/30. This place is located almost opposite the Venus, so the position is good. There's hot water and the rooms, with bath and air-con, are clean.

Hotels – West Bank

Although the West Bank is a more pleasant place to be than the town, there is only a limited selection of budget accommodation and it is all much pricier than in town. Which is better depends on whether you want the bustle and bright lights of the town or a peaceful sojourn in the Egyptian countryside.

Habu Hotel *(☎ 372 477, Kom Lolah)* Singles/doubles E£25/40. With its small, vaulted rooms and stunning views over the entrance to Medinat Habu temple complex, this could be a gem of a hotel if the management bothered to take care of it. The three upstairs rooms with a terrace overlooking the temple gate almost make it worth staying here, despite the state of the bathrooms. But it's probably better to pay E£6 for a beer up here rather than shell out the accommodation costs.

Queen's Hotel *(☎ 384 854, Kom Lolah)* Singles/doubles E£30/50. Queen's is overpriced but, like the Habu, it is locally run. There are great views from the roof terrace but the rooms need renovating. It's a toss-up whether it or the Habu has the most uncomfortable beds.

Marsam Hotel *(☎ 372 403, 311 603, e marsam@africamail.com, Gurna)* Singles/doubles E£25/50. Also known as Ali Abd al-Rasul Hotel or Sheikh Ali Hotel, this is the best place to stay on the West Bank in this price range. A local institution, the hotel was originally built for American archaeologists in the 1920s. In the 1960s it became a retreat for Egyptian artists (*marsam* means 'a place for drawing' in Arabic) – you can still see the odd sculpture in the shady courtyard. It belonged to Sheikh Ali Abdul Rasul, who was a member of the clan who helped discover the Tomb of Seti I. Following his death, his son took over the hotel. It is currently under the management of a friendly Australian woman, Natasha, and has improved vastly in recent years. There are 23 rooms (with shared bath) altogether, 10 in the main concrete building and the remainder in two mud-brick buildings.

Osiris Hotel *(☎ 310 685, Gurna)* E£20 per person. The Osiris is a small new hotel (no sign) off the road between the Ramesseum and Hatshepsut's temple. It has reasonably nice rooms with baths, high ceilings and fans. The roof terrace is not well finished but it has stunning views over the mountains. Breakfast costs E£5.

Abu al-Kasem Hotel *(☎ 310 319, At-Taref)* Singles/doubles with bath E£35/50. Near the Temple of Seti I on Sharia Wadi al-Melouk is this hotel which, although basically clean, is looking a bit scruffy and has 20 dusty rooms. The best ones overlook the mountains and there's a great view from the roof. The owner, the Abu al-Kasem family, also has an alabaster factory attached to the hotel and rents bicycles for E£5 a day, or donkeys for E£10.

Wadi al-Melouk Hotel *(☎ 310 175, At-Taref)* Singles/doubles E£20/35. On the east side of Al-Fadlya canal, this hotel is run-down and overpriced, although some effort has been made to improve things. Rooms have balconies but no fans. There is a wonderful roof terrace but it doesn't offset the state of the bathrooms. Bargaining with the old man who runs it might be possible.

PLACES TO STAY – MID-RANGE

Many mid-range places dropped their prices substantially following the decline in tourism after the Luxor massacre; many have jacked them back up again but the glut of similar places has meant others have been forced to keep prices down.

East Bank

Karnak Hotel (*☎ 376 155, fax 374 155, Sharia el-Nil*). Singles/doubles US$35/45, 20% discount June-Sept. This hotel is about 3km north of the town centre, opposite the Hilton, with comfortable rooms, a garden and a clean pool. It's a good place to be if you want to be out of the bustle of Luxor, but stay on the East Bank, and it has received rave reviews from some travellers.

Windsor Hotel (*☎ 372 847, fax 373 447*) Singles/doubles E£80/120. The Windsor Hotel has 120 rooms in a small alley just off Sharia Nefertiti. It has a pool but some of the rooms are a little shabby and others are decidedly gloomy and dark. It's popular with European tour groups.

Merryland Hotel (*☎/fax 381 746*) Singles/doubles in low season E£50/65, doubles in high season E£80. Across from the Windsor, off Sharia Nefertiti, Merryland has 32 rooms. All have TV, phone, air-con, bath and balcony, making it a reasonable deal. The rooftop bar has spectacular views over the Nile. However, be careful if you have a late departure; some readers report having had their bags tampered with when left at reception for the day.

Philippe Hotel (*☎ 373 604, fax 380 050, Sharia Nefertiti*) Singles/doubles E£70/100. Between the Corniche and Sharia Karnak is this upper mid-range hotel with clean, carpeted rooms, although those in its new wing are far superior to those in the old. All the rooms have powerful air-con, TV, mini-fridge and bathrooms with bathtubs. There's a pleasant roof garden with a small bar and pool. As this was one of the few hotels to be full during the post-massacre tourist slump, reservations are recommended.

Emilio Hotel (*☎ 373 570, fax 370 000, Sharia Yousef Hassan*) Singles/doubles US$50/55. This is a very good upper mid-range hotel with 48 rooms, all with bath, air-con, mini-fridge and TV with a hotel video channel. The astro-turfed roof terrace has plenty of shade, reclining chairs and a popular pool. Reservations are needed here in winter, when it is often taken over by travel groups.

St Mark Hotel (*☎/fax 373 532, Sharia Karnak*) Singles/doubles E£35/60. Around the corner from the Emilio, the St Mark has small but clean rooms with air-con, bath, TV and fridge. It's a friendly place and there's a small roof bar where beer is served.

Mina Palace Hotel (*☎ 372 074, Corniche el-Nil*) Singles/doubles E£60/80. The Mina Palace is just opposite the entrance to the Mummification Museum. Although it is getting slightly run-down, the Nile views are great. Rooms feature air-con and private bath. The management will drop prices considerably during the low season. Make sure you ask for a corner room with two balconies – one looking towards Luxor Temple and the other over the Nile.

Horus Hotel (*☎ 372 165, fax 373 447, Sharia Karnak*) Singles/doubles E£30/40. About a block north of Sharia al-Mahatta, you'll see the Horus. Rooms seem reasonably comfortable, but few people seem to stay here. The front rooms are definitely better than the others but they face a mosque, which means an early wake-up call each morning.

Luxor Wena Hotel (*☎ 380 018, fax 379 849, Sharia Karnak*) Singles/doubles US$30/40. Near Luxor Temple, this hotel is at the centre of a long-running court battle and as a result is looking a bit dilapidated. It has a swimming pool and a variety of restaurants.

New Radwan Hotel (*☎ 385 502, fax 385 501, Sharia Abdel Moneim al-Adasi*) Singles/doubles E£55/70. A three-star hotel at two-star prices; spotless rooms with bath and air-con make this an excellent deal. It's centrally located, and has a roof terrace, a garden restaurant and a bar.

Arabesque Hotel (*☎ 371 299, fax 372 193, Sharia Mohammed Farid*) Singles/doubles E£70/100. This hotel is not far from the main post office, and has a pool and roof garden with good views over Luxor Temple and the Nile. It's central, but the rooms (with air-con and very small beds) suffer a little from street noise. It has its own Internet cafe, but at E£20 per hour, you'd do better to try elsewhere.

Shady Hotel *(☎/fax 374 859, Sharia Televizyon)* Singles/doubles E£60/80. This is a reasonable deal, with decent air-con rooms. However, the much-vaunted pool is often murky and unusable and there have been complaints about the restaurant and the management.

Golden Palace Hotel *(☎ 382 972, fax 382 974, Sharia Televizyon)* Singles/doubles E£60/100. Further down Sharia Televizyon from Shady Hotel is this blue-and-yellow hotel with clean rooms featuring air-con, TV, fridge and telephone. It also has a reasonably sized pool.

Tutotel *(☎ 377 990, fax 372 671, Sharia Salah ad-Din)* Singles/doubles low season US$32/44. This small four-star hotel has a rooftop pool and all the usual facilities.

St Joseph Hotel *(☎ 381 707, fax 381 727)* Singles/doubles US$30/40. This popular, well-run, three-star hotel is just past the Club Med Belladona Resort, off Sharia Khaled ibn al-Walid. Rooms feature TV, air-con, phone and bath. It also has a pool and basement bar.

Flobater Hotel *(☎ 374 223, fax 370 618)* Singles/doubles not including 5% taxes US$16/22. Next to the St Joseph, off Sharia Khaled ibn al-Walid, the rather oddly named Flobater has similar, comfortable rooms with TV, fridge, a token pool and pleasant roof garden.

West Bank

Nur el-Gurna *(☎ 311 430, Gurna)* Singles/doubles E£60/70, suites E£100. This unique little hotel is in a mud-brick house in a palm grove just across the road from the Antiquities Inspectorate ticket office. It has large rooms with fans, each slightly different, with small stereos, simple, locally made furniture and nice tiled baths. All beds have mosquito nets, which are both practical and decorative. This is one of the nicest hotels in the area and is highly recommended.

Pharaohs Hotel *(☎ 310 702, fax 310 110, Gurna)* E£50 per person, single or double. This is the oldest mid-range place to stay on the West Bank, with 14 old rooms (which are currently being used by police officers billeted in the area) and 15 new ones, all with air-con and bath. Although it's not beautiful, the location can't be beat. There is also a garden restaurant that serves Stella for E£6 and has kebab meals starting at E£10.

Amenhotep Hotel *(☎/fax 311 228, Kom Lolah)* Singles/doubles E£75/130. This quiet new hotel, in a large building near the Medinat Habu temple complex, has spotless, comfortable rooms, a nice rooftop restaurant and friendly management. Most of the rooms have fans but the management promises air-con in the near future.

Amon al-Gezira Hotel *(☎ 310 912, Al-Gezira)* Doubles with air-con E£60-70. This is a small, spotlessly clean, family run hotel presided over by Ahmed Mahmoud Suleiman. Five of the nine rooms here have their own bathrooms and there is a terrace on each floor as well as a great roof terrace. To get there follow the signs to the Pharaoh's Stables.

Al-Gezira Hotel *(☎/fax 310 034, Al-Gezira)* Singles/doubles E£40/60. This is a new addition on the West Bank; it has 11 rooms, some with great Nile views, all with private baths and either air-con or ceiling fans. There is also a very pleasant rooftop restaurant overlooking the Nile where you can eat a filling Egyptian meal for E£20. Stella is available for E£7. To get to the hotel take the small track that goes beside the bicycle hire and video rental shop just up from the local ferry landing. The hotel is about 50m away on the left.

PLACES TO STAY – TOP END

The hotels in this price range start at about US$50 for a single and generally have all the usual attributes of big international hotels. Unless specified, the rates listed in this section include breakfast and taxes (up to 26%).

Club Med Belladona Resort *(☎ 380 850, fax 380 879, Sharia Khaled ibn al-Walid)* Singles/doubles US$75/106. This four-star resort has tacky, prefab architecture but a nice pool overlooking the Nile. It's popular with French package tourists.

Gaddis Hotel *(☎ 382 838, fax 382 837, Sharia Khaled ibn al-Walid)* Singles/doubles US$60/80. This is a small, very comfortable hotel with friendly staff. Unfortunately it's not on the Nile but it has three restaurants, a bar, disco and pool.

Hilton Hotel *(☎ 374 933, fax 376 571, Sharia el-Nil)* Singles/doubles US$120/130. Prices do not include taxes. The Hilton is 1km north of the Karnak temple complex. Buses are on hand to shuttle guests into the centre of town.

Hotel Mercure *(☎ 380 944, fax 384 912, Corniche el-Nil)* Singles/doubles US$105/124, with Nile views US$124/156. Prices do not include taxes. In summer (May to September) prices are reduced by 10% to 15%. A US$15 supplement is applied to the high-season rate between 23 December and 4 January. This well-located but soulless hotel is managed by the famous French chain of the same name. It's popular, not surprisingly, with French package tourists.

Isis Hotel *(☎ 372 750, fax 372 923, Sharia Khaled ibn al-Walid)* Singles/doubles in low season US$80/100. This five-star hotel is an eyesore of a building set in a lush garden setting with manicured hedges, two pools and Italian and Chinese restaurants. It also has great views over the Nile.

Mercure Inn *(☎ 373 321, fax 370 051, Sharia Karnak)* Singles/doubles with garden view US$53/70, with pool view US$77/94. This is another four-star hotel belonging to the French chain, with comfortable, if tackily decorated rooms, and the usual air-con, satellite TV and pool.

Mövenpick Jolie Ville *(☎ 374 855, fax 374 936, ⓔ jolie.ville@movenpick-lxr.com.eg, Crocodile Island)* Singles/doubles US$170/200. On Crocodile Island, 4km south of town, this is a five-star, Swiss-managed place with swimming pool, tennis courts and sailing boats. There is also a mini zoo and a playground, making it a popular choice for families with young children. There are 320 reasonably good rooms set out in bungalow style amid lush tropical gardens. The hotel motorboat shuttles guests to and from the centre of town.

Novotel Luxor *(☎ 380 925, fax 380 972, Corniche el-Nil)* Singles/doubles US$91/120. This is a squat high-rise at the southern tip of the Corniche with an indoor atrium, great Nile views and a floating swimming pool.

Sheraton Luxor Resort *(☎ 374 544, fax 374 941, Sharia Khaled ibn al-Walid)* Singles/doubles US$55/80, with Nile views US$75/100. The Sheraton is a secluded three-storey building at the southern end of Sharia Khaled ibn al-Walid. The hotel sits on the edge of the Nile and has some great views. It also has one of the best pools in town.

Sonesta St George Hotel *(☎ 382 575, fax 382 571, ⓔ reservations@sonesta-hotel-luxor.com, Sharia Khaled ibn al-Walid)* Singles/doubles with Nile views US$175/220. This 224-room marble-filled hotel had the distinction of opening its doors only days before the 1997 massacre decimated tourism in Luxor. It offers comfortable rooms, some with great views, a business centre, pool with faux Pharaonic columns, and other five-star comforts.

Old Winter Palace and ***New Winter Palace*** *(☎ 380 422, fax 374 087, ⓔ h1661@accor-hotels.com, Corniche el-Nil)* Singles/doubles standard Nile & garden view US$304/274, deluxe Nile & garden view US$369/334, new wing Nile & garden view US$190/166. These hotels stand side by side on the Corniche, but the new section is not nearly as interesting and romantic as the old, which was built to attract the aristocracy of Europe and is one of Egypt's famous historic hotels. A lovely Victorian pile, with fabulous views over the Nile, it also has a large garden with exotic trees and shrubs, a nice swimming pool, table-tennis tables and tennis court.

El-Moudira *(mobile ☎ 012-325 1307, Daba'iyya, West Bank)* Rooms US$120-250. Prices do not include taxes. The finishing touches were being put on this palatial new 54-room hotel at the time of writing.

Built to resemble a series of Damascene courtyard houses, each of the huge rooms has a trompe l'oeil theme and a richness that brings to mind ancient Italian villas. The large, airy bathrooms are bigger than the rooms in some of Luxor's shoddier places and details such as the incorporation of old doors and wrought-iron balconies make this a truly special place. Set in the desert about 5km from the bridge, this is destined to be one of Egypt's most beautiful hotels.

PLACES TO EAT

Budget Dining

Sharia al-Mahatta has a number of good sandwich stands and other cheap eats possibilities, as well as a few juice stands at its Luxor Temple end. The other area for low-priced food is Sharia Televizyon.

Sayyida Zeinab *(Sharia Televizyon)* Dishes E£1.50-2.50. This tiny but spotless place is one of Luxor's best kushari joints.

Salt & Bread Cafeteria *(Midan al-Mahatta)* Dishes E£4-10. Cheap meals are served here, across from the train station. It offers many dishes, including kebab, pigeon and chicken. The menu also includes six kinds of omelette – one wonders how different they can be.

Mensa Restaurant *(☎ 385 726, Sharia al-Mahatta)* Dishes E£8.50. This place serves slightly overpriced basic food, including sandwiches, chicken and pigeon stuffed with rice.

Abu Ashraf *(☎ 380 209, Sharia al-Mahatta)* Dishes E£2-9. This large, popular takeaway restaurant is just down from the station. It serves roasted chicken, kushari and shwarma.

Chicken Hut Dishes E£E2-5. On the corner of Sharias as-Souq and Karnak, this Egyptian fast-food restaurant offers chicken shwarmas, kofta and other sandwiches. It's popular with locals and tourists.

Al-Hussein *(Sharia Karnak)* Mains E£5-28, not including service. This restaurant does a good fish in a tomato and basil sauce and pizzas, starting at E£8.

Amoun Restaurant *(Sharia Karnak)* Mains E£8-25. Next door to the Al-Hussein and marginally more popular, the Amoun serves oriental kebab, chicken, fish and various rice and vegetable dishes at slightly lower prices than the Hussein. These are two of the town's most popular eating houses for tourists.

Ali Baba Cafe *(☎ 380 018)* Dishes E£3-10. Although part of the Luxor Wena Hotel, on the corner of Sharias Mohammed Farid & Karnak, this cafe has its own street entrance and offers reasonably priced mezze and meals such as shish kebab and *shish tawouq* (grilled chicken on skewers). You can also get *sheeshas* (water pipes) for about E£3. It's popular with locals and tourists alike.

Mish Mish *(☎ 380 407, Sharia Televizyon)* Mains E£7-10. Mish Mash is a long-standing travellers favourite, with good pizza, salads and stews.

Sultana Restaurant *(Sharia Televizyon)* Mains E£7-11. This tiny place is popular with travellers. Try the vegetable stew *(bram)*, served steaming in a clay pot, or pizzas.

Chez Omar *(mobile ☎ 012-282 0282, Midan Hassan)* Mains E£6-15. This outdoor cafe is a small oasis of green, with 10 tables under umbrellas. It's a pleasant lunch spot, with basic Egyptian dishes, salads and French fries.

Restaurants

East Bank Unfortunately there are no really fine restaurants in Luxor – the food at the Winter Palace does not live up to expectations and if you want a culinary treat you'd be better off at one of the other five-star hotels. ***Mövenpick Jolie Ville*** is famous for its breakfast buffets but its other meals are also highly recommended. For something totally different, the new ***Sonesta St George*** has a Japanese restaurant that has received excellent reviews from local residents. For something slightly cheaper, there is also a small restaurant at the ***New Radwan Hotel***, near the station, which has steaks and chicken curry for under E£20.

Dawar al-Umda Restaurant *(☎ 373 321, Sharia Karnak)* Mains E£16-20. Set in the garden of the Mercure Inn, this pleasant outdoor restaurant serves Egyptian specialities, with a decent selection of mezze in addition to the usual kebab and kofta. There is often a belly dancer or folkoric show during the high season.

Marhaba Restaurant *(☎ 372 282, Corniche el-Nil)* Mains E£20-50. This rooftop restaurant is beloved of tour groups and serves the usual Egyptian salads and mezze, with overcooked grills and chicken. However, the view over the Nile and Luxor Temple almost makes up for the less than inspiring food.

Jamboree Restaurant *(mobile ☎ 010-146 1712, Sharia al-Montazah)* Mains E£22-35. This is a new restaurant, just behind the Mena Palace Hotel, with British owners. It serves a mixture of Egyptian and international fare that's way above the usual Luxor standard and has been the subject of much praise from readers. It has a (safe) salad bar, a roof terrace and air-con but no liquor licence (yet).

Peace Abouzeid Restaurant *(☎ 372 419, Corniche el-Nil)* Mains E£25-50. Next to the Karnak temple complex, this is one of Luxor's few Nile-side restaurants that isn't part of a hotel. Although the lunch-time buffet tends to be mobbed by dazed tourists on bus trips from Hurghada, at night its tables are frequented by Egyptians and foreigners who want dinner and a sheesha by the Nile. It offers a wide selection of seafood and Egyptian specialities; try the grilled pigeon.

Esquire Restaurant Mains E£8-30. This restaurant is attached to Pub 2000, off Sharia Khaled ibn al-Walid. It has pub-style food similar to the Kings Head but not quite as successful. However, prices are more reasonable and you can roll in or out to the pub next door for happy hour (from 7.30pm to 8.30pm).

Kings Head Pub *(☎ 371 249, Sharia Khaled ibn al-Walid)* Mains E£10-30. Near the passport office, the King's Head continues to be one of Luxor's most popular bar/eateries. This place is England through and through – except that it's open 24 hours and the king in question is Akhenaten wearing a Tudor hat. It's a laid-back place to spend an afternoon catching up on foreign newspapers or tucking into toasted sandwiches and chips. They even have a roast beef and Yorkshire pudding lunch-time special on Sunday. Beer is reasonably priced and there's a huge array of cocktails (E£15 each) and spirits.

Ritz Restaurant *(☎ 370 912)* Mains E£10-20. In a small alleyway off Sharia Khaled ibn al-Walid between the Sonesta St George and Isis Hotels, this is a new place that offers a variety of mains and has soups starting at E£3.50.

Jem's *(☎ 383 604, Sharia Khaled ibn al-Walid)* Mains E£15-35. Khaled ibn al-Walid has become Luxor's restaurant strip and Jem's does very good Egyptian or European meals, including a vegetarian set menu. Filling appetisers and salads are cheaper at about E£8.

Tudor Rose *(Sharia Khaled ibn al-Walid)* Mains E£20-30. Underneath Jem's, Tudor Rose is presumably hoping to cash in on the success of the King's Head – it also offers English food, including roast beef and Yorkshire pudding. Prices are similar to those at the King's Head but it lacks the ambience.

La Mama *(☎ 374 544, Sheraton Luxor Resort)* Mains $18-45. The Italian restaurant on the terrace at the entrance to the Sheraton is a good bet if you've got kids in tow. Apart from a range of the usual Italian specialities such as pizza and pasta, there's a pelican that wanders around and chases you if you get too close.

West Bank Some of the best, or at least most atmospheric, meals in Luxor can be found on the West Bank rather than across the river in town.

Tutankhamun Restaurant *(☎ 310 118, Al-Gezira)* Mains E£10-25. This small restaurant is on the riverside just north of the local ferry dock. It's run by Aam Mahmoud, a former cook at one of the French archaeological missions in Luxor, who serves up excellent *tagins* (stews) and other dishes.

Anna's Kitchen *(mobile ☎ 012-416 3267, Al-Gezira)* Snacks E£5-15. This tiny, spotless little teashop/cafe is on the main road to Gurna. It's run by the eponymous Anna, a Welsh woman living in Al-Gezira, who serves delicious omelettes, home-made cakes, English-style tea and cold drinks from 11am to 6.30pm.

Al-Gezira Hotel *(☎ 310 034, Al-Gezira)* Mains E£15-35. This hotel serves Egyptian specialities such as the infamous *molokhiyya* (for more details, see Food in the Facts for the Visitor chapter) and *mahshi kurumb* (stuffed cabbage leaves). The covered rooftop restaurant has great views over the Nile and the bright lights of Luxor beyond. Beer is available for E£7.

Marsam Hotel *(☎ 382 403, Gurna)* Mains E£14-18. The Marsam, near the Antiquities Inspectorate ticket office, serves surprisingly good, fresh food on its tree-filled terrace. Lunch dishes are usually Egyptian specialities, such as stuffed pigeon and lentil soup, while in the evenings Western-style dishes are served. It has a set menu and it is a good idea to call ahead. Beer is not available.

Nur el-Gurna *(☎ 311 430, Gurna)* Meals E£15-20. Stuffed pigeon, duck and other hearty local dishes are served under a palm-reed shade or in a cool room, depending on the season. Near the Antiquities Inspectorate ticket office, this is a friendly and pleasant place to eat, but beer is not available.

Restaurant Mohammed *(☎ 311 014)* Mains E£12-30. Open noon-10pm daily. Next to Pharaohs Hotel, this restaurant is in a large, recently renovated room attached to owner Mohammed Abdel Lahi's mud-brick house, with a shady outdoor terrace. This is the venue for the annual Gourna Festival (for more information, see Special Events earlier in this chapter) and is very popular with French archaeologists and other foreign residents in the area. There is no menu (you are told what's on offer that day) but you can usually get good, basic Egyptian food (the home-made white cheese is great), as well as standard chicken and French-fry platters. Portions are generous and Stella can be had for E£7.

Hatshepsut Restaurant *(☎ 310 469, Gurna)* Mains E£15-35. Open 11am until late daily. This 2nd-floor, shaded, rooftop restaurant is above an alabaster shop and has great views over Hatshepsut's temple and the Theban hills. It serves a mixture of Egyptian and Western dishes. The food is reasonable and the atmosphere in the evenings can be good, especially in the cooler months, when Saidi music and dancing takes place.

Self-Catering

If you want to buy your own food for meals or snacks, you will find a wide range on sale in Luxor. The best place for fruit and vegetables is the ***souq***, although the good stuff sells out early in the morning. On either side of the main street are little shops selling fruit and veg throughout the day.

On these streets you'll also find small ***grocery shops***, or *ba'als*, that stock canned goods, some Western-style cereals, imported cheese such as Edam (called *felamenk*) as well as local white cheese and *gibna rumi* (Roman cheese). If you're over by Sharia Televizyon, look for the ***Barghouti*** grocery store on the west side of the street, just south of Mish Mish restaurant. It has a good selection of yogurts and cheeses kept in clean, functioning fridges, as well as an excellent selection of dry foods. Near Barghouti, on Sharia Medina al-Manawwara, ***Omar*** is a larger, Western-style mini-market, which has a better range of imported goodies.

Luxor has a number of ***bakeries*** but one of the best is a no-name bakery at the beginning of Sharia Ahmed Orabi that makes delicious cookies and breads, and has prices in English. Also good is the large bakery at the beginning of Sharia Karnak, where locals go to buy buns and bread sticks.

Those in search of a few takeaway beers can go to the ***Al-Ahram Beverages*** *(☎ 372 445)* just north of the train station. It's open from 8am until midnight daily and stocks local beer and wine at the best prices in town. On the corner of the same block is ***Mahall Hosny and Refat***, which stocks the same products at slightly higher prices. Opening hours are from 1pm to 1am Monday to Saturday.

ENTERTAINMENT

With tourism booming in Luxor, the town is busy at night. This is not the place to go clubbing, unless you're into dancing to outmoded disco music with a group of other tourists, but there are some bars with a decent atmosphere. Most of the larger hotels put on a folkloric show several times each week, depending on the season and number of tour groups around. For a more authentic experience, you can head over to the calm of the West Bank, although you'll need to ensure that you have transport back to wherever you're staying.

Bars

If you want a drink, there are several bars in Luxor, apart from ***Kings Head Pub*** (see Restaurants under Places to Eat earlier for more details).

Old Winter Palace *(☎ 380 422, Corniche el-Nil)* The terrace in front of the Winter Palace is the most elegant place in Luxor to watch the sun slowly set over the Theban hills. Starched collars and gin and tonics are the rule here, but you can order afternoon tea if you prefer. The service is usually slow but the silver tableware and white tablecloths soothe away the frustrations of the souq and make the high prices worthwhile.

Pub 2000 *(☎ 370 076)* Off Sharia Khaled ibn al-Walid, on a side street about 200m south of the Novotel, Pub 2000 has a popular happy hour between 7.30pm and 8.30pm when Stellas go for E£5. It also has a good selection of meals, including reasonably priced daily specials in conjunction with the Esquire Restaurant next door.

St Joseph Bar *(☎ 381 707)* The bar at the St Joseph Hotel has its own happy hour between 10pm and 11pm. Beer is reduced by 30% and spirits by 50%. It's popular with tourists from neighbouring hotels.

Over on the West Bank, beer is available at ***Habu Hotel***, in the garden of ***Pharaohs Hotel***, ***Hatshepsut Restaurant*** and at ***Restaurant Mohammed***.

Nightclubs, Discos & Shows

Dawar al-Umda *(☎ 373 321, Sharia Karnak)* This restaurant, in the garden of the Mercure Inn, has a folkloric show that includes a belly dancer, *rababa* music (for more on rababa music, see the boxed text 'Saidi Music' later in this chapter), and occasionally a snake charmer. With its reasonably priced Egyptian food, it is very popular. The show does not have a regular schedule and depends on the number of tourists on hand, but it usually takes place twice a week in the high season. Call the hotel for information.

Mövenpick Jolie Ville *(☎ 374 855, Crocodile Island)* presents an extravagant floor show. You are dressed in a *galabiyya* (traditional Egyptian man's robe), taken for a felucca ride at sunset, introduced to 'peasants', and then fed and entertained in a tent by the Nile. Call the resort for up-to-date information on the schedule.

The ***Isis*** and ***Winter Palace*** hotels have folkloric and belly-dance performances as well as discos. There is no schedule to these events and you should call and check beforehand.

If you'd rather move about on the dance floor yourself instead of watching someone else gyrate, the disco at ***Tutotel*** *(☎ 377 990)* is one of the more popular options, while at ***Hotel Mercure*** *(☎ 380 944)*, nonguests must pay a minimum charge of E£20 to get into the Sabil disco. This covers you for the belly dancer at 11.30pm too.

An authentically sleazy nightclub/restaurant with belly dancing, ***Mandaria*** is frequented by local businessmen and the few Arab tourists who venture to Luxor. Regular patrons buy a bottle of Johnny Walker that sits in the centre of the table and the level in the bottle goes down as the evening progresses. The show starts sometime around midnight and continues into the early hours of the morning. It's off Sharia Khaled ibn al-Walid, down an alleyway almost opposite Isis Hotel.

If you want to avoid the bright lights of the town, the West Bank is the place to be, although the jumpy police have put a damper on some of the more interesting night-time experiences to be enjoyed here. Pharaoh's Stables (see under Donkey, Horse & Camel Rides earlier in this chapter) arranges evening desert barbecues for groups of 10 or more and sometimes puts on a horse-dancing show. Bakri or Nasser will be able to tell you if this is possible again.

Saidi Music

Upper Egyptians (or Saidis) may be ridiculed as country bumpkins by the relatively sophisticated Cairenes, but their sometimes stubborn adherence to tradition has preserved some of Egypt's most distinctive regional culture. This is especially true when it comes to music, and with its strong rhythms and simple instruments Saidi music is a welcome change from the tinny Cairo pop that you hear throughout the country.

People in Luxor will tell you of four different types of Saidi music, although categories blur. First is the very popular *medah*, which comes from traditional Sufi *zikr* (devotional singing) and often involves repetitive chanting. Second is *kaff al-Saidi*, which is usually performed by one or two singers accompanied by handclapping (*kaff* means palm) instead of instruments. Third is *muzmar*, named after a reed instrument and often used to accompany horse dancing or belly dancing. Finally, there's *rababa*, named after an instrument that looks and sounds a bit like a home-made, single-string violin.

Many of the musicians come from the small towns around Luxor and get their start at village weddings or Sufi zikrs and sometimes you can hear their music on weekend nights on the West Bank.

A few of the most famous and, to Western ears, most accessible Saidi musicians include Sheikh Ahmed Birrin, a blind sheikh hailing from Esna with an addictive, reedy voice; Rayyis Nessim, a student of Birrin; Yousef Bakash, a famous rababa musician who has been 'discovered' and is now famous in France (and is one of the few Saidi musicians whose work is available on CD); Gamal al-Esnawi, one of the younger generation of medah singers; and Sayyed ad-Dawy, who sings the famous epic, the *Sira al-Hilalawi*.

Their cassettes (which cost about E£7 each) can be bought in Luxor at the Hani w'Hanafon tape shop opposite the post office on Sharia al-Mahatta. The owners are happy to let you listen before you buy.

Hatshepsut Restaurant (*☎ 310 469, Gurna*) On Sunday and Wednesday there is a popular belly-dancing and Saidi music show that usually includes an exhibition of *tahtib*, or stick dancing.

On Thursday nights, especially in the summer, you can often hear the music from a local wedding or a Sufi zikr wafting across the fields – if you follow your ears you will usually be welcomed.

SHOPPING

Pretty much the whole range of standard Egyptian souvenirs can be bought in Luxor, although the variety is not nearly as great as in Cairo. One exception is alabaster. You will notice a plethora of alabaster shops on the West Bank. The alabaster is mined about 80km north-west of the Valley of the Kings, and some of the handmade cups, vases and other articles make sturdy and original souvenirs. Take care when buying, however; the quality can be poor and in some cases what passes for stone is in fact wax with stone chips.

The clay pots *(tawagen*, singular *tagen)* that are used in local cooking make a more unusual buy. Extremely practical, they can be used to cook on top of the stove or in the oven and they look good on the table too. Before they are used they must be 'cured' using a mixture of molasses and oil in a very low oven for about 30 minutes. They aren't exactly light, but they come in various sizes and prices start at E£5. They are on sale just beside the police station in Luxor.

Hand-carved wooden bowls from Hegaza, a village just north of Luxor, are another locally produced handicraft. Made of lemon, orange and tamarisk wood, they are light and beautifully finished. The security measures around Luxor mean that it's difficult to visit the village itself, but there is a display of the products in the shop at the Mövenpick Jolie Ville on Crocodile Island.

Winter Akhmeem Gallery (☎ 380 422), beside the staircase to the Old Winter Palace, has beautiful handmade cotton, linen and silk from Akhmin, near Sohag. Prices are steep, averaging E£40 to E£80 per metre, but this is still cheaper than you'd pay for something comparable in most other countries. They will also make made-to-measure galabiyyas and shirts.

GETTING THERE & AWAY

Air

The EgyptAir (☎ 380 580) office is on the Corniche, next to AmEx. EgyptAir flies daily between Cairo, Luxor and Aswan. A one-way ticket to Luxor from Cairo costs E£459 and there are frequent daily departures. There are also daily flights from Luxor to Aswan (E£199 one way) and three flights per week to Sharm el-Sheikh (E£393 one way). There are two flights a week to Hurghada (E£210 one way).

Bus

The bus station (☎ 372 118) is behind Luxor Temple on Sharia Karnak (the garage on Sharia Televizyon is not an official pick-up point).

From Luxor, there is only one daily departure to Cairo and it leaves at 7pm (E£60, 10 to 11 hours). Seven buses leave for Aswan (E£8, four to five hours) between 6.30am and 8pm but only the last one has air-con. Some of these are through-services from Qena and Hurghada, so there may not always be seats. The same buses go to Esna (E£2.50) and Edfu (E£4).

To Hurghada (E£13 to E£20, five hours), there are seven daily buses, from 6.30am to 8pm. All stop in Safaga (E£11 to E£17) and all except the last two stop in Suez (E£31 to E£40).

There are 11 buses to Qena between 6.30am and 8pm that cost from E£3 to E£5, but you may not be allowed to take them because of the jittery police.

There are buses to Kharga via Asyut at 8.30am (E£28) and 11pm (E£12). There is also a direct bus to Dahab at 5pm for E£90 (14 to 16 hours). However, some travellers have reported that 'direct' means going via Cairo on a nightmarish 24-hour odyssey. Check with the tourist office if you have any doubt about the routing.

Train

The train station at Luxor has a post office (which has express mail service, cardphones, left-luggage, telex and telegraph facilities) and a tourist information office that is often closed.

If you want to take a sleeper to Cairo, the only option is the wagons-lit train (see under Train in the Getting Around chapter for more details). Berths have to be booked two or three days in advance. The ticket window (☎ 372 015) for these is open only between 9am and 2pm and 5pm and 8pm and the fare is E£362 one way. The train leaves Luxor at about 9pm and reaches Cairo at 7am. There is no student discount.

Otherwise, there are only three other Cairo trains that foreigners are allowed to take. The first departs at 8.15am and costs E£56/31 (E£36/24 for students) in 1st/2nd class. It stops in Balyana for those who wish to visit Abydos. The next train departs at 8:50pm and arrives in Cairo at 6am; fares are E£60/33 (E£36/24 for students). There is also a train at 11.10pm, which arrives in Cairo at 8.30am; fares are E£60/36 (E£46/28 for students). There are, of course, many more trains heading north and you can hop on any one of them without a reservation. The police are not usually overly zealous about stopping you.

To Aswan (three to four hours) it costs E£27/18 (E£20/15 for students) on the 7.30am train and E£22/14 on the 5.40pm service.

There is a train to Kharga every Thursday at 7am, which has 3rd class only and no air-con. It is supposed to take seven hours but reportedly can take up to 10. Tickets cost E£9.80 (E£4.90 for students).

For tickets, the 3rd-class window is on your left when facing the tracks; other tickets are sold at the windows on the right.

Car

No matter where you want to go these days, getting out of Luxor by road usually involves going in police convoy. Current convoy times to Hurghada are 6am, 8am, 2pm and 5.30pm; to Aswan they leave at 11am and 3pm. Check these times with the tourist office before travelling.

Vehicles congregate at the road behind the 25 January Hotel about 30 minutes before the convoy time. Day trips to Dendara and Abydos leave with the 8am convoy and branch off at Qena with their own escort. Those heading south can also wait at the checkpoint just before the bridge.

Service Taxi

The service taxi station is on a street off Sharia Karnak, a couple of blocks inland from Luxor Museum. Regular destinations include Aswan (E£8, 3½ hours), Esna (E£2, 45 minutes), Edfu (E£4, two hours), Kom Ombo (E£8, 2½ hours) and Qena (E£2).

The drivers are always ready to bargain for special trips down the Nile to Aswan, stopping at the sights on the way – reckon on about E£100 for the car. Keep in mind that you may have to travel in a convoy. You should arrive at the service taxi station about 30 minutes before the convoy is due to leave.

Those planning a trip from Luxor to Kharga via the new direct road will have to go via Asyut until the police deem the road secure. Taxis are reluctant to undertake the trip and their current asking price is E£700 for the car (maximum seven people). You're better off suffering the long bus or train ride.

Cruise Ship

For information on the 250 cruise boats that ply the Nile between Luxor and Aswan see the Getting Around chapter.

Felucca

You can take a felucca from Luxor to Aswan but very few people do it because it means going against the Nile's very strong flow. Unless you have a strong wind, it can take days to go more than a few kilometres. It's better to do it from Aswan. For more information, see the boxed text 'Felucca Trips' in the Nile Valley – Esna to Abu Simbel chapter.

GETTING AROUND

To/From the Airport

Luxor airport is 7km east of town and you cannot get a taxi for less than E£20, although they'll usually ask for more. There are no buses to or from the airport into town.

Motorcycle

A few hotels have started renting out motorcycles for about E£40 to E£60 per day. If you are interested, hunt around a bit and check the condition of the bikes carefully.

Bicycle

Luxor is bursting with bicycle rental shops and almost all hotels rent out bikes. Some of the better places even have children's bikes. Depending on the quality of the bike, how good business is and the determination of your bargaining, they can cost from E£6 to E£15 per day. You are often asked to

Brooke Hospital for Animals

Desert rides and horse-drawn carriages are a memorable part of any trip to Egypt but the way some of the animals are treated shocks many visitors. However, there are people who are working to combat cruelty to animals. Although not really a tourist sight, the Brooke Hospital, open from 8am to 1.30pm and 4pm to 6pm October to April, from 8am to 1.30pm and 6pm to 8pm May to September, is part of a worldwide network of clinics aiming to provide at least minimum care for animals, especially those put to work. It's up the road from the Mina Palace Hotel, and has been operating in Luxor for more than three decades (although the original hospital was on a different site). You might like to visit and see what they do for the horses that used to pull the hantours through the streets of Luxor. Just as importantly, they have a notice board of dos and don'ts on the treatment of horses, which includes not tipping drivers for pushing the animals into going too fast.

If you are particularly interested in its work, it also has clinics in Cairo (☎ 02-364 9312; head office), Alexandria, Edfu and Aswan.

leave your passport or student identification card.

Bicycles can also be rented on the West Bank, near the local ferry landing, but the choice of bicycle is better in the town itself and the prices on the West Bank are sometimes inflated.

Hantour

For about E£20 per hour you can get around by horse and carriage. Rates are subject to haggling and, occasionally, screaming.

Felucca

There are, of course, a multitude of feluccas to take you on short trips around Luxor. They leave from various points all along the river. How much you pay depends on your bargaining skills, but you're looking at about E£15 to E£20 for an hour of sailing.

Nile Valley – Esna to Abu Simbel

Although southern Upper Egypt has a history as ancient as anywhere else in the country, it is most famous for its Graeco-Roman monuments.

Following the death of Alexander the Great, his huge empire was divided between his Macedonian generals. For 300 years the Greek-speaking Ptolemies ruled Egypt as pharaohs, respecting the traditions and religion of the Egyptians and setting an example to the Romans who succeeded them.

Their centre of power tied them to Alexandria and the coast but the Ptolemies also pushed their way south, extending Graeco-Roman power into Nubia (the land that straddles what is now the border between Egypt and Sudan) through their politically sensible policy of assimilation rather than subjugation.

In Upper Egypt, the Ptolemies raised temples honouring the local gods, building them in grand Pharaonic style to appease the priesthood and earn the trust of the people. Although well preserved and beautiful, somehow these imitations lost something in the translation; in many ways they were stilted, unimaginative edifices lacking the artistic brilliance that marked the truly Egyptian constructions they copied.

In southern Upper Egypt, south of Luxor, the major Graeco-Roman works were a series of riverside temples at Esna, Edfu, Kom Ombo and Philae, admirable as much for their strategic locations (all either overlook ancient trade routes or were built at key commercial centres) as for their actual artistic or architectural merit.

Beyond Edfu the ribbon of cultivation on the east bank gives way to the Eastern Desert. At Silsila, 145km south of Luxor, the Nile passes through a gorge, once thought to mark a cataract. Further on from here there are early dynastic and New Kingdom ruins, including on Elephantine Island and at Abu Simbel; there's also the city of Aswan, the great High Dam and Lake Nasser, which mark the end of Egypt proper.

Highlights

- Stand in awe of ancient and modern engineering in front of the Great Temple of Ramses at Abu Simbel, arguably Egypt's most stunning monument.
- Visit the Nubian Museum at Aswan and get some idea of what was lost when the High Dam was built.
- Sail on a felucca through Upper Egypt on one of the world's greatest rivers.
- Admire the stark beauty of Lake Nasser from the comfort of a luxury cruise boat – not cheap but worth it.
- Wander through the Temple of Horus at Edfu, one of the last great Pharaonic monuments to be built in Egypt.
- Watch as 2000 camels are bought and sold at Daraw, the end of one of the world's historic camel caravans.

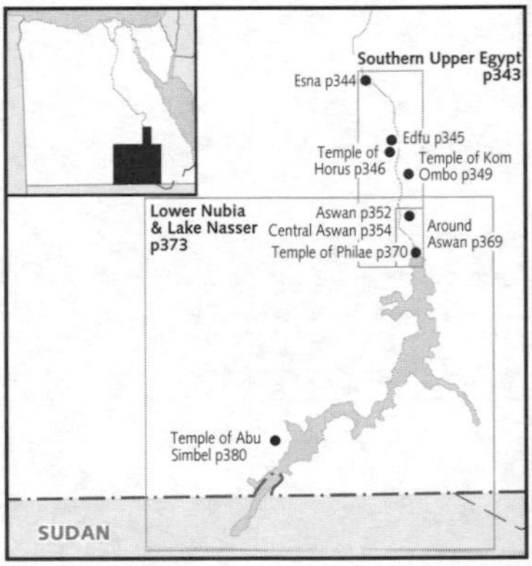

SOUTHERN UPPER EGYPT

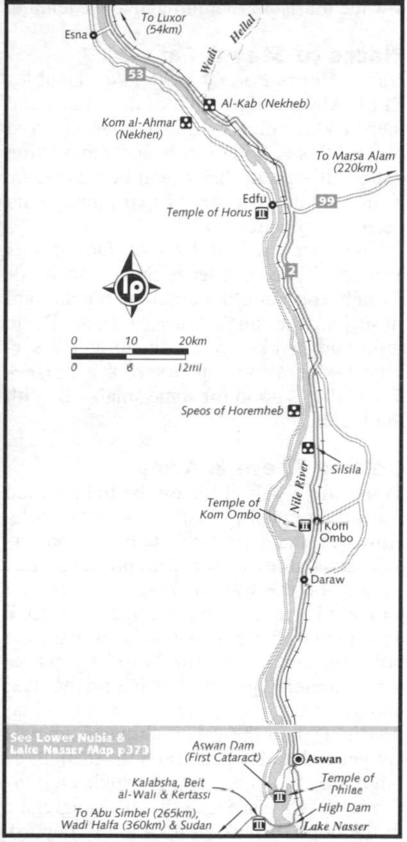

ESNA

☎ 095

The Graeco-Roman Temple of Khnum is the main attraction of Esna, a busy little farming town on the west bank of the Nile, 54km south of Luxor. Wandering around the town's dusty streets it's hard to believe that only a century ago Esna was the den of iniquity. Here Flaubert encountered the famous erotic dancer Kuchuk Hanem and forced her to dance the Bee – a striptease where the dancer removes her clothes to release a fictitious trapped bee. Nowadays there's not much happening apart from the usual relentless hassle of the bazaar touts.

> **Travelling in the South**
>
> In the aftermath of the Luxor massacre, police in the heavily travelled area between Luxor and Aswan instituted security measures designed to protect tourists. What this means for an individual traveller is that your freedom of movement can be severely curtailed as you are forced to travel by convoy, prevented from taking buses or service taxis and forbidden from wandering about in villages or back lanes.
>
> Some people feel more secure when surrounded by a phalanx of policemen pointing machine guns at the general populace; others don't. Fortunately, this is Egypt and no rule is hard and fast – sometimes you will be left alone to walk around wherever you want, other times you will be politely (or not so politely) escorted to the nearest train station and put on the first train out.
>
> As there have been no violent incidents involving Islamists since 1997, those who chafe under the measures can only hope that the security forces will soon lighten their heavy-handed tactics.

The post office and a branch of the Bank of Alexandria are on the street that leads to the Nile from the canal. On Saturday, there's an animal market here too. The tourist police office (☎ 400 686) is in the bazaar near the temple.

Temple of Khnum

All that has been excavated of the Temple of Khnum *(admission E£8; open 6am-5.30pm Oct-May, 6am-6.30pm June-Sept)* is the hypostyle hall. This sits rather incongruously in its huge excavation pit among the houses and narrow alleyways in the middle of town.

Dedicated to Khnum, the ram-headed creator god who fashioned humankind on his potter's wheel using Nile clay, the temple was begun by Ptolemy VI and built over the ruins of earlier temples. The hypostyle hall, as it stands today, was built by the

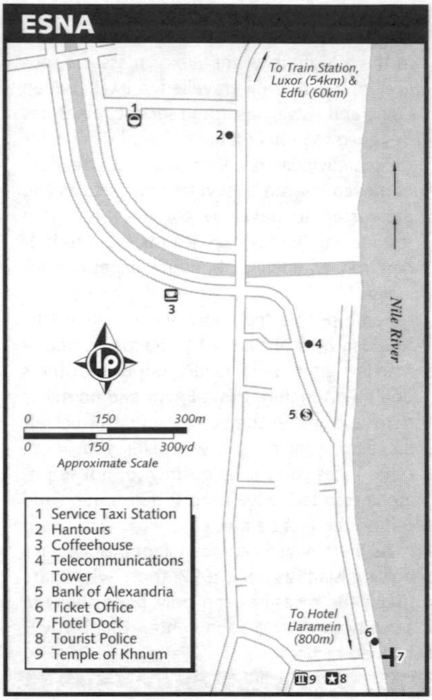

Romans. Parts of the decoration date from as late as the 3rd century AD. The quay connecting the temple to the Nile was built by Marcus Aurelius (AD 161–180).

The intact roof of the hall is supported by 24 columns decorated with the pharaoh making offerings to the gods. Inside the front corners, beside the smaller doorways, are two hymns to Khnum. The first is a morning hymn to awaken Khnum in his shrine, and the second is a wonderful 'hymn of creation' that acknowledges Khnum as creator of all – even foreigners – 'all are formed on his potter's wheel, their speech different in every region…but the lord of the wheel is their father too…'.

The back wall, to the north-east, is the only remaining part of the original Ptolemaic temple and features reliefs of two Ptolemaic pharaohs, Ptolemy VI Philometor and Ptolemy VIII Euergetes II.

The ticket office is on the river itself, about 1km upriver from the main bridge across the Nile. You buy your ticket and follow the tourist bazaar through to the temple.

Places to Stay & Eat

Hotel Haramein (☎ *400 340*) Doubles E£14. About 800m south of the temple and then 100m inland, via another covered bazaar, this is Esna's only accommodation option. It's pretty basic, and because Esna is an easy day trip from Luxor, there is no need to stay here.

There are a few of the usual ***food stands*** around if you're after a cheap snack, although you should watch out for the odd rip-off in the small tourist bazaar. Basic food and drinks are available at the service taxi station, and there's a ***coffeehouse*** that's good for some small talk with the locals.

Getting There & Away

Trains are a pain, because the train station is on the opposite (east) bank of the Nile. However, there are frequent buses and service taxis from Luxor. The bus stops frequently on the way, making a service taxi (sometimes in the form of a microbus; E£3, 45 minutes) the best option. However, the police in Luxor are unlikely to let you take a bus, preferring you to take a private taxi and go in convoy. Esna's service taxi station is next to the canal, although arrivals are generally dropped off on the main thoroughfare into town along which *hantour* (horse-drawn carriage) drivers congregate in the hope of picking up a fare. They ask E£5 each way for the five- to 10-minute ride to the temple.

If you'd prefer to walk to the temple from the service taxi drop-off point, head straight (south) down the main road, cross a small bridge over the canal and continue for 50m until you come to a small green-domed building on your left. Turn left after the building and follow this lane for 100m until you get to a telecommunications tower. Turn right and continue along this road (which eventually meets up with the Nile) for about 800m. You'll see the ticket office next to the mooring for the Nile cruisers. The temple is 50m inland, up through the tourist bazaar.

AL-KAB & KOM AL-AHMAR

Between Esna and Edfu are the scattered ruins of two settlements, both dating back over 5000 years, with traces of even earlier habitation.

Al-Kab (ancient Nekheb) is the site of predynastic and Pharaonic settlements; the huge mud-brick walls that surrounded the ancient settlement area date to the Late Period (747–332 BC). To the north of the walls is an Old Kingdom cemetery and New Kingdom rock-cut tombs for the local governors. The most important of these tombs is the Tomb of Ahmose, son of Ebana (tomb No 5), who took part in the war to reunite Egypt and drive out the Hyksos, and who left a long, detailed biographical inscription to tell of his bravery.

As home of Nekhbet (the vulture goddess of Upper Egypt), Al-Kab also has several sandstone temples, mostly located within the mud-brick enclosure wall. The first temples existed by the early dynastic period (c. 3100 BC), with later temples built by the pharaohs of the Middle Kingdoms, however, the remains seen today are from the New Kingdom through to the Graeco-Roman period.

To the north of the town walls are the remains of a small chapel built by Tuthmosis III, and to the east a small Ptolemaic temple partly carved into the rock face. Further east into the desert, some 3.5km away, is the small temple of Hathor and Nekhbet built by Amenhotep III as a way station for Nekhbet's cult statue when she visited the area. Her protective influence was no doubt appreciated, as this was one of the supply routes to the gold mines that gave Egypt much of its wealth.

On the opposite site of the river is Nekhen (now known as Kom al-Ahmar) or, in Greek, Hierakonpolis, 'City of the Falcon', home of the falcon god Nekheny, an early form of Horus. Although there is little to see of what was once Egypt's most important city in predynastic times, recent excavations have revealed a large settlement (with Egypt's earliest brewery!) and a cemetery site dating from around 3400 BC, together with the site of Egypt's earliest known temple, a large timber-framed structure fronted by 12m-high imported wood pillars. A century ago, archaeologists discovered within the sacred enclosure a whole range of ritual artefacts, including the Narmer Palette and a superb, gold falcon head that are now both in Cairo's Egyptian Museum.

Close by stands Egypt's oldest standing brick building, the enigmatic mud-brick enclosure thought to have been built by Khasekhemy (c. 2686 BC). Testament to Nekhen's continued importance during the dynastic period, there are also a series of impressive rock-cut tombs of New Kingdom dignitaries.

Al-Kab and Kom al-Ahmar are 26km south of Esna.

EDFU

☎ 097

The Temple of Horus at Edfu is the most completely preserved Egyptian temple, and is definitely worth a visit if you can make it. One of the last great Egyptian attempts at monument building on a grand scale, the temple dominates this west-bank town, 53km south of Esna, although Edfu's more modest structures crowd in on its enclosure

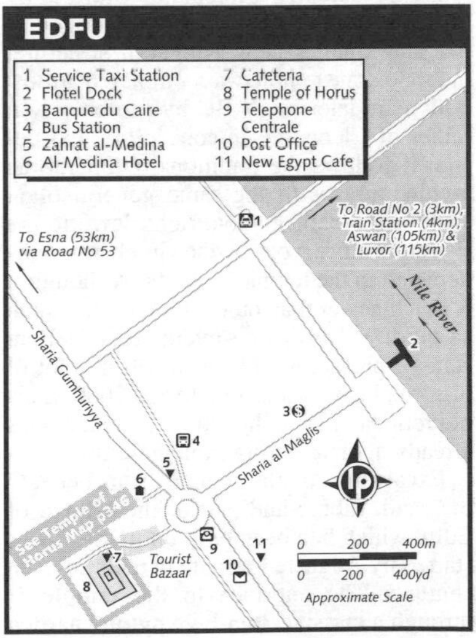

wall. Because the town and temple were established on a rise above the broad river valley around them, they escaped the disastrous Nile floods that occurred from time to time.

Modern Edfu, a centre for sugar and pottery, is a very friendly place. Although it is an agricultural town, tourism is the biggest money earner and everyone in the town seems to have a shop in the tourist bazaar, which all visitors must brave in order to reach the temple. Just before the bazaar is a square that is the nerve centre of the town. A large, new telephone centrale sits on the southern side of the square and the post office is behind it, just along the first street off to the left. The bus and minibus station is about 100m along the street off to the right. Service taxis can be found at the entrance to town, next to the bridge over the Nile.

Temple of Horus

Although Edfu was a settlement and cemetery site from as early as around 3000 BC and, as the cult centre of the falcon god Horus, would have had a cult temple throughout the dynastic period, the Temple of Horus *(admission E£20; open 7am-4pm Oct-May, 7am-5pm June-Sept)* you see today is actually Ptolemaic. Started by Ptolemy III in 237 BC on the site of an earlier and smaller New Kingdom structure, the sandstone temple was completed almost 200 years later in 57 BC by Ptolemy XII, father of Cleopatra. In conception and design it follows the traditions of Pharaonic architecture, with the same general plan, scale and ornamentation, right down to the Egyptian attire worn by the Greek pharaohs depicted in the temple's reliefs. Although it is much newer than other cult temples, such as those at Luxor or Abydos, its excellent state of preservation helps to fill in a lot of historical gaps – it is, in effect, a 2000-year-old replica of an architectural style that was already archaic during Ptolemaic times.

Excavation of the temple from beneath the sand, rubble and part of the village of Edfu, which had been built on its roof, was started by Auguste Mariette in the mid-19th century. The entrance to the temple is through a massive 36m-high **pylon** guarded by two huge and splendid granite falcons and decorated with colossal reliefs of Ptolemy XII grasping the hair of his enemies in order to smash their skulls in. This is the classic propaganda pose of the all-powerful pharaoh.

Beyond this pylon is the **great court**, where offerings were once made to Horus. The walls are decorated with reliefs, including the 'Feast of the Beautiful Meeting' just inside the entrance, depicting Horus of Edfu and Hathor of Dendara who were brought together each year amid great celebrations.

TEMPLE OF HORUS

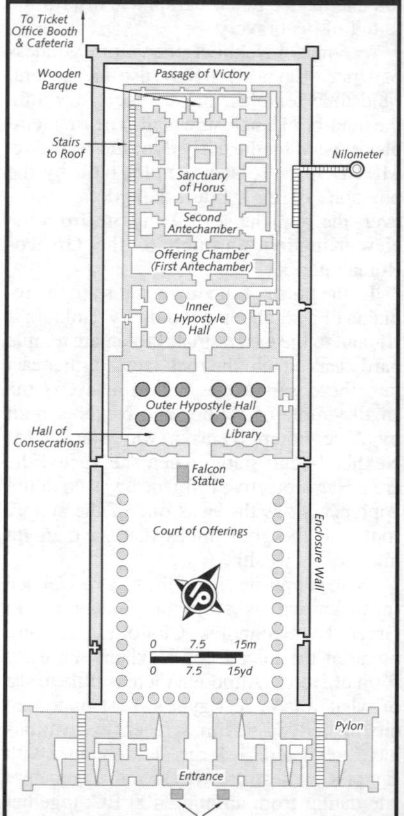

A second set of Horus statues (in the form of a falcon) in black granite once flanked the entrance to the temple's first or outer hypostyle hall, although today only one remains. Inside the entrance of the **hypostyle hall**, to the left and right, are two small chambers: The one on the right was the temple library where the ritual texts were stored, and the chamber on the left was the hall of consecrations, a type of vestry where the priests' freshly laundered robes and ritual vases were kept. The hall itself has 12 columns, and the walls are decorated with reliefs of the temple's founding.

The **second hypostyle hall** again has 12 columns, and in the top left part of the room is perhaps this temple's most interesting room: the temple laboratory. Here, all the necessary perfumes and incense recipes were carefully brewed up and stored, and their ingredients were listed on the walls.

On either side of the hall are doorways that exit into the narrow **Passage of Victory**, which runs between the temple and its massive protective enclosure walls. This narrow ambulatory is decorated with scenes that are of tremendous value to Egyptologists in trying to understand the nature of the ancient temple rituals. Reliefs here show the dramatic re-enactment of the battle between Horus and Seth at the annual Festival of Victory. Throughout the conflict, Seth is shown in the form of a hippopotamus, his tiny size rendering him less threatening, and at the culmination of the drama the priests cut up a hippo-shaped cake and ate it to destroy Seth completely.

Back in the inner hypostyle hall, exit through the large central doorway to enter the **offering chamber**, or first antechamber, which has an altar where daily offerings of fruit, flowers, wine, milk and other foods were once left. On the west side are 242 steps leading up to the rooftop, giving a fantastic view of the Nile and the surrounding fields. You may have to pay the guard a bit of baksheesh if you want to go up here.

The second chamber gives access to the **sanctuary of Horus**, which still contains the polished-granite shrine that once housed the gold cult statue of Horus. Created during the reign of Nectanebo II (360–343 BC), the statue was reused by the Ptolemies in their newer temple. All around Horus' sanctuary are the smaller shrines of other gods, including Hathor, Ra and Osiris, and, at the very back, a modern reproduction of the wooden barque in which Horus' statue would be taken out of the temple in procession during festive occasions.

Places to Stay & Eat

Al-Medina Hotel *(☎ 711 326)* Singles/doubles E£40/20. This place, just off Sharia Gomhuriyya, is a little overpriced for a basic hotel with spartan furniture and erratic hot water. However, the large breakfasts are the pride of owner Taha Osman, and several travellers have sung its praises.

As well as the expensive cafeteria in the temple grounds, there are a few kebab places on the square, and the ***Zahrat al-Medina*** cafeteria opposite the Al-Medina, which serves basic chicken and vegetable dishes. At all these places you should ask how much dishes cost before you order.

Getting There & Away

Trains, buses and service taxis stop frequently in Edfu. However, the train station is on the east bank of the Nile, about 4km from town. To get to the town, you must first take a covered pick-up truck to the bridge, then another into town. Each costs 25pt. Alternatively, you can hire an entire pick-up to take you to the main square for about E£5.

Buses travelling between Luxor and Aswan sometimes only stop on the east bank, which can be a real pain. Again, pick-ups are your main option and as you're already on the main road you will only need to take one. Leaving Edfu is not so bad, as you can at least take a bus from the station in town. The fare is E£5 to Luxor and E£2.50 to Aswan.

Service taxis are again the best option, but at the time of writing foreigners were forbidden by the police to take them. Drivers say that their licences are confiscated if they violate this rule. Should this change, the trip to Luxor (two hours) costs about E£5, and to Aswan (1½ hours) it costs about E£3.

If you've had enough of the Nile, tombs and temples, you can exit east and head straight for Marsa Alam on the Red Sea. The daily bus servicing this route originates in Aswan and passes Edfu at about 8am to 8.30am. However, it does not usually stop at the bus station in town. Instead, it pulls up for 30 minutes at a cafe on the east bank of the river at the start of the desert road. The trip takes three hours to Marsa Alam and costs E£8.

Most feluccas end their journey at Edfu on their way north from Aswan. Very patient travellers, who prefer to travel against the current, can get a felucca heading south.

SILSILA

At Silsila, about 42km south of Edfu, the Nile narrows considerably to pass between steep sandstone cliffs that are cluttered with ancient rock stelae and graffiti. Known in Pharaonic times as Khenu (Place of Rowing), the gorge also marks the change from limestone to sandstone in the bedrock of Egypt. The local Silsila quarries were worked by thousands of men throughout the New Kingdom and Graeco-Roman periods to provide the sandstone used in temple building.

On the west bank of the river is the **Speos of Horemheb**, a rock-hewn chapel dedicated to Pharaoh Horemheb (1323–1295 BC) and seven deities, including the local god Sobek.

At present, you can only get to Silsila if you are on a cruise boat or have a private vehicle. Should the security situation change, you may be able to hire a taxi from Aswan or Kom Ombo to take you there.

KOM OMBO

☎ 097

The fertile, irrigated sugar-cane and corn fields around Kom Ombo, 65km south of Edfu, support not only the original community of fellaheen (farmers) but also a large population of Nubians displaced from their own lands by the creation of Lake Nasser. It's a pleasant little place easily accessible en route between Aswan and Luxor. If you're not stopping here on a felucca trip it's possibly best visited on a day trip from Aswan, which is 40km to the south.

In ancient times, Kom Ombo was known as Pa-Sebek (Land of Sobek), after the crocodile god of the region. It became important in Ptolemaic times when it was made the capital of the first nome of Upper Egypt during the reign of Ptolemy VI Philometor (180–145 BC). Kom Ombo was an important military base and trading centre between Egypt and Nubia, not only for the all-important gold, but also for the African elephants the Ptolemies needed to counteract the Indian elephants used by their long-term rivals the Seleucids, who ruled the largest chunk of Alexander's former empire to the east of Egypt. The main attraction these days, however, is the unique river-side Temple of Kom Ombo, about 4km from the centre of the town.

Temple of Kom Ombo

The Temple of Kom Ombo *(admission E£10; open 8am-4pm daily)* or, more precisely, the dual Temple of Sobek and Haroeris (a form of Horus), stands on a promontory at a bend in the Nile, where in ancient times sacred crocodiles basked in the sun on the river bank. Although there is evidence of earlier Pharaonic structures at the site, the sandstone temple dates from Ptolemaic times – part of the ambitious building plans of Ptolemy VI. Although its spectacular riverside setting resulted in the erosion of part of its partly Roman forecourt and outer sections, most of the temple has survived and is very similar in general plan to the other Ptolemaic temples of Edfu and Dendara, albeit smaller. The temple is unusual in that, architecturally, everything is doubled and perfectly symmetrical along the main axis of the temple. There are twin entrances, twin courts, twin colonnades, twin hypostyle halls, twin sanctuaries and, in keeping with the dual nature of the temple, there was probably a twin priesthood. The left side of the temple was dedicated to Haroeris, the right half to Sobek, the local crocodile-headed god.

Entry to the temple is through the damaged gateway that was built by Cleopatra

TEMPLE OF KOM OMBO

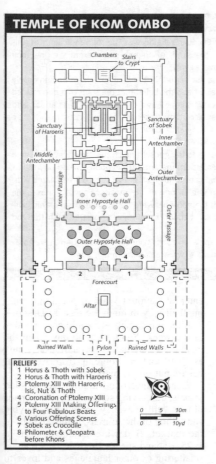

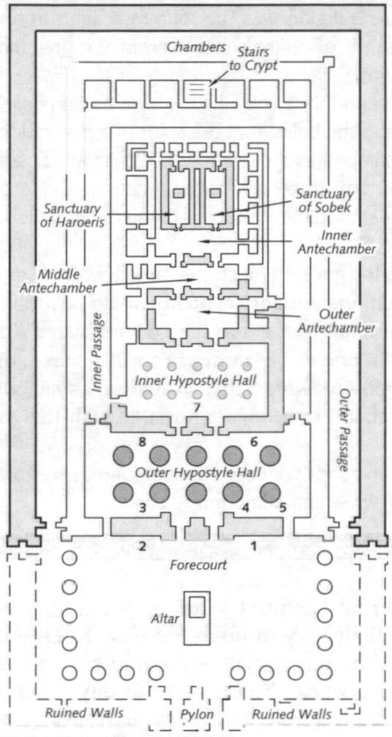

RELIEFS
1 Horus & Thoth with Sobek
2 Horus & Thoth with Haroeris
3 Ptolemy XIII with Haroeris, Isis, Nut & Thoth
4 Coronation of Ptolemy XIII
5 Ptolemy XIII Making Offerings to Four Fabulous Beasts
6 Various Offering Scenes
7 Sobek as Crocodile
8 Philometer & Cleopatra before Khons

VII's father, Ptolemy XII. Close to this entrance, to the right of the temple wall, is a small shrine to Hathor, used to store a collection of **mummified crocodiles** dug up from a nearby sacred-animal cemetery. Four of the collection are on display. On the opposite side of the compound, to the left (south-west) corner of the temple are the remains of a small **birth house**, decorated with relief scenes, including one depicting Ptolemy VIII Euergetes (170–116 BC) in a boat in a reed thicket before the god Min. Beyond this to the north is the deep well that supplied the temple's water, and close by is a small pool in which crocodiles, Sobek's sacred animal, were raised.

Passing into the temple's **forecourt**, where the reliefs are divided east-west between the two gods, there is a double altar in the centre of the court for both gods. Beyond are the two hypostyle halls, each with 10 columns, leading into antechambers and then to the unique double sanctuary arrangement. Notice the controversial scene on the inside of the left-hand corner of the temple's back wall; usually described as a collection of 'surgical instruments' – they could equally well be the implements used during temple rituals.

Places to Stay & Eat

Radwan Hotel *(☎ 501 827)* Beds E£4. This place, situated on the main road, is pretty grimy, and you can even smell the bathrooms from outside the front door. It's better to press on to Aswan or Luxor.

Al-Noba Restaurant Meals E£5-12. On the main road, a little way north of the service taxi station, is the only sit-down eatery in this part of town. It's cheap, relatively clean, and serves chicken, rice and vegetable dishes. Otherwise, there are the usual ***ta'amiyya*** and ***kebab stands***.

Snacks can be bought at one of the cafeterias situated on the bank of the Nile between the temple and the boat landing. Of the two, ***Cafeteria Venus*** has the best atmosphere, serving burgers, kofta and beer in a pleasant garden setting.

Getting There & Away

If you're coming by road, the police usually insist that you visit Kom Ombo as part of a convoy. Should this change, a service taxi or minibus from Aswan to the town of Kom Ombo takes between 45 minutes and one hour, and costs E£1.50. The Luxor-Aswan buses also frequently stop in the town. As you approach Kom Ombo from Aswan, you can ask the driver to drop you off at the road leading to the temple – look for the sign. From here it's about a 2km walk or else you can hitch. If you are heading back to Aswan, it shouldn't be hard to get a lift or flag down a passing service taxi or microbus once on

Sacred Cows (& Cats & Crocodiles)

One of the more bizarre by-products of ancient Egyptian religion was the mummification of animals. From ibises to gazelles and hawks to bulls, thousands of animals were carefully mummified and placed in specially dedicated catacombs all over Egypt.

Animals were worshipped throughout the Pharaonic period, but animal cults became immensely popular during Graeco-Roman rule. Central to the cult was the belief that the spirit of a god resided in a certain type of animal. So the god Sobek was worshipped as a crocodile, Thoth as an ibis and Bastet as a cat. A specific animal would be chosen according to certain mystical criteria and while that animal was alive it would be worshipped as a living embodiment of its particular god. When it died, it was mummified and another one took its place.

Animal mummies were also used as votive offerings to the gods. In much the same way that some Christians buy and light candles as a form of intercession, the ancient Egyptians would buy mummified animals and place them in specially devoted catacombs as a gift to the god associated with them. Apart from the crocodile cemetery at Kom Ombo, one of the most spectacular sites is the Serapeum in Saqqara, where bulls associated with the god Apis were buried in colossal granite sarcophagi. Another such site is the enormous ibis and baboon catacombs associated with the god Thoth at Tuna al-Gebel in Middle Egypt.

You can find out more about animal mummies, and even adopt your own to help fund the restoration of animal mummies in the Egyptian Museum, at W www.animalmummies.com.

the highway. Should you want to head to the Red Sea from here, the daily bus from Aswan to Marsa Alam calls in at about 7am. Tickets are E£12.

Trains are another option. Although less frequent than service taxis, they are your best option if you want more freedom.

Otherwise, to get to the temple from Kom Ombo town, take a covered pick-up (25pt) to the boat landing on the Nile about 800m north of the temple, then walk the remainder of the way. Pick-ups to the boat landing leave from the service taxi station.

A private taxi between the town and temple should cost about E£7 return. Feluccas travelling between Aswan and Luxor often stop at the temple itself.

DARAW

The main reason to stop in this otherwise unremarkable village 8km south of Kom Ombo is to see its famous **camel market** *(souq al-gamaal)*. Most of the camels are brought up in caravans from Sudan along the 40 Days Rd to just north of Abu Simbel, from where they're trucked to Daraw. The rest walk to the market in smaller groups, entering Egypt at Wadi al-Alagi and making their way through the Eastern Desert.

Although camels are sold here each day of the week, Sunday is the day when the main group of camels (sometimes as many as 2000) that has come up from Abu Simbel are put on the market.

Wandering around among the hobbled camels, and giving some order to the chaos of men yelling as they go about the buying and selling of the animals, is the 'sheikh' of the market, Badawi, a character born in 1925. Badawi speaks English, Greek and a smattering of other languages and loves to relate stories about how he worked for (and sometimes against) the British during their occupation of Egypt early in the 20th century. He walks around the market with a long stick covered in what looks suspiciously like donkey fur and will give you a self-addressed envelope to send back the photos he insists you take of him.

Also worth seeing in Daraw is a Nubian house called **Hosh al-Kenzi**. Built in 1912 by the father of the current resident, Haj Muhammed Eid Mohammed Hassanein, it is constructed in traditional Nubian style and decorated with Nubian artefacts. To get

Taking Camels to Market

For hundreds of years camels from Sudan have been brought to Egypt in large caravans along the 40 Days Rd (Darb al-Arba'een), the treacherous desert route thought to have been named for the number of days it took for the journey from Sudan's Darfur province to southern Egypt.

In the centuries following the introduction of camels into the region – thought to have been by the Persians in the 6th century BC – the animals brought slaves, ostrich feathers, precious stones, animal skins and other goods to Egypt, where they were used by the country's Pharaonic overlords or, in later times, distributed to the great empires in Greece, Persia, Rome and Europe. But by the 18th and 19th centuries, the gradual introduction of steamers and trains in Egypt and Sudan meant that camels were no longer the most efficient way to get goods from south to north. The establishment of airlinks between the two countries seemed to seal the fate of the caravans as relics of a bygone age.

But the camels have continued to come. Now, however, they themselves are the cargo. Some are used for agricultural work, others are exported to other Middle Eastern countries, but many – if not most – are destined for the dinner tables of poor Egyptians (yes, that cheap kebab does taste a bit strange…).

Once the camels get to Daraw they spend two days in quarantine, where they are inoculated against a number of diseases. After they have been sold, most go on to the camel market in Birqash, about 35km north-west of Cairo, and from here they are either shipped on to other countries in the region or are sent to the slaughterhouse.

there, ask for the Gar Rasoul Mosque on Sharia al-Kunuz. The house is clearly visible next door.

Getting There & Away

The service taxis and minibuses running between Aswan and Kom Ombo stop in Daraw (if passengers indicate that they want to get off). The fare is the same as for the whole stretch – E£1.50. The camel market is 2km off the east side of the main road. You may be forced to go in a convoy to Daraw, which is usually arranged via the tourist office in Aswan. Unfortunately it normally goes on a Tuesday.

Aswan

☎ 097

Over the centuries Aswan, Egypt's southernmost city, has been a garrison town and frontier city, the gateway to Africa and the now-inundated land of Nubia, a prosperous marketplace at the crossroads of the ancient caravan routes and, more recently, a popular winter resort.

In ancient times the area was known as Swenet, meaning 'Trade', a name that later became the Arabic 'As-Suan', meaning 'Market'. The main town and temple area of Swenet was on the southern end of the island called Yebu (meaning both 'Elephant' and 'Ivory'), which the Greeks later renamed Elephantine Island. A natural fortress protected by the turbulent river, Aswan became the capital of the first Upper Egyptian nome and a base for military expeditions into Nubia, Sudan and Ethiopia. From those foreign parts, right up into Islamic times, the city was visited by great caravans of camels and elephants laden with slaves, gold, ivory, spices, cloth and other exotic wares.

Pharaonic and Ptolemaic leaders each took their turn through history to guard the southern reaches of Egypt from the customary routes of invasion; their fleets patrolled the river as far as the Second Nile Cataract at Wadi Halfa and their troops penetrated several hundred kilometres into Sudan. Aswan was also, to a certain extent, the Siberia of the Roman Empire, one of those far-flung garrisons where troublesome generals were sent in order to protect the interests of the emperor.

The modern town of Aswan lies on the east bank of the Nile, opposite Elephantine

Island. The town is at the northern end of the First Nile Cataract, one of six rocky outcrops (the remaining five are all in Sudan) situated between Aswan and Khartoum in Sudan.

Aswan is the perfect place for a break from the rigours of travelling in Egypt. Although its ancient temples and ruins are not as outstanding as others in the country, Aswan does have a few things to offer the traveller, one of which is the town's superb location on the river. The Nile is magically beautiful here as it flows down from the dams and around the giant granite boulders and palm-studded islands that protrude from the cascading rapids of the First Nile Cataract. Aswan's Corniche is one of the most attractive of the country's Nile-side boulevards.

While you can visit Pharaonic, Graeco-Roman, Coptic, Islamic and modern monuments, a good museum, superb botanical gardens, the massive High Dam, Lake Nasser and one of the most fascinating souqs outside Cairo, by far the best thing to do in Aswan is to sit by the Nile and watch the feluccas gliding by at sunset.

The best time to visit Aswan is in winter, when the days are warm and dry, with an average temperature of about 26°C. In summer, the temperature is around 38° to 45°C and it's too hot to do anything other than sit by a fan and swat flies or flop into a swimming pool.

ORIENTATION

It's quite easy to find your way around Aswan because there are only three main avenues and most of the city is along the Nile or parallel to it. The train station is at the northern end of town, only three blocks east of the river and the Corniche el-Nil.

The street running from north to south in front of the train station is Sharia as-Souq (also occasionally signposted as Sharia Saad Zaghloul). This is Aswan's splendid

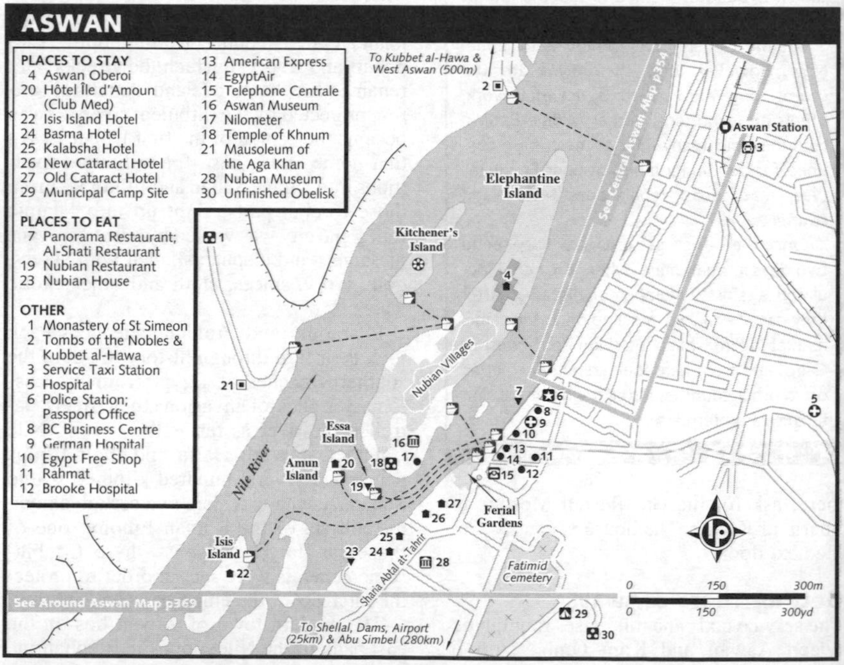

market street, where the souqs overflow with colourful, tempting and aromatic wares. Running parallel to it is Sharia Abtal at-Tahrir, where you'll find the youth hostel and a few hotels. Most of Aswan's government buildings, banks, travel agencies, restaurants and top-end hotels are on the Corniche, and from there you can see the rock tombs on the west bank, as well as Elephantine Island.

INFORMATION

Visa Extensions

The passport office (☎ 317 006) is on the Corniche and is open from 8.30am to 1pm and from 6pm to 8pm Saturday to Thursday.

Tourist Offices

There are two tourist offices; one (☎ 312 811) is next to the train station and the other (☎ 323 297) is on a side street, one block in from the Corniche. Shukri Saad and his assistant, Hakeem Hussein, can usually be found at the office next to the station, and are among the most helpful tourist officials in Egypt. They will assist in booking accommodation and can give you official prices for taxis and felucca trips – although lower prices are usually obtainable with some haggling.

Both offices are open from 8.30am to 2pm and 6pm to 8pm Saturday to Thursday, and from 10am to 2pm and 6pm to 8pm on Friday.

Money

The main banks have their branches on the Corniche. Banque Masr and the Banque du Caire will issue cash advances on both Visa and MasterCard. There are ATMs at both Banque Masr and the National Bank of Egypt. The Bank of Alexandria accepts Eurocheques. Banque Masr has a foreign-exchange booth (open from 8am to 3pm and from 5pm to 8pm daily) next to its main building.

There is an American Express office (AmEx; ☎ 306 983) on the Corniche, open from 9.30am to 5pm daily. Thomas Cook (☎ 304 011, fax 306 209), also on the Corniche, is open from 8am to 5pm daily.

Telephone & Fax

The main post office is on the Corniche, next to the municipal swimming pool. However, poste restante must be collected from the smaller post office on Sharia Abtal at-Tahrir, opposite Victoria Hotel. Both post offices are open from 8am to 2pm Saturday to Thursday.

There are cardphones along the Corniche and at the train station, or you can make international calls at the centrale, which is on the Corniche towards the southern end of town, just past the EgyptAir office. There are cardphones at the centrale and usually stocks of cards too. Telexes and faxes can also be sent from here, and there is a post office stamp counter that is occasionally open. The office is open from 8am to 10pm daily.

Back up the road, next to Photo Sabri, is the BC Business Centre, from where you can send faxes.

Email & Internet Access

At the time of writing there was only a small group of Internet cafes in Aswan, but the number is likely to grow in the near future. At present, the best is the Aswanet Internet Cafe at the Keylany Hotel. A local Internet service provider, Aswanet has the fastest lines and cheapest rates in town, at E£10 per hour, with a minimum of E£5. It is open from 9am until midnight daily. The Rowing Club on the Corniche also has an Internet cafe, although at the time of writing it was being renovated and rates were not available. The Cleopatra Hotel has a terminal in its lobby that you can use for E£20 per hour. The Nubian Oasis, Noorhan (E£15 per hour) and Rosewan (55pt per minute) hotels also have terminals that you can use.

Bookshops

Only the top-end hotels such as the New Cataract and the Basma have bookshops selling foreign-language material. If you're after international newspapers and magazines, try the newsstand near the Philae Hotel on the Corniche.

Medical Services & Emergencies

The German Hospital (☎ 317 176) has staff who speak foreign languages and is the best place to go if you get ill in Aswan. It's on the Corniche next to the Egypt Free shop. The other option is the General Hospital (☎ 302 855, 314 151). As elsewhere in Egypt, if you need an ambulance, call ☎ 123.

The tourist police (☎ 303 163) have an office at the northern end of the Corniche; the regular police (☎ 302 043) are further south, near Thomas Cook. In either case, it is a good idea to contact the tourist office first to help with translation.

THE TOWN & EAST BANK

The exotic atmosphere of Aswan's backstreet **souqs** is definitely one of the highlights of the city. Although the fabulous caravans no longer pass this way, the colour and activity of these markets and stalls recall those romantic times. Just wander through the small, narrow alleyways and you'll see, hear, smell and, if you want, taste life as it has been for many centuries in these parts.

Unfortunately, Sharia as-Souq itself is very much a tourist market nowadays. Nubian baskets, T-shirts, perfume, spices, beaded *galabiyyas* (men's robes) and grotesque stuffed crocodiles and desert creatures are all for sale. Although the traders here are not as persistent as those in Luxor, they can still be irritating.

Fresh and live produce, including fruit, vegetables, chickens and pigeons, are traded in the street stretching to the south of the Happi Hotel.

Walking along the Corniche and watching the sun set over the desert on the far side of the Nile is another favourite pastime in Aswan. If you want to sit down to watch the sun work its magic, the **Ferial Gardens** *(admission free)* at the southern end of the Corniche is a peaceful place.

Nubian Museum

One of the highlights of a visit to Aswan is the Nubian Museum *(☎ 313 826; admission E£20; open 9am-1pm & 5pm-9pm daily)*, opposite the Basma Hotel, where the history, art and culture of Nubia from prehistoric times to the present is showcased. It is a very small and belated thanks to the sacrifice

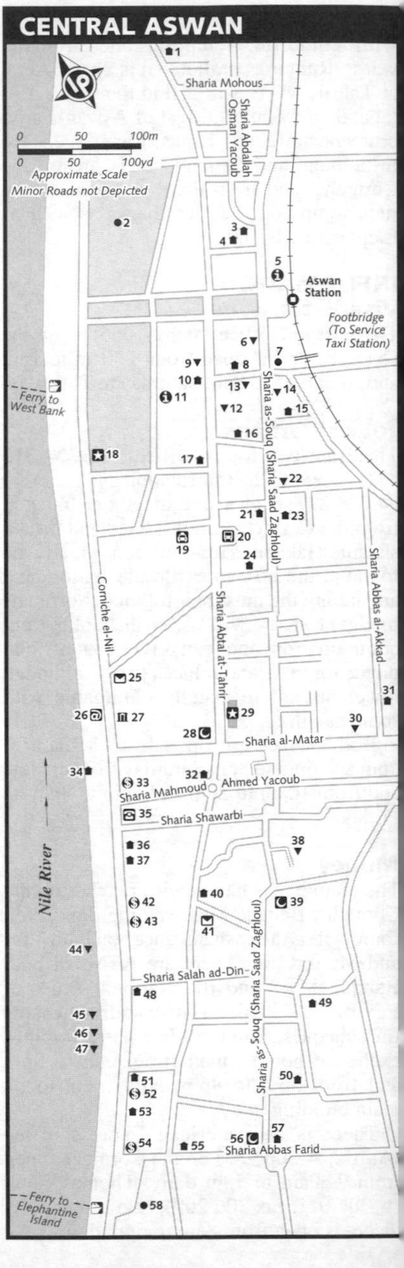

CENTRAL ASWAN

PLACES TO STAY
- 1 New Abu Simbel Hotel
- 3 Queen Hotel
- 4 Rosewan Hotel
- 8 Marwa Hotel
- 10 Youth Hostel
- 15 Noorhan Hotel; Yassin Hotel
- 16 Al-Amin Hotel
- 17 Ramses Hotel
- 21 Cleopatra Hotel
- 23 New Brethren Hotel
- 24 Nubian Oasis Hotel
- 31 Oscar Hotel
- 32 Happi Hotel
- 34 Isis Hotel
- 36 Al-Salaam Hotel
- 37 Hathor Hotel
- 40 Victoria Hotel
- 48 Horus Hotel
- 49 Keylany Hotel; Aswanet Internet Cafe
- 50 Hotel Orabi
- 51 Memnon Hotel
- 53 Philae Hotel
- 55 Al-Amir Hotel
- 57 Abu Shelib Hotel

PLACES TO EAT
- 6 Restaurant Derwash
- 9 Al-Dar
- 12 Esraa
- 13 An-Nasr
- 14 Chef Khalil
- 22 Medina Restaurant
- 30 Al-Masry Restaurant
- 38 Al-Sayyida Nefissa
- 44 Saladin Restaurant
- 45 Aswan Moon Restaurant
- 46 Emy Restaurant
- 47 Monalisa Restaurant

OTHER
- 2 Governorate Building
- 5 Tourist Office
- 7 Samah (Ta'amiyya Stand)
- 11 Tourist Office; Nile Valley Navigation Office
- 18 Tourist Police
- 19 Service Taxi Stand
- 20 Bus Station
- 25 Main Post Office
- 26 Rowing Club
- 27 Palace of Culture
- 28 Mosque
- 29 Police Station
- 33 Banque Masr (ATM)
- 35 Cardphones
- 39 Mosque
- 41 Post Office (Poste Restante)
- 42 Banque du Caire
- 43 Bank of Alexandria
- 52 National Bank of Egypt (ATM)
- 54 Banque du Caire
- 56 Mosque
- 58 Thomas Cook

made by the Nubian people for the Aswan Dam. The exhibits are beautifully displayed, and clearly written explanations take you from 4500 BC through to the present day.

At the entrance to the main exhibition hall is a model of the Nile Valley and the main temple sites. Among the highlights are the 6000-year-old painted pottery bowls and a stunning quartzite statue of a 25th-dynasty Kushite priest of Amun. Distinct from the Pharaonic artefacts are the cases filled with objects from burials dating to the Ballana period (5th to 7th century BC). Examples of weaponry and armour, including a complete set of horse armour displayed on a model horse, found in Ballana tombs show the sophistication of artisanship during this brief ascendancy. Beautifully worked silver crowns and other jewellery attest to its wealth.

There is also a fascinating display tracing the development of irrigation along the Nile, from the earliest attempts to control the flow of the river, right up to the building of the Aswan Dam. Detailed displays also explain the massive Unesco project to move Nubia's most important historic monuments away from the rising waters of Lake Nasser following the building of the dam. A model of a Nubian house, complete with old furniture and mannequins wearing traditional silver jewellery, attempts to convey modern Nubian folk culture.

All this is housed in a well-designed modern building, loosely based on traditional Nubian architecture. In the museum garden there is a reconstructed Nubian house (which you can't enter, unfortunately) and a small 'cave' in which prehistoric petroglyphs of giraffes and other wild animals once indigenous to the region have been placed. The site also incorporates an 11th-century Fatimid tomb, as well as a number of other tombs of sheikhs.

The museum entrance is about a 10-minute walk from the EgyptAir office.

Fatimid Cemetery

Behind the Nubian Museum, to the left of the road to the airport, is a vast cemetery with a collection of low, mud-brick buildings with domed roofs. Many of the graves here are modern, but some of the mausoleums clustered towards the back of the cemetery date from the 9th century. Although the graves are in very bad shape, they show the progression of tomb architecture from simple open enclosures to complex domes built on cubes. In a feature unique to southern Egypt, some of the domes are built on a drum with corners sticking out like horns. Many of the tombs had marble inscriptions attached to them until the late 19th century, when a freak rainstorm caused them to fall away. In a misguided attempt to preserve them, the inscriptions were collected and taken to Cairo without any record of which tomb they were originally attached to. Unfortunately, this means that the dates of the tombs' construction and the names of their inhabitants are lost forever. A few of the domes towards the outer edges of the cemetery have flags outside them and are in much better shape than the others. These are the graves of local saints and sometimes you can see local people circumambulating the sarcophagus and praying for the saint's intercession.

The municipality of Aswan is building a large, green, metal fence around the cemetery. The main entrance is a five-minute to 10-minute walk from the roundabout where the road to the airport forks off the Corniche. You can walk right through the cemetery and join the road to the Unfinished Obelisk on the other side – just aim for the three-storey building facing the back of the cemetery.

Unfinished Obelisks

Aswan quarries were Egypt's main source of granite, a stone only found in this southerly region. Of the numerous quarrying sites around here, the most important were the Northern Quarries to the south of town, as well as the quarries on the islands of Elephantine and Sehel, and at Shellal opposite Philae. From these places, the ancient Egyptians hacked out most of the hard stone used in their statuary and to embellish temples and pyramids.

In the former **Northern Quarries** *(admission E£12)*, which now lie about 1.5km from town opposite the Fatimid Cemetery, is a huge discarded obelisk. Three sides of the shaft, which is nearly 42m long, were completed except for the inscriptions. Had it been completed, the obelisk would have been, at 1168 tonnes, the single heaviest piece of stone ever fashioned. However, a flaw appeared in the rock. So it lies where the disappointed stonemasons abandoned it, still partly attached to the parent rock and with no indication of what it was intended for.

No service taxis run past the site, but you can get one to the junction on Sharia Kisr al-Haggar and then walk (about 10 minutes). Private taxis will charge about E£5. You can also walk through the Fatimid Cemetery. Most people simply visit the obelisk at the end of an organised day trip to Abu Simbel.

Another unfinished obelisk lies in the quarry of **Gebel Simaan**, on the opposite bank of the Nile in the desert west of the Monastery of St Simeon. It was made on the orders of the 19th-dynasty pharaoh, Seti I, and there was already decoration on three sides of its apex when it was abandoned. You'll need a guide, preferably on a camel, to find it.

Sculpture Park

This little-known park houses the sculptures made each spring at Aswan's International Sculpture Symposium. Each year, sculptors from around the world come to Aswan and spend a month creating works on the terrace at the Basma Hotel. Their work is exhibited near the old granite quarries. To get here, take the road to Shellal. Instead of turning right towards the ferry to Philae, take the road up the hill. Continue until you reach the top; on the left is the quarry, on the right the sculptures.

THE RIVER

Feluccas & Ferries

As you will quickly discover if you spend any time near the Nile, feluccas are the traditional canvas-sailed boats of the Nile. The river is at its most picturesque in Aswan and no visit would be complete without at least an hour spent sailing around the islands in one of these graceful little boats. One of the most scenic sections of the river is around the southern end of Elephantine Island. Here you'll probably encounter a troop of young boys furiously hand-paddling their minuscule self-made boats in pursuit of larger vessels in order to score some baksheesh from passers-by. One enterprising child sings in whichever language the tourists in the nearest boat speak, belting out everything from Italian arias to 'Three Blind Mice'.

In case you've miraculously avoided them, felucca touts hang out on the Corniche. The prices for boats are negotiable and vary widely according to the effectiveness of your bargaining and the time of year – if they're having a bad season, they may be willing to take people out for less than they would normally find acceptable. The best strategy is to first show that you are interested and then begin to walk away. The official government price for hiring a felucca capable of seating up to eight people is E£15 per hour, but nobody will take you for that price if business is good; if business is slack, you may be able to bargain down the price to less than this. A three- or four-hour tour costs about E£35 to E£45. A three-hour trip down to Sehel Island costs about E£35.

If you simply want to get from A to B, the best deal in town is the public ferry. For only 25pt, you can get to Elephantine Island, departing either the landing opposite the telephone centrale or the one across from Thomas Cook. There is another ferry that leaves from a landing in front of the governorate building and takes you over to the Tombs of the Nobles on the West Bank, also for 25pt. When the river is low the ferry leaves from just north of the tourist police station. Note that women sit up front, men towards the back.

To get to Kitchener's Island you can incorporate it into a felucca tour or you can take the northernmost ferry to Elephantine and walk through the edge of the village to the other side of the island. You'll find a couple of little feluccas at the edge of the lush palm gardens overlooking the entrance to Kitchener's Island. From here you can also go to the landing for the Monastery of St Simeon on the west bank. You'll have to bargain hard, though; you're a captive audience and will be unlikely to get the captain down to less than E£4 or E£5 for a one-way trip. For details on taking an overnight felucca trip down the Nile, see the boxed text 'Felucca Trips' under Getting There & Away later in this chapter.

Elephantine Island

Elephants lived all over Egypt as late as 4000 BC and are thought to have survived in the south until around 2600 BC. Throughout the dynastic period elephant ivory was traded by Nubians on Elephantine Island – hence the name. It's also true that the numerous, giant, grey granite boulders in the river around the island resemble a herd of elephants bathing.

As well as being Egypt's frontier town, where the island officials were known as keepers of the Gate of the South, Elephantine was the cult centre of ram-headed Khnum – creator of humankind and god of the cataracts who controlled the Nile's water level – and his companion goddesses Satis (his wife) and Anukis (his daughter).

Nowadays the island is a more modest place. The extensive ruins of Yebu take up the southern end of the island, and to the north are two colourful Nubian villages, Siou and Koti. Although the villages are not tourist attractions, the inhabitants are friendly and the alleyways are worth exploring, as are the lush, peaceful palm groves.

Taking up much of the northern end of the island, the deluxe and famously ugly Aswan Oberoi Hotel (with an appalling protrusion resembling an airport control tower) has its own private ferry and a 3m-high fence around it to keep the tourists in and away from the local Nubians. Construction on an extension to the hotel on the island's northern tip has been stopped by a lawsuit, but the concrete shell looks set to remain for several years while the matter is fought out in the courts.

Aswan Museum At the south-eastern end of the island, overlooking the ruins of the original town and situated next to an attractive flower and spice garden, this museum *(admission E£10; open 8am-5pm Sun-Thur Oct-May, 8am-6pm Sun-Thur June-Sept)* houses a collection of antiquities discovered in Aswan and Nubia. Most of the Nubian artefacts were found and rescued before the construction of the old Aswan Dam, while the annexe houses objects found in the excavations on Elephantine. The weapons, pottery, utensils, statues, encased mummies and sarcophagi date from predynastic to late Roman times, and everything is labelled in Arabic and English. The sarcophagus and mummy of a sacred ram, the animal associated with Khnum, are in a room by themselves to the right of the main entrance, while four mummies can be seen to the left of the entrance.

The older part of the museum dates back to 1898 and was a rest house for Sir William Willcocks, the architect of the Aswan Dam. It has been a museum since 1912. The newer extension was added in the early 1990s. You'll probably be shepherded around the well-tended gardens.

Ruins of Yebu Excavation of Yebu began at the start of the 20th century and is still being carried out by a German team. Numbered plaques and reconstructed buildings lead you through a fascinating history spanning from around 3000 BC until the 14th century AD. The largest structure in the site is the partially reconstructed **Temple of Khnum**, which was built in the Old Kingdom but added to and used for over 1500 years before being extensively enlarged and rebuilt in Ptolemaic times. Some other highlights include a small 3rd-dynasty **step pyramid**, a tiny **Ptolemaic chapel** reconstructed from the Temple of Kalabsha (which is now just south of the High Dam), a **temple** dedicated to the goddess Statet, a **cemetery** for sacred rams and the ruins of an Aramaic Jewish colony dating from the 5th century BC.

Perhaps the most famous and impressive sight is the **Nilometer**. Heavenly portents and priestly prophecies aside, in ancient times the Nilometer gave the only sure indication of the likelihood of a bountiful harvest. Descending to the water's edge from beneath a sycamore tree near the museum, the shaft of the ancient Nilometer measured the height of the Nile. Although it dates from the New Kingdom, it was rebuilt by the Romans, and restored last century.

When the Nilometer recorded that the level of the river was high, it meant that the approaching annual flood would be heavy and therefore sufficient for the irrigation vital to a good harvest. It also affected the taxation system, for the higher the river, the better the harvest and the more prosperous the fellaheen and merchants – and therefore, the higher the taxes.

You can enter the Nilometer from the river or down the steps from near the Aswan Museum, or just view it from a felucca on the water.

A booklet detailing the long history of Yebu and the monuments that remain is available in English, German and Arabic at the Aswan Museum or, when it is open, at the excavation house, adjacent to the site.

Kitchener's Island

This island to the west of Elephantine is one of the most delightful places in Aswan. It was given to Lord Horatio Kitchener in the 1890s when he was consul general of Egypt and commander of the Egyptian army. Indulging his passion for beautiful flowers, Kitchener turned the entire island into a **botanic garden** *(admission E£5)*, importing plants from the Far East, India and parts of Africa. The only ugly part of the island is the area with caged animals, including monkeys. The gardens are perfect for a peaceful stroll, but avoid Friday when the island is invaded by picnicking crowds with stereos.

THE WEST BANK

To get to the sights on the west bank, you can either incorporate them into a felucca tour or you can take a ferry from Elephantine across to the landing for the Monastery of St Simeon. To get to the Tombs of the Nobles, there is a public ferry that leaves from outside the governorate building. See Feluccas & Ferries under The River earlier in this chapter for more details.

Mausoleum of the Aga Khan

Aswan was the favourite wintering place of Mohammed Shah Aga Khan, the 48th imam, or leader, of the Ismaili sect of Islam. When he died in 1957, his wife, the begum, oversaw the construction of his domed granite-and-sandstone mausoleum, which is partway up the hill on the west bank opposite Elephantine Island.

Modelled on the Fatimid tombs, the interior, which incorporates a small mosque, is more impressive than the exterior. The sarcophagus, made from Carrara marble, is inscribed with text from the Quran and stands in a vaulted chamber in the interior courtyard. Part of the sarcophagus was reserved for the begum, who died in 2000. Until her death she used to place a red rose on her husband's sarcophagus each day.

At the time of writing the tomb was closed to visitors. Nobody knows whether it will open again, but its hours used to be 8am to 4pm Tuesday to Sunday and admission was free. If you are able to visit, dress modestly and remove your shoes as you enter the mausoleum.

Monastery of St Simeon

This 7th-century monastery *(Deir Amba Samaan; admission E£12; open 7am-5pm daily)* is one of the best preserved of the original Christian strongholds in Egypt. Confusingly, the original monastery foundations were dedicated to a local saint named Hadra, but the monastery survived under the name of St Simeon until Salah ad-Din destroyed it in 1173.

Surrounded by desert sands, except for a glimpse of the fertile belt around Aswan in the distance, the monastery has stunning views and bears more resemblance to a fortress than to a religious sanctuary. It once provided accommodation for about 300 resident monks plus a further 100 or so pilgrims. Built on two levels, the lower level of stone and the upper level of mud brick, it was surrounded by 10m-high walls and contained a church, shops, bakeries, offices, a kitchen, dormitories, stables and workshops. Mud-brick architecture buffs will love the long vault in the upper enclosure. Off the vault are the monks' cells with their mastaba, or bench, beds. The last room on the right still has graffiti from the Muslim pilgrims who stayed here en route to Mecca.

To get to the monastery from the boat landing, you can either negotiate with the camel drivers (expect to pay about E£25 for an hour) or scramble up the desert track (about 25 minutes). Alternatively, you can take the ferry to the Tombs of the Nobles and ride a camel or donkey from there.

Tombs of the Nobles

The high cliffs opposite Aswan, just north of Kitchener's Island, are honeycombed with the tombs *(admission E£12; open 8am-4pm Oct-May, 8am-5pm June-Sept)* of the princes, governors, keepers of the Gate of the South and other dignitaries of ancient Yebu. The tombs date from the Old and Middle Kingdoms and although most of them are in a sorry state of disrepair, there are a few worth visiting.

Tombs of Mekhu & Sabni (Nos 25 & 26) The adjoining tombs of father and son, Mekhu (Tomb No 25) and Sabni (Tomb No 26), both overseers of Upper Egypt, date from the extraordinarily long reign of the 6th-dynasty pharaoh Pepi II (2278–2184 BC). The reliefs in No 26 record a tale of tragedy and triumph. Mekhu was killed on an expedition into Africa, so his son Sabni led the army into Nubia to punish the tribe responsible. Sabni recovered his father's body and sent a messenger to the pharaoh in Memphis to inform him that the enemy had been taught a lesson. On his return to Aswan he was met by priests, professional mourners and some of the royal embalmers, all sent by the pharaoh himself to show the importance that was accorded to the keepers of the kingdom's southern frontier.

Tomb of Sarenput II (No 31) Sarenput, the local governor and commander of the frontier garrison of the south under the 12th-dynasty pharaoh Amenemhat II (1922–1878 BC), has one of the best-preserved tombs. There are statues of the prince and wall paintings depicting Sarenput and his son hunting and fishing.

Tomb of Harkhuf (No 34) A governor of the south under Pepi II, Harkhuf led three trading expeditions south into Nubia. The most remarkable thing about his tomb is the long biographical text to the right of the entrance, which includes a copy of a letter Harkhuf received from Pharaoh Pepi, who was then still a boy of eight. Having heard that Harkhuf had obtained a 'dancing pygmy' on his travels, the young pharaoh was so keen to see the pygmy that he advised Harkhuf to keep a careful watch on him day and night in case he should fall off the boat and into the Nile! Look carefully to see the tiny hieroglyph figure of the pygmy several times in the text.

Tomb of Pepinakht (No 35) Also called Hekaib, Pepinakht was the overseer of foreign soldiers during the reign of the 6th-dynasty pharaoh Pepi II. Pepinakht was sent to quell rebellions in both Nubia and Palestine, and was even deified after his death as is revealed by the small shrine of Hekaib built on Elephantine Island during the Middle Kingdom (c. 1900 BC). His tomb has a columned facade and some fine reliefs showing fighting bulls and hunting scenes.

Tomb of Sarenput I (No 36) Sarenput I was the grandfather of Sarenput II and was a regional governor during the 12th-dynasty reign of Sesostris I (1965–1920 BC). On the rear wall of a columned court, to the left of the door, he is shown being followed by his dogs and sandal-bearer, and there are other scenes of his three sons and of women bearing flowers.

Kubbet al-Hawa

Also on the west bank is Kubbet al-Hawa, a small tomb constructed for a local sheikh at the top of the hill. If you climb up to it, you'll be rewarded with fantastic views of the Nile and the surrounding area.

SWIMMING

Aswan is a hot place, and sometimes a swim seems just the way to escape the worst of it. Short of joining the local kids and jumping into the Nile to cool off (which is definitely not advised – see the boxed text 'Bilharzia' under Health in the Facts for the Visitor chapter for more details), there are a few hotels with swimming pools open to the public, generally from 9am to sunset. The cheapest by far is the small pool at the Cleopatra Hotel, which costs E£10, but it's small and overlooked by other buildings. The Basma Hotel has a pool that nonguests can use for E£25, while the Aswan Oberoi and Isis Island Hotel charge E£30. Some readers have reported that you can use the New Cataract's pool for free, as long as you order lunch. The municipal pool next to the main post office does not admit tourists.

ORGANISED TOURS

Small hotels and travel agencies arrange day tours of the area's major sights. Half-day tours usually include the Temple of Isis at Philae, the unfinished obelisk and the High Dam, and start at US$27 with AmEx (per person with three to five people) or Thomas Cook. It is far cheaper and just as easy to simply hire a taxi to take you on the same circuit, incorporating the Nubian Museum and perhaps even the Temple of Kalabsha. This will cost about E£75. Travel agencies will also arrange felucca trips to Elephantine Island and the botanic garden for about E£35 per person, based on a group of three to five people.

PLACES TO STAY

As in Luxor, prices for accommodation vary greatly depending on the season. The high season officially extends from October to April, however, its zenith is December and January when many Egyptians come here in groups. In the low season, and even until early November, you'll have no trouble finding a room, and haggling is part of the game. All the prices listed in the Budget and Mid-Range entries here are low-season rates, so expect prices to be higher if you're here in winter. The prices in the Top-End range are high season rates.

If you arrive by train, you'll invariably be met by hotel touts each postulating the best deal in town and often claiming to be the

ANDERS BLOMQVIST

The outer court of the Temple of Isis at Philae shows reliefs of Ptolemy XII smiting his enemies.

CHRISTINE OSBORNE

This view of Elephantine Island and Aswan was taken from the west bank of the Nile.

TROY FLOWER

Two huge statues of Ramses II guard the entrance to his rock-cut temple at Abu Simbel.

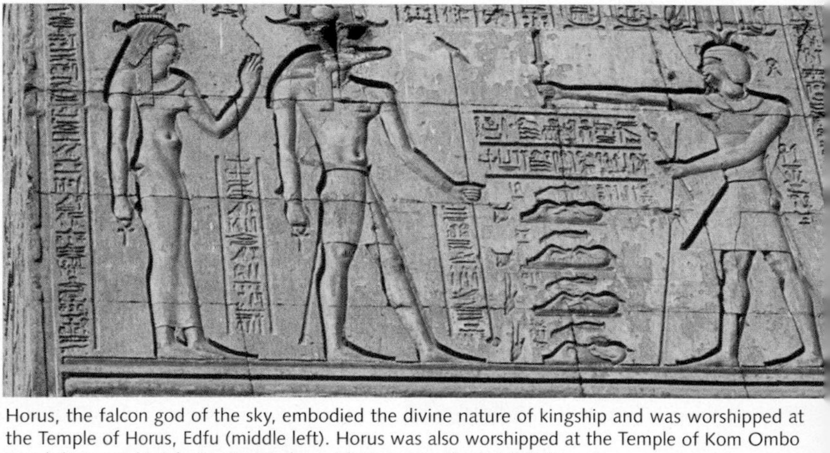

ALL PHOTOGRAPHS BY SARA-JANE CLELAND

Horus, the falcon god of the sky, embodied the divine nature of kingship and was worshipped at the Temple of Horus, Edfu (middle left). Horus was also worshipped at the Temple of Kom Ombo (top left, top right & bottom) together with the crocodile god Sobek.

owner of a particular place. Unless you want to be hassled by them for the rest of your stay in Aswan, it's best to give these guys a wide berth and find your own place to stay.

PLACES TO STAY – BUDGET

Camping

Municipal Camp Site Camping per motorcycle/person/car/van E£2/3/5/10. The official site is next to the unfinished obelisk, a 20- to 25-minute walk from the area around EgyptAir. Facilities here are basic (filthy toilets and cold showers only), but there are grassy spaces for setting up tents and a few trees to provide shade. Bright lamps and guards keep the place secure, but the lights can make it difficult to sleep.

Hostels

Youth Hostel *(☎/fax 302 235, Sharia Abtal at-Tahrir)* Dorm beds members/nonmembers E£7.60/8.60. This place is not far from the train station at the side entrance of the governorate-run hostel that, just to confuse you, also calls itself a youth hostel. The freshly painted rooms have fans, the showers and toilets are clean and, if you avoid Egyptian university breaks, the place is generally empty. It makes a point of keeping foreigners separate from the locals.

Hotels

Rosewan Hotel *(☎ 304 497, e rosewan20@hotmail.com)* Singles/doubles/triples E£12/22/31. This has been popular with budget travellers for quite a few years but it is now a bit overpriced. It's near the station and has fairly clean, simple, but rather small rooms. All have shower, toilet, fan and tiled floors. The staff is very friendly and the owner, Farouk Nasser, is a self-taught artist, poet and all-round character. Internet use is available for 55pt a minute. Prices include breakfast.

Queen Hotel *(☎ 326 069, Sharia Atlas)* Singles/doubles E£30/45, with air-con E£35/50. This newly opened and spotlessly clean small hotel is close to the station but far enough away to avoid the noise. Some rooms have Nile views and all prices include breakfast.

Marwa Hotel Beds in 3-bed or 4-bed room E£5. This hotel is entered from an alley off Sharia Abtal at-Tahrir, directly across the street from the youth hostel. The rooms are simple and a little cramped, but it is a fairly popular place. Each room has a fan and there's hot water in the communal showers. A few rooms have air-con, for which you pay E£2 more. Breakfast is E£1 extra.

Al-Amin Hotel *(☎ 314 189, fax 309 214, Sharia Abtal at-Tahrir)* Singles/doubles E£13/25. This hotel offers gloomy but reasonably clean rooms with small toilet/shower combinations. Despite its Abtal at-Tahrir address, the entrance to the hotel is actually on a side street just across from the Ramses Hotel.

Nubian Oasis Hotel *(☎ 312 126, fax 312 124, 234 Sharia as-Souq)* Singles/doubles E£20/25. Just off Sharia as-Souq, this remains one of Aswan's most popular travellers' haunts, although on our visits the staff was consistently rude. Otherwise, it has clean rooms with bath and air-con; prices include breakfast. There's a large lounge area and a roof garden where beer is served. As in most budget places, staff can be pushy about the hotel's own organised excursions and felucca trips.

Noorhan Hotel *(☎ 316 069, Sharia as-Souq)* Doubles with fan/air-con E£15/20. On the eastern side of Sharia as-Souq, Noorhan Hotel has had mixed reviews from travellers. The hotel touts can be aggressive and will try to sell you its organised trips. However, the rooms (with bath) aren't bad, Internet use is available for E£15 per hour, and Stellas are E£6.

Yassin Hotel *(☎ 317 109)* Dorm beds E£8, doubles E£25. Yassin has a complicated pricing system, depending on which floor you're staying, but it offers clean rooms with fan or air-con and bath; double rooms include breakfast. The Yassin is in a three-storey building off Sharia as-Souq, next door to the Noorhan.

New Brethren Hotel *(☎ 310 466, Sharia as-Souq)* Singles/doubles E£15/30. This hotel may have an off-putting Islamic name to some, but it's central and not too bad if you're stuck for a place to stay. Rooms have a shared bath and include breakfast. However, it should be avoided by single women.

Victoria Hotel *(☎ 313 870, Sharia Abtal at-Tahrir)* Singles/doubles E£8/15. The Victoria boasts rickety wooden balconies, high ceilings, ceiling fans, iron bed frames and a wonderful sweeping staircase. Unfortunately, the shared facilities are full of a less welcome kind, in the form of grime and insect life. Prices include breakfast.

Abu Shelib Hotel *(☎ 303 051, Sharia Abbas Farid)* Singles/doubles E£18/25. This hotel is at the southern end of the street, next to a mosque. Rooms are dark but clean and simple, with fan and/or air-con and toilet/shower combination (some have big bathrooms). You may be able to negotiate the price, depending on the size of the rooms and whether or not they have showers. It's popular with overland travel groups.

Hotel Orabi *(☎/fax 317 578)* Doubles without/with breakfast E£16/20, doubles with air-con & breakfast E£25. On a quiet side street just off Sharia as-Souq, the Orabi has a central location that is an advantage for exploring the souq and the Corniche. The staff is friendly, and the rooms are modern and comfortable, and the communal bathrooms are fairly clean. Some rooms also have big balconies.

Keylany Hotel *(☎/fax 317 332, ⓔ mohamed@aswanet.com.eg, 25 Sharia Keylany)* Doubles with fan/air-con E£30/35. This is probably the best option in the budget range, with 21 simple but clean rooms, each with ceiling fan or air-con, pine furniture and a spotless bathroom. Prices include breakfast. The attached Internet cafe is very good.

PLACES TO STAY – MID-RANGE

Prices include service and taxes, unless noted otherwise.

Ramses Hotel *(☎ 324 000, fax 315 701, Sharia Abtal at-Tahrir)* Singles/doubles E£60/84. Rooms have shower, toilet, air-con, colour TV, mini-fridge and Nile views. It's not a bad deal, but the rooms are looking a bit grotty and readers have complained about the pushy staff. It's popular with tour groups from Europe.

Happi Hotel *(☎ 314 115, fax 307 572, Sharia Abtal at-Tahrir)* Singles/doubles E£55/75. A few blocks down from the Ramses, the Happi has 64 clean rooms with spotless bathrooms. The rooms have air-con and some also have balconies, TV and double beds. Ask for a room with a Nile view. The owner also runs the Cleopatra Hotel, so guests can use the Cleopatra's pool for a discounted price.

Oscar Hotel *(☎/fax 306 066, 5 Sharia Abbas al-Akkad)* Singles/doubles E£40/70. The Oscar has become a travellers' favourite, although the renovations currently underway mean that room prices are less likely to be negotiable in the future. Clean and friendly, it's a good deal in the middle of town. There's also a rooftop terrace where beers (E£7) are available.

New Abu Simbel Hotel *(☎ 306 096, Sharia Abtal al-Tahrir)* Singles/doubles E£35/45. This hotel is several blocks north of the train station and, although it's out of the centre, the management is friendly, and there's a pleasant garden where you can cool off with a beer. Air-con rooms with Nile views and balconies are the best. Prices include breakfast.

Al-Salaam Hotel *(☎ 312 651, 313 649, Corniche el-Nil)* Singles/doubles E£25/40, with air-con & breakfast E£35/50. Most of the freshly painted rooms here have baths and some have great views of the Nile, although they somehow manage to be a bit dark. Still, its a fair deal for the price.

Hathor Hotel *(☎ 314 580, fax 303 462, Corniche el-Nil)* Singles/doubles E£20/40, with air-con E£30/50. The Hathor has 36 rooms, most with air-con but some are tiny. Still, they are clean and the roof terrace has a small swimming pool and spectacular views over the Nile. It's a good deal for the price.

Horus Hotel *(☎/fax 313 313, Corniche el-Nil)* Singles/doubles E£40/50. This hotel has large and comfortable rooms with air-con and bath. Some rooms have great Nile views. Ask for a room that has been renovated. There is also a rooftop bar and restaurant.

Kalabsha Hotel *(☎ 322 666, fax 325 974, Sharia Abtal at-Tahrir)* Singles/doubles no ncluding taxes US$40/60. The four-star Kalabsha is another modernist affair, with an excellent view of the First Nile Cataract. t's nowhere near as good as the surrounding hotels, but it's considerably cheaper and guests can use the swimming pool at the New Cataract Hotel for free.

Philae Hotel *(☎ 312 090, Corniche el-Nil)* Singles/doubles E£40/60, with Nile view E£50/80. Taxes are extra. Partially enovated and with ill-fitting carpets and lusty hallways, this place is only worth staying in if you can get a room with a Nile view and if the Horus and Hathor are empty.

Memnon Hotel *(☎ 300 483, Corniche el-Nil)* Singles/doubles E£45/50. This hotel is above the National Bank of Egypt but can only be entered through a back alley. The eception is on the 2nd floor. The rooms are clean, and have air-con, bath and comfortable beds. There is a small pool on the roof. Staff can be a bit pushy when it comes to rying to sell felucca trips.

Al-Amir Hotel *(☎ 314 735, Sharia Abbas Farid)* Singles/doubles E£85/115. A street back from the Corniche, this threestar hotel claims to have Nile views (apparent only if you strain your neck). It's popular with Gulf Arabs (Saudi emblems emblazon the stationery and brochures) and has 28 clean rooms with a TV, air-con and phone. It's next to a mosque, and somewhat overpriced considering that it's not on he Nile.

Cleopatra Hotel *(☎ 314 003, fax 314 002, Sharia as-Souq)* Singles/doubles US$48/62. Not far from the train station, this hotel s well situated for exploring the old souq area. All 109 rooms are clean and comfortable and have air-con, bath and telephone, although they don't quite live up to the promise of the lobby. There's also a rooftop pool that is overlooked by the surrounding buildings.

PLACES TO STAY – TOP END

Aswan has a good selection of luxury hotels, including the famous Old Cataract. Unless otherwise noted, prices quoted here are for the high season and include service and taxes. During the summer months (June to September), or between European holidays, you may be able to negotiate the price down considerably.

Old Cataract Hotel *(☎ 316 000, fax 316 011, Sharia Abtal at-Tahrir)* Standard doubles US$167, deluxe rooms with terrace US$296, suites US$493-1217. This is one of Egypt's most famous and historic hotels. An impressive Moorish-style building, it is surrounded by gardens on a rise above the river, and has splendid views of the Nile and across the southern tip of Elephantine Island to the Mausoleum of the Aga Khan. The hotel's exterior was used in the movie of Agatha Christie's *Death on the Nile*, in part because Christie once did some writing here. Many people complain that the standard of food and service here is not worth the high cost of the rooms (prices do include breakfast), but the setting is unparalleled. The hotel is worth visiting just to enjoy a cool Stella or a cocktail on the veranda; however, after large groups of package tourists began treating the hotel and its guests as a tourist attraction, the management closed the terrace to nonguests. You may be able to sneak in by saying that you're staying at the New Cataract Hotel.

New Cataract Hotel *(☎ 316 002, fax 316 011, Sharia Abtal at-Tahrir)* Singles/doubles US$94/128, with Nile views US$106/140. This is a high-rise lump next door to the old hotel; however, if you stay here, you have the advantage of not having to look at it, and the rooms overlooking the Nile have stunning views. This hotel has none of the style of the Old Cataract, and its rooms are in need of refurbishment, but it has a large pool and tennis courts and shares the Old Cataract's gardens.

Basma Hotel *(☎ 310 901, fax 310 907, Sharia Abtal at-Tahrir)* Singles/doubles US$103/141. Another four-star hotel, Basma is at the top of the hill just past the Kalabsha Hotel. Its garden terrace has great views over the southern end of Elephantine Island and the Mausoleum of the Aga Khan. Less offensive aesthetically than the Kalabsha and New Cataract, it has the usual four-star amenities and prices include breakfast.

Aswan Oberoi *(☎ 314 667, fax 313 538, Elephantine Island)* Singles/doubles not including taxes US$150/193. This is the disfiguring blot that rises from Elephantine Island. It has two hotel launches that ferry guests and visitors from the east bank. However, once you're there, you have magnificent views, good-sized rooms, a spa, a pool and beautiful gardens.

Isis Hotel *(☎ 324 744, fax 326 893, Corniche el-Nil)* Singles/doubles US$90/112. Although its shoddily built rooms are hardly beautiful, this four-star place has a prime location on the river in the centre of town. Prices include breakfast.

Isis Island Hotel *(☎ 317 400, fax 317 405, Isis Island)* Singles/doubles US$125/155. Controversy surrounded the construction of this enormous five-star place, as it was built within a few metres of a nature reserve on a group of islands that are home to the only original Nile vegetation remaining in Egypt. An ostentatious launch ferries guests (and outsiders wanting to use the pool) from the east bank in front of the EgyptAir office. Prices include breakfast.

Hôtel Île d'Amoun *(☎ 313 800, fax 317 193, Amun Island)* Singles/doubles E£180/240. This salmon-toned hotel is on a neighbouring islet. It's operated by Club Med, which took over the original building years ago and transformed it into an idyllic garden paradise. The hotel's modest motorboats leave from in front of the EgyptAir office. Prices include breakfast.

PLACES TO EAT

Restaurants in Aswan don't have the turnover found in many other Egyptian resorts. Few new ones open and old stalwarts don't close, even if they seem to have few customers. Still, while the selection may not be wide or diverse, there's something for all budgets.

Budget Dining

Along Sharia as-Souq is a smorgasbord of small restaurants and cafes in the midst of the lively atmosphere of the souqs. There are also plenty of cafes around the train station.

Restaurant Derwash Dishes E£6-10. On the south side of the midan in front of the station, this place has been recommended by some travellers. It offers the usual basic chicken, rice and vegetable dishes.

A block from the station is ***Samah***, a little ta'amiyya stall. Down a side street, a bit further on, is ***An-Nasr***, which has pizza, as well as fried fish and chicken.

Al-Dar Dishes E£6-10. Next to the Youth Hostel, this is an OK place that does full meals for E£6.

Esraa Dishes E£3-12. This tiny kofta place is just down the road from the Al-Dar.

Medina Restaurant *(Sharia as-Souq)* Dishes E£4.50-12. Across from the Cleopatra Hotel, this place is recommended for its kofta and kebab deals, and is often patronised by travellers. It also does a vegetarian meal, as well as good stuffed courgette and cabbage leaves.

Al-Sayyida Nefissa Dishes E£2-11. Tucked away in a side alley in the heart of the souq is this good-value place serving kofta, soup and meals of rice, salad, vegetables and bread.

Restaurants

Al-Masry Restaurant *(☎ 302 576, Sharia al-Matar)* Meals E£8-30. This is one of Aswan's better-known restaurants. It is famous for kebabs and kofta, but also serves pigeon and chicken. The meat is excellent and comes with bread, salad and tahini. It's a popular place with local families. No beer is served.

At the following three places on the Corniche you can sit out on a barge in the river and get decent food and beers.

Aswan Moon Restaurant *(☎ 316 108, Corniche el-Nil)* Meals E£7-35. This is the best of the trio and a popular hang-out for both foreigners and Egyptians. After a few days in Aswan you're likely to recognise the regulars. It has generous soups and pizzas, and a good *daoud basha* (meatballs in tomato sauce). Down on the river, with a laid-back atmosphere and slow but reasonable service, it is a good place to sit and sip wine or beer while watching the Nile flow slowly past.

Emy Restaurant *(Corniche el-Nil)* Meals E£9-12. Next door to the Aswan Moon, the Emy prepares especially nice fruit cocktails, as well as serving the usual selection of meals. The view from the top deck at sunset is bliss, and there is a discount available for those with student cards.

Saladin Restaurant *(Corniche el-Nil)* Meals E£8-15. The third barge belongs to the Saladin and while it's pleasant enough for a drink, the food is nothing to rave about. It's less popular than the other two and rarely full.

Chef Khalil *(☎ 310 142, Sharia as-Souq)* Meals E£8-45. This new fish restaurant just along from the station serves very fresh fish from Lake Nasser as well as the Red Sea. The fish is sold by weight, and is served with salad and rice or French fries. It's a small place, but worth the wait if it's full.

On the Nile side of the Corniche there are several other restaurants floating on pontoons on the river, all offering a similar range of dishes at virtually the same prices. They include ***Monalisa Restaurant***, ***Panorama*** and ***Al-Shati***. Panorama has some greenery and is particularly nice for a riverside lunch. Most of their meals are cooked in huge, clay pots and it has a wide selection of herbal teas on offer.

Nubian Restaurant *(☎ 302 465, Essa Island)* Meals E£55. This place offers set Nubian meals with an after-dinner folkloric show, which some people enjoy but others find kitsch. Wine and beer are served, at a price. The restaurant sits on a tiny island south of Elephantine Island and offers a free boat that leaves from opposite EgyptAir.

Nubian House *(☎ 326 226)* Meals E£8-20. This small, pleasant restaurant is on a hill behind the Basma Hotel. Its vantage point on the edge of the cliffs affords stunning views over Elephantine Island and the river.

Garden Restaurant *(☎ 316 002, New Cataract)* Meals E£57. This place serves set meals that are billed as Nubian but are in reality Egyptian and Lebanese. You get generous servings of food, with several dishes of mezze followed by servings of potatoes, rice, chicken, meat and fish cooked in clay pots. The wooden gazebo-type setting is nice if the weather is cool, but it's hot in the summer.

Alternatively, you can partake of a buffet dinner at one of the hotels. The ***Hôtel Île d'Amoun*** has a good spread for E£58.

Self-Catering

The souq is the best place to head if you want to buy your own food. On the main street, as well as some of the small alleyways, there are a number of small grocery shops that stock canned goods, cheese and UHT milk. As you can see on a quick stroll through the market, fruit and vegetables are abundant when in season. They are best bought in the morning, when they are fresh. To buy local beer and wine, head to the Egypt Free shop on the Corniche (☎ 314 939). It is open from 9am to 2pm and from 6pm to 10pm daily.

ENTERTAINMENT

Palace of Culture *(☎ 313 390, Corniche el-Nil)* Between October and February/March, Aswan's folkloric dance troupe sporadically performs Nubian *tahtib* (stick dancing) and songs depicting village life. If tour groups demand performances and the troupe is not travelling, they begin their performances at around 9pm Saturday to Thursday. The show lasts about two hours and admission is E£10. The centre also sometimes presents other traditional Upper Egyptian and Nubian music performances.

Nubian shows are also performed at the Aswan Oberoi and the New Cataract hotels, although they are expensive and sometimes veer into kitsch. If you are lucky, you may be invited to a Nubian wedding on a weekend night. Foreign guests are deemed auspicious additions to the ceremony, but don't be surprised if you're asked to pay a E£10 'fee' to help defray the huge costs of the band and the food.

Otherwise, strolling along the Corniche, watching the moon rise as you sit at a rooftop terrace and having a beer at one of the floating restaurants is about all that most travellers get up to in Aswan at night. The top-end hotels all have discos and nightclubs, but they're fairly empty.

SHOPPING

Aswan's famous souq may be more touristy than it used to be but it's still a good place to pick up souvenirs and crafts. Colourful Nubian skullcaps are popular and go for about E£5 each. More bulky are the baskets and trays that you can see around town. Prices vary according to size and age; expect to pay about E£50 for an old, medium-sized tray. Small round discs go for around E£10.

The spices and indigo powder prominently displayed are also good buys, and most of the spice shops sell the dried hibiscus used to make the refreshing drink *karkadey*. However, beware of the safflower that is sold as saffron. Aswan is also famous for the quality of its henna powder and its delicious roasted peanuts. The higher grade of the latter go for E£6 a kilogram.

GETTING THERE & AWAY

Air

The EgyptAir office (☎ 315 000) is at the southern end of the Corniche. There are daily flights from Cairo to Aswan (E£627 one way, 1¼ hours). The one-way trip to Luxor is E£199. The return flight from Aswan to Abu Simbel costs E£550.80 and includes bus transfers between the airport and the temple site.

Felucca Trips

Watching the dark waters of the Nile slide by from the deck of a felucca is one of the highlights of any trip to Egypt. Aswan is the best place to arrange overnight trips, largely because you'll be going with the current and won't find yourself marooned if the wind dies.

The most common trips are to Kom Ombo (two days, one night) or, the most popular option, Edfu (three days, two nights). A typical itinerary is to set sail in the morning and to spend the day heading towards the town of Kom Ombo. Many of the captains are Nubian and will take you for tea in their village along the way. Nights are spent on the boat or camping on an island in the Nile. Night-time entertainment ranges from star-gazing to partying, depending on you and your fellow passengers. Once you arrive you can either return to Aswan or head up to Luxor by service taxi.

Arranging a felucca trip can seem daunting when you face the legions of touts on Aswan's Corniche. The small hotels can be just as aggressive in trying to rope you in. While it is easier to let them do the organising, remember that the hotels get a percentage, which either comes out of the captain's fee or your food allowance. If you want to be sure of what you're getting it's best to do it yourself.

Officially, feluccas can carry a minimum of six passengers and a maximum of eight; it costs E£25 per person to Kom Ombo, E£45 to Edfu, E£50 to Esna or E£60 to Luxor. On top of this add E£5 for police registration, plus there's the cost of food supplies. You can get boats for less than the official rate, but take care; if it's much cheaper you'll either have a resentful captain and crew, or you'll be eating little more than bread and fuul for three days.

Finding a good captain is essential, especially if you are a woman travelling alone or in a group of women. Some women travellers have reported sailing with felucca captains who had groping hands and there have been some rare reports of assault. There are more than 600 feluccas plying the waters around Aswan, so you have plenty of choice. Many of the better captains can be found having a *sheesha* (water pipe) in Nile-side restaurants such as the Aswan Moon or near the Panorama restaurant further south. If you want help, Shukri Saad and his assistant Hakeem Hussein at the tourist office can recommend some reputable people, or at least advise you against some who are shady.

When dealing with a felucca captain, there are a few things to look out for:

- Ensure that the captain has what appears to be a decent, functioning boat, with some blankets and cooking implements, a sunshade and something comfortable to sit on. There should also

Bus

The bus station is in the middle of town on Sharia Abtal at-Tahrir. In their zeal to 'protect' foreigners, some policemen have been forbidding foreigners from taking buses out of Aswan. There seem to be no hard and fast rules, although at the time of writing, Abu Simbel buses were definitely off limits to tourists. Check with the tourist office or ask around before you buy your ticket.

A direct bus to Cairo (E£55, 12 hours) leaves at 3.30pm daily. A second bus leaving three hours later costs E£41. Both buses supposedly have air-con, video and toilet.

There are hourly buses to Kom Ombo (E£1.50/5 without/with air-con, one hour), Edfu (E£3/10, two hours), Esna (E£4.50/15, three hours) and Luxor (E£6.50/15, four to five hours).

There are five buses going the whole way through to Hurghada (seven hours). The 6am and 8am buses each cost E£25 and continue to Suez (E£37); the 3.30pm bus is a Pullman (E£40) that goes on to Cairo but does not stop in Suez. The 5pm bus (E£35) stops in Suez (E£45) and the 6.30pm bus (E£25) goes on to Cairo via Suez (E£40) – a 15-hour long haul. A bus for Marsa Alam (E£12, five hours) leaves from Aswan at 6.30am.

Felucca Trips

be a place to lock up valuables. If a different boat is foisted on you at the last minute, be firm in refusing to take it. Likewise with the captain himself – many travellers agree to sail with one man and find themselves with someone else when they get on the boat. If you have a problem with a captain, report it to the tourist office in Aswan. They will act as an intermediary with the tourist police.

- Establish whether the price includes food and, if so, go with whomever does the shopping to see just what you are getting. Otherwise, set a price without food and get your own.
- Agree on the number of passengers before you go and don't be talked into taking 'a few others on board later downriver', otherwise you'll find yourselves sharing limited supplies of food, water and space.
- Decide on the drop-off point before you set sail. Although you may think you're going to Edfu, many felucca captains stop 30km short of the town, in the villages of Hammam, Faris or Ar-Ramady and arrange for 'special' shared taxis – which take you straight to a hotel of the captain's choice in Luxor for E£10 per person (instead of the E£5 it usually costs).
- Don't hand over your passport. Often captains, or more likely middlemen, like to take them so that they have a couple of passengers in the bag. They then scour around for other people. A photocopy will do for the permit. It's advisable to accompany the captain to the police when organising permission.
- Take plenty of bottled water for the trip; otherwise the captain may dip into the Nile for cooking and drinking water.
- Bring a sleeping bag – it can get bitterly cold at night, and the supply of blankets on board won't be enough. Insect repellent is a good idea. A hat is essential.
- Think ahead – accidents occasionally happen with feluccas. We've heard a report of a felucca capsizing and sinking within minutes. Obviously, you should think twice about taking such a trip if you cannot swim. Packing all your belongings in sealed plastic bags will not only keep them dry, it will help them to float to the surface in the case of an accident. Keeping your important documents on you in a moneybelt is another common-sense tip.
- Take your rubbish with you when you leave if you camp overnight on an island or beach. After all, nobody wants to spend their trip sitting in a garbage dump.

Train

There is a handful of trains running daily between Cairo and Aswan but only three of them can be used by foreigners. However, if you try climbing aboard another train and buying your ticket on board then usually nobody will stop you. If you want to stop off in Daraw or some of the other smaller towns between Aswan and Luxor this is probably the best way unless you go in the convoy.

The most expensive is the wagons-lit (sleeper) train (No 85) that costs E£362 one way to Cairo and departs at 6.15pm.

The other two trains deemed 'safe' by the security forces are express train Nos 981 and 997 to Cairo, which have to be booked in advance. They both have air-con and a restaurant and leave at 5am and 8pm, respectively. The fare is E£69/38 (students E£45/29) for 1st/2nd class. The trip to Cairo is scheduled to take about 15 hours but has been known to take more than 20 hours.

Tickets for the train to Luxor (four hours) cost E£16/11 in 1st/2nd class in the morning, and E£20/15 in the evening. Both trains also stop at Kom Ombo (E£7/5 or E£10/9) and Edfu (E£10/7 or E£14/11).

Other trains northbound leave at 7am, 10.45am, 3.45pm and 7pm. Because foreigners are, strictly speaking, not allowed to take these trains, they cannot book seats in advance, buy a ticket on board instead.

Car & Motorcycle

Driving north or south means going in a police convoy. Convoys north congregate in front of the Officer's Club, north of the governorate building on the Corniche, and leave at 8am and 1.30pm. You should get there about 15 minutes in advance. Convoys south to Abu Simbel leave at 4am and, if there are enough tourists, at 11am. Check with the tourist office to see whether rules have been relaxed or convoy times have changed.

Service Taxi

At the time of writing, the police in Aswan were forbidding foreigners from taking service taxis, often turning them back at the checkpoint just north of town. As with all such directives, people do get around the rules. However, in general it's better to take the train, or else get a group of people together and hire a private taxi. If things change (check with the tourist office), the service taxi station is across the train tracks on the east side of town. Just off Sharia as-Souq, one block south of the train station, is an overpass over the tracks. Climb the overpass and walk to the end of the street on the other side (about 10 minutes). Turn right and walk about 500m to the service taxi station. Alternatively, just follow the tracks south to the tunnel: The service taxi station is on the other side of the railway line.

Boat

For details about the five-star cruisers that sail between the High Dam and Abu Simbel, see Getting There & Away under Lower Nubia & Lake Nasser later in this chapter. There is a hydrofoil that runs between Aswan and Abu Simbel, although at the time of writing it had no set schedule and was dependent on demand from tour groups. The tourist office or any travel agency should be able to tell you if it is running. A return ticket, with breakfast, lunch, entry to the temple and a guide costs about US$90.

For details on boat transport to Sudan see under Sea in the Getting There & Away chapter.

GETTING AROUND

To/From the Airport

The airport is 25km south-west of town and the taxi fare is about E£25.

Taxi

A taxi tour that includes Philae, the High Dam and the unfinished obelisk near the Fatimid Cemetery costs around E£30 for five to six people. Taxis can also take you on day trips to Daraw and/or Kom Ombo for about E£80. Remember that you have to join the convoy to do this.

Bicycle

There are a few places at the train station end of Sharia as-Souq where you can hire bicycles for about E£5 a day – try around the Marwa and Ramses Hotels.

Around Aswan

ASWAN DAM

When the British constructed the Aswan Dam above the First Nile Cataract at the turn of the 19th century it was the largest of its kind in the world. The growing population of Egypt had made it imperative to put more land under cultivation and the only way to achieve this was to regulate the flow of the Nile. The dam was built between 1898 and 1902; it measures 2441m across, and is made almost entirely of local Aswan granite.

Although its height had to be raised twice to meet the demand, the dam not only greatly increased the area of cultivable land but also provided the country with most of its hydroelectric power. Now completely surpassed both in function and as a tourist attraction by the High Dam 6km upstream, it is still worth a brief visit, as the area around the First Nile Cataract below it is extremely fertile and picturesque.

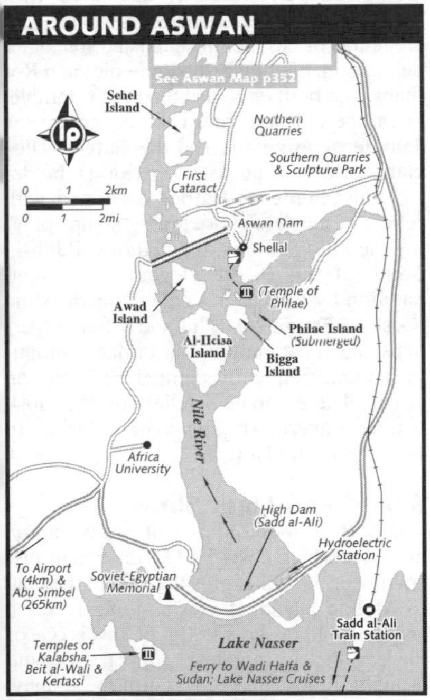

The road to the airport and all trips to Abu Simbel by road include a drive across this dam.

SEHEL ISLAND

Sehel, the large island north of the old Aswan Dam, was sacred to the goddess Anukis. As a destination for an extended felucca trip on this part of the Nile, Sehel Island is a good choice, although there isn't much to see apart from a friendly Nubian village and a great many rock inscriptions dating from Middle Kingdom to Graeco-Roman times.

TEMPLE OF PHILAE

The romantic and majestic aura surrounding the temple complex of Isis *(admission E£20; open 8am-4pm Oct-May, 7am-5pm June-Sept)* on the island of Philae (fee-**li**) has been luring pilgrims for thousands of years. During the 19th century the ruins were one of Egypt's legendary tourist attractions. From the start of the 20th century, Philae and its temples became swamped for six months of every year by the high waters of the reservoir created by the construction of the old Aswan Dam. It seemed that they were destined to be lost forever, and travellers took to rowing boats to glide among the partly submerged columns and peer down through the translucent green to the wondrous sanctuaries of the mighty gods below.

In the 1960s, with the approaching completion of the High Dam, a rescue of the temple complex was organised by Unesco. The massive complex was disassembled and removed stone by stone from Philae between 1972 and 1980. The temples were reconstructed 20m higher on nearby Agilkia Island, which was even landscaped to resemble the sacred isle of Isis, in positions corresponding as closely as possible to their original layout.

By Roman times, Isis had become the greatest of all the Egyptian gods, worshipped right across the Roman Empire even as far as Britain. Her much older cult rivalled the new-fangled cult of Christianity. Indeed, well after Rome and its empire

TEMPLE OF PHILAE

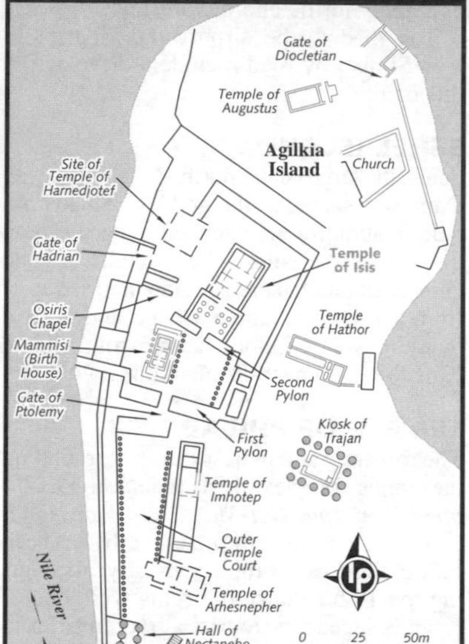

accepted Christianity, Isis was still being worshipped at Philae as late as AD 550, when her temple was closed by the emperor Justinian.

Although Isis worship at Philae dates back to around 690 BC at least, the earliest visible remains of the temple date from the reign of Nectanebo I (380–362 BC). Most of the rest was initiated by Ptolemy II Philadelphus (285–246 BC) and added to for the next 500 years until the reign of Diocletian (AD 284–305). The early Christians also added their bit by transforming the main temple's hypostyle hall into a chapel, building some churches and defacing the pagan reliefs. Their inscriptions were in turn vandalised by the early Muslims.

Touring the Temple

The boat across to the temple leaves you at the base of the **Hall of Nectanebo**, the oldest part of the Philae complex. Heading north, you walk down the **outer temple court**, which has colonnades running along both sides, to the entrance of the Temple of Isis, marked by the 18m-high towers of the **first pylon** with their reliefs of Ptolemy XII (Cleopatra's father) smiting enemies.

In the central court of the **Temple of Isis** is the *mammisi* (birth house) dedicated to Horus. Successive pharaohs reinstated their legitimacy as the mortal descendants of Horus by taking part in the mammisi rituals, which celebrated the god's birth.

The **second pylon** leads to a 10-columned hypostyle hall and beyond into the **Inner Sanctuary of Isis** where the goddess' gold statue once stood inside a red-granite shrine carved on the orders of Ptolemy VIII Euergetes (170–116 BC). Although the stone shrine is now in the British Museum, the stone base that once held the barque in which the statue travelled remains, and is inscribed with the names of Ptolemy III (246–221 BC) and his wife Berenice. A staircase, on the western side, leads up to the **Osiris Chapel**, which is decorated with scenes of mourners; and everywhere there are reliefs of Isis, her husband and son, other deities and, of course, the Ptolemies and Romans who built or contributed to the temple.

On the northern tip of the island are the **Temple of Augustus** and the **Gate of Diocletian**; east of the second pylon is the delightful **Temple of Hathor** decorated with reliefs of musicians (including an ape playing the lute) and Bes, the god of childbirth. South of this is the elegant, unfinished pavilion by the water's edge, known as the **Kiosk of Trajan** (or 'Pharaoh's Bed'), perhaps the most famous of Philae's monuments and frequently painted by Victorian artists. The completed reliefs on the kiosk feature Emperor Trajan making offerings to Isis, Osiris and Horus.

Sound-and-Light Show

There is a sound-and-light show in the evening, which costs E£33 (no student discount) for the ticket plus the cost of the boat to Agilkia Island. If you're going to see a sound and light show in Egypt, this is one of the least kitschy, and just being on the island at night almost makes it worth the money.

Times vary according to the season. In winter (29 September to 27 April) shows are at 6.30pm, 7.45pm and 9pm; in summer (28 April to 28 September) they're at 8pm, 9.15pm and 10.30pm; and during Ramadan at 7.30pm, 8.45pm and 10pm. Double-check this schedule at the tourist office.

day	show 1	show 2	show 3
Monday	English	French	–
Tuesday	French	English	French
Wednesday	French	English	French
Thursday	French	Spanish	Arabic
Friday	English	French	–
Saturday	English	Italian	–
Sunday	French	German	–

Getting There & Away

The boat landing for the Philae complex is at Shellal, south of the old Aswan Dam. The only easy way to get there is by taxi or organised trip (arranged by most travel agencies and major hotels in town, but possibly for more money than you may pay otherwise). The return taxi fare for a group of six costs about E£30 without bargaining. It is possible, if you can get a ride to the old Aswan Dam, to walk along the water's edge to Shellal. From here, a small motorboat to the island costs E£20 (during the day) or E£22 (in the evening) divided between however many of you there are (maximum eight). If there are more than eight, each person simply pays E£2.50 for the return trip. These fares are paid directly to the boatmen.

HIGH DAM

Egypt's contemporary example of construction on a monumental scale contains 18 times the amount of material used in the Great Pyramid of Khufu. The controversial High Dam or Sadd al-Ali, 17km south of Aswan, is 3600m across, 980m wide at its base and 111m high at its highest point. About 35,000 people helped build this enormous structure and 451 of them died during its construction.

When it was completed the water that collected behind it became Lake Nasser, the world's largest artificial lake.

As early as the 1940s it was evident that the old Aswan Dam, which only regulated the flow of water, was not big enough to counter the unpredictable annual flooding of the great river. But it wasn't until Nasser came to power in 1952 that the plans were drawn up for the new dam, 6km south of the British-built dam. Originally scoffed at as an impossible dream, the building of the dam was fraught with political, as well as engineering, difficulties. In 1956, after the USA, the UK and the World Bank suddenly refused the financial backing they had offered for the project, Nasser ordered the nationalisation of the Suez Canal precipitating the Suez Crisis in which France, the UK and Israel invaded the canal region. They were eventually restrained by the United Nations. The Soviet Union then offered the necessary funding and expertise, and work began on the High Dam in 1960. It was completed in 1971.

The benefits of building the dam have been enormous. Egypt's area of cultivable land has increased by 30%; the High Dam's hydroelectric station has doubled the country's power supply; and a rise in the Sahara's water table has been recorded as far away as Algeria.

On the other hand, the dam prevents the flow of the silt that was so critical to the Nile Valley's fertility. The effects of this are being felt all over Egypt. Heavy use of artificial fertilisers has led to increasing salinity of the ground water in agricultural areas. At the Nile's mouth in the Mediterranean, shrimp beds and fishing grounds have almost disappeared. The now perennially full irrigation canals have led to endemic infection with the bilharzia parasite, which is a huge public health problem. The authorities are also faced with the problem that silt could eventually fill the lake.

Most people get to the High Dam as part of an organised trip to the sights around Aswan. For the privilege of driving part of the way along the dam to a small pavilion that has a couple of displays detailing the dimensions and the construction of the dam, you pay E£5. If you come by foot from the train station you'll still have to pay 50pt.

Many visitors are disappointed by the visit, expecting views more spectacular than those they actually get, so perhaps you should not hope for too much. Video cameras and zoom lenses cannot be used, although nobody seems to police this.

A stone monument honouring Soviet-Egyptian friendship and cooperation is on the west side of the dam.

Getting There & Away

The cheapest way to get to the High Dam, which is 13km south of Aswan, is to take a train (E£1), which leaves almost every hour from 6am to 4pm to Sadd al-Ali station, the end of the Cairo-Aswan line. The station is near the docks for the boat to Sudan, and from there you can either walk for a long way or try to get a service taxi to the dam.

If you're planning to take a taxi across the top of the dam, then you might also consider continuing on to the Temple of Kalabsha, which is visible from the dam on the west side of Lake Nasser. It's about 3km from the western end of the dam.

Lower Nubia & Lake Nasser

For countless centuries before the Aswan and High Dams irrevocably changed the topography of the area, the rocky cataract at Aswan marked the dividing line between Egypt and its southern neighbour, Nubia, which held the land that lay between Aswan and Khartoum. As the Nile changed here, so too did the territory along its shores. Whereas the land to the north was under continuous cultivation, to the south it was more rugged, with rocky desert cliffs and sand forcing its way down to the water's edge and separating the pockets of agricultural land.

Nowadays all this lies deep under the waters of Lake Nasser. Instead, the landscape is dominated by the contrast of smooth desert and calm, green-brown water. Apart from the beauty of the lake itself, the main attraction of this region is the temples that were so painstakingly moved away from the floodwaters in the 1960s (see the boxed text 'Saving Nubia's Monuments' later in this chapter for more about this mammoth cultural rescue mission).

History

The ancient Egyptians called Nubia 'Ta-Seti' (Land of the Bow), after the weapons for which the Nubians were famous. The modern name is thought to have come from the ancient Egyptian word *nbw* meaning 'gold', which was extensively mined in the north-eastern part of the country in Pharaonic and Graeco-Roman times. It is ironic that our name for this now lost land comes from ancient Egyptian, as much of Nubia's long history was dominated by its more powerful northern neighbour. When Egypt was strong it either annexed or aggressively exploited the natural resources of its weaker neighbour; by contrast, times of turmoil and anarchy in Egypt tended to coincide with periods of indigenous growth and development in Nubia.

There is evidence of settlements in northern Nubia 10,000 years ago, and at Nabta Playa, some 100km west of Abu Simbel, archaeologists have recently found evidence of housing, sculpted monoliths and the world's oldest calendar made of small standing stones dating from around 6000 BC. Until 3500 BC it seems that Nubia and southern Egypt developed in roughly similar ways, with the growing domestication of animals, the development of crops and the gradual adoption of permanent settlements. But there were also important differences. Although the two were ethnically linked, the darker-skinned Nubians had more African features than the Egyptians. Furthermore, their language was Nilo-Saharan, while ancient Egyptian was Afro-Asiatic.

With its unification in around 3100 BC, Egypt developed rapidly. Throughout the Old Kingdom, trading and mining expeditions were sent to extract Nubian mineral wealth, establishing a pattern that was to last nearly 5000 years. When centralised authority collapsed in Egypt during the First Intermediate Period, a new culture began to establish itself in Nubia and relations between the two neighbours appear to have

LOWER NUBIA & LAKE NASSER

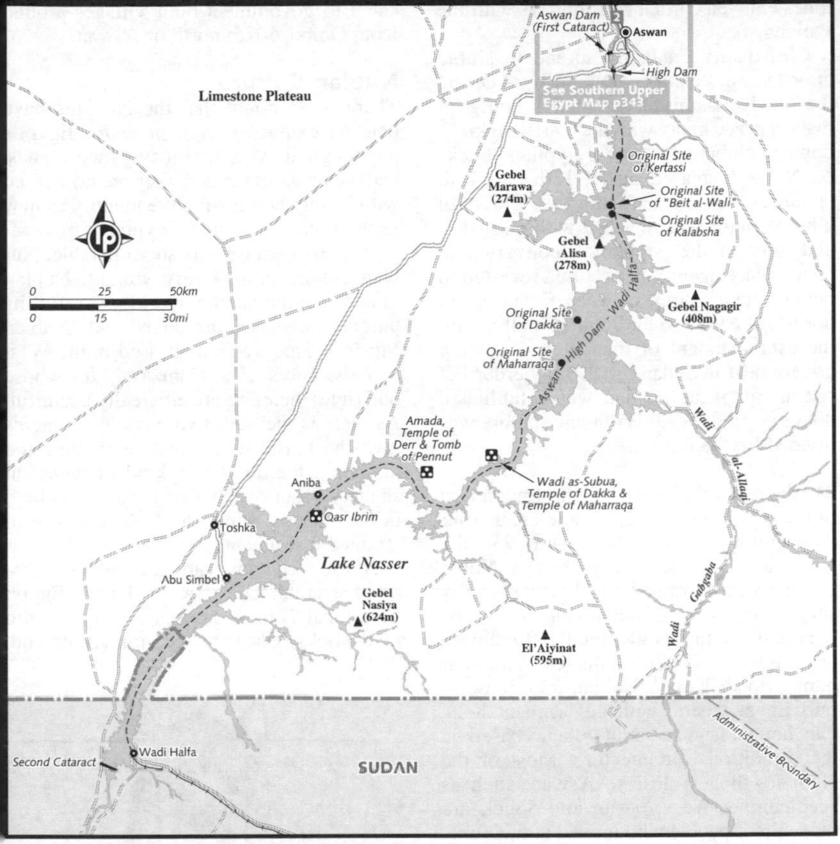

been good. But with the reunification of Egypt at the start of the Middle Kingdom, Lower Nubia (roughly the area between the First and Second Nile Cataracts) was once again annexed as a province and a chain of mud-brick fortresses was built at strategic points along the Nile to safeguard trade.

During the New Kingdom, instead of fortresses the Egyptians built temples in Nubia, dividing the whole of the region into five administrative districts, or nomes, ruled on the pharaoh's behalf by his viceroy, who took the title King's Son of Kush (Kush being the southern province of Nubia). Taking advantage of Egypt's political disunity during the Third Intermediate Period, the tables were turned and Nubia forged north, ruling Egypt for a century as the 25th Kushite dynasty (747–656 BC). They ruled in the traditional manner as pharaohs, built in the Egyptian style, worshipped Amun and the other gods, and in many ways were more Egyptian than the Egyptians.

The 25th dynasty ended with the Assyrian invasion of Egypt in 671 BC. Over the next several centuries, as Egypt suffered a succession of invasions, Nubia sometimes warred with the conquerors to the north (as in the case of the Persians) and at other times enjoyed cordial relations (as with the Ptolemies).

Christianity gradually spread to Nubia after the 5th century AD, and by AD 652 the newly Islamised authorities in Egypt made a peace treaty with the Christian kingdoms in Nubia. However, Egyptian attacks on Nubia increased in the 12th and 13th centuries, and in 1315 the last Christian king of Nubia was replaced with a Muslim and most of the population converted to Islam. Once again Lower Nubia reverted to being a transit point between Egypt to the north and Africa to the south. Finally, with the establishment of the Anglo-Egyptian government in Sudan in 1899, a border between Egypt and Sudan was established 40km north of Wadi Halfa and Nubia was divided for the last time.

Modern Nubia Following the completion of the Aswan Dam in 1902, and again after its height was raised in 1912 and 1934, the water level of the Nile in Lower Nubia gradually rose from 87m to 121m, partially submerging many of the monuments in the area and, by the 1930s, totally flooding a large number of Nubian villages. With their homes flooded, many Nubians moved north into Egypt where, with government help, they bought land and built villages based on their traditional architecture. Most of the Nubian villages close to Aswan, such as Elephantine, West Aswan and Sehel, are made up of people who moved at this time.

However, the majority of Nubians, assuming that the Nile's new shoreline would not change again, decided to stay in their homeland and build new houses on higher land. The rising waters imposed huge changes on those who stayed – the date plantations that had been central to their economy were destroyed and would take years to replace, so many Nubian men were forced to search for work in the north, leaving the women behind to run the communities.

Less than 30 years later, the building of the High Dam meant that those who had stayed were forced to move again. In the 1960s, 50,000 Egyptian Nubians were relocated to government-built villages around Kom Ombo, 50km north of Aswan.

Nubian Culture

There is no doubt that the Nubians have paid an extremely high price for Egypt's greater good. After first losing their homes, and then their homeland, they are now faced with losing their distinctive identity as new generations grow up as Egyptians.

Perhaps because it is so vulnerable, Nubian culture is also very vibrant. Nubian music is famous the world over for its unique sound (see the boxed text 'Nubian Music'). This was popularised in the West by musicians such as Hamza ad-Din, whose oud (lute) melodies are ethereally beautiful. As well as the oud, two basic instruments give the music its distinctive rhythm and harmony: the *douff* is a kind of wide but shallow drum or tabla that musicians hold in their hands, while the *kisir* is a type of stringed instrument.

Not so well known abroad is Nubia's distinctive architecture. As in Upper Egypt, traditional Nubian houses are made with mud bricks. But here the similarities end.

Traditional Nubian mud-brick houses are often covered with pictures and decorations, differentiating them from other Egyptian houses.

Nubian Music

It's one of those strange quirks, but it's almost easier to hear and buy Nubian music in the West than it is in Egypt. The city folk of Cairo and Alexandria have an aversion to anything that comes from south of the capital and, with few exceptions, Nubian music is conspicuously absent from national TV and radio. You won't find it in the Downtown (Cairo) cassette shops either. Yet, while mainstream Egyptian pop icons such as Amr Diab dream of reaching an audience beyond the Arab world, Nubian artists sell CDs by the rackload in Europe and play to sell-out audiences.

The biggest name is Ali Hassan Kuban, a septuagenarian former tillerman from a small village near Aswan. He grew up playing at weddings and parties, and he made the leap to a global audience after being invited to perform at a Berlin festival in 1989. Since then, he has toured all over Europe as well as in Japan, Canada and the USA. He has several CDs out on the German Piranha record label (W www.piranha.de), including *From Nubia to Cairo* and *Walk Like a Nubian*.

What makes Kuban's music appealing to a Western audience is that unlike Arabic music, with its jarring use of quarter tones, the Nubian sound is extremely accessible. It has a rhythmic quality that's almost African, which mixes simple melodies and soulful vocals. It's an incredibly warm sound. This can be heard at its best on a series of CDs by a loose grouping of musicians and vocalists recording under the name Salamat. Look out especially for *Mambo al-Soudani* (again on Piranha).

A slightly different facet of Nubian music is represented by Hamza ad-Din, a Nubian composer born in Wadi Halfa in 1929 and widely respected in the West for his semiclassical compositions written for the oud (lute). Inspired by his Sufi beliefs, Ad-Din's work is extremely haunting, especially 'Escalay' (The Waterwheel), which you can find in a recording by the composer himself, or there's an excellent version of it by the Kronos Quartet on their CD *Pieces of Africa*.

Other names to look out for are the now retired Sayyed Gayer, who sings poems and love songs accompanied only by the *douff* (drum), and Ahmed Monieb and Mohammed Hamam.

The one place in Egypt you might be able to pick up cassettes by some of these artists is in Aswan; there are several cassette shops in the souq and the sales assistants are happy to pull out their Nubian collections and let you listen.

Lower Nubian houses sometimes have domed or vaulted ceilings and houses from further south usually have a flat, split-palm roof. They are plastered or whitewashed and covered with pictures and decorations, including ceramic plates. The basic forms of these houses can be seen in the Nubian villages around Aswan and in Ballana, near Kom Ombo.

Nubians also have their own marriage customs. Traditionally, wedding festivities lasted up to 15 days but nowadays they have devolved to a three-day affair. On the first night, the bride and groom celebrate separately with their respective friends and families. On the second night, the bride takes her party to the groom's home and both groups dance to traditional music until the wee hours. Then the bride returns home and her hands and feet are painted with beautiful designs in henna. The groom will also have his hands and feet covered in henna but without any design. On the third day, the groom and his party walk slowly to the bride's house in a *zaffa* or procession, singing and dancing the whole way. Traditionally the groom will stay at the bride's house for three days before seeing his family. The couple will then set up home.

Women visitors who want to get a taste of Nubian culture can have henna 'tattoos' put on their hands (or feet or stomachs) at some of the Nubian villages around Aswan – it looks great and you get to spend time with Nubian women. The villages of West Aswan, just north of the Tombs of the Nobles, are a good place to try. In Aswan, a half-Nubian woman named Rahmat is famed among Nubian brides for her high-quality designs. She works from her very simple house that is in the last alley on left, just past the Brooke Hospital Clinic on Sharia Sultan Abu'l Ela. Her house is the last on the right. She can also be reached by phone (☎ 301 465). You're looking at anywhere between E£15 and E£30 per tattoo, depending on the size of the design.

Getting There & Away

Although all the sites except Qasr Ibrim have roads leading to them (or soon will), foreigners are currently forbidden to drive to any except Kalabsha, Beit al-Wali and Kertassi. The road to Abu Simbel has reopened, however foreigners are at present only allowed to travel in buses or microbuses in a police convoy, and no private vehicles or taxis are allowed to make the journey. Abu Simbel can be reached by plane from Aswan, Luxor or Cairo. For more details on travelling to Abu Simbel, see Getting There & Away under Abu Simbel later in this chapter.

For the moment, the rest of the sites can only be reached by boat, which is in any case one of the best ways of seeing Lake Nasser's dramatic monuments. There are six boats currently sailing on Lake Nasser, but two stand out far above the rest. The *Eugénie* and *Qasr Ibrim* are both run by the same company, Belle Epoque Travel, and were the brainchild of Mustafa al-Guindi, a Cairene of Nubian origin who is almost single-handedly responsible for getting Lake Nasser opened to tourists. The boats are stunningly designed: *Eugénie* is modelled on an early 20th-century hunting lodge; *Qasr Ibrim* is all 1930s Art-Deco elegance. Both have pools, *hammams* (bathhouse) and fantastic French cuisine. In addition, passengers are pampered with treats such as evening cocktails and classical music in front of the temples at Abu Simbel. Trips on the cruises can be arranged through the company's Cairo office (☎ 02-516 9654/6, fax 516 9546). A standard room costs at least US$90 per person per day on a three- or four-day trip, including all meals and temple visits.

The other cruise boats are neither as plush nor as tasteful, but they are slightly cheaper and easier to book at late notice. They include the *Prince Abbas* (☎ 097-314 660, mobile 012-220 6747), *Queen Abu Simbel* (☎ 097-306 512, mobile 012-224 8658), the *Nubian Sea* (mobile ☎ 012-322 2065) and the *Tania* (☎ 097-316 393, 304 786); the latter is run by Travco Tours.

LAKE NASSER

Looking out over Lake Nasser's wide expanses of calm green-blue water, it's hard to believe that it is a human-made creation. As the world's largest artificial lake, its statistics are staggering – with an area of 5250 sq km, it stretches 510km in length and between 5km and 35km in width. On average it contains some 135 billion cubic metres of water, of which an estimated six billion are lost each year to evaporation. Its maximum capacity is 157 billion cubic metres of water. This was reached in 1996 after heavy rains in Ethiopia occasioned the opening of a special spillway at Toshka, about 30km north of Abu Simbel, for the first time since the dam was built. The Egyptian government has since embarked on a controversial project to build a new canal and irrigate thousands of acres in what is now the Nubian Desert between Toshka and the New Valley.

Numbers aside, the contrast between this enormous body of water and the remote desert stretching away on all sides makes Lake Nasser a place of austere beauty. Because the level of the lake fluctuates it has been difficult to build any settlements around its edges. Instead the lake has become a place for migrating birds to rest on their long journeys north and south. Gazelle, fox and several types of snake (including the deadly horned viper) live on its shores. Many species of fish live in its waters, including the enormous Nile perch. Crocodiles – some reportedly up to 5m long – and monitor lizards also live in the lake's shallows. The main human presence here, apart from the few tourists who visit, is limited to the 5000 or so fishermen who spend up to six months at a time in small rowing boats, altogether catching about 50,000 tonnes of small fish each year.

Fishing in the Desert

For most people, fishing is the last thing that comes to mind when they think of southern Egypt. However, the size of the fish in Lake Nasser is legendary. Living in the silt-rich depths of the lake, with few predators apart from the crocodiles that roam the murky waters, the fish are growing to gigantic proportions – the record for a Nile perch is almost 100kg. Not surprisingly, fishing enthusiasts from around the world are lining up to come here and reel in their own record-breaker.

At the moment there are two companies running fishing trips on the lake. Both are led by guides with years of experience on the lake and the fish they catch are returned to the waters after weighing. The African Angler (☎ 097-316 052) is run by a former Kenyan safari guide, Tim Bailey. He has seven fishing boats and two supply boats, and runs weekly safaris from September to December and February to June. He also operates through Abercrombie & Kent in Cairo (☎ 02-394 7735) and through agencies specialising in fishing throughout Europe and Australia. Wild Nuba (☎/fax 097-309 191, ⓔ wildnuba@yahoo.com) is a new company run by Pascal Artieda, who developed a passion for fishing in Lake Nasser during his three years as manager of the *Eugénie* cruise boat, and Sayed Gharib, a Nubian who has been on the lake for most of his life. As well as fishing on the lake from their two comfortable boats, they offer overland safaris in the little-travelled southern part of the Eastern Desert.

KALABSHA, BEIT AL-WALI & KERTASSI

As a result of the massive Unesco effort, these three temples *(admission E£12; open 8am-4pm daily)* were transplanted from a now submerged site about 50km south of Aswan. The new site is on the west bank of Lake Nasser just south of the High Dam.

The Temple of Kalabsha was started in the late Ptolemaic period and completed during the reign of Emperor Augustus, between 30 BC and AD 14. It was dedicated to the composite Egyptian-Nubian god Horus-Mandulis and to Isis and Osiris. Later, it was used as a church.

The then West German government financed the transfer and reconstruction of the 13,000 blocks of the temple and was presented with the temple's west pylon, which is now in the Berlin Museum. During the rescue operation, evidence was found of even older structures, dating from the times of Amenhotep II and Ptolemy IX.

An impressive stone causeway leads from the lake up to the first pylon of the temple, beyond which are the colonnaded court and the eight-columned hypostyle hall. Inscriptions on the walls show various emperors or pharaohs in the presence of gods and goddesses. Just beyond the hall are three chambers, with stairs leading from one up to the roof. The view of Lake Nasser and the High Dam, across the capitals of the hall and court, is fantastic. An inner passage, between the temple and the encircling wall, leads to a well-preserved Nilometer.

The Temple of Beit al-Wali (House of the Holy Man) was rebuilt with assistance from the US government and was placed just north-west of the Temple of Kalabsha. Most of Beit al-Wali, which had been cut into a sandstone cliffside and fronted by a brick pylon, was built by Ramses II and dedicated to Amun-Ra. On the walls of the forecourt are several fine reliefs detailing the pharaoh's victory over the Nubians (on the south wall) and his wars against the Libyans and Syrians (on the north wall). Ramses is gripping the hair of his enemies prior to smashing their brains while women plead for mercy. The most beautiful scenes are those detailing the tribute being paid by the defeated Nubians. The reliefs show Ramses sitting on his throne and receiving, among other things, leopard skins, gold, elephant tusks, feathers, cattle, a monkey and an ostrich.

Just north of the Temple of Kalabsha are the remains of the Temple of Kertassi. Two Hathor (or cow-headed) columns, a massive architrave and four columns decorated with intricate capitals are the only pieces that were salvaged from Lake Nasser.

Strewn about the area between these two temples are a jumble of rocks with prehistoric

Saving Nubia's Monuments

As plans for building the Aswan Dam were drawn up, attention worldwide focused on the antiquities that would be lost by the creation of a huge lake behind the dam. A great many valuable and irreplaceable ancient monuments were doomed by the waters of Lake Nasser.

Teams from the Egyptian Department of Antiquities and archaeological missions from many countries descended on Nubia to set in motion the Unesco-organised projects aimed at rescuing as many of the threatened treasures as possible. Necropolises were excavated, all portable artefacts and relics were removed to museums and, while some temples disappeared beneath the lake, 14 were salvaged and moved to safety.

Ten of them, including the temple complexes of Philae, Kalabsha and Abu Simbel, were dismantled stone by stone and rebuilt on higher ground. The other four were donated to the countries that contributed to the rescue effort; they include the splendid Temple of Dendur, which has been reconstructed in a glass building in the Metropolitan Museum of Art in New York.

The preservation of the temples at Abu Simbel, 280km south of Aswan, must rank as the greatest achievement of the Unesco rescue operation. Hewn as they were out of solid rock, the modern technology involved in cutting, moving and rebuilding the incredible temples and statues at least paralleled the skill of the ancient artisans who chiselled them out of the cliff face in the first place.

A worldwide appeal for the vital funding and expertise needed to salvage these Abu Simbel monuments was launched in the 1960s. The response was immediately forthcoming and a variety of conservation schemes were put forward. Finally, in 1964 a cofferdam was built to hold back the already encroaching water of the new lake, while Egyptian, Italian, Swedish, German and French archaeological teams began to move the massive structures.

At a cost of about US$40 million, the temples were cut up into more than 2000 huge blocks, weighing from 10 to 40 tonnes each, and were reconstructed inside a specially built mountain 210m away from the water and 65m higher than the original site. The temples were carefully oriented to face in the correct direction and the landscape of their original environment was recreated on and around the concrete, dome-shaped mountain.

The project took just over four years. The temples of Abu Simbel were officially reopened in 1968, while the sacred site they had occupied for over 3000 years disappeared beneath Lake Nasser. A plaque to the right of the temple entrance eloquently describes this achievement: 'Through this restoration of the past, we have indeed helped to build the future of mankind'.

carvings and paintings, some amazingly well preserved, that were salvaged along with the temples.

You'll need a boat to get to the temple; motorboats can be found near the shipyard on the western side of the High Dam. It costs about E£25 to hire a boat to take you there and back.

WADI AS-SUBUA

The temples of Wadi as-Subua, Dakka and Maharraqa were all moved to this site *(admission E£12)*, about 4km west of the original Wadi as-Subua (now submerged beneath Lake Nasser), by the Egyptian Department of Antiquities between 1961 and 1965.

Wadi as-Subua means 'Valley of Lions' in Arabic and refers to the avenue of 10 sphinxes that stood in front of the **Temple of Ramses II**. Yet another monument dating from the reign of the energetic pharaoh, the rear part of the temple was hewn from rock and the front portion was freestanding. At the entrance to the temple itself are the remains of colossal statues of Ramses. The scenes on the pylon show Ramses II smiting the enemies of Egypt before Amun-Ra. Behind the pylon is a court featuring 10 more statues of the pharaoh, beyond which lies a 12-pillared hall and the sanctuaries, all cut out of the rock face. Although the middle sanctuary was once carved with relief scenes of Ramses making offerings to the temple's gods, it was converted in Christian times into a church and the pagan reliefs plastered over and painted with saints. With part of the plaster having fallen away, Ramses II now appears to be making offerings to St Peter!

About 1km to the north are the remains of the **Temple of Dakka**, begun by the Nubian pharaoh Arkamani (218–200 BC) and continued under Ptolemies VI and VIII and the Romans Augustus and Tiberius. Originally situated 40km north of here, it is dedicated to the god of wisdom, Thoth, and is notable for its 12m-high pylon, which you can climb for great views of the lake and the surrounding temples.

The **Temple of Maharraqa**, the smallest of the three at this site, originally stood 50km north of here near the village of Ofendina. Thought to have been dedicated to Serapis, the Alexandrian god, its decorations were never finished and the walls seem very bare. In the north-east corner of the main hall a spiral staircase leads up to the roof, the only spiral staircase in any ancient Egyptian structure. There is some evidence that the temple was later used as a church, but little of it remains.

AMADA

Situated around 180km south of the High Dam there are two temples and a tomb at the Amada site *(admission E£12)*. The **Temple of Amada**, moved about 2.5km from its original location between 1964 and 1975, is the oldest surviving monument on Lake Nasser. It dates from the 18th-dynasty reigns of Tuthmosis III and his son Amenhotep II, with a hypostyle hall added by his son Tuthmosis IV and with later Ramessid additions. Dedicated, like many temples in Nubia, to the gods Amun-Ra and Ra-Harakhty, it has some of the finest reliefs in any Nubian monument and contains two important historical inscriptions. The first text is to be found on a stele at the left (north) side of the entrance and describes the unsuccessful Libyan invasion of Egypt in the fourth year (1232 BC) of the pharaoh Merneptah's rule. The second inscription, again carved on a stele, is on the back wall of the sanctuary and dates to the third year of the reign of Amenhotep II (1424 BC). It describes the pharaoh's military campaign to Palestine and details his ruthless murder of prisoners of war. It was no doubt designed to impress upon the Nubians that political opposition to the powerful Egyptians was useless.

On the very top of the temple facade you can see crudely carved camels that are thought to have been the work of either Bedouin or travellers during the Middle Ages.

Unlike the other Nubian temples, the rock-cut **Temple of Derr** was situated on the river's east bank due to the reversal of its course in this area. Although the front of the building is damaged, there are some well-preserved reliefs in the pillared hall, portraying Ramses II once again, worshipped as a living god, as at Abu Simbel. In the scenes on either side of the doorway you can see him killing his enemies, followed by his famous pet lion. Following cleaning, many of the scenes are once again brightly coloured.

Five minutes' walk from the Temple of Derr is the small rock-cut **Tomb of Pennut**, which was originally situated at Aniba, 40km south-west of Amada. Pennut was the chief administrator of Lower Nubia during the reign of Ramses VI. Consisting of a small offering chapel with a niche at the rear, some of its reliefs, which depict events and personalities from Pennut's life, including a scene showing him being presented with a gift by Ramses VI himself, still have traces of colour.

QASR IBRIM

The only Nubian monument visible on its original site, Qasr Ibrim sits with water lapping at its edges on what was once the top of a 70m-high cliff about 60km north of Abu Simbel. The unusual name of this fortress is derived from the ancient name, Pedeme, which became Primis in Greek, Phrim in Coptic and finally Ibrim in Arabic (there's no 'p' in Arabic).

Early history of the site is obscure. Situated at a strategic point overlooking the Nile, archaeologists have so far found evidence of a fortification here dating back to 1000 BC. However, it is possible that there was some sort of garrison at the site as much as 800 years earlier, when the Egyptians built a series of mud-brick fortresses along the Nile to maintain their control over Lower Nubia.

In about 680 BC the 25th-dynasty Nubian pharaoh of Egypt, Taharka, built a mud-brick temple here and about 700 years later the first fortification wall was built. During Roman times the area appears to have been a bastion of paganism as Christianity spread in Nubia. As many as six temples, including a mud-brick temple to Isis, are thought to have existed on its two-hectare site. The area finally converted to Christianity more than 200 years after the rest of Egypt and Taharka's temple became a church. By the 13th century, Ibrim had become one of Lower Nubia's principal Christian centres and it held out against Islam until the 16th century, when a group of Bosnian mercenaries working for the Ottomans came and occupied the site. They stayed on and married into the local Nubian community, using part of the cathedral as a mosque. Their descendants were driven out by panicked Mamluks fleeing Mohammed Ali's purges in the early 19th century.

Apart from the structural remains, of which a 8th-century sandstone cathedral is the most prominent, many written documents have been found at Qasr Ibrim. At the time of writing extensive archaeological work was being carried out and the site was closed to visitors.

ABU SIMBEL

☎ 097

The village of Abu Simbel lies 280km south of Aswan and only 40km north of the Sudanese border. A small settlement with breeze-block buildings and a few basic workers' cafes, there is little to keep you here other than the colossal temples for which it is famous. Few tourists linger more than a few hours, although there are four hotels that try to lure visitors for overnight stays. There is a post office and a new hospital (☎ 499 237). The tourist police have an office opposite the Nobaleh Ramses Hotel.

Admission to both temples is E£36 (E£18 for students), including a mandatory fee for a guide, whether you want one or not.

Great Temple of Ramses II

While the fate of his colossal statue at the Ramesseum in Luxor no doubt gnaws at the spirit of Ramses II, the mere existence, in the 21st century AD, of his great temple at Abu Simbel must make Ramses shake with laughter and shout 'I told you so'.

Carved out of the mountain on the west bank of the Nile between 1274 and 1244 BC, the temple was dedicated to the gods Ra-Harakhty, Amun and Ptah and, of course, to the deified pharaoh himself. But mostly, with its four colossal statues of Ramses II addressing the river, it was designed as a show of strength, an awesome quarteted sentinel watching over any boats sailing into the pharaoh's lands from the south.

However, over the centuries both the Nile and the desert sands imperceptibly shifted until the temple was lost to human memory. It was rediscovered by chance in 1813 by the Swiss explorer Jean-Louis Burkhardt – only one of the heads was completely showing above the sand, the next head was

TEMPLE OF ABU SIMBEL

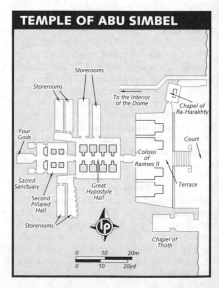

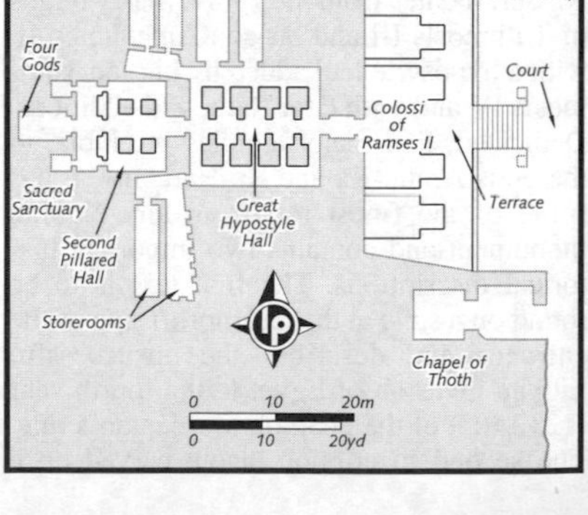

broken off and, of the remaining two, only the crowns could be seen. There's a superb and often reproduced etching of this scene made by David Roberts, who visited about 25 years after Burkhardt. Sufficient sand was cleared away in 1817 by Giovanni Belzoni for the temple to be entered.

From the temple's forecourt, a short flight of steps leads up to the terrace in front of the massive rock-cut facade, which is about 30m high and 35m wide. Guarding the entrance, the four famous colossal statues of Ramses II sit majestically, staring out across the desert as if looking through time itself. Actually, only three still sit majestically, as the inner left statue collapsed in antiquity and its upper body lies on the ground, left like this when the temple was moved. Each complete statue is more than 20m high and is accompanied by smaller, though much larger than life-size, statues of the pharaoh's mother Queen Tuya, his wife Nefertari and some of their children.

Above the entrance, between the central throned colossi, is the figure of the falcon-headed sun god Ra-Harakhty. Unfortunately, the sun god has been subjected to the trials of time and now lacks part of a leg and foot.

The roof of the large hall is supported by eight columns, each fronted by a 10m-high statue of Ramses. The roof is decorated with vultures, which are protective figures symbolising the goddess Nekhbet, and the reliefs on the walls depict the pharaoh in various battles, trampling over his enemies, victorious as usual. In the next hall, the four-columned vestibule, Ramses and Nefertari are shown in front of the gods and the solar barques that carry the dead to the underworld.

The innermost chamber is the sacred sanctuary, where the four gods of the Great Temple sit on their thrones carved in the back wall and wait for dawn. The temple is aligned in such a way that on 22 February and 22 October every year, the first rays of the rising sun reach across the Nile, penetrate the temple, move along the hypostyle hall, through the vestibule and into the sanctuary, where they illuminate the somewhat mutilated figures of Ra-Harakhty, Ramses II and Amun. Ptah, to the left, is never illuminated. (Until the temples were moved, this phenomenon happened one day earlier.)

Temple of Hathor

The other temple at the Abu Simbel complex is the rock-cut Temple of Hathor, which is fronted by six massive standing statues, each about 10m high. Four of them represent Ramses, the other two represent his beloved wife, Queen Nefertari, and they are all flanked by the smaller figures of the Ramessid princes and princesses.

The six pillars of the hypostyle hall are crowned with Hathor capitals and its walls are adorned with scenes depicting: Nefertari before Hathor and Mut; the queen honouring her husband; and Ramses, yet again, being valiant and victorious. In the vestibule and adjoining chambers there are colourful scenes of the goddess and her sacred barque. In the sanctuary there is a weathered statue of Hathor as a cow emerging from the rock.

Sound & Light Show

A sound-and-light show is performed at Abu Simbel each night. Tickets are E£50, plus E£5 sales tax. In summer (28 April to 28 September) the shows are at 8pm, 8.45pm and 9.30pm; in winter (29 September to 27 April) at 7pm, 7.45pm and 8.30pm. At the time of writing the schedule was as follows, but you should double-check it with the tourist office in Aswan.

day	show 1	show 2	show 3
Monday	English	French	Spanish
Tuesday	English	French	Japanese
Wednesday	English	French	German
Thursday	English	French	Arabic
Friday	English	French	Italian
Saturday	English	French	German
Sunday	English	French	Italian

Places to Stay & Eat

There are currently four hotels in Abu Simbel, all but one at the upper end of the price scale. Keep in mind that prices are usually slashed during the summer months. Apart from at Abu Simbel Village, hotel rates quoted here include taxes.

Nefertari Hotel *(☎ 400 508/9, fax 400 510)* Singles/doubles US$70/80. This four-star hotel is ideally located about 400m from the temples in a relatively lush setting overlooking Lake Nasser. The rather small rooms have lake views, air-con, full carpeting and fridge. There's also a swimming pool. The ***restaurant*** is open year-round, and offers breakfast/lunch/dinner for E£23/35/40. During winter, reservations are recommended.

Mercure Seti Abu Simbel *(☎ 400 720, fax 400 829)* Singles/doubles US$130/175. This is another overpriced five-star hotel, with air-con, satellite TV and a swimming pool. Breakfast is E£42.

Nobaleh Ramses Hotel *(☎ 400 294, fax 400 381)* Singles/doubles with half board US$60/95. This state-run hotel is about 1.5km from the temple site. The 39 rooms are clean and bright, with bath, TV, air-con and fridge. The buffet breakfast here costs E£14, lunch is E£25 and dinner E£35.

Abu Simbel Village *(☎/fax 400 092, 400 179)* Singles/doubles $35/40. This newly opened, cheaper option is a few hundred metres from the temple. All rooms have bath and air-con.

The line-up of cheap cafes in town, such as ***Nubian Oasis*** and ***Wadi el-Nil*** offers little incentive to diners.

Getting There & Away

Although the road from Aswan to Abu Simbel has reopened, at present foreigners are only allowed to travel in buses or microbuses (ie, no private vehicles or taxis) in police convoys. There is at least one convoy each day each way, more if the volume of traffic demands, but you should check with the tourist office in Aswan before making plans.

EgyptAir has flights to Abu Simbel from Aswan – see Getting There & Away under Aswan earlier in this chapter for flight details. You can also take a same-day return flight from Cairo to Abu Simbel for E£234.60.

Organised Tours Travel agencies and hotels in Aswan offer trips to Abu Simbel. Generally the trips begin between 4am and 5am, with minibuses picking up guests from various hotels around town. They aim to get to the temple by about 8.30am, before it gets too hot, and leave at about 10am. In general, those on the short trip will be back by about 2.30pm; long-haulers will be looking at about 5pm. Admission fees are not always included in the price of the trip, so make sure you check when booking. Also, on many cheaper trips the minibuses do not have air-con, which can be extremely uncomfortable in summer, especially if the organisers have packed in too many people (which they often try to do).

Alternatively, most of the larger travel agents in Aswan send air-con coaches and minibuses to Abu Simbel. Try Thomas Cook, AmEx, Travco or one of the other reputable agencies in town. Their bus trips will be a lot more expensive, but you will be comfortable. To take one of their day trips by plane, you're looking at about US$60 per person, including admission to the temples and air fare.

The larger travel agencies also organise trips to Abu Simbel by hydrofoil. The return trip, including breakfast, lunch, temple admission and a guide, costs in the region of US$90.

Western Oases

'There are deserts and there are deserts', the explorer Ralph Bagnold famously said. But the Western (or Libyan) Desert, a vast expanse that starts at the western banks of the Nile and continues well into Libya, is the desert of deserts. Covering a total of 2.8 million sq km and bordered by Libya in the west, Sudan in the south and the Mediterranean in the north, it is a world of desolation and beauty – and one of the few places in Egypt where you can go for days at a time without seeing a soul.

Five isolated but thriving oases dot this otherwise uninhabited expanse: Kharga, Dakhla, Farafra, Bahariyya and, to the north-west of these, Siwa. Herodotus called these small settlements the 'Islands of the Blest', and after a long camel trek through the desert they must certainly have appeared so. Despite their remoteness, the five oases have long and surprisingly rich histories. Recent research in the area has unearthed a wealth of prehistoric artefacts, pointing to habitation at the very dawn of human history. In late Pharaonic and Roman times, the oases were the bustling hubs on trade routes between Africa and the Mediterranean.

In more recent history, since the time of Nasser, the Egyptian authorities have formulated grandiose plans to conquer the desert through land reclamation and intensive agriculture. The oases were to form a new alternative to the Nile Valley for Egypt's burgeoning population, and landless farmers and inner-city families were encouraged to settle there. In the late 1950s, the oases of Kharga, Dakhla and Farafra were grouped into the New Valley Governorate; the first new inhabitants arrived on 3 October 1959 – this date is now an annual public holiday throughout the New Valley. But although some of the New Valley projects were successful, many were not. As of the last census in 1996, only 143,000 people lived within the governorate boundaries – far short of original plans.

Highlights

- Visit the Roman hilltop ruins, many of which doubled as protective fortresses, at Kharga Oasis.
- Wander through the ancient mud-brick town of Al-Qasr in Dakhla, where narrow, labyrinthine streets repelled sandstorms and marauders for centuries.
- Marvel at the White Desert – the only desert in the world where the sand looks like snow and surreal white sculptures arise.
- Explore the isolated palm-filled Siwa Oasis, famed for its fiercely independent inhabitants, with their unique language and distinctive culture.

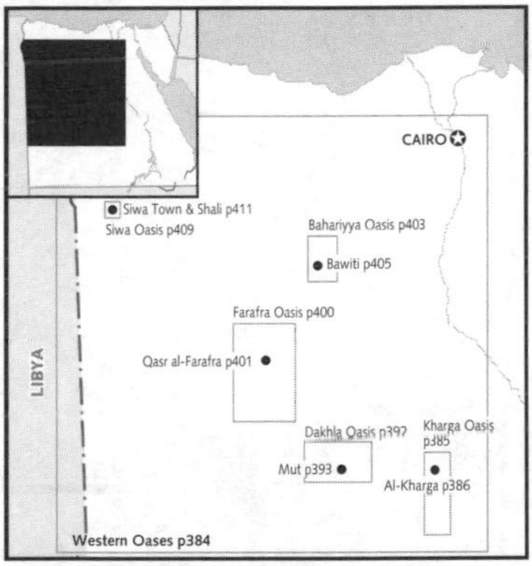

Although the oases are attracting more and more travellers, their increased popularity has not diminished the adventure of exploring this remote region. The towns and villages are dotted with archaeological sites that are easily accessible to most travellers, and a safari into the open desert beyond is one of the last great trips that can be taken in Egypt. The ideal time to visit is in late autumn (October to November) or early spring (March to April), because summer (June to August) temperatures can soar as

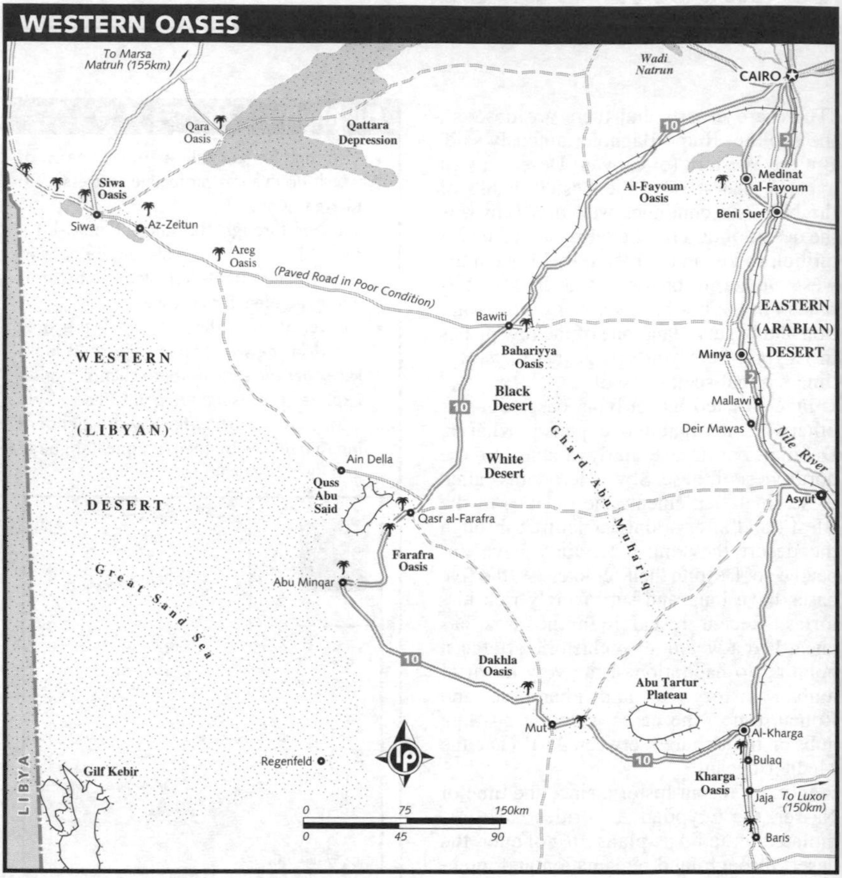

high as 52°C (125°F), though humidity rarely exceeds 9%. Winter is very pleasant with average daytime highs of between 20 and 25°C from December to February, and sometimes March, but it can get very nippy (down to 2°C at times) at night.

Asphalt roads link all the oases. Kharga is also linked by road to Luxor and Asyut. Note, however, that while you can drive from Kharga to Luxor, it is not always possible to do the reverse, due to the nervous Luxor police.

Siwa is usually reached by road from Marsa Matruh on the north coast. Although there is road access from Bahariyya to Siwa, there is no public transport as yet. For more information see Getting There & Away under Siwa later in this chapter.

KHARGA OASIS

☎ 092

Kharga, the largest and most developed of the oases, is situated in a desert depression about 30km wide and 200km long. The chief town is Al-Kharga, 233km from Asyut. It was originally a way station on the Darb al-Arba'een (40 Days Rd), the caravan route between Sudan and Egypt. But unlike the other oasis towns, which have retained something of their original character, this place (the capital of the New Valley) reflects the dreams of Egyptian planners in the 1960s. Enormous concrete-and-glass modernist structures stand on wide, shadeless boulevards that speak of a brave new world of agri-business and mass population movement rather than desert heat and date plantations.

Even though the town itself is faceless and uninteresting, there are several things worth seeing nearby.

Orientation

The bus station is in the south-east of Al-Kharga, near what's left of the old centre, and it's a fair hike to most of the hotels. If you're coming from Dakhla, decide where you want to stay before arriving – you may want to be let off at Sharia al-Adel rather than having to trudge all the way back again.

Those arriving from Asyut will be treated to a spectacular panorama as the road descends the escarpment before passing one of Egypt's most notorious prisons at Al-Munira, about 23km north of Al-Kharga. Once in town you'll come to Midan Nasser, marked by a large statue of a woman (representing Egypt) holding her children (the oases).

Information

The tourist office (☎ 921 206, fax 921 205) on Midan Nasser is open from 8.30am to 3pm Saturday to Thursday and for variable periods in the evening. Staff members are friendly but don't always have the most recent information. Another local information source is the New Valley Tourist Friends Association (☎ 921 451) at Midan Basateen, near the Ministry of Culture. It's open from 5pm to 10pm Saturday to Thursday.

The local branches of Banque du Caire and Banque Masr both change cash and travellers cheques; Banque Masr also gives cash advances on credit cards – the only place in the oases to do so. The post office, on Sharia Abdel Moniem Riad, is open from 8am to 2.30pm Saturday to Thursday. The telephone centrale, on Sharia al-Gomhuriya, is open 24 hours a day.

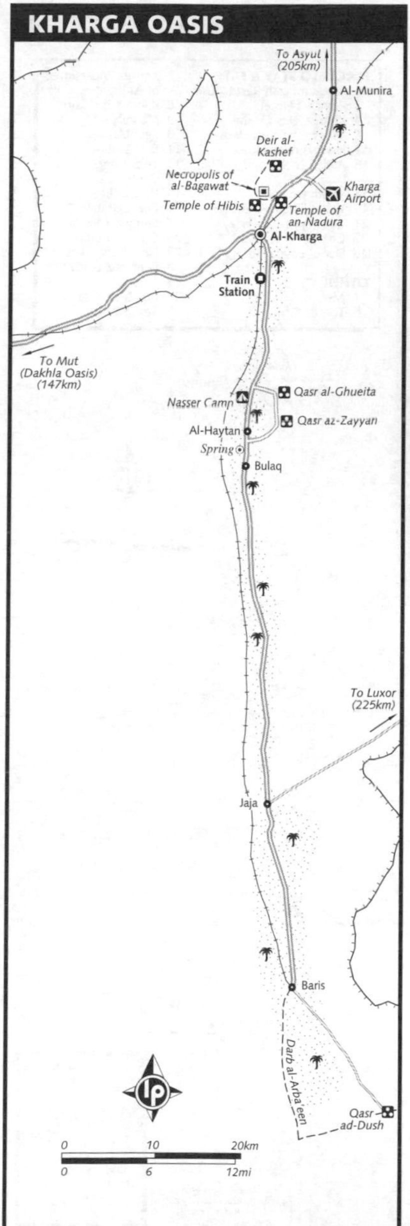

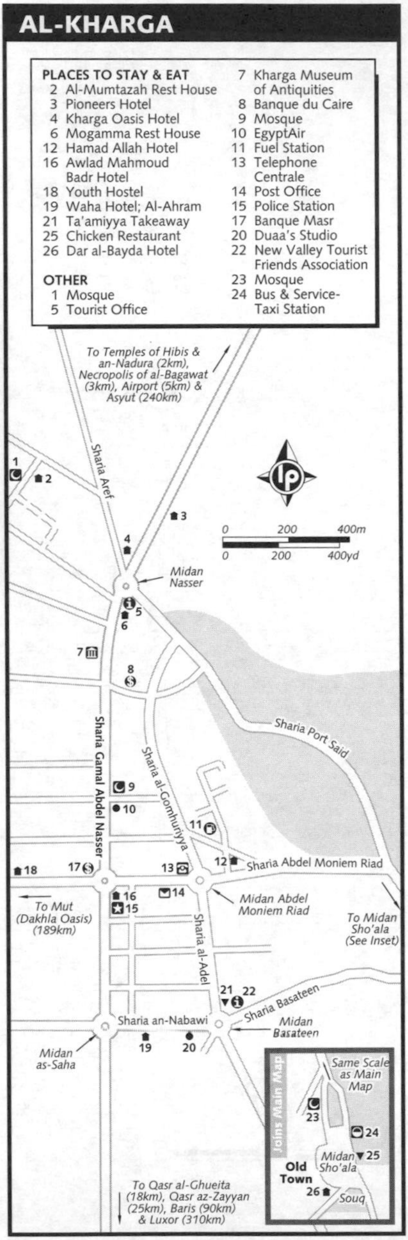

Duaa's Studio, a little place on Sharia an-Nabawi between the Waha Hotel and the Midan Basateen, usually has some Kodak and Agfa film.

Kharga Museum of Antiquities

This museum *(Sharia Gamal Abdel Nasser; admission E£20; open 8am-4pm daily)*, down the road from the tourist office, houses archaeological exhibits from various ancient sites around Kharga and Dakhla Oases. Particularly good is the small display in the room to the right of the entrance hall. Sponsored by a Canadian museum, it traces the prehistory of the oases in both English and Arabic and has four vitrines filled with prehistoric artefacts. As well as this, there is a wide selection of Pharaonic, Ptolemaic and early Christian displays.

Temple of Hibis

Restored by the Metropolitan Museum in the early 20th century, the Temple of Hibis *(admission E£16; open 8am-5pm Oct-Apr, 8am-6pm May-Sept)* is the largest of the Kharga temples and is dedicated to Amun. Built using the local limestone, it was begun possibly during the reign of the 25th dynasty, but was certainly decorated by the Persian king Darius I. A colonnade was also added by Nectanebo II and there were further additions by the Ptolemies. A sphinx-lined avenue leads to a series of gateways, the colonnade of Nectanebo and then a court, a hypostyle hall (with graffiti left by 19th-century European travellers, including the famous Western Desert explorer, Gerhard Rohlfs) and an inner sanctuary. Relief scenes include the pharaoh offering lettuce to the fertility god Min, and Seth battling with the evil serpent Apophis.

Although it's well preserved, the temple is threatened by rising ground water, and is currently enshrouded in scaffolding in preparation for being moved to higher ground 300m away. Until the work is completed it remains closed to the public, but you can still walk around the outside. The temple is 2km north of town just to the left off the main road. If it's too hot to walk from the town, pick-ups (50pt) heading to

The Real English Patient (& Other Desert Explorers)

Anyone familiar with the book or film *The English Patient* may be intrigued to know that the character played by Ralph Fiennes – the 'english patient' of the title – is not a fictional creation; neither was he English, nor was he ever a patient crippled by burns and a broken heart.

Ladislaus 'Laszlo' Almasy was a Hungarian aristocrat who arrived in Cairo during the interwar years. Adventurer, explorer and sometime spy, he worked for the British-run Egyptian Desert Survey Department conducting arial surveys. Flying above the Western Desert in his Gypsy Moth, Almasy did make the discoveries attributed to him in the book and the film, most notably finding a way to the top of the Gilf Kebir and the Cave of the Swimmers in Uwaynat. When WWII broke out, Almasy enlisted with the pro-German Hungarian air force and found himself attached to Rommel's Afrika Korps teaching desert survival. Famously in 1942, Almasy led a German spy on a gruelling overland trek across the Western Desert to get him into Egypt undetected by the British.

But although Almasy has received all the attention in recent years, he was only one of the many extraordinary modern heroes of the Western Desert. Even as recently as the late 19th century, vast swathes of this huge and mysterious territory remained uncharted because the distance between water sources was too great for camels to manage. In 1874, German geographer Gerhard Rohlfs began to map the area, in the process making an epic and near-fatal journey of 676km through the Great Sand Sea without being able to water his camels. In what is now a classic moment in the annals of desert travel, he had given himself up for dead when a freak rainstorm saved his party and his camels. He and his companion built a cairn on the top of the nearest dune and named it Regenfeld (Rainfield). In 1876, he published an account of his explorations *Drei Monate in der Libyschen Wust*, still one of the most important works on the Western Desert.

In 1923, Egyptian explorer Ahmed Hassanein made the first crossing of the Western Desert in modern times, travelling an incredible 3572km from Sallum on the Mediterranean coast to Fasher in Sudan via the oasis of Kufra (now in Libya). In between his long marches he managed to discover Gebel Uwaynat in the south-west corner of the country, later describing it in his book *The Lost Oases*.

But it was the introduction of the car that allowed desert exploration to really take off. In 1923, Prince Kamal ad-Din, another Egyptian, took three custom-made Citroën caterpillars into the Great Sand Sea. Over the next couple of years he mapped the remote south-west corner of the desert.

Like Almasy, British employees of the Desert Survey, such as PA Clayton and GW Murray, did much to chart the desert. During WWII, Clayton was joined by other desert enthusiasts who formed the Long Range Desert Group – the gang loosely portrayed in *The English Patient*. The group spent the war years patrolling the Western Desert for the allies, using the expertise they'd gained in years of travel in the area to mount daring raids and help prevent the German and Italian armies from advancing into Egypt. Ralph Bagnold, one of its members, tells how he and his army buddies got started on their desert trips in the classic *Libyan Sands: Travel in a Dead World*. He later went back to England and continued his desert exploration by building a wind tunnel and studying the effect of wind on sand. The outcome was his book *The Physics of Blown Sand and Desert Dunes*, which was later used by NASA to interpret satellite pictures of Mars.

Mounira pass this way; just make sure that you tell the driver that you want to get off at *el ma'abad* (the temple).

Temple of an-Nadura

This temple, on the main road at the north end of town, also doubled as a fortress and was built to protect the oasis by Roman emperor Antonnius Pius in AD 138. Inside are the remains of a sandstone temple, with hieroglyphic inscriptions. It was later used as a fortress by the Ottomans.

Entry to the temple is free. You can't miss the ruins, perched on a rise off to the right of the main road, shortly before the Temple of Hibis becomes visible. Follow the road to the right for 500m and scramble up the potsherd-strewn hill. Although the temple is ruined, it has sweeping views of the desert and oasis, and is a great place to watch the sunset.

Necropolis of al-Bagawat

About 1km north of the Temple of Hibis, this necropolis *(admission E£20; open 8am-5pm Oct-Apr, 8am-6pm May-Sept)* is probably the most interesting of the three sights clustered just north of the town. If you're on foot, just cut across the desert from the main road when you see the necropolis to your left. By car, you'll have to drive 1km or so up the road to the entrance. Most of the several hundred mud-brick tombs in this Christian cemetery date from the 4th to the 6th centuries AD. They are traditional domed Coptic tombs, some of which have interesting, but rapidly disappearing, wall paintings of biblical scenes. You will be dogged by someone anxious to become your guide; if you want to get inside some of the more colourful tombs, he's your man. Ask to see the Chapel of Peace, which has figures of the apostles on the squinches of the domes, just visible through the Greek graffiti. The Chapel of the Exodus has the best-preserved paintings, with a dome full of Old Testament biblical stories and graffiti dating back to the 9th century. Also worth seeing are tomb No 25 and a small tomb that the site guard has named the Chapel of the Grapes (Anaeed al-Ainab) after the grapevines that cover the walls.

Deir al-Kashef

Dominating the cliffs to the north of Bagawat is the ruined Monastery of al-Kashef, named after Mustafa al-Kashef or Mustafa the Tax Collector. To get there, walk or drive on the left-hand track from the ticket office at the Necropolis of al-Bagawat. The track snakes behind the hill on which the cemetery is built, passing below the ugly concrete rest house of the famous oasis archaeologist Ahmed Fakhry, and the small, rock-cut tombs that honeycomb the mountain. After about 1km you will come upon the imposing mud-brick ruins. Strategically placed to overlook what was once one of the most important crossroads of the Western Desert, the point where the Darb al-Ghabari from Dakhla crossed the Darb al-Arba'een, the magnificent remains date back to the early Christian era, although the site was occupied as early as the Middle Kingdom. Once five storeys high, much of it has collapsed but you can see the tops of the arched corridors that crisscrossed the building. On the plain below are other ruins, including a small church with some barely visible wall paintings on the west wall and the remains of the tiny cells where the monks once slept.

Places to Stay

Camping Given the vast expanses of empty desert surrounding Kharga, it seems counter-intuitive to camp in the town, which is why there are few options here. Keep in mind that if you do choose to camp here, the mosquitoes can be bad.

Kharga Oasis Hotel *(☎ 921 500, Midan Nasser)* E£7 per person. You can camp in the grounds of the Kharga Oasis and use the toilet and shower inside. Although the palm-filled garden is pleasant, it is filled with mosquitoes.

Hotels Kharga has few hotels, none of which are particularly outstanding. But as they seem to be half empty most of the time, it isn't usually a problem to find a room. Some hotels offer half board, which includes breakfast and dinner, while full board prices include breakfast, lunch and dinner.

Youth Hostel *(☎ 922 640, Sharia Abdel Moniem Riad)* Beds in 5-bed dorm E£6. This is inconveniently located at the eastern end of town, but is very clean. Each dorm has its own bathroom.

Dar al-Bayda Hotel *(☎ 921 717, Midan Sho'ala)* Singles/doubles E£15, doubles with bath E£22. This clean and pleasant budget place is just to the left off Midan Sho'ala, where the buses and service taxis are based. Most rooms have fans and there is a restaurant on top. Breakfast is E£5 extra.

Awlad Mahmoud Badr Hotel *(☎ 922 689, Sharia Gamal Abdel Nasser)* Singles/doubles E£15/20, with bath E£20/30. This is a newly built clean budget place at the southern end of the main street.

Waha Hotel *(☎ 920 393, Sharia an-Nabawi)* Singles/doubles E£8/16, with bath E£18/25. Singles are cramped and windowless and the shared bathrooms can be filthy. On the plus side, the rooms have fans, the water is hot and the staff is friendly. If you're coming in from Dakhla, the bus can drop you off at the entrance.

Mogamma Rest House *(☎ 921 206, fax 921 205, Sharia Gamal Abdel Nasser)* Rooms E£17.30 per person. Mogamma, behind the tourist office, is the best of several government rest houses in Al-Kharga. It consists of four chalets, one of which can sleep 10 people. The rooms, have a fridge, kitchen and TV, and are very clean. Rooms are reserved through the tourist office.

Al-Mumtazah Rest House *(☎ 921 206, fax 921 205)* E£9 per bed. A huge modernist affair with five large rooms, Al-Mumtazah is cheaper than, but not nearly as good as, the Mogamma. It is also inconveniently located off Sharia Aref. Rooms are reserved through the tourist office.

Hamad Allah Hotel *(☎ 920 638, fax 925 017)* Singles/doubles E£53/75. Located off Sharia Abdel Moniem Riad this hotel is popular with overland tour groups. The air-con rooms are clean, but dark and gloomy. They come with breakfast, and also have a bath, fridge and TV.

Kharga Oasis Hotel *(☎ 921 500, Midan Nasser)* Singles/doubles E£65/87. Another modern homage to concrete, Kharga Oasis does have a nice palm-filled garden and terrace. A favourite stopping-off point for desert adventurers, it's a good place with air-con rooms, although it often seems sadly empty. Prices include breakfast and taxes.

Pioneers Hotel *(☎ 927 982, fax 927 983, Sharia Gamal Abdel Nasser)* Singles/doubles half board US$95/124. The first five-star hotel in the oases, Pioneers opened its lacquered doors in November 1998. A salmon pink, 90-room low-rise, it is more appropriate to the mass tourism of the Nile Valley than the oases, and bills itself as 'a short-cut to modern life'. This is the place to be if you can't live without satellite TV and central air-con. The swimming pool can be used by nonguests for E£30.

Places to Eat

Restaurants are few and far between in Al-Kharga and the best places to eat here are the hotels. Your only other option is the small fuul and ta'amiyya places scattered around Midan Sho'ala and Sharia al-Adel. There's a cheap ***chicken place*** a few doors down from the bus station on Midan Sho'ala. There's also a ***ta'amiyya takeaway*** joint on Sharia al-Adel near Midan Basateen, and a ***juice stand*** just opposite.

Hamad Allah Hotel *(☎ 920 638, fax 925 017)* Set lunch E£17, dinner E£19. Just off Sharia Abdel Moniem Riad, this place has mediocre food, but there is a bar.

Kharga Oasis Hotel *(☎ 921 500, Midan Nasser)* Set lunch E£21, dinner E£25. This is marginally better than the Hamad Allah, particularly if you can brave the mosquitoes and sit in the outdoor bar overlooking the tranquil garden.

Pioneers Hotel *(☎ 927 982, fax 927 983, Sharia Gamal Abdel Nasser)* Meals E£25-80. This hotel has the usual overpriced Egyptian hotel food, with lots of pseudo-continental dishes on offer. However, it also has a well-stocked bar and an outdoor terrace.

Al-Ahram Restaurant *(Sharia an-Nabawi)* Meals E£5-15. This small roast chicken and kofta place at the front of the Waha Hotel, has the usual basic salads, grilled meat and vegetable dishes.

Getting There & Away

Air EgyptAir (☎ 920 838) flies from Cairo to Al-Kharga and back again on Sunday and Wednesday; the fare is E£510 one way. The EgyptAir office is on Sharia Gamal Abdel Nasser, just by the big mosque. The airport is 5km north of town. A taxi ride to the airport costs between E£10 and E£15.

Bus The bus station is in the south-east of the town (see under Orientation earlier). There are three buses to Cairo: 6am (E£23), 9pm (E£37) and 11pm (E£37). The 6am bus goes via Asyut and takes the Nile Valley agricultural road, allowing you to stop in Minya or Beni Suef, but lengthening the trip to Cairo to 11 hours or more. The 9pm and 11pm buses originate in Dakhla and take the desert road all the way, making the trip from Al-Kharga in seven to eight hours.

There are several buses from Al-Kharga to Asyut (E£7 to E£8, three to four hours) leaving at 1am, 6am, 7am, 11am, 2pm, 5pm and 10pm. Two other buses pass through Al-Kharga en route from Dakhla to Asyut.

Buses to Dakhla (E£7, three hours) leave at 3am, 4am, 7am, 11am, 1pm and 2pm.

Train There is a train from Al-Kharga to Luxor at 7am every Friday. The trip takes about seven hours and tickets (3rd class only) cost E£9.80. A branch line has been inaugurated to Baris but there is no scheduled service as yet.

Service Taxi A service taxi is a convenient way to travel to Al-Kharga from Asyut. The trip takes from three to four hours and costs E£8 per person. To Dakhla, the trip takes three hours and costs E£7.

Special Taxi At the time of writing, special taxis are about the only vehicles using the new Kharga-Luxor road (via Jaja). You'll be looking at about E£500 for the trip (maximum seven people). There might be the odd truck going this way but hitching isn't recommended.

Getting Around

Covered pick-up trucks act as the local transport in Al-Kharga. They run up and down Sharia Gamal Abdel Nasser, and between Midan Sho'ala and Midan Nasser, as well as servicing various other routes around town. Expect to pay between 25pt and 50pt, depending on the distance travelled.

SOUTH TO BARIS

Heading south from Al-Kharga is an asphalt road leading to Baris, the southernmost town in the oases. The road passes through a number of newly established villages with names like Revolution – all part of the numerous projects designed to turn the desert around here green. As you follow the road there are a number of easily accessible sites.

Qasr al-Ghueita & Qasr az-Zayyan

Dominating the hillside on the east side of the Baris road, about 18km south of Al-Kharga, are the remains of Qasr al-Ghueita, or Palace of the Beautiful One, *(adults/students E£16/8)* a temple from the 25th dynasty dedicated to the Theban triad Amun, Mut and Khons. Inside the mud-brick walls there is a well-preserved Ptolemaic temple with reliefs showing scenes of Hapy, god of the Nile. An asphalt road leads the 2km to the temple from the main road. About 7km further south are the remains of Qasr az-Zayyan *(admission E£16)*, another Roman temple built inside a fortress. Close to a modern village, it doesn't have the remote feel of most of the other temple-fortresses in the area, but it is still worth a visit.

If you don't have a vehicle you can get to the temples by taking a bus heading for Baris or a covered pick-up going to Bulaq. Ask the driver to let you off at the asphalt road leading to the temples. There is also an asphalt road linking the two, but 7km is a long hike if you're on foot. If you are planning to walk between the sites, take lots of water.

Baris

Baris, 90km south of Al-Kharga, is the fourth town of the New Valley Governorate, but there is little here to remind you that it was once one of the most important trading centres along the Darb al-Arba'een. Other than a few kiosks selling fuul and ta'amiyya there is little of note apart from the uninhabited mud-brick houses of Baris al-Gedida, about 2km north of the original town. Designed in traditional oasis style by Egypt's most famous modern architect, Hassan Fathy, Baris al-Gedida was supposed to be a model for other new settlements. However, the Six Day War of 1967 intervened and the village was never completed.

About 23km to the south-east of Baris is **Qasr ad-Dush** *(admission E£16; open 8am-5pm Oct-Apr, 8am-6pm May-Sept)*, a temple-fortress built by the Romans and completed around AD 177. Originally the gateway to Egypt from the south, it was an important stopping point on the Darb al-Arba'een and may also have been used to guard the Darb al-Dush, an east-west track to the Esna and Edfu Temples in the Nile Valley. The sandstone temple abutting the eastern side of the fortress is dedicated to Isis and Serapis, and was built by Domitian in the 1st century AD. Few decorations remain but the temple was renowned for once having been partially covered with gold. The European travellers who visited Qasr ad-Dush in the 19th century left their names inscribed for posterity, and they can still be seen in the gateway, next to the original inscriptions of Roman emperors. Although the temple now stands alone in a dramatic landscape, as you walk down the hill to leave you can see the outlines of walls that formed a substantial settlement abutting the fortified structure.

There is an asphalt road to the temple, and to get there from Baris you can either get dropped off by the bus from Al-Kharga, leaving you without a way of getting back to town, or negotiate for a special ride out with a covered pick-up, usually available for about E£20, including waiting time.

Places to Stay

Baris is not a good place to stay the night, and you're better off staying in Al-Kharga.

Nasser Camp (☎ 927 982, fax 927 983, Kharga-Dush Rd) Canvas tents E£12 per person, bungalows E£50 per person. Just south of Qasr al-Ghueita, 20km south of Al-Kharga, this camp site is owned by Pioneers Hotel in Al-Kharga. Its tents and overpriced, stuffy prefab bungalows are set in a straggling garden beside a spring.

Getting There & Away

There are two buses each day between Al-Kharga and Baris (E£1.75), leaving from Al-Kharga at 7am and 2pm, and Baris at 6am and 3pm. At 7am and 2pm each day a local bus heads down to Baris, stopping at all the villages on the way; it will take you to Qasr ad-Dush and other outlying villages (also for E£1.75). The frequent microbuses and pick-up trucks are a more convenient option between Al-Kharga and Baris, and cost about E£3.

DAKHLA OASIS

☎ 092

Dakhla, about 189km west of Kharga, was created from more than 600 natural springs and ponds. Its picturesque mud-brick villages, many built upon much older settlements, sit among impossibly lush fields and orchards. The oasis is home to about 70,000 people and produces rice, wheat, mangoes, oranges, olives and dates, as well as apricots, the latter being dried and then sold mainly during Ramadan. As they drive about on donkey carts and work the fields, farmers wear straw hats, giving the place a strange, Latin American air.

Recent research in Dakhla has shown that is has been lived in continuously since prehistory. In Neolithic times it was the site of a huge lake, and prehistoric rock paintings show that elephants, buffaloes and ostriches wandered along its shores. As the lake dried up, the human population is thought to have migrated eastwards to become among the earliest settlers in the Nile Valley.

The bus from Asyut and Al-Kharga drops you off at Mut (population 13,000), the largest town in the oasis, from where you can take a service taxi to Al-Qasr, the other town of interest in the area. The bus coming from Farafra Oasis can drop you at Al-Qasr or Mut.

Information

Omar Ahmed is one of the most helpful tourist information officers in Egypt. He is a mine of knowledge about the oases and is very obliging. There are two tourist offices, both in Mut, and Omar flits between them. One office (☎ 821 686) is on Sharia as-Sawra al-Khadra, the other (☎ 820 404) is in the same building as the Government Rest House, just by the bus station. Both are open from 8am to 3pm daily.

Banque Masr in Mut exchanges cash and travellers cheques. It is open from 8am to 3pm and 6pm to 9pm Saturday to Thursday.

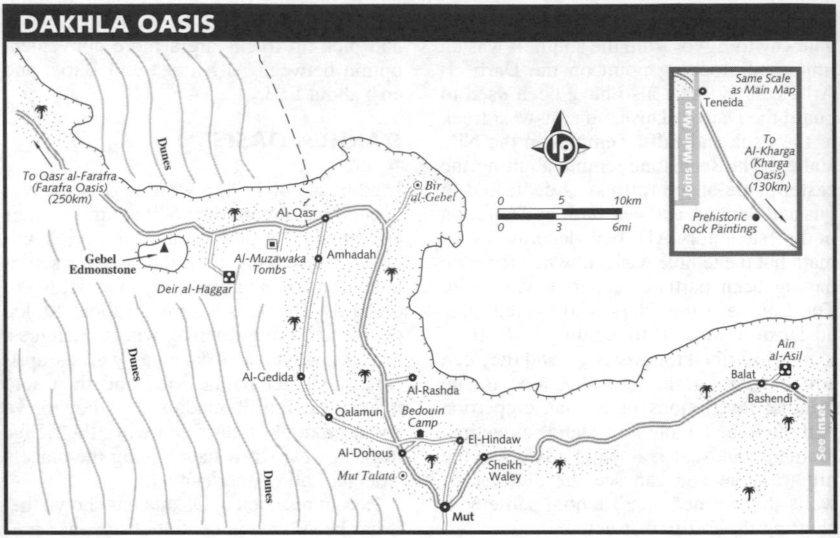

The post office is behind the mosque at the bus station and is open from 8am to 2pm Saturday to Thursday. There is another post office on Sharia as-Salam, which is also open from 8am to 2pm Saturday to Thursday. The 24-hour telephone centrale handles international traffic (but there are no cardphones).

There is a hospital in Mut (☎ 821 555, ambulance 123). The police station (☎ 821 500) is close to the microbus stand on Sharia 10th of Ramadan.

Ethnographic Museum

This museum *(Sharia as-Salam; admission E£2)* is attached to Dar al-Wafdeen Government Hotel. If you want to see displays on oasis life, ask at one of the tourist offices to have it opened. Or you can go to the Cultural Palace (☎ 821 311) on Sharia al-Wadi and ask for the museum's manager, Ibrahim Kamel. He is usually in his office between 8am and 2pm Saturday to Thursday.

Old City of Mut

Often ignored by passing travellers, the labyrinth of mud-brick houses and winding lanes, which clings to the slopes of the hill leading to the old citadel, is worth exploring. You can climb up to the remains of the **citadel**, which used to be the town proper (but is now used as a dump and has been taken over by goats), for views of the town against the backdrop of desert cliffs and dunes. On the right of Sharia al-Wadi, which leads into the new town centre, is a former medieval **Islamic cemetery**.

Hot Springs

There are several hot sulphur pools around the town of Mut, but the easiest to reach is the official tourist spring 3km down the road to Al-Qasr from Mut. Called **Mut Talata** (Mut Three) the spring is the site of a small hotel (see Places to Stay later in this chapter), so unless you can afford to pay the inflated prices to stay there, you have to dip in the very exposed 1.5m-deep pool just outside the hotel's pink walls. The pool's rust-coloured water may not look very inviting (and it can stain clothes) but it is very hot and relaxing.

Bir al-Gebel (Mountain Spring) is a pleasant hot spring that can be reached via a turn-off about 25km north of Mut; from the turn-off it's about another 5km to the

JULIET COOMBE

The mud-brick remains of the 13th-century fortress of Shali dominate the town of Siwa.

SARA-JANE CLELAND

Siwan mud-brick architecture

JULIET COOMBE

Transport Siwa-style

JULIET COOMBE

The surrounding Western Desert has kept Siwa isolated from the rest of Egypt for centuries.

CHRIS BARTON

SIMON BRACKEN

The deserts of Egypt stretch for hundreds of kilometres, endless seas of sand that occasionally give way to lush oases. The White Desert is full of bizarre and beautiful forms shaped by the wind (top), while the Western Desert (bottom) is part of the mass of sand known as the Sahara.

spring. During the day, women should only bathe here wearing baggy T-shirts over their bathing suits. A sign states that there is a rest house, but it is not operating.

Sand Dunes & Camel Rides

A few kilometres out past the bus station you can have a roll around in sand dunes said to have been there since Roman times. They are not the most spectacular of dunes, but are easy to reach for people without their own transport. Head out towards the airport and you'll see the dunes off to the right of the road. Sunset camel rides out to the dunes can also be arranged – ask at the Bedouin Camp (see Places to Stay later), Abu Mohammed Restaurant or one of the tourist offices.

Rock Paintings

On the south-west side of the Kharga-Dakhla road, about 55km south-east of Mut you can see **prehistoric rock paintings**. At a bend in the road beyond Teneida there are strangely shaped rock formations, just next to the last of Dakhla's cultivated land. One of the largest and closest to the road has well-preserved pictures of giraffes, antelopes and fish. The place was a major

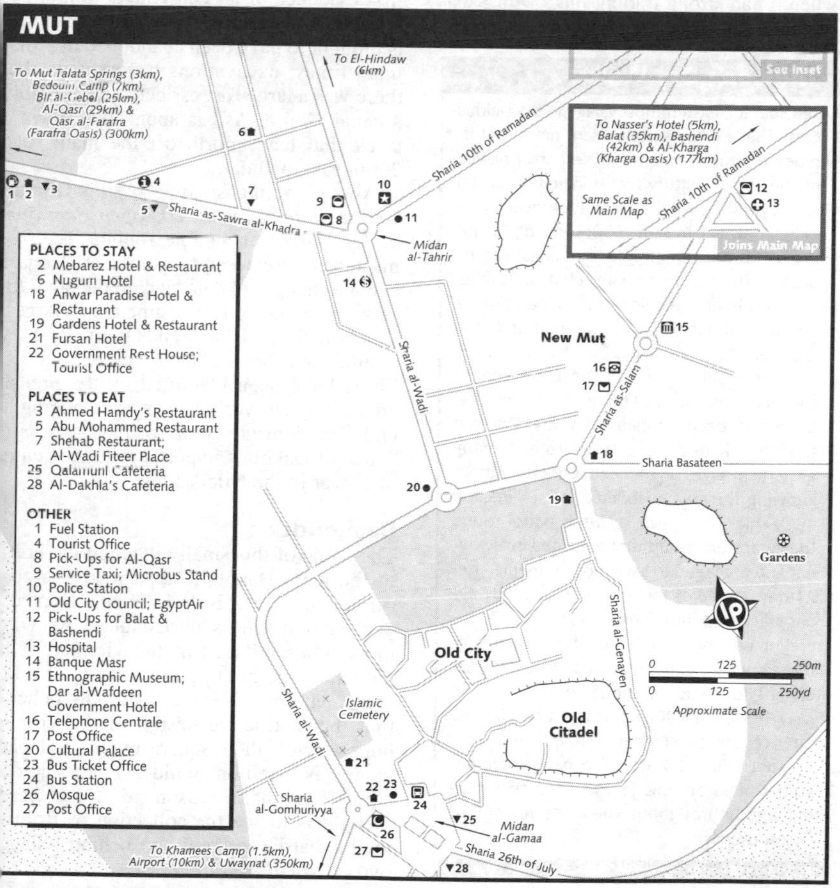

caravan stop and marked an intersection between two major trade routes, the Darb al-Ghabari, which ran between Dakhla and Kharga and another, now lost, track that linked the village of Teneida with the Darb al-Arba'een to the south.

Balat

About 35km east of Mut on the road to Al-Kharga is Balat, another town that has retained much of its medieval Islamic character. Although the oldest houses here date back to medieval times, there has been a town on the site since Old Kingdom times, when it had strong trading links with Kush (Nubia). The covered streets in the town, with their moulded benches, smoothly rounded mud-plaster walls and tiny doors look almost African; they were built this way to confuse would-be invaders and keep the inhabitants cool. There is not much to do but wander through the picturesque alleys and see how little has changed here over the centuries. A pick-up from near the hospital in Mut costs E£1.

If you have your own vehicle you may want to explore a couple of nearby sites that date back to Pharaonic times. **Ain al-Asil**, or the Spring of the Origin, is an Old Kingdom settlement that provided historians with the first evidence of an Old Kingdom link between Dakhla and the Nile Valley. The site is thought to have been abandoned in Ptolemaic times; excavations have shown that there was a large fortress here, and possibly a canal. Ain al-Asil is about 2km down a track that leads north off the main road 200m east of Balat.

About 1.5km past Ain al-Asil is **Qila al-Dabba** *(admission E£20; open 8am-5pm daily)*, Balat's ancient necropolis. The five mastabas here resemble those at Saqqara and are thought to date back to the 6th dynasty. Although all are ruined, the largest stands at least 10m high. Originally they would have been clad in fine limestone. Three have been identified by the French archaeologists working here as belonging to Old Kingdom governors of the oasis, evidence of Dakhla's importance to the centre of power in the Nile Valley.

The Long Dry Walk

Teneida, the easternmost village in the Dakhla Oasis, has existed since ancient times, but its modern fame comes from the part it played in one of this century's most incredible desert journeys. When the Italians took over Kufra Oasis (now in Libya) in 1930, some of the nomads of the area preferred to risk death in the desert rather than be subjected to foreign rule. With no time for real preparation, a group of about 500 men, women and children set out on a risky 322km journey across the Great Sand Sea and the Gilf Kebir to Uwaynat. They arrived there only to find that there had been no rain for years. Without food for themselves or their camels many gave themselves up for dead. Others, without knowing the area, wandered in the direction of Dakhla. By chance, a British patrol found the emaciated group that remained in Uwaynat and managed to save most of them. After 21 days, three of the men who'd left Uwaynat staggered into Teneida and a rescue operation was mounted to find the remainder of the refugees wandering in the desert. According to a report in the *Times* of London in May 1931, some 300 nomads reached Dakhla after covering a staggering 676km of desert on foot without water. The newspaper described it as an epic journey that few have managed throughout the long history of desert travel.

Bashendi

The name of this small village to the north of the main Dakhla-Kharga road is a corruption of the words Pasha Hindi, the medieval sheikh who's buried here. As with most other villages in the vicinity, it is thought to be built upon the ruins of a far older settlement. Some historians believe that the distinctive design of the village houses, with their square pillars and balconies, is based on an older, Pharaonic design. The main reason to come here though, is to see the collection of Roman tombs that lie in the desert behind village two of which are of interest.

Tomb of Pasha Hindi may be from the Islamic era, but the dome was added to a pre-existing Roman structure, clearly visible from the inside of the building. Locals make pilgrimages to pray for the saint's intercession.

Tomb of Kitanes *(admission E£16; open 8am-5pm daily)* was lived in by Sanussi soldiers during WWI, and occupied by a village family after that. Nevertheless, its funerary reliefs are still intact and depict the 2nd century AD official meeting of the gods Min, Seth and Shu.

Al-Qasr

On the edge of lush vegetation at the foot of high limestone cliffs is the medieval town of Al-Qasr, a charming little place that reminds you what the other oasis towns must have been like before the New Valley development projects changed the face of the area. Some 700 people live in the town although at one time it contained 4500. It is now forbidden for newcomers to settle in the old section of Al-Qasr.

The town was built on Graeco-Roman foundations. The gateway to a temple to Thoth (buried) is now the front of a private house, and inscribed blocks from the temple have been used in other local buildings. Otherwise, the architecture has retained much of its medieval character. The narrow covered streets retain their cool in the hot summer months and also serve to protect, to some extent, their inhabitants from desert sandstorms. You can see quite a few entrances to old houses that go back to Ottoman and Mamluk times, some marked by beautiful **lintels** – acacia beams situated above the door, and carved with the names of the carpenter, the owner of the house, the date and a verse from the Quran. There are 54 lintels in the village, the earliest of which dates to AD 924, but one of the finest is above the Tomb of Sheikh Nasr ad-Din inside the old mosque, which is marked by a 12th-century mud-brick minaret (it was rebuilt in the 19th century). The Supreme Council for Antiquities has recently renovated the town's **Ayyubid madrassa**, a school where Islamic law is taught. The madrassa also did double duty as a town hall and courthouse, and near the door is a stake where prisoners would be shackled. Adjoining it is **Nasr ad-Din Mosque**, with a 21m-high minaret. Also of interest is **House of Abu Nafir**, another recently restored building. A dramatic pointed arch forms the entrance to the house, under which is a huge studded wooden door. Built of mud brick, but on a grander scale than the surrounding houses, it is thought to have been built on a temple, probably dating back to Ptolemaic times. Huge blocks from the earlier structure, most covered in hieroglyphic reliefs, can be seen in the walls of the house and some of the other buildings in the vicinity. Other buildings of interest include the **pottery factory** and a huge old **corn mill**. You can still see people making mud bricks in the time-honoured way, as well as men working an antique bellows in a tiny foundry.

There are pick-ups to Al-Qasr from near the police station in Mut for 50pt. Heading back to Mut from Al-Qasr, take the secondary road for a change of scenery. You can visit several **tombs** near the ruined village of Amhadah, dating from the 22nd century BC. About 15km further towards Mut is the Mamluk village of **Qalamun** that has a cemetery from where there is a good view of the surrounding area.

Al-Muzawaka Tombs

About 3km west of Al-Qasr, you'll find a turn-off to the left (south) leading 1km to a hillside riddled with hundreds of tombs. Two of these stand out for their beautifully coloured frescoes, from which the tombs take their name *(muzawaka* means 'decorated' in Arabic). Dated to the 2nd century AD by Ahmed Fakhry, the Egyptian archaeologist who surveyed many of the monuments in the Western Desert, they blend Roman and Egyptian painting styles and motifs, giving a fascinating glimpse at the transition between the two eras. The **Tomb of Petosiris** has amazing blonde figures standing in Pharaonic-style profile, chubby, curly haired angels and a zodiac. In the single-roomed **Tomb of Patubastis**, Anubis and

Osiris (who is standing in judgment) share wall space with Janus. Both tombs were restored in the 1980s, but in 1998 the ceilings threatened to collapse and they were closed to the public. Check with the tourist office in Mut to see if restoration is complete.

With a little baksheesh, the custodian will probably show you a rough-cut tomb, just to the left of the two main tombs, that contains four adult mummies.

Deir al-Haggar

About 7km west of Al-Qasr, at the checkpoint on the road to Farafra Oasis, there's a signposted turn-off to the temple site of Deir al-Haggar. From the turn-off it's another 5km to the restored **sandstone temple** *(admission E£20)*. Dedicated to the Theban triad of Amun, Mut and Khons, as well as to Seth, the brother of Osiris (who can be seen with a falcon's head) and god of the oasis, it was built between the reigns of Nero (AD 54–68) and Domitian (AD 81–96). The cartouches of Nero, Vespasian and Titus (Domitian's father and elder brother respectively) can be seen in the hypostyle hall, which has also been inscribed by almost every 19th century explorer who passed through the oasis. If you look carefully you can see the names of the entire expedition of Gerhard Rohlfs (of Regenfeld fame – see the boxed text 'The Real English Patient' earlier in this chapter for more on this intrepid explorer). Also visible are the names of Edmonstone, Drovetti, Houghton and other famous desert travellers.

The temple has been enclosed by a wall to help prevent wind and sand erosion, and at the entrance is a display room outlining its history and the restoration process.

Organised Tours

Like every other oasis, Dakhla has its share of would-be desert guides. Most of the hotels and restaurants can dig up 4WDs to take you on a trek around the area. As an example, Hamdy at Ahmed Hamdy's Restaurant will take you on a day trip around Dakhla that includes Qalamun, Al-Gedida, a drive through the dunes, visits to a spring, Al-Qasr and Al-Muzawaka tombs, among other things, for E£100. He takes up to six people. An overnight trip around the same area, with Bedouin music, will cost about E£350, including food. The owner of the Bedouin Camp (see Places to Stay later in this chapter) also arranges camel and jeep trips into the desert around Dakhla. You're looking at about E£100 to E£150 per person per day, including a guide, all meals and bedding.

Places to Stay

Camping It's possible to camp near the dunes west of Mut or in Al-Qasr, on a plateau just north of town, where the night sky is a spectacular field of stars, but you should check with the tourist office in Mut first.

Rest Houses Like many of the Western Desert Oases, Dakhla has a number of government rest houses that were until recently, the only accommodation on offer in the area. Usually very basic, they are only of use when everything else is full.

Government Rest House *(☎ 820 404, Midan al-Gamaa, Mut)* Beds E£4.35. Near the bus station (in the same building as the tourist office) this place is pretty basic, and the question of running water problematic but it's cheap.

Dar al-Wafdeen Government Hotel is reserved for officials only.

Hotels As in most of the oases, the majority of Dakhla's hotels are in the budget category Even the more expensive hotels tend to be small and friendly, making up for what they lack in amenities. Some hotels offer hal board, which includes breakfast and dinner

Al-Qasr Hotel *(☎ 876 013, Al-Qasr)* E£ per person. The only option in Al-Qasr, thi friendly place on the main road near the entry to the old town has four big screened rooms with narrow balconies. Shared bath rooms are clean and, contrary to the norm have hot water only. It also has a ground floor coffeehouse and a restaurant tha serves good basic fare such as chicken, rice fuul and salad. Breakfast costs E£2.

Gardens Hotel *(☎ 821 577, Sharia al Genayen, Mut)* Singles/doubles E£15/19 with bath E£18/23. A reasonable deal in convenient location. The showers sometimes have piping-hot water, but the shared bathrooms can be pretty dire and single women may feel uncomfortable. The palm-filled courtyard out the back is a peaceful spot to relax. Breakfast is extra and the hotel rents bicycles for E£6.

Khamees Camp *(☎ 821 577, Mut)* Doubles E£20. This new camp on the south edge of town is run by the management of Gardens Hotel. It has small, simple chalet-style rooms with screens, oasis-style wooden locks, and shared toilet and showers. Difficult to reach without your own transport, Khamees is off the road leading to the airport in Mut.

Anwar Paradise Hotel *(☎ 820 070, Sharia Basateen, Mut)* Singles/doubles E£20/40. This new hotel is above the successful restaurant of the same name. It has friendly management and clean, comfortable rooms with baths in a convenient location.

Nasser's Hotel *(☎ 820 767, Sheikh Waley)* E£15 per person. On the edge of Sheikh Waley, a village about 5km east of Mut on the road to Kharga Oasis (or 20 minutes by bicycle from Mut), this is another cheap alternative; the rate includes breakfast. It's about 400m off the main road to the left and is signposted. The young and likeable owner, Nasser, built this simple, peasant-style mud-brick house over a period of two years. He has five rooms. Nasser usually meets the buses from Kharga and Farafra but if you don't find him and are interested in staying there, you can contact him at Ahmed Hamdy's Restaurant in Mut (owned by his brother).

Fursan Hotel *(☎ 821 343, fax 822 870, Sharia al-Wadi, Mut)* Singles/doubles E£15/25, with bath E£20/35. Practically inside the cemetery on the edge of the old city, it has fairly comfortable rooms at a good price that includes breakfast. It also has an outdoor cafeteria where meals are available for E£12 to E£15.

Bedouin Camp *(☎ 830 604/5, Al-Dohous)* E£15 per person. Bedouin Camp (currently signposted as Bedwen Camp) is a new place 7km north-west of Mut, on a desert hilltop near the small desert village of Al-Dohous. Run by Bedouin who settled in the area a generation ago, the eight reed huts and three mud-brick rooms are simple, but very clean and quiet and have great views. The shared bathrooms are also clean, but have cold water only. The price includes breakfast. A large sitting area with rugs and cushions on the floor serves as the dining area, and is sometimes used for parties at which Bedouin music is played.

Mut Talata *(☎ 821 530, fax 927 983, Mut Talata Springs)* Singles/doubles half board US$52/90. The only three star in town, Mut Talata is operated by the Pioneers Hotel in Al-Kharga, with what are evidently the Pioneer's signature salmon-pink walls. It has six 'chalets', three canvas tents with mattresses, a villa with five rooms, and a restaurant. It's overpriced but it does have a pleasant deep pool fed by warm water from a nearby spring (see under Hot Springs earlier).

Mebarez Hotel *(☎/fax 821 524, Sharia as-Sawra al-Khadra)* Singles/doubles E£28/42, with bath & air-con E£44/58. This hotel has reasonably comfortable rooms with clean shared facilities and is popular with groups on oasis tours. It also has an international phone line (but there's a 30% mark-up on normal tariffs).

Nugum Hotel *(☎ 823 084, Mut)* Singles/doubles E£32/42, with air-con E£50/57. A new hotel close to the tourist office in Mut, it is clean and comfortable and slightly better than the Mebarez, if a little inconveniently located.

Places to Eat

There are a few restaurants in Mut, all serving pretty much the same selection of street food or basic chicken/kebab and rice meals.

Al-Dakhla's Cafeteria *(Midan al-Gamaa)* Dishes E£2-8. This is a basic cafeteria near the bus station.

Qalamuni Cafeteria *(Midan al-Gamaa)* Dishes E£2-10. Another basic cafeteria, it has a reasonable choice of fuul, ta'amiyya and vegetable dishes.

Ahmed Hamdy's Restaurant *(☎ 820 767, Sharia as-Sawra al-Khadra)* Dishes E£3-15. Ahmed Hamdy's is popular with travellers

Desert Safaris

Going on a trek through the desert is one of the last great adventures available to travellers in Egypt. But heading off into remote areas takes serious planning, reliable equipment and a guide with years of experience. For a truly memorable safari you also need someone who will not only show you beautiful vistas, but who understands that the desert is a fragile environment. As well as following such basic environmentally friendly practices as taking all garbage away with you and burning all toilet paper, this includes being aware of the vulnerability of many antiquities sites that dot remote areas in Egypt. Guides who allow tourists to help themselves to flint arrowheads or spray water on prehistoric rock paintings so that their holiday snaps look clearer are destroying a link to humankind's earliest history.

Apart from local guides available from the oases themselves (see under Organised Tours in Dahkla, Bahariyya and Siwa), a number of other adventure travel outfits have sprung up in recent years. Unfortunately, the majority are more concerned with profit and self-promotion than protecting the desert, and tales of company names inscribed on rocks and piles of rubbish left behind are all too common. The ones listed here have been chosen for their concern for the environment, as well as their experience in desert travel.

Amr Shannon
(☎ 02-519 6894, ⓔ ashannon@internetegypt.com) Shannon is an artist who has been leading small groups through Egypt's deserts for more than 20 years. Famous in Egypt for his *Desert Stories* television programs, in which he tries to educate Nile Valley dwellers about the importance of conserving their unique desert environment, he leads groups of up to 12 people. He has three 4WDs and camping equipment, and can help with rental of extra vehicles if needed. He charges a flat rate of US$300 per day, so the more people you can gather together, the cheaper the rate per person. Food is extra.

Badawiyya
(☎ 02-345 8524, ⓔ badawya@link.com.eg) Although owner Saad and his brothers are from Farafra, they have also established an office in Cairo and they arrange highly recommended camel, jeep and walking treks throughout the Western Desert and other areas of Egypt.

Egyptian Desert Pioneers Society
(in Cairo ☎ 02-419 7268, fax 393 1440 , ⓔ desertsociety@link.net) A new Cairo-based non-government organisation of Egyptian desert lovers and safari enthusiasts, who are worried about

and serves chicken, kebab, vegetables and a few other small dishes, plus excellent, freshly squeezed lime juices and, if requested, beer.

Abu Mohammed Restaurant *(☎ 821 431, Sharia as-Sawra al-Khadra)* Dishes E£3-10. This restaurant has good and seemingly unending serves of soups, vegetables, rice, kebabs, salads, sweets and nonalcoholic beer all from a pristine kitchen.

Anwar Paradise Restaurant *(☎ 820 070, Sharia Basateen)* Dishes E£2-15. A popular cafe/restaurant that is below the hotel of the same name. Near the Gardens Hotel, Anwar Paradise serves up ta'amiyya and fuul, in addition to the more substantial chicken and rice combo, and is quite popular with locals.

Gardens Hotel Restaurant *(☎ 821 577 Sharia al-Genayen)* Dishes E£5-12. The Gardens serves a range of meat dishes, rice omelettes and salad, plus a very tasty mixed vegetable dish baked and served in an earthenware pot. Prices are low, but it's best to eat here in the evening when the head chef is around.

Mebarez Hotel Restaurant *(☎ 821 524 Sharia as-Sawra al-Khadra)* Breakfast E£5 lunch E£16, dinner E£20. This place serves similar food to the others but it is a slightly higher quality. Beer is also served.

Other places worth investigating are ***Shehab Restaurant*** and, next door, ***Al-Wad Fiteer Place***, where you can get a sweet fiteer (Egyptian pancake/pizza).

Desert Safaris

the damage being done to Egyptian deserts, has just been established. Its members can advise on safari operators, types of trips, flora and fauna, mechanics in far-flung locations and other useful information. Its Web site is under construction.

Khalifa Expedition

(☎ 011-802 542, ⓔ info@khalifa-exp.com) With well over a decade of experience, Khaled and Rose-Maria Khalifa run camel and jeep tours throughout the Western Desert out of their base in Bahariyya Oasis. They also offer 'meditation' tours for those more interested in communing with nature than looking at antiquities. There's a minimum of four people required.

Lama Expeditions

(☎ 49-69-447 897, fax 499 0767 in Frankfurt, Germany) Samir Lama is the undisputed king of the Western Desert explorers. Although he now lives in Germany he organises several long-range desert expeditions each year. Lasting from 15 to 21 days the trips head into the far south-west of Egypt and beyond into Sudan. Lama usually takes small groups of six to eight people but will take special groups of up to 12 people.

Getting There & Away

Air EgyptAir flies from Mut to Cairo every Sunday and Wednesday. A one-way ticket will cost you E£510. The airport is 10km south of Midan al-Gamaa on the road to Uwaynat.

Bus The services to Cairo (E£30 to E£40, eight to 10 hours) via Kharga Oasis (E£8) and Asyut (E£15) leave every day at 6am, 7pm and 9pm. You can also go to Cairo via Farafra Oasis (E£15) and Bahariyya Oasis at 6am for E£35.

Other buses to Asyut (E£15) via Al-Kharga (E£7) leave at 8.30am 5pm and 10pm daily. There is another bus to Farafra Oasis (E£15) at 6pm.

Service Taxi These leave from the station on Sharia as-Sawra al-Khadra, and cost E£7 to Al-Kharga and E£10 to either Farafra Oasis or Asyut. There are not many, so try in the morning. There are also microbuses to Farafra Oasis for E£8 and to Cairo for E£50.

Getting Around

Pick-Up Most of the small towns and villages are linked by pick-up, but working out where they all go can be difficult and they can be ridiculously crowded. Those heading to Al-Qasr (50pt) depart from near the police station. You can take pick-ups to Balat and Bashendi from in front of the hospital for E£1. It may prove easier on occasion to bargain for a 'special' pick-up.

WESTERN OASES

Bicycle Abu Mohammed Restaurant and Gardens Hotel rent out a few clattering bicycles for E£5.

FARAFRA OASIS

☎ 019

The main town of Farafra Oasis, the smallest oasis in the Western Desert, is Qasr al-Farafra. It's named after the town's fort of which little remains. As in the other old oasis towns, the villagers would retreat into the fort when they were attacked, and each family was assigned a room where they stored provisions. Although the town is linked by a 300km paved road to Mut (Dakhla Oasis) and another 185km stretch to Bahariyya Oasis, the 2900 people who live there are still quite isolated from most of the world. For better or for worse, that is starting to change as the population increases annually by about 1.8% and new constructions, in the New Valley breeze-block, four-storey mould, start to take shape.

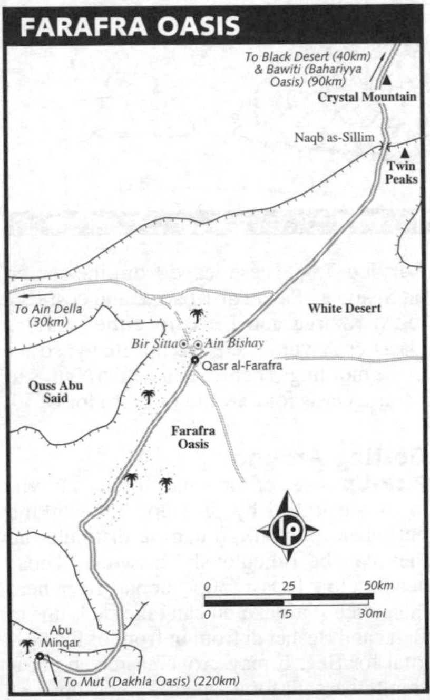

Many of the Farafrans are Bedouin, who still adhere to some of the age-old traditions of their culture. The small mud-brick houses of the town all have wooden doorways with medieval peg locks, and some of the walls are painted with verses of the Quran and murals of ships and planes – references to the haj (pilgrimage to Mecca) journeys of their inhabitants. The Bedouin women of Farafra produce beautifully embroidered dresses and shirts, although most of the work is for their own personal use and not for sale. Olives and olive oil are a speciality of the region, but the rich oasis also produces dates, figs, apricots, guavas, oranges, apples and sunflower seeds. Wheat and rice are the main crops.

There are more than 100 springs and wells around the oasis, many sunk in the mid-1960s as part of the government's program to attract outsiders to the region. Not all of the springs are open to travellers but there are some that can be visited.

The calm and simplicity of this place will enchant you, especially if you're coming from Cairo or Kharga. There's precious little to do but wander around town and its beautiful gardens, then head out into the desert.

Information

There is no tourist office as such but Farafra's mayor, Mohammed Rifaat, is an informed chap who can be of great assistance to travellers and often extends an invitation to his chambers at the town council. The nearby post office is open from 8.30am to 2.30pm Saturday to Thursday. The telephone centrale next door is open from 6am to noon daily for national calls only.

There is nowhere to change money here.

Badr's Museum

This museum *(admission free, donations appreciated)* is Farafra's only 'sight', and it's worth seeing. It has no set opening hours and is the showpiece of Badr, a very expressive artist who paints and sculpts not-so-subtle works of village people in daily life. His distinctive style has won him foreign admirers; he exhibited successfully in Europe in the early 1990s and later in Cairo. His museum's latest addition is a desert garden

Bir Sitta

A popular stop on most itineraries is Bir Sitta, or 'Well Number Six', a sulphurous hot spring just 6km north-west of Qasr al-Farafra. Hot water gushes from a pipe into a Jacuzzi-sized concrete pool and then spills out into a larger tank. This is a great place for a night-time soak under the stars, and you can also camp here, although the imminent opening of a hotel overlooking the spring may change the character of the place.

Ain Bishay

This roman spring bubbles forth on a hillock on the north-west edge of town. It has been developed into an irrigated grove of date palms together with citrus, olives, apricots and carob trees, and is a cool haven amid the arid landscape. Several families tend the crops here; you should seek someone out and ask permission before wandering around.

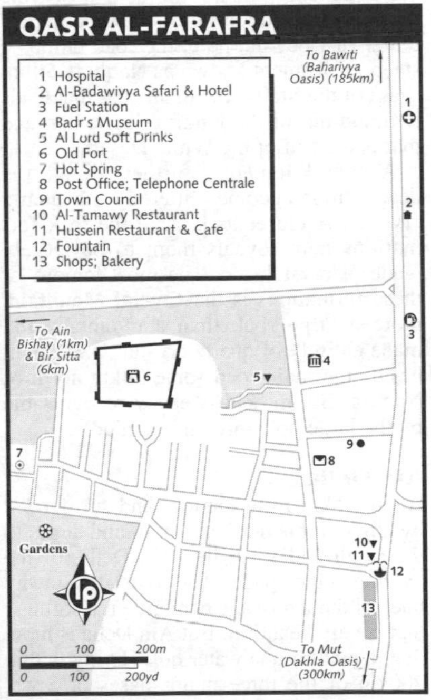

Places to Stay

For now you can ***camp*** at Bir Sitta, but it is frequently used and once the new hotel opens you may not be allowed. Ask in town before heading out there.

Al-Badawiyya Safari & Hotel *(in Cairo ☎ 345 8524, mobile 012-214 8343, e badawya@link.com.eg)* Beds in 4-bed room E£10, doubles E£15 per person, large doubles/triples with bath, sitting area & TV E£80/90. The tastefully designed mud-brick Al-Badawiyya Safari is one of the best hotels in the oases and is a nerve centre for travellers and campers passing through the Western Desert. Its rooms come in different styles and are spotlessly clean. It's popular with small safari groups as well as individual travellers, so you may need to reserve in advance. Breakfast costs between E£5 to E£8. Its owners, Saad Ali and his brothers, Hamdy and Atef – Farafrans of Bedouin origin – also lead camel and jeep trips into the Western Desert (see the boxed text 'Desert Safaris' earlier in this chapter).

Youth Rest House on the same road is for Egyptians only.

Places to Eat

The choice of where to eat is limited in Farafra. There are some shops and a bakery at the southern end of the main road and, surprisingly, a shop, ***Al Lord Soft Drinks***, in the old part of the town that sells beer.

Al-Tamawy Restaurant Dishes E£2-10. This is a cafe/restaurant on the main road that has basic food on offer along with the usual tea and coffee.

Hussein Dishes E£3-10. This is one of the only restaurants in town, but even here most of the pots are empty by 7pm, so come early. Make sure you check your bill – they've been known to overcharge.

Al-Badawiyya Safari & Hotel *(in Cairo ☎ 345 8524)* Dishes E£5-30. The food here is more expensive than the cafeterias, but is fresh and good. Choose from a plate of spaghetti (with fresh tomato sauce, not just the usual tomato paste) to a full chicken or meat meal. All vegetables are organic and grown on the hotel's own farm. It also serves beer and wine.

Shopping
'Mr Socks' is a local character who knits socks, scarves and other woollies out of camel hair. He and his wares can usually be found at the Al-Badawiyya Safari & Hotel, where camel- and sheep-hair rugs are also on sale.

Getting There & Away
There are buses from Farafra to Cairo (E£27, eight to 10 hours) via Bahariyya (E£10, 2½ hours) at 10am and 10pm. There are two buses a day from Farafra to Dakhla (E£15, four to five hours) – the first leaves between 1pm and 2pm and the other between 1am and 2am. The bus originates in Cairo so the times are approximate.

Buses stop at the Al-Tamawy Restaurant, the petrol station and at Al-Badawiyya. Tickets are bought from the conductor. As usual, you should check the latest schedules for all these buses.

Microbuses to Dakhla leave from in front of Al-Tamawy Restaurant whenever they have a full load. There's not a lot of traffic between the two oases, however, and you're better off going early in the morning. Sometimes you can hitch a ride from Farafra to Dakhla, but don't count on this.

FARAFRA TO BAHARIYYA OASIS
The desert between the Farafra and Bahariyya Oases offers some of the most varied and amazing terrain in the Western Desert. From the snow-like ergs of the White Desert to the Black Desert's eerie black cones, the landscape never disappoints. Because the major sights are relatively easy to access the area is a favourite destination for safari outfits in Qasr al-Farafra and Bawiti.

White Desert
The White Desert (Sahra al-Beida) is an otherworldly region of blindingly white rock formations shaped by wind erosion. Beginning about 20km north-east of Farafra you can see the first formations on the east side of the road. As you approach the white outcroppings they take on surreal forms – you can make out ostriches, camels, hawks and other bizarre shapes. In a country with fewer natural and man-made sights, these would be a national monument on a par with the Grand Canyon in the USA. They are best viewed at sunrise or sunset, when the sun turns the white into chalk pink and orange – rather like a Salvador Dali painting – or under a full moon, which gives the landscape an eerie arctic appearance. The sand around the outcroppings is littered with quartz and different varieties of deep black iron pyrites, as well as thousands of small fossils.

On the other side of the road, away from the wind-eroded shapes, there are small canyons formed by white, clifflike chalk monoliths called inselbergs. Less dramatic than the odd shapes in other areas, they are nevertheless beautiful and eerie to walk around. The shade and privacy they provide also makes them good camping spots.

About 50km north of here, on the south-east side of the road are two flat-topped mountains known as the **Twin Peaks**. Prominent landmarks in Farafra, they are surrounded by small rounded, bowl-like hills and are a favourite destination of local tours. Just beyond here, the road climbs a steep escarpment known as **Naqb as-Sillim** (Pass of the Stairs) the main pass that leads into and out of the Farafra depression and marks the end of the White Desert.

A few kilometres further along, the desert floor becomes littered with quartz crystals. A closer look at all the rock formations here reveals them to be largely made of crystal, too. The most famous of these formations is the **Crystal Mountain**, more a large rock than a mountain and made entirely of quartz crystal. It sits right beside the main road some 24km north of Naqb as-Sillim, and is easily recognisable by the large hole through its middle.

Ain Della
About 75km from Farafra, and surrounded by cliffs on the north and east, and dunes to the south and west, lies Ain Della, or the 'Spring of the Shade'. The contrasting tawny hues of the landscape here give it a softness that is very beautiful. But Ain Della is more than a picturesque water hole. Lying within 200km of the three major oases of Siwa,

Bahariyya and Farafra, it has been a strategic and extremely important source of water for desert travellers since ancient times. Most famously, the lost army of Cambyses is thought by many to have disappeared in the dunes near here on its ill-fated journey to destroy the Temple of the Oracle in Siwa Oasis. (For more information see Aghurmi under Siwa Oasis later in this chapter.) During WWII, the British Army's Long Range Desert Group stored fuel and supplies here and used it as a jumping off place for their raids behind German and Italian lines.

Ain Della's position is still considered vital to controlling vast swathes of the Western Desert: It is from here that the Egyptian army patrols search the desert for drugs and arms smugglers. As a result, anyone coming here *must* have a military permit (obtained through desert guides; see the boxed text 'Desert Safaris' earlier in this chapter).

Black Desert

About 50km south of Bawiti, the desert floor turns from beige to black. This is the beginning of the Black Desert, formed over the millennia as wind eroded the mountains and spread a fine black powder over the ground. It ends with small black, volcano-shaped mountains, part of a fault that runs through Bahariyya Oasis. The Black Desert is a favourite off-road destination for tours out of Bahariyya as there are a number of sights here. **Gebel Gala Siwa** is a pyramid-shaped mountain that was a lookout post for caravans coming from Siwa. **Gebel az-Zuqaq** is a mountain known for the red, yellow and orange streaks in its limestone base. An easily climbed path leads to the top. About 10km south of Bawiti is the domed **Tomb of René Michel**, a Swiss man who retired to Bahariyya in 1981 and was the first to take tourists on safaris in the surrounding desert. He died in 1986.

Getting There & Away

Regular vehicles can drive the first kilometre or so off the road and into the White or Black Deserts, but only 4WD vehicles can advance deeper into the area. Some travellers simply get off the bus and take themselves off into the White Desert – but be sure to have adequate supplies, and remember that traffic either way is not very heavy. Venturing to Ain Della is more of an expedition, and needs a guide and permits.

There are plenty of safari outfits that can take you through these sights. Al-Badawiyya Safari & Hotel (see Places to Stay under Farafra Oasis earlier in this chapter) is one of the best outfits in the Western Desert. The three Bedouin brothers who run it have years of experience in desert travel and offer short- and long-range trips by camel or 4WD. For more local safari operators, see Organised Tours under Bahariyya Oasis, or the boxed text 'Desert Safaris' earlier in this chapter.

BAHARIYYA OASIS

☎ 011

Bahariyya Oasis is situated in a 2000-sq-km depression about 330km south-west of Cairo. Although a major agricultural centre

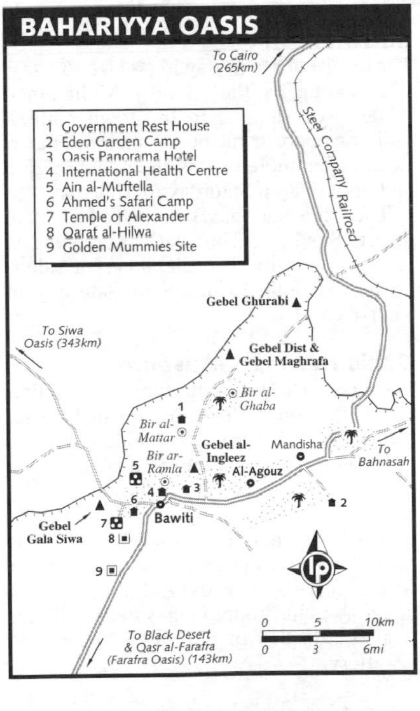

as far back as the Middle Kingdom, most of the ancient monuments around here date from New Kingdom to Roman times. None of the main ancient trade routes passed through the oasis, but it was prosperous until the 4th century AD, when attacks from marauding tribes and the decline of Roman rule left much of its once-rich agricultural land to be reclaimed by the surrounding desert.

Nowadays the Bahariyya is part of the Giza Governorate, unlike the oases to the south, and is linked to both Cairo and Qasr al-Farafra by paved roads across the desert. There is also a road to Siwa.

There are several little villages spread throughout the oasis, but the main one, with a population of about 30,000, is Bawiti. The main street of the town has got the same squat modern buildings as the rest of the oases but a walk in almost any direction will lead you to the more traditional mud-brick houses in which many of the inhabitants still live.

Information

The tourist office in Bawiti (☎ 802 167, 803 035) is run by the friendly Muhammed Abdel Ader and is in the town council building opposite the police station. The office is open more or less from 8am to 2pm and 5pm to 8pm Saturday to Thursday.

There is a National Bank, open from 8am to 2pm Sunday to Thursday, where you can change cash only. The telephone centrale is open from 8am to midnight Saturday to Thursday.

Oasis Heritage Museum

The Oasis Heritage Museum is a smaller, newer version of the museum in Farafra, and is about 1km from the police station on the road to Cairo. Set up in a small house by a young artist called Mahmoud Eed, it features unbaked clay figurines set in scenes from traditional village life, such as men playing *siga* (a game played in the dirt with clay balls or seeds) and a man crying in agony as his injured leg is treated. There is also a display of old oasis dresses and jewellery.

Hot & Cold Springs

The closest springs to central Bawiti are the so-called Roman springs, known as **Al-Beshmo**, about a 10-minute walk from the Popular Restaurant. The view over the oasis gardens and the desert beyond is wonderful, but the spring is not suitable for swimming. An equally useless place for swimming is **Bir al-Muftella**, about 3km from the centre of town. It's an interesting walk out through the town, but don't go for the water alone. Take the Siwa road and keep asking. If you pass a big, white conical structure (a sheikh's tomb) on your right, you will know you're on the right track.

The hot sulphurous spring of **Bir ar-Ramla** is OK if you're into scalding (45°C) baths, but you may feel a bit exposed to the donkey traffic passing to and fro. Women especially should think twice and stay well covered. It's about a 3km walk north from the centre of the town.

The best spot is **Bir al-Ghaba**, about 15km north-east of Bawiti. There is nothing quite like a moonlit hot bath on the edge of the desert. The Alpenblick Hotel (see under Places to Eat later) runs a rudimentary camp site there, so you can often arrange with them to go there for a bath, or you may prefer to just stay in the camp for a couple of days. Be sure to bring supplies with you, though, as there's nothing there.

At **Bir al-Mattar**, 7km north-east of Bawiti, cold springs pour into a viaduct and then down into a concrete pool where you can splash around.

Antiquities

Since the discovery of the 'golden mummies' (see the boxed text 'Mummies of Gold') interest has grown in Bahariyya's ancient past. In addition to the gilded mummies in the antiquities inspectorate, which serves as a museum for the mummies, a small number of sites have been opened to the public. All can be visited with one ticket (E£30), which is sold at the antiquities inspectorate (open from 8.30am to 2pm daily). Apart from admitting you to see the 'golden mummies', the ticket allows you to visit the following sights.

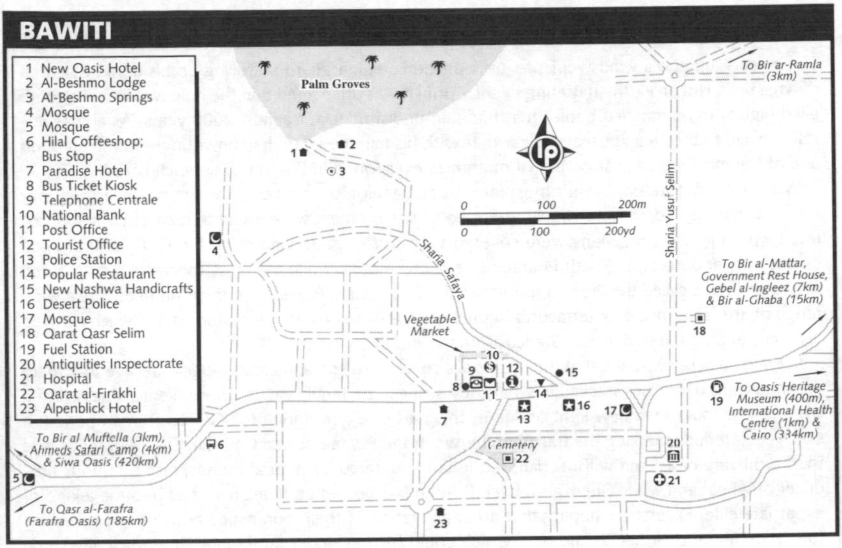

Qarat Qasr Salim This small mound amid the houses of Bawiti, is likely to have been built upon the debris of centuries. There are two 26th-dynasty tombs here. Both were robbed in antiquity and reused as collective burial sites in Roman times. The **Tomb of Zed-Amunerankh** is currently closed but there are plans to open it in the near future. The **Tomb of Bannentiu**, his son, is open. Consisting of a four-columned burial chamber with an inner sanctuary, it is covered in fine but faded reliefs depicting Bannentiu in various positions with the gods. The most interesting pictures flank the entrance to the burial chamber. On one side, the journey of the moon is shown, with the moon, in the form of the god Khons, depicted as a source of life and is flanked by goddesses Isis and Nephthys. On the other side of the entrance, the journey of the sun is shown.

Temple of Alexander South-west of Bawiti, just beyond Ahmed's Safari Camp, is the only place in Egypt where Alexander the Great's image and cartouche have been found (although since they were uncovered by archaeologists in the late 1930s they have been worn away by the wind). As Alexander is not known to have passed through Bahariyya, despite its link to Siwa, the representation puzzles archaeologists. Victim of an appalling restoration in recent years, in addition to the corrosive desert winds, the temple is in a sorry state and gives few clues as to its origins.

Chapels of Ain al-Muftella Slightly south of the spring here are four 26th-dynasty chapels that are unusual because they don't conform to any known temple plan. All have been extensively restored and have been given wooden roofs to protect them from the elements. The walls are patchily covered with reliefs, including some depicting the dwarf god Bes, usually protector of childbirth and the home, but sometimes also the patron of musicians and dancers.

Qarat al-Hilwa This sandstone ridge is about 3km south of Bawiti, north-west of the road to Farafra. In the New Kingdom, this was a necropolis, a burial place of successive governors who, as representatives of the pharaoh, were the most powerful figures in the oasis. The 18th- or 19th-

Mummies of Gold

Three years ago, on a windswept site just outside Bawiti, a guard patrolling on his donkey slipped down a hole. Not an earth-shattering event – until it was discovered that the hole was in fact a tomb piled high with mummified bodies that had lain undisturbed for almost 2000 years. As archaeologists rushed to the area, it became clear that with his fall, the guard had unwittingly stumbled upon one of the most spectacular caches of mummies ever found in this antiquities-rich country.

When Dr Zahi Hawass, Egypt's most famous archaeologist, excavated the site he unearthed four kinds of mummy. Some were simply wrapped in linen, others were inside terracotta coffins decorated with human faces. Many were covered with *cartonage* (a kind of pasteboard made of linen or papyrus) and decorated with Pharaonic religious motifs, while the most spectacular had gilded masks and were called the 'golden mummies' by Dr Hawass. Buried with the mummies was a wide range of artefacts, including terracotta figures of Egyptian gods, jewellery and coins (which allowed his team to date the find to the Graeco-Roman period).

Surveys have since shown that the necropolis covers 6 sq km, and archaeologists believe that there are thousands of corpses stacked in what they suspect are family vaults. These silent witnesses of a bygone age could shed new light on life in this part of Egypt during the Graeco-Roman period, a 600-year interlude marking the transition between the Pharaonic and Christian eras. Bahariyya was then a thriving oasis, and with its rich, fertile land, watered by natural springs, was a famous producer of wheat and wine. Greek and, later, Roman families set up home here and became a kind of expatriate elite. Experts are hoping that an examination of their mummified remains will reveal information about their health and diet, which could help us understand more about daily life some 2000 years ago.

dynasty **Tomb of Amenhotep** is the only inscribed tomb left in the necropolis and, as the oldest tomb found in the oasis, is an important source of information about Bahariyya's ancient past. Unfortunately, the reliefs here have faded but you can see traditional burial scenes, with the governor Amenhotep making offerings to the gods. On the eastern wall are scenes showing corn and wine being gathered for tribute to the pharaoh.

Qarat al-Firakhi This hill, translated as 'Ridge of the Chicken Merchant', features several underground galleries containing signs of ibis burials. Ibis were sacred birds and their mummified bodies were used as offerings to the gods, similar to the way that Christians today place candles in churches. Check with the tourist office to make sure the site is open.

Other Sights Around Bahariyya Oasis

There are a number of other sights around Bahariyya that are included as part of a tour by the many 'safari' operators in town. Most can also be done on foot if the weather is cool. **Gebel Mandisha** is a ridge capped with black dolorite and basalt that runs for 4km behind the village of the same name just west of Bawiti.

Clearly visible from the road to Cairo is **Gebel al-Ingleez**, also known as the Black Mountain in English. It's a flat-topped hill with the remains of a WWI castle built by a British officer named Captain Williams to monitor the movements of Libyan Senussi tribesmen. To get here, go out along the road to Cairo and turn off onto the track heading to Bir al-Ghaba and the Government Rest House at Bir al-Mattar. Keep the mountain in sight and follow village tracks out to it. The walk takes about an hour.

Also near Bir al-Ghaba, **Gebel Dist** is a pyramid-shaped mountain that can be seen from most of the oasis. Called the Magic Mountain by many of the locals because of the way the light plays on the surface, it is a local landmark and is famous for its fossils. Dinosaur bones were found here in the early part of the 20th century, disproving the previously held theory that dinosaurs only lived in North America. Palaeontologists continue to dig here. About 100m away is **Gebel Maghrafa**, or the 'Mountain of the Ladle'.

Organised Tours

There is fierce competition among the few hotels in town to arrange desert trips, but somehow everyone charges more or less the same price – the big distinction is whether or not you stay near the asphalt road. A trek in a 4WD with one night and two days in the White Desert is E£350, with a maximum of four people, if you stay on or near the road. This rises to E£800 or E£900 for three days and two nights off-road, including food, blankets and tents. Most of the operators in town also offer three- or four-day trips to Siwa for about E£700 for a maximum of four people, but this does not necessarily include camping in the desert. Badri at the New Nashwa Handicrafts (☎ 802 276) is one of the more reliable guides. Others include Lutfi Abd al-Sayed (☎ 802 092), whose English is limited but who knows the area well and is equipped to do longer trips, and Red Abd al-Razzoul (☎ 802 934), a geography and history teacher. Whoever you pick, ensure that you see the car before you head out into the sand and check that you have adequate water in case of a breakdown. For other safari information, see the boxed text 'Desert Safaris' earlier in this chapter.

Places to Stay

Government Rest House *(☎ 802 600)* Beds E£5. This place is very basic and in need of renovation. It's 7km out of town near Bir al-Mattar. Ask at the tourist office or the Paradise Hotel. The price includes transport.

Paradise Hotel *(☎ 802 600, Bawiti)* Beds E£5. This small hotel behind a lush garden in the centre of town has six clean rooms, each with three beds. Breakfast on the small vine-covered terrace is an extra E£2.

Ahmed's Safari Camp *(☎/fax 802 090)* Doubles with breakfast & bath E£12.50 per person, newer rooms with breakfast & bath E£25 per person, rooms with shared bathroom E£5 per person, reed huts E£4 per person, roof E£3 per person. About 4km west of the centre, Ahmed's has become a bit of a favourite among travellers and trans-Africa groups. There are cool, pleasant, domed double rooms or basic ones; you can sleep under the stars on the roof or in two large new rooms with vaults and full bathrooms. Basic meals and beer are available. If you can't get a lift and want to walk, take the Siwa fork and keep asking your way there. Alternatively, you could try to rent a bike from the New Nashwa Handicrafts shop in town for E£10 per day (see under Shopping later).

Eden Garden Camp *(☎ 802 345)* Rooms without/with breakfast E£15/20 per person. Eden is a new camp, with eight conical reed huts and 10 more under construction in the desert about 3km off the road to Cairo, to the south east of Bawiti. With clean shared bathrooms, a 'pool' of mineral water from a nearby spring and an outdoor fire pit for the evenings, it's a good option if you want to relax in peaceful surroundings.

Alpenblick Hotel *(☎ 802 184, Bawiti)* Doubles without/with bath E£35/46, budget rooms E£17, huts E£10. This is a relatively attractive two-storey place with a variety of clean rooms; breakfast is included in the price of the double rooms and costs an extra E£5 if staying in the budget rooms. The hotel also has 15 huts with mattresses out at Bir al-Ghaba. The enclosure is watched by a warden, who will also help out with tea and firewood. It is very peaceful, and you must bring your own food.

Al-Beshmo Lodge *(☎/fax 802 177, Bawiti)* Singles/doubles US$28/32. Beside the Al-Beshmo springs, this hotel has 20 comfortable rooms, some with air-con, and the price includes a buffet breakfast. The shared bathrooms are big and spotless and there is also a cafe just outside the hotel entrance.

New Oasis Hotel *(☎/fax 803 030, Bawiti)* Singles/doubles B&B E£25/50. This new 22-room hotel on the edge of the date palms, near the Al-Beshmo springs, is comfortable but not as good as Al-Beshmo Lodge.

Oasis Panorama Hotel *(☎ 802 894, Bawiti)* Doubles/triples B&B E£75/105. This newly built hotel on the main road to Cairo has tacky decor but its rooms are clean and comfortable, with fans and phones.

International Health Centre *(☎ 802 322)* Singles/doubles US$45/70. About 1km outside town on the road to Cairo, this German-run three-star spa resort has forgettable architecture. It has 27 rooms and eight chalets built around a hot spring. As well as a deep pool of therapeutic spring water there's a gym, sauna and restaurant.

Places to Eat

Other than the Popular Restaurant, the only alternatives are the hotels or to make your own meals. There are several grocery stores where you can pick up supplies for a few nights out in the desert.

Popular Restaurant *(☎ 802 322)* Dishes E£5-15. Just off the main road in Bawiti, this mall roadside restaurant, also known as Bayoumi's, serves a selection of dishes such as chicken, soup, rice and vegetables. It's open for breakfast.

Shopping

New Nashwa Handicrafts *(☎ 802 276, Sharia Safaya, Bawiti)* Opposite the Popular Restaurant off the main road, this shop sells white camel-hair blankets for about E£100, as well as camel-hair woollies and rugs. Badri, the owner, also rents bicycles for E£10 per day.

Getting There & Away

Bus There are four daily buses to Cairo (E£12.50) at 7am, noon, 3pm and between midnight and 1am. The 7am and 3pm buses originate at the ticket kiosk (in front of the telephone centrale) in Bawiti and the others come from Dakhla and Farafra and stop at the Hilal Coffeeshop at the western end of town, as well as at the ticket kiosk.

Heading to Farafra (E£15) you can pick up one of the buses from Cairo that are supposed to leave Bahariyya at 11.30am, 1pm and 7.30pm. Passengers are usually dropped off at the Popular Restaurant before the bus continues down the street to one of the coffeehouses at the western end of town, where it stops for about 30 minutes.

Note that only some bus tickets can be booked from the Bawiti ticket kiosk. As most of the buses don't originate here, you either have to book in Cairo or take your chances on standing. Ticket office opening hours are erratic – try from 9am to 1pm or after the evening prayer until about 11pm. The tourist office will also have up-to-date schedule information.

Service Taxi Supposedly, there's always a service taxi going to Sayyida Zeinab in Cairo between 3pm and 4pm, but this could be earlier or later and not every day. Ask at Popular Restaurant. A service taxi to Farafra (and they're not very frequent) will also cost E£11. Microbuses to either place cost about the same but are more frequent. They can be caught opposite the desert police station or, again, ask at Popular Restaurant.

If you want to get a taxi to Siwa, expect to pay at least E£550.

SIWA OASIS

The lush and productive Western Desert oasis of Siwa, famous throughout the country for its dates and olives, is 305km south-west of Marsa Matruh and 550km west of Cairo, near the Libyan border. It is 12m below sea level in a depression (ranging from 9 to 28km in width) that stretches for 80km.

The Siwa Oasis is undoubtedly one of the most picturesque and idyllic places in Egypt. Against the awesome backdrop of eroded hills and a sea of sand dunes, Siwa appears like the proverbial mirage. It's a wealth of green date palms shading mud-brick villages that are connected by streams and springs and irrigated gardens.

Siwa is situated on the ancient date caravan route via Qara, Qattara and Kerdassa (near Cairo) that ended at Memphis. However, for centuries, few outsiders ventured to Siwa, apart from the desert caravans of ancient times or the occasional pilgrim who journeyed there to visit the famed **Temple of Amun**. Although Islam and Arabic did eventually reach this far into the desert, Siwa's solitary location had until recently allowed the predominantly Berber-speaking inhabitants to preserve many of their ancient traditions and customs, including their own language, which is still spoken.

That is all changing now, and some observers feel the onslaught of the Egyptian state and tourists will all but wipe out this unique place. The road linking the oasis to Marsa Matruh has now been joined by another road linking the Siwa Oasis to the Bahariyya Oasis, to the south-east. What started as a trickle of travellers venturing down the new road from Marsa Matruh is becoming a flood. Even tour buses find their way down there now.

The least visitors can do to help preserve Siwa's culture is to respect local sensibilities and act accordingly – do not bring alcohol to the oasis or, as the tourist office puts it, show 'displays of affection' in public. Modest dress is also required. Women travellers should make sure they cover their upper arms and their legs, and should wear more than just bathing suits to dip in the numerous springs. Otherwise, they will find themselves feeling very out of place.

Life for Siwan women is very secluded. Siwan girls are often married by the time they're 17, after which they may speak to male members of their immediate family only. In public, Siwan women must wear a demure blue/grey shawl, known as a *tarfodit*, which totally covers their face and upper body.

History

Siwa's original Berber settlers were attracted to this island of green in a desolate sea of sand many centuries ago, when they discovered several freshwater springs in the area.

The most illustrious of Siwa's early visitors was the young conqueror Alexander, who led a small party on an eight-day trek through the desert in 331 BC to seek out the oracle of the Temple of Amun. Alexander's goal, which he apparently attained, was to seek confirmation that he was the son of Zeus, and also to uphold the traditional belief that, as the new pharaoh of Egypt, he was also the son of Amun.

Apart from a Greek traveller who visited in AD 160, the people of Siwa did not see another European until 1792, when several

SIWA OASIS

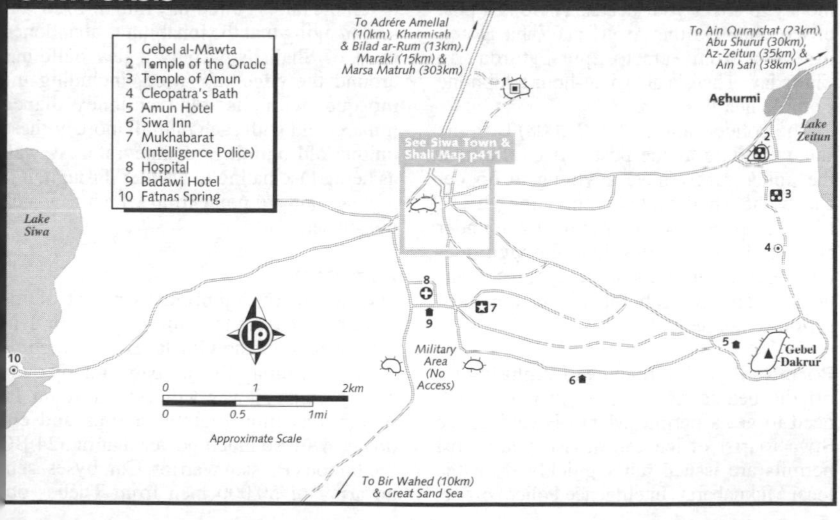

Europeans narrowly escaped with their lives after trying to visit Siwa. The Siwans thus gained a reputation of being fiercely independent and hostile to non-Muslim outsiders. Throughout the 19th century, the Egyptian government also had problems trying to gain the loyalty of the oasis. Then in WWII, the British and Italian/German forces chased each other in and out of Siwa and Jaghbub, 120km west in Libya, until Rommel decided not to bother with it any more. By then the Siwans were fully incorporated into Egypt, but the oasis remained isolated until the asphalt road connected it to Marsa Matruh in the 1980s. As a result, Siwans still speak their own distinct Berber dialect and have a local culture separate from that of the rest of Egypt.

Information

The tourist office (☎ 460 2883) is across from the Arous al-Waha Hotel. The very helpful and knowledgable Mahdi Hweiti can help arrange trips to some of the surrounding villages. The office is generally open from 8am to 2pm Saturday to Thursday. Mahdi can also be reached at home (☎ 460 2130).

There is no bank in Siwa, so bring enough money to cover your needs. There is a post office opposite the Arous al-Waha Hotel; it's open from 8am to 2pm Saturday to Thursday. There's also a 24-hour telephone centrale nearby.

The police station (☎ 460 2008) is in the same building as the post office, although the police rarely have anything to do because the sheikhs from the nine Siwan tribes keep law and order in the town under control. There is a hospital, although doctors are rarely in residence and most Siwans go to Marsa Matruh for all but the most serious emergencies.

Permits If you're thinking of venturing far off the beaten track from Siwa, you will need to get a permit. Mahdi Hweiti at the Siwa tourist office can advise you. Most permits are issued fairly quickly from the local Mukhabarat (Intelligence Police) office. You'll need one photo and your passport, plus a photocopy.

Siwa Town

Siwa is a pleasant, sleepy little town consisting of little more than a market surrounding the main square, with roads leading off into the palm groves. The few sights are near the centre of the town. Around the corner from the local council offices is the small **House of Siwa Museum** *(admission E£1.50; open 10am-noon Sat-Thur)*, which contains a modest display of traditional clothing, implements and so on. It was inspired by a Canadian diplomat who feared the disappearance of Siwan culture and its mud-brick houses would occur in a flood of concrete and modernity. You can also arrange to see the museum through the tourist office.

The centre of the town is dominated by the mud-brick remains of the 13th-century fortress enclave of **Shali**. Built from a material known locally as *kershef*, large chunks of salt mixed with rock and plastered in local clay, the labyrinthine buildings originally rose up to four or five storeys and housed hundreds of people. For centuries, few outsiders were admitted inside – and even fewer came back out again to tell the tale. A three-day rain in 1926 was so damaging that the inhabitants abandoned most of Shali. Now only a few buildings around the edges are used, including the mosque with its old, chimney-shaped minaret and with each rainfall more of these unique old buildings disintegrate. As well as being fascinating to wander through, it is a great vantage point from which to watch the sunset.

Aghurmi

On the hill of Aghurmi, 4km east of the town of Siwa, are the ruins of the 26th dynasty **Temple of the Oracle**. Built sometime in the 6th century BC, probably on top of an earlier temple, it was dedicated to Amun. Its oracle was immediately famous and endowed with so much power that in 524 BC the famous Persian warrior, Cambyses, sent an army of 50,000 men from Thebes ou

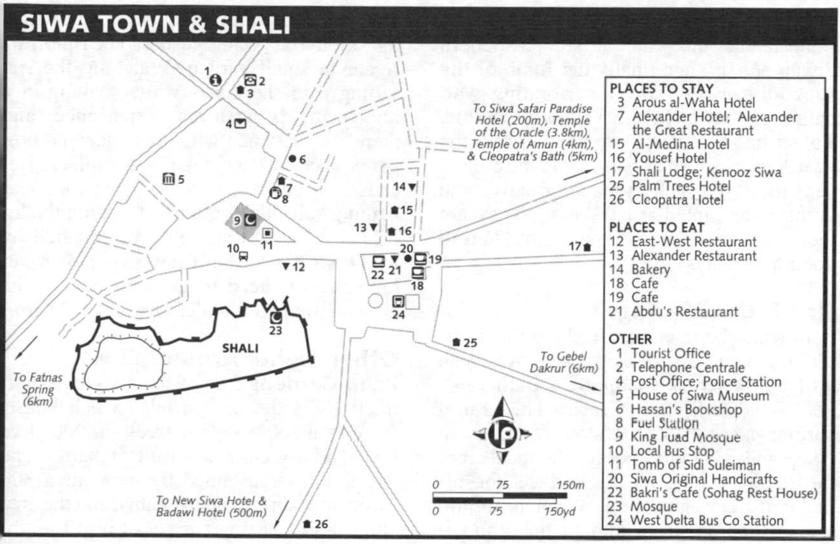

into the desert to destroy it. The legendary army never arrived at its destination and was lost to the sands of the desert somewhere between Kharga and Siwa. A couple of centuries later Alexander the Great made his perilous desert journey specifically to consult with the oracle. Satisfied with its answer (it conveniently confirmed his own assertions that he was a god), he is then thought to have returned to the Mediterranean and continued his conquering campaigns throughout the region.

Today the Temple of the Oracle sits in the north-west corner of the ruins of Aghurmi village (look for the signs). It is in bad shape, and was the victim of a poor restoration in the middle of the last century, but the ruined village around it is evocative and worth a clamber through. It also affords stunning views of the surrounding oasis.

About 200m further along the track is the almost totally ruined **Temple of Amun** (also known as the Temple of Umm Ubaydah). All that's left standing is part of a wall covered with inscriptions, thanks to an Ottoman governor who blew up the temple in 1896 to get building material. However, thanks to earlier drawings, historians have learned that the original structure was built by Nectanebo during the 30th dynasty.

Gebel al-Mawta

Gebel al-Mawta means 'Mountain of the Dead' and this small hill at the northern end of town is honeycombed with rock tombs, most dating back to Ptolemaic and Roman times. Only 1km from the centre of town, the tombs were used by the Siwans as shelters when the Italians bombed the oasis in WWII. Many new tombs were discovered at this time but were not properly excavated. In his book on Siwa, Ahmed Fakhry recalls British soldiers paying Siwan families a few piastres to cut away large chunks of the tomb paintings to keep as souvenirs.

Despite the damage, there are still some tomb paintings left. The best are in the **Tomb of Si Amun**, where beautifully coloured reliefs portray the dead man, thought to be a wealthy Greek landowner or merchant, making offerings and praying to Egyptian gods. Also interesting are: the unfinished **Tomb of Mesu-Isis**, which contains a mummified skull, although not of its original inhabitant; the **Tomb of Niperpathot**, with inscriptions and crude drawings in the same reddish ink you can see on modern Siwan pottery; and finally the **Tomb of the Crocodile**, with badly deteriorating wall paintings that include a yellow crocodile. To get into the tombs you need to find the guardians. As well as possessing the crucial keys they are usually very informative and deserve the hinted-at baksheesh. They are there between 7am and 2pm daily (7am to noon on Fridays).

Hot & Cold Springs

Following the track that leads to the Temple of Amun through the palm groves, you will come across **Cleopatra's Bath** (also known as the Spring of Juba). The natural spring water pours into a stone pool, which is a popular bathing spot for the locals, but the scum floating on the surface doesn't make it very appealing. Women should think twice about swimming here, and if they decide to risk the stares then they should only bathe with their clothes on. At the time of writing Abdu Restaurant was building changing rooms and a sitting area beside the pool and they've also promised to clean the water.

There's a similar, but more pleasant and secluded pool at **Fatnas Spring** (sometimes called Fantasy Island), an oasis ringed by the saltwater Lake Siwa, which is accessible across a narrow causeway. The pool, about 6km from Siwa town, is in an idyllic setting amid palm trees and lush greenery. Although it is a safer place for a swim than Cleopatra's Bath, women going alone should be wary and, again, should leave their bikinis for the beach. There's a small cafe among the palms, and sitting and puffing on a *sheesha* (water pipe) or sipping tea and watching the sun set over the lake is one of Siwa's magical experiences. To get there go past the council building and take the road to the left at the first fork. Follow it around the base of Shali – at the next intersection of possible confusion a sign points the way.

Bir Wahed is a hot spring out in the dunes on the edge of the Great Sand Sea. A favourite excursion of local guides, there is a tub the size of a large jacuzzi into which the sulphurous water gushes. The runoff irrigates a small garden. Watching the sun setting over the dunes while soaking in a hot spring is a surreal experience, and there's a custodian who brews tea and prepares sheeshas to make it complete. Because it's far from town, women can wear bathing suits here without offending the locals. Bir Wahed can only be reached by 4WD, so if you don't have your own vehicle, you'll need to go with one of the guides listed later under Organised Tours.

Other Sights Around Siwa

Palm Gardens One of Siwa's greatest attractions is the oasis itself, which boasts more than 300,000 palm trees, 70,000 olive trees and a great many fruit orchards. The vegetation is sustained by more than 300 freshwater springs and streams, and the area attracts an amazing variety of bird life, including quails and falcons.

Gebel Dakrur About 4km from town, this mountain is a popular place with rheumatism sufferers. From July to September people flock here to be plopped into a bath of very hot sand for 20 minutes at a time, and then extracted and given hot tea. Three days of this, local guides say, and no more rheumatism. The mountain also supplies the oasis with the reddish-brown pigment used to decorate Siwan pottery.

Outlying Villages There are a few interesting villages to the north-west of the main town of Siwa. **Kharmisah** and **Bilad ar-Rum** (City of the Romans) are 15km from town and can be reached by local bus. They are Berber villages, and the latter has about 100 tombs cut into the rock of the nearby hills.

About 2km west of these villages is **Maraki**, where a Greek archaeologist claimed in 1995 to have found the tomb of Alexander the Great. She was proven wrong, however, and the site remains off limits.

To the east of Siwa are some more springs. **Ain Qurayshat** is 27km out from the town and **Abu Shuruf**, said by locals to be the biggest and cleanest spring in the oasis, is 7km further east from Ain Qurayshat at the next palm thicket. The clear water here is about 3m deep and spills into Lake Zeitun, another huge saltwater lake. Another 5km brings you to **Az-Zeitun**, an abandoned mud-brick village, beaten by the sand and wind, which sits alone on the sandy plain. Hundreds of Roman-era tombs have been discovered about 2km beyond Az-Zeitun and are currently under excavation, although little of interest has been found.

From Az-Zeitun, another 3km brings you to **Ain Safi**, the last human vestige before the overwhelming wall of desert dunes that stretch for hundreds of kilometres, all the way south to the Kharga Oasis. Some 30 Bedouin families live at Ain Safi.

To visit the sights east of Siwa you'll need your own sturdy vehicle. Mahdi Hweiti from the tourist office, and every restaurant and hotel in town, organises trips.

Organised Tours

Every restaurant and hotel in Siwa offers tours ranging from half a day in the desert around Siwa, to a full five- or six-day safari. The tourist office can be a great help in organising trips around the oasis. Abdallah Baghi at the Siwa Original Handicrafts shop is also very helpful. Almost all desert trips require permits, which cost E£10.50 and are usually obtained by your guide. Prices and itineraries vary, but one of the most common day trips takes you to the desert hot spring at Bir Wahed at the edge of the Great Sand Sea. Here you can have a simple meal or tea, then move on to the nearby springfed lake, where you can take a dip in the summer. Usually you will do a spot of dune driving, stop at fossil sites and see some fantastic desert vistas before returning to Siwa. This day trip costs about E£50. Abu Bakr at the East-West Restaurant and Salah at the Alexander the Great Restaurant also do similar tours at competitive prices.

There are no camels in Siwa so all trips are done by 4WD. As with any desert trip, ensure you have enough water and that the vehicle is roadworthy before you set out.

Special Events

Gebel Dakrur is the scene of the annual Siyaha festival. For three days around the October full moon, thousands of Siwans gather to celebrate friendship and togetherness, presumably burying all the hatchets that they may have taken up in the previous year. All Siwans, no matter what their financial or social standing, eat together at a huge feast after the noon prayer each day during the festival. The festival is intertwined with Sufism, and each evening, hundreds of men form a circle and join together in a *zikr*, a long session of dancing, swaying and singing repetitive songs in praise of God. Siwan women do not attend the festivities, although girls up to about the age of 12 are present until sunset. Each year hundreds of non-Siwans, Egyptians and foreigners attend the festival.

Once a year, just after the corn harvest, the small tomb shrine of Sidi Suleiman, behind the King Fuad mosque in the centre of town, is the scene of a *moulid* (religious festival), known in Siwi as the Moulid en Tagmigra. Banners announce the moulid and zikrs are performed outside the tomb.

Occasionally on Thursday nights, after the evening prayer, local sufis of the Arusiya order gather near the tomb for a zikr and they don't mind the odd foreigner watching.

Places to Stay

Camping As with most places in Egypt since the Luxor massacre, the police here are jittery about people camping out. However, you can go to the **Amun Hotel** on Gebel Dakrur and ask if you can pitch your tent in the hotel grounds. You can also check with the tourist office to see if things have loosened up.

Hotels Siwa's hotel selection is growing slowly but steadily, which means the choice of accommodation is better than in the other oases. Stiff competition among the cheaper options means that the standard of budget hotels is higher here, too. Hotels offering half board include breakfast and dinner in the price; those with full board include breakfast, lunch and dinner.

Yousef Hotel *(☎ 460 2162, Siwa Town)* Beds E£5. In close competition with the Palm Trees Hotel, Yousef Hotel is in the town centre. Some of the rooms here really are tiny, but everything is clean, the beds are comfortable and the showers steaming with hot water. The owner is very helpful and, like everyone else, rents bikes for E£8 to E£10 per day.

Badawi Hotel Beds E£5. This place, 1km from Siwa Town, opens only when everything else is full. Its no-frills rooms have fans. Couples wanting to stay here must be able to show their marriage certificate.

Al-Medina Hotel *(Siwa Town)* Beds E£5. Next door to Yousef Hotel is the oasis' longtime hotel. It's considerably more grotty than its neighbour. Both places are close to mosques.

Amun Hotel *(Gebel Dakrur)* Beds E£5. This hotel is generally only used by people seeking rheumatism cures during the height of summer. There's not much in the way of food out here. Call Mahdi Hweiti at the tourist office for reservations.

Palm Trees Hotel *(☎ 460 2204, Siwa Town)* Doubles without/with bath E£6/7 per person. Just off the main square, the Palm Trees is a popular place to stay. It has reasonably clean rooms with screened windows, fans and small balconies. There's plenty of hot water and the bathrooms are clean. Best of all, it has a shady, tranquil garden with date-palm furniture where you can relax, and there are also quite a few good bicycles to rent for E£8 to E£10 per day.

Cleopatra Hotel *(☎ 460 2148, Siwa Town)* Singles/doubles E£10/13, with bath E£18/25, chalet rooms with bath E£35/54. Directly south of the main square, this hotel is an old building consisting of basic rooms, and the new, much better, addition of more-expensive chalets, where rooms have a ceiling fan and simple wooden furniture.

Alexander Hotel *(☎ 460 0512, Siwa Town)* Singles/doubles E£12/25. Just off the main square, this hotel has 17 spotless rooms with baths and an inside staircase leading to the Alexander the Great Restaurant below.

Arous al-Waha Hotel *(☎/fax 460 2100, Siwa Town)* Singles/doubles B&B E£54/72, extra beds E£15, suites E£60. The 20-room Arous al-Waha is opposite the tourist office. Although it resembles a modern government building rather than a hotel, the management is friendly and helpful. Rooms have fans and bathrooms with constant hot water.

Siwa Inn *(☎ 460 2287)* Singles/doubles B&B E£106/152. This is a small hotel on the edge of the desert just outside of Siwa Town which has 10 simple but comfortable rooms and its own organic garden and mineral spring. It is not as aesthetically pleasing as Shali Lodge, but is a good alternative option.

Shali Lodge *(☎ 460 1299, fax 460 1799, Siwa Town)* Singles/doubles B&B E£150/200. This is a tiny but beautiful new mudbrick hotel among the palm groves about 300m from Shali's main square. The palms are kept as a feature of the building wherever possible and the seven huge rooms are arranged courtyard style around a small stone-lined pool. Tasteful and quiet, this is how small hotels should be.

Siwa Safari Paradise Hotel *(☎ 460 2289/90, fax 460 2286, Siwa Town)* Singles/doubles half board E£295/467, bungalows E£242/354, huts E£30 per person. This is a three-star place set in palm groves about 200m down the road to the Temple of Amun. The architecture does not live up to its picturesque garden setting, however and the prices are too high. All rooms have air-con, a TV and a fridge. Bungalows have no air-con. The tiny reed huts in another part of the hotel are without fans and are way overpriced.

Adrére Amellal *(in Cairo ☎ 02-340 0052, fax 341 3331, Sidi Ja'afar).* Doubles full board US$300. About 17km from the centre of Siwa, at the flat-topped White Mountain on the way to Bilad ar-Rum, Adrére Amellal (which means 'White Mountain' in Siwa) is Egypt's first ecolodge. Constructed using almost-forgotten traditional Siwan building techniques, it has stunning views over the lake to the oasis and to the edge of the Great Sand Sea and beyond. The owner, environmentalist Mounir Naematalla, claims that the site is mystical and after spending time there you begin to think that he may be right. With its simple but beautiful rooms and suites, a natural spring tucked in among the date palms and innovative food that uses local produce from its own organically farmed garden, it is one of the best, and certainly the most innovative, places to stay in the country. The price includes desert excursions.

Places to Eat

There's a handful of restaurants and cafes in Siwa catering to tourists and, less so, to locals. With one exception, they all offer a fairly similar menu, so trial and error is probably the only way of searching out any differences in quality.

Kenooz Siwa *(☎ 460 1299, Subukha)* Dishes E£3-20. Attached to Shali Lodge, it serves simple but good dishes such as vegetable stews, soups, salads and meat dishes (including special orders of stuffed lamb and free-range turkey), on a shady terrace among the palms. You can also recline on cushions and smoke a sheesha for E£4. It is by far the best restaurant in town.

Abdu Restaurant *(Siwa Town)* Dishes E£5-15. Abdu, the longest-running restaurant in town, is across the road from Yousef Hotel. Ever popular, it serves a range of traditional dishes, vegetable stews, couscous and roasted chickens. It also serves tasty pizza, although you might wait an hour or so for it.

Alexander Restaurant *(Siwa Town)* Dishes E£5-15. Just off the main square, opposite Al-Medina Hotel, it has pretty much the same pizzas, veggie stews and chicken as everywhere else.

Alexander the Great Restaurant *(☎ 460 0512, Siwa Town)* Dishes E£4-20. Run by the original chef of the Alexander Restaurant,

WESTERN OASES

Siwan Crafts

Siwa's rich culture is easily identified these days by the abundance of traditional crafts that are still made for local use as well as for tourists. Unfortunately, an estimated 98% of the older artefacts – such as jewellery, wooden chests and other family heirlooms – have become collectors' items and, over the years, have been sold to investors from around the world. With most of the original artisans now dead, these pieces of Siwan heritage are now lost to the Siwans themselves.

With the exception of the Nubians, Siwans adorn themselves with the biggest and most ornate pieces of jewellery to be found in Egypt. Although Siwan women only wear the heavy silver jewellery on special occasions these days, several interesting pieces are still made (unfortunately outside the oasis). Modern replicas of these traditional designs can be bought at craft shops for between E£50 and E£150.

Siwan wedding dresses are famous for their red, orange, green and black embroidery, which is often embellished with shells and beads. The black silk *(asherah nazitaf)* and the white cotton *(ahserah namilal)* dresses can both be found on the local market and can cost anywhere from E£250 to E£400. As with other handicrafts, old ones with finer workmanship will cost more.

Baskets from the oasis are also distinctive and are still made here, woven from date-palm fronds by women and girls. You can spot old baskets by their finer workmanship and the use of silk or leather instead of polyester and vinyl. The *tarkamt*, a woven plate that features a red leather centre, is traditionally used for serving sweets and sells for between E£5 and E£50, depending on the size. The largest basket is the *tghara*, which is used for storing bread. You can buy one for between E£100 and E£250. Smaller baskets include the *aqarush* and the red and green silk tasselled *nedibash*, which start at E£10 and go up in price according to size.

Local clays are mixed with straw and coloured with pigment from Gebel Dakrur to make pottery water jugs, drinking cups and incense burners. The *maklay*, a round-bottomed cup, and the *adjra*, used for washing hands, are among the most popular buys, as are *timjamait,* or incense burners. The smaller ones can be bought for about E£5.

it offers much the same fare as the others, including the curries that appeared on all the town's menus after three Pakistanis spent a month in the oasis a few years back. It also has a lot of vegetarian dishes. Many people insist that the chef is the reason that the Alexander became popular in the first place; you'll have to make up your own mind.

East-West Restaurant *(Siwa Town)* Dishes E£4-15. Another restaurant in the Abdu/Alexander vein, it's not as popular as the others, but serves pretty much the same quality of food.

There are two ***cafes*** on the square where ta'amiyya is cooked early every morning. Hot bread can be bought from the little ***bakery*** just off the square; there's also a market on the square each Friday morning. There are several places dotted around the square where you can have a sheesha or a cup of coffee and play some backgammon. ***Bakri's Cafe*** (also known as Sohag Rest House) next to Abdu Restaurant is one of the most popular.

Shopping

Several little craft shops around town compete for the tourist trade and sell replicas of old Siwan baskets, jewellery, pottery and the blue shawls worn by the local women (see the boxed text 'Siwan Crafts' for more information). Compare prices and goods at the tiny shop at the back of Palm Trees Hotel, the shop just off the main square on the road towards Cleopatra Hotel, and at Hassan's Bookshop. Siwa Original Handicrafts, next to Abdu Restaurant, has set prices, which can make things easier. Owners Abdallah Baghi and his cousin Suleiman have also saved some old pieces in an effort to conserve at least part of Siwa's unique cultural heritage. They will allow you to look through them, but they're not for sale.

Siwa is also known for its dates and olives and they are available in the shops around town. Usually someone will open a jar so you can try the olives to find the recipe you like. Everyone has their favourite brand of dates but the Jawhara dates are particularly good.

Getting There & Away

The West Delta bus station is on the main square. There are buses at 7am, 5pm and 10pm that go to Marsa Matruh (E£12), and on to Alexandria (E£27). You should book ahead for these services. There is an additional daily service to Marsa Matruh at 2pm that costs E£10; no bookings are taken.

There is no service-taxi station, but those making the trip to Marsa Matruh (E£10) leave from the area in front of Abdu's Restaurant. The taxis tend to leave in the evening, but you'll need to ask around to confirm this.

Although there is a road linking the oases of Siwa and Bahariyya, there is no public transport. The road, which passes through some stunning desert landscapes, is asphalted, but it is in bad shape and a permit is needed to take it. Some entrepreneurial types in town will take you if you can manage the E£550 they're charging.

To/From Libya At the time of writing it was illegal to cross into Libya and go on to the town of Jaghbub, about 120km away. Although the border is only 50km away it is reportedly mined, so things are unlikely to change soon. Should it become possible to cross, there is a paved road from Jaghbub to the Libyan coast.

Getting Around

There is a local bus to Kharmisah and Bilad ar-Rum once or twice a day, usually at 7am and 2pm, departing from near the King Fuad Mosque. It costs E£1 and returns about 45 minutes after completing its route so it's best to catch the morning bus and come back on the afternoon bus. Should anything happen to the afternoon bus, you may be stranded overnight and you'll have to bunk with the locals as there's nothing in the way of accommodation or provisions in either of these places.

A better bet is one of the pick-up trucks plying the route between Siwa and Bilad ar-Rum. You'll be expected to pay between 50pt and E£1, depending on where you get off. Alternatively, you can get a group together and rent a pick-up. Mahdi Hweiti a the tourist office or any of the restaurants will be able to help.

Bicycles are a terrific way to get around and can be rented from several sources, including Palm Trees Hotel, the small shop opposite Abdu Restaurant, and Arous al-Waha Hotel. The standard rate is about E£5 per day.

Hiring a *careta*, a donkey-drawn cart, can be a more amusing, if less practical, way to get around. Expect to pay about E£10 for half a day.

BEYOND SIWA

Qara Oasis

About 120km east of Siwa, near the Qattara Depression, is another oasis, Qara. The remote oasis is home to some 250 Berbers who, like the Siwans, built their fortress-like town on top of a mountain. According to legend, the harsh environment and scarce resources in the area meant that whenever a child was born in Qara an older person would have to leave in order to keep the population at a sustainable level. Whether or not this is true, it is no longer practised, but the Qarans remain small in number and their life is harsh. Unlike in Siwa, the old fortress is still inhabited, but increasingly the people are building new concrete houses down below. To get there, take the narrow asphalt road that branches off the Siwa–Marsa Matruh road at the rest house, 150km from Siwa. You can either rent a pick-up to take you there for about E£250 or talk to the many people in town offering desert safaris.

Great Sand Sea

One of the world's largest dune fields, the Great Sand Sea straddles Egypt and Libya, stretching over 800km south to the Gilf Kebir. There are 18 sand seas around the world, four of them in North Africa. The Great Sand Sea begins south of the Mediterranean coast. A branch splits off in Libya, south of Siwa, forming the Calanscio Sand Sea; the rest carries on south-east within Egypt. Sitting on a rise in the desert floor and covering a colossal 72,000 sq km, it

Dunes for Beginners

Formal classification of the types of sand dune was made in the 1970s, when scientists could examine photographs of dune fields taken on an early space mission. They identified five types of dune, four of which are found in Egypt.

Parallel Straight Dunes
Called *seif* or 'sword' in Arabic because they resemble the blades of curved Arab swords, these dunes are formed by wind and are primarily found in the Great Sand Sea and the northern Western Desert. Usually on the move, they will even fall down an escarpment, reforming at its base.

Parallel Wavy (or Barchan) Dunes
These are crescent-shaped dunes, with a slip face on one side. They are as wide as they are long and are usually found in straight lines with flat corridors between them. Usually on the move, they can travel as far as 19m in one year. They are predominant in the Kharga and Dakhla Oases and are also found in the Great Sand Sea.

Star Dunes
Created by wind blowing in different directions, these dunes are usually found alone. Instead of moving, they tend to build up within a circle. They are rare in Egypt.

Crescent (or Whaleback) Dunes
These are hill-like dunes formed when a series of smaller dunes collide and piggyback one another. Distinctive, with sides pointing in different directions, they can be seen in the area between the Kharga and Dakhla Oases.

contains some of the largest recorded dunes in the world, including one that is 140km long. Crescent, *seif* (sword) and parallel wavy dunes are found here (see the boxed text 'Dunes for Beginners'), some of which are on the move while others remain in place. Undulating and beautiful, the dunes are treacherous and have challenged desert travellers for hundreds of years. The Persian king Cambyses is thought to have lost an army here, while the British Long Range Desert Group spent months trying to find a way through its impenetrable sands. Aerial surveys and expeditions have tried to chart this vast expanse and it remains one of the least explored areas on earth.

The Great Sand Sea is not a place to go wandering on a whim, and you will need military permits as well as good preparation. Guides will take you to the edges of the Great Sand Sea from Siwa and most of the safari outfits listed in the boxed text 'Desert Safaris' earlier in this chapter will take you on expeditions that skirt the area. Remember that you don't need to penetrate far into the desert in order to feel the isolation, beauty and enormous scale of the dunes.

Alexandria & the Mediterranean Coast

On the north coast of Egypt, west of where the Rosetta branch of the Nile leaves the Delta and where the desert meets the sparkling waters of the Mediterranean Sea, is the charming – although somewhat jaded – city of Alexandria, once the shining gem of the Hellenistic world. Nearby is the famous town of El Alamein, where the tide of the African campaign during WWII was changed in favour of the Allies, and west beyond that are the Mediterranean resorts of Sidi Abdel Rahman and Marsa Matruh. The rest of this region is sparsely populated. The road westward beyond Matruh to the Libyan border runs along an almost deserted coast that greets the sea with craggy cliffs or smooth sandy beaches.

Highlights

- Eat excellent grilled fish at one of Alexandria's open-air street restaurants.
- Indulge in some strong coffee and cold Stella at some of Alexandria's wonderful period cafes and bars.
- Visit the Catacombs of Kom ash-Shuqqafa, a series of subterranean tombs straight from a horror film.
- Explore Rosetta with its date palms, fishing boats and stunning old Turkish houses.

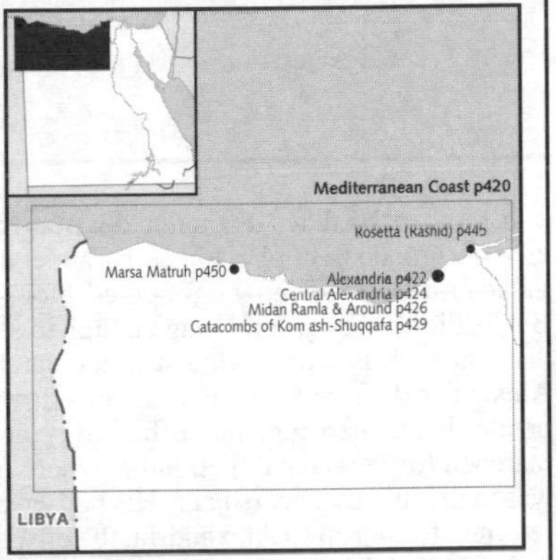

Alexandria

☎ 03

Alexandria (Iskendariyya) is often said to be the greatest historical city with the least to show: founded by Alexander the Great, yet it bears no trace of him; site of one of the wonders of the ancient world, but there's barely a notable monument remaining; ruled by Cleopatra and a rival of Rome, it's now a provincial city, overcrowded with people but short on prestige.

The reality of modern-day Alexandria can be a little disappointing, but to judge the city on first appearances is to sell it short. It's a city of nuances and shades, with plenty to be discovered if you're prepared to invest the time. Come here to kick back for a couple of days, hang out in atmospheric old watering holes, eat decent food and lose yourself in nostalgic meanderings.

HISTORY

Alexandria's history is the bridging link between the pharaohs and Islam. The city gave rise to the last great Pharaonic dynasty (the Ptolemies), provided the entry into Egypt for the Romans and nurtured early Christianity, then rapidly faded into near obscurity when Islam's invading armies passed it by to set up camp on the site that would later become Cairo.

The city began with the conquests of Alexander the Great. Having had his right to rule Egypt confirmed by the priests of Memphis, the Macedonian general followed the Nile up to the Mediterranean. There, on the shores of the sea very familiar to him, he chose a fishing village as the site on which he would found a new city. The foundations for Alexandria were laid in 331 BC.

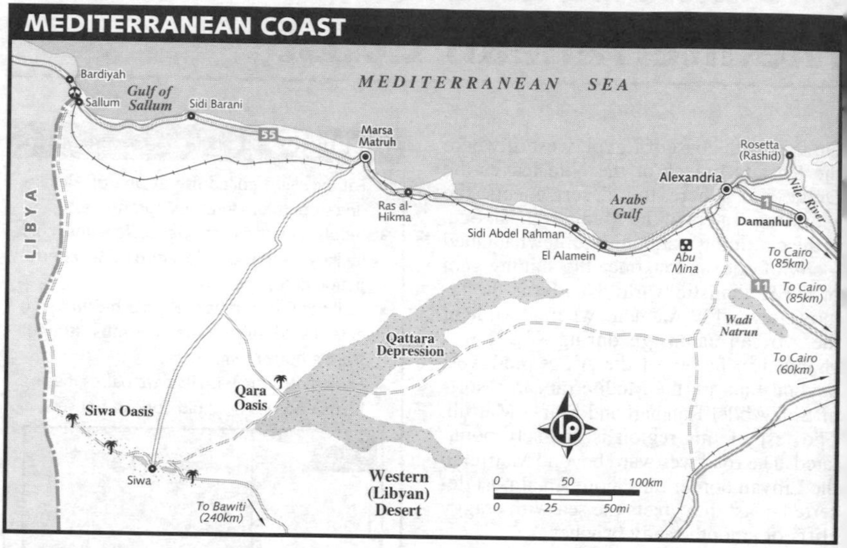

It's recorded that Alexander devised the city's original street plan himself – a rectangular grid divided into regimented blocks. But he didn't stay around long enough to see his vision set in stone. Almost immediately Alexander departed for Siwa to consult the oracle there, then regathered his army and marched for Persia and then India, where he was to die just two years later. His body was returned for burial to Alexandria, the city he had conceived as the cultural and political centre of his empire.

Instead, it was one of Alexander's generals, Ptolemy, who presided over the development of the city. Under Ptolemy's direction Alexandria was filled with architecture every bit as impressive as that of Rome or Athens. To create a sense of continuity between his rule and that of the Pharaonic dynasties, Ptolemy made Alexandria look at least superficially Egyptian by adorning his city with sphinxes, obelisks and statues scavenged from the old sites of Memphis and Heliopolis.

Alexandria developed into a major port on the trade routes between Europe and Asia. More notably, its economic wealth was matched by its intellectual standing. Alexandria became a renowned centre for scientific, philosophical and literary thought and learning, attracting some of the finest artists and scholars of the time. Its famed library contained 500,000 volumes, and its research institute, the Mouseion, produced some of the most scholarly works of the age.

A grand tower, the Pharos, built on an island just offshore, acted as both a beacon to guide ships entering the booming harbour and, at a deeper level, served as an ostentatious symbol of the city's greatness. Such were the massive dimensions of the Pharos that ancient scholars counted it as one of the Seven Wonders of the World.

During the reign of its most famous regent, Cleopatra, Alexandria rivalled Rome in everything but military power – a situation that Rome found intolerable and was eventually forced to act upon (see History in the Facts about Egypt chapter for more information).

Once under Roman control, Alexandria remained the capital of Egypt. It was still regarded as the most learned place on earth and with nearly a million inhabitants it was second only to Rome in size.

During the 4th century AD, however, insurrection, civil war, famine and disease ravaged Alexandria's populace, and although the city later became a centre of Christianity, it never returned to its former glory. At the end of the century, the city's cultural importance was almost wiped out as Christianity became the official religion of the Roman Empire. All pagan temples were razed and learned institutes (including the Mouseion), along with the theatre, were smothered.

Alexandria's decline was sealed when the conquering Muslim armies swept into Egypt in the 7th century AD and ignored the Mediterranean city to establish their new capital further south on the Nile.

All through the Middle Ages Alexandria dwindled, superseded in importance as a seaport by the nearby town of Rosetta. Its monuments were destroyed by earthquakes and their ruins quarried for building materials. The former great classical city physically shrank to little more than a fishing village on the peninsula between the two harbours (now Anfushi) with a population of less than 10,000.

The turning point in Alexandria's fortunes came with Napoleon's invasion of 1798; recognising the city's strategic importance, he initiated its revival. During the subsequent reign of the Egyptian reformist Mohammed Ali, a new town was built directly on the top of the old one, with a canal linking the city to the Nile.

Alexandria once more became one of the Mediterranean's busiest ports and attracted an influx of wealthy Turkish-Egyptian traders, followed by Jews, Greeks, Italians and other Mediterranean races. French and British interests and investments increased with the advent of the Suez Canal. Multicultural, buoyant on the gains of commerce and built on the foundations of antiquity, Alexandria took on an almost mythical quality and served as the muse for a new string of poets, writers and intellectuals (see the boxed text 'Literary Alexandria' later in this chapter).

But it was a bright flame that burned briefly. The revolution that brought Gamal Abdel Nasser to power in 1952 also struck a death knell for Alexandria's cosmopolitan days. Foreigners flooded out of the country, many minus their properties and businesses, which had all been hastily sold off before they could be nationalised by the new government.

Since that time, the character of the city has changed completely. From a population of 300,000 in the 1940s (of which around 40% were foreigners), Alexandria is now home to an almost exclusively Egyptian population of some five million, filled by a steady migration of rural dwellers to the city.

ORIENTATION

Alexandria is a true waterfront city, nearly 20km long from east to west and only about 3km wide. The city centre faces the Eastern Harbour, which is almost closed by two spindly promontories.

The focal point of the city is Midan Ramla, also known as Mahattat Ramla (Ramla Station) because this is the central terminus for many of the city's tram lines. Immediately adjacent is Midan Saad Zaghloul, a large square running back from the seafront and joining Midan Ramla at the corner. Around these two midans, and in the streets to the south and west, are the central shopping area, the tourist office, airline offices, restaurants and most of the cheaper hotels.

To the west of this central area are the older quarters of the city, such as Anfushi, while in the other direction are a succession of newer districts stretching right out to Montazah, with its palace and gardens, which marks the eastern extent of the city.

The whole strip, from Anfushi to Montazah, is connected by the seafront Corniche (also known in some parts as Sharia 26th of July and Sharia al-Geish) and by Tariq al-Horreyya (*tariq* means 'avenue'), which runs parallel to the seafront about 1km inland.

Note that whereas in Cairo *sharia* is translated as 'street', in Alexandria French still rules and sharia means *rue*.

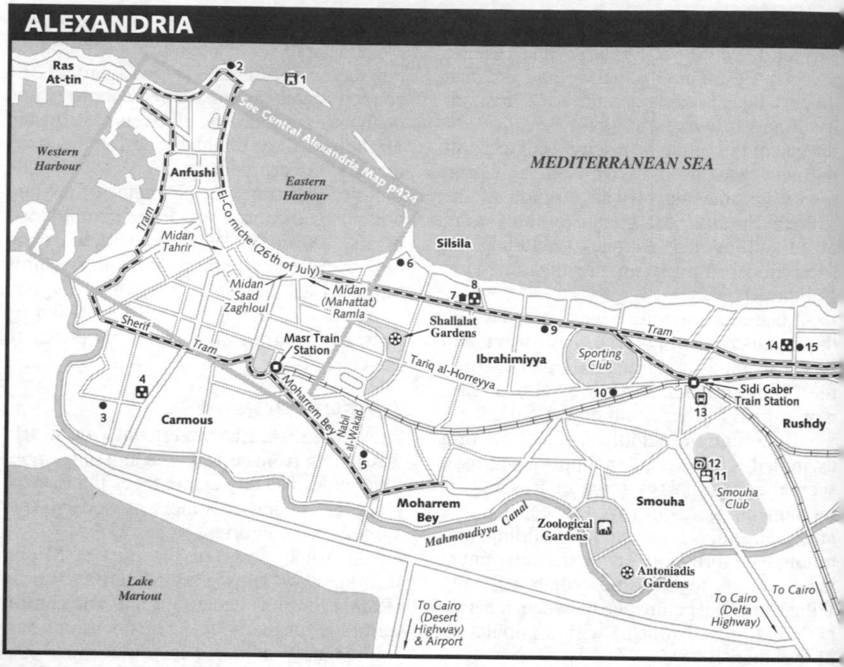

INFORMATION

Visa Extensions

The passport office is at 28 Talaat Harb. You'll need one photo and a photocopy of the relevant pages of your passport (available from the machines out front) as well as the passport itself. The office is open from 8am to 1.30pm Saturday to Thursday.

Tourist Office

The main tourist office (☎ 807 9885) is on the south-west corner of Midan Saad Zaghloul. It's open from 8am to 6pm daily. The central Alexandria branch of the tourist police (☎ 487 3378) is upstairs from the main tourist office.

There is also a tourist office at Masr train station on platform one.

Money

For changing cash or cashing travellers cheques, the simplest option is to use one of the many exchange bureaus on the side streets between Midan Ramla and the Corniche (el-Corniche). There are also dozens of currency exchange offices along Talaat Harb.

ATMs are scarcer in Alex than in Cairo. The most reliable ATM (and the one most likely to accept foreign cards) belongs to the HSBC (☎ 487 2839) at 47 Sultan Hussein, a five-minute walk east of the centre. There are also several ATMs on Salah Salem, including one belonging to the EAB.

American Express (AmEx; ☎ 541 0177, fax 545 7363) is at 34 Al-Moaskar ar-Romani, some distance from the centre, in Rushdy. It's open from 8.30am to 5pm Saturday to Thursday. This office is also a travel agency, and you can have mail forwarded here. The main Thomas Cook office (☎ 484 7830, fax 487 4073, ⓔ tcalex@attmail.com) is much more conveniently located at 15 Sharia Saad Zaghloul, and it's open from 8am to 5pm Saturday to Thursday.

If you need to have money wired to you, Western Union has two offices in town –

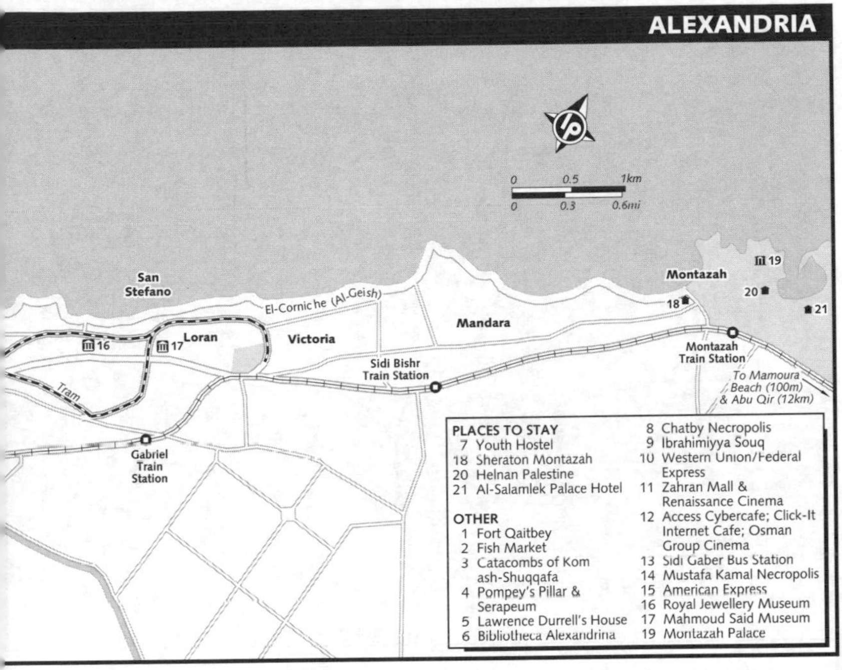

see International Transfers under Money in the Facts for the Visitor chapter.

Post

The main post office is about 200m east of Midan Orabi. There's an Express Mail Service (EMS) office round the side. Several other post offices are dotted around the city, including one adjacent to the Masr train station (to the left as you exit the station) and another at Midan Ramla (open to 6pm). Most are open 8am to 3pm Saturday to Thursday.

To pick up poste restante, go to the mail sorting centre one block west of Midan Orabi and a block north of Midan Tahrir. It's a decrepit little stone building opposite a new 15-storey high-rise; enter around the back on Sharia Sahafa. It's open from about 6.30am to 6pm Saturday to Thursday.

Email & Internet Access

At the time of writing, Alex has only one centrally located Internet cafe – the Zawiya. If this is no longer in business then the next best option is one of the two cafes out in the eastern district of Smouha.

Access Cybercafe (☎ 425 5766, W www.cyberaccess.com.eg) 1st floor of the shopping mall beside the new Zahran Mall in Smouha; open from 9am to midnight daily; E£10 per hour

Click-It Internet Cafe (☎ 311 7520) Ground floor of the shopping mall beside the new Zahran Mall in Smouha; open from 10.30am to 1am daily; E£12 per hour

Zawiya Internet Cafe (☎ 484 8014) Sharia Dr Hassan Fadaly, off Safiyya Zaghloul, just south of Midan Ramla; open from 10am to 1am daily, 2pm to 1am Friday; E£5 per hour

To get to the Internet places located in Smouha, catch a minibus from in front of the Cecil Hotel to the Sidi Gaber bus station, head south, away from the train station, until you hit the main road, where you take a right. After 200m you'll reach a roundabout at which you take the second left. The shopping mall with the Internet cafes is between the

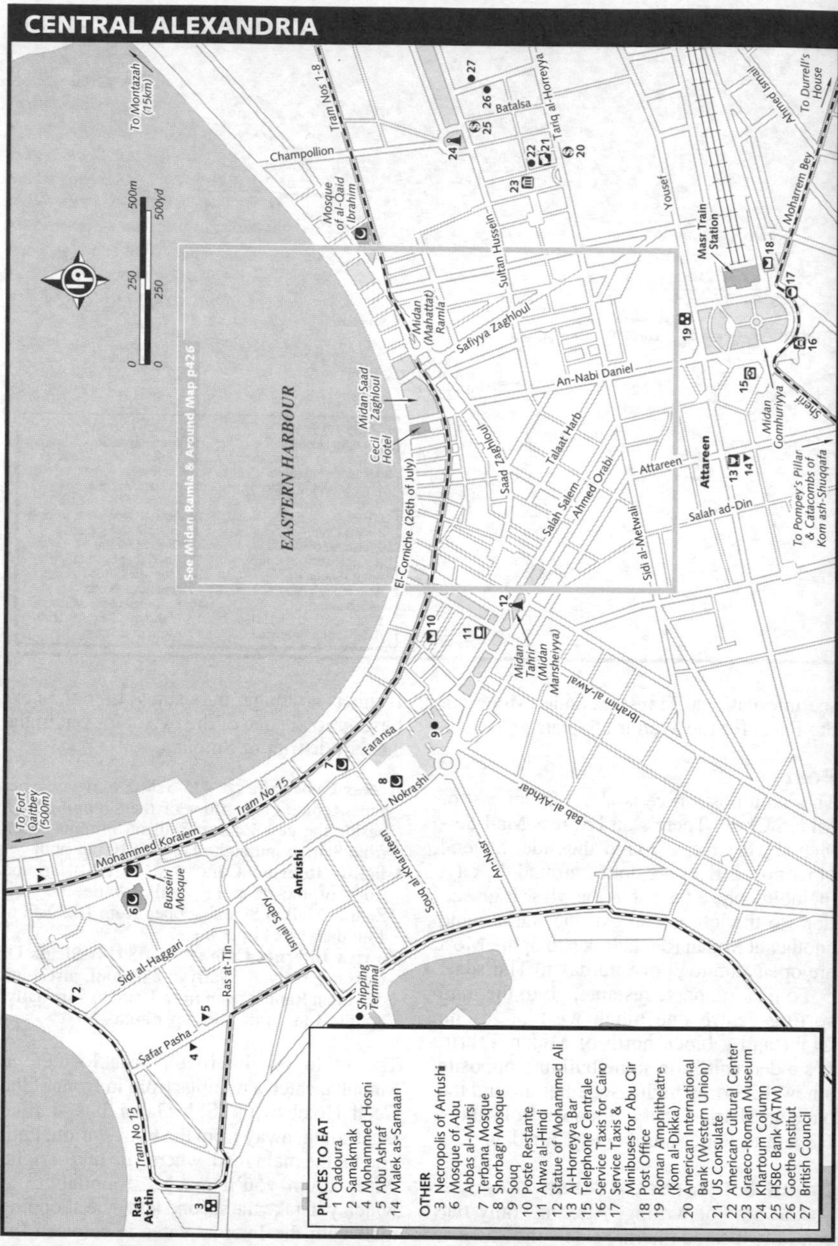
CENTRAL ALEXANDRIA
ALEXANDRIA
EASTERN HARBOUR
See Midan Ramla & Around Map p426
0 250 500m
0 250 500yd
To Fort Qaitbey (500m)
To Montazah (15km)
To Durrell's House
To Pompey's Pillar & Catacombs of Kom ash-Shuqqafa
Ras At-tin
Anfushi
Attareen
Tram No 15
Tram Nos 1-8
Mohammed Koraiem
Busseiri Mosque
Sidi al-Haggari
Ras at-Tin
Safar Pasha
Ismail Sabry
Shipping Terminal
Souq al-Khaiteen
Nokrashi
Faransa
An-Nasr
Bab al-Akhdar
Ibrahim al-Awal
Midan Tahrir (Midan Mansheiyya)
El-Corniche (26th of July)
Cecil Hotel
Midan Saad Zaghloul
Midan (Mahattat) Ramla
Mosque of al-Qaid Ibrahim
Champollion
Saad Zaghloul
Safiyya Zaghloul
Talaat Harb
Salah Salem
Ahmed Orabi
Sidi al-Metwali
Attareen
Salah ad-Din
An-Nabi Daniel
Sultan Hussein
Batalsa
Tariq al-Horreyya
Yousef
Masr Train Station
Ahmed Ismail
Moharrem Bey
Sherif
Midan Gomhuriyya
PLACES TO EAT
1 Qadoura
2 Samakmak
4 Mohammed Hosni
5 Abu Ashraf
14 Malek as-Samaan
OTHER
3 Necropolis of Anfushi
6 Mosque of Abu Abbas al-Mursi
7 Terbana Mosque
8 Shorbagi Mosque
9 Souq
10 Poste Restante
11 Ahwa al-Hindi
12 Statue of Mohammed Ali
13 Al-Horreyya Bar
15 Telephone Centrale
16 Service Taxis for Cairo
17 Service Taxis & Minibuses for Abu Qir
18 Post Office
19 Roman Amphitheatre (Kom al-Dikka)
20 American International Bank (Western Union)
21 US Consulate
22 American Cultural Center
23 Graeco-Roman Museum
24 Khartoum Column
25 HSBC Bank (ATM)
26 Goethe Institut
27 British Council

ountain in front of Alexandria's Mosque of Abu Abbas al-Mursi

BOTH PHOTOGRAPHS BY CHRISTINE OSBORNE

Colourful fishing boats moored in the Eastern Harbour of Alexandria, a true waterfront city

MARK ECCLESTON

In Alexandria, Fort Qaitbey was built on the foundations of the ancient Pharos lighthouse.

SIMON BRACKEN

Fishing among the ruins at Alexandria

INDRA KILFOYLE

The Commonwealth War Cemetery, El Alamein

mosque and the modern, green multistorey Zahran Mall. It's a 10-minute walk in all.

Bookshops

Alexandria has no good English-language bookshops; the small selection of English-language titles carried by Al-Ahram Bookshop on the corner of Tariq al-Horreyya and Sharia an-Nabi Daniel is about the best there is. It's open from 9am to 4pm Saturday and Monday to Thursday and 9am to 1pm on Sunday. Alternatively, Al-Mustaqbal Bookshop across from the Cinema at 32 Sharia Safiyya Zaghloul has a reasonable selection of AUC Press publications, as well as other locally produced Alexandria guides.

For second-hand books, you could trawl the stalls lining the southern end of Sharia an-Nabi Daniel or visit the stand outside the Amir Cinema on Tariq al-Horreyya, but either way the pickings are slim.

The situation with foreign-language newspapers and magazines is better – the newsstand at Midan Ramla gets everything from *Elle* (English, French and Italian) to the *Economist*, *Der Spiegel* and *Le Monde*.

Cultural Centres

Most of the city's cultural centres run libraries and organise occasional films, lectures, exhibitions and performances – see *Egypt Today* for notices of what's on. Take along your passport as you may have to show it before entering.

American Cultural Center (☎ 486 1009, fax 487 3811, ⓔ aca@internetalex.com) 3 Sharia al-Pharaana (behind the consulate); open from 10am to 4pm Sunday to Wednesday

British Council (☎ 486 0199, ⓦ www.britishcouncil.org) 9 Sharia Batalsa, Bab Sharqi; open from 10am to 8pm Sunday to Wednesday, 10am to 3pm Thursday & Saturday

French Cultural Centre (☎ 492 0804) 30 An-Nabi Daniel; open from 9am to noon and 5pm to 7.30pm Sunday to Thursday

Goethe Institut (☎ 487 9870) 10 Sharia Batalsa, Bab Sharqi

Medical Services

There's no shortage of pharmacies in Alexandria, especially along Sharia Saad Zaghloul. The one opposite Midan Ramla, next to the Baskin Robbins ice-cream shop, is open until midnight.

ANCIENT ALEXANDRIA

Ancient Alexandria is almost as intangible to us as Atlantis. It's a place of legendary status associated in the mind with half-remembered tales of Cleopatra, the Seven Wonders of the World and the Great Library. It borders on the mythological. Only an odd column or two or a gateway hints that it might once all have been real. But thanks to ongoing archaeological research, more and more evidence is continually being unearthed to give physical shape to the ancient city. Much remains inaccessible – the Alexandria of Cleopatra's time lies buried 6m underground – but every now and then the city gives up some of its secrets, such as the honeycomb of Graeco-Roman tombs accidentally exposed in 1997 by a road-building crew. In recent years the sea has also thrown up some dramatic finds – see the boxed text 'Cleopatra's Palace' for more information.

For the most part, it's still necessary to employ a little imagination. If you stand at the intersection of Sharia an-Nabi Daniel and Tariq al-Horreyya, for instance, with the Al-Ahram bookshop on one side and a patisserie on the other, you are at the crossroads of the ancient city. What's now Horreyya avenue was then the Canopic Way, extending from the city's Gate of the Sun in the east to the Gate of the Moon in the west. According to a 5th-century account it was adorned with 'a range of columns…from one end of it to the other'.

A little way south of this intersection, along Sharia an-Nabi Daniel, the Ptolemaic-era Street of the Soma, is what's believed to be the site of the renowned Mouseion and library, where the greatest philosophers, writers and scientists gathered. It's thought these great institutions were on the west side of the road – the right as you head away from Al-Horreyya. But it's what may have lain – what may still lie, claim some – beneath the modern and fairly unnoteworthy **Mosque of an-Nabi Daniel** on the east side

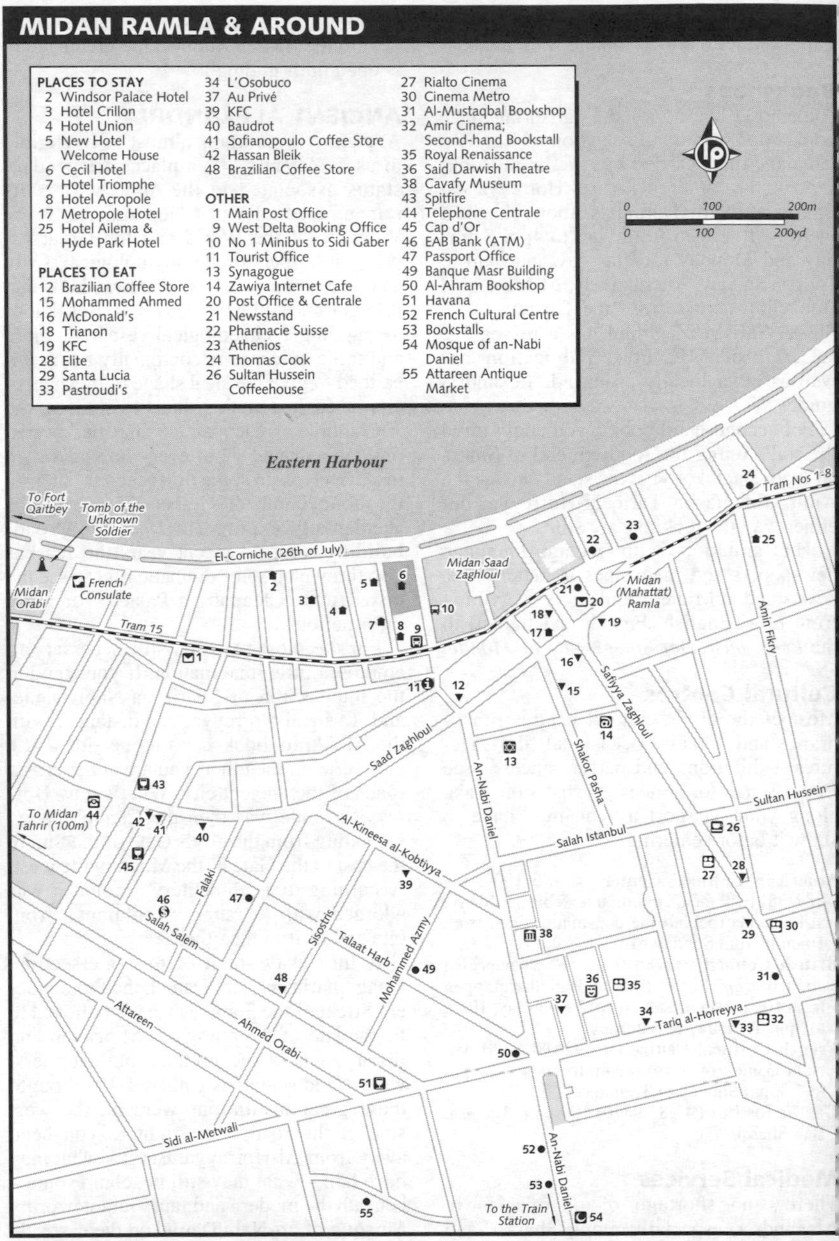
MIDAN RAMLA & AROUND
PLACES TO STAY
2 Windsor Palace Hotel
3 Hotel Crillon
4 Hotel Union
5 New Hotel Welcome House
6 Cecil Hotel
7 Hotel Triomphe
8 Hotel Acropole
17 Metropole Hotel
25 Hotel Ailema & Hyde Park Hotel
PLACES TO EAT
12 Brazilian Coffee Store
15 Mohammed Ahmed
16 McDonald's
18 Trianon
19 KFC
28 Elite
29 Santa Lucia
33 Pastroudi's
34 L'Osobuco
37 Au Privé
39 KFC
40 Baudrot
41 Sofianopoulo Coffee Store
42 Hassan Bleik
48 Brazilian Coffee Store
OTHER
1 Main Post Office
9 West Delta Booking Office
10 No 1 Minibus to Sidi Gaber
11 Tourist Office
13 Synagogue
14 Zawiya Internet Cafe
20 Post Office & Centrale
21 Newsstand
22 Pharmacie Suisse
23 Athenios
24 Thomas Cook
26 Sultan Hussein Coffeehouse
27 Rialto Cinema
30 Cinema Metro
31 Al-Mustaqbal Bookshop
32 Amir Cinema; Second-hand Bookstall
35 Royal Renaissance
36 Said Darwish Theatre
38 Cavafy Museum
43 Spitfire
44 Telephone Centrale
45 Cap d'Or
46 EAB Bank (ATM)
47 Passport Office
49 Banque Masr Building
50 Al-Ahram Bookshop
51 Havana
52 French Cultural Centre
53 Bookstalls
54 Mosque of an-Nabi Daniel
55 Attareen Antique Market
0 100 200m
0 100 200yd
Eastern Harbour
To Fort Qaitbey
Tomb of the Unknown Soldier
El-Corniche (26th of July)
Midan Orabi
French Consulate
Tram 15
Midan Saad Zaghloul
Midan (Mahattat) Ramla
Tram Nos 1-8
Amin Fikry
Safiyya Zaghloul
Saad Zaghloul
Shakor Pasha
An-Nabi Daniel
Sultan Hussein
Salah Istanbul
To Midan Tahrir (100m)
Al-Kineesa al-Kobtiyya
Falaki
Salah Salem
Sisostris
Talaat Harb
Mohammed Azmy
Attareen
Ahmed Orabi
Tariq al-Horreyya
Sidi al-Metwali
To the Train Station

of the street that causes hearts to quicken. The tomb of Alexander the Great has never been found and historical sources indicate that it lies under his Egyptian capital. Certain scholars, amateur archaeologists and romantics believe, hope and dream that it lies in crypts deep below the mosque. Trial excavations revealed that the mosque does indeed rest on the site of a 4th-century Roman temple but religious authorities have placed a halt on any further digging. However, other leading authorities contend that a more likely site for the tomb is east of the centre, near the Shallalat Gardens, a site occupied today by extensive Greek graveyards.

Pending further discoveries, the best of Alexandria's treasures are on display at the city's Graeco-Roman Museum.

Graeco-Roman Museum

This excellent small museum *(☎ 487 6434, 5 Al-Mathaf ar-Romani; admission E£16; open 9am-4pm Sat-Thur, 9am-11.30am & 1.30pm-4pm Fri)* contains about 40,000 valuable relics dating from as early as the 3rd century BC. Unfortunately, as is so typically the case in Egypt, labelling is next to nonexistent. Things to look out for include, in the very first room (Room 6), three carved heads of Alexander the Great, the city's founder. These are overpowered by two impressive wall-hung mosaics, discovered in the Delta region and dating from about 100 years after Alexander, both portraying Queen Berenice, wife of Ptolemy III.

At the other end of the room, past the giant Apis bull found at the Serapeum, are two carvings of the god Serapis, one in wood, the other in marble. Serapis is a wholly Alexandrian creation, a divinity part-Egyptian (the husband of Isis) and part-Greek, with echoes of Zeus and Poseidon. Pharaoh Ptolemy I invented him as a way of bringing together his Egyptian and Greek subjects in shared worship. It worked, and the museum is full of Serapises (the Apis bull is Serapis in another guise).

Room 9 contains a mummified crocodile, which would have been carried in processions devoted to Sobek the crocodile god. Beside the mummy is a carved wooden door that belongs to a temple discovered in Al-Fayoum, now rebuilt and exhibited in the museum's garden.

Room 12 has more examples of the melding of Greek and Egyptian – in this case pink granite statues of Egypt's Greek-Ptolemaic kings are depicted wearing Pharaonic dress and crowns in an attempt to legitimise them as heirs to the rule of the pharaohs. The fine statue at the centre of the room is of the Roman emperor Marcus Aurelius who visited Alexandria in AD 175. It was found during the digging of the foundations for the Said Darwish Theatre, just off Tariq al-Horreyya.

In Room 18, the fourth cabinet on the left contains just about the only historical depictions of the Pharos in Alexandria; these come in the shape of several small terracotta lanterns dating back to the 3rd century BC and showing the three stages of the tower (see the boxed text 'The Pharos of Alexandria' later in this chapter).

In the coin room (Room 24), there are several examples of coins from Alexander's time, displaying a portrait of the Macedonian (panels 36–43) and several bearing profiles of Cleopatra VII (panel 88) – the Cleopatra of Shakespearian and Hollywood fame (although it has to be said, she looks more Virginia Woolf than Elizabeth Taylor).

The last few rooms contain objects from Egypt's Coptic period. The most striking is a huge, 4th-century marble capital carved with a basketwork design (Room 2). It was discovered near Midan Ramla in central Alex and is believed to have come from one of the city's earliest churches.

For anyone with more than just a passing interest, we strongly recommend that you pick up the well-illustrated *A Short Guide to the Graeco-Roman Museum* by Jean-Yves Empereur. It should be available at the museum bookshop.

Roman Amphitheatre (Kom al-Dikka)

The well-preserved 13 white marble terraces of the only Roman amphitheatre *(Kom*

Cleopatra's Palace

Cleopatra VII

In recent years, Alexandria has been giving up some of her hidden treasures. Underwater excavations have been going on for a decade or so in the Eastern Harbour, and in 1998 the work finally started to pay off with some high-profile discoveries that placed the Mediterranean city back in the international spotlight.

There are two separate dive sites currently under exploration: one is the area around Fort Qaitbey; the other is in the south-east part of the Eastern Harbour, where archaeologists had long suspected lay a submerged Ptolemaic-era royal quarter.

The Qaitbey dive has recorded hundreds of objects including sphinx bodies (their heads tugged off by the motion of the sea), columns and capitals, and fragments of obelisks. The divers have also discovered giant granite blocks, some of them broken as if by a fall from a great height – it's thought that these blocks are likely to be the remains of the Pharos.

Over in the royal quarter area, another joint French-Egyptian diving team has discovered platforms, pavements and red granite columns that they speculate were part of a former palace ('Cleopatra's Palace' is what they're calling it), as well as the remains of a 5th-century wooden pier and a remarkably complete shipwreck that has been carbon dated to between 90 BC and AD 130. But what has really captured the interest of the media and the public at large are the statues. In October 1998, in front of a crowd of international journalists and cameramen, the archaeologists raised from the water a beautiful black granite statue of a priest of Isis holding the Canopic emblem of Osiris, followed by a diorite sphinx adorned with the face of what's thought to be Ptolemy XII, father of Cleopatra.

A small, independent agency, Alexandra Dive (☎ 012-327 1993, W www.alexandra-dive.com), has recently begun offering diving tours of the submerged harbour sites, and there's talk of establishing an underwater museum (the world's first) with a Plexiglas tunnel through which visitors could walk 5m below the sea's surface and view the palace complex. At the moment it's nothing more than a fine idea and there's no sign of anything happening any time soon. But if it ever does get off the drawing board then Alexandria may well be able to lay claim once more to possessing one of the wonders of the world.

al-Dikka; ☎ 490 2904, Sharia Yousef; admission E£6; open 9am-4pm daily) in Egypt were discovered in 1964, when the foundations for a new apartment building were being dug off Midan Gomhuriyya. Although the scale of the thing is unprepossessing, the terraces, arranged in a semicircle around the arena, are excellently preserved. The area under excavation has now shifted to the north of the site (known as Kom al-Dikka, or 'Mound of Rubble'), where a team is still working on exposing the remains of Roman-era baths and a villa.

Large floor mosaics have been uncovered here and restored, including a nine-panel masterpiece depicting several colourful birds. The mosaic should be open to the public by the time you read this.

Pompey's Pillar & the Serapeum

This massive yet unimpressive 30m-high pink granite column *(☎ 484 5800, Carmous; admission E£6; open 9am-4pm daily)*, which the Crusaders mistakenly credited to the Roman general Pompey rises out of the disappointing remains of the acropolis known as the Serapeum. In Ptolemaic times, this was a rocky outcrop with 100 steps that led up to a great temple devoted to Serapis, the man-made god of Alexandria (see Graeco-Roman Museum earlier in this chapter). One of the city's major sites of worship, it was surrounded by subsidiary shrines and included a second great library. It's now a great earthen mound, pocked by trenches and holes, with a few sphinxes (originally from Heliopolis), a Nilometer and the pillar.

The pillar, which has a circumference of 9m, was erected in AD 293 amid the Serapeum complex for Diocletian, not Pompey. During the final assault on the pagan intellectuals of Alexandria in about AD 391, the Christians destroyed the Serapeum and library, leaving only the pillar. It is, in fact, the only ancient monument that remains whole and standing in Alexandria.

To get here walk west from Midan Gomhuriyya (the train station square) following the tram tracks west along Sharia Sherif and turn left where they do; this should bring you onto a busy market street and the entrance to the Serapeum is 300m ahead on the right. It's about a 1.5km walk.

Catacombs of Kom ash-Shuqqafa

Kom ash-Shuqqafa *(☎ 484 5800, Carmous; admission E£12; open 9am-4pm daily)* is about five minutes' walk south-west of Pompey's Pillar. Follow the wall around to the right after you leave the Serapeum and keep going straight ahead. The entrance to the catacombs is on the left about 150m beyond the small midan.

These catacombs, the largest-known Roman burial site in Egypt, were discovered accidentally in 1900 when a donkey disappeared through a hole in the ground. They consist of three tiers of tombs and chambers cut out of the rock to a depth of about 35m. The bottom level is flooded and inaccessible, but the areas that can be visited are impressive.

Enter by descending the spiral staircase cut into a circular shaft; the bodies of the dead would have been lowered on ropes down the centre of the shaft. The staircase leads off to a **rotunda** with a central well piercing down into the gloom of the flooded lower level. When the catacombs were originally constructed in the 2nd century AD, probably as a family crypt, the rotunda would have led to the triclinium (to your

CATACOMBS OF KOM ASH-SHUQQAFA

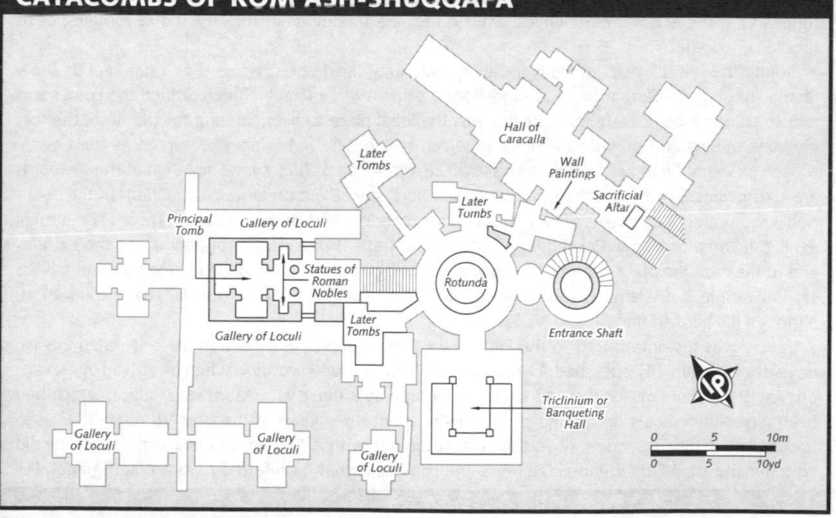

left) and the principal tomb chamber (straight ahead) only, but over time more chambers were hacked out until the complex had expanded to accommodate more than 300 corpses.

The **triclinium** is a banqueting hall where grieving relatives paid their last respects with a funeral feast. Diners would have reclined on the raised benches at the centre of the room around a low table. When the first archaeologists entered this chamber they found tableware and wine jars.

Back in the rotunda, head down the stairs to the **principal tomb**, the centrepiece of the catacombs – and a prototype for a horror film set. A miniature funerary temple featuring an antechamber with columns and a pediment leading through to an inner sanctum, it's decorated with a weird synthesis of ancient Egyptian, Greek and Roman death iconography. For instance, as you enter the inner chamber, on either side of the doorway are carved figures representing Anubis, the Egyptian god of the dead, but dressed as a Roman legionary and with a serpent's tail representative of Agathodaemon, a Greek divinity.

It's not known who is buried here, but one theory is that it's the man and woman standing in the niches in the antechamber, who may have been Roman nobles.

Literary Alexandria

A few years ago, there was a nationwide survey conducted through the press and bookshops in the UK to find the country's all-time 100 most popular books. *The Alexandria Quartet* by Lawrence Durrell came in somewhere in the 40s. It's probably safe to say then that more people have visited Alexandria through that book than they have by physically stepping foot in the city. Alexandria – which somebody once called the 'city of the literary cross-reference' – is better known through its literature and writers than through any stone-built monuments or other tourist sites.

It's somewhat ironic then that outside of serious poetry fans and Alexandriophiles, the city's finest writer, Constantine Cavafy, is these days so little known. Born of Greek parents, Cavafy (1863–1933) lived all but a few of his 70 years in Alexandria, spending most of his working life as a clerk for the Ministry of Public Works, occupying an office above the still existent Trianon patisserie. Never collected during his lifetime, but since widely translated and published, his poems resurrect events and figures from the era of the Ptolemies, while others are fragments of the city and its routines, or of recalled encounters.

During the last 25 years of his life, Cavafy lived in a 2nd-floor apartment at 4 rue Lepsius (now Sharia Sharm el-Sheikh) above a ground-floor brothel. With a Greek church around the corner and a hospital opposite, Cavafy thought this was the ideal place to live, catering for the flesh, the forgiveness of sins and providing a place in which to die. The flat is now preserved as the *Cavafy Museum (Sharia Sharm el-Sheikh; admission E£8; open 10am-3pm Tues-Sun)*. Two of the six rooms are arranged as Cavafy kept them, while in the others, spread out on tables, are editions of the poet's publications and photocopies of his manuscripts, notebooks and correspondence. There's also a small exhibit devoted to fellow Alexandrian-Greek writer Stratis Tsirkas, author of poems and short stories and of the monumental *Drifting Cities*, a weighty trilogy centred around Greek underground politics set in wartime Jerusalem, Cairo and Alexandria. It is available in an English-language translation, although it's hard to find.

Cavafy was first introduced to the English-speaking world by EM Forster, the celebrated English novelist who'd already published *A Room with a View* and *Howards End* when he arrived in Alexandria in 1916. Working for the Red Cross (for a time as a nurse at a Montazah Palace, which had been requisitioned as a military hospital), Forster spent three years in the city. Although it failed to find a place in his subsequent novels (he was struggling with *A Passage to India* at the time), he did write for the local English-language press and compiled what he referred to as an 'anti-guide'. His

From the antechamber a couple of short passages lead to a large U-shaped chamber lined with the pigeonholes – or to give them their proper name, loculi – in which the bodies were placed. After the body (or bodies, as many of the loculi held more than one) had been placed inside, the small chamber was then sealed with a plaster slab.

Back up in the rotunda there are four other passageways leading off to small clusters of tombs. One of these gives access to an entirely different complex, known as the **Hall of Caracalla**. This hall had its own staircase access (long-since caved in) and has been joined to the Kom ash-Shuqqafa, which it predates, by the efforts of tomb robbers who hacked a new passageway into the complex.

For further information Jean-Yves Empereur's *A Short Guide to the Catacombs of Kom el Shoqafa* has some great photos and very readable text.

CENTRAL ALEXANDRIA

'Like Cannes with acne' was Michael Palin's verdict on Alexandria's looping **Corniche** (in his book of the TV series *Around the World in 80 Days*). But among the many blemishes are some real beauty spots, foremost of which is the **Cecil Hotel**, overlooking Midan Saad Zaghloul. Built in 1930, it's an Alexandrian institution and a

Literary Alexandria

Alexandria: A History & Guide (sadly, now out of print) was intended, he explained, as a guidebook to things not there, based on the premise that 'the sights of Alexandria are in themselves not interesting, but they fascinate when we approach them from the past'.

The guide provided an introduction to the city for Lawrence Durrell, arriving in Egypt 22 years after Forster's departure. Durrell had been evacuated from Greece and resented both Cairo, where he first settled, and then Alex, which he regarded as 'a broken-down version of Naples'. But this was 1942 to 1945, and Durrell found great distraction in the slightly unreal air of decadence and promiscuity engendered by the uncertainties and transience caused by the ongoing desert war. He worked as a press attache and lived in the tower room of a great house in Moharrem Bey at 19 Sharia Maamoun, which is where he entertained, and wrote poetry and his short novel *The Dark Labyrinth*. On our last visit in 2001, the house and its turret (which is illustrated on the cover of the Faber & Faber edition of the collected *Quartet*) still stood, but developers – who have recently demolished the adjacent villa and replaced it with an apartment block – are just itching to haul it down. It may be gone by the time you read this, but if you want to have a look then starting at Masr train station walk south-east down Sharia Moharrem Bey until the very end where there's a small midan at which the road swings to the right; at the midan, you turn left, into Sharia Nabil al-Wakad, and Sharia Maamoun is a couple of hundred metres along on the right. It's a few kilometres in all.

In truth, those Egyptians that are aware of Durrell's opus are not particularly fond of the book. It deals with a city they don't recognise. Durrell felt little affinity with the locals and instead his narrative is peopled by Greeks, Jews and expatriates. The odd Copt aside, Egyptians don't figure much at all. The heavy eroticism and sensual nature that underlies the work – providing much of the appeal to readers – has also always had far more to do with Durrell himself than it did with the reality of Alexandria. Certainly, anyone who visits today with visions of the city gleaned from the *Quartet* will gain as much satisfaction as they would visiting London in order to look for the world of Mary Poppins.

Instead, they'd do better to read *Miramar* by Naguib Mahfouz. Most of the Nobel prize–winning Egyptian author's novels and stories are set in his home city of Cairo, but *Miramar* uses post-Revolutionary Alexandria as its setting. A story of a murder of passion recounted from the varying viewpoints of four Egyptian residents of a shabby pension, it is supremely evocative of a living city, unlike the city of memories, ghosts and myths presented by Alexandria's more famous European visitors.

memorial to the city's *belle époque* when guests included Somerset Maugham, Noel Coward and Winston Churchill, and the British Secret Service operated out of a suite on the 1st floor.

The area around **Midan Ramla** is full of snapshots of the city's cosmopolitan past – take a look in the **Pharmacie Suisse** with its beautiful dark wood and glass cabinets painted with skull and crossbones and the warning *substances toxique*. Next door is **Athenios**, a once-grand tearoom frequented by Greek girls and besuited Egyptian pashas. Athenios has faded but, diagonally across the midan, the **Trianon** still possesses a wonderfully grand Art Deco dining room with fabulous murals (it's currently unused and you need to ask to see it) and pulls a select crowd to breakfast on coffee, croissants and other European pastries.

Incidentally, Midan Ramla is located roughly on the site of the Caesareum, a large sanctuary and temple initiated by Cleopatra in honour of the deified Julius Caesar, and continued by Augustus, first Roman ruler of Egypt. To mark the entrance to the complex, Augustus had two great obelisks brought up from Heliopolis. They stood just in front of where the Trianon stands today. Long after the Caesareum disappeared, the obelisks remained standing – or at least one of them did, the other toppled over during an earthquake in 1301 – and were frequently sketched by visitors who nicknamed them 'Cleopatra's Needles'. In 1877 one of the obelisks was removed to Britain to stand beside the Thames River in London; the other was carted off to New York to be re-erected in Central Park.

A short walk away from the midan, west along Sharia Saad Zaghloul and then left opposite the Brazilian coffee store into Sharia an-Nabi Daniel, you'll find Alexandria's chief **synagogue**. It was built over a century ago to serve a thriving Jewish community of about 15,000, but since the wars with Israel it now opens each Shabbat to only a handful of elderly people, mainly women. It's a fabulous Italian-built structure with pink marble pillars, although casual visitors aren't usually admitted.

About 200m south of the synagogue, off Sharia an-Nabi Daniel, is the side street leading to the Cavafy Museum (see the boxed text 'Literary Alexandria' earlier in this section), but for more grandeur bear right at the fork and head down to the junction with Sharia Talaat Harb and the wonderful **Banque Masr Building**. It's a working bank so you can stick your nose in and take a look at the church-like interior with its high-backed benches, Gothic arches and stained glass. It's absolutely beautiful. Just around the corner, at 1 Rue Tousoum Pasha, is the building where in 1942, Lawrence Durrell worked as part of the British propaganda bureau. Next door at No 2, a plaque marks the first trading company established by native Alexandrians, the Al-Fayed brothers, one of whom is slightly more infamous now as father of the late Dodi (partner of the late Diana Princess of Wales), and as the owner of Harrod's in London. From here head one block south to Salah Salem and then east to its end and Midan Tahrir, and then to Anfushi beyond.

Midan Tahrir & Anfushi

Midan Tahrir More popularly known as Midan Mansheiyya, Midan Tahrir was laid out in 1830 as the centrepiece of Mohammed Ali's new Alexandria. It is Mohammed Ali who is depicted in the equestrian statue standing high on a plinth at the centre of the midan. There's some fine architecture around the big open space, which is now looking quite impressive after a recent spruce up.

Souqs At the north-west end of the midan the grand architecture switches scale to something more intimate as you enter the city's souq district. Two main streets head into the market: to the left, Sharia Nokrashi and to the right, Sharia Faransa. Sharia Nokrashi runs for about a kilometre and it's one long, heaving bustle of fruit, vegetables, fish and meat stalls, bakeries, cafes and sundry shops selling every imaginable household item. Sharia Faransa begins with cloth, clothes and all things connected with dressmaking. The tight weave of covered alleys running off to the south-west are collectively known as Zinqat as-Sittat, or 'The Women's Squeeze'. Here you'll find buttons, braid, baubles, bangles, beads and much more, from junk jewellery to those enormous padded bras. Beyond the haberdashery is gold and silver, and then herbalists and spice vendors.

Anfushi At the junction of Faransa and Souq al-Kharateen is the interesting little **Terbana Mosque**. Built in the late 17th century, it incorporates bits of ancient Alexandria in its structure – look around the side for the two classical columns that support the minaret. The red-and-black painted brickwork on the facade is a common Delta style. **Shorbagi Mosque**, nearby on Sharia Nokrashi, is also built with salvaged remnants of antiquity.

At this point, you're deep into Anfushi, the old Turkish part of town. While Midan Ramla and the Midan Tahrir area were developed along the lines of a European model in the 19th century, Anfushi remained an untouched, indigenous quarter. Standing in counterpoint to the new cosmopolitan city, it was considered a bit beyond the pale. This is where Durrell's characters came in search of prostitutes and a bit of rough trade. Today it remains one of the poorest parts of the city, with a high population density squeezed into old, decaying buildings, many of which seem on the verge of collapsing.

If you continue along Sharia Faransa north of Ras at-Tin, the street becomes much narrower, opening suddenly into a midan dominated by the large white **Mosque of Abu Abbas al-Mursi**. Built in 1943 on the site of an earlier mosque that had been constructed over the tomb of a 13th-century Muslim saint, this is a modern but impressive example of Islamic architecture. On feast days and during Ramadan, this is the place to come as thousands of people converge here to enjoy the night-time festivities.

From the mosque, Fort Qaitbey is just over 1km along the Corniche. Alternatively, if you're keen on tombs, 1km to the west there's the **Necropolis of Anfushi** *(Sharia Ras at-Tin; admission E£12; open 9am-4pm daily)*, five tombs dating back to around 250 BC. The two main ones contain some much-faded wall decoration, supposedly imitating marble, but they're not nearly as interesting as the Catacombs of Kom ash-Shuqqafa.

Fort Qaitbey

Fort Qaitbey *(☎ 480 9144, Eastern Harbour; admission E£20; open 9am-4pm daily)* is unfortunate in that it looks like a piece of Toytown architecture. Its greatest point of interest is that it occupies the site of the much more famous Pharos lighthouse (see the boxed text 'The Pharos' later in this chapter).

The lighthouse had been gone for a century when, in about 1480, the Mamluk sultan Qaitbey ordered the fortification of the city's harbour peninsulas and the construction of a fort and mosque. Naturally, debris from the Pharos was used. Mohammed Ali modernised the fort in the 19th century, for which we can blame its twee appearance. However, if you get up close to the outer walls you can pick out some great pillars of red granite, which in all likelihood came from the ancient lighthouse.

These days the three floors of the fort house a small naval museum with various displays, including Ottoman weaponry, and bits and pieces recovered from Napoleon's unhappy fleet that was savaged by Nelson in 1798. Even if you aren't interested in entering the fort, do make the walk out here for the view back across the harbour, with a foreground of small bobbing fishing boats and, in the distance, the sun-like disk of the new library. There's also a pungent fish market nearby.

To walk to the fort from the Ramla area along the Corniche takes about 30 to 45 minutes. It's a pleasant walk, but if you don't quite feel up to it, take yellow tram No 15 from Midan Ramla for 20pt or flag down any of the microbuses barrelling along the Corniche. A taxi should cost about E£2.

The Pharos

According to classical accounts, the Egyptian coast was notoriously treacherous, with hidden rocks and sand banks, and a flat, featureless shoreline offering little in the way of navigational aids. Therefore, Ptolemy I ordered a great tower to be built, one that took 12 years to complete and was finally inaugurated in 283 BC. The finished structure was of such massive proportions and of such a unique nature that ancient scholars regarded it as one of the Seven Wonders of the World.

In its original form, the Pharos was a simple marker, probably topped with a statue, as was common at the time. Historians believe that the tower became a lighthouse in the 1st century AD, when the Romans added a beacon, probably in the form of an oil-fed flame that was reflected by sheets of polished bronze. Some excellent descriptions of the Pharos exist from as late as the 12th century. It had a square base, an octagonal central section and a round top (which is the form seen in early minarets, leading some historians to speculate that the Pharos was the original inspiration for this Islamic structure). Contemporary images of the Pharos still exist, most notably in a mosaic in St Mark's cathedral in Venice and in two little terracotta representations displayed in Alexandria's Graeco-Roman Museum.

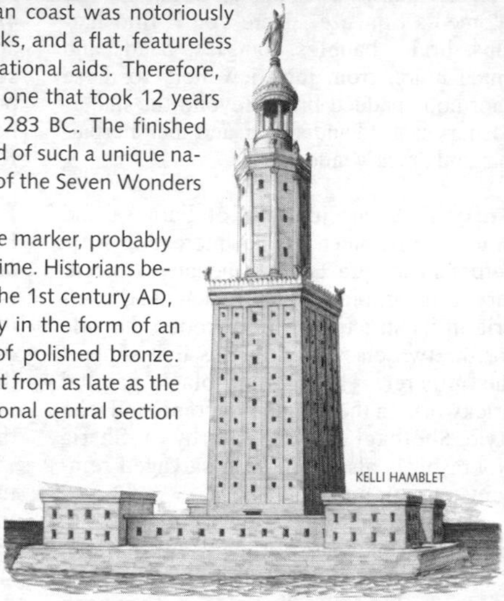

The Pharos lighthouse was one of the Seven Wonders of the World in ancient times.

In all, the Pharos withstood winds, floods and the occasional tidal wave for a total of 17 centuries. However, in the year 1303, a violent earthquake rattled the entire eastern Mediterranean, from Egypt to Greece, and the Pharos was toppled. A century later the Mamluk sultan Qaitbey quarried the ruins for the fortress that he built on the same site.

EASTERN SUBURBS

Bibliotheca Alexandrina

A mammoth piece of 21st-century architecture, the new Alexandria library – officially known as the Bibliotheca Alexandrina – is an attempt to put the city back on the world cultural map. The new library was inspired by the original Great Library, founded in the early 3rd century BC, shortly after the city itself. Acclaimed as the greatest of all classical institutions, this library is said to have held as many as half a million texts. Legend has it that every vessel entering the city's harbour had to hand over any manuscripts for copying.

The new library is intended to hold eight million books in its vast rotunda space. The design, which resembles a gigantic discus embedded into the ground at an angle, is intended to represent a second sun rising beside the Mediterranean. The ancient wealth of learning is lyrically evoked on the curved exterior walls, which are carved with giant letters, pictograms, hieroglyphs, and symbols from every known alphabet. Besides books, other facilities are to include exhibition spaces, a science museum and a planetarium, which is a separate, spherical structure on the outside plaza and resembles the Death Star from the movie *Star Wars*. Visually, it's all highly impressive, but it remains to be seen how the whole thing will function as the opening date, initially set for 2000, has repeatedly been pushed back and currently stands at October 2002.

Chatby & Mustafa Kamal Necropolises

If you haven't had enough of tombs, there are two more sets of them. The **Chatby necropolis** *(Sharia Port Said, Chatby; admission E£6; open 9am-4pm daily)*, next to the youth hostel, is considered to be the oldest necropolis found in Alexandria. Discovered in 1904, the burials here date from the 4th century BC, soon after the city's founding, and belong to the first generations of Alexandrians. Further east, opposite AmEx, is the **Mustafa Kamal necropolis** *(Sharia al-Moaskar ar-Romani, Rushdy; admission E£12; open 9am-4pm daily)*. Two of the four tombs are interesting for the Doric columns at their centre.

Bus No 218 from Midan Ramla will drop you near the Chatby necropolis. To get to the Mustafa Kamal necropolis, take tram No 1 or No 2 to the Mustafa Kamal as-Sughayyer stop and walk east a couple of blocks to Al-Moaskar ar-Romani. Turn left here (towards the sea) and walk a couple more blocks. The necropolis is on the left.

Royal Jewellery Museum

Farouk, the last king of Egypt, was a man known for extravagance and excess. He gambled away $150,000 in a single sitting (even though the majority of his subjects struggled in poverty), and society hostesses reputedly hid away their daughters when the king turned up at their parties. The 1952 Revolution would no doubt have happened without him, but his supremely decadent behaviour can only have hastened the demise of the royals. This **museum** *(☎ 586 8348, 27 Sharia Ahmed Yehia Pasha, Glym; admission E£20; open 9am-4pm daily)* is a testament to royal excess. It houses a glitzy collection of personal and family heirlooms. Aside from the standard stuff (medals, jewels etc), the exhibits include diamond-encrusted garden tools, jewelled watches with hand-painted miniature portraits and a golden chess set. The collection is housed in a beautiful villa formerly belonging to the family of Farida, Farouk's first queen. It retains some wonderfully eclectic decor: One corridor is lined with a series of floor-to-ceiling painted-glass windows depicting a bright parade of waltzing courtesans; the ceilings are crowded with pink cherubs on cottonwool clouds; but best of all are the pictorially tiled bathrooms – tasteful they are not.

To get to the museum, take tram No 2 from Midan Ramla and get off at the Qasr as-Safa stop, beside the Faculty of Fine Arts building, then look for the big white villa surrounded by a high wall.

Mahmoud Said Museum

Unknown outside his home country, Mahmoud Said (1897–1964) was one of the finest Egyptian artists of the 20th century. He was a judge by profession and painted only as a sideline, but he was part of an influential group of sophisticates who in the 1920s and 1930s experimented with forging an Egyptian artistic identity. Said's work has echoes of the past (some of his portraits resemble the Graeco-Roman Fayoum Portraits), but is blended with European and American influences and techniques such as cubism and social realism. The **museum** *(☎ 582 1688, 6 Sharia Mohammed Said Pasha, Gianaclis; admission E£10; open 9am-1.30pm & 5pm-9pm Sat-Thur)* presents about 40 of his works (although some of his signature pieces are held in the National Museum of Modern Egyptian Art in Cairo) housed in the beautiful Italianate villa in which he once lived. Best of all are the nudes of honey-toned, earthy women depicted against richly coloured backgrounds. The paintings are well worth the trip out here. To get to the museum, take tram No 2 from Midan Ramla to the San Stefano stop – a ride of about 20 minutes – then cross the tracks and walk up the steps to the raised road. Go right and Sharia Mohammed Said Pasha is a short distance along on the left.

Montazah Palace Gardens

Montazah is a royal palace built as a summer retreat for Khedive Abbas Hilmy (r. 1892–1914). On a rocky bluff overlooking the sea, it's designed in a vaguely Moorish style but with a definite Florentine twist (the tower is a direct steal from the Palazzo

Vecchio). Now used by Egypt's presidents, it's off limits to the public but the surrounding lush groves and gardens, planted with pine and palms, are accessible (admission E£4) and they're a favourite place for picnicking locals. There's also an attractive sandy cove with a semiprivate beach (admission E£9.50) although it's not particularly clean, and an eccentric Victorian-style bridge running out to a small island. It's all very pretty and makes for a pleasant escape from the traffic and concrete. A second royal residence, known as the Salamlek and built in an Austrian style as a hunting lodge, has recently been refurbished and opened as a luxury hotel.

The simplest way to get to the palace is to stand on the Corniche or on Tariq al-Horreyya and flag down a service (microbus); when it slows, shout 'Montazah' and if it's going that way (and most of them are) it'll stop and you can jump in. Most of these services originate at Midan al-Gomhuriyya, the square in front of Masr train station, so you could also catch one from there. You can also reach Montazah on the local train from Masr or Sidi Gaber stations on the way to Abu Qir but services are infrequent and slow.

BEACHES

There are a few public or semipublic beaches along Alexandria's waterfront, but most of the ones between the Eastern Harbour and the Montazah are usually crowded and very grubby. **Mamoura Beach**, about 1km east of Montazah Palace, is better – it even has a few small waves rolling in. It is also the only beach where women are likely to feel comfortable stripping down to a one-piece swimsuit. The local authorities are trying to keep this beach suburb exclusive by charging everyone who enters the Mamoura area a fee of E£3, payable at the toll booth as you drive in off Sharia Abu Qir. To get here jump in an Abu Qir microbus at Midan al-Gomhuriyya.

PLACES TO STAY

The summer months of June to September are the high season in Alexandria, when half of Cairo seems to decamp here in a bid to escape the heat in the capital. They mainly occupy the masses of holiday apartments out along the Corniche in the eastern suburbs but at the peak of the season, in August, you may have difficulty finding a hotel room even at some of the budget places.

For general information on places to stay see Accommodation in the Facts for the Visitor chapter.

PLACES TO STAY – BUDGET

Unless stated otherwise, these prices include taxes and breakfast.

Hostels

Youth Hostel *(☎ 597 5459, 13 Sharia Port Said, Chatby)* Beds in 8-bed room E£12, double rooms E£20-24, nonmembers E£4 extra. This is a very unappealing option with shabby rooms and is poorly located well out of the centre (neither do the rooms have sea views). To get here take any blue tram from Midan Ramla and get off at the Chatby Casino, in front of the College of St Mark; cross to the waterfront side of the college and walk back west a short way along Sharia Port Said.

Hotels

Almost all of Alexandria's budget hotels are located in the side streets off the Corniche in the Midan Ramla area, particularly in the streets just behind the Cecil Hotel. Most of these hotels at least partly front onto the Corniche, so don't settle for a room that doesn't have a sea view – one of the best things about staying in Alex is pushing open the shutters in the morning to get a face full of the Mediterranean.

The hotels below are listed in order from cheapest to more expensive.

New Hotel Welcome House *(☎ 480 6402, 8 Gamal ad-Din Yassin)* Doubles E£25. On the street behind the Cecil, this is one of three cheapies occupying the top two floors of this building (beware, the lift doesn't work), and the only one of the trio we would consider staying at. Its rooms are variable in quality, but an attempt has been made to look after them. Try to get one of the three doubles that overlook the harbour; these have their own shower and toilet units.

Hotel Triomphe *(☎ 480 7585, 5th floor, 2 Gamal ad-Din Yassin)* Singles/doubles E£20/35. A poor relation to the Acropole across the road, the Triomphe has grubby, dust-coated rooms at negotiable prices – management was prepared to come down to E£25 for a double. Nonc of the rooms have views. An option for only the most impecunious.

Hotel Acropole *(☎ 480 5980, 4th floor, 1 Gamal ad-Din Yassin)* Singles/doubles E£25/40. A long-time budget favourite, the Acropole has a shabby appeal. Rooms are reasonably clean, as are the shared bathrooms. None overlook the harbour directly, but several have superb views over Midan Saad Zaghloul.

Hyde Park Hotel *(☎ 487 5666, 6th floor, 21 Amin Fikry)* Singles E£30-35, doubles E£35-45. Note breakfast is not compulsory and the rooms are E£5 cheaper without it. While the hotel is too far back from the harbour to properly benefit from the sea, looking down on all the activity around Midan Ramla is a buzz (the view from room 44 is especially good). The higher-priced rooms come with their own bathroom.

Hotel Ailema *(☎ 484 7011, 7th floor, 21 Amin Fikry)* Singles E£30-40, doubles E£40-60. Comments on the Hyde Park regarding the views also apply here, but the Ailema also has an endearing, shuffling, sepia-toned quality. If you've read Mahfouz, then the Ailema is a ringer for the Pension Miramar in the book of the same name. The more expensive rooms come complete with brand new shower and toilet cubicles.

Hotel Union *(☎ 480 7312, fax 480 7350, 5th floor, 164 Sharia 26th of July)* Singles/doubles without bath E£35/50, with bath E£45/60. One block to the west of the Cecil, the Union offers good value, although breakfast seems to be mandatory and adds E£8. The rooms are some of the cleanest in Alex with sparkling tiled bathrooms. Some have balconies and harbour views. Reservations are recommended.

Hotel Crillon *(☎ 480 0330, 4th floor, 5 Sharia Adib Ishaq)* Doubles with shower E£53, doubles with bath E£67. Two blocks west of the Cecil, the Crillon used to be a good second choice if the Union was full but standards have slipped. Readers have complained of unwashed bed linen and unemptied ashtrays. Still, we do like the lovely pre-Revolutionary reception/lounge area and those rooms with polished wooden floors and French windows that open on to balconies with that great harbour view.

PLACES TO STAY – TOP END

Alexandria has a dearth of mid-range accommodation. The few options that do exist tend to be strung out in the eastern suburbs along the Corniche, which is no-man's land as far as sights, shops and other conveniences go. Nor are these hotels particularly well looked after. They represent poor value for money, which is why none of them are listed here. The situation may change very soon as the municipality has announced its intention to create more beds in advance of the October 2002 opening of the Bibliotheca Alexandrina. In the meantime, if somewhere like the budget-oriented Union (around US$15 a night) isn't quite up to requirements, then it's a huge leap of at least a further US$85 if you want to move up to something better.

Cecil Hotel *(☎ 487 7173, fax 484 0368, Midan Saad Zaghloul)* Singles US$120-150, doubles US$133-168. Alexandria's most famous establishment seems to be overtrading on past glories (see Central Alexandria for more information). Although managed by the international Sofitel chain and benefiting from several refits over the years, bedrooms are grimy and threadbare, and hardly consistent with the hotel's purported four-star status. Common areas such as the lobby and bar have also been stripped of elegance and charm. On the plus side, the sea views are unbeatable and there's a very good Chinese restaurant on the roof. Breakfast is included in the price.

Helnan Palestine *(☎ 547 4033, fax 547 3378,* e *resh@helnan.com, Montazah*

Palace Gardens) Singles US$105-132, doubles US$132-190. This brutal 1970s hotel in the otherwise lovely Montazah Palace grounds blights the view for everyone else, but offers superb Mediterranean vistas to its guests. Its great distance from the city centre is a drawback.

Metropole Hotel *(☎ 484 1465, fax 484 2040, 52 Sharia Saad Zaghloul)* Singles/doubles from US$100/120. The Metropole has a good, central location with most rooms overlooking either Midan Ramla or Midan Saad Zaghloul, and the harbour. It's a classy old joint that has been recently renovated, earning itself a four-star rating. The lobby is horrendously overdone, but the high-ceiling rooms are fine and the staff meticulously polite.

Al-Salamlek Palace Hotel *(☎ 547 7999, fax 547 3585, e salamlek@sangiovanni.com, w www.sangiovanni.com, Montazah Palace Gardens)* Doubles from US$215. Neighbouring the presidential summer palace, this is a former royal hunting lodge built by Khedive Abbas II for his Austrian mistress. Rooms are opulently furnished in swanky period style, and there's a casino and two quality restaurants (ties are required for male diners). The park setting is fantastic, but the big drawback is its distance from the city centre.

Sheraton Montazah *(☎ 548 0550, fax 540 1331, e smontaza@rite.com, el-Corniche, Montazah)* Doubles from US$135. At least the Al-Salamlek and Helnan Palestine are within the palace grounds with its beautiful garden setting, but the Sheraton is outside the walls surrounded only by concrete. So while facilities are good, the location here is dreadful.

Windsor Palace Hotel *(☎ 480 8256, fax 480 9090, 17 Sharia ash-Shohada)* Singles/doubles from US$120/150. Another old Alex institution, built in 1907, the Windsor Palace has recently been bought by Paradise Inns and given a much-needed smartening up (including an awful pink paint job). Thankfully, the wonderful old elevators have been retained. Most rooms have wonderful sea views thanks to the excellent Corniche-front location.

PLACES TO EAT

One of the great pleasures of visiting Alexandria is sitting around in its various cafes and gorging yourself on the abundant, fresh seafood.

Fast Food

Most of the fast-food joints are out in the more fashionable suburbs such as Rushdy, Smouha and Mamoura, but ***McDonald's*** has a city centre branch on Sharia Safiyya Zaghloul, just south of Midan Ramla, while ***KFC*** is around the corner on the midan itself. There's another KFC on Sharia al-Kineesa al-Kobtiyya, just off An-Nabi Daniel.

Budget Dining

The place for cheap eating is around the area where Sharia Safiyya Zaghloul meets Midan Ramla, and along Sharia Shakor Pasha, one street over to the west. There are plenty of little fuul and ta'amiyya places here, as well as sandwich shops.

Mohammed Ahmed *(17 Sharia Shakor Pasha).* Dishes E£2-10. Reckoned by all to be the best of the lot, it specialises in fuul, but also does ta'amiyya, omelettes and fried cheese, plus all the usual salad and dip accompaniments. The food is a bit greasy but Alexandrians swear by it and the place is always packed. There are both takeaway and sit-in sections.

Hassan Bleik *(18 Sharia Saad Zaghloul).* Dishes E£6-20. Open noon-6pm daily. Next to the Sofianopoulo Coffee Store, this venerable Lebanese restaurant is nestled behind a patisserie. Never mind the grubby tablecloths, it has an excellent menu of traditional Levantine dishes such as *kibbeh* (meat-filled cracked-wheat croquettes) in yogurt sauce, *fatta* (a bed of rice and bread in a garlicky, vinegary sauce) with chickpeas and lamb, and chicken livers.

Havana *(☎ 487 0661, Tariq al-Horreyya)* Opposite the Sednaoui store, this is primarily a bar (see Bars under Entertainment later in this chapter), but it also does great food. There is a menu with standards such as fried calamari (superb) and pizza, but ask about the specials of the day, which could be anything from roast beef and Yorkshire pudding to chicken curry, depending on what the owner/chef picked up at the market that morning. Prices are very reasonable.

Restaurants

City Centre Most of the better places to eat are either on or just off Tariq al-Horreyya, especially around the junction with Safiyya Zaghloul near Midan Ramla.

Au Privé *(☎ 484 1881, Rue de Verdi)* Bar dishes E£10-40, restaurant E£30-40 plus cover charge. Open noon-2am daily. Tucked away down the little alley just east of the junction of Sharia an-Nabi Daniel and Tariq al-Horreyya, this is a hip bar/restaurant with bar snacks and a la carte menus. The bar menu includes lots of dips, salads and burgers, plus a wide variety of seafood. The other is a more heavy-hitting menu with a strong French slant, including dishes of duck and rabbit, plus seafood and steaks, all in rich sauces.

Elite *(☎ 486 3592, 43 Sharia Safiyya Zaghloul)* Dishes E£4.50-30. Open 11am-late daily. Near the Cinema Metro, this is another of those Alexandrian time-warp affairs. Faintly resembling an old US diner, it seems sealed in a 1950s bubble, under the spell of the elderly but formidable Madame Christina, the ever-present proprietress. The menu is displayed outside, beside the door, and ranges from spaghetti bolognese to grilled meats.

Malek as-Samuun E£6 per bird. Open 8pm-late daily. Just south of the junction with Sharia Yousef and off Sharia Attareen in central Alexandria, by day this is a small, courtyard clothes market; by night it's an open-air restaurant serving one thing and one thing only – quail. Diners sit under an awning on a rough dirt floor and tuck into grilled birds served with rice and salad. It's a bit hard to find, but look for a sign painted with a small bird.

L'Osobuco *(☎ 487 2506, 14 Tariq al-Horreyya)* Two courses E£30-50. Open 11am-3am daily. Run by the same people as Cairo's L'Aubergine (see Places to Eat in the Cairo chapter) this is a chic bar/restaurant on two floors (boozing downstairs, candle-lit dining upstairs) with a frequently changing, wide-ranging world menu. The quality of the food is very good and there are plenty of vegie options.

Santa Lucia *(☎ 486 4240, 40 Sharia Safiyya Zaghloul)* Two courses E£40-60. Open 11am-11pm daily. Santa Lucia was for a long time one of Alexandria's best restaurants; standards have slipped but it remains a big favourite with Alexandrians of a certain age. The French menu leans heavily towards tarted-up seafood dishes such as *spaghetti aux fruits de la mer* (spaghetti with seafood) and *crevettes à l'indienne.*

Anfushi Some of Alexandria's best restaurants for straightforward good value and street-side dining can be found in the Anfushi district. Head for Sharia Safar Pasha, which is lined with maybe a dozen places all crackling and flaming with grills barbecuing meat and fish. You could chance a table at any of them and probably come away satisfied, but those mentioned below are the ones we've tried and liked.

Abu Ashraf *(☎ 481 6597, 28 Safar Pasha)* Open 24 hrs daily. Abu Ashraf is one of this wonderful street's fish specialists. Make your selection from the day's catch then take a seat under the green awning and watch it being cooked. Prices are determined by weight and choice, eg, grey mullet E£30 per kilogram or jumbo prawns E£120.

Mohammed Hosni *(☎ 485 6216, 48 Safar Pasha)* Two courses E£16-24. Unlike most of the other restaurants on this street, which do either fish or meat, Mohammed Hosni does both, plus quail. Seating is in a semi–open air courtyard.

Qadoura *(☎ 480 0405, 33 Bairam al-Tonsi)* Open 24 hrs daily. Fish around E£35 per kilogram, prawns E£80 per kilogram. Pronounced 'Adora', this place has long been regarded as Alex's premier fish restaurant. It's a semioutdoor place two blocks in from the Corniche, where you pick your fish from the ice-packed selection that usually includes, at the least, sea bass, red and grey mullet, bluefish, sole, squid and shrimp. A selection of mezze comes with all orders (there's no menu).

Samakmak *(☎ 481 1560, 42 Qasr Ras as-Tin)* Dishes E£30-50. Samakmak is owned by the retired queen of the Alexandrian belly-dancing scene, Zizi Salem. Her restaurant places itself upmarket from Abu Ashraf and Qadoura, and although you can have grilled or fried fish, the place is better known for its seafood specials, such as crayfish, an excellent crab *tajine* (crab cooked slowly in an earthenware dish) and a delicious spaghetti with clams. In summer, a large tented area supplements the indoor seating.

Cafes

Alex has at least five 'must-visit' cafes. The best known is ***Pastroudi's*** *(☎ 496 9609, 39 Tariq al-Horreyya)*, founded in 1923 by Greeks and immortalised in Durrell's *The Alexandria Quartet*. It's no longer the haunt of any sort of smart or literary set, and is in fact a bit fusty, but the pavement tables on its south side are a pleasant late afternoon spot for some reading over lemon tea and pastries (which will comfortably ease you over the E£5 minimum charge). The ***Trianon*** *(☎ 486 0986, 56 Midan Saad Zaghloul)*, which faces Midan Ramla, was a favourite of the poet Cavafy, who worked in the offices above. It's still immensely popular and a good place for a continental breakfast (although the coffee is lousy).

Much better coffee can be had at the ***Brazilian Coffee Store*** *(Sharia Saad Zaghloul)*, or at the ***Sofianopoulo Coffee Store*** *(Sharia Saad Zaghloul)*, down at the western end of the same street. Both of these places are dominated by huge, silver coffee grinders, and boxes, cases and sacks of the shiny dark aromatic beans. The drawback is that neither has any seating so you have to drink your coffee standing up. There's a second branch of the Brazilian Coffee Store on Sharia Salah Salem that does have some chairs.

Not far away from Sofianopoulo's is ***Baudrot*** *(Sharia Saad Zaghloul)*, which is completely dead in the winter (December to February) but a must in the summer (June to August) for its garden with vine-laden trellises, and wicker chairs and tables.

Self-Catering

For fruit and vegetables, either head for Souq Nokrashi on the street of the same name just north-west of Midan Tahrir, or the Ibrahimiyya Souq, which is a couple of stops east of Midan Ramla on any tram – get off at the Al-Moaskar stop. These two areas are also the best for *ba'als* (grocers) selling cheese, olives, yogurt, bread and the like. Takeaway beer is available in the centre at a dedicated Stella shop just off Midan Saad Zaghloul, below the Acropole.

ENTERTAINMENT

Alexandria's cultural life has never really recovered from the exodus of the Europeans and Jews in the 1940s and 1950s. Since that time, Cairo has been the selfish proprietor of the arts, resulting in Alexandria playing host to just one theatre, one concert hall, no galleries, no opera house and, up until 1998, it had had no new cinema screens built since the Revolution. It does have at least two of the best bars in the country, though.

Ahwas

During the summer the whole 20km length of the Corniche from Ras at-Tin to Montazah becomes one great strung out *ahwa*, or coffeehouse. Generally speaking though, these are not good places – they're catering for a passing holiday trade and so they tend to overcharge. Instead, our favourite is the ***Sultan Hussein***, a good, no nonsense friendly ahwa with excellent *sheesha* (water pipe); it's popular with chess players, and has a separate 'family' area. It's the one with yellow awnings on the corner of Sharias Sultan Hussein and Safiyya Zaghloul. For an odd, atmospheric place – which is admittedly a bit scruffy – take a look at the ***Ahwa al-Hindi*** in the central courtyard of the big, battered old building on the corner where Midan Orabi meets Midan Tahrir. You have to squeeze through a passageway almost closed by clothes stalls to find it.

Bars

Fifty years ago – pre-Revolution – Alexandria was full of Greek tavernas and divey little watering holes. Sadly, that's no longer the case but one or two fine places do survive.

Havana *(☎ 487 0661, Tariq al-Horreyya)* Open noon-2am Sat-Thur. Opposite the Sednaoui store, this gets our vote for best bar in Egypt. It's run by Nagy, whose father bought the place from a departing Greek in the 1950s. Since that time some of the details may have changed, but a cosmopolitan, laissez faire air still prevails at its six tables. Nagy is also a great cook – see Places to Eat earlier. There's no sign and the door is usually kept locked, but just knock and you'll be made welcome – that is, as long as you obey the old rules, posted up in Arabic, which read, 'No entry in pyjamas and no spitting on the floor'.

Cap d'Or *(☎ 487 5177, 4 Sharia Adib)* Open noon-3am daily. Almost as good as the Havana is Cap d'Or, which is just off Sharia Saad Zaghloul. With stained glass windows, a big high marble-topped bar and plenty of old bits and pieces hanging on the walls, it has the feel of an Andalusian tapas bar. Plenty of people come here to eat calamari, shrimp or fish, all of which are excellent, but it's an equally fine place just to pull up a stool and settle in for a Stella.

Spitfire *(☎ 480 6503, 7 rue de L'Ancienne Bourse)* Open noon-midnight daily. The Spitfire, just north of Sharia Saad Zaghloul, has a reputation as a sailors' bar and the walls are plastered with stickers for shipping lines and photos of drunk regulars.

Another old Alex bar worth investigating is ***Al-Horreyya*** on Sharia Attareen, just south of the junction with Sharia Yousef. You can also drink without having to eat at ***Elite*** (see Places to Eat earlier), which has the appeal of large windows so you can street-watch while drinking your Stella.

Cinemas

The following cinemas regularly screen English-language films:

Amir Cinema *(☎ 491 7972, 42 Tariq al-Horreyya)* In central Alexandria, this place has two screens, both of which usually show movies a year or two old. It's a nice enough cinema though.

Cinema Metro *(☎ 487 0432, 26 Safiyya Zaghloul)* In central Alexandria, this is an absolutely beautiful old place, and is very well looked after – pity the movies it screens are always so bad.

Osman Group Cinema *(☎ 424 5897, Smouha Shopping Centre)* Fairly new cinema in the central court of the Smouha shopping centre, next to the Zahran Mall in Smouha. For how to get here, see the directions to the Smouha Internet cafes under Internet & Email Access earlier in this chapter. Alternatively, a taxi from the centre will cost about E£3.

Renaissance *(☎ 424 0844, Zahran Mall, Smouha)* Alexandria's newest cinema, it has four screens all showing first-run Hollywood films. For how to get here, follow the same directions as for the Osman Group Cinema.

Rialto *(☎ 486 4694, Safiyya Zaghloul)* Slightly scruffy old downtown cinema that has recently taken to showing first release English-language films.

Royal Renaissance *(mobile ☎ 012-227 5493)* An old cinema off Tariq al-Horreyya and beside the Said Darwish Theatre. It has recently been upgraded and two of its three screens are usually devoted to English-language films.

Music, Theatre & Dance

There is virtually nothing going on in Alexandria in the way of theatre or music. The Elite restaurant usually sticks up notices advertising anything that's happening; otherwise have a look at *Egypt Today*. Also, check the French Cultural Centre (see Cultural Centres earlier in this chapter), as it is behind most of the few performances that do go on.

Said Darwish Theatre *(☎ 486 5602, 22 Tariq al-Horreyya)* This is Alexandria's modestly sized but splendid old opera house, and what little classical music and performance art there is usually gets staged here.

SHOPPING

There's the souq just west of Midan Tahrir, and Sharias Safiyya Zaghloul and Saad Zaghloul are lined with an assortment of poky old stores, but overall Alexandria is not a great place to shop. Not, that is, unless you like shopping for antiques and other miscellaneous historical debris. The confusion of backstreets and alleys of the **Attareen**

district make up an antique market of world renown. When Alexandria's European high society was forced en masse to make a hasty departure from Egypt following the Revolution in 1952, they largely went without their personal belongings and much of what they left behind has over the years found its way into the shops of Attareen. But while there are some wonderful finds, there are few bargains. Dealers here know their stuff. Their bedtime reading are the Christie's and Sotheby's catalogues. Some of these guys even have branches in Paris and the regular clientele are largely rich Egyptians and collectors from the Gulf, the US and Europe. Still, there are good buys around and there's no charge for just looking.

GETTING THERE & AWAY

Air

There are direct international flights from Alexandria to Athens (Olympic Airways) and Frankfurt (Lufthansa Airlines), and to Saudi Arabia and Dubai (EgyptAir). Airline offices in Alexandria include:

Air France (☎ 487 8901) 22 Salah Salem
British Airways (☎ 487 6668) 15 Midan Saad Zaghloul
EgyptAir (☎ 487 3357) 19 Midan Saad Zaghloul
KLM-Royal Dutch Airlines (☎ 486 8547) 6 Tariq al-Horreyya
Lufthansa Airlines (☎ 487 7031) 6 Talaat Harb
Olympic Airways (☎ 486 1014) 19 Midan Saad Zaghloul
SAS (☎ 487 3973) 32 Tariq al-Horreyya, opposite the Amir Cinema
TWA (☎ 487 6482) 2 Tariq al-Horreyya

Air travel to Alexandria from within Egypt is expensive; the one-way fare for the 40-minute flight from Cairo is E£204. Unless you are in a tremendous hurry, it is best to get to and from Alexandria by bus, taxi or train. In fact, by the time you take getting to and from airports into account, you're not likely to save any time whatsoever.

Bus

Long-distance buses all leave from one garage behind Sidi Gaber train station and the No 1 minibus from outside the Cecil Hotel connects this train station with the city centre. (If you get dropped off at the front of the train station you need to take the underpass to the platform on the far side of the tracks, then go down another flight of steps to get out.)

The main companies operating from Sidi Gaber are Superjet (☎ 428 9092), whose ticket office and bays are almost immediately behind the train station, and West Delta (☎ 427 0916), who are about 100m to the east. Between these two are several little cabins beside the road that house the East Delta and Upper Egypt bus ticket offices.

West Delta also has a city centre booking office (☎ 480 9685) on Midan Saad Zaghloul, close to the main tourist office.

Cairo Superjet has buses to Cairo (also stopping at Cairo airport) every 30 minutes from 5am to 10pm. The trip takes 2½ hours and costs from E£20 to E£25 until 5.30pm after which it goes up and costs from E£22 to E£31. There's also a 1am service to the airport only (E£31).

West Delta also has buses to Cairo every 30 minutes between 5am and 2am (5.30am to 1am in winter) and charges E£16 to E£20, with prices rising by E£1 after 5pm, and jumping to E£25 after 11.30pm. The Superjet buses are a bit bigger and more modern, but all the Cairo services have air-con and a toilet on board.

North Coast & Siwa Oasis West Delta has around 20 buses a day to Marsa Matruh (E£15 to E£23, depending on the bus) between 7am and 2.30am. Almost all of these buses continue on to Sallum (E£23, nine hours) on the Libyan border. Three services go on to Siwa (E£30, nine hours) – those at 8.30am, 11am and 2pm. Otherwise just take any Marsa Matruh bus and change there.

Most of the Matruh buses stop in El Alamein (E£10, one hour), and will stop at Sidi Abdel Rahman (E£6) if you want to get off there.

Superjet has buses to Marsa Matruh (E£24) only in the summer, departing daily at 7.15am and 4pm.

Sinai Superjet has a daily 6.30pm service to Sharm el-Sheikh (E£77, seven hours).

Suez Canal & Red Sea Coast Superjet has one bus daily to Port Said (E£22, four hours) at 6.45am, and one to Hurghada (E£80, nine hours) at 8pm. West Delta has four services a day to Port Said (E£17 to E£20), two to Ismailia (E£17) at 7am and 2.30pm, and two to Suez (E£20) at 6.30am and 2.30pm. The Upper Egypt Bus Company also has three Hurghada (E£55) buses a day that continue on down to Port Safaga (E£60).

International Buses West Delta and Superjet both run buses to Benghazi and Tripoli in Libya. Superjet's bus leaves at 8am daily and costs US$60 to Benghazi and US$123 for the 32-hour trip to Tripoli. The West Delta bus leaves at 1pm, costs E£75 and terminates 17 hours later in Benghazi from where you can get another bus on to Tripoli.

Train

Alexandria's main train terminal is Masr Station (Mahattat Masr; for information ☎ 392 0010), although Sidi Gaber (for information ☎ 427 7363), which serves the populous eastern suburbs, is almost as busy. At Masr Station, 1st-class and 2nd-class air-con tickets must be bought from the ticket office next to the tourist information booth; 3rd-class and 2nd-class ordinary tickets are purchased from the front hall.

Cairo-bound trains leave from Masr Station at least hourly, from about 5am to 10pm (there's also one at 3.25am), stopping five minutes later at Sidi Gaber station. The best trains, the *Turbini* and *Espani,* don't stop again until 2½ hours later when they arrive in Cairo. They depart Masr Station at 7am, 8am, 2pm, 3pm, 7pm, 7.30pm and 10.15pm and tickets for 1st-class/2nd-class air-con cost E£30/22.

The next best train, the *Faransawi*, stops at Damanhur, Tanta and Benha taking three hours to get to Cairo; it departs at 6am, 8.15am, 11am, 1pm, 3.30pm, 5pm and 8pm and 1st-class/2nd-class tickets cost E£23/14.

Two trains a day leave Alexandria for Marsa Matruh (about six hours) at 6.45am and 1pm, but they are not a good option; there's no 1st class, only 2nd/3rd class that costs E£6.40/2.80. The bus service on this route is faster and more comfortable.

Service Taxi

The service taxi depot is across the midan from the Masr train station. The fares are between E£8 and E£10 to Cairo or Marsa Matruh, depending on whom you talk to. To more local destinations, some sample fares are: Zagazig E£8; Tanta E£5; Mansura E£8; Abu Qir 50pt. There's also a second, bigger service taxi station at Moharrem Bey.

Boat

At the time of writing, there are absolutely no passenger boats operating out of Alexandria. They used to sail regularly up the coast to Beirut in Lebanon, Lattakia in Syria, and on up to İstanbul and even Odessa in Russia. There was also a regular ferry between Alex and Athens. But cheap airfares have taken away the trade and the last boats quit in 1997. This situation is not expected to change.

GETTING AROUND

To/From the Airport

Alexandria's airport (information ☎ 427 1036) has been relocated to 60km west of the city centre at an old military airfield called Burg al-Arab. To get there, you can take bus No 555 from in front of the Cecil Hotel. A taxi should cost no more than E£30. Inquire before heading out there, however, because rumour has it that once the old airport has been fixed up (possibly by 2002) it'll be brought back into service.

Bus & Minibus

As a visitor to Alex, you may find that you won't use the buses at all – the trams and microbuses are a much better way of getting around.

Train

About the only conceivable service you might use in Alexandria is the slow 3rd-class train from Masr Station to Abu Qir that stops, among other places, at Sidi Gaber, Montazah and Mamoura. The fare is 40pt.

Tram

The tram is the best way to travel in Alex. Mahattat Ramla is the main tram station and from here lime-yellow coloured trams go west:

tram no	destination
No 14	Masr station and Moharrem Bey
No 15	past the Mosque of Abu al-Abbas Mursi and Fort Qaitbey to Ras at-Tin

Blue coloured trams travel east:

tram no	destination
Nos 1&2	Victoria via Rushdy and Sidi Gaber
Nos 3 & 7	Sidi Gaber North
Nos 4 & 6	Sidi Gaber South
Nos 5 & 8	San Stefano

Some trams have two or three carriages and one of them is usually reserved for women. It causes considerable amusement when an unsuspecting foreigner gets in the wrong carriage. The standard fare is 20pt.

Taxi

You can expect to pay for taxis in Alexandria what you would pay in Cairo. A short trip, say from Midan Ramla to Masr train station, will cost E£2, while between E£3 and E£4 is reasonable for a trip to the eastern beaches.

Around Alexandria

ABU QIR

☎ 03

This coastal town, 24km east of central Alexandria, is historically important for two major 18th-century battles between the French and English. During the Battle of the Nile in 1798, Admiral Nelson surprised and destroyed the French fleet in the bay at Abu Qir. Although Napoleon still controlled Egypt, his contact with France by sea was effectively severed. The British landed 15,000 Turkish soldiers at Abu Qir in 1799, but the French force of 10,000 men, mostly cavalry led personally by Napoleon, forced the Turks back into the sea, drowning at least 5000 of them.

It is best to go to Abu Qir during the week to avoid the crowds of Alexandrians who flock there on the weekends. If you're into seafood, this is definitely a good place to go.

There are plenty of buses from central Alexandria to Abu Qir every day (for example bus Nos 260 and 261 or minibus No 729 from Midan Orabi), but it's probably easier to take a microbus for 60pt from in front of Masr train station. Note that Abu Qir is pronounced 'Abu ear'.

ABU MINA

☎ 03

St Mina is said to have fallen victim to anti-Christian feeling in the Roman Empire of the early 4th century. Born in West Africa, he did a stint in the Roman army before deserting and finally being tortured and beheaded for his faith. He was buried at a place near the present site of Abu Mina, which eventually became a place of pilgrimage. Churches and even a basilica were built, but all have been subsequently destroyed. In the 14th century, a Mamluk army supposedly rediscovered the site and the bones of St Mina, which could not be burned, proving to the Mamluks that they belonged to a saint.

A German team has been working at Abu Mina since 1969 (excavations have uncovered the early medieval Church of the Martyr, where St Mina's remains are believed to be buried), and there are grand plans for a museum and archaeological park. At present the site is not open to visitors.

ROSETTA (RASHID)

☎ 03

Rosetta, also known by its newer name of Rashid, is 65km east of Alexandria, where the western branch of the Nile empties into the Mediterranean, some 6680km from its source at Lake Victoria.

Warning

Do not visit Rosetta if it has rained any time during the last few days – the town's streets are unsurfaced and after a downpour the whole place becomes one big mud bath.

Founded in the 9th century, the town is nost famous as the place of discovery of the tone stele that provided the key to deci›hering hieroglyphs (see the boxed text The Rosetta Stone') but, during the 17th and 8th centuries, it was also Egypt's most vital ›ort. Then, as Alexandria staged its come›ack in the 19th century, Rosetta fell into lecline, to the point where today it's a sleepy ittle provincial town sustained by fishing and lates. There are more donkey carts and horses ınd traps on the streets than there are cars.

The Nile here is particularly beautiful, vide and full; boat builders line the Rosetta Corniche and little palms dot the far bank.

Ottoman Houses

Rosetta's main attraction is its fine old Ottoman-era merchants' houses. These are built in a distinctive Delta style, with small flat bricks painted alternately red and black. They tend to be three storeys high with each of the upper floors sticking out slightly from the one below it, and there's a lot of jutting *mashrabiyyas* – the intricately assembled wooden screens that serve for windows. The houses are beautiful things and there are at least 22 of them, all within 500 sq metres. Most have either been restored or are presently undergoing restoration work, and about eight are currently open to the public. Theoretically, there's a small admission fee, but on our last visit the ticket office (which is in the small park in front of the museum) was closed and we didn't have to pay anything.

Ramadan House The most impressive of all of Rosetta's fine architecture is the

ROSETTA (RASHID)

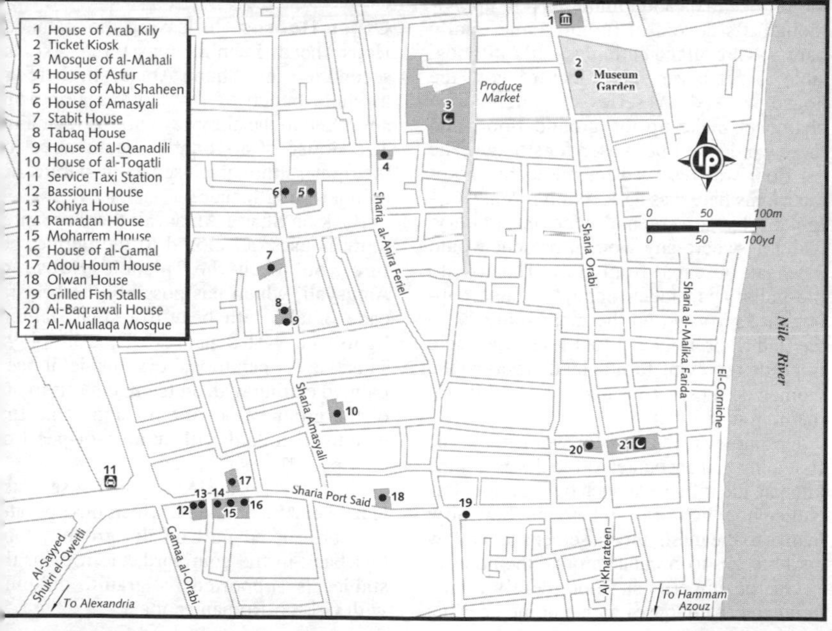

The Rosetta Stone

Now a crowd-pulling exhibit at the British Museum in London, the Rosetta Stone is regarded as one of the key finds of Egyptology. Unearthed in 1799 by Napoleon's soldiers while refortifying old Arab battlements near Rosetta, the stone is part of a large black stele dating from the reign of Ptolemy V (c. 196 BC). The inscription that covers the stone was supposedly written by the priests of Memphis in commemoration of the pharaoh's accession to the throne but, more crucially, it's executed in three languages: Egyptian hieroglyphs, demotic Egyptian (a shorthand form of hieroglyphs) and Greek. It was quickly realised that a comparison of the texts would potentially provide a key to the as yet indecipherable script found on the walls of Egypt's ancient temples and tombs.

In 1801 the Rosetta Stone was conceded to the British and the first attempts were made to decode the hieroglyphs. An Englishman, Thomas Young, established the direction in which the hieroglyphs should be read, and discovered that the hieroglyphs enclosed within oval rings (cartouches) were in fact the names of royalty.

However, it was Frenchman Jean François Champollion who, in 1822, achieved the breakthrough and established a complete list of signs with their Greek equivalents. Champollion was the first Egyptologist to perceive that signs could be alphabetic, syllabic or determinative, and also established that the hieroglyphs inscribed on the Rosetta Stone were actually a translation from the Greek, and not the other way around. His obsessive work not only solved the mystery of Pharaonic script but also contributed significantly to a modern understanding of ancient Egypt.

Ramadan House, which is part of the grouping immediately east of the midan where the service taxis and minibuses pull up. Although it's devoid of furniture and totally bare – as are all the buildings – it's still possible to get a very clear idea of how the house worked. A series of rough stone chambers make up the ground floor, and these would have been used for storage. The 1st floor was reserved for the men; one of the rooms here was a reception room, overlooked by a screened wooden gallery, which is where any women present would have sat, obscured from view. The stair to the gallery is hidden behind a false cupboard. As you go up the main staircase to the 2nd floor, notice at foot level that there is a little revolving turntable; this was so the women could serve tea and coffee while remaining invisible.

Upstairs was the area for women and the first thing you encounter, off to the left, is the kitchen, identifiable as such by the huge flue. Notice how light it is up here and how airy, thanks to the mashrabiyya screens that allow cool breezes to circulate around the house.

On the uppermost floor there's a tiny *hammam* (bathhouse) with a domed ceiling into which would have been set pieces c coloured glass.

Other Houses On leaving the Ramada House head downhill (east) and take th second left into Sharia Amasyali; there ar a whole bunch of fine houses along thi street and in the alleyways off to either side The **House of al-Toqatli** (second street o the right), although closed to the public, ha an interesting facade.

Back on Sharia Amasyali there are thre more houses, all closed to the public, be fore you reach the splendid **House c Amasyali**, which has possibly the best fa cade of all, with beautiful small lanter lights and vast expanses of mashrabiyya This one is open to visitors. Inside, it has painted ceiling with an Islamic motif in or of the ground floor rooms, and some fir woodwork inlaid with mother-of-pearl o the upper floors.

Next door to the Amasyali house is th **House of Abu Shaheen**, which incorporate a reconstructed mill on the ground floo Out back in the courtyard, the roof of th stables is supported by granite colum with Graeco-Roman capitals.

Mosque of al-Mahali

[There are more recycled ancient columns at [t]his mosque, about 100m north-east of the [A]bu Shaheen house. An absolute forest of [t]hem fills the interior and nearly all of them [a]re different – fluted, carved, Doric, Corinth[i]an – posing the question: What were the [b]uildings that they originally supported? We [c]an only wonder. But chances are the col[u]mns were scavenged from Alexandria in [t]he Middle Ages when that city was a ghost [o]f its former Ptolemaic self and Rosetta was [b]ooming. The mosque's doorways are exe[c]uted in the Delta style and are beautiful, as [i]s the central tomb chamber inside the [p]rayer hall.

Museum

[T]he museum was closed for renovation at [t]he time of our last visit but it occupies the **[H]ouse of Arab Kily**, the former residence of [t]he governor during Rosetta's heyday. In the [g]ardens in front of the museum is the ticket [k]iosk (again, closed when we visited) from [w]here tickets are bought to enter the houses.

From the museum head directly south, parallel to the river. This will take you past the [b]ack of the interesting **Al-Muallaqa Mosque**, [w]hich is raised up on ancient Graeco-[R]oman columns with the ground floor un[d]erneath used for storage and stalls. Continue [a]long the same street and after about 200m [y]ou'll come to the **Hammam Azouz**.

[H]ammam Azouz

[T]he hammam, or public bath, is the two-[s]torey, beige-yellow building with a broken [c]olumn lying beside the doorway. It should [b]e open to the public but if the door is [l]ocked and nobody answers your knocking, [j]ust hang around and somebody will run off [a]nd find the custodian. It's worth persever[i]ng because although the hammam hasn't [y]et been restored in any way, it can have [o]nly fallen out of use in recent history be[c]ause it's in a remarkably complete state.

You first enter into a chamber with a cen[t]ral fountain and raised platforms around the [p]eriphery; this is where bathers would first [d]isrobe and where they'd later return, after [s]crubbing and steaming, to lie around, sip tea and chat. Notice, again, more recycled bits of antiquity – in this case the pink granite column. If you then go through the little doorway on the right, you pass through a warren of steam rooms with black-and-white marble floors, and these lead into a beautiful domed chamber, the ceiling of which is inset with coloured glass. The four small rooms at the corners are for washing in and some still have their stone basins.

Bathhouses such as this were in common use until very recently, but now that most houses in Egypt have some form of plumbing they've nearly all closed down.

Getting There & Away

Although buses and trains operate between Alexandria and Rosetta, the easiest way to do the trip is by minibus. From in front of Alexandria's Masr train station jump in one for Abu Qir (60pt). After leaving Alex behind, you travel a long open road with the train track to the left and fields to the right; you need to get out at the point where the minibus swings a sharp left, crossing the tracks. On the north side of the tracks there's a little lot that is where the Rosetta minibuses stand (E£1.50, 45 minutes). Coming back, it's possible to get a minibus (E£2.50) from Rosetta straight in to central Alexandria (they travel the length of the Corniche, passing Midan Saad Zaghloul).

Mediterranean Coast

The stretch of coastline between El Alamein and Alexandria has largely disappeared under a spew of ugly concrete 'tourist villages' – the places that the moneyed classes of Cairo flock to through the wickedly hot summer months.

EL ALAMEIN

☎ 03

The small coastal village of El Alamein, 105km west of Alexandria, is famous as the scene of a decisive Allied victory over the Axis powers during WWII.

In June 1942, the German general Erwin Rommel, nicknamed the 'Desert Fox', launched an offensive from Tobruk, Libya, in an attempt to push his troops and 500 tanks all the way through the Allied lines to Alexandria and the Suez Canal. It was not the first attempt in what had been two years of seesaw battles, but this time the Axis forces were confident of a breakthrough. However, the Allies, under the command of General Bernard Montgomery, stopped their advance with a line of defence stretching southward from El Alamein to the Qattara Depression. On 23 October 1942, Montgomery's eighth army swooped down from Alexandria with a thousand tanks, and within two weeks routed the German and Italian forces, driving Rommel and what was left of his Afrika Korps back to Tunis.

More than 80,000 soldiers were killed or wounded at El Alamein and the subsequent battles for control of North Africa. The thousands of graves in the three massive war cemeteries in the vicinity of the town are a bleak and moving reminder of the war.

The town's two hotels, museum, Commonwealth cemetery, and so on, are actually along a side road that leaves the main highway at the Greek War Memorial and rejoins it again after passing right through the town. Should you need to make a phone call there's a telephone centrale a little way beyond the museum.

Though it's possible to stay overnight, El Alamein is best visited as a day trip from Alexandria, as there really isn't much here that would detain any but the most enthusiastic of military historians.

War Museum

This museum *(Medinat el-Alamein; admission E£5, photography E£5; open 8am-6pm daily)* contains a good collection of uniforms, memorabilia and pictorial material relating to the Battle of El Alamein and the North African campaigns in general. Maps and explanations of various phases in the campaign in Arabic, English, German and Italian complement the exhibits, and there's a 30-minute Italian-made documentary that you can watch. Outside the museum is a collection of tanks, artillery and hardwar from the fields of battle.

Commonwealth War Cemetery

The cemetery, on the eastern side of towr is a haunting place where more than 700 tombstones cover a slope overlooking th desert battlefield of El Alamein. Soldier from the UK, Australia, New Zealanc France, Greece, South Africa, East an West Africa, Malaysia and India wh fought for the Allies lie here. The cemeter is maintained by the War Graves Commis sion, and admission is free. Outside is small separate memorial to the Australia contingent, and a little further east is th Greek War Memorial.

German & Italian War Memorial

About 7km west of El Alamein, on a blu overlooking the sea, is what looks like hermetically sealed sandstone fortres Inside this silent but unmistakable re minder of war lie the tombs of Germa servicemen and, in the centre, a memori obelisk.

About 4km further on is the Italia memorial with, as its focal point, a tal slender tower. Before reaching the Germa memorial, you may notice on the left side c the road what seems a little like a glorifie milestone. On it is inscribed in Italian wit *Mancò la fortuna, non il valore* – 'We wer short on luck, not on bravery'.

Places to Stay & Eat

Al-Amana Hotel *(☎ 493 8324, Medina el-Alamein)* Singles/doubles E£20/30. Al most opposite the museum, this place ha simple double rooms that are nothing spe cial – but a damn sight better than rooms i the rest house down the road. It also has small cafeteria where you can get chicke and rice meals, omelettes and fuul, as we as drinks and biscuits.

El Alamein Rest House *(☎ 430 278 Medinat el-Alamein)* This was once *th* place to stay but it's now extremely dilap dated and not recommended.

Hotel Atic *(☎ 492 1340, Mediterranea Coast Rd)* Doubles E£120. Around 15kı east of El Alamein, this is the nearest of the many beach resorts that blight this stretch of coastline.

It may be possible to ***camp*** on the beaches, but you'll have to hunt around for the police and attempt to get a *tasreeh* (permit).

Getting There & Away

Bus Catch any of the Marsa Matruh buses from Sidi Gaber in Alexandria (see Getting There & Away under Alexandria earlier in this chapter). You'll be dropped on the main road about 200m down the hill from the museum.

Service Taxi Service taxis leave from the lot in front of Alexandria's train station and cost about E£6. More often than not they are of the microbus variety. It's easy to pick up one of these from El Alamein to get back to Alexandria or to head further west to Sidi Abdel Rahman. For other destinations, the traffic is reasonably regular, but remember to bring water with you, as the heat can be sweltering.

SIDI ABDEL RAHMAN

☎ 03

The fine, white sandy beach and the sparkling turquoise of the Mediterranean make this stunning place, 23km west of El Alamein, a real, and as yet unspoilt, coastal beauty spot – though the developers can't be far away.

Bedouin occasionally congregate in a small village about 3km in from the beach. They belong to the Awlad Ali tribe, who came into the region several hundred years ago from Libyan Cyrenaica and subdued the smaller local tribes of the Morabiteen. There are now five main tribes subdivided into clans, each of which has several thousand members. The Egyptian government has been attempting to settle these nomads, so nowadays most of the Bedouin have forsaken their tents and herd their sheep and goats from the immobility of government-built stone and concrete houses.

The beach, the Bedouin and an expensive hotel are about all there is to Sidi Abdel Rahman.

Places to Stay & Eat

El Alamein Hotel *(☎ 492 1228, fax 492 1232)* Doubles E£440. This place is ridiculously overpriced. It's about 3km further west of town and there is a turn-off for Hanna Beach (Shaat al-Hanna), where during summer you might find a few tents set up for passers-by, but don't count on it. You may well be able to camp further along the beach, but again, technically at least, you will need to have a permit.

Getting There & Away

The same buses that can drop you at El Alamein en route to or from Marsa Matruh can also drop you here. They generally stop for a break just after the Hanna Beach turn-off. There are service taxis operating between El Alamein and Sidi Abdel Rahman and to places further west, but nothing much happens after early afternoon.

RAS AL-HIKMA

☎ 03

About 48km short of Marsa Matruh, this is little more than another small Bedouin village with some attractive beaches. There is supposedly an official camping site here. Ordinary buses between Alexandria and Marsa Matruh can let you off here, or you can pick up the occasional service taxi to Marsa Matruh.

MARSA MATRUH

☎ 046

The large waterfront town of Marsa Matruh, built around a charming bay of stunning turquoise waters and clean, white, sandy beaches, is a popular summer destination with Egyptians. This is a problem in that the place is packed in summer and the beaches – at least those close to town – are pandemonium. Away from the sand, the town itself, with a population of about 80,000, is dull and very unattractive. Outside of the summer season, it's also completely dead, and while this means empty expanses of gleaming white beach, it also means that many of the town's hotels and restaurants are closed. Still, this may be preferable to the chaos of the summer.

Orientation & Information

There are really only two streets in Marsa Matruh that you need to know about: the Corniche (el-Corniche), which runs all the way around the waterfront, and Sharia Iskendariyya, which runs perpendicular to the Corniche, towards the hill behind the town. The more expensive hotels are along the Corniche. Others are dotted around the town, mostly not too faraway from Sharia Iskendariyya. The bulk of the restaurants and shops are on or around Sharia Iskendariyya.

The passport office (☎ 493 5351) is just off Sharia Iskendariyya, a couple of blocks north-west of the train station. It's open from 8.30am to 2pm and from 6pm to 9pm June to April, from 5pm to 8pm in October to May. The tourist office (☎ 493 1841) is on the ground floor of the governorate building one block west of Sharia Iskendariyya on the corner of the Corniche and Sharia Omar Mukhtar. It's open from 8.30am to 9pm June to April and from 8.30am to 6pr October to May. The tourist police (☎ 49 5575) are next door.

There are two banks in Marsa Matrul You can change cash and cheques at th National Bank of Egypt, a few blocks wes of Sharia Iskendariyya and south of th Corniche. The Banque Masr branch o Sharia al-Galaa will usually accept Visa o MasterCard for a cash advance. There ar also several exchange bureaus on Shari al-Galaa.

The main post office is on Sharia ash Shaata, a block south of the Corniche an two blocks east of Sharia Iskendariyya. It' open from 8.30am to 3pm Sunday to Fri day. The 24-hour telephone centrale i across the street.

The Hotel Beau Site has a computer ter minal where you can use the Internet fo E£30 per hour.

There is a general hospital (☎ 493 3355 that is best avoided. In emergencies, you'r

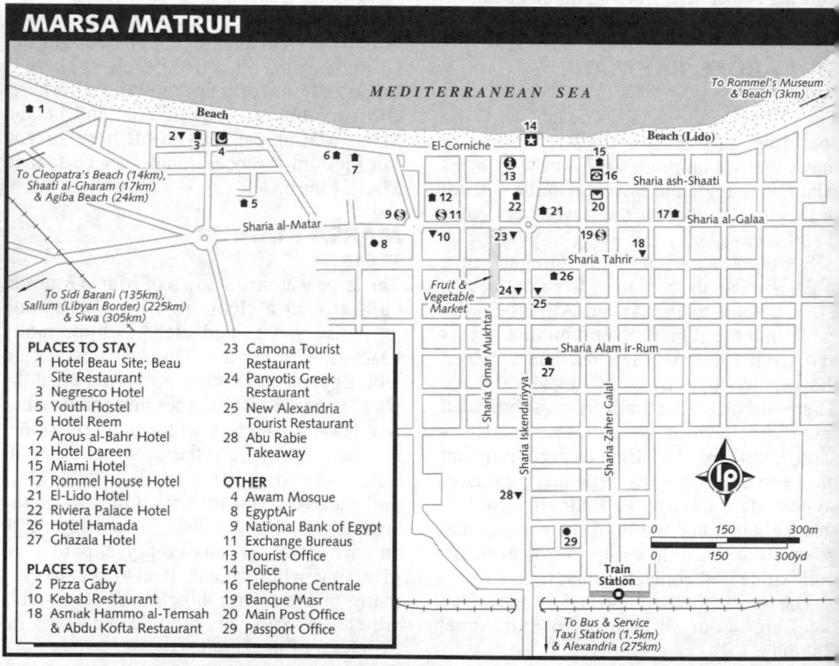

more likely to be taken to the marginally better Military Hospital (☎ 493 5286) at the eastern end of Sharia al-Galaa.

Rommel's Museum & Beach

Set in the caves Rommel used as his headquarters during part of the El Alamein campaign, this rather poor excuse for a museum (*admission E£5, open 9.30am-4pm June-Apr)* contains a few photos, a bust of the Desert Fox, some ageing German, Italian and British military maps and what is purported to be Rommel's greatcoat. The museum is about 3km east of the town centre, out by the beach of the same name. The turn-off to the museum and beach is signposted. You can arrange to see it in winter through the tourist office or the staff at the governorate building.

Rommel's Beach, a little east of the museum, is supposedly where the field marshal took time off from tanks and troops to have his daily swim. It's popular with holidaying Egyptians in summer, and women will feel uncomfortable bathing here. To get here you can walk around the little bay (or hire a bike or *careta* (E£5), the donkey-drawn carts that serve as taxis in Marsa Matruh), or get a boat from the landing about 300m east of Sharia Iskendariyya.

Other Beaches

The stunning azure water of the Mediterranean would be even better if the town and its hotels were not here. But further away the water is just as nice and you can still find a few places where human encroachment is minimal. Unfortunately, during the hot summer months, women cannot bathe in swimsuits, unless they enjoy being the object of intense harassment and ogling. For better or worse, this is working-class Egypt's favoured holiday destination and most women enter the water in galabiyya-like robes. The exception is the private beach at Hotel Beau Site.

If you do manage to avoid the masses and get into the turquoise waters, offshore lies the wreck of a German submarine, and sunken Roman galleys reputedly rest in deeper waters off to the east.

The **Lido**, the main beach in town, is no longer an attractive swimming spot, and although Rommel's Beach is OK, it is often too crowded for comfort.

The next choice is either **Cleopatra's Beach** or **Shaati al-Gharam** (Lovers' Beach), which are about 14km and 17km respectively west of town. The rock formations here are certainly worth a look and you can wade to Cleopatra's Bath, a natural pool where the great queen and Marc Antony are supposed to have bathed. A boat from near Hotel Beau Site goes across the bay to Cleopatra's Beach and Shaati al-Gharam. Like most things in Marsa Matruh, the boats only run in summer. Taxis will charge about E£60 to bring you here and they will wait while you enjoy the beach.

Agiba means 'miracle' and **Agiba Beach**, about 24km west of Marsa Matruh, is just that. It is a small but spectacular beach, accessible only by a path leading down from the cliff top. There is a cafe nearby (open in summer only) where you can get light refreshments, and the hassle potential for women who want to strip down to a swimsuit is considerably lower here than elsewhere.

Places to Stay

The accommodation situation in Marsa Matruh is bad. The hotels are all generally crummy and way overpriced, but demand for rooms over summer is such that hoteliers really don't need to try very hard. There are a huge number of places, especially if you head out of town, but we just list a few of the better central options.

Prices vary greatly from winter to summer, and substantial discounts are sometimes available until mid-June. Hotels with half board include accommodation, breakfast and dinner.

Places to Stay – Budget

Although there are no official camp sites, it may be possible to pitch a tent along the beach or at Rommel's Beach – check with the tourist office.

Youth Hostel *(☎ 493 2331)* Bunk beds members E£9, nonmembers E£10. Open May-Oct only. A couple of blocks south of the Awam Mosque, this hostel has comfortable bunks in cramped rooms that have their own kitchenettes. The toilets are fairly clean.

***Ghazala Hotel** (☎ 493 3519, Sharia Alam ir-Rum)* Beds E£10 per person. This is the most popular backpackers stop. The entry is sandwiched between some shops and is easily overlooked. Beds are basic but clean. Most rooms have balconies (but no view to speak of) and the shared toilet/shower combinations are clean, if lacking in hot water.

***Hotel Hamada** (☎ 493 3300)* Singles/doubles with shared bath E£15/20. The Hamada has a great central location just off Sharias Iskendariyya and Tahrir. While basic (no hot water), it's reasonably clean.

Places to Stay – Mid-Range & Top End

Town Centre The advantage of staying in the town centre is that you are close to the few shops and restaurants, but you've a long way to go to find a decent beach.

***Hotel Dareen** (☎ 493 5607, fax 493 0808)* Singles/doubles E£42/62. Off Sharia ash-Shaati, the Dareen has friendly management and reasonable rooms that are not very well maintained but are clean; there's also hot water in the en suite bathrooms. The price is E£12 more from June to September and includes breakfast.

***El-Lido Hotel** (☎ 493 2249, fax 493 2248, Sharia al-Galaa)* Singles/doubles without breakfast E£30/35, with breakfast E£35/44 (50% more expensive June to September). On the corner of Sharia Iskendariyya and Sharia al-Galaa, El-Lido has poky rooms with TV, phone and bath.

***Rommel House Hotel** (☎ 493 5466, fax 493 2485, Sharia al-Galaa)* Singles/doubles June-Sept E£70/117, with obligatory half board Oct-May E£43.50/63. East of Sharia Iskendariyya, this hotel's rooms have bath, TV and refrigerator, and the price includes breakfast.

***Riviera Palace Hotel** (☎ 493 3045, fax 493 0004, Sharia Iskendariyya)* Doubles Oct-May E£170. From June to September it is block-booked by groups from Cairo. One of the better places in this category, the recently renovated Riviera Palace has decent large rooms with partial views of the bay. The price includes breakfast.

***Miami Hotel** (☎ 493 1400, fax 493 2083, Sharia Zaher Galal)* Singles/doubles June-Sept E£162/200, Oct-May E£120/144. This is a large, very gloomy three-star place that does at least benefit from a Corniche setting. It's way overpriced though.

Along the Corniche There is a string of places along the waterfront west of Sharia Iskendariyya and there is little to choose between them. They all have good sea views but little else in the way of nearby amenities.

***Arous al-Bahr Hotel** (☎ 493 4420, fax 493 4419, el-Corniche)* Singles/doubles half board June-Sept E£36.50/48.50, Oct-May E£24.50/36.50. Another bland hotel here with clean, but not great, rooms with baths; some also have balconies and breakfast is included.

***Hotel Reem** (☎ 493 3605, fax 493 3608, el-Corniche)* Singles/doubles June-Sept E£70/100, Oct-May E£35/70. Hotel Reem has unremarkable but clean rooms with balconies. There are good views from the sea-facing rooms. The price includes breakfast.

***Negresco Hotel** (☎ 493 4491/2, fax 493 3960, el-Corniche)* Singles/doubles half board June-Sept E£160/250, Oct-May E£75/110. While a bit on the expensive side, the Negresco has spotless rooms and decent facilities; breakfast is included.

***Hotel Beau Site** (☎ 493 8555, fax 493 3319, el-Corniche)* Singles/doubles half board June-Sept E£487/688, half board Oct-May E£243/344. This is easily Matruh's most attractive option – if you have the money. The food here is good and 'luxury' rooms on the beach come with breakfast, air-con and satellite TV. There are some tiny rooms with great balconies available above the disco, but little else for substantially cheaper rates. The Beau Site also boasts the only private beach in Matruh.

Places to Eat

The dining situation in Matruh is also significantly less than impressive. When we last visited, which was admittedly in winter, we had a hard time getting anything to eat at all.

Camona Tourist Restaurant *(Sharia al-Galaa)* Dishes E£2-10. Camona Tourist, on the corner of Sharias Al-Galaa and Iskendariyya, and another corner ***kebab restaurant***, about 200m west of that, are the main budget options. The latter also serves fiteer, the Egyptian pancake/pizza.

There's also a good takeaway in ***Abu Rabie*** at the train station end of Sharia Iskendariyya. It does fuul, ta'amiyya, salads and good *gambari* (shrimp) or calamari sandwiches for about E£1.25 each.

New Alexandria Tourist Restaurant (Sharia Iskendariyya) Dishes E£5-20. This is an excellent-value restaurant, with a full fish meal for E£15.

Asmak Hammo al-Temsah & Abdu Kofta Restaurant *(Sharia Tahrir)* Dishes E£5-15. An exception to the restaurant situation in Matruh, this outdoor grill dips the fish of your choice in a spice mixture before grilling. The delicious result is brought to you at the Abdu's Kofta Restaurant next door, where you can have the usual *baba ghanoug* (grilled-aubergine puree), with rice and bread as an accompaniment.

Pizza Gaby *(el-Corniche)* Pizzas E£8-19. Open June-Sept only. Not a beautiful place to sit, but the pizzas here are good.

Panyotis Greek Restaurant *(Sharia Iskendariyya)* Dishes E£10-20. No longer Greek owned and perhaps not as good as it was, this is Matruh's oldest restaurant and offers seafood accompanied by tahini and other salads, and beer.

Beau Site Restaurant *(☎ 493 8555, el-Corniche)* Dishes E£5-60. In the hotel of the same name, the Beau Site is famous for its food (although admittedly it is not hard to shine in Marsa Matruh). Meals are a mixture of Egyptian and standard Mediterranean, with lots of fish.

Getting There & Away

Air EgyptAir (☎ 493 4398) has flights twice weekly between Cairo and Marsa Matruh in the summer months of June to September. Tickets are about E£350 one way. The EgyptAir office is on Sharia al-Matar.

Bus For details on buses from Cairo or Alexandria to Marsa Matruh, see under Getting There & Away in those cities.

Matruh's bus station is 2km out of town on the main coastal highway. Expect to pay about E£3 for a taxi from the town centre.

Superjet has two services a day that run only in summer, one to Alexandria (E£24, four hours) at 2.30pm and one to Cairo (E£37, five hours) at 3pm. These leave from the tourist office station.

West Delta (☎ 493 2027) has frequent services from Marsa Matruh to Alexandria (E£15 to E£23). Buses going to Cairo leave at 7.30am, noon, 3.30pm and 6pm. All have air-con and ticket prices range from E£28 to E£33. Buses to Sallum (four hours) run throughout the day and most of the night. Tickets are E£10.

Buses to Siwa leave at 7.30am, 1.30pm, 4pm and 7.30pm. All have air-con and the journey takes three to four hours.

Train Between June and September there is a daily luxury sleeper train between Cairo and Marsa Matruh. Trains leave Matruh at 11pm and arrive in Cairo at 6am. Tickets are E£225 per person in a double cabin, E£356 for a single. Reservations can be made at the station in Matruh (☎ 493 3036) or in Cairo (☎ 02-738 3682/4).

Otherwise, avoid the rails. Even the station master at Matruh says that the trains are 'horrible'. Should you choose to ignore his advice, there are two per day to Alexandria, departing at 7am and 3.40pm with 2nd-class/3rd-class tickets costing E£6.40/2.80. The journey takes anywhere from six to seven hours. There is nothing heading west to Sallum.

Service Taxi The service taxi lot is beside the bus station, 2km out of town. Service taxis to Siwa cost E£10, if there are enough passengers. Other fares include: El Alamein (E£10), Alexandria (E£10), Cairo (E£10 to E£20), Sallum (E£10) and Sidi Barani (E£6).

Getting Around

Caretas, or donkey carts, are the most common form of transport around the streets of

Marsa Matruh. Some are like little covered wagons with colourful canvas awnings. A ride across town should cost no more than E£3. From the centre to Rommel's Museum is E£5.

Private taxis or pick-ups can be hired for the day, but you must negotiate and bargain aggressively, especially in the summer.

In summer there are supposedly regular buses to Cleopatra's and Agiba Beaches from Sharia Iskendariyya.

SIDI BARANI

☎ 046

About 135km west of Marsa Matruh on the way to Libya is this small but busy Bedouin town. It serves as a bit of a food and petrol way-station for traffic coming into Egypt from Libya. But that's about it. There's a small hotel and just a few unsanitary places to eat.

SALLUM

☎ 046

Nestled at the foot of Gebel as-Sallum on the gulf of the same name, Sallum (pronounced sa-**loom**) is in the proverbial middle of nowhere. The dearth of Western travellers coming through here means there is little sign of the hassling so common elsewhere in the country. There is a post office here and a branch of the National Bank of Egypt.

As usual, the water is crystal clear, but in town the rubbish on the beach detracts from it. Head east for a while and you can pick yourself out some secluded stretch of sand, but ask first if the spot you've chosen is OK. Some parts of the beach are government property. And remember that being on the beach without a permit after about 5pm can get you into strife.

On the eastern entrance to the town is a WWII Commonwealth War Cemetery, a somewhat more modest version of the El Alamein cemetery.

You really don't want to stay in Sallum, but if you have no choice ***Hotel al-Ahram*** *(☎ 480 0148)* is the best of a terrible bunch. It costs E£6/12 for basic rooms. When there is water, it's cold. There are a couple of ***lokandas*** (basic, cheap places to doss) with their names in Arabic only.

At the border, 12km further on, is ***Hotel at-Ta'un*** (name in Arabic only). There are one or two modest fuul stands around, but ask first how much the food costs.

Getting There & Away

There are buses and the odd service taxi from Alexandria and Marsa Matruh; see the relevant Getting There & Away sections.

From Sallum, buses for Marsa Matruh (E£8, four hours) depart three times a day; some of these go on to Alexandria (E£20, eight hours). A service taxi to Marsa Matruh will cost about E£10.

Libya The border crossing point of Amsaad, just north of the Halfaya Pass, is 12km west of Sallum. Service taxis run up the mountain between the town and the Egyptian side of the crossing for E£2 to E£3. Once through passport control and customs on both sides (you walk through), you can get a Libyan service taxi on to Al-Burdi for about LD1. From there you can get buses on to Tobruk and Benghazi.

Note, it is not possible to get a Libyan visa at the border.

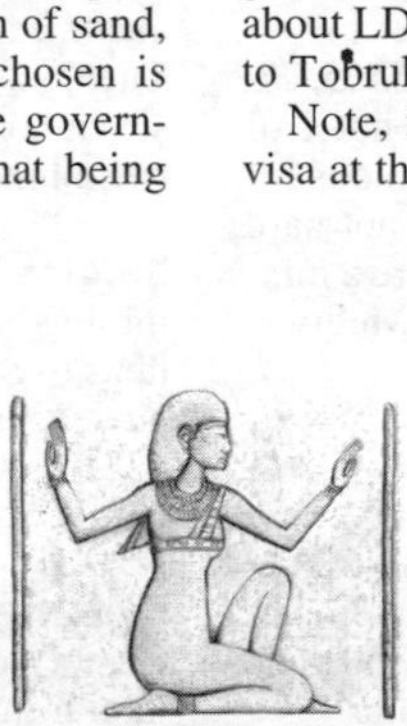

Suez Canal

The Suez Canal – one of the greatest feats of modern engineering – represents the culmination of centuries of effort to enhance trade and expand the empires of Egypt by connecting the Red Sea with the Mediterranean Sea. Although the modern canal was by no means the first project of its kind, it was the only one to bypass the Nile, excavating instead across the Isthmus of Suez to provide a major shipping route between Europe and Asia.

Construction of the first recorded canal was begun by Pharaoh Necho between 610 and 595 BC. The canal stretched from the Nile Delta town of Bubastis, near present-day Zagazig, to the Red Sea via the Bitter Lakes. After reputedly causing the death of more than 100,000 workers, the construction of the canal was abandoned. The project was picked up again and completed about a century later under Darius, one of Egypt's Persian rulers. The canal was improved by the Romans under Trajan, but over the next several centuries it was either neglected and left to silt up, or dredged by various rulers for limited use depending on the available resources.

The canal was again briefly restored in AD 649 for a period of 20 years by Amr ibn al-As, the Arab conqueror of Egypt.

Following the French invasion in 1798, the importance of some sort of sea route south to Asia was again recognised. For the first time, digging a canal directly from the Mediterranean Sea to the Red Sea, across the comparatively narrow Isthmus of Suez, was considered. The idea was abandoned, however, when Napoleon's engineers mistakenly calculated that there was a 10m difference between the two sea levels.

British reports corrected that mistake several years later, but it was Ferdinand de Lesseps, the French consul to Egypt, who pursued the Suez Canal idea through to its conclusion. In 1854 de Lesseps presented his proposal to the Egyptian khedive Said Pasha, who authorised him to excavate the canal. Work began in 1859.

Highlights

- Watch supertankers appear to glide through the desert as they make their way through one of the world's most famous canals.
- Admire Port Said's waterfront architecture – more New Orleans than Mediterranean.
- Stroll through Egypt's colonial past in Ismailia's old European quarter.

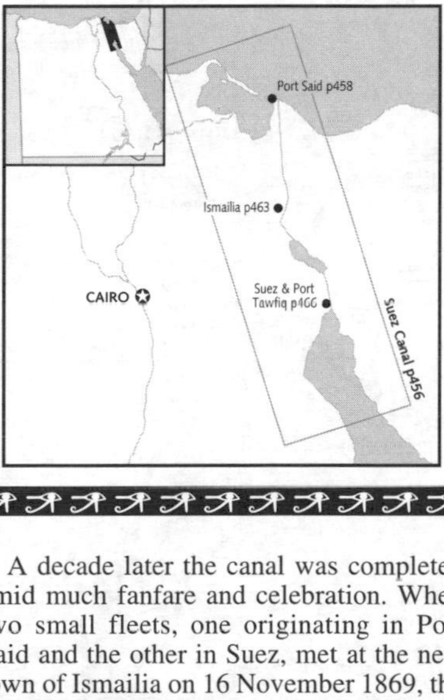

A decade later the canal was completed amid much fanfare and celebration. When two small fleets, one originating in Port Said and the other in Suez, met at the new town of Ismailia on 16 November 1869, the Suez Canal was declared open and Africa was officially severed from Asia.

Ownership of the canal remained in French and British hands for the next 86 years, until, in the wake of Egyptian independence, President Nasser nationalised the canal in 1956. The two European powers, in conjunction with Israel, invaded Egypt in an ungallant attempt to retake the waterway by force. In what came to be known as the 'Suez Crisis', they were forced to retreat in the face of widespread international condemnation.

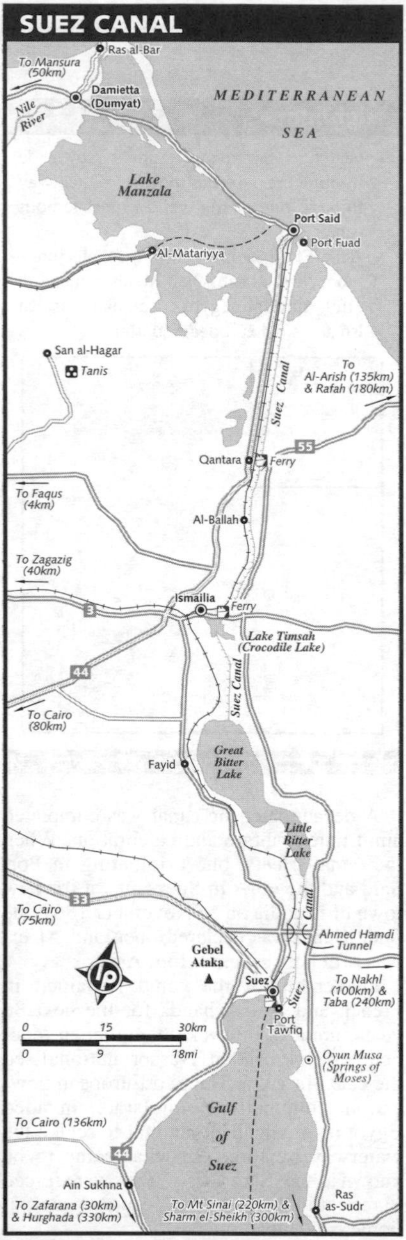

The canal remains one of the world's most heavily used shipping lanes and toll revenues represent one of the biggest contributors to the Egyptian state coffers.

PORT SAID

☎ 066

The main attraction of Port Said, and the reason for its establishment on the Mediterranean, is the Suez Canal. The spectacle of the huge ships and tankers lining up to pass through the northern entrance of the canal is something to be seen. Port Said's status as a duty-free port means that of all the canal cities it is the most flourishing.

The city was founded in 1859 by its namesake, the khedive Said Pasha, when excavation for the Suez Canal began. Much of the city is an island, created by filling in part of Lake Manzala, to the west, with sand from the canal site. Upon completion of the canal 10 years later, Port Said was the scene of the opening ceremony for the festivities that followed, reported in the international press as 'the party of the century'.

The city continued to grow until 1956, when much of it was bombed during the Suez Crisis. It suffered again during the 1967 and 1973 wars with Israel. Damage from the wars can still be seen, but most of the city, which these days is home to about 400,000 people, has been rebuilt.

Egyptians think of Port Said as a summer resort, and hundreds of beach bungalows line the coast along the city's northern edge.

Orientation

Port Said is connected to the mainland by a bridge to the south and a causeway to the west. There is also a ferry across Lake Manzala to Al-Matariyya, and another between Port Said and its sister town Port Fuad, which is on the other side of the canal.

Most of the banks and important services are on Sharia Palestine, which runs along the canal, or on Sharia al-Gomhuriyya, which is two blocks inland.

Information

Visa Extensions If you need to get a visa extension, the passport office is in the governorate building (left wing, 4th floor, window seven) and is open from 8am to 2pm Saturday to Thursday.

Customs Port Said was declared a duty-free port in 1976, so everyone must pass through customs when entering and leaving the city. Be sure to have your passport with you, and if you are given the choice of declaring cameras and electronic goods on entering, then do so. If you do want to buy anything, check in the shop whether or not duty must be paid on a particular item – some, including a few electrical items, can be taken out of Port Said without any problem; varying rates of tax apply. Duty free in Egypt doesn't necessarily mean that all items are tax free.

Tourist Offices The tourist office (☎ 235 289) at 8 Sharia Palestine has maps and information about the Suez Canal and the port. It's open from 9am to 1.30pm and from 3pm to 8pm Saturday to Thursday. There's also a branch office at the train station.

Money There are a number of banks on Sharia al-Gomhuriyya. The National Bank of Egypt seems to be the least complicated at which to change travellers cheques.

Thomas Cook (☎ 227 559), 43 Sharia al-Gomhuriyya, is open from 9am to 6pm daily. Nearby, in the MenaTours office, an American Express (AmEx; ☎ 230 939) agency opens from 10am to 3pm daily. It doesn't have foreign exchange facilities.

Post & Communications The main post office, opposite the Ferial Gardens one block north of Sharia al-Gomhuriyya is open from 9am to 5pm Saturday to Thursday.

There are two telephone centrales: one is on Sharia Palestine one block north-west of the tourist office; the other is behind the governorate building. Both are open 24 hours.

Suez Canal House

If you've ever seen a picture of Port Said, it was probably of the striking green domes of Suez Canal House. One of the best views of the Suez Canal used to be from this white-columned building, south-west of the ferry terminal and tourist office, which was built in time for the inauguration of the canal in 1869. It is off-limits to visitors, although you could try to talk your way past the guards and go up to the central dome.

Town Centre

For many, Port Said is a boring stop on their trip through Egypt, and few bother to visit it at all. However, the five-storey buildings with their wooden balconies and high verandas in grand *belle époque* style are one of those little surprises that should be fascinating to anyone with an interest in architecture or the life of late-19th-century colonial centres. Take a wander down Sharia Memphis, in particular, with its old Woolworth's building (now a souvenir emporium), and around the streets just north of the Commercial Basin. There are some wonderfully odd colonial remnants, such as the old

Liberty on the Canal

A little-known fact about New York's Statue of Liberty is that it was originally to have stood at the entrance to the Suez Canal in Port Said. Inspired by the colossal statues at Abu Simbel, French sculptor Frédéric-Auguste Bartholdi formulated the idea of a huge statue of a woman bearing a torch. She was to represent progress – 'Egypt carrying the light of Asia', to use Bartholdi's own words. He presented his idea to Khedive Ismail, who loved the idea of the grand gesture and was thrilled with the concept.

However, after two years of sketching and making models, Bartholdi was told that Ismail had decided (somewhat uncharacteristically) that the project was too expensive. The 'Light of Asia' was then sent to New York, where she became Lady Liberty. In her place, a less idealistic statue of Ferdinand de Lesseps was erected at the head of the canal. It was ripped off its pedestal when Colonel Nasser, leader of the revolutionary Free Officers, announced the nationalisation of the Suez Canal in 1956. Although the statue was restored at the expense of the French government in the early 1990s, it has yet to be re-erected.

PORT SAID

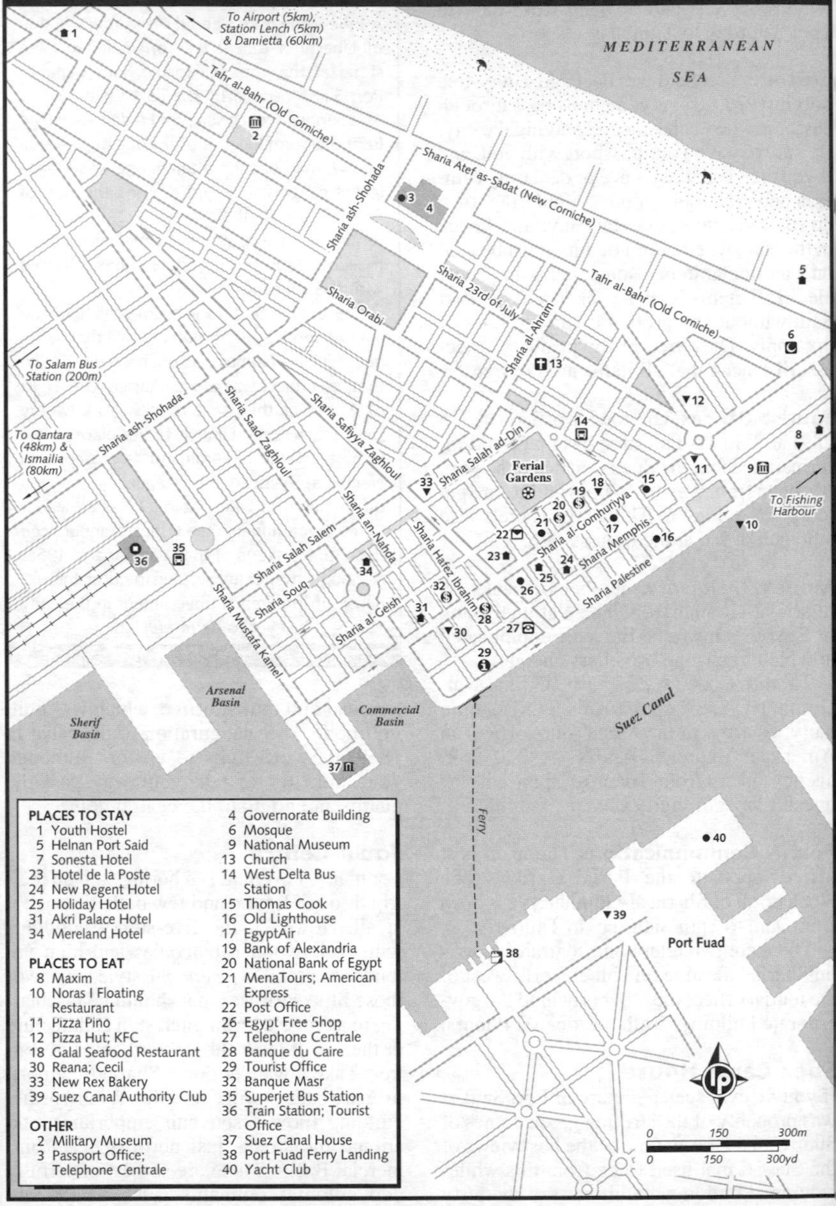
To Airport (5km), Station Lench (5km) & Damietta (60km)
MEDITERRANEAN SEA
Tahr al-Bahr (Old Corniche)
Sharia Atef as-Sadat (New Corniche)
Sharia ash-Shohada
Sharia Orabi
Sharia 23rd of July
Sharia al-Ahram
To Salam Bus Station (200m)
To Qantara (48km) & Ismailia (80km)
Sharia Saad Zaghloul
Sharia Safiyya Zaghloul
Sharia Salah ad-Din
Ferial Gardens
Sharia al-Gomhuriyya
Sharia Memphis
Sharia Palestine
To Fishing Harbour
Sharia an-Nahda
Sharia Hafez Ibrahim
Sharia Salah Salem
Sharia Souq
Sharia al-Geish
Sharia Mustafa Kamel
Arsenal Basin
Sherif Basin
Commercial Basin
Suez Canal
Ferry
Port Fuad
0 150 300m
0 150 300yd

PLACES TO STAY
1 Youth Hostel
5 Helnan Port Said
7 Sonesta Hotel
23 Hotel de la Poste
24 New Regent Hotel
25 Holiday Hotel
31 Akri Palace Hotel
34 Mereland Hotel

PLACES TO EAT
8 Maxim
10 Noras I Floating Restaurant
11 Pizza Pino
12 Pizza Hut; KFC
18 Galal Seafood Restaurant
30 Reana; Cecil
33 New Rex Bakery
39 Suez Canal Authority Club

OTHER
2 Military Museum
3 Passport Office; Telephone Centrale
4 Governorate Building
6 Mosque
9 National Museum
13 Church
14 West Delta Bus Station
15 Thomas Cook
16 Old Lighthouse
17 EgyptAir
19 Bank of Alexandria
20 National Bank of Egypt
21 MenaTours; American Express
22 Post Office
26 Egypt Free Shop
27 Telephone Centrale
28 Banque du Caire
29 Tourist Office
32 Banque Masr
35 Superjet Bus Station
36 Train Station; Tourist Office
37 Suez Canal House
38 Port Fuad Ferry Landing
40 Yacht Club

Postes Françaises; a sign for the ship chandlers of the pre-Soviet 'volunteer Russian fleet' and another for the Bible Society. Perhaps the oddest sight is the Italian consulate building, erected in the 1930s and adorned with a piece of engraved propaganda to the Fascist dictator Benito Mussolini: 'Rome – once again at the heart of an Empire'.

At the very northern end of Sharia Palestine, near the new Sonesta Hotel, is a huge stone plinth that once held a statue of de Lesseps, until it was torn down in 1956 (see the boxed text 'Liberty on the Canal').

National Museum

Opened in 1987, this museum *(☎ 237 419, Sharia Palestine; admission E£12; open 9am-4pm Sat-Thur, 9am-11am & 1pm-4pm Fri)*, at the top end of Sharia Palestine, houses a varied collection representative of most periods in Egyptian history. The ground floor is dedicated to prehistory and the Pharaonic period. You can see statuary, utensils, pottery and a couple of mummies and colourful sarcophagi. The 1st floor contains a modest display of Islamic and Coptic exhibits, including textiles, manuscripts and coins. There is also a room full of memorabilia of the khedival family that oversaw the construction of the canal.

Military Museum

This small museum *(☎ 224 657, Sharia 23rd of July; admission E£6; open 9am-2pm Sat-Thur)* has some interesting relics from the 1956 Suez Crisis and the 1967 and 1973 wars with Israel. There are captured US tanks with the Star of David painted on them, a couple of unexploded bombs and various other reminders of recent wars, as well as a small display relating to ancient Pharaonic and Islamic conflicts.

Al-Matariyya Ferry

Aboard the Al-Matariyya Ferry *(E£2 one way)* you can chug west across shallow lakes and lagoons to the Delta town of Al-Matariyya, perhaps watching as becalmed feluccas are taken in tow along the way. There's nothing to do at Al-Matariyya but wait for the return boat. To get to the ferry, you must first go to Station Lench, about 15 minutes by taxi towards Damietta (Dumyat), north-west of the town centre.

Port Fuad

Across the canal from Port Said, Port Fuad, founded in 1925, is really a suburb of civil servants. The yacht club in Port Fuad is the place to go to find a passage or work on a vessel plying the canal, as the captains are sometimes looking for crew members. Free ferries from Port Said to Port Fuad offer a great view of the canal, and leave about every 10 minutes from a terminal near the tourist office.

Although not as interesting as canal-side central Port Said, a short visit and a stroll around the streets near the quay is worth the effort. Sprawling residences with lush gardens and sloping tiled roofs are a refreshing sight after seeing nothing but standard Middle Eastern poured-concrete boxes, and are a reminder of the one-time European presence here.

Places to Stay – Budget

The area around the canal used to be crawling with little dives, but most seem to be losing out to the gradual gentrification of Sharia al-Gomhuriyya.

Youth Hostel *(☎ 228 702, Sharia 23rd of July)* Beds E£3.25 members, nonmembers E£4.25. Near the stadium, this is the cheapest place to stay in Port Said. It has basic bunk beds, with 20 beds per room. It's not bad, but suffers from a highly inconvenient location some distance from the town centre.

Akri Palace Hotel *(☎ 221 013, 24 Sharia al-Gomhuriyya)* Singles/doubles E£20/25, doubles with bath E£37. The Greek-owned Akri Palace has reasonably clean rooms with a bit of charm. The rooms are nicely furnished and have balconies, but hot water can be unreliable. Breakfast is extra.

Mereland Hotel *(☎ 227 020)* Singles/doubles E£15/20, with bath E£24/35. Two blocks north-west from the Akri, the Mereland is in a lane between Sharia Saad Zaghloul and Sharia an-Nahda. It offers big clean rooms and the showers are hot. Breakfast is extra.

Places to Stay – Mid-Range & Top End

In the early 20th century, Port Said boasted one of the most famous hotels in the country in the form of the mammoth, seven-storey Eastern Exchange, which stood roughly opposite to where the Banque du Caire is today. But that was in the days when passenger liners regularly docked here and the town was a global transit point. Few beds are needed in the town these days.

Hotel de la Poste *(☎ 224 048, 42 Sharia al-Gomhuriyya)* Singles/doubles US$8/12, with balcony & bath US$10/14. This place has a fading elegance that the management has attempted to salvage through careful renovation. Some rooms have TV and a fridge. There's also a restaurant, bar and patisserie downstairs.

New Regent Hotel *(☎ 235 000, fax 224 891, 27 Sharia al-Gomhuriyya)* Singles/doubles US$27/34. This is a smart, modest-sized three-star hotel with a fine location in a lane just off Sharia al-Gomhuriyya, a block in from the canal. Prices include breakfast.

Holiday Hotel *(☎ 220 711, fax 220 710, 23 Sharia al-Gomhuriyya)* Singles/doubles US$40/50. A largish modern block on the main street, the Holiday has a chic-ish cafe on the ground floor. It is probably the smartest place to stay aside from the two big five-star hotels up at the north end of town.

Sonesta Hotel *(☎ 325 511, fax 324 825, W www.sonesta.com/egypt_portsaid, Sharia Sultan Hussein)* Singles/doubles US$120/150, with canal views US$150/185. A fairly modest, but pleasant, low-rise five-star chain hotel. It overlooks the canal and has an adjacent shopping centre.

Helnan Port Said *(☎ 320 890, fax 323 762, e reshps@helnan.com, W www.helnan.com, Sharia Atef as-Sadat)* Singles/doubles US$175/225. On the beach front at the north end of town, the Helnan gets a five-star rating from the tourist office, but thumbs down from us for being hulking, grim, characterless and an eyesore to boot. Prices include breakfast.

Places to Eat

Not surprisingly, there are plenty of seafood restaurants in Port Said.

Galal Seafood Restaurant Dishes E£12-24. One of the cheapest eateries in town, Galal is a big local favourite serving the likes of fried calamari and fish with Greek mezze, such as dolmades (stuffed vine leaves). There are a few tables outside, but beer is only served indoors. It's on the corner of Sharias al-Gomhuriyya & Gaberti.

Pizza Pino *(☎ 239 949, Sharia al-Gomhuriyya)* Dishes E£12-30. This is a local attempt at a Pizza Express joint, ie pizza and pasta in smart, attractive, non-plastic surrounds. Not bad at all.

Reana *(Sharia al-Gomhuriyya)* Dishes E£15-35. This place offers passable attempts at Chinese or Korean dishes with a seafood slant. Below is the ***Cecil*** bar for a pre- or post-dinner Stella.

Maxim *(☎ 234 335, 1st floor, Sonesta Shopping Centre, Sharia Palestine)* Fish dishes E£30. A fine seafood restaurant and one of the few upmarket places in town, Maxim is, however, a bit lacking in atmosphere.

Suez Canal Authority Club *(Port Fuad)* Dishes E£7-30. Serving lunch only, you can dine on chicken or meat with rice and salad for E£7 on the club's breezy terrace. The big drawcard, however, is the great, unobstructed view of the canal and passing ships. The club is immediately to your left once you get off the ferry; the entrance is opposite the tennis courts and there's a E£1 entry ticket.

Noras I Floating Restaurant *(☎ 32… 804, Sharia Palestine)* Dishes E£36-60. From its canal mooring near the National Museum, the *Noras I* departs daily at 3pm and 8.30pm for a 1¼ hour tour of the canal during which a predominantly seafood lunch or dinner is served.

Three blocks north of Sharia al-Gomhuriyya, there's a lively fruit and vegetable market on Sharia Souq. For bread and pastries, try the popular ***New Rex Bakery*** at the intersection of Sharias Souq and Safiyya Zaghloul.

Shopping

Almost anything can be bought in Port Said, although cheap electronics and designer jeans seem to be the biggest-selling items. Since the government began liberalising the economy in the mid-1990s, the merchandise is geared more towards sailors passing through the town. The best deals can be found along Sharia al-Gomhuriyya; try the Egypt Free Shop on this street.

Getting There & Away

You must go through a customs check before leaving Port Said, so be sure to leave enough time to do this. The train and bus stations all have customs halls.

If you don't want to risk a service taxi or spend the night in town, then beware – the last train and buses for Cairo all depart Port Said by 6.05pm.

Air EgyptAir (☎ 222 870) has an office at 39 Sharia al-Gomhuriyya, but it does not offer flights to Port Said.

Bus There are three bus terminals. The Superjet buses to Cairo (E£15, three hours) leave 11 times a day from a terminal in front of the train station. Superjet also has a bus to Alexandria (E£22, four hours) at 4.30pm daily. Bookings are advisable.

West Delta goes to destinations outside the Delta (as well as to Tanta in the Delta for some reason) from its terminal (also known as the 'Lux' terminal) near the Ferial Gardens. Buses to Cairo depart hourly between 6am and 6pm daily and fares range from E£13 to E£15. The most expensive buses don't make stops, usually shaving about 30 minutes off the three- to 3½-hour ride. There are four buses to Alexandria (E£17 to E£22) via Damietta at 7am, 9am, 2.30pm and 4.30pm daily. Buses south to Ismailia (E£5) depart hourly between 6am and 6pm daily. Buses to Suez (E£7.50, 2¼ hours) depart at 6am, 10am, 1pm and 4pm daily. For Al-Arish on the Sinai peninsula, you must first go to Ismailia or Qantara and take a bus or service taxi from there.

The other terminal, known as the Salam bus station, is on Sharia an-Nasr, north-west of the train station. Buses to destinations within the Delta (except Tanta) depart from here. Every hour on the half-hour daily, a bus also goes south to Qantara (E£2.50).

Train There are five trains departing daily to Cairo. These take four hours and are the slowest, but can also be the cheapest, way to get there. There are no 1st-class services. Fares for 2nd-class air-con/2nd-class ordinary/3rd class are E£14/5.50/3. The train stops in Ismailia.

There are an additional five trains that travel daily to Ismailia only (E£6/2.30/1). Two of these trains continue on making a long loop via Zagazig to Alexandria (E£28/8.50/4).

Service Taxi Service taxis depart from a garage about 2km west of the centre. The only way to get out there is by taxi – ask for 'al-mahattat servees'. Destinations and fares include Cairo (E£10), Ismailia (E£5), Qantara (E£3.50) and Suez (E£6).

Boat A number of ships ply the waters between Port Said and Limassol (Cyprus), although most are five-star cruisers offering package tours to Egypt and Israel. They sail between April and October. For more information on prices and schedules, contact MenaTours (☎ 225 742) on Sharia al-Gomhuriyya.

In Cyprus you can contact Paradis Island Tours (☎ 357-237 4699) or Louis Tours (☎ 357-237 4699). From Limassol, you can connect with vessels heading on to Haifa in Israel or to several Greek islands, but this is quite an expensive way of getting around the area.

Getting Around

The best and most enjoyable way to tour Port Said, especially around sunset, is by *hantour* (horse-drawn carriage). A carriage and driver can be hired for about E£10 per hour. Otherwise there are plenty of blue-and-white taxis.

Cruising the Canal

Although hundreds of ships cruise the Suez Canal each week, canal enthusiasts who want to do the same will find that it's not that easy. The port authorities do not appreciate people just hopping on a freighter for the ride and organised trips do not exist. However, there are one or two ways of seeing this famous waterway from the deck of a boat.

If you're in Suez you can rent a private boat for a cruise up to Port Said. Mohammed Moseilhy of Damanhur Shipping (☎ 062-572 177) can arrange this for you, but he needs a few days' notice. Expect to pay at least E£500 for a boat that holds a maximum of 12 people.

A cheaper option is the passenger ferry at Qantara, 35km north of Ismailia. Two ferries cross the canal throughout the day and can do so even when a convoy is passing through – if you're lucky you'll get a close-up view of a supertanker. The passenger ferry is free and is virtually opposite the town, while the vehicle ferry crosses further to the south. Be prepared to join a stampede of people, chickens, donkeys and bicycles for a space on this ferry.

The *Noras I* Floating Restaurant, docked at the top of the canal in Port Said, offers a 1¼-hour tour of the canal for E£10, including a soft drink. It departs daily at 3pm and 8.30pm. You can also have a decent seafood meal on board – see Places to Eat under Port Said earlier in this chapter.

If you do manage to get on some sort of vessel, remember that taking photographs may not be appreciated as there is a strong military presence all along the canal. Some travellers have had their film confiscated after inadvertently snapping a sensitive site.

QANTARA

The only reason to visit the town of Qantara, 50km south of Port Said, is to cross to the east side of the canal, then leave again as quickly as possible (see the boxed text 'Cruising the Canal'). Service taxis leave from the east bank – you'll be looking at paying about E£7 to reach Al-Arish (150km). A bridge across the canal is being built here.

Most of Qantara was destroyed during the 1973 war with Israel and the town's buildings still have evidence of bullet holes.

ISMAILIA

☎ 064

Ismailia was founded by and named after Pasha Ismail, khedive of Egypt in the 1860s while the Suez Canal was being built. Ferdinand de Lesseps, the director of the Suez Canal Company, also lived in the city until the canal was completed.

As in Port Said, a stroll around the elegant colonial streets of Ismailia can be an unexpected pleasure. We're not talking great monuments, but there are some beautiful old villas laid out in a shady, Western-style grid. Apart from the architecture, it's interesting to see how this canal city grew in the image of the British and French masters who were pulling the strings in Egypt in the 19th century and first half of the 20th century.

Orientation

Ismailia is perhaps the most picturesque of the new canal towns, yet it has been quickly developing, or rather, devolving, into an urban mess. This city of about 300,000 people is divided by the train line, which marks a boundary between well-tended streets on one side and a veritable disaster area on the other.

If the old European quarter of Ismailia, south of the tracks, can be said to have a main street, it's probably Sharia Sultan Hussein, which runs between the train line and the Sweetwater Canal. The central square, Midan al-Gomhuriyya, is a quiet affair, and in fact, this entire side of town is rather exceptional in that it is all comparatively peaceful. The thoroughfare beside the Sweetwater Canal is known by three names: Mohammed Ali Quay, the Promenade and Sharia Salah Salem.

On the northern side of the train tracks you'll find the modern city, full of potholed streets, horn-honking maniacs and smoking piles of garbage.

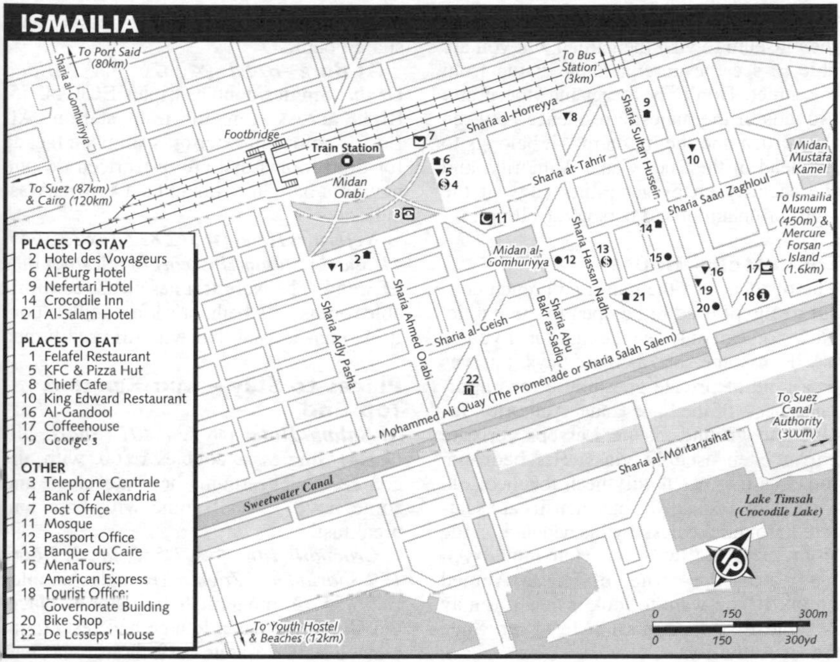

Information

Visa Extensions The passport office is on Midan al-Gomhuriyya and it is open from 8am to 2pm Saturday to Thursday.

Tourist Offices The tourist office (☎ 321 072) is in the governorate building on Mohammed Ali Quay. It is open from 8am to 3pm Saturday to Thursday, but has little to offer besides the standard glossy brochures.

Money There's a Bank of Alexandria on Midan Orabi across the square from the train station and a Banque du Caire on Sharia Hassan Nadh. AmEx (☎ 324 361) has a branch in the MenaTours office at 12 Sharia Sultan Hussein.

Post & Communications The main post office is just north up the tracks from the train station. A 24-hour telephone centrale is across from the train station on Midan Orabi, virtually opposite the Bank of Alexandria.

Ismailia Museum

This small but interesting museum *(☎ 322 749, Mohammed Ali Quay; admission E£6; open 9am-3pm Sat-Thur)*, several blocks north-east of the governorate building, has more than 4000 objects from Pharaonic and Graeco-Roman times. There are statues, scarabs, stelae and records of the first canal, built between the Bitter Lakes and Bubastis by the Persian ruler Darius. The highlight of the collection is a 4th-century AD mosaic depicting characters from Greek and Roman mythology. At the top, Phaedra is sending a love letter to her stepson, Hippolytus (who ended up in a bad way after his father set Poseidon onto him). Below, Dionysus, the god of wine, tags along on a chariot driven by Eros. The bottom section recounts the virtues of Hercules, demigod and son of Jupiter.

Garden of the Stelae

Just south-west of the museum is a garden containing a poor little sphinx from the time of Ramses II. You need permission from the museum to visit the garden, but you are able to see the unremarkable statue from the street. Don't try to get into the pretty grounds of the majestic residence between the garden and the museum – it belongs to the head of the Suez Canal Authority, and the security chaps get rather edgy at the sight of unauthorised persons strolling in.

De Lesseps' House

The residence of the one-time French consul to Egypt used to be open to the public. Now you can only see the interior if you're a VIP of some sort, as these days it serves as a kind of private guesthouse for important guests of the Suez Canal Authority. Inside the grounds is de Lesseps' private carriage encased in glass. His bedroom looks as if it has hardly been touched; old photos, books and various utensils are scattered around the desk by his bed and on the floor. The house is on Mohammed Ali Quay near the corner of Sharia Ahmed Orabi. If you want to look inside you may be able to get permission from the Suez Canal Authority.

Beaches

There are several good beaches around Lake Timsah, 12km south-east of the town, but as these have become highly popular among middle-class Cairenes, using them involves paying to get into one of the clubs and hotels that dot the shore. Entrance fees vary but on average they are E£20, and some include a buffet lunch as part of the admission price. All fees include access to a private swimming beach.

Places to Stay – Budget

Youth Hostel *(☎ 322 850, Lake Timsah)* Beds in 2-bed/4-bed/6-bed rooms E£18/15/8. This high-rise hostel on a beach by the lake has comfortable rooms and fine views. The white-tiled toilets and showers are blindingly clean. Prices include breakfast.

Hotel des Voyageurs *(Travellers Hotel; ☎ 228 304, 22 Sharia Ahmed Orabi)* Singles/doubles E£10/16. A short walk from the train station, this is big, derelict place offers basic but acceptable rooms with shared bath.

Al-Burg Hotel *(☎ 326 327, Midan Orabi)* Singles/doubles/triples E£30/50/75. Right across from the train station, Al-Burg's colourful exterior is simply a facade for drab rooms that are overpriced despite having a bath, air-con and a TV. Breakfast is E£5.

Nefertari Hotel *(☎ 322 822, fax 322 645, 41 Sharia Sultan Hussein)* Singles/doubles E£36/54. The Nefertari has clean, comfortable rooms with bath, breakfast and air-con. It also has a small bar with dim red lights.

Places to Stay – Mid-Range & Top End

Al-Salam Hotel *(☎ 324 401, Sharia al-Geish)* Singles & doubles E£60, with air-con E£75. The rooms here are clean and some have TV; all come with bath and breakfast.

Crocodile Inn *(☎ 331 555, fax 331 666, 179 Sharia Saad Zaghloul)* Singles/doubles E£55/75. A modernish five-storey place, the Crocodile has a lounge and restaurant, as well as a 24-hour coffeehouse and bar. There are some renovated rooms for E£90/130 but they're hardly worth the extra money. Prices include breakfast.

Mercure Forsan Island *(☎ 338 040, fax 338 043, Gezirat Forsan)* Singles/doubles US$97/150. About 1.6km south-east of the old centre of town, the Mercure sits on its own island. It has a fine beach and all the amenities of a four-star hotel. For around E£20 per day nonguests can use the swimming pool and beach, but on Friday you have to pay for the buffet as well – E£47 all up.

Places to Eat

The ***Mercure Forsan Island*** does a good buffet lunch and also has a couple of reasonable restaurants. Otherwise, places to eat are concentrated on and around Sharia Sultan Hussein.

Al-Gandool *(Sharia Sultan Hussein)* Dishes E£8-35. Al-Gandool would like to sell you 1kg of mixed grilled meats for E£35, but you can settle for a plate of spaghetti for just a few pounds instead.

George's *(☎ 337 327, 11 Sharia Sultan Hussein)* Dishes E£12-40. Open noon-midnight daily. One of our favourite restaurants in Egypt, Greek-run George's has been around since 1950 and little has changed in the intervening half century. Pick your fish from an iced display in the back kitchen or order meat from the menu. It also includes a wonderful old bar.

King Edward Restaurant *(☎ 325 451, 171 Sharia at-Tahrir)* Dishes E£15-30. Open 11am-late daily. Meat and fish are offered here with a few surprises – if available the chicken curry is quite good and makes a nice change from the usual fare. Pizzas start at E£6.50.

Close to the train station on Sharia at-Tahrir is a good little ***felafel restaurant*** where you can dine in or takeaway. The tiny ***Chief Cafe*** on Sharia al-Horreyya specialises in an unusual combination of kushari, cakes and chocolates. All are very good and the kushari is cheap. There are tables on the pavement only.

Just east of Sharia Sultan Hussein, near the end of the pedestrian mall, is an old ***coffeehouse*** under a great spreading tree that has a very welcoming atmosphere.

Getting There & Away

Bus Ismailia is served by a large new bus station some 3km north-west of the old quarter. Taxis between the bus station and the town centre cost about E£3. From the station West Delta has frequent departures to Cairo (E£6, 2½ hours), and two buses a day at 7am and 2.30pm to Alexandria (E£17, three hours). East Delta also has frequent buses to Cairo for E£6; buses to Port Said leave every 30 to 45 minutes and cost E£4; to Suez they leave every 15 to 20 minutes and cost E£3.50.

Buses to Sinai also leave from here. There are buses every hour or so to Al-Arish (three hours) from 8am to 5pm. They usually cost E£7, but be aware that prices may fluctuate for buses passing through from Cairo. There are buses to Sharm el-Sheikh (E£25) at 6.30am, noon, 2.30pm, 3.30pm, 9pm, 10pm, 11pm and midnight daily.

Train About 10 trains arrive in Ismailia every day from Cairo (via Zagazig). Tickets cost E£8/4.40/1.80 in 2nd-class air-con/2nd-class ordinary/3rd class; the trip can easily take more than three hours.

To Port Said, there are nine trains per day (E£6/2.30/1 in 2nd-class air-con/2nd-class ordinary/3rd class, 1½ hours). There are also frequent trains to Suez (E£2.40/1.10 in 2nd/3rd class). The train is a painfully slow way to travel, and once you reach Suez, the station is a long way out of the town.

Trains to Alexandria (E£15/6.70/3 in 2nd-class air-con/2nd-class ordinary/3rd class, five hours) leave at 8.30am and 7.50pm daily.

Service Taxi These depart from the new bus station. Destinations include Suez (E£3), Port Said (E£3.50), Zagazig (E£3), Cairo (E£5), Mansura (E£5.50) and Al-Arish (E£7).

Getting Around

Ismailia's parks and tree-lined streets are good cycling territory. There is a bike shop behind the Al-Gandool Restaurant that rents bicycles for E£5 per day.

SUEZ

☎ 062

Suez sprawls around the shores of the gulf where the Red Sea meets the southern entrance of the Suez Canal. It's a city going through a metamorphosis. It was all but destroyed during the 1967 and 1973 wars with Israel, although today there is little obvious evidence of the devastation. The revamped main streets, however, are mostly a facade hiding a sordid mess of backstreet slums. A memorial on Sharia al-Galaa commemorates both wars.

The town itself is divided between Suez proper and Port Tawfiq. The latter is at the mouth of the canal and is a good place for watching the ships go by. It also has a few streets with gracious old colonial buildings that managed to escape the bombing. It is joined to the town itself by Sharia al-Geish, a wide highway that cuts through an industrial area before cutting through the heart of

SUEZ & PORT TAWFIQ

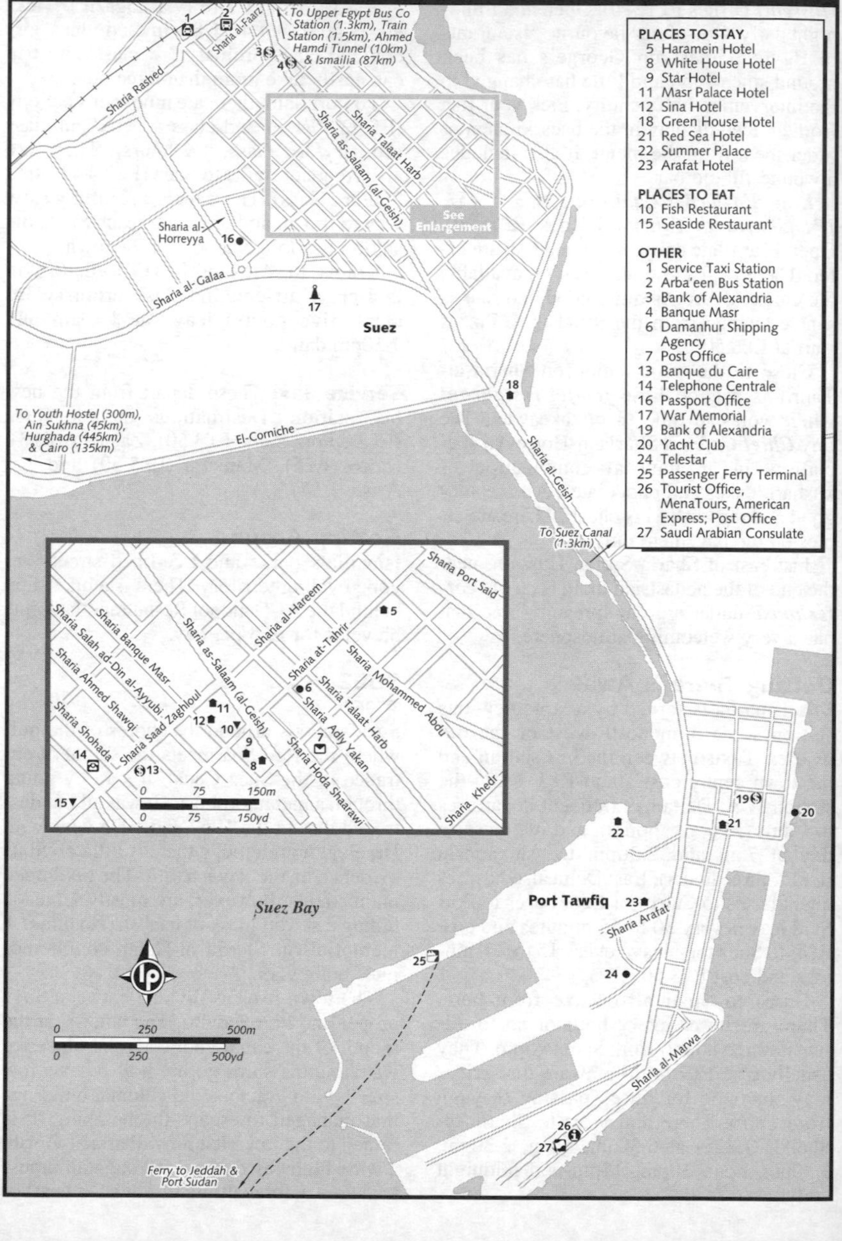

To Upper Egypt Bus Co Station (1.3km), Train Station (1.5km), Ahmed Hamdi Tunnel (10km) & Ismailia (87km)
Sharia al-Faarz
Sharia Rashed
Sharia Talaat Harb
Sharia as-Salaam (al-Geish)
See Enlargement
Sharia al-Horreyya
Sharia al-Galaa
Suez
To Youth Hostel (300m), Ain Sukhna (45km), Hurghada (445km) & Cairo (135km)
El-Corniche
Sharia al-Geish
To Suez Canal (1.3km)
Sharia Port Said
Sharia al-Hareem
Sharia Banque Masr
Sharia Salah ad-Din al-Ayyubi
Sharia Ahmed Shawqi
Sharia Shohada
Sharia Saad Zaghloul
Sharia at-Tahrir
Sharia Mohammed Abdu
Sharia Talaat Harb
Sharia Adly Yakan
Sharia Hoda Shaarawi
Sharia Khedr
0 75 150m
0 75 150yd
Suez Bay
Port Tawfiq
Sharia Arafat
Sharia al-Marwa
0 250 500m
0 250 500yd
Ferry to Jeddah & Port Sudan
PLACES TO STAY
5 Haramein Hotel
8 White House Hotel
9 Star Hotel
11 Masr Palace Hotel
12 Sina Hotel
18 Green House Hotel
21 Red Sea Hotel
22 Summer Palace
23 Arafat Hotel
PLACES TO EAT
10 Fish Restaurant
15 Seaside Restaurant
OTHER
1 Service Taxi Station
2 Arba'een Bus Station
3 Bank of Alexandria
4 Banque Masr
6 Damanhur Shipping Agency
7 Post Office
13 Banque du Caire
14 Telephone Centrale
16 Passport Office
17 War Memorial
19 Bank of Alexandria
20 Yacht Club
24 Telestar
25 Passenger Ferry Terminal
26 Tourist Office, MenaTours, American Express; Post Office
27 Saudi Arabian Consulate

Suez. Here, too, there are one or two old buildings left, but they are fast being lost to the ubiquitous shoddily built high-rises.

There is nothing at all to do in either Suez or Port Tawfiq. They are basically just transit points, not only for the great tankers, cargo vessels and private yachts en route to or from the Mediterranean, but also for the Muslim faithful who pass through here each year on their way to Saudi Arabia for the haj.

Information

If you want to extend your visa, the passport office is in Suez just off Sharia Saad Zaghloul on Sharia al-Horreyya. There is a tourist office (☎ 223 589) of sorts in Port Tawfiq, whose staff is keen to provide information about the city, canal and surrounding sites. It's open from 8am to 6pm Saturday to Thursday and from 8am to 2pm on Friday.

Most of the main Egyptian banks have branches in Suez, while the MenaTours office (☎ 220 269) at 3 Sharia al-Marwa, next to the tourist office, houses representation for AmEx.

The main post office is on Sharia Hoda Shaarawi. There is also another small post office in Port Tawfiq, next to the tourist office. The centrale is on the corner of Sharias Shohada and Saad Zaghloul.

Foreign Consulates The Saudi Arabian consulate (☎ 222 461) in Port Tawfiq (around the corner from the tourist office) is open from 9am to 3pm Saturday to Thursday. There are separate sections for work and haj visas, but transit or tourist visas seems to fall between the two stools. Getting any sort of visa here can take up to one month – at a minimum you'll need to show an air ticket plus a letter from your embassy. If you're stopping over in Jeddah, you will also be asked to get a letter from the company issuing the ongoing ticket. Given the hoops you have to jump through, you're best off going through MenaTours (☎ 336 888), which will simplify the lengthy process and make sure you have the correct documents in advance.

Places to Stay – Budget

During the month of the haj, budget places tend to fill up with passengers travelling to and from Saudi Arabia by sea.

Youth Hostel *(☎ 221 945, Suez)* Beds members/nonmembers E£5/E£6. On the main road heading west out of Suez, the Youth Hostel is cheap, grungy and a long way from anything.

Haramein Hotel *(☎ 320 051, Sharia at-Tahrir, Suez)* Singles/doubles E£6/10. Near the end of the street, the Haramein is one of the cheapest in this area, with extremely dingy rooms (no fan, no air-con). For the truly impecunious only.

Star Hotel *(☎ 228 737, 17 Sharia Banque Masr, Suez)* Doubles E£20-25. A wide assortment of rooms is available at the Star, although all are fairly grotty. All have fans but no air-con, and the shared bathrooms can be dirty.

Sina Hotel *(☎ 334 181, 21 Sharia Banque Masr, Suez)* Singles/doubles E£25/34. The Sina has reasonable rooms all with ceiling fan, although you can pay E£5 extra for air-con. Bathroom facilities are shared but clean.

Arafat Hotel *(☎ 338 355, Sharia Arafat, Port Tawfiq)* Singles/doubles/triples E£15/22/33, with bath E£24/30/37. Off Sharia al-Geish, Arafat Hotel is just about the only budget option in the vicinity of the port. The hotel has recently been renovated and is well run and spotlessly clean.

Places to Stay – Mid-Range & Top End

Masr Palace Hotel *(☎ 223 031, 2 Sharia Saad Zaghloul, Suez)* Singles/doubles E£25/35. The Masr Palace has 101 beds in rooms of varying price, standard and degree of cleanliness. Rooms feature bath and air-con, and the price includes breakfast. It's good value without being spectacular.

White House Hotel *(☎ 227 599, fax 223 330, 322 Sharia as-Salaam, Suez)* Singles/doubles E£32/40. Clean, respectable and popular, if a little worn around the edges, the rooms here all have showers. Prices include breakfast.

Green House Hotel *(☎ 331 553, fax 331 554, Sharia Port Said, Suez)* Singles/doubles

US$38/48. This place has good views of the canal, a 24-hour restaurant, a pool (E£3 for nonguests), a bar and a branch of the Banque du Caire. Rooms are comfortable with bath, air-con, TV, fridge and balcony. It's on the road out of Suez to Port Tawfiq, on the corner of Sharias Port Said and Al-Geish.

Summer Palace *(☎ 224 475, fax 321 944, Port Tawfiq)* Singles/doubles US$34/44. This place has ordinary motel-style rooms, which in our opinion are ridiculously expensive. You're paying for the Gulf views and the seawater pools, which you can use for E£10 if you're not a hotel guest. It has an ordinary restaurant (open 24 hours) and a tranquil waterfront bar where you can get a reasonably priced Stella.

Red Sea Hotel *(☎ 334 302, fax 334 301, 13 Sharia Riad, Port Tawfiq)* Singles US$42-50, doubles US$50-58. The city's premier establishment, the Red Sea's 81 rooms have TV, bath, phone and air-con and are comfortable and clean. It has a 6th-floor restaurant with a great panoramic view of the canal.

Places to Eat

For the cheap old favourites such as ta'amiyya and shwarma, take a wander around the streets bounded by Sharia Talaat Harb, Sharia Abdel as-Sarawat, Sharia Banque Masr and Sharia Khedr. There are also a few juice stalls, and plenty of cafes and coffeehouses around here. There's another clump of small restaurants in the streets west of the Arba'een bus station. The ***White House Hotel*** also has a decent enough restaurant specialising in – what else? – fish.

Fish Restaurant *(Sharia as-Salaam, Suez)* Dishes E£25-40. Open noon-2am daily. Just north of the White House Hotel, this restaurant is exactly what it says on the name board. It sells the day's catch by weight; pick your fish, then wait for it to be grilled.

Seaside Restaurant *(Sharia Saad Zaghloul, Suez)* Dishes E£12-24. Open 24 hrs daily. The Seaside offers basic food such as grilled chicken and kebabs.

For a late afternoon soft drink, you could join the locals at the string of little ***drink kiosks***, all with outdoor chairs and tables and loud music, along Sharia al-Galaa near the war memorial.

There is also a series of ***cafes*** down in Port Tawfiq, if you happen to stumble off a boat and want to sit down for a breather.

Getting There & Away

Bus Buses to Cairo, Alexandria and the other canal cities leave from the East Delta Bus Co's Arba'een bus station on Sharia al-Faarz, not far from the centre of town. Buses to Cairo (E£6.50 to E£7.50, two hours) leave every 30 minutes from 6am to 8pm daily. Buses to Ismailia (E£3.50) depart every 15 to 20 minutes. There are three buses directly to Port Said (E£7.50) at 7am, 9am and 3.30pm, and two to Alexandria (E£20) at 7am and 2.30pm.

Buses to the Sinai peninsula also leave from the Arba'een station. If you want to go to Al-Arish, it's best to go to Ismailia and catch another bus from there. Alternatively, you can catch the bus for Nakhl (pronounced Nekhl; E£8) at 3pm and try to make a connection from there. However, very few vehicles use the road between Nakhl and Al-Arish, so there's a good chance you'll be waiting a long time for a ride. The same bus goes on to Taba (E£30, five hours) and Nuweiba (E£25, six hours).

Five buses go nonstop to Sharm el-Sheikh (E£26 to E£35, 5½ hours) taking the direct route down the Gulf of Suez. They go on to Dahab (E£23, 6½ hours) and Nuweiba (E£25). A bus leaves for St Katherine's Monastery (E£17, five hours) via Wadi Feran at 11am daily.

Buses to nearby towns of Oyun Musa (one hour), Ras as-Sudr (E£7 to E£8, 1¼ hours), Hammam Fara'un (1¾ hours) and Al-Tor (four hours) leave at odd intervals throughout the day. The 11am and 3pm services to Sharm el-Sheikh, and the 11am bus to St Katherine's Monastery can let you off at these places along the way.

Minibuses sometimes run to destinations in Sinai, too. You'll be looking at about E£15 per person to St Katherine's Monastery, E£20 to Sharm el-Sheikh or Nuweiba and E£35 to Dahab. Ask around at the bus station for more details.

Buses for the Red Sea coast, Luxor and Aswan depart from the Upper Egypt Bus Co's station about 3km north of the town, just before the train station. There are buses heading to Hurghada (E£25 to E£35) almost every hour. You can ask to be let off at either Ain Sukhna or Zafarana (both E£8). Most of these go on to Qena (E£26 to E£30, nine to 10 hours) via Port Safaga.

Six buses a day go to Luxor (E£35 to E£37, 10 hours); three continue to Aswan (E£40 to E£45, 14 hours). You can also catch an Upper Egypt Bus Co service en route to Cairo (E£10) from Red Sea destinations at around noon, 2.30am and 3am daily; book ahead.

Departure times are always subject to change, so remember to check them in advance with the staff at the bus station.

Train Only a masochist would want to travel to or from Suez by train. The train station is 2km west of the Arba'een bus station; a microbus shuttles between them and costs 25pt. Six Cairo-bound trains depart daily from here (E£2.60/1.05 in 2nd/3rd class, 2¼ hours) and only make it as far as Ain Shams, 10km north-east of central Cairo.

There are nine very slow trains to Ismailia (E£2.40/1.10 in 2nd/3rd class, 2½ hours).

Service Taxi Service taxis depart from near the bus station to many of the destinations that are also serviced by buses and trains.

No structured service-taxi system exists in Sinai, which partly explains why it is so outrageously expensive to get there by taxi. Destinations include Cairo (E£5), Ismailia (E£3), Port Said (E£6) and Hurghada (E£20, 3½ to four hours). The only place in Sinai that service taxis service is Al-Tor (E£10).

With a group of seven people you can hire a 'special' taxi to get you to St Katherine's Monastery on the Sinai peninsula (E£175 to E£200), the Ain Sukhna hot springs 45km south of Suez (E£100/150 one way/return), or to the Red Sea monasteries (return E£350).

Boat While it used to be possible to travel by boat between Suez and Port Sudan (Sudan), this service is no longer running. However, if you're desperate to take this laborious journey, there are services available from Jeddah to Port Sudan.

Should you find a boat, the Suez-Jeddah leg of the trip takes about two days. There are boats departing daily from Jeddah at 1pm (you are supposed to be there a full five hours before departure time). Fares are E£270 in 1st class, E£230 in 2nd class, E£175 in Pullman and E£125 in deck class.

You can book tickets to Jeddah through Telestar in Suez (☎ 326 251) or MenaTours (☎ 228 821) in Tawfiq. Or alternatively call Mohammed Moseilhy at the Damanhur Shipping Agency (☎ 572 177).

Apparently it's impossible to get a ticket during the haj, and you won't be sold a ticket if you don't already have the necessary visas which, considering the difficulty of getting them, is quite sensible.

Sometimes you can find private yachts that will take you with them on their way south. Occasionally travellers have found passage on yachts to India, South Africa and even Australia. Mohammed Moseilhy can help you with this.

Getting Around

There are regular microbus services along Sharia as-Salaam from the Arba'een bus station to Port Tawfiq. They stop to pick you up or drop you off wherever you want along the route and cost 25pt.

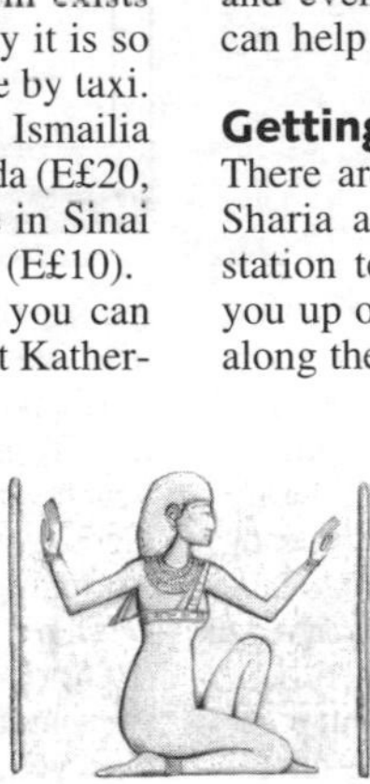

Red Sea Coast

Egypt's Red Sea coast stretches for more than 800km from Suez in the north to the village of Bir Shalatein near the disputed border with Sudan in the south. Famed for its brilliant turquoise waters, splendid coral and exotic creatures of the deep, the Red Sea coast attracts hundreds of thousands of tourists annually. It's Egypt's most rapidly developing area, and more hotels and resorts have been constructed here in the last few years than anywhere else in the country.

Unfortunately, much of the development during the freewheeling boom of the last decade has gone unchecked, resulting in massive environmental damage. An estimated 60% to 80% of the coral reefs around the coast's premier resort town, Hurghada, have been damaged due to illegal landfill operations by developers and irresponsible use of the reef by tourist operators. In some places the coast has simply eroded away due to developers building solid concrete jetties that have altered the natural shoreline. Though recently enacted laws have made many of these practices illegal, there appears to be little to contain the speculative boom based on the area's future as a major source of tourist growth. Even towns south of Hurghada, including Safaga and picturesque Al-Quseir, are showing signs of going the same way.

Highlights

- Plunge into the turquoise waters off the Red Sea coast and marvel at the famed coral and marine life.
- See where Christian monasticism got its start at the monasteries of St Anthony and St Paul.
- Laze on a beach at one of Hurghada's huge seaside resorts.
- Imagine yourself a spice trader in the narrow lanes of historic Al-Quseir, site of the last remaining Ottoman fortress on the Red Sea coast.
- Watch the sun set over the rocky mountains of the Eastern Desert.

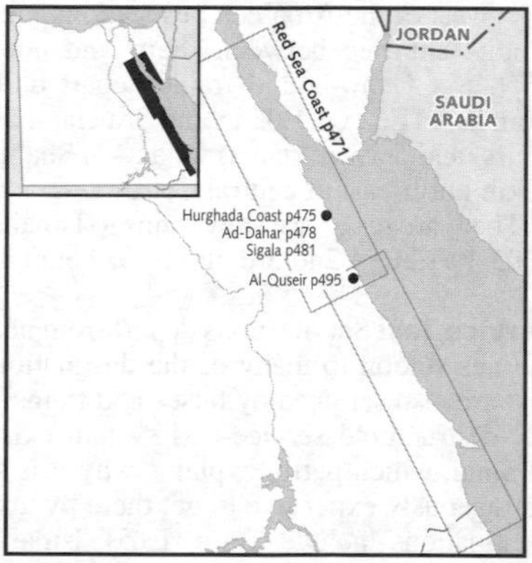

AIN SUKHNA

☎ 062

Ain Sukhna, which simply means 'Hot Spring', is the site of springs originating from within Gebel Ataka, the northernmost mountain in the Eastern Desert. There's not much to the place, but it is quite an attractive bit of coast. The road squeezes along between the water and the hills that slope almost down to the relatively clean beach. Unfortunately, developers are currently carving it up and the entire coastline between here and Zafarana to the south is becoming a series of concrete resorts. To make matters worse, the government is also planning a massive industrial port just to the north.

It's possible to visit Ain Sukhna on a day trip from Cairo (via Suez), but as all the beaches are being taken over by tourist villages, you'll have to pay for the pleasure of stretching out on the sand.

There are three buses a day from Suez (E£5). However, there's little in the way of refreshments, so, unless you bring some food with you, you'll have to dine at the hotels.

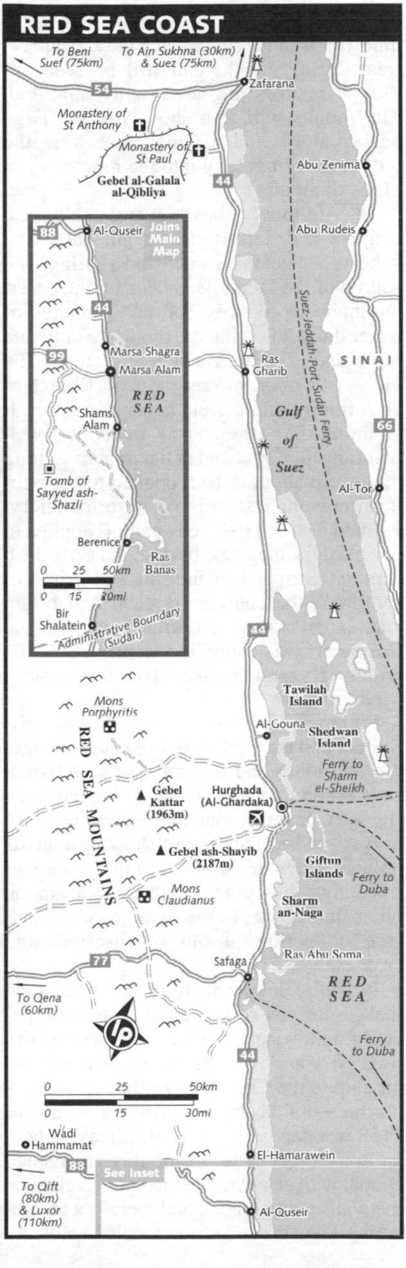

If you want to stay longer there is a choice of resorts, all geared to weekending Cairenes, and all pretty much the same.

As-Sukhna Portrait Hotel *(☎ 325 561, fax 322 003)* Doubles half board E£250. This is a glitzy hotel/time-share resort.

Hilton Ain Sukhna Resort *(☎ 290 500, fax 290 515)* Chalets E£250 weekends, E£180 midweek. Rates are for double occupancy and breakfast. Like the rest of the places here, it is geared to large Egyptian families.

ZAFARANA

This town, 62km south of Ain Sukhna and 150km east of Beni Suef on the Nile, is little more than a way-station for visits to the isolated Coptic monasteries of St Anthony and St Paul in the mountains overlooking the Gulf of Suez, although this may change since a huge number of resorts are under construction here. Should you want to stay overnight, there is the choice of ***Sahara Inn Motel*** or the five-star ***Sol y Mar Zafarana*** *(mobile ☎ 012-228 8399)*, both on the Red Sea coast road, with singles/doubles at US$60/106, including breakfast. Given that the beaches aren't stellar, we'd recommend that you keep going to Hurghada.

Buses running between Suez and Hurghada will drop you at Zafarana. There's also one bus a day from Beni Suef.

MONASTERIES

The Coptic Christian monasteries of St Anthony and St Paul are Egypt's – and Christendom's – oldest monasteries. As the crow flies, they are only about 35km apart, but thanks to the cliffs and plateau of Gebel al-Galala al-Qibliya (which lies between 900m and 1300m above sea level) they're around 82km apart by road.

Information

The monasteries are open to visitors between 9am and 5pm. It's possible to stay overnight at St Paul's, but you'll need permission from its residence in Cairo (☎ 02-590 0218), which is at 26 Al-Keneesa al-Morcosia, off Klot Bey, in the area just south of Midan Ramses. The monks at St

Warning

There's a heavy military presence along much of the coast and some areas contain mines. Although some of these are clearly marked with signs and barbed wire, others are not, particularly in the south. Any area demarcated by barbed wire, no matter how broken or old, should be treated with caution. If you decide to check out that secluded beach, always look for tyre tracks or footprints – better still, check with local authorities to be sure. Because of the military installations along the Red Sea coast, be prudent about where you aim your cameras, too.

Anthony's are reluctant to accept tourists overnight, preferring to reserve rooms for Coptic pilgrims, and permission must be given at their residences (same address and number as for St Paul's). The monks won't accept visitors during Lent (February to the beginning of Easter, generally in April), although if you show up they will sometimes let you in.

Monastery of St Anthony

The establishment of the fortified religious community of St Anthony's, hidden away in the barren cliffs of the Eastern Desert, represented the beginning of the Christian monastic tradition. Built in the 4th century AD by the disciples of St Anthony, the walled village at the foot of Gebel al-Galala al-Qibliya is the largest of the Coptic monasteries in Egypt.

This founding monastic order sprang up around the son of a merchant who had given up his worldly possessions to devote his life to God. Anthony actually retreated into the desert in about AD 294. While his followers adopted an austere communal life at the foot of the mountain, Anthony lived in a cave, high above the developing monastery village, until the ripe old age of 105.

Despite its isolation, the monastery suffered Bedouin raids in the 8th and 9th centuries, attacks from irate Muslims in the 11th century, and a revolt by bloodthirsty servants in the 15th century, which resulted in the massacre of the monks. The small mud-brick citadel into which they would retreat during attacks can still be seen, although visitors are not usually admitted. The monks will also show you the large basket and wooden winch that were the only means of getting into the monastery in times of attack.

St Anthony's has several churches, chapels and dormitories, a guesthouse, a bakery, a vegetable garden and a spring. The source of the latter, deep beneath the desert mountains, produces 100 cubic metres of water daily, allowing the monks to cultivate olive and date trees and a few crops. The oldest part of the monastery is the **Church of St Anthony**, built over the saint's tomb. It contains the largest array of Coptic wall paintings in Egypt and at the time of writing they were about to be reopened to the public after being restored to their former glory. Painted in *secco* (whereby paint is applied to dry plaster), they date back to the early 13th century. Stripped of the dirt and grime of centuries, the colours are clear and bright and, experts say, demonstrate how medieval Coptic art was connected to the arts of the wider Byzantine and Islamic eastern Mediterranean.

Following the example set by St Anthony, St Paul and their followers 16 centuries ago, the 60 monks and five novices who live at St Anthony's today have dedicated their lives to poverty, chastity, obedience and prayer – when they're not showing tourists around. They are currently in the process of finishing a museum that will contain, among other things, part of the monastery's extensive collection of old manuscripts and crosses.

If you're hiking in from the main road make sure you're properly equipped, especially with water, as it's a long, hot and dry walk. If you do get this far you should also hike up to the **Cave of St Anthony**, which is north-east of the monastery, some 300m – or 1158 wooden steps – up a cliff. It takes about an hour to get there. Inside there is a small chapel with an altar. The medieval graffiti on the walls is fascinating and there is a breathtaking view of the hills and valley below.

The Father of Monasticism

Although St Paul was the earliest Christian hermit (or, at least, the first we know of), it is St Anthony who takes the credit for founding monasticism. Born around AD 251, this shy son of a provincial landowner from a small Upper Egyptian town near Beni Suef was a reluctant religious leader. Orphaned with his sister at the age of 18 he was already more interested in the spiritual than the temporal, and soon gave away his share of the inheritance to the poor. After studying with local holy men he then went into the Eastern Desert, living in a cave and hoping for solitude and spiritual salvation. However, word soon spread about the holy man, and would-be disciples came flocking and tried to copy his ascetic existence. By default he became their spiritual leader.

After a brief spell in Alexandria ministering to Christians imprisoned under Emperor Maximus Daia in the early 300s, he returned to the desert. Once again, he was pursued by eager supplicants. Eventually, after fleeing even further into the sandy wastes in search of solitude, he established himself in a cave on a remote mountain. His would-be imitators formed a loose community at its base, and so the first Christian monastery was born.

The trend spread like wildfire; only decades after Anthony's death, travellers reported how every town in Egypt was surrounded by hermitages. Soon the whole of the Byzantine Empire was alive with monastic fever and only a century later there were many monasteries throughout Italy and France.

It is ironic that for all his influence, Anthony spent his life seeking to escape others. When he died, his wish was finally respected and the location of his grave kept secret for generations.

Monastery of St Paul

St Paul was born in Alexandria late in the 3rd century and fled to the Eastern Desert to escape Roman persecution. The most fascinating part of this large complex, founded in the cliffs of Gebel al-Galala al-Qibliya shortly after St Paul's death, is the **Church of St Paul**, cluttered with altars, candles, ostrich eggs (the symbol of the Resurrection) and colourful murals representing saints and biblical stories. It was built in and around the cave where Paul lived for nearly 90 years, during the 4th century after founding the monastery as a show of devotion to St Anthony. Legend has it that the latter outlived his younger devotee and at the age of 90 made the difficult trek through the mountains to bury him. The **fortress**, above the church, was where the monks retreated during Bedouin raids.

Visitors are more than welcome, and a couple of the monks, who speak excellent English, give guided tours. St Paul's has two guesthouses, one inside the monastery for men and one outside for women. Food and lodging are provided free of charge, so don't abuse the monks' hospitality.

Hiking Between the Monasteries

It is possible to hike between the two monasteries along a trail across the top of the plateau. However, hiking this uncharitable land, commonly known as 'Devil's Country', is only for the fit and experienced and should be done with a guide. In 2001 a lone tourist attempting the walk died of thirst after losing his way here, so it is not a trip to undertake lightly. Those who have made the hike recommend starting from St Paul's; ideally, you should be able to reach St Anthony's in two days.

Getting There & Away

Buses running between Suez and Hurghada will take you to Zafarana (price negotiable with the driver), but direct access to the monasteries is limited to private vehicles and tour buses from Cairo or Hurghada. The easiest way is to join one of the tours from Hurghada.

St Anthony's is 45km inland from the Red Sea. To get there follow the road that runs between Zafarana and Beni Suef. The turn-off to the monastery is about 30km from Zafarana and from there it's a 13km walk south through the desert to St Anthony's.

To get to St Paul's you can take one of the buses that run between Suez and

Hurghada and get off after Zafarana at the turn-off to the monastery, which is south of the Zafarana lighthouse. Buses between Suez and Qena go along the Red Sea coast road and can also drop you at the turn-off. It's then a 13km hike along the badly surfaced road through the desert.

Another alternative is to hire a taxi from Suez or Hurghada to the monasteries. Otherwise you'd be better off with your own transport to make this journey.

AL-GOUNA

A fully self-contained resort town built by one of Egypt's biggest tycoons, Al-Gouna, about 20km north of Hurghada, boasts, among other things, six hotels, an airport, a hospital, an open-air amphitheatre, a golf course, a brewery and several outdoor shopping malls. A playground for Egypt's rich and famous, it often hosts concerts and sporting events. Despite being a purpose-built resort, its airbrushed 'traditionally inspired' architecture is more tasteful than almost anywhere else in Hurghada and if you only want to laze on a beach, staying here avoids the hassle of the town.

Al-Khan Hotel *(☎ 545 062, fax 545 061, Kafr al-Gouna)* Singles/doubles US$46/68. A tasteful, small hotel complete with domes and arches in the style of Egypt's most famous architect, Hassan Fathy, this is one of the best three-stars in Egypt. Prices include breakfast.

Dawar al-Umda *(☎ 545 060, fax 545 561, Kafr al-Gouna)* Singles/doubles US$49/74. Also influenced by Hassan Fathy, this beautifully decorated four-star has a pool and is in the heart of 'downtown' Al-Gouna. Prices include breakfast.

Sheraton Miramar *(☎ 545 606, fax 545 608, Al-Gouna)* Doubles from US$70. A five-star, pastel-coloured, postmodern desert fantasy, the Sheraton was designed by well-known architect Michael Graves, with all the luxury features you'd expect, as well as access to Al-Gouna's other amenities. It is also participating in a pilot program to develop environmentally friendly practices in hotels on the Red Sea. Prices include breakfast.

HURGHADA

Little more than a decade and a half ago Hurghada had two hotels separated by nothing more than virgin beach. A once isolated and modest fishing village, it's now home to more than 35,000 people and packed with more than 100 resorts and hotels catering to sun seekers and diving enthusiasts on package tours from the world over. But while the crystal-clear waters and fascinating reefs have made Hurghada, or Al-Ghardaka as it is called in Arabic, Egypt's most popular resort town, if you're not into beaches, or diving or snorkelling with thousands of holiday-makers, then this ever-developing strip of hotels and beach resorts has little to offer.

Much of the town is marred by chunks of concrete, iron rods and empty oil drums – the results of the ongoing construction boom. Every spare bit of dirt or sand in the town is being turned into a building site. For more than 20km to the south, a dense band of concrete in the form of four- and five-star resorts has created the kind of disaster that you can also see on the southern shores of Europe.

Even worse is that developers, not content with having all but destroyed this part of the Red Sea coast, are repeating their mistakes further and further south. Russian dancers, fast food restaurants and shoddy hotels are the norm, and during the peak season of November to April, it feels as if half of Eastern and Western Europe has flown in on cheap sun-and-sea package holidays.

One of the few positive observations that can be made about all this is that the destruction of the environment has been so alarming that action is finally being taken to try and control future construction. The Egyptian National Parks Office has belatedly established an office in the Ad-Dahar area, and a nongovernmental organisation, the Hurghada Environmental Protection & Conservation Association (Hepca), is also helping to address many of the local environmental problems. Its office is in Sigala. (See the boxed text 'Rescuing the Red Sea' later in this chapter.)

Orientation

The town is split into three main areas. **Ad-Dahar**, where virtually all the budget accommodation is located and many of the locals live, is at the northern end of the stretch of resorts that makes up the whole area. Many of the buildings here remain unfinished and side streets are unpaved, but the souq, such as it is, is vibrant. The main inland road through Ad-Dahar is Sharia an-Nasr, which is part of the main north-south route on the Red Sea coast.

Separated from Ad-Dahar by a sandy mountain called Gebel al-Afish is **Sigala**, the fastest-growing part of town, where resort hotels jostle for sea frontage and smaller two-star and three-star hotels fill the spaces inland. The main thoroughfare through Sigala is Sharia Sheraton, named after the round Sheraton building that was one of Hurghada's first hotels but is now, confusingly, owned by Le Meridien. Most of Hurghada's best restaurants are clustered at the northern end of Sharia Sheraton, and the area is very lively at night. This is also where you'll find the port for ferries to Sharm el-Sheikh and Duba.

South of Sigala, a road winds down along the coast through the **resort strip**. At the five-star Magawish Tourist Village, about 15km south of Ad-Dahar, the road meets another a few kilometres inland to head down past the newer resorts and the rapidly growing shells of future pleasure domes on the way to Safaga.

Information

Visa Extensions You can obtain visa extensions and re-entry visas at the passports section in the Passports & Immigration office (☎ 546 727) at the northern end of Ad-Dahar on Sharia an-Nasr. It's open from 8am to 2pm Saturday to Thursday.

Tourist Offices Hurghada's tourist office (☎ 444 421), on the main road near the beginning of the resort strip, is open from 8.30am to 8pm Saturday to Thursday.

Money In Ad-Dahar, branches of Banque Masr, the National Bank of Egypt (with an

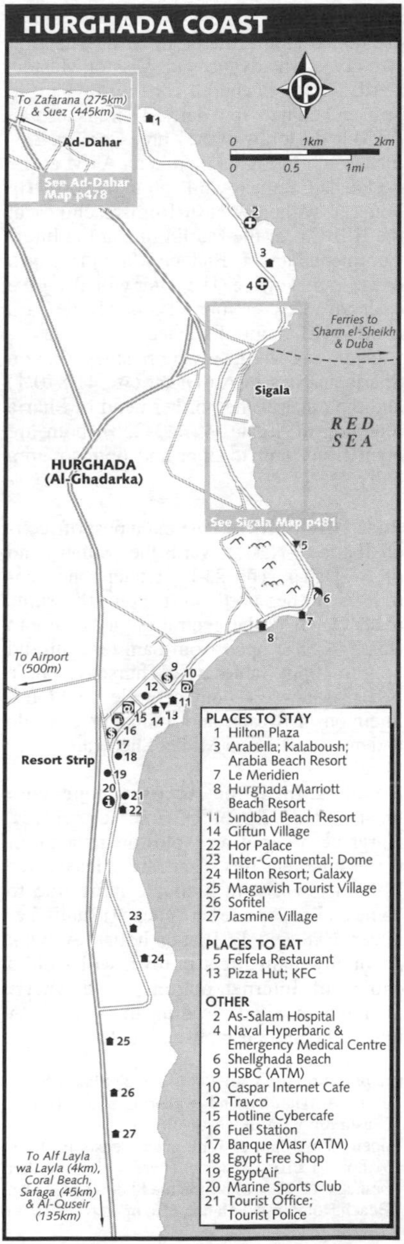

ATM machine) and the Bank of Alexandria are dotted along Sharia an-Nasr. The first two give cash advances on Visa or MasterCard. They are generally open from 9am to 1pm and 6pm to 9pm daily. There is also an ATM in the lobby of the Three Corners Empire Hotel. In Sigala there's an ATM at the Le Pacha Cataract, while on the resort strip you can withdraw cash from machines at the HSBC near the Marlin Inn, at the Inter-Continental and at Banque Masr just north of the tourist office. The latter will also give cash advances on your Visa or MasterCard if the ATM is out of service.

Thomas Cook has two branches, one on Sharia an-Nasr in Ad-Dahar (☎ 541 870/1) and the other at the northern end of Sharia Sheraton in Sigala (☎ 443 338); both are open from 9am to 2pm and 6pm to 9pm daily.

Post & Telephone The main post office is on Sharia an-Nasr, towards the southern end of Ad-Dahar. The 24-hour telephone centrale is further north-west along the same road. Opposite the centrale is a fax booth (fax 544 581) open from 8am to 2pm and 8pm to 10pm Saturday to Thursday. There is also a new 24-hour centrale on Sharia Sheraton in Sigala, and a smaller centrale and a post office on Midan Shedwan.

Email & Internet Access Along with most other Egyptian tourist centres, Hurghada has seen an explosion in the number of Internet cafes. There are at least three ISPs in town, with a couple more due to come on line, so rates are cheap (usually between E£8 and E£10 per hour). A walk down any main street in town will yield a choice of Internet options, with Sharia Sheraton in Sigala leading the charge. A few of the more established include:

Caspar Internet Cafe (☎ 442 375) Sharia Sheraton. A friendly and well-run place beside Mashrabiyya Village on the resort strip. It's open from 10am to 1am; access costs E£3 per ¼ hour, E£10 per hour. There's also another branch (☎ 540 870) beside the Shedwan Golden Beach Hotel in Ad-Dahar, also open from 10am to 1am.

Down Town Internet Cafe (☎ 548 777) Sharia an-Nasr. Four terminals in an airy first-floor room. It's open from 9.30am to midnight; access costs E£3 per ¼ hour.

Elbess Bookshop Internet Cafe (☎ 540 748) Sharia Sayyed al-Qorayem. First Internet cafe in town and convenient for those staying in or around the Three Corners Empire. It's open from 9.30am to 1am; access costs E£4 per ¼ hour, E£15 per hour.

Hotline (☎ 446 512, Villa 11012) Sharia Sheraton. Comfortable, air-con room and good connections. It's opposite the Royal Hotel and is open 24 hours. Access costs E£3 per ¼ hour, E£8 per hour.

Oznet (☎/fax 447 780) Sharia Sheraton. One of Hurghada's ISPs (call for up-to-date subscription rates), so connections are good. It's open from 10am to 5pm daily.

Travel Agencies There are at least 45 travel agencies in Hurghada, so you've got lots of choice. For details on the trips they offer, see Organised Tours later in this chapter. Masr Travel (☎ 546 600) has an office in Ad-Dahar near the main mosque. Travco (☎ 442 231), another reliable agency, runs the ferries to Sharm el-Sheikh. Thomas Cook (☎ 546 799) in Sigala can organise general travel arrangements and, like the others, runs excursions on land or sea.

Bookshops There's not a lot on offer if you're looking for books in Hurghada. Elbess Bookshop & Internet Cafe, opposite the Market Place shopping centre in Ad-Dahar, has a small, dusty selection of English, French, German and Egyptian literature, as well as maps, guidebooks, foreign newspapers and postcards. It is open from 9.30am to 1am daily, but hours can be erratic.

Newspapers & Magazines *Hurghada Bulletin* is a free magazine that you can find on stands around Hurghada or at the tourist office. Even better is *Red Sea Life*, a pocket guide to the Red Sea's tourist offerings. Both are free and have listings of what's happening around town. With the odd exception the articles are pretty useless but they can help for finding out about the clubs and discos of the moment, special events and restaurants.

Medical Services & Emergency There are four hospitals in the Hurghada area. The best two are the private hospital at Al-Gouna (☎ 580 014), 20km north of Hurghada, and the As-Salam Hospital (☎ 548 785/6/7), about halfway between Ad-Dahar and Sigala, beside the Arabia Beach Resort, where there is a 24-hour emergency department. Less reliable are Al-Saffa Hospital (☎ 546 965) on Sharia an-Nasr, Ad-Dahar, and the public hospital (☎ 546 740) near Shedwan Golden Beach Hotel, Ad-Dahar.

For diving emergencies, there are also two decompression chambers in Hurghada. One is in Al-Gouna (☎ 580 011), while the other is at the Naval Hyperbaric & Emergency Medical Centre (☎ 544 195, 549 525).

Other emergency telephone numbers include: ambulance (☎ 546 490/123), police (☎ 546 303) and tourist police (☎ 447 774).

Aquarium

If you've ended up in Hurghada and don't want to put your head under the water, you can still get an idea of some of the life teeming in the waters of the Red Sea by paying a visit to the aquarium *(☎ 548 557, el-Corniche; admission E£5; 9am-10pm Sat-Thur, 9am-noon & 1pm-10pm Fri)*. Just north of the public hospital in Ad-Dahar, the aquarium has a reasonable selection of fish and various other odd-looking marine creatures. Bear in mind, though, that this is not a well-funded institution; the tanks are small and their occupants would doubtless have been better off left in the sea.

Beaches & Pools

Hurghada's beaches are not the most stunning in the world; in fact, they're often quite bare and stark. This has not stopped developers from coveting every square centimetre, however, and the few spaces left between tourist villages are garbage-strewn sites slated for construction. This means you've got little choice but to join the hordes at one of the resorts if sun, sand and sea are what you want (and why else would you stay here?).

A Word of Caution

Despite being Egypt's premier resort, Hurghada is filled with young men from Upper Egypt and is thus a traditional town. Local sensibilities must be considered when you move away from the beach area. Many tourists have taken to wandering around the market quarter in Ad-Dahar in shorts and skimpy tops, and the trend seems to be growing. If you do this, don't be surprised if you are grabbed, pinched or otherwise harassed.

There are other options, though, including the two public beaches. The one in Ad-Dahar is garbage strewn and unpleasant. Any women who brave the mess tend to attract a crowd, making it uncomfortable unless you enjoy swimming in a long T-shirt and leggings. Much better is the newly opened public beach next to Al-Sakia restaurant in Sigala, which boasts a good stretch of clean sand, sunshades, lounge chairs and a kiosk selling soft-drinks. Admission is E£3.50 and it is open from 8am until sunset.

Al-Sakia restaurant in Sigala allows you to stretch out on a reasonable piece of sand for a minimum charge of E£15 (including a drink). Access to the better, but smaller, Shellghada Beach, to the north of the Meridien, costs E£10; it's free if you eat at their restaurant. Also good is The Chill, the beach bar/restaurant in front of the Roma Hotel at the southern end of Sharia Sheraton. E£30 gets you onto the beach for the day, where you can loll in hammocks, order beers or simply enjoy the sun. If you're feeling energetic enough you can join local diving and water sports instructors each Tuesday in their weekly volleyball tournament.

If you've got kids, you could head to Fun Sport Beach next to the Seagull Resort on Sharia Sheraton in Sigala. Bouncing castles line the way to the sand and there's a new windsurfing centre where you can rent a board and sail for E£50 per hour. However, entrance for the day is a pricey E£40 for adults, E£20 for children.

AD-DAHAR

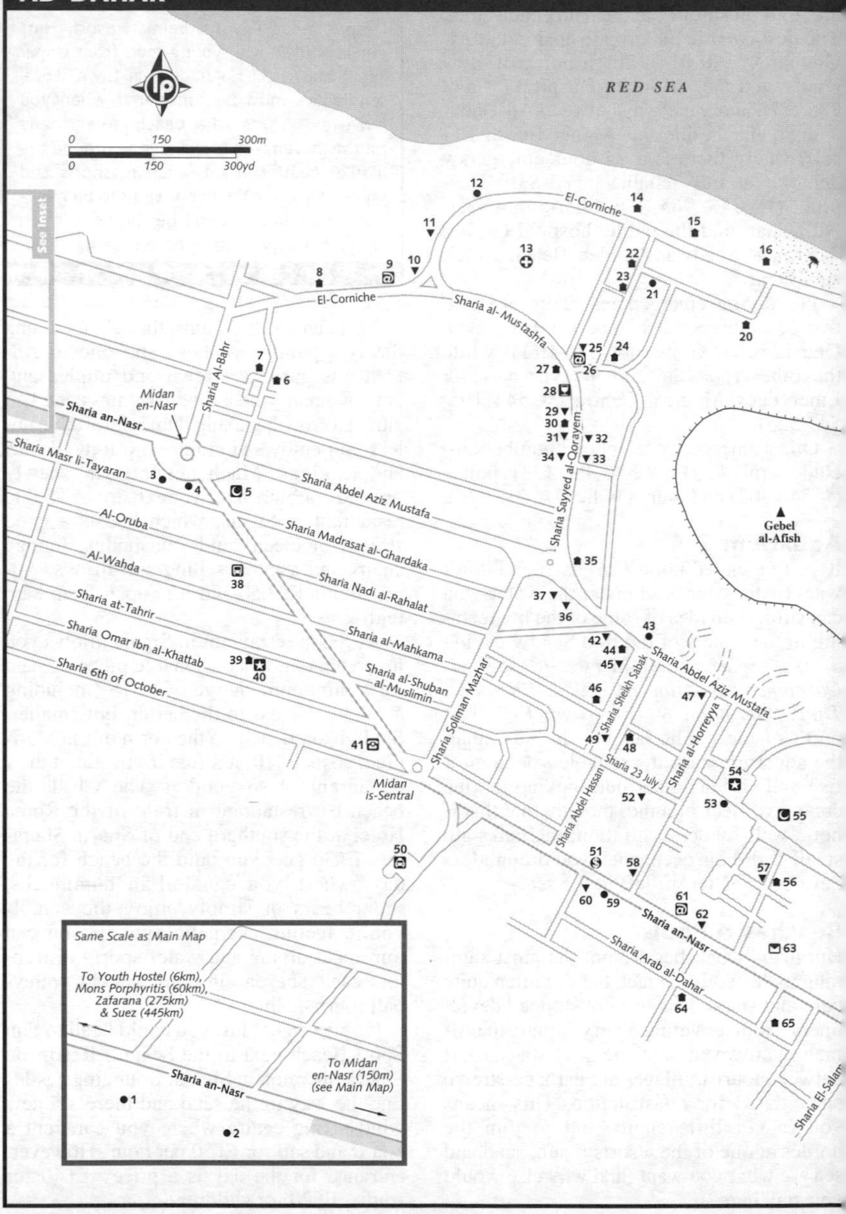
RED SEA
0
150
300m
0
150
300yd
See Inset
El-Corniche
Sharia al- Mustashfa
Sharia Al-Bahr
Midan en-Nasr
Sharia an-Nasr
Sharia Masr li-Tayaran
Sharia Abdel Aziz Mustafa
Al-Oruba
Sharia Madrasat al-Ghardaka
Al-Wahda
Sharia Nadi al-Rahalat
Sharia at-Tahrir
Sharia al-Mahkama
Sharia Omar ibn al-Khattab
Sharia al-Shuban al-Muslimin
Sharia 6th of October
Sharia Sayyed al-Qorayem
Sharia Soliman Mazhar
Sharia Sheikh Sabak
Sharia al-Horreyya
Sharia 23 July
Sharia Abdel Hassan
Sharia Abdel Aziz Mustafa
Midan is-Sentral
Sharia an-Nasr
Sharia Arab al-Dahar
Sharia El-Salam
Gebel al-Afish
Same Scale as Main Map
To Youth Hostel (6km), Mons Porphyritis (60km), Zafarana (275km) & Suez (445km)
To Midan en-Nasr (150m) (see Main Map)
Sharia an-Nasr
1
2
3
4
5
6
7
8
9
10
11
12
13
14
15
16
20
21
22
23
24
25
26
27
28
29
30
31
32
33
34
35
36
37
38
39
40
41
42
43
44
45
46
47
48
49
50
51
52
53
54
55
56
57
58
59
60
61
62
63
64
65

You may be able to sneak onto one of the paying beaches at the resorts if you act confidently enough, but it's not difficult for staff to spot the person who doesn't have hotel-issued towels. Paying will make life easier. Daily fees for access to pools and beaches range from E£25 to about E£60. Magawish Tourist Village has a good, large beach (E£60). Shedwan Golden Beach Hotel in Al-Dahar, Jasmine Village on the resort strip, and Coral Beach, to the south of the resort strip, have small reefs that allow you to combine snorkelling with sunbathing.

Snorkelling

Although there is some easily accessible coral at the beach south of the Sheraton, the best reefs are offshore, and the only way to see them is to take a boat and make a snorkelling or diving excursion for at least one day.

For years, **Giftun Islands** have been one of the most popular sites. The islands have been incorporated into the Red Sea Protectorate and access is restricted. A daytime resort/restaurant called Mahmya Protectorate has been opened on the larger island (see Places to Eat later in this chapter for details). For US$50, you are taken there by boat. You have the run of the island's pristine beaches, are given an hour-long guided snorkelling trip and eat a full lunch buffet. All garbage and waste water is removed from the island by specially equipped boats. Trips leave the Sheraton Marina at 8.45am and arrive back there at about 4.30pm.

Other day trips to Giftun include transport to and from the harbour, two stops on a reef, snorkelling gear and lunch on the boat; prices start at US$30. Overnight trips are also possible; however, you'll need to carefully choose the captain and crew. Groups of women may face unwanted advances or worse from their male 'guides'.

You will find no shortage of places offering these kinds of trips. The best advice is to shop around a little and see where you can get a deal that suits you. Simply relying on your hotel (and many of the smaller hotels work hard to get you to join the

Rescuing the Red Sea

Conservationists estimate that more than 600 pleasure boats and almost as many fishing boats ply the waters between Hurghada and the many reefs situated within an hour of the town. Until recently, there was nothing to stop these boats' captains from anchoring to the coral, or snorkellers and divers breaking off a colourful chunk to take home. But thanks largely to the efforts of the Hurghada Environmental Protection & Conservation Association (Hepca) and the belatedly established Egyptian National Parks Office in Hurghada, the Red Sea's reefs are at last being protected.

Set up in 1992 by 15 of the town's larger and more reputable dive companies, Hepca's program to conserve the Red Sea's reefs is manifold. Public-awareness campaigns are underway, direct community action has been taken and the Egyptian government has been lobbied to introduce appropriate laws. Now the whole coast south of Suez Governorate is known as the Red Sea Protectorate.

Environmental protection measures already undertaken include the installation of more than 450 mooring buoys at popular dive sites around Hurghada and further south, enabling boat captains to drop anchor on a buoy rather than on the coral itself. Marine rangers from the Egyptian National Parks Office police the waters, and captains found mooring to the reef rather than to the buoys are prosecuted.

The Egyptian National Parks Office is also trying to establish new dive sites to ease the pressure on existing sites, as well as trying to reduce the number of new boats licensed in the Red Sea. Finally, a symbolic 'reef conservation tax' of E£1 has been introduced and is payable by anyone using the reefs for diving, snorkelling or any other boating activity. It is designed to make the public aware that the reefs and offshore islands are now protected areas, rather than as a source of revenue. For details of the rules for marine protectorates see the boxed text 'Code of Ethics for Reef Protection' in the Diving the Red Sea chapter.

Both Hepca and the Egyptian National Parks Office encourage visitors to take an active role in helping to protect Hurghada's beleaguered reefs. The Egyptian National Parks Office is opposite the Sindbad Seaview Hotel, beside the public beach in Al-Dahar. You can drop by the office and pick up a brochure or call ☎ 598 339 or 540 720 between 8.30am and 2pm for information on the office's slide shows of Hurghada's reefs.

Hepca, just up from the old port in Sigala, sells a guide to the main dive sites around Hurghada and Safaga for about E£70; proceeds go towards the cost of setting up and maintaining mooring buoys. If you have any questions about safe diving practices or about how you can help Hepca in its efforts to protect the Red Sea's reefs, call ☎ 445 035 or 446 674 between 9am and 4pm Saturday to Thursday.

trips for which they are getting a commission) may not be the best way to do things. Several travellers have complained of not getting everything they thought they would. Eliminating at least one intermediary might reduce the risk of disappointment. Some of the more reputable dive clubs also take snorkellers out and, by going with one of them, you're almost assured of environmental reef protection practices being observed.

Take your passport with you on any boat excursion, as you may have to show it at the port.

Remember to use sun screen when swimming and snorkelling. It is probably a good idea to wear a T-shirt too, as the sun's rays easily penetrate the surface of the water. For more information about marine life and possible snorkelling sites, see the Diving the Red Sea chapter.

Other Water Sports

Plenty of the bigger resorts cater for most tastes in water sports. The best-known **windsurfing** places in the area are Three Corners Village, Jasmine Village or Giftun Village. Keep in mind that the huge amount of construction along the coast has affected the wind here, so if you're a windsurfing buff, you're better off in Sinai or further south along the coast at Safaga. If you decide to do it here, you're looking at about E£120 for an hour's lesson, with equipment, or about E£660 to E£700 for a week's equipment rental.

Paragliding, **paraskiing** and **water-skiing** are also available at some resorts. Magawish Tourist Village and Jasmine Village also offer **kite surfing**.

Hot-Air Ballooning

German-run **Cast Ballooning Egypt** *(☎ 444 928, mobile 012-218 2355; US$185 per person)* offers hot-air-balloon trips in the desert behind Hurghada. A five- or six-hour trip includes a one-hour balloon ride, plus jeep safari and breakfast at a Bedouin camp.

Flying

Tours with **Sharm Air** *(mobile ☎ 010-554 4400; US$80 for 20 minutes)* take you over the Red Sea coast in a single-engine prop plane. A certified instructor will let you take the controls. The price includes insurance and transfers to and from hotels.

Organised Tours

A wide range of organised excursions from Hurghada is available. Most of the bigger hotels and most travel agencies organise some or all of the following tours, many of them aimed at people flying in directly on charters and not planning on travelling through the rest of the country.

For those with a lot of stamina, the more ambitious tours include a whirlwind one-day tour to Cairo for E£200, or a slightly more leisurely two-day tour for E£450. A one-day jaunt to Luxor costs around E£250.

More feasible are some of the desert jeep safaris, which tend to include visits to at least one of two Roman sites: Mons Porphyritis and Mons Claudianus. These trips cost about E£150. A full-day excursion to the monasteries of St Paul and St Anthony costs about E£150. A half-day desert safari, including a one-hour camel trek, is about

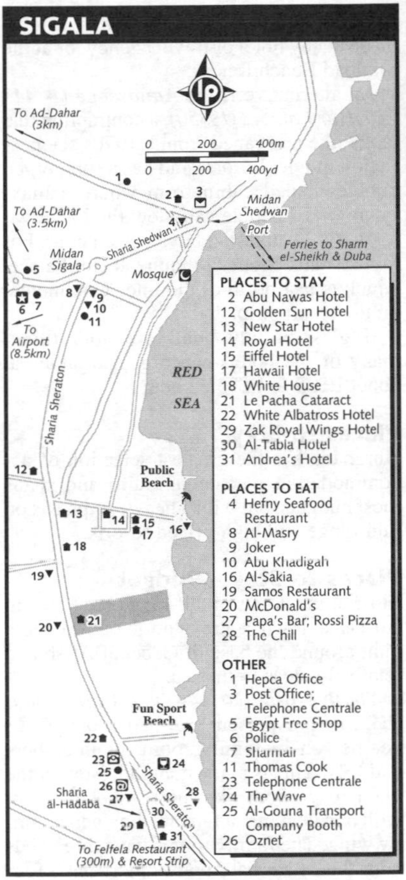

US$35; an evening excursion into the desert, including a sunset drive, camel ride and BBQ dinner, costs at least E£75.

A minimum number of people is needed for most of these trips, so it's best to inquire several days in advance.

A ride in ***Sindbad Submarine*** *(☎ 444 688, Sindbad Beach Resort; US$50 per person)* is one way to plumb the depths and stay bone dry. This yellow submarine can carry 46 people to a depth of 22m. This is a 'two-hour' trip; however, an hour of this is spent on a boat travelling between Sindbad Beach Resort and the site where the submarine is moored. Bookings can be made at any hotel or travel agency, or at the Sindbad Beach Resort.

An alternative is the ***Aquascope*** *(☎ 443 710, Hor Palace; US$50)*, a contraption that looks like it escaped from a 1970s science-fiction movie. It floats and has a submerged bubble-shaped cabin from where a maximum of 10 people can view the underwater world. Admission buys you an hour. For more details phone or inquire at Hor Palace, which is just north of the Inter-Continental on the resort strip.

If glass-bottom boats are your thing, many of the hotels can organise jaunts at about E£25 to E£35 an hour.

Places to Stay

Hurghada has the greatest selection of accommodation outside of Cairo and spans most budgets, but with a heavy emphasis on mid-range and high-priced resorts.

Places to Stay – Budget

Most of the hotels in this range are either in Ad-Dahar town centre or north of the centre, built around the base of Gebel al-Afish and relatively close to the sea.

Youth Hostel *(☎ 544 989, Cairo road)* E£23.10 per person in 4-bed room, E£28 per person in family room, nonmembers add E£1. This is a newly built hostel on the main road about 5km north of Ad-Dahar, with a male wing, a female wing and a family wing. The family rooms have three beds with their own bathroom; others have four beds to a bathroom. Lunch here is E£10, dinner E£4. Though it seems a bit pricey for a youth hostel and inconvenient without a car, the spacious rooms and the fact that is has its own beach actually make it a good deal.

Ad-Dahar Centre Hurghada's budget accommodation is concentrated in the souq area. Keep in mind that the market can be noisy at night.

Happy House *(☎ 549 611, Main Square)* Singles/doubles without bath E£30/40, doubles with bath E£50. Spotlessly clean pension on the main square by the mosque in the centre of Ad-Dahar. It is small, with only five double rooms with fans, as well as a kitchen and fridge. Prices include breakfast.

St George's Hotel *(☎ 548 246)* Singles/doubles E£20/30, with bath E£25/35. Off Sharia Sheikh Sebak, this hotel is run by a Coptic family and is popular with Copts. It has dark, but very clean rooms (which can be noisy because of the adjacent souq).

Shakespear Hotel *(☎ 546 256, Sharia Sayyed al-Qorayem)* Doubles without/with bath E£35/45. This place has some spacious, if dingy, doubles with communal baths and fans. Ask to see a few rooms to compare, because some are much better than others. Breakfast is not available.

Gobal Hotel *(☎ 546 623, Sharia Sheikh Sebak)* Singles/doubles E£15/25. The Gobal has shabby rooms in the centre of the souq. It's mostly used by Egyptian men, so women travelling alone should avoid it. Prices include breakfast and sometimes private bath.

Happy Land Hotel *(☎ 547 373, Sharia Sheikh Sebak)* Doubles without/with bath E£25/30. All the rooms here have phones and are clean, but because of the location in the souq it can be noisy.

Hotel Sosna *(☎ 546 647, Sharia Arab al-Dahar)* Doubles without/with bath E£20/35. There are also a couple of rooms with air-con for another E£10. It's off the tourist track and inconveniently located, but the rooms are fairly clean and the price is reasonable.

Ramses Ghardaka *(☎/fax 548 941, Sharia Arab al-Dahar)* Singles/doubles E£45/55, with air-con E£55/65. This place has large, clean rooms with telephones and fridges. Prices include breakfast.

Ad-Dahar Seaside You'll find quite a family of little hotels in the dirt lanes between the Market Place shopping centre and the sea. Though relatively close to the water, very few rooms in these places have sea views.

California Hotel *(☎ 549 101, fax 541 566)* Doubles without/with bath E£20/25. Friendly and popular, although the rooms are cramped and slightly grubby, this place sports exotic murals and has a roof terrace with a sea view. It's off Sharia Sayyed al-Qorayem; prices include breakfast.

Four Seasons *(☎ 549 882, fax 545 456)* Doubles E£35. This small, friendly hotel is just down the road from Aboudi Bookshop, off Sharia Sayyed al-Qorayem. It has 14 recently renovated rooms with private bath and air-con. For E£5 you can also use the beach at the Geisum Village Hotel. Prices include breakfast.

Alaska Hotel *(☎ 548 413)* Doubles E£20, with bath E£30. This small, reasonable hotel is on the slope behind the Aboudi Bookshop. Unfortunately, the rooms are dark and the staff somewhat shifty. Prices include breakfast.

Casablanca Hotel *(☎ 548 292, el-Corniche)* Singles/doubles E£15/25, with air-con & bath E£25/40. Close to the public beach, this place has large, bright rooms, some of which overlook the sea. However, we've had reports about the staff harassing women here, so it may be best avoided by lone females. Prices include breakfast.

Pharaohs Hotel *(☎ 547 577)* Doubles with/without bath E£35/25. Off Sharia Sayyed al-Qorayem, this place has large, freshly painted (but unfortunately carpeted) rooms. It's clean, but slightly dark. Nevertheless, a good deal for the price.

Snafer Hotel *(☎ 540 260, fax 545 456)* Doubles with fan/air-con E£45/55. The Snafer, off Sharia Sayyed al-Qorayem, is a small, new, friendly place at the top of the budget range. It has big and bright, clean rooms with their own bath, some with sea views. A good deal for the price, which includes breakfast.

Ritz Hotel *(☎ 547 031, fax 543 845, Sharia at-Tahrir)* Singles/doubles E£30/60. Also at the top end of this price range, this is a laid-back place with air-con rooms, but it's inconveniently located. There's a restaurant and bar, and you get access to the beach at the Sand Beach hotel for E£5. Prices include breakfast.

Sigala If you're on a budget you're better off in Ad-Dahar than Sigala, where mid-priced and expensive hotels and resorts proliferate. But if you can't bear to be away from the area's hectic nightlife, there are one or two reasonable places to choose from.

Abu Nawas Hotel *(☎ 442 830)* Singles/doubles E£20/30. Although usually empty, this is a local landmark off Midan Shedwan. Reasonably priced rooms have fans and communal baths, but this place is really only worth it if you need to be close to the port.

White House *(☎ 443 688, fax 442 085, Sharia Sheraton)* Singles E£35-48, doubles E£55-65. This is a friendly, long-standing (for Hurghada) hotel, which is losing out to the fierce competition in the area. All rooms have air-con; those overlooking the street are more expensive Guests get free access to the beach at Giftun Village on the resort strip. Prices include breakfast.

New Star Hotel *(☎ 442 588, Sharia Sheraton)* Singles/doubles E£25/40. Just down the road from the White House, the New Star has stuffy rooms with air-con. Not great, but one of the cheapest options in Sigala. Prices include breakfast.

Places to Stay – Mid-Range

Ad-Dahar There are some good mid-range options in Ad-Dahar, many of them beachfront tourist villages that have lowered their rates due to competition from the newer, better-appointed places to the south.

Sea Horse Hotel *(☎/fax 547 016, Sharia al-Bahr)* Singles/doubles E£65/85. This is a reasonable three-star that, as do of its ilk, caters mainly to Eastern European tour groups. The hotel has its own beach and most rooms have air-con, TV, phone and wall-to-wall carpet. Prices include breakfast.

Horus Hotel *(☎/fax 549 801)* Singles/doubles E£85/115. Across from the Sea Horse, off Sharia al-Bahr, this six-storey hotel has kitsch decor and comfortable rooms with air-con, TV and fridge. There is also a rooftop pool. It's popular with Western and Eastern European tour groups. Prices include breakfast.

Three Corners Empire Hotel *(☎ 549 200, fax 549 213, ⓔ info@threecorners.com, Sharia Sayyed al-Qorayem)* Singles/

doubles US$35/50. Just up from the sea, this enormous 366-room hotel looks more like a public housing block. Nevertheless it has the advantage of a central location and is only two minutes from the beach at the Three Corners Village. Prices include breakfast.

Three Corners Village *(☎ 547 816, fax 547 514, el-Corniche)* Singles/doubles US$38/56. This is a slightly shabby holiday village near the heart of Al-Dahar's seaside area. Its low-cost rooms are popular with Eastern European package tourists. Prices include breakfast.

Three Corners Terrace *(☎ 546 618, fax 548 617, Sharia Sayyed al-Qorayem)* Doubles US$30. This is another in the Three Corners' growing empire, but more intimate, with friendly management. Rooms are smaller but otherwise similar to those in the Empire next door. Price includes breakfast.

Al-Arousa Hotel *(☎ 548 434, fax 549 190)* Doubles with breakfast E£100, half board E£130. Overlooking the sea but from behind the Corniche, this is a good deal in this price range if you want to avoid the group mentality of the holiday villages. It has immaculate air-con rooms all with private bath, TV, phone and balconies with sea views. It has an indoor pool (E£10 for nonguests) and a poolside bar, and guests have free access to the beach at the close-by Geisum Village. Bookings are recommended as it's popular with divers.

Geisum Village *(☎ 548 048, fax 547 995, el-Corniche)* Singles/doubles half board E£90/155. This is a large holiday village but one of the cheapest of the three places right on the beach.

Sand Beach *(☎ 547 992, fax 547 822, el-Corniche)* Singles/doubles US$35/60. A four-star holiday village with its own beach and diving centre, this place has comfortable rooms with air-con and all the usual four-star amenities. It's popular with Russian groups.

Sea View *(☎ 545 959, fax 546 779, el-Corniche)* Singles/doubles E£80/110. On the other side of the road, facing the public beach, is this latest addition to Hurghada's Sindbad empire. It has 30 rooms with air-con and satellite TV and it also has a small indoor pool. A free shuttle bus ferries guests to the beach at the Sindbad Beach Resort (also free).

Sigala There's a large array of mid-range places on and around Sharia Sheraton, but while the place is hopping at night, the hotels don't live up to their exteriors. If you're here for the beach (and there's little else to keep you in Hurghada), you'd be better off at one of the cheaper tourist villages in Ad-Dahar or along the resort strip.

Golden Sun Hotel *(☎ 444 403, fax 443 862)* Singles/doubles E£60/75. Just behind La Mera off Sharia Sheraton is this friendly place where you can get spotless, air-con rooms. The management makes an effort here: There are flowers on the towels and an Egyptian 'cafe' with *sheeshas* (water pipes) has been set up in the courtyard. Prices include breakfast.

White Albatross Hotel *(☎/fax 442 519, 162 Sharia Sheraton)* Singles/doubles E£75/90. This 40-room family-owned hotel with air-con rooms. Prices include breakfast. For E£10 you can use the beach at the Le Pacha Cataract just down the road.

Royal Hotel *(☎ 447 728, fax 447 195)* Singles/doubles E£60/110. Rooms in this five storey orange-and-blue concrete box off Sharia Sheraton come with air-con and bath, and some have sea views. Guests get free access to the nearby public beach. Prices include breakfast.

Eiffel Hotel *(☎ 444 570, fax 444 572)* Singles/doubles E£60/90. This is a large (132-room) hotel off Sharia Sheraton with comfortable rooms complete with TV and air-con. It's used by Eastern European tour groups. Guests have free use of the adjacent public beach. Prices include breakfast.

Hawaii Hotel *(☎ 445 101, fax 445 702)* Singles/doubles E£45/80. Just behind the Royal Hotel, off Sharia Sheraton, this place has spotless rooms and free access to the public beach. Prices include breakfast.

Zak Royal Wings Hotel *(☎/fax 446 012, Sharia Sheraton)* Singles/doubles E£85/113. This oddly named hotel, beside Papas Bar, has clean, air-con rooms (with TVs and phones) clustered around a pool. Prices include breakfast.

Andrea's Hotel *(☎ 442 551, fax 442 251, Sharia al-Hadaba)* Singles/doubles US$20/30. Across the road from Zak Royal Wings Hotel, this hotel is owned by an Italian-trained chef. It is associated with the Sheraton Hotel's diving centre and there's a free shuttle bus between the two hotels. Prices include breakfast.

Al-Tabia Hotel *(☎ 442 350, fax 442 351, Sharia al-Hadaba)* Singles/doubles half board US$18/30. Just beside Andrea's is the kitsch Al-Tabia, with its castle-like crenellations. The best thing about this place is its beach bar/restaurant, The Chill (see Places to Eat and Entertainment later in this chapter for more information).

Resort Strip Reminiscent of Benidorm, or any of the other package-tourist nightmares of Mediterranean Europe, is the long strip of resorts that leads south from Sharia Sheraton. While most are in the top-price bracket, some are cheaper, catering to Eastern European groups or cut-price all-inclusive package tours from Europe.

Giftun Village *(☎ 442 665, fax 442 666)* Singles/doubles half board E£175/£240. Another of Hurghada's older resorts, with 380 newly renovated, comfortable chalet rooms. There's also a popular German-run diving and windsurfing centre.

Jasmine Village *(☎ 446 443, fax 446 441)* Singles/doubles half board US$47/68. Another of Hurghada's older establishments, its 434 bungalow-style air-con rooms cater mainly to German, Russian and Polish groups. There is disabled access, a playground and a full water-sports centre, which includes a reputable diving club and windsurfing facilities.

Magawish Tourist Village *(☎ 442 621, fax 442 759, ⓔ magawish@link.com.eg)* Singles/doubles half board US$39/58. This may not be the best hotel in Hurghada, but its spaceship architecture is priceless. A former Club Med with a children's play area, a huge beach and decent sports facilities, it's operated by Masr Travel, so you can get more information, and details of possible discounts, from their branches throughout the country.

Hor Palace *(☎ 443 350, 710 fax 442 603)* Singles/doubles half board US$30/50. This is one of the older tourist villages along the strip, with competitive prices and a snigger-invoking name. It has its own beach, reasonable air-con rooms and, like most of these places, is filled with low-end European package tourists.

Places to Stay – Top End

With the exception of Cairo, Hurghada has the greatest concentration of four- and five-star hotels and resorts in all of Egypt and the number is increasing as developers swallow the land further south. Most of these places are on the resort strip, which starts just south of Sigala and stretches for 20-odd kilometres down the coast, but there are also some along the beach between Ad-Dahar and Sigala. In keeping with the character of the city, most of the resorts here are cheaply built and meant to appeal to the package tourist, so don't expect much in the way of pleasing aesthetics.

The following is a short list of some of the better places on offer. Keep in mind that travel agencies in Europe and Cairo can offer reductions if you book in advance, and that prices fluctuate according to the season and state of the tourism industry. Prices include breakfast unless otherwise indicated.

Arabella *(☎ 065 545 087, fax 545 090, ⓔ reservation@iberotelarabella.com, el-Corniche)* Singles/doubles half board US$75/100. A warren of tasteful, white-washed domes on the beach between Sigala and Al-Dahar, Arabella has a famous disco and a good selection of restaurants.

Coral Beach *(☎ 447 160/2, fax 443 577)* Singles/doubles half board US$80/100. This is the last place on the resort strip – at least until the next one is finished. While it is far from town (a blessing if you want to look at your surroundings instead of other concrete resorts), it has well-appointed rooms, good sports facilities and a large beach with a reef. It's popular with Italians.

The burgeoning development at Hurghada makes you wonder at times whether you're at a beach or a building site.

Hilton Plaza *(☎ 549 745, fax 547 597, ⓔ hrghitw@hilton.com, el-Corniche)* Singles/doubles US$105/120. This plush five-star place near the centre of town has a good dive centre and very comfortable rooms.

Hilton Resort *(442 116, fax 442 113, ⓔ hurghada_resort@hilton.com)* Singles/doubles US$93/114. Older and slightly cheaper than its sister *Plaza*, with a lively bar and nightlife. Half board is US$14 per person extra.

Inter-Continental *(446 911, fax 446 910, ⓔ hrgha-resvn@interconti.com,)* Singles/doubles US$140/160. Taxes are 20% extra. One of Hurghada's most luxurious hotels, the Inter-Continental is built in the style of an Arab fort. It has a large marina and an indifferent beach, but it's well managed and very comfortable. Special deals are often available in off-peak seasons.

Le Pacha Cataract *(☎ 444 150, fax 443 705, ⓔ shrouk5@hotmail.com, Sharia Sheraton)* Singles/doubles US$50/80. This is a beige, Moorish-style resort in the centre of Sigala, with its own small beach and a shopping mall. Half board is US$10 extra.

Hurghada Marriott Beach Resort *(☎ 446 950, fax 446 970)* Singles/doubles US$79/84. This conveniently located six-storey luxury hotel is near the beginning of the resort strip. It's well managed and has a small beach, a pool and all the usual five-star amenities.

Le Meridien *(☎ 442 000, fax 443 333, Sharia Sheraton)* Site of the former Sheraton, which was the first resort to be built on the strip and gave one of Hurghada's main streets its name. It has a circular, modernist design that seventies architecture buffs will enjoy, but most people dislike. However, it's about to be renovated and expanded and will no doubt soon look exactly like all the other resorts around here. It was closed for renovation at the time of writing, but is due to reopen in early 2002.

Shedwan Golden Beach Hotel *(☎ 547 007, fax 548 045, el-Corniche, Ad-Dahar)* Singles/doubles US$130/150. This place is conveniently located near the centre of Ad-Dahar. It has 370 plain rooms, a vast swimming pool with a water slide, a decent beach and reportedly good food. It's popular with German and French tourists, but overpriced for a three-star.

Sofitel *(☎ 447 261, fax 442 260, ⓔ H18 15-gm@accor-hotels.com)* Singles/doubles

US$131/145. This is one of the more exclusive hotels in town, with 312 plush rooms clustered into 12 Arabesque-style blocks. It offers extensive water sports and has a 700m-wide beach, as well as a kids club, jogging track, tennis and squash courts and a selection of restaurants and bars.

Places to Eat

The beginning of April to mid-October is lobster-spawning season and during this period it is illegal to catch lobsters. Even so, you may see some unscrupulous restaurants offering them at this time.

Budget Dining Most of the budget dining options are found in Ad-Dahar, with a handful of places in Sigala.

Ad-Dahar Centre Many of the cheap eateries around the tourist souq have transformed into yet more souvenir shops but there are a few places opposite the Happy House Hotel, including one called ***Zeko*** which, like many others, specialises in grilled chicken. You'll also find a couple of ***coffeehouses*** around here.

La Torta *(☎ 549 504, Sharia Sheikh Sabak)* Pastries E£1-10. This is a pristine little cafe that serves filter coffee and a small selection of pastries at six small tables.

Pizza Tarboush *(☎ 548 456, Sharia Abdel Aziz Mustafa)* Meals E£9-18. A popular pizzeria with a variety of topping choices, most of which seem to taste the same.

Bell Riviera *(Sharia Abdel Aziz Mustafa)* Dishes E£4-40. Not to be confused with its more expensive sister restaurant with the similar name across the road, this place has excellent lentil soup, spaghetti, pizzas and calamari. You can also get breakfast here.

Egyptian Corner *(Sharia Abdel Aziz Mustafa)* Dishes E£4-20. Next door to the Bell Riviera, this is a tiny little place popular with travellers. It has a very limited menu that includes breakfast, spaghetti bolognaise and simple meals such as chicken or vegetable stew.

Ad-Dahar Seaside Sharia Sayyed al-Qorayem, the road running from the Shakespear Hotel right around to the Shedwan Golden Beach Hotel (on the Corniche), is lined with shops and restaurants. For self-caterers, the Al-Saby ***supermarket*** is reasonably well stocked. The nearby ***souq*** is a good source of fruit and vegetables, and there is a good 24-hour bakery, ***Sweet Hut***, on the corner of Sharia an-Nasr next to the Red Sea I restaurant. Local beer and wine can be found in the souq close to the tourist-police booth.

Norhan *(Sharia Sayyed al-Qorayem)* Dishes E£5-15. This is an unpretentious little diner with a few terrace tables and a limited menu. Meals such as shepherds pie or chicken come with a complimentary soft drink (no beer is served).

Amon Grill *(☎ 544 404, Sharia Sayyed al-Qorayem)* Dishes E£1.50-15. Kebabs, shwarma and other Egyptian fast-food staples are served in this tiny restaurant.

Jukebox *(el-Corniche)* Dishes E£6-20. Reasonably priced kebabs, pizzas and sandwiches are served here. It's next to the popular Papas II bar.

Cafe Cheers *(el-Corniche)* Dishes E£4-20. This is a tiny 24-hour cafe/bar that serves sandwiches, pizzas and burgers as well as cold beer.

Sigala There may not be a large selection of budget restaurants at Sigala, but the area does have two excellent traditional Egyptian places that compensate for the lack of variety.

Abu Khadigah *(☎ 443 768, Sharia Sheraton)* Meals E£6-10. This is a basic, no-frills restaurant famous for its excellent koftas, stuffed cabbage leaves and other Egyptian staples. It's filled with an intriguing mix of workers and local businessmen, as well as the odd tourist.

Al-Masry *(☎ 443 398)* Dishes E£1.50-48. Off Sharia Sheraton, this is a famous old restaurant with basic Egyptian dishes such as stuffed pigeon, *kebab hala* (meat stew) and stuffed vegetables. It also serves good soups for only E£1.50.

McDonald's *(Sharia Sheraton)* is a good landmark and a refuge for those who like familiarity.

Restaurants Restaurants abound in Ad-Dahar and Sigala, and on the resort strip.

Ad-Dahar There are a number of mid-priced restaurants in ad-Dahar, most centred on the souq. The food here is generally mediocre, but it's convenient for the many tourists that spill out of the hotels and resorts each evening.

Young Kang *(Sharia Sheikh Sabak)* Dishes E£10-17. Young Kang does surprisingly good far-Eastern cuisine in a small space. Try the fried rice and sweet-and-sour chicken.

Hurghada Fish Place Restaurant *(☎ 549 782, Sharia an-Nasr)* Dishes E£5-30. This is a small cafe with a good selection of fruit drinks and a basic selection of fish dishes.

Scruples *(☎ Sharia an-Nasr)* Dishes E£6-30. Across from the National Bank, this is a 'pub and steak house' that has a couple of other outlets around Ad-Dahar. It looks like a 1980s singles bar from the outside, but it serves a reasonable fillet of beef with rice and vegetables. The same management also runs a pool hall, ***Scruples Biliardeni***, near the end of Sharia Abdel Aziz Mustafa, where the same menu is available, plus beer for E£7.

Red Sea I Restaurant *(☎ 547 704)* Dishes E£6-40. In a street off Sharia an-Nasr, this restaurant is popular with package tourists wanting a night away from their resorts – the rooftop terrace gets quite crowded in the evenings. With a wide selection of seafood, plus Egyptian dishes and pizza, you can tailor the menu to fit most budgets.

Pharaoh's Restaurant *(☎ 546 306, Souq area)* Dishes E£7-30. Just around the corner from the Red Sea I, Pharaoh's has Egyptian food, including a decent kebab hala. Beer is available for E£8.

Red Sea Restaurant II (☎ 549 630, Sharia Sayyed al-Qorayem) Dishes E£6-40. This branch of the successful Red Sea I Restaurant, in the seaside area, has a roof terrace accessed from the adjacent side street. It offers the same selection of safe but uninspired seafood, steaks and poultry as its sister restaurant.

Lo Scarabeo *(mobile ☎ 012-364 6927, Sharia Sayyed el-Qorayem)* Dishes E£10-30. This Italian-run pizzeria and restaurant has a good selection of pastas and pizzas and huge salads. Delicious bread comes topped with a dusting of oregano. Despite the view of the enormous Three Corners Empire opposite, the terrace is a pleasant place to sit.

Portofino *(☎ 546 250, Sharia Sayyed al-Qorayem)* Dishes E£10-65. Across the road from the Red Sea II, this friendly place serves good, medium-priced Italian (and some Egyptian) food. Its pasta dishes are about the best in town. Most evenings the gregarious owner wanders around talking to customers.

Belgian Restaurant *(☎ 547 816, Sharia Sayyed al-Qorayem)* Dishes E£15-50, set menus E£45 & E£65. Nice but bland restaurant that serves similar food. The three-course set menus are a good deal, however, and the pizzas aren't bad.

Sigala As the number of hotels in Sigala mushrooms, so too does the number of restaurants.

Joker *(☎ 543 146, Midan Sigala)* Mains E£8-60. This is a deservedly popular fish restaurant at the beginning of Sharia Sheraton. You can choose your own fish, priced by the kilo. The food is fresh and unpretentious and served with bread and salads. It's very popular with locals and tourists. No alcohol is served here.

Al-Sakia *(☎ 442 497)* Mains E£15-25, beer E£8. Off Sharia Sheraton, this place is right down on the water's edge and has a wonderful view of the fishing boats in the old port. The food, a mixture of seafood and Egyptian cuisine, is good. If nothing else, it's a pleasant place to sit outside and enjoy a beer.

Samos Restaurant *(mobile ☎ 012-233 8027, Sharia Sheraton)* Meals E£10-40. This long-standing, popular Greek restaurant halfway down Sharia Sheraton has the usual salads, moussaka and souvlakia.

Rossi Pizza *(☎ 446 012, Sharia Sheraton)* Meals E£9-35. Located just at the point where Sharia Sheraton forks, this is a popular hang-out for divers and expat Hurghada residents. It serves a variety of pizza toppings on crispy crusts, as well as pasta dishes. The service is laid-back and women on their own can relax without being hassled.

Hefny Seafood Restaurant *(mobile ☎ 012-393 3122)* Meals E£6-35. This basic but very good seafood restaurant is frequented by locals. It's just up from the port off Midan Shedwan. A wide variety of fish is served with salads and rice.

The Chill *(mobile ☎ 012-382 0694, Sharia Sheraton)* Meals E£18-20. This is a laid-back beach bar/tent serving lunches and dinner. The small menu changes daily and features an interesting mixture of Eastern European and standard Italian/Mediterranean dishes. The atmosphere may not be authentically Egyptian, but this is by far the hippest place in town.

Resort Strip A couple of kilometres along the road, past the Moon Valley Village, is the best-located branch of Cairo's Felfela restaurant in the country.

Felfela Restaurant *(☎ 442 410, Sharia Sheraton)* Dishes E£3-35. Sitting on a rise and gentle bend in the coastline and overlooking the turquoise sea, this is a splendid place for a modestly priced Egyptian meal, but be prepared for the extra charge for bread (an absurd E£1 per piece). Beers are a little more pricey than the food, at E£10 for a local Stella. Further along on the resort strip you'll find ***Pizza Hut*** and ***KFC***.

Mahmya *(☎ 444 806, Giftun Islands)* Boat & lunch US$30. Half-day 9.30am-3pm. If you fancy lunch on an island, a daytime resort/restaurant has been opened on Giftun Islands, despite the fact that it is a protected area. The owners claim that they do not leave any garbage, and all waste water is supposedly returned by a special tank. There are tents and showers provided for daytime use (no overnight stays are allowed).

Entertainment

With its many hotels and so many sunburned punters looking for action, Hurghada has a lively nightlife. The large community of resident dive instructors, tour guides, hotel employees and other fun-loving foreigners also means that there is more on offer than in most other Egyptian towns, including Cairo.

Bars Almost all the three-star to five-star hotels and tourist villages have at least one, and in some cases, multiple bars. In addition, there are a number of independent places catering to the town's large community of foreign residents or to those tourists who have had enough of their hotels.

Peanuts Bar *(☎ 549 200, Hospital St)* Open 24 hrs daily. Stellas E£8.50, German beers on tap from E£11. Haunt of dive instructors and package tourists from the nearby Three Corners Empire, this is a popular bar. Those with the munchies can stuff themselves on an unlimited supply of unshelled peanuts. On Tuesday night there are specials for divers.

Papa's Bar *(mobile ☎ 010-512 9051, Sharia Sheraton)* Popular Dutch-run bar attached to Rossi Pizza in Sigala. Filled with diving instructors and other foreign residents, it is lively and has a great atmosphere most nights.

Papas II *(mobile ☎ 012-251 6511, el-Corniche, Ad-Dahar)* The formula of Papa's Bar has been replicated here, and as well as the dark wooden interior and cold beers, it offers live music several nights a week.

Jukebox *(el-Corniche, Ad-Dahar)* Upstairs from Papa's II, with less atmosphere but a nice view from the rooftop terrace and well-priced beers.

Cafe Cheers *(el-Corniche, Ad-Dahar)* Small, 24-hour cafe/bar where you can continue the party when the DJ has gone home, or satisfy the late-night munchies with a sandwich.

Hilton Pub *(☎ 549 739, Resort Strip)* This is a popular bar with live music six nights a week (beware: Sunday is karaoke night). Thursday night is Divers Night with limited free beer and food.

The Chill *(mobile ☎ 012-382 0694, Sharia Sheraton)* Another popular drinking destination with the diving fraternity, as well as with tourists looking for something away from the pseudo-European pubs that dominate Hurghada.

Check the *Red Sea Life* pocket guide or the *Hurghada Bulletin* for listings of all the latest events and live music.

Discos & Nightclubs Most of the bigger hotels offer some sort of spectacle – usually a Russian show – as well as belly-dancing performances in their clubs.

Alf Layla wa Layla *(☎ 446 571)* Dinner US$15-20, US$10 with soft drink only. If spectacle is what you like, try this kitsch place. It's at the southern end of the resort strip; tickets (which include transport) are on sale at most hotels.

If you want to dance, Hurghada is probably the best place to be in Egypt; although the music tends to be pretty mainstream, there is a good choice of places. Check *Red Sea Life* for the most popular venue of the moment. Keep in mind that things don't heat up until at least 11pm.

Kalaboush *(☎ 545 087, Arabella)* This has been the most popular disco in town for a couple of years now. It's decorated to resemble a jail. Most nights have a theme, but a wide variety of music is played. For some reason Tuesday is the most popular night.

The Chill *(mobile ☎ 012-382 0694, Sharia Sheraton)* This popular beach bar holds dance parties every Thursday, Friday and Saturday. It occasionally brings DJs out from Europe and once a month puts on 'full-moon parties'. Sunday, Monday and Tuesday are the nights to'lounge, chill and relax'.

The Wave *(Sharia Sheraton)* South of the Pacha Cataract, this is a new dance place with a good DJ and theme nights.

Almost all Hurghada's larger hotels also have discos. The most popular remain ***The Dome*** at the Inter-Continental, the ***Jungle Disco*** across from the Grand Hotel, and ***Galaxy*** at the Hilton Resort. There are also events held at ***The Arena*** or the ***Zeituna Beach Bar*** out at Al-Gouna, often with transport laid on.

Casinos At the ***Inter-Continental,*** on the resort strip, there's a casino. Admission is free, but you might be asked to show your passport. Smart casual dress is required and only foreign currencies are accepted.

Shopping

Hurghada is no shopper's paradise, with little on offer except overpriced T-shirts, snorkels and fins. With the influx of Russian and Eastern European tourists to Hurghada in the past few years, the trade in marine curios has taken off. Despite raids by the police, there is an alarming number of stalls and shops in Ad-Dahar selling everything from stuffed sharks to lamps made out of triggerfish. Avoid those who still try to flog their wares at the expense of the reefs.

Tax-free goods and local beer and wine are available at the ***Egypt Free Shop*** opposite the EgyptAir office on the resort strip or at the new pyramid-shaped branch at the roundabout in Sigala.

Getting There & Away

Air There are two EgyptAir offices in Hurghada. One (☎ 546 788) is near the Superjet bus station in Ad-Dahar, and the other (☎ 447 503) is on the resort strip almost opposite the Marine Sports Club. There are daily flights between Hurghada and Cairo (E£472 one way), plus several flights per week to Sharm el-Sheikh (E£218).

There are charter flights from various European cities to Hurghada throughout the winter. If you want to head directly to Europe, it is a good idea to check around to see what charters are available for the one-way flight.

Orascom Aviation (☎ 547 934) flies a turbo-prop from Cairo to Al-Gouna airport every Thursday afternoon and returns to Cairo on Saturday evening. Flights cost approximately US$140 return.

Bus Three bus companies operate services from Hurghada. Superjet (☎ 547 686) has its office and terminal near the main mosque in Ad-Dahar. It has three buses a day to Cairo (E£47, six hours) departing at noon, 2.30pm and 6pm. There's also a daily 2.30pm bus to Alexandria (E£75, nine hours).

The Upper Egypt Bus Co (☎ 547 582) operates from the main bus station at the southern end of Ad-Dahar, from where it runs buses every couple of hours to Cairo (E£30 to E£50 depending on the on-board services and the time of day, six hours) from 8am to 2.15am. The 7pm Pullman goes on to Alexandria (E£60, at least nine hours). A couple of these set down passengers in Suez as well, but some bypass it. There are other buses bound only for Suez (E£25 to E£35, five hours) leaving throughout the day.

About 10 Upper Egypt Bus Co buses go daily to Qena (E£8, three hours), starting at 6am and finishing at 11pm. There are eight daily buses to Luxor (E£15 to E£22, five hours), most of which go on to Aswan (E£35 to E£40, eight hours). There are buses to Al-Quseir (E£10 to E£15, two hours) via Safaga (E£5) at 5am, 3.30pm, 7.30pm, 8.30pm, 12.30am and 2am. All except the 3.30pm and 2am go on to Marsa Alam (E£20, four hours) and Bir Shalatein (E£35, five hours).

There are also daily services to Beni Suef (E£25), Minya (E£30), Sohag (E£16) and Asyut (E£20), and regular buses to Qift and Qus.

These details should be checked with the staff at the bus station, as changes are more than likely. It is a good idea to book ahead for long-distance journeys such as Luxor and Cairo.

Al-Gouna Transport (☎ 440 410) operates a regular minibus service to Safaga, leaving from the centrale in Ad-Dahar or from the duty-free shop in Sigala and stopping at all the tourist villages in Safaga. They leave Ad-Dahar at 7.30am, 10am, noon, 2.30pm, 4pm, 6pm and 11pm. Minibuses leave Safaga for Hurghada at the same times, with the exception of the last bus, which is at 8pm. Tickets cost E£10 and can be issued on the bus.

Service Taxi The service taxi station is near the centrale in Ad-Dahar. Taxis go to Cairo (E£30 per person, six hours). Others go to Safaga (E£3, 45 minutes), Al-Quseir (E£7, two hours), Qena (E£10, three hours), Marsa Alam (E£15, four hours) and Suez (E£20, 3½ to four hours). They don't go to Luxor or Aswan, except on a private basis with a police convoy. If you bargain, it'll cost about E£200 to get to Luxor in a car that seats seven people.

Police Convoys Whether you're going by taxi or private car, if you're heading across to the Nile Valley you'll be forced to go in a police convoy. They leave from Hurghada's southernmost checkpoint outside the Alf Layla wa Layla nightclub at 6am, 9am and 5pm, but you should check with the tourist office to make sure the times haven't changed.

Boat Until EgyptAir improves air links, boat remains the quickest way to get between Hurghada and Sharm el-Sheikh. A luxury high-speed ferry operated by Travco (☎ 445 037, 443 231) departs Hurghada every Monday (5am), Tuesday (5am), Thursday (8am) and Saturday (8am). It leaves from the old port in Sigala (US$40 or E£100 per person, vehicles E£150 to E£250 depending on engine size, 1½ hours). The boat is air-con. The trip can take longer when seas are rough. For more information you can also call the reservation office at the Sand Beach (☎ 545 147).

There is also a 'flying boat' from Hurghada to Duba in Saudi Arabia (E£180 or US$100 to US$200 per car, three hours). Daily departures are at noon, but you must be at the port at least three hours in advance. Call Amco Tours (☎ 447 571) for more information.

Getting Around

To/From the Airport The airport is close to the resort strip. A taxi to downtown Ad-Dahar should cost E£25.

Microbus In the mornings, microbuses full of labourers run back and forth along Sharia an-Nasr. Throughout the day, microbuses regularly run from central Ad-Dahar at least as far south as the Inter-Continental for

E£1. This appears to be the terminus. Short rides around Ad-Dahar cost 25pt to 50pt.

Al-Gouna Transport (☎ 440 410) now operates an efficient minibus network throughout Hurghada, with brightly coloured stops clearly visible around town. Buses within town run every 15 minutes and a weekly unlimited ticket on all four routes costs US$10 (available on the bus). Routes are colour coded. The yellow route runs from Al-Gouna all the way south to the Coral Beach Resort. One-way tickets cost E£5. The orange route does a small circle on the eastern end of Sigalla, while the blue route does a circuit around Ad-Dahar. One-way tickets on either cost E£2. (For information on the brown route, which goes to Safaga, see under bus in Getting There & Away earlier in this chapter.)

Taxi From central Ad-Dahar, taxis will take you as far south as the Sheraton for a ridiculous E£10 (or more if there are plenty of tourists around).

Bicycle These can be rented in Ad-Dahar from Boho, next to Al-Shaymaa Sea Trips on Sharia Abdel Aziz Mustafa, for E£3/10 per hour/day. Be warned, though, strong headwinds can make cycling very hard going.

Hitching While it is possible to hitch around town or out to the beaches, it is not recommended. Lone women shouldn't even attempt it.

AROUND HURGHADA

Mons Porphyritis

About 40km into the desert, along a side track off the main coast road 20km north of Hurghada, lie ancient porphyry quarries worked by the Romans. The precious white-and-purple crystalline stone was mined for use in sarcophagi, columns and other decorative work. The quarries were under the direct control of the imperial family in Rome, which had encampments, workshops and even temples built for the workers and engineers here. Evidence of this quarry town can still be seen, albeit not much of it standing. An increasing number of tours out of Hurghada make the trip out here. Failing that you'll have to hire a taxi.

Sharm al-Naga

About halfway down to Safaga, this is a fairly low-key beach resort used mainly by divers, though those with their own tent can also camp. Day-trippers wanting to use the beach (there's some good snorkelling here) must pay E£10. Masr Travel (☎ 546 600) in Hurghada often runs snorkelling excursions to this spot. For diving details, see Hurghada & Red Sea Coast under Clubs in the Diving the Red Sea chapter.

Ras Abu Soma

In an attempt to replicate the success of Al-Gouna, a number of similar 'resort clusters' are being built along the Hurghada-Safaga coast. Ras Abu Soma was the first to open and so far boasts a golf course and two luxury hotels.

Soma Bay Sheraton *(☎ 545 845, fax 545 885, e sales_soma_bay@sheraton.com).* Doubles US$110. The more famous of the luxury hotels is the 298-room Soma Bay Sheraton. As you sit in air-conditioned luxury of the pseudo-Pharaonic building here, you can feel good about the hotel's participation in a US Agency for International Development–sponsored pilot project to help hotels become environmentally friendly. Price includes breakfast.

If you don't have your own vehicle, Al-Gouna Transport's brown route runs through here several times a day (see Getting There & Away under Hurghada earlier in this chapter for more information).

SAFAGA

☎ 065

Safaga (sometimes referred to as Port Safaga) is 53km south of Hurghada and is first and foremost a port for the export of phosphates from local mines (and from the mines at Abu Tartur hundreds of kilometres away in the New Valley). During the haj, plenty of pilgrims from the Nile Valley embark here on their voyage to Mecca.

Despite the turquoise waters and the reefs that lie offshore, it is an unattractive town that barely stretches beyond a few flyblown streets off a main thoroughfare. Unless you're into windsurfing or diving and are thus staying at one of the beach resorts at the northern end of the bay, it is hardly worth stopping here, particularly if you're on a budget (cheap accommodation is geared to truck drivers, not tourists). Although the plague of construction around Hurghada is repeated on a smaller scale here, Safaga does have its own small resort strip and there are plans for many more holiday villages along the coast to the north and the south.

Orientation & Information

Sharia al-Gomhuriyya, the main road on the waterfront, has most of the services you might need. The bus station is near the southern end of town. Heading north there is a motley collection of small, cheap eateries and tacky souvenir stalls, and beyond them the post office. About 2km north of the bus station is the service taxi station. Next to it is the main centrale and next to this are branches of Banque Masr and Banque du Caire. Further north, next to Maka Hotel, is the Bank of Alexandria. You can catch a microbus up and down Sharia al-Gomhuriyya for 25pt; when heading south many of these vehicles will drop you about 400m north of the bus station. Microbuses also shuttle back and forth between the town and the northern resorts.

Windsurfing

Safaga is a famously windy place – the wind here comes along the coast from the north – and a number of the resort hotels have windsurfing centres. The construction boom has not affected Safaga as it has in Hurghada. **Shams Safaga Village**, north of Safaga, is probably the best-known place for windsurfing and has a German-run Mistral windsurfing centre. It also offers **kitesurfing**.

Places to Stay & Eat

Maka Hotel *(☎ 251 866, Hurghada-Safaga road)* Doubles E£30. The budget options here, including the Maka, all seem to be used by truckers waiting for their cargo to arrive at the port. At the northern end of town near the turn-off to Qena, this is a rip-off with shabby rooms (all with fan) and dirty bathrooms.

El-Ezz *(☎ 252 312, Hurghada-Safaga road)* Doubles E£20. Another very basic hotel with rooms with fan and none-too-clean shared bathrooms, but marginally better than the Maka.

Cleopatra ASI Hotel *(☎/fax 253 926, Hurghada-Safaga road)* Singles/doubles E£69/99. A few hundred metres further north of the Maka, this place is pricier but much better than the others. All rooms have a bath.

Safaga Marina Hotel *(☎ 251 133, fax 452 670)* Singles/doubles US$21/36. An ugly concrete building with air-con rooms and a small marina, it's about 200m up from the Cleopatra on the northern edge of town off the Hurghada-Safaga road. Prices include breakfast.

Heading north out of town there are at least six resorts: ***Menaville*** and ***Lotus Bay*** are on the main road while ***Sun Beach Camp***, ***Shams Paradise***, ***Holiday Inn*** and ***Shams Safaga*** are all on a side road leading around a bay.

Lotus Bay Resort *(☎ 251 040, fax 251 042)* Singles/doubles half board US$52/72. One of the cheaper options, with chalets set amid lush gardens.

Holiday Inn Resort *(☎ 252 821, fax 252 825)* Singles/doubles half board US$70/110. This is at the other end of the scale, with a large pool, a decent-sized beach and the usual Holiday Inn amenities.

Shams Safaga *(☎ 251 781, fax 251 780)* Singles/doubles half board US$42/60. One of the better hotels on the strip, with competitive prices and excellent water sports.

There is a string of cheap cafeterias heading north from the bus station along Sharia al-Gomhuriyya, otherwise, you could try the small pizzeria attached to ***Cleopatra Hotel*** (which, incidentally, also has a bar), or the expensive resort restaurants.

Getting There & Away

Bus There are five buses a day passing through Safaga en route to Cairo (E£35 to

E£45, about eight hours). Some of these buses stop in Suez, or there are Suez services (E£22 to E£30, about five hours) every hour or two, all of which stop in Hurghada (E£5, 45 minutes to an hour). Buses to Al-Quseir (E£5, about two hours) leave at 1.30am, 2am, 6am, 4pm and 9pm. All except the 1.30am and 4pm continue to Marsa Alam (E£10 to E£15, three hours). Regular services to Qena cost between E£8 and E£10. There are six buses to Luxor (E£13 to E£17) and four to Aswan (E£25 to E£35) each day at 1am, 2am (Luxor only), 11am, 2pm (Luxor only), 4.30pm and 11.30pm.

Service Taxi The taxis basically do three routes. Hurghada takes about 40 minutes and costs E£5. The trip to Al-Quseir (try asking early in the morning) costs E£5, and to Marsa Alam it's E£15. To Suez costs E£25, while to Cairo it's E£35. Because of the convoy system, you can only get to the Nile Valley (ie, Qena, Luxor and Aswan) by hiring the entire taxi. Expect to pay about E£200 but be prepared to haggle.

Boat The only passenger boats from Safaga are those going to Duba. There's a daily boat, *Al-Salam al-Seoudi*, which leaves at 11pm. For details, see the Getting There & Away chapter. There is no regular service from Safaga to Jeddah, except during the haj.

AROUND SAFAGA

Mons Claudianus

About 40km along the Qena road, a track breaks off north towards a one-time Roman granite quarry/fortress complex. This stark and impossibly remote place was the end of the line for Roman prisoners brought to hack the granite out of the barren mountains, and was a hardship post for the soldiers sent to guard them. More a concentration camp than a quarry you can still see the remains of the tiny cells that these unfortunates inhabited. There is also an immense cracked pillar, left where it fell 2000 years ago, a small temple and some other remains. You really need a guide for this trip, but the bigger hotels organise excursions. If you have your own vehicle and manage to avoid the convoy, there's a turn-off of sorts to the right on the Qena road. Follow the old broken asphalt as it winds through the mountains and you'll eventually get there.

AL-QUSEIR

☎ 065

The port town of Al-Quseir is 85km south of Safaga and about 160km east of Qift on the Nile. Although its history stretches back to Pharaonic times, when it was the launching point for boats sailing to Punt, its ancient port is now silted up and lies some 8km north of town. Still, the 'modern' town is just as interesting. Until the 10th century, it was one of the most important ports on the Red Sea and a major exit point for pilgrims travelling to Mecca. It was also a thriving centre of trade and export between the Nile Valley and the Red Sea and beyond. Even in decline it remained a vibrant port and was sufficiently important for the Ottomans to fortify the town in the 16th century. Later the British beat the French for control of it and at one point it was the point of importation for all spices going to Britain from India. However, the opening of the Suez Canal in 1869 put an end to all that, and the town's decline sped up, with only a brief burst of prosperity as a phosphate-processing centre in the early decades of the 20th century.

With its long history and sleepy present, Al-Quseir has a charm absent from Egypt's other Red Sea towns. Dominated by an Ottoman fortress, old coral-block buildings with wooden balconies surround the waterfront in the centre of town and are interspersed by the domed tombs of a number of saints – mostly pious pilgrims who died en route to or from Mecca. Because large-scale tourist development has not quite reached this far south (although it's only a matter of time) local people tend to be friendlier and less aggressive than in Hurghada or Safaga, making the town well worth visiting.

Orientation & Information

A branch of the National Bank of Egypt is just north-west of the main roundabout on

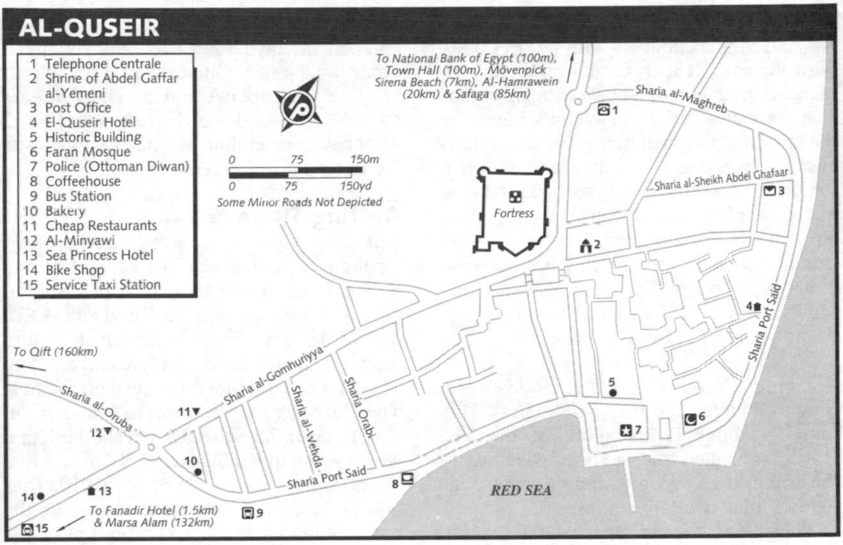

the way into town from Safaga. The 24-hour centrale is right on the roundabout, while the post office is off to the east, down towards the waterfront.

Things to See

The 16th-century Ottoman **fortress** is the town's most important remaining building. It was modified by the French, and some 6000 British cannonballs rained upon it during a heated battle in the 19th century. The British then added a fortified gate to make sure nobody else could take it away from them. At the time of writing, the restoration work on the building was complete but it had not yet been opened. When it does, it will house a visitors centre with displays on local history, Red Sea mining, monasteries and trade, and the history of the haj.

Just across from the fortress is the 19th-century **shrine** of a Yemeni sheikh, Abdel Gaffar al-Yemeni, with the old gravestone in a niche in the wall.

If you wander down to the waterfront you will see the picturesque **police station**, originally an Ottoman *diwan* (council chamber) and later the town hall. Because of its present function you cannot take pictures and you're unlikely to be allowed inside, but there is talk of moving the police to a new location and restoring the building.

Behind here is another fortresslike building, formerly a **quarantine hospital** built during the reign of the Ottoman sultan Selim II. Just next to it is the **Faran Mosque**, which dates back to 1704.

If you continue your walk along the waterfront, you will see a newly restored **merchant's house** dating back to the 1920s. It has been turned into a small hotel, the El-Quseir Hotel (see Places to Stay following).

Places to Stay

Sea Princess Hotel (☎ *331 880*) Singles/doubles E£15/20. Taxes are extra. This is the only choice in Al-Quseir for those travelling on a tight budget. Just west of the bus station, it has small, grubby cabinlike rooms with fan. The toilet/shower combinations can be a bit smelly, but hot water is reliable. The management claims to be about to undertake some much-needed upgrading of the rooms, so prices may go up in the near future. Breakfast costs E£5 extra.

El-Quseir Hotel *(☎/fax 332 301, Port Said St)* Singles/doubles with fan E£60/90, with air-con E£80/120. A highly recommended, rare gem of a hotel with six rooms in a renovated 1920s merchant's house on the sea front. Original narrow wooden staircase, high wooden ceilings and wooden lattice-work on the windows make staying inside a pleasure. Because the original structure has been respected, bathrooms are shared between three rooms, but are spacious and spotless. There are also stunning views from the sea-front rooms. The friendly manager, from Al-Quseir, is a good source for local history.

Fanadir Hotel *(☎ 330 861, fax 331 415).* Singles/doubles half board US$35/60. This hotel is about 1.5km south of the Sea Princess. Named after a rocky islet just to the south, it has 55 adjoining domed bungalows, plus two large villas.

Mövenpick Sirena Beach *(☎ 332 100, fax 332 128)* Singles/doubles from US$35/185. Top of the range in Al-Quseir, 7km to the north. This low-set, domed ensemble is one of the best seaside resorts along the coast – if not the whole country – and is designed to harmoniously blend in with the desert environment. Although it boasts excellent food and the usual five-star amenities, it avoids the glitz so common in Egyptian hotels – evenings are accompanied by the lapping of the waves against the shore rather than a thumping disco beat. The management is famous for its environmentally conscious approach and will haul guests out of the sea if it finds them breaking off coral on the hotel's reef. With a Subex diving centre and wide range of sports on offer, this is the place to go if you want total comfort and relaxation in a beautiful setting. Prices include breakfast.

Places to Eat

Foodwise, the options are very limited. There are the usual ta'amiyya and fish joints around the seafront and the bus station. There is also a ***bakery*** close to the bus station. The nicest place to have a cup of coffee is at the ***coffeehouse*** on the waterfront. ***Al-Minyawi***, on the road to Qift, is a small truckers' cafe that has the best chicken in town for E£10, but you must order in advance. Other than that, you will have to stick to the hotels. The ***Fanadir*** *(☎ 430 861)* and the ***Mövenpick*** *(☎ 432 100)* have buffet dinners open to nonguests for E£60 and E£80 respectively.

Getting There & Away

Bus There are four buses that go all the way through to Cairo (E£55, 11 hours) via Safaga (E£5 during the day, E£8 at night, one to two hours) and via Hurghada (E£10 during the day, E£15 at night); departure times are 5am, 5.30am, 7.45pm and 8.30pm. The 5am and 7.45pm buses also go to Suez. There are three buses south to Marsa Alam (E£5) at 3am, 7.30am, 10.30pm and 11.30pm, which go on to Bir Shalatayn. There are five buses daily to Qena (E£8 to E£10, four hours) via Qift. There's talk of moving the bus station to a new purpose-built place off the road to Safaga, but nobody seems in a hurry to leave the town centre.

Service Taxi The service taxi station is at the southern end of town. The officially prescribed fares are Cairo E£40, Suez E£25, Qena E£15, Hurghada E£8 and Safaga E£5. As in Hurghada and Safaga you have to hire the entire taxi for the trip to Luxor, Qena or Aswan. Drivers ask for about E£250, but you may be able to bargain them down. Because of the security situation, you have to go via Safaga.

Getting Around

There is a no-name bike shop virtually opposite the service taxi station. The owner asks E£15 for a day's bike rental, but this can probably be bargained down.

AROUND AL-QUSEIR

Wadi Hammamat

About halfway along the road connecting Al-Quseir to the town of Qift, Wadi Hammamat contains a fascinating but rarely visited collection of **Pharaonic graffiti**. The wayward chisellings of Wadi Hammamat were first extensively examined by the Russian Egyptologist Vladimir Golenischeff late in the 19th century. The high, smooth walls of the wadi have made it an ideal resting place for travellers through the ages, and indeed there is graffiti dating from Pharaonic times right down to Egypt's 20th-century King Farouk. The road runs on an ancient trade route, and remains of old wells and other evidence of the trail's long history can also be seen. In Graeco-Roman times, watch towers were built along the trail at short enough intervals for signals to be visible. Many of them are still intact on the barren hilltops on either side of the road.

The police are very nervous about foreigners taking this road these days so you may not be able to go. But you could try to get the early bus from either Al-Quseir or Qena (one leaves each way at 7am) to drop you at Wadi Hammamat, and try to get a lift on the next one either way about four or five hours later. Other than that you will have to bargain with a taxi driver.

Places to stay

If you're heading down the coast towards Marsa Alam there are a couple of places to look out for.

Utopia Beach Club Singles/doubles half board US$40/70. Some 20km from Al-Quseir and easily spotted from the road, thanks to a green Nile cruiser that was brought here a few years ago and converted into a diving centre, this place has a nice beach and good reef.

Mangrove Bay *(☎ 02 748 6748, fax 02 760 5458)* half board US$50/80. This is a comfortable three-star 30km south of Al-Quseir with white sandy beaches, good reefs and a dive centre.

MARSA ALAM

Marsa Alam is a fishing village 132km south of Al-Quseir. A road also connects the village with Edfu, 230km across the desert to the west. Phosphate mining is the big thing in this part of the country, although it is fast being overtaken by tourism. The village is basically a T-junction of the road from Edfu with the coast road. South of the junction is the bulk of the village with a small, incongruous looking shopping arcade that has a pharmacy, a school and a centrale, from where you can sometimes call overseas.

Although there is little else here now, the cement mixers have already hit the coast to the north and south of town. Construction will start in earnest when the new airport here is complete (so far it's a couple of years late). In the meantime, divers are signing up to come here in increasing numbers in an effort to avoid the hordes on reefs further north. The ubiquitous tourist villages are not far behind them, so hurry if you want to see the last stretch of unspoiled Egyptian coastline. The landscape here is barren and wilder than further north, with coral shelves abutting the land and few beaches to soften the transition between land and sea. Quite how the developers will change the topography so that tourists have sand to lay on remains to be seen.

A military pass (issued from Cairo) is currently required for travel south of Shams Alam, 50km south of town.

Information

Emergency If you do come here, whether to dive or simply to enjoy the scenery, keep in mind that the only decompression chamber is at Marsa Shagra, 20km north of Marsa Alam. It can be reached at emergency VHF code 16, satellite phone ☎ 0195-100 262 or mobile ☎ 012-218 7550.

Other than this, emergency services are almost nonexistent. Although dive centres and most hotels have a satellite phone for emergencies, there's not much else for the moment.

Tomb of Sayyed ash-Shazli

About 145km south-west into the desert at Wadi Humaysara is the **Tomb of Sayyed ash-Shazli**, a 13th-century sheikh who is revered by many as one of the more important Sufi leaders. His followers believe that he wanted to die in a place where nobody had ever sinned. Evidently it was difficult to find because the site was a journey of several days from either the Nile Valley or the coast. His tomb was restored under the orders of King Farouk in 1947 and there is now an asphalt road leading to it, but you may not make it through the checkpoints. His *moulid* (religious festival), on the 15th of the Muslim month of Shawal, is attended by thousands of Egyptians and, according to locals, a plane load of Germans, each year.

Places to Stay

Coral Cove Beach Safari *(☎ 364 7970, Coral Cove)* Camp sites E£15, half board E£55, full board, E£70. About 7km north of the town, draped around two azure bays, this camp has 10 semipermanent 'tents' and a communal shower block with very limited water. If you do stay here, don't walk along the beach north of the main headland – it's definitely mined. To get there (and to the other camps) you can either bargain for a taxi (E£10 to E£15, 10 minutes) from Marsa Alam or you can get the bus.

Red Sea Diving Safari *(in Cairo ☎ 02-337 1833, fax 749 4219, e redseasaf@gega.net, w www.redseadivingsafari.com, Marsa Shagra)* Doubles in tents/huts/stone chalets US$35/44/55 per person. At Marsa Shagra, 20km north of Marsa Alam, this place is owned by Hossam Helmi, lawyer, committed environmentalist and diving enthusiast. He has 10 tents, 10 huts and 10 stone chalets. All are spotlessly clean and more comfortable than anything else available on this stretch of coast. All prices are for full board. Nondivers in search of beautiful vistas and tranquillity are welcome, too.

Red Sea Diving Safari has another camp with the same prices at ***Marsa Nakari***, 18km to the south of Marsa Alam. In 2001, it built another camp in ***Wadi Lahami***, a remote mangrove bay just north of Ras Banas. At the moment, accommodation here is in tents only, at US$40 per person in a double (full board). There are live-aboards based in each of the three boats used for offshore diving. With his legal qualifications, Helmi has also developed a quirky sideline in underwater weddings.

Kahramana *(in Cairo ☎ 02-760 4820, 748 0883, e sales@kahramanaresort.com)* Singles/doubles half board US$65/90. This place, 6km south of Marsa Allam, has 55 rooms in ochre-coloured buildings around a stunning beach. A pool, air-con, bars and restaurants make remote living very comfortable. The diving centre is run by Red Sea Diving Safari.

Shams Alam *(☎ 02-417 0046, fax 417 0158)* Singles/doubles half board US$70/100. The most southerly resort on Egypt's Red Sea coast (for now), this place specialises in diving trips to local and less-frequented southern reefs. There are 70 comfortable rooms in domed and vaulted two-storey chalets, and there is a pool as well as a nice beach.

Places to Eat

In town there are a couple of ***cafes*** at the junction where you can occasionally get some dubious looking ta'amiyya, and there is a pair of grocery shops with scant supplies. The only other option is the ***cafeteria*** next to the service station. The young owner is very friendly, but the choice of food is limited to stale sandwiches, packet soups and frozen hamburgers. There's a ***bakery*** next door.

Getting There & Away

The bus from Aswan to Marsa Alam (E£10.50) departs from Aswan at 6.30am, passes through Edfu (E£9) between 8am and 8.30am, and arrives in Marsa Alam at around noon. It continues on to Bir Shalatein but, at the time of writing, it was unlikely you'd get past the military checkpoint south of Marsa Alam. The bus going back to Aswan via Edfu leaves from the cafes at the T-junction of the Edfu and coast roads at about 7am.

There are three buses to Al-Quseir (E£5, 1½ hours), departing at 4am, 12.30pm, 2pm, 4pm and 5pm, from where there are more frequent connections to northern destinations.

BERENICE

The military centre and small port of Berenice, 150km south of Marsa Alam, was founded in 275 BC by Ptolemy II Philadelphus and was an important trading post until the 5th century AD. Near the town, the ruins of the **Temple of Seramis** can be seen.

The US Navy occasionally brings its aircraft carriers here. Apparently, this is one of the staging areas for the US Rapid Deployment Forces. As a military permit is required for land travel south of the Shams Alam, it may not be possible to get this far south down the coast.

BIR SHALATEIN

This tiny village 90km south of Berenice marks the administrative boundary between Egypt and Sudan, although Egypt at least considers the political boundary to be another 175km south-east, beyond the town of Halaib, a once important Red Sea port that has long since fallen into obscurity.

Some of the best dive sites in the Red Sea are located in this area and dive companies from further north are increasingly organising boat safaris to the region (see Hurghada & Red Sea Coast under Clubs in the Diving the Red Sea chapter for more information). Divers and the odd desert trekker are about the only civilians who make it this far south these days, as all the necessary permits are either arranged well in advance, or hastily put together thanks to a bit of baksheesh by the various dive clubs.

Diving the Red Sea

From mountains of coral that rise from the sea bed to shallow reefs swarming with fish; from sheer drop-offs that descend to unknown depths to coral-encrusted shipwrecks – the Red Sea is a diver's paradise. In 1989 an international panel of scientists and conservationists selected the northern portion of this 1800km-long body of water as one of the Seven Underwater Wonders of the World. Since then its popularity as a diving destination has taken off and thousands of visitors come here each year.

Surrounded by desert on three sides, the Red Sea was formed some 40 million years ago when the Arabian Peninsula split from Africa, allowing the waters of the Indian Ocean to rush in. Bordered at its southern end by the 25km-long Bab al-Mandab Straits, the Red Sea is the only tropical sea that is almost entirely closed. No river flows into it and the influx of water from the Indian Ocean is slight. These unique geographical features combined with the arid desert climate and extremely high temperatures make the sea extremely salty. It is also windy; on average the sea is flat for only 50 days a year.

Diving tends to be concentrated at the northern end of the Egyptian Red Sea. The most popular destinations are around the southern tip of the Sinai Peninsula, most famously the thin strip of land that juts out into the sea and forms **Ras Mohammed National Park** – often called the jewel in the crown of the Red Sea. Another major diving area is the **Straits of Tiran**, which form the narrow entrance to the Gulf of Aqaba. The currents sweeping through the deep, narrow channel here allow coral to grow prolifically and attract all manner of marine life. The reefs further north along the Egyptian shores of the Gulf of Aqaba are also popular. On the western side of the Sinai Peninsula lie the **Straits of Gubal**, a series of coral pinnacles that lie just beneath the surface of the sea and are famous for snagging ships trying to navigate their way north to the Suez Canal. This is where you will find the majority of Egypt's shipwrecks, including the famous World War II freighter, *The Thistlegorm*.

Heading south along the Red Sea coast, the best reefs are found around the proliferation of offshore islands and reefs. Although most shore reefs near Hurghada have been damaged by uncontrolled tourist development, pristine dive sites further south can still be reached from the shore.

Highlights

- Marvel at the coral and the teeming fish life at Ras Mohammed National Park, one of the world's most famous marine parks.
- Explore the remains of *The Thistlegorm*, bombed in WWII, then rediscovered by Jacques Cousteau and now one of the most sought-after wreck-dives in the world.
- Experience the strong currents, dramatic seascape and abundant fish life of the Straits of Tiran.
- Visit the remote islands south of Berenice (the Southern or Far Islands), where the reefs are stunning, the coral lush and the pelagic fish plentiful.

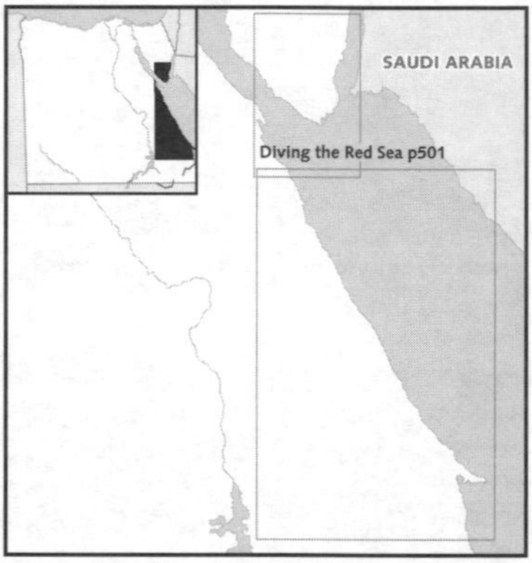

DIVING THE RED SEA

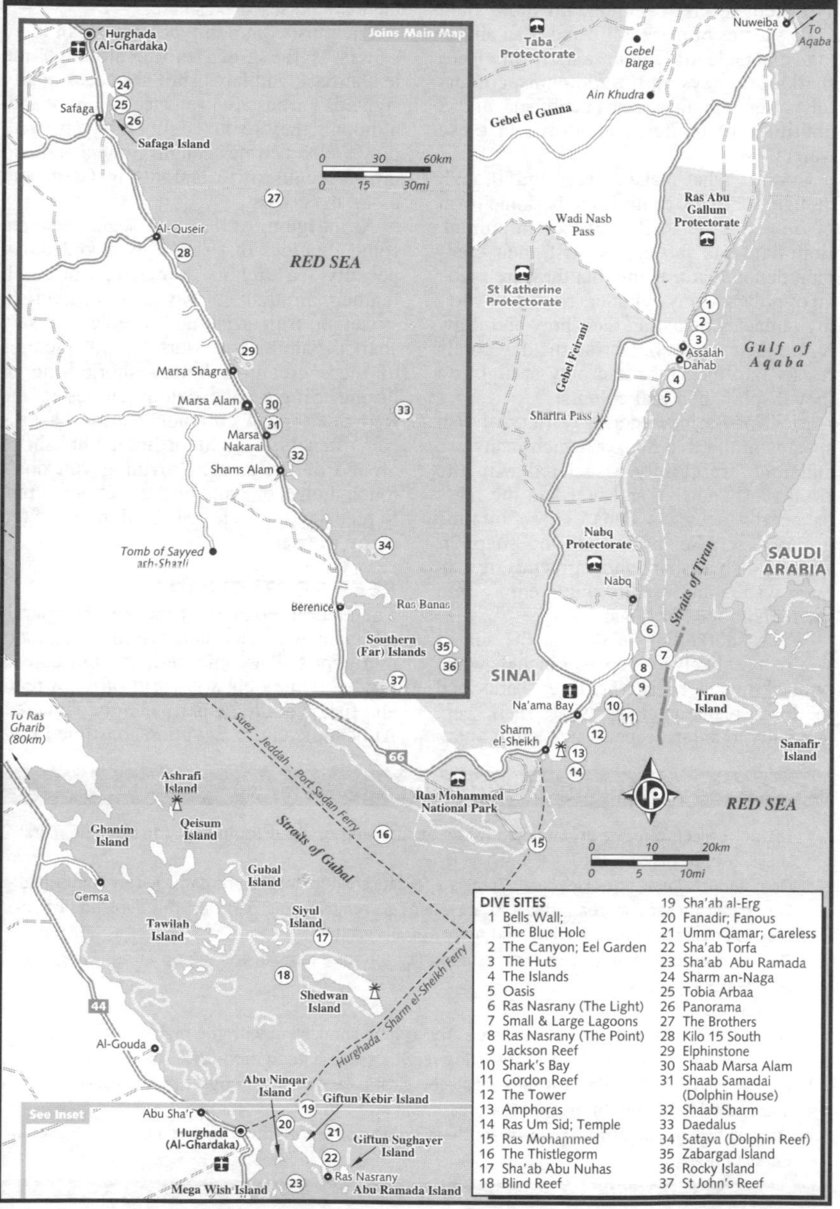

MARINE LIFE

The Red Sea is teeming with more than 1000 species of marine life and is an amazing spectacle of colour and form. Reef sharks, stingrays, turtles, dolphins, colourful corals, sponges, sea cucumbers and a multitude of molluscs all thrive in these waters.

Coral is what makes a reef and, though thought for many centuries to be some form of flowering plant, it is in fact an animal. Both hard and soft corals exist, their common denominator being that they are made up of polyps – tiny cylinders ringed by waving tentacles that sting their prey and draw it into their stomach. During the day corals retract into their tube and only at night do they display their real colours.

Most of the bewildering variety of fish species in the Red Sea, of which many are endemic, are closely associated with the coral reef, and live and breed in the reefs or nearby seagrass beds. These include grouper, wrasse, parrotfish and snapper. Others, such as shark and barracuda, live in open waters and usually only venture into the reefs to feed or breed.

When snorkelling or diving, the sharks you're most likely to encounter include white or black-tipped reef sharks. Tiger sharks, and the huge, plankton-eating whale sharks, are generally found in deeper waters only. Shark attacks in the Red Sea are extremely rare, and there are no sea snakes here.

The most common type of turtle in these waters is the green turtle, although the leatherback and hawksbill are occasionally sighted. Turtles are protected in Egypt and, although they're not deliberately hunted, they are sometimes caught in nets and end up on menus in restaurants in Cairo and along the coasts.

As intriguing as they may seem, there are some creatures that should be avoided, especially sea urchins, blowfish, fire coral, feathery lionfish, moray eels, turkeyfish, stonefish, triggerfish and, needless to say, sharks. Familiarise yourself with pictures of these creatures before snorkelling or diving. Single-page colour guides to the Red Sea's most common marine hazards can often be bought in hotel bookshops around diving areas. Providing you don't touch things, or stand on the reef or attempt to feed a moray eel, you shouldn't have too many worries.

REEF PROTECTION

The natural wonders of the Red Sea parallel (many would say surpass) the splendours of Egypt's Pharaonic heritage, but care is needed if the delicate world of coral reefs and fish is not to be permanently damaged. Almost the entire Egyptian coastline in the

Code of Ethics for Reef Protection

- Do not collect, remove or damage any material, living or dead (including, for example, coral, shells, fish, plants or fossils).
- Do not touch, kneel on or kick coral. Coral is a delicate creature that can be damaged when touched.
- Do not stir up sand as coral uses a lot of energy to remove sand particles; this depletion of energy interferes with their feeding and reduces their growth.
- Do not disturb any part of the reef community by, for example, picking up and playing with sea creatures.
- Do not litter.
- Do not walk or anchor on any reef area. Try to time snorkelling with the high tide, so that you can swim, rather than walk, over the living reef to get to a good drop-off.
- Do not feed fish. This disturbs the reef's ecological balance and can upset the digestive system and natural behaviour of marine creatures.
- Do not fish or spearfish. If you see others doing so, report them to the Egyptian National Parks Office.

Gulf of Aqaba is now a protectorate, as is the Red Sea coast from Hurghada south to Sudan. This means you could be liable to penalties if you violate any of the rules listed in the code of ethics outlined in the boxed text 'Code of Ethics for Reef Protection'. Divers and snorkellers should heed the requests of instructors *not* to touch or tread on coral. If you kill the coral, you'll eventually kill or chase off the fish, too.

The same principle applies with paying baksheesh to do something you shouldn't be doing, such as breaking off a bit of coral or collecting shells to take home as souvenirs. Doing so is illegal and you can be prosecuted. Don't be tempted to flaunt these rules just because you can bribe someone to get around them. As the Egyptian National Parks Office gets more clout it is cracking down on offenders and checking bags at the country's exit points. You can be fined and in some cases forbidden from diving here again.

The code outlined in the boxed text 'Code of Ethics for Reef Protection' should be kept in mind by all divers, but if there's one paramount guideline, it's that you should *take nothing with you, leave nothing behind*. In addition to the code of ethics, there are a few other things to remember when diving that will help preserve the ecology and beauty of reefs:

- Do not wear gloves. As you're not touching marine life you won't need them anyway. The wearing of gloves is banned in Ras Mohammed National Park and around the southern islands, but some dive clubs are lax in enforcing this rule.
- Be conscious of your fins. Even without contact the surge created from heavy fin strokes near the reef can damage delicate organisms. When treading water in shallow reef areas, take care not to kick up clouds of sand. Settling sand can easily smother the delicate organisms of the reef.
- Practice and maintain proper buoyancy control. Major damage can be done by divers descending too fast and colliding with the reef. Because the Red Sea is so salty you'll need to add extra weight to overcome the increased buoyancy. Make sure you are correctly weighted and that your weight belt is positioned so that you stay horizontal. If you have not dived for a while, have a practice dive in a pool before taking to the reef. Be aware that buoyancy can change over the period of an extended trip: Initially you may breathe harder and need more weight; a few days later you may breathe more easily and need less weight.
- Take great care in underwater caves. Spend as little time within them as possible as your air bubbles may be caught within the roof and thereby leave previously submerged organisms high and dry. Taking turns to inspect the interior of a small cave will lessen the chances of damaging contact.
- Resist the temptation to collect or buy corals or shells. Aside from the ecological damage, taking home marine souvenirs depletes the beauty of a site and spoils the enjoyment of others. The same goes for marine archaeological sites (mainly shipwrecks). These sites are protected by Egyptian law and the authorities are cracking down on violators.
- Ensure that you take home all your rubbish and any litter you may find as well. Plastics in particular are a serious threat to marine life. Turtles can mistake plastic for jellyfish and eat it.

DIVE SITES

The following list of dive sites is not exhaustive but does include the most popular destinations from north to south:

Dahab Area

Bells Wall This dive is just north of The Blue Hole, which is reached through a small chute. Rich coral and marine life are here, with large fish and rays.

The Blue Hole An 80m-deep pool in the reef, only a few metres out from shore. This infamous, deep dive has claimed the lives of many divers due to nitrogen narcosis or improper use of equipment (which isn't difficult at such a depth). It can't be stressed enough that it is only for very experienced divers, and even they should be wary – many of those who have lost their lives here have been instructors or divemasters. There is nothing to see down there and, according to some dive club managers, it's way overrated.

The Canyon A popular dive but, to an inexperienced diver, it will seem somewhat harrowing at first. From the shore, you snorkel along the reef before diving, past a wall of coral, to the edge of The Canyon and into a cavern under the sea bed. It is dark, narrow and seems capable of swallowing you.

Eel Garden About a 15-minute walk north of the lighthouse area in Assalah, this is a popular snorkelling spot that is also good for learner divers. The maximum depth is 17m and there's a sandy bottom.

The Huts Also known as Abu Talha, The Huts has huge corals in the shallows, with rich marine life and unusual formations. Good for all levels. Often combined with a drift dive to Abu Helal, 4km north of Dahab.

The Islands A collection of colourful coral pinnacles just south of Dahab before the lagoon. Despite its proximity to Dahab, fish are abundant here.

Oasis A secluded spot excellent for a variety of marine life, 8km south of Dahab. Nearby are the Three Pools.

Sharm el-Sheikh & Na'ama Bay Area

Ras Nasrany There are two sites worth noting here: The Light and The Point. There are 40m drop-offs and heaps of reef and pelagic fish.

Small & Large Lagoons Off the north-west tip of Tiran Island, featuring a shallow reef and the wreck of the *Sangria*. The currents are strong here, and there is a mooring so that boats don't have to drop anchor onto the reef. The Large Lagoon has reef and sand fish.

Jackson Reef Midway between Tiran Island and the mainland, home to sharks and large pelagic fish. There is a 70m drop-off, but be warned: This site is not for beginners. The currents are dangerous.

Shark's Bay A good shore entry dive for beginners, but with plenty for more-advanced divers, with a sloping reef and deep canyon offshore. Famous for manta rays.

Gordon Reef Close to Ras Nasrany and a popular site with experienced divers. There are sharks and open-water fish here and a wreck on the reef. Thomas and Woodhouse reefs also have some good diving.

The Tower South of Na'ama Bay, this is a remarkable wall dropping 60m into the depths just offshore and is frequented by (among other amazing fish) sea horses and ghost-pipe fish. Its deep colours are very good for photography.

Amphoras Also known as Mercury. A Turkish galleon lies at the bottom of the sea here. Evidence of its cargo of mercury can still be seen in among the coral. Other dives between here and Ras Um Sid include Turtle Bay, Paradise and Fiasco.

Ras Um Sid A prime diving site to a deep, sloping wall, easily accessible near the lighthouse. The beautiful coral garden has lots of colourful fan coral and a great variety of fish. Because the small beach here is divided between a number of hotels, nonguest divers and snorkellers must use the access path to the left of the lighthouse.

> **Warning**
>
> ! Note that Sanafir Island is off limits to divers. Visitors should also be aware that landing on Tiran Island is strictly prohibited – there are land mines on the island.

Temple Three large pinnacles rising to the surface from a depth of about 20m, just around the point.

Ras Mohammed Without doubt, one of the best diving sites in the world. In an attempt to protect the Ras Mohammed National Park, the number of boats that can bring in divers is subject to limits and water access is restricted to designated areas. You'll have to organise dives here through the dive clubs. There are 20 dive sites within the park, including Shark Observatory, Stingray Station and Eel Garden (see Activities under Ras Mohammed National Park in the Sinai chapter for more information). There's a shipwreck (at 10m to 15m) that scattered hundreds of toilet bowls on the ocean floor, and off to the south-west is the wreck of the *Dunraven*, a British vessel that went down (and turned over) in 1876 on a voyage from Bombay to Newcastle in England. Many dive clubs combine diving this wreck with that of *The Thistlegorm*. When you're diving here remember that there are designated access points to reduce damage to reefs.

The Thistlegorm Sinai's most prized wreck was discovered by Jacques Cousteau in the 1950s. It was a British war ship that sank with a full consignment of war supplies, including tanks, jeeps and guns, after being bombed during WWII. Rediscovered in 1993, laying at a depth of 17m to 35m to the north-west of Ras Mohammed, it is currently the wreck to explore in the Red Sea (though it has already been stripped of much of its wartime memorabilia). It's best dived on an overnight trip, as it takes 3½ hours each way from Sharm el-Sheikh by boat. It is often too rough to dive here.

Sha'ab Abu Nuhas A group of small submerged islands at the southern entrance to the Straits of Gubal that have snagged more ships than any other reefs since the opening of the Suez Canal in 1869. One of the most famous in this marine graveyard is the *Carnatic*, which went down in 1879 and, with its rotting wooden beams, is now almost a reef in itself. It's a popular site among divers, along with the nearby wrecks of two Greek cargo ships, the *Giannus D* and the *Chrisoula K*, which both sank in the early 1980s. The three are about 45 minutes by boat from the point of Ras Mohammed, but can also be visited from Hurghada, about two hours away.

ALL PHOTOGRAPHS BY MARK WEBSTER

The Red Sea is a diver's paradise, teeming with brightly coloured fish and coral-encrusted wrecks. t has been voted by an international panel to be one of the Seven Underwater Wonders of the World, and divers must take care not to disturb the precious and delicate coral or other marine life.

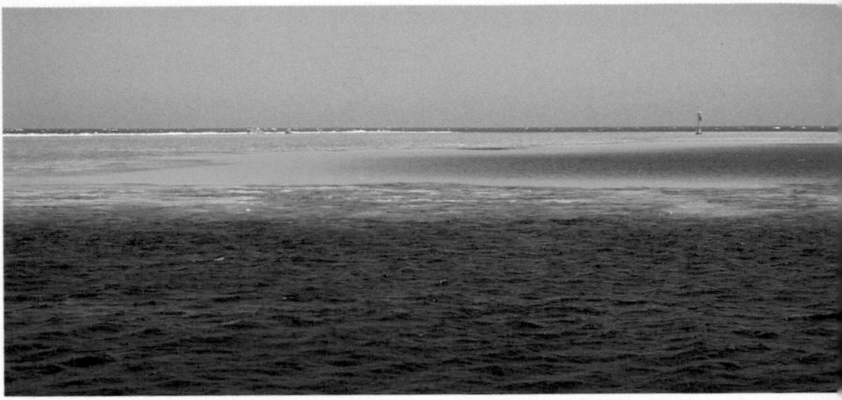

JEAN-BERNARD CARILLET

MARK WEBSTER

MARK WEBSTER

MARK WEBSTER

Things aren't always what they seem in the Red Sea. Sha'ab Abu Nuhas (top) looks idyllic, but its submerged islands have wrecked countless ships. The crown-of-thorns starfish (middle) looks beautiful, but it eats coral. The lionfish (bottom left) is poisonous, but the clownfish (bottom right) is harmless.

Hurghada & Safaga

The reefs close to Hurghada have been all but trashed by the unfettered touristic development of the past few years and experienced divers these days look for sites further afield, often sailing at least two hours from Hurghada. Some simply opt for dive clubs further down the coast. With conservation efforts finally being put into place, there is a chance the situation around Hurghada will improve. Some of the best sites near Hurghada and Safaga include:

Shedwan Island This is a 25km-long island with long sheer walls that attract sharks and other pelagic fish. At its northern end is Blind Reef, another deep wall. Accessible by boat from Hurghada.

Sha'ab al-Erg Horseshoe shaped reef with a shallow lagoon about 1½ hours north of Hurghada. Famous for dolphins and manta rays. Among the many other species around here you can sometimes find whitetips.

Fanadir Popular reef close to Hurghada. Coral gardens lead above a ledge that drops off into the depths. Teeming with many different species of fish, but known for stonefish and scorpionfish. Also frequented by dolphins.

Fanous Made up of two reefs, Fanous East and Fanous West, located about 45 minutes from Hurghada. Known for dolphins and occasional rare-fish sightings, as well as beautiful coral pinnacles.

Umm Qamar Long, thin reef about 1½ hours north of Hurghada, with a vertical wall plunging down on the east side. Three coral towers just off the wall are swathed in beautiful purple soft coral and surrounded by glassfish.

Careless A mid-sea reef 5km north of Giftun Islands and often off limits because of strong, unpredictable currents. Famous for its two ergs on a plateau leading to a spectacular drop-off. The ergs are surrounded by a forest of coral around which swim swarms of fish, including a group of moray eels.

Giftun Islands A short boat ride from Hurghada and very popular dive destinations, the islands of Giftun Kebir and Giftun Sughayer (Big Giftun and Little Giftun) are surrounded by a number of spectacular reefs teeming with marine life. They include Hamda, Banana Reef, Sha'ab Sabrina and Erg Somaya.

Sha'ab Torfa Long crescent reef in the strait between the Giftun Islands, with several types of coral teeming with fish, including clownfish.

Sha'ab Abu Ramada About 11km south-east of Hurghada and nicknamed The Aquarium because of its enormous schools of fish.

Tobia Arbaa Just south of Ras Abu Soma, a group of seven 12m-high ergs with stunning coral and fish life.

Gamul Sughayar Only 15 minutes from Safaga and the second in a chain of reefs stretching north from Safaga Island. Diveable in any weather and famous for a hollow pillar of coral with gorgonian inside – and, of course, its abundant marine life.

Panorama Surrounds a small island with a beacon just over one hour outside Safaga. A plateau at 15m to 25m leads down to a dramatic drop-off. Large fish abound here and you can see turtles, schools of barracuda, and various species of sharks, rays and dolphins.

South Coast

As tourist development moves further and further south, so too does diving. But while the cement mixers are working down here, this part of the coast remains remote. Much of the diving here is done from live-aboards and some of the sites are difficult to dive because of high winds and strong currents. But the reefs are spectacular and the fish, especially pelagics, copious. Some of the most famous sites include:

Kilo 15 South As the name suggests this reef is situated 15km south of Al-Quseir. It is accessed through a smooth tunnel from 5m to 7m, leading to a canyonlike passage between steep vertical walls. This site boasts many hard coral species, and is frequented by sharks, including reef whitetips and guitar sharks.

Elphinstone Long, fingerlike reef opposite Marsa Shagra, some 20km north of Marsa Alam. The steep reef walls are covered with soft corals and the strong currents and rich fish life make it ideal for sharks. Seven species reportedly frequent its waters. Legend has it that a large arch in the reef, between 50m and 70m down, contains the sarcophagus of an unknown pharaoh. Adding to the mystery, divers have reported seeing a coral-encrusted rectangular shape at about 60m.

Shaab Marsa Alam Large reef adjacent to Marsa Alam. Rich coral gardens, with schools of snappers, jacks, goat fish and banners.

Shaab Samadai (Dolphin House) Horsehoe-shaped reef about 18km south of Marsa Alam at Marsa Nakarai. The reef is wrapped around a shallow lagoon that is home to a school of dolphins. There are beautiful corals along its outer walls and a large group of pinnacles (rich with reef fish) rises from its western tip.

Shaab Sharm Large, kidney-shaped offshore reef just south of Shaab Samadai with steep walls hosting rich corals. Currents are strong here but fish life is excellent, with barracuda, grouper, snapper and large yellowmargin and yellowmouth moray eels.

Daedalus Reef Large reef (topped with a lighthouse) with steep walls covered in a profusion of corals. Strong currents make diving here tricky, but perseverance pays off; big pelagics and a huge variety of fish.

Sataya or Dolphin Reef About 28km north of Ras Banas, Dolphin is the main reef of Fury Shoal. The horseshoe-shaped reef has steep walls leading down to a sandy slope scattered with coral heads. There is a wide variety of corals, particularly in the top 10m. Fish life here is particularly rich. There are several species of sharks, as well as dolphins.

St John's Reef Large, beautiful reef close to the Sudanese border. Consisting of different islets and coral reefs, it is filled with hard coral and rich pelagic fish life. Difficult to reach and often impossible to dive because of high winds and currents, but worth the trouble.

Southern (Far) Islands

As Egypt's dive sites become increasingly popular, divers are looking further afield for new underwater vistas. Four islands down in Egypt's southernmost waters, **The Brothers** (*Big Brother* and *Little Brother*), **Zabargad** and **Rocky**, are said to offer some of the best diving in the Red Sea and are coveted destinations for divers. They reopened to divers in the late 1990s after a three-year hiatus, during which a conservation and management plan was drawn up and mooring buoys installed. Access here is strictly regulated. Divers going here must have completed a minimum of 50 dives. Night diving or landing on the islands is prohibited and national park rules apply, so fishing, spearfishing and the use of gloves are banned. Permission must be given for each trip and a park ranger will often accompany boats to ensure that the rules are being enforced and to monitor the site. In order to take divers, boats must have special safety equipment and National Park and Red Sea governorate officials inspect them before each trip. There are currently between 130 and 140 boats licensed to go to the islands and about 12 sail each week.

If you've been offered a trip to these remote areas, you might want to call the Egyptian National Parks Office in Hurghada or Sharm el-Sheikh to check that the boat is licensed; if you are caught on an unlicensed boat you could have your own equipment or belongings confiscated and find yourself in custody. Even if you do make it to the islands, the strong currents and choppy seas often mean you can't even get in the water. But if you do, you'll be rewarded by spectacular and rarely visited reefs and amazing marine life. As veterans of these islands will tell you, once you've dived there nothing else will compare.

Big Brother The most northerly of the two 'brothers', with a small lighthouse and two wrecks lying on its walls, one a freighter and the other an Italian ship called the *Aida II.* Currents are strong here and the soft corals are amazing. As you'd expect, the marine life is rich, and large pelagic fish are frequently sighted.

Little Brother The smaller island with a long reef protruding at its northern end. Sharks cruise here in the strong current. Elsewhere there are huge fan corals, caves and overhangs. Pelagic fish throng the waters to the south-east, including thresher sharks, silver tips, hammerheads and grey reef sharks.

Zabargad Island Large mountain emerging from the sea, which has snagged at least two ships that now lie beneath the surface. Surrounded by a lagoon, which is in turn circled by a reef, there is also rich coral and marine life.

Rocky Island A small, rocky protrusion just south of Zabargad. Steep walls, strong currents and incredibly rich offerings of reef fish, soft corals and pelagics.

DIVE CLUBS

As Egypt's Red Sea and Sinai coasts continue to develop at a break-neck speed, the number of dive clubs is mushrooming. Almost all of the large resorts in Sinai and along the Red Sea coast have a dive centre. There are also smaller places, some of which have been around for years and some of which are fly-by-night outfits set up by those wanting to cash in on the popularity of the area for divers. Given the huge choice, there is something to suit everyone. Some clubs are laid-back and informal, others are slick and structured, but two considerations should be uppermost in your mind when deciding on which one to use: the club's attention to safety and its sensitivity to the environmental issues.

Safety Concerns

There is no regulatory body responsible for overseeing dive clubs in Egypt and although most are well equipped and staffed by professionals, some are not. Accidents do occasionally happen as a result of neglect so it is important to check a club carefully before diving with them. A few common sense safety measures include:

- Take your time when choosing clubs and dive sites – don't let yourself be pressured into accepting something, or someone, you're not comfortable with.
- Don't choose a club based solely on cost. Safety should be your paramount concern and if a dive outfit cuts corners to keep prices low, you could be in danger.
- If you haven't dived for more than three months, take a check-out dive. This is for your own safety and the cost is usually put towards your later dives.
- If you're taking lessons, ensure that the instructor speaks your language well. If you can't understand him/her, request another.
- Make sure all equipment is clean and stored away from the sun.
- Check all hoses, mouthpieces and valves for cuts and leakage.
- Make sure wet suits are in good condition. Some divers have reported getting hypothermia because of dry, cracked suits.
- Make sure that there is oxygen on the dive boat in case of accidents.
- If you're in Sinai, ask if the club donates US$1 per diver each day to the decompression chamber; this is often a reflection of the club's safety consciousness.

Diving Courses

Dive clubs in Egypt offer a variety of certifications. PADI, NAUII, SSI and CMAS are all taught here, although PADI is the most popular. Prices vary but not greatly. PADI open-water dive courses, which usually take five (intensive) days, cost between US$250 and US$330. When comparing prices, check to see whether the certification fee is included. If not, it is an extra US$30.

Beginner courses are designed to drum into you things that have to become second nature when you're underwater. They usually consist of classroom work, where you learn the principles and basic knowledge needed to dive, followed by training in a confined body of water, such as a pool, before heading out to the open sea. If you've never dived before and want to give it a try before you commit yourself, all dive clubs offer introductory dives for between US$35 and US$50, including equipment.

Most of the well-established clubs on the Red Sea coast also offer a variety of more-advanced courses. An advanced open-water course will cost in the region of US$220, while you're looking at about US$80 to US$100 for a one-day Medic First Aid course. Some of the clubs offer professional level courses or training in technical diving. Again, prices vary but most charge about US$500 for a dive-master course.

Equipment

Operators all rent scuba and snorkelling equipment, usually at competitive prices. Some divers prefer to bring their own masks, snorkels and fins, and some like to have their own regulator, but all these are available for rent. Masks and snorkels usually go for US$4 and US$1 per day respectively. Full scuba equipment is about US$20 to US$35 per day.

Despite the intense desert heat of the Egyptian coast, the waters of the Red Sea are surprisingly cool and you'll need some sort of wetsuit for diving, even in summer. In winter you may even need a dry suit. Again, although many people like to bring their own, these are all available for between US$6 and US$20 per day, depending on the type and size.

Trips

When you agree to dive with a club, make sure you know where they are going to take you. Apart from seeing the best coral, it is important to ensure that you are experienced enough for the site. Sometimes dive centres will put a novice on a boat going to reefs that demand a high level of expertise. A reputable dive club should not do this but if you feel unsure of yourself, ask to go somewhere else.

If you're going to Ras Mohammed or the Nabq Protectorate remember that you may have to pay the US$5 park fees in addition to the cost of the dive. Make sure you bring your passport with you too. There are often supplementary charges for going to the wrecks in the Straits of Gubal. Usually you're looking at US$15 to US$20 extra for a dive at the *Dunraven*. Day trips from Sharm el-Sheikh to *The Thistlegorm* go for US$75 to US$100, depending on whether food is included.

Many clubs organise dive safaris to remote sites ranging from one night to two weeks. When it comes to 'live-aboard' dive safaris, the cost varies according to the boat. The choice, especially around Hurghada, is wide and although you can negotiate directly with captains, arrangements are usually made through the dive clubs, many of which have at least one or two boats of their own. Make sure you see the boat before agreeing to sail on it. Also, if a trip is very cheap, check whether or not the cost of diving and food are included.

Clubs

Sharm el-Sheikh & Na'ama Bay Area

There are dozens of dive clubs around this area, which is not surprising considering its popularity with divers. The following are just a few of the more respectable ones:

African Divers (☎/fax 660 307, ⓔ african@sinainet.com.eg) PADI, CMAS, SSI. Run by Claude and Liza Antoine and with its own live-aboards, this is a reputable and long-standing club that is good at catering to individuals.

Anemone (☎ 600 995, ⓔ anemone@sinainet.com.eg) PADI, NAUI, SSI. Laid-back but reputable centre based at the Pigeon House Hotel.

Aquamarine Diving Centre (☎ 600 276, fax 600 176) PADI. Based at the Novotel, this is a popular, reputable club offering a wide variety of diving possibilities. It runs courses through the Red Sea Diving College.

Camel Dive Club (☎ 600 700, fax 600 601, ⓔ reservations1@cameldive.com) PADI, CMAS, NAUII, SSI. Just up from the Sanafir, a highly respected club owned by longtime Sinai diver Hisham Gabr. It also has facilities for disabled divers.

Divers International (☎ 600 865, ⓦ www.diversintl.com) PADI. Large diving outfit with branches in Taba, Dahab, Sharm el-Sheikh, Hurghada and Safaga. Offers a wide range of courses and dive excursions.

Emperor Divers (☎ 601 734, fax 601 735, ⓔ info.sharm@emperordivers.com) PADI. Five-star outfit with offices at the Rosetta Hotel, as well as at the Nuweiba Hilton. PADI open-water certificate costs US$325 and there are courses that teach breathing underwater to children as young as eight.

Oonas Diving Centre (☎ 600 581, ⓦ www.oonasdivers.com) PADI. At the northern end of the bay. This is a popular, cheery centre and, for those following a course, it offers reasonably cheap (by Sharm el-Sheikh standards) accommodation: Air-con rooms cost US$40/60, including breakfast. Operates dive camps in the far south of the Red Sea with Red Sea Diving Safari. See also Organised Tours in the Getting There & Away chapter.

Red Sea Diving College (☎ 600 313, fax 600 312, ⓔ college@sinainet.com.eg, ⓦ www.redseacollege.com) PADI. Operates in conjunction with Scuba Pro International, which provides one of the world's best diving curricula. It runs courses only and also has reasonably cheap accommodation for course members: B&B in an air-con dorm (eight beds) for U$10.

Sinai Divers (☎ 600 150, ⓔ sinai_divers@sinainet.com.eg) PADI, SSI, Barrakuda and BSAC. One of Sharm el-Sheikh's most established dive centres, based at the Ghazala Hotel. Offers 20% discounts to members of the Cairo Divers Group.

Subex (☎ 600 100) CMAS. Swiss-based dive club at the Mövenpick Hotel with years of experience in the Red Sea.

Dahab Apart from the very good local reefs, the advantage to diving here is the camel/dive safaris on offer. Most involve a day trip by jeep and camel along the desert shore to a remote offshore dive site. You can spend the night or return the same day. It's a great way of combining desert travel with underwater adventure. There are currently at least 40 dive clubs in Dahab, although not all of them have reputable safety records. The following dive clubs have the best reputations:

Club Red (☎ 640 380, e clubred@intouch.com) PADI. Offers technical diving certificates as well as regular diving packages. There's a New Age element with massage and yoga on offer, but they swear it helps with the diving.

Fantasea Dive Centre (☎/fax 640 043, e fdc@intouch.com) PADI, SSI. Owned by Chris Harding and Mohammed Rafaie, an Australian/Egyptian couple who recently set up on the northern end of Assalah. It does one-day camel/diving safaris for US$85.

Inmo (☎ 640 370, fax 640 372, w www.inmodivers.com.com) PADI. Run by Mohammed and Ingrid al-Kabany, this was one of the first dive clubs to start operating in Dahab. It has an attractive domed complex, with hotel accommodation and restaurant, and offers the full range of diving services. Its three-day camel/diving safari goes to dive sites south of Dahab and starts at US$115 per day.

Nesima Dive Centre (☎ 640 320, fax 640 321, e nesima@intouch.com, w orca-tech-diving.com) PADI. A well-managed and highly reputable club owned by local environmental activist and veteran diver Sherif Ebeid. Also has a very pleasant hotel attached (see Places to Stay under Dahab in the Sinai chapter). One-day camel/diving safaris begin at US$85.

Orca Dive Club (☎/fax 640 020, e orcadive_eg@yahoo.com) PADI, TDI. Only club in Dahab to offer technical diving instruction up to instructor level. Managed by an ex-merchant marine officer, Wael Derballa. Supports local Bedouin through its camel-dive safaris.

Sphinx Dive Centre (☎ 640 458, fax 640 032, e info@sphinxdivers.de, w www.sphinxdivers.com) PADI. Long-standing five-star PADI centre with a good reputation. Managed by the energetic Arman Gazeryan and attached to the Sphinx House and New Sphinx Hotels.

Nuweiba Nuweiba doesn't have as much diving on offer as the resorts further south, but there are three centres to choose from, if you happen to find yourself there.

Diving Camp Nuweiba (☎ 500 402, e dcn@sinainet.com.eg) PADI, CMAS. Operated by Hartmut Janssen and Sylvia May at the Helnan Nuweiba Hotel, it offers the usual courses, but is considerably more expensive than dive clubs in Dahab or Na'ama Bay. PADI certificate courses for beginners cost US$300; the manual, log books and certificate are US$25 extra.

Emperor Divers (☎ 520 321, fax 520 327, w www.emperordivers.com) PADI. Situated at the Nuweiba Hilton Coral Resort, this place is part of the four-branch Emperor empire, offering five-star PADI service. Open-water courses cost US$295.

Scuba Divers La Siréne (☎ 500 701, fax 500 702, e SCUBA@gega.net) SSI. German-run centre that does shore diving as well as two-day to seven-day dive safaris for a minimum of two people for about US$115 per day.

Hurghada & Red Sea Coast Because the offshore reefs of Hurghada are not as rich as they once were, this is the place for 'live-aboards': Dive safaris, usually of several days to a week, which take in distant sites ranging from the relatively close Shedwan Island to the distant shores south of Marsa Alam. With more than 125 dive centres to choose from, the following is only a small sample.

Aquanaut Red Sea (☎ 549 891, fax 547 045, e info@aquanaut.net) PADI, VDTL. Founding member of the Hurghada Quality Dive Club, a group of clubs that tries to maintain basic standards of safety and service. This club has multilingual staff and two custom-built live-aboards.

Divers Lodge (☎ 446 911, e Tek@DiversLodge.com, w www.divers-lodge.com) PADI, BSAC, TDI. Based at the Inter-Continental with a branch in El-Gouna, offers a choice of live-aboards as well as training.

Jasmin Diving Center (☎/fax 446 455, e info@jasmin-diving.com) PADI, SSI. At the Jasmin Hotel, this is another member of the Hurghada Quality Dive Club. Runs dive safaris from its own live-aboards.

Red Sea Diving Center (☎ 442 960, fax 442 234, e wrkneip@intouch.com) PADI, SSI, CMAS. Highly reputable long-standing diving centre in Hurghada, formerly known as Rudi Kneip. Another founder of the Hurghada Quality Dive Club. Has six live-aboards and gives instruction in English and German.

Red Sea Diving Safari (in Cairo ☎ 02-337 1833, fax 749 4219, e redseasaf@gega.net). Run by environmentalist and longtime diver Hossam Hassan. Hassan pioneered diving in the Red Sea's deep south, and has years of experience here. He runs three dive camps: one at Marsa Shagra, 20km north of Marsa Alam; another in Marsa Nakari, 18km to the south of Marsa Alam. In 2001, he established another camp in Wadi Lahami, a mangrove bay just north of Ras Banas. There are live-aboards based in each of the three for offshore diving. Trips can also be booked through Oonas Diving Centre (see the Sharm el-Sheikh earlier).

Red Sea Scuba Schools (☎ 444 854, e info hurghada@emerordivers.com) PADI. At the Hilton Resort in Hurghada. Has a branch in Sharm el-Sheikh and is also known as Emperor Divers.

Shams Safaga Diving Center (☎ 451 781, fax 451 780) PADI. Reputable diving centre in Shams Safaga Resort that is about to open a new divers lodge some 40km south of Marsa Alam.

Sharm al-Naga Dive Center (☎ 444 109, e willys@red-sea.com) PADI, CMAS, NAUI. Dutch-managed diving centre, on a secluded bay between Hurghada and Safaga at Sharm al-Naga on Safaga road, gives instruction in six languages. There is tented accommodation on the beach for divers; also offers safaris.

Sub Aqua (☎ 442 473, e subaqua@red-sea.com, w www.subaqua-diveteam.de) PADI, NAUI, CMAS. Branch of Diveteam Sub Aqua at the Sofitel Hotel, Hurghada, which specialises in diving around the world.

Subex This well-known Swiss outfit has three branches on the coast: Subex Hurghada (☎ 547 593, fax 547 471) is in Ad-Dahar; Subex Paradiso (☎ 547 934, fax 547 933) is out at Al-Gouna; and Subex Quseir (☎ 432 100, fax 432 124) is at the Mövenpick in Al-Quseir.

TIPS FOR SAFE DIVING IN THE RED SEA

You've chosen your club, you've got your gear and you've memorised reef protection measures, so there's just one more thing to remember – use your head.

There were more than 22 diving fatalities around Sinai in 1997 and most were due to divers forgetting some of the basic rules. In Dahab, where the majority of accidents occurred, drink and drugs often played a starring role in these tragic and largely avoidable deaths. Many of those who lost their lives were experienced divers who should have known better than to go beyond safety limits or dive under the influence. Others were divers who were not experienced enough for the situations they found themselves in – next time you complain about having to take a check-out dive, remember that dive clubs have a reason to be cautious.

The following are a few common-sense tips for safe diving:

- Don't drink and dive. Of 160 serious cases seen by the folks at the decompression chamber in Sharm el-Sheikh in 1997, 46% involved people who'd been drinking the night before. Alcohol dehydrates, especially in a dry climate such as Egypt's, and increases your susceptibility to decompression sickness.
- If you are taking any prescription drugs, inform your medical examiner that you intend to be diving. Sometimes drugs can affect your metabolism and your dosage might need to be changed.
- Dive within your scope of experience. The Red Sea's clear waters and high visibility often lull divers into going too deep. The depth limit for sports divers is 30m. Stick to it.
- Do not fly within 24 hours of diving. You should not climb above 300m either, so don't take that trip to St Katherine's Monastery or into the Eastern Desert mountains the day after a dive.
- Make sure you can recognise your boat from in the water. Some dive sites get crowded and boats can look similar from underneath. It's not unknown for divers to get left behind because they didn't realise that their boat had left without them.
- Be insured. The most reputable clubs will make insurance a condition for diving with them. If something happens to you, treatment in the decompression chamber can cost as much as US$6000. If you hadn't planned to dive before arriving in Egypt, many of the better clubs can provide insurance. The chamber in Sharm el-Sheikh can help too.

Emergency Information

Note, the VHF emergency channel is 16.

Hurghada Decompression Chamber (☎ 065-580 011), El-Gouna

Naval Hyperbaric & Emergency Medical Centre (☎ 065-549 525, 544 195) El-Corniche, Hurghada

Sharm el-Sheikh Hyberbaric Medical Center (☎ 069-660 922/3, mobile ☎ 012-212 4292) Run by Dr Adel Taher and Dr Ahmed Sakr.

Sharm el-Sheikh International Hospital (☎ 069-661 625, 660 894/5) New computerised hyperbaric chamber at the pyramid-shaped hospital.

The following people are hyperbaric specialists in Hurghada: Dr Hossam Nasef (mobile ☎ 012-218 7550), Dr Ehab (☎ 442 519), Willy Schmidhamer (☎ 065-444 109).

Further Information

Diving & Snorkeling Red Sea, published by Lonely Planet, is an excellent guide to all the dives available on the Red Sea.

Hurghada's first (and so far only) environmental NGO, the Hurghada Environmental Protection & Conservation Association (Hepca), has published its own guide to the sites around Hurghada and Safaga: *The Official HEPCA Dive Guide*. Available at Hepca's office in Hurghada (see the Hurghada section for more information), it costs E£70 and the proceeds go towards maintaining the mooring buoys they have installed throughout the area. The guide details 46 sites with artists' drawings and diagrams; it also has a small fish index.

There's no shortage of glossy coffee-table books with beautiful photos of Red Sea flora and fauna on sale at hotel bookshops around Egypt's Red Sea resorts.

The Red Sea Association for Diving and Watersports (☎ 065-444 801, **W** www.rsdass.com), at Sharia Sheraton in Hurghada, is a new NGO concerned about the unregulated nature of diving the Red Sea. Established in early 2001, it is hoping to raise the quality of diving centres and other water sports throughout the Red Sea governorate with such measures as standardised testing and identity cards for all dive masters and a rating system for dive centres. After only four months it had 420 members, including some of the most respected divers in Egypt. Their quarterly magazine, *H2O*, will be distributed for free throughout the governorate and will have news about diving, environmental developments and general tourism issues. They encourage feedback from visiting divers about their experiences, whether good or bad.

The Egyptian government's Virtual Dive Center on the Web has excellent, detailed descriptions of more than 73 dive sites, along with ratings of the level of expertise needed to dive there (although they tend to underestimate the difficulty slightly). Go to **W** www.touregypt.net and click on the Red Sea Virtual Diving Center. Some of the dive centre Web sites listed earlier also have descriptions of dive sites. Go to **W** www.red-sea.com for an index of dive centres and live-aboards as well as some other information on the Red Sea.

Sinai

Sinai, a region of awesome and incredible beauty, has been a place of refuge, conflict and curiosity for thousands of years. Wedged between Africa and Asia, its northern coast is bordered by the Mediterranean Sea, and its southern peninsula by the Red Sea Gulfs of Aqaba (east side) and Suez (west side). Row upon row of barren, jagged, red-brown mountains fill the southern interior, surrounded by relentlessly dry, yet colourful, desert plains. From the palm-lined coast and the dunes and swamps of the north to the white-sand beaches and superb coral reefs of the Red Sea, Sinai is full of contrasts.

In Pharaonic times, the quarries of Sinai provided enormous quantities of turquoise, gold and copper. The great strategic importance of this 'Land of Turquoise' also made it the goal of empire builders and the setting for countless wars.

Sinai is the 'great and terrible wilderness' of the Bible across which the Israelites journeyed in search of the Promised Land, having been delivered from the Egyptian army by the celebrated parting of the Red Sea that allowed the 'Children of Israel' safely to gain access to the dry land of Sinai. It was here that God is said to have first spoken to Moses from a burning bush and it was at the summit of Mt Sinai that God delivered his Ten Commandments to Moses:

> Tell the children of Israel; Ye have seen what I did unto the Egyptians…If ye will obey my voice and keep my covenant, then ye shall be a peculiar treasure unto me above all people: for all the earth is mine. And ye shall be unto me a kingdom of priests, and a holy nation.
>
> And Mount Sinai was altogether in smoke, because the Lord descended upon it in fire; and the whole mount quaked greatly…And the Lord came down upon Mount Sinai…and called Moses up to the top of the mount…And God spoke all these words, saying, I am the Lord thy God, which have brought thee out of the land of Egypt, out of the house of bondage. Thou shalt have no other gods before me…
>
> **Exodus 19:4–6; 19:18–20:3**

Highlights

- Spend the night on the slopes of Mt Sinai where Moses received the Ten Commandments.
- Discover hidden oases and mountain springs on a trek through the rugged Sinai desert.
- Listen to the eerie silence and admire the subtle desert palette of one of Sinai's most famous rock formations, the Coloured Canyon.
- Combine desert and underwater adventure on a camel and dive safari with the help of the Bedouin of Dahab.
- Lose yourself in another world diving among the underwater wonders at Ras Mohammed National Park.
- See how far the pharaohs would go for turquoise at Serabit al-Khadim, a remote temple and ancient mine.

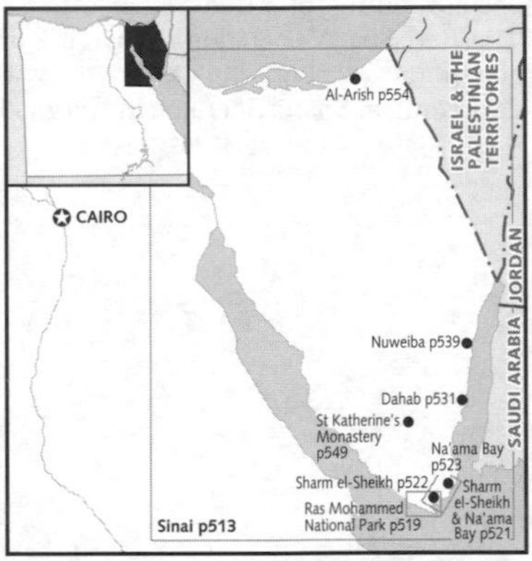

In recent years Sinai has become the focus of development and 'reconstruction' in much the same way as the New Valley in the Western Desert was during the 1970s and 1980s, when landless fellaheen (peasant farmers) from an overcrowded Nile Valley were encouraged to move to the oases.

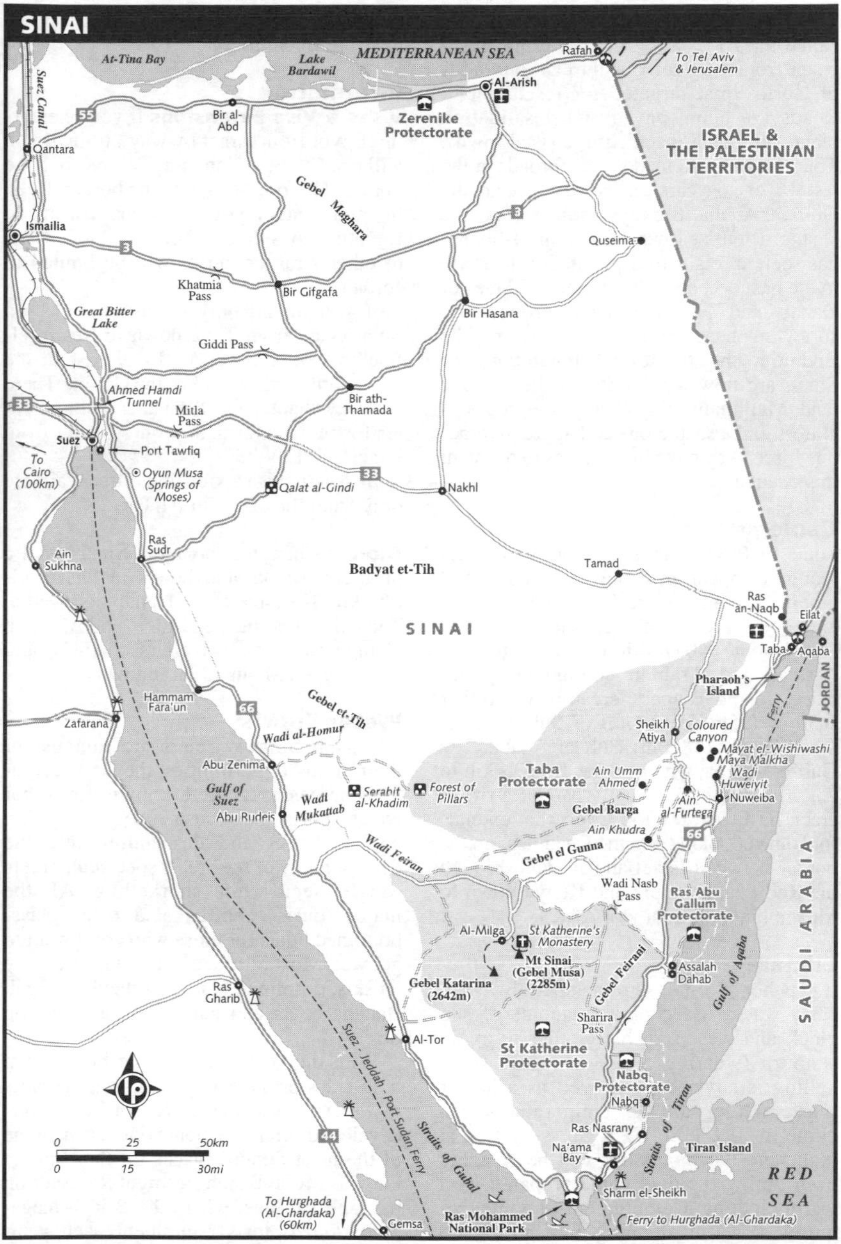
SINAI
MEDITERRANEAN SEA
At-Tina Bay
Lake Bardawil
Suez Canal
Rafah
Al-Arish
To Tel Aviv & Jerusalem
Bir al-Abd
Zerenike Protectorate
ISRAEL & THE PALESTINIAN TERRITORIES
Qantara
Gebel Maghara
Ismailia
Quseima
Khatmia Pass
Bir Gifgafa
Bir Hasana
Great Bitter Lake
Giddi Pass
Ahmed Hamdi Tunnel
Bir ath-Thamada
Mitla Pass
Suez
Port Tawfiq
To Cairo (100km)
Oyun Musa (Springs of Moses)
Qalat al-Gindi
Nakhl
Ras Sudr
Ain Sukhna
Badyat et-Tih
Tamad
Ras an-Naqb
Eilat
SINAI
Taba
Aqaba
Pharaoh's Island
JORDAN
Ferry
Hammam Fara'un
Gebel et-Tih
Zafarana
Wadi al-Homur
Sheikh Atiya
Coloured Canyon
Mayat el-Wishiwashi
Maya Malkha
Abu Zenima
Taba Protectorate
Ain Umm Ahmed
Wadi Huweiyit
Gulf of Suez
Serabit al-Khadim
Forest of Pillars
Wadi Mukattab
Ain al-Furtega
Nuweiba
Abu Rudeis
Gebel Barga
Ain Khudra
Wadi Feiran
Gebel el Gunna
Wadi Nasb Pass
Ras Abu Gallum Protectorate
Al-Milga
St Katherine's Monastery
Mt Sinai (Gebel Musa) (2285m)
Gebel Katarina (2642m)
Gebel Feirani
Assalah
Dahab
Gulf of Aqaba
SAUDI ARABIA
Ras Gharib
Sharira Pass
Al-Tor
St Katherine Protectorate
Suez - Jeddah - Port Sudan Ferry
Nabq Protectorate
Nabq
Straits of Tiran
Straits of Gubal
Ras Nasrany
Na'ama Bay
Tiran Island
RED SEA
Sharm el-Sheikh
0 25 50km
0 15 30mi
To Hurghada (Al-Ghardaka) (60km)
Gemsa
Ras Mohammed National Park
Ferry to Hurghada (Al-Ghardaka)
55
3
33
66
44

SINAI

The government has built a new pipeline, called the Al-Salam Canal, to bring freshwater from the Suez Canal to various areas of North Sinai targeted for resettlement. Roads are being paved and desalination plants are being installed in coastal towns. Tourism, too, has made great inroads in the last 15 or so years, especially around the Gulf of Aqaba. Surveys estimate that the southern tourist town of Sharm el-Sheikh has seen an eight-fold population increase in the past decade, and the small villages of Dahab and Nuweiba have grown into sprawling beach-front tourist towns. The Bedouin, the traditional inhabitants of Sinai, are now a minority in their native land. Marginalised by Cairo-based tour operators and a suspicious and aggressive police force, they have little means to resist all this change.

Geology

Some of Egypt's most striking geological features appear in Sinai. Sandstone and granitic mountains are cut by deep wadis, and coral reefs embrace the peninsula. Here, some 40 million years ago, the African and Arabian continental plates began to move apart, creating the rather shallow (95m deep) Gulf of Suez and the much deeper (1800m) Gulf of Aqaba. The Gulf of Aqaba, which varies from 14km to 25km in width, is actually part of a rift (a crack in the earth's top layer) that extends for some 6000km from the Dead Sea, on the border between Israel and Jordan, through the Red Sea, Ethiopia and Kenya down to Mozambique in Southern Africa.

Climate

It gets hot in Sinai, so remember always to carry water, use copious amounts of sun block and wear sensible clothes to avoid sunburn (wearing a T-shirt while snorkelling is advisable), as well as a hat or scarf. While summer temperatures can climb to 50°C (120°F), it gets very cold at night and the mountains can be freezing even during the day; come prepared with warm clothing. Camping out in winter requires a warm sleeping bag and good jacket – snow is frequent at this time of year on Mt Sinai.

Information

Visas & Visa Extensions If you're entering Egypt from Israel by way of Sinai, you will need an Egyptian visa. This can only be obtained before you get to the border. Keep in mind that if you get your visa at the Egyptian consulate in Tel Aviv, your visits to other Arab countries will be limited to Jordan.

If you intend only to visit the eastern Sinai coast from Taba down to Sharm el-Sheikh, you can get a 14-day pass at the Taba border crossing. See the Getting There & Away chapter and Taba later in this chapter for more information on crossing from Israel into Egypt.

In Sinai, visa extensions are available only from the office in Al-Tor.

Money Changing money in Sinai is not a problem. Banks and hotels in Sharm el-Sheikh, Na'ama Bay, Dahab, Nuweiba, Taba, St Katherine (Al-Milga) and Al-Arish change cash and travellers cheques, and there are ATMs in all large towns.

Water Sports

Although Sinai's waters are famous for their diving opportunities, they are becoming increasingly well known for other water sports. For those wary of donning oxygen tanks and descending into the depths, many of the area's spectacular reefs can be seen while snorkelling. All the major tourist centres also offer glass-bottomed boats for those who don't want to get wet. Most of the resort towns also have jet skis, despite the fact that they're illegal. Banana boats and parasailing are also on offer.

With the steady winds that blow down both sides of the Sinai peninsula, the parts of Sinai's coast that have not been overdeveloped offer excellent windsurfing. One of the most famous places for those in the know is Moon Beach Resort at Ras Sudr on the Gulf of Suez, where the British magazine *Boards* tests equipment each year.

Balancing Sinai's Ecosystem

Although much of Sinai is hot dry desert, it is not devoid of life. A very delicate ecosystem is in place. It is, however, under direct threat from the onslaught of tourism.

Sinai is a unique land of craggy mountains sliced by dry gravel wadis in which the odd acacia tree or clump of gnarled tamarisk manages to survive. On the edges are the coastal dunes where a variety of plants tenuously holds onto life in loose, sandy soil. Once every few years, when storm clouds gather over the mountains and dump colossal amounts of water on this parched landscape, the entire scene is transformed into a sea of greenery. Seeds that have lain dormant in the soil for years suddenly burst into life. For Sinai's wildlife, such as the gazelle and rock hyrax (as well as for the goats herded by local Bedouin), these rare occasions are times of plenty.

Until relatively recently, the only people to wander through this region were Bedouin on camels; nowadays, groups of tourists looking for outback adventure and pristine spots are ploughing their way through in 4WD vehicles and quads (four-wheeled motorcycles), which churn up the soil, uproot plants and contribute to erosion.

Aware of the danger this poses to Sinai's ecosystem, the authorities have banned vehicles from going off-road in certain areas, such as Ras Mohammed National Park and the protected areas of Nabq and Ras Abu Gallum. Soon these rules will also apply to the new Taba Protectorate, site of the Coloured Canyon and other popular off-road trips. But banning something and actually enforcing it in areas as vast as these are two different things. Rangers do patrol protectorates, but it's largely up to tourists themselves to follow the rules. So try not to be persuaded by over-eager guides wanting to show you something that's off the beaten track. If you really want to explore the region in depth, do it in the age-old fashion – go by foot or hire a camel.

A much more obvious impact of tourism is rubbish. Each year, volunteer clean-ups of beaches and reefs yield several tonnes of garbage. In 1997, a month-long cooperative effort by local dive centres and nongovernmental organisations to clear Dahab of garbage yielded a colossal 5000 cubic tons of debris. In late 1998, Lonely Planet helped fund a cleanup in the Ras Abu Gallum Protectorate. A total of 640kg of garbage was found on the reef alone. Even more was found on land. Why ruin a beautiful place by leaving garbage in the water, on the beach or in the mountains? Carry out all rubbish with you, and dispose of it thoughtfully.

On the bright side, isolated efforts are being made to resist the tide of junk. Apart from the cleanups, the establishment of protectorates in St Katherine and around Taba, and the increasingly strict enforcement of national park–rules in other protected areas are helping these vulnerable sites cope with the onslaught of tourism. It's still far from perfect, but any sign of improvement is welcome. Treat Sinai, above and below the sea, with care and do what you can to preserve the natural beauty of this very special place.

Dahab is also famous for its offshore winds. See the relevant sections for hotels offering windsurfing.

Getting Around

The few paved roads through the desert and hills link only the permanent settlements, and transport is not as regular as elsewhere in Egypt. You can get to most places by bus, but in many cases there are only a couple of connections a day – and sometimes only one. Service taxis, in the organised sense of the word, do not exist. As drivers in Suez will tell you, beyond the coast route to Al-Tor, you can only get hold of a service taxi by bargaining and paying far more than would be the case over similar distances elsewhere in Egypt. The reason is simple: There are not enough locals around in need of a fully developed transport system.

If you are driving yourself, you will see occasional signs forbidding foreigners to leave the roads. This is now rarely enforced, but you should still exercise caution. Stick to tracks when going off the road; there are still mines left over from the wars with Israel. When at the wheel in winter, remember that it rains in Sinai more than you might think, and that flash floods often wash out paved roads, particularly around Wadi Feiran. Taxi drivers will often know of any trouble spots.

OYUN MUSA

Oyun Musa, or the 'the Springs of Moses', is said to be the place where Moses, on discovering that the water there was too bitter to drink, took the advice of God and threw a special tree into the springs, miraculously sweetening the water.

Seven of the 12 original springs still exist and, around them, a small settlement has grown up. Most of the palm trees are burnt stumps, their crowns blown off in various Sinai wars.

Oyun Musa is about 25km south of the Ahmed Hamdi Tunnel, which goes under the Suez Canal near Suez. Completed in 1982, the 1.6km-long tunnel is named after a martyr of the 1973 war and is now open 24 hours. Camping at Oyun Musa is possible but, as the spring water is too brackish, there is no drinkable water – and there's no sign of the special tree that Moses used.

Getting There & Away

The buses from Cairo (10 per day) and from Suez to Sharm el-Sheikh and St Katherine's Monastery pass through Oyun Musa.

RAS SUDR

☎ 069

Ras Sudr, or Sudr, is about 60km south of the Ahmed Hamdi Tunnel. The town developed around one of Egypt's biggest oil refineries, yet because of its proximity to Cairo, it has also become a resort area.

At the time of research, a large number of new tourist villages were under construction starting at about 35km south of the tunnel and stretching south of Sudr towards the turn-off to St Katherine's monastery. There are no reefs to speak of here and, apart from the windsurfing opportunities that are appreciated by a small group of Egyptian and foreign enthusiasts, the resorts are largely filled with time-share villas geared to families from Cairo.

Places to Stay & Eat

There are no budget places on offer here – those that did exist are currently being refurbished to compete with the new places opening up – and few of the upscale resorts are worth stopping for. If you do stay, there's little to do away from the hotels, all of which offer rooms on a half-board basis. The following are the best on offer.

Helnan Royal Beach Hotel *(☎ 400 101, fax 400 108, New Corniche Rd, Ras Sudr)* Singles/doubles US$41/31 per person. Just south of Sudr, this has the usual resort amenities and the inevitable time-share villas surrounded by nice gardens. It advertises itself as a windsurfing destination, but the winds are choppy and unreliable because of the enormous amount of construction.

Moon Beach Resort *(☎ 401 500/1/2, fax 401 503, in Cairo ☎/fax 02-336 5103,* W *www.gybemasters.co.uk)* Singles/doubles US$60/90. About 38km from Ras as-Sudr, on a quiet sandy beach, this three-star hotel offers beachfront bungalows with balconies, air-con and fridges. The hotel is overpriced for the facilities on offer (although sometimes you can negotiate), but is well worth it if you're a windsurfer, thanks to its uninterrupted winds mostly blowing at force 5 or 6 (see Water Sports earlier).

Moon Beach Resort offers windsurfing lessons for E£80 per hour, with equipment; the price goes down with the number of hours reserved. Kitesurfing will soon be on offer too, and deals are available to windsurfers who book from outside Egypt. In the UK you can book on ☎ 01580-753824.

Getting There & Away

All buses from Cairo and Suez to Sharm el-Sheikh and St Katherine's Monastery pass through Ras Sudr. The journey from Suez takes about 1½ hours.

QALAAT AL-GINDI & NAKHL

About 80km south-east of the Ahmed Hamdi Tunnel is Qalaat al-Gindi, which features the 800-year-old Fortress of Saladin (Salah ad-Din). In the 12th century AD, Muslims from Africa and the Mediterranean streamed across Sinai on their way to Mecca. As the three caravan routes they followed all converged at Qalaat al-Gindi, Saladin built a fortress here to protect the pilgrims making their haj. He also planned to use the fort, which is still largely intact, as a base from which to launch attacks on the Crusaders, who had advanced as far as Jerusalem. As it turned out, Saladin managed to evict the Crusaders from the Holy City even before the completion of his fortress.

Qalaat al-Gindi is definitely off the beaten track and is rarely visited. From the coast, you must turn off at Ras Sudr. There is no public transport, so you must either have your own vehicle or hire a taxi.

Continuing north from Qalaat al-Gindi for about 20km you'll reach the turn-off for Nakhl, another 60km east. This little community sits almost smack in the centre of the Sinai peninsula and is surrounded by a vast wilderness. It boasts a population of about 60 people, and has a hotel (of sorts) for the odd traveller who passes this way, a petrol station, supermarket and bakery.

HAMMAM FARA'UN

Hammam Fara'un, or 'the Pharaoh's Bath', is about 50km south of Ras Sudr. The hot springs are used by Bedouin as a cure for rheumatism and a big sign at the entrance to the area proclaims that a huge five-star spa is to be built here. The springs themselves are in a cave beside the beach, but are too hot for all but the most dedicated hot-tub fans. It is more comfortable to swim in the warm sea around the cave, although the garbage-strewn beach and crowds of day-tripping families from Suez make the prospect uninviting. Unless you're into being stared at by hordes of leering youths, women who brave the waters should avoid swimming in anything more daring than leggings and a baggy T-shirt.

Sinai buses to/from Cairo and Suez can drop you off at the turn-off to Hammam Fara'un (about 1¾ hours from Suez). The beach is not too far from the main road.

Land Mines

! Despite what local tour operators may tell you, some areas of the Sinai landscape are still littered with land mines left from the wars with Israel. Don't rely on tourist operators, signs or barbed wire to alert you to a potentially dangerous area, and be very wary about going off the beaten track as there are no warnings. Two American tourists were killed in mid-1995 after leaving the track with a guide in the area around the well-travelled Nabq Protectorate. Flash floods sometimes carry mines away from their original location so that even Bedouin who know the area occasionally fall victim. Wherever you go, stick to tracks and don't explore that pristine beach until you've checked with locals that it's safe.

SERABIT AL-KHADIM

Several of Egypt's Sinai development schemes are being implemented along this 90km stretch of coastline beside the Gulf of Suez. Most relate to the offshore oil fields; consequently the area is marred by jumbled masses of pipes, derricks and machinery.

The community of **Abu Zenima** has a manganese processing plant and a rest house on the highway where buses stop.

Just past Abu Zenima is a track signposted in Arabic that leads to the old turquoise mines and dramatic Pharaonic temple remains at **Serabit al-Khadim**. Despite its remote location, turquoise was mined here as far back as the Old Kingdom. The temple dates back to the 12th dynasty and is dedicated to the goddess Hathor; next to it is a New Kingdom shrine to Sopdu, god of the Eastern Desert. Throughout the temple's many courts, inscriptions list the temple's benefactors, who included Hatshepsut and Tuthmosis III. It is thought to have been abandoned during the reign of Ramses VII.

Serabit al-Khadim can also be reached from the road through Wadi Feiran via **Wadi Mukattab** (the Valley of Inscriptions). Here Sinai's largest collection of rock inscriptions and stelae, some dating back to the 3rd dynasty, give further evidence of turquoise mining that was carried out here. Unfortunately, many of the workings and stelae were damaged when the British tried – and failed – to revive the mines in 1901.

Heading inland from Serabit al-Khadim another track takes you through the colourful wadis of **Gebel Foga** to the cliffs that edge Gebel et-Tih and the **forest of pillars**, a naturally occurring phenomenon accessible via a long track by 4WD and camel.

All of these destinations require guides. Most of the outfits in Na'ama Bay offer jeep trips. Or, if you are travelling in your own vehicle, you can head into the village of Sheikh Barakat and get your own guide. To get there if you're coming from Ras Sudr, follow the road/track that leads off into the desert, just south of Abu Zenima, for about 39km. When you see a white dome on your right, take the track to your left. After about 3km you'll come to Sheikh Barakat (where you can also camp). There you can find a guide to take you the remaining 7km to the trail leading up to the temple. At the end of this you will have to park your vehicle and climb for about an hour. Make sure you stick to the trails – some of the areas near here are mined – and bring plenty of water. If you are coming from Wadi Feiran, you can negotiate for a guide in the village of Feiran. Keep in mind that you will need a 4WD, so you will need to get a guide who has one, bring your own, or rent one in Sharm el-Sheikh.

AL-TOR

☎ 069

Al-Tor, also known as **Tur Sinai**, is the administrative capital of the South Sinai Governorate. There's little here but government buildings and a windy Corniche bisected by a broad central avenue bordered by new apartments. If you're staying at any of south Sinai's resorts, this is the closest place where you can extend your visa – which can be done at the town's Mogamma, the large administrative building on the main road in the centre of town. Other than that, there's little reason to linger. If you do decide to stay there are a couple of uninspiring hotels in town.

Delmon Hotel *(☎/fax 771 060, Sharia Manshiyya)* Singles/doubles E£60/70. This is probably your best bet in Al-Tor, rooms have baths and air-con. Breakfast is an extra E£8.

Tur Sinai *(☎/fax 770 059, Midan Mahatat al-Otobees)* Singles/doubles E£45/60. This hotel is scruffy but almost inside the bus station, so easy to find.

RAS MOHAMMED NATIONAL PARK

About 20km before the town of Sharm el-Sheikh on the road from Al-Tor lies the headland of Ras Mohammed. Named by local fisherman for a cliff that resembles a man's profile, it is famous to divers the world over as the jewel in the crown of the Red Sea. A peninsula forming Sinai's most southern point, Ras Mohammed was declared a marine reserve in 1983 and became Egypt's first (and to date only) fully fledged national park in 1989. It occupies a total of 480 sq km of land and sea, including the desert in and around the Ras (or peninsula), Tiran Island and the shore lines between Sharm el-Sheikh harbour and Nabq Protectorate. At the time of its declaration, the park was the subject of much controversy, but the project has been very successful in preventing the area's fragile environment from being destroyed by the sort of development that has transformed the Sharm el-Sheikh coast. Hotels cannot develop the area, and only 12% of the park is accessible to visitors. In addition, a ceiling has been applied to the number of dive boats allowed into the area.

However, despite these limitations, Ras Mohammed is the catch cry of nearly every tourist operator in Sharm el-Sheikh, and the park is inundated with more than 50,000 visitors each year. It's not hard to see why. Inside the park boundaries are some of the world's most spectacular coral reef ecosystems. The most ancient of these are fossil reefs dating back some 2 million years. Because they are similar in composition and structure to present day reefs, they are an invaluable source of scientific information about changing sea levels and past climatic conditions. For nonscientists, the profusion of coral species (as many as 150 can be seen) is overwhelming and the area teems with marine life like nowhere else. Most, if not all, of the Red Sea's 1000 species of fish can be seen here, including large pelagic fish such as sharks, making it a mecca for divers. Because many of the reefs can be easily reached from the shore, Ras Mohammed is also a great place to snorkel.

Remember to take your passport. Visitors on Sinai-only permits cannot go to Ras Mohammed because it is beyond the Sharm el-Sheikh boundary, but should not have any problem on boat dive trips. Check with the dive clubs if you have any doubts. For more information about dive sites at Ras Mohammed National Park, see Sharm el-Sheikh & Na'ama Bay Area in the Diving the Red Sea chapter.

Activities

The entrance to the park is about 20km from the reefs. A **visitors centre** *(open 10am-sunset Sat-Thur)* with a restaurant is clearly marked to the left of the main access road in an area known as Marsa Ghoslane. Videos are shown here, and you may be able to pick up an interesting booklet highlighting the park's fauna. The park is laid out with colour-coded trails and clearly marked pictograms of what each site offers. At the park's laboratory, a pink trail leads to **Khashaba Beach** and a camping area. Yellow arrows lead to the sandy beaches and calm waters of **Marsa Bareika**, excellent for snorkelling and safe for children. Blue arrows takes you to **Main Beach**, which gets crowded with day-trippers but remains one of the best places to see vertical coral walls. Brown arrows lead to **Aqaba Beaches**, which border the **Eel Garden**, named after a colony of garden eels 20 metres down. This is a great area for snorkelling in calm weather. Just beyond here, orange arrows lead to **Shark Observatory**, a clifftop area where you can sometimes see sharks as they feed off Ras

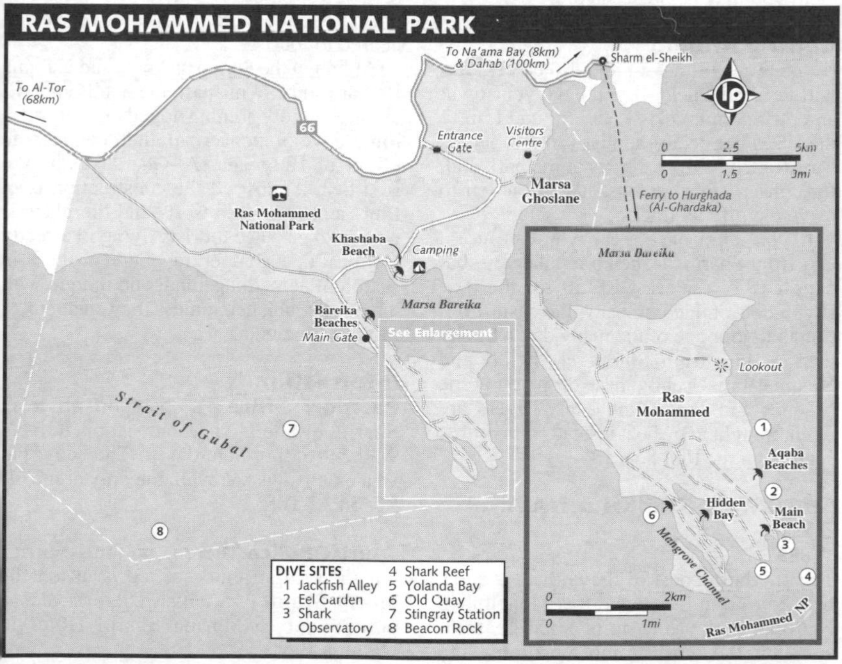

Mohammed's rich offerings. The red arrows lead to **Yolanda Bay**, another beach with good snorkelling and diving, and green arrows lead to the **Mangrove Channel** and **Hidden Bay** (both good for bird-watching) and to **Old Quay**, a spectacular vertical reef teeming with fish and accessible to snorkellers as well as divers. Offshore, some of the most popular dive sites here include **Jackfish Alley**, **Shark Reef**, **Stingray Station** and **Beacon Rock**.

Camping permits (E£5 per person per night) are also available from the entrance gate or the visitors centre but camping is allowed only in designated areas. Bring everything you'll need with you; the nearest shops are in Sharm el-Sheikh. If you are going to camp, respect the environment you're in and clean up after yourself. Do not bury toilet paper or garbage; the relentless winds here mean that nothing stays under the sand for long. Camp rules are enforced by rangers and if you're caught violating them you may be prosecuted.

Getting Around

If you want to move around the park you will need a vehicle. If you have your own, an entry permit costs US$5 (in addition to the US$5 per person admission), but access is restricted to certain parts of the park and, for conservation reasons, it's forbidden to leave the official tracks.

If you don't have a car, you can hire a taxi from Sharm el-Sheikh to take you, but expect to pay at least E£150 for the day. If you don't mind company, the easiest option is to join one of the many day tours by jeep or bus from Sharm el-Sheikh and Na'ama Bay. Usually these drop you at the beaches and snorkelling sites. Divers are often brought in by boat instead from tourist centres on the Red Sea.

SHARM EL-SHEIKH & NA'AMA BAY

☎ 069

The southern coast of the Gulf of Aqaba, between Tiran Island and Ras Mohammed National Park at the tip of Sinai, features some of the world's most brilliant and amazing underwater scenery. The crystal-clear water, the rare and lovely reefs and the incredible variety of exotic fish darting in and out of the colourful coral have made this a snorkelling and scuba-diving paradise, attracting people from all over the globe.

Unfortunately, the resort of Sharm el-Sheikh, comprising two adjacent bays – Na'ama Bay and Sharm al-Maya – does not reflect this underwater beauty. Na'ama is a string of resorts that has grown from virtually nothing in the early 1980s to a Las Vegas–style strip with all the charm of a shopping mall. Loud music, fast food, unimaginative architecture and hordes of aimlessly wandering package tourists make an unimpressive mixture for anyone looking to get away from it all. Sharm el-Sheikh (also known as 'Sharm') was initially developed by the Israelis during their occupation of the peninsula (1967–1982). While it is a relatively long-standing settlement and feels a little more Egyptian than the glitzy plastic of Na'ama Bay, it is still very much geared to tourists.

Although the Sharm al-Maya and Na'ama Bay are some 6km apart, the hotels and villas are rapidly joining together to form a long development strip that echoes the blight of Hurghada (Al-Ghardaka) on the Red Sea. Almost all the construction is of four- and five-star resorts and the place is geared to package tourists flying in directly from Europe. Budget travellers, or those in search of something small and unique, will have little luck here unless they spend most of their time under water.

Information

Passport Office The passport office in Sharm el-Sheikh harbour is open from 9.30am to 2pm Saturday to Thursday, but visa extensions are available only at the office in Al-Tor.

Tourist Police There is no tourist office but the tourist police office is up on the hill in Sharm el-Sheikh. There is also a booth next to Marina Sharm Hotel in Na'ama Bay.

SIMON BRACKEN

The coastal towns of the Red Sea, mostly fishing villages, have experienced the impact of tourism.

THOMAS HARTWELL

Shark Observatory at Ras Mohammed National Park is a fragile environment that needs protection.

CHRIS BARTON

Mt Sinai is believed to be where God delivered the Ten Commandments to Moses.

JOHN BORTHWICK

St Katherine's Monastery was established in the 4th century AD and is still in operation.

BRETT SHEARER

The mountains provide a dramatic backdrop to the seaside town of Dahab in Sinai.

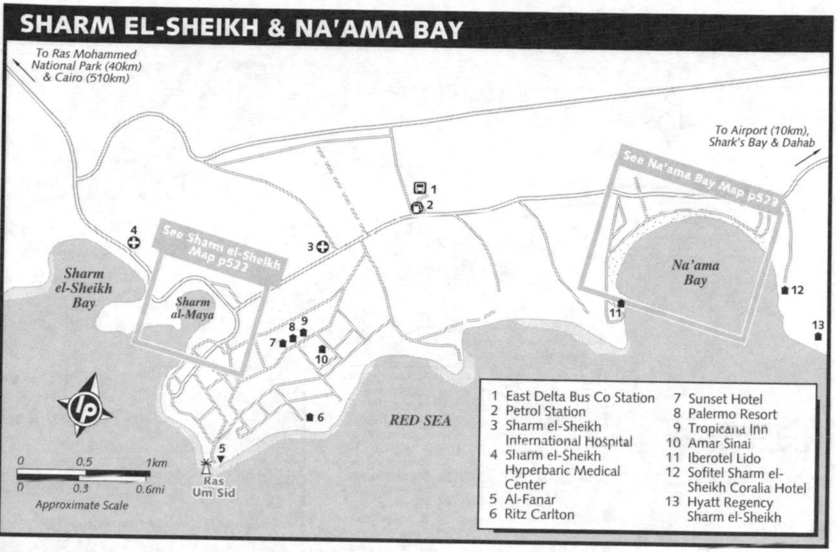

Money Banque Masr, the Bank of Alexandria and the National Bank of Egypt all have branches in Sharm el-Sheikh (on the hill) and in Na'ama Bay. Banque Masr handles MasterCard and the Bank of Alexandria handles Visa. There are a number of ATMs in Na'ama Bay; HSBC, in the mall beside McDonald's, has one, and there are others in the lobby of the Mövenpick Hotel, at the entrance to the Sanafir Hotel and outside Banque Masr (under Best Tours) in the shopping bazaar. In Sharm, there's one at the Banque Masr beside the telephone centrale.

Western Union (☎ 640 466) shares an office with DHL at the Rosetta Hotel on the main road in Na'ama Bay, and is open from 9am to 9pm Sunday to Thursday.

American Express (AmEx) operates through the Egyptian American Bank (EAB) in the shopping bazaar just off the mall at Na'ama Bay; it's open from 8.30am to 2pm and 6pm to 9pm Sunday to Thursday, and from 10am to 1pm and 6pm to 9pm Friday and Saturday.

Thomas Cook (☎ 601 808) has an office in the Gafy Mall, opposite the Gafy Land Resort on the main road in Na'ama Bay, open from 9am to 2pm and 5pm to 10pm daily.

Post The post office is in Sharm el-Sheikh on the hill; it is open from 8am to 3pm Saturday to Thursday.

Telephone The nearby telephone centrale is open 24 hours. There are a number of cardphones in Na'ama Bay – one at the Shamandura supermarket and at least two on the beachfront promenade (one in front of the Red Sea Diving College). Cards can be bought everywhere but watch out for overcharging by shopkeepers.

Email & Internet Access There are Internet cafes all over Sharm and more spring up each month. Almost all charge E£10 to E£15 per hour, or E£3 to E£5 for 15 minutes. Most are clustered in the hotels and shops in Na'ama Bay. Neama Internet (☎ 602 372), open from 9am to midnight, is in the Shamandura Mall, next to McDonald's, and there are others in Sanafir Hotel (open from 10am to midnight) and the Hilton Fayrouz Village (☎ 600 136), open from noon to 9pm. Global Services Internet, in Al-Zohoor Centre (☎ 603 332), which is open from 10am to midnight, is another option. In Sharm al-Sheikh there are fewer

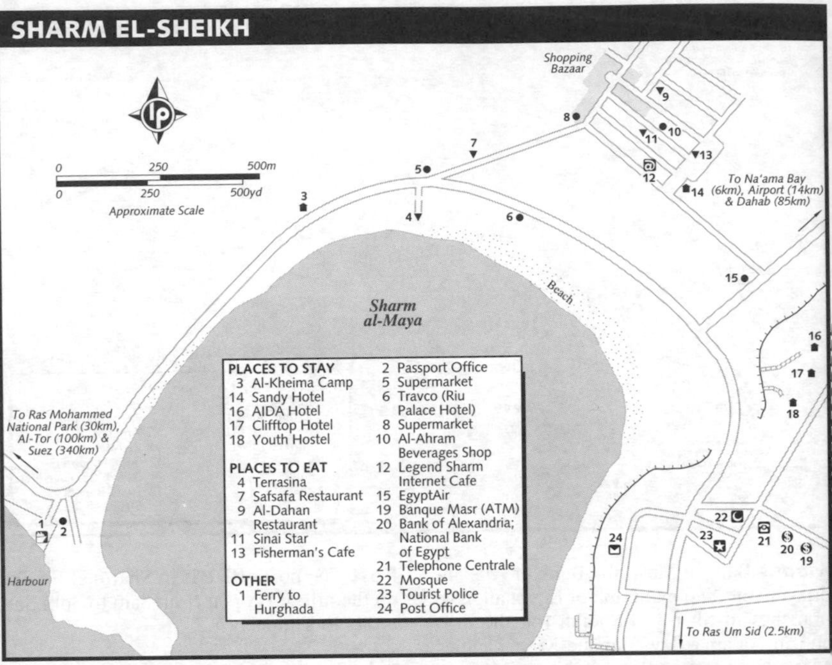

choices. Legend Sharm Internet Cafe (☎ 662 243) at the edge of the 'old' market is open from 10am to 11pm. Amar Sinai, a hotel near Ras Um Sid, also has an Internet cafe (☎ 662 223).

Bookshops There are bookshops in the Hilton Fayrouz Village and the Mövenpick Hotel stocked with the usual tourist books and glossy guides to diving in the Red Sea. There is a better selection at the Al-Ahram Bookshop on the main road between Na'ama and Sharm. Newspapers can be bought at a number of kiosks along the beach strip.

Underwater Photography Underwater cameras are easy to come by in Na'ama Bay. Most of the dive clubs rent out cameras to snap some underwater memories. Wide Angle Productions has branches next to Camel Dive Club and on the promenade in front of the Red Sea Diving College. It rents specialist underwater cameras, which start at US$20 per day, and video cameras which start at US$60.

Medical Services & Emergencies For an ambulance call ☎ 600 554. Sharm el-Sheikh International Hospital (☎ 661 625, 660 894/5) has a 24-hour emergency clinic. Mount Sinai Clinic (☎ 600 100, mobile 012-218 9889), at the Mövenpick Hotel, is a private clinic that specialises in diving-related medical problems as well as ordinary ailments. Other private clinics include the Sonesta Medical Clinic (☎ 600 258) at the Sonesta Beach Resort, and the Sharm Medical Center (☎ 661 744). There are two hyperbaric decompression chambers in Sharm (see Emergency Information in the Diving the Red Sea chapter for addresses and telephone numbers).

Snorkelling

Na'ama Bay itself has reefs, but far better are the stunning Near and Middle Garden

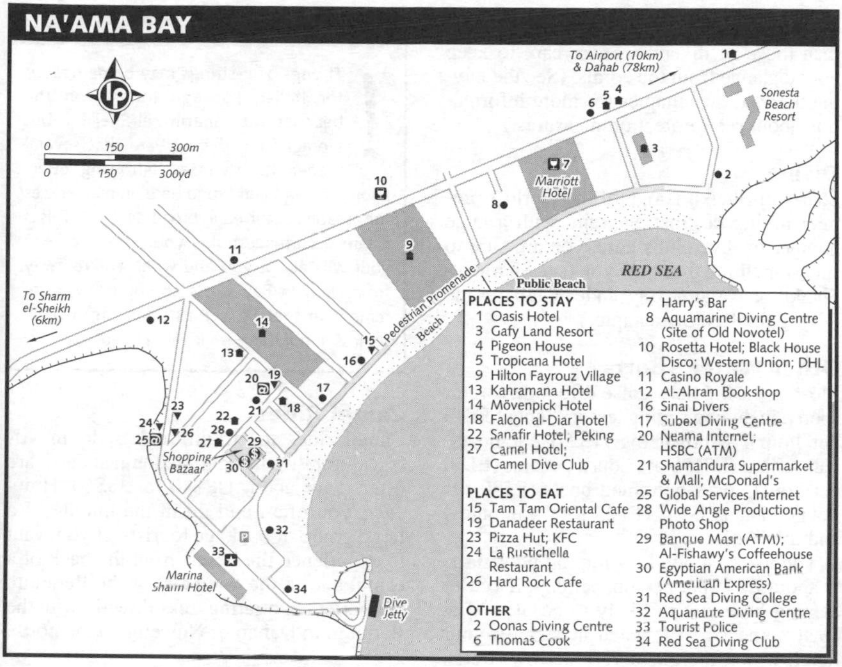

and the even more incredible Far Garden. The Near Garden is around the point at the northern end of the bay just below the Sofitel hotel, and the Middle and Far Gardens are below the Hyatt. Because of all the hotel construction, it can be difficult to walk to the reefs. If access is blocked you may have to take a boat organised by one of the diving centres. No matter how you get there, remember to take plenty of drinking water and sun block with you.

Another excellent spot for snorkelling is Ras Um Sid near the lighthouse at Sharm el-Sheikh. The small beach is parcelled up between a number of resorts and gets quite crowded. The area near the lighthouse used to be a public beach but is now part of the Al-Fanar restaurant; entry to the beach is E£20, which goes towards the cost of drinks and a meal. Apart from Ras Um Sid Reef (known for its fan corals and plethora of fish), the popular Temple and Fiasco Reefs are within easy swimming distance, and while they're primarily dive destinations, snorkellers can still get a taste of their flora and fauna.

It's possible to get to some of the more distant sites by joining a dive boat – inquire at some of the dive clubs in town. You should expect to pay between US$20 to US$50 for a day trip. Many of the clubs also do snorkelling trips to Ras Mohammed National Park, with prices starting at US$50. There is some excellent snorkelling in the park but make sure that you head to a suitable site; good dive destinations are not always great for snorkellers and some areas have strong currents that are not for the faint-hearted (see Ras Mohammed National Park earlier in this chapter and the Diving the Red Sea chapter for more information).

Most of the dive clubs rent masks, snorkels and fins. Remember that if you do snorkel, the same reef protection rules apply to you as they do to divers. As snorkellers tend to stick to shallower waters, their fins often do more damage to reefs than those of divers, so take care to keep your distance from the corals. (See the Diving the Red Sea chapter for more information about reef protection measures.)

Diving
Sharm el-Sheikh is one of the world's premier diving destinations, and with a huge number of dive clubs here, you are sure to find something that suits you (see Sharm el-Sheikh & Na'ama Bay under Clubs in the Diving the Red Sea chapter).

Other Water Sports
Most of the big hotels also offer other water sports, including sailing lessons (about E£45 per hour), windsurfing (E£50 per hour), parasailing (E£150 per hour), pedalos (E£30 per hour), glass-bottomed boats (E£30 per hour), banana boats (E£25 for 15 minutes) and the like.

The use of a hotel swimming pool starts at about E£45 per person, per day. If you're staying here you're likely to be offered at least some sort of beach access by your hotel. If not, there is a very narrow stretch of public beach between the Hilton and the old Novotel site on Na'ama Bay, but it is crammed with chairs that are rented for E£3.50 per day. Other than this, all of the beach space around Na'ama Bay has been taken up by hotels. Not all the hotels take much notice of nonguests using their beach, but many do, so if you're unable to blend in with the crowd you'll have to pay. Keep in mind that it's illegal to swim off Na'ama Bay after 11pm, and that despite all the development, the beaches and waters of Na'ama Bay are part of the Ras Mohammed National Park and its regulations apply here (see Reef Protection in the Diving the Red Sea chapter for more details).

In Sharm al-Maya there is a good stretch of public beach. However, while a hoarding announces a cleanup of the bay by the Egyptian National Parks Office, the water remains polluted. Other public beaches are being opened along the newest resort strip between Ras Um Sid and Na'ama Bay, including one close to the Ritz Carlton.

Warning
! Thongs or g-strings may be *de rigueur* for Italian package tourists on the beaches at Sharm el-Sheikh, but women should be aware that several readers have written harrowing letters about having been raped here. In many cases the assaults occurred in broad daylight. This is a rare occurrence but if you are alone keep your wits about you and when you're away from Na'ama Bay, dress appropriately. Also, remember that as well as offending people, topless sunbathing is illegal in Egypt.

Camel Rides
Camel rides to 'traditional Bedouin villages' for 'traditional Bedouin meals' are offered for about US$40 to US$60. However, you often end up in the middle of a large group of package tourists. If you want to experience the desert from the back of a camel and in the company of the Bedouin, it's better negotiating treks directly with the Bedouin in Dahab or Nuweiba to the north.

Horse Riding
There are a couple of hotels that offer horse rides in the desert. However, you're looking at a minimum of US$15 per hour – far more than anywhere else in Egypt. If the price doesn't dissuade you, try the Oasis, Sofitel or Sanafir hotels in Na'ama Bay.

Quads
These four-wheel motorbikes are immensely popular in Sharm el-Sheikh; two-hour trips to the desert cost about E£150. However, think before you roar off into the sand: The large wheels churn up the desert and do immense damage to the fragile environment.

Organised Tours
Most bigger hotels and travel agencies are organising a growing range of things to do out of the water. Jeep or bus trips to St Katherine's Monastery or such desert sights as the Coloured Canyon (see Camel & Jeep Treks under Nuweiba later in this chapter) are available for about US$45 or more. If

you're heading up to Dahab or Nuweiba, better deals can be had there.

For those only visiting Sinai, quick excursions are also organised to Cairo.

Places to Stay – Budget

Sharm el-Sheikh If you're on a budget there's little choice in Sharm.

Youth Hostel *(☎/fax 660 317)* Beds in 8-bed dorm members E£18.60, nonmembers E£19.60. Up on the hill, this is the cheapest, but by no means the best, place to stay in an area geared to tourists with comparatively fat wallets. Breakfast is included; lunch costs E£8.50 and dinner is E£4.

Al-Kheima Camp *(☎ 660 167, fax 660 166, Sharm al-Maya)* Bamboo-covered huts singles/doubles E£40/55, with air-con E£125/140. One of the first places you pass on your way from the port, but looking shabby of late and rooms are overpriced. Huts are the best bet if you're on a tight budget. Breakfast costs E£8.

Na'ama Bay If your budget is tight, there's even less choice at Na'ama Bay than at Sharm el-Sheikh.

Pigeon House *(☎ 600 996, fax 600 965)* Singles/doubles/triples thatched huts with fan E£38/56/76, small rooms E£65/85/105, rooms with air-con & bath E£120/170/205. This is a popular budget option with a good atmosphere. Guests get a 10% discount at the Anemone Dive Centre. It's often fully booked, so reserve ahead.

Oasis Hotel *(☎/fax 601 602)* Singles/doubles with air-con & bath E£100/150, concrete & reed huts with fan E£45/65. This place has reasonable rooms but no ambience and is only worth staying at if the nearby Pigeon House is full. Prices include breakfast.

Red Sea Diving College and ***Oonas Diving Centre*** also offer cheap(ish) accommodation but only for people taking their diving courses.

Places to Stay – Mid-Range

Sharm el-Sheikh A new strip of hotels is emerging from the construction sites in the Ras Um Sid area above Sharm el-Sheikh. Although most are, like everything else here, fairly pricey, a few are not so bad. Prices include breakfast and taxes unless otherwise stated.

Clifftop Hotel *(☎ 660 251, fax 602 036, Clifftop Area)* Singles/doubles US$35/45. One of the original hotels in the area and showing its age, it remains one of the most reasonably priced options for a good room with breakfast, TV, air-con, fridge, phone and bath. You also get the use of the beach at Marina Sharm Hotel.

AIDA Beach Hotel *(☎ 660 719, fax 660 722, Clifftop Area)* Doubles from US$60. Reasonable double-storey rooms, all with air-con and satellite TV, are built around a large swimming pool. This hotel's main claim to fame is its 10-lane bowling alley.

Sunset Hotel *(☎/fax 661 673/4, ⓔ sunset@sinainet.com.eg, Clifftop Area)* Singles/doubles E£100/120. This is another reasonable three-star with decent rooms and use of the beach at Ras Um Sid.

Palermo Resort *(☎ 661 561, fax 661 562, Clifftop Area)* Singles/doubles US$25/31. This is a well-priced three-star hotel with a large pool and a shuttle bus to the beach at nearby Ras Um Sid.

Tropicana Inn *(☎ 661 384, fax 661 380, Clifftop Area)* Singles/doubles US$60/70. The hotel has 70 simple but clean rooms with kitchenettes and 16 villas, all with air-con. Guests have beach use in Na'ama, with hourly buses laid on.

Sandy Hotel *(☎ 661 177, fax 660 377, Sharm al-Maya)* Singles/doubles E£85/120. This hotel has a pool and air-con rooms, but is close to the market and the main road in Sharm el-Sheikh itself, so it is noisy.

Amar Sinai *(☎ 662 222, fax 660 233, Clifftop Area)* Singles/doubles US$30/44. This is an 88-room addition to a burgeoning hotel strip inland from Ras Um Sid, featuring domes and brick architecture in contrast to the white concrete elsewhere. The hotel has its own Internet cafe, pool and Jacuzzi.

Na'ama Bay It's wall-to-wall hotels at Na'ama Bay, and they're all competing for beach frontage. Most are four- and five-star resorts and even those back from the sea have their own stretch of beach for guests.

Sanafir Hotel *(☎ 600 197, fax 600 196)* Singles/doubles/triples with air-con US$82/98/126. Taxes are extra. The nerve centre of Na'ama Bay, Sanafir Hotel has two classes of rooms and seasonal rates. With a pool and the addition of new rooms, it's no longer the intimate place that it used to be but the older rooms, with their whitewashed walls, domed ceilings, and beds raised two or three steps above the floor are pleasant, if noisy due to the nightly partying at Bus Stop (see Entertainment later). Guests receive a free pass to use the beach at Aquanaute Diving Centre.

Kahramana Hotel *(☎ 601 071, fax 601 076)* Singles/doubles US$70/95. One block away from the beach is this reasonable four-star hotel with the usual amenities. Deals are available if you book in advance.

Tropicana Hotel *(☎ 600 652, fax 600 649)* Singles/doubles US$73/90. This is best described as a cheap imitation of Sanafir Hotel (though its rooms are more expensive). Although located on the western side of the main road, guests have access to the beach on Na'ama Bay and there is a small pool from where you get good views of the mountains. Rooms feature air-con, TV and phone.

Gafy Land Resort *(☎ 600 210, fax 600 210, Ⓦ www.daysinngafy.com)* Singles/doubles US$52/74. Virtually across the road from Tropicana Hotel and offering its own beach, the Gafy Land Resort has modern rooms with low ceilings, TV, air-con, minibar and a big bath. It is under management of the American chain Days Inn.

Places to Stay – Top End

The entire coast north of Na'ama Bay has been subject to an incredible construction boom over the past few years. There is now a golf course and a line of resorts, some of them enormous, terracing the cliffs down to the sea. Having used most of the available land between here and the airport some 10km away, developers have turned their attention to the area near Ras Um Sid. Most of these places are geared to package tourists and, as in Hurghada, are considerably cheaper if booked from outside Egypt or as part of a package. Unless stated otherwise, prices for the following places include breakfast but not taxes.

Ritz Carlton *(☎ 661 919, fax 661 920, Ⓔ res_ress@sinainet.com.eg, Ras Um Sid)* Rooms from US$260. No single rate. The first Ritz in Africa is referred to locally as Sharm's only seven-star hotel. Large rooms, Internet access through the TV, good gym facilities, a spa, cigar lounge and other top-of-the-line amenities make up for the uninspiring architecture.

Camel Hotel *(☎ 600 700, fax 600 601, Ⓦ www.cameldive.com, Na'ama Bay)* Single/double superior rooms US$91/108, regular rooms US$78/96, dorm beds in quad US$30 per person. This is a small but well-appointed hotel attached to the dive centre of the same name in the heart of Na'ama Bay. It is well run and quiet, despite its proximity to the area's nightlife, with five rooms specially equipped for guests in wheelchairs. There is a 20% discount if you book in advance by email, which can be done via the hotel's Web site.

Falcon al-Diar Hotel *(☎ 600 827, fax 600 826, Na'ama Bay)* Singles/doubles US$65/100. This hotel is smaller than many of its bigger neighbours, but with the usual pool, beach and restaurant facilities. Guests recommend its buffet meals.

Mövenpick Hotel *(☎ 600 100/5, fax 600 111, Ⓦ www.movenpick-sharm.com, Na'ama Bay)* Singles/doubles from US$150/180. If you like sprawling resorts, you'll be happy at this place. Tacky architecture and astroturf predominate but it remains a popular spot along the Na'ama Bay waterfront. It's divided into three zones: Villa Area (facing the promenade), Front Area (between the Villa Area and the road) and the so-called Sports Area (spilling into the desert across the highway).

Iberotel Lido *(☎ 602 603, fax 602 099, Na'ama Bay)* Singles/doubles from US$77/102. This recent addition at the far end of Na'ama Bay has pleasant rooms and great views.

Hilton Fayrouz Village *(☎ 600 137, fax 601 040, Ⓔ fayrouz@sinainet.com.eg, Na'ama Bay)* Singles/doubles from

US$120/150. Although it has less than beautiful architecture, this sprawl of deluxe aircon bungalows along the promenade is well located and somehow feels a little more intimate than some of its giant neighbours. As you'd expect of a Hilton, it has the usual pools, restaurants and beach facilities.

Sofitel Sharm el-Sheikh Coralia Hotel *(☎/fax 600 081, e reservations@sofitel sharm-redsea.com, Na'ama Bay)* Singles/doubles US$160/208. Dominating the bay's northern cliffs, this is one of the more tasteful luxury hotels to open in the area. The vaguely Moorish-looking whitewashed rooms have tasteful wooden furniture and stunning views over the bay, as do some of the bars and restaurants.

Hyatt Regency Sharm el-Sheikh *(☎ 601 234, fax 603 600, w www.sharm.hyatt.com)* Rooms start at US$140. There is no single rate. Luxury perched above the rich corals of the Near Garden reef, with all the usual five-star facilities, seaviews and some good bars and restaurants.

Places to Eat

Sharm el-Sheikh There are a number of fuul and ta'amiyya places around the Sharm market, and self-caterers will find several well-stocked supermarkets in the bazaar. Beer and wine can be bought at the Al-Ahram beverages shop (☎ 663 133) next door to Sinai Star.

Sinai Star *(☎ 660 323, Sharm al-Maya)* Dishes E£12-45. This popular restaurant serves some excellent fish meals in no-nonsense surroundings. It doesn't have beer but will bring some from the Al-Ahram beverages shop next door.

Fisherman's Cafe Mains E£10-40. Chicken or fish are served with generous portions of rice, salad, tahini and bread. Beers are E£10.

Safsafa Restaurant *(☎ 660 474, Sharm al-Maya)* Mains E£10-45. In the old Sharm 'mall' and one of the best places in this area, this is a small, eight-table, family run affair, and local residents say the fish here is the freshest in Sharm. The clientele is a mixture of families and divers. Try the calamari and rice, with tahini and *baba ghanoug* (puree of grilled aubergines with tahini and olive oil). Whole fish is priced at E£45 per kilogram. No alcohol is served.

Al-Dahan Restaurant *(☎ 660 840/1, Sharm al-Maya)* Meals E£10-60. Small 'Oriental' restaurant serving good Egyptian/Middle Eastern food, with the emphasis on mezze and meat.

Al-Fanar *(☎ 662 218, Ras Um Sid)* Meals E£30-55. With an excellent seafront location at the base of the lighthouse, this is an open-air, Bedouin-style restaurant with sunken alcoves and a wide selection of Italian food. Prices are on the steep side but the view of the sea is marvellous, the food is good and the beers, which start at E£10, are well chilled.

Terrasina *(mobile ☎ 010-116 6662, Sharm al-Maya)* Meals E£15-50. Open 8am-late. This is a new seafood restaurant/beach club at Sharm al-Maya, where the beach is clean and has shade. You can sit here for E£10 or come for lunch. Evenings under the stars can be pleasant and there is sometimes a disco.

Na'ama Bay There are a lot of places to eat here, but don't expect to dine cheaply (by the standards of the rest of the country, anyway). The hotels have a wide range of restaurants, offering everything from seafood to Thai dishes, although few of these places suit a budget traveller's pocket.

Tam Tam Oriental Cafe *(☎ 600 150, Ghazala Hotel)* Dishes E£3-20. This is one of the cheapest restaurants in Na'ama Bay and is deservedly popular. Jutting out onto the beach, it's a laid-back place where you can delve into a range of Egyptian fare including mezze, kushari and roast pigeon, and wash it all down with a cold beer. *Sheeshas* (waterpipes) are E£3.50.

Danadeer Restaurant *(☎ 600 321, Shamandura Mall)* Dishes E£8-45. This is another Egyptian/Arab restaurant, just along from the Sanafir. It offers a selection of seafood and Egyptian dishes, with fish meals starting at about E£35.

Andrea *(☎ 600 972)* Meals E£9-12. You will find reasonably priced Egyptian food from this Cairo-based chain, which is opposite the Hard Rock Cafe, making this one of the better-value meals in Na'ama.

Peking *(☎ 600 179, Sanafir Hotel)* Dishes E£8-45. This branch of the popular Cairo restaurant has decent, if unauthentic, Chinese food.

Mashy Caf *(☎ 600 197, Sanafir Hotel)* Dishes E£4-45. This decent Lebanese restaurant is on the sidewalk outside the Sanafir. The food is reasonable, but beware the tacky 'Oriental Lights of 1001 Nights' show at 10pm every night except Thursday (when it becomes a disco instead).

Tandoori *(☎ 600 700, Camel Hotel)* Dishes E£10-60. This small but very good and peaceful Indian restaurant is in the courtyard of the Camel Hotel.

Hard Rock Cafe *(☎ 602 665)* Dishes E£20-55. One of Sharm's most popular nightspots, this hamburgers-and-beer place becomes a throbbing disco at midnight. It also has a children's menu.

Sala Thai *(601 234, Hyatt Regency Hotel)* Dishes E£30-80. Sala Thai has expensive but excellent Thai food and nice aesthetics with teak/wooden decor.

La Rustichella Restaurant *(mobile ☎ 010-116 0692)* Meals E£30-55. Open for lunch & dinner. This is an excellent Italian restaurant that is popular with Sharm's many resident and visiting Italians, who praise the home-style cooking. Fish dishes are especially good.

The usual fast food outlets are also represented: ***McDonald's*** *(☎ 602 110)*, which does home delivery, ***KFC*** *(☎ 603 036)* and ***Pizza Hut*** *(☎ 603 034)* are clustered in or around the malls at the southern end of Na'ama Bay.

SINAI

Entertainment

With so many tourists milling around in the evenings, Sharm el-Sheikh has a vibrant nightlife. The party is concentrated around Na'ama Bay and tends to start late but many bars have early evening happy hours to bring in the punters. Some of the dive schools along the beach have small bars too – look out for specials advertised along the promenade. Keeping up with the scene is difficult given the number of new bars and discos that spring up each month, but the following are solid favourites.

Pirates Bar *(☎ 600 140, Hilton Fayrouz Village)* This is a cosy, pub-style bar where divers congregate for an early evening drink or bar meal. There's a happy hour between 5.30pm and 7.30pm, when drinks are discounted by 30%.

Pigeon House Bar *(☎ 600 996, Na'ama Bay)* This popular laid-back bar is the best place to start the evening – drink specials keep the prices reasonable.

Harry's Pub *(☎ 600 190, Marriott Hotel)* This expensive pseudo-English pub has a large selection of beers on tap. There are occasional special nights with unlimited draught beer for only E£25.

Rooftop Bar *(☎ 600 197, Sanafir Hotel)* This is a popular place to have a drink while reclining on cushions and looking at the stars. The minimum charge is E£8.

La Folie Bar *(☎ 602 603, Iberotel Lido)* This is a quiet, pleasant bar overlooking the bright lights of Na'ama Bay.

Bus Stop *(☎ 600 197, Sanafir Hotel)* Admission E£20. Open 10pm-6am. This hotel remains the hub of Sharm's nightlife, and Bus Stop is its most popular venue. Each Thursday is House Nation night and the disco spills outside. Owner Adli Mestakawi also holds **Echo Temple Concerts** in the desert outside Sharm, bringing big name singers such as Khaled to play to audiences of thousands under the stars. There's no set schedule so you'll have to check with the hotel or check out its Web site at W www.sanafirhotel.com.

Hard Rock Cafe *(☎ 602 655, Na'ama Bay)* This is an immensely popular late-night disco/bar. Dancing starts at midnight and goes on until late.

Black House Disco *(☎ 601 888, Rosetta Hotel)* This is a popular place to go and continue dancing in the wee hours when you're sick of the DJ at Bus Stop.

Mövenpick's Casino Royale *(☎ 600 100, Mövenpick Hotel)* This is the first of a growing number of casinos in the area where visitors (no Egyptians allowed) can gamble away their dollars and yen (no Egyptian pounds, thank you very much).

Getting There & Away

Air EgyptAir (☎ 661 056) has an office in Sharm al-Maya near the start of the road to Na'ama Bay and another in the Mövenpick Hotel (☎ 600 314) in Na'ama Bay. It has daily fights to Cairo (E£472), Saturday flights to Hurghada (E£374), and Saturday and Thursday flights to Luxor (E£393).

Charter flights from various European cities run virtually all year round.

Bus & Minibus Superjet bus company (☎ 601 622) has a bus to Cairo (E£55) leaving at 11pm from its terminus next to East Delta Bus Co. If you want to reserve tickets (which is advisable), the office is open from 10am to 2pm and again from 6.30pm to 11pm.

The East Delta Bus Co station (☎ 649 250) is in Hay an-Nur, behind the Mobil petrol station halfway between Na'ama Bay and Sharm el-Sheikh. Buses heading for Dahab and beyond occasionally stop on the highway in Na'ama Bay, but don't count on it. Seats to Cairo can and should be booked ahead. Keep in mind that schedules change; always double-check before your trip.

Direct services to Cairo (about seven hours) run at 7.30am, 10.30am, 11.30am, 12.30pm, 1.30pm, 3pm, 4.30pm, 10pm, 11pm and midnight. Tickets cost between E£50 and E£65.

It is cheaper, but more time consuming, to get a bus to Suez and then another bus or service taxi from there to Cairo (the same is also true in reverse). Buses to Suez (E£26 or E£35, 5½ hours) depart almost every hour throughout the day, starting at 7am and finishing at 11pm.

Nine buses go to Dahab (1½ hours), beginning at 6.30am and ending at 12.30am. Tickets cost E£10. Services at 8am, 9am, 2.30pm and 5pm go on to Nuweiba (E£25), with the 9am bus continuing all the way to Taba (E£35). There is no longer a bus to St Katherine's Monastery; you have to go to Dahab and change.

There is a bus to Hurghada (E£65) at 6pm that goes on to Luxor (E£85).

Minibuses also cover the route between Sharm el-Sheikh and Suez and Cairo, as well as north to Dahab, but they're not all that common or frequent – ask around at the bus station.

Boat Travco (☎ 660 764) operates a high-speed air-con ferry that travels between Sharm and Hurghada in 1½ hours (although some travellers have said that it can take much longer). The boat departs at 6pm on Monday, Thursday and Saturday. A one-way ticket costs US$40 (vehicles start at E£175) and you must be at the port with your passport one hour before departure. You can buy tickets at the port or, to be sure of a place, book them in advance.

Getting Around

To/From the Airport The airport is about 10km north of Na'ama Bay at Ras Nasrany; a taxi will cost about E£20.

Bus & Taxi Getting between Na'ama Bay and Sharm can be expensive. Toyota pick-ups and minibuses carry workers about town, but tend to charge an absurd E£5 to let foreigners go along. Likewise, taxis charge a minimum of E£10 to take you anywhere within the town. Many of the hotels up by Ras Um Sid have their own shuttles to Na'ama Bay, so you can try your luck with them. Other than that, it is quite possible to hitch, as there is a fair amount of traffic on the roads. The usual warnings about hitching apply; women should avoid it completely.

Car Many of the big-name car rental companies have offices in Na'ama Bay, usually in one of the bigger hotels. Avis (☎ 600 979) is at the Sonesta Beach Resort, Hertz (☎ 600 197) is at Sanafir Hotel, and Max Europcar (☎ 600 686) is at the Hilton Fayrouz Village. Sanafir Hotel rents 4WD jeeps for US$95 per day while Fox Safari (☎ 601 074, ext 510), also in Na'ama Bay, has them for US$120 including a driver.

Bicycle Normal and cross-country bicycles can be hired from stands along the promenade in Na'ama Bay for E£25 or more per day.

Boat Sharm el-Sheikh's marina is just west of Sharm el-Sheikh. Some dive clubs operating out of Na'ama Bay bring their boats around to the jetty on Na'ama Bay early each morning; others ferry passengers to the marina. It's possible to hitch a ride either way on one of these vessels – ask around at the marina or on the jetty in Na'ama Bay at about 6.30am. You can also check with one of the dive clubs.

SHARK'S BAY

☎ 069

Shark's Bay, or Beit al-Irsh, used to be a quiet, low-key resort camp about 6km north of Na'ama Bay (look for the unmarked asphalt turn-off), but unfortunately the giant Pyramisa Hotel has colonised half of the beach and Italians doing aerobics to loud music interrupt the solitary bliss of the place. Still, from its pebbly beach you can walk into some quite good snorkelling and diving. The place is particularly popular with Germans and Israelis, most of whom dive in a nearby 15m- to 20m-deep canyon with the Embarak dive club there. There remains a good stretch of public beach here, however, and for E£2 admission you can spend the day here.

Places to Stay & Eat

Shark's Bay Camp *(☎ 600 947, fax 600 943, Shark's Bay)* Singles/doubles with fans on the beach E£60/75, huts higher up on the hillside with air-con E£100/150. This two-star camp has clean and comfortable huts built up on the beach, clean toilets and showers with hot water. There is also a mini-market and a Bedouin-style restaurant with meals starting at E£20.

Getting There & Away

The only way to get here is to take a taxi. Expect to pay E£20 each way.

NABQ

Thirty-five kilometres north of Sharm el-Sheikh lies the largest coastal protectorate on the Gulf of Aqaba, Nabq (officially called the Nabq Protectorate). Named after an oasis that lies within its boundaries, it straddles 600 sq km of land and sea between the Straits of Tiran and Dahab. Nabq is the site of the world's most northerly **mangrove forest**, which stands along the shoreline at the mouth of Wadi Kid. Mangrove root systems filter most of the salt from sea water and help to stabilise shorelines, at the same time providing an important habitat for birds and fish. Just inland from the mangrove stand are the dunes of Wadi Kid, in which stand one of the Middle East's largest stands of **Arak bushes** (Arak twigs were traditionally used by Bedouin to clean teeth). Gazelles, rock hyraxes and Nubian ibexes can be seen in the protectorate and it is home to two villages of Bedouin from the Mizena tribe.

Offshore, there are rich reefs with easy access, although visibility can be poor because of sediment from the mangroves.

Because it is less frequently visited than Ras Mohammed, Nabq is a good place to see Sinai as it was before mass tourism all but destroyed its coastline. There is a visitors centre, several hiking trails, clearly marked snorkelling spots and designated camping areas. As at Ras Mohammed, there is a US$5 entrance fee.

To get here you'll need a vehicle or you'll have to join a tour from one of the resorts. Most of the dive centres in Dahab have dive safaris to Nabq, some by camel. If you drive, remember that vehicles are strictly forbidden from leaving the tracks. Apart from threatening the 134 plant species that are unique to the area, there are still some mines left over from the wars with Israel.

DAHAB

☎ 069

A village beach resort 85km north of Sharm el-Sheikh, Dahab is the wannabe Koh Samui of the Middle East. Banana fritters and Bob Marley, stoned travellers in tie-dyes and shops with names such as 'Laughing Buddha' offering tarot card readings – it's all here. Accommodation virtually on the beach can cost as little as E£6 per night and common is the backpacker who pitches

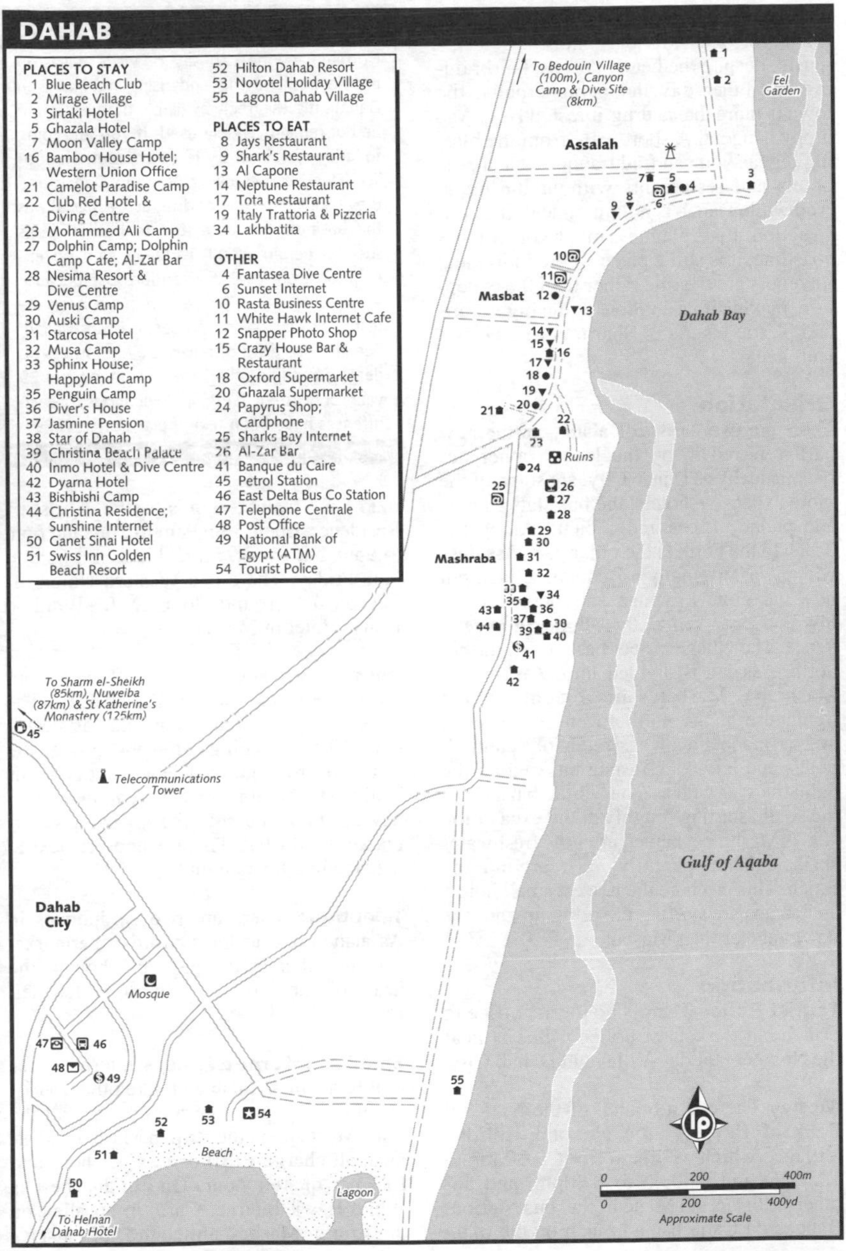
DAHAB
PLACES TO STAY
1 Blue Beach Club
2 Mirage Village
3 Sirtaki Hotel
5 Ghazala Hotel
7 Moon Valley Camp
16 Bamboo House Hotel; Western Union Office
21 Camelot Paradise Camp
22 Club Red Hotel & Diving Centre
23 Mohammed Ali Camp
27 Dolphin Camp; Dolphin Camp Cafe; Al-Zar Bar
28 Nesima Resort & Dive Centre
29 Venus Camp
30 Auski Camp
31 Starcosa Hotel
32 Musa Camp
33 Sphinx House; Happyland Camp
35 Penguin Camp
36 Diver's House
37 Jasmine Pension
38 Star of Dahab
39 Christina Beach Palace
40 Inmo Hotel & Dive Centre
42 Dyarna Hotel
43 Bishbishi Camp
44 Christina Residence; Sunshine Internet
50 Ganet Sinai Hotel
51 Swiss Inn Golden Beach Resort
52 Hilton Dahab Resort
53 Novotel Holiday Village
55 Lagona Dahab Village
PLACES TO EAT
8 Jays Restaurant
9 Shark's Restaurant
13 Al Capone
14 Neptune Restaurant
17 Tota Restaurant
19 Italy Trattoria & Pizzeria
34 Lakhbatita
OTHER
4 Fantasea Dive Centre
6 Sunset Internet
10 Rasta Business Centre
11 White Hawk Internet Cafe
12 Snapper Photo Shop
15 Crazy House Bar & Restaurant
18 Oxford Supermarket
20 Ghazala Supermarket
24 Papyrus Shop; Cardphone
25 Sharks Bay Internet
26 Al-Zar Bar
41 Banque du Caire
45 Petrol Station
46 East Delta Bus Co Station
47 Telephone Centrale
48 Post Office
49 National Bank of Egypt (ATM)
54 Tourist Police
To Bedouin Village (100m), Canyon Camp & Dive Site (8km)
Eel Garden
Assalah
Masbat
Dahab Bay
Ruins
Mashraba
To Sharm el-Sheikh (85km), Nuweiba (87km) & St Katherine's Monastery (125km)
Telecommunications Tower
Gulf of Aqaba
Dahab City
Mosque
Beach
Lagoon
To Helnan Dahab Hotel
0 200 400m
0 200 400yd
Approximate Scale

up here for a night or two and ends up staying on for weeks, if not months.

But, despite the henna tattoos, hairbraiding and other traveller paraphernalia, the town is more than a drug-infested New Age hippy hangout. A short walk from the blaring reggae you can find tranquil beach-side hotels and restaurants without the hype. And while Dahab is not immune to the construction that plagues much of Sinai's coastline, it is still a place where individual travellers are the rule rather than the exception, making it an antidote to the big groups and plastic resorts of Sharm el-Sheikh and Hurghada.

Orientation

There are two parts to Dahab – in the new part, referred to by the locals rather euphemistically as Dahab City, are some of the more expensive hotels, the bus station, post and phone offices and a bank. Along the beach to the north is the other part, **Assalah**, which was originally a Bedouin village but now has more Egyptian entrepreneurs and low-budget travellers than Bedouin in residence. The village proper has moved further north. Assalah is divided into **Masbat** and **Mashraba**. Masbat starts roughly at the lighthouse at the northern end of Assalah and is made up of a stretch of 'camps', hotels and laid-back restaurants among the palm trees, as well as a busy little bazaar. To the south, starting roughly at the excavation site, is Mashraba, named after the freshwater springs that apparently exist around the beach. This is where the newest small hotels and camps are starting to spring up and it is much quieter than Masbat.

Drugs & Dahab

Nothing anyone can say or write will stop people from buying and using marijuana in Dahab. It's less freely available than it used to be but remains widely used. If you are going to indulge, at least try to be discreet. The police have been cracking down in Dahab and they take a dim view of drug use, especially as the business has escalated to harder drugs such as heroin. You'll certainly gain no exemption from police attention just because you're a tourist – Westerners have been arrested in Dahab for possession, and jailed. Penalties for drug offences are high in Egypt; dealing and smuggling attract sentences of 25 years or death by hanging. Executions for such offences have been taking place since 1989.

Information

Tourist Police There's no tourist office in Dahab but the tourist police office is near the Novotel Holiday Village in Dahab City.

Money There is a branch of the National Bank of Egypt at the Novotel Holiday Village, which is open from 9.30am to 12.30pm and 6.30pm to 8.30pm, and another with an ATM near the bus station. Banque du Caire has a branch on the main road in Assalah, opposite the Christina Residence, open from 9am to 2pm and 6pm to 9pm, but from 9am to 11am and 6pm to 9pm Friday. There is a Western Union office on the ground floor of the Bamboo House Hotel in Masbat.

Post The post and telephone offices are opposite the bus station in Dahab City. The latter is open 24 hours a day and has a cardphone. To save going to the post office, you can also drop stamped letters into the air mail postal box (supposedly emptied every day at 10am) outside the Ghazala supermarket in Masbat. There is another next to the Neptune Restaurant.

Telephone There are two cardphones in Assalah – one at the Oxford supermarket and the other at the papyrus shop in the heart of the bazaar, both of which sell phonecards.

Email & Internet Access Internet cafes proliferate in Assalah and, like other tourist centres in Egypt, more are opening all the time. Most are on the strip in Masbat and almost all charge E£10 or less per hour and E£3 per quarter hour. One of the best is White Hawk Internet Cafe, in an alley on the strip in Masbat, although it often stays

Warnings

Tap water in Dahab is not drinkable, but plenty of shops sell bottled water. When you buy water check that the seal on the bottle is not broken.

shut until lunchtime. Rasta Business Center (☎ 640 183) is nearby and opens at 10am. Shark's Bay Internet (☎ 500 752), opposite Nesima Resort, only charges E£8 per hour. Further down Mashraba's main street, at the Christina Residence, Sunshine Internet (☎ 640 669) has four terminals in a bright and airy room.

Diving

After loafing around, diving is the most popular activity in Dahab. There are over 40 dive clubs, all offering a full range of diving possibilities; however, you should choose your club carefully as some places have lousy reputations when it comes to safety standards (see the Diving the Red Sea chapter for more information).

Snorkelling

Although you can snorkel in the reefs off Assalah, they are often strewn with litter. If you can ignore the garbage, the reef at the northern end of **Mashraba** has nice table corals and teeming fish life. There are also reefs off the southern end of Mashraba, just before the lagoon. At the northern tip of Assalah, **Lighthouse Reef** is also a good, sheltered snorkelling site. More popular, though is the **Eel Garden**, just north of Assalah, where a colony of eels lives on the sandy seabed. About 6km further north are the **Canyon** and **Blue Hole** dive sites. Despite their intimidating reputation as danger zones for careless divers, the top of the reefs are teeming with life, making them fine for snorkelling. Most of the dive centres organise dive safaris to the **Ras Abu Gallum and Nabq Protectorates**. Although most cater to divers, some will take snorkellers along. (See the Diving the Red Sea chapter for more information.)

You can hire snorkelling gear from all the dive centres and many other places in Masbat for about E£20 to E£30 per day. Keep in mind that some of the reefs have unexpected currents. After watching a dramatic rescue at a reef close to the Eel Garden, one reader discovered that several people had drowned there.

Other Water Sports

The usual pedalos (E£25 per hour) and kayaks (E£10 per hour) can be rented at the north end of Masbat and at the holiday villages on the lagoon. There's a very good, German-run windsurfing club at Ganet Sinai Hotel, with equipment and instruction for children who want to windsurf. The Novotel Holiday Village and the Hilton and Helnan hotels also have good windsurfing centres and the bay there is excellent for it. Windsurfers can also be rented at the northern end of Dahab Bay, although the wind tends to be gusty here. Kitesurfing is also starting to take off in Dahab, although the offshore winds limit the areas where it can be done. The Helnan, Hilton and Novotel hotels are all planning to offer kitesurfing in the near future.

There's no 'beach' to speak of in Assalah itself; instead the rocky coastline leads straight out onto the reef. For the golden sands, after which Dahab (Gold) was named, you must go down to the lagoon area where the resorts are clustered.

Camel Treks

Many of the local Bedouin organise camel trips to the interior of Sinai. In the morning, camel drivers and their camels congregate along the waterfront in the village. Register with the police before beginning the trek, and don't pay the camel driver until you return to the village. Prices for a one-day trip start at E£70. As all drivers seem to have agreed among themselves on this price, bargaining will probably get you nowhere. The price includes food but not always water.

Jeep Treks

All the hotels, dive centres and travel agencies arrange jeep trips to the Coloured Canyon (see Camel & Jeep Treks under Nuweiba later in this chapter for details) and

Ras Abu Gallum. When choosing who to go with, try to find a Bedouin – or at least someone who works with Bedouin – because many are excluded from the tourist industry, which tends to be dominated by migrants from the Nile Valley. Centre for Sinai (☎ 640 702, W www.centre4sinai.com.eg) is one outfit that tries to promote knowledge of the local culture as well as showing visitors the sights. Nesima, Club Red and Orca Diving Centres also use local guides for their excursions. Itineraries are pretty much custom-designed but, as an example of prices, you'll be looking at E£15 per person (with a minimum of four people) for a morning of snorkelling at the Blue Hole or E£35 and up for an evening trip into the mountains with dinner at a Bedouin camp.

Horse Riding

If you want to ride a horse just wait on the beach in Mashraba for one of the Bedouin who walk up and down with horses for hire. Expect to pay about E£25 per hour. You can also ask around the camps. From the Novotel Holiday Village you can ride around the lagoon on horseback for E£55.

Places to Stay – Budget

Most, if not all, low-budget travellers head straight for Assalah. There's a plethora of so-called camps there, which are basically compounds with spartan stone, cement or reed huts, usually with two or three mattresses tossed on the floor, and communal bathroom facilities. The camps south of Nesima Resort tend to be the best as they are away from the noise of Masbat, are sheltered from the wind and have more space. Some have attractive waterfront areas shaded by palm groves.

Many of the camps are starting to introduce proper rooms with private bathrooms. These are considerably more expensive than the huts, but prices are often negotiable.

When hunting for a good place remember that concrete huts with iron roofs are hotter than those made of reeds, but the latter may be less secure; ask for a padlock. Check that there's electricity and running water – some places have hot water – as well as decent mattresses, fly screens and fans.

SINAI

The following list is by no means exhaustive. Keep in mind that prices can often be negotiated in low season.

Auski Camp *(☎ 640 474)* Ordinary room without/with fan E£10/15, big rooms with bath E£25, newly built rooms with air-con & bath E£40-60. This is a popular camp next to Starcosa Hotel, run by the amiable Nasser. There's hot water and access to the beach.

Camelot Paradise Camp *(☎ 640 136, Masbat)* Single/double huts E£7/10, with fan & bath E£20/30. If the camp is full you can sleep on the roof of its hotel building for E£3. This is a small camp/hotel that can be reached by an alley running beside the Ghazala supermarket. There is a kitchen that you can use as well as a laundry area. Breakfast starts at E£3.

Dolphin Camp *(☎ 640 018, Mashraba)* Single/double huts E£10/15, with fan E£20, rooms with bath E£40. Although the facilities are good, some travellers have reported theft here, so make sure you lock up all your valuables.

Happyland Camp *(☎ 640 207)* Huts E£7 per person, doubles with fan & bath E£20 per person, rooms with air-con E£40 per person. Next to Sphinx House, this camp has basic rooms and is suffering from the growing competition, but it is still recommended by some travellers. There is a nice beach restaurant with umbrellas.

Mirage Village *(☎ 640 341, fax 640 332 Assalah)* Singles/doubles E£40/70, with bath E£60/85. On the waterfront just north of the lighthouse area, this place is run by the very helpful Salama and is very friendly and secure but, like many camps, it has become more like a hotel. All the rooms have fly screens, a fan and a cupboard. Meals and beers are available – breakfast costs E£10.

Mohammed Ali Camp *(☎ 640 268, fax 640 380, Masbat)* Camp-style rooms E£5, rooms E£15, singles/doubles with fan & bath E£40/60, double rooms with air-con & bath E£80. In the centre of Assalah, this is the largest and longest running of the camps. Its huts are long gone and it now boasts 128 rooms. Although clean, the place is often noisy, but remains popular. You can see its layout and range of room types on the Club Red diving centre's Web site at W www.club-red.com.

Moon Valley Camp *(mobile ☎ 010-520 8936, Masbat)* Huts E£10 per person, rooms with fan & bath E£25. This reasonably long-standing camp is in the thick of things along the restaurant strip (so it can be noisy at night).

Musa Camp *(☎ 640 268, fax 640 380, Mashraba)* Doubles E£40. The rooms have baths and screened windows but the huts are cheaper. The nice palm grove gives lots of shade to the gravel-coated beach.

Penguin Camp *(☎ 640 320, Mashraba)* Single/double huts E£7/10. This is another new camp on the waterfront in Mashraba. It is clean, with friendly staff and a good beach area beside a palm grove.

Star of Dahab *(☎/fax 640 130, Mashraba)* Singles/doubles E£15/20. This hotel has beds in small, apricot-toned rooms or in beehive-shaped reed huts (which have candles only) near the water. The communal bathrooms are reasonably clean and there's hot water as well as a small laundry. If you have a tent you can sometimes camp on the gravel-coated waterfront area for E£5 per person, although there's only room for two small tents and there's no shade.

Venus Camp Single/double huts E£7/15, rooms with bath E£15/30. This is a popular new camp on the beach next to Auski Camp in Mashraba with plenty of sunshades and a beachfront restaurant.

Places to Stay – Mid-Range

As camps replace huts with concrete, there's an increasing number of mid-range hotels available in Dahab.

Bamboo House Hotel *(☎ 640 263, fax 640 466, Masbat)* Rooms E£120. The large rooms are double only, with minibar, air-con and good-sized bathrooms. It's above a dive shop and a Western Union office.

Blue Beach Club *(☎/fax 640 413, Assalah)* Singles/doubles US$30/40. Back in town, north of Masbat, this new hotel has very clean rooms with fan and breakfast. It is popular with Swiss and German groups.

Canyon Camp & Dive Resort *(☎/fax 640 197, The Canyon)* Rooms US$20 per person, with air-con & bath US$25. This camp is right in front of the dive site of the same name, about 8km north of Dahab. It's a reasonable option if diving is your passion and you don't mind being away from the action. Prices included breakfast.

Ghazala Hotel *(mobile ☎ 012-224 3845, in Cairo fax 02-337 4686, Masbat)* Rooms low season E£$30-50, high season E£35-70. This is a new hotel in Masbat with good sea views and clean, air-con rooms with attached bathrooms. There is an Internet cafe and good Italian restaurant attached.

Divers House *(☎/fax 640 451, e DiversHouse@gmx.de, Mashraba)* Singles/doubles with fan E£35/50, with air-con & sea view E£60/70. This small, very clean hotel on the waterfront has nice rooms and gives preferential treatment to divers.

Jasmine Pension *(☎ 640 370, fax 640 372, Mashraba)* Doubles E£60-80. This is a small, well-run hotel in a building on the seafront; rooms have air-con and private bath.

Sirtaki Hotel *(☎/fax 640 314, Assalah)* Singles/doubles US$40/60. This four-star hotel has an attached diving centre that sticks out on the point near the lighthouse, spoiling the view on the north end of Dahab Bay. Still, the views looking out over the sea are nice. All rooms have air-con, TV and a balcony. Prices include breakfast.

Club Red Hotel *(☎/fax 640 380, W www.club-red.com, Masbat)* Doubles/triples/quads with fan, breakfast & bath E£40/60/80, doubles E£15. There is a 15% discount on the room if you dive with Club Red; you can see the room layout on the Web site.

Sphinx House *(☎ 640 032, e sphinx_d@intouch.com)* Singles/doubles US$28/37. Rooms have air-con and bath; prices include breakfast.

New Sphinx Hotel *(☎ 640 032, e sphinx_d@intouch.com)* Singles/doubles US$42/47. Rooms here are large and there is a pool, a restaurant and billiard room. There is also a seafront bar with well-priced beer and wine.

Christina Residence *(☎ 640 390, fax 640 296, Mashraba)* Singles/doubles E£70/85. Small Swiss-run hotel set back from the beach. All rooms are spotless and have fan and bath; breakfast costs from E£3 to E£10. The same management team runs the newly built Christina Beach Palace.

Christina Beach Palace *(☎ 640 390, fax 640 296, Mashraba)* Singles/doubles E£100/130. This hotel is on the beach.

Inmo Hotel *(☎ 640 370, fax 640 372, Mashraba)* Singles/doubles US$18/25 for divers, US$20.70/28.80 for nondivers, with bath US$41/52 for divers, US$47.15/59.80 for nondivers. With colourful rooms with fans, domed ceilings and attractive furniture, this hotel mainly caters to people on diving packages from Europe, especially Germany, although it does take in stray travellers if there's some room. There are a few mountain bikes for guests to use.

Dyarna Hotel *(☎ 640 120, fax 640 122, Mashraba)* Singles/doubles with fan E£60/95, with air-con E£85/125. The 42-room Dyarna has a variety of rooms on offer. Its name means 'our home' in Arabic but, unfortunately, it's nothing special, though the staff are very friendly and people enjoy staying here. There's a pool, two restaurants, a roof bar and a disco.

Lagona Dahab Village *(☎ 640 352, fax 640 351, Near Dahab City)* Singles/doubles US$30/48. For now this resort remains on its own on the beach between Dahab City and Assalah, but construction sites seem set to surround it imminently. It's a comfortable enough place with air-con, dome-shaped rooms and the feel of a resort. There's a restaurant but alcohol is not served. Prices include breakfast.

SINAI

Places to Stay – Top End

Most of Dahab's higher priced accommodation is grouped around the beach near Dahab City.

Nesima Resort *(☎ 640 320, fax 640 321, ⓔ nesima@menanet.net, Mashraba)* Singles/doubles US$45/55. Overlooking the beach in Mashraba, this highly recommended hotel has simple but very comfortable domed rooms. Calm yet central, it also has a fantastic pool with a juice bar overlooking the beach. Child care is available and divers at the Nesima Dive Centre get a discount; breakfast is included in the price.

Novotel Holiday Village *(☎/fax 640 301, Resort Strip)* Singles US$50-90, doubles US$68-116. Nonguests can use the beach for E£50. There is also a dive club; breakfast is included in the price.

Hilton Dahab Resort *(☎ 640 310, fax 640 424, Resort Strip)* Singles/doubles US$140/180. Comfortable rooms in whitewashed, domed two-storey villas. There are two pools, a nice beach and the usual five-star amenities; prices include breakfast.

Swiss Inn Golden Beach Resort *(☎ 640 472, fax 640 470, Resort Strip)* Singles/doubles US$105/130. This is a four-star hotel with a gigantic marble lobby and whitewashed buildings spread down to the beach. You can use the beach for E£35; breakfast is included in the price.

Ganet Sinai Hotel *(☎ 640 440, fax 640 441, Resort Strip)* Singles/doubles/triples US$45/60/75. Furthest south (until the next resort is built) is this hotel on the bay in Dahab City. Popular with groups from Cairo, the small, chalet-style rooms are comfortable, but really overpriced, and the grounds have sparse vegetation. However, there is a good windsurfing centre (see Other Water Sports earlier in this chapter).

Helnan Dahab Hotel *(☎ 640 427, fax 640 428)* Singles/doubles with half board US$40/60. South of Dahab City, this hotel is on its own around the bay with a swimming pool, bars, restaurants and a Club Mistral windsurfing centre.

Places to Eat

There is a string of places to eat at along the waterfront in Assalah, and touts have an annoying habit of hanging around in front of most of them trying to entice you in. They serve breakfast, lunch and dinner and most seem to have identical menus hanging up out the front. A meal will generally cost between E£6 and E£25, with the intense competition keeping the prices far lower than elsewhere in Egypt. A few, including

Al Capone and ***Crazy House***, serve fish meals, displaying their catch out the front and selling by weight. It's best not to turn up with a raging hunger as service can be slow. Generally, people hang out in these places all day, occasionally summoning the strength of mind and soul to flop into the sparkling waters of the Gulf of Aqaba for a while and then emerge to collapse back into a state of idyllic inertia and order either a tea or cola.

Jays Restaurant *(mobile ☎ 012-335 3377, Masbat)* Dishes E£4-6. Open for dinner Sat-Thur. This British-run restaurant, a perennial favourite, serves a mixture of Egyptian and Western fare at very good prices. The menu changes each week and dishes such as coconut rice and curried vegetables make a welcome change from the usual offerings. No alcohol is served.

Shark's Restaurant *(mobile ☎ 010-561 0023, Masbat)* Mains E£5-15. Open for dinner only. Next door to Jays and also deservedly popular, Shark's has an extensive choice of main courses and serves a vegetarian special most days. No alcohol is served.

Neptune Restaurant *(☎ 640 262, Masbat)* Dishes E£10-35. This is a good Chinese restaurant with beer on offer.

Tota Restaurant *(☎ 640 014, Masbat)* Meals E£6-30. This boat-shaped place in the heart of Assalah has a good Italian kitchen. It serves excellent soup complete with garlic bread, large doughy pizzas (which are a bit light on toppings) and a range of other meals and desserts. The top 'deck' is a good place to watch the sunset while sipping a cold beer, especially during the 5pm to 7pm happy hour, when you can get a Stella Artois for E£6.

Tratoria Pizzeria *(☎ 640 173, Masbat)* Dishes E£8-25. Two doors along, next to the Oxford Supermarket, this two-storey pizzeria does arguably better pizzas than anyone else. If you prefer a thin crust, this is your place. Other Italian dishes also on offer.

Dolphin Camp Cafe *(☎ 640 018, Mashraba)* Dishes E£6-15. Balti and other Indian dishes are served on the waterfront. Beer and wine are reasonably priced.

Nesima Resort *(☎ 640 320, Mashraba)* Dishes E£20-65. If eating in front of the parade of people on the strip doesn't appeal to you, this restaurant is intimate. It also serves very good food. The steaks here are famous around Sinai.

Jasmine Pension *(☎ 640 370, Mashraba)* Meals E£15-55. This popular restaurant on the water offers home-cooked food from the open kitchen.

Lakhbatita *(mobile ☎ 010-196 4120, Mashraba)* Dishes E£8-30. This eccentric beachfront restaurant at the southern end of Mashraba is decorated with old Egyptian furniture and doors. The food reflects the decor and includes traditional Egyptian dishes as well as Asian- and European-influenced meals. No alcohol is served.

The big hotels down by the lagoon also have restaurants, but you'll pay considerably more to eat there and the food will not necessarily be any better.

Entertainment

If it's beer, wine or billiard tables you're after, try ***Crazy House*** *(Masbat)*. Beers cost only E£6. ***Al-Zar Bar***, next to Dolphin Camp, has cold Stellas at E£6 and loud music, but can be a pleasant hangout. The ***New Sphinx Bar*** *(Sphinx House)* is a good bar away from the Masbat scene. It also has a happy hour from 5pm to 8pm, with Stellas for E£7. Popular with divers and others is the ***Shipwreck Bar*** *(☎ 640 320, Nesima Resort)*. In summer you can drink on the rooftop terrace and it has a happy hour from 7pm to 9pm. It also has popular parties with dancing every Friday night.

Away from Assalah there are also bars at the big resort hotels.

There are plenty of other wholesome activities available. Nesima, Club Red Hotel and Blue Beach Club occasionally offer yoga and massage. Or you can simply buy the Dahab traveller look and have your hair braided or your newly tanned body adorned with a henna tattoo. Both are offered by almost every shop in Masbat. Prices vary wildly but braids start at about E£35 for short hair and tattoos start at E£15 for the most simple designs.

Getting There & Away

Bus The East Delta Bus Co station (☎ 640 250) is in Dahab City. The most regular connection is to Sharm el-Sheikh (E£10, 1½ hours) with buses every hour or so throughout the day. Buses to Nuweiba (E£10) leave at 9.30am, 10.30am, 3pm, 4pm, 5.30pm and 6.30pm. The 9.30am and 10.30am services go on to Taba (E£20). There is a 9.30am bus to St Katherine (E£15). Buses to Cairo (nine hours) leave at 8.30am, 1pm and 2pm (all E£55), and at 10pm (E£70). Buses for Suez (E£30 to E£40, 6½ hours) depart at 8am and 4pm. Note that the departure times posted at the bus station are not always correct, so you should double-check the schedule with the ticket office.

Service Taxi As a rule, service taxis are much more expensive than buses – they know you're only using them because the bus doesn't suit and hitching possibilities are limited. Travellers are a captive market. Although a trip to, say, St Katherine can cost as little as E£10 per person, it will often cost closer to E£20. An entire taxi (with a maximum of seven passengers) to Nuweiba or Sharm el-Sheikh costs about E£70 to E£80, and to Taba it's about E£15 per person.

Getting Around

Pick-ups go up and down the main street in Assalah and, less frequently, around the resort strip. The usual fare is E£1, but if you want to go between Assalah and Dahab City, expect to pay more.

SINAI

RAS ABU GALLUM PROTECTORATE

Covering 400 sq km of the coastline between Dahab and Nuweiba is Ras Abu Gallum Protectorate. Picturesque, with high coastal mountains, narrow valleys, sand dunes and fine gravel beaches, it also has a number of excellent diving and snorkelling sites. Scientists describe Abu Gallum as 'floristic frontier' in which Mediterranean conditions are influenced by a tropical climate. With 165 plant species, 44 of which are not found elsewhere in Sinai, in addition to a large number of mammals and reptiles, it has enormous environmental significance and is a fascinating place to visit. As in Nabq, Bedouin of the Mizena tribe live within the protectorate confines. They continue to fish here as they have done for centuries (although this is now regulated by the protectorate) and you can hire Bedouin guides and camels through the ranger house at the edge of Wadih Rasasah. There is a designated camping area as well as several hiking trails.

Dive centres and travel agencies in Nuweiba and Dahab offer excursions to Abu Gallum, usually as part of a diving safari. If you are driving, remember that all vehicles should stick to tracks.

NUWEIBA

☎ 069

Strung out over a long distance, with no real centre and little ambience, Nuweiba can hardly be called Sinai's most beautiful resort. During the Israeli occupation, it was the site of a major *moshav* (farming settlement), which has been converted into a residence for Egyptian government officials. In recent times, Israelis have formed the bulk of the tourist trade, which means that the town has suffered greatly with the outbreak of the Palestinian Intifada in September 2000, which all but stopped Israeli tourism in Egypt. However, the ferry between Nuweiba and Aqaba means that there is a continual flow of people and vehicle traffic through the port, and many hotels are trying to attract European tourists. Construction around here is continuing at a furious pace as the Egyptian state crams as many hotels along the beaches as possible, particularly on the road north to Taba.

Orientation

Nuweiba is divided into three parts. To the south is the port, with a large bus station, banks, a couple of fairly awful hotels and the Hilton Coral Resort. About 8km further north is 'Nuweiba City', a small but spread-out settlement with a variety of accommodation options, a bazaar with tourist shops, and several cheap places to eat. As more hotels are being built the 'city' is gradually linking

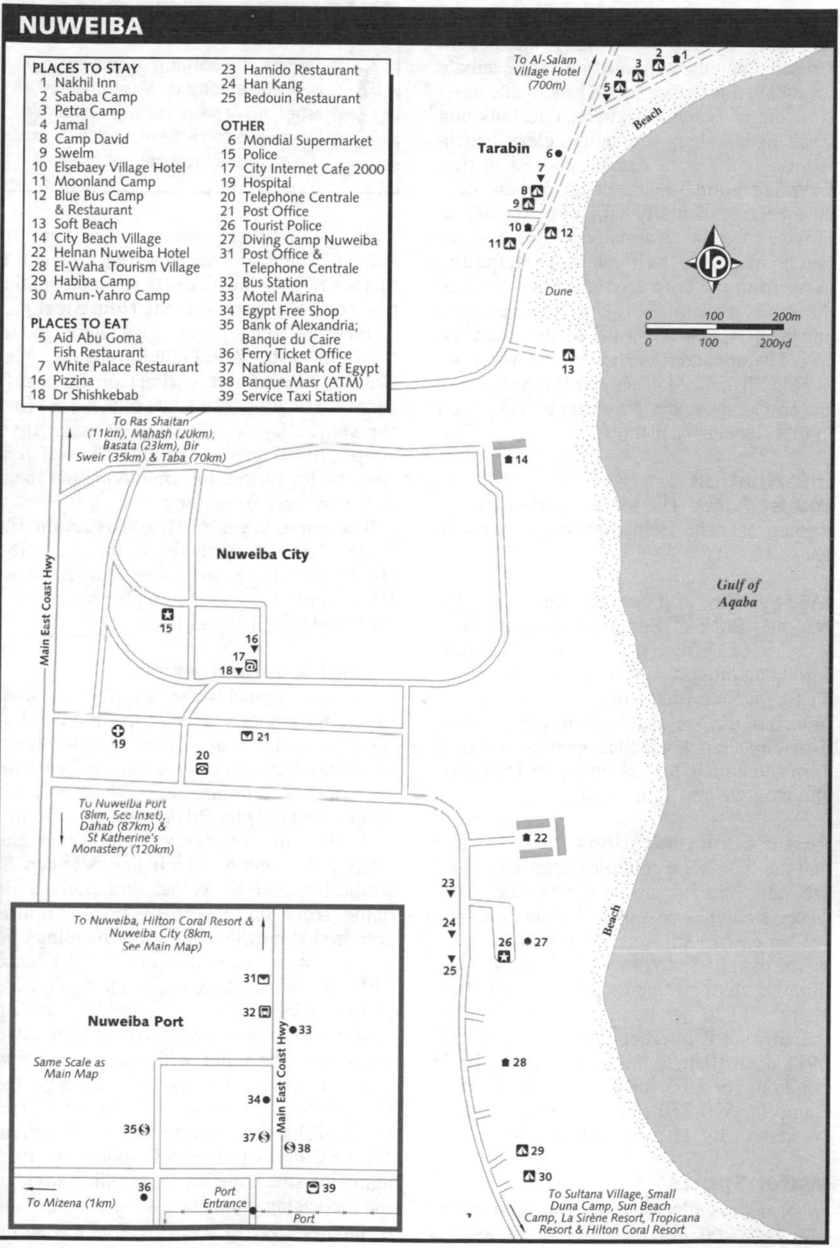
NUWEIBA
PLACES TO STAY
1 Nakhil Inn
2 Sababa Camp
3 Petra Camp
4 Jamal
8 Camp David
9 Swelm
10 Elsebaey Village Hotel
11 Moonland Camp
12 Blue Bus Camp & Restaurant
13 Soft Beach
14 City Beach Village
22 Helnan Nuweiba Hotel
28 El-Waha Tourism Village
29 Habiba Camp
30 Amun-Yahro Camp
PLACES TO EAT
5 Aid Abu Goma Fish Restaurant
7 White Palace Restaurant
16 Pizzina
18 Dr Shishkebab
23 Hamido Restaurant
24 Han Kang
25 Bedouin Restaurant
OTHER
6 Mondial Supermarket
15 Police
17 City Internet Cafe 2000
19 Hospital
20 Telephone Centrale
21 Post Office
26 Tourist Police
27 Diving Camp Nuweiba
31 Post Office & Telephone Centrale
32 Bus Station
33 Motel Marina
34 Egypt Free Shop
35 Bank of Alexandria; Banque du Caire
36 Ferry Ticket Office
37 National Bank of Egypt
38 Banque Masr (ATM)
39 Service Taxi Station
To Al-Salam Village Hotel (700m)
Beach
Tarabin
Dune
0 100 200m
0 100 200yd
To Ras Shaitan (11km), Mahash (20km), Basata (23km), Bir Sweir (35km) & Taba (70km)
Nuweiba City
Main East Coast Hwy
Gulf of Aqaba
To Nuweiba Port (8km, See Inset), Dahab (87km) & St Katherine's Monastery (120km)
Beach
To Nuweiba, Hilton Coral Resort & Nuweiba City (8km, See Main Map)
Nuweiba Port
Same Scale as Main Map
Main East Coast Hwy
To Mizena (1km)
Port Entrance
Port
To Sultana Village, Small Duna Camp, Sun Beach Camp, La Sirène Resort, Tropicana Resort & Hilton Coral Resort

SINAI

up with the port. Further north still is Tarabin, a 15-minute walk along the beach. Draped along the northern end of Nuweiba's calm bay, this once tranquil beach-side oasis is a line of bamboo-and-concrete huts and small hotels along a none-too-clean beach. Although the area can be packed during Egyptian holidays, the camp owners here have been particularly hard hit by the dearth of Israeli tourists. Normally, though, it has a party atmosphere, so if you want tranquillity away from the crowds you'll have to go to the sandy beaches between Nuweiba City and the port, or head further north to the clusters of camps and small hotels on the beaches of Ras Shaitan, Mahash and Bir Sweir (see Beach Camps under Nuweiba to Taba later in this chapter for listings).

Information

Tourist Police The tourist police office is located near the Helnan Nuweiba Hotel in Nuweiba City.

Money At the port there are branches of the National Bank of Egypt and Banque Masr with an ATM (note that neither will handle Jordanian dinars), a Masr Travel office and an Egypt Free (duty-free) shop. There is a branch of the National Bank of Egypt inside the Helnan hotel, which is open from 9am to 1pm and 7pm to 9pm Saturday to Thursday, and from 9am to 11am Friday.

Post & Communications The post office and the telephone centrale (open 24 hours) are near the hospital in Nuweiba City. There's another post office at the port.

Compared with other tourist towns, Nuweiba has sparse Internet offerings. In Tarabin, the Mondial Supermarket (☎ 500 108) charges E£20 per hour. In Nuweiba City, the tiny City Internet Cafe 2000 (☎ 500 091), open 10am to midnight, charges E£25 per hour, or E£6 for 15 minutes. Habiba Camp (☎ 500 770), on the beach south of Nuweiba City, charges similar prices.

Water Sports

Once again, underwater delights are the feature attraction, although they're not as dramatic as at other resorts on the Gulf of Aqaba. There are shallow reefs offshore that are reasonable places to snorkel, but the best snorkelling is the **Stone House** reef just south of the town. Divers based here tend to head out to Ras Abu Gallum (see Ras Abu Gallum Protectorate earlier) or other offshore destinations but some of these are fine for snorkellers too. Check at local dive shops, listed in the Diving the Red Sea chapter, for further information about local dive sites and excursions.

Those into kayaking should ask at the El-Waha Tourism Village or the Nuweiba Hilton Coral Resort, where kayaks cost US$6 per hour. The Hilton also has jet skis for US$15 for 10 minutes.

> **Warning**
>
> Topless sunbathing is increasingly common among visitors to Nuweiba, especially Israelis staying in Tarabin. Not only is this little more than a strip show for the local men, it is illegal.

Camel & Jeep Treks

Nuweiba is probably the best place in Sinai to arrange camel and jeep trips into the dramatic mountains that line the coast here. There are hundreds of stunningly beautiful sites in the Sinai mountains, although most people visit only the 20 or so on the 'circuit'.

At the top of every itinerary is the **Coloured Canyon**, which lies between St Katherine and Nuweiba, and derives its name from the layers of bright, multi-coloured stones that resemble paintings on its very steep, narrow walls. Total silence (the canyon is sheltered from the wind) adds to the eeriness. This is a popular day trip from Sinai's resorts and it's often difficult to appreciate the quiet with the groups that crowd in here every day. Fortunately, the Coloured Canyon falls inside the boundaries of the Taba Protectorate and the Egyptian National Parks Office will soon start managing the site, hopefully controlling some of the increasing numbers who visit here. Talk of paying a fee to enter the area has so far

The Dolphin of Nuweiba

A few years ago, a young, mute Bedouin named Abdullah from Mizena, the tiny village about 1km south of Nuweiba port, noticed a lone dolphin frequenting the bay over which his village looks. He started to befriend her, swimming out into the turquoise water and diving to her depths. Although he was unable to talk to humans, Abdullah was somehow able to communicate with the dolphin, which he named Holeen, and she began to turn up regularly and take Abdullah for a swim. In the months and years that have followed, the two have become 'an item'.

This incredible bonding between a human and a wild marine mammal has, of course, attracted plenty of onlookers and eager participants, and visitors are now swamping Abdullah's village in the hope of swimming with Holeen. To ensure her return to the bay each day the villagers now feed her. They also charge visitors E£10 to go for a swim and E£10 to rent a mask and snorkel.

If you do take the plunge, remember to take off any jewellery or sharp items before entering the water and try to be content with viewing rather than chasing and grabbing at Holeen. One flick of her tail is enough to propel her away from unwanted suitors, but if the attention becomes too much this graceful creature of the deep is just as likely to go back from where she came.

led nowhere, but it is possible that you will have to pay in the near future. The canyon is about 5km from the main road; vehicles can drive to within 100m of it.

One company that organises camel and jeep treks is **Abanoub Travel** (☎ 062-520 201, fax 520 206). It is headed by Dr Rabia, a medical doctor who fell in love with Sinai and whose Nuweiba-based company has been leading tours there ever since. Jeep tours cost about US$35 per person per day, including food. Camel treks are about US$45.

Places to Stay

Nuweiba Port There are only three hotels close to the port, and these are overpriced and scruffy. Better to head into the camps of Tarabin or the hotels of Nuweiba City.

Nuweiba Hilton Coral Resort *(☎ 520 320, fax 520 327, Nuweiba Port)* Singles/doubles from US$125/160. This large resort has lush gardens and good water sports and is the only real option in the port area. Prices include breakfast.

Nuweiba City Although far from a city, this stretch of Nuweiba is slowly becoming the town's tourist hub, with an increasing number of hotels in all price ranges.

Helnan Nuweiba Hotel *(☎ 500 401, fax 500 407)* Singles/doubles US$50/65. This hotel caters mainly to package tourists or middle class Cairenes. Prices include breakfast. There is also the cheaper ***Helnan Holiday Camp***, where singles/doubles in scruffy cabins with shared bathroom cost E£50/70, including breakfast.

El-Waha Tourism Village *(☎ 500 420 fax 500 421, ⓔ elwaharesort@hotmail.com)* Singles/doubles in air-con bungalow-style rooms with bath E£90/115, doubles in wooden huts with fan E£55. South of Nuweiba City, this place has a nice beach bar for cold beers. The rooms have satellite TV.

Habiba Camp *(☎ 500 770, fax 500 565, ⓔ habiba@nuweiba.net)* Double bungalow-style rooms with bath E£120, singles/doubles in wooden cabins E£40/80, singles/doubles in huts E£30/60. South of Nuweiba City, this camp has fairly large huts and there is an excellent beachfront restaurant where Bedouin bread is made and buffet lunches served. The only disadvantage is that groups on day trips from Sharm stop here for lunch. Still, the beach is beautiful and it's a calm place to hang out.

Amun-Yahro Camp *(☎ 500 307, fax 500 244)* Singles/doubles from E£15/30. South of Nuweiba City, this camp has huts with electricity and clean bathrooms on raised concrete platforms on a nice beach.

Sultana Village *(☎ 500 490, fax 500 491)* Doubles/triples US$22/30, doubles with air-con & bath US$30. Rooms here are small stone huts on the beach, each with electricity and couch-style beds, but a little

Sinai's Bedouin

Fifty thousand Bedouin live in Sinai's harsh desert, the majority in the north of the peninsula. They belong to 14 distinct tribes, most with ties to Bedouin in the Negev, Jordan and northern Saudi Arabia. The Sukwarka, living along the northern coast, near Al-Arish, are the largest tribe. The Tarabin, who have territory in both northern and southern Sinai, and the Tyaha, in the centre of the peninsula, both originated in Palestine. The Haweitat, centred in an area south-east of Suez, came from the Hejaz in Arabia, as *Lawrence of Arabia* buffs might remember.

The seven tribes in the south are known collectively as the Towara, or 'Arabs of Al-Tor', the provincial capital. Of these, the first to settle in Sinai were the Aleiqat and the Suwalha, who arrived in the peninsula soon after the Muslim conquest of Egypt. The largest southern tribe is the Mizena, which is concentrated in the coastal areas between Sharm el-Sheikh and Nuweiba. Members of the tiny Jabaliyya tribe, centred in the mountains around St Katherine, are descendants of Macedonians sent by the Emperor Justinian to build and protect the monastery in the sixth century.

Centuries of living in the harsh conditions of Sinai have helped the Bedouin develop a sophisticated understanding of their environment. Strict laws and traditions govern the use of precious resources. Water use is closely regulated and vegetation carefully conserved, as revealed in the Bedouin adage, 'killing a tree is like killing a soul'.

But despite their long history and immense knowledge of the peninsula, Sinai's original inhabitants are being left behind in the race to build up the coast. Viewed with distrust because of their ties to tribes in neighbouring countries, especially Israel & the Palestinian Territories, their strong traditions, respect for their environment, and proud nomadic past are given short shrift by Nile Valley dwellers who treat the peninsula as a goldmine to be exploited. With their coastal landholdings sold out from under them by the state, their fishing grounds polluted by uncontrolled development and their nomadic past turned into a Disney-like caricature of packaged camel rides and desert dinners, they are increasingly marginalised in their own land.

overpriced for what you get. There is also a restaurant.

Small Duna Camp *(☎ 500 198)* Beds in beach huts E£10. This camp is simple but quiet. It's run by a Bedouin from the local Mizena tribe.

Sun Beach Camp *(☎ 500 163)* Huts E£10 per person. This is another camp along the sandy beach south of Nuweiba City that will suit refugees from the noise of Tarabin.

La Sirène Resort *(☎/fax 500 701)* Singles/doubles US$45/64. Further down the beach, this resort has 40 tasteful, whitewashed rooms with air-con, telephone, bath and TV. There is also a beach restaurant – room prices include breakfast – and bar and a German-run diving centre.

Tropicana Resort *(☎ 500 056, fax 500 022)* Doubles from US$70. This four-star chain hotel has comfortable rooms and a nice sandy beach; prices include breakfast.

City Beach Village *(☎ 500 307, fax 500 146)* Camp sites E£7, double reed huts E£30, singles/doubles in stone bungalows with air-con & bath E£50/70. Halfway between Nuweiba City and Tarabin, this is not a bad option if you just want to sit all day on a tranquil beach; it has a fish restaurant and bar. Prices for huts and bungalows include breakfast.

Tarabin As Tarabin develops along Dahab lines, the choice of accommodation is becoming wider. You can get a mattress in a bamboo or concrete hut at one of the camps for as little as E£5, and there are a couple of hotels.

Camps Judge for yourself which camps have the more solid huts – the differences are not great. Most of these places have cafes selling food and drinks. A few are run by Sudanese, with their own special laid-back touch. Tarabin has been badly hit by the lack of Israeli tourists in 2000–01 and prices have either remained static or even fallen from previous years. The following camps are listed from north to south.

Sababa Camp *(☎ 500 855)* Huts E£10. This camp is Sudanese-run, with small, clean huts and shared facilities.

Petra Camp (*☎ 500 086*) Beds in bungalows E£10. There are 35 bungalows with fan and shared bathroom. Although it's generally tidy, the bathrooms are not as great as they could be.

Jamal *(☎ 500 066)* Double rooms E£60, double huts E£20. This large place is popular with young Israelis; all the signs are in Hebrew. It has 40 rooms with air-con and bath and 40 huts jammed into a small area; some rooms are located on the roof. There is a 24-hour restaurant on the ground floor.

Camp David *(☎ 500 010)* Huts with fans & shared bath E£20, rooms with air-con & bath E£50.

Swelm *(☎ 500 025)* Beds in huts E£10. This popular camp is run entirely by Sudanese.

Blue Bus Camp *(☎ 500 172)* Beds in huts E£10. One of Tarabin's original establishments, this is more a place to eat than a camp. However, it does have a few huts with fans and rickety old reed recliners.

Moonland Camp *(☎ 500 610)* Beds in huts E£10. This has been recommended as one of the cleaner camps with good, friendly management.

Soft Beach Single/double huts E£10/15. This is a 30-hut camp at the dunes end of Tarabin and is run by Sudanese. The outdoor showers have cold water only, although they swear that there is hot water available in the winter. There are horses for rent next door at E£20 to E£40 per hour.

Hotels Tarabin may be known for camps but small hotels are springing up here for those who want the scene but like their comfort.

Elsebaey Village Hotel *(☎ 500 373)* Doubles E£50-85. This small, clean hotel in the heart of Tarabin has 15 tiled rooms with fan, cupboard and a double bed, plus shared bathroom facilities. More expensive rooms have air-con and private bathroom. There is also a rooftop bar, a ground floor restaurant and a supermarket.

Nakhil Inn *(☎ 500 879, fax 500 878, e surf@sinainet.com.eg)* Singles/doubles US$30/45. This is a small new hotel at the northern end of Tarabin. Spacious, well-appointed rooms have air-con and satellite TV; prices include breakfast. The inn has its own beach and dive centre.

Al-Salam Village *(☎ 500 440)* Singles/doubles US$30/40. This spacious 100-room place occupies the point at the northern end of Nuweiba Bay. However, it is away from the action and overpriced for the slightly shabby prefab rooms that feature air-con, TV and refrigerator; prices include breakfast.

Places to Eat

If you're staying at either the port or Tarabin, dining options are limited mainly to the hotels and camps. At the port, you'll also find a line of fuul and ta'amiyya places about 150m off to your left (with your back to the port entrance). In Tarabin there's a ***supermarket*** in front of Elsebaey Village Hotel selling junk food and basic groceries. ***Mondial Supermarket***, between Palm beach camp and Al-Salam camp, also sells food supplies and has an international cardphone outside.

Blue Bus Camp *(☎ 500 172, Tarabin)* Meals E£10-20. This long-standing, popular restaurant is on the beach at the beginning of Tarabin and serves pizzas, pastas and fish meals.

Aid Abu Goma Fish Restaurant *(Tarabin)* Dishes E£15-45. A small but popular fish restaurant, this place serves fresh fish dishes, but has suffered from the downturn in tourism.

Dr Shishkebab *(☎ 500 273, Bazaar, Nuweiba City)* Dishes E£8-40. This immensely popular place offers a generous spread of ta'amiyya, salad, fried aubergine and hummus with all meals; the *daoud pasha* (meatballs in a rich tomato sauce) and rice is very good. Although famous for meat dishes, this place has cheap vegetarian meals too. The unmistakable 'doctor' is a big, white-turbaned, cheerful man wandering from table to table, attentively waiting on all those who eat here. Sometimes he and his friends will bring out their tablas and hold an impromptu concert.

Pizzina *(☎ 500 608, Bazaar, Nuweiba City)* Dishes E£8-25. This tiny restaurant has excellent pizzas with fresh toppings. Takeaway is also available.

Hamido Restaurant *(☎ 500 604, Nuweiba City)* Meals E£10-45. One of a row of restaurants opposite the Helnan hotel, this place offers excellent fish meals and Egyptian mezze.

Han Kang *(☎ 500 970, Nuweiba City)* Dishes E£15-50. This is a good Chinese–Korean restaurant that's open for lunch and dinner.

Bedouin Restaurant *(☎ 500 082)* Dishes E£20-65. Serving fish and mezze with a Bedouin touch, this place attracts tour groups as well as individuals.

Habiba Camp *(☎ 500 770)* Meals E£15-50. Open 11am-midnight. This beachfront restaurant south of Nuweiba City serves excellent buffet lunches.

Getting There & Away

Bus There is an East Delta Bus Co station at the port in Nuweiba (☎ 520 371), but getting a bus out of Nuweiba can be a bit confusing, especially if you're staying in nearby Tarabin. Buses going to or from Taba pass down the highway and turn at the hospital to do a circuit past the Helnan Holiday Camp and Dr Shishkebab, before heading out again and proceeding on their way. They usually also call in at the port, stopping at either the bus station or in front of the Motel Marina just opposite. You can pick the buses up at any of these places (you can certainly get off). However, if possible, make sure you check the routing for your specific bus with a local, as the pick-up points have been known to change.

Buses to Cairo leave the port at 9am, 11am (via Taba) and 3.30pm. Tickets cost E£50 in the morning and E£55 in the afternoon. Tickets to Taba cost E£10 and there are buses at 6am (continuing to Suez), noon and 1pm, in addition to the 11am Cairo service. There is an 8am bus to St Katherine (E£10) and services to Sharm el-Sheikh (E£20) via Dahab (E£10) at 5.30am, 8am, 10am, 2.30pm and 4pm. The afternoon buses also call in at Helnan hotel.

Car Rental vehicles are available from Europcar at the Hilton Coral Resort.

Service Taxi There is a big service taxi station by the port but unless you get there when the ferry has arrived from Aqaba in the afternoon, you'll have to wait a long time for the car to fill up. If you are in luck, it costs E£25 to go to Sharm or St Katherine (or E£150 for the entire car), E£12 to Dahab (E£80 if you are alone) and E£60 to Cairo.

As Tarabin's popularity has escalated, service taxis here take people directly out on the road north to Israel & the Palestinian Territories or south to Dahab, St Katherine's Monastery or Sharm el-Sheikh.

Boat For detailed information about ferries and speedboats to Aqaba in Jordan, see Jordan under Sea in the Getting There & Away chapter.

Getting Around

In Tarabin, service taxis ask an outrageous E£5 to E£10 for the few kilometres between Tarabin and Nuweiba City, and E£15 to E£20 to the port. The only other option here for getting to one of the bus stops in Nuweiba City is to walk the 2km.

AROUND NUWEIBA

Another popular destination, **Ain al-Furtega**, is a palm-filled oasis some 16km north of Nuweiba, and easily accessible by regular car. **Mayat el-Wishwashi** is a large cistern hidden between two boulders in a canyon. It used to be the largest cistern in Sinai; it now only has a trickle of water, except after floods. Close by is **Mayat Malkha**, a palm grove fed by the waters of Mayat el-Wishwashi and set amid colourful sandstone. It is accessible by camel or on foot only. **Wadi Huweiyit** is a colourful sandstone canyon with lookouts giving panoramic views over to Saudi Arabia. It is accessible by 4WD and camel. **Ain Hudra** (more properly called Ain Khudra or 'the Green Spring') is where Miriam was supposed to have been struck by leprosy for criticising Moses. Famously beautiful, it is an easy day trip by 4WD vehicle, or a longer trip by camel. The picturesque **Ain Umm Ahmed** is the largest oasis in eastern Sinai, with lots of palms, Bedouin houses and a famous stream that becomes an icy river in the winter months. It can be visited by camel or 4WD. Further afield, **Wadi Sheikh Atiya** is named after the father of the Tarabin tribe – the largest tribe in the area – who lies buried here under a white dome. There is an oasis here and Bedouin frequently come on pilgrimage. **Gebel Barga** is a mountain that is difficult to climb yet affords stunning views over the mountains of eastern Sinai.

Almost every camp and supermarket in Tarabin offers these trips, but take care that whoever you pick is a local Bedouin – not only are they marginalised by tour operators from the Nile Valley and therefore need the work, but there have been some nasty tales of travellers lost without water in the desert because their so-called guides didn't know where they were going. Travellers have recommended Am Salem at Moonland Camp, who charges about E£90 per day for a camel trip, including food and water, for a minimum of three days. Jeep trips are marginally cheaper. Also worth contacting is Salama at the Mondial supermarket (☎ 500 108), who does trips for about E£70 per day including food, camels and a guide, but not water. Other Bedouin guides can also be hired at Basata, the recommended camps in Bir Sweir, or at a small hut on the highway near Ras Shaitan, where many of the trips begin (see Beach Camps under the Nuweiba to Taba later in this chapter).

Abanoub Travel *(☎ 520 201, fax 520 206, Mizena)* Jeep treks US$35 per person per day including food, camel treks US$45. Dr Rabiya, the owner of the agency, has lived in Sinai for years and works with local Bedouin. He is also affiliated with Wind, Sand and Stars, a British agency that specialises in environmentally aware treks through Sinai.

For more information on jeep and safari options, see the boxed text 'Desert Safaris' in the Western Oases chapter).

Before choosing a guide, keep in mind that if you want to go into the high mountain area of central south Sinai, better for hiking on foot, you can also arrange Bedouin guides from St Katherine. Remember also that most areas listed here are within the confines of either the St Katherine or Taba Protectorates, so their rules apply (see the boxed text 'St Katherine Protectorate' later in the chapter for more information).

NUWEIBA TO TABA

☎ 069

Along the stunning coastline north of Nuweiba, especially near Taba, are many large, expensive 'tourist villages' in various stages of completion. Although most of them have been designed with at least some modesty (no skyscrapers here), they mar the wild beauty of this desert coast, as indeed will the planeloads and busloads of package tourists they are hoping to attract.

Beach Camps

There are still some empty beaches backed by stunning blue waters and pockets of fringing reefs to be found along this stretch of road, but they are becoming rare with the race to cover the entire coastline with wall-to-wall resorts. Controversially, many of the Bedouin were turfed off their land here to make way for large developers, and the small camps with huts have been forced into what the Ministry of Tourism terms 'clusters'. Driving along the road it's often difficult to distinguish where one cluster ends and another begins, but these places remain laid-back and quiet. Unless otherwise noted, they all charge between E£10 to E£20 per person in a hut. The only way to get to them is by service taxi, hitching, or bus (but you'll probably have to pay the full Nuweiba to Taba fare).

Maagana Beach About 8km north of Nuweiba, you will find the first cluster of camps, with names such as ***Freedom Beach***, ***Bedaya*** and ***Blue Wave***. Although the beach is nice, it is close to the road and exposed to wind.

Ras Shaitan No more than 3km on lies a rocky point jutting out into the water point that is known locally as Ras Shaitan (Satan's Head). On its northern side is a group of simple Bedouin-run camps.

Ayyash Camp *(mobile ☎ 010-575 6064)* This place is owned by a local Bedouin and has Bedouin tents and simple huts, but no electricity.

Castle Beach *(mobile ☎ 012-317 4754)* This camp sits beside the 'ras' or point. Run by a local Bedouin and his Israeli wife, a large wall and the beginnings of construction mean that it may transform itself into a hotel but for now it retains its calm air.

Mahash About 20km north of Nuweiba lies another camp cluster on a nice beach. Many of the camps here are new and are trying to conform to Ministry of Tourism requirements, which gives them a uniform look. Nevertheless, some of them are pleasant places to spend a couple of days. ***Yasmina Camp***, ***Eden Camp*** and ***Mayyan*** are owned by local Bedouin, while the popular ***Escapeland*** is run by Sudanese.

Bawaki Beach Hotel *(☎ 500 470)* Singles/doubles US$30/40. About 3km further on is this quite isolated three-star hotel where you can walk virtually from your beachfront hut straight into some great snorkelling sites.

Basata *(☎ 500 481, in Cairo ☎ 02-358 1829, Nuweiba-Taba road)* Bamboo huts E£30 per person, beach sleep E£15 per person. You can come and use the beach here if the hotel is not crowded, but there is a E£10 daily entrance charge. This is one of the most famous hotels/camps in Sinai and is about 23km north of Nuweiba. Basata means 'simplicity' in Arabic, and this simple, clean, ecologically minded travellers' settlement reflects its name. Owner Sherif Ghamrawy is an environmentalist who recently started Nuweiba's first recycling program. His concern for the environment is reflected in the philosophy of the hotel, where the produce is organically grown and guests separate their garbage into marked bins for recycling. There are 18 huts, a common kitchen hut, a bakery and a camping ground. There is great snorkelling in the bay, but scuba diving is not allowed. It's advisable to book ahead as it gets very crowded on Egyptian and Israeli holidays.

Club Aquasun *(☎ 530 392, fax 530 390, Nuweiba-Taba road)* Singles/doubles/triples US$24/35/40. About 5km north of Basata is this 90-room resort. Like most of these beach hotels/camps it has a great beach and wonderful reef. It's also a good place to arrange jeep or camel safaris to the interior. Just beyond it is its newer spin off, ***Aquasun Ghazaly***, which has beach huts and a dive centre. Prices include breakfast.

Sally Land Holiday Village *(☎ 530 380, fax 530 381, Nuweiba-Taba road)* Singles/doubles US$50/65. This two-star village just beyond Aquasun is frequented by New Age tourists from Europe who have meditation sessions on the beach. Prices include breakfast.

Bir Sweir Some 35km south of Taba, just beyond Sally Land, is another row of camps on a lovely beach. With names such as ***Sayal***, ***Nirvana*** and ***Lama Beach***, they charge the usual E£15 to E£20 per person in a hut. Most have no electricity.

Taba Heights

A massive development 17km south of Taba, Taba Heights is a grouping of luxury hotels, not all of which are currently up and running, along a 5km stretch of beach. When complete it will house a casino, numerous shops, bars, restaurants, a medical clinic and extensive water-sports facilities, making it a highlight of thc Egyptian plans to create a 'Red Sea Riviera'. To see more, check its Web site at W www.tabaheights.com.

Hyatt Regency *(in Cairo ☎ 02-574 8474, fax 574 913)* Rooms from US$150. This is a tasteful desert pastel hotel designed by the American designer and architect Michael Graves. It features balconies, modem jacks, minibars, children's facilities, three pools and a large health centre.

Inter-Continental *(in Cairo ☎ 02-570 2373, fax 570 2358)* Another Michael Graves–designed hotel, this time in a vaguely Moorish vein; it's due to open in mid-2001. All the usual facilities, including tennis and squash courts and a Turkish bath.

The Fjord

This small, protected bay is a natural harbour and popular sunbathing spot about 15km south of Taba.

Salima Motel *(☎ 530 130/1, Nuweiba-Taba road)* Singles/doubles E£40/60. The motel is up on the rise to the north of the bay and run by the amiable Mohammed Magdi. It has six basic rooms with none-too-clean bathrooms. Note that the phone usually works only in the evenings. Meals are available and breakfast/lunch/dinner cost E£10/20/25.

Pharaoh's Island

Only 7km short of Taba, Pharaoh's Island *(Gezirat Fara'un; adult/child US$6/3; open 9am-5pm daily)* lies about 250m off the Egyptian coast. The islet is dominated by the much restored Castle of Salah ad-Din, a fortress actually built by the Crusaders in 1115, but captured and expanded by Saladin in 1170 as a bulwark against feared Crusader penetration south from Palestine. At the height of Crusader successes, it was feared they might attempt to head for the holy cities of Mecca and Medina. Some of the modern restoration is painfully obvious (concrete was not a prime building material in Saladin's time), but the island is a pleasant place for a half-day trip. The limpid aqua waters are extremely inviting, and a lot of Israeli pleasure boats carrying divers cruise down here from nearby Eilat. From the island you can see the Taba Hilton and the port city of Aqaba in Jordan.

A return boat ride to the island is an outlandish US$4. Tickets for the boat are available in the cafeteria next to the Salah ad-Din Hotel, and tickets for the island are available on landing.

Salah ad-Din Hotel *(☎ 530 340/2, fax 530 343)* Singles/doubles US$35/45. Opposite Pharaoh's Island, this hotel has 120 low-key rooms. All have air-con and bath and there's a restaurant where dinner is served for US$15. There is also a fairly pricey cafe on Pharaoh's Island.

TABA

☎ 069

Until 1989, Taba – a few hundred metres of beach, a luxury hotel and a coffee shop on the Israel-Egypt border – was a minor point of contention between the two countries. After several years of squabbling and formal arbitration, the land was returned to Egypt. Since 1982, when the rest of Sinai was returned by Israel, Taba has served as a busy border crossing. The border is open 24 hours a day, except from sunset Friday to Saturday night, the Jewish Sabbath.

There is a small post and telephone office in the 'town', along with a hospital, bakery and an EgyptAir office (often closed). You can change money at booths of Banque du Caire (which has unreliable opening hours) and Banque Masr (open 24 hours), both 100m before the border, or at the Taba Hilton Hotel.

Places to Stay & Eat

Taba Hilton *(☎ 530 300, in Cairo fax 02-578 7044, Taba Beach)* Singles/doubles US$160/208. This 11-storey luxury hotel dominates the surrounding landscape and has a diving centre.

Nelson Village *(☎ 530 140, fax 530 301, Taba Beach)* Singles/doubles US$185/233. This is a pricey new addition to the Hilton complex.

There's not a lot on offer when it comes to eating. There are a few cafes and some overpriced supermarkets around the bus station, and there's an even more overpriced mall across the road with a small restaurant where you can get meals for E£3 to E£10.

Getting There & Away

Air EgyptAir has flights from Cairo to Ras an-Naqb airport, 38km from Taba, each Monday for E£547.40. Once the gigantic

SINAI

Taba Heights development gets working, Orascom Air will also have flights here.

Bus East Delta Bus Co (☎ 530 250) has a kiosk a couple of hundred metres from the border and runs several buses from Taba. Buses to Nuweiba (E£10) leave at 7am, 7.30 am, 9am, 1pm, 2pm and 3pm. The 7am continues to St Katherine (E£25) and Suez (E£45). Buses to Cairo leave at 7.30am (E£50), 9am (E£50) and 2pm (E£70). Buses to Sharm el-Sheikh (E£25) via Dahab (E£20) leave at 8.30am, 1pm and 3pm.

Getting Around

Car The only rental car option here is Europcar (☎ 379 222, fax 379 660) at the Taba Hilton.

Service Taxi Peugeot taxis and minibuses congregate by the border crossing waiting for passengers. If business is slack (as in 2001), you may have a long wait for the vehicle to fill up. Alternatively, you can bargain to pay the equivalent of all seven fares and leave immediately. Getting to Nuweiba costs E£10 per person, to Dahab E£25 and to Sharm el-Sheikh E£40. St Katherine is E£45, while to Cairo you're looking at E£50 to E£60 per person. Your bargaining power increases if the bus is not too far off.

SINAI

ST KATHERINE'S MONASTERY

☎ 069

There are 22 Greek Orthodox monks living in this ancient monastery at the foot of Mt Sinai near Al-Milga village. The monastic order was founded in the 4th century AD by the Roman empress Helena, who had a small chapel built beside what was believed to be the burning bush from which God spoke to Moses.

The chapel is dedicated to St Katherine, the legendary martyr of Alexandria, who was tortured on a spiked wheel and then beheaded for her Christianity. Her body was supposedly transported by angels away from the torture device (which spun out of control and killed the pagan onlookers) and onto the slopes of Gebel Katarina, the highest mountain in Egypt, which is about 6km south of Mt Sinai. The body was 'found' about 300 years later by monks from the monastery.

In the 6th century, Emperor Justinian ordered the building of a fortress, with a basilica and a monastery, as well as the original chapel, to serve as a secure home for the monks of St Katherine's and as a refuge for the Christians of southern Sinai. Since then it has been visited by Christian pilgrims from throughout the world, many of whom braved extremely difficult and dangerous journeys in order to get to this isolated place.

Nowadays, the hazards accompanying a trip here have disappeared and the monastery and Mt Sinai can be choked with tour buses and people, especially in the morning. When you visit, remember that this is still a functioning monastery, not a museum piece. The only parts of the monastery to which members of the public are admitted are the chapel and a rather macabre room full of the bones of deceased monks; you are also permitted to view part of a splendid collection of icons and jewelled crosses. St Katherine's Monastery is open to visitors from 9am to noon Monday to Saturday except on holidays.

Orientation & Information

The monastery is about 3.5km from the village of Al-Milga (which is also called Katreen but known as the 'Meeting Place' by local Jabaliyya Bedouin), or 2km from the large roundabout on the road between the two. At Al-Milga there is a bank, telephone centrale (open 24 hours), police station, tourist police office (next to the mosque), several hotels and a variety of shops and cafes. The Banque Masr will change cash or travellers cheques and may accept Visa and MasterCard for a cash advance. It's open from 9am to 2pm and 6pm to 9pm daily.

Mt Sinai

Although some archaeologists and historians dispute Mt Sinai's biblical claim to fame, it is revered by Christians, Muslims and Jews, all of whom believe that God delivered his Ten Commandments to Moses at its summit.

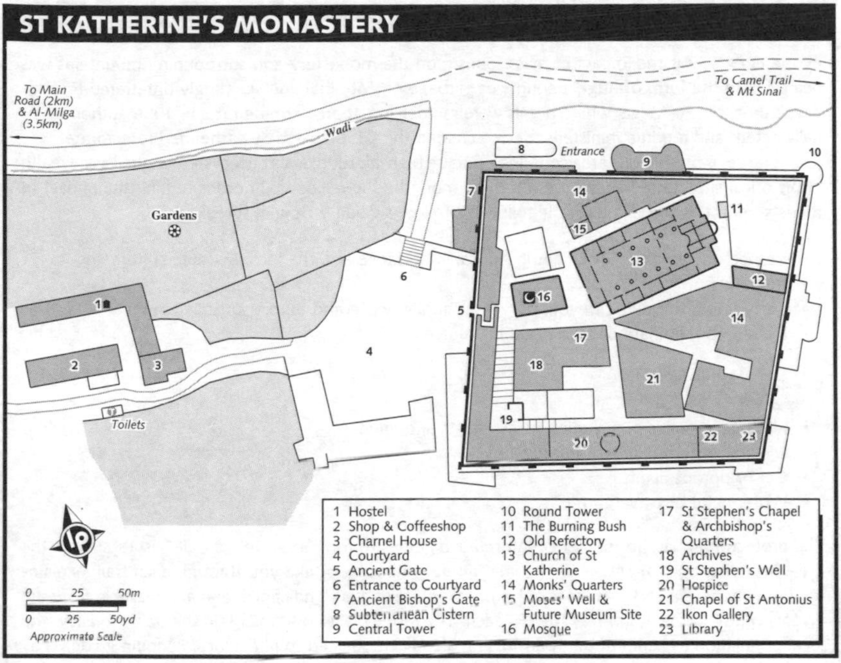

At a height of 2285m, Mt Sinai (Gebel Musa is the local name) towers over St Katherine's Monastery. It is easy to climb and there are two well-defined routes to the summit – the camel trail and the Steps of Repentance. Mt Sinai is not, however, the mountain directly up the valley behind the monastery; that one is far lower! And from the top of Mt Sinai you can look across to the even higher summit of Gebel Katarina.

The camel trail is the easier route; this takes about two hours. Usually there are at least four or five tea and Coca-Cola stands on the trail for those who need caffeine. At the stand where the camel trail meets the steps, a full breakfast is sometimes available.

The alternative path to the summit, the taxing 3750 Steps of Repentance, was laid by one monk as a form of penance. If you want to try both routes, it's best to take the path on the way up and the steps on the way back down, particularly if you want a great view of the monastery.

During the summer, you should avoid the heat by beginning your hike at 2am or 3am. This way, you'll also see the sunrise. Although stone signs have been placed on the trail to guide you, it can be a bit difficult in parts, so a torch (flashlight) is essential.

Because of the sanctity of the mountains and the tremendous pressure that large groups place on the desert environment, the Egyptian National Parks Office has instituted a few much-needed rules. Apart from the basic trekkers code (see the boxed text 'St Katherine Protectorate'), if you spend the night on the mountain, you are asked to sleep just below the summit at the small plateau known as Elijah's Basin. It is dominated by a 500-year-old cypress tree, marking the spot where the prophet Elijah heard the voice of God. Five composting toilets have been put here to prevent pollution of the site. You can climb to the summit to watch the sunrise.

If you do plan to spend the night on the summit, make sure you have plenty of food

St Katherine Protectorate

By the early 1990s the impact of mass tourism on the monastery and surrounding mountains was being felt in the form of huge amounts of garbage on Mt Sinai and seemingly unfettered touristic development in Al-Milga, where hotels were multiplying at an alarming rate. In 1996 authorities finally acted, and a prime ministerial decree created the 4350-sq-km St Katherine Protectorate.

This large, mountainous area contains a unique high-altitude desert ecosystem as well as a wealth of historical sites sacred to the world's three monotheistic religions. In order to limit the impact of tourists upon this special place, the following Trekkers Code is now in force:

- Respect the area's religious and historical importance and the local Bedouin culture and traditions.
- Carry your litter out with you, bury your bodily waste and burn your toilet paper.
- Do not contaminate or overuse water sources.

It is illegal to:

- Remove any object, including rocks, plants and animals.
- Disturb or harm animals or birds.
- Cut or uproot plants.
- Write, paint or carve graffiti.

The protectorate has also published informative guides to four 'interpretive trails' established in the area, including one for Mt Sinai. The well-produced booklets take you through each trail, explaining flora and fauna as well as sites of historical and religious significance, and are available from the visitors centre at the monastery for E£5 each. The money is used to maintain the trails. To allow the local population to benefit from tourism, you are also requested to hire a local Bedouin guide. They can be found in Al-Milga and charge about E£20 to E£30 for a half-day's walk. Also on sale at the visitors centre is *Wild Sinai*, an illustrative booklet describing the wildlife of the area. An interactive CD-ROM with maps and pictures of key sites, flora and fauna will also be available soon.

and water. As it gets cold and windy, even in summer, you will also need warm clothes and a sleeping bag (there is no space to pitch a tent). Sometimes you can rent a blanket for E£1 to E£2. As late as mid-May, be prepared to share the summit with hordes of tourists, some bearing stereos, others carrying Bibles and hymn books. With the music and singing, and people nudging each other for a space on the holy mountain, don't expect to get much sleep, especially in the wee small hours before sunrise.

On the summit itself are a Greek Orthodox chapel containing beautiful paintings and ornaments, and a small mosque. However, these were so desecrated by tourists in the 1980s that they're usually kept locked. The summit also offers spectacular views of the surrounding bare, jagged mountains and plunging valleys where, throughout the day, the rocks and cliffs change colour as if they were stone chameleons.

Trekking Around St Katherine

Sitting in the centre of South Sinai's high mountain region, St Katherine is the ideal place to begin a mountain trek. These can be as short as a half day or as long as a week (or more if you prefer). Much of the terrain is too rugged for vehicles, so treks are done either on camel or on foot. Even if you decide to walk, you'll need at least one camel for your food and baggage.

One of the most common circuits goes to the **Galt al-Azraq** (Blue Pools) and takes three or four days. The trail leaves Al-Milga via the man-made **Abu Giffa Pass** and goes through **Wadi Tubug**, taking a detour around **Wadi Shagg**, where there are springs, water holes and lush, walled gardens or *bustans*. The walk then goes through the picturesque **Wadi Zuweitin** (Valley of the Olives), where there are ancient olive trees said by local Bedouin to have been planted by the founder of the Jebaliyya tribe. The first night is usually spent here and there is a small stone hut in which hikers can sometimes sleep. The hike continues through **Wadi Gibal**, through high passes and along the valleys of **Farsh Asara** and **Farsh Arnab**. Many hikers then climb either **Ras Abu Alda** or **Gebel Abu Gasba**, before heading to the spring of **Ein Nagila** and the ruins of a Byzantine monastery at **Bab ad-Dunya** (Gate of the World). On the third day the trail leads to the crystal clear, icy waters of the **Galt al-Azraq**, a deep, dramatic pool in the rock. On the fourth day the trail leads through more dramatic wadis to a camel pass on **Gebel Abbas Basha**. A one-hour hike up a fairly easy, if steep path, leads to the ruined palace that the 19th-century viceroy Abbas Hilmi I built here. The panoramic views at the summit (2304m) are awesome. The trail then goes back to Wadi Zuweitin and retraces its way to Al-Milga.

Some other destinations include **Sheikh Awad**, where there are a Sheikh's tomb and Bedouin settlement; the **Nugra Waterfall**, a difficult-to-reach, rain-fed cascade some 20m high, which is reached through a winding canyon called **Wadi Nugra**; and **Naqb al-Faria'**, a camel path with rock inscriptions. Shorter trips include hiking to the top of **Gebel Katarina**, Egypt's highest peak at 2642m. It takes about five hours to reach the summit along a reasonably easy, but tiring, trail. The views from the top are breathtaking, and the panorama can even include the mountains of Saudi Arabia on a clear day. The **Blue Valley**, given its name after a Belgian artist painted the rocks here blue some years ago, is another popular day trip.

All treks must be done with a Bedouin guide and most are arranged through **Sheikh Musa**, a member of the local Jabaliyya tribe, whose office is in Al-Milga, a few hundred metres from the shops and banks that form the touristic centre. He will take your passport, register you with the police and arrange a guide from the local Jabaliyya tribe for E£50 per day. E£50 more goes to Sheikh Musa and camels cost E£50 per day each. He can also provide food and utensils at a negotiable price, usually around E£30 per day. You can buy firewood here at E£1 per kilo (sold by the protectorate to discourage destruction of the few trees in the mountains). Other guides can be found at the Fox of the Desert Camp (see Places to Stay) or at Sheikh Hamed, near the turn-off to Nuweiba. It is also worth picking up the protectorate's trail guides to Gebel Abbas Pasha, Gebel Safsafa, and Wadi I'tlah and Wadi Tala' (see the boxed text 'St Katherine Protectorate' earlier for more information). They are designed to complement a Bedouin guide and give historical and ecological background to help you get even more out of your trip.

Whoever you go with, make sure you bring water purification tablets, unless you want to rely on the mountain springs. You'll also need good, comfortable walking boots, a hat and sunglasses, sun block, a warm jacket, a good sleeping bag and toilet paper. Keep in mind that it can get very cold at night – frost, and even snow, are common in the winter.

A simple **ecolodge** adapted from an old Bedouin stone hut is due to open in Sheikh Awad at the end of 2001. Established by St Katherine Protectorate but run by Bedouin, it is designed to give basic shelter to trekkers in the area. Call the office in St Katherine (☎ 470 032) for information about reservations and prices.

Places to Stay

Fox of the Desert Camp *(☎ 470 344, fax 470 034, Al-Milga)* E£10 per person in room or Bedouin tent; E£5 per person camping. St Katherine's only budget option, this new camp is run by local Bedouin, Soliman and Farag al-Gebaly. It is a calm, relaxed place with simple but clean facilities and friendly staff. Located about 200m from the main roundabout, Farag also does desert safaris for about E£75 per person each day, with a minimum of 3 people.

Monastery Hostel *(☎ 470 353, fax 470 343, St Katherine's Monastery)* Beds in 5-bed dorm US$20, singles/doubles US$35/60. This is one of the better options in town, but no longer the cheap place it used to be. Recently renovated, comfortable rooms have baths; prices are for half board. Heaters and blankets are provided to keep out the mountain chill. Meals are reasonable and you can get beer and wine in the restaurant. The hostel will sometimes let you leave your baggage in one of the rooms while you hike up Mt Sinai.

St Katherine's Tourist Village *(☎ 470 333, fax 470 325, Al-Milga)* Singles/doubles US$75/100. This hotel has bungalow-style rooms that blend in with the surrounding landscape, right by the roundabout 2km west of the monastery. The air-con rooms, all with TV and bathroom, have views of the distant monastery; prices include breakfast and dinner.

Daniela Village *(☎/fax 470 379, Al-Milga)* Singles/doubles US$44/56. This three-star hotel has comfortable rooms in stone bungalows, a restaurant and one of the only bars in town; prices include breakfast.

Al-Wadi al-Mouqudus *(☎/fax 470 225, Al-Milga)* Singles/doubles E£120/150. This two-star hotel is next door to Daniela Village; prices include breakfast.

Catherine Plaza Hotel *(☎ 470 289, fax 470 292, Al-Milga)* Singles/doubles half board US$60/90. A totally incongruous and flashy 128-room place, this hotel has a pool and several restaurants and bars.

Morgenland Village *(☎ 470 331, in Cairo fax 02-356 4104)* Singles/doubles US$80/102. In the unlikely event that other places are full, this inconveniently located tourist village 6km along the Nuweiba road has stone bungalow-style rooms.

Places to Eat

In Al-Milga there's a ***bakery*** opposite the mosque and a couple of well-stocked ***supermarkets*** in the shopping arcade. Just behind the bakery are a few simple restaurants. Other than these, your only option is to eat at one of the hotels.

Kafeteria Ikhlas *(☎ 470 455, Al-Milga)* Dishes E£6-15. This simple and friendly restaurant with carpets and low tables under palm fronds serves good hearty breakfasts and chicken, rice and vegetable meals. It is located behind the mosque, next to the bakery.

Katrien Rest House *(☎ 470 374, Al-Milga)* Dishes E£1-10. Open for lunch & dinner. Just by the bus stop, this restaurant serves filling chicken, rice and vegetable meals either inside or on a veranda.

Shopping

Authentic Bedouin crafts are sold at a fair-trade shop called **Bedouin House**. Supported by the St Katherine Protectorate, it is the first company owned and run by Bedouin women and sells embroidery, bead jewellery and stone carvings. It is open 9am to 3pm daily except Friday; contact the protectorate (☎ 450 155) for details.

Getting There & Away

Bus You can ask the driver to drop you off at the roundabout, which is closer to the monastery. Buses leave from the square in front of the mosque in Al-Milga. There is a bus to Cairo at 6am (E£50) and another at 1pm that goes via Dahab (E£10), Nuweiba (E£15) and Taba (E£20) before heading to Cairo via Nakhl.

Service Taxi These travel in and out of the village irregularly and infrequently. If you are lucky, you might be able to find a taxi driver who is willing to take you all the way to Cairo for about E£300 for the taxi (up to seven people). A similar taxi to Suez will cost about E£200, after intense bargaining. At the monastery taxis often wait for people coming down from Mt Sinai in the early afternoon. Count on between E£10 and E£20 per person to Dahab or Nuweiba.

WADI FEIRAN

This long valley serves as the main drainage route for the entire high mountain into the

Gulf of Suez. Sinai's largest oasis, it is lush and very beautiful, containing more than 12,000 date palms, and Bedouin from all Sinai's tribes. Stone walls surround the date palms and the bustans, and the rocky mountains on each side of the wadi have subtly different colours that stand out at sunrise and sunset, making the landscape even more dramatic.

Feiran has a Biblical significance, as it is reputed to be the first Christian stronghold in Sinai. An extensively rebuilt early Christian convent remains from this time, although you need permission from St Katherine's Monastery if you want to visit.

The valley is also a good spot from which to trek into the surrounding mountains. To the south, Gebel Serbal (2070m high and thought by early Christians to have been the real Mt Sinai) is a challenging six-hour hike along a track also known as Ssikket ar-Reshshah. Those who persevere are rewarded with fantastic panoramic views.

St Katherine's Protectorate is hoping to open a Bedouin tourist office here in the near future to help arrange for treks in the area.

AL-ARISH

☎ 068

Much of the north coast of Sinai, from Port Fuad most of the way to Al-Arish, is dominated by the swampy lagoon of Lake Bardawil, separated from the Mediterranean by a limestone ridge, making the area hardly attractive for swimming. The road follows what must be one of history's oldest march routes, used by the pharaohs to penetrate into what is now Israel & the Palestinian Territories and then on to Jordan and Syria, and by the Persians, Greeks, Crusaders, Arab Muslims and many others coming the other way.

Al-Arish, beyond Lake Bardawil, is the capital of North Sinai Governorate and has a population of about 40,000. Its greatest asset, a palm-fringed beach, is becoming increasingly fragmented by expanding construction along the coast. The place, at present, is not heavily visited by either Egyptians or foreign tourists, except in the height of summer, when middle-class Cairo moves in en masse.

Orientation & Information

The main coastal road, Sharia Fuad Zikry, forms a T-junction with Sharia 23rd of July, which runs a couple of kilometres south (changing name to Sharia Tahrir on the way) to the bus and service taxi stations.

The tourist police office (☎ 361 016) is next to a tourist information kiosk on Sharia Fuad Zikry, just down from the Sinai Beach Hotel. There is little information on offer, however, and opening hours are erratic.

The National Bank of Egypt, on Sharia Tahrir, is open from 9am to 2.30pm Sunday to Thursday. Nearby, a street back from Sharia Tahrir, is Banque Masr. The Bank of Alexandria and Banque du Caire both have branches on Sharia 23rd of July.

The post office, open from 8.30am to 2.30pm Saturday to Thursday, is a block east of Banque Masr. The 24-hour telephone centrale is around the corner from the post office.

There is a public hospital (☎ 360 010, which is to be avoided except in the direst emergencies. The Mubarak Military Hospital (☎ 324 018), near the governorate building, is a better bet. For an ambulance call ☎ 123.

Things to See & Do

The **Zerenike Protectorate** *(admission US$5 per person; open sunrise-sunset)* is a haven for migrating birds that was established by the Egyptian National Parks Office in 1985. It covers a 220-sq-km area running along the coast from the eastern part of Lake Bardawil until about 25km east of Al-Arish. The entrance to the protectorate is about 35km east of Al-Arish. Inside the gates there is a visitors centre with a cafeteria and information about the protectorate and some of the many species of birds that stop here on their journey between Europe and Africa.

The **Sinai Heritage Museum** *(Coast road; admission E£1; camera/video E£5/25; open 9.30am-2pm Sat-Thur)*, on the coastal road to Rafah on the outskirts of Al-Arish, was established several years ago to inform people about life in Sinai. The museum's displays include items such as

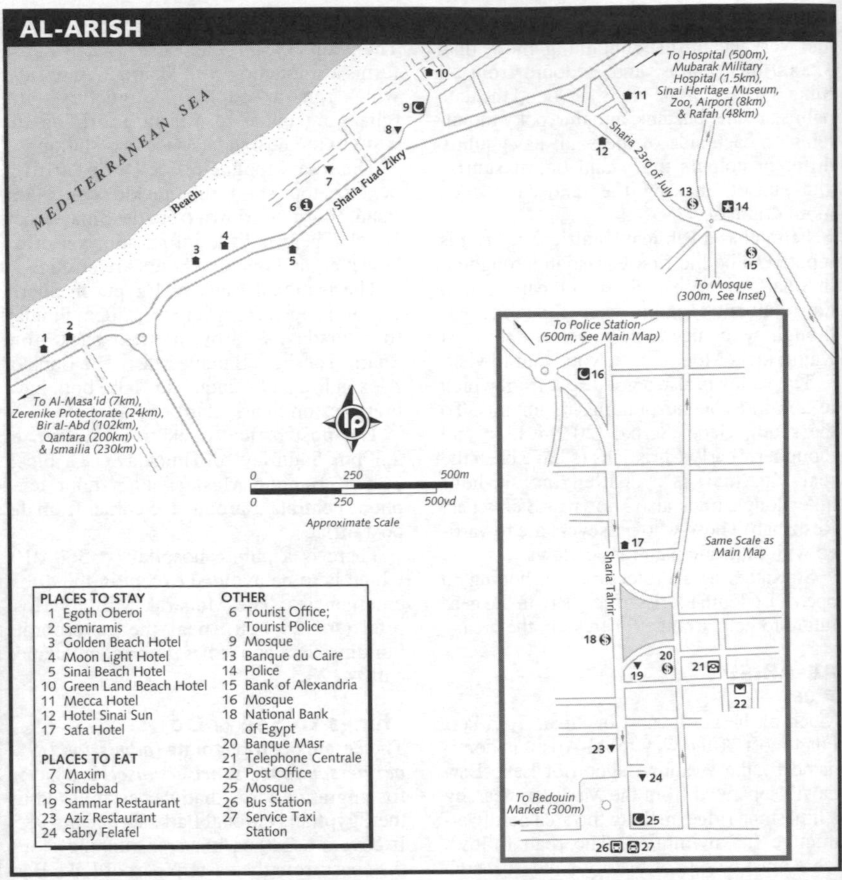

Bedouin handicrafts, tools, clothing and traditional medicines, supplemented by the odd English explanation.

Next door is a miserable **zoo**; among its unhappy inmates is a range of nocturnal desert creatures that are kept in barred cages, unprotected from the blazing sun. There's not even a darkened antechamber where they can secrete themselves. This is simply a disgrace.

Every Thursday, when the **souq** is held in the oldest part of town, Bedouin come in from the desert in pick-up trucks or on camels. The veiled women trade silver, beadwork and embroidered dresses, while the men sell camel saddles. Although the crafts can be fine, the savvy women save their best items for the large numbers of middlemen who buy up their wares for Cairo shops. They tend to palm off substandard stuff to tourists. Still, it is a sight to see the women arrive and bargain. Sometimes you can see them buying gold after having sold their handiwork.

The other main attraction is the **beach**. The parade of palms, fine white sand and clean water (even the odd small wave) make this one of the nicer Mediterranean spots in Egypt. As is unfortunately so often the case, women may feel somewhat uncomfortable swimming here unless they're in the confines of the Oberoi. There is supposedly a beach curfew after dark.

Places to Stay – Budget

***Golden Beach Hotel** (☎ 362 270, Sharia Fuad Zikry)* Beds in 3-bed dorm E£15. A conglomeration of drab cement bungalows makes up this place. It also has cold showers.

***Moon Light Hotel** (☎ 341 362, Sharia Fuad Zikry)* Singles/doubles E£15/30. This hotel is well placed on the beach with newly renovated rooms. Prices include breakfast.

***Mecca Hotel** (☎ 352 632 fax, 352 632, Sharia Al-Salam)* Singles/doubles E£38/48. Behind the New Golden Beach Hotel off Sharia Fuad Zikry is this friendly, good, clean place that has rooms with fan and hot water. Prices include breakfast.

***Safa Hotel** (☎ 353 798, Sharia 23rd of July)* Singles/doubles E£15/20. This hotel has reasonable rooms with bath and fan. There's a roof restaurant from which you can just about see the beach.

***Green Land Beach Hotel** (☎ 360 601, Sharia Fuad Zikry)* Singles/doubles E£40/60. Virtually on the beach, this is one of the better deals. Most of the clean and comfortable rooms have terraces and all have bathrooms. Prices include breakfast.

Places to Stay – Mid-Range & Top End

***Hotel Sinai Sun** (☎/fax 361 855, Sharia 23rd of July)* Singles/doubles Oct-May US$14/18, June-mid-Sept US$21/25. This is a reasonable place and the rooms come with bath, TV, phone and air-con. Breakfast is E£5.

***Sinai Beach Hotel** (☎/fax 361 713, Sharia Fuad Zikry)* Singles/doubles US$30/35. This hotel is slightly better than Hotel Sinai Sun, with balconies overlooking the sea in some rooms. It also has a restaurant and a coffee shop, and breakfast is included in the price.

***Semiramis** (☎/fax 364 167, Sharia Fuad Zikry)* Singles/doubles US$45/60. This hotel has comfortable rooms, but they are not great because most are away from the beach; the suites facing the sea are much more expensive. Prices include breakfast. The pool costs E£15 for nonguests.

***Egoth Oberoi** (☎ 351 321, fax 352 352, Sharia Fuad Zikry)* Singles/doubles US$103/128. This is the only five-star hotel in north Sinai. All rooms have sea views, balconies and the usual amenities. The Oberoi also has sandpit therapy for rheumatism, fresh- and sea-water pools and the only bar in town. Those not staying at the hotel can use the pool for E£30.

Places to Eat

There's not a huge range of places to eat in Al-Arish. Apart from the Oberoi and summer resorts, most are fairly basic, nondescript kofta places where no alcohol is served.

***Aziz Restaurant** (Sharia Tahrir)* Meals E£2-10. This is about the best you'll find in the budget range. Aziz serves good meals of fuul and ta'amiyya as well as grilled chicken, kofta, rice and spaghetti. It is also open for breakfast.

***Sabry Felafel** (Sharia Tahrir)* Dishes 50pt-E£5. Opposite Aziz Restaurant in the back corner of a little square, you'll find the best ta'amiyya in town at Sabry.

***Sammar Restaurant** (Sharia Tahrir)* Dishes E£5-20. This kofta and kebab joint is signposted in Arabic.

***Sindebad** (Sharia Fuad Zikry)* Dishes 50pt-E£3. This is another popular fuul and ta'amiyya place.

***Maxim** (☎ 340 850)* Dishes £25-40. This nice fish restaurant, among the palms on the beach, serves good food but is open in summer only.

Getting There & Away

Bus Buses for Cairo (five hours) leave Al-Arish at 7am (E£25) and 4pm (E£35). There are buses to Ismailia (E£7, three hours) via Qantara (E£5) almost hourly until 7pm. Some of these go on to Mansura (E£12), and the 7am, 7.45am, 9am and 3pm buses go to Zagazig (E£10). For Suez, you have to first go to Ismailia and take another bus from there.

There are buses to Rafah (E£2) at 7am, 10.30am and 3pm (although the schedule was about to change at the time of research, so this should be double-checked at the bus station). The bus bypasses Rafah town and takes you directly to the Egyptian border post, at which point you disembark with your bags and go through passport control. After this you are forced to take a shuttle bus to the border post for Israel and the Gaza Strip (you're prohibited from walking). You have to pay a tax of about E£18 before continuing on to Rafah.

Service Taxi A cheaper alternative to the expensive Sinai buses to Cairo is a service taxi, which costs about E£20 per person. Service taxis to Qantara cost E£5, to Ismailia E£6, and to the border (or vice versa) they like to charge anything from E£5 to E£7.

Getting Around

There is a regular stream of buses, microbuses and service taxis (huge US limousines dating back to the 1960s at least) running between the bus station and the satellite residential area of Al-Masa'id to the south-west. It'll cost you between E£3 and E£5 to take a taxi. Microbuses shuttle between the bus station and the beach for 25pt.

RAFAH

This coastal town, 48km north of Al-Arish, marks the border with the Gaza Strip and Israel. Although the town fathers apparently feel the warm Mediterranean location could make it an ideal resort, it has no hotels (there are some chalets). The nearest cheap hotel is in Sheikh Zuweid, 17km short of Rafah.

The border crossing is 4km from the town.

Getting There & Away

A couple of local buses run between Rafah town and Al-Arish for E£1. For border crossing details see the Getting There & Away chapter.

SINAI

Language

Arabic is the official language of Egypt. However, the Arabic spoken on the streets differs greatly from the standard Arabic written in newspapers, spoken on the radio or recited in prayers at the mosque.

Egyptian Colloquial Arabic (ECA) is fun, but difficult to learn. It is basically a dialect of the standard language but so different in many respects as to be virtually another language. As with most dialects, it is the everyday language that differs the most from that of Egypt's other Arabic-speaking neighbours. More specialised or educated language tends to be pretty much the same across the Arab world, although pronunciation may vary considerably. An Arab from, say, Jordan or Iraq, will have no problem having a chat about politics or literature with an Egyptian, but might have more trouble making themselves understood in the bakery.

There is no official written form of the Egyptian Arabic dialect, although there is no practical reason for this – Nobel Prize-winning author Naguib Mahfouz has no trouble writing out whole passages using predominantly Egyptian (or Cairene) slang. For some reason though, foreigners specifically wanting to learn the Egyptian dialect (instead of Modern Standard Arabic, or MSA, the written and spoken lingua franca common to all Arabic-speaking countries) are told that it can't be written, and then presented with one system or other of transliteration – none of them totally satisfactory. If you're getting a headache now, that will give you some idea of why few non-Arabs and non-Muslims embark on the study of the language.

Nevertheless, if you take the time to learn even a few words and phrases, you'll discover and experience much more while travelling through the country. For a more comprehensive guide to the language, get hold of Lonely Planet's *Egyptian Arabic phrasebook*.

Pronunciation

Pronunciation of Arabic can be somewhat tongue-tying for someone unfamiliar with the intonation and combination of sounds. Pronounce the transliterated words and phrases slowly and clearly.

The following guide should help, but it isn't complete because the myriad rules governing pronunciation and vowel use are too extensive to be covered here.

Short Vowels

a	as in 'had' (sometimes very short)
e	as in 'bet' (sometimes very short)
i	as in 'hit'
o	as in 'hot'
u	as the 'oo' in 'book'

Long Vowels

Long vowels are indicated by a macron (stroke above the letter).

ā	as the 'a' in 'father'
ē	as the 'e' in 'ten', but lengthened
ī	as the 'e' in 'ear', only softer
ō	as the 'o' in 'four'
ū	as the 'oo' in 'food'

You may also see long vowels transliterated as double vowels, eg, 'aa' (**ā**), 'ee' (**ī**) and 'oo' (**ū**).

Diphthongs

aw	as the 'ow' in 'how'
ay	as the 'y' in 'by'
ei	as the 'a' in 'cake'

These last two are tricky, as one can slide into the other in certain words, depending on who is pronouncing them. Remember these rules are an outline and are far from exhaustive.

Consonants

Pronunciation for all Arabic consonants is covered in the alphabet table on the following page. Note that when double consonants occur in transliterations, each consonant is

The Arabic Alphabet

Final	Medial	Initial	Alone	Transliteration	Pronunciation
ـا			ا	**ā**	as the 'a' in 'father'
ـب	ـبـ	بـ	ب	**b**	as in 'bet'
ـت	ـتـ	تـ	ت	**t**	as in 'ten'
ـث	ـثـ	ثـ	ث	**th**	as in 'thin'
ـج	ـجـ	جـ	ج	**g**	as in 'go'
ـح	ـحـ	حـ	ح	**H**	a strongly whispered 'h', almost like a sigh of relief
ـخ	ـخـ	خـ	خ	**kh**	as the 'ch' in Scottish *loch*
ـد			د	**d**	as in 'dim'
ـذ			ذ	**dh**	as the 'th' in 'this'
ـر			ر	**r**	a rolled 'r', as in the Spanish word *caro*
ـز			ز	**z**	as in 'zip'
ـس	ـسـ	سـ	س	**s**	as in 'so', never as in 'wisdom'
ـش	ـشـ	شـ	ش	**sh**	as in 'ship'
ـص	ـصـ	صـ	ص	**ṣ**	emphatic 's'
ـض	ـضـ	ضـ	ض	**ḍ**	emphatic 'd'
ـط	ـطـ	طـ	ط	**ṭ**	emphatic 't'
ـظ	ـظـ	ظـ	ظ	**ẓ**	emphatic 'z'
ـع	ـعـ	عـ	ع	**'**	the Arabic letter 'ayn; pronounce as a glottal stop – like the closing of the throat before saying 'Oh oh!' (see Other Sounds on p.559)
ـغ	ـغـ	غـ	غ	**gh**	a guttural sound like Parisian 'r'
ـف	ـفـ	فـ	ف	**f**	as in 'far'
ـق	ـقـ	قـ	ق	**q**	a strongly guttural 'k' sound; in Egyptian Arabic often pronounced as a glottal stop
ـك	ـكـ	كـ	ك	**k**	as in 'king'
ـل	ـلـ	لـ	ل	**l**	as in 'lamb'
ـم	ـمـ	مـ	م	**m**	as in 'me'
ـن	ـنـ	نـ	ن	**n**	as in 'name'
ـه	ـهـ	هـ	ه	**h**	as in 'ham'
ـو			و	**w**	as in 'wet'; or
				ū	long, as the 'oo' in 'food'; or
				aw	as the 'ow' in 'how'
ـي	ـيـ	يـ	ي	**y**	as in 'yes'; or
				ī	as the 'e' in 'ear', only softer; or
				ay	as the 'y' in 'by' or as the 'ay' in 'way'

Vowels Not all Arabic vowel sounds are represented in the alphabet. See Pronunciation on p.557 for a list of all Arabic vowel sounds.

Emphatic Consonants To simplify the transliteration system used in this book, the emphatic consonants have not been included.

pronounced. For example, *el-hammam*, (bathhouse), is pronounced 'el-ham-mam'.

Other Sounds

Arabic has two sounds that are very tricky for non-Arabs to produce, the 'ayn and the glottal stop. The letter 'ayn represents a sound with no English equivalent that comes even close – it is similar to the glottal stop (which is not actually represented in the alphabet) but the muscles at the back of the throat are gagged more forcefully and air is allowed to escape, creating a sound that has been described as reminiscent of someone being strangled! In many transliteration systems 'ayn is represented by an opening quotation mark, and the glottal stop by a closing quotation mark. To make the transliterations in this language guide (and throughout the rest of the book) easier to use, we have not distinguished between the glottal stop and the 'ayn, using the closing quotation mark to represent both sounds. You'll find that Arab speakers will still understand you.

Transliteration

Converting what for most outsiders is just a bunch of squiggles into meaningful words (ie, those written using the Roman alphabet) is a tricky business – in fact no really satisfactory system of transliteration has been established, and probably never will be. For this edition, an attempt has been made to standardise some spellings of place names and the like. There is only one article in Arabic: *al* (the). It is also sometimes written as 'il' or 'el' and sometimes modifies to reflect the first consonant of the following noun. For example, in Saladin's name, *Salah ad-Din* (righteousness of the faith), the 'al' has been modified to 'ad' before the 'd' of 'Din'. The use of *el* is seen only in a few circumstances such as well-known places (El Alamein, Sharm el-Sheikh) or where locals have used it in restaurant and hotel names.

The whole business is fraught with pitfalls, and in a way there are no truly 'correct' answers. The locals themselves can only guess at how to make the conversion – and the result is often amusing. The fact that French and English have had a big influence (though the latter has all but 'conquered' the former in modern Egypt) has led to all sorts of interesting ideas on transliteration. Egypt's high rate of illiteracy doesn't help either. Don't be taken aback if you start noticing half a dozen different spellings for the same thing.

For some reason, the letters 'q' and 'k' have caused enormous problems, and have been interchanged willy-nilly in transliteration. For a long time, Iraq (which in Arabic is spelled with what can only be described in English using its nearest equivalent: 'q') was written, even by scholars, as 'Irak'. Other examples of an Arabic 'q' receiving such treatment are *souq* (market), often written 'souk'; *qasr* (castle), sometimes written 'kasr'; and the Cairo suburb of Doqqi, often written 'Dokki', although the Egyptian habit of swallowing 'q' and pronouncing the place name 'Do'i' is a dead giveaway. It's a bit like spelling English 'as she is spoke' – imagine the results if Australians, Americans, Scots and Londoners were all given free rein to write as they pronounce!

Greetings & Civilities

Arabic is more formal than English, especially with greetings; thus even the simplest greetings, such as 'hello', vary according to when and how they are used. In addition, each greeting requires a certain response that varies according to whether it is being said to a male, female or group of people.

The Transliteration Dilemma

TE Lawrence, when asked by his publishers to clarify 'inconsistencies in the spelling of proper names' in *Seven Pillars of Wisdom* – his account of the Arab Revolt in WWI – wrote back:

'Arabic names won't go into English. There are some 'scientific systems' of transliteration, helpful to people who know enough Arabic not to need helping, but a washout for the world. I spell my names anyhow, to show what rot the systems are.'

Hello.
salām 'alēkum
(lit: peace upon you)
(response)
wa 'alēkum es salām
(lit: and peace upon you)
Hello/Welcome.
ahlan wa sahlan
(response)
ahlan bīk (to m)
ahlan bīkī (to f)
ahlan bīkum (to group)
Pleased to meet you. (when first meeting)
tasharrafna (polite)
fursa sa'īda (informal)
Good morning.
sabāH al-khēr
(response)
sabāH an-nūr
Good evening.
misa' al-khēr
(response)
misa' an-nūr
Good night.
tisbaH 'ala khēr (to m)
tisbaHī 'ala khēr (to f)
tisbaHu 'ala khēr (to group)
(response; also used as 'Good afternoon' in the late afternoon)
wenta bikhēr (to m)
wentī bikhēr (to f)
wentū bikhēr (to group)
Goodbye.
ma'as salāma (lit: go in safety)

Basics

There are three ways to say 'Please' in Egyptian Arabic, each of which is used somewhat differently:

min fadlak/fadlik/fadlukum (to m/f/group), when asking for something in a shop; *law samaHt/samaHtī/samaHtu* (to m/f/group), similar, but more formal; *tfaddal/tfaddalī/tfaddalū* (to m/f/group), when offering something, for example, a chair or bus seat, or when inviting someone into your home or to join in a meal. The same words preceded by 'i' (eg, *itfaddal*) can be used to mean much the same thing or 'Please, go ahead' (and do something).

Excuse me.
'an iznak, esmaHlī (to m)
'an iznik, esmaHīlī (to f)
'an iznukum, esmaHūlī (to group)
Thank you.
shukran
Thank you very much.
shukran gazīlan
No thank you.
la' shukran
You're welcome.
'afwan, al-'affu
Yes.
aywa or *na'am* (more formal)
No.
la'
Sorry.
'assif

A useful words to know is *imshī*, which means 'Go away'. Use this at the pyramids or at other tourist sites when you are being besieged by children. Do not use it on adults; instead, just say, *la' shukran* ('No thank you').

Small Talk

How are you?
izzayyak? (to m)
izzayyik? (to f)
izzayyukum? (to group)
I'm fine.
kwayyis ilHamdu lillah
(to m, lit: fine, thanks be to God)
kwaysa ilHamdu lillah (to f)
kwaysīn ilHamdu lillah (to group)

(On their own, *kwayyis*, *kwaysa* and *kwaysīn* literally mean 'good' or 'fine', but they are rarely heard alone in response to 'How are you?')

What's your name?	*ismak ēh?* (to m)
	ismīk ēh? (to f)
My name is ...	*ismī ...*
Where are you from?	*enta/entī minayn?* (m/f)
I'm from ...	*ana min ...*
America	*amrīka*
Australia	*ustralya*
Canada	*kanada*

England	*inglaterra*
France	*fransa*
Germany	*almanya*
Italy	*itāliyya*
Japan	*al-yaban*
Netherlands	*holanda*
Spain	*isbanya*
Sweden	*as-swīd*
Switzerland	*swīsra*

Language Difficulties

Do you speak English?	*enta bititkallim inglīzī?* (to m) *entī bititkallimī inglīzī?* (to f)
I understand.	*ana fāhem/fahma* (m/f)
I don't understand.	*ana mish fāhem/ fahma* (m/f)

Getting Around

bicycle	*'agala, bīcīklēt*
boat	*markib*
car	*sayyāra/'arabiyya*
ferry	*ma'atiya*
camel	*gamal*
donkey	*Humār*
horse	*Husān*

Where is the ...?	*fein ...?*
airport	*matār*
bus station	*maHattat al-otobīs*
railway station	*maHattat al-'atr*
ticket office	*maktab at-tazāker*
street	*ash-shāri'*
city	*al-medīna*
village	*al-qarya*
bus stop	*maw'if al-otobīs*
station	*al-maHatta*

When does the ... leave/arrive?	*emta qiyam/wusuul...?*
bus	*al-otobīs*
train	*al-'atr*
boat	*al-markib*

How far is ...?	*kam kilo li ...?*
I want to go to ...	*ana 'ayiz arūH ...*
Which bus goes to...?	*otobīs nimra kam yerūH...?*
Does this bus go to ...?	*al-otobīs da yerūH ...?*

Signs

Entry	مدخل
Exit	خروج
Toilets (Men)	حمام للرجال
Toilets (Women)	حمام للنساء
Hospital	مستشفى
Police	الشرطة
Prohibited	ممنوع

How many buses per day go to ...?	*kam otobīs fil yōm yerūH...?*
Please tell me when we arrive in ...	*min fadlak, ullī emta Hanūsel ...*
What is the fare to ...?	*bikam at-tazkara li ...?*
May I/we sit here?	*mumkin eglis/neglis hena?*
Stop here, please.	*wa'if/hassib hena, min fadlak*
Please wait for me.	*mumkin tantazarnī*
Where can I rent a bicycle?	*fein e'aggar 'agala?*
Wait!	*istanna!*

Directions

Where is the hotel ...?	*fein al-funduq ...?*
Can you show me the way to the hotel ...?	*mumkin tewarrīnī at-tarīqlil-funduq ...?*
Where?	*fein?*
here	*hena*
there	*henek*
this address	*al-'anwān da*
north	*shimāl*
south	*ganūb*
east	*shark*
west	*gharb*

Around Town

Where is the ...?	*fein ...?*
bank	*al-bank*
barber	*al-Hallē'*
beach	*al-plā/ash-shaata*

Emergencies

Help!	*el-Ha'nī!*
Call a doctor!	*itassal-ī bi-doktōr!*
Call an ambulance!	*ittasal-ī bil-is'āf!*
Call the police!	*itassal bil-bolīs!*
I've been robbed.	*ana itsara't*
Thief!	*Harāmi!*
I'm lost.	*ana tāyih/tāyha*
Go away!	*imshī!*
Where are the toilets?	*fein al-twalēt?*

citadel	*al-'ala*
embassy	*as-sifāra*
female toilet	*twalēt al-Harīmī*
market	*as-sūq*
male toilet	*twalēt ar-ragel*
monastery	*dēr*
mosque	*al-gāme'*
museum	*al-matHaf*
old city	*al-medīna/al-'adīma*
palace	*al-'asr*
police station	*al-bolīs*
post office	*al-bōsta/ maktab al-barīd*
restaurant	*al-mat'am*
university	*al-gam'a*
zoo	*Hadīqat al-Haywān*

Accommodation

I'd like to see the rooms.	*awiz ashūf al-owad*
May I see other rooms?	*mumkin ashūf owad tānī?*
How much is the room per night?	*kam ugrat al-odda bil-laila?*
Do you have any cheaper rooms?	*fī owad arkhas?*
It's too expensive.	*da ghālī 'awī*
This is fine.	*da kwayyis*
air-conditioning	*takyīf hawa*

Shopping

Where can I buy ...?	*fein mumkin ashtirī ...?*
How much is this/that ...?	*bikam da ...?*
It costs too much.	*da ghālī 'awī*
Do you have ...?	*fī 'andak ...?*

Money

The Egyptians have a collection of names for their own money, used in most everyday transactions.

pound	*guinay*
½ pound (50 pt)	*nuss guinay*
¼ pound (25 pt)	*ruba' guinay*
20 pt	*riyal*
10 pt	*barisa*
5 pt	*shilling*

I want to change ...	*ana 'ayiz usarraf ...*
money	*fulūs*
travellers cheques	*shīkāt siyaHiyya*

US$	*dolār amrikānī*
UK£	*guinay sterlīnī*
A$	*dolār ustrālī*
€	*ūrō 'urubbī*

Time & Dates

What time is it?	*sā'ah kam?*
When?	*emta?*
day	*yom*
month	*shaher*
today	*el nharda*
tomorrow	*bokra*
week	*esbuwa*
year	*sana*
yesterday	*mberrah*
early	*badrī*
late	*mut'akhar*
daily	*kull yōm*

Sunday	*(yōm) al-aHadd*
Monday	*(yōm) al-itnīn*
Tuesday	*(yōm) at-talāt*
Wednesday	*(yōm) al-arba'a*
Thursday	*(yōm) al-khamīs*
Friday	*(yōm) al-gum'a*
Saturday	*(yōm) as-sabt*

East of Egypt, in addition to the Hejira calendar, there is also another set of names for the Gregorian calendar. In Egypt the names of the months are virtually the same as their European counterparts and are easily recognisable.

Numbers

Arabic numerals are simple to learn and, unlike the written language, run from left to right. Pay attention to the order of the words in numbers from 21 to 99.

0	٠	*sifr*
1	١	*wāHid*
2	٢	*itnein*
3	٣	*talāta*
4	٤	*arba'a*
5	٥	*khamsa*
6	٦	*sitta*
7	٧	*sab'a*
8	٨	*tmanya*
9	٩	*tis'a*
10	١٠	*'ashara*
11	١١	*Hidāshar*
12	١٢	*itnashar*
13	١٣	*talattāshar*
14	١٤	*arba'tāshar*
15	١٥	*khamastāshar*
16	١٦	*sittāshar*
17	١٧	*saba'tāshar*
18	١٨	*tamantāshar*
19	١٩	*tisa'tāshar*
20	٢٠	*'ishrīn*
21	٢١	*wāHid wi 'ishrīn*
22	٢٢	*itnein wi 'ishrīn*
30	٣٠	*talatīn*
40	٤٠	*arba'īn*
50	٥٠	*khamsīn*
60	٦٠	*sittīn*
70	٧٠	*sab'īn*
80	٨٠	*tamanīn*
90	٩٠	*tis'īn*
100	١٠٠	*myya*
101	١٠١	*myya wi wāHid*
200	٢٠٠	*mītein*
300	٣٠٠	*talāt mia*
1000	١٠٠٠	*'alf*
2000	٢٠٠٠	*'alfein*
3000	٣٠٠٠	*talāttalāf*

Ordinal Numbers

first	*'awwal*
second	*tānī*
third	*tālit*
fourth	*rābi'*
fifth	*khāmis*

January	*yanāyir*
February	*fibrāyir*
March	*māris*
April	*abrīl*
May	*māyu*
June	*yunyu*
July	*yulyu*
August	*aghustus*
September	*sibtimbir*
October	*'uktūbir*
November	*nufimbir*
December	*disimbir*

For a list of Hejira calendar months, see the Public Holidays & Special Events section in the Facts for the Visitor chapter.

Health

I need a doctor.	*'awiz doktōr*
Where is the hospital?	*fein al mustashfa?*
My friend is ill.	*sadīqi 'ayan*
I'm allergic ...	*'andī Hasasiyya ...*
to antibiotics	*min mudād Hayawi*
to penicillin	*min binisilīn*
I'm ...	*'indī ...*
asthmatic	*azmit rabū*
diabetic	*is sukkar*
epileptic	*sara'*
antiseptic	*mutahhir*
aspirin	*asbirin*
Band-Aids	*blāstir*
condoms	*kabābīt*
diarrhoea	*is-hāl*
fever	*sukhūna*
headache	*sudā'*
hospital	*mustashfa*
pharmacy	*agzakhana*
pregnant	*Hāmel*
prescription	*roshetta*
sanitary	*napkins*
stomachache	*waga' fil batn*
tampons	*hifāz al-'āda al-shahriyya*

Glossary

abd – servant of
abeyya – women's gown
abu – father, saint
ahwa – coffee or coffeehouse
ain – well, spring

bab – gate or door
bahr – river
baksheesh – tip
baladi – local, rural
bawwab – doorman
beit – house
bey – term of respect
bir – spring, well
birket – lake
Book of the Dead – funerary texts inscribed on *papyrus* consisting of 'spells' or chapters to guide ancient Egyptians through the afterlife
burg – tower

caliph – Islamic ruler; also spelt khalif
Canopic jars – pottery jars that held the embalmed internal organs and viscera (liver, stomach, lungs, intestines) of the mummified pharaoh
capital – top, decorated part of a column
caravanserai – merchants' inn
careta – donkey cart
cartouche – oval-shaped figure enclosing the *hieroglyphs* of royal or divine names in ancient Egypt
cenotaph – symbolic tomb, temple or place of cult worship that was additional to the pharaoh's actual burial place
Coffin Texts – funerary texts inscribed on the coffins of ancient Egyptian officials in the Middle Kingdom

dahabiyya – houseboat
darb – track, street
deir – monastery, convent

effendi – gentleman
eid – feast
emir – Islamic ruler, military commander or governor

false door – fake, seemingly half-open *ka* door in a tomb wall that enabled the pharaoh's spirit, or life force, to come and go at will
fellaheen – the peasant farmers or agricultural workers who make up the majority of Egypt's population; fellaheen literally means ploughman or tiller of the soil
filoos – money
finial – top part of a minaret
funerary complex – a pharaoh's last resting place; it usually comprised: a pyramid that was the pharaoh's tomb and the repository for all his household goods, clothes and treasure; a funerary temple on the east side of the pyramid that served as a cult temple for worship of the dead pharaoh; pits for solar barques; a valley temple on the banks of the Nile; and a massive causeway from the river to the pyramid

galabiyya – full-length robe worn by men
gebel – mountain or mountain range
gezira – island
ghawazee – cast of dancers who travelled with storytellers and poets and performed publicly or for hire
guinay – pound

haj – pilgrimage to Mecca; all Muslims should make the journey at least once in their lifetime
haji – one who has made the *haj* to Mecca
hammam – bathhouse
hantour – horse-drawn carriage
haram – anything forbidden by Islamic law
harem – the women of the household or family
hara – small lane, alley
Heb-Sed Festival – also known as the Jubilee Festival, this was a five-day celebration of symbolic royal rejuvenation held after 30 years of a pharaoh's reign and then every three years thereafter
Heb-Sed Race – traditional re-enactment, held during the Heb-Sed Festival, of a pharaoh's coronation

Hejira – Islamic calendar; Mohammed's flight from Mecca to Medina in AD 622
hieratic – ancient Egyptian short-hand version of *hieroglyphs* used for day-to-day transactions
hieroglyphs – ancient Egyptian form of writing, which used pictures and symbols to represent objects, words or sounds
higab – woman's headscarf
hypostyle hall – imposing hall in temples characterised by densely packed columns

ibn – son of
iconostasis – screen with doors and icons set in tiers, used in Eastern Christian churches
imam – a man schooled in Islam and who often doubles as the *muezzin*
iwan – vaulted hall, opening into a central court, in the *madrassa* of a mosque

al-jeel – a type of music characterised by a hand-clapping rhythm overlaid with a catchy vocal; translates as 'the generation'

ka – in ancient Egypt, the spirit, or 'double' that came into existence with the birth of an individual, and which continued to live after a person's death
kershef – building material made of large chunks of salt mixed with rock and plastered in local clay
khamsi – a dry, hot wind from the Western Desert
khan – another name for a *caravanserai*
khanqah – Sufi monastery
khedive – Egyptian viceroy under Ottoman suzerainty
khwaga – foreigner
kineesa – church
kubri – bridge
kuttab – Quranic school

lotus – white water lily regarded as sacred by the ancient Egyptians

madrassa – school where Islamic law is taught
mahattat – station
malqaf – angled wind catchers on the roof that direct the prevailing northerly breezes down into the building
mammisi – birth house; in these small chapels or temples, erected in the vicinity of a main temple, the rituals of the divine birth of the living pharaoh were performed
maristan – hospital
mashrabiyya – ornate carved wooden panel or screen; a feature of Islamic architecture
Masr – Egypt (also means Cairo)
mastaba – Arabic word for 'bench'; mudbrick structure in the shape of a bench above tombs that was the basis for later pyramids
matar – airport
midan – town or city square
mihrab – niche in the wall of a mosque that indicates the direction of Mecca
minaret – mosque tower
minbar – pulpit in a mosque
moulid – festival celebrating the birthday of a local saint or holy person
muezzin – mosque official who calls the faithful to prayer five times a day from the minaret
mufti – Muslim legal expert or leader of the religious community
mugzzabin – Sufi followers who participate in *zikrs* in order to achieve unity with Allah
mukwagee – laundry man
muqarnas – stalactite-like stone carving used to decorate doorways and window recesses of Islamic religious buildings

nai – reed pipe
naos – sanctuary containing a god's statue in ancient Egyptian temples
natron – whitish mineral of hydrated sodium carbonate that occurs in saline deposits and salt lakes and acts as a natural preservative; it was used in ancient Egypt to pack and dry a body during mummification
Nilometer – pit descending into the Nile containing a central column marked with graduations; the marks were used to measure and record the level of the river, especially during the inundation
nomarch – local governor or governor of a *nome*
nome – administrative division or province of ancient Egypt, introduced during the Old Kingdom era; there were 22 nomes in Upper Egypt and 20 in Lower Egypt

obelisk – monolithic stone pillar with square sides tapering to a pyramidal, often gilded, top, which was used as a monument in ancient Egypt; obelisks were usually set in pairs at the entrance to a tomb or temple
Opet Festival – celebration held in Luxor (Thebes) during the Nile inundation season where the pharaoh restored his own divine powers when he 'met' with the god Amun
oud – a type of lute

papyrus – plant identified with Lower Egypt; writing material made from the pith of this plant; a document written on such paper
pasha – lord, but also a term used more generally to denote someone of standing
porphyry – from Greek *porphyros* (purple); a reddish-purple rock highly resistant to erosion; many *sarcophagi* were made from this rock
pylon – monumental gateway at the entrance to a temple
Pyramid Texts – paintings and reliefs on the walls of the internal rooms and burial chamber of pyramids and often on the *sarcophagus* itself; used only for royalty

qa'a – reception room
qala'a – fortress
qasr – palace

Ramadan – ninth month of the lunar Islamic calendar during which Muslims fast from sunrise to sunset
ras – headland

sabil – public drinking fountain
sakia – water wheel
sarcophagus – huge stone or marble coffin used to encase other wooden coffins and the mummy of the pharaoh or queen
scarab – dung beetle regarded as sacred in ancient Egypt and represented on amulets or in *hieroglyphs* as a symbol of the sun god Ra
serapeum – network of subterranean galleries constructed as tombs for the mummified sacred Apis bulls; the most important temple of the Graeco-Egyptian god Serapis
serdab – hidden cellar in a tomb, or a stone room in front of some pyramids, containing a coffin with a lifesize, life-like, painted statue of the dead pharaoh; serdabs were designed so that the pharaoh's *ka* could communicate with the outside world
servees – service taxi
shabti – servant figure used in ancient Egypt
shadouf – water wheels used for irrigation purposes
sharia – Arabic for road or street
Shari'a – Islamic law, the body of doctrine that regulates the lives of Muslims
sharm – bay
sheesha – waterpipe
solar barque – wooden boat placed in or around the pharaoh's tomb; used to carry the sun god and the deceased pharaoh through the underworld
souq – market
speos – rock-cut tomb or chapel
stele (pl: stelae) – stone or wooden commemorative slab or column decorated with inscriptions or figures
Sufi – follower of any of the Islamic mystical orders that emphasise dancing, chanting and trances in order to attain unity with God

tabla – small hand-held drum
tarboosh – the hat known elsewhere as a fez
towla – backgammon

ulema – group of Muslim scholars or religious leaders; a member of this group
umm – mother of
uraeus – the characteristic symbol of Egyptian royalty, representing the cobra goddess Wadjet, worn on the pharaoh's forehead or crown

wadi – desert watercourse, dry except in the rainy season
waha – oasis
wikala – another name for a *caravanserai*

zikr – long sessions of dancing, chanting and swaying usually carried out by *Sufi mugzzabin* to achieve oneness with God

Thanks

Many thanks to the following travellers who used Egypt and wrote to us with helpful hints, useful advice and interesting anecdotes about travelling in Egypt.

Dagmar & Richard Abbott, Fares Abdel Aziz, Chris Abernethy, Vistor Abrash, Paul Adams, Sumanth Addagaria, Penelope Aitken, Sabah Akbar, Jane Akshar, Francesca Albertini, Lamont Albertson, Zahid Ali, Charles Allen, Colin Allin, Adam Allouba, Tim Allratt, Dan Andrews, S Andrews, Siobhan Andrews, Stephen & Sally Andrews, Julie Anne Justus, Bob Applebaum, Marianne Aral, Thomas Arbs, Barbara & Graham Archer, J Argentin, Jonathan Ariel, Maggie Armstrong, Ben Arnott, Katy Aros, Frozan Arsalan, Wahid Arsalan, Ian Ashbridge, Cathy Atkinson, MJ Bache, Henry Bacon, Carminia Banares, Melinda Banki, Lode Baptist, Roger Barlow, Danielle Baron, Geary Bartmess, Mark Bartolo, RN Barton, Billy-Jo Basinger, Louise Bater, Stephen Bateson, Anita Batistic, Marcus Bechtold, Wolfram Beck, Trudy Bedard, John Bedford, AJ Beekman, John S Bell, Shawn Bell, Sue Bellamy, Kate Belton, Maria & Tony Benfield, Connie J Bennett, Olaf Berggren, Alp Berker, Genevieve Bernard, Patricia Bernard, Paul Berry, Rachel Berry, W Berryman, Bob Berthiaume, C & F Beudeker-Prochaska, Nicola Beyfus, Laurent Bianchi, Al Biery, GM Bilgig, Annacarin & Nils Billing, Justin Blake, Tina Blakeney, Jan Blazek, Heather Blumberg, Joanna Blunt, Eric Blyboon, Jacqui Boardman, Julien Bodart, Harry Boehme, Andi & Ronki Bonin, Peter Boodell, Rob Boord, Dominic Booth, Christine Borcher, Frans Borst, Eric Boudin, Jane Boxall, Oliver Bradley, Marijana Brajac, Carlo Brand, Kim Brattinga, Lance Brendish, Dana Brigham, Kees Brink, Gidon Bromberg, Michelle Bromley, Daniel Brons, Jodie Brooks, Colin Brougham, Karen Brown, Andeas Bruckmeier, Gunner Brunke, Todd Bryan, Janice Buckley, Geoff Budd, Omar Buklin, N Burczyk, Chris & Daphne Burford, Sandi Burford-Poole, Julie Burnett, Delia Burrage, Sally Burrows, Henning Busboom, Harald Busch, Maret Busch, Luc Buseyne, Jonathon Butchard, Paola Buzi, Joshua Byrne, Meral Caktu, Tina Calov, Libby Cameron, Mark Cameron, Rees Cameron, Philip Camilleri, Elizabeth Campbell, Paola Capris, Mariana Carneiro, M Caroe, Deborah Carr, Michael Carroll, Jon & Sonja Carter, Wes Carter, Tom Cauchon, Peter Ceulemans, Ken Chamberlain, Beryl & Patrick Chambers, Colleen Chan, Jayne Chater, Jon Chion, Kwok Chor-ying, G Chow, Alfred Choy, Stephen Chubb, Fernando Ciria, Ann Clark, Rosemary & Rodney Clark, Sylvia Clark, Amy Clifton, Alice Coelho, Basil Condos, Marlene Cook, Eric Cooper, Ian Cooper, Tarquin Cooper, Colin Cotterill, Tom Coughlan, George Coulouris, Steven Coulson, Jeff Crandall, Amanda Cranmer, A Cressaty, Angeline Croft, Anne Lady Crofton, Russell Cronk, Edwin N Cross, Vanessa Cross, Anne Croxford, Rob Curry, Megan Curtis, Andrew Cusick, Warren Da Costa, Marques Da Silva, Dan Dahlberg, Lee D'Alterio, Laura Danforth, Silva Danieli, Tim Daniell, Susan Daniels, Anjana Das, RAH Davies, Simon Davies, Martin Davis, Waldo de Oliveira, Geert De Sitter, Judith De Wevek, Katherine Deal, Paul Deering, Roland Degoux, Rob Delacour, Julie Delahunt, Romas DelaRosa, Melanie Delieu, Coeno den Engelsman, Peter Denby, Patrick Dennis, Spencer Denyer, M Denys, Mieke Denys, Romain Desrousseaux, Patrick Dielissen, Karlheinz Dienelt, Jacqueline Diffey, David & Alison Dixon, Rachel Dodds, Sarah Dodson, R Doherty, Kari Dolezal, Mike Dolota, M Donahue, Michael Donnellan, Shirley Doss, Kate Douglas, Mervyn Douglas, John Downing, Martin Doyle, Robert Dress, Lorrie Drumm, Margaret Dudley, Alison Dudney, Tilman Duerbeck, AL Duffy, Audrey Duffy, Alistair Duncan, Yvonne Duncan, Laura Dunham, David Dunkley, Rosemary Dunning, Phil Dunnington, Sean Egypt, Hussein Elazm, Dr Ahmed Elgohary, Amro Elio, Bruce Elliott, Kari Eloranta, Andreas Engelmayer, A Engels, Paul England, Kerrieann Enright, Hans Erlandsson, Michael Esinger, Angharad Evans, Tim Eyre, Marc Fabien, Sue Fabre, Adel Fahmy, Lisa Farrelly, Jerry Felix, Tammy Fellin, Lyndon Ferguson, Marylene Ferguson, Robyn Ferguson, Grada Ferreira, Sandra Fichetti, Pierangelo Filigheddu, Scott Fincham, Emma Finlay, Jonah Fisher, Margaret Fisher, Teresa Fisher, Tim Fisher, Elier Flagraklett, Mike Fleming, A Flett, Lisa Flynn, Stephanie Folk, Jeroen Fontein,

Sulveigh Ford, John Fowler, Franca Franceschini, Ellen Frankel, Trish Franks, Sean Fraser, Ines Freuz, P Wayne Frey, Per-Axel Frielingsdorf, Simon Froehling, Edith Fronczek, Adam Fry, Cindy Fry, Christopher Fuller, Dave Fuller, Julianne Fuller, Scott Furness, J Gage, Michelle Gallagher, Ross Galvin, Marzia Gandini, Robert Gardner, Belinda Gaskell, Stefan Gasser, EPG Gearon, Anne Gebauer, Sandra Geisler, Charl Gerber, Stefan Gerke, Helen Gibbs, Mark Giddens, Ritchie Gifford, Maria Gil, Kirk & Pamela Gilbert, Sarah Gilbert, Richard Gillingham, Paul W Gioffi, Katherine A Giuffre, Christian Glossner, Angela Godfrey, David Goldberg, Leigh Goldstein, Diane B Goodpasture, Annie Gordon, Philipe Gossaert, Wolf Gotthilf, Louise Goulding, Nadia Graham, John Grainger, Jonathan Granger, Lee Greathouse, Zach Greig, Emily Grew, Daniel Groeber, Alexander Groenewege, Xavier Gros, Ed Gruhl, Steve Gudgeon, Matteo Guidotti, Dr Arun Gupta, Ralph Gurski, Pamela Hagedorn, Mike Hale, Mitch Hale, Barnabas Hamerlik, Jana Hamplova, Steve Hancock, Marisa Handler, Bev Handley, David Hannam, Teresa Hannon, Florian Hanslik, Garth Hargreaves, Lisa Harper, J Harris, Mandy Harris, Amanda Harvey, Meik Haselbach, Sue Haskins, Mike Hayes, Chris Heal, Andrew Hecht, Marijke de Heer, AJ Hellard, Roos Hermans, Patricia M & Eric Hicks, Maria Hidalgo, Mark Higgins, Karsten Hilbert, Joseph Hill, Karen Hillick, Lana Hinton, Andrew Hirsch, Michael Hoeppner, Maud Hoezen, Catherine Hogue, Aashild Hoiseth, Chris Holliday, Clark Holloway, Liban & Malene Holm, Markus Holmberg, Cynthia Holmes, Melainie Holten, Alexander Holtom, John Holtzclaw, Lee & Mei Hook, David Hooper, Glyn Hopkins, James Hopper, Richard Hornsby, Ian Horrocks, James Howlett, Vita Hribar, Petr Hruska, Andrew Hubbard, N & S Hundal, Frances B Hunt, John Hunt, A Hurley, Maha Hussain, PJ Hyland, Sylwia Hyzopska, Ameer Ibrahi, Kirby Inwood, Jan Iversen, Kate Jackson, Keith G Jackson, Thomas I Jacobs, Adrian James, Graham James, Sonan Janzan Vertregt, Rita Jaouich, Pete & Barbara Jeene, Juliette Jeffries, Farouk Jehan, Steen B Jensen, Esther Jilovsky, Stephen Johnson, Meg Jolliffe, Peter Jona, Don Jones, Elwynn Jones, Kirsten Jones, Margie Jones, Peter Jones, Kevin Jordon, Malene Jorgensen, Ralf & Michaela Juetter, Milos Jusko, Oscar Kafati, Gyorg Kalmory, Douglas Kandt, Salimah Kassam, Amanda Kauters, Steve Kay, Tim Kealy, Catherine Kean, Kate Keen, Wendy Keeney, AA Kelly, Dave Kento, Khammany Keovichith, Susanne Kerner, Lee Kessler, Korosh Khalili, Sittichai Khantiyanuwat, Roshdy Khattab, Hanan J Kisch, Prof Hanan J Kisch, Heidi Klaschka, Joachim Klein, Alexander Klupp, John Knight, Frithjof Koepp, Koe Kok Hau, Heidi Korhonen, Peter Koutsoukos, Joost Kremers, Mike Krosin, Dale & Debbie Krumreich, Felicia Kruse, Peter Kurze, Arthur van der Laak, Nadya Labib, Gilles Lamere, Alexandra Lang, Mary-Justine Lanyon, Tony Lattari, Paul Lau, Espen Lauritzen, Luc Lauwers, Brenda Lee, Darren Lee, Joanne Lee, Dieter Lehmann, Andreas Leininger, Paul Lelievre, Sue LeMarchant, Gina Lennox, C Leonidas, Ruud Leukel, Ian Lewis, Simon Li, Veerle Libberecht, Cas Liber, Henry YM Lim, Simon Lim, Nina Lincoln, Jenny Linde, Eric Linder, Daniel Lindhagen, Robert Lipske, Helen Little, Natalie & Mark Little, Angela Lloyd, Rainer Lodes, Beth Logan, Laura Logan, Heidi Long, Fabrizio Loschi, Laura Losee, T Lout, Clare Loveday, Graham Low, Roger Low Puay Hwa, Hans Lubbinje, K Luchs, Joanna Maciejewska, Paul MacLeod, Maryse Maes, Dan Magnus, Livia Magyar, Ahmed Mahran, Julie Main, Catherine Maingaud, Jamie Maler, Julie Malkin, Yasser Mamdouh, M Marchini, Susan Mares-Pilling, Andrew Margolin, Cheinan Marks, Ben Marsden, Andrew Marshall, Jean-Denis Martin, Jessica Martin, Nigol Martin, Yves Maselis, Neil Masey, Clare Mason, Stana Matousova, Paul Mattock, Bernhard Matz, Richard Maurice, Kathleen McCann, Jason McGrath, Maureen McGuire, James McKechne, Jane McKenzie, John McKie, Chelsea McKinny, J Mclellan, Ian McLeod, Ged McPhail, Jo Measure, Kuwakubo Megumi, Stefan Meier, Mari Mellum, Robert Merrision, M & S Merz-Kubesch, Wendy Meskes, Simon Messing, Richard Meyrian, Sarah Michael, Michael Middleton, Sharon Midge, Fizh Mike, Ian Millard, Robert Miller, Eric Milsom, Lorenzo Minutelli, C Mitchell, Gilbert Moase, Mario Moeller, Amanda Mohabir, Fiona Monahan, Dore Montes, David Montgomery, Anita Montvazski, Robyn Moore, Guy Moorhouse, Toni Mooy, Cathleen Moran, Steffi Morjan, Robert Morris, Mohamed Moseilhy, Dry Mousseau-Gershman, Hal Mozer, Dietrich Mulder, Samuel Mullerstraat, Brennan Mulligan, Graham Munn, Roelant van der Munnik, Franklin Murillo, Phil Murphy, Sean & Carol Murphy, Phil Muscutt, Timothy Nagy, Lorenzo Nastasi, Simon

Neal, Paul D Nelson, Michael S Newman, Ben Nicholls, Alex & Diane Nikolic, Carmalina Nizzardi, Tracey Nock, Sara Nolan, Stuart Norgrove, Padraig O'Blivion, Pat O'Brien, Emma O'Connell, Caren Ogland, Anna Olsson, Lars Oltrogge, Amanda O'Neill, Gerdiego Ontiveros, Stefanie Opper, Denise Orel, Elizabeth Osbourne, Tony Ostersen, Patrick Ostyn, Valentina Othmacic, Andrea Den Otter, Charles Owen, Shawn Owen, Ben Owens, J Oxley, Tina Pachero, Jason Palmer, Martin Panek, Nicolette Papastefanou, Jennifer Parkes, James Parsons, Alesandro Pascale, Debra & Bharat Patel, Ostyn Patrick, Cliff Patridge, Bostjan Payntan, Katy Peacock, Emily Peckham, Pieter Peeters, Jimmy Pegg, Ian Penberthy, Lucien Peron, Jane Perry, Remco Petersen, Dana Petric, Katja & Henry Petzold, Larissa Pfeifer, Daniel Pfund, Frank Phelan, Julia Phillips, P Phillips, Paul Phillips, Susan Picard, Nick Picton, Serena Pirrotta, Constant Piscart, Sean Plamondon, Anna Plandiura Riba, Shirley Porsche, John Potterat, Jo Price, Matthew Price, Tony Pringle, Wim Pronk, Peter & Erika Pucsok, Leon Punt, Marie-Lise Quaradeghini, Ambrogio Radaelli, Sarah Raine, Tim Rampey, Zeena Rasheed, Scott Redinger, Charles Reeve, Melissa Reid, Hayo Reinders, Laszlo Reisch, Dr Mark Rembrandt, Paula Reynolds, David Roberts, Lorraine Roberts, Maurice Roberts, Jacob Rode, Ingrid Roder, Howard Roe, Vincent Roger-Machart, Graham Rogers, Michael Rohaly, Renatus Rohde, Pilar Rojo, Diana Rose, Darren Ross, Micheal Rotherman, Caroline Rousseau, David Rowe, Krysztof Rybak, Aimee Sacks, Tarek Sadek, Silvia Salem, Errol Salvador, Monique Samsen, Sharon Saunders, Keith Savory, Barbara Sawyer, Sam Schaeffer, Ulrike Schenk, Matthias Schluter, Judith Schmidt, Monique Schoone, Robert Schriek, Mariah Schug, David Schultze II, Diana Schumacher, Howard Schwartz, Robert Schwarz, Erica Sefton, Grzegorz Serowka, Christine Shalaby, Peter & Florence Shaw, Victor Sheahan, Stephan Siemer, Thomas Siffer, Don Silver, Janna Silverstein, Nathalie Silvestre, Katia Simonov, Amelia Simpson, Helen Simpson, John Simpson, Jass Sio, Agnete Skaarup, Jan Skaarup, BJ Skane, Richard Skilton, Bob Skinner, John Skuthorpe, Mirjam Skwortsow, Alex Sky, Stuart Slater, Fiona Slaw, Judith Slot, Doris Smith, Gavin Smith, Louise Smith, Paul Smith, Rebecca Smith, Stephen Smith, Sarah Smyth, Annette Snow, Robert Snyder, Helena Soderlind, Andrea Solotar, Ralph Somma, Martin Ulf Sorensen, Ricardo Sosa, Steve Sosa, Zoe Sowden, Andy Sparrow, Carole Spiers, Damien Spry, Tomasz Stafiej, Rana J Standal, Sheri Stanford Driver, Joesph T Stanik, John Stapleton, Bjorn Staschen, Jochen Stegmaier, Peter Stein, Aly Stevens, I Stevens, Neil Stevenson, Niels Stougaard, Bill & Ann Stoughton, Ida Strasser, Dr Thomas Straub, Thomas Straub, Thorsten Strufe, Paul Stuart, R Sturgeon, Craig Summers, Mari Swanston, J Swinden, John Sylvester, Barry & Wanda Syner, Zara Tai, Toshiaki Takahashi, Grant Tarliang, Fiona Tarpey, John M Taylor, Ruud Teeuwen, Antje Temler, Martin Terber, Robert Thiel, Lee Thienny, Simon & Erika Thijs de Feber, Ernest Thompson, Ruth Thompson, S Thorsoe, Sarah Thurston, Alfred J Tinao, Louise Tomblin, Eleanor Tonkin, Gerhard Topper, Monique Tortrat, Julie Toth, Darin Triplett, Kevin Turley, Paul Turner, Kuba Tymula, RG Ulderink, Dr Z Ungvari, Adriana Valencia, Adele Valsesia, Ramses Valvekens, Wourt Van Amerongen, Sashia van Brierner, Michel J van Dam, Famke van der Duin, Erwin van Engelen, Jeanette van Everdingen, Jean-Louis van Gelder, Bart van Meyer, Carolien van Zoest, Arlette Vanderheijden, Thomas Vaughan, Marja Veen, Tamara Veenendaal, Johan Verheyden, Vincent Vermeire, Igor Verton, Hugo Vet, Anthony Vickers, Sonya Virtu, Dre Visscher, Hayco J Volkers, Mikiel von Glaub, Ulrike von Ruecker, Radim Vovesny, J Wagenaar, Carl Wahlen, Louise Walker, Kevin & Andrea Wall, Siobhan Wall, Kerry & John Wallace, Olga & Ron Wallace, Daniel Wallis, Ayesha Walmsley, Sue Wang, Chris Ward, Michael Ward, Trevor Ward, Joanna Warr, Lisa Warren, Phil Watmough, Paul & Joanne Watson, Nick Watt, Stuart Weatherley, Sheila Weinberg, Kathryn Weir, Dawid & Kathy Welgemoed, Barry Wellman, Cuyler W Wenberg, Andre Went, Izak Wessels, Karl Westerholt, Kate Whittington, Chris Wicke, Damien Wilhelm, Craig Wilkinson, Andy Williams, Craig Williams, Sam Williams, Kirsten Willoughby, Toni Wills, Diana Wilson, Jennifer P Wilson, Yvonne Wilson, Matt Wingett, Gerda Wink, Debra Winters, A Wodford, Dan Wolf, Carolien Wolff, Daniel Worsley, Patrick Wullaert, Eduardo & Marjorie Xavier, Faisal Yafai, Deannie Yew, Fran Yniguez, T Yousuff, Haseena Zachariah, RA Zambardino, Paola Zancanaro, Jane Z Zhang, Jaka Zibrat, Peter Zidar, Erik Zoonlief, Aleksandra Ztobinska, Daan Zuyderland, Jum Zwijnenburg

Lonely Planet Guides by Region

Lonely Planet is known worldwide for publishing practical, reliable and no-nonsense travel information in our guides and on our Web site. The Lonely Planet list covers just about every accessible part of the world. Currently there are 16 series: Travel guides, Shoestring guides, Condensed guides, Phrasebooks, Read This First, Healthy Travel, Walking guides, Cycling guides, Watching Wildlife guides, Pisces Diving & Snorkeling guides, City Maps, Road Atlases, Out to Eat, World Food, Journeys travel literature and Pictorials.

AFRICA Africa on a shoestring • Botswana • Cairo • Cairo City Map • Cape Town • Cape Town City Map • East Africa • Egypt • Egyptian Arabic phrasebook • Ethiopia, Eritrea & Djibouti • Ethiopian Amharic phrasebook • The Gambia & Senegal • Healthy Travel Africa • Kenya • Malawi • Morocco • Moroccan Arabic phrasebook • Mozambique • Namibia • Read This First: Africa • South Africa, Lesotho & Swaziland • Southern Africa • Southern Africa Road Atlas • Swahili phrasebook • Tanzania, Zanzibar & Pemba • Trekking in East Africa • Tunisia • Watching Wildlife East Africa • Watching Wildlife Southern Africa • West Africa • World Food Morocco • Zambia • Zimbabwe, Botswana & Namibia
Travel Literature: Mali Blues: Traveling to an African Beat • The Rainbird: A Central African Journey • Songs to an African Sunset: A Zimbabwean Story

AUSTRALIA & THE PACIFIC Aboriginal Australia & the Torres Strait Islands •Auckland • Australia • Australian phrasebook • Australia Road Atlas • Cycling Australia • Cycling New Zealand • Fiji • Fijian phrasebook • Healthy Travel Australia, NZ & the Pacific • Islands of Australia's Great Barrier Reef • Melbourne • Melbourne City Map • Micronesia • New Caledonia • New South Wales • New Zealand • Northern Territory • Outback Australia • Out to Eat – Melbourne • Out to Eat – Sydney • Papua New Guinea • Pidgin phrasebook • Queensland • Rarotonga & the Cook Islands • Samoa • Solomon Islands • South Australia • South Pacific • South Pacific phrasebook • Sydney • Sydney City Map • Sydney Condensed • Tahiti & French Polynesia • Tasmania • Tonga • Tramping in New Zealand • Vanuatu • Victoria • Walking in Australia • Watching Wildlife Australia • Western Australia
Travel Literature: Islands in the Clouds: Travels in the Highlands of New Guinea • Kiwi Tracks: A New Zealand Journey • Sean & David's Long Drive

CENTRAL AMERICA & THE CARIBBEAN Bahamas, Turks & Caicos • Baja California • Belize, Guatemala & Yucatán • Bermuda • Central America on a shoestring • Costa Rica • Costa Rica Spanish phrasebook • Cuba • Cycling Cuba • Dominican Republic & Haiti • Eastern Caribbean • Guatemala • Havana • Healthy Travel Central & South America • Jamaica • Mexico • Mexico City • Panama • Puerto Rico • Read This First: Central & South America • Virgin Islands • World Food Caribbean • World Food Mexico • Yucatán
Travel Literature: Green Dreams: Travels in Central America

EUROPE Amsterdam • Amsterdam City Map • Amsterdam Condensed • Andalucía • Athens • Austria • Baltic States phrasebook • Barcelona • Barcelona City Map • Belgium & Luxembourg • Berlin • Berlin City Map • Britain • British phrasebook • Brussels, Bruges & Antwerp • Brussels City Map • Budapest • Budapest City Map • Canary Islands • Catalunya & the Costa Brava • Central Europe • Central Europe phrasebook • Copenhagen • Corfu & the Ionians • Corsica • Crete • Crete Condensed • Croatia • Cycling Britain • Cycling France • Cyprus • Czech & Slovak Republics • Czech phrasebook • Denmark • Dublin • Dublin City Map • Dublin Condensed • Eastern Europe • Eastern Europe phrasebook • Edinburgh • Edinburgh City Map • England • Estonia, Latvia & Lithuania • Europe on a shoestring • Europe phrasebook • Finland • Florence • Florence City Map • France • Frankfurt City Map • Frankfurt Condensed • French phrasebook • Georgia, Armenia & Azerbaijan • Germany • German phrasebook • Greece • Greek Islands • Greek phrasebook • Hungary • Iceland, Greenland & the Faroe Islands • Ireland • Italian phrasebook • Italy • Kraków • Lisbon • The Loire • London • London City Map • London Condensed • Madrid • Madrid City Map • Malta • Mediterranean Europe • Milan, Turin & Genoa • Moscow • Munich • Netherlands • Normandy • Norway • Out to Eat – London • Out to Eat – Paris • Paris • Paris City Map • Paris Condensed • Poland • Polish phrasebook • Portugal • Portuguese phrasebook • Prague • Prague City Map • Provence & the Côte d'Azur • Read This First: Europe • Rhodes & the Dodecanese • Romania & Moldova • Rome • Rome City Map • Rome Condensed • Russia, Ukraine & Belarus • Russian phrasebook • Scandinavian & Baltic Europe • Scandinavian phrasebook • Scotland • Sicily • Slovenia • South-West France • Spain • Spanish phrasebook • Stockholm • St Petersburg • St Petersburg City Map • Sweden • Switzerland • Tuscany • Ukrainian phrasebook • Venice • Vienna • Wales • Walking in Britain • Walking in France • Walking in Ireland • Walking in Italy • Walking in Scotland • Walking in Spain • Walking in Switzerland • Western Europe • World Food France • World Food Greece • World Food Ireland • World Food Italy • World Food Spain **Travel Literature:** After Yugoslavia • Love and War in the Apennines • The Olive Grove: Travels in Greece • On the Shores of the Mediterranean • Round Ireland in Low Gear • A Small Place in Italy

Lonely Planet Mail Order

Lonely Planet products are distributed worldwide. They are also available by mail order from Lonely Planet, so if you have difficulty finding a title please write to us. North and South American residents should write to 150 Linden St, Oakland, CA 94607, USA; European and African residents should write to 10a Spring Place, London NW5 3BH, UK; and residents of other countries to Locked Bag 1, Footscray, Victoria 3011, Australia.

INDIAN SUBCONTINENT & THE INDIAN OCEAN Bangladesh • Bengali phrasebook • Bhutan • Delhi • Goa • Healthy Travel Asia & India • Hindi & Urdu phrasebook • India • India & Bangladesh City Map • Indian Himalaya • Karakoram Highway • Kathmandu City Map • Kerala • Madagascar • Maldives • Mauritius, Réunion & Seychelles • Mumbai (Bombay) • Nepal • Nepali phrasebook • North India • Pakistan • Rajasthan • Read This First: Asia & India • South India • Sri Lanka • Sri Lanka phrasebook • Tibet • Tibetan phrasebook • Trekking in the Indian Himalaya • Trekking in the Karakoram & Hindukush • Trekking in the Nepal Himalaya • World Food India **Travel Literature:** The Age of Kali: Indian Travels and Encounters • Hello Goodnight: A Life of Goa • In Rajasthan • Maverick in Madagascar • A Season in Heaven: True Tales from the Road to Kathmandu • Shopping for Buddhas • A Short Walk in the Hindu Kush • Slowly Down the Ganges

MIDDLE EAST & CENTRAL ASIA Bahrain, Kuwait & Qatar • Central Asia • Central Asia phrasebook • Dubai • Farsi (Persian) phrasebook • Hebrew phrasebook • Iran • Israel & the Palestinian Territories • Istanbul • Istanbul City Map • Istanbul to Cairo • Istanbul to Kathmandu • Jerusalem • Jerusalem City Map • Jordan • Lebanon • Middle East • Oman & the United Arab Emirates • Syria • Turkey • Turkish phrasebook • World Food Turkey • Yemen **Travel Literature:** Black on Black: Iran Revisited • Breaking Ranks: Turbulent Travels in the Promised Land • The Gates of Damascus • Kingdom of the Film Stars: Journey into Jordan

NORTH AMERICA Alaska • Boston • Boston City Map • Boston Condensed • British Columbia • California & Nevada • California Condensed • Canada • Chicago • Chicago City Map • Chicago Condensed • Florida • Georgia & the Carolinas • Great Lakes • Hawaii • Hiking in Alaska • Hiking in the USA • Honolulu & Oahu City Map • Las Vegas • Los Angeles • Los Angeles City Map • Louisiana & the Deep South • Miami • Miami City Map • Montreal • New England • New Orleans • New Orleans City Map • New York City • New York City City Map • New York City Condensed • New York, New Jersey & Pennsylvania • Oahu • Out to Eat – San Francisco • Pacific Northwest • Rocky Mountains • San Diego & Tijuana • San Francisco • San Francisco City Map • Seattle • Seattle City Map • Southwest • Texas • Toronto • USA • USA phrasebook • Vancouver • Vancouver City Map • Virginia & the Capital Region • Washington, DC • Washington, DC City Map • World Food New Orleans **Travel Literature**: Caught Inside: A Surfer's Year on the California Coast • Drive Thru America

NORTH-EAST ASIA Beijing • Beijing City Map • Cantonese phrasebook • China • Hiking in Japan • Hong Kong & Macau • Hong Kong City Map • Hong Kong Condensed • Japan • Japanese phrasebook • Korea • Korean phrasebook • Kyoto • Mandarin phrasebook • Mongolia • Mongolian phrasebook • Seoul • Shanghai • South-West China • Taiwan • Tokyo • Tokyo Condensed • World Food Hong Kong • World Food Japan **Travel Literature**: In Xanadu: A Quest • Lost Japan

SOUTH AMERICA Argentina, Uruguay & Paraguay • Bolivia • Brazil • Brazilian phrasebook • Buenos Aires • Buenos Aires City Map • Chile & Easter Island • Colombia • Ecuador & the Galapagos Islands • Healthy Travel Central & South America • Latin American Spanish phrasebook • Peru • Quechua phrasebook • Read This First: Central & South America • Rio de Janeiro • Rio de Janeiro City Map • Santiago de Chile • South America on a shoestring • Trekking in the Patagonian Andes • Venezuela **Travel Literature**: Full Circle: A South American Journey

SOUTH-EAST ASIA Bali & Lombok • Bangkok • Bangkok City Map • Burmese phrasebook • Cambodia • Cycling Vietnam, Laos & Cambodia • East Timor phrasebook • Hanoi • Healthy Travel Asia & India • Hill Tribes phrasebook • Ho Chi Minh City (Saigon) • Indonesia • Indonesian phrasebook • Indonesia's Eastern Islands • Java • Lao phrasebook • Laos • Malay phrasebook • Malaysia, Singapore & Brunei • Myanmar (Burma) • Philippines • Pilipino (Tagalog) phrasebook • Read This First: Asia & India • Singapore • Singapore City Map • South-East Asia on a shoestring • South-East Asia phrasebook • Thailand • Thailand's Islands & Beaches • Thailand, Vietnam, Laos & Cambodia Road Atlas • Thai phrasebook • Vietnam • Vietnamese phrasebook • World Food Indonesia • World Food Thailand • World Food Vietnam

ALSO AVAILABLE: Antarctica • The Arctic • The Blue Man: Tales of Travel, Love and Coffee • Brief Encounters: Stories of Love, Sex & Travel • Buddhist Stupas in Asia: The Shape of Perfection • Chasing Rickshaws • The Last Grain Race • Lonely Planet ... On the Edge: Adventurous Escapades from Around the World • Lonely Planet Unpacked • Lonely Planet Unpacked Again • Not the Only Planet: Science Fiction Travel Stories • Ports of Call: A Journey by Sea • Sacred India • Travel Photography: A Guide to Taking Better Pictures • Travel with Children • Tuvalu: Portrait of an Island Nation

Index

Text

Bold indicates maps.

Bold indicates maps.

C

Bold indicates maps.

N

Bold indicates maps.

U

V

Boxed Text

MAP LEGEND

CITY ROUTES

- Freeway ... Freeway
- Highway ... Primary Road
- Road ... Secondary Road
- Street ... Street
- Lane ... Lane
- On/Off Ramp
- Unsealed Road
- One Way Street
- Pedestrian Street
- Stepped Street
- Tunnel
- Footbridge

REGIONAL ROUTES

- Tollway, Freeway
- Primary Road
- Secondary Road
- Minor Road

BOUNDARIES

- International
- State
- Disputed
- Fortified Wall

TRANSPORT ROUTES & STATIONS

- Train
- Underground Train
- Metro
- Tramway
- Cable Car, Chairlift
- Ferry
- Walking Trail
- Walking Tour
- Path
- Pier or Jetty

HYDROGRAPHY

- River, Creek
- Canal
- Lake
- Dry Lake; Salt Lake
- Spring; Rapids
- Waterfalls

AREA FEATURES

- Building
- Park, Gardens
- Market
- Sports Ground
- Beach
- Christian Cemetery
- Islamic Cemetery
- Campus

POPULATION SYMBOLS

- CAPITAL ... National Capital
- CAPITAL ... State Capital
- CITY ... City
- Town ... Town
- Village ... Village
- Urban Area

MAP SYMBOLS

- Place to Stay
- Airstrip; Airport
- Bank
- Bus Stop/Terminal
- Coffeehouse
- Camping
- Cave
- Church
- Cinema
- Embassy
- Gate
- Place to Eat
- Golf Course
- Hospital
- Information
- Internet Cafe
- Islamic Monument
- Lighthouse
- Lookout
- Monument
- Mosque
- Museum
- National Park
- Oasis
- Parking
- Petrol
- Police Station
- Post Office
- Pub or Bar
- Ruins
- Shopping Centre
- Synagogue
- Point of Interest
- Taxi
- Telephone
- Temple
- Theatre
- Toilet
- Tomb
- Tourist Information
- Transport
- Zoo

Note: not all symbols displayed above appear in this book

LONELY PLANET OFFICES

Australia
Locked Bag 1, Footscray, Victoria 3011
☎ 03 8379 8000 fax 03 8379 8111
email: talk2us@lonelyplanet.com.au

USA
150 Linden St, Oakland, CA 94607
☎ 510 893 8555 TOLL FREE: 800 275 8555
fax 510 893 8572
email: info@lonelyplanet.com

UK
10a Spring Place, London NW5 3BH
☎ 020 7428 4800 fax 020 7428 4828
email: go@lonelyplanet.co.uk

France
1 rue du Dahomey, 75011 Paris
☎ 01 55 25 33 00 fax 01 55 25 33 01
email: bip@lonelyplanet.fr
www.lonelyplanet.fr

World Wide Web: www.lonelyplanet.com *or* AOL keyword: lp
Lonely Planet Images: lpi@lonelyplanet.com.au